psychology

psychology

FIFTH EDITION

LESTER M. SDOROW
Arcadia University

CHERYL A. RICKABAUGH
University of Redlands

Boston   Burr Ridge, IL   Dubuque, IA   Madison, WI   New York   San Francisco   St. Louis
Bangkok   Bogotá   Caracas   Kuala Lumpur   Lisbon   London   Madrid   Mexico City
Milan   Montreal   New Delhi   Santiago   Seoul   Singapore   Sydney   Taipei   Toronto

McGraw-Hill Higher Education

*A Division of The **McGraw-Hill** Companies*

PSYCHOLOGY, FIFTH EDITION

Published by McGraw-Hill, a business unit of The McGraw-Hill Companies, Inc., 1221 Avenue of the Americas, New York, NY 10020. Copyright © 2002, 1998, 1995, 1993, 1990 by The McGraw-Hill Companies, Inc. All rights reserved. No part of this publication may be reproduced or distributed in any form or by any means, or stored in a database or retrieval system, without the prior written consent of The McGraw-Hill Companies, Inc., including, but not limited to, in any network or other electronic storage or transmission, or broadcast for distance learning.

Some ancillaries, including electronic and print components, may not be available to customers outside the United States.

This book is printed on acid-free paper.

International 1 2 3 4 5 6 7 8 9 0 QPV/QPV 0 9 8 7 6 5 4 3 2 1
Domestic   2 3 4 5 6 7 8 9 0 QPV/QPV 0 9 8 7 6 5 4 3 2

ISBN 0–07–235832–7
ISBN 0–07–112157–9 (ISE)

Editorial director: *Jane E. Karpacz*
Senior sponsoring editor: *Melissa Mashburn*
Developmental editor: *Mindy De Palma*
Senior marketing manager: *Chris Hall*
Project manager: *Mary E. Powers*
Production supervisor: *Enboge Chong*
Design manager: *Stuart D. Paterson*
Cover/interior designer: *Rokusek Design*
Cover image: *Stone*
Senior photo research coordinator: *Lori Hancock*
Photo research: *Toni Michaels*
Supplement producer: *Jodi K. Banowetz*
Media technology senior producer: *Sean Crowley*
Compositor: *Electronic Publishing Services, Inc. (TN)*
Typeface: *10/12 Times Roman*
Printer: *Quebecor World Versailles Inc.*

The credits section for this book begins on page C-1 and is considered an extension of the copyright page.

Library of Congress Cataloging-in-Publication Data

Sdorow, Lester M.
    Psychology / Lester M. Sdorow, Cheryl A. Rickabaugh. — 5th ed.
        p.   cm.
    Includes bibliographical references and indexes.
        ISBN 0–07–235832–7 — ISBN 0–07–112157–9 (ISE)
    1. Psychology. I. Rickabaugh, Cheryl A. II. Title.

BF121 .S39   2002
150—dc21
                                              2001031481
                                              CIP

INTERNATIONAL EDITION ISBN 0–07–112157–9
Copyright © 2002. Exclusive rights by The McGraw-Hill Companies, Inc., for manufacture and export. This book cannot be re-exported from the country to which it is sold by McGraw-Hill. The International Edition is not available in North America.

www.mhhe.com

To Jan and Her
Wonderful Pride
Les

To Mom and Dad
Cheryl

About the Authors

Les Sdorow is a visiting professor of psychology at Arcadia University (formerly Beaver College). He received his B.A. from Wilkes College and his M.A. and Ph.D. from Hofstra University. He was chairperson of the Department of Behavioral Science at St. Francis College (Pa.) and the Department of Psychology at Allentown College (now DeSales University). Les was named Outstanding Educator at St. Francis College and Teacher of the Year at Allentown College. He also co-founded (with Richmond Johnson of Moravian College) the Lehigh Valley Undergraduate Psychology Research Conference and served as president of the Pennsylvania Society of Behavioral Medicine and Biofeedback. His research interests are in psychophysiology, sport psychology, and health psychology. Les has made numerous presentations on the teaching of psychology at local, regional, and national conferences. He teaches introductory psychology, research methods, history of psychology, sport psychology, and health psychology.

Cheryl Rickabaugh is professor of psychology and department chair at the University of Redlands. She received her B.A. from California State University, Los Angeles, and her M.A. and Ph.D. in social-personality psychology at the University of California, Riverside. She has received two Outstanding Faculty Awards for teaching during her thirteen years at the University of Redlands. Cheryl teaches introductory psychology, research methods, social psychology, health psychology, and psychology of gender. She also teaches an interdisciplinary course, women, wellness, and sport, in the University of Redlands Women's Studies program. She has published research in social psychology, health psychology, psychology of gender, and teaching undergraduate psychology, and is the author of *Sex and Gender: Student Projects and Exercises* (1998).

Brief Contents

Contents

CHAPTER 3

Behavioral Neuroscience 56

CHAPTER 4

Human Development 94

CHAPTER 5

Sensation and Perception 132

CHAPTER 6

Consciousness   176

CHAPTER 9

Thinking and Language 276

CHAPTER 10

Intelligence 302

CHAPTER 11

Motivation 326

CHAPTER 12

Emotion 350

CHAPTER 13

Personality 374

CHAPTER 14

Psychological Disorders 400

CHAPTER 15

Therapy 428

CHAPTER 17

Social Psychology 478

Preface

From psychology's inception as a separate discipline, authors of introductory psychology textbooks have been confronted with the need to convey a broad discipline to students in a book of reasonable length. To accomplish all that Les originally intended, this book could easily have been twice as long as it is now. A century ago, William James, disturbed at the length of his now-classic *Principles of Psychology,* gave his own stinging review of it. He called it, among other things, "a bloated tumescent mass." Though this comment might have been written during one of James's frequent bouts with depression, it indicates the challenge of synthesizing a vast quantity of information. Given that psychology has become an even broader discipline and has accumulated an enormous information base, Les quickly discovered that he would somehow have to manipulate a kind of intellectual "Rubik's cube" of six goals to avoid producing a bloated, tumescent mass (or what textbook reviewers often, perhaps euphemistically, refer to as an "encyclopedic" book). Our goals in writing the fifth edition could only be achieved by considering each goal in light of the others.

If you have not adopted this book in the past, we believe that you, too, will find that your students will be eager to read and to learn from it. You will find that the book achieves this while also accomplishing the following goals:

- Portraying psychology as a science
- Demonstrating the superiority of science over common sense
- Showing that psychological research occurs in a sociocultural context
- Illustrating the relevance of psychology to everyday life
- Encouraging critical thinking in all aspects of life, particularly in the media
- Placing psychology in its intellectual, historical, sociocultural, and biographical contexts

To ensure that students will find the book appealing, we have made every effort to write clearly and concisely and to include interesting content. To make our prose as clear as possible, we have taken care that every sentence, paragraph, and section in the book presents a crisp, logical flow of ideas. To make the content more interesting, we have included many engaging examples of concepts and issues throughout the book. Because we find books that provide vivid examples of the concepts and issues they cover are more readable, we have included concrete examples from psychological research and from virtually every area of life, including art, literature, history, biography, entertainment, sports, politics, and student life.

Though a textbook should be readable, for students to respect psychology as a science the textbook they use must be scholarly. Though popular examples are sprinkled throughout this text, they are not used as substitutes for evidence provided by scientific research. If you skim the reference list at the end of the book, you will note that it is up-to-date in its coverage of research studies, yet does not slight classic studies.

THEMES GUIDING *PSYCHOLOGY,* FIFTH EDITION

The fifth edition of *Psychology* includes special features that advance the six main goals of this text.

Portraying Psychology as a Science

Over the years, several of our colleagues have expressed frustration that many people—including students—do not realize that psychology is a science, instead believing that it is based on common sense and the opinions of experts called "psychologists." Because of this, one of the primary goals of this book is to show the student reader that psychology is, indeed, a science. Psychologists do have opinions, but as scientists they try their best to hold opinions that do not come out of thin air but, rather, are supported by empirical data.

Yet a psychology textbook should provide students with more than research findings. It should discuss "how we know" as well as "what we know." To give students enough background to appreciate the research process, in Chapter 2 we introduce psychology as a science, the methods of psychological research, and the statistical analysis of research data. The chapter includes a concrete example of the scientific method that shows how it relates to an engaging, classic research study on interpersonal attraction. The chapter also includes data from a hypothetical experiment on the effects of melatonin on sleep and explains how to calculate descriptive statistics using that data.

Beginning with Chapter 2, each chapter features an in-depth discussion of a research study. This **Anatomy of a Research Study** feature (retained from the fourth edition) highlights the rationale, methods, results, and interpretation of research studies in a manner accessible to beginning psychology students. The studies have been chosen for both their appeal and their ability to illustrate the scientific method. These studies include the following:

- David Buss and colleagues' (1992) evolutionary psychology study of emotional and sexual jealousy (Chapter 3)
- Nicholas Spanos and Erin Hewitt's (1980) study of hypnosis as an altered state of consciousness (Chapter 6)
- Lewis Terman's longitudinal study, the Genetic Studies of Genius (Chapter 10)

Demonstrating the Superiority of Science over Common Sense

Many psychology professors we have known have stressed the need to demonstrate that psychology is more than formalized common sense. Though common sense is often correct and functionally useful, unlike science it is not self-correcting. False commonsense beliefs might survive indefinitely—and might be held tenaciously by introductory psychology students—despite being wrong. The text provides numerous examples of the failure of commonsense beliefs to stand up to scientific challenge. Chapter 2 provides research evidence contradicting the commonsense belief that students should not change their answers on multiple-choice exams and the commonsense belief that basketball coaches should call time out to "psych out" opposing players who are about to shoot foul shots near the end of games.

To demonstrate the superiority of the scientific approach, we also have included a *new feature,* **Psychology Versus Common Sense.** This feature challenges widely held commonsense beliefs by evaluating them scientifically.

- Chapter 2 presents a study that showed how scientific research has countered the commonsense belief (upheld even in high-court decisions) that we can reliably determine if someone is legally drunk by observing their behavior.
- Chapter 5 discusses a research study indicating that it might be impossible for baseball players to follow the commonsense directive to "keep your eye on the ball" when they are at bat.
- Chapter 6 presents evidence that we do, in fact, need to sleep in order to maintain our physical health.

Showing That Psychological Research Occurs in a Sociocultural Context: Enhanced, Integrated Coverage of Culture, Ethnicity, and Gender

Perhaps the most distinctive addition in the fifth edition, primarily due to the contributions of a new co-author, Cheryl Rickabaugh, is the comprehensive, integrated coverage of psychology in regard to the sociocultural variables that affect people's lives. The presentation of psychology's social-cultural perspective has been markedly enhanced by integrating the influence of culture, ethnicity, sexual orientation, and gender throughout the text, unlike texts that include it primarily in boxes or separate chapters. For example, Chapter 2 includes a discussion of a research study that found that responses to rating scales might depend in part on one's cultural background. The discussion considers the possible cultural basis for this difference in the students' response tendencies. And Chapter 6 reports gender and ethnic differences in some aspects of the sleep cycle, noting that these differences may be attributable to variables that could vary with gender and ethnicity, such as stress levels and sleep environments.

Psychology in Everyday Life

We enjoy books that give us a sense of the author by providing "coloration" for the typically sober material that is presented. We believe that the examples we use in showing the relevance of psychology to everyday life provide this coloration. These examples come from virtually every area of life, including art, literature, history, biography, entertainment, sport, politics, and student life and are interwoven into the body of the text. For example:

- Research-based suggestions for overcoming insomnia (Chapter 6)
- How operant conditioning is used to train animals (Chapter 7)
- Ways to improve one's memory and study habits (Chapter 8)

Encouraging Critical Thinking in All Aspects of Life

If students learn nothing else from the introductory psychology course, they should learn to think more critically—that is, to be skeptical rather than gullible or cynical. Chapter 2 describes formal steps in thinking critically, and critical thinking is encouraged throughout the book. Students will find that the ability to think critically benefits them in their daily lives when confronted with claims made by friends, relatives, politicians, advertisers, or anyone else. Every chapter of the book gives the student repeated opportunities to critically assess popular claims portrayed in the media, provide alternative explanations for research findings, and think of possible implications of research findings.

In a senior seminar course that Les has taught over the years, entitled "Current Issues in Psychology," students read many journal articles and some popular articles on a host of controversial topics, which they then discussed or debated. Because of the success of this course—students enjoyed sinking their teeth into controversial issues—we have adapted its rationale for this book in the topics covered in the *new feature,* **Thinking Critically About Psychology and the Media,** throughout the book. The topics chosen for this feature promote critical thinking by showing how psychologists use reason and empirical data to tackle controversies. Some of the topics covered include the following:

- The furor over Einstein's preserved brain (Chapter 3)
- The validity of recovered memories of childhood abuse (Chapter 8)
- The controversy over *The Bell Curve* (Chapter 10)

Psychology Has a Variety of Contexts

Psychology does not exist in a vacuum. It must consider sociocultural factors, has an intellectual heritage, reflects its times, and is the product of individual human lives. That is, psychology has a variety of contexts: sociocultural, intellectual, historical, and biographical. This is stressed throughout the book.

Psychology in Sociocultural Context

Throughout the text, cross-cultural and gender differences are discussed within the context of human universals. Critical thinking about group differences must include consideration of the magnitude of these differences as well as the variables on which groups do not differ appreciably. For example, Chapter 12 reports cross-cultural differences in the experience and socialization of emotion along with studies reporting remarkable cross-cultural similarity in self-reported happiness and well-being. Moreover, the power of gender roles is emphasized in many instances when discussing gender differences. For example, in Chapters 11 and 17 we include a discussion of the influence of gender roles on body satisfaction, eating disorders, physical attractiveness, and mate selection among heterosexual women and men, lesbians, and gay men.

Psychology in Intellectual Context

Students need to realize that psychology is not intellectually homogeneous. Psychologists favor a variety of perspectives, including the psychoanalytic, the behavioristic, the cognitive, the humanistic, the biopsychological, and the social-cultural. Our text's attention to each of these perspectives reflects our belief that an introductory psychology textbook should introduce students to a variety of perspectives, rather than reflect the author's favored one. That is, the introductory psychology textbook should be fair in representing psychology's intellectual context—while being critical of the various perspectives when research findings merit it. Students are introduced to the major psychological perspectives in Chapter 1 and continue to encounter them throughout the book, most obviously in the chapters on personality, psychological disorders, and therapy.

The text takes particular topics and shows how the psychologists who represent different perspectives would approach them. For example, Chapter 14 includes a discussion of how psychologists who favor the psychoanalytic, behavioristic, cognitive, humanistic, biopsychological, and social-cultural perspectives differ in their views of the possible causes of depression.

Psychology is diverse not only in its intellectual perspectives but also in its intellectual fields. Our students often express amazement at the breadth of psychology. It's not just about "crazy people." One psychologist might devote a career to using brain-scanning techniques in studying cerebral hemispheric functions; another might devote a career to studying the relationship of childhood attachment patterns to adult romantic relationships. And while one member of a psychology department studies the causes of human aggression, another studies the nature of so-called flashbulb memories. Because of this breadth, we were forced to be selective in the topics, studies, and concepts that are included in the book. Nonetheless, we believe the book presents a representative sampling of the discipline of psychology.

Psychology in Historical Context

An article in the June 1991 issue of the *American Psychologist,* dealing with psychology and the liberal arts curriculum, stressed that providing students with the historical context of psychology is an essential goal in undergraduate psychology education. Introductory psychology textbooks should not present psychology as though it developed in "ivory towers" divorced from a historical context. Throughout this book, you will find many ways in which topics are given a historical grounding. Chapter 1 includes a discussion of the contributions made by women psychologists to the early growth of psychology—as well as the obstacles they faced. Chapter 3, by drawing a connection between Galvani's work on electricity, Mary Shelley's Frankenstein, and views on the nature of neural conduction, reveals how over the centuries activity in one area of scientific endeavor can influence theorizing in another. And Chapter 10 traces the nature-nurture debate regarding intelligence back to the work of Francis Galton in the late 19th century.

Psychology in Biographical Context

Psychology is influenced not only by the intellect of the psychologist but also by his or her own life experiences. We have attempted to show that psychology is a human endeavor, practiced by people with emotions as well as intellects, and that scientific progress depends on serendipity as well as on purposeful scientific pursuits. Evidence of this is presented throughout the text. For example, Chapter 3 tells how the first demonstration of the chemical basis of communication between nerve cells came to Otto Loewi in a dream. And Chapter 7 explains why the name *Pavlov* rings a bell but the name *Twitmyer* does not. Students tend to find this biographical information engaging, making them more likely to read assigned material in the text.

CHAPTER-SPECIFIC CHANGES

There were a number of specific changes to this edition:

Chapter 1: The Nature of Psychology

- Integrated The Role of Women in the Early History of Psychology into its own subsection in the history section of the chapter. Additional women psychologists were also included.
- The social-cultural perspective was developed, including ethnic psychology.

Chapter 2: Psychology as a Science

- Made examples/definition of external validity more inclusive and developed the section on meta-analysis as a tool for understanding group differences and similarities.
- Changed coverage of Sources of Knowledge to a comparison of common sense and science.
- Added basic description of meta-analysis to statistics section.
- Integrated Ethics of Psychological Research by moving it from the chapter-ending Thinking About Psychology section to its own section.

Chapter 3: Behavioral Neuroscience

- Added coverage of evolutionary psychology (also developed in Chapters 10, 11, 13 and 17), including evolutionary psychology's hypotheses and research findings on human mate selection.
- Integrated Hemispheric Specialization by moving it from the chapter-ending Thinking About Psychology section to its own subsection in the Brain section of the chapter.
- Added discussion of SPECT and SQUID in section on Techniques for Studying the Brain
- Added additional studies that considered moderating variables—the extent to which women are denied power in certain cultures as well as individual differences in tolerance of gender inequality.
- Added section on gender differences on hemispheric lateralization. Also included coverage of fetal environments differing hormonally to set the stage for the lateralization discussion as well as the gender differences section in the next chapter.

Chapter 4: Human Development

- Integrated Sex Differences by moving it from the chapter-ending Thinking About Psychology feature to its own section.
- The prenatal sexual differentiation, puberty, and aging sections were rewritten to include females (in the former), and gender differences and similarities in physical development.
- Cutting-edge research on hormone replacement therapy and women's cognitive abilities in old age was added.
- Attention is devoted to developing the relationship of gender to physical health and aging.
- Cross-cultural studies were added throughout. The attachment section was extensively rewritten to include fathers and multiple attachments. Research on ethnic identity was also introduced.
- One of the most extensive changes was reconceptualizing the definition of families and couple relationships.

Chapter 5: Sensation and Perception

- Cross-cultural studies have been added. The feature on cultural differences in pain perception introduces the experience of childbirth.
- Color blindness was discussed more in depth in terms of being a sex-linked trait.

Chapter 6: Consciousness

- Added discussion of an interesting study (Maquet et al., 2000) that used the PET scan to demonstrate that REM sleep helps in the processing of memories of daytime events.
- Integrated the unconscious by moving it from the chapter-ending Thinking About Psychology feature to the opening section of the chapter.
- Added discussion of MDE and MDMA, two of the new "club drugs."
- The section on sleep and dreams was edited considerably to include social-cultural factors.

Chapter 7: Learning

- Integrated Biofeedback (condensed) by moving it from the chapter-ending Thinking About Psychology feature to its own section.

Chapter 8: Memory

- Integrated Eyewitness Testimony by moving it from the chapter-ending Thinking About Psychology feature to its own section. This section contains considerable cross-cultural evidence for differences and similarities. In addition, research evidence was added for eyewitness error in identifying out-group targets, a difference that is consistent across the ethnic groups mentioned in the text.
- Cross-cultural studies as well as research in gender schema were introduced.

Chapter 9: Thinking and Language

- Integrated Language in Apes by moving it from the chapter-ending Thinking About Psychology feature to its own section.
- Added studies on gender and cultural differences in creativity. The cross-cultural research also included the study of differential processing of click consonants among speakers of African tone languages.
- Moved language acquisition from caregiver-child dyads to the polyadic relationships in other cultures. The addition of Hyde's classic study of nonsexist language feature was also an important addition.

Chapter 10: Intelligence

- Added discussion of Claude Steele's notion of stereotype threat as a factor in African Americans' performance on IQ tests.
- Integrated Nature, Nurture, and Intelligence by moving it from the chapter-ending Thinking About Psychology feature to its own section.
- Added Helen Thompson Woolley and Leta Stetter Hollingworth and the history of assessing gender differences in IQ and added gender differences in studies of genius, emphasizing sociohistorical factors underlying cohort differences.
- Added findings of research in behavioral genetics.

Chapter 11: Motivation

- Integrated Sport Psychology by including material from the chapter-ending Thinking About Psychology feature into the Arousal Motive and Achievement Motive sections of the chapter.
- Introduced research on the interaction of gender and sexual orientation.
- Examples of the influence of gender, ethnicity, and sexual orientation are discussed in the section on body image as well as cross-cultural differences in the prevalence of eating disorders.
- Included discussion of Baumeister's recent article on erotic plasticity and Diamond's work on sexual minority women.

Chapter 12: Emotion

- Integrated the Lie Detector section by moving it from the chapter-ending Thinking About Psychology feature to its own subsection within the Biopsychology of Emotion section.
- Added discussion of an interesting study (Hariri et al., 2000) using functional MRI to show activity changes in the amygdala and frontal lobes related to different emotional states.
- Increased the number of studies investigating the role of gender and culture in emotion, including extensively revising coverage of the relation of gender-role socialization to perceivers' responses to men's and women's emotional expression.
- Included cross-cultural studies that investigate differences in the socialization of emotion as well as similarities in happiness and well-being.

Chapter 13: Personality

- Added a section on Horney's theory of Feminine Psychology and a section on Schema Theory.
- Integrated the Personality Consistency section by moving it from the chapter-ending Thinking About Psychology feature to its own subsection within the Dispositional Approach to Personality section.
- Increased the visibility of women in the discussion of the neo-Freudians, cross-cultural studies of the validity of personality trait models, and the development of schema theory.
- Introduced Markus and Kitayama's model of culture and the self and included changes relevant to cross-cultural psychology focusing on the dimension of collectivism-individualism.

Chapter 14: Psychological Disorders

- Moved Insanity Defense section from chapter-ending Thinking About Psychology feature to a Thinking About Psychology and the Media section early in the chapter.
- Added discussion of Borderline Personality Disorder.
- Increased coverage of the social-cultural perspective. Inclusiveness was increased substantially.
- Research in this chapter discusses the influence of ethnicity, culture, and gender on psychopathology.

Chapter 15: Therapy

- Added discussion of the National Multicultural Training Conference that introduces the concept of cultural competence, which has been woven throughout the text's coverage of different therapeutic models.
- Cultural competence is discussed in terms of cross-cultural studies and studies of sexual and ethnic minorities.

Chapter 16: Psychology and Health

- Integrated Type A Behavior by moving it from the chapter-ending Thinking About Psychology section to the section on Stress and Cardiovascular Disease.
- Studies of gender and ethnic differences in health-related attitudes and behaviors are integrated throughout this chapter, including discussion of the prevalence of HIV infection among heterosexual women.
- The relation of gender and ethnicity to the types of stressors people experience also was included.

Chapter 17: Social Psychology

- Included cutting-edge cross-cultural research in social cognition.
- Discussion of gendered aggression was included in this chapter.

PEDAGOGICAL FEATURES

Chapter Features

- *New!* **Psychology Versus Common Sense:** This is an interesting feature that examines commonsense notions in light of research. It presents the scientific backing (or the lack of) behind them.
- *New!* **Thinking Critically About Psychology and the Media:** This cutting-edge feature focuses on various types of media. It examines the validity of media reports by using actual research studies on the topic. The idea is to teach students to evaluate information critically—to never accept what you read at face value.
- **Anatomy of a Research Study:** Based on the popular *Anatomy of a Classic/Contemporary Research Study,* this feature focuses on contextualizing theories, showing students how scientists arrive at findings and how research evolves. The last edition presented one of each research study in each chapter. This edition has integrated many of those studies into the text and reported new studies that continue to present a balance of both classic and contemporary studies. It is found once in Chapters 2–17 and has multiple headings to help organize the material: Rationale, Method, and Results.
- *New!* **Web Icons:** Ten web icons appear in the margins of each chapter. The icons direct the reader to websites that contain material complementing information presented in the chapter.
- *New!* **Thought Questions:** At the end of each chapter is a list of applied and critical thinking questions based on the material in the chapter. This reinforcing exercise provides feedback to students about their comprehension of the chapter content.

Chapter Pedagogy

- **Staying on Track:** Each of the major sections within the chapter ends with a self-quiz called *Staying on Track.* These quizzes encourage readers to pause and assess whether they can recall and comprehend important information from the relevant section. The quizzes include factual, conceptual, and applied questions. Answers to all of the questions are provided at the end of the book.
- **Chapter Summary:** Each chapter ends with a bulleted *Chapter Summary* that captures the essential points made in the major sections of the chapter. The summaries provide quick overviews that will help students master what they have read.
- **Key Concepts and Key Contributors:** Each chapter includes lists of *Key Concepts* and *Key Contributors* that were discussed in the chapter. The lists are arranged alphabetically and indicate the pages on which the terms and contributors were discussed. The lists should help students in reviewing and studying for their exams.
- **Illustrations:** We selected or helped design all of the illustrations in this book. In doing so, we tried to make each of them serve a sound pedagogical purpose. Though the illustrations make the book aesthetically more appealing, they were chosen chiefly because their visual presentations complement material discussed in the text.
- **Running Marginal Glossary:** A running marginal glossary is integrated throughout the book. Terms that are printed in boldface in the text are defined in the margins. The marginal definitions are also collected in a page-referenced glossary at the end of the book.

ACKNOWLEDGMENTS

We would like to thank our McGraw-Hill editors who have helped us with the fifth edition. They include Joe Terry, Sylvia Shepherd, Hélène Greenwood, Mindy DePalma, and Melissa Mashburn. Special thanks go to Mary Powers, who guided the production of the book under tight deadlines while somehow managing to maintain her pleasant, friendly manner and being helpful to us in every possible way. The physical attractiveness of the book owes much to the expertise of book designer Stuart Paterson, and photo editor Lori Hancock. The book also benefited from the input of our conscientious permissions editor Terri Hampton and our outstanding photo researcher Toni Michaels.

We would also like to thank those who contributed to the supplements that are available with this book: Jody Davis, Sue Frantz, Jeff Greene, and Jan Kottke.

Thanks to Paul Levy for writing the excellent appendix on industrial/organizational psychology.

The quality of the book was enhanced by input from the many reviewers who provided us with thoughtful advice on each of the chapters.

Thanks to the following reviewers of the Fifth Edition:

Ute Johanna Bayen, *University of North Carolina, Chapel Hill*
Bethany Neal-Beliveau, *Indiana University–Purdue University Indianapolis*
Dennis Cogan, *Texas Technical University*
Ken Cramer, *University of Windsor*
Richard Cribs, *Motlow State Community College*
Hank Davis, *University of Guelph*
Scott Dickman, *University of Massachusetts, Dartmouth*
Karen Kopera-Frye, *University of Akron*
Larry Fujinaka, *Leeward Community College*

Preston E. Garraghty, *Indiana University*
Janet Gebelt, *University of Portland*
Sandy Grossman, *Clackamas Community College*
Deanna Julka, *University of Portland*
Janet L. Kottke, *California State University, San Bernardino*
Joan B. Lauer, *Indiana University– Purdue University Indianapolis*
Ting Lei, *Borough of Manhattan Community College*
Dennis Lorenz, *University of Wisconsin*
James Mottin, *University of Guelph*
Christopher Pagano, *Clemson University*
Richard Pisacreta, *Ferris State University*

Karen Quigley, *Pennsylvania State University*
Robert W. Ridel, *Maryhurst University*
Linda Robertello, *Iona College*
Sonya M. Sheffert, *Central Michigan University*
NC Silver, *University of Nevada, Las Vegas*
Lisa Valentino, *Seminole Community College*
Frank Vattano, *Colorado State University*
Amy Wilkerson, *Stephen F. Austin State University*
Michael Zicker, *Bowling Green University*

Thanks to the following reviewers of the Fourth Edition:

Ronald Baenninger, *Temple University*
Robert C. Beck, *Wake Forest University*
John Benjafield, *Brock University*
Linda Brannon, *McNeese State University*
John B. Connors, *Canadian Union College*
Stanley Coren, *University of British Columbia*
Randolph Cornelius, *Vassar College*
Verne C. Cox, *University of Texas at Arlington*
Deanna L. Dodson, *Lebanon Valley College*
Donald K. Freedheim, *Case Western Reserve University*

Ajaipal S. Gill, *Anne Arundel Community College*
Morton G. Harmatz, *University of Massachusetts, Amherst*
Debra L. Hollister, *Valencia Community College*
Daniel Houlihan, *Mankato State University*
Lera Joyce Jonson, *Centenary College*
Stanley K. Kary, *St. Louis Community College at Florrissant Valley*
Richard Lippa, *California State University, Fullerton*
Gerald McRoberts, *Stanford University*

Ralph Miller, *State University of New York, Binghamton*
Joel Morgovsky, *Brookdale Community College*
Ian Neath, *Purdue University*
Brent D. Slife, *Brigham Young University*
Michael D. Spiegler, *Providence College*
George T. Taylor, *University of Missouri, St. Louis*
Benjamin Wallace, *Cleveland State University*
Wilse Webb, *University of Florida, Gainsville*
Ian Wishaw, *University of Lethbridge*

Les would like to thank his colleagues at Arcadia University—especially his department chairperson, Barbara Nodine—for providing him with the opportunity to teach in a psychology department that is dedicated to excellence in undergraduate psychology. Les also has benefited from the continued support of his brother Eric Sdorow and his sister-in-law Connie Sdorow; his cousins Caryn Stark, Joel Steinger, and Dawna Gold; his aunt and uncle Shirley and Harold Lustbader; and his friends Herb Millman, John Dwyer, Carla Fuentes, Lino Fuentes, Phillip Lloyd Powell, Vincent Ceglia, Jan Witte, Paul Witte, Charles Olson, Martha Boston, Annette Benert, Gregg Amore, and Michael Lange. A special thank you goes from Les to Janis Landgraf and her wonderful children Amanda, Emily, Jameson, Joshua, Luke, Jordan, and Peter, who always bring a ray of sunshine into his life.

Cheryl also thanks her colleagues at the University of Redlands, especially Susan Goldstein who cheerfully shared her expertise in cross-cultural psychology and Sandi Richey for her help in researching the text. Cheryl also thanks her parents, John and Marcella Rickabaugh; her sister, Gail Rickabaugh; and her friends Jill Borchert, Emily Culpepper, Kathie Jenni, Susanne Johnston, Susanne Pastuschek, and Judy Tschann for their love and support.

SUPPLEMENTS

Students

Making the Grade Student CD-ROM

Packaged for FREE, this user-friendly CD-ROM gives students an opportunity to test their comprehension of the course material in a manner that is most comfortable and beneficial to them. The CD-ROM opens with a Learning Style/Study Skills questionnaire. Also included are practice tests that cover topics in the introductory psychology course, an Internet primer, and a statistics primer.

In-Psych CD-ROM

In-Psych sets a new standard for introductory psychology multimedia. Every **In-Psych** CD-ROM is organized according to the textbook the CD accompanies and features 70 interactive exercises chosen to illustrate especially difficult core introductory psychology concepts. Each exercise showcases one of three types of media assets—an audio clip, a video clip, or a simulation—and includes a pre-test, follow-up assignments, and web resources. **In-Psych** also includes chapter quizzes, a student research guide, and an interactive timeline that puts events, key figures, and research in psychology in historical perspective. A learning style assessment tool helps students identify what kind of learners they are—kinesthetic, auditory, or visual—and then provides them with study tips tailored to their own particular learning style.

Student Study Guide

For each chapter of the text, the student is provided with Learning Objectives, Chapter Outline (new), Key Concepts (new), Key Contributors (new), Guided Review (for each section), Mini Review (matching), Practice Test, Essay Questions, Fill-in labels (new), and Transparency Masters (new).

Online Learning Center

The official website for the text contains Chapter Outlines, Practice Quizzes that can be emailed to the professor, internet exercises based on all boxed features in the book, Interactive Exercises, Links to Working the Web sites, Recommended Readings, Internet Primer, Becoming a Psychology Major, and a Statistics Primer. www.mhhe.com/Sdorow5

Instructors

Instructor's Manual

This instructor's manual provides many useful tools to enhance your teaching. For each chapter you will find Learning Objectives, Chapter Outlines, Key Concepts (new), Key Contributors (new), Teaching the Chapter, Lecture/Discussion suggestions, Classroom Activities (new), Experiencing Psychology boxed feature (new), Critical Thinking questions, Video/Media Suggestions, References, and Sources of Biographical Information.

Test Bank

A *Test Item File* with questions for all seventeen chapters will be available to instructors who adopt *Psychology, 5e.* The questions in the *Test Item File* are also available on **Diploma Testing Software,** a powerful but easy-to-use test-generating program by Brownstone Research Group. Diploma is available for your use in a cross-platform CD-ROM. With its Test Generator, On-Line Testing Program, Internet Testing, and Grade Management Systems, Diploma is instructor-friendly software.

PowerPoint® Lectures

Available on the book's website and the Instructor's Resource CD, these presentations cover the key points of the chapter and include charts and graphs from the text where relevant. They can be used as is or modified to meet your personal needs.

Overhead Transparencies

Over 70 key images drawn directly from this textbook are available for the instructor upon adoption. In addition, the *Introductory Psychology Transparency Set* provides over 100 additional transparencies illustrating key concepts in general psychology.

Online Learning Center

This collection of Student and Instructor resources contains a wealth of additional materials. The password-protected Instructor side of the site contains the Instructor's Manual, Power-Point Presentations, Experiencing Psychology feature, Web Links, Image Gallery, and other teaching resources.

Instructor's Resoure CD

Includes the contents of the Instructor's Manual, Test Bank, Image Gallery, and PowerPoint® slides. The Instructor's Resource CD provides an easy-to-use interface for the design and delivery of multimedia classroom presentations.

PageOut- Build your own course website in less than an hour.

You don't have to be a computer whiz to create a website, especially with an exclusive McGraw-Hill product called PageOut™. It requires no prior knowledge of HTML, no long hours of coding, and no design skills on your part. With PageOut even the most inexperienced computer user can quickly and easily create a professional-looking course website.

Realizing that the ideal textbook might be approached but never achieved, we welcome your comments about the book and suggestions for improving it. Just as user comments improved the previous editions, more comments will improve the next edition. Please send your correspondence to Psychology Editor, McGraw-Hill College Division, 699 Boylston Street, Boston, MA 02116.

Les Sdorow
Cheryl Rickabaugh

To the Students

PSYCHOLOGY VERSUS COMMON SENSE

This is an interesting feature that examines commonsense notions in light of research. It presents the scientific backing (or the lack of) behind these issues.

Psychology Versus Common Sense

Can Baseball Batters Really Keep Their Eyes on the Ball?

Professional athletes make faster smooth-pursuit eye movements than amateurs do (Harbin, Durst, & Harbin, 1989). This is important because, for example, a professional baseball batter might have to track a baseball thrown by a pitcher at more than 90 miles an hour from a distance of only 60 feet. Ted Williams, arguably the greatest hitter in the history of baseball, called hitting a baseball the most difficult single task in any sport. Given this, is there any scientific support for the commonsense suggestion to batters, "Keep your eye on the ball"? Let's look at a study by Terry Bahill and Tom LaRitz (1984), of the University of Arizona, in which they sought the answer to this question. Bahill and LaRitz rigged a device that propelled a ball toward home plate along a string at up to 100 miles an hour on a consistent path. A photoelectric device recorded the batter's eye movements as he tracked the ball. Several professional baseball players took part in the study.

Eye-movement recordings indicated the batters were able to track the ball until it was about 5 feet from home plate. Over the last few feet they could not keep the ball focused on their foveae—it simply traveled too fast over those last few degrees of visual arc. Thus, the commonsense advice to keep your eye on the ball is well intentioned, but it is impossible to follow the ball's movement all the way from the pitcher's hand to home plate. The reason some hitters, including Ted Williams, claim they can see the ball strike the bat is that, based on their extensive experience in batting, their brains automatically calculate both the speed and the trajectory of the ball. This allows them to anticipate the point in space where the bat will meet the ball, and make a final eye movement to that exact point. Years later Bahill likewise presented research evidence contradicting the commonsense belief that fastballs can "rise" (Bahill & Karnavas, 1993). To baseball players, as well as other people, "seeing is believing." Nonetheless, scientists insist that objective evidence from research is superior to common sense as a source of knowledge.

Your Eye on the Ball
...sense idea that batters can "keep their eye... ...s not supported by research. Professional ...s Sammy Sosa, anticipate the point in ...the bat will meet the ball and make a final ...t to that point.

...pter 3), which transmits visual infor- ...tinal information about objects in the ...and retinal information about objects ...tal lobe. The visual cortex integrates ...e (Buechel et al., 1998) and distance ...999), brightness (Rossi, Rittenhouse, ...999).

visual cortex
The area of the occipital lobes that processes visual input.

Thinking Critically About Psychology and the Media

Does the Insanity Defense Let Many Violent Criminals Escape Punishment?

Spurred by the media's coverage of the successful insanity plea of John Hinckley, Jr., following his attempted assassination of President Ronald Reagan in 1981, many people have criticized the insanity defense as a miscarriage of justice. But do the Hinckley case and other cases portrayed in the media indicate that many people have gotten away with murder by using the insanity defense?

◀ **The Insanity Defense**
John Hinckley, Jr., was found not guilty (by reason of insanity) of his attempted assassination of President Reagan.

insanity
A legal term attesting that a person is not responsible for his or her own actions, including criminal behavior.

The Nature of the Insanity Defense

Insanity is a legal, not a psychological or psychiatric, term attesting that a person is not responsible for his or her own actions. The insanity defense was formalized in 1843 in the case of Daniel M'Naghten, a paranoid schizophrenic man who had tried to murder the English prime minister Robert Peel. But M'Naghten killed Peel's secretary Edward Drummond by mistake. After a controversial trial, M'Naghten was ruled not guilty by reason of insanity and was committed to a mental hospital. *The M'Naghten rule* became a guiding principle in English law. The rule states that a person is not guilty if, at the time of a crime, the person did not know what she or he was doing or did not know that it was wrong.

Today the most widely used standard for determining insanity in the United States comprises two rules. First, the *cognitive rule,* similar to the M'Naghten rule, says that a person was insane at the time of a crime if the person did not know what he or she had done or did not know that it was wrong. Based on this rule, some defendants who have killed a person while sleepwalking have been acquitted of murder charges (Thomas, 1997).

Second, the *volitional rule* says that a person was insane at the time of a crime if the person was not in voluntary control of her or his behavior. In 1857, in an early use of the volitional rule, Abraham Lincoln—then an attorney in Illinois—prosecuted a case in which defense attorneys claimed a defendant was insane at the time he committed a murder because he was under the influence of chloroform, a drug that can induce anesthesia (Spiegel & Suskind, 1998).

THINKING CRITICALLY ABOUT PSYCHOLOGY AND THE MEDIA

This cutting-edge feature focuses on various types of media. It examines the validity of media reports by using actual research studies on the topic. The idea is to teach students to evaluate information critically—to never accept what you read at face value.

Anatomy of a Research Study

Can the Immune Response Be Altered by Classical Conditioning?

Rationale

Certain chemicals can enhance or suppress the immune response. Researcher Robert Ader wondered whether such a chemical could be used as the basis for classically conditioning the immune response. He reasoned that a neutral stimulus paired with the chemical might come to have the same effect on the immune response. This possibility inspired him to test his hypothesis experimentally.

Method

Ader and his colleague Nicholas Cohen (1982) used the drug cyclophosphamide, which suppresses the immune system, as the unconditioned stimulus. When mice were injected with the drug, they experienced both nausea and immunosuppression—dual effects of the drug. Ader and Cohen used saccharin-flavored water as the neutral stimulus. They hoped that if the mice drank it before being injected with the drug, the taste of sweet water would suppress their immune response to an antigen.

Results and Discussion

As Ader and Cohen expected, the mice developed an aversion to sweet-tasting water, because they associated it with nausea caused by the drug. But when some of them were later forced to drink sweet-tasting water, several developed illnesses and died. Ader and Cohen attributed this to conditioned suppression of the mice's immune response, with the sweet-tasting water having become a conditioned stimulus after being paired with the drug (see Figure 16.3). Many subsequent studies have provided additional evidence that the immune response is subject to classical conditioning (Exton et al., 2000). Animal research indicates that epinephrine and norepinephrine mediate conditioned immunosuppression (Lysle, Cunnick, & Maslonek, 1991).

▶ **Figure 16.3**
Conditioned Immunosuppression
When Ader and Cohen (1982) paired saccharin-sweetened water with cyclophosphamide, a drug that suppresses the immune response, they found that the sweet-tasting water itself came to elicit immunosuppression. (See Chapter 7 for a discussion of the relationship between the UCS, UCR, CS, and CR.)

Step 1

UCS ⟶ UCR
(drug) (immunosuppression)

Step 2

CS + UCS ⟶ UCR
(sweet-tasting water + drug) (immunosuppression)

Step 3

CS ⟶ CR
(sweet-tasting water) (immunosuppression)

◆ **FACTORS THAT MODERATE THE STRESS RESPONSE**

More than 2,000 years ago, Hippocrates recognized the relationship between individual factors and physiological responses when he observed that it is more important to know what sort of person has a disease than to know what sort of disease a person has. Because of variability among individuals, a given stressor will not evoke the same response in every person. Our reactions to stress are moderated by a variety of factors. These include *physiological reactivity, cognitive appraisal, explanatory style, perceived control, psychological hardiness,* and *social support.*

ANATOMY OF A RESEARCH STUDY

This feature focuses on contextualizing theories—showing students how scientists arrive at findings and how research evolves. The last edition presented one of each research study in each chapter. This edition has integrated many of those studies into the text and reported new studies that continue to present a balance of both classic and contemporary studies. It has multiple headings to help organize the material: Rationale, Method, and Results and Discussion.

ILLUSTRATIONS

We selected or helped design all of the illustration in this book. In doing so, we tried to make each of them serve a sound pedagogical purpose. Though the illustrations make the book aesthetically more appealing, they were chosen chiefly because their visual presentations complement material discussed in the text.

Table 5.1	Sound Levels (Decibels) of Some Everyday Noises	
Harmful to Hearing	140	Jet engine (25 m distance)
	130	Jet takeoff (100 m away)
		Threshold of pain
	120	Propeller aircraft
Risk Hearing Loss	110	Live rock band
	100	Jackhammer/pneumatic chipper
	90	Heavy-duty truck
		Los Angeles, third-floor apartment next to freeway
		Average street traffic
Very Noisy	80	Harlem, second-floor apartment
Urban	70	Private car
		Boston row house on major avenue
		Business office
		Watts—8 miles from touch down at major airport
	60	Conversational speech or old residential area in L.A.
Suburban and Small Town	50	San Diego—wooded residential area
	40	California tomato field
		Soft music from radio
	30	Quiet whisper
	20	Quiet urban dwelling
	10	Rustle of leaf
	0	Threshold of hearing

Source: Reprinted with permission from *Science News*, the weekly newsmagazine of science. Copyright 1982 by Science Service, Inc.

WEB ICONS

Ten Web icons appear in the margins of each chapter. The icons direct the reader to websites that contain material complementing information presented in the chapter.

H.E.A.R: Hearing Education and Awareness for Rockers
www.mhhe.com/sdorow5

RUNNING MARGINAL GLOSSARY

A running marginal glossary is integrated throughout the book. Terms that are printed in **boldface** in the text are defined in the margins. The marginal definitions are also collected in a page-referenced glossary at the end of the book.

conduction deafness
Hearing loss usually caused by blockage of the auditory canal, damage to the eardrum, or deterioration of the ossicles of the middle ear.

hearing. In contrast, the typical 90-year-old in rural African tribes, whose surroundings only occasionally produce loud sounds, has better hearing than the typical 30-year-old North American (Raloff, 1982).

In extreme cases, individuals can lose more than their high-frequency hearing. They can become deaf. In **conduction deafness,** there is a mechanical problem in the outer or middle ear that interferes with hearing. The auditory canal might be filled with wax, the eardrum might be punctured, or the ossicles might be fused and inflexible. Conduction deafness caused by deterioration of the ossicles can be treated by surgical replacement with plastic ossicles. Conduction deafness is more often overcome by hearing aids, which amplify sound waves that enter the ear.

STAYING ON TRACK: *Body Senses*

1. What is the kinesthetic sense?
2. What is the role of the vestibular sense in motion sickness?

Answers to Staying on Track start on p. ST-3.

◆ EXTRASENSORY PERCEPTION

extrasensory perception (ESP)
The alleged ability to perceive events without the use of sensory receptors.

parapsychology
The study of extrasensory perception, psychokinesis, and related phenomena.

As you have just read, perception depends on the stimulation of sensory receptors by various kinds of energy. But you have certainly heard claims that support the possibility of perception independent of sensory receptors, so-called **extrasensory perception (ESP)**. The field that studies ESP and related phenomena is called **parapsychology** (*para-* means "besides"). The name indicates its failure to gain widespread acceptance within mainstream psychology. Parapsychological abilities are typically called *paranormal*.

Despite scientific skepticism about paranormal abilities, a survey found that more than 99 percent of American college students believed in at least one paranormal ability and that more than 65 percent claimed a personal experience with at least one (Messer & Griggs, 1989). Moreover, mainstream journals in psychology, philosophy, and medicine periodically publish articles on paranormal abilities. Public belief in paranormal abilities was exemplified in a 1986 lawsuit in which a Philadelphia woman who made a living as a psychic sued a hospital, insisting that a CT scan of her head made her lose her ESP abilities. A jury, impressed by the testimony of police officers who claimed she had helped them solve

STAYING ON TRACK

Each of the major sections within the chapter ends with a self-quiz called *Staying on Track.* These quizzes encourage readers to pause and assess whether they can recall and comprehend important information from the relevant section. The quizzes include factual, conceptual, and applied questions. Answers to all of the questions are provided at the end of the book.

CHAPTER SUMMARY

Each chapter ends with a bulleted *Chapter Summary* that captures the essential points made in the major sections of the chapter. The summaries provide quick overviews that will help students master what they have read.

Chapter Summary

SENSORY PROCESSES

• Sensation is the process that detects stimuli from one's body or environment.
• Perception is the process that organizes sensations into meaningful patterns.
• Psychophysics is the study of the relationship between the physical characteristics of stimuli and the conscious psychological experiences they produce.
• The minimum amount of stimulation that can be detected is called the absolute threshold.
• According to signal-detection theory, the detection of a stimulus depends on both its intensity and the physiological and psychological state of the receiver.
• Research on subliminal perception investigates whether participants can unconsciously perceive stimuli that do not exceed the absolute threshold.
• The minimum amount of change in stimulation that can be detected is called the difference threshold.

• The lens focuses light onto the rods and cones of the retina.
• Visual input is transmitted by the optic nerves to the brain, ultimately reaching the visual cortex.
• During dark adaptation the rods and cones become more sensitive to light, with the rods becoming significantly more sensitive than the cones.
• The trichromatic theory of color vision considers the interaction of red, green, and blue cones.
• Opponent-process theory assumes that color vision depends on activity in red-green, blue-yellow, and black-white ganglion cells and cells in the thalamus.
• Color blindness is usually caused by an inherited lack of a cone pigment.

VISUAL PERCEPTION

• Form perception depends on distinguishing figure from ground.
• In studying form perception, Gestalt psychologists identified the principles of proximity, similarity, closure, and continuity.

Key Concepts

THE NATURE OF CONSCIOUSNESS
attention 178
automatic processing 180
conscious mind 177
consciousness 177
controlled processing 180
perception without awareness 179
preconscious mind 181
subliminal psychodynamic activation 181
unconscious mind 181

SLEEP
biological rhythms 183

circadian rhythms 183
insomnia 191
narcolepsy 191
NREM sleep 185
phase advance 183
phase delay 183
pineal gland 183
REM sleep 185
sleep apnea 191

DREAMS
activation-synthesis theory 196
dream 192
latent content 194
lucid dreaming 194
manifest content 194

nightmare 193
night terror 193

HYPNOSIS
age regression 201
dissociation 199
hidden observer 199
hypermnesia 198
hypnosis 196
neodissociation theory 199
posthypnotic suggestions 198

PSYCHOACTIVE DRUGS
amphetamines 205
barbiturates 203
caffeine 204

cannabis sativa 206
cocaine 205
depressants 202
entactogens 207
ethyl alcohol 202
hallucinogens 205
LSD 206
nicotine 205
opiates 204
psychoactive drugs 201
stimulants 204
synesthesia 206

KEY CONCEPTS AND KEY CONTRIBUTORS

Each chapter includes lists of *Key Concepts* and *Key Contributors* that were discussed in the chapter. The list is arranged alphabetically and indicate the pages on which the terms and contributors were discussed. The list should help students in reviewing and studying for their exams.

Key Contributors

SENSORY PROCESSES
Gustav Fechner 134
Ernst Weber 134

VISUAL SENSATION
Russell de Valois 144
Hermann von Helmholtz 144
Ewald Hering 145

George Wald 145
Thomas Young 144

VISUAL PERCEPTION
James J. Gibson 147
David Hubel and Torsten Wiesel 148
Max Wertheimer 147

HEARING
Georg von Békésy 159
Ernest Wever 159

CHEMICAL SENSES
Linda Bartoshuk 163

SKIN SENSES
Ronald Melzack and Patrick Wall 166

EXTRASENSORY PERCEPTION
James Randi 171
J. B. Rhine 171
Gertrude Schmeidler 172

THOUGHT QUESTIONS

At the end of each chapter is a list of applied and critical thinking questions based on the material in the chapter. This reinforcing exercise provides feedback to students about their comprehension of the chapter content.

Thought Questions

1. Why is it conceivable that creatures on planets in other solar systems have evolved sensory receptors that detect radio and television waves?
2. How does the opponent-process theory of color vision explain afterimages?

3. Why are both frequency and place theories needed to explain pitch perception?
4. Why do psychologists tend to discount the existence of paranormal abilities?

Possible Answers to Thought Questions start on p. PT-2.

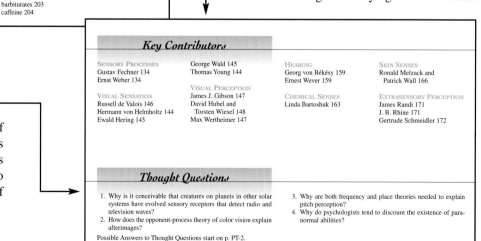

psychology

The Nature of Psychology

CHARLES OLSON
Recognition, 1993

On April 20, 1999, Americans were shocked when two students went on a shooting rampage at Columbine High School in Littleton, Colorado. The students, Eric Harris, age 18, and Dylan Klebold, age 17—armed with pistols, rifles, shotguns, and homemade bombs—held their fellow students and teachers hostage and over the course of several hours, coldly, and with apparent pleasure, killed one teacher and 12 students and wounded 23 other students. The two then committed suicide. It took days for the police to defuse about thirty bombs Harris and Klebold had planted in the school to maim or kill would-be rescuers. Harris and Klebold were members of the so-called Trench Coat Mafia, an "antijock" group of students who wore black clothing and ridiculed students who conformed to traditional social norms.

◀ **Psychology and Violence**
Psychologists are interested in discovering the causes of violence and preventing it, as in deadly rampages such as the one at Columbine High School in Colorado in 1999.

What would lead two intelligent teenagers from apparently stable, affluent families to commit such heinous acts? How can we prevent other incidents like it? How can we help the survivors cope with the tragedy? School violence has become an important issue. What happened at Columbine High School was not an isolated incident. Similar tragedies have occurred at other American schools in the past few years—in towns such as Pearl, Mississippi; West Paducah, Kentucky; Jonesboro, Arkansas; and Springfield, Oregon. Because violence of all kinds pervades many societies, it is of great concern to psychologists.

The science of *psychology* seeks answers to questions about violence and other aspects of human and animal behavior, such as these: Do attachment patterns in infancy predict attachment patterns in dating relationships? Do eyewitnesses give accurate testimony? Can chimpanzees learn to use language? Do lie detectors really detect lies? Is there a heart-attack-prone personality? These are some of the hundreds of questions about human and animal behavior discussed in upcoming chapters.

But what is psychology? The word *psychology* was coined in the 16th century from the Greek terms *psyche*, meaning "soul," and *logos*, meaning "the study of a subject." Thus, the initial meaning of *psychology* was "the study of the soul" (Lapointe, 1970). This reflected the early interest of theologians in topics that are now considered the province of psychologists. Psychology has continued to be defined by its subject matter, which has changed over time. By the late 19th century, when psychology emerged as a science, it had become "the Science of Mental Life" (James, 1890/1981, Vol. 1, p. 15).

Beginning in the second decade of the 20th century, many psychologists—believing that a true science can study only directly observable, measurable events—abandoned the study of the mind in favor of the study of overt behavior. This meant that most psychologists moved from studying mental experiences, such as thirst or anger, to studying their observable manifestations, such as drinking or aggression. Consequently, by the 1920s psychology was commonly defined as "the scientific study of behavior." This definition was dominant until the 1960s, when there was a revival of interest in studying the mind. As a result, **psychology** is now more broadly defined as "the science of behavior and mental processes."

What makes psychology a science? Psychology is a science because it relies on the *scientific method*. Sciences are "scientific" because they share a common method, not because they share a common subject matter. Physics, chemistry, biology, and psychology differ in what they study, yet each uses the scientific method. While a chemist might use the scientific method in studying the effects of toxic pollutants, a psychologist might use it in studying the behavior or mental experiences of a person suffering from severe depression. The role of the scientific method in psychology is discussed in Chapter 2.

◆ THE HISTORY OF PSYCHOLOGY

Like any other science, psychology has evolved over time. It has been influenced by developments in other disciplines and by its social, cultural, and historical contexts. To appreciate the state of psychology today, you should understand its origins (Danziger, 1994).

The Roots of Psychology

Psychology's historical roots are in philosophy and science. When scientists of the late 19th century began to use the scientific method to study the mind, psychology became an independent scientific discipline. Though scientists and philosophers alike rely on systematic observation and reasoning as sources of knowledge, philosophers rely more on reasoning. For example, whereas a philosopher might use reasoning to argue whether we are ever truly altruistic (that is, completely unselfish) in helping other people, a psychologist might approach this issue by studying the emotional and situational factors that determine whether one person will help another (see Chapter 17).

The Philosophical Roots of Psychology

The philosophical roots of psychology reach back to the philosophers of ancient Greece, most notably Plato (c. 428–347 B.C.) and his pupil Aristotle (384–322 B.C.), who were especially interested in the origin of knowledge. Plato noted that our senses can deceive us, as in illusions like the apparent bending of a straight stick partly immersed in a pool of water. Downplaying knowledge gained through the senses, Plato believed human beings enter the world with inborn knowledge—a position called **nativism.** Psychologists today study the extent to which infant cognitive development is affected by inborn factors versus life experiences (Spelke, 1998). Plato also believed reasoning gives us access to inborn knowledge, a philosophical approach called **rationalism**.

Though Aristotle accepted the importance of reasoning, he was more willing than Plato to accept sensory experience as a source of knowledge—a philosophical approach called

Chapter One

empiricism. Yet he recognized the frailty of sensory data, as in "Aristotle's illusion." To experience it for yourself, cross your middle finger over your index finger and run a pen between them. You will feel two pens instead of one. Aristotle was one of the first thinkers to speculate on psychological topics, as indicated by the titles of his works, including *On Dreams, On Sleep and Sleeplessness, On Memory and Reminiscence,* and *On the Senses and the Sensed.*

During the early Christian and medieval eras, answers to psychological questions were given more often by theologian philosophers than by secular philosophers like Plato or Aristotle. The dominant Western authority was Saint Augustine (354–430), who lived almost all of his life in what is now Algeria. Augustine wrote of his views on memory, emotion, and motivation in the self-analysis he presented in his classic autobiographical *Confessions.* He anticipated Sigmund Freud in providing insight into the continual battle between our human reason and our animal passions, especially the powerful sex drive (Gay, 1986).

During the Middle Ages, when the Christian West was guided largely by religious dogma, and those who dared to conduct empirical studies risked punishment, scientific investigations became almost solely the province of Islamic intellectuals. The most noteworthy of these was the Persian scientist and philosopher Abu Ibn Sina (980–1037), better known in the West as Avicenna, who kept alive the teachings of Aristotle (Afnan, 1958/1980). With the revival of Western intellectual activity in the late Middle Ages, scholars who had access to Arabic translations of the Greek philosophers rediscovered Aristotle. But most of these scholars limited their efforts to reconciling Aristotle's ideas and Christian teachings.

With the coming of the Renaissance, which extended from the 14th to the 17th century, Western authorities once again relied less on theology and more on philosophy to provide answers to psychological questions. The spirit of the Renaissance inspired René Descartes (1596–1650), the great French philosopher-mathematician-scientist. Descartes, the first of the modern rationalists, insisted we should doubt everything that is not proved self-evident by our own reasoning. In fact, in his famous statement "I think, therefore I am," Descartes went to the extreme of using reasoning to prove to his own satisfaction that he existed. Descartes contributed to the modern intellectual outlook, which opposes blind acceptance of proclamations put forth by authorities—religious or otherwise. Church leaders felt so threatened by Descartes's challenge to their authority that they banned his works.

Other intellectuals, though favoring empiricism instead of rationalism, joined Descartes in rejecting the authority of theologians to provide answers to scientific questions. Chief among these thinkers was the English politician-philosopher-scientist Francis Bacon (1561–1626). Bacon inspired the modern scientific attitude that favors skepticism, systematic observation, and verification of claims by other observers (Hearnshaw, 1985). He was also a founder of applied science, which seeks practical applications of research findings. In support of this, Bacon asserted, "to be useless is to be worthless." Ironically, his interest in the application of scientific findings cost him his life. While studying the possible use of refrigeration to preserve food, he experimented by stuffing a chicken with snow—and caught a severe chill that led to a fatal case of pneumonia.

Following in Francis Bacon's empiricist footsteps was the English philosopher John Locke (1632–1704). According to Locke (borrowing a concept from Aristotle), each of us is born a blank slate—or *tabula rasa*—on which are written the life experiences we acquire through our senses. While nativists like Descartes believe much of our knowledge is inborn, empiricists like Locke believe knowledge is acquired solely through life experiences. Concern about the relative importance of heredity and life experiences is known as the *nature versus nurture* controversy. Because Locke's views were incompatible with the prevalent belief in the inborn right of certain people to be rulers over others, you can appreciate why Locke's writings helped inspire the American and French Revolutions. The nature-versus-nurture issue, a recurring theme in psychological theory and research, appears in later chapters in discussions about a host of topics, including language, intelligence, personality, and psychological disorders.

empiricism
The philosophical position that true knowledge comes through the senses.

▲ **Francis Bacon (1561–1626)**
"If a man will begin with certainties, he shall end in doubts; but if he will be content to begin with doubts, he shall end in certainties."

The German philosopher Immanuel Kant (1724–1804) offered a compromise between Descartes's extreme rationalism and Locke's extreme empiricism. Kant was the ultimate "ivory tower" intellectual, never marrying and devoting his life to philosophical pursuits. Despite his international acclaim, he never left his home province—and probably never saw an ocean or a mountain (Paulsen, 1899/1963).

Kant taught that knowledge is the product of inborn mental faculties that organize and interpret sensory input from the physical environment. For example, though the specific language you speak (whether English or another) depends on experience with your native tongue, your ability to speak any language depends on inborn brain mechanisms. If it did not, other animals that can hear speech and that have a vocal apparatus might develop a spoken language when exposed to one.

Despite studying psychological topics, Kant would have claimed psychology could not be a science. He believed this because the mind is not tangible: it cannot be directly observed, measured, or manipulated. Moreover, its contents are in a constant state of flux. And, most important, the very act of examining one's mind alters its contents. For example, suppose you are asked to report your mental experience while you are angry. The very act of observing your own anger might weaken it, making your verbal report of your anger experience inaccurate. Because of these shortcomings, according to Kant, the study of the mind can never be objective—a prerequisite for any science.

The Scientific Roots of Psychology

By the 19th century, scientists were making progress in answering questions about the nature of psychological processes that philosophers were having difficulty with. As a consequence, intellectuals began to look more and more to science for guidance in the study of psychological topics. For example, in the mid 19th century, popular belief, based on reasoning, held that nerve impulses travel the length of a nerve as fast as electricity travels along a wire—that is, almost instantaneously—and were too fast to measure. This claim was contradicted by research conducted by the German physiologist Hermann von Helmholtz (1821–1894), arguably the greatest scientist of the 19th century.

In studying nerve impulses, Helmholtz found they took a measurable fraction of a second to travel along a nerve. In one experiment, he had participants release a telegraph key as soon as they felt a touch on their foot or thigh. A device recorded their reaction time. Participants reacted slower to a touch on the foot than to a touch on the thigh. Helmholtz attributed this difference in reaction time to the longer distance nerve impulses must travel from the foot to the spinal cord and then on to the brain. This indicated that nerve impulses are not instantaneous. In fact, Helmholtz found that in human beings they traveled at the relatively slow speed of 50 to 100 meters per second.

Helmholtz's scientific contemporaries made important discoveries about brain functions that could not be discovered by philosophical speculation. The leading brain researcher was the French physiologist Pierre Flourens (1794–1867), who studied the effects of damage to specific brain structures on animal behavior. For example, he found that damage to the cerebellum, a large structure at the back of the brain, caused motor incoordination. This led him to conclude, correctly, that the cerebellum helps regulate the coordination of movements.

Other 19th-century scientists were more interested in the scientific study of mental processes, apart from the brain structures that served them. The most notable of these researchers was the German mystic-physician-scientist Gustav Fechner (1801–1887). In his scientific research, Fechner used the methods of **psychophysics,** one of the first fields of psychological research. Psychophysics was the intellectual offspring of the German physicist Ernst Weber (1795–1878), whose writings influenced Fechner. Fechner, inspired to do so by a daydream, used psychophysical methods to quantify the relationship between physical stimulation and mental experience. This accomplishment would have surprised his predecessor Immanuel Kant, who believed it was impossible to study the mind scientifically. Psychophysics considers questions such as these: How much change in the intensity of a light is necessary for a person to perceive a change in its brightness? And how much change in the intensity of a sound is necessary for a person to perceive a change in its loudness? Psychophysics contributed to psychology's maturation from being a child of philosophy and

▲ **Gustav Fechner (1801–1887)**
"... body and mind parallel each other; changes in one correspond to changes in the other."

psychophysics
The study of the relationship between the physical characteristics of stimuli and the conscious psychological experiences that are associated with them.

Chapter One

science to being an independent discipline with its own subject matter, and it has had important applications during the past century. For example, the researchers who perfected television relied on psychophysics to determine the relationship between physical characteristics of the television picture and the viewer's mental experience of qualities such as color and brightness (Baldwin, 1954).

Psychologists of the late 19th century also were influenced by the theory of evolution, put forth by the English naturalist Charles Darwin (1809–1882). Darwin announced his theory in *On the Origin of Species* (Darwin, 1859/1975), which described the results of research he conducted while studying the plants and animals he encountered during a 5-year voyage around the world on HMS *Beagle.* Though thinkers as far back as ancient Greece had proposed that existing animals had evolved from common ancestors, Darwin (along with fellow English naturalist Alfred Russell Wallace) was the first to propose a process that could account for it. According to Darwin, through *natural selection* physical characteristics that promote the survival of the individual are more likely to be passed on to offspring, because individuals with these characteristics are more likely to live long enough to reproduce.

Darwin's theory had its most immediate impact on psychology through the work of Darwin's cousin, the Englishman Francis Galton (1822–1911). In applying Darwin's theory of evolution, Galton argued that natural selection could account for the development of human abilities. Moreover, he claimed that individuals with the most highly developed abilities, such as vision and hearing, would be the most likely to survive. This led him to found the field of **differential psychology,** which studies variations among human beings in physical, personality, and intellectual attributes. Galton's impact on the study of intelligence is discussed in Chapter 10.

Differential psychology was introduced to North America by the psychologist James McKeen Cattell (1860–1944), who studied with Galton in England. In 1890 Cattell coined the term *mental test,* which he used to refer to various tests of vision, hearing, and physical skills that he administered to his students. After being banished from academia for opposing America's entrance into World War I, Cattell started his own business, the Psychological Corporation, which to this day is active in the development of tests that assess abilities, intelligence, and personality. Thus, Cattell was a pioneer in the development of psychology as both a science and a profession (Landy, 1997).

The Growth of Psychology

Cattell was the first psychology professor in the world (that is, he was the first person to hold such a position independent of an academic biology or philosophy department). He began his professorship little more than a century ago, a fact that supports a remark made by Hermann Ebbinghaus (1850–1909), a pioneer in psychology: "Psychology has a long past, but only a short history" (Boring, 1950, p. ix). By this, Ebbinghaus meant that though intellectuals have been interested in psychological topics since the era of ancient Greece, psychology did not become a separate discipline until the late 19th century.

Psychologists commonly attribute the founding of this new discipline to the German physiologist Wilhelm Wundt (1832–1920). In 1875 Wundt set up a psychology laboratory at the University of Leipzig in a small room that had served as a dining hall for impoverished students. Wundt's request for a more impressive laboratory had been rejected by the school's administrators, who did not want to promote a science they believed would drive students crazy by encouraging them to scrutinize the contents of their minds (Hilgard, 1987). Beginning in 1879 Wundt's laboratory became the site of formal research conducted by many students who later became some of the most renowned psychologists in the world. More than thirty American psychologists took their Ph.D.'s with Wundt (Benjamin et al., 1992). Psychologists recognized Wundt's accomplishment by celebrating 1979 as psychology's centennial year.

The early growth of the new science founded by Wundt was marked by the rise of competing approaches championed by charismatic leaders, many of whom were trained in both philosophy and science. These approaches were known as *schools* of psychology, and included *structuralism, functionalism, behaviorism, Gestalt psychology,* and *psychoanalysis.*

History of Psychology
www.mhhe.com/sdorow5

differential psychology
The field of psychology that studies individual differences in physical, personality, and intellectual characteristics.

The University of Akron Psychology Archives
www.mhhe.com/sdorow5

structuralism

The early school of psychology that sought to identify the components of the conscious mind.

analytic introspection

A research method in which highly trained participants report the contents of their conscious mental experiences.

▲ **Edward B. Titchener (1867–1927)**

"Since all the sciences are concerned with the one world of human experience, it is natural that scientific method, to whatever aspect of experience it is applied, should be in principle the same."

The schools differed in three significant ways: (1) in their object of study (the conscious mind, the unconscious mind, or overt behavior); (2) in their goal of study (analyzing the contents of the mind, examining the functions of the mind, or observing the effect of the environment on behavior); and (3) in their method of study (having participants report the contents of their minds, or observing overt behavior).

Structuralism

The first school of psychology—**structuralism**—arose in the late 19th century. Structuralists were inspired by the efforts of biologists, chemists, and physicists to analyze matter and categorize it into cells, molecules, and atoms. Following the lead of these scientists, structuralists tried to analyze the mind into its component elements and discover how the elements interact.

Structuralism was named and popularized by Wundt's student Edward Titchener (1867–1927), who favored a more narrow approach to psychology than Wundt's (Zehr, 2000). Titchener, an Englishman, introduced structuralism to the United States after receiving his Ph.D. from Wundt in 1892 and then joining the faculty of Cornell University later that year. To study the mind, Titchener had his participants use **analytic introspection,** a procedure aimed at analyzing complex mental experiences into what he believed were the three basic mental elements: images, feelings, and sensations. In a typical study using analytic introspection, Titchener would present a participant with a stimulus (for example, a repetitious sound produced by a metronome) and then ask the participant to report the images, feelings, and sensations evoked by it. Based on his research, Titchener concluded that there were more than 40,000 mental elements, the vast majority of them visual (Lieberman, 1979).

Among Titchener's contributions was research that analyzed tastes, which led to the discovery that even complex tastes are mixtures of the four basic tastes of sour, sweet, salty, and bitter (Webb, 1981). Despite Titchener's renown, structuralism became not only the first school of psychology to appear, but the first to disappear. This was caused, in part, by its being limited to the laboratory. In fact, Titchener frowned on psychologists who tried to apply the new science of psychology to everyday life (White, 1994).

But the demise of structuralism owed more to its reliance on introspection, which limited it to the study of conscious mental experience in relatively intelligent, adult human beings with strong verbal skills. Psychologists also found introspection to be unreliable, because introspective reports in response to a particular stimulus by a given participant were inconsistent from one presentation of the stimulus to another. Similarly, introspective reports in response to the same stimulus were inconsistent from one participant to another. And, perhaps most important, the very act of introspection changed the conscious experience that was being reported—a point that Kant had made many years earlier. Though the shortcomings of analytic introspection made it fade into oblivion, many psychologists today rely on the related research procedure of having their participants give verbal reports of their mental processes—without necessarily trying to analyze them into their components.

Functionalism

The American school of psychology called **functionalism** arose chiefly as a response to structuralism. Functionalists criticized the structuralists for limiting themselves to analyzing the contents of the mind. The functionalists preferred, instead, to study how the mind affects what people do. Whereas structuralists might study the mental components of tastes, functionalists might study how the ability to distinguish different tastes affects behavior. This reflected the influence of Darwin's theory of evolution, which stressed the role of inherited characteristics in helping the individual adapt to the environment. The functionalists assumed that the mind evolved because it promoted the survival of individual human beings. (Your conscious mind permits you to evaluate your current circumstances and select the best course of action to adapt to them. Recall a time when you tasted food that had gone bad. You quickly spit it out, vividly demonstrating the functional value of the sense of taste.)

The most prominent functionalist was the American psychologist and philosopher William James (1842–1910). In his approach to psychology, James viewed the mind as a stream, which, like a stream of water, cannot be meaningfully broken down into discrete elements. Thus, he believed the mind—or *stream of consciousness*—is not suited to the kind of analytic study favored by structuralists. In 1875, the same year as Wundt established his laboratory at Leipzig, James established a psychology laboratory at Harvard University. But, unlike Wundt, James used the laboratory for demonstrations, not for experiments. He urged psychologists, instead, to study how people function in the world outside of the laboratory. James and Wundt were so influential that a recent survey of several major Canadian universities found that 48 percent of their psychology faculty members could trace their intellectual lineage through key faculty members back to James or Wundt (Lubek et al., 1995).

Though he conducted few experiments, James made several contributions to psychology. His classic textbook *The Principles of Psychology* (1890/1981) highlighted the interrelationship of philosophy, physiology, and psychology. The book is so interesting, informative, and beautifully written that it is one of the few century-old psychology books that is still in print. An abridged version of the book, *Psychology: Brief Edition*, became a leading introductory psychology textbook. William James also contributed a theory of emotion (discussed in Chapter 12) that is still influential today. And his views influenced later research in self psychology (Coon, 2000), which is discussed in Chapter 13.

As a group, the functionalists broadened the range of subjects used in psychological research by including animals, children, and people suffering from mental disorders. The functionalists also expanded the subject matter of psychology to include such topics as memory, thinking, and personality. And unlike the structuralists, who limited their research to the laboratory, the functionalists, in the tradition of Francis Bacon, applied their research to everyday life. The functionalist John Dewey (1859–1952) applied psychology to the improvement of educational practices. But the functionalist credited with founding the field of applied psychology was Hugo Münsterberg (1863–1916), who became a tragic figure in the history of psychology. Münsterberg had been under extreme stress after being ostracized by his colleagues for trying to promote good relations between America and Germany during the years leading up to World War I (Spillmann & Spillmann, 1993), and he died after suffering a stroke while lecturing in class.

In 1892 William James, tiring of the demands of running the psychology laboratory at Harvard, hired Münsterberg, who had earned his Ph.D. under Wilhelm Wundt in 1885 and had become a renowned German psychologist, to take over the laboratory. Münsterberg quickly gained stature in America. During the first decade of the 20th century, Münsterberg was second only to James in his fame as a psychologist. Ironically, though he was hired to run the Harvard psychology laboratory, Münsterberg's main contributions were in his role as a founder of applied psychology (Van De Water, 1997). He conducted research and wrote books describing how psychology could be applied to law, industry, education, psychotherapy, and film criticism.

▲ **William James (1842–1910)**
"Consciousness, then, does not appear to itself chopped up in bits. Such words as *chain* or *train* do not describe it fitly as it presents itself in the first instance. It is nothing jointed; it flows. A *river* or a *stream* are the metaphors by which it is most naturally described. *In talking of it hereafter, let us call it the stream of thought, of consciousness, or of subjective life.*"

▲ **Francis Sumner (1895–1954)**
When he received his doctorate from Clark University in 1920, Francis Sumner, a functionalist, became the first African American to receive a Ph.D. in psychology in the United States (Sawyer, 2000). Sumner went on to develop the undergraduate psychology program at Howard University, which has graduated more African Americans who have become psychologists than has any other school. Sumner was also one of the most prolific contributors to *Psychological Abstracts*, the basic library research tool for scholars and students of psychology. Proficient in several languages, he wrote almost 2,000 abstracts of articles written in English, French, Spanish, German, and Russian (Bayton, 1975).

behaviorism
The early school of psychology that rejected the study of mental processes in favor of the study of overt behavior.

▲ **John B. Watson (1878–1958)**
"Psychology . . . needs introspection as little as do the sciences of chemistry and physics."

Because Münsterberg and his functionalist colleagues dared to move psychology out of the laboratory and into the everyday world, they felt the wrath of structuralists, such as Titchener, who insisted psychology could be a science only if it remained in the laboratory. Despite Titchener's criticisms, most psychologists would applaud the functionalists for increasing the kinds of research methods, research participants, and research settings used by psychologists (Yancher, 1997).

Behaviorism

In 1913 a leading functionalist published an article entitled "Psychology as the Behaviorist Views It." It included the following proclamation:

> ▶ Psychology as the behaviorist views it is a purely objective experimental branch of natural science. Its theoretical goal is the prediction and the control of behavior. Introspection forms no essential part of its methods, nor is the scientific value of its data dependent on the readiness with which they lend themselves to interpretation in terms of consciousness. (Watson, 1913, p. 158)

This bold statement by the American psychologist John B. Watson (1878–1958) heralded the rise of **behaviorism,** a school of psychology that dominated the discipline for half a century. Watson rejected the position shared by structuralists and functionalists that the mind is the proper object of study for psychology. He and other behaviorists were emphatic in their opposition to the study of mental experience. To Watson, the proper subject matter for psychological research is observable behavior. Unlike mental experiences, overt behavior can be recorded and subjected to verification by other scientists. For example, some psychologists might study the mental experience of hunger, but behaviorists would prefer to study the observable behavior of eating. Though Watson denied that mental processes could cause behaviors, he did not deny the existence of the mind. Thus, he would not have denied that human beings have the mental experience called "hunger," but he would have denied that the mental experience of hunger causes eating (Moore, 1990). Instead, he would have favored explanations of eating that placed its causes in the body (such as low blood sugar) or in the environment (such as a tantalizing aroma) instead of in the mind (such as feeling famished).

Watson impressed his fellow psychologists enough to be elected president of the American Psychological Association in 1915. Watson was an attractive and charismatic person who popularized his brand of psychology by giving speeches and writing books and articles. Though he wrote about both heredity and environment, he placed great faith in the effect of environmental stimuli on the control of behavior, especially children's behavior (Horowitz, 1992). His "stimulus-response" psychology placed him firmly in the empiricist tradition of John Locke and is best expressed in his famous pronouncement on child development:

> ▶ Give me a dozen healthy infants, well-formed, and my own specified world to bring them up in and I'll guarantee to take any one at random and train him to become any type of specialist I might select — doctor, lawyer, artist, merchant-chief and, yes, even beggar man and thief, regardless of his talents, penchants, tendencies, abilities, vocations, and race of his ancestors. (Watson, 1930, p. 104)

Apparently, no parents rushed to offer their infants to Watson. Nonetheless, his views on child rearing became influential. Despite some of their excessive claims, behaviorists injected optimism into psychology by fostering the belief that human beings are minimally limited by heredity and easily changed by experience. In favoring nurture over nature, behaviorists assumed that people, regardless of their hereditary background, could improve themselves and their positions in life. Watson and his fellow behaviorists were more than willing to suggest ways to bring about such improvements. Watson even hoped to establish a utopian society based on behavioristic principles (Morawski, 1982).

Behaviorism dominated psychology through the 1960s (O'Neil, 1995). In fact, from 1930 to 1960 the term *mind* rarely appeared in psychological research articles (Mueller, 1979). But during the past four decades, the mind has returned as a legitimate object of study. The weakened influence of orthodox behaviorism is also shown by renewed respect for the constraints heredity places on learning (a topic discussed in Chapter 7).

Gestalt Psychology

The structuralists' attempt to analyze the mind into its component parts and the behaviorists' view of the human being as a passive responder to environmental stimuli were countered by German psychologist Max Wertheimer (1880–1943), who founded the school of **Gestalt psychology.** Wertheimer used the word *Gestalt*, meaning "form" or "shape," to underscore his belief that we perceive wholes rather than combinations of individual elements. A famous tenet of Gestalt psychology asserts: "The whole is different from the sum of its parts" (Wertheimer & King, 1994). Because of this basic assumption, Wertheimer ridiculed structuralism as "brick-and-mortar psychology" for its attempt to analyze mental experience into discrete elements.

The founding of Gestalt psychology can be traced to a vacation trip taken by Wertheimer in 1912. While aboard a train he daydreamed about the **phi phenomenon**—apparent motion in the absence of actual motion (as in a motion picture). At a stop Wertheimer left the train and bought a toy stroboscope, which, like a motion picture, produces the illusion of movement by rapidly presenting a series of pictures that are slightly different from one another. On returning to his laboratory, he continued studying the phi phenomenon by using a more sophisticated device called a tachistoscope, which flashes visual stimuli for a fraction of a second. Wertheimer had the tachistoscope flash two lines in succession, first a vertical one and then a horizontal one. When the interval between flashes was just right, a single line appeared to move from a vertical to horizontal orientation.

According to Wertheimer, the phi phenomenon shows that the mind does not respond passively to discrete stimuli, but instead organizes stimuli into coherent wholes. Thus, perception is more than a series of individual sensations. This is in keeping with Immanuel Kant's notion of the mind as an active manipulator of environmental input. If the mind responded passively to discrete stimuli, in observing Wertheimer's demonstration you would first see the vertical line appear and disappear and then the horizontal line appear and disappear.

For another example of how the mind can create a whole different from the sum of its parts, consider a melody. A given melody, such as "Yankee Doodle Dandy," can be recognized regardless of whether it is sung, hummed, or whistled; whether it is played on a banjo or by a symphony orchestra; and whether it is played in any of a variety of keys. Thus, a melody is not simply the product of a series of particular sensations produced by a particular source. Instead, a melody depends on the mind's active processing of sensations that can be produced by a variety of sources. Gestalt psychology gave a new direction to psychology by stressing the active role of the mind in organizing sensations into meaningful wholes (Epstein & Hatfield, 1994).

Though founded by Wertheimer, Gestalt psychology was popularized by his colleagues Kurt Koffka (1886–1941), the most prolific and influential writer among the Gestalt psychologists, and Wolfgang Köhler (1887–1967), who promoted Gestalt psychology as a natural science (Henle, 1993) and applied it to the study of problem solving. Koffka and Köhler introduced Gestalt psychology to the United States after fleeing Nazi Germany. Kohler, a Christian college professor, had provoked the Nazis by writing and speaking out against their oppression of his Jewish colleagues. He became a respected psychologist and in 1959 was elected president of the American Psychological Association. In his presidential address, Kohler (1959) urged Gestalt psychologists and behaviorists to create a psychology that included the best aspects of both of their schools. As you will read later in this chapter, psychologists who favor the cognitive perspective have followed Kohler's advice.

Psychoanalysis

Unlike Gestalt psychology and the other early schools of psychology, which originated in universities, **psychoanalysis** originated in medicine. Sigmund Freud (1856–1939), the founder of psychoanalysis, was an Austrian neurologist who considered himself "a conquistador of the mind" (Gay, 1988). His theory, which views the human being as first and foremost an animal, owes a debt to Darwin's theory of evolution (Dunn, 1993). Psychoanalysis grew, in part, from Freud's attempts to treat patients suffering from physical symptoms, such as paralyzed legs, inability to speak, or loss of bodily sensations, that had no

▲ **Max Wertheimer (1880–1943)**
"... the comprehension of whole-properties and whole-conditions must precede consideration of the real significance of parts."

► **Sigmund Freud (1856–1939)**

Freud is shown here with a group of eminent psychologists during his only visit to the United States, in 1909, when he came to attend the famous Clark University psychology conference. (*Seated, left to right:* Freud, host G. Stanley Hall, and Carl Jung. *Standing, left to right:* Abraham Brill, Ernest Jones, and Sandor Ferenczi.)

psychic determinism

The Freudian assumption that all human behavior is influenced by unconscious motives.

▲ **"Good morning, beheaded—uh, I mean beloved."**

apparent physical causes. Based on his treatment of patients suffering from symptoms of *conversion hysteria,* Freud concluded that the disorder was the result of unconscious psychological conflicts about sex caused by cultural prohibitions against sexual enjoyment. These conflicts were "converted" into the physical symptoms seen in conversion hysteria, which often provided the patient with an excuse to avoid engaging in the taboo behaviors.

Freud's case studies of patients led him to infer that unconscious conflicts, usually related to sex or aggression, were prime motivators of human behavior. Freud believed that all behavior—whether normal or abnormal—is influenced by psychological motives, often unconscious ones. This belief is called **psychic determinism.** In his book *The Psychopathology of Everyday Life,* Freud (1901/1990) explained how even apparently unintentional behaviors could be explained by psychic determinism. Psychic determinism explains misstatements, popularly known as "Freudian slips," like that of the radio announcer who began a bread commercial by saying, "For the breast in bed . . . I mean, for the best in bread . . . ." As a leading psychologist has noted, the concept of psychic determinism meant that "the forgotten lunch engagement, the slip of the tongue, the barked shin could no longer be dismissed as accident" (Bruner, 1956, p. 465).

In addition to shocking the public by claiming human beings are motivated chiefly by unconscious—often sexual—motives, Freud made the controversial claim that early childhood experiences were the most important factors in personality development. Freud believed memories of early childhood experiences stored in the unconscious mind continue to affect behavior throughout life. According to Freud, these unconscious influences explain the irrationality of much human behavior and the origins of psychological disorders.

Freudian psychoanalysis has been so extraordinarily influential that a 1981 survey of chairpersons of graduate psychology departments found that they considered Freud to be the most important figure in the history of psychology (Davis, Thomas, & Weaver, 1982). Nonetheless, psychoanalysis has been the target of severe attacks. Critics have pointed out that the unconscious mind can be too easily used to explain any behavior for which there is no obvious cause. William James had expressed this concern even before Freud's views had become widely known. James warned that the unconscious "is the sovereign means for believing whatever one likes in psychology and of turning what might become a science into a tumbling ground for whimsies" (James, 1890/1981, Vol. 1, p. 166). Though John B. Watson was fascinated by Freud's theory, he, like James, rejected the notion that human behavior could be motivated by unconscious mental processes (Rilling, 2000).

Psychoanalysis has also been subjected to criticism for failing to provide adequate research evidence for its claims of the importance of sexual motives, unconscious processes, and early childhood experiences. In fact, Freud never tested his theory experimentally.

Table 1.1	Early Schools of Psychology		
School	**Object of Study**	**Goal of Study**	**Method of Study**
Structuralism	Conscious experience	Analyzing the structure of the mind	Analytic introspection
Functionalism	Conscious experience	Studying the functions of the mind	Introspection and measures of performance
Behaviorism	Observable behavior	Controlling behavior	Observation and experimentation
Gestalt Psychology	Conscious experience	Demonstrating the holistic nature of the mind	Introspection and demonstrations
Psychoanalysis	Unconscious motivation	Understanding personality	Clinical case studies

Instead, he based his theory on notes written after seeing patients, which made his conclusions subject to his own memory lapses and personal biases. Moreover, Freud violated good scientific practice by generalizing to all people the results of his case studies of a relative handful of people with psychological disorders.

Despite these shortcomings, Freud's views have influenced the psychological study of topics as diverse as dreams, creativity, motivation, development, personality, and psychotherapy. Freud's views have also inspired the works of artists, writers, and filmmakers, including Eugene O'Neill's play *Mourning Becomes Electra* (1931) and the classic science fiction film *Forbidden Planet* (1956). Freud's contributions to a variety of psychological topics are discussed in several other chapters. Table 1.1 summarizes the major characteristics of psychoanalysis and the other early schools of psychology.

The Role of Women in the Growth of Psychology

In 1980 Florence Denmark, then president of the American Psychological Association, remarked that "women have contributed a great deal to the growth and development of the discipline of psychology. . . . For the most part, however, women have been unrecognized, undervalued, and invisible in our recorded history" (Denmark, 1980, p. 1057). Since its founding little more than a century ago, psychology has been more hospitable to women than any other science has been, yet obstacles prevented some women from pursuing careers as psychologists, and many women who were pioneers in psychology have not been accorded the degree of recognition they deserve (Bohan, 1993).

Early Obstacles to Women in Psychology

To appreciate the obstacles women faced in the early years of psychology, one must delve into the social and cultural factors that affected them. The chief factor that limited professional opportunities for women was the notion of "separate spheres" for men and women. The primary roles in a woman's sphere included being a good daughter, wife, and mother. In contrast, though a man was expected to be devoted to his family, his sphere included a variety of career choices, including the possibility of becoming a scientist. Women who pursued careers as scientists typically had to forsake (or at least postpone) marriage and parenthood, or faced customs and policies aimed at preventing them from leaving their sphere. This, coupled with beliefs that women simply lacked the personal and intellectual abilities needed to profit from higher education, kept many capable women from entering the sciences, including psychology.

Moreover, women who wanted to pursue higher education were refused admission by many colleges and universities, were ineligible for financial aid, and were less likely to be offered faculty positions at prestigious universities after graduation. Women also were excluded from professional circles that helped scientists advance in their careers. For example, in 1904 Edward Titchener, appalled at what he believed was the American Psychological Association's movement toward applied psychology, established a psychological research society called the Experimentalists. Its bylaws excluded women, allegedly to permit men to engage in masculine activities, including smoking and "man talk." Ironically, Titchener's doctoral program in psychology at Cornell University was more hospitable to women than any other doctoral psychology program. In fact, about one-third of his Ph.D. students were women, and he championed their efforts to find academic positions at Cornell and elsewhere.

But Titchener's banning of women from the Experimentalists prevented them from making the same useful professional connections as their male colleagues. The leading psychologist who opposed this exclusion was Christine Ladd-Franklin (1847–1930), who studied with Hermann von Helmholtz in Germany and became known for her evolutionary theory of color vision (Furumoto, 1992). For more than two decades, Ladd-Franklin acted as a gadfly, trying unsuccessfully to gain membership for women in the Experimentalists. She even accused Titchener of hypocrisy for admitting men who were not true experimentalists while excluding women who were (Furumoto, 1988). No woman was admitted until 1929, two years after Titchener's death and a year before Ladd-Franklin's.

The first woman member was Margaret Floy Washburn (1871–1939), the leading comparative psychologist of her day and author of the most widely used textbook on animal psychology, *The Animal Mind* (Washburn, 1908). In 1894 she became Titchener's first female doctoral student; in 1921 she became the second female president of the American Psychological Association. Washburn became active in editing journals and in running professional organizations. But perhaps her greatest contribution was the development of the psychology program at Vassar College (Scarborough & Furumoto, 1987).

Given the roadblocks they faced, how did women find ways to become pioneers in psychology and other sciences? Oftentimes they had parents who supported education for women and would help them financially. The minority who married typically had supportive husbands. And many were championed by prominent psychologists who helped them advance in their careers. To illustrate several of these factors and to appreciate the accomplishments of women pioneers in psychology, consider Mary Whiton Calkins (1863–1930), arguably the first great woman psychologist.

The Life and Work of Mary Whiton Calkins

In 1903 Calkins, along with Margaret Floy Washburn and Christine Ladd-Franklin, was listed in a ranking by James McKeen Cattell of the fifty most eminent American psychologists (O'Connell & Russo, 1990). Calkins was one of William James's students. But as pointed out by Laurel Furumoto (1980), an authority on Calkins, being a student of the most renowned psychologist of her time did not guarantee Calkins an easy path to a career as a psychologist.

Calkins, a resident of Newton, Massachusetts, was a descendant of the famous John and Priscilla Alden of Plymouth Colony. Her parents encouraged her to pursue a professional career. In 1885, after earning a bachelor's degree from Smith College, she became a Greek instructor at Wellesley College. In 1890 Wellesley's founder decided to introduce the new science of psychology to the school. Because there were too few psychologists to staff all the psychology departments sprouting up in North America, Calkins, an outstanding teacher, was asked to take graduate courses to prepare her to become Wellesley's first psychology professor.

Calkins sought admission to nearby Harvard University. Though Harvard did not let women enroll in its courses, Calkins's father, a respected minister, convinced Harvard's president to let her audit courses. Despite this initial good fortune, she suffered discrimination throughout her years at Harvard. In her autobiography, Calkins (1930) describes her first course, a seminar offered by William James, from which the other students—all men—withdrew. Given that James was a popular professor and Harvard students had expressed alarm in the campus newspaper at the possible intrusion of women into their classes (Scarborough & Furumoto, 1987), one is left with the strong suspicion that they withdrew because they disapproved of her presence in the course. As was her custom, Calkins saw the glass as half full rather than half empty and basked in her memories of the time she spent alone with the great William James in front of a library fireplace, discussing psychology and using his just-published *Principles of Psychology* as the textbook.

Calkins also took courses offered by Edmund Clark Sanford, a leading psychologist, at Clark University. They collaborated on one of the earliest experimental studies of dreams,

▲ **Laurel Furumoto**

"Despite their presence in psychology's past, women psychologists have been a well-kept secret in the history of the discipline."

Chapter One

recounted in Chapter 6, which produced findings that have held up remarkably well over the years. In 1891, with Sanford's and James's help, Calkins founded the psychology laboratory at Wellesley College, the first at a women's school (O'Connell & Russo, 1990). By 1895 she had completed the course work and doctoral dissertation necessary for a Ph.D. in psychology. Her dissertation was based on research on memory she had carried out with Hugo Münsterberg; while conducting this research, she invented the paired-associates technique, which became one of the main tools of memory researchers.

In 1895, several eminent members of the Harvard faculty, including James and Münsterberg, gave Calkins the customary opportunity to defend her dissertation. James called her performance "the most brilliant examination for the Ph.D. that we have had at Harvard." Münsterberg, her dissertation sponsor, petitioned the Harvard administration to grant her the Ph.D. she had earned. His request was denied. In 1902 Calkins was offered a Ph.D. from Radcliffe College, Harvard's sister school. She rejected it, insisting she would not honor Harvard's discriminatory policy by accepting a degree from a school she had not attended. In 1927 several eminent Harvard alumni who had become leading psychologists petitioned Harvard to finally grant Calkins the degree she had earned three decades earlier. Once again, the request was denied (Furumoto, 1980).

▲ Mary Whiton Calkins (1863–1930)

"I am more deeply convinced that psychology should be conceived as the science of the self, or person, as related to its environment, physical and social."

The lack of a doctorate did not deter Calkins from becoming a prominent psychologist. In 1905 she became the first woman president of the American Psychological Association. In her presidential speech, she defended her own theoretical creation, self psychology, and put it forth as an alternative to the competing schools of structuralism and functionalism. She urged psychologists to study the conscious mind, the environment (both physical and social), and the relationship between the conscious mind and the environment (Calkins, 1906). She made self psychology the theme of her popular introductory psychology textbook (Calkins, 1901).

Calkins also wrote the first article that criticized John B. Watson's call for a behaviorist approach to psychology (Calkins, 1913). She insisted that ignoring the mind might be fine for the study of animals but was inadequate for the study of human beings. Unlike Watson, who viewed the human being as a passive responder to environmental stimuli, Calkins viewed the human being as active and purposive. One historian of psychology has suggested that Calkins's relatively unknown self psychology was more prophetic of where psychology is now headed than was Watson's well-known behaviorist theory (Samelson, 1981). The increased attention to theories of the self (see Chapter 13) is in keeping with the direction, if not necessarily the content, of her theory.

Calkins was beloved by her students and colleagues alike. They found her to be a warm, open-minded, and devoutly religious person. She also remained an active champion of women's rights. At a national suffrage convention in Baltimore, Calkins gave a speech in favor of granting women the right to vote. She also insisted that allegedly inborn intellectual and personality differences between men and women were more likely the products of gender-role socialization (Scarborough & Furumoto, 1987).

Like her mentor William James, Calkins developed an increasingly active interest in philosophy. In 1918, her fellow philosophers showed their respect for her by electing her president of the American Philosophical Association. In 1929, the year in which women were first admitted to Titchener's society of experimental psychologists, Calkins retired from Wellesley College to write and to care for her mother, only to die of cancer the following year. Though an outstanding psychologist in her day, she, like many other women psychologists, taught at a women's college that lacked a graduate program. This prevented her theories from being carried forth by graduate-student disciples in their own research, publications, and professional presentations—one of the ways in which psychologists build their reputations.

Calkins would be pleased women are now at least as likely as men to pursue careers in psychology. In fact, in the United States the trend in recent years has been for more women than men to earn doctorates in psychology (Denmark, 1998).We also are beginning to recognize the contributions of women to the early development of particular fields of psychology, such as industrial/organizational psychology (Koppes, 1997). Women contributors to psychology are more recognized, valued, and visible today than they were when Mary Whiton Calkins fought the odds and became a pioneer in psychology.

▲ B. F. Skinner (1904–1990)

"I am a radical behaviorist simply in the sense that I find no place in the formulation for anything which is mental."

scientific paradigm

A model that determines the appropriate goals, methods, and subject matter of a science.

behavioral perspective

The psychological viewpoint, descended from behaviorism, that stresses the importance of studying the effects of learning and environmental factors on overt behavior.

▲ Melanie Klein (1882–1960)

"The infant's emotional life, the early defenses built up under the stress of the conflict between love, hatred, and guilt, and the vicissitudes of the child's identifications—all these are topics which may well occupy analytical research for a long time to come."

STAYING ON TRACK: *The History of Psychology*

1. Why would the success of psychophysics have surprised Kant?
2. What were the contributions of functionalism to psychology?
3. What is the role of psychic determinism in Freudian theory?
4. How were the Experimentalists an illustration of the difficulties faced by women trying to advance their careers in psychology?

Answers to Staying on Track start on p. ST-1.

◆ CONTEMPORARY PSYCHOLOGICAL PERSPECTIVES

According to Thomas Kuhn (1970), an influential philosopher of science, as a science matures it develops a unifying **scientific paradigm,** or model, that determines its appropriate goals, methods, and subject matter. Though there are no longer separate schools of psychology, with charismatic leaders and loyal followers, psychology still lacks a unifying scientific paradigm to which most psychologists would subscribe (Kenrick, 2001). Instead, there are rival psychological perspectives. They include the *behavioral perspective,* the *psychoanalytic perspective,* the *humanistic perspective,* the *cognitive perspective,* the *biopsychological perspective,* and the *social-cultural perspective.*

The Behavioral Perspective

The **behavioral perspective** descended from behaviorism (Staats, 1994). Its leading proponent was the American psychologist B. F. Skinner (1904–1990). As a young man, Skinner pursued a career as a writer, and even spent 6 months living in Greenwich Village to soak up its creative Bohemian atmosphere. After discovering he was not cut out to be a fiction writer, and being excited by the writings of John B. Watson, he decided to become a psychologist (Keller, 1991). Though Skinner eventually became the most prominent psychologist in the world (Korn, Davis, & Davis, 1991), it took many years for him to achieve that standing. In fact, by the end of World War II, in 1945, his landmark book *The Behavior of Organisms* (which had been published in 1938) had sold only eighty copies.

Like John B. Watson, Skinner urged psychologists to ignore mental processes and to limit psychology to the study of observable behavior. Many behaviorists still refuse to treat verbal reports of mental experiences as appropriate subject matter for psychological research. But in contrast to Watson, Skinner stressed the role of the consequences of behavior, rather than environmental stimuli, in controlling behavior. He noted that animals and people tend to repeat behaviors that are followed by positive consequences. Consider your performance in school. If your studying (a behavior) pays off with an A on an exam (a positive consequence), you will be more likely to study in the future. In Skinner's terms, your behavior has been "positively reinforced."

Skinner, like Watson, was a utopian. In 1948 Skinner—showing he did, in fact, have the ability to write fiction—published *Walden Two,* a still-popular book that describes an ideal society based on behavioral principles. In Skinner's utopia, society is run by benevolent behaviorists who control its citizens by providing positive consequences for desirable behaviors. The tiny community of Twin Oaks, Virginia, was founded on principles presented in *Walden Two.* Though there is still no behavioral utopia, the behavioral perspective has contributed to improvements in education, child rearing, industrial productivity, and therapy for psychological disorders. These are discussed in later chapters.

Despite Skinner's efforts, the influence of the behavioral perspective has waned in recent years in the face of growing dissatisfaction with the lack of attention behaviorists typically give to mental processes. This has prompted some behaviorists to study the relationship between mental processes such as thoughts or images, which cannot be directly observed, and overt behavior, which can. These psychologists are called cognitive behaviorists; one of their most influential leaders has been Albert Bandura. The views of Skinner and Bandura are discussed further in Chapter 7.

The Psychoanalytic Perspective

Like the behavioral perspective, the **psychoanalytic perspective** is a descendant of an early school of psychology—psychoanalysis. The decline of Freudian psychoanalysis began when two of Freud's followers, Carl Jung (1875–1961) and Alfred Adler (1870–1937), developed psychoanalytic theories that contradicted important aspects of Freud's theory. Jung, Adler, and other so-called neo-Freudians placed less emphasis on the biological drives of sex and aggression and more emphasis on the importance of social relationships. Jung developed his own theory of personality, which included the concepts of the inner-directed *introvert* and the outer-directed *extravert*. Adler based his personality theory on his belief that each of us tends to compensate for natural childhood feelings of inferiority by striving for superiority, as in the case of students who study long hours to earn the necessary grades for admission to medical school, or athletes who train for Olympic competition.

Other neo-Freudians also contributed to the psychoanalytic perspective. Anna Freud (1895–1982), Sigmund Freud's daughter, was a leader in the field of child psychoanalysis, as was her intellectual rival Melanie Klein (1882–1960), who developed the technique of play therapy. The views of influential neo-Freudians are discussed in later chapters, particularly in Chapters 4 and 13.

Though the psychoanalytic perspective downplays the importance of biological drives, it accepts the importance of early childhood experiences and the unconscious mind. During the past two decades researchers have devised techniques—some of them ingenious—that permit the scientific study of unconscious mental processes (Hornstein, 1992). (You can read about research on the unconscious mind in Chapter 6.) Those who favor the psychoanalytic perspective believe, "No psychological model that seeks to explain how human beings know, learn, or behave can ignore the concept of unconscious psychological processes" (Shevrin & Dickman, 1980, p. 432).

The Humanistic Perspective

Because it provided the first important alternative to the psychoanalytic and behavioral perspectives (DeCarvalho, 1992), the **humanistic perspective** has been called the "third force" in psychology. It was founded in the 1950s by American psychologists Abraham Maslow (1908–1970) and Carl Rogers (1902–1987) to promote the idea that human beings have free will and are not merely pawns in the hands of unconscious motives or environmental stimuli. Maslow, who served as president of the American Psychological Association in 1967, had begun as a behaviorist but later rejected behaviorism's narrow focus on observable behavior and the effects of the environment. He stressed the human being's natural tendency toward *self-actualization,* which was his term for the fulfillment of one's potentials (Frick, 2000).

Maslow's views were echoed by Rogers. And both assumed that the subject matter of psychology should be the individual's unique subjective mental experience of the world. In favoring the study of mental experience, Maslow and Rogers showed their intellectual kinship to William James. Whereas Maslow and Rogers considered the study of subjective mental experience to be one of several aspects of humanistic psychology, such study is the overriding concern of the branch of humanistic psychology called **phenomenological psychology.** Humanistic psychology's assumption that human beings have free will is central to **existential psychology.** This branch of humanistic psychology favors the study of how human beings respond to the basic givens of reality, including the responsibility of personal freedom, the isolation of one person from another, the need to find meaning in one's life, and the realization that we eventually will die.

Humanistic psychology has been a prime mover in the field of psychotherapy, most notably through the efforts of Carl Rogers. His person-centered therapy, one of the chief kinds of psychotherapy, is discussed in Chapter 15. Though person-centered therapy has been the subject of extensive scientific research, other aspects of humanistic psychology, such as techniques that promote personal "growth experiences" and "consciousness raising," have been criticized for having little scientific support (Wertheimer, 1978). This lack of scientific rigor might be one reason why humanistic psychology has had only a relatively

▲ **Abraham Maslow (1908–1970)**
"I suppose it is tempting, if the only tool you have is a hammer [that is, the behaviorist's sole reliance on studying overt behavior], to treat everything as if it were a nail."

▲ **Herbert Simon (1916–2001)**
"On the American side of the Atlantic Ocean, there was a great gap in research on human thinking from the time of William James almost down to World War II. . . . Cognitive processes . . . were hardly mentioned, and the word *mind* was reserved for philosophers, not to be uttered by respectable psychologists."

cognitive perspective
The psychological viewpoint that favors the study of how the mind organizes perceptions, processes information, and interprets experiences.

biopsychological perspective
The psychological viewpoint that stresses the relationship of physiological factors to behavior and mental processes.

behavioral genetics
The study of the effects of heredity and life experiences on behavior.

minor impact on academic psychology, a fact lamented by Rogers (1985) near the end of his life. Despite its scientific shortcomings, humanistic psychology has made a valuable contribution in promoting the study of positive aspects of human experience, including love, altruism, and healthy personality development. Moreover, many humanistic psychologists have become more willing to use experimentation to test their theories (Rychlak, 1988).

The Cognitive Perspective

Recent decades have witnessed a so-called cognitive revolution in psychology (Gardner, 1985), leading to the emergence of a **cognitive perspective.** The cognitive perspective combines aspects of Gestalt psychology and the behavioral perspective. Like Gestalt psychologists, cognitive psychologists stress the active role of the mind in organizing perceptions, processing information, and interpreting experiences. And like behavioral psychologists, cognitive psychologists stress the need for objective, well-controlled, laboratory studies. Thus, cognitive psychologists infer mental processes from observable responses, without relying on verbal reports alone. But unlike strict behavioral psychologists, who claim that mental processes, such as thoughts, cannot affect behavior, many cognitive psychologists believe they can.

The cognitive perspective is illustrated in the work of the Swiss biologist-psychologist Jean Piaget (1896–1980), who put forth a cognitive theory of the child's mental development based on his interviews with children as they solved various problems. Piaget's research is discussed in Chapter 4. The cognitive perspective also has been influenced by the computer revolution of the past three decades, which stimulated research on the human brain as an information processor. A leader in this field was Herbert Simon (1916–2001), a psychologist who won the 1978 Nobel Prize in economics, the field in which he worked early in his career (Hilgard, 1993). Some cognitive psychologists use computer programs to create models of human thought processes; others use their knowledge of human thought processes to improve computer programs, like those for computer chess games.

Since about 1980 the cognitive perspective has surpassed the behavioral perspective and the psychoanalytic perspective in its influence on psychology (Robins, Gosling, & Craik, 1999). As you will realize while reading upcoming chapters, the cognitive perspective pervades almost every field of psychology. For example, the concept of cognitive schemas, or specialized knowledge structures, has been applied to the study of human development, memory, thought and language, personality, and social behavior.

The Biopsychological Perspective

Though the schools of psychology that appeared in the early 20th century had their roots in 19th-century physiology, there was never a strictly biopsychological school of psychology. In recent decades, growing interest in the biological basis of behavior and mental processes, combined with the development of sophisticated research equipment, has led to the emergence of a **biopsychological perspective.**

Psychologists who favor this perspective are interested in studying the brain, the hormonal system, and the effects of heredity on psychological functions. Though most biopsychology researchers rely on animals as subjects, some of their most important studies have used human participants. For example, in the course of surgery on the brains of epilepsy victims to reduce their seizures, Canadian neurosurgeon Wilder Penfield (1891–1976) mapped the brain by using weak electrical currents to stimulate points on its surface. He found that stimulation of particular points on one side of the brain caused movements of particular body parts on the opposite side.

In 1981, American biopsychologist Roger Sperry (1913–1994) was awarded a Nobel Prize for his studies of the functions of the left and right brain hemispheres of epilepsy victims whose hemispheres had been surgically separated to reduce their seizures. In conducting research on the brain, Sperry and his colleagues found that each hemisphere was superior to the other in performing particular psychological functions. Chapter 3 describes the research of Penfield, Sperry, and other contributors to biopsychology. Because of the increasing influence of this perspective, psychology might be moving toward an even broader definition as "the science of behavior and mental processes, and the physiological processes underlying them."

| **Chapter One**

Some biopsychologists work in the field of **behavioral genetics,** which studies the relative influence of hereditary and environmental factors on human and animal behavior. Chapter 3 discusses the use of behavioral genetics in explaining differences in human intelligence and personality. Many of those who study the role of heredity rely on Charles Darwin's theory of evolution as the inspiration for their research (Snyder, 2000). They champion the relatively new approach called **evolutionary psychology.** For example, evolutionary psychologists interpret gender differences as the product of natural selection, in which traits and behaviors that have had survival value for men and women are passed from generation to generation. According to evolutionary psychology, men tend to be more physically aggressive than women in large part because physical aggression has had greater survival value for men than for women. Chapter 3 discusses a study on the possible evolutionary basis of gender differences in sexual and emotional jealousy, and Chapter 17 considers evolutionary psychology's explanation of gender differences in the attributes that women and men find attractive in potential romantic partners.

The Social-Cultural Perspective

Though Wilhelm Wundt is most famous for founding psychology as a laboratory science, he stressed the importance of considering social-cultural influences on human psychology (Cahan & White, 1992). In fact, his ten-volume *Folk Psychology*, which was published during the years 1900 to 1920, anticipated the **social-cultural perspective.** This perspective has developed over the past three decades as a reaction against what its proponents believe is the unfortunate tendency to presume that psychological research findings, obtained chiefly from research conducted in Europe and North America, are automatically generalizable to other cultures and other social groups. As leading social-cultural psychologists have commented:

▶ The typical psychology text contains hundreds of concepts, terms, and theories. . . . Most of these abstractions are used as if it has already been established that they are applicable everywhere. This is a premature if not dangerous assumption to make. (Lonner & Malpass, 1994, p. 2)

Throughout this text you will read about many studies that have attempted to determine whether research findings obtained in one culture are, in fact, applicable to other cultures. Also, you will read about studies of the influence of social-cultural variables such as gender, ethnicity, and sexual orientation on the many aspects of human behavior and thought processes studied by psychologists. Harry Triandis (1990), one of the founders of the social-cultural perspective, takes a position that would be favored by functionalists. He suggests we avoid ethnocentrism (viewing other cultures by using ours as the ideal standard of comparison) and instead view each culture as the outcome of attempts by its members to adapt to particular ecological niches. Then we would realize that, had we been born in another culture, our views about what is normal and desirable might fit that culture's norms.

What has accounted for the relatively recent surge of interest in the social-cultural perspective? Perhaps the greatest influence has been the "shrinking" of our planet. Today people on opposite sides of the world can communicate instantly with one another using a variety of means, including telephone, radio, television, and computer networks. Other factors include tourism, immigration, international trade, and ethnic conflict. Thus, it behooves people from different cultures to be less ethnocentric so they can better understand one another.

But there are disagreements among supporters of the social-cultural perspective about how to carry out their research. Some study **cross-cultural psychology.** Cross-cultural psychologists employ unique research methods designed to make comparisons between two or more cultures in an attempt to discover universal psychological principles. Others believe that human behavior and mental processes are so molded by culture that we should be most concerned with studying how specific cultures influence human behavior and mental processes. They are less interested in cross-cultural comparisons. Their approach is known as **cultural psychology** (Saraswathi, 1998). A related field, **ethnic psychology,** employs culturally appropriate methods to describe the experience of members of groups that historically

▲ **Roger Sperry (1913–1994)**
"The new mentalist position of behavioral and cognitive science seems to hold promise, not only as a more valid paradigm for all science but also for all human belief."

 International Psychology
www.mhhe.com/sdorow5

evolutionary psychology
The study of the evolution of behavior through natural selection.

social-cultural perspective
The psychological viewpoint that favors the scientific study of human behavior in its social-cultural context.

cross-cultural psychology
An approach that tries to determine the extent to which research findings about human psychology hold true across cultures.

cultural psychology
An approach that studies how cultural factors affect human behavior and mental experience.

 Cultural Psychology Links
www.mhhe.com/sdorow5

ethnic psychology
The field that employs culturally appropriate methods to describe the experience of members of groups that historically have been underrepresented in psychology.

 The Society for the Psychological Study of Ethnic Minority Issues
www.mhhe.com/sdorow5

▲ **William E. Cross, Jr.**
"We have just begun to understand the vast diversity that constitutes the Black experience."

have been underrepresented in psychology. For example, pioneers Mamie and Kenneth Clark and ethnic psychologist William E. Cross, Jr., have studied the development of African Americans' self-concept and mental health (Phillips, 2000).

Putting the Perspectives in Perspective

To appreciate the differences among the psychological perspectives, consider how each might explain the massacre at Columbine High School. A behavioral psychologist might wonder whether the murderers had received positive reinforcement for being cruel and violent during their lives and perhaps sought to gain the world's attention before dying by committing their heinous act. A psychoanalytic psychologist might wonder whether they had developed an abundance of repressed hostility over the years that eventually erupted from their unconscious minds and provoked them to engage in extreme violence. A humanistic psychologist might wonder whether they had been blocked by parental domination from pursuing self-actualization and, angered by this, had chosen to identify with an outcast group and pursue an antisocial means of expressing their anger. A cognitive psychologist might wonder whether they had developed an irrational pattern of beliefs about being persecuted by teachers and fellow students, leading them to lash out against their presumed oppressors. A biopsychologist might wonder whether they had a brain disorder, such as an imbalance in hormones or neurotransmitters, that contributed to their becoming extraordinarily angry and violent. And a social-cultural psychologist might wonder whether the prevalence and celebration of violence in the American media might have influenced them to act in the violent manner they had seen in countless movies and television shows.

While reading the upcoming chapters, you should keep in mind that many psychologists are eclectic—that is, they accept aspects of more than one perspective in guiding their own research or practice. This is in keeping with the wishes of William James, who insisted a century ago that while they seek to unify psychology, psychologists should also revel in its diversity (Viney, 1989).

STAYING ON TRACK: *Contemporary Psychological Perspectives*

1. Why is the humanistic perspective called the "third force"?
2. In what way does the cognitive perspective combine aspects of Gestalt psychology and the behavioral perspective?
3. Why has the social-cultural perspective become influential?

Answers to Staying on Track start on p. ST-1.

◆ PSYCHOLOGY AS A PROFESSION

As psychology has evolved as a science, its fields of specialization have multiplied and its educational and training requirements have become formalized. Today psychologists work in a wide variety of fields in both academic and professional settings (see Figure 1.1). The development of psychology has led to the appearance of numerous academic and professional fields of specialization. A 1997 report by the National Science Foundation found that graduate school enrollments in all subfields of psychology had increased more than 10 percent during the previous 6 years (Chamberlin, 2000).

Academic Fields of Specialization

Most of the chapters in this book discuss academic fields of specialization in psychology, usually practiced by psychologists working at colleges or universities. In fact, colleges and universities are the main employment settings for psychologists. Because each field of psychology contains subfields, which in turn contain sub-subfields, a budding psychologist has hundreds of potential specialties from which to choose. For example, a psychologist

 American Psychological Association
www.mhhe.com/sdorow5

 American Psychological Society
www.mhhe.com/sdorow5

Canadian Psychological Association
www.mhhe.com/sdorow5

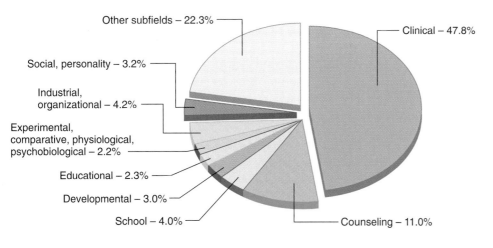

Other subfields – 22.3%

Social, personality – 3.2%

Industrial, organizational – 4.2%

Experimental, comparative, physiological, psychobiological – 2.2%

Educational – 2.3%

Developmental – 3.0%

School – 4.0%

Clinical – 47.8%

Counseling – 11.0%

◀ **Figure 1.1**
Fields of Specialization in Psychology
This pie graph presents the percentages of members of the American Psychological Association working in major fields of specialization (American Psychological Association, 1999).

 The Society for the Psychological Study of Social Issues (SPSSI)
www.mhhe.com/sdorow5

basic research
Research aimed at finding answers to questions out of theoretical interest or intellectual curiosity.

applied research
Research aimed at improving the quality of life and solving practical problems.

experimental psychology
The field primarily concerned with laboratory research on basic psychological processes, including perception, learning, memory, thinking, language, motivation, and emotion.

specializing in the field of sensation and perception might be interested in the subfield of vision, with special interest in the sub-subfield of color vision.

Psychology researchers typically conduct either **basic research,** which is aimed at contributing to knowledge, or **applied research,** which is aimed at solving a practical problem. Note that basic research and applied research are not mutually exclusive. Many psychologists conduct both kinds of research, and findings from basic research can often be applied outside of the laboratory. For example, basic research findings on learned taste aversions in rats have been applied to preventing cancer chemotherapy patients from becoming nauseated by food, which can make them lose their appetite and, as a result, become weak and emaciated (see Chapter 7).

The largest field of academic specialization in psychology is **experimental psychology.** Experimental psychologists restrict themselves chiefly to laboratory research on basic psychological processes, including perception, learning, memory, thinking, language, motivation, and emotion. Though this field is called experimental psychology, it is not the only field that uses experiments. Psychologists in almost all fields of psychology conduct experimental research. Figure 1.2 shows examples of experimental research involving human participants and animal subjects.

Consider some of the topics tackled by experimental psychologists that will be discussed in upcoming chapters. Chapter 5 describes how perception researchers determine whether human beings can identify others by their odor. Chapter 8 explains how memory

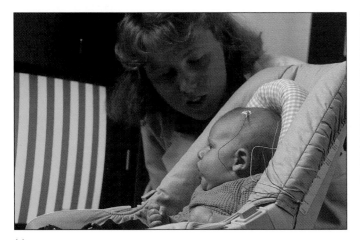

(a)

(b)

▲ **Figure 1.2**
Psychological Research
Psychologists conduct research on human participants and animal subjects, such as *(a)* measuring the brain's response to changing patterns of visual stimulation in infancy, and *(b)* training dolphins to communicate with human beings.

behavioral neuroscience
The field that studies the physiological bases of human and animal behavior and mental processes.

comparative psychology
The field that studies similarities and differences in the physiology, behaviors, and abilities of different species of animals, including human beings.

developmental psychology
The field that studies physical, perceptual, cognitive, and psychosocial changes across the life span.

personality psychology
The field that focuses on factors accounting for the differences in behavior and enduring personal characteristics among individuals.

social psychology
The field that studies how the actual, imagined, or implied presence of other people affects one another's thoughts, feelings, and behaviors.

clinical psychology
The field that applies psychological principles to the prevention, diagnosis, and treatment of psychological disorders.

counseling psychology
The field that applies psychological principles to help individuals deal with problems of daily living, generally less serious ones than those treated by clinical psychologists.

psychiatry
The field of medicine that diagnoses and treats psychological disorders by using medical or psychological forms of therapy.

school psychology
The field that applies psychological principles to help improve the academic performance and social behavior of students in elementary, middle, and high schools.

educational psychology
The field that applies psychological principles to help improve curriculum, teaching methods, and administrative procedures.

researchers assess the effect of our moods on our ability to recall memories. And Chapter 12 discusses how emotion researchers demonstrate the effect of facial expressions on emotional experiences.

Psychologists in the field of **behavioral neuroscience** study the physiological bases of behavior and mental processes. Chapter 3 discusses research by behavioral neuroscientists on the effects of natural opiates in the brain and the differences in functioning between the left and right hemispheres of the brain. In Chapter 6 you will learn of research by behavioral neuroscientists on the effects of psychoactive drugs on mind and behavior.

The related field of **comparative psychology** studies similarities and differences in the physiology, behaviors, and abilities of animals, including human beings. Comparative psychologists study motives related to eating, drinking, aggression, courtship, mating, and parenting. Chapter 9 discusses how comparative psychologists even study whether apes can learn to use language.

The field of **developmental psychology** is home to psychologists who study the factors responsible for physical, cognitive, and social changes across the life span. Chapter 4 presents research showing that infants are born with better perceptual skills than you might assume and that many gender differences might be smaller than is commonly believed.

Personality psychology is concerned with differences in behavior among individuals. As noted in Chapter 13, this field seeks answers to questions such as these: Are our personalities determined more by nature or by nurture? To what extent do people behave consistently from one situation to another? Personality psychologists also devise tests for assessing personality, such as the famous Rorschach "inkblot test."

Psychologists in the field of **social psychology** study the effects people have on one another and the power of social situations. In Chapter 17 you will learn how social psychologists study the factors affecting interpersonal attraction, the problem of "groupthink" in making important decisions, and the reasons people are often all too willing to follow orders to harm other human beings.

Professional Fields of Specialization

Professional psychologists commonly work in settings outside of college or university classrooms and laboratories. As indicated in Figure 1.1, two of the largest fields of professional psychology are **clinical psychology** and **counseling psychology,** which deal with the causes, prevention, diagnosis, and treatment of psychological disorders. Counseling psychologists tend to deal with problems of everyday living related to career planning, academic performance, and personal relationships. In contrast, clinical psychologists typically treat more serious disorders, including phobias, alcoholism, drug abuse, and severe depression. Chapter 15 discusses the various techniques used by clinical and counseling psychologists, as well as research concerning this important question: Is psychotherapy effective?

Clinical psychology and counseling psychology are distinctly different from the medical field of **psychiatry.** A psychiatrist is not a psychologist, but a physician who has served a residency in psychiatry, which takes a medical approach to the treatment of psychological disorders. Because psychiatrists are physicians, they may prescribe drugs or other biomedical treatments. Chapter 15 considers the various biopsychological treatments, including drugs to treat schizophrenia, psychosurgery to calm agitated patients, and electroconvulsive therapy to relieve depression.

Psychology has other well-established professional fields. One of the oldest is **school psychology,** founded almost a century ago in part through the efforts of functionalist G. Stanley Hall (Good, Simmons, & Smith, 1998). School psychologists work in elementary schools, middle schools, and high schools. School psychologists help improve students' academic performance and school behavior. For example, school psychologists take part in programs to prevent violence in schools (Li, 1994), to improve reading ability (Good, Simmons, & Smith, 1998), and to increase homework completion (Olympia et al., 1994).

The allied field of **educational psychology** tries to improve the educational process, including curriculum, teaching, and the administration of academic programs. For example, educational psychologists hope to improve medical education by studying the ways in

Chapter One

(a)

(b)

(c)

▲ **Figure 1.3**
Emerging Fields of Professional Psychology

In recent years, several new fields of professional psychology have emerged. Professionals in the field of *(a) sport psychology* help amateur and professional athletes, such as slalom skiers, improve their performance. Practitioners of *(b) health psychology* contribute to the prevention of physical illness by promoting adherence to healthy behaviors, including regular aerobic exercise, such as rowing. And *(c) environmental psychology* applies research findings to improve the physical environment, as in designing neighborhoods to reduce noise, crowding, and other sources of stress.

which medical students acquire their expertise (Schmidt & Boshuizen, 1993). Educational psychologists are usually faculty members at colleges or universities.

Psychologists who practice **industrial/organizational psychology** work to increase productivity in businesses, industries, government agencies, and virtually any other kind of organization. They do so by improving working conditions, methods for hiring and training employees, and management techniques of administrators. Industrial/organizational psychology began in North America, but it has spread to countries as far away as New Zealand (Inkson & Paterson, 1993). Appendix B discusses this important field of psychology.

Specialists in **engineering psychology** are experts in *human factors* (Stone & Moroney, 1998), the aspects of human body structure, behavior, and mental processes that must be considered when designing equipment, instruments, and other artificial aspects of the environment. Topics of concern to engineering psychologists include the improvement of warning signs (Wogalter & Laughery, 1996) and the design of instrument displays in automobiles (Ward & Parkes, 1994). Like other psychologists, engineering psychologists might need to consider social-cultural differences, as in helping to promote the effective interaction of the many personnel—often from different cultures—responsible for air-traffic safety (Maurino, 1994).

Psychologists who practice **forensic psychology** apply psychology to the legal system. The topics they study include the jury deliberation process and the best ways to select jurors. Some forensic psychologists train police to handle domestic disputes, negotiate with hostage takers, and cope with job-related stress. They also help in the development of simulators to teach officers good judgment in the use of firearms (Seymour et al., 1994). Chapter 8 describes another important issue: What is the best way to obtain eyewitness testimony from children? Figure 1.3 illustrates three emerging fields of professional psychology: **sport psychology, health psychology,** and **environmental psychology.**

STAYING ON TRACK: *Psychology as a Profession*

1. What is the difference between basic and applied research?
2. How does psychiatry differ from psychology?

Answers to Staying on Track start on p. ST-1.

industrial/organizational psychology
The field that applies psychological principles to improve productivity in businesses, industries, and government agencies.

engineering psychology
The field that applies psychological principles to the design of equipment and instruments.

forensic psychology
The field that applies psychological principles to improve the legal system, including the work of police and juries.

sport psychology
The field that applies psychological principles to help amateur and professional athletes improve their performance.

health psychology
The field that applies psychological principles to the prevention and treatment of physical illness.

environmental psychology
The field that applies psychological principles to help improve the physical environment, including the design of buildings and the reduction of noise.

Chapter Summary

THE HISTORY OF PSYCHOLOGY
- Psychology is the scientific study of behavior and mental processes.
- The roots of psychology are in philosophy and science.
- The commonly accepted founding date for psychology is 1879, when Wilhelm Wundt established the first formal psychology laboratory.
- Structuralism sought to analyze the mind into its component parts.
- Functionalism favored the study of how the conscious mind helps the individual adapt to the environment.
- Behaviorism rejected the study of the mind in favor of the study of observable behavior.
- Gestalt psychology favored the study of the mind as active and perception as holistic.
- Psychoanalysis studied the influence of unconscious motives on behavior.
- Despite obstacles presented by laws and customs, women contributed to the growth of psychology.

CONTEMPORARY PSYCHOLOGICAL PERSPECTIVES
- To date, psychology has no unifying scientific paradigm, only competing psychological perspectives.

- The behavioral perspective is a descendant of behaviorism, though cognitive behaviorists accept the study of mental processes.
- The psychoanalytic perspective accepts the role of unconscious and early childhood experiences, but places less emphasis on the sex motive than did the school of psychoanalysis.
- The humanistic perspective, which favors the study of conscious mental experience and accepts the reality of free will, arose in opposition to psychoanalysis and behaviorism.
- The cognitive perspective views the individual as an active processor of information.
- The biopsychological perspective favors the study of the biological bases of behavior, mental experiences, and cognitive processes.
- The social-cultural perspective insists psychologists must study human beings in their social and cultural contexts.

PSYCHOLOGY AS A PROFESSION
- Academic fields of specialization are chiefly concerned with conducting basic research.
- The professional fields of specialization in psychology are chiefly concerned with applying psychological research findings.

Key Concepts

psychology 4

THE HISTORY OF PSYCHOLOGY
analytic introspection 8
behaviorism 10
differential psychology 7
empiricism 5
functionalism 9
Gestalt psychology 11
nativism 4
phi phenomenon 11
psychic determinism 12
psychoanalysis 11
psychophysics 6

rationalism 4
structuralism 8

CONTEMPORARY PSYCHOLOGICAL PERSPECTIVES
behavioral genetics 19
behavioral perspective 16
biopsychological perspective 18
cognitive perspective 18
cross-cultural psychology 19
cultural psychology 19
ethnic psychology 19
evolutionary psychology 19
existential psychology 17

humanistic perspective 17
phenomenological psychology 17
psychoanalytic perspective 17
scientific paradigm 16
social-cultural perspective 19

PSYCHOLOGY AS A PROFESSION
applied research 21
basic research 21
behavioral neuroscience 22
clinical psychology 22
comparative psychology 22
counseling psychology 22

developmental psychology 22
educational psychology 22
engineering psychology 23
environmental psychology 23
experimental psychology 21
forensic psychology 23
health psychology 23
industrial/organizational psychology 23
personality psychology 22
psychiatry 22
school psychology 22
social psychology 22
sport psychology 23

Key Contributors

THE HISTORY OF PSYCHOLOGY
Aristotle 4
Saint Augustine 5
Avicenna 5
Francis Bacon 5

Mary Whiton Calkins 14
James McKeen Cattell 7
Charles Darwin 7
René Descartes 5
John Dewey 9
Hermann Ebbinghaus 7

Gustav Fechner 6
Pierre Flourens 6
Sigmund Freud 11
Francis Galton 7
William James 9
Immanuel Kant 6

Kurt Koffka 11
Wolfgang Köhler 11
Christine Ladd-Franklin 14
John Locke 5
Hugo Münsterberg 9
Plato 4

Francis Sumner 10
Edward Titchener 8
Hermann von Helmholtz 6
Margaret Floy Washburn 14
John B. Watson 10
Ernst Weber 6
Max Wertheimer 11

Wilhelm Wundt 7

CONTEMPORARY
PSYCHOLOGICAL
PERSPECTIVES
Alfred Adler 17
Albert Bandura 16

Mamie and Kenneth Clark 20
William E. Cross, Jr. 20
Anna Freud 17
Carl Jung 17
Melanie Klein 17
Abraham Maslow 17
Wilder Penfield 18

Jean Piaget 18
Carl Rogers 17
Herbert Simon 18
B. F. Skinner 16
Roger Sperry 18
Harry Triandis 19

Thought Questions

1. How would nativists and empiricists differ in their opinion of early-childhood intervention projects, such as Head Start?
2. In the late 19th century and early 20th century, many Americans believed women's and men's lives should be lived in "separate spheres." How did this notion limit women's contributions to psychology?

3. Suppose you find that your professor is an unusually "happy" person—smiling, cracking jokes, and complimenting students on their brilliant insights. How would the different psychological perspectives explain this behavior?

Possible Answers to Thought Questions start on p. PT-1.

OLC Preview

For additional quizzing and a variety of interactive resources, visit the book's Online Learning Center at www.mhhe.com/sdorow5.

Psychology as a Science

TUSCAN EVENING
Vincent Ceglia, 1995

As discussed in Chapter 1, psychology is a science that studies human and animal behavior and mental processes. This means that psychology deals with topics of great interest to people, making them also of particular interest to the media. But the media are at times more interested in attracting readers, viewers, and listeners than in the objective reporting of scientific findings. This often leads the media to exaggerate or sensationalize research findings. Consider the media's coverage of the supposed effects of the hormone melatonin.

Is Melatonin Effective in Overcoming Insomnia?

In November 1995, *Newsweek* magazine published a cover story (Cowley, 1995) about a craze involving the alleged beneficial physical and psychological effects of a "natural wonder drug": the hormone melatonin. Melatonin, secreted by the pineal gland (located in the center of the brain), was touted in the article as a cure for aging, insomnia, and jet lag. And *Newsweek* was not alone. Reports by magazines, newspapers, radio stations, and television networks across the United States added to the excitement about melatonin.

The effect of the media was so powerful that many health-food stores could not keep up with the demand for melatonin pills. At the time the *Newsweek* article was published, a book praising the effects of melatonin was third on the *New York Times* best-sellers list. Though the craze has subsided since 1995, the media still include periodic reports on the effects of melatonin—and the Internet is brimming with websites praising the alleged benefits of melatonin, while just so happening to offer melatonin for sale.

Should readers have accepted the claims about melatonin's amazing effects simply because they appeared in a popular news weekly? Psychologists, being scientists, do not accept such claims unless they are supported by sound scientific research findings. As you read this chapter, you will learn how a psychologist might use the scientific method to conduct an experiment to test the effects of melatonin. But you must first understand the nature of psychology as a science.

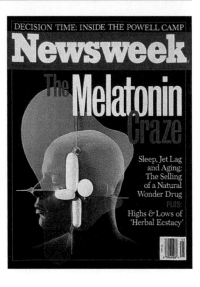

◀ **Science Versus Pseudoscience**
Should we accept media reports as strong evidence for popular claims, such as melatonin's alleged ability to promote sleep, overcome jet lag, and slow the aging process? Scientists require more rigorous standards of evidence than that.

*I*n discussing psychology as a science, this chapter will answer questions such as these: Why do psychologists use the scientific method? What are the goals of psychological research? How do psychologists employ the scientific method in their research? The answers to these questions will help you appreciate the scientific basis of the issues, theories, research findings, and practical applications presented throughout this book.

Theoretical and Philosophical Psychology

www.mhhe.com/sdorow5

◆ Sources of Knowledge

Psychologists and other scientists favor the scientific method as their means of obtaining knowledge, such as knowledge about the effects of melatonin. To appreciate why they do, you need to appreciate the shortcomings of the everyday alternative to the scientific method: *common sense.*

Common Sense

When you rely on common sense, you assume that the beliefs you have obtained from everyday life are trustworthy. Commonsense beliefs come from a variety of sources, including statements by recognized authorities, your own reasoning about things, and observations from your personal experience. Unfortunately, many college students view psychology as little more than common sense—until they are presented examples of how their commonsense beliefs are false (Osberg, 1993). The photograph of the student changing an answer on a multiple-choice exam provides an example of the shortcomings of common sense that might surprise you.

As another example of the frailty of common sense, consider the practice of calling time-outs during the last few minutes of a close basketball game when an opposing player is about to shoot free throws. This is done to make the player "choke" and miss the shots. The effectiveness of this commonsense strategy was examined in a study of the archival records of 1,237 men's NCAA Division I basketball games from 1977 to 1989. A perusal of the play-by-play records of the games revealed—in accordance with common sense—that when the score became closer and the time remaining decreased, the opposing coaches became more likely to call time-outs when an opposing player was about to shoot free throws. But contrary to common sense, this strategy proved ineffective; in fact, free-throw percentages tended to *increase* after time-outs (Kozar et al., 1993).

Even the judicial system, which strives for objectivity in courtroom deliberations, at times relies more on common sense than on scientific research to settle important issues, such as jurors' ability to disregard prejudicial information they have gained from pretrial media publicity (Studebaker & Penrod, 1997). But note that scientists do not discount the possibility that commonsense beliefs might be true. According to Harold Kelley, a leading researcher on commonsense thinking, "Discarding our commonsense psychology baggage would require us needlessly to separate ourselves from the vast sources of knowledge gained in the course of human history" (Kelley, 1992, p. 22). In other words, common sense can inspire scientific research, even though it cannot substitute for it. The Psychology Versus Common Sense feature illustrates how scientific research findings can contradict commonsense beliefs.

The Scientific Method

Because of the weaknesses of common sense, scientists prefer the *scientific method*, which is based on certain assumptions and follows a formal series of steps. The fact that the scientific method is the dominant research method in psychology owes much to psychology's origins in 19th-century natural science.

Assumptions of Science

Scientists share some basic assumptions that guide their thinking about physical reality. Two of the most important of these assumptions are *determinism* and *skepticism*.

Determinism and Lawfulness. Albert Einstein was fond of saying, "God does not play dice with the universe." In using the scientific method, psychologists and other scientists share his belief that there is order in the universe, meaning that the relationships among events are lawful, rather than haphazard. In looking for these lawful relationships, scientists also share the assumption of **determinism,** which holds that every event has physical, potentially measurable, causes. This rules out free will and supernatural influences as causes of behavior.

Yet, as pointed out a century ago by William James, scientists might be committed to determinism in conducting their research, while being tempted to assume the existence of free will in their everyday lives (Immergluck, 1964). They might succumb to this temptation because, if carried to its logical extreme, the assumption of strict determinism would lead them to unpalatable conclusions—for example, that Mother Teresa did not deserve praise for her work with the poor and that Adolph Hitler did not deserve blame for his acts of genocide, because neither was free to choose otherwise. This also means that strict determinism is incompatible with the legal system, which assumes the existence of free will in order to hold criminals responsible for their actions. Despite centuries of philosophical debate, neither side of the determinism versus free will debate has won the battle. And psychologists are probably no more likely than philosophers to resolve this controversy, though some still try (Slife & Fisher, 2000).

Skepticism and Critical Thinking. Aside from assuming the universe is an orderly place in which events—including behaviors—are governed by determinism, scientists today, like René Descartes before them, insist that open-minded **skepticism** is the best predisposition when judging the merits of any claim. Open-minded skepticism requires the maintenance of a delicate balance between cynicism and gullibility. As Mario Bunge, a leading philosopher of science, has said, skeptics "do not believe anything in the absence of evidence, but they are willing to explore bold new ideas if they find reasons to suspect that they have a chance" (Bunge, 1992, p. 380). This skeptical attitude requires supportive evidence before accepting any claim. The failure to maintain a skeptical attitude leads to the acceptance of phenomena, such as ESP, that have inadequate empirical support (Stanwick, 1998).

Skepticism is important in psychology, because many psychological "truths" are tentative, in part because psychological research findings depend on the times and places in which the research takes place. What is generally true of human behavior in one era or culture might be false in another era or culture. For example, gender differences in behavior in Western cultures have changed dramatically over the past few decades, and gender differences observed in Western cultures might be unlike those in non-Western cultures. More than two decades

determinism
The assumption that every event has physical, potentially measurable, causes.

 International Network of Skeptical Organizations
www.mhhe.com/sdorow5

skepticism
An attitude that doubts all claims not supported by solid research evidence.

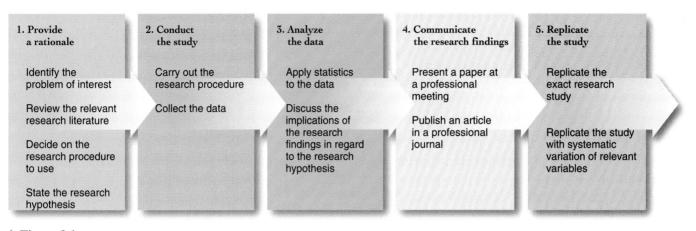

▲ **Figure 2.1**
The Scientific Method

Critical Thinking on the Web
www.mhhe.com/sdorow5

scientific method
A source of knowledge based on the assumption that knowledge comes from the objective, systematic observation and measurement of particular variables and the events they affect.

hypothesis
A testable prediction about the relationship between two or more events or characteristics.

statistics
Mathematical techniques used to summarize research data or to determine whether the data support the researcher's hypothesis.

replication
The repetition of a research study, usually with some alterations in its methods or setting, to determine whether the principles derived from that study hold up under similar circumstances.

before the social-cultural perspective (see Chapter 1) achieved its current widespread acceptance in North American psychology, Anne Anastasi (1972), in her presidential address to the American Psychological Association, showed foresight in urging psychologists not to confuse their ethnocentric personal beliefs and values with scientific "truths."

Skepticism is valuable not only for scientists, but for all of us in our everyday lives, including in your academic courses (Carlson, 1995). Skepticism is the basis of critical thinking—the systematic evaluation of claims and assumptions. The following steps in critical thinking will serve you well as you evaluate claims made in your everyday life:

- *First,* identify the claim being made. Ask yourself if the claim is based on empirical data (which would be subject to scientific evaluation) or on personal values, opinions, or religious beliefs (which would be less subject to scientific evaluation).
- *Second,* examine the evidence in support of the claim. Is the evidence accurate? If so, does it logically support the claim?
- *Third,* consider possible alternative explanations of the claim. Perhaps there is a better explanation than the one that has been given.

Steps in Conducting Scientific Research

Because psychologists are skeptical about claims not supported by research findings, they employ the **scientific method** as their means of gaining knowledge. Though scientists vary in their approach to the scientific method, ideally they follow a formal series of steps (as shown in Figure 2.1).

Step 1. The first step is to provide a *rationale* for the study. The scientist identifies the problem, reviews the relevant research literature, decides on the research method to use, and states the research **hypothesis**. A hypothesis (from the Greek word for "supposition") is a testable prediction about the relationship between two or more events or characteristics.

Step 2. The second step is to *conduct* the study. The scientist carries out the research procedure and collects data.

Step 3. The third step is to *analyze* the data, usually by using logical, mathematical techniques called **statistics,** and discussing the implications of the research findings.

Step 4. The fourth step is to *communicate* the research findings. The scientist presents papers at professional meetings and publishes articles in professional journals. In doing so, the scientist includes the rationale for the research, the exact method that was used, the results of the research, and a discussion of the implications of the results.

Step 5. The fifth step is to *replicate* the study. **Replication** involves repeating the study, exactly or with some variation. Successful replications of research studies strengthen confidence in their findings.

These steps were used by psychologist Donn Byrne and his colleagues (Byrne, Ervin, & Lamberth, 1970) in a classic research study of an issue regarding interpersonal attraction:

Can We Reliably Detect When Someone Is Drunk?

In the landmark 1961 Zane decision, a New Jersey court stated, "Whether the man is sober or intoxicated is a matter of common observation not requiring special knowledge or skill" (Langenbucher & Nathan, 1983, p. 1071). This is an important assumption, because state laws in the United States, based on the commonsense belief that drunkenness is easily detected, hold people, such as party hosts and tavern owners, legally responsible for the actions of people who become drunk at their homes or businesses. The ability to detect drunkenness was tested in a scientific study by alcohol researchers James Langenbucher and Peter Nathan (1983).

Langenbucher and Nathan had 12 bartenders, 49 social drinkers, and 30 police officers observe drinkers and judge whether they were legally drunk or sober. The drinkers in each case were two male and two female young adults. Each drinker consumed one of three types of drinks: tonic water, moderate doses of vodka (but not enough to become legally drunk), or high doses of vodka (enough to become legally drunk). A breathalyzer assured that the desired blood-alcohol levels were achieved for participants in the two vodka conditions.

The bartenders observed their participants being interviewed in a cocktail lounge. The social drinkers observed their participants being interviewed in the Alcohol Behavior Research Laboratory at Rutgers University. And the police officers observed their participants in a simulated nighttime roadside arrest in which they were given 3 minutes to determine whether the motorist they had pulled over was drunk or sober.

Langenbucher and Nathan used statistics to analyze their data. They found that the observers correctly judged the drinkers' level of intoxication only 25 percent of the time. Not a single legally drunk person was identified as such by a significant number of the observers. Of the 91 persons who served as judges, only 5 were consistently accurate—and all of them were members of a New Jersey State Police special tactical unit for the apprehension of drunk drivers. Those 5 police officers had received more than 90 hours of training in the detection of drunkenness. The results implied that without special training, even people with extensive experience in observing drinkers might be unable to determine whether a person is legally drunk or sober. The social implication of these findings is that common sense is wrong in assuming that people with experience in observing drinkers can detect whether someone is drunk. We are even more confident in the findings of this study because they were replicated in a different experiment conducted by a different researcher, using different participants, in a different research setting (Beatty, 1984). Perhaps bartenders, police officers, and habitual party givers should obtain special training similar to that given the 5 police officers who performed well in the study.

▲ **The Detection of Drunkenness**
Scientific research contradicts the commonsense belief that we can easily detect when someone is legally drunk.

Do opposites attract? Or do birds of a feather flock together? In his study, the problem concerned the relationship between interpersonal similarity and interpersonal attraction. After reviewing the research literature relevant to the problem, Byrne decided to conduct a *field experiment* in which college students were studied in a real-life setting instead of in a laboratory. In fact, his study was a replication conducted to determine whether the results of previous laboratory studies on the effects of attitude similarity on social attraction would generalize to a field setting. Based on his review of the literature, Byrne hypothesized that heterosexual men and women with similar attitudes would be more likely to be attracted to each other.

Byrne had his participants complete a 50-item questionnaire that assessed their attitudes as part of a computer-dating service. He told them their responses would be used to pair them with an opposite-sex student who shared their attitudes. But the students were actually paired so that some partners were similar in attitudes and others were dissimilar. Their similarity on the questionnaire provided a concrete definition of "similarity." The 44 couples, selected from 420 volunteers, were then sent to the student union for a snack. After this 30-minute get-acquainted date, they were asked to rate their partners, which provided Byrne with his research data.

Byrne then analyzed the data. Like almost all researchers, he used statistics to summarize his data and to determine whether they supported his hypothesis. In this case, Byrne found that the data did support the hypothesis. Partners who were similar in attitudes were more likely to recall each other's name, to have talked with each other since the date, and to desire to date each other again. Thus, in this study, the use of the scientific method found that birds of a feather tend to flock together.

Byrne communicated his findings by publishing them in a professional journal. He also might have shared his findings by presenting them at a research conference. Even undergraduate psychology researchers can present the results of their research studies at undergraduate psychology research conferences held each year.

STAYING ON TRACK: *Sources of Knowledge*

1. What are the basic assumptions of science?
2. What is critical thinking?
3. What are the formal steps in the scientific method?

Answers to Staying on Track start on p. ST-1.

♦ GOALS OF SCIENTIFIC RESEARCH

In conducting their research, psychologists and other scientists share common goals. They pursue the goals of *description, prediction, control,* and *explanation* of behavior and mental experiences.

Description

To a scientist, *description* involves noting the observable characteristics of an event, object, or individual. For example, we might note that participants who take daily doses of melatonin report they sleep longer.

Psychologists, following in the intellectual tradition of Francis Bacon, discussed in Chapter 1, are *systematic* in what they describe. Instead of arbitrarily describing everything they observe, they describe only things that are relevant to their research problem. Thus, good observational skills are essential to psychologists. The need to be systematic in what you describe is expressed well in a statement about criminal investigations made by the fictional detective Sherlock Holmes to his friend Dr. Watson:

> ▶ A fool takes in all the lumber [facts] that he comes across, so that the knowledge which might be useful to him gets crowded out, or at best is jumbled up with a lot of other things. . . . It is of the highest importance, therefore, not to have useless facts elbowing out the useful ones. (Doyle, 1930)

In science, descriptions must be more than systematic; they must be precise. Precise descriptions are concrete, rather than abstract. This typically involves **measurement,** the use of numbers to represent events or characteristics. According to Francis Galton, one of the pioneers of psychology, "Until the phenomena of any branch of knowledge have been submitted to measurement . . . it cannot assume the status and dignity of a science" (Cowles, 1989, p. 2). Thus, describing a friend as "generous" would be acceptable in everyday conversation but would be too imprecise for scientific communication.

measurement
The use of numbers to represent events or characteristics.

Scientists solve this problem by using **operational definitions,** which define behaviors or qualities in terms of the procedures used to measure or produce them. Donn Byrne did this when he defined *similarity* according to participants' responses to a questionnaire in his study of interpersonal attractiveness. More than a century ago, Francis Galton, in studying audience behavior at plays and lectures, operationally defined *boredom* by recording the number of fidgets by audience members. You might operationally define *generous* as "donating more than 5 percent of one's salary to charity." A common operational definition of *drunk* is "a blood-alcohol level of at least 0.1 percent." Though operational definitions are desirable, psychologists sometimes find it difficult to agree on acceptable ones. For example, a recent journal article was devoted to arguments about how best to operationally define *psychological child abuse* by parents (Gorey & Leslie, 1997).

Prediction

Psychologists are not content just to describe things. They also make predictions in the form of hypotheses about changes in behavior, mental experiences, or physiological processes. A hypothesis is usually based on a **theory,** which is a set of statements that summarize and explain research findings and from which research hypotheses can be derived. For example, Sigmund Freud's theory of psychoanalysis integrates many observations he had made of the characteristics of people suffering from psychological disorders. Theories provide coherence to scientific research and suggest applications of research findings, making science more than the accumulation of isolated facts (Kukla, 1989).

Because we cannot know all the factors that affect a person or an animal at a given time, psychologists are never certain about their theories or the predictions made in their research hypotheses. In fact, it would be pointless to conduct a research study whose outcome would be certain. Moreover, scientific predictions about human participants or animal subjects are usually more accurate when applied to many people or animals than when applied to a specific case. For example, your automobile insurance company can more accurately predict the percentage of people in your age group who will have an accident this year than it can predict whether you will have one. Likewise, though melatonin might prove effective in treating insomnia for most people, we would be unable to predict with certainty whether a particular person would benefit from it.

Psychology has nothing to apologize for in being limited to probabilistic prediction, because this situation is no different in the other sciences, which can make predictions only with certain probabilities of being correct (Hedges, 1987). Your physician might prescribe an antibiotic that, based on medical research, is effective 98 percent of the time in treating pneumonia, but she or he cannot guarantee it will cure your pneumonia. Similarly, seismologists know that regions along geological faults are more likely to experience earthquakes, but they cannot accurately predict the day, or even the year, when an earthquake will occur in a given region. For example, the U.S. Geological Survey estimates there is a 76 percent chance of a powerful earthquake of 6.7 or larger on the Richter seismic scale in northern California before the year 2030 (Perlman, 1999). But seismologists are far from being able to predict that "a magnitude 7.3 earthquake will strike 18 miles northeast of San Francisco in the spring of 2014." In the same vein, in regard to interpersonal attraction, people who are similar to each other will probably—but not always—be more attracted to each other than are people who are different from each other. We cannot predict with certainty whether two specific people who are similar to each other will be attracted to each other.

Control

Psychologists go beyond describing and predicting changes in behavior, mental experiences, and physiological processes. They also try to control them by manipulating factors that affect them. The notion of control is used in two ways (Cowles, 1989). First, as you will read in the upcoming discussion of methods of psychological research, *control* is an essential ingredient in the conduct of experiments. Second, psychologists try to apply their

operational definition
The definition of behaviors or qualities in terms of the procedures used to measure or produce them.

theory
An integrated set of statements that summarizes and explains research findings, and from which research hypotheses can be derived.

research findings to the control of behavior in everyday life. Thus, melatonin might be prescribed to control insomnia by inducing sleep, and young adults might be advised to find romance by seeking people who share their values and interests.

Explanation

The ultimate goal of psychology is *explanation*—the discovery of the causes of overt behaviors and mental experiences. If it is demonstrated that people who ingest melatonin do overcome insomnia, the next step might be explaining how melatonin affects the brain to trigger sleep. And even though we know that interpersonal similarity promotes interpersonal attraction, we would still need to explain why we prefer people who are similar to us.

As discussed in Chapter 1, a psychologist's favored perspective determines where she or he looks for explanations of psychological events. Psychologists who favor the cognitive, humanistic, or psychoanalytic perspective will look for causes in the mind. Psychologists who favor the behavioral perspective will look for causes in the environment. Psychologists who favor the biopsychological perspective will look for causes in the brain or hormonal system. And psychologists who favor the social-cultural perspective will look for causes in the social or cultural context of the event.

STAYING ON TRACK: *Goals of Scientific Research*

1. Why do scientists use operational definitions?
2. In what way are psychology and other sciences probabilistic?
3. What is the nature of scientific explanation in psychology?

Answers to Staying on Track start on p. ST-1.

◆ METHODS OF PSYCHOLOGICAL RESEARCH

Given that psychologists favor the scientific method as their primary source of knowledge, how do they use it in their research? And once they have collected their data, how do they make sense of it? As shown in Table 2.1, psychologists use research methods that permit them to describe, predict, control, or explain relationships among variables. *Descriptive research* pursues the goal of description, *correlational research* pursues the goal of prediction, and *experimental research* pursues the goals of control and explanation.

Descriptive Research

Descriptive research is descriptive because the researcher simply records what he or she has systematically observed. Descriptive research methods include *naturalistic observation, case studies, surveys, psychological testing,* and *archival research.*

Naturalistic Observation

In **naturalistic observation,** people or animals are observed in their natural environment. Researchers who use naturalistic observation study topics as diverse as gender differences in flirtation (McCormick & Jones, 1989) and the ability to recall where one has parked one's car

PsycINFO Direct
www.mhhe.com/sdorow5

Psychological Research on the Net
www.mhhe.com/sdorow5

descriptive research
Research that involves the recording of behaviors that have been observed systematically.

naturalistic observation
The recording of the behavior of people or animals in their natural environments, with little or no intervention by the researcher.

Table 2.1	The Goals and Methods of Psychology	
Goal	**Research Method**	**Relevant Question**
Description	Descriptive	What are its characteristics?
Prediction	Correlational	How likely is it?
Control	Experimental	Can I make it happen?
Explanation	Experimental	What causes it?

Chapter Two

(Lutz, Means, & Long, 1994). To make sure their observations represent natural behavior, observers refrain as much as possible from influencing the individuals they are observing. In other words, the observer remains *unobtrusive*. If you were studying the eating behavior of students in your school cafeteria, you would not announce your intention over the loudspeaker. Otherwise, your participants might behave unnaturally; a person who normally gorged on cake, ice cream, and chocolate pudding for dessert might eat Jello instead.

Naturalistic observation is also used in studying animal behavior. Some of the best-known studies employing naturalistic observation have been conducted by Jane Goodall, who has spent more than three decades observing chimpanzees in Gombe National Park in Tanzania. To prevent chimpanzees from acting unnaturally because of her presence, Goodall spends her initial observation periods letting them get used to her.

The study of animal behavior in the natural environment, as in Goodall's research, is called **ethology.** One of the advantages of an ethological approach is the potential discovery of behaviors not found in more artificial settings, such as zoos and laboratories. Goodall has reported observations of chimpanzee behavior that have not been made in captivity, such as cannibalism, infanticide, and unprovoked killing of other chimpanzees (Goodall, 1990).

ethology

The study of animal behavior in the natural environment.

case study
An in-depth study of an individual.

survey
A set of questions related to a particular topic of interest administered to a sample of people through an interview or questionnaire.

▲ **The Case Study**
In the movie *Sybil*, Sally Field portrayed a young woman with sixteen different personalities. The movie was based on the case study of a woman who developed a dissociative identity disorder, apparently as a consequence of extreme childhood abuse. This photograph shows Sybil (Field, *wearing glasses*) and her psychotherapist (as portrayed by Joanne Woodward).

But researchers who use naturalistic observation, like those who use other research methods, must not be hasty in generalizing their findings. Even the generalizability of Jane Goodall's observations must be qualified. The behavior of the Gombe chimpanzees differs from the behavior of chimpanzees in the Mahali Mountains of western Tanzania. For example, female Mahali chimpanzees hunt more often than female Gombe chimpanzees do (Takahata, Hasegawa, & Nishida, 1984).

Naturalistic observation cannot determine the causes of the observed behavior, because there are simply too many factors at work in a natural setting. So you could not determine *why* female chimpanzees hunt more in one part of Tanzania than in another—is it due to differences in prey, in climate, or in topography, or in another factor, or some combination of factors? It would be impossible to tell just by using naturalistic observation.

Case Studies

Another descriptive research method is the **case study**—an in-depth study of a person, typically conducted to gain knowledge about a psychological phenomenon that is rare or that would be unethical to study experimentally (such as the effects of brain damage). The case study researcher obtains as much relevant information as possible about a host of factors, including the person's thoughts, feelings, life experiences, and social relationships. The case study is often used in clinical studies of people suffering from psychological disorders. In fact, Sigmund Freud based his theory of psychoanalysis on data he obtained from clinical case studies.

More recently, a best-selling book and a television movie presented the case study of a woman called Sybil, who suffered from the rare psychological disorder known as *dissociative identity disorder,* in which the person shifts from one distinct personality to another. Sybil reportedly had sixteen separate personalities, including men and women and adults and children. In seeking help, Sybil attended 2,354 psychotherapy sessions, during which she and her psychiatrist discovered that her disorder was apparently the result of a childhood filled with physical and psychological torture inflicted by her mother.

Because a person's behavior is affected by many variables, the case study method cannot determine the particular variables that caused the behavior being studied. Though it might seem reasonable to assume that Sybil's traumatic childhood experiences caused her to defend herself from intense emotional distress by developing multiple personalities, that assumption might be wrong. Other factors, unrelated to how she was treated by her mother, might have caused her disorder. It is even conceivable that Sybil's mother began torturing her only *after* discovering she had multiple personalities.

Another shortcoming of the case study is that the results of a single case study, no matter how dramatic, cannot be generalized to all people. Even if Sybil's disorder was caused by traumatic childhood experiences, other people with dissociative identity disorder might not have had traumatic childhoods. However, as you will learn in Chapter 14, numerous case studies have shown that people with dissociative identity disorder usually have had traumatic childhoods—making it more likely, but not certain, that a traumatic childhood is a cause of the disorder.

Surveys

When psychologists wish to collect information about behaviors, opinions, attitudes, life experiences, or personal characteristics of many people, they use the descriptive research method called the *survey.* A **survey** asks participants a series of questions about the topic of interest, such as product preferences or political opinions. Surveys deal with topics as varied as the use of condoms to prevent AIDS (Albarracin et al., 2000) and the factors involved in physical attacks on baseball umpires (Rainey, 1994).

Surveys are commonly in the form of personal *interviews* or written *questionnaires.* You have probably been asked to respond to several surveys in the past year, whether enclosed in the "You May Have Already Won!" offers that you receive in the mail or conducted by your student government association to get your views on campus policies. The prevalence of surveys, and the annoyance they can induce, is not new. A century ago, William James (1890/1981) was so irritated by the seeming omnipresence of surveys that he called them

◀ **The Survey**

Just as biased sampling affected the results of polls on voter preference during the 1936 presidential campaign, it did the same in 1948. The editor of the *Chicago Daily Tribune* had so much confidence in a Gallup poll that placed Thomas Dewey well ahead of Harry Truman that on the night of the election he published an edition proclaiming Dewey the winner. He was more than a little embarrassed when Truman won. The photograph shows Truman gleefully displaying the premature headline after learning that he had won. The Gallup poll was accused of making Dewey's supporters too confident, so that many failed to vote on election day, giving the election to Truman. Criticism that polls can have such an effect on voters has continued to this day.

"one of the pests of life." Today, the most ambitious of these "pests" is the U.S. Census, which is conducted every 10 years. Others you might be familiar with include the Gallup public opinion polls and Nielsen television ratings survey.

Good surveys use clearly worded questions that do not bias the respondent to answer in a particular way. But surveys are limited by respondents' willingness to answer honestly and by social desirability—the tendency to give appropriate responses. You can imagine the potential effect of social desirability on responses to surveys on delicate topics such as child abuse, academic cheating, or sexual practices.

Still another issue to consider in surveys is the effect of social-cultural differences between test takers. You are certainly familiar with questionnaires that ask you to respond on a scale from, say, 1 to 7, with 1 meaning "strongly agree" and 7 meaning "strongly disagree." A study of high school students from several countries found they differed in the degree to which they were willing to use the extreme points on scales like this. Students from Japan and Taiwan were more likely to use the midpoint than were students from Canada and the United States. This finding might be attributable to the greater tendency toward individualism in North American cultures and the greater tendency toward collectivism in East Asian cultures (Chen, Lee, & Stevenson, 1995). Consequently, researchers who use these kinds of scales must consider the cultural backgrounds of their participants when interpreting their survey findings.

Because of practical and financial constraints, surveys rarely include everyone of interest. Instead, researchers administer a survey to a **sample** of people who represent the target **population.** In conducting a survey at your school, you might interview a sample of 100 students. But for the results of your survey to be generalizable to the entire student population at your school, your sample must be representative of the student body in age, sex, and any other relevant characteristics. This is best achieved by **random sampling,** which makes each member of the population equally likely to be included in the sample.

The need for a sample to be representative of its population was dramatically demonstrated in a notorious poll conducted by the *Literary Digest* during the 1936 U.S. presidential election. The *Literary Digest*'s presidential poll, based on millions of ballots, had accurately predicted each presidential election from 1916 through 1932. In 1936, based on that poll, the editors predicted that Alf Landon, the Republican candidate, would easily defeat Franklin Roosevelt, the Democratic candidate. Yet Roosevelt defeated Landon in a landslide.

What went wrong with the poll? Evidently the participants included in the survey were a *biased sample,* not representative of those who voted. Many of the participants were selected from telephone directories or automobile registration lists, in an era when telephones and automobiles were luxuries to many people and those who had telephones or automobiles

sample
A group of participants selected from a population.

population
A group of individuals who share certain characteristics.

random sampling
The selection of a sample from a population so that each member of the population has an equal chance of being included.

▲ **Anne Anastasi**

"The test user cannot properly evaluate a test without having some familiarity with the major steps in test construction and some knowledge of the psychometric features of tests, especially as they pertain to norms, reliability, and validity."

psychological test
A formal sample of a person's behavior, whether written or performed.

standardization
1. A procedure assuring that a test is administered and scored in a consistent manner. 2. A procedure for establishing test norms by giving a test to large samples of people who are representative of those for whom the test is designed.

norm
A score, based on the test performances of large numbers of participants, that is used as a standard for assessing the performances of test takers.

reliability
The extent to which a test gives consistent results.

validity
The extent to which a test measures what it is supposed to measure.

tended to be wealthier than those who did not. Because Republican candidates attracted wealthier voters than did Democratic candidates, people who had telephones or automobiles were more likely to favor the Republican, Landon, than the Democrat, Roosevelt. The previous polls did not suffer from this bias because economic differences among voters did not significantly affect their party allegiances until the 1936 election.

Psychological Testing

A widely used descriptive research method is the **psychological test,** which is a formal sample of a person's behavior, whether written or performed. The advantage of good tests is that they can help us make more unbiased educational, vocational, or other decisions about individuals. There are many psychological tests, including tests of interests, attitudes, abilities, creativity, intelligence, and personality. As noted by Anne Anastasi (1985), who has been an influential authority on psychological testing for the past few decades, a good test reflects important principles of test construction: *standardization, reliability,* and *validity.*

There are two kinds of **standardization.** The first kind assures that the test will be administered and scored in a consistent manner. In giving a test, all test administrators must use the same instructions, the same time limits, and the same scoring system. If they do not, a test taker's score might misrepresent her or his characteristics. The second kind of standardization establishes **norms,** which are the standards used to compare the scores of test takers. Without norms, a score on an intelligence test would be a meaningless number. Norms are established by giving the test to samples of hundreds or thousands of people who are representative of the people for whom the test is designed. If a test is to be used in North America, samples might include representative proportions of homosexual and heterosexual men and women; people from all ethnic groups; lower-, middle-, and upper-class individuals; and urban, rural, and suburban dwellers.

The use of testing norms became popular beginning in the early 20th century, in part because of the introduction of the Stanford-Binet Intelligence Scale in 1916 by Lewis Terman. In one case, Terman used the scale's norms to prevent the execution of a mentally retarded young man who had committed a heinous murder. Should he have been tried as an adult and, therefore, as responsible for his actions? Or was he so intellectually limited that he should not have been held responsible? The man's score on the Stanford-Binet indicated that his mental age was equivalent to that of a 7-year-old child. Terman testified as a defense witness in opposition to the prosecution's expert witness, who claimed that the young man could perform various activities only an adult could perform. But he presented no more evidence than his own opinion. Terman convinced the jury, using his intelligence scale's norms as objective evidence, that the activities noted by the prosecution witness could easily be performed by a child of 7 or 8 years of age. The jury accepted that the man was mentally retarded and ruled out the death penalty in his case (Dahlstrom, 1993).

An adequate psychological test must also be *reliable.* The **reliability** of a test is the degree to which it gives consistent results. Suppose you took an IQ test and scored 105 (average) one month, 62 (mentally retarded) the next month, and 138 (mentally gifted) the third month. Because your level of intelligence would not fluctuate that much in 3 months, you would argue that the test is unreliable.

One way to determine whether a test is reliable is to use the *test-retest method,* in which the same test is given to a group of people on two occasions. The greater the consistency of the scores on the tests from one occasion to the other, the higher the reliability of the test. Intelligence tests typically have high reliability, but personality tests typically have low to moderate reliability. The uses of intelligence testing and personality testing are discussed in Chapters 10 and 13, respectively.

A reliable test would be useless if it were not also valid. **Validity** is the extent to which a test measures what it is supposed to measure. An important kind of validity, *predictive validity,* indicates that the test accurately predicts behavior related to what the test is supposed to measure. A test of mechanical ability with predictive validity would accurately predict who would perform better as an automobile mechanic. The behavior or characteristic that is being predicted by a test, whether baking, automobile repair, or academic performance, is called a *criterion.* One of the first studies of the predictive validity of a formal test was conducted by Francis Galton. He collected the civil service exam scores of hundreds of Englishmen who had taken the test in 1861 and compared them to their salaries 20 years later. He found that the exam had good predictive validity, in that those who had scored higher had higher salaries (the criterion) than did those who had scored lower.

Archival Research

The largest potential source of knowledge from descriptive research is **archival research,** which examines collections of letters, manuscripts, tape recordings, video recordings, or similar materials. The uses of archival research are virtually without limit. Do right-handed people live longer than left-handed people (Aggleton, Kentridge, & Neave, 1993)? The answers to this, and other, questions asked by archival research studies are presented in upcoming chapters.

Archives also are valuable sources of historical information. Chiefly through the efforts of John Popplestone and Marion McPherson, the Archives of the History of American Psychology at the University of Akron, which is the main repository of records related to the growth of American psychology, have provided insight into the major issues, pioneers, and landmark events in the history of American psychology (Popplestone & McPherson, 1976). And consider this question: What changes have there been in gender roles? One archival study of articles published in psychology journals found that the proportion of women listed as first authors and journal editors increased from 1970 to 1990 (Gannon et al., 1992). This indicates that women may have played a progressively greater role in psychology over that period. But note that, as is true of all descriptive research, archival research does not permit definite causal statements about the findings. For example, the archival study just described does not present enough information to let you determine *why* women were publishing more frequently or more likely to hold editorial positions.

Correlational Research

When psychologists want to predict changes in one variable from changes in another, rather than simply describe something, they turn to **correlational research.** A **correlation** refers to the degree of relationship between two or more *variables*. A **variable** is an event, behavior, condition, or characteristic that has two or more values. Examples of possible variables include age, height, temperature, and intelligence.

Kinds of Correlation

A **positive correlation** between two variables indicates that they tend to change values in the same direction. That is, as the first increases, the second increases, and as the first decreases, the second decreases. A **negative correlation** between two variables indicates that they tend to change values in opposite directions. For example, as age increases in adulthood, visual acuity decreases. Correlations range in magnitude from zero, meaning that there is no systematic relationship between the variables, to 1.00, meaning that there is a perfect relationship between them. Thus, a perfect positive correlation would be $+1.00$, and a perfect negative correlation would be -1.00.

Consider the relationship between obesity and exercise. The more people exercise, the less they tend to weigh. This indicates a negative correlation between exercise and body weight: as one increases, the other decreases. But it is essential to realize that when two variables are correlated, one can be used to *predict* the other, but it does not necessarily *cause* the other. That is, *correlation* does not necessarily imply **causation.** Even though it is plausible that exercise causes lower body weight, it is also possible that the opposite is true: Lower body weight might cause people to exercise. Lighter people might exercise more because they find it less strenuous, less painful, and less embarrassing than heavier people do.

Causation Versus Correlation

As another example, there is a positive correlation between educational level and the likelihood of developing a deadly form of skin cancer called malignant melanoma ("Melanoma Risk and Socio-Economic Class," 1983). This means that as educational level rises, the

Evaluation, Measurement, and Statistics
www.mhhe.com/sdorow5

archival research
The systematic examination of collections of letters, manuscripts, tape recordings, video recordings, or other records.

correlational research
Research that studies the degree of relationship between two or more variables.

correlation
The degree of relationship between two or more variables.

variable
An event, behavior, condition, or characteristic that has two or more values.

positive correlation
A correlation in which variables tend to change values in the same direction.

negative correlation
A correlation in which variables tend to change values in opposite directions.

causation
An effect of one or more variables on another variable.

▲ Causation Versus Correlation

People who exercise regularly tend to be thinner than those who do not. But is exercise the cause of thin physiques? Perhaps not. Thin people might simply be more likely to exercise than people who are overweight. So, a negative correlation between exercise and body weight does not imply that exercise causes weight loss. Only experimental research can determine whether there is such a causal relationship.

experimental method

Research that manipulates one or more variables, while controlling other factors, to determine the effects on one or more other variables.

independent variable

A variable manipulated by the experimenter to determine its effect on another, dependent, variable.

dependent variable

A variable showing the effect of the independent variable.

experimental group

The participants in an experiment who are exposed to the experimental condition of interest.

control group

The participants in an experiment who are not exposed to the experimental condition of interest.

probability of getting the disease also rises. You would be correct in predicting that people who attend college will be more likely, later in life, to develop malignant melanoma than will people who never go beyond high school.

But does this mean that you should drop out of school today to avoid the disease? The answer is no, because the positive correlation between educational level and malignant melanoma does not necessarily mean that attending college causes the disease. Other variables common to people who attend college might cause them to develop the disease. Perhaps they increase their risk of malignant melanoma by exposing themselves to the sun more than do those who have only a high school education. College students might be more likely to spend spring breaks in Florida, find summer jobs at beach resorts, or go on Caribbean vacations after finding full-time jobs. Instead of dropping out of college to avoid the disease, students might be wiser to spend less time in the sun.

Psychologists are careful not to confuse causation and correlation. They are aware that if two variables are positively correlated, the first might cause changes in the second, the second might cause changes in the first, or another variable might cause changes in both. Because of the difficulty in distinguishing causal relationships from mere correlational ones, correlational research has stimulated controversies in important areas of research. Does televised violence cause real-life aggression? A review of research on that question found a significant positive correlation between watching televised violence and exhibiting aggressive behavior. But this does not indicate that televised violence *causes* aggressive behavior (Freedman, 1984). Perhaps people who are aggressive for other reasons simply prefer to watch violent television programs.

Experimental Research

The research methods discussed so far do not enable you to discover causal relationships between variables. Even when there is a strong correlation between variables, you cannot presume a causal relationship between them. To determine whether there is a causal relationship between variables, you must use the **experimental method** (Miller, Chaplin, & Coombs, 1990).

Experimental Method

As in correlational research, the components of an experiment are called variables. Every experiment includes at least one *independent variable* and one *dependent variable*. The **independent variable** is manipulated by the experimenter, which means that she or he determines its values before the experiment begins. The **dependent variable** shows any effects of the independent variable. In terms of cause-and-effect relationships, the independent variable would be the *cause* and changes in the dependent variable would be the *effect*. Thus, in a hypothetical experiment on the effects of drinking on driving, the independent variable of alcohol intake would be the cause of changes in the dependent variable of, say, steering accuracy.

The simplest experiment uses one independent variable with two values (an experimental condition and a control condition) and one dependent variable. A group of participants, the **experimental group,** is exposed to the experimental condition, and a second group of participants, the **control group,** is exposed to the control condition. The control condition is often simply the absence of the experimental condition. For example, the experimental condition might be exposure to a particular advertisement, and the control condition might be nonexposure to the advertisement. The dependent variable might be the number of sales of the advertised product. The control group provides a standard of comparison for the experimental group. If you failed to include a control group in the suggested experiment on the effects of advertising, you would be unable to determine whether the advertising accounted for changes in the volume of sales. The introduction of control groups in psychological research in the early 20th century contributed to psychology's development as a science (Dehue, 2000).

To appreciate the nature of the experimental method, imagine you are a psychologist interested in conducting an experiment on the effect of melatonin on nightly sleep duration. A basic experiment on this topic is illustrated in Table 2.2. Assume that introductory psychology students volunteer to be participants in the study. Members of the experimental

Table 2.2	A Basic Experimental Research Design	
Group	**Independent Variable**	**Dependent Variable**
(Participants are randomly assigned to groups)	(Drug)	(Sleep)
Experimental	Takes melatonin	Hours of sleep
Control	Does not take melatonin	Hours of sleep

group receive the same dose of melatonin nightly for 10 weeks; members of the control group receive no melatonin. As the experimenter, you would try to keep constant all other factors that might affect the two groups. By treating both groups the same except for the condition to which the experimental group is exposed, you would be able to conclude that any significant difference in average sleep duration between the experimental group and the control group was probably caused by the experimental group receiving doses of melatonin. Without the use of a control group, you would have no standard of comparison and would be less secure in reaching that conclusion.

In the experiment on melatonin and nightly sleep duration, the independent variable (drug condition) has two values: melatonin and no melatonin. The experimenter is interested in the effect of the independent variable on the dependent variable. The dependent variable in this case is nightly sleep duration, with many possible values: 6 hours and 2 minutes, 7 hours and 48 minutes, and so on.

As an experimenter, you would try to hold constant all factors other than the independent variable, so that the effects of those factors are not confused with the effect of the independent variable. In the melatonin experiment, you would not want differences between the experimental group and the control group in diet, drugs, and other relevant factors to cause changes in the dependent variable that you would mistakenly attribute to the independent variable.

Internal Validity

An experimenter must do more than simply manipulate an independent variable and record changes in a dependent variable. The experimenter must also promote the **internal validity** of the experiment by *controlling* any extraneous factors whose effects on the dependent variable might be confused with those of the independent variable. Such extraneous factors are called **confounding variables,** because their effects are confused, or *confounded,* with those of the independent variable. A confounding variable might be associated with the experimental situation, participants, or experimenters involved in an experiment.

Situational Variables. In carrying out the procedure in the melatonin experiment, you would not want any confounding variables to affect nightly sleep duration. You would want the participants to be treated the same, except that those in the experimental group would receive the same dose of melatonin nightly over a 10-week period. But suppose that some participants in the experimental group decided to take sleeping pills, to exercise more, or to practice meditation. If, at the end of the study, the experimental group had a longer nightly sleep duration than the control group, the results might be attributable not to the melatonin but to confounding variables—that is, differences between the groups in the extent to which they used sleeping pills, exercised, or practiced meditation.

As an example of the importance of controlling potential confounding variables, consider what happened when the Pepsi-Cola company conducted one of its "Pepsi Challenge" taste tests, an example of *consumer psychology* ("Coke-Pepsi Slugfest," 1976). Coca-Cola drinkers were asked to taste each of two unidentified cola drinks and state their preference. The drinks were Coca-Cola and Pepsi-Cola. The brand of cola was the independent variable, and the preference was the dependent variable. To keep the participants from knowing which cola they were tasting, they were given Pepsi-Cola in a cup labeled "M" and Coca-Cola in a cup labeled "Q." To the delight of Pepsi-Cola stockholders, most of the participants preferred Pepsi-Cola.

internal validity
The extent to which changes in a dependent variable can be attributed to one or more independent variables rather than to a confounding variable.

confounding variable
A variable whose unwanted effect on the dependent variable might be confused with that of the independent variable.

The Pepsi-Cola company proudly—and loudly—advertised this as evidence that even Coca-Cola drinkers preferred Pepsi-Cola. But knowing the pitfalls of experimentation, the Coca-Cola company replicated the experiment, this time filling both cups with Coca-Cola. Most of the participants still preferred the cola in the cup labeled "M." Evidently, the Pepsi Challenge had not demonstrated that Coca-Cola drinkers preferred Pepsi-Cola. It had demonstrated only that Coca-Cola drinkers preferred the letter *M* to the letter *Q*. The effect of the letters on the dependent variable (the taste preference) had been confounded with that of the independent variable (the kind of cola).

If you were asked to design a Coke-Pepsi challenge, how would you control the effect of the letter on the cup? Pause to think about this question before reading on. One way to control it would be to use cups without letters. Of course, the experimenter would have to keep track of which cup contained Coke and which contained Pepsi. A second way to control the effect of the letter would be to label each of the colas "M" on half of the taste trials and "Q" on the other half. Thus, two ways to control potential confounding variables are to eliminate them or to ensure that they affect all conditions equally.

Participant Variables. Experimenters must likewise control potential confounding participant variables that might produce effects that would be confused with those of the independent variable. Suppose that in the melatonin experiment the participants in the experimental group initially differed from the participants in the control group on several variables, including their nightly sleep duration, psychoactive drug habits, and daily exercise practices. These differences might carry over into the experiment, affecting the participants' nightly sleep duration during the course of the study and giving the false impression that the independent variable (melatonin versus no melatonin) caused a significant difference on the dependent variable (nightly sleep duration) between the two groups.

Experimenters increase the chance that the experimental group and the control group will be initially equivalent on as many participant variables as possible by relying on *random assignment* of participants to groups. In **random assignment,** participants are as likely to be assigned to one group as to another. Given a sufficiently large number of participants, random assignment will make the two groups initially equivalent on many, though not necessarily all, participant variables.

After randomly assigning participants to the experimental group and the control group, you would still have to control other participant variables. One of the most important of these is **participant bias,** the tendency of people who know they are participants in a study to behave differently than they normally do. As in the case of naturalistic observation, you might choose to be unobtrusive, exposing people to the experimental condition without their being aware of it. If this were impossible, you might choose to misinform the participants about the true purpose of the study. (The ethical issues involved in using deception are discussed later in this chapter.)

Experimenter Variables. Experimenters must control not only potential confounding variables associated with the research procedure or the research participants, but also potential confounding variables associated with themselves. *Experimenter effects* on dependent variables can be caused by the experimenter's personal qualities, actions, and treatment of data. Experimenter effects have been studied most extensively by Robert Rosenthal and his colleagues, who have demonstrated them in many studies since the early 1960s (Harris & Rosenthal, 1985). Rosenthal has found that the experimenter's personal qualities—including sex, attire, and attractiveness—can affect participants' behavior (Barnes & Rosenthal, 1985).

Also of concern is the effect of the experimenter's actions on the recording of data or on participants' behavior, as in the **experimenter bias effect.** This occurs when the results are affected by the experimenter's expectancy about the outcome of a study, which is expressed through her or his unintentional actions. The tendency of participants to behave in accordance with experimenter expectancy is called *self-fulfilling prophecy.* Actions that might promote self-fulfilling prophecy include facial expressions (perhaps smiling at participants in one group and frowning at those in another), mannerisms (perhaps shaking hands with participants in one group but not with those in another), or tone of voice (perhaps speaking in an animated voice

random assignment
The assignment of participants to experimental and control conditions so that each participant is as likely to be assigned to one condition as to another.

participant bias
The tendency of people who know they are participants in a study to behave differently than they normally would.

experimenter bias effect
The tendency of experimenters to let their expectancies alter the way they treat their participants.

▲ **Robert Rosenthal**
"Recent experiments have shown that an investigator's expectation can . . . come to serve as a self-fulfilling prophecy."

Anatomy of a Research Study

Can Experimenter Expectancies Affect the Behavior of Laboratory Rats?

Rationale

Robert Rosenthal noted that, in the early 20th century, Ivan Pavlov had found that each succeeding generation of his animal subjects learned tasks faster than the preceding one. At first he presumed this supported the (since-discredited) notion of the inheritance of acquired characteristics. But he came to believe that the animals' improvement was caused by changes in the way in which his experimenters treated them. Rosenthal decided to determine whether experimenter expectancies could likewise affect the performance of laboratory animals.

Method

Rosenthal and his colleague Kermit Fode had 12 students act as experimenters in a study of maze learning in rats conducted at Harvard University (Rosenthal & Fode, 1963). Six of the students were told that their rats were specially bred to be "maze bright," and 6 were told that their rats were specially bred to be "maze dull." In reality, the rats did not differ in their inborn maze-learning potential. Each student was given 5 albino rats to run in a T-shaped maze, with one horizontal arm of the maze painted white and the other painted gray. The rats received a food reward whenever they entered the gray arm. The arms were interchanged on various trials so that the rats had to learn to respond to the color gray rather than to the direction left or right. The students ran the rats 10 times a day for 5 days and recorded how long it took them to reach the food.

Results and Discussion

As shown in Figure 2.2, the results indicated the apparent influence of experimenter expectancy: On the average, the "maze-bright" rats ran faster than the "maze-dull" rats. Because there was no evidence of cheating or misrecording of data by the students, the researchers attributed the results to experimenter expectancy. The students' expectancies apparently influenced the manner in which they trained or handled the rats, somehow leading the rats to perform in accordance with the expectancies. For example, those who trained "maze-bright" rats reported handling them more, and more gently, than did those who trained "maze-dull" rats. Confidence in the experimenter expectancy effect with animal subjects was supported in a replication by a different researcher, using different rats, and involving a different task (Elkins, 1987). This indicates that those responsible for handling animals during an experiment should, if possible, be kept unaware of any presumed differences among the animals.

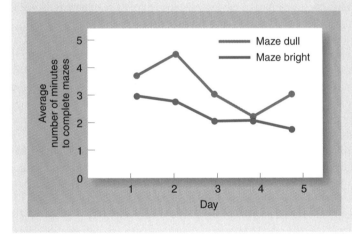

◀ **Figure 2.2**
Experimenter Bias
The graph shows the results of the Rosenthal and Fode (1963) experiment, which found that allegedly maze-bright rats ran mazes faster than allegedly maze-dull rats.

to participants in one group and speaking in a monotone to those in another). Self-fulfilling prophecy is especially important to control in studies of psychotherapy, because therapist expectancies, rather than therapy itself, might affect the outcome of therapy (Harris, 1994).

In a widely publicized study of self-fulfilling prophecy, Rosenthal found that elementary school teachers' expectancies for the performance of their students affected how well the children performed. Students whose teachers were led to believe they were fast learners performed better than students whose teachers were led to believe they were slow learners. Yet the students did not differ in their initial ability (Rosenthal & Jacobson, 1968). This became known as the *Pygmalion effect,* after the story in which an uneducated woman improves herself because of the faith her mentor has in her. The Pygmalion effect can also occur between parents and children, therapists and patients, and even employers and workers (McNatt, 2000). In the Anatomy of a Research Study feature, you can read about a classic research study that demonstrated that experimenter expectancies can even affect the behavior of animals.

How might experimenter bias affect the results of the melatonin experiment? The experimenter might act more friendly and encouraging toward the participants in the experimental group, perhaps motivating them to sleep better than they would have otherwise. Participants with a higher need for social approval would be especially susceptible to experimenter expectancy effects like this (Hazelrigg, Cooper, & Strathman, 1991). One way to control experimenter bias would be to have those who interact with the participants be unaware of the research hypothesis, eliminating the influence of the experimenter's expectancies on the participants' performance.

At times both participant bias and experimenter bias might become confounding variables. This might prompt experimenters to use the **double-blind technique,** in which neither the experimenter nor the participants know the conditions to which the participants have been assigned. This is a common technique in studies of the effectiveness of drug treatments for psychological disorders. Consider studies of drug treatments for depression. The experimental group would receive the drug and the control group would receive a **placebo**—a similar looking and tasting pill, tablet, or capsule that is inactive. Neither the experimenter nor the participants would know which individuals were in each group. In the melatonin experiment, instead of giving one group melatonin and the other nothing, it would be wise to give one group melatonin and the other a placebo. Neither the experimenter nor the participants would know which participants received the melatonin and which received the placebo.

External Validity

Though experimenters are chiefly concerned with matters of internal validity, they are also concerned with matters of **external validity**—the extent to which they can generalize their research findings to other populations, settings, and procedures. Because psychology relies heavily on college students as research participants, external validity is an important consideration (Sears, 1986). As stressed by Stanley Sue (1999) and other psychologists who favor the social-cultural perspective, the results of a research study done in one culture will not necessarily be generalizable to another culture or ethnic group. Researchers must identify the specific populations to which their research findings may be applied.

In regard to external validity, an experimenter might ask, "Will the findings of my melatonin experiment with students here at Grimley College hold true for other people? using different doses of melatonin? in other cultures?" The experimenter might also ask, "Will people who suffer from insomnia benefit from melatonin?" and "Will melatonin be more effective in helping participants fall asleep or in helping them stay asleep?"

Another problem affecting external validity is the use of volunteer participants. Those who volunteer to take part in a given experiment might differ from those who refuse, possibly limiting the generalizability of the research findings. In a study using volunteer participants, male and female undergraduates were given the choice of participating in either a study in which they would take a personality test or a study in which they would report their responses to sexual films. The results indicated that, in comparison to those who volunteered to take the personality test, men and women who volunteered for the sexual experiment were more sexually experienced. This means that those who participate in sexual experiments might not be representative of people in general, limiting the confidence with which sex researchers can generalize their findings (Saunders et al., 1985).

Of course, differences between volunteers and nonvolunteers do not automatically mean the results lack external validity. The best way to determine whether the results of research studies do have external validity is to replicate them (Thompson, 1994). Replication also enables researchers to determine whether the results of laboratory studies will generalize to the world outside of the laboratory. Most replications are approximate; they rarely use the same setting, participants, or procedures. For example, confidence in the Pygmalion effect was strengthened when it was replicated by different researchers, using different teachers, with different students, in a different school (Meichenbaum, Bowers, & Ross, 1969). The ideal would be to replicate studies systematically several times, varying one aspect of the study each time (Hendrick, 1990). Thus, you would be more confident in your ability to generalize the findings of the melatonin experiment if people with insomnia, of a variety of ages, in several different cultures, succeeded in sleeping longer after taking melatonin.

double-blind technique

A procedure that controls experimenter bias and participant bias by preventing experimenters and participants from knowing which participants have been assigned to particular conditions.

placebo

An inactive substance that might induce some of the effects of the drug for which it has been substituted.

external validity

The extent to which the results of a research study can be generalized to other people, animals, or settings.

▲ Stanley Sue

"When theories and models applied to different populations are examined, important ethnic and cultural differences are often found."

Now that you have been introduced to the descriptive, correlational, and experimental methods of research, you should be able to recognize them as you read about research studies described in later chapters. As you read particular studies, try to determine which kind of method was used, as well as its possible strengths and weaknesses—most notably, any potential confounding variables and any limitations on the generalizability of the research findings. You are now ready to learn how psychologists analyze the data generated by their research methods.

Experimental Psychology
www.mhhe.com/sdorow5

STAYING ON TRACK: *Methods of Psychological Research*

1. Why is it important to use random samples in doing surveys?
2. What is validity in psychological testing?
3. What is an independent variable?
4. What is internal validity?

Answers to Staying on Track start on p. ST-1.

◆ STATISTICAL ANALYSIS OF RESEARCH DATA

How would you make sense out of the data generated by the melatonin experiment? In analyzing the data, you would have to do more than simply state that Ann Lee slept 9.1 hours, Steve White slept 7.8 hours, Sally Ramirez slept 8.2 hours, and so on. You would have to identify overall patterns in the data and whether the data support the research hypothesis that inspired the experiment.

As mentioned earlier, to make sense out of their data, psychologists rely on statistics. The term *statistics* was originally used to refer to the practice of recording quantitative political and economic information about European nation-states (Cowles, 1989). Over the past few decades, the use of statistics to analyze research data has become increasingly more prevalent in articles published in psychology journals (Parker, 1990). Psychologists use *descriptive statistics* to summarize data, *correlational statistics* to determine relationships between variables, and *inferential statistics* to test their research hypotheses. Appendix A presents an expanded discussion of statistics and their calculation.

Descriptive Statistics

You would summarize your data by using **descriptive statistics.** An early champion of the use of descriptive statistics was Florence Nightingale (1820–1910), one of the founders of modern nursing. She urged that hospitals keep medical records on their patients. As a result, she demonstrated statistically that British soldiers during times of war were more likely than the enemy to suffer death from disease and unsanitary conditions. She also was a pioneer in the use of graphs to support her conclusions. Her work led to reforms in nursing and medicine and to her being made a fellow of the Royal Statistical Society and an honorary member of the American Statistical Association (Viney, 1993). Descriptive statistics include *measures of central tendency* and *measures of variability.*

descriptive statistics
Statistics that summarize research data.

Measures of Central Tendency

A **measure of central tendency** is a single number used to represent a set of scores. The measures of central tendency include the mode, the median, and the mean. Psychological research uses the mode least often, the median somewhat more often, and the mean most often.

The **mode** is the most frequent score in a set of scores. As shown in Table 2.3, in the melatonin experiment the mode for the experimental group is 8.6 hours and the mode for the control group is 8.9 hours. The **median** is the middle score in a set of scores that have been arranged in numerical order. Thus, in the melatonin experiment the median score for each group is the fifth score. The median for the experimental group is 8.8 hours and the

measure of central tendency
A statistic that represents the "typical" score in a set of scores.

mode
The score that occurs most frequently in a set of scores.

median
The middle score in a set of scores that have been ordered from lowest to highest.

median for the control group is 7.8 hours. You are most familiar with the **mean,** which is the *arithmetic average* of a set of scores. You use the mean when you calculate your grade point average, batting average, or average gas mileage. In the melatonin experiment, the mean for the experimental group is 8.9 hours and the mean for the control group is 7.9 hours.

One of the problems in the use of measures of central tendency is that they can be used selectively to create misleading impressions. Suppose you had the following psychology exam scores: 23, 23, 67, 68, 69, 70, 91. The mode (the most frequent score) would be 23, the median (the middle score) would be 68, and the mean (the average score) would be 58.7. In this case, you would prefer the median as representative of your performance. But what if you had the following scores: 23, 67, 68, 69, 70, 91, 91? The mode would be 91, the median would be 69, and the mean would be 68.4. In that case, you would prefer the mode as representative of your performance.

Product advertisers, government agencies, and political parties are also prone to this selective use of measures of central tendency, as well as other statistics, to support their claims. But the use of statistics to mislead is not new. Its prevalence in the 19th century prompted British Prime Minister Benjamin Disraeli to declare, "There are three kinds of lies: lies, damned lies, and statistics." Even a basic understanding of statistics will make you less likely to be fooled by claims based on their selective use.

Measures of Variability

To represent a distribution of scores, psychologists do more than report a measure of central tendency. They also report a **measure of variability,** which describes the degree of dispersion of the scores. That is, do the scores tend to bunch together, or are they scattered? Commonly used measures of variability include the *range* and the *standard deviation.* The **range** is the difference between the highest and lowest score in a set of scores. In Table 2.3 the range of the experimental group is $9.9 - 7.8 = 2.1$ hours, and the range of the control group is $9.5 - 6.2 = 3.3$ hours. But the range can be misleading, because one extreme score can create a false impression. Suppose that a friend conducts a similar experiment and reports that the range of sleep duration among the 15 participants in his experimental group is 4 hours, with the longest duration being 9.3 hours and the shortest duration being 5.3 hours. You might conclude that there was a great deal of variability in the distribution of scores. But what if he then reported that only one participant slept less than 9.1 hours? Obviously, the scores would bunch together at the high end, making the variability of scores much less than you had presumed.

Because of their need to employ more meaningful measures of variability than the range, psychologists prefer to use the standard deviation. The **standard deviation** represents the degree of dispersion of scores around their mean and is the square root of a measure of variability called the *variance.* The **variance** is a measure based on the average deviation of a set of scores from their group mean. Table 2.3 shows that the standard deviation of the experimental group is 0.59 hours, whereas the standard deviation of the control group is 1.02 hours. Thus, the distribution of scores in the experimental group has a larger mean, but the distribution of scores in the control group has a larger standard deviation.

Correlational Statistics

If you were interested in predicting one set of scores from another, you would use a *measure of correlation.* The concept of correlation was put forth in 1888 by Francis Galton, who wanted a way to represent the relationship between parents and offspring on factors, such as intelligence, presumed to be affected by heredity. While the mean and standard deviation are useful in describing individual sets of scores, a statistic called the coefficient of correlation is useful in quantifying the degree of association between two or more sets of scores. The **coefficient of correlation** was devised by the English mathematician Karl Pearson (1851–1926) and is often called *Pearson's r* (with the *r* standing for "regression," another name for correlation). As you learned earlier, a correlation can be positive or negative, and can range from zero to $+1.00$ or -1.00. In a *positive correlation* between two sets of scores,

| **Chapter Two**

Table 2.3 — Descriptive Statistics from a Hypothetical Experiment on the Effect of Melatonin on Average Nightly Sleep Duration

Experimental Group (Melatonin)				Control Group (No Melatonin)			
Participant	Duration	d	d^2	Participant	Duration	d	d^2
1	9.1	0.2	0.04	1	7.4	−0.5	0.25
2	8.6	−0.3	0.09	2	8.2	0.3	0.09
3	8.6	−0.3	0.09	3	9.5	1.6	2.56
4	8.8	−0.1	0.01	4	8.9	1.0	1.00
5	7.8	−1.1	1.21	5	6.7	−1.2	1.44
6	9.9	1.0	1.00	6	8.9	1.0	1.00
7	8.6	−0.3	0.09	7	7.5	−0.4	0.16
8	9.7	0.8	0.64	8	6.2	−1.7	2.89
9	9.0	0.1	0.01	9	7.8	−0.1	0.01
	Sum = 80.1		Sum = 3.18		Sum = 71.1		Sum = 9.40

Mode = 8.6 hours

Median = 8.8 hours

Mean = $\frac{80.1}{9}$ = 8.9 hours

Range = 9.9 − 7.8 = 2.1 hours

Variance = $\frac{\text{sum of } d^2}{\text{no. of participants}} = \frac{3.18}{9} = 0.35$

Standard deviation = $\sqrt{\text{Variance}}$
$= \sqrt{0.35}$
$= 0.59$ hours

Mode = 8.9 hours

Median = 7.8 hours

Mean = $\frac{71.1}{9}$ = 7.9 hours

Range = 9.5 − 6.2 = 3.3 hours

Variance = $\frac{\text{sum of } d^2}{\text{no. of participants}} = \frac{9.40}{9} = 1.04$

Standard deviation = $\sqrt{\text{Variance}}$
$= \sqrt{1.04}$
$= 1.02$ hours

Note: d = deviation from the mean.

relatively high scores on one set are associated with relatively high scores on the other, and relatively low scores on one set are associated with relatively low scores on the other. For example, there is a positive correlation between height and weight and between high school and college grade point averages.

In a *negative correlation* between two sets of scores, relatively high scores on one set are associated with relatively low scores on the other. For example, there is a negative correlation between driving speed and gas mileage. A *zero correlation* indicates that there is no relationship between one set of scores and another. You would find an approximately zero correlation between the intelligence levels of two groups of randomly selected strangers. The types of correlations are illustrated graphically in Figure 2.3.

The higher the correlation between two variables, the more the scores on one variable will be accurate predictors of scores on the other. For example, suppose you found a correlation of .83 between the number of milligrams of melatonin that people take each night and their nightly sleep duration. This relatively strong correlation would make you fairly confident in predicting that as the dose of melatonin increases, the average nightly duration of sleep would increase. If, instead, you found a relatively weak correlation of .17, you would have less confidence in making that prediction.

Inferential Statistics

In the melatonin experiment, the experimental group had a longer average nightly sleep duration than the control group. But is the difference in average nightly sleep duration between the two groups large enough for you to conclude with confidence that melatonin was responsible for the difference? Perhaps the difference happened by chance—that is,

In a *positive correlation,* scores on the measures increase and decrease together. An example is the relationship between SAT verbal scores and college grade point average (GPA). In a *negative correlation,* scores on one measure increase as scores on the other measure decrease. An example is the relationship between age and nightly sleep. In a *zero correlation,* scores on one measure are unrelated to scores on the other. An example is the relationship between the number of times people brush their teeth each day and the number of houseplants they have.

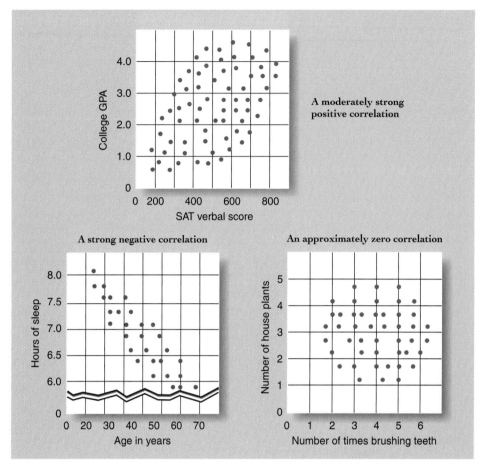

inferential statistics
Statistics used to determine whether changes in a dependent variable are caused by an independent variable.

statistical significance
A low probability (usually less than 5 percent) that the results of a research study are due to chance factors rather than to the independent variable.

because of a host of random factors unrelated to melatonin. To determine whether the independent variable, rather than chance factors, caused the changes in the dependent variable, psychologists use **inferential statistics.** By permitting psychologists to determine the causes of events, inferential statistics help them achieve the goal of explanation. Inferential statistics are "inferential" because they enable experimenters to make inferences from the sample used in their experiment to the population of individuals they represent. Two of the most important topics related to inferential statistics are *statistical significance* and *meta-analysis.*

Statistical Significance

If there is a low probability that the difference between groups on the dependent variable is attributable to chance (that is, to random factors), the difference is **statistically significant** and is attributed to the independent variable. The concept of statistical significance was put forth by the English mathematician Ronald Fisher (1890–1962) when he sought a way to test a noblewoman's claim that she could tell whether tea or milk had been added to her cup first (Tankard, 1984). Though he never carried out the demonstration, he proposed presenting her with a series of cups in which tea was sometimes added first and milk was sometimes added first. He assumed that if she could report the correct order at a much greater than chance level, her claim would be verified. To rule out simple lucky guessing, she would have to be correct significantly more than 50 percent of the time—the chance level of guessing between two events.

In the melatonin experiment, you would expect that chance factors would account for some changes in the sleep duration of participants in both groups during the course of the study. As a result, for the difference in average sleep duration between the two groups to be statistically significant, it would have to be significantly larger than would be expected by chance alone. Psychologists usually accept a difference as statistically significant when there is less than a 5 percent (5 in 100) probability that the difference is the product of chance factors—the so-called .05 level.

Nonetheless, even when the analysis of research data reveals statistical significance, the best way to determine whether research findings are generalizable is to replicate them (Falk, 1998). Two real experiments did, in fact, "replicate" the findings of the imaginary melatonin experiment described earlier. These experiments, which used the double-blind technique, found that participants who took melatonin slept longer than participants who took the placebo—regardless of whether the participants were normal sleepers (Waldhauser, Saletu, & Trinchard, 1990) or insomnia sufferers (MacFarlane et al., 1991). Thus, there is some scientific support for the claims made in the *Newsweek* cover story discussed at the opening of the chapter.

Meta-analysis

Still another approach to assessing generalizability is to use the relatively new statistical technique called *meta-analysis*. **Meta-analysis** combines research findings from many, perhaps hundreds, of related studies and goes beyond simply determining statistical significance. After gathering the studies under analysis, the researcher computes the average size of the effect of the independent variable on the dependent variable

Because meta-analyses consider a large number of published, and often unpublished, studies, other factors influencing research findings can be evaluated in addition to effect sizes. For example, a meta-analysis of altruism found that men were more likely to help in risky situations, particularly when others were present (Eagly & Crowley, 1986). Thus, this gender difference might be attributable to the male gender role. Meta-analyses also enable psychologists to compare effect sizes across time, thus assessing the effect of social-cultural change. Two meta-analyses of gender differences in verbal and mathematics ability compared the effect sizes of studies published before and after 1973 (Hyde, Fennema, & Lamon, 1990; Hyde & Lynn, 1988). In both analyses, gender differences declined over the years.

Meta-analyses have been useful to psychologists interested in distilling the results of a large number of studies. However, the use of meta-analysis cannot overcome the methodological limitations of the studies on which they are based. Most important, studies that rely upon selective recruitment of participants and poor assessment procedures are not improved by the use of meta-analysis (Halpern, 1995). Proponents, such as Janet Shibley Hyde (1994), assert that meta-analyses are helpful in understanding group differences, the effects of social roles and other situational factors on behavior, and how variables such as gender and ethnicity can influence each other. Psychologists have used the results of meta-analyses to shed light upon a number of topics, including the effectiveness of psychotherapy (Smith, Glass, & Miller, 1980) and ethnic differences and similarities in measures of mental health (Hall, Bansal, & Lopez, 1999).

As you read the research studies discussed in later chapters, keep in mind that virtually all were analyzed by descriptive statistics, correlational statistics, or inferential statistics. You should also note that statistical significance does not necessarily imply practical or social significance (Favreau, 1997; Rachman, 1993). For example, a number of studies have reported small, but consistent, gender differences in social influence (Eagly, 1983). Though studies have found statistically significant differences in women's and men's behavior, these differences might not be of practical significance. In other words, they might not be large enough to account for the observed differences in the lives of individual men and women.

STAYING ON TRACK: *Statistical Analysis of Research Data*

1. What are measures of central tendency?
2. What are measures of variability?
3. What is statistical significance?
4. How does meta-analysis summarize the results of many research studies?

Answers to Staying on Track start on p. ST-1.

meta-analysis
A technique that combines the results of many similar studies to determine the effect size of a particular kind of independent variable.

 Vassar Stats: Website for Statistical Computation
www.mhhe.com/sdorow5

◆ THE ETHICS OF PSYCHOLOGICAL RESEARCH

Psychologists must be as concerned with the ethical treatment of their data and human participants and animal subjects as they are with the quality of their research methods and statistical analyses. A serious ethical violation in the treatment of data is falsification. Thus, in the melatonin experiment, you would have to record your data accurately—even if it contradicted your hypothesis. During the past few decades there have been several notorious cases in which medical, biological, or psychological researchers have been accused of falsifying their data. Chapter 10 discusses a prominent case in psychology, in which Sir Cyril Burt, an eminent psychologist, was so intent on demonstrating that intelligence depends on heredity that he apparently misrepresented his research findings (Tucker, 1997). Though occasional lapses in the ethical treatment of data have provoked controversy, there has been even greater concern about the ethical treatment of humans and animals in psychological research.

Ethical Treatment of Human Participants

The first code of ethics for the treatment of human participants in psychological research was developed in 1953, partly in response to the Nuremberg war crimes trials following World War II (Reese & Fremouw, 1984). The trials disclosed the cruel medical experiments performed by Nazi physicians on prisoners of war and concentration camp inmates. Today, the U.S. government requires institutions that receive federal research grants to establish committees that review research proposals to assure the ethical treatment of human participants (McGaha & Korn, 1995).

The APA's Code of Ethics

The code of ethics of the American Psychological Association (APA) contains specific requirements for the treatment of human participants.

- First, the researcher must inform potential participants of all aspects of the research procedure that might influence their decision to participate. In the melatonin experiment, you would not be permitted to tell participants they will be given melatonin and then give them a placebo instead, unless they have been informed of the possibility. This requirement, *informed consent,* can be difficult to ensure, because participants might be unable to give truly informed consent. Perhaps the participants cannot comprehend the language used on informed consent forms (Ogloff & Otto, 1991) or suffer from a serious psychological disorder, such as schizophrenia (Stephens, 2000).
- Second, potential participants must not be forced to participate in a research study. This could become a problem with prisoners or hospitalized patients who fear the consequences of refusing to participate (Rosenthal, 1995).
- Third, participants must be permitted to withdraw from a study at any time. Of course, when participants withdraw, it can adversely affect the study, because those who remain might differ from those who drop out. The loss of participants can therefore limit the ability to generalize research findings from those who complete the study to the desired target population (Trice & Ogden, 1987).
- Fourth, the researcher must protect the participants from physical harm and mental distress. Again, the use of deception might violate this provision by inducing mental distress.
- Fifth, if a participant does experience harm or distress, the researcher must try to alleviate it. But some critics argue that it is impossible to routinely determine whether attempts to relieve distress produce long-lasting benefits (Norris, 1978).
- Sixth, information gained from participants must be kept confidential. This becomes a major issue in research on sensitive topics, such as drug use among students (Bjarnason & Adalbjarnardottir, 2000), because laws might force researchers to reveal information that their participants presumed was confidential.

The Issue of Deception in Research

Despite their code of ethics, in their treatment of human participants psychologists sometimes confront ethical dilemmas, as in the use of deception to reduce participant bias. Psychologists might fail to inform people that they are participating in a study or might misinform participants about the true nature of a study. This is of concern, in part because it violates the ethical norm of informed consent. Recall that the computer-dating study by Donn Byrne and colleagues (Byrne, Ervin, & Lamberth, 1970) used deception by falsely claiming that all participants would be matched with partners who shared their attitudes. Today, for this to be considered ethical, the researcher would have to demonstrate to an institutional research review committee that the experiment could not be conducted without the use of deception and that its potential findings are important enough to justify the use of deception (Fisher & Fyrberg, 1994). Moreover, at the completion of the study, each participant would have to be debriefed. In **debriefing** participants, the researcher explains the reasons for the deception and tries to relieve any distress that might have been experienced.

Some psychologists worry that deceptive research will make potential participants distrust psychological research (Sharpe, Adair, & Roese, 1992). And Diana Baumrind (1985), a critic of deceptive research, argues that not even the positive findings of studies that use deception outweigh the distress of participants who learn they have been fooled. Arguments against deceptive research have been countered by psychologists who argue that it would be unethical not to conduct deceptive studies that might produce important findings (Christensen, 1988).

While some psychologists argue about the use of deception, others try to settle the debate over deceptive research by using the results of empirical research. In one study, undergraduates who had participated in deceptive experiments rated their experience as more positive than did those who had participated in nondeceptive ones. Moreover, those in deceptive experiments did not rate psychologists as less trustworthy. Any negative emotional effects reported by participants seemed to be relieved by debriefing. The researchers concluded that debriefing eliminates any negative effects of deception, perhaps because the participants learn the importance of the research study (Smith & Richardson, 1983).

But this interpretation of the findings has been criticized. You might wish to pause now and see if you can think of an alternative explanation of why participants in deceptive experiments responded more positively. One possibility is that the procedures used in deceptive experiments are more interesting and enjoyable than those used in nondeceptive ones (Rubin, 1985). Remembering that psychology, as a science, resolves issues through empirical research instead of through argument alone, how might you conduct a study to determine whether this assumption is correct? One way would be to conduct experiments whose procedures have been rated as equally interesting, and use deception in only half of them. If participants still rate the deceptive experiments more positively, then the results would support Smith and Richardson (1983). If participants rate the deceptive experiments less positively, then the results would support Rubin (1985).

▲ Diana Baumrind
"Deceptive practices do not succeed in accomplishing the scientific objectives that are used to justify such deception any better than methods that do not require deception."

debriefing
A procedure, after the completion of a research study, that informs participants of the purpose of the study and aims to remove any physical or psychological distress caused by participation.

Ethical Treatment of Animal Subjects

At the 1986 annual meeting of the APA in Washington, D.C., animal rights advocates picketed in the streets and disrupted talks, including one by the prominent psychologist Neal Miller, a defender of the use of animals in psychological research. The present conflict between animal rights advocates and psychologists who conduct laboratory research with animals is not new. In the early 20th century, animal rights activists attacked the work of leading psychologists, including John B. Watson. In 1925, in part to blunt these attacks, the APA's Committee on Precautions in Animal Experimentation established a code of regulations for the use of animals in research (Dewsbury, 1990).

Animal Rights Versus Animal Welfare

Many *animal rights* advocates oppose all laboratory research using animals, regardless of its scientific merit or practical benefits. Thus, they would oppose testing the effects of melatonin on animal subjects. A survey of demonstrators at an animal rights march in Washington,

D.C., in 1990 found that almost 80 percent of animal rights advocates valued animal life at least as much as human life, and 85 percent wanted to eliminate all animal research (Plous, 1991). Animal rights advocates go beyond *animal welfare* advocates, who would permit laboratory research on animals as long as the animals are given humane care and the potential benefits of the research outweigh any pain and distress caused to the animals. Thus, they would be more likely to approve the use of animals in testing the effects of melatonin on sleep. Bernard Rollin, an ethicist who has tried to resolve the ethical conflict between animal researchers and animal rights advocates, would permit animal research but urges that, when in ethical doubt, experimenters should err in favor of the animal (Bekoff et al., 1992).

The APA's current ethical standards for the treatment of animals are closer to those of animal welfare advocates than to those of animal rights advocates. The standards require that animals be treated with respect, housed in clean cages, and given adequate food and water. Researchers must also ensure that their animal subjects experience as little pain and distress as possible; when it is necessary to kill the animals, researchers must do so in a humane, painless way. Moreover, all institutions that receive research grants from the U.S. government must have committees that judge whether research proposals for experiments using animal subjects meet ethical standards (Holden, 1987). The Canadian government likewise regulates the treatment of research animals in universities, government laboratories, and commercial institutions (Rowsell, 1988).

Reasons for Using Animals in Research

But with so many human beings available, why would psychologists be interested in studying animals?

- First, some psychologists are simply intrigued by animal behavior and wish to learn more about it. To learn about the process of echolocation of prey, you would have to study animals like bats rather than college students.
- Second, it is easier to control potential confounding variables that might affect the behavior of an animal. You would be less likely to worry about participant bias effects, for example, when studying pigeons.
- Third, developmental changes across the life span can be studied more efficiently in animals. If you were interested in the effects of the complexity of the early childhood environment on memory in old age, it could take you 75 years to complete an experiment using human beings, but only 3 years to complete one using rats.
- Fourth, research on animals can generate hypotheses that are then tested using human participants. B. F. Skinner's research on learning in rats and pigeons stimulated research on learning in human beings.
- Fifth, research on animals can benefit animals themselves. For example, as described in Chapter 7, psychologists have developed techniques to make coyotes feel nauseated by the taste of sheep; perhaps these can someday be used to protect sheep from coyotes, and coyotes from angry sheep ranchers.
- Sixth, because of an assumption that animals do not have the same moral rights as human beings (Baldwin, 1993), certain procedures that are not ethically permissible with humans are ethically permissible under current standards with animal subjects. Thus, if you wanted to conduct an experiment in which you studied the effects of surgically removing a particular brain structure, you would be limited to the use of animals.

The Continuing Controversy

But these reasons have not convinced animal rights advocates of the merits of psychological research on animals. Animal rights advocates argue that the benefits of laboratory research that submits animals to painful procedures do not outweigh the suffering they induce (Bowd, 1990). During the past few decades some animal rights advocates have even vandalized animal research laboratories and stolen animals from their laboratory cages. The vast majority of advocates, however, have been content to lobby for stronger laws limiting animal research or to picket meetings of animal researchers. Prior to the meeting at which he was harassed, Neal Miller (1985) had pointed out that for every dog and cat used in laboratory

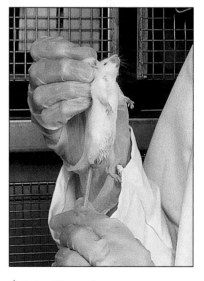

research, 10,000 are abandoned by their owners, and that, in contrast, few psychology experiments inflict pain or distress on animals. He urged animal rights advocates to spend more time helping the millions of abandoned pets that are killed in pounds, starve to death, or die after being struck by motor vehicles.

Miller (1985) has also cited ways in which animal research contributes to human welfare. Findings from animal research have contributed to progress in the treatment of pain; the development of behavior therapy for phobias; the rehabilitation of victims of neuromuscular disorders, such as Parkinson's disease; the understanding of neurological disorders associated with aging, such as Alzheimer's disease; and the development of drugs for treating anxiety, depression, and schizophrenia. Nonetheless, Miller's critics accuse him of exaggerating the benefits of animal research (Kelly, 1986).

Though reasonable people can disagree about the ethical limits of psychological research on animals, the attention given to such research might be out of proportion to its extent and to the pain and distress it causes. Only 5 percent of psychologists conduct research with animals. Of their animal subjects, 95 percent are mice, rats, and birds; less than 1 percent are dogs, cats, monkeys, and chimpanzees—the kinds of animals to which people feel the greatest kinship (Gallup & Suarez, 1985). Moreover, few psychological studies on animals inflict pain or distress (Coile & Miller, 1984). And despite the special attention that psychological research receives from animal rights advocates, a government report praised the American Psychological Association's ethical standards for the care and use of animals in research as being superior to those of any other science (Fisher, 1986).

No responsible psychologist would condone a cavalier disregard for the pain and suffering of laboratory animals. Nonetheless, it seems that animal rights advocates have been more effective than animal researchers in influencing the public and lawmakers. Thus, it might be wise for animal researchers to communicate more through the popular media to argue that a moderate position on animal research is better than either extreme position (King & Viney, 1992). Moreover, there seems to have been a recent decline in popular interest in the ethics of animal research. An archival study of popular magazine articles found that the number of articles about animal rights peaked in 1990 and declined over the following few years (Herzog, 1995). But others disagree, claiming instead that the animal rights movement might be as influential as ever even if media coverage of it has declined (Rowan & Shapiro, 1996). Regardless of the extent of media coverage of the animal rights movement today, a comparison of a survey of animal rights activists in 1990 and 1996 found a shift to relatively greater concern about the treatment of animals used in agriculture than about their treatment in laboratories (Plous, 1998).

Trends in Animal Research
www.mhhe.com/sdorow5

▲ **Animal Research**
Those who favor animal research note the medical and psychological benefits it produces for human beings and, in some cases, animals.

STAYING ON TRACK: *The Ethics of Psychological Research*

1. Why has the use of deception in research provoked controversy?
2. What is debriefing in psychological research?
3. How do animal rights and animal welfare differ from one other?

Answers to Staying on Track start on p. ST-1.

Chapter Summary

SOURCES OF KNOWLEDGE

- Psychologists prefer the scientific method to common sense as a source of knowledge.
- The scientific method is based on the assumptions of determinism and skepticism.
- In using the scientific method to conduct research, a psychologist first provides a rationale for the research, then conducts the research study, analyzes the resulting data, and, finally, communicates the results to other researchers.
- Replication of research studies is an important component of the scientific research process.

GOALS OF SCIENTIFIC RESEARCH

- In conducting research, psychologists pursue the goals of description, prediction, control, and explanation.
- Scientific descriptions are systematic and rely on operational definitions.
- Scientific predictions are probabilistic, not certain.
- Scientists exert control over events by manipulating the factors that cause them.
- Scientific explanations state the probable causes of events.

METHODS OF PSYCHOLOGICAL RESEARCH

- Psychologists use descriptive, correlational, and experimental research methods.
- Descriptive research methods pursue the goal of description through naturalistic observation, case studies, surveys, psychological testing, and archival research.
- Correlational research pursues the goal of prediction by uncovering relationships between variables.
- In using correlational research, psychologists avoid confusing correlation with causation.
- Experimental research pursues the goals of control and explanation by manipulating an independent variable and measuring its effect on a dependent variable.
- Experimenters promote internal validity by controlling confounding variables whose effects might be confused with those of the independent variable.
- Confounding variables might be associated with the experimental situation, the participants in the experiment, or the experimenter.
- Random assignment is used to make the experimental group and control group equivalent before exposing them to the independent variable.
- Experimenters must also control for participant bias and experimenter bias.

- Another concern of experimenters is external validity: whether their results are generalizable from their participants and settings to other participants and settings.
- Experimenters rely on replication to determine whether their research has external validity.

STATISTICAL ANALYSIS OF RESEARCH DATA

- Psychologists typically make sense of their data by using mathematical techniques called statistics.
- Psychologists use descriptive statistics to summarize data, correlational statistics to determine relationships between variables, and inferential statistics to test their experimental hypotheses.
- Descriptive statistics include measures of central tendency (including the mode, median, and mean) and measures of variability (including the range and standard deviation).
- Correlational statistics let researchers use the values of one variable to predict the values of another.
- Inferential statistics examine whether numerical differences between experimental and control groups are statistically significant.
- Meta-analysis involves computation of the average effect size across a number of related studies.
- Statistical significance does not necessarily indicate social or practical significance.

THE ETHICS OF PSYCHOLOGICAL RESEARCH

- American and Canadian psychologists have ethical codes for the treatment of human participants and animal subjects.
- In research using human participants, researchers must obtain informed consent, not force anyone to participate, let participants withdraw at any time, protect participants from physical harm and mental distress, alleviate any inadvertent harm or distress, and keep information obtained from the participants confidential.
- The use of deception in research has been an especially controversial issue.
- The use of animals in research has also been controversial.
- Many animal rights supporters oppose all research on animals.
- Animal welfare supporters approve of research on animals as long as the animals are treated humanely and the potential benefits of the research outweigh any pain and distress caused to the animals.
- Though relatively few psychologists conduct research on animals, most psychologists support the use of animals in research because of the benefits of such research to both human beings and animals.
- Few psychologists treat their animal subjects in a less than humane way.

Key Concepts

Key Contributors

Thought Questions

1. How would a skeptical attitude toward ESP, UFOs, and similar topics differ from either a cynical or a gullible attitude?
2. How would the four goals of science influence research on violence?
3. In what way are medical treatments, weather forecasting, horse-race handicapping, college admissions decisions, and psychological child-rearing advice "probabilistic"?
4. Why is the experimental method considered a better means of determining causality than nonexperimental methods?
5. Why do many psychologists believe that animal research in psychology has been the unfair target of animal rights activists?

Possible Answers to Thought Questions start on p. PT-1

OLC Preview

 For additional quizzing and a variety of interactive resources, visit the book's Online Learning Center at www.mhhe.com/sdorow5.

Behavioral Neuroscience

ROBERTO MATTA
Listen to Living, 1941

A 64-year-old, right-handed man was awakened by the sense that there was something strange in his bed. Opening his eyes, he observed to his horror that there was a strange arm reaching toward his neck. The arm approached nearer, as if to strangle him, and the man let out a cry of terror. Suddenly, he realized that the arm had on its wrist a silver-banded watch, which the man recognized to be his own. It occurred to him that the arm's possessor must have stolen his watch sometime during the night. A struggle ensued, as the man attempted to wrestle the watch off of the arm. During the struggle, the man became aware that his own left arm was feeling contorted and uncomfortable. It was then that he discovered that the strange arm in fact was his own. The watch was his, and it was on his own left wrist. He was wrestling with his own arm! (Tranel, 1995, p. 885)

unilateral neglect
A disorder, caused by damage to a parietal lobe, in which the individual acts as though the side of her or his world opposite to the damaged lobe does not exist.

behavioral neuroscience
The field that studies the physiological bases of human and animal behavior and mental processes.

What could account for such bizarre behavior? It was caused by a stroke that damaged the right side of the man's brain. This made him exhibit **unilateral neglect,** which involves difficulty in attending to one side (usually the left side) of one's body and of one's immediate environment (Deouell, Haemaelaeinen, & Bentin, 2000). Victims of unilateral neglect often act as though one side of their world, including one side of their bodies, does not exist. A man with unilateral neglect might shave the right side of his face, but not the left, and might eat the pork chop on the right side of his plate but not the potatoes on the left. Figure 3.1 shows self-portraits painted by an artist, Anton Raederscheidt, whose paintings illustrate the effects of unilateral neglect. As in his case, unilateral neglect is usually self-limiting, typically lasting weeks or months (Harvey & Milner, 1999). Though unilateral neglect is more often found after damage to the right side of the brain, it is sometimes found in people with damage to the left side of the brain; they show neglect for objects in the right half of their spatial world (Weintraub et al., 1996).

Such profound effects of brain damage on physical and psychological functioning indicate that abilities we often take for granted require an intact, properly functioning brain. If you have an intact brain, as you read this page your eyes inform your brain about what you are reading. At the same time, your brain interprets the meaning of that information and stores some of it in your memory. When you reach the end of a right-hand page, your brain directs your hand to turn the page. But how do your eyes inform your brain about what you are reading? How does your brain interpret and store the information it receives? And how does your brain direct the movements of your hand? The answers to these questions are provided by the field of **behavioral neuroscience,** which studies the relationship between neurological processes (typically brain activity) and psychological functions (such as memory, emotion, and perception). Some behavioral neuroscientists are particularly interested in the influence of heredity on behavior.

▲ **Charles Darwin (1801–1882)**
"I have called this principle, by which each slight variation, if useful, is preserved, by the term Natural Selection."

◆ HEREDITY AND BEHAVIOR

Interest in behavioral neuroscience is not new. William James (1890/1981), in his classic psychology textbook *The Principles of Psychology,* stressed the close association between biology and psychology. James declared, "I have felt most acutely the difficulties of understanding either the brain without the mind or the mind without the brain" (Bjork, 1988, p. 107). James was influenced by Charles Darwin's (1859/1975) theory of evolution, which holds that individuals who are biologically well adapted to their environment are more

 Milestones in the History of Neuroscience
www.mhhe.com/sdorow5

▶ **Figure 3.1**
Unilateral Neglect

These self-portraits painted by the German artist Anton Raederscheidt were painted over a period of time following a stroke that damaged the cortex of his right parietal lobe. As his brain recovered, his attention to the left side of his world returned (Wurtz, Goldberg, & Robinson, 1982).

likely to survive, reproduce, and pass on their physical traits to succeeding generations through their genes. Thus, the human brain has evolved into its present form because it helped human beings in thousands of earlier generations adapt successfully to their surroundings and survive long enough to reproduce. Because of its remarkable flexibility in helping us adapt to different circumstances, the brain that helped ancient people survive without automobiles, grocery stores, or electric lights helps people today survive in the arctic, outer space, and New York City.

Evolutionary Psychology

To what extent are you the product of your heredity, and to what extent are you the product of your environment? This issue of "nature versus nurture" has been with us since the era of ancient Greece, when Plato championed nature and Aristotle championed nurture. Plato

Anatomy of a Research Study

Do Predispositions Molded by Evolution Affect Romantic Relationships?

Rationale

This study (Buss et al., 1992) tested David Buss's belief that evolution has left its mark on human behavior, even in the area of heterosexual romance. Women can be sure that their newborns are truly theirs, but men cannot, so Buss hypothesized that men would exhibit more jealousy in response to an intimate partner's sexual infidelity than to her emotional infidelity. Because prehistoric women were, on the average, physically weaker and more responsible for caring for their children, and depended on men to support them after giving birth, Buss hypothesized that women would exhibit more jealousy in response to an intimate partner's emotional infidelity than to his sexual infidelity. Buss assumes that these differences are the product of thousands of generations of natural selection.

Method

Participants were 202 male and female undergraduate students. They were asked which of the following two alternatives would distress them more: their romantic partner forming a deep emotional attachment to someone else or that partner enjoying passionate sexual intercourse with someone else. The participants also were asked to respond to a similar dilemma in which their romantic partner either fell in love with another person or tried a variety of sexual positions with that person.

Results and Discussion

The results showed that for the first dilemma 60 percent of the male participants reported greater jealousy over their partner's potential sexual infidelity. In contrast, 83 percent of the female participants reported greater jealousy over their partner's potential emotional infidelity. The second dilemma brought out the same pattern of responses. Of course, cultural interpretations of male sexual jealousy and female emotional jealousy are possible. But the researchers pointed to the commonness of these gender differences in sexual and emotional jealousy as evidence of its possible hereditary basis.

These findings have been replicated in research studies across different cultures: men tend to be more sexually jealous and women tend to be more emotionally jealous (Buss et al., 1999; Wiederman & Kendall, 1999). But the degree of the difference in female and male responses to sexual and emotional infidelity varies across cultures and ideologies. In one study, for example, gender differences in the two kinds of jealousy were stronger in the United States than in Germany or the Netherlands (Buunk et al., 1996). Another study found that gender differences in sexual and emotional jealousy were greater among undergraduates who believed in gender inequality (Pratto & Hegarty, 2000). As you can see, research findings can be equally compatible with an evolutionary interpretation and a social-cultural interpretation (Wood & Eagly, 2000).

---

believed we are born with some knowledge; Aristotle believed that at birth our mind is a blank slate (or *tabula rasa*) and that life experiences provide us with knowledge.

In modern times, the argument became even more heated after Charles Darwin put forth his theory of evolution in the mid 19th century. Darwin noted that animals and human beings vary in their physical traits. Given the competition for resources (including food and water) and the need to foil predators (by defeating them or escaping from them), animals and human beings with physical traits best adapted to these purposes would be the most likely to survive long enough to produce offspring, who would likely also have those traits. As long as particular physical traits provide a survival advantage, those traits will have a greater likelihood of showing up in succeeding generations. Darwin called this process *natural selection.* Psychologists who champion **evolutionary psychology** employ Darwinian concepts in their research and theorizing. The possible role of evolution in human social relationships inspired the study by evolutionary psychologist David Buss and his colleagues Randy Larsen, Drew Westen, and Jennifer Semmelroth at the University of Michigan (Buss et al., 1992) that you can read about in the Anatomy of a Research Study feature.

Human Behavior and Evolution Society
www.mhhe.com/sdorow5

evolutionary psychology
The study of the evolution of behavior through natural selection.

Behavioral Genetics

behavioral genetics

The study of the effects of heredity and life experiences on behavior.

Beginning in the 1970s, psychology has seen the growth of **behavioral genetics,** which studies how heredity affects behavior. Research in behavioral genetics has found evidence of a hereditary basis for characteristics as diverse as divorce (Jocklin, McGue, & Lykken, 1996), empathy (Plomin, 1994), and intelligence (Petrill & Wilkerson, 2000).

To appreciate behavioral genetics, it helps to have a basic understanding of genetics itself. The cells of the human body contain 23 pairs of *chromosomes,* which are long strands of *deoxyribonucleic acid (DNA)* molecules. (Unlike the other body cells, the egg cell and sperm cell each contains 23 single chromosomes.) DNA molecules are ribbon-like structures composed of segments called *genes.* Genes direct the synthesis of *ribonucleic acid (RNA).* RNA, in turn, directs the synthesis of proteins, which are responsible for the structure and function of our tissues and organs.

Though our genes direct our physical development, their effects on our behavior are primarily indirect (Mann, 1994). There are, for example, no "motorcycle daredevil genes." Instead, genes influence physiological factors, such as hormones, neurotransmitters, and brain structures. These factors, in turn, make people somewhat more likely to engage in particular behaviors. Perhaps people destined to become motorcycle daredevils inherit a less physiologically reactive nervous system, making them experience less anxiety in dangerous situations. Moreover, given current trends in molecular genetics, behavioral geneticists are on the threshold of identifying genes that affect behavior (Plomin & Crabbe, 2000). For example, the ambitious Human Genome Project aims to identify the structure and functions of all human genes, with scientists estimating that there are more than 30,000 genes to be identified. Most researchers in behavioral genetics prefer to search for the effects of interactions among these genes, rather than single-gene effects, as influences on behavior (Wahlsten, 1999). This holds promise for the prevention and treatment of physical and psychological disorders with possible genetic bases, such as obesity (see Chapter 11) and schizophrenia (see Chapter 14).

 Human Genome Project Information
www.mhhe.com/sdorow5

Our outward appearance and behavior might not indicate our exact genetic inheritance. In recognition of this, scientists distinguish between our genotype and our phenotype. Your **genotype** is your genetic inheritance. Your **phenotype** is the overt expression of your inheritance in your appearance or behavior. For example, your eye color is determined by the interaction of a gene inherited from your mother and a gene inherited from your father. The brown-eye gene is *dominant,* and the blue-eye gene is *recessive.* Dominant genes take precedence over recessive genes. Traits carried by recessive genes show up in phenotypes only when recessive genes occur together. If you are blue-eyed, your genotype includes two

genotype

An individual's genetic inheritance.

phenotype

The overt expression of an individual's genotype (genetic inheritance) in his or her appearance or behavior.

Chapter Three

blue-eye genes (both recessive). If you have brown eyes, your genotype could include two brown-eye genes (both dominant) or one brown-eye gene (dominant) and one blue-eye gene (recessive).

In contrast to simple traits like eye color, most characteristics are governed by more than one pair of genes—that is, they are *polygenic*. With rare exceptions, this is especially true of genetic influences on human behaviors and abilities. Your athletic, academic, and social skills depend on the interaction of many genes, as well as your life experiences. For example, your muscularity (your phenotype) depends on both your genetic endowment (your genotype) and your dietary and exercise habits (your life experiences).

If you understand the concept of heritability, you will be able to appreciate research studies that try to determine the relative contributions of heredity and environment to human development. **Heritability** refers to the proportion of variability in a trait across a population attributable to genetic differences among members of the population (Turkheimer, 1998). For example, human beings differ in their intelligence (as measured by IQ tests). To what extent is this variability caused by heredity, and to what extent is it caused by experience? Heritability values range from 0.0 to 1.0. If heritability accounted for none of the variability in intelligence, it would have a value of 0.0. If heritability accounted for all of the variability in intelligence, it would have a value of 1.0. In reality, the heritability of intelligence, as measured by IQ tests, is estimated to be between .50 (Chipuer, Rovine, & Plomin, 1990) and .70 (Bouchard et al., 1990). This indicates that the variability in intelligence is strongly, but not solely, influenced by heredity. Environmental factors also account for much of the variability. Note that heritability applies to groups, not to individuals. The concept cannot be used, for example, to determine the relative contributions of heredity and environment to your own intelligence. Research procedures that assess the relative contributions of nature and nurture involve the study of relatives. These include studies of families, adoptees, and identical twins reared apart.

heritability
The proportion of variability in a trait across a population attributable to genetic differences among members of the population.

Family Studies

Family studies investigate similarities between relatives with varying degrees of genetic similarity. These studies find that the closer the genetic relationship (that is, the more genes that are shared) between relatives, the more alike they tend to be on a variety of traits. For example, the siblings of a person who has schizophrenia are significantly more likely to have schizophrenia than are the person's cousins. Though it is tempting to attribute this to their degree of genetic similarity, one cannot rule out that it is instead due to their degree of environmental similarity.

The best kind of family study is the *twin study,* which compares identical (or *monozygotic*) twins to fraternal (or *dizygotic*) twins. This kind of study was introduced by Francis Galton (1822–1911), who found more similarity between identical twins than between fraternal twins—and attributed this to heredity. Identical twins, because they come from the same fertilized egg, have the same genetic inheritance. Fraternal twins, because they come from different fertilized eggs, do not. They merely have the same degree of genetic similarity as non-twin siblings. Moreover, twins, whether identical or fraternal, are born at the same time and share similar environments. Because research has found that identical twins reared in similar environments are more psychologically similar than fraternal twins reared in similar environments, it is reasonable to attribute the greater similarity of identical twins to heredity. Twin studies have been consistent across cultures in supporting the heritability of psychological characteristics, as in studies of the personality of twins in Russia (Saudino et al., 1999), sexual orientation and conformity to gender roles in Australian twins (Bailey, Dunne, & Martin, 2000), and schizophrenia in twins in Finland (Cannon et al., 1999). Nonetheless, there is an alternative, environmental explanation. Perhaps identical twins become more psychologically similar because they are treated more alike than fraternal twins are.

Adoption Studies

Superior to family studies are *adoption studies,* which measure the correlation in particular traits between adopted children and their biological parents and between those same adopted children and their adoptive parents. Adoption studies have found that adoptees are more similar to their biological parents than to their adoptive parents in traits such as body fat (Price & Gottesman, 1991), drug abuse (Cadoret et al., 1995), vocational interests (Lykken et al., 1993), and religious values (Waller et al., 1990). These findings indicate that, with regard to such traits, the genes that adoptees inherit from their biological parents affect their development more than does the environment they are provided with by their adoptive parents.

Yet the environment cannot be ruled out as an explanation for the greater similarity between adoptees and their biological parents. As explained in Chapter 4, prenatal experiences can affect children's development. Perhaps adoptees are more like their biological parents, not because they share the same genes, but because the adoptees spent their prenatal months in their biological mother's womb, making them subject to their mother's drug habits, nutritional intake, or other environmental influences. Moreover, their experiences with their biological parents in early infancy, before they were adopted, might affect their development, possibly making them more similar to their biological parents.

Studies of Identical Twins Reared Apart

Perhaps the best procedure is to study *identical twins reared apart.* Research on a variety of traits consistently finds higher positive correlations between identical twins reared apart than between fraternal twins reared together. Because identical twins share identical genes, virtually identical prenatal environments, and highly similar neonatal environments, this provides strong evidence in favor of the nature side of the debate. This has been supported by a widely publicized study conducted at the University of Minnesota, which has examined similarities between identical twins who were separated in infancy and reunited later in life. As part of the University of Minnesota study of twins reared apart, researchers administered a personality test to 71 pairs of identical and 53 pairs of fraternal adult twins reared apart and 99 pairs of identical and 99 pairs of fraternal adult twins reared together. The results found that the heritability estimate for personality was 0.46, indicating that heredity plays an important, but not dominant, role in personality (Bouchard et al., 1998).

The University of Minnesota study has found some uncanny similarities in the habits, abilities, and physiological responses of the reunited twins (Bouchard et al., 1990). For example, one pair of twins at their first reunion discovered that they "both used Vademecum toothpaste, Canoe shaving lotion, Vitalis hair tonic, and Lucky Strike cigarettes. After that meeting, they exchanged birthday presents that crossed in the mail and proved to be identical choices, made independently in separate cities" (Lykken et al., 1992, p. 1565).

But some of these similarities might be due to coincidence or being reared in similar environments or having some contact with each other before being studied. In fact, research

Chapter Three

on even unrelated people sometimes show moderately strong similarities in their personality traits (Wyatt, 1993). Moreover, identical twins look the same and might elicit responses from others that indirectly lead to their developing similar interests and personalities. Consider how we treat obese people, muscular people, attractive people, and people with acne. Thus, identical twins who share certain physical traits might become more similar than ordinary siblings who do not share such traits—even when reared in different cultures (Ford, 1993). As you can see, no kind of study is flawless in demonstrating the superiority of heredity over environment in guiding development.

Regardless of the influence of heredity on development, behavioral genetics researcher Robert Plomin reminds us that life experiences are also important. In one study, personality test scores of identical and fraternal twins were compared at an average of 20 years of age and then at 30 years of age. The conclusion was that the stable core of personality is strongly influenced by heredity but that personality change is overwhelmingly influenced by environment (McGue, Bacon, & Lykken, 1993). Thus, heredity might have provided you with the intellectual potential to become a Nobel Prize winner, but without adequate academic experience in childhood you might not perform well enough even to graduate from college.

STAYING ON TRACK: *Heredity and Behavior*

1. What is behavioral neuroscience?
2. Why are the greater physical, cognitive, and personality similarities among relatives than among nonrelatives not enough to demonstrate conclusively that they are the product of heredity?

Answers to Staying on Track start on p. ST-1

◆ COMMUNICATION SYSTEMS

Biopsychological activity is regulated by two major bodily communication systems: the *nervous system* and the *endocrine system.* These systems regulate biopsychological functions as varied as hunger, memory, sexuality, and emotionality.

The Nervous System

The brain is part of the **nervous system,** the chief means of communication within the body. The nervous system is composed of **neurons,** cells that are specialized for the transmission and reception of information. As illustrated in Figure 3.2, the two divisions of the nervous system are the *central nervous system* and the *peripheral nervous system.*

The Central Nervous System

The **central nervous system** comprises the *brain* and the *spinal cord.* The brain, protectively housed in the skull, is so important in psychological functioning that most of this chapter and many other sections of this book are devoted to it. As you will learn, the **brain** is intimately involved in learning, thinking, language, memory, emotion, motivation, body movements, social relationships, psychological disorders, perception of the world, and even immune-system activity.

The **spinal cord,** which runs through the boney, protective spinal column, provides a means of communication between the brain and the body. Motor output from the brain travels down the spinal cord to direct activity in muscles and certain glands. Sensory input from pain, touch, pressure, and temperature receptors in the body travels up the spinal cord to the brain, informing it of the state of the body. Damage to the spinal cord can have catastrophic effects. You might know people who have suffered a spinal-cord injury in a diving, vehicular, or contact-sport accident, causing them to lose the ability to move their limbs or feel bodily sensations below the point of the injury. Emotional reactions to spinal cord injuries

nervous system
The chief means of communication in the body.

neuron
A cell specialized for the transmission of information in the nervous system.

central nervous system
The division of the nervous system consisting of the brain and the spinal cord.

brain
The structure of the central nervous system that is located in the skull and plays important roles in sensation, movement, and information processing.

spinal cord
The structure of the central nervous system that is located in the spine and plays a role in bodily reflexes and in communicating information between the brain and the peripheral nervous system.

The Organization of the Nervous System
The nervous system comprises the brain, spinal cord, and nerves.

reflex
An automatic, involuntary motor response to sensory stimulation.

peripheral nervous system
The division of the nervous system that conveys sensory information to the central nervous system and motor commands from the central nervous system to the skeletal muscles and internal organs.

nerve
A bundle of axons that conveys information to or from the central nervous system.

somatic nervous system
The division of the peripheral nervous system that sends messages from the sensory organs to the central nervous system and messages from the central nervous system to the skeletal muscles.

Spinal Cord Injury Links
www.mhhe.com/sdorow5

▲ **Spinal Cord Damage**
A fall from a horse broke the neck and severed the spinal cord of Christopher Reeve, famous for portraying Superman in several movies. The accident left him a quadriplegic, with little or no feeling or voluntary movement in his limbs.

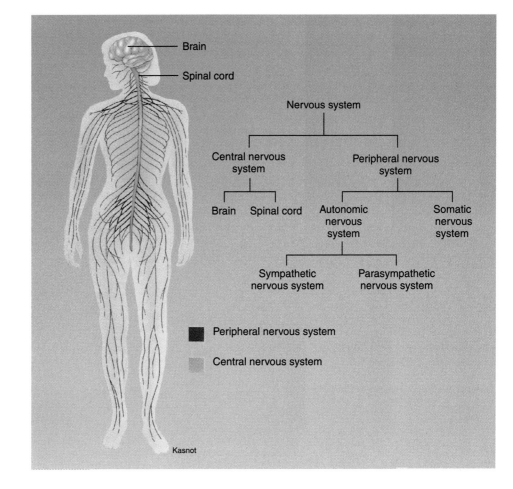

show the influence of gender and culture. Two studies of people with spinal cord injuries in Southern California found that the men reported more distress over interpersonal problems than did the women (Krause, 1998). Moreover, severe depression was more common among Latinos than among European Americans or African Americans (Kemp, Krause, & Adkins, 1999). Recent research on the transplantation of healthy nerve tissue into damaged spinal cords of animals indicates that scientists might be on the threshold of discovering effective means of restoring motor and sensory functions to people who have suffered spinal cord injuries (Kim et al., 1999).

As discussed in the next section, the spinal cord also plays a role in limb reflexes. A **reflex** is an automatic, involuntary motor response to sensory stimulation. Thus, when you step on a sharp, broken shell at the beach, you immediately pull your foot away. This occurs at the level of the spinal cord; it does not require input from the brain.

The Peripheral Nervous System

The **peripheral nervous system** contains the **nerves,** which provide a means of communication between the central nervous system and the sensory organs, skeletal muscles, and internal bodily organs. The peripheral nervous system comprises the *somatic nervous system* and the *autonomic nervous system.* The **somatic nervous system** includes *sensory nerves,* which send messages from the sensory organs to the central nervous system, and *motor nerves,* which send messages from the central nervous system to the skeletal muscles. The **autonomic nervous system** controls automatic, involuntary processes (such as sweating, heart contractions, and intestinal activity) through the action of its two subdivisions: the *sympathetic nervous system* and the *parasympathetic nervous system.* The **sympathetic nervous system** arouses the body to prepare it for action, and the **parasympathetic nervous system** calms the body to conserve energy.

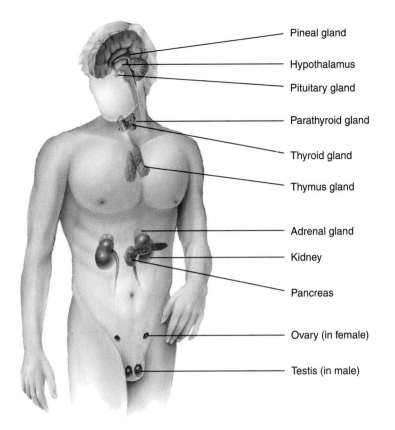

◀ **Figure 3.3**
The Endocrine System
Hormones secreted by the endocrine glands affect metabolism, behavior, and mental processes.

Pineal gland

Hypothalamus

Pituitary gland

Parathyroid gland

Thyroid gland

Thymus gland

Adrenal gland

Kidney

Pancreas

Ovary (in female)

Testis (in male)

Imagine that you are playing a tennis match. Your sympathetic nervous system speeds up your heart rate to pump more blood to your muscles, makes your liver release sugar into your bloodstream for quick energy, and induces sweating to keep you from overheating. As you cool down after the match, your parasympathetic nervous system slows your heart rate and constricts the blood vessels in your muscles to divert blood for use by your internal organs. Chapter 12 describes the role of the autonomic nervous system in emotional responses and includes a diagram (Figure 12.1) illustrating its effects on various bodily organs. Chapter 16 explains how chronic activation of the sympathetic nervous system can contribute to the development of stress-related diseases.

The Endocrine System

The glands of the **endocrine system,** the other major means of communication within the body, exert their functions through chemicals called **hormones.** The endocrine glands secrete hormones into the bloodstream, which transports them to their site of action. The actions of the endocrine system are slower, longer lasting, and more diffuse than those of the nervous system. This contrasts with *exocrine glands,* such as the sweat glands and salivary glands, which secrete their chemicals onto the body surface or into body cavities. Endocrine secretions have many behavioral effects, but exocrine secretions have few. Figure 3.3 illustrates the locations of several endocrine glands. Hormones can act directly on body tissues, serve as neurotransmitters, or modulate the effects of neurotransmitters.

The Pituitary Gland

The **pituitary gland,** an endocrine gland protruding from underneath the brain, regulates many of the other endocrine glands by secreting hormones that affect their activity. This is why the pituitary is known as the "master gland." The pituitary gland, in turn, is regulated by the brain structure called the *hypothalamus.* Feedback from circulating hormones stimulates the hypothalamus to signal the pituitary gland to increase or decrease their secretion.

Pituitary hormones also exert a wide variety of direct effects. For example, *prolactin* stimulates milk production in lactating women. Because an elevated prolactin level is also

autonomic nervous system
The division of the peripheral nervous system that controls automatic, involuntary physiological processes.

sympathetic nervous system
The division of the autonomic nervous system that arouses the body to prepare it for action.

parasympathetic nervous system
The division of the autonomic nervous system that calms the body and performs maintenance functions.

endocrine system
Glands that secrete hormones into the bloodstream.

hormones
Chemicals, secreted by endocrine glands, that play a role in a variety of functions, including synaptic transmission.

pituitary gland
An endocrine gland that regulates many of the other endocrine glands by secreting hormones that affect the secretion of their hormones.

associated with both infertility and psychological stress, prolactin might be involved in stress-related infertility. This indicates that women who are highly anxious about their inability to become pregnant might enter a vicious cycle in which their anxiety increases the level of prolactin, which in turn makes them less likely to conceive (Edelmann & Golombok, 1989). This might explain anecdotal reports of couples who, after repeatedly failing to conceive a child, finally adopt a child, only to have the woman become pregnant soon after—perhaps because her anxiety decreased after the adoption.

Growth hormone, another pituitary hormone, aids the growth and repair of bones and muscles. A child who secretes too much growth hormone might develop *giantism,* marked by excessive growth of the bones. A child who secretes insufficient growth hormone might develop *dwarfism,* marked by stunted growth. Giantism and dwarfism do not impair intellectual development. Though it might seem logical to administer growth hormone to increase the height of very short children who are not diagnosed with dwarfism, this is unwise because the long-term side effects are unknown (Tauer, 1994).

Other Endocrine Glands

Among the other psychologically relevant endocrine glands are the *adrenal glands* and the *gonads.* The **adrenal glands,** which lie on the kidneys, secrete important hormones. The *adrenal cortex,* the outer layer of the adrenal gland, secretes hormones, such as *aldosterone,* that regulate the excretion of sodium and potassium, which contribute to proper neural functioning. The adrenal cortical hormone *cortisol* helps the body respond to stress by stimulating the liver to release sugar. People under chronic stress, perhaps from jobs in which they have little control over their workload, might show an increase in their secretion of cortisol (Steptoe et al., 2000).

In response to stimulation by the sympathetic nervous system, the *adrenal medulla,* the inner core of the adrenal gland, secretes *epinephrine* and *norepinephrine,* which function as both hormones and neurotransmitters. Epinephrine increases heart rate; as noted earlier, norepinephrine is the neurotransmitter in the sympathetic nervous system that arouses the body to take action. For example, married couples (especially wives) show increases in epinephrine and norepinephrine during conflicts with their spouses (Kiecolt-Glaser et al., 1996).

The **gonads,** the sex glands, affect sexual development and behavior. The **testes,** the male gonads, secrete *testosterone,* which regulates the development of the male reproductive system and secondary sex characteristics. The **ovaries,** the female gonads, secrete *estrogens,* which regulate the development of the female reproductive system and secondary sex characteristics. The ovarian hormone *progesterone* regulates changes in the uterus that can maintain pregnancy. During prenatal development sex hormones also affect certain structures and functions of the brain. The effects of sex hormones, including their possible role in psychological gender differences (Berenbaum & Snyder, 1995), are discussed in Chapters 4 and 11.

Anabolic steroids, synthetic forms of testosterone, have provoked controversy during the past few decades. They have been used by athletes, bodybuilders, and weightlifters to promote muscle development, increase endurance, and boost self-confidence. Yet studies have shown inconsistent effects of steroids on physical strength. For example, it is unclear whether anabolic steroids directly increase strength or do so through a placebo effect, in which users work out more regularly and more vigorously simply because they have faith in the effectiveness of steroids (Maganaris, Collins, & Sharp, 2000). Moreover, anabolic steroids appear to have dangerous side effects, including increased aggressiveness. For example, male weightlifters who go on and off steroids are more verbally and physically abusive toward their wives and girlfriends when they are using steroids than when they are not (Choi & Pope, 1994).

STAYING ON TRACK: *Communication Systems*

1. What are the divisions of the nervous system?
2. What is the difference between exocrine glands and endocrine glands?
3. What are the effects of adrenal hormones?

Answers to Staying on Track start on p. ST-1.

adrenal glands
Endocrine glands that secrete hormones that regulate the excretion of minerals and the body's response to stress.

gonads
The male and female sex glands.

testes
The male gonads, which secrete hormones that regulate the development of the male reproductive system and secondary sex characteristics.

ovaries
The female gonads, which secrete hormones that regulate the development of the female reproductive system and secondary sex characteristics.

Anabolic Steroids
www.mhhe.com/sdorow5

♦ THE NEURON

You are able to read this page because *sensory neurons* are relaying input from your eyes to your brain. You will be able to turn the page because *motor neurons* from your spinal cord are sending commands from your brain to the muscles of your hand. **Sensory neurons** send messages to the brain or spinal cord. **Motor neurons** send messages to the glands, the cardiac muscle, and the skeletal muscles, as well as to the smooth muscles of the arteries, small intestine, and other internal organs. Illnesses that destroy motor neurons, such as *amyotrophic lateral sclerosis* (also known as Lou Gehrig's disease, after the great baseball player struck down by it), cause muscle paralysis (Andreassen et al., 2000).

The nervous system contains 10 times more *glial cells* than neurons. **Glial cells** provide a physical support structure for the neurons (*glial* comes from the Greek word for "glue"). Glial cells also supply neurons with nutrients, remove neuronal metabolic waste, and help regenerate damaged neurons in the peripheral nervous system. Recent research indicates that glial cells might even facilitate the transmission of messages by neurons (Coyle & Schwarcz, 2000).

To appreciate the role of neurons in communication within the nervous system, consider the functions of the spinal cord. Neurons in the spinal cord convey sensory messages from the body to the brain and motor messages from the brain to the body. In 1730 the English scientist Stephen Hales demonstrated that the spinal cord also plays a role in limb reflexes. He decapitated a frog (to eliminate any input from the brain) and then pinched one of its legs. The leg reflexively pulled away. Hales concluded the pinch had sent a signal to the spinal cord, which in turn sent a signal to the leg, eliciting its withdrawal. We now know that this limb-withdrawal reflex involves sensory neurons that convey signals from the site of stimulation to the spinal cord, where they transmit their signals to **interneurons** in the spinal cord. The interneurons then send signals to motor neurons, which stimulate flexor muscles to contract and pull the limb away from the source of stimulation—making you less susceptible to injury.

To understand how neurons communicate information, it will help to become familiar with the structure of the neuron (see Figure 3.4). The **soma** (or *cell body*) contains the nucleus, which directs the neuron to act as a nerve cell rather than as a fat cell, a muscle cell, or any other kind of cell. The **dendrites** (from the Greek word for "tree") are short, branching fibers that receive neural impulses. The dendrites are covered by bumps called *dendritic spines,* which provide more surface area for the reception of neural impulses from other neurons. The **axon** is a single fiber that sends neural impulses. Axons range from a tiny fraction

sensory neuron
A neuron that sends messages from sensory receptors to the central nervous system.

motor neuron
A neuron that sends messages from the central nervous system to smooth muscles, cardiac muscle, or skeletal muscles.

glial cell
A kind of cell that provides a physical support structure for the neurons, supplies them with nutrition, removes neuronal metabolic waste materials, facilitates the transmission of messages by neurons, and helps regenerate damaged neurons in the peripheral nervous system.

interneuron
A neuron that conveys messages between neurons in the brain or spinal cord.

soma
The cell body, the neuron's control center.

dendrites
The branchlike structures of the neuron that receive neural impulses.

axon
The part of the neuron that conducts neural impulses to glands, muscles, or other neurons.

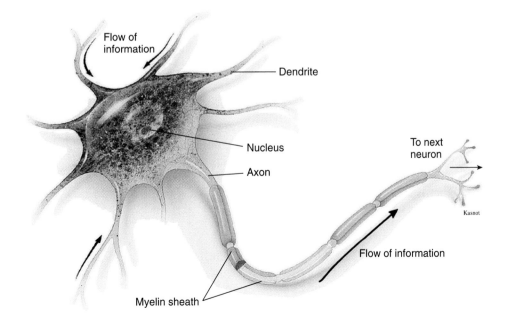

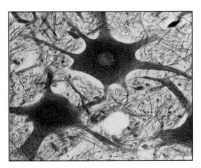

◄ **Figure 3.4**
The Neuron

Both the drawing and the photograph show the structure of the motor neuron. Neurons have dendrites that receive signals from other neurons or sensory receptors, a cell body that controls cellular functions, and an axon that conveys signals to skeletal muscles, internal organs, or other neurons.

of an inch (as in the brain) to more than 3 feet in length (as in the legs of a 7-foot-tall basketball player). Just as bundles of wires form telephone cables, bundles of axons form the nerves of the peripheral nervous system. A nerve can contain motor neurons or sensory neurons, or both.

The Neural Impulse

How does the neuron convey information? It took centuries of investigation by some of the most brilliant minds in the history of science to find the answer. Before the neuron was discovered in the 19th century, scientists were limited to studying the functions of nerves. In these studies, they typically were influenced by their other research interests. The first significant discovery regarding nerve conduction came in 1786, when Italian physicist Luigi Galvani (1737–1798) gave demonstrations hinting that the nerve impulse is electrical in nature. Galvani found that by touching the leg of a freshly killed frog with two different metals, such as iron and brass, he could create an electrical current that made the leg twitch. He believed he had discovered the basic life force—electricity. Some of Galvani's followers, who hoped to use electricity to raise the dead, obtained the fresh corpses of hanged criminals and stimulated them with electricity. To the disappointment of these would-be resurrectors, they failed to induce more than the flailing of limbs (Hassett, 1978). Not much later, another of Galvani's contemporaries, Mary Shelley, applied what she called "galvanism" (apparently, the use of electricity) to revive the dead in her classic novel, *Frankenstein.*

Though Galvani and his colleagues failed to demonstrate that electricity was the basic life force, they put scientists on the right track toward understanding how neural impulses are conveyed in the nervous system. But it took almost two more centuries of research before scientists identified the exact mechanisms. We now know that neuronal activity, whether involved in hearing a doorbell, throwing a softball, or recalling a childhood memory, depends on electrical-chemical processes, beginning with the *resting potential.*

The Resting Potential

In 1952, English scientists Alan Hodgkin and Andrew Huxley, using techniques that let them study individual neurons, discovered the electrical-chemical nature of the processes that underlie **axonal conduction,** the transmission of a *neural impulse* along the length of the axon. In 1963 Hodgkin and Huxley won the Nobel Prize for physiology and medicine for their discovery (Lamb, 1999). Hodgkin and Huxley found that in its inactive state, the neuron maintains an electrical **resting potential,** produced by differences between the *intracellular fluid* inside of the neuron and the *extracellular fluid* outside of the neuron. These fluids contain *ions,* which are positively or negatively charged molecules. In regard to the resting potential, the main positive ions are *sodium* and *potassium,* and the main negative ions are *proteins* and *chloride.*

The *neuronal membrane,* which separates the intracellular fluid from the extracellular fluid, is *selectively permeable* to ions. This means that some ions pass back and forth through tiny *ion channels* in the membrane more easily than do others. Because ions with like charges repel each other and ions with opposite charges attract each other, you might assume the extracellular fluid and intracellular fluid would end up with the same relative concentrations of positive ions and negative ions. But, because of several complex processes, the intracellular fluid ends up with an excess of negative ions and the extracellular fluid ends up with an excess of positive ions. This makes the inside of the resting neuron negative relative to the outside, so the membrane is said to be *polarized,* just like a battery. For example, at rest the inside of a motor neuron has a charge of -70 millivolts relative to its outside. (A millivolt is one one-thousandth of a volt.)

The Action Potential

When a neuron is stimulated sufficiently by other neurons or by a sensory organ, it stops "resting." The neuronal membrane becomes more permeable to positively charged sodium ions, which, attracted by the negative ions inside, rush into the neuron. This makes the inside of the neuron less electrically negative relative to the outside, a process called *depolarization.*

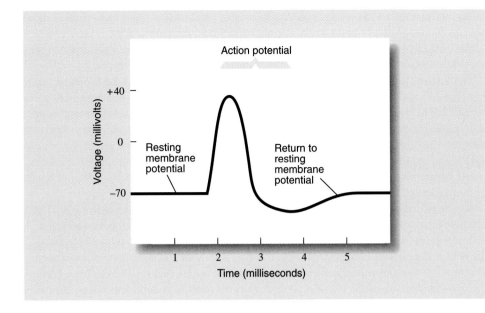

Action potential

Resting membrane potential

Return to resting membrane potential

Voltage (millivolts)

+40

0

−70

1   2   3   4   5

Time (milliseconds)

◀ **Figure 3.5**
The Action Potential

During an action potential, the inside of the axon becomes electrically positive relative to the outside, but quickly returns to its normal resting state, with the inside again electrically negative relative to the outside.

As sodium continues to rush into the neuron, and the inside becomes less and less negative, the neuron reaches its *firing threshold* (about −60 millivolts in the case of a motor neuron) and an *action potential* occurs at the point where the axon leaves the cell body.

An **action potential** is a change in the electrical charge across the axonal membrane, with the inside of the membrane becoming more electrically positive than the outside and reaching a charge of +40 millivolts. Once an action potential has occurred, that point on the axonal membrane immediately restores its resting potential through a process called *repolarization*. This occurs, in part, because the sudden excess of positively charged sodium ions inside the axon repels the positive potassium ions, driving many of them out of the axon. This loss of positively charged ions helps return the inside of the axon to its negatively charged state relative to the outside. The restored resting potential is also maintained by chemical "pumps" that transport sodium and potassium ions across the axonal membrane, returning them to their original concentrations. Figure 3.5 illustrates the electrical changes that occur during the action potential.

If an axon fails to depolarize enough to reach its firing threshold, no action potential occurs—not even a weak one. If you have ever been under general anesthesia, you became unconscious because you were given a drug that prevented the axons in your brain that are responsible for the maintenance of consciousness from depolarizing enough to fire off action potentials (Nicoll & Madison, 1982). When an axon reaches its firing threshold and an action potential occurs, a neural impulse travels the entire length of the axon at full strength, as sodium ions rush in at each successive point along the axon. This is known as the **all-or-none law.** It is analogous to firing a gun: If you do not pull the trigger hard enough, nothing happens; but if you do pull the trigger hard enough, the gun fires and a bullet travels down the entire length of its barrel.

Thus, when a neuron reaches its firing threshold, a neural impulse travels along its axon, as each point on the axonal membrane depolarizes (producing an action potential) and then repolarizes (restoring its resting potential). This process of depolarization/repolarization is so rapid that an axon might conduct up to 1,000 neural impulses a second. The loudness of sounds you hear, the strength of your muscle contractions, and the level of arousal of your brain all depend on the number of neurons involved in those processes and the rate at which they conduct neural impulses.

The speed at which the action potential travels along the axon varies from less than 1 meter per second in certain neurons to more than 100 meters per second in others. The speed depends on several factors, most notably whether sheaths of a white fatty substance called **myelin** (which is produced by glial cells) are wrapped around the axon (Miller, 1994). At frequent intervals along myelinated axons, tiny areas are nonmyelinated. These are called

action potential

A series of changes in the electrical charge across the axonal membrane that occurs after the axon has reached its firing threshold.

all-or-none law

The principle that once a neuron reaches its firing threshold, a neural impulse travels at full strength along the entire length of its axon.

myelin

A white fatty substance that forms sheaths around certain axons and increases the speed of neural impulses.

▲ **Santiago Ramón y Cajal (1852–1934)**

"For all those who are fascinated by the bewitchment of the infinitely small, there wait in the bosom of the living being millions of palpitating cells which, for the surrender of their secret, and with it the halo of fame, demand only a clear and persistent intelligence to contemplate, admire, and understand them."

synaptic transmission

The conveying of a neural impulse between a neuron and a gland, muscle, sensory organ, or another neuron.

synapse

The junction between a neuron and a gland, muscle, sensory organ, or another neuron.

nodes. In myelinated axons, such as those forming much of the brain and spinal cord, as well as the motor nerves that control our muscles, the action potential jumps from node to node, instead of traveling from point to point along the entire axon. This explains why myelinated axons conduct neural impulses faster than nonmyelinated axons.

If you were to look at a freshly dissected brain, you would find that the inside appeared mostly white and the outside appeared mostly gray, because the inside contains many more myelinated axons. You would be safe in concluding that the brain's white matter conveyed information faster than its gray matter. Some neurological disorders are associated with abnormal myelin conditions. In the disease *multiple sclerosis,* portions of the myelin sheaths in neurons of the brain and spinal cord are destroyed, causing muscle weakness, sensory disturbances, memory loss, and cognitive deterioration as a result of the disruption of normal axonal conduction (Bitsch et al., 2000).

To summarize, a neuron maintains a *resting potential* during which its inside is electrically negative relative to its outside. Stimulation of the neuron makes positive sodium ions rush in and *depolarize* the neuron (that is, make the inside less negative relative to the outside). If the neuron depolarizes enough, it reaches its *firing threshold* and an *action potential* occurs. During the action potential, the inside of the neuron becomes electrically positive relative to the outside. Because of the *all-or-none law,* a *neural impulse* is conducted along the entire length of the axon at full strength. Axons covered by a *myelin sheath* conduct impulses faster than other axons. After an action potential has occurred, the axon *repolarizes* and restores its resting potential.

Synaptic Transmission

If all the neuron did was conduct a series of neural impulses along its axon, we would have an interesting, but useless, phenomenon. The reason we can see a movie, feel a mosquito bite, think about yesterday, or ride a bicycle is because neurons can communicate with one another by the process of **synaptic transmission**—communication across gaps between neurons. Many psychological processes, such as detecting the direction of a sound by determining the slight difference in the arrival time of sound waves at the two ears, require rapid and precisely timed synaptic transmission (Sabatini & Regehr, 1999).

The question of how neurons communicate with one another provoked a heated debate in the late 19th century. Spanish anatomist Santiago Ramón y Cajal (1852–1934) argued that neurons were separate from one another (Koppe, 1983). He won the debate by showing that neurons do not form a continuous network (Ramón y Cajal, 1937/1966). In 1897, the English physiologist Charles Sherrington (1857–1952) had coined the term **synapse** (from the Greek word for "junction") to refer to the gaps that exist between neurons. Synapses also exist between neurons and glands, between neurons and muscles, and between neurons and sensory organs.

Mechanisms of Synaptic Transmission

As is usually the case with scientific discoveries, the observation that neurons were separated by synapses led to still another question: How could neurons communicate with one another across these gaps? At first, some scientists assumed that the neural impulse simply jumped across the synapse, just as sparks jump across the gap in a spark plug. But the correct answer came in 1921—in a dream.

The dreamer was Otto Loewi (1873–1961), an Austrian physiologist who had been searching without success for the mechanism of synaptic transmission. Loewi awoke from his dream and carried out the experiment it suggested. He removed the beating heart of a freshly killed frog, along with the portion of the *vagus nerve* attached to it, and placed it in a solution of salt water. By electrically stimulating the vagus nerve, he made the heart beat slower. He then put another beating heart in the same solution. Though he had not stimulated its vagus nerve, the second heart also began to beat slower. If you had made this discovery, what would you have concluded? Loewi concluded, correctly, that stimulation of the vagus nerve of the first heart had released a chemical into the solution. It was this chemical, which he later identified as *acetylcholine,* that slowed the beating of both hearts.

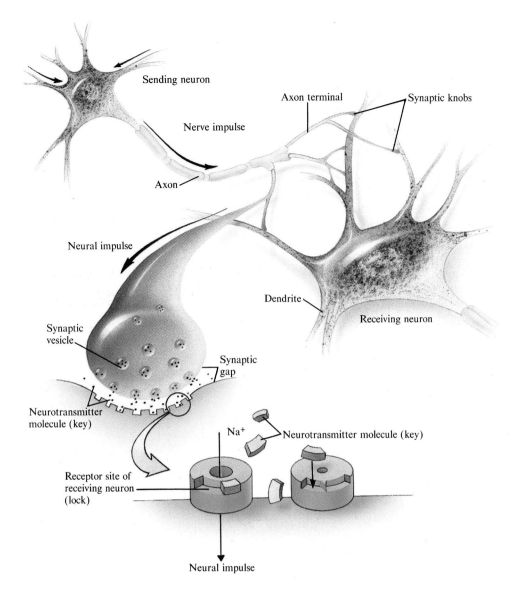

Sending neuron

Nerve impulse

Axon terminal

Synaptic knobs

Axon

Neural impulse

Dendrite

Receiving neuron

Synaptic vesicle

Synaptic gap

Neurotransmitter molecule (key)

Na⁺

Neurotransmitter molecule (key)

Receptor site of receiving neuron (lock)

Neural impulse

◀ **Figure 3.6**

Synaptic Transmission Between Neurons

When a neural impulse reaches the end of an axon, it stimulates synaptic vesicles to release neurotransmitter molecules into the synapse. The molecules diffuse across the synapse and interact with receptor sites on another neuron, causing sodium ions to leak into that neuron. The molecules then disengage from the receptor sites and are broken down by enzymes or taken back into the axon.

Acetylcholine is one of a group of chemicals called **neurotransmitters,** which transmit neural impulses across synapses. Neurotransmitters are stored in round packets called *synaptic vesicles* in the intracellular fluid of bumps called *synaptic knobs* that project from the end branches of axons. The discovery of the chemical nature of synaptic transmission led to a logical question: How do neurotransmitters facilitate this transmission? Subsequent research revealed the processes involved (see Figure 3.6):

- First, when a neural impulse reaches the end of an axon, it induces a chemical reaction that makes some synaptic vesicles release neurotransmitter molecules into the synapse.
- Second, the molecules diffuse across the synapse and reach the dendrites of another neuron.
- Third, the molecules attach to tiny areas on the dendrites called *receptor sites.*
- Fourth, the molecules interact with the receptor sites to excite the neuron; this slightly depolarizes the neuron by permitting sodium ions to enter it. But for a neuron to depolarize enough to reach its firing threshold, it must be excited by neurotransmitters released by many neurons. To further complicate the process, a neuron can also be affected by neurotransmitters that inhibit it from depolarizing. Thus, a neuron will fire an action potential only when the combined effects of *excitatory neurotransmitters* sufficiently exceed the combined effects of *inhibitory neurotransmitters.*

neurotransmitters

Chemicals secreted by neurons that provide the means of synaptic transmission.

▲ **Curare, Acetylcholine, and Hunting**

Natives of the Amazon jungle use curare-tipped darts to paralyze, and thereby suffocate, their prey. Curare blocks receptor sites for the neurotransmitter acetylcholine, causing flaccid paralysis of the muscles.

▲ **Parkinson's Disease**

Actor Michael J. Fox is an advocate for Parkinson's research. In September, 2000 he testified on Capitol Hill with other people suffering from Parkinson's disease in support of federal funding for medical research.

Alzheimer's disease

A brain disorder characterized by difficulty in forming new memories and by general mental deterioration.

Parkinson's disease

A degenerative disease of the dopamine pathway, which causes marked disturbances in motor behavior.

• Fifth, neurotransmitters do not remain attached to the receptor sites, continuing to affect them indefinitely. Instead, after the neurotransmitters have done their job, they are either broken down by chemicals called *enzymes* or taken back into the neurons that had released them—in a process called *reuptake.*

Neurotransmitters and Drug Effects

Of the neurotransmitters, acetylcholine is the best understood. In the peripheral nervous system, this is the neurotransmitter at synapses between the neurons of the parasympathetic nervous system and the organs they control, such as the heart. Acetylcholine also is the neurotransmitter at synapses between motor neurons and muscle fibers, where it stimulates muscle contractions. *Curare,* a poison Amazon Indians put on the darts they shoot from their blowguns, paralyzes muscles by preventing acetylcholine from attaching to receptor sites on muscle fibers. The resulting paralysis of muscles, including the breathing muscles, causes death by suffocation.

In the brain, acetylcholine helps regulate memory processes (Levin & Simon, 1998). The actions of acetylcholine can be impaired by drugs or diseases. For example, chemicals in marijuana inhibit acetylcholine release involved in memory processes, so people who smoke it might have difficulty forming memories (Carta, Nava, & Gessa, 1998). **Alzheimer's disease,** a progressive brain disorder that strikes in middle or late adulthood, is associated with the destruction of acetylcholine neurons in the brain (Albert & Drachman, 2000). Because Alzheimer's disease is marked by the inability to form new memories, a victim might be able to recall her third birthday party but not what she ate for breakfast this morning. Alzheimer's disease also is associated with severe intellectual and personality deterioration. Though we have no cure for Alzheimer's disease, treatments that increase levels of acetylcholine in the brain—most notably drugs that do so by preventing its breakdown and deactivation in synapses—delay the mental deterioration that it brings (Francis et al., 1999).

Since the discovery of acetylcholine, dozens of other neurotransmitters have been identified. Your ability to perform smooth voluntary movements depends on brain neurons that secrete the neurotransmitter *dopamine.* **Parkinson's disease,** which is marked by movement disorders, is caused by the destruction of dopamine neurons in the brain. Drugs, such as L-dopa, that increase dopamine levels provide some relief from Parkinson's disease symptoms (Schrag et al., 1998). Based on recent research findings, there also is hope that the transplantation of healthy dopamine-secreting neural tissue into the brains of Parkinson's victims will be effective in treating the disorder (Barker & Dunnett, 1999).

Dopamine has psychological, as well as physical, effects. Positive moods are maintained, in part, by activity in dopamine neurons (Kumari et al., 1998). Elevated levels of dopamine activity are found in the serious psychological disorder called *schizophrenia.* Drugs that block dopamine activity alleviate some of the symptoms of schizophrenia (Reynolds, 1999); and drugs, such as amphetamines, that stimulate dopamine activity can induce symptoms of schizophrenia (Castner & Goldman-Rakic, 1999).

Our moods vary with the level of the neurotransmitter *norepinephrine* in the brain. A low level is associated with depression. Many antidepressant drugs work by increasing norepinephrine levels in the brain (Anand & Charney, 2000). Like norepinephrine, the neurotransmitter *serotonin* is implicated in depression. In fact, people who become so depressed that they try suicide often have unusually low levels of serotonin (Mann et al., 2000). Drugs that boost the level of serotonin in the nervous system relieve depression (Heiser & Wilcox, 1998). Antidepressant drugs called *selective serotonin reuptake inhibitors,* such as Prozac, relieve depression by preventing the reuptake of serotonin into the axons that release it, thereby increasing serotonin levels in the brain (Racagni & Brunello, 1999).

Some neurotransmitters are amino acids. The main inhibitory amino acid neurotransmitter is *gamma aminobutyric acid* (or GABA). GABA promotes muscle relaxation and reduces anxiety (Crestani et al., 1999). So-called tranquilizers, such as Valium, relieve anxiety by promoting the action of GABA (Costa, 1998). As discussed in Chapter 8, the main excitatory amino acid neurotransmitter, *glutamic acid,* helps in the formation of memories (Newcomer et al., 1999).

Endorphins

Another class of neurotransmitters comprises small proteins called *neuropeptides*. The neuropeptide *substance P* has sparked interest because of its apparent role in the transmission of pain impulses, as in migraine headaches (Nakano et al., 1993) and sciatic nerve pain (Malmberg & Basbaum, 1998). During the past few decades, neuropeptides called **endorphins** have been the subject of much research and publicity because of their possible roles in relieving pain and inducing feelings of euphoria.

The endorphin story began in 1973, when Candace Pert and Solomon Snyder of Johns Hopkins University discovered opiate receptors in the brains of animals (Pert & Snyder, 1973). Opiates are pain-relieving drugs (or *narcotics*)—including morphine, codeine, and heroin—derived from the opium poppy. Pert and Snyder became interested in conducting their research after finding hints in previous research studies by other scientists that animals might have opiate receptors. Pert and Snyder removed the brains of mice, rats, and guinea pigs. Samples of brain tissue then were treated with radioactive morphine and naloxone, a chemical similar in structure to morphine that blocks morphine's effects. A special device detected whether the morphine and naloxone had attached to receptors in the brain tissue.

Pert and Snyder found that the chemicals had bound to specific receptors (opiate receptors). If you had been a member of Pert and Snyder's research team, what would you have inferred from this observation? Pert and Snyder inferred that the brain must manufacture its own opiatelike chemicals. This would explain why it had evolved opiate receptors, and it seemed a more likely explanation than that the receptors had evolved to take advantage of the availability of opiates such as morphine in the environment. Pert and Snyder's findings inspired the search for opiatelike chemicals in the brain.

The search bore fruit in Scotland when Hans Kosterlitz and his colleagues found an opiatelike chemical in brain tissue taken from animals (Hughes et al., 1975). They called this chemical *enkephalin* (from Greek terms meaning "in the head"). Enkephalin and similar chemicals discovered in the brain were later dubbed "endogenous morphine" (meaning "morphine from within"). This was abbreviated into the now-popular term *endorphin*. Endorphins function as both neurotransmitters and *neuromodulators*—neurochemicals that affect the activity of other neurotransmitters. For example, endorphins serve as neuromodulators by inhibiting the release of substance P, thereby blocking pain impulses.

Once researchers had located the receptor sites for the endorphins and had isolated endorphins themselves, they then wondered: Why has the brain evolved its own opiatelike neurochemicals? Perhaps the first animals blessed with endorphins were better able to function in the face of pain caused by diseases or injuries, making them more likely to survive long enough to reproduce and pass this physical trait on to successive generations (Levinthal, 1988). Evidence supporting this speculation has come from both human and animal experiments.

▲ **Candace Pert**

"Our brains probably have natural counterparts for just about any drug you could name."

endorphins
Neurotransmitters that play a role in pleasure, pain relief, and other functions.

◀ **The Runner's High**

The euphoric "exercise high" experienced by long-distance runners, such as these athletes competing at the Sydney Olympics, might be caused by the release of endorphins.

In one experiment, researchers first recorded how long mice would allow their tails to be exposed to radiant heat from a lightbulb before the pain made them flick their tails away from it. Those mice then were paired with more aggressive mice, which attacked and defeated them. The losers' tolerance for the radiant heat was then tested again. The results showed that the length of time the defeated mice would permit their tails to be heated had increased, which suggests that the aggressive attacks had raised their endorphin levels. But when the defeated mice were given naloxone, which (as mentioned earlier) blocks the effects of morphine, they flicked away their tails as quickly as they had done before being defeated. The researchers concluded that the naloxone had blocked the pain-relieving effects of the endorphins (Miczek, Thompson, & Shuster, 1982). Other studies have likewise found that endorphins are associated with pain relief in animals (Spinella et al., 1999).

Endorphin levels also rise in response to vigorous exercise (Harbach et al., 2000), perhaps accounting for the "exercise high" reported by many athletes, including runners, swimmers, and bicyclists. This was supported by a study that found increased endorphin levels after aerobic dancing (Pierce et al., 1993). Further support came from a study of bungee jumpers. After jumping, their feelings of euphoria showed a positive correlation with changes in their endorphin levels (Hennig, Laschefski, & Opper, 1994).

STAYING ON TRACK: *The Neuron*

1. What are the major structures of the neuron?
2. What is the basic process underlying neural impulses?

Answers to Staying on Track start on p. ST-2.

◆ THE BRAIN

"Tell me, where is fancy bred, in the heart or in the head?" (*The Merchant of Venice,* act 3, scene 2). The answer to this question from Shakespeare's play might be obvious to you. You know that your brain, and not your heart, is your feeling organ—the site of your mind. But you have the advantage of centuries of research, which have made the role of the brain in all psychological processes obvious even to nonscientists. Of course, the cultural influence of early beliefs can linger. Just imagine the response of a person who received a gift of Valentine's Day candy in a box that was brain-shaped instead of heart-shaped.

The ancient Egyptians associated the mind with the heart and discounted the importance of the apparently inactive brain. In fact, when the pharaoh Tutankhamen ("King Tut") was mummified to prepare him for the afterlife, his heart and other bodily organs were carefully preserved, but his brain was discarded. The Greek philosopher Aristotle (384–322 B.C.) also

The Whole Brain Atlas
www.mhhe.com/sdorow5

▶ **The Human Brain**

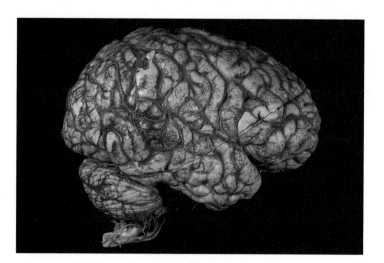

believed the heart was the site of the mind, because when the heart stops, mental activity stops (Laver, 1972). But the Greek physician-philosopher Hippocrates (460–377 B.C.), based on his observations of the effects of brain damage, did locate the mind in the brain:

▶ Some people say that the heart is the organ with which we think and that it feels pain and anxiety. But it is not so. Men ought to know that from the brain and from the brain alone arise our pleasures, joys, laughter, and tears. (quoted in Penfield, 1975, p. 7)

Techniques for Studying the Brain

Later in this chapter you will learn about the function of the different substructures of the brain. But how did scientists discover them? Today, they rely on *clinical case studies, experimental manipulation, recording of electrical activity,* and *brain imaging.* But some techniques that scientists have used for studying the brain have fallen out of favor, as described in the Thinking Critically About Psychology and the Media feature.

Thinking Critically About Psychology and the Media

What Can We Infer from the Size of the Brain?

"Research on Einstein's Brain Finds Size Does Matter" (CBC *Newsworld,* June 19, 1999)
   "Einstein Was Bigger Where It Counts, Analysis Shows" (*Sydney Morning Herald,* June 18, 1999)
   "Peek into Einstein's Brain" (*Discovery Online,* June 18, 1999)
   "The Roots of Genius" (*Newsweek,* June 24, 1999)
   "Part of Einstein's Brain 15 Percent Bigger Than Normal" (National Public Radio, June 18, 1999).

As you can gather from these headlines, the international media responded with excitement when researchers at McMaster University in Ontario, Canada, announced that the brain of scientific genius Albert Einstein was anatomically distinct. That is, a particular region of it, the parietal lobe, was larger than that same region in other people.

The media reports were based on a study of Einstein's preserved brain published in *The Lancet,* a respected British medical journal. Einstein, who is famous for his theory of relativity, is considered one of the outstanding scientists in history. The reports attributed his scientific genius to that unusually large region of his brain—a region associated with spatial and mathematical ability. It seemed to be a matter of common sense: if you know the function of a brain structure, and that structure is unusually large in a particular person, then that person must have excelled in that function. But attempts to assess intellectual and personality functions by studying the size (and shape) of specific areas of the brain are not new—and typically have been fruitless, as in the case of the practice known as **phrenology** (Greek for "science of the mind").

The Misguided "Science" of Phrenology

"You need to have your head examined!" is a refrain heard by many people whose ideas and behavior upset other people. Today, this is simply a figure of speech, but for most of the 19th century and well into the early 20th century it was common practice for people to—literally—have their heads examined. This pseudoscience, phrenology, was perhaps the most dramatic example of the commonsense practice of inferring personal characteristics from the size and shape of the brain.

Phrenology began when the respected Viennese physician-anatomist Franz Joseph Gall (1758–1828) proclaimed that particular regions of the brain controlled specific psychological functions. Gall not only believed that specific brain sites controlled specific mental faculties, but assumed that the shape of specific sites on the skull indicated the degree of development of the brain region beneath it. To Gall it was simply a matter of common sense to assume that a bumpy site would indicate a highly developed brain region; a flat site would indicate a less developed brain region.

But what did Gall use as evidence to support his practice? Much of his evidence came from his own casual observations. For example, as a child he had noted, with

The History of Phrenology on the Web
www.mhhe.com/sdorow5

phrenology
A discredited technique for determining intellectual abilities and personality traits by examining the bumps and depressions of the skull.

some envy, that classmates with good memories had bulging eyes. He concluded that their eyes bulged because excess brain matter pushed them out of their sockets. This led to the commonsense conclusion that memory ability is controlled by the region of the brain just behind the eyes. Thus, phrenology was supported by commonsense reasoning about isolated cases, which is frowned upon by scientists because of its unreliability. Though phrenology had its scientific shortcomings and disappeared in the early 20th century, it sparked interest in the localization of brain functions (Miller, 1996).

The Furor over Einstein's Brain

But what of Einstein's brain? If it did not make scientific sense to infer the size of brain areas and the degree of development of their associated functions from the shape of the skull, is it any more scientifically credible to infer brain functions from the size of particular brain structures? When Einstein died in 1955 at the age of 76 in Princeton, New Jersey, his body was cremated and his ashes spread over the nearby Delaware River, but his brain had been removed and was kept by the pathologist, Thomas Harvey, who did the autopsy. Harvey took the brain with him when he moved to Wichita, Kansas, where he kept it in two mason jars. Most of it had been cut into sections that looked like cubes of tofu.

Over the years, Harvey had mailed small sections of the brain to scientists who wished to study its microscopic structure. But the 1999 study was the first to examine the structure of the brain as a whole. The researchers compared Einstein's brain with the preserved brains of 35 men and 56 women who were presumably of normal intelligence when they died. Einstein's brain was the same weight and overall size as those of the other men, including 8 who died at about the same age as Einstein. Though Sandra Witelson, the neuroscientist who led the research team, found that Einstein's brain was normal in size, she found more specific differences between Einstein's brain and those of the other men. The lower portion of the parietal lobe was 15 percent wider than normal. This led Witelson to conclude there might have been more neural connections in that region of Einstein's brain.

"That kind of shape was not observed in any of our brains and is not depicted in any atlas of the human brain," noted Witelson (Ross, 1999, p. A-1). Because research has indicated that the parietal region is involved in spatial and mathematical functions, Witelson inferred that this might account for Einstein's superiority as a physicist and mathematician—especially given that Einstein always insisted he did his scientific thinking spatially, not verbally.

But what can we make of this research report? Witelson warned that overall brain size is not a valid indicator of differences in intelligence. But she noted that the more specific anatomical differences between Einstein's brain and the others might indicate that mathematical genius is, at least to some extent, inborn. "[W]hat this is telling us is that environment isn't the only factor" (Ross, 1999, p. A-1). Nonetheless, Witelson added that she would not discount the importance of the environment in governing brain development. Perhaps Einstein was born with a brain similar to those of the people his was compared to, but a lifetime of thinking scientifically and mathematically (not to mention other experiences, such as diet and personal health habits) altered his brain and created distinctive anatomical differences between it and the others.

The media will always seek the most interesting, controversial research studies to report. Scientific consumers are well advised to go beyond popular reports and articles and think critically about what they claim, perhaps even reading some of the scientific literature itself when it relates to topics of personal importance. One of the goals of this textbook is to help you become that kind of critical consumer of information—whether the information is presented by a scientist or a news reporter.

Clinical Case Studies

For thousands of years human beings have noticed that when people suffer brain damage from accidents or injuries, they might experience physical and psychological changes. Physicians and scientists sometimes conduct *clinical case studies* of such people. For example, later in the chapter you will read about a clinical case study of Phineas Gage, a man who lived on after a 3-foot-long metal rod pierced his brain. Neurosurgeon Oliver Sacks has written several books based on clinical case studies of patients who suffered brain damage that produced unusual—even bizarre—symptoms, including a man who lost the ability to recognize familiar faces. This disorder, *prosopagnosia,* is discussed in Chapter 5.

Experimental Manipulation

Clinical case studies involve individuals who have suffered brain damage from illness or injury. In contrast, techniques that involve *experimental manipulation* involve purposefully damaging the brain, electrically stimulating the brain, or observing the effects of drugs on the brain.

When scientists use brain lesioning, they destroy specific parts of animal brains and, after the animal has recovered from the surgery, look for changes in behavior. Since the early 19th century, when the French anatomist Pierre Flourens formalized this practice, researchers who employ this technique have learned much about the brain. As described in Chapter 11, for example, researchers in the late 1940s demonstrated that destroying a specific part of the brain structure called the *hypothalamus* would make a deprived rat starve itself even in the presence of food, whereas destroying another part of the hypothalamus would make a rat insatiable and overeat until it became obese.

Some researchers, instead of destroying parts of the brain to observe the effects on behavior, use electrical stimulation of the brain (ESB). They use weak electrical currents to stimulate highly localized sites in the brain and observe any resulting changes in behavior. Perhaps the best-known research using ESB was conducted by neurosurgeon Wilder Penfield, who, in the course of operating on the brains of people with severe epilepsy, meticulously stimulated the surface of the brain. As discussed later in the chapter, Penfield thereby discovered that activity in specific brain sites controls specific body movements and that specific sites are related to sensations from specific body sites.

Some researchers, instead of using ESB, observe the behavioral effects of drugs on the brain. Earlier in this chapter, you learned that animal subjects, when given the drug naloxone, do not show a reduction in pain following attack. Because naloxone blocks the effects of opiates, this supported research implicating endorphins as the body's own natural opiates. In a discussion later in this chapter, you will learn of a technique that involves injecting a barbiturate into an artery serving the left or right side of the brain and then observing any resulting effects. When the drug affects the left side of the brain, but rarely when it affects the right side, the person will lose the ability to speak. This supports research indicating that the left half of the brain regulates speech in most people.

Recording Electrical Activity

Consider the **electroencephalograph (EEG),** which records the patterns of electrical activity produced by neuronal activity in the brain. The EEG has a peculiar history, going back to a day at the turn of the 20th century when an Austrian scientist named Hans Berger fell off a horse and narrowly escaped serious injury. That evening he received a telegram informing him that his sister felt he was in danger.

The telegram inspired Berger to investigate the possible association between *mental telepathy* (the alleged, though scientifically unverified, ability of one mind to communicate with another by extrasensory means) and electrical activity from the brain (La Vague, 1999). In 1924, after years of experimenting on animals and his son Klaus, Berger succeeded in perfecting a procedure for recording electrical activity in the brain. He attached small metal disks called *electrodes* to Klaus's scalp and connected them with wires to a device that recorded changes in the patterns of electrical activity in his brain.

Though Berger failed to find physiological evidence in support of mental telepathy, he found that specific patterns of brain activity are associated with specific mental states, such as coma, sleep, and wakefulness (Gloor, 1994). He also identified two distinct rhythms of electrical activity. He called the relatively slow rhythm associated with a relaxed mental state the *alpha rhythm* and the relatively fast rhythm associated with an alert, active mental state the *beta rhythm.* Berger also used the EEG to provide the first demonstration of the stimulating effect of cocaine on brain activity. He found that cocaine increased the relative proportion of the beta rhythm in EEG recordings (Herning, 1985).

electroencephalograph (EEG)
A device used to record patterns of electrical activity produced by neuronal activity in the brain.

The red areas of these PET scans reveal the regions of the brain that have absorbed the most glucose, indicating that they are the most active regions during the performance of particular tasks (Phelps & Mazziotta, 1985).

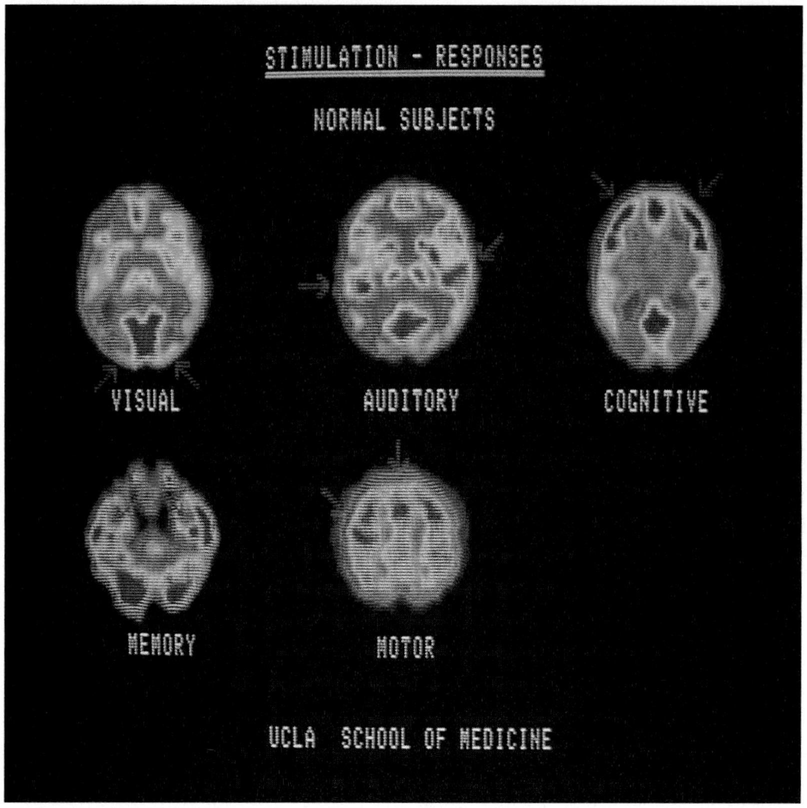

Berger's method of correlating EEG activity with psychological processes is still used today. In one study, for example, researchers determined the EEG patterns that accompanied mental fatigue in white-collar workers. The ultimate aim of the researchers was to maximize workers' productivity by determining the optimal length of work periods and rest breaks (Okogbaa, Shell, & Filipusic, 1994). The EEG even has been used to distinguish differences in brain-wave patterns in responses of listeners to different kinds of music (Panksepp & Bekkedal, 1997).

Brain-Imaging Techniques

The computer revolution has given rise to a major breakthrough in the study of the brain: brain-imaging techniques. Brain imaging involves scanning the brain to provide pictures of brain structures or "maps" of ongoing activity in the brain. Brain imaging has been used to assess brain abnormalities in psychological disorders (Gordon, 1999), brain activity while performing arithmetic thinking (Dehaene et al., 1999), and brain processes involved in storing memories (Glanz, 1998).

positron-emission tomography (PET)
A brain-scanning technique that produces color-coded pictures showing the relative activity of different brain areas.

Perhaps the most important kind of brain scan to psychologists is **positron-emission tomography (PET),** which lets them measure ongoing activity in particular regions of the brain. In using the PET scan, researchers inject radioactive glucose (a type of sugar) into a participant. Because neurons use glucose as a source of energy, the most active region of the brain takes up the most radioactive glucose. The amount of radiation emitted by each region is measured by a donut-shaped device that encircles the head. This information is analyzed by a computer, which generates color-coded pictures showing the relative degree of activity in different brain regions. As illustrated in Figure 3.7, PET scans are useful in revealing the precise patterns of brain activity during the performance of motor, sensory, and cognitive tasks (Phelps & Mazziotta, 1985). For example, a study of severe stutterers as they read aloud used the PET scan to identify brain pathways that might be involved in stuttering (De Nil et al., 2000). The PET scan has also found lasting alterations in the functioning of particular brain structures in users of the illegal drug Ecstasy, also known as MDMA (Obrocki et al., 1999).

Two other brain-scanning techniques, which are more useful for displaying brain structures than for displaying ongoing brain activity, are **computed tomography (CT)** and **magnetic resonance imaging (MRI).** The CT scan takes many X rays of the brain from a variety of orientations around it. Detectors then record how much radiation has passed through the different regions of the brain. A computer uses this information to compose a picture of the brain. The MRI scan exposes the brain to a powerful magnetic field, and the hydrogen atoms in the brain align themselves along the magnetic field. A radio signal then disrupts the alignment. When the radio signal is turned off, the atoms align themselves again. A computer analyzes these changes, which differ from one region of the brain to another, to compose an even more detailed picture of the brain. Figure 3.8 illustrates an MRI image.

Traditional CT and MRI scans have been useful in detecting structural abnormalities. For example, degeneration of brain neurons in people with Alzheimer's disease has been verified by CT scans and MRI scans (Wahlund, 1996). In the past few years, a technique called *functional MRI* has joined the PET scan as a tool for measuring ongoing activity in the brain. This ultrafast version of the traditional MRI detects increases in blood flow to brain regions that are more active at the moment. Functional MRI has been used to study brain activity involved in processes such as eating (Liu et al., 2000) and short-term memory (D'Esposito et al., 1998).

A more recent version of computed tomography, **single photon emission computed tomography (SPECT),** does more than provide images of brain structures; it creates images of regional cerebral blood flow. SPECT has been used in assessing brain activity in sensory processes such as hearing (Ottaviani et al., 1997), cognitive activities such as language (McMackin et al, 1998), and psychological disorders such as schizophrenia (Chen & Ho, 2000).

The electrical activity produced by neuronal action potentials induces changing magnetic fields. Changes in these magnetic fields can be detected by the **superconducting quantum interference device,** or **SQUID,** a recent addition to the behavioral neuroscientist's arsenal of brain-imaging techniques. SQUID uses these changes in magnetic fields to trace pathways of brain activity associated with different processes such as hearing or movement. SQUID even has been used to reveal the pattern of brain activity involved in memory processing (Glanz, 1998).

Functions of the Brain

The human brain's appearance does not hint at its complexity. Holding it in your hands, you might not be impressed by either its 3-pound weight or its walnutlike surface. You might be more impressed to learn it contains billions of neurons. And you might be astounded to learn that any given brain neuron might communicate with thousands of others, leading to an enormous number of pathways for messages to follow in the brain. Moreover, the brain is not homogeneous. It has many separate structures that interact to help you perform the myriad of activities that let you function in everyday life.

Though the functions of brain structures are similar across human beings, there are cultural differences in brain functioning (Shrivastava & Rao, 1997). For example, culturally disadvantaged preschool children in Mexico have been found to display brain-wave patterns different from those of nondisadvantaged children (Otero, 1997). When discussing brain functions, it is customary to categorize areas of the brain as the *brain stem,* the *limbic system,* and the *cerebral cortex* (see Figure 3.9).

The Brain Stem

Your ability to survive from moment to moment depends on your *brain stem,* located at the base of the brain. The brain stem includes the *medulla,* the *pons,* the *cerebellum,* the *reticular formation,* and the *thalamus.*

The Medulla. Of all the brain stem structures, the most crucial to your survival is the **medulla,** which connects the brain and spinal cord. At this moment your medulla is regulating your breathing, heart rate, and blood pressure. Because the medulla supports basic life functions, the absence of neurological activity in the medulla is sometimes used as a

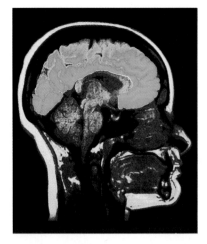

▲ Figure 3.8
The MRI Scan

The illustration shows a color-enhanced MRI scan of a healthy human brain presenting a high-definition view of the brain stem.

computed tomography (CT)
A brain-scanning technique that relies on X rays to construct computer-generated images of the brain or body.

magnetic resonance imaging (MRI)
A brain-scanning technique that relies on strong magnetic fields to construct computer-generated images of the brain or body.

single photon emission computed tomography (SPECT)
A brain-imaging technique that creates images of cerebral blood flow.

superconducting quantum interference device (SQUID)
A brain-imaging technique that uses changes in magnetic fields to trace pathways of brain activity associated with processes such as hearing or movement.

medulla
A brain stem structure that regulates breathing, heart rate, blood pressure, and other life functions.

▶ Figure 3.9
The Structure of the Human Brain
The structures of the brain stem, limbic system, and cerebral cortex serve a variety of life-support, sensorimotor, and cognitive functions.

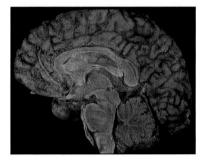

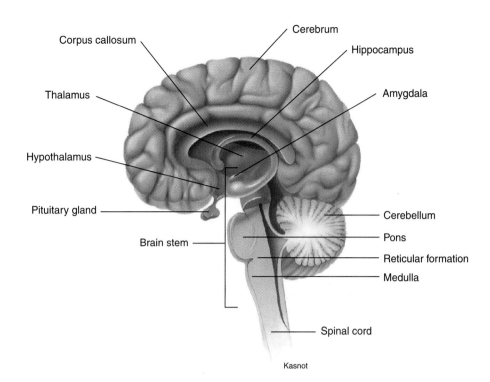

Corpus callosum

Cerebrum

Hippocampus

Thalamus

Amygdala

Hypothalamus

Pituitary gland

Cerebellum

Pons

Brain stem

Reticular formation

Medulla

Spinal cord

Kasnot

sign of brain death by physicians (Sonoo et al., 1999). When called upon, your medulla also stimulates coughing, vomiting, or swallowing. By inducing vomiting, for example, the medulla can prevent people who drink too much alcohol too fast from poisoning themselves. The medulla is also important in regulating the transmission of pain impulses (Urban, Coutinho, & Gebhart, 1999).

pons

A brain stem structure that regulates the sleep-wake cycle.

The Pons. Just above the medulla lies a bulbous structure called the **pons.** As explained in Chapter 6, the pons helps regulate the sleep-wake cycle through its effect on consciousness (Shouse et al., 2000). Surgical anesthesia induces unconsciousness by acting on the pons (Ishizawa et al., 2000). And if you have ever been the unfortunate recipient of a blow to the head that knocked you out, your loss of consciousness was caused by the blow's effect on your pons (Hayes et al., 1984).

cerebellum

A brain stem structure that controls the timing of well-learned movements.

The Cerebellum. The pons (which means "bridge" in Latin) connects the **cerebellum** (meaning "little brain") to the rest of the brain. The cerebellum controls the timing of well-learned sequences of movements that are too rapid to be controlled consciously, as in running a sprint, singing a song, or playing the piano (Kawashima et al., 2000). As you know from your own experience, you can disrupt normally automatic sequences of movements by trying to control them. Pianists who think of each key they are striking while playing a well-practiced piece would be unable to maintain proper timing. Recent research indicates that the cerebellum might even affect the smooth timing and sequencing of mental activities, such as the use of language (Fabbro, 2000). Damage to the cerebellum can disrupt the ability to perform skills that we take for granted, such as timing the opening of the fingers in throwing a ball (Timmann, Watts, & Hore, 1999).

reticular formation

A diffuse network of neurons, extending through the brain stem, that helps maintain vigilance and an optimal level of brain arousal.

The Reticular Formation. The brain stem also includes the **reticular formation,** a diffuse network of neurons that helps regulate vigilance and brain arousal. The role of the reticular formation in maintaining vigilance is shown by the "cocktail party phenomenon," in which you can be engrossed in a conversation but still notice when someone elsewhere in the room says something of significance to you, such as your name. Thus, the reticular formation acts as a filter, letting you attend to an important stimulus while ignoring irrelevant ones (Shapiro, Caldwell, & Sorensen, 1997). Experimental evidence supporting the role of the reticular formation in brain arousal came from a study by Giuseppe Moruzzi and Horace Magoun in which they awakened sleeping cats by electrically stimulating the reticular formation (Moruzzi & Magoun, 1949).

The Thalamus. Capping the brain stem is the egg-shaped **thalamus.** The thalamus functions as a sensory relay station, sending taste, bodily, visual, and auditory sensations on to other areas of the brain for further processing. The visual information from this page is being relayed by your thalamus to areas of your brain that process vision, and, at this moment the thalamus is processing impulses that will inform your brain if part of your body feels cold (Davis et al., 1999) or is in pain (Bordi & Quartaroli, 2000). The one sense whose information is not relayed through the thalamus is smell. Sensory information from smell receptors in the nose goes directly to areas of the brain that process odors.

The Limbic System

Surrounding the thalamus is a group of structures that constitute the **limbic system.** The word *limbic* comes from the Latin for "border," indicating that the limbic structures form a border between the higher and lower structures of the brain. The limbic system interacts with other brain structures to promote the survival of the individual and, as a result, the continuation of the species. Major components of the limbic system include the *hypothalamus,* the *amygdala,* and the *hippocampus.*

The Hypothalamus. Just below the thalamus, on the underside of the brain, lies the **hypothalamus** (in Greek the prefix *hypo-* means "below"), a structure that is important to a host of functions. The hypothalamus helps regulate eating, drinking, emotion, sexual behavior, and body temperature. It exerts its influence by regulating the secretion of hormones by the pituitary gland and by signals sent along neurons to bodily organs controlled by the autonomic nervous system.

   The importance of the hypothalamus in emotionality was discovered by accident. Psychologists James Olds and Peter Milner (1954) of McGill University in Montreal inserted fine wire electrodes into the brains of rats to study the effects of electrical stimulation of the reticular formation. They had already trained the rats to press a lever to obtain food rewards. When a wired rat now pressed the lever, it obtained mild electrical stimulation of its brain. To the experimenters' surprise, the rats, even when hungry or thirsty, ignored food and water in favor of pressing the lever—sometimes thousands of times an hour, until they dropped from exhaustion up to 24 hours later (Olds, 1956). Olds and Milner examined brain tissue from the rats and discovered that they had mistakenly inserted the electrodes near the hypothalamus and not into the reticular formation. They concluded they had discovered a "pleasure center." Later research studies showed that the hypothalamus is but one structure in an interconnected group of brain structures that induce feelings of pleasure when stimulated.

The Amygdala. The **amygdala** of the limbic system continuously evaluates information from the immediate environment, such as facial expressions and tone of voice, and helps elicit appropriate emotional responses (Killcross, 2000). If you saw a pit bull dog running toward you, your amygdala would help you quickly decide whether the dog was vicious, friendly, or simply roaming around. Depending on your evaluation of the situation, you might feel happy and pet the dog, feel afraid and jump on top of your desk, or feel relief and go back to studying.

   In the late 1930s, Heinrich Klüver and Paul Bucy (1937) found that lesions of the amygdala in monkeys led to "psychic blindness," an inability to evaluate environmental stimuli properly. The monkeys indiscriminately examined objects by mouth, tried to mate with members of other species, and acted fearless when confronted by a snake. Human beings who suffer amygdala damage can also exhibit symptoms of Klüver-Bucy syndrome (Hayman et al., 1998).

The Hippocampus. Whereas your amygdala helps you evaluate information from your environment, the limbic system structure that is most important in helping you form memories of that information (including what you are now reading) is the **hippocampus** (Nadel

thalamus
A brain stem structure that acts as a sensory relay station for taste, body, visual, and auditory sensations.

limbic system
A group of brain structures that, through their influence on emotion, motivation, and memory, promote the survival of the individual and, as a result, the continuation of the species.

hypothalamus
A limbic system structure that, through its effects on the pituitary gland and the autonomic nervous system, helps to regulate aspects of motivation and emotion, including eating, drinking, sexual behavior, body temperature, and stress responses.

amygdala
A limbic system structure that evaluates information from the immediate environment, contributing to feelings of fear, anger, or relief.

hippocampus
A limbic system structure that contributes to the formation of memories.

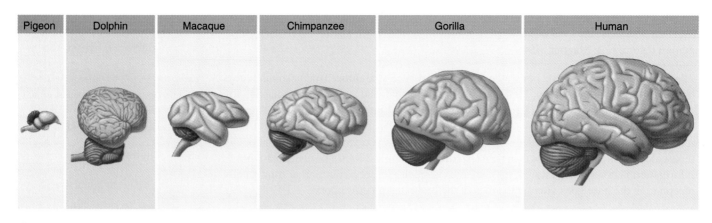

| Pigeon | Dolphin | Macaque | Chimpanzee | Gorilla | Human |

■ Cerebrum　　　　■ Cerebellum　　　　■ Brain stem

▲ **Figure 3.10**
The Evolution of the Brain
Animals that are more cognitively complex have evolved brains that are larger in proportion to their body sizes. Their cerebral cortex is also larger in proportion to the size of their other brain structures, which creates a more convoluted brain surface.

cerebral cortex
The outer covering of the brain.

cerebral hemispheres
The left and right halves of the cerebrum.

primary cortical areas
Regions of the cerebral cortex that serve motor or sensory functions.

association areas
Regions of the cerebral cortex that integrate information from the primary cortical areas and other brain areas.

frontal lobe
A lobe of the cerebral cortex responsible for motor control and higher mental processes.

motor cortex
The area of the frontal lobes that controls specific voluntary body movements.

& Moscovitch, 1998). Much of what we know about the hippocampus comes from case studies of people who have suffered damage to it. The most famous study is of a man known as "H. M." (Scoville & Milner, 1957), whose hippocampus was surgically removed in 1953—when he was 27—to relieve his uncontrollable epileptic seizures. Since the surgery, H. M. has formed few new memories, though he can easily recall events and information from before his surgery. You can read more about the implications of his case in regard to memory in Chapter 8. Damage to the hippocampus has been implicated in the memory loss associated with Alzheimer's disease. Victims of this disease suffer from degeneration of the neurons that serve as pathways between the hippocampus and other brain areas (Laakso et al., 2000).

The Cerebral Cortex

Covering the brain is the crowning achievement of brain evolution—the **cerebral cortex.** *Cortex* means "bark" in Latin. And just as the bark is the outer layer of the tree, the cerebral cortex is the thin, 3-millimeter-thick outer layer of the uppermost portion of the brain called the *cerebrum.* The cerebral cortex of human beings and other mammals has evolved folds called *convolutions,* which, as shown in Figure 3.10, give it the appearance of kneaded dough. The convolutions permit more cerebral cortex to fit inside the skull. This is necessary because evolution has assigned so many complex brain functions to the mammalian cerebral cortex that the brain has, in a sense, outgrown the skull in which it resides. If the cerebral cortex were smooth instead of convoluted, the human brain would have to be enormous to permit the same amount of surface area. The brain would be encased in a skull so large that it would give us the appearance of creatures from science fiction movies.

The cerebrum is divided into left and right halves called the **cerebral hemispheres.** Figure 3.11 shows that the cerebral cortex covering each hemisphere is divided into four regions, or *lobes:* the *frontal lobe,* the *temporal lobe,* the *parietal lobe,* and the *occipital lobe.* The lobes have **primary cortical areas** that serve motor or sensory functions. The lobes also have **association areas** that integrate information from the primary cortical areas and other brain areas in activities such as speaking, problem solving, and recognizing objects.

Motor Areas. Your tour begins in 1870, when the German physicians Gustav Fritsch and Eduard Hitzig (1870/1960) published their findings that electrical stimulation of a strip of cerebral cortex along the rear border of the right or left **frontal lobe** of a dog induced limb movements on the opposite side of the body. This is known as *contralateral control.* The area they stimulated is called the **motor cortex.** They were probably the first to demonstrate conclusively that specific sites on the cerebral cortex control specific body movements (Breathnach, 1992).

Figure 3.12 presents a "map" of the motor cortex of the frontal lobe, represented by a *motor homunculus* (*homunculus* is a Latin term meaning "small human"). Each area of the motor cortex controls a particular contralateral body movement. Certain sites on the motor cortex even show activity merely in anticipation of particular arm movements (Hyland,

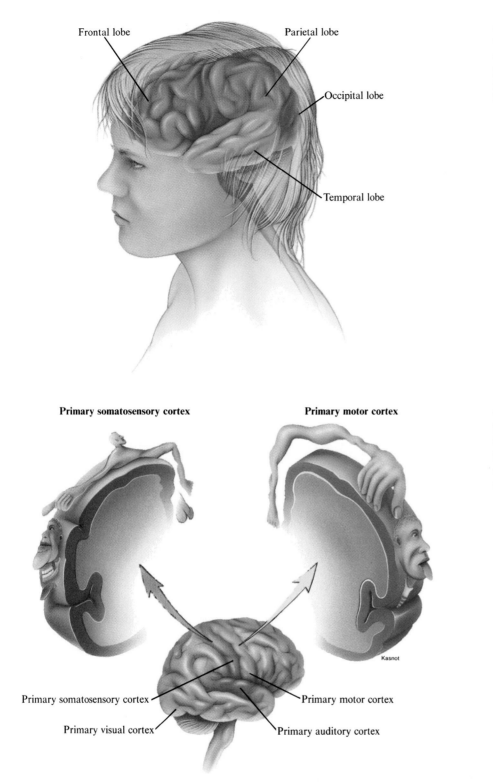

Frontal lobe

Parietal lobe

Occipital lobe

Temporal lobe

◀ **Figure 3.11**
The Lobes of the Brain

The cerebral cortex covering each cerebral hemisphere is divided into four lobes: the frontal lobe, the temporal lobe, the parietal lobe, and the occipital lobe.

Primary somatosensory cortex   **Primary motor cortex**

Kasnot

Primary somatosensory cortex   Primary motor cortex

Primary visual cortex   Primary auditory cortex

◀ **Figure 3.12**
The Motor Cortex and the Somatosensory Cortex

Both the motor cortex and the somatosensory cortex form distorted, upside-down maps of the contralateral side of the body.

1998). Note that the motor homunculus is upside down, with the head represented at the bottom and the feet represented at the top. You might also be struck by the disproportionate sizes of the body parts on the motor homunculus—each body part is represented in proportion to the precision of its movements, not in proportion to its actual size. Because your fingers move with great precision in manipulating objects, the region of the motor cortex devoted to your fingers is disproportionately large relative to the regions devoted to body parts that move with less precision, such as your arms.

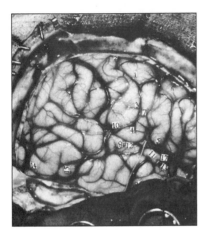

▲ **Mapping the Brain**
Wilder Penfield mapped the cerebral cortex while performing brain surgery on patients with epilepsy. The numbered tags on the exposed brain indicate sites that produced particular movements or mental experiences when electrically stimulated.

parietal lobe
A lobe of the cerebral cortex responsible for processing bodily sensations and perceiving spatial relations.

somatosensory cortex
The area of the parietal lobes that processes information from sensory receptors in the skin.

temporal lobe
A lobe of the cerebral cortex responsible for processing hearing.

▲ **Wilder Penfield (1891–1976)**
"The mind remains, still, a mystery that science has not solved."

Sensory Areas. The primary cortical areas of the frontal lobes control movements; the primary cortical areas of the other lobes process sensory information. You will notice in Figure 3.12 that the primary cortical area of the **parietal lobes** runs parallel to the motor cortex of the frontal lobes. This area is called the **somatosensory cortex,** because it processes information related to bodily senses such as pain, touch, and temperature. Certain sites even respond when the individual merely anticipates being touched (Drevets et al., 1995). As in the case of the motor cortex, the somatosensory cortex forms a distorted, upside-down homunculus of the body and receives input from the opposite side of the body. Each body part is represented on the *sensory homunculus* in proportion to its sensory precision rather than its size. This is why the region devoted to your highly sensitive lips is disproportionately large relative to the region devoted to your less sensitive back.

How do we know that a motor homunculus and a sensory homunculus exist on the cerebral cortex? We know because of research conducted by neurosurgeon Wilder Penfield (1891–1976), of the Montreal Neurological Institute, in the course of brain surgery to remove defective tissue causing epileptic seizures. Of his many contributions, his most important was the "Montreal procedure" for surgically removing scar tissue that caused epilepsy. In applying the procedure, he made the first use of Hans Berger's EEG, by comparing brain activity before and after surgery to see if it had been successful in abolishing the abnormal brain activity that had triggered his patients' seizures.

In using the Montreal procedure, Penfield made an incision through the scalp, sawed through a portion of the skull, and removed a large flap of bone—exposing the cerebral cortex. His patients required only a local anesthetic at the site of the scalp and skull incisions, because incisions in the brain itself do not cause pain. This let the patients remain awake during surgery and converse with him.

Penfield then administered a weak electrical current to the exposed cerebral cortex. He did so for two reasons. First, he wanted to induce an *aura* that would indicate the site that triggered the patient's seizures. An aura is a sensation (such as an unusual odor) that precedes a seizure. Second, he wanted to avoid cutting through parts of the cerebral cortex that serve important functions.

Penfield found that stimulation of a point on the right frontal lobe might make the left forefinger rise, and that stimulation of a point on the left parietal lobe might make the patient report a tingling feeling in the right foot. After stimulating points across the entire cerebral cortex of many patients, Penfield found that the regions governing movement and bodily sensations formed the distorted upside-down maps of the body shown in Figure 3.12. His discovery has been verified by research on animals as well as on human beings. For example, stimulation of points on the cerebral cortex of baboons produces similar distorted "maps" of the body (Waters et al., 1990).

The **temporal lobes** have their own primary cortical area, the **auditory cortex.** Particular regions of the auditory cortex are responsible for processing sounds of particular frequencies (Schreiner, 1998). This enables the temporal lobes to analyze sounds of all kinds, including speech (Binder et al., 2000). When you listen to a symphony, certain areas of the auditory cortex respond more to the low-pitched sound of a tuba, while other areas respond more to the high-pitched sound of a flute.

At the back of the brain are the **occipital lobes,** which contain the **visual cortex.** This region integrates input from your eyes into a visual "map" of what you are viewing (Swindale, 2000). Because of the nature of the pathways from your eyes to your visual cortex, visual input from objects in your *right visual field* is processed in your left occipital lobe, and visual input from objects in your *left visual field* is processed in your right occipital lobe. Damage to a portion of an occipital lobe can produce a blind spot in the contralateral visual field. In some cases, damage can produce visual hallucinations, such as the perception of parts of objects that are not actually present (Anderson & Rizzo, 1994).

Association Areas. In reading about the brain, you might have gotten the impression that each area functions independently of the others. That is far from the truth. Consider the association areas that compose most of the cerebral cortex. These areas combine information from other areas of the brain. For example, the association areas of the frontal lobes integrate

| **Chapter Three**

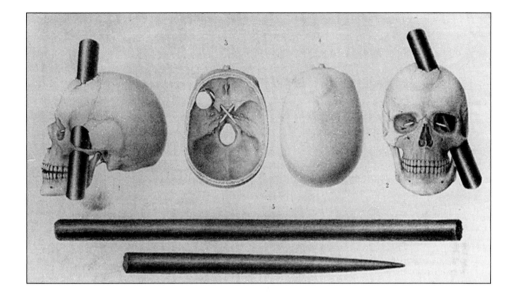

information involved in thinking, planning, and problem solving. The unusually large association areas of the human cerebral cortex provide more area for processing information. This contributes to human beings' greater flexibility in adapting to diverse circumstances.

Some of the evidence supporting the importance of the association areas of the frontal lobes in emotion and personality has come from case studies of people with damage to it, most notably the case of Phineas Gage (Harlow, 1993). On a fall day in 1848, Gage, the 25-year-old foreman of a Vermont railroad crew laying track, was clearing away rocks. While he was using an iron tamping rod to pack a gunpowder charge into a boulder, a spark ignited the gunpowder. The resulting explosion hurled the rod into Gage's left cheek, through his frontal lobes, and out the top of his skull.

Miraculously, Gage survived, recuperated, and lived 12 more years, with little impairment of his intellectual abilities. But there were dramatic changes in his personality and emotionality. Instead of remaining the friendly, popular, hardworking man he had been before the accident, he became an ornery, disliked, irresponsible bully. Gage's friends believed he had changed so radically that "he was no longer Gage."

The case study of Phineas Gage implies that the frontal lobe structures damaged by the tamping rod might be important in emotion and personality. But as explained in Chapter 2, it is impossible to determine causality from a case study. Perhaps Gage's emotional and personality changes were caused not by the brain damage itself, but instead by Gage's psychological response to his traumatic accident or by changes in how other people responded to him. Nonetheless, the frontal lobe's importance in emotion and personality has been supported by subsequent scientific research (Luv, Collins, & Tucker, 2000).

As in the case of Phineas Gage, damage to the frontal lobes causes the person to become less inhibited, which produces emotional instability, inability to plan ahead, and socially inappropriate behavior (Macmillan, 2000). This indicates the association areas of the frontal lobes are especially important in helping us adapt our emotions and behavior to diverse situations. A case study of a 50-year-old man with frontal lobe damage similar to Gage's showed intact cognitive abilities but difficulty inhibiting his behavior and trouble in behaving responsibly (Dimitrov et al., 1999).

Language Areas. The integration of different brain areas underlies many psychological functions. Consider the process of speech, one of the most distinctly human abilities. Speech depends on the interaction of the association cortex of the frontal and temporal lobes. In most left-handed people and almost all right-handed people, the left cerebral hemisphere is superior to the right in processing speech. The speech center of the frontal lobe, **Broca's area,** is named for its discoverer, the French surgeon and anthropologist Paul Broca (1824–1880). In 1861 Broca treated a 51-year-old man named Leborgne, who was given the nickname "Tan"

auditory cortex
The area of the temporal lobes that processes sounds.

occipital lobe
A lobe of the cerebral cortex responsible for processing vision.

visual cortex
The area of the occipital lobes that processes visual input.

The Phineas Gage Information Page
www.mhhe.com/sdorow5

Broca's area
The region of the frontal lobe responsible for the production of speech.

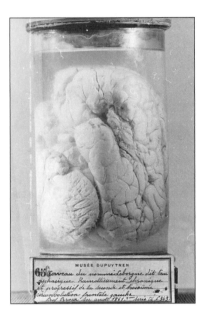

▲ Tan's Brain

Tan's brain, preserved for more than a century, shows the damage to Broca's area in the left frontal lobe that destroyed his ability to speak.

Wernicke's area

The region of the temporal lobe that controls the meaningfulness of speech.

because he had a severe speech disorder that made *tan* the only syllable he could pronounce clearly. After Tan died of an infection, Broca performed an autopsy and found damage to a small area of the left frontal lobe of his brain. Broca concluded that this area controls speech. Tan's speech disorder is now called *Broca's aphasia*. (*Aphasia* is the Greek word for "speechless.") Broca's observation was confirmed in later autopsies of the brains of people who had speech disorders similar to Tan's. CT scans have also verified that damage to Broca's area in living people is, indeed, associated with Broca's aphasia (Breathnach, 1989).

What is the nature of Broca's aphasia? Though its victims retain the ability to comprehend speech, they speak in a telegraphic style that can be comprehended only by listeners who pay careful attention. For example, when one victim of Broca's aphasia was asked about a family dental appointment, he said, "Monday . . . Dad and Dick . . . Wednesday nine o'clock . . . doctors and teeth" (Geschwind, 1979, p. 186). The speaker expressed the important thoughts but failed to express the connections between them. Nonetheless, you probably got the gist of the statement.

Speech also depends on a region of the temporal lobe cortex called **Wernicke's area,** named for the German physician Karl Wernicke. In contrast to Broca's area, which controls the production of speech, Wernicke's area controls the meaningfulness of speech. In 1874, Wernicke reported that patients with damage to the rear margin of the left temporal lobe spoke fluently but had difficulty comprehending speech and made little or no sense to even the most attentive listener. This became known as *Wernicke's aphasia.*

Consider the following statement by a victim of Wernicke's aphasia that is supposed to describe a picture of two boys stealing cookies behind a woman's back: "Mother is away here working her work to get her better, but when she's looking the two boys looking in the other part. She's working another time" (Geschwind, 1979, p. 186). The statement seems more grammatical than the telegraphic speech of the victim of Broca's aphasia, but it is impossible to comprehend—it is virtually meaningless.

The consensus among researchers is that speech production requires the interaction of Wernicke's area, Broca's area, and the motor cortex (Geschwind, 1979). Wernicke's area selects the words that will convey your meaning and communicates them to Broca's area. Broca's area then selects the muscle movements to express those words and communicates them to the region of the motor cortex that controls the speech muscles. Finally, the motor cortex communicates these directions through motor nerves to the appropriate muscles, and you speak the intended words. As you can see, speaking phrases as simple as *let's go out for pizza* involves the interaction of several areas of your brain (see Figure 3.13).

Cerebral Hemispheric Specialization

You may have noted reports in the popular media alleging that the cerebral hemispheres control different psychological functions, leading to the notion of "left-brained" and "right-brained" people. Though most researchers would not assign complete responsibility for any psychological function to just one hemisphere, they have reached agreement on some of the psychological functions for which each hemisphere is primarily responsible. The left hemisphere is somewhat superior at performing verbal, mathematical, analytical, and rational functions, and the right hemisphere is somewhat superior at performing nonverbal, spatial, holistic, and emotional functions (Springer & Deutsch, 1998). Some researchers believe we have evolved hemispheric specialization because it makes us more efficient in carrying out multiple activities at the same time, such as eating while remaining vigilant to potential threats (Rogers, 2000). Though each hemisphere has its own strengths, the hemispheres do not work in isolation. For example, the left hemisphere generally controls the production of speech, but the right hemisphere gives speech its appropriate emotional intonation (Snow, 2000).

But hemispheric specialization might differ between ethnic groups. A study comparing left- and right-hemispheric EEG patterns of natives of northeast Russia and immigrants to that region found significant differences between them during performance of tasks involving mental arithmetic and imagining a natural landscape (Rotenberg & Arshavsky, 1997). Moreover, there is some evidence of gender differences in cerebral lateralization. In one study, for example, men showed greater lateralization of language to the left hemisphere

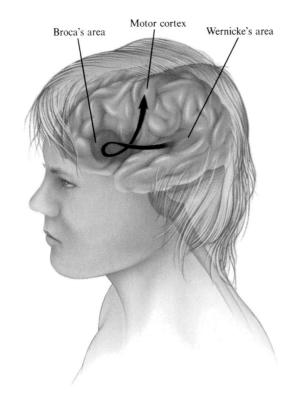

Broca's area   Motor cortex   Wernicke's area

◀ **Figure 3.13**
Speech and the Brain
Wernicke's area, Broca's area, and the
motor cortex interact in producing speech.

than did women (Jaeger et al., 1998). The size of this gender difference is small (Hiscock et al., 1995), however. In fact, other researchers have failed to find a gender difference at all (Frost et al., 1999).

Because about 90 percent of human beings are right-handed and, as a consequence, the manufactured environment favors right-handers, left-handers have some difficulties functioning in the everyday world. For example, left-handers have difficulty operating control panels designed for right-handers, especially under stressful conditions that can cause confusion, as in airplane cockpits. Because of this, human-factors engineers must consider left-handed people when designing control consoles (Garonzik, 1989). Nonetheless, left-handedness has some advantages. For example, a disproportionate number of competitive athletes are left handed, apparently because it provides a tactical advantage in sport competition (Grouios et al., 2000).

Because right-handedness is prevalent in virtually all cultures, heredity is evidently more important than life experiences in determining handedness and cerebral lateralization of functions. Additional evidence of this comes from research findings that even newborns show evidence of cerebral lateralization of psychological functions (Fein, 1990) and fetuses show a preference for sucking their right thumb while in the womb (Hepper, Shahidullah, & White, 1991). Yet cultural factors can override hereditary tendencies, as revealed in a survey of natives of the Amazon region of Colombia. All of the persons in the survey reported that they were right-handed. The researchers who did the survey concluded that those who had been born with initial tendencies toward left-handedness became right-handed as a result of cultural pressures to do so (Bryden, Ardila, & Ardila, 1993).

Perhaps the most controversial issue in recent years regarding handedness is whether right-handed people tend to live longer than left-handed people. There is no controversy about one fact: There are proportionately fewer left-handers among older adults than among younger adults. But as you will soon see, this does not necessarily mean that right-handers live longer. Two of the main proponents of the belief that right-handers do, in fact, live longer have been Stanley Coren and Diane Halpern.

Coren, a psychologist at the University of British Columbia, and Halpern, a psychologist at California State University at San Bernardino, pointed to earlier studies indicating that the percentage of right-handers was greater in older age groups (Coren & Halpern, 1991).

Gauche! Left-Handers in Society
www.mhhe.com/sdorow5

► **Figure 3.14**

Handedness and Longevity

As the graph indicates, when comparing different age groups the proportion of left-handers in the population decreases as the age of the group increases. Whereas about 15 percent of young adults are right-handers, almost none of those above age 80 are left-handers. It is unclear whether this decline reflects the greater longevity of right-handers or the forced change from left-handedness to right-handedness in some members of older age groups earlier in their lives.

Source: Coren, S. (1992). *The left-hander syndrome.* New York: Free Press.

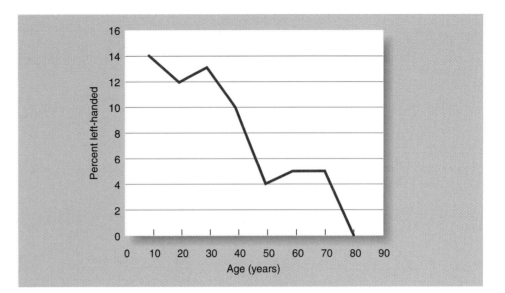

▲ **Stanley Coren and Diane Halpern**

"The absence of left-handedness in older age groups may be due to the elimination of this set of individuals through selective mortality."

Figure 3.14 illustrates the drastic change in the percentage of left-handers from younger age groups to older ones (Porac & Coren, 1981). Note that by age 80 there are virtually no left-handers in the population! To assess this handedness effect, Halpern and Coren (1988) conducted an archival study of longevity in professional baseball players, using the *Baseball Encyclopedia* as their source of data on more than 2,000 players. They found that, on the average, right-handers lived 8 months longer than left-handers. This inspired them to replicate that study to determine if their findings would generalize to people other than baseball players.

Coren and Halpern sent brief questionnaires to the next of kin of 2,875 persons who recently had died in two counties in southern California. The questionnaires asked questions about the deceased's handedness regarding writing, drawing, and throwing. Each person's age at death was obtained from death certificates. Despite the apparent intrusion of the questionnaires into the lives of grieving relatives, 1,033 questionnaires were returned. Of these, 987 were usable. Coren and Halpern determined whether the deceased had been right-handed or left-handed.

The results were startling: right-handers lived an average of 9 years longer than left-handers. Thus, this study found a much larger longevity gap than the study of baseball players found. Coren and Halpern attributed the gap to the earlier deaths of left-handers (the *elimination hypothesis*) rather than to cultural pressures to become right-handed (the *modification hypothesis*) affecting older generations more than younger ones. Coren and Halpern found that the most important factors accounting for this were a greater tendency for left-handers to have accidents, immune disorders, and evidence of neurological defects. For example, a Canadian study of people hospitalized for head injuries caused by automobile accidents found that victims were disproportionately left-handers (MacNiven, 1994).

Research findings have not consistently supported Coren and Halpern's findings. Even the allegedly longer life spans of right-handed baseball players have been called into question. A large-scale study of more than 5,000 professional baseball players found that left-handers actually lived an average of 8 months longer than right-handers (Hicks et al., 1994). Coren and Halpern's explanations for the apparent longevity difference favoring right-handers also have been called into question. For example, a study in the Netherlands found no relationship between accident proneness and handedness among undergraduate students (Merckelbach, Muris, & Kop, 1994). Moreover, research has been inconsistent on the relationship between handedness and immune disorders, with some even showing that right-handers are more susceptible to them (Bryden, 1993). And there is conflicting evidence about the greater likelihood of neurological disorders in left-handers (Bishop, 1990).

The strongest response to Coren and Halpern has come from Lauren Harris of Michigan State University, who believes the modification hypothesis is a better explanation for the decline in left-handers across the life span (Harris, 1993). According to Harris, today's older adults grew up at a time when left-handers were forced to use their right hands or simply chose to conform to a right-handed world. In contrast, over the past few decades left-handedness has lost its stigma, resulting in more left-handers remaining left-handed.

This was supported by a study in Norway. In keeping with Coren and Halpern's findings, the researchers found that about 15.2 percent of 21- to 30-year-olds were left-handed and only 1.7 percent of those more than 80 years old were left-handed. But the researchers found that the apparent decline in left-handedness across the life span was, in reality, due to the fact that many left-handers in earlier generations had switched to being right-handed (Hugdahl et al., 1993). Despite these findings, which contradict their position, Halpern and Coren (1993) insist that most scientifically sound studies support their belief that left-handers tend to die younger.

Several questions remain to be answered, but the main one is this: If we follow groups of young people as they grow older, will the left-handers tend to die sooner than the right-handers? If they do, it would support Coren and Halpern's explanation. If they do not, it would support Harris's explanation. Of course, this would take many decades to determine.

In addition to their interest in handedness, cerebral-laterality researchers study the psychological functions of the left and right hemispheres. They do so by studying the damaged brain, the intact brain, and the split brain.

Evidence of Hemispheric Specialization from the Damaged Brain. As you read earlier in the chapter, the earliest source of knowledge about cerebral hemispheric specialization was the study of unilateral brain damage; that is, damage to one cerebral hemisphere. If damage to one hemisphere of the brain produces symptoms that differ from symptoms produced by damage to the other hemisphere, researchers conclude that the damaged hemisphere plays more of a role in that function than does the other hemisphere.

Paul Broca, after finding that a specific kind of language disorder consistently followed damage to the left hemisphere, concluded that language depended more on the left hemisphere than on the right hemisphere (Harris, 1999). More recent research on brain damage has found that both hemispheres are involved in language, but that their particular roles differ. For example, though the left hemisphere is more important for the production and comprehension of speech, the right hemisphere is more important for processing aspects of speech unrelated to the spoken words themselves. For example, damage to the right hemisphere produces greater deterioration in the ability to interpret the speaker's tone of voice than does damage to the left hemisphere (Ross, Thompson, & Yenkosky, 1997).

Evidence of Hemispheric Specialization from the Intact Brain. Psychologists interested in hemispheric specialization have devised several methods for studying the intact brain. One of the chief methods has participants perform tasks while an EEG records the electrical activity of their cerebral hemispheres. Studies have found that people produce greater electrical activity in the left hemisphere while performing verbal tasks, such as solving verbal analogy problems, and greater electrical activity in the right hemisphere while performing spatial tasks, such as mentally rotating geometric forms (Loring & Sheer, 1984). Research using functional MRI has demonstrated activity in the language areas of the left hemisphere even in people using American Sign Language. But American Sign Language also involves greater involvement of the right hemisphere than does English (Bavelier et al., 1998).

A more recent approach to studying hemispheric specialization in the intact brain uses the PET scan to create color-coded pictures of the relative activity in regions of the left hemisphere and right hemisphere. Figure 3.15 shows the results of one such study. Another approach, the **Wada test,** studies human participants in whom a hemisphere has been anesthetized in the course of brain surgery to correct a neurological defect (Izac & Banoczi, 1999). This is done by injecting a barbiturate anesthetic into either the right or the left carotid artery, which provides oxygenated blood to the associated cerebral hemisphere. The injection anesthetizes that hemisphere. As you might expect, anesthetization of the left hemisphere, but only rarely of the right hemisphere, induces temporary aphasia—the patient has difficulty speaking (Mueller et al., 1998).

Wada test
A technique in which a cerebral hemisphere is anesthetized to assess hemispheric specialization.

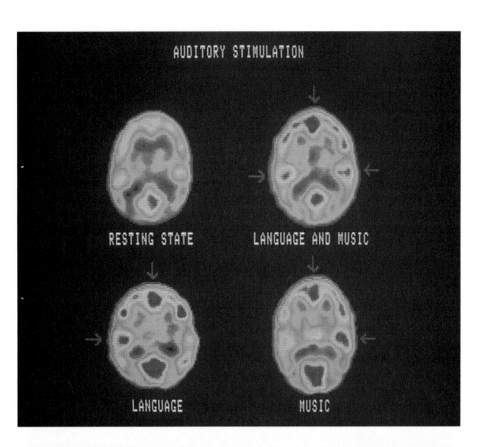

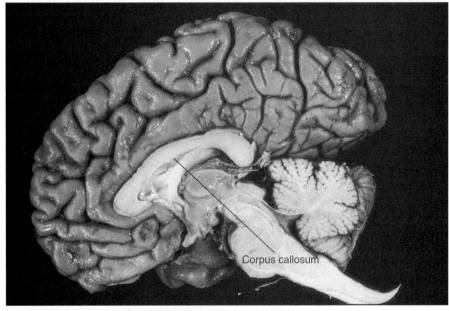

Corpus callosum

Evidence of Hemispheric Specialization from the Split Brain. Studies of damaged brains and intact brains have provided most of the evidence regarding cerebral hemispheric specialization, but the most fascinating approach has been **split-brain research.** This involves people whose hemispheres have been surgically separated from each other. Though split-brain research is only a few decades old, the idea was entertained in 1860 by Gustav Fechner, who was introduced in Chapter 1 as a founder of psychology. Fechner claimed that people who survived the surgical separation of their cerebral hemispheres would have two separate minds in one head (Springer & Deutsch, 1998). Decades later English psychologist William McDougall argued that such an operation would not divide the mind, which he considered

split-brain research
Research on hemispheric specialization
that studies individuals in whom the
corpus callosum has been severed.

Chapter Three

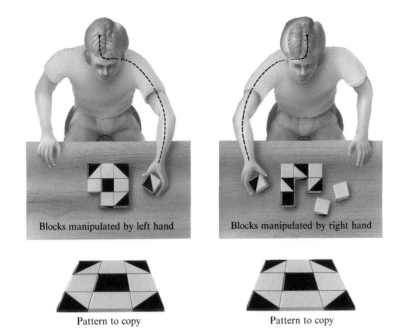

Blocks manipulated by left hand   Blocks manipulated by right hand

Pattern to copy   Pattern to copy

◀ **Figure 3.17**
A Split-Brain Study

Gazzaniga (1967) had a split-brain patient arrange multicolored blocks to match a design printed on a card in front of him. The patient's left hand performed better than his right, because the left hand is controlled by the right hemisphere, which is superior at perceiving spatial relationships. You would be able to perform a block-design task equally well with either your right or your left hand, because your intact corpus callosum would let information from your spatially superior right hemisphere help your left hemisphere control your right hand.

indivisible. McDougall even volunteered to test Fechner's claim by having his own cerebral hemispheres surgically separated if he ever became incurably ill.

Though McDougall never had split-brain surgery, it was performed on patients in the early 1960s, when neurosurgeons Joseph Bogen and Phillip Vogel severed the **corpus callosum** of epileptic patients to reduce seizure activity that had not responded to drug treatments. As illustrated in Figure 3.16, the corpus callosum is a thick bundle of axons that provides the means of communication of information between the cerebral hemispheres (Gazzaniga, 2000). Split-brain surgery works by preventing seizure activity in one hemisphere from spreading to the other. Split-brain patients behave normally in their everyday lives, but special testing procedures have revealed an astonishing state of affairs: Their left and right hemispheres can no longer communicate with each other (Reuter-Lorenz & Miller, 1998). Each acts independently of the other.

Roger Sperry (1982) and his colleagues, most notably Jerre Levy and Michael Gazzaniga, have been pioneers in split-brain research. In a typical study of a split-brain patient, information is presented to one hemisphere and the participant is asked to give a response that depends more on one hemisphere than on the other. In one study (Gazzaniga, 1967), a split-brain patient performed a block-design task in which he had to arrange multicolored blocks so that their upper sides formed a pattern that matched the pattern printed on a card in front of him. This is illustrated in Figure 3.17. When the participant performed with his left hand, he did well, but when he performed with his right hand, he did poorly. Can you figure out why that happened?

Because the left hand is controlled by the right hemisphere, which is superior in perceiving spatial relationships, such as those in designs, he performed well with his left hand. And because the right hand is controlled by the left hemisphere, which is inferior in perceiving spatial relationships, he performed poorly with his right hand—even though he was right-handed. At times, when his right hand was having a hard time completing the design, his left hand would sneak up on it and try to help. This led to a bizarre battle for control of the blocks—as if each hand belonged to a different person.

Despite the dramatic findings of split-brain studies, Jerre Levy (1983) believes that researchers, including Gazzaniga (1983), have exaggerated the extent to which each hemisphere regulates particular psychological processes, especially the supposed superiority of the left hemisphere. As always, only additional scientific research will resolve the Levy-Gazzaniga debate, which, you might note, is an example of the continual controversy over the degree to which psychological functions are localized in particular areas of the brain.

corpus callosum

A thick bundle of axons that provides a means of communication between the cerebral hemispheres, which is severed in so-called split-brain surgery.

▲ **Jerre Levy**

"Although the right hemisphere is nonlinguistic (except in unusual or pathological cases), the evidence is overpowering that it is active, responsive, highly intelligent, thinking, conscious, and fully human with respect to its cognitive depth and complexity."

1. What are the functions of the brain stem, the limbic system, and the cerebral cortex?
2. What roles do Broca's and Wernicke's area play in speech production?
3. What evidence is there for hemispheric specialization based on split-brain research?

Answers to Staying on Track start on p. ST-2.

Chapter Summary

HEREDITY AND BEHAVIOR

- The field of behavioral neuroscience studies the relationships between physiological processes and psychological functions.
- Psychologists who champion evolutionary psychology employ Darwinian concepts in their research and theorizing.
- Scientists who study behavioral genetics are interested in how heredity affects behavior.
- Heritability refers to the proportion of variability in a trait across a population attributable to genetic differences among members of the population
- Research procedures that assess the relative contributions of nature and nurture involve studies of families, adoptees, and identical twins reared apart.

COMMUNICATION SYSTEMS

- The nervous system is composed of cells called neurons and serves as the main means of communication within the body.
- The nervous system is divided into the central nervous system, which comprises the brain and the spinal cord, and the peripheral nervous system, which comprises the nerves of the somatic nervous system and the autonomic nervous system.
- The autonomic nervous system is subdivided into the sympathetic nervous system, which arouses the body, and the parasympathetic nervous system, which conserves energy.
- Hormones, secreted into the bloodstream by endocrine glands, also serve as a means of communication within the body.
- Most endocrine glands are regulated by hormones secreted by the pituitary gland, which, in turn, is regulated by the hypothalamus.
- Hormones participate in functions as diverse as sexual development and responses to stress.

THE NEURON

- The nervous system carries information along sensory neurons, motor neurons, and interneurons, as in the limb-withdrawal reflex mediated by the spinal cord.
- The neuron generally receives signals through its dendrites and sends signals along its axon.
- The axon maintains a resting potential during which it is electrically negative on the inside relative to its outside, as a result of a higher concentration of negative ions inside.
- Sufficient stimulation of the neuron causes the axon to depolarize (become less electrically negative) and reach its firing threshold.

- This produces an action potential, which causes a neural impulse to travel along the entire length of the axon.
- The neural impulses stimulate the release of neurotransmitter molecules into the synapse. The molecules cross the synapse and attach to receptor sites on glands, muscles, or other neurons. These molecules exert either an excitatory or an inhibitory influence.
- In recent years, the neurotransmitters known as endorphins have inspired research because of their role in pain relief and euphoria.

THE BRAIN

- The functions of the brain have been revealed by clinical case studies, experimental manipulation, recording of electrical activity, and brain-imaging techniques.
- The medulla regulates vital functions, such as breathing; the pons regulates arousal and attention; and the cerebellum controls the timing of well-learned sequences of movements.
- The reticular formation regulates brain arousal and helps maintain vigilance.
- The thalamus relays sensory information (except smell) to various regions of the brain for further processing.
- Within the limbic system, the hypothalamus regulates the pituitary gland, as well as emotion and motives such as eating, drinking, and sex.
- The amygdala continuously evaluates the immediate environment for potential threats, and the hippocampus processes information into memories.
- The cerebral cortex covers the brain and is divided into the frontal, temporal, parietal, and occipital lobes.
- Well-defined areas of the lobes regulate movements and process sensory information.
- Most areas of the cerebral cortex are association areas devoted to integrating information from different brain areas, such as those devoted to speech.
- Each cerebral hemisphere has psychological functions at which it excels, though both hemispheres influence virtually all functions.
- Studies of the degree of activity in each hemisphere, of the effects of damage to one hemisphere, and of people whose hemispheres have been surgically disconnected show that the left hemisphere is typically superior at verbal tasks and the right hemisphere is typically superior at spatial tasks.

Key Concepts

Key Contributors

Thought Questions

1. How do psychologists interested in behavioral genetics use studies of identical twins reared apart to assess the role of heredity in human development?
2. How would you determine whether the joy of a student who earns a 4.00 grade-point average is associated with an increase in endorphin levels?

Possible Answers to Thought Questions start on p. PT-1

3. Why do some psychologists believe that phrenology was an important but misguided approach to the localization of brain functions?
4. How does split-brain research provide evidence that the left cerebral hemisphere predominates in speech and the right cerebral hemisphere predominates in spatial relations?

OLC Preview

 For additional quizzing and a variety of interactive resources, visit the book's Online Learning Center at www.mhhe.com/sdorow5.

chapter four

4

Human Development

EDWARD POTTHAST
Children at Shore, 1919

In 1987 Hulda Crooks climbed Mount Whitney in the Sierra Nevada Mountains of California for the twenty-third time. This would be a noteworthy feat for any person, given that 14,495 Mount Whitney is the tallest mountain in the contiguous 48 states. What made it more impressive was that 5-foot-1-inch Hulda was 91 years old at the time, making her the oldest person ever to reach the summit. That year she also became the oldest woman to climb Mount Fuji, the tallest mountain in Japan. The Japanese sponsors of her ascent honored her with a banner reading "Grandma Fuji."

The following year Hulda decided to add the U.S. Capitol to her long list of conquests. She barely worked up a sweat as she ascended the 350-step staircase in the building's dome in just 30 minutes. Hulda, a physical fitness proponent who also held eight Senior Olympics world records in track and field at the time, made the climb to celebrate National Women in Sports Day (Connors, 1988). The climb was second nature to her, given that her typical training regimen involved climbing 60 steps 15 times.

In 1991 a peak near Mount Whitney was named Crooks Peak in Hulda's honor. "You have not only highlighted the importance of physical fitness for all Americans, but also served as a role model for senior citizens everywhere," wrote President George Bush in a letter recognizing her accomplishments. At the ceremony naming the peak, Hulda observed, "It's never too late to change your lifestyle if you realize it's not appropriate. I want to impress to young people that they're building their old age now" (Kuebelbeck, 1991).

Hulda, who died in 1997 at the age of 101, was a vegetarian who took up hiking in her forties following a bout with pneumonia. She did not scale her first peak until she was 66, an age at which many people are content to lead a more sedate life. Hulda advocated a healthful diet, vigorous exercise, and avoiding caffeine and alcohol. She also credited her healthy life to her spirituality as a devout member of the Seventh-Day Adventist Church. Hulda published her memoirs, *Conquering Life's Mountains,* as a testament to the importance of mental, physical, and spiritual well-being. At a book signing, she was treated as a celebrity. Mountaineers lined up to have her sign their copies. One of them laughed when he realized that he had retired from mountain climbing at 55, when he was more than 10 years younger than Hulda was when she began her climbing career (Fieckenstein, 1996).

▲ **Vigorous in Old Age**
Hulda Crooks, who climbed her first mountain in her mid sixties, illustrates the importance of maintaining physical fitness and a healthful lifestyle across the life span. Research indicates that physically and mentally active adults might age at a slower rate.

American Psychological Association, Division 7
www.mhhe.com/sdorow5

developmental psychology
The field that studies physical, perceptual, cognitive, and psychosocial changes across the life span.

maturation
The sequential unfolding of inherited predispositions in physical and motor development.

*H*ulda Crooks's accomplishments in old age contradict the stereotype of the elderly as frail and lacking in vitality. Psychologists who study the aging process find that severe mental and physical decline is not necessarily a characteristic of old age. As Hulda noted, by keeping mentally and physically active in adulthood we can have rich, rewarding lives throughout our later years. The field of **developmental psychology** is concerned with the physical, perceptual, cognitive, and psychosocial changes that take place across the life span. Though opinions about the nature of human development can be found in the writings of ancient Greek philosophers, the scientific study of human development did not begin until the 1870s. That decade saw the appearance of the "baby biography," usually written by a parent, which described the development of an infant. Though much of infant development depends on learning, it is also guided by physical **maturation**—the sequential unfolding of inherited predispositions (as in the progression from crawling to standing to walking). Developmental psychologists recognize that most aspects of human development depend on the interaction of genetic and environmental factors (Collins et al., 2000). The 1890s saw the beginning of research on child development after infancy (White, 1990), most notably at Clark University by G. Stanley Hall (1844–1924). Hall based his theories on Darwin's theory of evolution, earning him the title "the Darwin of the mind." He applied research findings to the improvement of education and child rearing, and today he is recognized as the founder of *child psychology.* Until the 1950s the study of human development was virtually synonymous with child psychology. During that decade, psychologists began to study human development across the life span.

◆ RESEARCH METHODS IN DEVELOPMENTAL PSYCHOLOGY

Though developmental psychologists often use the same research methods as other psychologists, they also rely on methods unique to developmental psychology. These include *longitudinal research* and *cross-sectional research,* which enable researchers to study age-related differences and changes in their participants.

Longitudinal Research

Longitudinal research follows the same participants over a period of time, typically ranging from months to years. The researcher looks for changes in particular characteristics, such as language, personality, intelligence, or perceptual ability. Suppose you wanted to study changes in the social maturity of college students. If you chose to use a longitudinal design, you might assess the social maturity of an incoming class of first-year students and then note changes in their social maturity across their 4 years in college. Longitudinal research has been used to study numerous topics, such as factors associated with risk of divorce in married couples (Karney & Bradbury, 1995), the effect of day care on children (Broberg et al., 1997), and the relative influence of genetic and environmental factors on problem behaviors in adopted children (van der Valk et al., 1998).

Though longitudinal research has the advantage of permitting us to study individuals as they change across their life spans, it has major weaknesses. First, the typical longitudinal study takes months, years, or even decades to complete. This often requires ongoing financial support and continued commitment by researchers—neither of which can be guaranteed. Second, the longer the study lasts, the more likely it is that participants will drop out. They might refuse to continue or move away or even die. If those who drop out differ in important ways from those who remain, the results of the research might be less generalizable to the population of interest. For example, a 14-year longitudinal study of changes in adult intelligence found that those who dropped out had scored lower on intelligence tests than did those who remained. This made it unwise to generalize the study's findings to all adults. Generalizing from only those who remained in the study would have led to the erroneous conclusion that as adults age they show a marked increase in intelligence (Schaie, Labouvie, & Barrett, 1973).

Cross-Sectional Research

The weaknesses of longitudinal research are overcome by **cross-sectional research,** which compares groups of participants of different ages at the same time. Each of the age groups is called a **cohort.** If you chose a cross-sectional design to study age-related differences in social maturity of college students, you might compare the current social maturity of four cohorts: first-year students, sophomores, juniors, and seniors. A cross-sectional research design was used in a study of age differences in male sexuality. The researchers compared samples of men in their thirties through nineties. The stereotype of old age as a time of asexuality was

▲ **G. Stanley Hall (1844–1924)**

"There is really no clue by which we can thread our way through all the mazes of culture and the distractions of modern life save by knowing the true nature and needs of childhood and adolescence."

longitudinal research

A research design in which the same group of participants is tested or observed repeatedly over a period of time.

cross-sectional research

A research design in which groups of participants of different ages are compared at the same point in time.

cohort

A group of people of the same age group.

countered by the finding that all of the participants in the oldest groups reported feelings of sexual desire (Mulligan & Moss, 1991). Cross-sectional research designs have been used to study topics as varied as age-related differences in personality in adulthood (Jang, Livesley, & Vernon, 1996) and the relationship between medical education and differences in moral reasoning across 4 years of medical school (Self & Baldwin, 1998).

Like longitudinal research, cross-sectional research has its own weaknesses. The main one is that cross-sectional research can produce misleading findings if a cohort in the study is affected by circumstances unique to that cohort. Thus, cross-sectional studies can identify differences between cohorts of different ages, but those differences might not hold true if cohorts of those ages were observed during another era. Suppose that you conduct a cross-sectional study and find that older adults score higher on a measure of ethnic prejudice than younger adults. Does this mean that we become more prejudiced with age? Not necessarily. Perhaps, instead, the cohort of older adults was reared at a time when prejudice was more acceptable than it is today. Members of the cohort simply might have retained attitudes they developed in their youth.

Longitudinal research and cross-sectional research have long been staples of life-span developmental research. Today, technology permits developmental psychologists to study ongoing developmental processes even before birth, during the prenatal period.

STAYING ON TRACK: *Research Methods in Developmental Psychology*

1. What is maturation?
2. What are the strengths and weaknesses of cross-sectional and longitudinal research designs?

Answers to Staying on Track start on p. ST-2.

◆ PRENATAL DEVELOPMENT

You, Julius Caesar, Oprah Winfrey, and anyone else who has ever lived began as a single cell. The formation of that cell begins the prenatal period, which lasts about 9 months and is divided into the *germinal stage,* the *embryonic stage,* and the *fetal stage.* Figure 4.1 illustrates prenatal development.

The Germinal Stage

The **germinal stage** begins with conception, which occurs when a *sperm* from the male unites with an egg (or *ovum*) from the female in one of her two *fallopian tubes,* forming a one-celled *zygote.* The zygote contains 23 pairs of chromosomes, one member of each pair coming from the ovum and the other coming from the sperm. The chromosomes, in turn, contain genes that govern the development of the individual. The zygote begins a trip down the fallopian tube, during which it is transformed into a larger, multicelled ball by repeated cell divisions. By the end of the second week, the ball attaches to the wall of the uterus. This marks the beginning of the embryonic stage.

germinal stage
The prenatal period that lasts from conception through the second week.

The Embryonic Stage

The **embryonic stage** lasts from the end of the second week through the eighth week of prenatal development. The embryo, nourished by nutrients that cross the placenta, increases in size and begins to develop specialized organs, including the eyes, heart, and brain. What accounts for this rapid, complex process? The development and location of bodily organs is regulated by genes, which determine the kinds of cells that will develop and also direct the

embryonic stage
The prenatal period that lasts from the end of the second week through the eighth week.

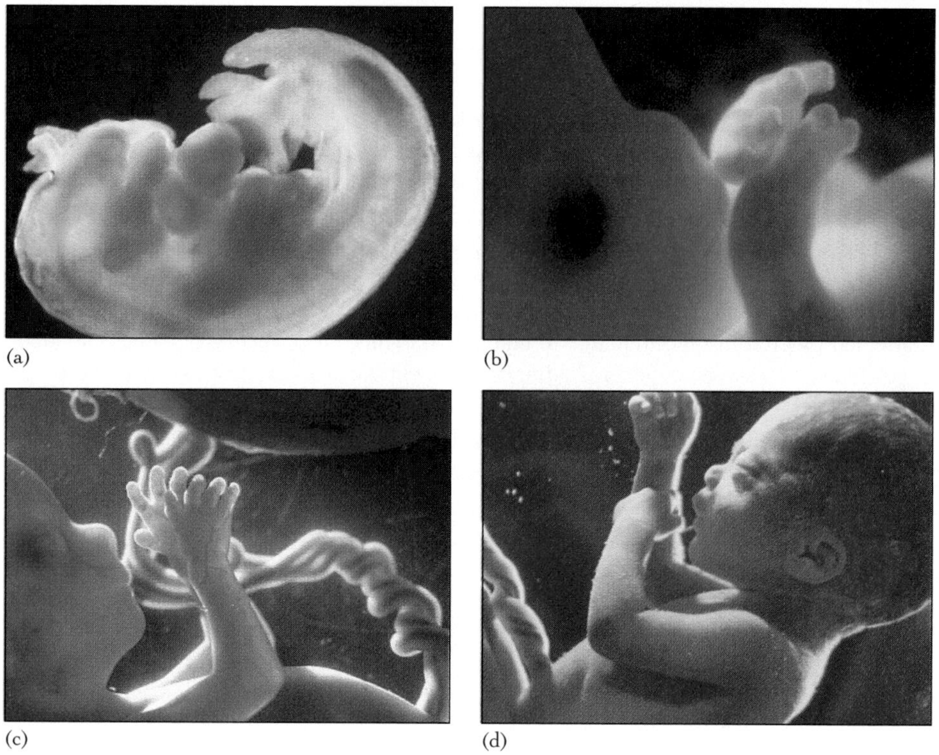

Prenatal Development

Prenatal development is marked by rapid growth and differentation of structures. *(a)* At 4 weeks, the embryo is about 0.2 inches long, has a recognizable head, arm buds, leg buds, and a heart that has begun beating. *(b)* At 8 weeks—the end of the embryonic stage—the embryo has features that make it recognizable as distinctly human, including a nose, a mouth, eyes, ears, hands, fingers, feet, and toes. This marks the beginning of the fetal stage. *(c)* At 16 weeks the fetus is about 7 inches long and makes movements that can be detected by the mother. The remainder of the fetal stage involves extremely rapid growth. *(d)* At 9 months the fetus is fully formed and ready to be born.

(a)   (b)

(c)   (d)

actions of *cell-adhesion molecules.* These molecules direct the movement of cells and determine which cells will adhere to one another, thereby deciding the size, shape, and location of organs in the embryo (Ronn et al., 2000). By the end of the embryonic stage, development has progressed to the point at which the heart is beating and the approximately 1-inch-long embryo has facial features, limbs, fingers, and toes.

But what determines whether an embryo becomes a male or a female? The answer lies in the 23rd pair of chromosomes, the sex chromosomes, which are designated *X* or *Y.* Embryos that inherit two X chromosomes are genetic females, and embryos that inherit one X and one Y chromosome are genetic males. The Y chromosome directs the development of testes; in the *absence* of a Y chromosome ovaries develop. Near the end of the embryonic period, the primitive gonads of male embryos secrete the hormone *testosterone,* which stimulates the development of male sexual organs. And the primitive gonads of female embryos secrete the hormones *estrogen* and *progesterone,* which stimulate the development of female sexual organs. Thus, the hormonal environments of female and male fetuses differ at the embryonic stage of development.

Prenatal hormones direct the differentiation of sexual organs and the brain, especially the hypothalamus (see Chapter 3). The secretion of testosterone directs the differentiation of the male sexual organs. In cases where testosterone is absent, female sexual organs differentiate. There is evidence, though, that estrogen plays a greater role in sexual differentiation of the female fetus than has been estimated in the past (Collaer & Hines, 1995).

The Fetal Stage

The presence of a distinctly human appearance marks the beginning of the **fetal stage,** which lasts from the beginning of the third prenatal month until birth. By the fourth month, pregnant women report movement by the fetus. And by the seventh month all of the major organs are functional, which means that an infant born even 2 or 3 months prematurely has a chance of surviving. The final 3 months of prenatal development are associated with most of the increase in the size of the fetus. Fetal behavioral patterns are related to the mother's socioeconomic status. For example, the fetuses of poor women tend to be less active (Pressman et al., 1998).

fetal stage

The prenatal period that lasts from the end of the eighth week through birth.

Chapter Four

Premature infants tend to be smaller and less physically and cognitively mature than full-term infants. For example, when an object approaches the eyes of a premature infant, the infant might not exhibit normal defensive blinking (Pettersen, Yonas, & Fisch, 1980).

Though prenatal development usually produces a normal infant, in some cases genetic defects produce distinctive physical and psychological syndromes. For example, the chromosomal disorder called Down syndrome (discussed in Chapter 10) is associated with mental retardation and abnormal physical development. Other sources of prenatal defects are **teratogens,** which are noxious substances or other factors that can disrupt prenatal development and prevent the individual from reaching her or his inherited potential. (The word *teratogen* was coined from Greek terms meaning, "that which produces a monster.") A powerful teratogen is the X ray. Prenatal exposure to X rays can disrupt the migration of brain cells, causing mental retardation (Schull, Norton, & Jensh, 1990).

Most teratogens affect prenatal development by first crossing the placenta. For example, a potent teratogen is the German measles (rubella) virus, which can cause defects of the eyes, ears, and heart—particularly during the first 3 months of prenatal development. Many drugs, both legal and illegal, can cross the placenta and cause abnormal physical and psychological development. These drugs include nicotine (Day & Richardson, 1994) and marijuana (Goldschmidt, Day, & Richardson, 2000). Pregnant women who drink alcohol can afflict their offspring with **fetal alcohol syndrome,** one of the leading causes of mental retardation in Western countries (Kaemingk & Paquette, 1999). Fetal alcohol syndrome is more common among women who drink heavily during pregnancy than among those who drink moderately (Polygenis et al., 1998). Fetal alcohol syndrome also is associated with facial deformities, hearing disorders, and attentional deficits. Figure 4.2 shows a child who suffers from fetal alcohol syndrome.

STAYING ON TRACK: *Prenatal Development*

1. What are cell-adhesion molecules?
2. What are the symptoms of fetal alcohol syndrome?

Answers to Staying on Track start on p. ST-2.

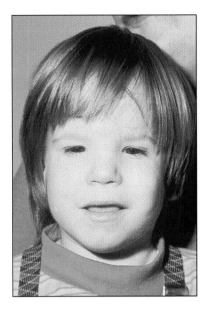

▲ **Figure 4.2**
Fetal Alcohol Syndrome
Prenatal exposure to alcohol can produce fetal alcohol syndrome, which is marked by mental retardation and facial deformities.

 National Organization on Fetal Alcohol Syndrome
www.mhhe.com/sdorow5

teratogen
A noxious substance, such as a virus or drug, that can cause prenatal defects.

fetal alcohol syndrome
A disorder, marked by physical defects and mental retardation, that can afflict the offspring of women who drink alcohol during pregnancy.

childhood
The period that extends from birth until the onset of puberty.

infancy
The period that extends from birth through 2 years of age.

◆ INFANT AND CHILD DEVELOPMENT

Childhood extends from birth until puberty and begins with **infancy,** a period of rapid physical, cognitive, and psychosocial development, extending from birth to age 2 years. Many developmental psychologists devote themselves to studying the changes in physical, perceptual, cognitive, and psychosocial development that occur during childhood.

Physical Development

Newborn infants exhibit reflexes that promote survival, such as blinking to protect their eyes from an approaching object and rooting for a nipple when their cheeks are touched. Through maturation and learning, the infant quickly develops motor skills that go beyond mere reflexes. The typical infant is crawling by 6 months and walking by 13 months. Though infant motor development follows a consistent sequence, the timing of motor milestones varies somewhat from one infant to another. Figure 4.3 depicts the major motor milestones.

Infancy is also a period of rapid brain development, when many connections between brain cells are formed and many others are eliminated. Though many of these changes are governed by maturation, research studies by Marian Diamond and her colleagues over the past few decades have demonstrated that life experiences can affect brain development (Diamond, 1988). One of these studies determined the effect of enriched and impoverished environments on the brain development of rats (Camel, Withers, & Greenough, 1986). A group of infant rats spent 30 days in an enriched environment and another group spent 30 days in an impoverished environment. In the enriched environment, the rats were housed

Infancy is a period of rapid motor development. The infant begins with a set of motor reflexes and, over the course of little more than a year, develops the ability to manipulate objects and move independently through the environment. The ages at which normal children reach motor milestones vary somewhat from child to child, but the sequence of motor milestones does not.

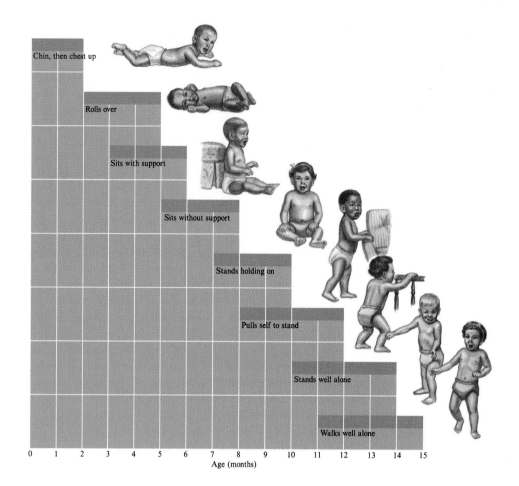

Chin, then chest up

Rolls over

Sits with support

Sits without support

Stands holding on

Pulls self to stand

Stands well alone

Walks well alone

0　1　2　3　4　5　6　7　8　9　10　11　12　13　14　15
Age (months)

together in two large, toy-filled cages, one containing water and one containing food, which were attached to the opposite ends of a maze. The pattern of pathways and dead ends through the maze was changed daily. In the impoverished environment, the rats were housed individually in small, empty cages.

Microscopic examination of the brains of the rats found that those exposed to the enriched environment had longer and more numerous dendrites (see Chapter 3) on their brain neurons than did those exposed to the impoverished environment. The increased size and number of dendrites would provide the rats exposed to the enriched environment with more synaptic connections among their brain neurons. The benefits of enriched environments on neural development have been replicated in other animal studies (Reed, 1993; Wallace et al., 1992).

After infancy, the child's growth rate slows, and most children grow 2 or 3 inches a year until puberty. The child's motor coordination also improves. Children learn to perform more sophisticated motor tasks, such as using scissors, tying their shoes, and riding bicycles. The development of motor skills even affects the development of cognitive skills. For example, children's ability to express themselves through language depends on the development of motor abilities that permit them to speak and to write.

Perceptual Development

A century ago, in describing what he believed was the chaotic mental world of the newborn infant, William James (1890/1981, Vol. 1, p. 462) claimed, "The baby, assailed by eyes, ears, nose, skin, and entrails at once, feels it all as one great blooming, buzzing confusion." But subsequent research has shown that newborn infants have more highly developed sensory, perceptual, and cognitive abilities than James believed. For example, though newborns cannot focus on distant objects, they can focus on objects less than a foot away—as though nature has programmed them to focus at the distance of the face of an adult who might be

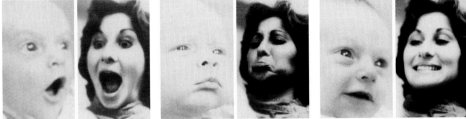

◀ **Figure 4.4**
Abilities of Newborn Infants

Newborn infants not only see better than has been traditionally assumed, they can also imitate facial expressions of surprise, sadness, and happiness.

holding them (Aslin & Smith, 1988). Newborn infants can use their sense of touch to discriminate between objects with different surface textures (Molina & Jouen, 1998). Newborn infants also have a more sophisticated sense of smell than James would have presumed. In one study, newborn infants were exposed to either the odor of amnionic fluid (which they experienced while in the womb) or another odor they had not been exposed to before. The results showed that the infants were more likely to turn their heads toward the odor of amnionic fluid than to the other odor (Schaal, Marlier, & Soussignan, 1998).

Ingenious studies have permitted researchers to infer what infants perceive by recording changes in their eye movements, head movements, body movements, sucking behavior, or physiological responses (such as changes in heart rate or brain-wave patterns). For example, a study of American newborns found they could discriminate between Japanese words with different pitch patterns as indicated by their sucking harder on a rubber nipple in response to particular pitch patterns (Nazzi, Floccia, & Bertoncini, 1998). Infant preferences can be determined by recording which targets they look at longer or by presenting them with a stimulus, waiting for them to *habituate* to it (that is, stop noticing it—as indicated by, for example, a stable heart rate), and then changing the stimulus. If they notice the change, they will show alterations in physiological activity, such as a *decrease* in heart rate.

Studies using these techniques have found infants have remarkably well developed sensory abilities. Tiffany Field has demonstrated that, as shown in Figure 4.4, infants less than 2 days old can imitate sad, happy, and surprised facial expressions (Field et al., 1982). Nonetheless, other studies have been inconsistent in their findings on neonatal imitation of facial expressions. The most consistent finding has been that neonates will respond to models who stick out their tongues by sticking out their own (Anisfeld, 1996). To read about the use of the "visual cliff" by Eleanor Gibson and Richard Walk in testing infant depth perception, see the Anatomy of a Research Study feature.

Infants also have good auditory abilities, including the ability to localize sounds. Between the ages of 8 and 28 weeks, infants can localize sounds that shift in location by only a few degrees, as indicated by head turns or eye movements in response to the shifts (Morrongiello, Fenwick, & Chance, 1990). Infants can even match the emotional tone of sounds to the emotional tone of facial expressions. In one study, 7-month-old infants were shown a sad face and a happy face. At the same time, they were presented with tones that either increased or decreased in pitch. When presented with a descending tone, they looked longer at a sad face than a happy face, as if they were equating the lower tones with a sad mood and the higher tones with a happy mood (Phillips et al., 1990). As the preceding studies attest, infants are perceptually more sophisticated than William James presumed.

Cognitive Development

Infancy also is a time of rapid cognitive development, during which infants show the unfolding of inborn abilities and their talent for learning. In regard to inborn abilities, for example, newborn infants can distinguish groups of objects that differ in number (Wynn, 1995). In regard to learning, by 4 or 5 months old an infant's response to the sound of its own name differs from its response to hearing other names (Mandel, Jusczyk, & Pisoni, 1995).

Jean Piaget (1896–1980), a Swiss biologist and psychologist, put forth the most influential theory of cognitive development. Piaget (1952) proposed that children pass through four increasingly sophisticated cognitive stages of development (see Table 4.1). According to Piaget, a child is not simply more ignorant than an adult; the child's way of thinking is

▲ **Tiffany Field**

"We now have evidence for both the discrimination and imitation of facial expressions at an even younger age, shortly after birth."

Anatomy of a Research Study

When Do Infants Develop Depth Perception?

Rationale

One of the most important perceptual abilities is depth perception. It lets us tell how far away objects are from us, preventing us from bumping into them and providing us with time to escape from potentially dangerous ones. But how early can infants perceive depth? This was the subject of a classic study by Eleanor Gibson and Richard Walk (1960).

Method

Gibson and Walk used a "visual cliff" made from a piece of thick, transparent glass set about 4 feet off the ground (see Figure 4.5). Just under the "shallow" side was a red and white checkerboard pattern. The same pattern was placed at floor level under the "deep" side. A one-foot-wide wooden board separated the sides. Participants were 36 infants, aged 6 to 14 months. The infants were placed, one at a time, on the wooden board. The infants' mothers called to them, first from one side and then from the other.

Results and Discussion

When placed on the board, 9 of the infants refused to budge. The other 27 crawled onto the shallow side toward their mothers. But only 3 of the 27 crawled onto the deep side. The remaining ones instead cried or crawled away from it. This indicated the infants could perceive the depth of the two sides—and feared the deep side. It also demonstrated that depth perception is present by 6 months of age. Replications of the study using a variety of animals found that depth perception develops by the time the animal begins moving about on its own—as early as the first day after birth for chicks and goats. This is adaptive, because it reduces their likelihood of harming themselves.

More recent research on human infants, using decreases in heart rate as a sign that they notice changes in depth, indicates rudimentary depth perception is present in infants as young as 4 months (Aslin & Smith, 1988). But research indicates human infants will not fear heights until they have had several weeks of crawling experience. Infants will not avoid the deep side of the visual cliff until they have had 6 to 8 weeks of crawling experience (Bertenthal, Campos, & Kermoian, 1994).

▶ **Figure 4.5**
The Visual Cliff

Eleanor Gibson and Richard Walk (1960) developed the *visual cliff* to test infant depth perception. The visual cliff consists of a thick sheet of glass placed on a table: The "shallow" end of the visual cliff has a checkerboard surface just below the glass. The "deep" end of the visual cliff has a checkerboard surface a few feet below the glass. An infant who has reached the crawling stage will crawl from the center of the table across the shallow end, but not across the deep end, to reach his or her mother. This indicates that by 6 months infants can perceive depth. Of course, this does not preclude the possibility that they can perceive depth even before they can crawl.

Table 4.1   Piaget's Stages of Cognitive Development

Stage	Description	Age Range
Sensorimotor	The infant progresses from reflexive, instinctual action at birth to the beginning of symbolic thought. The infant constructs an understanding of the world by coordinating sensory experiences with physical actions.	Birth–2 years
Preoperational	The child begins to represent the world with words and images; these words and images reflect increased symbolic thinking and go beyond the connection of sensory information and physical action.	2–7 years
Concrete Operational	The child now can reason logically about concrete events and can mentally reverse information.	7–11 years
Formal Operational	The adolescent reasons in more abstract, idealistic, and logical ways.	11–15 years

Source: From John W. Santrock, *Children,* 5th ed. Copyright © 1997 The McGraw-Hill Companies, Inc. All Rights Reserved. Reprinted by permission.

qualitatively different from the adult's. Moreover, infants are not passive in developing their cognitive views of the physical world. Instead, their views depend on their active interpretation of objects and events. Though Piaget assumed that complete passage through one stage is a prerequisite for success in the next one, research suggests that children can achieve characteristics of later stages without completely passing through earlier ones (Berninger, 1988). The issue of whether human cognitive development is continuous (gradual and quantitative) or discontinuous (in stages and qualitative) remains unresolved (Fischer & Silvern, 1985). The stages put forth by Piaget are the *sensorimotor stage, preoperational stage, concrete operational stage,* and *formal operational stage.* Some psychologists have criticized Piaget's theory for its assumption that cognitive development follows a universal pattern (Elkind, 1996). However, cross-cultural research indicates that children throughout the world tend to pass through these stages in the same order, though the timing varies (Segall et al., 1990).

Sensorimotor Stage

Piaget called infancy the **sensorimotor stage,** during which the child learns to coordinate sensory experiences and motor behaviors. Infants learn to interact with the world by sucking, grasping, crawling, and walking. In little more than a year, they change from being reflexive and physically immature to being purposeful, locomoting, and language using. By the age of 9 months, for example, sensorimotor coordination becomes sophisticated enough for the infant to grasp a moving object by aiming her or his reach somewhat ahead of the object instead of where the object appears to be at that moment (Hofsten, 1983).

Piaget claimed that experiences with the environment help the infant form **schemas,** which are mental models incorporating the characteristics of persons, objects, events, procedures, or situations. This means infants do more than simply gather information about the world. Their experiences actively change the way in which they think about the world. Schemas permit infants to adapt their behaviors to changes in the environment. But what makes schemas persist or change? They do so as the result of the interplay between **assimilation** and **accommodation.** We *assimilate* when we fit information into our existing schemas and *accommodate* when we revise our schemas to fit new information.

Young infants, prior to 6 months old, share an important schema in which they assume the removal of an object from sight means that the object no longer exists. If an object is hidden by a piece of cloth, for example, the young infant will not look for it, even after watching the object being hidden. As illustrated in Figure 4.6, to the young infant, out of sight truly means out of mind. As infants gain experience with the coming and going of objects in the environment, they accommodate and develop the schema of **object permanence**—the realization that objects not in view might still exist. Infants generally fail to search for objects that are suddenly hidden from view until they are about 8 months old (Munakata et al., 1997). But researchers have questioned Piaget's explanation that young infants fail to search for hidden objects because they lack object permanence. Perhaps, instead, they simply forget the location of an object that has been hidden from view (Bjork & Cummings, 1984).

The Jean Piaget Society
www.mhhe.com/sdorow5

sensorimotor stage
The Piagetian stage, from birth through the second year, during which the infant learns to coordinate sensory experiences and motor behaviors.

schema
A cognitive structure that guides people's perception and information processing that incorporates the characteristics of particular persons, objects, events, procedures, or situations.

assimilation
The cognitive process that interprets new information in light of existing schemas.

accommodation
The cognitive process that revises existing schemas to incorporate new information.

object permanence
The realization that objects exist even when they are no longer visible.

▶ Figure 4.6
Object Permanence

After young infants see an object being hidden from view, they act as though it no longer exists. This indicates that they lack the concept of *object permanence*—the realization that an object that is no longer in view may still exist.

preoperational stage

The Piagetian stage, extending from 2 to 7 years of age, during which the child's use of language becomes more sophisticated but the child has difficulty with the logical mental manipulation of information.

egocentrism

The inability to perceive reality from the perspective of another person.

concrete operational stage

The Piagetian stage, extending from 7 to 11 years of age, during which the child learns to reason logically about objects that are physically present.

transitive inference

The application of previously learned relationships to infer new relationships.

conservation

The realization that changing the form of a substance does not change its amount.

▲ Jean Piaget (1896–1980)

"As the child's thought evolves, assimilation and accommodation are differentiated and become increasingly complementary."

After the age of 8 months, most infants demonstrate their appreciation of object permanence by searching at other places for an object they have seen being hidden from view. At this point in their development they can retain a mental image of a physical object even after it has been removed from their sight, and they realize that the object might be elsewhere. This also signifies the beginning of *representational thought*—the use of symbols to stand for physical objects. But Piaget might have placed the development of object permanence too late, because infants as young as 3 or 4 months may show an appreciation of it (Baillargeon & DeVos, 1991).

Preoperational Stage

According to Piaget, when the child reaches the age of 2 years and leaves infancy, the sensorimotor stage gives way to the **preoperational stage,** which lasts until about age 7. The stage is called preoperational because the child cannot yet perform what Piaget called *operations*—mental manipulations of reality. For example, before about age 5 the early preoperational child cannot perform mental addition or subtraction of objects. During the preoperational stage, however, the child improves in the use of language, including a rapid growth in vocabulary and a more sophisticated use of grammar. Thus mental development sets the stage for language development. Unlike the sensorimotor-stage child, the preoperational-stage child is not limited to thinking about objects that are physically present.

During the preoperational stage the child also exhibits what Piaget called **egocentrism,** the inability to perceive reality from the perspective of another person. Egocentrism declines between 4 and 6 years of age (Ruffman & Olson, 1989). Children display egocentrism when they draw a picture of their family but fail to include themselves in the drawing. In some capital criminal cases, lawyers might gain a reduced sentence for a child defendant if they can convince the jury that the child had not progressed beyond egocentrism and therefore was unaware of the effect of the criminal act on the victim (Ellison, 1987).

Concrete Operational Stage

At about the age of 7, the child enters what Piaget calls the **concrete operational stage,** which lasts until about the age of 11. The child learns to reason logically but is at first limited to reasoning about physical things. For example, when you first learned to do arithmetic problems, you were unable to perform mental calculations. Instead, until perhaps the age of 8, you counted by using your fingers or other objects. An important kind of reasoning ability that develops during this stage is the ability to make **transitive inferences**—the application of previously learned relationships to infer new ones. For example, suppose that a child is told Pat is taller than Terry, and Terry is taller than Lee. A child who can make transitive inferences will correctly conclude Pat is taller than Lee. Though Piaget claimed the ability to make transitive inferences develops by age 8, research has shown that children as young as 4 can make them—provided they are given age-appropriate tasks (Pears & Bryant, 1990).

By the age of 8, the child in the concrete operational stage also develops what Piaget called **conservation**—the realization that changing the form of a substance or the arrangement of a set of objects does not change the amount. Suppose a child is shown two balls of clay of equal size. One ball is then rolled out into a snake, and the child is asked if either piece of clay has more clay. The child who has not achieved conservation will probably reply that

◀ Figure 4.7
Conservation

During the concrete operational stage, the child develops an appreciation of conservation. The child comes to realize that changing the form of something does not change its amount—for instance, that the glasses pictured here can hold the same amount of liquid. In a classic demonstration used by Piaget, a child is shown a tall, narrow container and a short, wide container that can hold equal amounts of a liquid. When the liquid in the short container is poured into the empty tall container, the preoperational child will perceive the tall container as holding more liquid than did the short container. In contrast, the concrete operational child realizes that the tall container now holds the same amount of liquid as did the short container.

the snake has more clay because it is longer. Figure 4.7 shows a classic means of testing whether a child has developed the schema of conservation. Conservation has implications for children as eyewitnesses. Children who have achieved conservation are less susceptible to leading questions than are children who have not achieved it (Muir-Broaddus et al., 1998).

The effect of different cultural experiences on the timing of conservation was demonstrated in a study of children in a Mexican village whose parents were pottery makers. The children who normally helped their parents in making pottery achieved conservation (at least of mass) earlier than other children (Price-Williams, Gordon, & Ramirez, 1969). Moreover, certain nonverbal variations of the conservation of liquid volume problem show that children might develop conservation earlier than indicated by studies that have used the traditional verbal demonstration procedure (Wheldall & Benner, 1993). In early adolescence, the concrete operational stage might give way to the formal operational stage, which is discussed in the section of this chapter devoted to adolescent development.

Psychosocial Development

Just as Piaget believed the child passes through stages of cognitive development, psychoanalyst Erik Erikson (1902–1994) believed the child passes through stages of psychosocial development. Erikson observed that, across the life span, we go through eight distinct stages. Each stage is marked by a conflict that must be overcome, as described in Table 4.2. Research has supported Erikson's belief that we pass through the stages sequentially—though people differ in the ages at which they pass through them (Vaillant & Milofsky, 1980). Erikson also was one of the first researchers to consider cultural differences in psychosocial development, noting that society, not just the family, affects the child's development (Eagle, 1997). This view was influenced by Erikson's studies of children in Sioux, Yurok, and other Native American cultures. You also should be aware that there might be cultural differences among peoples we normally might think of as members of a homogeneous cultural group.

Table 4.2	Erikson's Stages of Psychosocial Development	
Age	Conflict	Successful Resolution
First Year	Trust vs. mistrust	The infant develops a sense of security.
Second Year	Autonomy vs. shame and doubt	The infant achieves a sense of independence.
3–5 Years	Initiative vs. guilt	The child finds a balance between spontaneity and restraint.
6 Years–Puberty	Industry vs. inferiority	The child attains a sense of self-confidence.
Adolescence	Identity vs. role confusion	The adolescent experiences a unified sense of self.
Young Adulthood	Intimacy vs. isolation	The adult forms close personal relationships.
Middle Adulthood	Generativity vs. stagnation	The adult promotes the well-being of others.
Late Adulthood	Integrity vs. despair	The adult enjoys a sense of satisfaction by reflecting on a life well lived.

Source: Adapted from *Childhood and Society,* Second Edition, by Erik H. Erikson, by permission of W. W. Norton and Company, Inc. Copyright 1950, © 1963 by W. W. Norton and Company, Inc. Copyright renewed 1978, 1991 by Erik H. Erikson. Also Chatto and Windus, London, England.

▲ **Figure 4.8**
Social Attachment

Harry Harlow found that infant monkeys became more attached to a terry-cloth-covered wire surrogate mother than to a bare-wire surrogate mother. Even when fed only from a nipple protruding from the bare-wire surrogate mother, the infant monkeys preferred to cling to the terry-cloth-covered surrogate mother. Harlow concluded that social attachment might depend more on physical contact than on the provision of nourishment (Harlow & Zimmerman, 1959).

trust versus mistrust

Erikson's developmental stage in which success is achieved by having a secure social attachment with a caregiver.

social attachment

A strong emotional relationship between an infant and a caregiver.

Attachment: Theory and Research @ Stony Brook
www.mhhe.com/sdorow5

In Central Africa, for example, the infants of Ngandu farmers and the infants of neighboring Aka hunter-gatherers have markedly different experiences. Aka infants are more likely to be held and Nkandu infants are more likely to be left alone, possibly contributing to observed differences in infant behavior (Hewlett et al., 1998).

Early Attachment

Erikson found that the major social conflict of the first year of infancy is **trust versus mistrust.** One of the most important factors in helping the infant develop trust is **social attachment,** a strong emotional bond between an infant and caregivers that develops during the first year. Beginning in the 1930s, British psychiatrist John Bowlby (1907–1990) became interested in the effects of early maternal loss or deprivation on later personality development. Much of his theorizing was based on his study of World War II orphans. Bowlby favored an evolutionary viewpoint, suggesting that infants have evolved an inborn need for attachment because their survival depends on adult caregivers (Bowlby, 1988). Thus, infants seek physical contact and evoke responses from adults through crying, cooing, smiling, and clinging. Similarly, Sigmund Freud assumed that an infant becomes attached to his or her mother for a functional reason—she provides nourishment through nursing.

Freud's assumption was contradicted by research conducted by Harry Harlow and his colleagues on social attachment in rhesus monkeys. Harlow separated infant monkeys from their parents and peers and raised them for 6 months with two "surrogate mothers." The surrogates were wire monkeys with wooden heads. One surrogate was covered with terry cloth and the other was left bare. Harlow found the monkeys preferred to cling to the cloth-covered surrogate, even though milk was available only from a bottle attached to the bare-wire surrogate (see Figure 4.8). Harlow concluded that physical contact is a more important factor than nourishment in promoting infant attachment (Harlow & Zimmerman, 1959).

Harlow's research findings inspired interest in the possible role of attachment in human psychosocial development. Much of what we know about attachment in human infants comes from research by Mary Ainsworth (1913–1999) on the mother-infant relationship (Bretherton & Main, 2000). She was inspired by her long-time collaboration with Bowlby. Ainsworth conducted her first studies of infant-mother attachment patterns after visiting Uganda. She and others have found that the mother is more likely to be the primary caregiver in virtually all cultures (Best et al., 1994).

In assessing the mother's influence on the child, Ainsworth makes a distinction between *securely attached* and *insecurely attached* infants. This becomes an especially important issue at about 8 months of age, when infants show a strong preference for their mothers over strangers and show separation anxiety. To test this, Ainsworth developed the Strange Situation: The mother and infant are in a room together; the mother leaves the room, a stranger enters the room, the stranger then leaves and the infant's response to the mother is assessed when she then returns to the room. The securely attached infant seeks physical contact with the mother, yet, despite mildly protesting, freely leaves her to play and explore, using the mother as a secure base. In contrast, the insecurely attached infant clings to the mother, acts either apathetic or highly anxious when separated from her, and is either unresponsive or angry when reunited with her.

A meta-analysis of 21 studies using the Strange Situation with more than 1,000 infants found a moderately strong relationship between the mother's sensitivity and the infant's attachment security (De Wolff & van IJzendoorn, 1997). An infant whose mother is more sensitive, accepting, and affectionate will become more securely attached. Infants who are insecurely attached tend to show that style of relating in childhood, adolescence, and adulthood (Cassidy & Berlin, 1994). And research indicates the relationship between maternal responsiveness and the quality of infant attachment generalizes across cultures. Cultural differences have been observed, though, in the maternal and infant behaviors observed in the Strange Situation, especially in measures of *visual referencing*—infants' willingness to play at a distance while keeping mothers within eyesight—and physical proximity seeking, such as clinging and cuddling (Rothbaum et al., 2000).

Until recently, research on attachment has been limited to use of the Strange Situation in assessing the quality of attachment with the infant's primary caregiver (Field, 1996).

Researchers investigating the role of fathers in psychosocial development have found paternal sensitivity also promotes secure attachment in infants. Moreover, families may be described as reflecting a system of attachments between infants, young children, and family members who provide care and engage them in social interaction (van IJzendoorn & DeWolff, 1997).

One study assessed the quality of attachment between mothers, fathers, and two of their children. The Strange Situation was used to measure attachment in younger children (aged 18 to 24 months), and a questionnaire measure of attachment was used to measure attachment in older children (4 to 5 years of age). Parental caregiving was assessed through naturalistic observation and questionnaires. Results indicated that the majority of the children had developed secure attachments with both parents. Moreover, the quality of caregiving predicted secure attachment in only one case: between mothers and their younger children. Maternal caregiving was unrelated to the quality of attachment in older children. And paternal caregiving was unrelated to the quality of attachment of younger and older children (Schneider-Rosen & Burke, 1999). These findings suggest that caregiving is only one avenue by which parents, usually mothers, contribute to the development of a secure attachment in infancy. Moreover, the quality of attachment in older children appears to be related to other aspects of family interaction. And, though neglected by early research in attachment, fathers do contribute to the development of attachment in infancy and early childhood.

Researchers also have investigated the stability of attachment security across the life span. Two longitudinal studies found that attachment security is remarkably stable from infancy to adolescence (Hamilton, 2000) and early adulthood (Waters et al., 2000). In these studies, attachment category had been assessed in infancy. Later, participants completed questionnaires assessing the quality of their attachment or were interviewed by raters blind to their original classification. In both studies, the majority of the securely attached participants' classification was unchanged. But what predicts changes in attachment security? Attachment security can be adversely affected by negative life events that disrupt a family's functioning and the psychological well-being of adults in the household—and in turn their responsiveness and sensitivity to their offspring (Waters, Weinfield, & Hamilton, 2000).

According to Erikson, during the second year the child experiences a conflict involving **autonomy versus shame and doubt.** The child explores the physical environment, begins to learn self-care skills, such as feeding, and tries out budding motor and language abilities. In doing so, the child develops a greater sense of independence from her or his parents. This might account for the popular notion of the "terrible twos," when the child enjoys behaving in a contrary manner and saying no to any request. Parents who stifle efforts at reasonable independence or criticize the child's awkward efforts will promote feelings of shame and doubt. At 3 years of age, the child enters the stage that involves the conflict Erikson calls **initiative versus guilt.** The child shows initiative in play, social relations, and exploration of the environment. The child also learns to control his or her impulses, feeling guilt for actions that go beyond limits set by parents. So, at this stage, parents might permit their child to rummage through drawers but not to throw clothing around the bedroom. Thus, the stage of initiative versus guilt deals with the development of a sense of right and wrong.

At about the age of 6, and continuing until about the age of 12, Erikson observed, the child faces the conflict of **industry versus inferiority.** The industrious child who achieves successes during this stage is more likely to feel competent. This is important, because children who feel academically and socially competent are happier than other children (Blechman et al., 1985). A child who develops a sense of inferiority might lose interest in academics, avoid social interactions, or fail to participate in sports. The importance of this stage in psychosocial development has been demonstrated in both Western and non-Western countries, including the People's Republic of China (Wang & Viney, 1997).

Parent-Child Relationships

One of the most important factors in psychosocial development is the approach parents take to child rearing. Psychologist Diana Baumrind distinguished three kinds of parenting: *permissive, authoritarian,* and *authoritative.* Permissive parents set few rules and rarely punish

▲ **Mary Ainsworth (1913–1999)**
"Gaining an understanding of attachment over the whole life span will enrich psychologists' knowledge of human nature."

autonomy versus shame and doubt
Erikson's developmental stage in which success is achieved by gaining a degree of independence from one's parents.

initiative versus guilt
Erikson's developmental stage in which success is achieved by behaving in a spontaneous but socially appropriate way.

industry versus inferiority
Erikson's developmental stage in which success is achieved by developing a sense of competency.

misbehavior. Permissiveness is undesirable, because children will be less likely to adopt positive standards of behavior. At the other extreme, authoritarian parents set strict rules and rely on punishment. They respond to questioning of their rules by saying, "Because I say so!"

Authoritarian parents might also resort to physical discipline. Aside from the potential for injury to the child, child abuse is associated with lasting emotional effects. Abused children have lower self-esteem and are more socially withdrawn (Kaufman & Cicchetti, 1989), they tend to be more aggressive and less empathetic toward children in distress (Main & George, 1985), and they are more likely to become juvenile delinquents (Bowers, 1990).

Of great concern is the vicious cycle in which abused children become abusive parents. However, though most child abusers were abused as children, most abused children do not become abusers—a far cry from claims that being an abused child automatically makes one a future child abuser (Kaufman & Zigler, 1987). So, if you were unfortunate enough to have suffered child abuse, you may very well be able to break the vicious cycle when rearing your own children.

Authoritative Parenting. Baumrind has found that the best approach to child rearing is **authoritative parenting** (Baumrind, 1983). Authoritative parents tend to be warm and loving, yet insist their children behave appropriately. They encourage independence within well-defined limits, show a willingness to explain the reasons for their rules, and permit their children to express verbal disagreement with them. By maintaining a delicate balance between freedom and control, authoritative parents help their children internalize standards of behavior.

Children who have authoritative parents are more likely to become socially competent, independent, and responsible. They are less likely to use drugs (Jackson, Bee-Gates, & Henriksen, 1994), more likely to perform well in school (Steinberg et al., 1992), and more likely to be socially well adjusted (Durbin et al., 1993). But, as you were cautioned in Chapter 2, be wary of concluding parenting style *causes* these effects. Remember that only experimental, not correlational, research permits statements about causality. Perhaps the direction of causality is the opposite of what one would assume. For example, well-behaved children might evoke authoritative parenting.

Research tends to support a positive relationship between authoritative parenting and children's competence. But we still do not know how or why it does so (Darling & Steinberg, 1993). Moreover, we must be aware of cultural differences in child rearing—both between and within societies. Cultural beliefs about parental and child roles and the nature of child rearing influence parent-child interactions (Super & Harkness, 1997). For example, North Americans might see Chinese parenting as authoritarian and controlling. Chinese cultural beliefs about parenting stress the concept of *chiao shun,* or training the child to meet social expectations. Thus, parental control can have different meanings in different cultures (Chao, 1994).

Day Care. Another important, and controversial, factor in child rearing is day care. The number of American children placed in day care increased during the 1990s, with more than half of infants and toddlers spending at least 20 hours per week in the care of adults other than their parents (Singer et al., 1998). Though day care, overall, seems to have neither strong benefits nor strong detrimental effects (Lamb, 1996), research findings are contradictory in regard to the effects of day care on infants. On the negative side are studies finding that infant day care of more than 20 hours a week in the first year of life is associated with insecure attachment during infancy and greater noncompliance and aggressiveness in early childhood (Belsky, 1988), and that children who enter day care before age 2 perform more poorly in high school than do children who enter day care after age 2 (Ispa, Thornburg, & Gray, 1990). On the positive side are studies finding that infants in day care do not become insecurely attached (Burchinal et al., 1992) and they later do well in school and act less aggressively than do other children (Field, 1991). These contradictory findings reflect the complex nature of the issue, which involves numerous variables, including the characteristics of the infants, their parents, their caretakers, and their day-care settings.

authoritative parenting

An effective style of parenting, in which the parent is warm and loving, yet sets well-defined limits that he or she enforces in an appropriate manner.

The Temperament Project
www.mhhe.com/sdorow5

Chapter Four

Because many working parents have no choice but to place their infants in day care, it is reassuring to know that research indicates that high-quality infant day care is probably not harmful (Volling & Feagans, 1995). According to findings of the National Institute of Child Health and Human Development (NICHD) Study of Early Child Care, "high-quality" means that the number of children and the adult-child ratio are small; the adults practice nonauthoritarian caregiving; and the environment is safe, clean, and stimulating (NICHD Early Child Care Research Network, 1997). But the cost of high-quality day care—if it is, in fact, available—makes it unaffordable to many families. Nonetheless, even day care that is not optimal tends not to have damaging effects on most children. Heredity and home environment seem to outweigh the effects of day care on children, even when it is not of high quality (Scarr, 1998).

Parental Conflict. Children are affected not only by parenting and day-care practices but also by the quality of their parents' relationship. A meta-analysis of relevant studies (Erel & Burman, 1995) found that parental discord spills over into negative parent-child relationships. Moreover, marital discord can undermine the child's feeling of emotional security and lead to adjustment problems in childhood and marital discord in adulthood (Davies & Cummings, 1994).

In some cases marital discord leads to divorce. Because about half of all marriages in the United States end in divorce, many children spend at least part of their childhood primarily with one parent. Though it is easier for two adults to meet the stressful demands of providing the consistent, responsive caregiving that promotes children's well-being, research on single parents indicates that one responsible, emotionally available adult can provide the social and emotional bond essential to optimal development (Silverstein & Auerbach, 1999). More than one-third of American children born between the mid 1970s and the mid 1990s will experience parental divorce. And they will be more likely to suffer emotional problems, particularly depression (Aseltine, 1996). For example, a study that compared children with divorced parents to children from intact families in Quebec province found that children of divorce exhibit more problem behaviors (Kurtz, 1995).

Because divorce involves so many variables, including the age and economic status of the parents, the age of the children, and the custody arrangements, different combinations of these variables can have different effects on children. The effects of each combination remain to be determined. It should be noted, however, that children from divorced families have a greater

▶ **Child's Play**

Young children first engage in (a) parallel play before gradually shifting to (b) inter-active play with their peers.

(a)

(b)

▶ **Child's Play**

Young children first engage in (a) parallel play before gradually shifting to (b) inter-active play with their peers.

sense of well-being than children from intact families with intense parental conflict (Amato & Keith, 1991). Moreover, it is unclear whether the child's emotional distress is caused mainly by the divorce or by parental conflict prior to the divorce (Furstenberg & Teitler, 1994).

Interaction with Peers

Children are affected by their relationships with friends and siblings as well as those with their parents. Friendships provide the context for social and emotional growth. In fact, childhood friendships can have a bearing on adult emotional well-being. Consider a study that compared young adults who had a best friend in fifth grade and young adults who had no friends in fifth grade. Those who had a best friend had higher self-esteem than those who had no friends. And those who had no best friend were more likely to have symptoms of psychological disorders (Bagwell, Newcomb, & Bukowski, 1998). Of course, you must be careful not to assume there is a causal relationship in which friendships promote healthy personalities. Perhaps, instead, children with certain personalities are simply more likely to make friends and to have higher self-esteem.

Few children develop friendships before the age of 3, and 95 percent of childhood friendships are between children of the same sex (Hartup, 1989). Girls tend to have fewer, but more intimate, friendships than boys (Berndt & Hoyle, 1985). A meta-analysis of studies of children's peer relations found that socially and academically competent children are popular with their peers. In contrast, children who are withdrawn, aggressive, or academically deficient tend to be rejected by their peers (Newcomb, Bukowski, & Pattee, 1993).

Peer relationships in childhood involve play. A classic study (Parten, 1932) found that the interactive play of children gradually increased between 2 and 4 years of age, but throughout this period children engaged mainly in parallel play, as when two children in a sandbox play separately from each other with pails and shovels. The results of this study have been replicated. For example, a longitudinal study of children from 16 to 32 months old found a shift from parallel play to interactive play (Eckerman, Davis, & Didow, 1989). There also are cultural differences in play. For example, a study comparing American and Chinese children found Americans tended to be more competitive and individualistic (Domino, 1992).

Among our most important peers are our siblings. Sibling birth order is a factor in psychosocial development; firstborn children usually are less socially popular than later-born children. This might be because the firstborn interacts more with adults than with siblings, compared to the later-born, who interacts extensively with both parents and siblings. As a consequence, the later-born might be more likely to develop social skills that are well suited for interacting with peers (Baskett, 1984). As for the only child, the popular belief that she or he suffers because of the absence of siblings is unfounded. For example, an only child is usually superior to all except firstborn children and children from two-child families in intelligence and academic achievement (Falbo & Polit, 1986).

Gender-Role Development

One of the most important aspects of psychosocial development in childhood is the development of **gender roles,** which are behavior patterns that are considered appropriate for males or females in a given culture. Sigmund Freud put forth the first formal theory of gender-role development. He assumed that the resolution of what he called the *Oedipus complex* (in the case of boys) and *Electra complex* (in the case of girls)—both of which are discussed in Chapter 13—

gender roles

The behaviors that are considered appropriate for females or males in a given culture.

▲ **Eleanor Maccoby**

"Socialization pressures, whether by parents or others, do not by any means tell the whole story of the origins of sex differences."

Chapter Four

at age 5 or 6 led the child to internalize the gender role of the same-sex parent. The Oedipus and Electra complexes begin with the child's sexual attraction to the opposite-sex parent. According to Freud, because the child fears punishment for desiring the opposite-sex parent, the child identifies with the same-sex parent. But studies show that children develop gender roles even when they live in single-parent households. Because of the lack of research support for Freud's theory, most researchers favor more recent theories of gender-role development.

Social learning theory stresses the importance of observational learning, rewards, and punishment. Thus, social learning theorists assume the child learns gender-relevant behaviors by observing gender-role models and by being rewarded for appropriate, and punished for inappropriate, gender-role behavior. This process of gender typing begins on the very day of birth and continues through the life span. In one study, new parents were interviewed within 24 hours of the birth of their first child. Though there are no observable differences in the physical appearance of male and female newborns whose genitals are covered, newborn daughters were more likely than newborn sons to be described by their parents as cute, weak, and uncoordinated (Rubin, Provenzano, & Luria, 1974). But an influential review of research on gender differences by Eleanor Maccoby found that parents reported they did not treat their sons and daughters differently (Maccoby & Jacklin, 1974). Of course, parents might believe they treat their daughters and sons the same, while actually treating them differently. A recent meta-analysis, however, supported Maccoby by finding that gender-role development seems, at best, weakly related to differences in how parents rear their sons and daughters (Lytton & Romney, 1991).

Parents are not the only social influences contributing to gender-role development. As noted earlier in this chapter, children tend to socialize with same-sex peers and engage in sex-segregated play. Children reward each other for engaging in gender-appropriate activities and punish or exclude children who engage in cross-gender behavior. Moreover, this peer pressure is stronger for boys than for girls. Considering the inconsistent evidence for the role of differential parental reinforcement of children's behavior, it is very likely that peers wield a stronger influence on gender-role development than do parents (Bussey & Bandura, 1999).

An alternative to the social learning theory of gender-role development is Sandra Bem's (1981) **gender schema theory,** which combines elements of social learning theory and the cognitive perspective. Bem's theory holds that people differ in the schemas they use to organize their social world. People might have schemas relevant to age, ethnicity, gender, occupation, or any number of social categories. *Gender schemas* are cognitive structures that assimilate and organize information about women and men. Children are *gender schematic* if they categorize people, behavior, activities, and interests as masculine or feminine. In contrast, *gender aschematic* children do not categorize information into masculine and feminine categories. Gender-schematic individuals are likely to notice, attend to, and remember behavior and attributes that are relevant to gender. For example, one study found that gender-schematic adults recalled more gender-stereotypic information than did gender-aschematic adults (Renn & Calvert, 1993).

Gender schemas develop early. One study found that toddlers were able to label same-sex toys—operationally defined as touching a masculine or feminine toy—as early as 2 years of age (Levy, 1999). Social experience can modify the development of gender schemas, though, as shown in a study of traditional and egalitarian families. In the egalitarian families, mothers and fathers shared parental and child-rearing responsibilities equally. Children from egalitarian families adopted gender labels later and reported less knowledge of gender roles than did children from traditional families (Fagot & Leinbach, 1995). Gender schema theory provides a glimpse into the development of gender stereotypes and how gender stereotypes influence social behavior.

Moral Development

An often-overlooked aspect of life-span development is moral development. According to Sigmund Freud, moral values arise from the resolution of the Oedipus and Electra complexes. There is little research support for Freud's view of moral development (Hunt, 1979). Today, the most influential theory of moral development is Lawrence Kohlberg's (1981) cognitive-developmental theory.

The Society for the Psychology of Women
www.mhhe.com/sdorow5

social learning theory
A theory of learning that assumes that people learn behaviors mainly through observation and mental processing of information.

The Society for the Psychological Study of Men and Masculinity
www.mhhe.com/sdorow5

gender schema theory
A theory of gender-role development that combines aspects of social learning theory and the cognitive perspective.

▲ **Gender Roles**

According to social learning theory, children learn gender-role behaviors by being rewarded for performing those behaviors and by observing adults, particularly parents, engaging in them. Joel Vitart, who came to the United States from Paris in late 1980 after being invited to be one of the bakers for President Ronald Reagan's inauguration celebration, passes on his baking expertise to his son, Alexandre, at his bakery in New Hope, Pennsylvania.

▲ **Lawrence Kohlberg (1926–1986)**

"In the study of moral behavior, it is essential to determine the actor's interpretation of the situation and the behavior since the moral quality of the behavior is itself determined by that interpretation."

preconventional level

In Kohlberg's theory, the level of moral reasoning characterized by concern with the consequences that behavior has for oneself.

conventional level

In Kohlberg's theory, the level of moral reasoning characterized by concern with upholding laws and conventional values and by favoring obedience to authority.

postconventional level

In Kohlberg's theory, the level of moral reasoning characterized by concern with obeying mutually agreed upon laws and by the need to uphold human dignity.

Kohlberg's Theory of Moral Development. Kohlberg's theory, formulated in the 1960s, is based on Piaget's (1932) proposal that a person's level of moral development depends on his or her level of cognitive development (Carpendale, 2000). Piaget found that children, in making moral judgments, are at first more concerned with the consequences of actions. Thus, a young child might insist that accidentally breaking ten dishes is morally worse than purposely breaking one dish. As children become more cognitively sophisticated, they base their moral judgments more on a person's intentions than on the consequences of the person's behavior. Kohlberg assumed that as individuals become more cognitively sophisticated, they reach more complex levels of moral reasoning. Research findings indicate that adequate cognitive development is, indeed, a prerequisite for each level of moral reasoning (Walker, 1986).

Kohlberg, agreeing with Piaget, developed a stage theory of moral development based on the individual's level of moral reasoning. Kohlberg determined the individual's level of moral reasoning by presenting a series of stories, each of which includes a moral dilemma. The person must suggest a resolution of the dilemma and give reasons for choosing that resolution. The person's stage of moral development depends not on the resolution, but instead on the reasons given for that resolution. What is your response to the following dilemma proposed by Kohlberg? Your reasoning in resolving it would reveal your level of moral development:

▶ In Europe, a woman was near death from a very bad disease, a special kind of cancer. There was one drug that the doctors thought might save her. It was a form of radium that a druggist in the same town had recently discovered. The drug was expensive to make, but the druggist was charging 10 times what the drug cost him to make. He paid 200 dollars for the radium and charged two thousand dollars for a small dose of the drug. The sick woman's husband, Heinz, went to everyone he knew to borrow the money, but he could get together only about one thousand dollars, which was half of what it cost. He told the druggist that his wife was dying and asked him to sell it cheaper or let him pay later. But the druggist said, "No, I discovered the drug, and I am going to make money from it." So Heinz got desperate and broke into the man's store to steal the drug for his wife. (Kohlberg, 1981, p.12)

The levels of moral development represented by particular responses to this dilemma are presented in Table 4.3. Kohlberg identified three levels: the *preconventional,* the *conventional,* and the *postconventional.* Each level contains two stages, making a total of six stages of moral development. As Piaget noted, as we progress to higher levels of moral reasoning, we become more concerned with the actor's motives than with the consequences of the actor's actions. This was supported by a study of moral judgments about aggressive behavior, which found that high school and college students at higher stages of moral reasoning were more concerned with the aggressor's motivation than were students at lower stages (Berkowitz et al., 1986).

People at the **preconventional level** of moral reasoning, which typically characterizes children up to 9 years old, are mainly concerned with the consequences of moral behavior to themselves. In stage 1, the child has a punishment and obedience orientation, in which moral behavior serves to avoid punishment. In stage 2, the child has an instrumental-relativist orientation, in which moral behavior serves to get rewards or favors in return, as in "you scratch my back and I'll scratch yours."

People at the **conventional level** of moral reasoning, usually reached in late childhood or early adolescence, uphold conventional laws and values by favoring obedience to parents and authority figures. Kohlberg calls stage 3 the good boy–nice girl orientation, because the child assumes moral behavior is desirable because it gains social approval, especially from parents. Kohlberg calls stage 4 the society-maintaining orientation, in which the adolescent views moral behavior as a way to do one's duty, show respect for authority, and maintain the social order. These four stages have even been used to show differences in moral reasoning by members of the United States Congress about political issues (Shapiro, 1995).

At the end of adolescence, some of those who reach Piaget's formal operational stage of cognitive development also reach the **postconventional level** of morality. At this level of moral reasoning, people make moral judgments based on ethical principles that might conflict with their self-interest or with the maintenance of social order. In stage 5, the social-contract orientation, the person assumes that adherence to laws is in the long-term best interest of society but that unjust laws might have to be violated. The U.S. Constitution is

Table 4.3   Kohlberg's Theory of Moral Development

Levels	Stages	Moral Reasoning in Response to the Heinz Dilemma	
		In Favor of Heinz's Stealing the Drug	Against Heinz's Stealing the Drug
I. Preconventional Level: Motivated by Self-Interest	**Stage 1** *Punishment and obedience orientation:* Motivation to avoid punishment	"If you let your wife die, you will get in trouble."	"You shouldn't steal the drug because you'll be caught and sent to jail if you do."
	Stage 2 *Instrumental-relativist orientation:* Motivation to obtain rewards	"It wouldn't bother you much to serve a little jail term, if you have your wife when you get out."	"He may not get much of a jail term if he steals the drug, but his wife will probably die before he gets out, so it won't do him much good."
II. Conventional Level: Motivated by Conventional Laws and Values	**Stage 3** *Good boy–nice girl orientation:* Motivation to gain approval and to avoid disapproval	"No one will think you're bad if you steal the drug, but your family will think you're an inhuman husband if you don't."	"It isn't just the druggist who will think you're a criminal, everyone else will too."
	Stage 4 *Society-maintaining orientation:* Motivation to fulfill one's duty and to avoid feelings of guilt	"If you have any sense of honor, you won't let your wife die because you're afraid to do the only thing that will save her."	"You'll always feel guilty for your dishonesty and lawbreaking."
III. Postconventional Level: Motivated by Abstract Moral Principles	**Stage 5** *Social-contract orientation:* Motivation to follow rational, mutually agreed-upon principles and maintain the respect of others	"If you let your wife die, it would be out of fear, not out of reasoning it out."	"You would lose your standing and respect in the community and break the law."
	Stage 6 *Universal ethical principle orientation:* Motivation to uphold one's own ethical principles and avoid self-condemnation	"If you don't steal the drug, . . . you would have lived up to the outside rule of the law but you wouldn't have lived up to your own standards of conscience."	"If you stole the drug, . . . you'd condemn yourself because you wouldn't have lived up to your own conscience and standards of honesty."

Source: Table "Theory of Moral Development" from *Essays on Moral Development: The Philosophy of Moral Development* (Volume I) by Lawrence Kohlberg. Copyright © 1981 by Lawrence Kohlberg. Reprinted by permission of Harper Collins Publishers, Inc.

based on this view. Stage 6, the highest stage of moral reasoning, is called the universal ethical principle orientation. The few people at this stage assume that moral reasoning must uphold human dignity and their conscience—even if that brings them into conflict with their society's laws or values. Abolitionists who helped runaway American slaves flee to Canada in the early 19th century probably were acting at this highest level of moral reasoning.

Criticisms of Kohlberg's Theory. Kohlberg's theory has received mixed support from research studies. Children do appear to proceed through the stages he described in the order he described (Walker, 1989). And a study of adolescents on an Israeli kibbutz found, as predicted by Kohlberg's theory, their stages of moral development were related to their stages of cognitive development (Snarey, Reimer, & Kohlberg, 1985). But Kohlberg's theory has been criticized on several grounds. First, the theory explains moral reasoning, not moral action. A person's moral actions might not reflect her or his moral reasoning. Yet some research supports a positive relationship between moral reasoning and moral actions. One study found that people at higher stages of moral reasoning tend to behave more honestly and more altruistically (Blasi, 1980).

(a)

(b)

▲ Carol Gilligan

"Just as the conventions that shape women's moral judgment differ from those that apply to men, so also women's definitions of the moral domain diverge from that derived from studies of men."

A second criticism is that the situation, not just the person's level of moral reasoning, plays a role in moral decision making and moral actions. This was demonstrated in a study of male college students who performed a task in which their goal was to keep a stylus above a light moving in a triangular pattern—a tedious, difficult task. When provided with a strong enough temptation, even those at higher stages of moral reasoning succumbed to cheating (Malinowski & Smith, 1985).

Other critics insist Kohlberg's theory might not be generalizable beyond Western cultures, with their greater emphasis on individualism. This criticism has been countered by Kohlberg and his colleagues. They found that when people in other cultures are interviewed in their own languages, using moral dilemmas based on situations that are familiar to them, Kohlberg's theory holds up well. Moreover, in other cultures, the stages of moral reasoning unfold in the order claimed by Kohlberg. For example, a study of Taiwanese children and young adults found they progressed through the moral stages in the order and at the rate found in Americans (Lei, 1994). Nonetheless, postconventional moral reasoning is not found in all cultures (Snarey, Reimer, & Kohlberg, 1985).

Still another criticism of Kohlberg's theory is that it is biased in favor of a male view of morality. The main proponent of this criticism has been Carol Gilligan (1982). She points out that Kohlberg's theory was based on research on male participants, and she claims Kohlberg's theory favors the view that morality is concerned with detached, legalistic justice (an allegedly masculine orientation) rather than with involved, interpersonal caring (an allegedly feminine orientation).

Thus, Gilligan believes women's moral reasoning is colored by their desire to maintain interpersonal relationships, whereas men's moral reasoning is based on their desire to uphold rules and laws. The results of a study supported Gilligan's claim that men and women differ in their notions of morality. More than 600 undergraduates were asked to write an essay on the experience that was the most important in their moral development. As Gilligan would have predicted, more women than men described experiences related to a care orientation (Barnett, Quackenbush, & Sinisi, 1995).

Despite some research support for Gilligan's position (Garmon et al., 1996), there are no significant differences between men and women in their use of justice and care orientations (Page & Tyrer, 1996). This might hold true even for preschool children. A study presented American preschool children with moral dilemmas for them to solve. The children favored a care orientation and a justice orientation with equal likelihood (Cassidy, Chu, & Dahlsgaard, 1997). This failure to find gender differences in responses to moral dilemmas also held true in a study of Botswana high school students in South Africa (Maqsud, 1998).

Other critics claim that both Kohlberg's and Gilligan's theories are simplistic and do not consider enough of the factors that influence moral development. These critics believe that an adequate theory of moral development must consider the interaction of cultural, religious, and biological factors (Woods, 1996).

1. What has research discovered about infant depth perception?
2. What are Piaget's basic ideas about cognitive development?
3. What has research found about the importance of infant attachment to caregivers?
4. What are the differences between permissive, authoritarian, and authoritative parenting?

Answers to Staying on Track start on p. ST-2.

Adolescence: Change and Continuity
www.mhhe.com/sdorow5

◆ ADOLESCENT DEVELOPMENT

Adolescence is the transition period between childhood and adulthood. Change marks the entire life span, though it is more dramatic at certain stages than at others. Biological factors have a more obvious influence during adolescence and late adulthood than during early and middle adulthood. Social factors exert their greatest influence through the **social clock:** the typical or expected timing of major life events in a given culture. In Western cultures, for example, major milestones of the social clock include graduation from high school, leaving home, finding a job, getting married, having a child, and retiring from work. Being late in reaching these milestones can cause emotional distress (Rook, Catalano, & Dooley, 1989). There also is some evidence for cross-cultural and cohort differences in adults' beliefs about the timing of life events. For example, one study of Australian undergraduates found that the "best" ages associated with adult milestones differed from American age norms of the 1960s. Moreover, participants suggested later ages for marriage and grandparenthood and a wider age range for retirement (Peterson, 1996).

Cultural and historical factors can have different effects on different cohorts. Depending on your cohort, your adolescent and adult experiences might differ from those of other cohorts. Consider an 18-year-old first-year college student. College students in the late 1960s and early 1970s were influenced by the turmoil of the divisive Vietnam War, the cynicism generated by the Watergate scandal, the "psychedelic" style and music of groups like the Beatles and Jimi Hendrix, and television programs such as "All in the Family," which dealt with the formerly taboo topics of racism, sexism, and sexuality.

Today's traditional-age college students, whose childhood spanned the late 1980s and the 1990s, experienced the militarily successful Persian Gulf War, the demolition of the Berlin Wall and the downfall of communism, the commercially oriented music of performers like Madonna and M. C. Hammer, and television programs like "The Cosby Show," which portrayed African Americans in a more positive light than did earlier programs. Thus, as you read, keep in mind that whereas common biological factors and social clocks might make generations somewhat similar in their development, cultural and historical factors unique to particular cohorts can make them somewhat different from cohorts that precede or succeed them.

Adolescence is unknown in many nonindustrialized countries. Instead, adulthood begins with the onset of puberty and is commonly celebrated with traditional rites of passage. With the advent of universal free education and child labor laws in Western countries, children, who otherwise would have entered the adult work world by the time they reached puberty, entered a period of life during which they developed an adult body yet maintained a childlike dependence on parents.

Physical Development

Recall your own adolescence. What you might recall most vividly are the rapid physical changes associated with **puberty** (from the Latin word for "adulthood"). Puberty is marked by a rapid increase in height; girls show a growth spurt between the ages of 10 and 12, and boys show a spurt between the ages of 12 and 14. The physical changes of puberty also include the maturation of primary and secondary sex characteristics. Primary sex characteristics are hormone-induced physical changes that enable us to engage in sexual reproduction. These changes include growth of the penis and testes in males and the vagina, uterus, and

adolescence
The transition period lasting from the onset of puberty to the beginning of adulthood.

social clock
The typical or expected timing of major life events in a given culture.

puberty
The period of rapid physical change that occurs during adolescence, including the development of the ability to reproduce sexually.

► Puberty

Because adolescents enter puberty at different ages, groups of young adolescents include individuals who vary greatly in height and physical maturity. As a consequence, a typical middle school class might appear to include a wider age range than it actually does.

spermarche

The first ejaculation, usually occurring between the ages of 13 and 15.

menarche

The beginning of menstruation, usually occurring between the ages of 11 and 13.

ovaries in females. Secondary sex characteristics are stimulated by sex hormones but are unrelated to sexual reproduction. Pubertal males develop facial hair, deeper voices, and larger muscles. Pubertal females develop wider hips, larger breasts, and more rounded physiques, caused in part by increased deposits of fat.

These physical changes are triggered by a spurt in the secretion of the female sex hormone estrogen between ages 10 and 11 and the male sex hormone testosterone between ages 12 and 13. Boys generally experience **spermarche,** their first ejaculation, between the ages of 13 and 15, typically while asleep (so-called nocturnal emissions). Girls exhibit earlier physical maturation than boys and generally experience **menarche,** their first menstrual period, between the ages of 11 and 13 (Paikoff & Brooks-Gunn, 1991). The average age of menarche is lower than in the past; this has been attributed to improved health and nutrition. For example, the average age of menarche declined from 16.5 to 13.7 years over a span of 40 years in two rural counties of China. During this period of modernization, the health and living conditions of the rural Chinese population improved dramatically (Graham, Larsen, & Xu, 1999).

Though the dramatic physical changes of puberty are caused by hormonal changes, adolescent mood swings are not necessarily the by-products of hormones run wild. Hormone fluctuations affect the adolescent's moods, but life events have a greater effect (Brooks-Gunn & Warren, 1989). Of course, the physical changes of puberty, including acne, rapid growth, and genital maturation, can themselves produce emotional distress. This is especially true if the adolescent is unprepared for them or is made to feel self-conscious by peers or parents. Boys find it difficult enough to deal with scruffy facial hair, unwanted penile erections, and voices that crack, without being made more anxious about those changes. Girls, likewise, find it difficult to discover suddenly that they have enlarged breasts, experience their menstrual cycle, and possibly tower several inches above many of their male peers.

The timing of puberty also influences how adolescents respond to these physical changes. Early-maturing boys appear to negotiate the transition of puberty better than late-maturing boys. Early-maturing boys are more popular with their peers, more sociable, and more self-confident (Jones, 1965). Early-maturing girls, though, are more likely to experience puberty as a stressful transition. Though the timing of puberty does not *cause* behavior problems, early menarche has been found to exacerbate childhood behavioral problems (Caspi & Moffitt, 1991).

Cognitive Development

Adolescent cognitive development is less dramatic, with no obvious surge in mental abilities to match the surge in physical development. According to Piaget's theory, at about 11 years of age some adolescents pass from the concrete operational stage to the **formal operational stage.** A person who reaches this stage is able to reason about abstract, not just concrete, situations. The adolescent who has reached the formal operational stage can apply abstract principles and make predictions about hypothetical situations. In contrast, an ado-

formal operational stage

The Piagetian stage, beginning at about age 11, marked by the ability to use abstract reasoning and to solve problems by testing hypotheses.

lescent still in the concrete operational stage would rely more on blind trial and error than on a formal approach to problem solving.

To appreciate this, imagine you are given four chemicals and are asked to produce a purple liquid by mixing them—but it is left up to you to discover the proper mixture. People at the concrete operational level would approach this task in an unsystematic manner, hoping that through trial and error they would hit upon the correct combination of chemicals. In contrast, people at the formal operational level would approach it systematically, perhaps by mixing each possible combination of two of the chemicals, then each possible combination of three, and finally all four. Thus, people who reach the formal operational stage perform better on more complex intellectual pursuits. A study of adolescent students found those in transition between the concrete operational stage and the formal operational stage showed better understanding of abstract concepts presented in a physics textbook than did those still in the concrete operational stage (Renner et al., 1990).

Piaget found so few people who had reached the formal operational stage that he gave up his earlier belief that it was universal. Those who reach that stage are more likely to have been exposed to scientific thinking in their academic courses (Rogoff & Chavajay, 1995). Though educational interventions have effectively fostered the development of formal operational thought in developing countries such as Pakistan (Iqbal & Shayer, 2000), people from cultures that do not stress science in their school curricula are less likely to achieve the formal operational stage.

Psychosocial Development

Erik Erikson noted that psychosocial development continues through adolescence into adulthood and old age. Perhaps the most important psychosocial tasks of adolescence are the formation of a personal identity and the development of healthy relationships with peers and parents.

Identity Achievement

According to Erikson (1963), the most important feat of adolescence is the resolution of the conflict of **identity versus role confusion.** The adolescent develops a sense of identity by adopting her or his own set of values and social behaviors. Erikson believed this is a normal part of finding answers to questions related to one's identity, such as these: What do I believe is important? What are my goals in life?

identity versus role confusion
Erikson's developmental stage in which success is achieved by establishing a sense of personal identity.

Erikson's emphasis on the importance of the identity crisis might reflect, in large part, his own life history. He was born in Germany, the child of a Danish Christian mother and father. Erik's father abandoned his mother while she was pregnant with him. She then married a Jewish physician, Theodore Homburger. Erik was given his new father's surname, making him Erik Homburger. But it was not until Erik reached adolescence that he was told Homburger was not his biological father (Hopkins, 1995).

Erikson, uncomfortable among Jews and Christians alike, sought to find himself by traveling in European artistic and intellectual circles, as many young adults did in the 1920s. Eventually he met Anna Freud, Sigmund's daughter and an eminent psychoanalyst herself. Erikson underwent psychoanalysis with her almost daily for 3 years. In 1933 Erikson changed his name to Erik Homburger Erikson and left to pursue a career in the United States. His long, rich life was a testament to his success in finding his identity as a husband, writer, teacher, and psychoanalyst.

To appreciate the task that confronts the adolescent in developing an identity, consider the challenge of having to adjust simultaneously to a new body, a new mind, and a new social world. The adolescent body is larger and sexually mature. The adolescent mind can question the nature of reality and argue about abstract concepts regarding ethical, political, and religious beliefs. The social world of the adolescent requires achieving a balance between childlike dependence and adultlike independence. This also manifests itself in the conflict between parental and peer influences. Children's values tend to mirror their parents', but adolescents' values oscillate between those of their parents and those of their peers. Adolescents move from a world guided by parental wishes to a world in which they are confronted by a host of choices regarding sex, drugs, friends, schoolwork, and other things.

▲ Erik Erikson (1902–1994)
"If ever an identity crisis was central and long drawn out in somebody's life it was so in mine."

Erikson's theory has received support from longitudinal studies showing that adolescents typically move from a state of role confusion to a state of identity achievement (Streitmatter, 1993). There also is some evidence that Erikson's theory might generalize to adolescents' experiences across cultures. One study found that Hong Kong Chinese adolescents who achieved a sense of identity were more prosocial and exhibited fewer antisocial behaviors than adolescents who had not (Ma et al., 2000). And German adolescents who achieved a sense of identity reported more extensive exploration of career options and held broader vocational interests than adolescents who had not (Schmitt-Rodermund & Vondracek, 1999). Failure to achieve a sense of identity is associated with emotional distress, including feelings of emptiness and depression (Taylor & Goritsas, 1994).

But Carol Gilligan (1982) believes Erikson's theory applies more to male than to female adolescents. She points out that Erikson based his theory on studies of men, who tend to place a greater premium on the development of self-sufficiency than do women, who tend to place a greater premium on intimate relationships in which there is mutual caring. Thus, female adolescents who fail to develop an independent identity at the same time as their male age peers might unfairly be considered abnormal. One recent study compared self-descriptions and personality attributes of male and female undergraduates. Self-descriptions of men and women who had achieved identity were more similar than the self-descriptions of men and women who had not. However, gender differences were found in the relationship of personality variables that have been thought to contribute to identity development (Cramer, 2000). Though intimate relationships are important to both men's and women's well-being, psychologists studying gender differences in identity development believe women's identity development emphasizes the self in relation to others.

Psychologists also have investigated the nature of ethnic identity, particularly among immigrants and members of ethnic minority groups. Studies of ethnic and American identity in multiethnic samples have found ethnic identity is positively correlated with self-esteem—regardless of participants' ethnic backgrounds. Thus, positive attitudes toward one's ethnic group contribute to high self-esteem. Ethnic identity has been found to be positively correlated with measures of psychological adjustment, including optimism, mastery, and coping in a multiethnic sample of over 5,400 American adolescents (Roberts et al., 1999). This research has important implications for members of ethnic minority groups, many of whom consider themselves to be bicultural. One study assessed ethnic identity and measures of acculturation among 1,367 American undergraduates, most of whom were of Mexican origin. Ethnic identity was strongest for first-generation and less-acculturated participants. And higher levels of acculturation were associated with a diminished sense of ethnic identity and belongingness. More positive outcomes were associated with participants who were high in biculturalism—that is, feeling a part of both majority American and traditional Mexican cultures. Participants who scored high on a measure of biculturalism also had higher ethnic identity scores and were more socially oriented than participants who scored low on biculturalism (Cuéllar et al., 1997).

Once again, these findings demonstrate the importance of considering the cultural context of theoretical positions. For example, the Inuit people of Canada see personal identity as inseparable from the physical, animal, and human environments. The Inuits would find it maladaptive if members of their culture formed more individualistic identities (Stairs, 1992).

Social Relationships

Because the adolescent is dependent on parents while seeking an independent identity, adolescence has traditionally been considered a period of conflict between parents and children, or what G. Stanley Hall called a period of "storm and stress." Parents might be shocked by their adolescent's preferences in dress, music, and vocabulary. In trying out various styles and values, adolescents are influenced by the cohort to which they belong. Thus, male adolescents shocked their parents by wearing pompadours in the 1950s, shoulder-length hair in the 1970s, and spiked hairdos in the 1990s. Though parental conflict, moodiness, and a tendency for engaging in risky behavior is more common in adolescence, there are considerable cross-cultural differences. Adolescents in traditional cultures tend to maintain traditional values and practices—even those experiencing the rapid pace of modernization and globalization. Moreover, there are considerable individual differences in behavioral and mood disruptions among adolescents (Arnett, 1999).

Despite the conflicts between parental values and adolescent behaviors that might occur, most adolescents have positive relations with their parents. In general, adolescence is a time of only slightly increased parent-child conflict. Though the emotional intensity of parental-child conflicts is somewhat higher at puberty, the frequency of parent-child conflict declines over the adolescent years (Laursen, Coy, & Collins, 1998). Of course, some adolescents adopt negative identities that promote antisocial, or even delinquent, behaviors. This is more common in adolescents whose parents set few rules, fail to discipline them, and do not supervise them (Forehand et al., 1997). Conflicts also might be more frequent among first-generation immigrants and their children, due to differential rates of acculturation within the family. Compared to non-immigrant families, immigrant Armenian, Vietnamese, and Mexican parents were more likely to stress family obligations than their children. Moreover, among immigrant families, intergenerational discrepancies in familial values increased as a function of time spent living in the United States (Phinney, Ong, & Madden, 2000).

In regard to their friendships, adolescents have more intimate friendships than do younger children, possibly because they are more capable of sharing their thoughts and feelings and understanding those of other people. Though the level of intimate feelings expressed by boys and girls when interacting with their same-sex friends do not differ, there are gender differences in the ways adolescents establish intimate friendships. Adolescent girls tend to establish intimacy through self-disclosure whereas adolescent boys tend to establish intimacy through shared activities (McNelles & Connolly, 1999).

Adolescence is associated with an important biologically based psychosocial conflict between the powerful urge to engage in sexual relations and societal values against premarital sex. The proportion of American adolescents engaging in sex increased steadily from the 1930s, when less than 10 percent had premarital sex, to today, when most older adolescents engage in it. But the sexes differ in their sexual attitudes. Male adolescents are more willing to engage in casual sex; female adolescents are more likely to prefer sex as part of a committed relationship (Oliver & Hyde, 1993; also see Chapter 11).

Though American and European adolescents have similar levels of sexual activity, there are more unwanted pregnancies among Americans. This is attributable in part to the greater ignorance and recklessness of American youth in the use of contraception. This begins from the very first sexual experience, when most American adolescents do not use contraceptives—though the percentage who do use contraceptives increased during the 1980s (Poppen, 1994). Nonmonogamous sex and unprotected sex increase the risks of contracting sexually transmitted diseases such as herpes, syphilis, chlamydia, and AIDS. Moreover, irresponsible sexual activity in America leads to thousands of abortions, many fatherless offspring, and inadequate care for resulting offspring (Brooks-Gunn & Furstenberg, 1989).

Adolescence is also a period often involving widespread use of psychoactive drugs, including alcohol, nicotine, cocaine, and marijuana. Peer-group drug use is a factor in the promotion of adolescent drug use. For example, one study of a predominantly African American sample of urban high school students found that peer pressure and the frequency of peer drug use were associated with more frequent drug use, especially for girls (Farrell & White, 1998). Today alcohol is the main drug of choice among adolescents in many countries. A survey of more than 2,600 Canadian adolescents found alcohol use was associated with more problem behaviors than was the use of other drugs (Gfellner & Hundleby, 1994). Fortunately, despite the risks associated with sexual irresponsibility and drug and alcohol abuse, almost all adolescents enter adulthood relatively unscathed.

▲ **Identity Formation**
During adolescence our peers play a large role in the development of our sense of identity. Generation after generation, this has distressed North American parents–though, as adolescents, their stylistic choices may have upset their own parents.

STAYING ON TRACK: *Adolescent Development*

1. Why should adolescence researchers be concerned with cohort effects?
2. What is the formal operational stage?
3. According to Erikson, how does identity formation manifest itself in adolescents?

Answers to Staying on Track start on p. ST-2.

♦ GENDER DIFFERENCES AND HUMAN DEVELOPMENT

In the 19th century, scientific interest in gender differences was stimulated by Darwin's theory of evolution and promoted by Francis Galton. Galton assumed that women and men evolved physical and psychological differences that help them function in particular roles, and he insisted they should remain in those roles (Shields, 1975). Views like his were countered by some psychologists, such as Leta Stetter Hollingworth (1886–1939), who insisted gender differences were due to social factors.

The first major review of gender differences was published by Eleanor Maccoby and Carol Jacklin (1974). They reported that women were superior in verbal abilities and men were superior in spatial and mathematical abilities. They also found men were more aggressive than women. Nonetheless, they found fewer differences, and generally smaller differences, than were commonly believed to exist. Today, researchers are interested in identifying gender differences and similarities in cognitive abilities, personality, and social behavior. Many of these researchers have used a statistical technique, meta-analysis, which enables them to assess the magnitude of gender differences and situational factors that increase or decrease these effect sizes (see Chapter 2).

Cognitive Abilities

Researchers have studied gender differences primarily in three kinds of cognitive abilities. They ask: Are there gender differences in verbal abilities? in spatial abilities? in mathematical abilities?

Verbal Abilities

Research on children supports the popular belief in the verbal superiority of girls. Girls tend to be slightly superior to boys in speaking, spelling, vocabulary, and reading comprehension. Yet these differences decrease by adolescence. Overall, gender differences in verbal abilities have declined in size in recent decades until they are virtually negligible (Hyde & Plant, 1995). But what about talkativeness, which the popular stereotype holds to be the province of women? Research indicates that contrary to the stereotype men are consistently more talkative than women (Hyde & Linn, 1988).

Spatial Abilities

Research has tended to consistently find a large gender difference in one test of spatial abilities. Men are superior in the rotation of mental images (Hyde, Fennema, & Lamon, 1990). Gender differences in other spatial abilities, though, tend to be considerably smaller and inconsistent. Moreover, a meta-analysis of research studies of gender differences in spatial abilities found that the sizes of the differences have decreased in recent years (Voyer, Voyer, & Bryden, 1995). However, gender differences in spatial abilities are observed in early childhood (Levine et al., 1999) and in many settings. For example, when providing directions women are more likely to rely upon landmarks and right-left strategies whereas men are more likely to refer to north-south-east-west strategies (Halpern & LeMay, 2000).

Mathematical Abilities

Perhaps the most strongly established cognitive gender difference is that adolescent and adult males have higher average scores than adolescent and adult females on standardized mathematics tests. A national talent search by Camilla Benbow and Julian Stanley (1983) found that among seventh- and eighth-graders who took the mathematics subtest of the Scholastic Aptitude Test (SAT), the average score for boys was higher than the average score for girls. In fact, among those scoring higher than 700 (out of 800), boys outnumbered girls by a ratio of 13 to 1. Could this be attributable to boys' having more experience in mathematics? Benbow and Stanley said no, having found little difference in the number of mathematics courses

▲ **Gender Differences**

Physiological and social-cultural factors play an important role in girls' and boys' congnitive abilities.

taken by boys and girls. And because they found no other life experiences that could explain their findings, Benbow and Stanley concluded heredity probably accounts for the difference. This explanation has received some support from other researchers (Thomas, 1993).

But it has also provoked controversy. Critics argue the gender differences in mathematical abilities reported by Benbow and Stanley might be attributable to as yet unidentified differences in girls' and boys' experiences with mathematics. Also, boys do not have a higher average score than girls on all measures of mathematical ability. Though boys have higher average scores on mathematics achievement tests, which stress problem solving, girls receive higher grades in mathematics courses (Halpern, 2000b). A meta-analysis of more than 3 million participants in 100 studies found that, aside from higher average male scores on standardized tests, there is no overall gender difference in mathematics ability. If anything, there is a slight superiority in favor of girls in abilities such as calculating. Moreover, even male superiority in mathematical problem solving does not appear until adolescence (Hyde, Fennema, & Lamon, 1990). And even this might be attributable to differences in the number of advanced mathematics courses taken by males and females (Hyde & Plant, 1995).

It also is important to consider that gender differences in mathematics achievement are smaller than cross-cultural or ethnic differences in mathematics achievement (Kimball, 1995). In fact, the largest gender difference in mathematics ability is found among European-American samples (Hyde, Fennema, & Lamon, 1990). In cultures with comparatively smaller gender differences, parents are more likely to encourage academic achievement and advanced study in mathematics—for both sons and daughters (Hanna, Kundiger, & Larouche, 1990). As discussed in Chapter 17, people's beliefs about group differences can lead to a self-fulfilling prophecy, which ultimately influences their behavior. And research has shown participants' beliefs about group differences can affect their performance on cognitive tests (Steele, 1997). Thus, stereotypes about women's and men's cognitive abilities might contribute to gender differences in mathematics achievement.

Personality and Social Behavior

Researchers also study gender differences in personality and social behavior. They have been especially concerned with differences in personality traits and aggression.

Personality

Meta-analyses of research studies on personality differences have found men are more assertive whereas women are slightly more extraverted and more anxious, trusting, and, especially, tenderminded (that is, more caring and nurturing). These differences tended to be consistent across all ages and educational levels of participants, as well as across a variety of different cultures (Feingold, 1994). A recent meta-analysis found that male participants scored slightly higher on standardized measures of self-esteem than did female participants. The size of this small gender difference does increase—at least temporarily—in adolescence (Kling et al., 1999).

Researchers also have studied whether the stereotype that women are more self-disclosing than men is true. That is, do women reveal more of their private thoughts, feelings, and experiences than men? Contrary to popular belief, women are only marginally more likely to self-disclose than men (Dindia & Allen, 1992).

But what of the popular belief that women are more empathetic than men? This apparent gender difference depends on how empathy is measured. When asked to report their level of empathy, women score higher than men. But when empathy is measured by physiological arousal or overt behavior, gender differences disappear. Evidently, social expectations that women will be more emotionally sensitive than men create differences in their subjective views of themselves but not necessarily in their actual behavior or physiological responses (Eisenberg & Lennon, 1983). This hypothesis was tested in a recent meta-analysis that found women's empathy scores were higher than men's only when participants were aware their empathy was being assessed. This gender difference disappeared in experimental situations that lacked this demand characteristic (Ickes, Gesn, & Graham, 2000).

Aggression

Just as women are reputed to be more empathetic than men, men are reputed to be more aggressive than women. Research has found men are, indeed, more physically aggressive than women (Eagly & Steffen, 1986). Moreover, gender differences in aggression might be the product of gender roles. This was the conclusion of a study in which male and female participants were tested in the laboratory. When they were singled out as individuals, men were more aggressive than women. When they were deindividuated (that is, made to feel anonymous) men and women did not differ in aggression. The researchers attributed this difference to the power of gender roles: When we feel we are being noticed, we are more likely to behave according to gender expectations (Lightdale & Prentice, 1994). Moreover, as discussed in Chapter 17, when operational definitions of aggression are broadened to include behaviors that are more stereotypically female—such as indirect aggression—gender differences in aggression are minimized.

Explanations for Possible Gender Differences

If psychological gender differences exist, what might account for them? Researchers point to physiological factors and social-cultural factors.

Physiological Factors

Because of the obvious physical differences between men and women, researchers have looked to possible physiological factors to explain psychological gender differences. Evolutionary psychologist David Buss believes men and women inherit certain behavioral tendencies as a product of their long evolutionary history. According to Buss, "Men and women differ . . . in domains in which they have faced different adaptive problems over human evolutionary history. In all other domains, the sexes are predicted to be psychologically similar" (Buss, 1995, p. 164). Thus, men are more aggressive and women more nurturing because prehistoric males were more likely to be hunters and prehistoric females were more likely to be caregivers. They do not differ in traits unrelated to their prehistoric roles as males and females.

But how might heredity affect psychological gender differences? Evidence supporting the biological basis of gender differences in social behavior implicates hormonal factors. Girls whose adrenal glands secrete high prenatal levels of testosterone are slightly more likely to become "tomboys" who prefer rough play and masculine activities (though most tomboys do not have this adrenal disorder). The genitals of girls with this adrenal disorder look masculine at birth (though they are usually corrected by surgery), and this might make parents treat them as though they are more masculine, yet parents usually report they treat these girls the same as parents treat girls without the disorder (Berenbaum & Hines, 1992). There is some evidence, though, for a hormonal basis for cognitive gender differences (Kimura & Hampson, 1994). There also is evidence of a hormonal basis for gender differences in play behavior in childhood and fairly strong evidence for its effect on gender differences in physical aggressiveness during play (Collaer & Hines, 1995).

A second way heredity might affect gender differences is through brain development, but efforts to associate specific cognitive differences with differences in brain structures have produced mixed results. Some studies have found that men's brains might be more lateralized than women's brains. Studies of people with brain damage have found damage to men's left cerebral hemisphere is associated with impaired verbal skills and damage to men's right cerebral hemisphere is associated with impaired nonverbal skills. In contrast, women's verbal and nonverbal skills seem to be less influenced by the side of the brain damaged (Springer & Deutsch, 1998). Other studies, though, have failed to find gender differences in hemispheric lateralization (Snow & Sheese, 1985). And there are large individual differences in brain organization; biological sex is only one of many variables influencing brain organization (Kimura, 1987).

Social-Cultural Factors

The possibility that cognitive gender differences are caused more by social-cultural factors than by physiological factors is supported by studies that have found a narrowing of cognitive gender differences between North American male and female participants during the past

25 years (Hyde, Fennema, & Lamon, 1990; Voyer, Voyer, & Bryden, 1995). This might be explained in part by the cultural trend to provide female and male children with somewhat more similar treatment and opportunities (Jacklin, 1989). Even Camilla Benbow (1988) agrees that environmental, as well as hereditary, factors play an important role in cognitive abilities such as mathematics. After decades of extensive research, no gender differences have emerged that are large enough to predict with confidence how particular men and women will behave (Deaux, 1985). This has provoked a controversy about whether we should continue to study gender differences. Some psychologists, such as Roy Baumeister (1988), argue we should no longer study them. Why study differences that are too few or too small to have practical significance? And why study gender differences when reports of even small differences might support sex discrimination? But Baumeister's view was countered by researchers Alice Eagly (1995) and Diane Halpern (1994), who believe that objective scientific research on gender differences should continue, even if it might find differences that some people would prefer did not exist. A compromise position has been put forth by Janet Shibley Hyde, who favors studying gender differences but warns against relying on the results of studies that have not been replicated, interpreting gender differences as signs of female deficiencies, or automatically attributing such differences to inherited biological factors (Hyde & Plant, 1995).

STAYING ON TRACK: *Gender Differences and Human Development*

1. What is the best-established psychological gender difference?
2. Why do psychologists argue about the wisdom of studying gender differences?

Answers to Staying on Track start on p. ST-2.

Profile of Older Americans, 1999
www.mhhe.com/sdorow5

◆ ADULT DEVELOPMENT

In Western cultures, **adulthood** begins when adolescents become independent of their parents and assume responsibility for themselves. Interest in adult development accelerated in the 1950s after being inspired by Erikson's theory of life-span development (Levinson, 1986) and brought an increased realization that physical, cognitive, and psychosocial changes take place across the life span.

adulthood
The period beginning when the individual assumes responsibility for her or his own life.

Physical Development

Adults reach their physical peak in their late twenties and then begin a slow physical decline that does not accelerate appreciably until old age. Most athletes peak in their twenties, as is shown by the ages at which world-class athletes achieve their best performances (Schulz & Curnow, 1988). Beginning in our twenties, our basal metabolic rate (the rate at which the body burns calories when at rest) also decreases, accounting in part for the tendency to gain weight in adulthood. This makes it especially important for adults to pay attention to diet and exercise, which also can counter the tendency to experience lung, heart, and muscle deterioration in early and middle adulthood. A prime example of this is Kareem Abdul Jabbar, who, by meticulous attention to maintaining a healthy diet and a state of physical fitness, played 20 years of professional basketball.

Aging also brings sexual changes. As men age, their testosterone levels decline and they produce fewer sperm, yet they can still father children into old age. But they might have increasing difficulty in achieving penile erections. Typically beginning in their forties or fifties, women experience *menopause*—the cessation of their menstrual cycle. This is associated with a reduction in estrogen, cessation of ovulation, and consequently the inability to become pregnant. The reduction in estrogen can cause sweating, hot flashes, and brittle bones, as well as atrophy of the vagina, uterus, and mammary glands. Hormone replacement therapy sometimes is prescribed to reduce the physical symptoms of menopause. Menopause signals an end to the childbearing years, but it does not signal an end to sexuality. Postmenopausal

▲ **Aging and Physical Health**
These athletes show that diet and exercise can contribute to a healthy old age.

women can still have fulfilling sex lives and social lives. Moreover, a survey of 16,000 American women from five ethnic groups (European American, African American, Japanese American, Chinese American, and Latino) found that women's attitudes toward menopause were neutral to positive. Moreover, health status, not menopausal status, predicted the happiness of women in midlife (Sommer et al., 1999).

Middle-aged adults tend to become farsighted and require reading glasses, as evidenced by an increasing tendency to hold books and newspapers at arm's length. But marked changes in physical abilities usually do not occur until late adulthood. The older adult exhibits deterioration in heart output, lung capacity, reaction time, muscular strength, and motor coordination (Maranto, 1984). Old age also brings a decline in hearing, particularly of high-pitched sounds.

Eventually, no matter how well we take care of our bodies, all of us reach the ultimate physical change—death. Though the upper limit of the human life span seems to be about 120 years, few people live to even 100. But why is death inevitable? Death seems to be genetically programmed into our cells by limiting their ability to repair or reproduce themselves (Hayflick, 1980). Animal research indicates aging can be slowed by the reduction of daily caloric intake, which prevents the buildup of certain metabolic by-products that promote aging. For example, a study of rats found those who ate a low-calorie diet lived longer (Masoro et al., 1995). The effects of low-calorie diets on human aging and longevity remain unclear. Longevity also is influenced by physical activity. One longitudinal study of 70-year-old residents of western Jerusalem found mortality rates were significantly lower for participants who reported engaging in regular exercise. Moreover, walking as little as 4 hours per week was linked to increased survival (Stessman et al., 2000).

We do know, however, that the mere act of continuing to work is associated with slower aging. In a study supporting this, elderly people who continued to work or who retired but participated in regular physical activities showed a constant level of cerebral blood flow over a 4-year period. In contrast, elderly people who retired and did not participate in regular physical activities showed a significant decline in cerebral blood flow. Those who continued to work also scored better on cognitive tests than did the inactive retirees (Rogers, Meyer, & Mortel, 1990). One 30-year longitudinal study found that adults who were employed in occupations that required complex work—that is, thought and independent decision making—demonstrated higher levels of intellectual functioning compared to adults who were employed in less demanding occupations. Moreover, the beneficial effect of complex work was more pronounced in late adulthood compared to young adulthood (Schooler, Mulatu, & Oates, 1999). Thus, while physical aging is inevitable, people who maintain an active lifestyle might age at a slower rate. Note that these results do not conclusively demonstrate that activity causes a slowing of the effects of aging. Perhaps, instead, people who age more slowly are more likely to stay active.

Cognitive Development

One of the most controversial issues in developmental psychology is the pattern of adult cognitive development, particularly intellectual development. Early studies showed we experience a steady decline in intelligence across adulthood. But this apparent decline is found more often in cross-sectional studies than in longitudinal studies. Longitudinal studies have found a marked decline in intelligence does not begin until about age 60. This indicates that the decline in intelligence across adulthood found in cross-sectional studies might be a cohort effect (perhaps due to differences in early educational experiences) rather than an aging effect (Schaie & Hertzog, 1983). Moreover, the intellectual decline in old age does not encompass all facets of intelligence. Instead, it holds for *fluid intelligence* but not for *crystallized intelligence* (Ryan, Sattler, & Lopez, 2000). **Fluid intelligence** reflects the ability to reason and to process information; **crystallized intelligence** reflects the ability to gain and retain knowledge.

But what accounts for the decline in fluid intelligence in old age? The Seattle Longitudinal Study of 1,620 adults between 22 and 91 years of age conducted by K. Warner Schaie (1989) found the speed of information processing slows in old age. This has been replicated

fluid intelligence
The form of intelligence that reflects reasoning ability, memory capacity, and speed of information processing.

crystallized intelligence
The form of intelligence that reflects knowledge acquired through schooling and in everyday life.

| **Chapter Four**

◀ **Back to School**
The myth that intellectual decline is a normal aspect of aging is countered by the increasing number of older adults who enroll in undergraduate degree programs. In the case of memory and cognitive abilities, the adage "use it or lose it" might have validity.

in other research studies (Sliwinski & Buschke, 1999). This slowing is especially detrimental to short-term memory (Salthouse, 1991), which is the stage of memory that involves the conscious, purposeful mental manipulation of information.

Researchers have recently begun to question whether hormone replacement therapy can reduce the effects of aging on postmenopausal women's cognitive abilities, particularly short-term memory. Though the effects of hormone replacement therapy on older men's cognitive abilities are unknown, there is considerable evidence that hormone replacement therapy can reduce age-related declines in short-term memory and certain spatial skills. It also reduces postmenopausal women's risk of developing Alzheimer's disease (Halpern, 2000a). This research will have important implications for the growing population of older women. Women are more likely than men to experience physical frailty and psychological decline in late old age, primarily due to gender differences in longevity and living circumstances. Men have a shorter but healthier old age; women live longer but in poorer physical—and often psychological—health (Smith & Baltes, 1998).

The Nun Study
www.mhhe.com/sdorow5

Psychosocial Development

Psychosocial development continues through early, middle, and late adulthood. Keeping in mind that these divisions are somewhat arbitrary, assume that early adulthood extends from age 20 to age 40, middle adulthood from age 40 to age 65, and late adulthood from age 65 on. The similarities exhibited by people within these periods are related to the common social experiences of the "social clock." In recent decades, the typical ages at which some of these experiences occur have varied more than in the past. A graduate student might live at home with his parents until his late twenties, a woman working toward her medical degree might postpone marriage until her early thirties, and a two-career couple might not have their first child until they are in their late thirties. Of course, events unique to each person's life can also play a role in psychosocial development. Chance encounters in our lives, for example, contribute to our unique development (Bandura, 1982). You might reflect on chance encounters that influenced your choice of an academic major or that helped you meet your current boyfriend, girlfriend, husband, or wife.

Early Adulthood

Though Sigmund Freud paid little attention to adult development, he did note that normal adulthood is marked by the ability to love and to work. Erik Erikson agreed that the capacity for love is an important aspect of early adulthood, and he claimed that the first major task of adulthood is facing the conflict of **intimacy versus isolation.** Intimate relationships involve a strong sense of emotional attachment and personal commitment. A 20-year longitudinal study of a community sample supported Erikson's belief that the development of the capacity for intimacy depends on the successful formation of a psychosocial identity in

intimacy versus isolation
Erikson's developmental stage in which success is achieved by establishing a relationship with a strong sense of emotional attachment and personal commitment.

adolescence. The achievement of identity during adolescence contributed to the development of intimacy in young adulthood. Participants who were capable of a high degree of intimacy in young adulthood reported more successful romantic relationships and greater life satisfaction (Stein & Newcomb, 1999).

Establishing Intimate Relationships. About 95 percent of young adults eventually experience the intimate relationship of marriage. Of course there is a variety of family arrangements. And at any given time many adults are unmarried—they are either widowed, divorced, not ready, or committed to remaining single. A survey of never-married adults aged 20 to 30 found that the women were more motivated to marry than were the men. But whereas the men were especially concerned with future career considerations, the women were equally concerned with career and family considerations (Inglis & Greenglass, 1989).

A strong and consistent positive correlation has been found between marriage and psychological well-being. The World Values Survey, a survey of 159,169 adults in 42 countries, found married couples reported higher levels of life satisfaction than cohabiting couples and divorced or separated adults. Though there were significant cross-cultural differences, these differences were negligible. And men and women derive similar benefits from marriage (Diener et al., 2000). Unmarried status is correlated with greater physical and psychological risks, especially for men. A survey of more than 18,000 men conducted in England found unmarried middle-aged men of all kinds—single, widowed, divorced, or separated— had higher mortality rates than did married men (Ben-Shlomo et al., 1993). One reason for this is a greater risk of illness in the unmarried, in part because they have less contact with social networks that encourage healthy behavior and medical treatment (Burman & Margolin, 1992).

What characteristics do adults look for in potential mates? As you might expect, both women and men tend to seek partners who are kind, loyal, honest, considerate, intelligent, interesting, and affectionate. But men tend to be more concerned than women with the potential mate's physical attractiveness, and women tend to be more concerned than men with the potential mate's earning capacity (Buss et al., 1990). As discussed in Chapter 17, psychologists argue whether these preferences reflect the influence of evolution or of cultural factors that differentially affect men's and women's expectations.

What determines whether a relationship will succeed? An important factor is similarity—in age, religion, attitudes, ethnicity, personality, intelligence, and educational level (O'Leary & Smith, 1991). Willingness to talk about problems is another important factor, as found in a 2-year longitudinal study of newlyweds (Crohan, 1992). A 4-year longitudinal study found that high-quality, positive communication between spouses was associated with higher levels of marital satisfaction. Moreover, marital dissolution was associated with marital conflict and aggression—especially if present early in the marriage (Rogge & Bradbury, 1999).

Dissolving Intimate Relationships. Unfortunately, many married couples find happiness elusive, and they might eventually seek to divorce (Devine & Forehand, 1996). One of the hallmarks of an unhappy marriage is the tendency of spouses to consistently offer negative explanations for their spouse's behavior (Karney & Bradbury, 2000). In the United States, about half of first marriages are so unhappy they end in divorce. In fact, the United States has the highest divorce rate of any industrialized country (O'Leary & Smith, 1991). A study that interviewed over 1,300 persons found divorce has increased not because marriages were happier in the "good old days," but instead because barriers to divorce (such as conservative values or shared social networks) have fallen and alternatives to divorce (such as a wife's independent income or remarriage prospects) have increased. Thus, the threshold of marital happiness that will trigger divorce is lower than it was several decades ago.

The barriers to relationship dissolution associated with marriage are important in understanding the higher rate of relationship dissolution among gay and lesbian couples. One 5-year longitudinal study compared relationship satisfaction and dissolution rates among heterosexual, gay, and lesbian couples. Heterosexual married couples' satisfaction with their relationship was similar to that reported by cohabiting gay and lesbian couples. Whereas relationship satisfaction declined among all three groups, gay and lesbian couples were more likely to have ended their relationships. These results are attributed to the fact that gay and lesbian couples perceived fewer barriers to ending their relationship, such as cost of divorce or loss of insurance or health benefits (Kurdek, 1998).

Yet there is evidence that people might remain committed to spouses or partners who treat them poorly. You probably have known someone who sticks with a romantic partner who treats that person in a manner you would not tolerate. Consider a study of 86 married couples from central Texas, with an average age of 32 years and an average length of marriage of 6 years (Swann, Hixon, & De La Ronde, 1992). The spouses took personality tests measuring their self-concepts. They also measured how the spouses appraised each other and how committed they were to each other. The results revealed the degree of commitment to one's spouse depended on the degree of congruence between one's self-concept and how one was viewed by one's spouse. That is, those with positive self-concepts felt more committed when their spouses viewed them positively. Likewise, those with negative self-concepts felt more committed when their spouses viewed them negatively.

What could account for this finding, which runs counter to the commonsense notion that we all wish to be admired and treated well? The researchers found that though we might insist on being treated well in casual relationships, we insist on being treated in accordance with our self-concept within the intimacy of marriage. That is, we want our spouses to verify our self-concept so we are not confused about ourselves or about how other people will treat us. In addition, we will trust spouses more who do not try to "snow" us by telling us we're attractive when we feel ugly, intelligent when we feel stupid, and personally appealing when we feel socially inept. Moreover, whereas people with positive self-concepts might welcome high expectations of them, people with negative self-concepts might fear unrealistically high expectations that they could not meet.

Parenthood. For most people, parenthood is a major milestone in adulthood. Raising children can be one of the greatest rewards in life, but it can also be one of life's greatest stresses. Because women still tend to be the primary caregiver, their parental responsibilities tend to be especially stressful. But couples who share child-care responsibilities are more likely to successfully weather the stress of becoming new parents (Belsky & Hsieh, 1998). Overall, parents who live with their biological children show greater declines in marital happiness over time than do married, childless couples, or married couples living with stepchildren (Kurdek, 1999). Of course, some couples remain childless. They are not necessarily unhappy. In fact, especially if they are voluntarily childless, they might be happier than couples with children (Bell & Eisenberg, 1985). This is attributable, in part, to the fact they do not have the stress parents experience from money woes, children's illnesses, loss of sleep, and lack of recreational outlets.

But what of single parents? In the 1960s and 1970s, divorce was the chief cause of single parenting. This has been joined by planned or unplanned childbearing outside of marriage. Though single parents are usually women, one in five is male. Many single parents, given social and financial support, are successful in rearing children. For example, one study of single parents serving in the U.S. military found mothers and fathers readily used social, financial, and organizational resources to balance their family and work obligations (Heath & Orthner, 1999). But according to the U.S. Bureau of the Census, single-parent families, on the average, suffer disadvantages in regard to income, health, and housing conditions. The most disadvantaged are families consisting of children and a never-married mother (Bianchi, 1995).

Middle Adulthood

In 1850 few Americans lived beyond what we now call early adulthood; the average life span was only 40 years (Shneidman, 1987). But improved nutrition, sanitation, and health care have almost doubled that life span. What was the end of the life span more than a century ago is today simply the beginning of middle adulthood. Daniel Levinson (1978) found that during the transition to middle adulthood, men commonly experience a midlife crisis, in which they realize that their life goals will not be achieved or, even if achieved, will seem

generativity versus stagnation

Erikson's developmental stage in which success is achieved by becoming less self-absorbed and more concerned with the well-being of others.

transient in the face of the inevitability of death. Other studies indicate, however, that the midlife crisis is less intense than Levinson found in his research (Fagan & Ayers, 1982).

According to Erik Erikson, the main task of middle adulthood is the resolution of the conflict of **generativity versus stagnation.** Those who achieve generativity become less self-absorbed and more concerned about being a productive worker, spouse, and parent. They are more likely to report having learned lessons from past experiences and to enjoy talking to children or adolescents about life values (Pratt et al., 1999). They also are more satisfied with their lives (McAdams, de St. Aubin, & Logan, 1993). One way of achieving generativity is to serve as a mentor for a younger person, as your college professors may do for many of their students.

Middle adulthood also brings transitions affected by one's parental status. Couples who have children must eventually face the day when their last child leaves home. You might be surprised to learn that parents become more distressed and experience more marital unhappiness after their first child leaves home than after their last child leaves home. In fact, after the last child has left home, parents tend to be relieved and experience improved marital relations (Harris, Elliott, & Holmes, 1986). Perhaps the notion of an "empty nest syndrome" (after the last child has left home) should be replaced by the notion of a "partly empty nest syndrome" (after the first child has left home). Moreover, a growing trend in North America is the "crowded nest," caused by the return home of young adults who find it personally or financially difficult to live on their own (Ward & Spitze, 1996).

Late Adulthood

Now that more people are living into their seventies and beyond, developmental psychologists have become more interested in studying late adulthood. In 1900 only one person in thirty was over 65. By 2020 one person in five will be over 65 (Eisdorfer, 1983). Though this increase in the elderly population will create more concern about physical well-being in old age, it also will create more concern about psychosocial development in old age. Erikson found that the main psychosocial task of late adulthood is to resolve the crisis of **integrity versus despair.** A sense of integrity results from reflecting back on a meaningful life through a "life review." In fact, Erikson claimed pleasurable reminiscing is essential to satisfactory adjustment in old age. This was supported by a study of nursing home residents aged 70 to 88 years. Participants in the experimental group received a visitor who encouraged them to reminisce and engage in a life review. Participants in the control group

integrity versus despair

Erikson's developmental stage in which success is achieved by reflecting back on one's life and finding that it has been meaningful.

received a friendly visit. Participants who engaged in a life review scored higher on a questionnaire that measured their level of ego integrity, as long as 3 years after the intervention (Haight, Michel, & Hendrix, 2000).

And old age is not necessarily a time of physical decay, cognitive deterioration, and social isolation. For many, it is a time of physical activity, continued education, and rewarding social relations. Many elderly adults optimize their cognitive and physical functioning by capitalizing on their strengths and compensating for their weaknesses. For example, they might allot more time to perform tasks, practice old skills, or learn new skills. The use of these strategies by elderly adults has been found to be associated with successful aging, characterized by more positive emotions, enhanced well-being, and less loneliness (Freund & Baltes, 1998).

Eventually, many adults must confront one of the greatest psychosocial challenges of old age—the death of a mate. During the period immediately following the death of their spouse, bereaved spouses are more likely to suffer depression, illness, or death than are their peers with living spouses. This increased morbidity and mortality might stem from the loss of the emotional and practical support previously provided by the now-deceased spouse. One study tested this hypothesis with a sample of recently bereaved spouses. Widowers were more likely to experience greater deterioration in physical and mental health and receive less social support than were widows. However, there was no evidence that the loss of social support reported by widowers mediated this gender difference (Stroebe, Stroebe, & Abakoumkin, 1999). Thus, it is likely that other factors contribute to the poorer health and negative psychological outcomes experienced by bereaved widowers.

Though, as Benjamin Franklin observed, "in this world nothing's certain but death and taxes," we can at least improve the way in which we confront our own mortality. In old age, successful resolution of the crisis of ego integrity versus despair is associated with less fear of death (Goebel & Boeck, 1987). And a survey of 200 adults found that those with strong religious convictions and a greater belief in an afterlife have lower death anxiety (Alvarado et al., 1995).

Prior to the 20th century, death was accepted as a public part of life. People died at home, surrounded and comforted by loved ones. Today, people commonly die alone, in pain, in hospital rooms, attached to life-support systems. One of the most important developments to counter this approach to death and dying is the hospice movement, founded in 1958 by the British physician Cicely Saunders. She was motivated to do so by her colleagues' failure to respond sensitively to dying patients and their families. Hospices provide humane, comprehensive care for the dying patient in a hospital, residential, or home setting, with attention to alleviating the patient's physical, emotional, and spiritual suffering (Saunders, 1996).

What are the psychological experiences of the dying? The person who sparked interest in studying the experiences of dying persons was the Swiss psychiatrist Elisabeth Kübler-Ross (1969). She saw death and suffering as a young adult as she traveled through France and Poland to help victims of World War II and later when she worked as a physician in the United States (Gill, 1980). Based on her observations of dying patients, she identified five stages commonly experienced by terminally ill patients: denial, anger, bargaining, depression, and acceptance. At first, the patients deny their medical diagnoses, then become angry at their plight, bargain with God to let them live, suffer depression at the thought of dying, and finally come to accept their impending death. Kübler-Ross and others, however, have found that not all terminally ill patients go through all the stages or go through them in the same order (Kübler-Ross, 1974). Though flawed by subjective interpretations and unsystematic recording of patients' reactions to terminal illness, her research has inspired others to study the psychology of dying (Corr, 1993).

STAYING ON TRACK: *Adult Development*

1. What is the apparent relationship between caloric intake and aging?
2. What does research indicate about changes in intelligence in old age?
3. How do adults successfully resolve Erikson's conflict involving generativity versus stagnation?

Answers to Staying on Track start on p. ST-2.

(a)

(b)

▲ **Accomplishments in Old Age**

Old age is not necessarily a time of physical and mental deterioration. *(a)* Comedian George Burns (1896–1996) continued to be a popular performer into his nineties. *(b)* Senator John H. Glenn, Jr., one of the first astronauts in the U.S. space program, embarked on a second mission in his seventies.

RESEARCH METHODS IN DEVELOPMENTAL PSYCHOLOGY

- Research designs typical of developmental psychology include longitudinal research and cross-sectional research.

PRENATAL DEVELOPMENT

- The prenatal period is divided into the germinal, embryonic, and fetal stages.
- Cell-adhesion molecules direct the size, shape, and location of organs in the embryo.
- Teratogens can impair prenatal development.
- The consumption of alcohol, a teratogen, during pregnancy is associated with fetal alcohol syndrome.

INFANT AND CHILD DEVELOPMENT

- Childhood extends from birth until puberty.
- The first 2 years of childhood are called infancy.
- Motor development follows a consistent sequence, though the timing of motor milestones varies somewhat among infants.
- Jean Piaget found that children pass through cognitive stages of development.
- During the sensorimotor stage, the infant learns to coordinate sensory experiences and motor behavior, and forms schemas.
- The preoperational stage is marked by egocentrism. In the concrete operational stage, the child learns to make transitive inferences and achieves conservation.
- Erik Erikson believed the life span consists of eight psychosocial stages, each associated with a crisis that must be overcome.
- An important factor in infant development is social attachment, a strong emotional tie to caregivers.
- Permissive and authoritarian child-rearing practices are less effective than authoritative ones.
- Children who receive high-quality day care do not appear to suffer ill effects, though this might not be true of infants.
- Research on the effects of divorce on children has produced inconsistent results, with some studies finding no effects, others finding negative effects, and still others finding positive effects.
- Two influential theories of gender-role development are social learning theory and gender schema theory.
- The most influential theory of moral development has been Lawrence Kohlberg's cognitive-developmental theory, based on Piaget's belief that a person's level of moral development depends on his or her level of cognitive development.
- Kohlberg proposes we pass through preconventional, conventional, and postconventional levels of moral development.
- Carol Gilligan argues Kohlberg's theory is biased toward a male view of morality.
- Research has provided mixed support for Kohlberg and Gilligan's theories.

ADOLESCENT DEVELOPMENT

- Adolescence is a transitional period between childhood and adulthood that begins with puberty.
- In regard to physical development, the adolescent experiences the maturation of primary and secondary sex characteristics.
- In regard to cognitive development, some adolescents enter Piaget's formal operational stage, meaning they can engage in abstract, hypothetical reasoning.
- And, in regard to psychosocial development, Erik Erikson asserted adolescence is a time of identity formation.
- The adolescent also is increasingly influenced by peer values.

GENDER DIFFERENCES AND HUMAN DEVELOPMENT

- Though most psychological gender differences are small to moderate in size, males tend to have better mental rotation and mathematical abilities, especially after adolescence.
- Physiological explanations for psychological gender differences include our evolutionary history and the influence of sex hormones. Social-cultural explanations include social experience and expectations.
- Research on gender differences is controversial, because of fears that its findings might be used to promote and legitimize discrimination.

ADULT DEVELOPMENT

- Adulthood begins when adolescents become independent from their parents.
- In regard to physical development, adults reach their physical peak in their late twenties, at which point they begin a gradual decline that does not accelerate appreciably until old age.
- Middle-aged women experience menopause, which, contrary to popular belief, is rarely a traumatic event.
- In regard to cognitive development, though aging brings some slowing of cognitive processes, people who continue to be mentally active show less cognitive decline than do their peers who do not stay active.
- In regard to psychosocial development, Erik Erikson saw the main task of early adulthood as the establishment of intimacy. About 95 percent of adults marry, but half of the marriages in the United States will end in divorce.
- The most successful marriages are those in which the spouses discuss, rather than avoid, marital issues.
- Erikson saw the main task of middle adulthood as the establishment of a sense of generativity, which is promoted by parenting or mentoring children.
- After the last child leaves home, marital well-being improves.
- Erikson saw the final stage of life as ideally promoting a sense of integrity in reflecting on a life well lived.
- Eventually, all people must face their own mortality.
- The hospice movement, founded by Cicely Saunders, has promoted more humane, personal, and homelike care for the dying patient.
- Elisabeth Kübler-Ross stimulated interest in the study of death and dying.

Key Concepts

developmental psychology 95
maturation 95

Key Contributors

Thought Questions

1. How would you use a longitudinal research design and a cross-sectional research design to study whether college students become more tolerant of ethnic groups that are not their own between their admission to college and their senior year?
2. A child insists on going out to play without first doing his homework. How might parents respond differently in using authoritarian parenting, permissive parenting, and authoritative parenting?

3. What are some of the major physiological and social-cultural factors that contribute to the development of gender differences?
4. How might an adult successfully meet each of the last three conflicts in Erikson's theory of psychosocial development?

Possible Answers to Thought Questions start on p. PT-2.

OLC Preview

 For additional quizzing and a variety of interactive resources, visit the book's Online Learning Center at www.mhhe.com/sdorow5.

Sensation and Perception

GRANT WOOD
Fall Plowing, 1931

"He reached out his hand and took hold of his wife's head, tried to lift it off, to put it on. He had apparently mistaken his wife for a hat!" (Sacks, 1985, p. 10)

This bizarre scene was described in a case study presented in a best-selling book, *The Man Who Mistook His Wife for a Hat,* by neurologist Oliver Sacks. In the book, Sacks used case studies to illustrate the sometimes extraordinary effects of brain damage on human behavior. The man who mistook his wife for a hat, whom Sacks called "Dr. P.," was a talented singer and musician who taught at a music school. But his students began to notice that he could not recognize them from their faces. Yet when they spoke, he identified them immediately. Dr. P. also saw faces where they did not exist. As he strolled down a street, for example, he would kindly pat the tops of water hydrants and parking meters, mistaking them for the heads of children. At first people laughed and thought he was just joking—after all, he was known for his quirky sense of humor.

Did Dr. P. have a problem with his eyes? An eye examination found that he had good vision. Puzzled, the ophthalmologist sent Dr. P. for a neurological examination—to Dr. Sacks. After examining him, Sacks said, "His visual acuity was good: he had no difficulty seeing a pin on the floor" (Sacks, 1985, p. 9). But given that Dr. P. had normal vision, what accounted for his inability to recognize faces? Over time Sacks put the clues together to solve the mystery of Dr. P.'s peculiar problem. On one occasion, when Dr. P. perused an issue of *National Geographic,* he could identify individual details in scenes but not the scenes as a whole. When Sacks asked him to identify photographs of his family members, he could not—though he could identify their facial features. He identified his brother, Paul, based on his unusually large teeth. But Dr. P. did not recognize Paul's face. He simply inferred that it was Paul based on the size of the teeth.

Eventually, Sacks realized that Dr. P. suffered from brain damage (perhaps from an undetected stroke) that produced *visual agnosia* and *prosopagnosia.* In **visual agnosia,** the individual can see objects and identify their features, but cannot recognize them (Heider, 2000). When, for example, Dr. P. was shown a glove, he described it as being continuously curved, but he could not recognize it as a glove—until he put it on and used it. A person with **prosopagnosia** (a form of visual agnosia) can identify details of faces, but cannot recognize them as a whole (de Gelder & Rouw, 2000). Imagine a man with prosopagnosia. He might fail to recognize his wife's face, yet still recognize her voice. Every time they met, she would have to speak so he could identify her.

Prosopagnosia is caused by damage to the association cortex (see Chapter 3) running along the underside of the occipital and temporal lobes of the brain. Visual agnosia and prosopagnosia illustrate the difference between **sensation,** the process that detects stimuli from the environment, and **perception,** the process that organizes sensations into meaningful wholes.

visual agnosia
A condition in which an individual can see objects and identify their features but cannot recognize the objects.

prosopagnosia
A form of visual agnosia in which an individual can identify details of faces but cannot recognize faces as wholes.

sensation
The process that detects stimuli from the body or surroundings.

perception
The process that organizes sensations into meaningful patterns.

♦ SENSORY PROCESSES

The starting point for both processes is a *stimulus* (plural, *stimuli*), a form of energy (such as light waves or sound waves) that can affect sensory organs (such as the eyes or the ears). Visual sensation lets you detect the black marks on this page; visual perception lets you organize the black marks into letters and words. To appreciate the difference between

> ▶ **Figure 5.1**
> **Sensation and Perception**
> Do you see anything in this picture? Though *sensation* lets you see the pattern of light and dark in the picture, *perception* lets you organize what you sense into a meaningful pattern—a cow looking at you.

sensation and perception, try to identify the picture in Figure 5.1. Most people cannot identify it, because they sense the light and dark marks on the page but do not perceive a meaningful pattern.

Sensation depends on specialized cells called **sensory receptors,** which detect stimuli and convert their energy into neural impulses. This process is called **sensory transduction.** Receptors serve our visual, auditory, smell, taste, skin, and body senses. But some animals have receptors that serve unusual senses. The blind cave salamander has electroreceptors that detect electrical fields produced by prey (Schlegel & Roth, 1997). Whales and dolphins navigate by using receptors sensitive to the earth's magnetic field, and disruption of this sense might account for some of the periodic strandings of whales and dolphins on beaches (Weisburd, 1984).

sensory receptors

Specialized cells that detect stimuli and convert their energy into neural impulses.

sensory transduction

The process by which sensory receptors convert stimuli into neural impulses.

Sensory Thresholds

How intense must a sound be for you to detect it? How much change in light intensity must occur for you to notice it? Questions like these are the subject matter of **psychophysics,** the study of the relationship between the physical characteristics of stimuli and the corresponding psychological responses to them. Psychophysics was developed by the German scientists Ernst Weber (1795–1878) and Gustav Fechner (1801–1887). Fechner, after the publication of his classic *Elements of Psychophysics* in 1860, devoted the rest of his life to studying the relationship between physical stimulation and mental experiences. Psychophysics has been used to assess, among other things, the perceived slipperiness of floor tiles (Cohen & Cohen, 1994), gender differences in pain sensitivity (Fillingim, Maddux, & Shackelford, 1999), and the ability of monkeys and baboons to detect changes in the sweetness of sugar solutions (Laska et al., 1999).

psychophysics

The study of the relationship between the physical characteristics of stimuli and the conscious psychological experiences that are associated with them.

Absolute Threshold

The minimum amount of stimulation a person can detect is called the **absolute threshold,** or *limen.* For example, a cup of coffee would require a certain amount of sugar before you could detect a sweet taste. Weber used fine bristles to measure touch sensitivity by bending them against the skin. Because the absolute threshold for a particular sensory experience varies, psychologists operationally define the absolute threshold as the minimum level of stimulation that can be detected 50 percent of the time when a stimulus is presented. Thus, if you were presented with a low-intensity sound 30 times and you detected it 15 times, that

absolute threshold

The minimum amount of stimulation that an individual can detect through a given sense.

◄ The Magnetic Sense
Because whales and dolphins navigate by using receptors sensitive to the earth's magnetic field, disruption of this sense might account for some of the periodic strandings of whales and dolphins on beaches.

level of intensity would be your absolute threshold for that stimulus. The absolute thresholds for certain senses are remarkable. For example, you can detect the sweetness from a teaspoon of sugar dissolved in two gallons of water; the odor of one drop of perfume diffused throughout a three-room apartment; the wing of a bee falling on your cheek from a height of 1 centimeter; the ticking of a watch under quiet conditions at a distance of 20 feet; and the flame of a candle seen from a distance of 30 miles on a clear, dark night (Galanter, 1962). The absolute threshold is used, for example, in testing the ability of hearing-impaired people to detect speech (Nejime & Moore, 1998).

Signal-Detection Theory. The absolute threshold is also affected by factors other than the intensity of the stimulus. Because of this, researchers inspired by Fechner's work have devised **signal-detection theory,** which assumes that the detection of a stimulus depends on both its intensity and the physical and psychological state of the individual. One of the most important psychological factors is *response bias*—how ready the person is to report the presence of a particular stimulus. Imagine you are walking down a street at night. Your predisposition to detect a sound would depend partly on your estimate of the probability of being mugged, so you would be more likely to perceive the sound of footsteps in a neighborhood you believe to be dangerous than in a neighborhood you believe to be safe.

Signal-detection researchers study four kinds of reports a person might make in response to a stimulus. A *hit* is a correct report of the presence of a target stimulus. A *miss* is a failure to report the presence of a target stimulus that is, in fact, present. A *false alarm* is a report of the presence of a target stimulus that is not, in fact, present. And a *correct rejection* is a correct report of the absence of a target stimulus. Consider these four kinds of reports in regard to walking down a dark street at night. A hit would be perceiving footsteps when they actually occur. A miss would be failing to perceive footsteps when they actually occur. A false alarm would be perceiving footsteps when they do not occur. And a correct rejection would be failing to perceive footsteps when they do not occur.

Signal-detection theory has important applications to crucial tasks, such as identifying bombs put through airport X-ray machines. Signal-detection theory has been used to assess drivers' ability to detect an oncoming train by sight and sound as they approach a railroad crossing (Raslear, 1996). Even caregivers' responses to infants' cries can depend on their response biases. In one study, 38 mothers were presented with taped cries of infants they had been told were "easy" or "difficult." In reality, the infants were given these labels randomly. Cries of supposedly "difficult" infants elicited greater detection sensitivity from the mothers (Donovan, Leavitt, & Walsh, 1997).

Subliminal Perception. Research on **subliminal perception** investigates whether participants can unconsciously perceive stimuli that do not exceed the absolute threshold. Nonetheless, some research studies have failed to support the existence of subliminal perception (Fox &

signal-detection theory
The theory holding that the detection of a stimulus depends on both the intensity of the stimulus and the physical and psychological state of the individual.

subliminal perception
The unconscious perception of stimuli that are too weak to exceed the absolute threshold for detection.

Burns, 1993). Assuming that we might be able to perceive subliminal stimuli, could manufacturers make us buy their products by bombarding us with subliminal advertisements? This is the heart of a controversy that arose in the late 1950s after a marketing firm subliminally flashed the words *Eat Popcorn* and *Drink Coca-Cola* during movies shown at a theater in Fort Lee, New Jersey. After several weeks of this subliminal advertising, popcorn sales had increased 50 percent and Coke sales had increased 18 percent (McConnell, Cutter, & McNeil, 1958). Marketing executives expressed glee at this potential boon to advertising, but the public feared that subliminal perception might be used as a means of totalitarian mind control.

Psychologists, however, pointed out that the uncontrolled conditions of the study made it impossible to determine the actual reason for the increase in sales. Perhaps sales increased because better movies, hotter weather, or more appealing counter displays attracted more customers during the period when subliminal advertising was used. Another problem is that the limen varies from trial to trial for each participant. This makes it difficult to assess when stimulation has truly been subliminal (Miller, 1991). Thus, perhaps moviegoers were, at times, consciously aware of the supposedly subliminal messages about Coke and popcorn. Moreover, there is even evidence that the original study might have been a fabrication created by an overeager advertising executive (Pratkanis, 1992). And a recent meta-analysis found that subliminal advertising is ineffective in influencing consumers' product choices (Trappey, 1996).

What of the popular subliminal self-help audiotapes that supposedly help you to improve yourself? Manufacturers of subliminal self-help audiotapes claim they can help listeners do everything from smoke less to improve their study habits. People who listen to these audiotapes typically hear soothing music or nature sounds. Messages (such as "Study harder") presented on audiotapes below the auditory threshold supposedly motivate the listener to improve in the desired area. But consider an experiment that examined the effectiveness of subliminal audiotapes (Greenwald et al., 1991). Participants were 237 adults recruited from a university community. The study used audiotapes that the manufacturers claimed would improve memory or self-esteem. A double-blind technique was used, meaning neither the participants nor the experimenter knew which subliminal messages participants were listening to. The audible portions of the tapes consisted of classical music, popular music, or nature (surf or woodland) sounds. Participants were given tapes with labels indicating either that the tape would improve their memory or that it would improve their self-esteem. Participants listened to the tapes once a day for one month. They then were given memory and self-esteem tests to assess whether they had improved in those areas.

Though there was a tendency for participants to improve in memory and self-esteem, the improvement was not related to the subliminal message on the tape. Regardless of which subliminal message they *actually* listened to, participants' self-reports of improvement tended to reflect the subliminal message they *believed* they had listened to—even if the tapes had been mislabeled. Thus, testimonial reports that subliminal audiotapes are effective might be little more than placebo effects based on participants' expectations of improvement. This finding has been supported by other research studies (Moore, 1995). The topic of subliminal perception is explored in the Thinking Critically About Psychology and the Media feature.

Difference Threshold

In addition to detecting the presence of a stimulus, we must be able to detect changes in its intensity. The minimum amount of change in stimulation that can be detected is called the **difference threshold.** For example, you would have to increase or decrease the intensity of the sound from your CD player a certain amount before you could detect a change in its volume. Like the absolute threshold, the difference threshold for a particular sensory experience varies from person to person and from occasion to occasion. Therefore, psychologists formally define the difference threshold as the minimum change in stimulation that can be detected 50 percent of the time by a given person. The difference threshold has practical applications, as in a study of passengers' perception of differences in the comfort level of automobile rides based on changes in the intensity of vehicle vibrations (Mansfield & Griffin, 2000).

Weber and Fechner referred to the difference threshold as the **just noticeable difference (jnd).** They found the amount of change in intensity of stimulation needed to produce a jnd

difference threshold
The minimum amount of change in stimulation that can be detected.

just noticeable difference (jnd)
Weber and Fechner's term for the difference threshold.

Chapter Five

Can We Be Controlled by Subliminal Messages?

Since the 1950s the media periodically have created alarm by sensationalizing claims that we can be influenced by stimulation that does not exceed the absolute threshold (*subliminal stimulation*). This has provoked fears among citizens and government officials that subliminal stimulation could be used to control people's behavior. Over the years, concern has been raised in the media about subliminal messages presented in movies, on television, on audiotapes, in advertisements, and in rock music recordings. Subliminal stimulation even became part of the 2000 U.S. presidential election when Democrats complained that Republicans had superimposed the subliminal message, *RATS,* over a televised campaign advertisement attacking candidate Al Gore's Medicare plan. Given an unusually close election like that one, might subliminal messages sway enough voters to determine who wins?

As another example, after the John Travolta movie *Phenomenon* was released in 1996, the *Globe* quoted two disc jockeys from Flint, Michigan, as saying that the movie was filled with subliminal messages about Travolta's belief in the religion of Scientology (Baker, 1996). These messages were supposedly conveyed through *backmasking—* the superimposing of a soundtrack backward over a forward one. This controversy even merited attention on the television tabloid show *Extra.* It claimed, for example, that the movie's theme song, "I Have the Touch," sung by Peter Gabriel, includes the words, "Don't you miss Ron?" when played backward. Some took this as a reference to L. Ron Hubbard, the founder of Scientology, and author of *Dianetics,* the book that popularized it.

Parents of teenagers likewise have expressed concerns about the alleged subliminal messages in rock music recordings, such as Led Zeppelin's "Stairway to Heaven," that supposedly can be heard clearly when the recording is played backward. Despite the lack of evidence that such messages exist, fear that they might cause crime, suicide, Satanism, and sexual promiscuity led California and other states to pass laws requiring warnings on recordings that contained subliminal messages. Yet even if recordings (or movies) contain subliminal messages, there is no evidence that listeners will *obey* them like zombies any more than they will obey messages they are aware of (Vokey & Read, 1985). That is, subliminal *stimulation* should not be confused with subliminal *persuasion.*

◀ **Subliminal Perception**

In the 1960s certain songs by Bob Dylan and the Beatles supposedly contained subliminal messages. Opponents of rock music even warn that "Stairway to Heaven" by Led Zeppelin contains satanic subliminal messages that can be detected if the song is played backward. But virtually any song will have combinations of sounds that, when played backward, could be interpreted as satanic, sexual, or violent lyrics—especially if you are told what to listen for.

is a constant fraction of the original stimulus. This became known as **Weber's law** (Droesler, 2000). For example, because the jnd for weight is about 2 percent, if you held a 50-ounce weight you would notice a change only if there was at least a 1-ounce change in it. But a person holding a 100-ounce weight would require the addition or subtraction of at least 2 ounces to notice a change. Research indicates that Weber's law holds better for stimuli of moderate intensity than for stimuli of extremely low or high intensity.

Sensory Adaptation

Given that each of your senses is constantly bombarded by stimulation, why do you notice only certain stimuli? One reason is that if a stimulus remains constant in intensity, you will gradually stop noticing it. For example, on entering a friend's dormitory room, you might be struck by the repugnant stench of month-old garbage. A few minutes later, though, you might not notice it at all. This tendency of sensory receptors to respond less and less to an unchanging stimulus is called **sensory adaptation.**

Sensory adaptation lets us detect potentially important changes in our environment while ignoring unchanging aspects of it. For example, when vibrations repeatedly stimulate your skin, you stop noticing them (Hollins, Delemos, & Goble, 1991); and once you have determined that the swimming pool water is cold, it would serve little purpose to continue noticing it—especially when more important changes might be taking place elsewhere in your surroundings. Of course, you will not adapt completely to extremely intense sensations, such as severe pain or freezing cold. This is adaptive, because to ignore such stimuli might be harmful or even fatal.

STAYING ON TRACK: *Sensory Processes*

1. What is the difference between sensation and perception?
2. What is psychophysics?
3. What is sensory adaptation?

Answers to Staying on Track start on p. ST-2.

◆ VISUAL SENSATION

Because of our reliance on vision, psychologists have conducted more research on it than on all the other senses combined. **Vision** lets us sense objects by the light reflected from them into our eyes.

Light Waves

Light is the common name for the **visible spectrum,** a narrow band of energy within the *electromagnetic spectrum* (depicted in Figure 5.2). The wavelength of light corresponds to its *hue,* the perceptual quality that we call color. The wavelength is the distance between two

▶ **Figure 5.2**
The Visible Spectrum

The human eye is sensitive to only a narrow slice of the electromagnetic spectrum. This visible spectrum appears in rainbows, when sunlight is broken into its component colors as it passes through raindrops in the atmosphere.

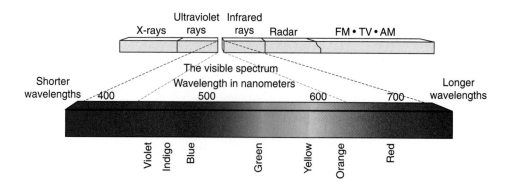

wave peaks, measured in nanometers (billionths of a meter). Visible light varies in wavelength from about 380 nanometers to about 760 nanometers. A light composed of short wavelengths of light appears violet; a light composed of long wavelengths appears red.

Though human beings have visual receptors that sense only the visible spectrum, certain animals have visual receptors that detect other forms of electromagnetic energy. Some fish and insects, as well as birds such as zebra finches (Bennett et al., 1996), have visual receptors that are sensitive to the relatively short wavelengths of *ultraviolet light,* which affects human beings chiefly by causing sunburn. Pythons have receptors located in pits below their eyes that are sensitive to the relatively long wavelengths of *infrared light,* which conveys heat. This lets pythons hunt at night by detecting the heat emitted by nearby prey (Grace et al., 2001). Police and soldiers sometimes use special infrared scopes and goggles to provide vision in the dark (Rabin & Wiley, 1994).

Returning to the visible spectrum, the height, or *amplitude,* of light waves determines the perceived intensity, or *brightness,* of a light. When you use a dimmer switch to adjust the brightness of a lightbulb, you change the amplitude of the light waves emitted by it. The purity of a light's wavelengths determines its *saturation,* or vividness. The narrower the range of wavelengths, the more saturated the light. A highly saturated red light, for example, would seem "redder" than a less saturated one.

Vision and the Eye

Vision depends on the interaction of the eyes and the brain. The eyes sense light reflected from objects and convey this information to the brain, where visual perception takes place. But what accounts for this? The eye (see Figure 5.3) is a fluid-filled sphere. The "white" of your eye is a tough membrane called the **sclera,** which protects the eye from injury. At the front of the sclera is the round, transparent **cornea,** which focuses light into the eye. Are you blue-eyed? brown-eyed? green-eyed? Your eye color is determined by the color of your **iris,** a donut-shaped band of muscles behind the cornea. At the center of the iris is an opening called the **pupil.** The iris controls the amount of light that enters the eye by regulating the size of the pupil, dilating it to let in more light and constricting it to let in less. Your pupils dilate when you enter a dimly lit room and constrict when you go outside into sunlight.

You can demonstrate the pupillary response to light by first noting the size of your pupils in your bathroom mirror. Next turn out the light for 30 seconds. Then turn on the light and look in the mirror. Notice how much larger your pupils have become and how quickly they constrict in response to the light.

sclera
The tough, white outer membrane of the eye.

cornea
The round, transparent area in the front of the sclera that allows light to enter the eye.

iris
The donut-shaped band of muscles behind the cornea that gives the eye its color and controls the size of the pupil.

pupil
The opening at the center of the iris that controls how much light enters the eye.

◀ **Figure 5.3**
The Human Eye

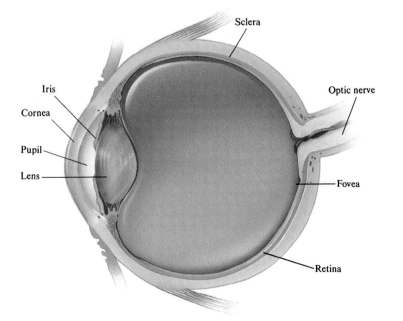

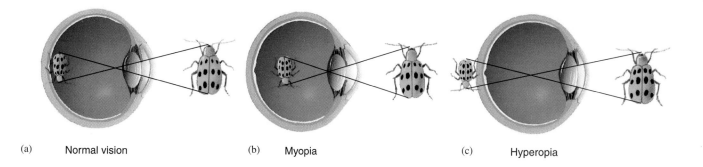

| (a) Normal vision | (b) Myopia | (c) Hyperopia |

▲ **Figure 5.4**
Visual Acuity
In normal vision, the lens focuses images on the retina. In myopia, the lens focuses images in front of the retina. In hyperopia, the lens focuses images at a point that would fall behind the retina.

lens
The transparent structure behind the pupil that focuses light onto the retina.

retina
The light-sensitive inner membrane of the eye that contains the receptor cells for vision.

accommodation
The process by which the lens of the eye increases its curvature to focus light from close objects or decreases its curvature to focus light from more distant objects.

myopia
Visual nearsightedness, which is caused by an elongated eyeball.

hyperopia
Visual farsightedness, which is caused by a shortened eyeball.

rods
Receptor cells of the retina that play an important role in night vision and peripheral vision.

cones
Receptor cells of the retina that play an important role in daylight vision and color vision.

The size of the pupil is also affected by a variety of psychological factors. When we are psychologically aroused, the sympathetic nervous system makes our pupils dilate. For example, the pupil dilates in response to painful stimulation (Oka, Chapman, & Jacobson, 2000) and to an increase in noise (Chapman et al., 1999). Regardless of the psychological phenomena associated with the pupil, its primary function is to regulate the amount of light that enters the eye. After passing through the pupil, light is focused by the **lens** onto the **retina,** the light-sensitive inner membrane of the eye. Tiny muscles connected to the lens control **accommodation,** the process by which the lens increases its curvature to focus light from close objects or decreases its curvature to focus light from more distant objects.

Today we know the image cast on the retina is upside down. This is illustrated in Figure 5.4. In the 15th century, Leonardo da Vinci (1452–1519) had rejected this possibility, because he could not explain how the brain saw a right-side-up world from an upside-down image. Why, then, do we not see the world upside down? The neural pathways in the brain simply "flip" the image to make it appear right side up.

Disruption of normal accommodation has important effects. As we age, the lens loses its elasticity, making it less able to accommodate when focusing on near objects. Adults typically discover this in their early forties, when they find themselves holding books and newspapers at arm's length to focus the print more clearly on their retinas. Many people, whether young or old, have conditions that make them unable to focus clear images on the retina. The two most common conditions are illustrated in Figure 5.4. In **myopia,** or *nearsightedness,* the lens focuses images of near objects on the retina, but focuses images of far objects at a point in front of the retina. In **hyperopia,** or *farsightedness,* the lens focuses images of far objects on the retina, but focuses images of near objects at a point that would fall behind the retina. Both of these conditions are easily corrected with prescription eyeglasses or contact lenses.

The Retina

As shown in Figure 5.5, the retina contains cells called *photoreceptors,* which respond when stimulated by light. There are two kinds of photoreceptors, **rods** and **cones,** whose names reflect their shapes. Each eye has about 120 million rods and about 6 million cones. The rods and cones stimulate *bipolar cells,* which in turn stimulate *ganglion cells.* The axons of the ganglion cells form the **optic nerves,** which convey visual information to the brain.

The rods are especially important in night vision and peripheral vision; the cones are especially important in color vision and detailed vision. Rod vision and cone vision depend on different pathways in the brain (Hadjikhani & Tootell, 2000). The rods are more prevalent in the periphery of the retina, and the cones are more prevalent in the center. You can demonstrate this for yourself by taking small pieces of colored paper and selecting one without looking at it. Hold it beside your head, and slowly move it forward while staring straight ahead. Because your peripheral vision depends on your rods and your color vision depends on your cones, you will notice the paper before you can identify its color. Peripheral vision has survival value. For example, we rely on it to help avoid traffic hazards when crossing a street.

A small area in the center of the retina, the **fovea,** contains only cones. One reason people differ in their visual acuity is that they vary in the number of foveal cones (Curcio et al., 1987). Because the fovea provides our most acute vision, we try to focus images on it when

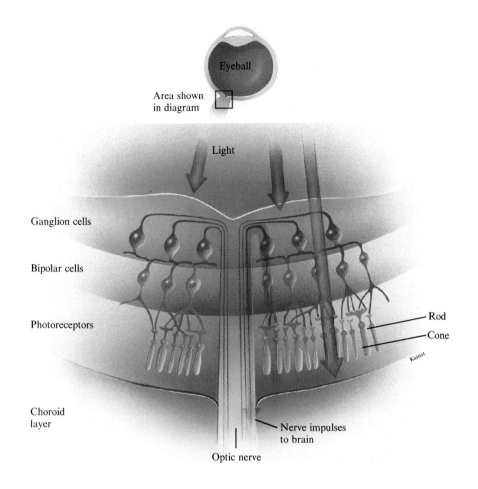

◀ **Figure 5.5**
The Cells of the Retina
Light must first pass through layers of
ganglion cells and bipolar cells before
striking the rods and cones. Neural
impulses from the rods and cones are
transmitted to the bipolar cells, which,
in turn, transmit neural impulses to the
ganglion cells. The axons of the ganglion
cells form the optic nerves, which transmit
neural impulses to the brain.

we want to see fine details. As you read this sentence, words focused on your cone-rich fovea look clear. Meanwhile, words focused on the cone-poor area around your fovea look blurred. One reason foveal vision is more acute is that each cone transmits neural impulses to one bipolar cell. This means that the exact retinal site of input from a given rod is communicated along the visual pathway. In contrast, neural impulses from an average of 50 rods are sent to a given bipolar cell (Cicerone & Hayhoe, 1990). Thus, the exact retinal site of stimulation of a given rod is lost. But in dim light the many rods sending their output to a given bipolar cell help make rod vision more sensitive than cone vision.

A ganglion cell might receive input from many rods and cones in a given area of the retina. The area of the retina that feeds input to a ganglion cell is called its *receptor field.* Some ganglion cells increase their activity when light strikes inside the relevant receptor field and reduce their activity when light strikes outside it. Other ganglion cells increase their firing when light strikes outside the relevant receptor field and reduce their activity when light strikes inside it. This makes the brain especially responsive to differences in adjacent lighter and darker areas, helping it distinguish one object from another by emphasizing their borders.

The retinal images of the words you read, or of any object on which your eyes are focused, are coded as neural impulses sent to the brain along the optic nerves. In the 17th century, French scientist Edmé Mariotte demonstrated the existence of the *blind spot,* the point at which the optic nerve leaves the eye (Riggs, 1985). He placed a small disk on a screen, closed one eye, stared at the disk, and moved his head until the image of the disk disappeared. It disappeared when it fell on the blind spot. The blind spot is "blind" because it contains no rods or cones. We do not normally notice the blind spot because the visual system fills in the missing area (Tripathy et al., 1995). To repeat Mariotte's demonstration, follow the procedure suggested in Figure 5.6.

optic nerve
The nerve, formed from the axons of ganglion cells, that carries visual impulses from the retina to the brain.

fovea
A small area at the center of the retina that contains only cones and provides the most acute vision.

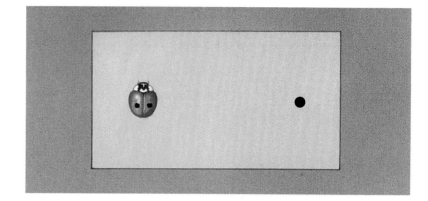

Figure 5.6
Finding Your Blind Spot

Because your retina has no rods or cones at the point where the optic nerve leaves the eye, your retina is "blind" at that spot. To find your blind spot, hold this book at arm's length, close your right eye, and focus your left eye on the black dot. Move the book slowly toward you. When the book is about a foot away, the image of the ladybug should disappear. It disappears when it becomes focused on your blind spot. You do not normally notice your blind spot because your eyes see different views of the same scene, your eyes are constantly focusing on different parts of the scene, and your brain fills in missing details of the scene.

smooth pursuit movements
Eye movements that track objects.

optic chiasm
The point under the frontal lobes at which some axons from each of the optic nerves cross over to the opposite side of the brain.

Eye Movements

We use **smooth pursuit movements** to keep moving objects focused on the foveae. One of the dangers of drinking and driving is that alcohol disrupts the ocular muscles, which control smooth pursuit movements (Freivalds & Horii, 1994). The Psychology Versus Common Sense feature illustrates how scientists studied these movements in testing everyday commonsense beliefs about hitting a baseball.

Vision and the Brain

Figure 5.7 traces the path of neural impulses from the eyeballs into the brain. The optic nerves travel under the frontal lobes of the brain and meet at a point called the **optic chiasm.** At the optic chiasm in human beings, axons from the half of each optic nerve toward the nose cross to the opposite side of the brain. Axons from the half of each optic nerve nearer the ears travel to the same side of the brain as they began on. Some axons of the optic nerves go to the specialized neurons in the brain that control visual reflexes like blinking. Most

Figure 5.7
The Visual Pathway

Images of objects in the right visual field are focused on the left side of each retina, and images of objects in the left visual field are focused on the right side of each retina. This information is conveyed along the optic nerves to the optic chiasm and then on to the thalamus. The thalamus then relays the information to the visual cortex of the occipital lobes. Note that images of objects in the right visual field are processed by the left occipital lobe and images of objects in the left visual field are processed by the right occipital lobe.

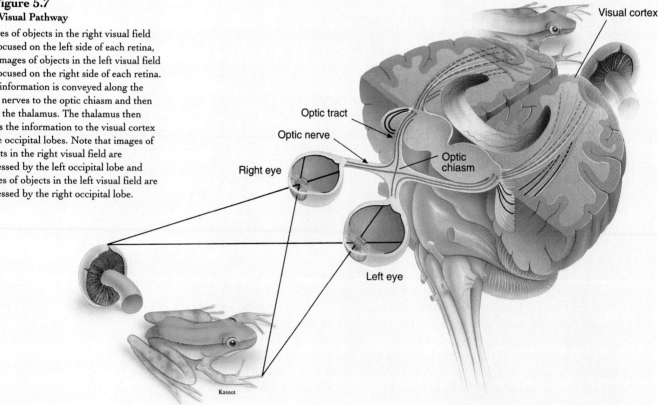

Can Baseball Batters Really Keep Their Eyes on the Ball?

Professional athletes make faster smooth-pursuit eye movements than amateurs do (Harbin, Durst, & Harbin, 1989). This is important because, for example, a professional baseball batter might have to track a baseball thrown by a pitcher at more than 90 miles an hour from a distance of only 60 feet. Ted Williams, arguably the greatest hitter in the history of baseball, called hitting a baseball the most difficult single task in any sport. Given this, is there any scientific support for the commonsense suggestion to batters, "Keep your eye on the ball"? Let's look at a study by Terry Bahill and Tom LaRitz (1984), of the University of Arizona, in which they sought the answer to this question. Bahill and LaRitz rigged a device that propelled a ball toward home plate along a string at up to 100 miles an hour on a consistent path. A photoelectric device recorded the batter's eye movements as he tracked the ball. Several professional baseball players took part in the study.

Eye-movement recordings indicated the batters were able to track the ball until it was about 5 feet from home plate. Over the last few feet they could not keep the ball focused on their foveae—it simply traveled too fast over those last few degrees of visual arc. Thus, the commonsense advice to keep your eye on the ball is well intentioned, but it is impossible to follow the ball's movement all the way from the pitcher's hand to home plate. The reason some hitters, including Ted Williams, claim they can see the ball strike the bat is that, based on their extensive experience in batting, their brains automatically calculate both the speed and the trajectory of the ball. This allows them to anticipate the point in space where the bat will meet the ball, and make a final eye movement to that exact point. Years later Bahill likewise presented research evidence contradicting the commonsense belief that fastballs can "rise" (Bahill & Karnavas, 1993). To baseball players, as well as other people, "seeing is believing." Nonetheless, scientists insist that objective evidence from research is superior to common sense as a source of knowledge.

◀ **Keeping Your Eye on the Ball**

The commonsense idea that batters can "keep their eye on the ball" is not supported by research. Professional hitters, such as Sammy Sosa, anticipate the point in space where the bat will meet the ball and make a final eye movement to that point.

---

axons of the optic nerves go to the *thalamus* (see Chapter 3), which transmits visual information to the **visual cortex** of the *occipital lobes*. Retinal information about objects in the right visual field is processed in the left occipital lobe, and retinal information about objects in the left visual field is processed in the right occipital lobe. The visual cortex integrates visual information about objects, including their shape (Buechel et al., 1998) and distance (Dobbins et al., 1998), as well as their color (Engel, 1999), brightness (Rossi, Rittenhouse, & Paradiso, 1996), and movement (Moore & Engel, 1999).

Because the visual cortex is covered by a "map" with a point-by-point representation of the retinas, people who have gone blind because of damage to their eyes or optic nerves might someday have their vision restored by devices that directly stimulate the visual cortex. Researchers have invented an electronic system that consists of a video camera connected to a microprocessor, which in turn is connected to a matrix of electrodes attached to the visual cortex. Stimulation of these electrodes produces a pattern of spots of light called *phosphenes* that can be used to represent the outlines of objects seen by the camera. In one

visual cortex
The area of the occipital lobes that processes visual input.

experiment, people with normal vision were able to negotiate around walls and objects in a maze using this system (Cha, Horch, & Normann, 1992). Perhaps more sophisticated devices will one day permit blind people to use prosthetic vision to read textbooks, paint pictures, and drive automobiles.

Basic Visual Processes

People with normal vision can see because of processes taking place in their retinas. Visual sensations depend on chemicals called **photopigments.** Rod vision depends on the photopigment *rhodopsin,* and cone vision depends on three kinds of photopigments called *iodopsin.* Until the late 19th century, when the role of photopigments was first discovered, prominent scientists, including Thomas Young, claimed vision depended on light rays striking the retina, making the optic nerves vibrate (Riggs, 1985).

Today we know that when light strikes the rods or cones it breaks down their photopigments. This breakdown begins the process by which neural impulses are eventually sent along the optic nerves to the brain. After being broken down by light, the photopigments are resynthesized—more rapidly in dim light than in bright light. The cones function better than the rods in normal light, but the rods function better than the cones in dim light. Because of this, in normal light we try to focus fine details on the fovea. But if you were to look directly at a star in the night sky, you would be unable to see it because it would be focused on the fovea. To see the star, you would have to turn your head slightly, thereby focusing the star on the rod-rich periphery of the retina. The photoreceptors are also important in the processes of *dark adaptation* and *color vision.*

Dark Adaptation

When you enter a darkened movie theater, you have difficulty finding a seat because your photoreceptors have been bleached of their photopigments by the light in the lobby. But your eyes adapt by increasing their rate of synthesis of iodopsin and rhodopsin, gradually increasing your ability to see the seats and people in the theater. The cones reach their maximum sensitivity after about 10 minutes of dim light. But your rods continue to adapt to the dim light, reaching their maximum sensitivity in about 30 minutes. So, you owe your ability to see in dim light to your rods. **Dark adaptation** is the process by which the eyes become more sensitive to light. Impaired dark adaptation, which accompanies aging (Jackson, Owsley, & McGwin, 1999), has been implicated in the disproportionate number of nighttime driving accidents that involve older adults. Dark adaptation also explains why motorists should dim their high beams when approaching oncoming traffic and why passengers should not turn on the dome light to read maps. High beams shining into the eyes or dome lights illuminating the inside of the vehicle bleach the rods, impairing the driver's ability to the see objects that might be ahead. You should also note that the cones are most sensitive to the longer wavelengths of the visible spectrum (which produce the experience of red) and the rods are most sensitive to the medium wavelengths (which produce the experience of green). This explains why at dusk (when we shift from cone vision to rod vision) a red jacket looks dull while a patch of green grass looks vibrant.

Color Vision

Color enhances the quality of our lives, as manifested by our concern with the colors of our clothing, furnishings, and automobiles. Color also contributes to our survival, as exemplified by the orange or yellow life rafts used at sea that make search and rescue easier (Donderi, 1994). Primates such as apes, monkeys, and human beings have good color vision. Most other mammals, including dogs, cats, and cows, have poor color vision. They lack a sufficient number or variety of cones. Most birds and fish have good color vision. But fish that live in the dark depths of the ocean lack color vision, which would be useless to them because cones function well only in bright light (Levine & MacNichol, 1982).

Theories of Color Vision. What processes account for color vision? One answer was offered in 1802 when British physicist Thomas Young presented the **trichromatic theory** of color vision, which was championed in the 1850s by German scientist Hermann von Helmholtz

photopigments
Chemicals, including rhodopsin and iodopsin, that enable the rods and cones to generate neural impulses.

dark adaptation
The process by which the eyes become more sensitive to light when under low illumination.

trichromatic theory
The theory that color vision depends on the relative degree of stimulation of red, green, and blue receptors.

▲ A *Green* Fire Truck?
Because the rods are more sensitive to the green region of the visible spectrum than to the red region, green objects look brighter in dim light than do red objects. So, though red fire trucks look bright in the daylight, they look grayish in dim light. This has led some fire departments to increase the evening visibility of their trucks by painting them a yellowish green color.

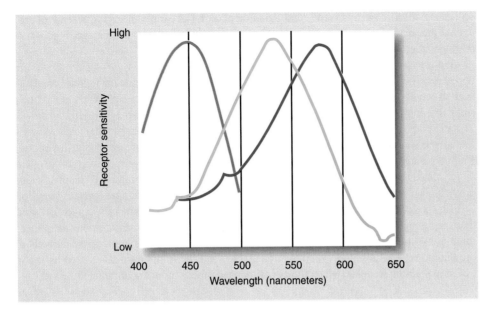

◀ **Figure 5.8**
Relative Sensitivity of the Cones

Each of the three kinds of cones (blue, green, and red) responds to a wide range of wavelengths of light. But each is maximally sensitive to particular wavelengths. The blue cones are maximally sensitive to short wavelengths, the green cones to medium wavelengths, and the red cones to long wavelengths. According to trichromatic theory, the perceived color of a light depends on the relative amount of activity in each of the three kinds of cones.

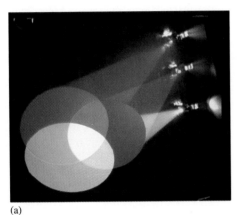

(a)

(b)

◀ **Figure 5.9**
Color Mixing

In additive mixing, lights of different colors are combined. As you can see, (a) mixing red, green, and blue lights of equal intensity yields white. In subtractive mixing, pigments of different colors are combined. Because each color absorbs certain wavelengths of light, (b) mixing red, yellow, and blue pigments of equal intensity yields black.

(1821–1894). Young and Helmholtz found that red, green, and blue lights could be mixed into any color, leading them to conclude that the brain pools the input of three receptors. Today the trichromatic theory is also called the *Young-Helmholtz theory*. It assumes that the retina has three kinds of receptors (which we now know are cones), each of which is maximally sensitive to red, green, or blue light (Chichilnisky & Wandell, 1999).

A century after Helmholtz put forth his theory, George Wald (1964) provided evidence for it in research that earned him a Nobel Prize. Wald found that some cones respond maximally to red light, others to green light, and still others to blue light (see Figure 5.8). The colors we experience depend on the relative degree of stimulation of the cones. Figure 5.9 illustrates the principles of mixing colored lights and mixing colored pigments, which differ from each other. Mixing colored lights is an additive process: Wavelengths added together stimulate more cones. For example, mixing red light and green light produces yellow. Mixing pigments is a subtractive process: Pigments mixed together absorb more wavelengths than does a single pigment. For example, mixing blue paint and yellow paint subtracts those colors and leaves green to be reflected into the eyes. More recent research has lent support to the trichromatic theory (Jacobs et al., 1996).

In the 1870s, German physiologist Ewald Hering (1834–1918) proposed an alternative explanation of color vision, **opponent-process theory.** He did so, in part, to explain the phenomenon of **color afterimages**—images that persist after the removal of a visual stimulus. If you stare at a red or blue surface for a minute and then stare at a white surface, you

opponent-process theory
The theory that color vision depends on red-green, blue-yellow, and black-white opponent processes in the brain.

color afterimage
A visual image that persists after the removal of a visual stimulus.

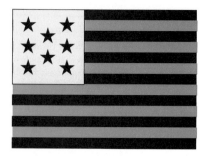

▲ **Figure 5.10**
Color Afterimages

If you stare at this image for a minute and then stare at a white surface, you will see an afterimage in which the flag appears in familiar colors-red, white, and blue.

color blindness

The inability to distinguish between certain colors, most often red and green.

sex-linked traits

Traits controlled by genes located on the sex chromosomes.

will see an afterimage that is the complementary color. For example, staring at red will produce a green afterimage, and staring at blue will produce a yellow afterimage. See Figure 5.10 for a demonstration of an afterimage.

Opponent-process theory assumes that there are *red-green, blue-yellow,* and *black-white* opponent processes (with the black-white opponent process determining the lightness or darkness of what we see). Stimulation of one process inhibits its opponent. When stimulation stops, the inhibition is removed and the complementary color is seen as a brief afterimage. This explains why staring at red leads to a green afterimage and staring at blue leads to a yellow afterimage. It also explains why we cannot perceive reddish greens or bluish yellows: Complementary colors cannot be experienced simultaneously because each inhibits the other.

Psychologist Russell de Valois and his colleagues (de Valois, Abramov, & Jacobs, 1966) provided evidence that supports opponent-process theory. For example, certain ganglion cells in the retina and certain cells in the thalamus send impulses when the cones that send them input are stimulated by red and stop sending impulses when the cones that send them input are stimulated by the complementary color, green. Other ganglion cells and cells in the thalamus send impulses when the cones that send them input are stimulated by green and stop sending impulses when the cones that send them input are stimulated by red.

Color Deficiency. Opponent-process theory also explains another phenomenon that the trichromatic theory cannot explain by itself: **color blindness.** People with normal color vision are *trichromats*—they have three kinds of iodopsin (red, blue, and green). Most color-blind people are *dichromats*—they have a normal number of cones but lack one kind of iodopsin (Shevell & He, 1997). The most common form of color blindness is the inability to distinguish between red and green. People with red-green color blindness have cones with blue iodopsin, but their red and green cones have the same iodopsin, usually green. Because many people suffer from red-green color blindness, traffic lights always have the red light on top so that color-blind people will know when to stop and when to go. Figure 5.11 presents an example of one of the ways of testing for color blindness, the Ishihara color test (Birch, 1997).

Color blindness is a *sex-linked trait.* Genes on the sex chromosomes control the expression of **sex-linked traits.** Because color blindness is a recessive trait carried on the X (female) chromosome, men are more likely than women to be color blind. For traits carried on the X chromosome, a woman would inherit two genes (one on each X chromosome) controlling the trait. Men, because they have only one X chromosome, inherit a single gene controlling the trait. This is because the Y (male) chromosome is small relative to the X chromosome, and lacks the gene controlling this trait. A woman must inherit two recessive genes to be color blind. If a man inherits only one recessive gene on his single X chromosome, he will be color blind. Few dichromats have blue-yellow color blindness. And even fewer people are *monochromats*—completely color blind.

▶ **Figure 5.11**
Color Deficiency

A person with red-green color blindness would not be able to read the number (9) contained in this design.

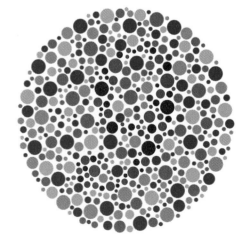

Chapter Five

But how does color blindness support opponent-process theory? It does so because, though dichromats cannot distinguish between the complementary colors of red and green or blue and yellow, they never fail to distinguish between red and blue, red and yellow, green and blue, or green and yellow. Today trichromatic theory and opponent-process theory are combined in explaining color vision this way (Boynton, 1988): Impulses from the red, green, and blue cones of the retina are sent to the opponent-process ganglion cells and then further integrated in the thalamus and visual cortex.

◆ VISUAL PERCEPTION

Visual sensations provide the raw materials that are organized into meaningful patterns by *visual perception.* Do we have to learn through experience to convert sensations into accurate perceptions? This is the basic assumption of the *constructionist theory* of Hermann von Helmholtz. Or, instead, does visual perception depend mainly on inborn mechanisms that automatically convert sensations into perceptions of stimuli? This is the basic assumption of the *direct perception theory* of James J. Gibson (1904–1979). According to Gibson (1979), evolution has endowed us with brain mechanisms that create perceptions directly from information provided by the sense organs. Thus, we do not need to rely on experience to help us perceive this information properly (Nakayama, 1994). Recent research, discussed in Chapter 4, on the sophisticated inborn perceptual abilities of newborn infants supports Gibson's theory. But most perception researchers believe that we "construct" our perceptions based on what Helmholtz called *unconscious inferences* that we make from our sensations (Cutting, 1987). These inferences are based on our experience with objects in the physical environment.

The Max Wertheimer Page
www.mhhe.com/sdorow5

Form Perception

To perceive *forms* (meaningful shapes or patterns), we typically must distinguish a *figure* (an object) from its *ground* (its surroundings), though there is some evidence that form perception can precede the segmentation into figure and ground (Peterson & Gibson, 1994).

figure-ground perception
The distinguishing of an object (the figure) from its surroundings (the ground).

Figure-Ground Perception

Research on the monkey visual cortex has found cells that respond more to a stimulus when it is perceived as a figure than to a stimulus when it is perceived as a ground (Lamme, 1995). Gestalt psychologist Edgar Rubin (1886–1951) called this **figure-ground perception.** For example, the words on this page are figures against the ground of the white paper. Gestalt psychologists stress that form perception is an active, rather than a passive, process. Your expectancies might affect what you see in an ambiguous figure, for example. If you were first shown pictures of pottery and were then shown Figure 5.12, you would be more likely to perceive a vase; if you were first shown pictures of faces, you would be more likely to perceive two profiles. The idea that our expectations impose themselves on sensations to form perceptions (so-called *top-down processing*) runs counter to the idea that we construct our perceptions strictly by mechanically combining sensations (so-called *bottom-up* processing). In fact, participants do not spontaneously reverse ambiguous figures. They must have experience with reversible figures or be informed that the figures are reversible before they will reverse them (Rock, Gopnik, & Hall, 1994). There is evidence that top-down and bottom-up processes interact in producing figure-ground perception (Vecera & O'Reilly, 1998).

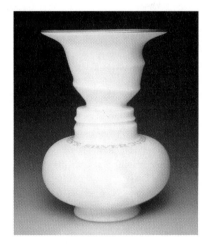

▲ **Figure 5.12**
Figure-Ground Perception

As you view this picture you will note that it seems to reverse. At one moment you see a vase, and at the next you see the profiles of two faces. What you see depends on what you perceive as figure and what you perceive as ground.

Gestalt Principles

Gestalt psychologists, including Max Wertheimer, Kurt Koffka, and Wolfgang Köhler, were the first to study the principles that govern form perception. Research has shown that these principles are more relevant to perceiving complex figures (Gillam, 1992). The principle of *proximity* states that stimuli that are close together tend to be perceived as parts of the same form. The principle of *closure* states that we tend to fill in gaps in forms. The principle of *similarity* states that stimuli similar to one another tend to be perceived as parts of the same

Gestalt Principles of Form Perception
These patterns illustrate the roles of
(a) closure, *(b)* proximity, *(c)* similarity,
and *(d)* continuity in form perception.

(a)

(b)

(c)

(d)

feature-detector theory

The theory that we construct
perceptions of stimuli from activity in
neurons of the brain that are sensitive
to specific features of those stimuli.

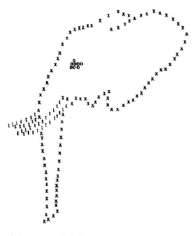

▲ **Figure 5.14**
**The Whole Is Different from the
Sum of Its Parts**

According to Gestalt psychologists, you
see a picture of an elephant instead of a
random grouping of marks because your
brain imposes organization on what it
perceives. Your perception of the elephant
depends on each of the Gestalt principles
of similarity, proximity, closure, and
continuity. As discussed later in this
chapter, your perception of the elephant
also depends on your prior experience.
A person from a culture unfamiliar with
elephants might fail to perceive the marks
as a meaningful form.

form. And the principle of *continuity* states that we tend to group stimuli into forms that follow continuous lines or patterns. These principles are illustrated in Figure 5.13. The principles only recently have been subjected to experimental research, with initial support for the role of similarity, continuity, and proximity in grouping stimuli into coherent patterns (Alais & Blake, 1999; Han, Humphreys, & Chan, 1999).

According to Gestalt psychologists, forms are perceived as wholes, rather than as combinations of features (Westheimer, 1999). This might prompt you to recall the famous Gestalt saying, mentioned in Chapter 1, that "the whole is different from the sum of its parts." Thus, in Figure 5.14 you see an image of an elephant rather than a bunch of black marks. To a Gestalt psychologist, you see a picture of an elephant instead of a random grouping of black marks (bottom-up processing) because your brain, based on your experience seeing real elephants and pictures of elephants, imposes organization on what it perceives (top-down processing). A person who has never seen a picture of an elephant might fail to perceive the marks as a meaningful form. How does your perception of the elephant depend on each of the Gestalt principles of similarity, proximity, closure, and continuity?

Feature Analysis

Though some research findings support the Gestalt position that forms are perceived holistically (Navon, 1974), other research findings suggest forms can be perceived through the analysis of their features (Oden, 1984). Consider the letter *A*. Do we perceive it holistically as a single form, or analytically as a combination of lines of various lengths and angles? Gestalt psychologists would assume we perceive it holistically. But the **feature-detector theory** of David Hubel and Torsten Wiesel (1979) assumes we construct it from its components. Hubel and Wiesel base their theory on studies in which they implanted microelectrodes into single

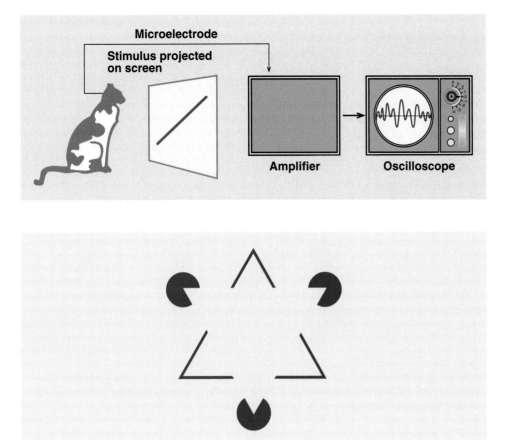

◀ **Figure 5.15**
Feature Detectors
David Hubel and Torsten Wiesel
implanted microelectrodes in the
visual cortex of cats. They found that
specific cells responded to lines with
certain features, such as being tilted at
a particular angle. An oscilloscope
displayed increases in the activity of
these "feature-detector" cells.

◀ **Figure 5.16**
Illusory Contours
Seeing a complete triangle when only its
corners exist is an example of the Gestalt
principle of closure. Feature-detector cells
in the visual cortex respond to such illusory contours as if they were real. This
supports the Gestalt position that the brain
imposes organization on stimuli.

cells of the visual cortex of cats and then presented them with lines of various sizes, orientations, and locations. Certain cells responded to specific features of images on the retina,
such as a line of a certain length, a line at a certain angle, or a line in a particular location.
Hubel and Wiesel concluded that we construct our visual perceptions from activity in such
feature-detector cells. For their efforts, Hubel and Wiesel won a Nobel Prize in 1981. More
recent studies indicate that whereas some *feature-detector cells* respond to component features of forms, others respond to whole forms (Wenderoth, 1994). Other neurons combine
input from feature detectors into more complex patterns such as letters, faces, or objects.
Figure 5.15 illustrates Hubel and Wiesel's procedure for identifying feature-detector cells
in the visual cortex.

Some feature-detector cells in the visual cortex respond to remarkably specific combinations of features. Different cells in the visual cortex of sheep respond to the faces of
sheep, sheepdogs, or human beings (Kendrick & Baldwin, 1987). Feature-detector cells
in the visual cortex even provide an anatomical basis for the illusory contours shown in
Figure 5.16, responding to nonexistent contours as if they were the edges of real objects
(Purghe & Coren, 1992).

Depth Perception

If we lived in a two-dimensional world, form perception would be sufficient. Because we
live in a three-dimensional world, we have evolved **depth perception**—the ability to judge
the distance of objects. Given that images on the retina (such as the image of a helicopter
landing pad) are two-dimensional, how can we perceive depth? That is, how can we determine the distance of an object (the *distal stimulus*) from the pattern of stimulation on our
retinas (the *proximal stimulus*)? Researchers in the tradition of Helmholtz's constructionist
theory maintain that depth perception depends on the use of *binocular cues* (which require
two eyes) and *monocular cues* (which require one eye).

depth perception
The perception of the relative distance
of objects.

Binocular Depth Cues

binocular cues

Depth perception cues that require input from the two eyes.

The two kinds of **binocular cues** involve the interaction of both eyes. These cues permit us to engage in everyday activities such as grasping objects (Watt & Bradshaw, 2000). A study of accidents involving Canadian taxi drivers found that those with binocular depth perception problems tended to be involved in more crashes than those without such problems (Maag et al., 1997).

One binocular cue is *retinal disparity,* the degree of difference between the images of an object that are focused on the two retinas. The closer the object, the greater the retinal disparity. To demonstrate retinal disparity for yourself, point a forefinger vertically between your eyes. Look at the finger with one eye closed. Then look at it with the other closed. You will notice that the background shifts as you view the scene with different eyes. This demonstrates that the two eyes provide different views of the same stimulus. The "View-master" device you might have used as a child creates the impression of visual depth by presenting slightly different images to the eyes at the same time—mimicking retinal disparity. Retinal disparity is greater when an object is near you than when it is farther away from you. Certain cells in the visual cortex detect the degree of retinal disparity, which the brain uses to estimate the distance of an object focused on the retinas (Grunewald & Grossberg, 1998).

The second binocular cue to depth is *convergence,* the degree to which the eyes turn inward to focus on an object. As you can confirm for yourself, the closer the object, the greater the convergence of the eyes. Hold a forefinger vertically in front of your face and move it toward your nose. You should notice an increase in ocular muscle tension as your finger approaches your nose. Neurons in the cerebral cortex translate the amount of muscle tension into an estimate of the distance of your finger (Takagi et al., 1992). Using a computer terminal for hours can induce eye fatigue caused by continuous convergence (Watten, Lie, & Birketvedt, 1994).

Monocular Depth Cues

monocular cues

Depth perception cues that require input from only one eye.

There are many more monocular cues than binocular cues. **Monocular cues** require only one eye, so even people who have lost the sight in one eye still can have good depth perception. One monocular cue is *accommodation,* which, as explained earlier, is the change in the shape of the lens to help focus the image of an object on the retina. Specialized brain neurons respond so that the greater the accommodation of the lens, the closer the object appears (Judge & Cumming, 1986).

A second monocular cue is *motion parallax,* the tendency to perceive ourselves as passing objects faster when they are closer to us than when they are farther away. You notice this when you drive on a rural road, perceiving yourself as passing nearby telephone poles faster than you are passing a distant farmhouse. Animal research indicates particular brain cells might respond to motion parallax. For example, the cat's brain has cells whose firing rate varies with the degree of motion parallax (Mandl, 1985).

The remaining monocular cues are often called *pictorial cues* (see Figure 5.17) because artists use them to create depth in their drawings and paintings. They include interposition, relative size, linear perspective, elevation, shading patterns, aerial perspective, and texture gradient. Leonardo da Vinci formalized pictorial cues in the 15th century in teaching his students how to use them to make their paintings look more realistic (Haber, 1980). He noted that an object that overlaps another object will appear closer, a cue called *interposition.* Because your psychology professor overlaps the blackboard, you know she or he is closer to you than the blackboard is. Comparing the *relative size* of familiar objects also provides a cue to their distance (Higashiyama & Kitano, 1991). If you know two people are about the same height and one casts a smaller image on your retina, you will perceive that person as farther away.

You probably have noticed that parallel objects, such as railroad tracks, seem to get closer together as they get farther away (and farther apart as they get closer). This pictorial cue is called *linear perspective.* During World War II, naval aviation cadets flying at night sometimes crashed into airplanes ahead of them, apparently because of a failure to judge the distance of those planes. Taking advantage of linear perspective solved the problem.

Chapter Five

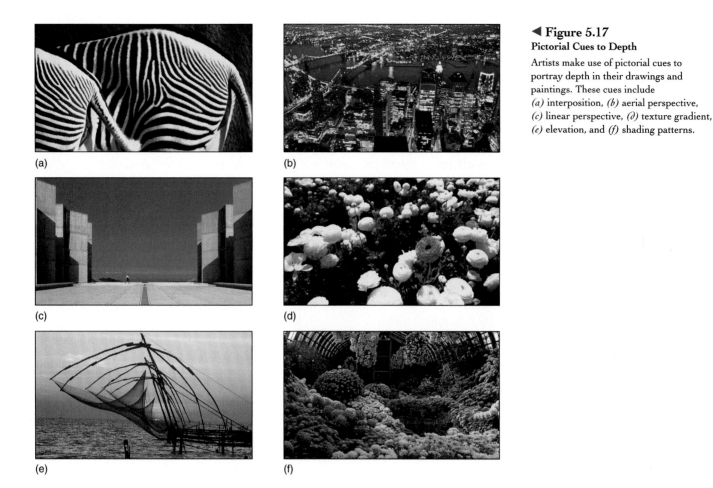

(a)

(b)

(c)

(d)

(e)

(f)

◀ **Figure 5.17**
Pictorial Cues to Depth

Artists make use of pictorial cues to portray depth in their drawings and paintings. These cues include *(a)* interposition, *(b)* aerial perspective, *(c)* linear perspective, *(∂)* texture gradient, *(e)* elevation, and *(f)* shading patterns.

Two taillights set a standard distance apart replaced the traditional single taillight. As a result, when pilots noticed that the taillights of an airplane appeared to move farther apart, they realized they were getting closer to it (Fiske, Conley, & Goldberg, 1987).

An object's *elevation* provides another cue to its distance. Objects that are higher in your visual field seem to be farther away. If you paint a picture, you can create depth by placing more distant objects higher on the canvas. *Shading patterns* provide cues to distance (Curran & Johnston, 1994) because areas in shadow tend to recede, whereas areas that are in light tend to stand out. Painters use shading to make balls, balloons, and oranges appear round. *Aerial perspective* refers to the fact that objects that are closer to us seem clearer than more distant ones. A distant mountain will look hazier than a near one (O'Shea, Govan, & Sekuler, 1997).

The final monocular cue, *texture gradient,* affects depth perception because the nearer an object, the more details we can make out, and the farther an object, the fewer details we can make out. When you look across a field, you can see every blade of grass near you, but only an expanse of green far away from you. Even 7-month-old infants respond to texture-gradient cues. When presented with drawings that use texture gradient to make some objects appear to be in the foreground and others in the background, infants will reach for an object in the foreground (Arterberry, Yonas, & Benson, 1989).

Perceptual Constancies

The image of a given object focused on your retina can vary in size, shape, and brightness. Yet, because of *perceptual constancy,* you will continue to perceive the object as stable in size, shape, and brightness. There is evidence that size and shape constancy are present at birth (Slater, 1992). This is adaptive, because it provides you with a more visually stable world, making it easier for you to function in it.

Size Constancy

The size of the object on your retina does not, by itself, tell you how far away it is. As an object gets farther away from you, it produces a smaller image on your retina. If you know the actual size of an object, **size constancy** makes you interpret a change in its retinal size as a change in its distance rather than as a change in its size. When you see a car a block away, it does not seem smaller than one that is half a block away, even though the more distant car produces a smaller image on your retina. Size constancy can be disrupted by alcohol. In one study, young adults drank alcohol and then were asked to estimate the size of an object. They consistently underestimated its size. Disruption of size constancy might be one way alcohol intoxication promotes automobile accidents (Farrimond, 1990).

Shape Constancy

Shape constancy assures that an object of known shape will appear to maintain its normal shape regardless of the angle from which you view it. Close this book and hold it at various orientations relative to your line of sight. Unless you look directly at the cover when it is on a plane perpendicular to your line of vision, it will never cast a rectangular image on your retinas, yet you will continue to perceive it as rectangular. Shape constancy occurs because your brain compensates for the slant of an object relative to your line of sight (Wallach & Marshall, 1986).

Shape constancy is subject to top-down processes, in that viewers' expectations can affect it. This is especially true for young children, as in a study in which 4- to 7-year-old children viewed a luminous circular disc oriented at a slant and presented in a darkened chamber. The children tended to overestimate the circularity of the disc when they knew the object was really a circle. This effect was greater in the younger children. In contrast, children who viewed an identical shape that they knew was an actual ellipse did not overestimate its circularity. Thus, the children's expectations affected their perception of the figure (Mitchell & Taylor, 1999).

Brightness Constancy

Though the amount of light reflected from a given object can vary, we perceive the object as having a constant brightness. This is called **brightness constancy.** A white shirt appears equally bright in dim light or bright light, and a black shirt appears equally dull in dim light or bright light. But brightness constancy is relative to other objects. If you look at a white shirt in dim light in the presence of nonwhite objects in the same light, it will maintain its brightness. But if you look at the white shirt by itself, perhaps by viewing a large area of it through a hollow tube, it will appear dull in dim light and brighter in sunlight.

Visual Illusions

In Edgar Allen Poe's story "The Sphinx," a man looks out his window and is horrified by what he perceives to be a monstrous animal on a distant mountain. He learns only later that the "monster" was actually an insect on his window. Because he perceived the animal as far away, he assumed it was relatively large. And because he never had seen such a creature, he assumed it was a monster. This shows how the misapplication of a visual cue, in this case perceived size constancy, can produce a **visual illusion.** Visual illusions provide clues to the processes involved in normal visual perception (Gordon & Earle, 1992).

As with most illusions, the Ponzo illusion (see Figure 5.18) is caused by the misapplication of perceptual cues. As you read earlier, linear perspective is a cue to depth. Because the train tracks appear to come together in the distance, the horizontal bar higher in the figure appears farther away than the one lower in the figure. If you measure the bars, you will find that they are equal in length. Because the bars produce images of equal length on your retinas, the bar that appears farther away seems to be longer. And Figure 5.19 describes an example of a remarkable visual illusion, the Ames room.

Here is another example: From ancient times to modern times, people have been mystified by the **moon illusion,** illustrated in Figure 5.20, in which the moon appears larger when it is at the horizon than when it is overhead. This is an illusion because the moon is the same

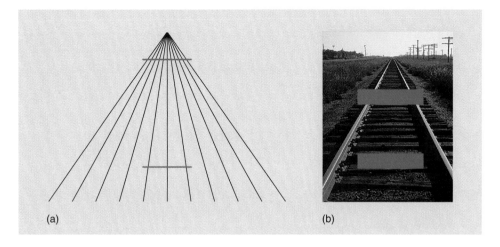

(a) The two horizontal lines are actually the same length. (b) Likewise, the two bars are the same length.

(a)   (b)

▲ **Figure 5.19**
The Ames Room

(a) The "giant" children on the right are actually shorter than the "tiny" adult on the left. (b) The floor plan of the Ames room shows that the persons on the left are farther away than the ones on the right, and the floor-to-ceiling height is greater on the left than on the right. The window on the left is also larger than the one on the right. This makes each of the persons seem like they are standing the same distance away from the viewer in a rectangular room. The illusion occurs because the persons on the right fill more of the space between the floor and the ceiling and because we assume that when two objects are the same distance away, the object that produces a smaller image on our retinas is, in fact, smaller.

◀ **Figure 5.20**
The Moon Illusion

Psychologists have put forth several theories to explain why the moon looks larger when it is at the horizon than when it is high up in the sky.

▲ **Figure 5.21**
The Müller-Lyer Illusion

Perhaps the most widely studied illusion was developed a century ago by Franz Müller-Lyer. Note that the vertical line on the right appears longer than the one on the left. If you take a ruler and measure the lines, you will find they are equal in length. Though no explanation has achieved universal acceptance (Mack et al., 1985), a favored one relies on size constancy and the resemblance of the figure on the right to the inside corner of a room and the resemblance of the figure on the left to the outside corner of a building. Given that the lines project images of equal length onto the retina, the line that appears farther away will be perceived as longer. Because an inside corner of a room appears farther away than an outside corner of a building, the line on the right appears farther and, therefore, longer than the line on the left (Gillam, 1980).

distance from us at the horizon as when it is overhead. Thus, the retinal image it produces is the same size when it is at the horizon as when it is overhead. The Greek astronomer Ptolemy put forth the earliest explanation of the moon illusion in the 2nd century. His explanation, based on the principle of size constancy, is called the *apparent-distance hypothesis* (Kaufman & Rock, 1962). Ptolemy assumed that we perceive the sky as a flattened dome, with the sky at the horizon appearing *farther* away than it does overhead. Because the image of the moon on the retina is the same size whether the moon is overhead or at the horizon, the brain assumes the moon must be *larger* at the apparently more distant location—the horizon. But modern research has found that under certain conditions the sky can look farther away overhead than at the horizon. So, if the apparent-distance hypothesis were correct, the moon would appear larger overhead than it does at the horizon (Baird & Wagner, 1982).

Despite hundreds of studies of the moon illusion, researchers have yet to agree on the best explanation of it, though a modified version of the relative-size hypothesis will probably turn out to be the best candidate (Baird, Wagner, & Fuld, 1990). Moreover, researchers have found that a variety of factors interact to create the moon illusion, so efforts to find a single explanation for it will most likely fail (Plug & Ross, 1994).

Figure 5.21 depicts the Müller-Lyer illusion, another illusion that has stimulated many research studies. This illusion, developed a century ago by Franz Müller-Lyer, is perhaps the most widely studied of all illusions. Look at the two vertical lines with normal arrowheads and inverted arrowheads on the extreme right. The line on the right should appear longer than the one on the left. If you take a ruler and measure the lines, you will find they are actually equal in length. The Müller-Lyer illusion can even impair our accuracy in estimating driving distances while reading maps when roads form patterns similar to those found in the illusion (Binsted & Elliott, 1999).

Experience, Culture, and Perception

As you have just read, visual perception depends on the interaction of the eyes and the brain. But it also depends on experience. Even the visual pathways themselves can be altered by life experiences, as demonstrated by the following study.

The Effect of Experience

As we discussed earlier, David Hubel and Torsten Wiesel found that feature detectors in the visual cortex respond to lines of particular orientations. Other researchers (Hirsch & Spinelli, 1970) reared kittens with one eye exposed to vertical stripes and the other eye exposed to horizontal stripes. When the kittens later were exposed to lines of either orientation with one eye, certain feature-detector neurons in their visual cortexes responded only to lines of the orientation to which that eye had been exposed. But what would occur if kittens were reared in an environment that exposed both eyes to either only vertical or only horizontal stripes? This was the question addressed in a study by Colin Blakemore and Graham Cooper (1970) of Cambridge University in England. Blakemore and Cooper reared kittens from the age of 2 weeks to the age of 5 months in darkness, except for 5 hours a day in a lighted, large cylinder with walls covered by either vertical or horizontal black and white stripes. Because the kittens also wore large saucer-shaped collars, they could not even see their own legs or bodies. This prevented their being exposed to lines other than the vertical or horizontal stripes.

After 5 months the kittens' vision was tested under normal lighting by waving a rod in front of them, sometimes vertically and sometimes horizontally. Kittens that had been exposed to vertical lines swatted at the vertical rod but not at the horizontal rod. And kittens that had been exposed to horizontal lines swatted at the horizontal rod but not at the vertical rod. Recordings of the activity in certain neurons in the visual cortex showed that particular neurons acted as feature detectors by responding to either vertical or horizontal lines, depending on the stripes to which the kittens had been exposed during the previous 5 months (Blakemore & Cooper, 1970). Later studies indicated that neurons in the visual cortex that are responsive to lines of different orientations are present at birth. But in an individual who is not exposed to lines of a particular orientation, the neurons responsive to that orientation will degenerate (Swindale, 1982).

Another source of evidence for the effect of experience on perception comes from studies of people blind from birth who have gained their sense of vision years later. German physiologist Max von Senden (1932–1960) reviewed all the studies of people who had been born blind because of lens cataracts and who gained their vision after surgical removal of the cataracts. He found that the newly sighted were immediately able to distinguish colors and to separate figure from ground, but had difficulty visually recognizing objects they had learned to identify by touch. They did, however, show gradual improvement in visual object recognition (Dember & Bagwell, 1985).

Cultural Influences on Perception

Visual perception also can be influenced by cultural factors. This was demonstrated by the anthropologist Colin Turnbull (1961), who studied the Bambuti Pygmies of central Africa. Turnbull drove one of the Pygmies, Kenge, who lived in a dense forest, to an open plain. Looking across the plain at a herd of grazing buffalo, Kenge asked Turnbull to tell him what kind of insect they were. Turnbull responded by driving Kenge toward the herd. As the image of the "insects" got bigger and bigger on his retinas, Kenge accused Turnbull of witchcraft for turning the insects into buffaloes. Because he had never experienced large objects at a distance, Kenge had a limited appreciation of size constancy. To him the tiny images on his retinas could only be insects. Because of his understandable failure to apply size constancy appropriately, Kenge mistook the distant buffalo for a nearby insect (in contrast to the man in Poe's short story, who mistook the nearby insect for a distant monster).

Experiences with monocular cues to depth, such as linear perspective, even affect responses to the Ponzo illusion (Fujita, 1996). Rural Ugandan villagers, who have little experience with monocular cues in two-dimensional stimuli, are less susceptible to the Ponzo illusion than are Ugandan college students, who have more experience with such cues in art, photographs, and motion pictures (Leibowitz & Pick, 1972). But research finding that infant monkeys respond to pictorial depth cues indicates that learning from exposure to these Western forms of depth representation is not necessary to produce such illusions (Gunderson et al., 1993). Moreover, even pigeons and horses are affected by the Ponzo illusion (Timney & Keil, 1996), making it less likely that it is simply the product of being exposed to Western art (Fujita, Blough, & Blough, 1993).

STAYING ON TRACK: *Visual Sensation and Visual Perception*

1. What structures do light waves pass through on their way from the cornea to the retina?
2. What is the trichromatic theory of color vision?
3. What are the Gestalt principles of form perception?
4. What are two binocular cues to depth perception?

Answers to Staying on Track start on p. ST-2.

◆ HEARING

audition
The sense of hearing.

Like the sense of vision, the sense of hearing (or **audition**) helps us function by informing us about objects at a distance from us. Unlike vision, audition informs us about objects we cannot see because they are behind us, hidden by darkness, or blocked by another object. On average, women have better hearing sensitivity and experience greater deterioration from exposure to high-frequency noise. Men are better at sound localization and detecting specific sounds from among other sounds. Because these gender differences are not found in women who have a male twin, they have been attributed to prenatal exposure to male sex hormones, which might androgenize the auditory system of the female twin (McFadden, 1998).

Sound Waves

Sound is produced by vibrations carried by air, water, or other mediums. Because sound requires a medium through which to travel, it cannot travel in a vacuum. Sound vibrations create a successive bunching and spreading of molecules in the sound medium. A sound wave is composed of a series of these bunching-spreading cycles. The height of a sound wave is its *amplitude,* and the number of sound-wave cycles that pass a given point in a second is its *frequency.* Sound-wave frequency is measured in *hertz (Hz),* named for the 19th-century German physicist Heinrich Hertz. A 60-Hz sound would have a frequency of 60 cycles a second. Figure 5.22 illustrates the main properties of sound waves that affect perceived pitch and loudness.

▼ **Figure 5.22**
Sound Waves and Hearing
The amplitude of a sound wave affects loudness (volume) and the frequency affects pitch.

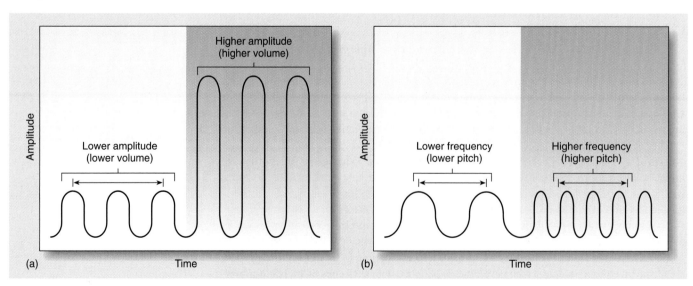

| **Chapter Five**

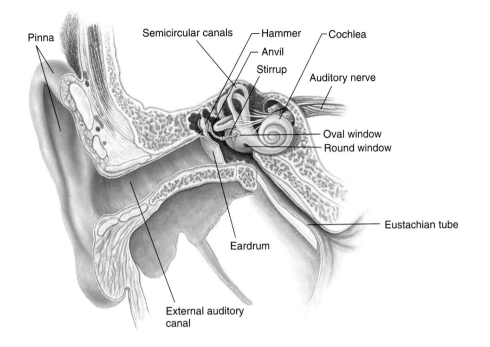

The Auditory System

Sound waves are sensed and perceived by the *auditory system,* which begins at the ear. The structure of the ear is illustrated in Figure 5.23. The ear is divided into an outer ear, a middle ear, and an inner ear.

The Outer Ear

The *outer ear* includes the *pinna,* the oddly shaped flap of skin and cartilage that we commonly call the "ear." Though the pinna plays a small role in human hearing, some animals, such as cats and deer, have large, movable pinnas that help them detect and locate faint sounds (Populin & Yin, 1998). Sound waves gathered by the pinna pass through the *external auditory canal* and reach the **tympanic membrane,** better known as the *eardrum.* Sound waves make the eardrum vibrate, and our hearing is responsive to even the slightest movement of the eardrum. If our hearing were any more acute, we would hear the air molecules that are constantly bouncing against the eardrum (Békésy, 1957).

The Middle Ear

The eardrum separates the outer ear from the *middle ear.* Vibrations of the eardrum are conveyed to the bones, or ossicles, of the middle ear. The ossicles are three tiny bones connected to one another by ligaments. The Latin names of the ossicles reflect their shapes: the *malleus* (hammer), the *incus* (anvil), and the *stapes* (stirrup). Infections of the middle ear must be taken seriously; in children they can produce hearing losses that adversely affect language ability and intellectual development (Roberts & Schuele, 1990).

Connecting the middle ear to the back of the throat are the *eustachian tubes,* which permit air to enter the middle ear to equalize air pressure on both sides of the eardrum. You might become painfully aware of this function during airplane descents, when the pressure increases on the outside of the eardrum relative to the inside. Chewing gum can help open the eustachian tubes and equalize the pressure.

The Inner Ear

Vibrations of the stapes are conveyed to the *oval window* of the *inner ear.* The oval window is a membrane in the wall of a spiral structure called the **cochlea** (from a Greek word meaning "snail"). Vibrations of the oval window send waves through a fluid-filled chamber that runs the length of the cochlea. These waves set in motion the **basilar membrane,** which

tympanic membrane
The eardrum; a membrane separating the outer from the middle ear that vibrates in response to sound waves that strike it.

cochlea
The spiral, fluid-filled structure of the inner ear that contains the receptor cells for hearing.

basilar membrane
A membrane running the length of the cochlea that contains the auditory receptor (hair) cells.

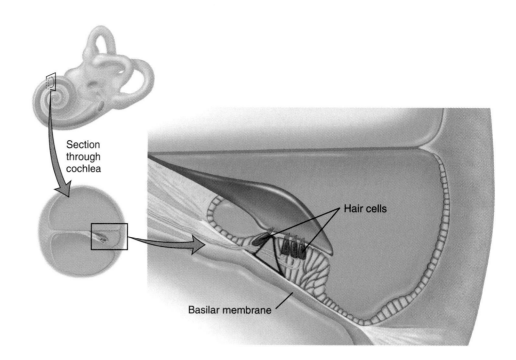

▶ Figure 5.24

The Cochlea

Vibrations of the oval window send waves through a fluid-filled chamber that runs the length of the cochlea. These waves set in motion the basilar membrane, which causes bending of hair cells. The bending triggers impulses that travel along the auditory nerve.

Section through cochlea

Hair cells

Basilar membrane

auditory nerve

The nerve that conducts impulses from the cochlea to the brain.

auditory cortex

The area of the temporal lobes that processes sounds.

also runs the length of the cochlea. The movement of the basilar membrane causes bending of *hair cells* that protrude from it. The bending triggers impulses that travel along the axons of the neurons that form the **auditory nerve.** Auditory impulses eventually reach the thalamus, where some processing takes place (Edeline & Weinberger, 1991). Input to the thalamus is then relayed to the **auditory cortex** of the temporal lobes of the brain, the ultimate site of sound perception (Hirata, Kuriki, & Pantev, 1999).

People with schizophrenia who experience auditory hallucinations show increased activity in their auditory cortex (David et al., 1996). Even communication by sign language depends on the auditory cortex, as though the "listener" is hearing what is being signed. PET scans show increased activity during sign language communication even in the auditory cortex of the temporal lobes of "listeners" who have been deaf since birth (Nishimura et al., 1999). The effects of damage to the auditory cortex depend on the precise location of the damage. Damage that spares the perception of speech and environmental sounds, for example, might profoundly impair the perception of tunes and voices (Peretz et al., 1994). Figure 5.24 shows the inner structures of the cochlea.

Auditory Perception

How do vibrations conveyed to the basilar membrane (the proximal stimulus) create a complex auditory experience regarding their source (the distal stimulus)? Your ability to perceive sounds of all kinds depends on *pitch perception, loudness perception, timbre perception,* and *sound localization.*

Pitch Perception

The frequency of a sound is the main determinant of its perceived *pitch,* whether the low-pitched sounds of a tuba or the high-pitched sounds of a flute. When you use the tone control on a CD player, you alter the frequency of the sound waves produced by the vibration of the speakers. This, in turn, alters the pitch of the sound. People with *absolute pitch* can identify and produce tones of a specific pitch. This ability appears to be learned best before the age of 6, and becomes difficult or impossible to develop afterward (Crozier, 1997).

Human beings and other animals vary in the range of frequencies they can hear. Human beings hear sounds that range from 20 Hz to 20,000 Hz. Because elephants can hear sounds only up to 10,000 Hz, they cannot hear higher-pitched sounds that human beings can hear.

Dogs, in turn, can hear sounds up to about 45,000 Hz (Heffner, 1983). Because dog whistles produce sounds between 20,000 and 45,000 Hz, they are audible to dogs but not to human beings.

Place Theory. What accounts for **pitch perception?** In 1863 Hermann von Helmholtz put forth **place theory,** which assumes that particular points on the basilar membrane vibrate maximally in response to sound waves of particular frequencies. Georg von Békésy (1899–1972), a Hungarian scientist, won a Nobel Prize in 1961 for his research on place theory. He took the cochleas from the ears of guinea pigs and human cadavers, stimulated the oval window, and, using a microscope, noted the response of the basilar membrane through a hole cut in the cochlea. He found that as the frequency of the stimulus increased, the point of maximal vibration produced by the traveling wave on the basilar membrane moved closer to the oval window. And as the frequency of the stimulus decreased, the point of maximal vibration moved farther from the oval window (Békésy, 1957).

Frequency Theory. But place theory fails to explain pitch perception much below 1,000 Hz, because such low-frequency sound waves do not make the basilar membrane vibrate maximally at any particular point. Instead, the entire basilar membrane vibrates equally. Because of this limitation, perception of sounds below 1,000 Hz is explained best by a theory first put forth by English physicist Ernest Rutherford (1861–1937) in 1886. His **frequency theory** assumes the basilar membrane vibrates as a whole in direct proportion to the frequency of the sound waves striking the eardrum. The neurons of the auditory nerve will, in turn, fire at the same frequency as the vibrations of the basilar membrane. But because neurons can fire only up to 1,000 Hz, frequency theory holds only for sounds up to 1,000 Hz.

Volley Theory. Still another theory, the **volley theory** of psychologist Ernest Wever (Wever & Bray, 1937), explains pitch perception between 1,000 Hz and 5,000 Hz. Volley theory assumes that sound waves in this range induce certain groups of auditory neurons to fire in volleys. Though no single neuron can fire at more than 1,000 Hz, the brain might interpret the firing of volleys of particular auditory neurons as representing sound waves of particular frequencies up to 5,000 Hz (Zwislocki, 1981). For example, the pitch of a sound wave of 4,000 Hz might be coded by a particular group of five neurons, each firing at 800 Hz. Though there is some overlap among the theories, frequency theory best explains the perception of low-pitched sounds, place theory best explains the perception of high-pitched sounds, and volley theory best explains the perception of medium-pitched sounds.

Loudness Perception

Sounds vary in intensity, or *loudness,* as well as pitch. The loudness of a sound depends mainly on the amplitude of its sound waves. When you use the volume control on a CD player, you alter the amplitude of the sound waves leaving the speakers. **Loudness perception** depends on both the number and the firing thresholds of hair cells on the basilar membrane that are stimulated. Because hair cells with higher firing thresholds require more intense stimulation, the firing of hair cells with higher thresholds increases the perceived loudness of a sound. A region of the auditory cortex processes differences in the intensity of sounds (Palomaeki et al., 2000).

The unit of sound intensity is the *decibel (dB).* The decibel is one-tenth of a Bel, a unit named for Alexander Graham Bell, who invented the telephone. The faintest detectable sound has an absolute threshold of 0 dB. For each change of 10 decibels, the perceived loudness doubles. Thus, a 70-dB sound is twice as loud as a 60-dB sound. Table 5.1 presents the decibel levels of some everyday sounds. Exposure to high-decibel sounds promotes hearing loss. Chronic exposure to loud sounds first destroys hair cells nearest the oval window, which respond to high-frequency sound waves. A study of the effects of loud music found significant hearing loss among rock fans who listened to personal stereos for more than 7 hours a week. In addition, two-thirds of the participants who attended rock concerts at least twice monthly exhibited symptoms of hearing loss (Meyer-Bisch, 1996). Elderly North Americans, after a lifetime of exposure to loud sounds, tend to have poor high-frequency

pitch perception
The subjective experience of the highness or lowness of a sound, which corresponds most closely with the frequency of the sound waves that compose it.

place theory
The theory of pitch perception that assumes that hair cells at particular points on the basilar membrane are maximally responsive to sound waves of particular frequencies.

frequency theory
The theory of pitch perception that assumes that the basilar membrane vibrates as a whole in direct proportion to the frequency of the sound waves striking the eardrum.

volley theory
The theory of pitch perception that assumes that sound waves of particular frequencies induce auditory neurons to fire in volleys, with one volley following another.

loudness perception
The subjective experience of the intensity of a sound, which corresponds most closely with the amplitude of the sound waves composing it.

Table 5.1	Sound Levels (Decibels) of Some Everyday Noises	
Harmful to Hearing	140	Jet engine (25 m distance)
	130	Jet takeoff (100 m away)
		Threshold of pain
	120	Propeller aircraft
Risk Hearing Loss	110	Live rock band
	100	Jackhammer/pneumatic chipper
	90	Heavy-duty truck
		Los Angeles, third-floor apartment next to freeway
		Average street traffic
Very Noisy	80	Harlem, second-floor apartment
Urban	70	Private car
		Boston row house on major avenue
		Business office
		Watts—8 miles from touch down at major airport
	60	Conversational speech or old residential area in L.A.
Suburban and Small Town	50	San Diego—wooded residential area
	40	California tomato field
		Soft music from radio
	30	Quiet whisper
	20	Quiet urban dwelling
	10	Rustle of leaf
	0	Threshold of hearing

Source: Reprinted with permission from *Science News,* the weekly newsmagazine of science. Copyright 1982 by Science Service, Inc.

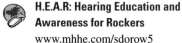

H.E.A.R: Hearing Education and Awareness for Rockers
www.mhhe.com/sdorow5

conduction deafness
Hearing loss usually caused by blockage of the auditory canal, damage to the eardrum, or deterioration of the ossicles of the middle ear.

nerve deafness
Hearing loss caused by damage to the hair cells of the basilar membrane, the axons of the auditory nerve, or the neurons of the auditory cortex.

timbre
The subjective experience that identifies a particular sound and corresponds most closely to the mixture of sound waves composing it.

hearing. In contrast, the typical 90-year-old in rural African tribes, whose surroundings only occasionally produce loud sounds, has better hearing than the typical 30-year-old North American (Raloff, 1982).

In extreme cases, individuals can lose more than their high-frequency hearing. They can become deaf. In **conduction deafness,** there is a mechanical problem in the outer or middle ear that interferes with hearing. The auditory canal might be filled with wax, the eardrum might be punctured, or the ossicles might be fused and inflexible. Conduction deafness caused by deterioration of the ossicles can be treated by surgical replacement with plastic ossicles. Conduction deafness is more often overcome by hearing aids, which amplify sound waves that enter the ear.

In **nerve deafness,** a problem of the inner ear, there is damage to the basilar membrane, the auditory nerve, or the auditory cortex. Victims typically lose the ability to perceive sounds of certain *frequencies.* Nerve deafness responds poorly to surgery or hearing aids. But *cochlear implants* (pictured in Figure 5.25) which provide electronic stimulation of the neurons leaving the basilar membrane, promise to restore at least rudimentary hearing in people with nerve deafness caused by the destruction of basilar membrane hair cells. Some recipients of cochlear implants hear well enough to perceive simple speech and to produce intelligible speech (Svirsky et al., 2000).

Timbre Perception

Sounds vary in *timbre,* as well as in pitch and loudness. **Timbre** is the quality of a sound, which reflects a particular mixture of sound waves. This is especially apparent, for example, in the complex sounds produced in orchestral music (Pressnitzer et al., 2000). Middle C on

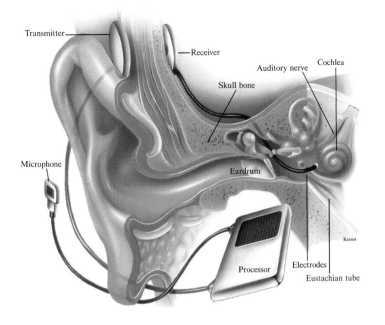

Transmitter

Receiver

Auditory nerve

Cochlea

Skull bone

Microphone

Eardrum

Kasnot

Processor

Electrodes

Eustachian tube

◀ **Figure 5.25**
The Bionic Ear
Cochlear implants involve electrodes attached to different points along the basilar membrane. A microphone worn behind the ear picks up sounds and transmits them to a microprocessor. The microprocessor then analyzes the sounds into their component frequencies and sends impulses through the electrodes to stimulate the places on the basilar membrane that respond to those frequencies (Loeb, 1985).

the piano has a frequency of 256 Hz, but it has a distinctive timbre because of overtones of varying frequencies. Timbre lets us identify the source of a sound, whether a voice, a musical instrument, or even—to the chagrin of students—a fingernail scratching across a chalkboard. The timbre of that spine-chilling sound is similar to that of the warning cry of macaque monkeys. Perhaps our squeamish reaction to it reflects a vestigial response inherited from our common distant ancestors who used it to signal the presence of predators (Halpern, Blake, & Hillerbrand, 1986).

Timbre lets us not only identify musical instruments, but evaluate their relative quality. Because musical notes of the same frequency differ in timbre when played on different instruments, no two instruments produce exactly the same sounds. Two instruments playing the same note would also produce different mixtures of accompanying sound waves. This helps you to tell a violin from a guitar and a cheap violin from an expensive one (Hutchins, 1981).

Cochlear Implant Association, Inc.
www.mhhe.com/sdorow5

Sound Localization

We need to localize sounds, as well as identify them. **Sound localization** involves discerning where sounds are coming from. Human beings have an impressive ability to localize sounds, whether of voices at a crowded party or of instruments in a symphony orchestra. Some animals have especially impressive sound localization ability. A barn owl can capture

sound localization
The process by which the individual determines the location of a sound.

◀ **Rocking His Way to Deafness**
The cumulative effect of exposure to loud noises may become apparent in middle age and beyond. Pete Townsend, lead guitarist of the Who, suffers from significant hearing loss induced by decades of exposure to the band's loud music.

a mouse in the dark simply by following the faint sounds produced by its movements (Knudsen, 1981). The ability to localize sound is important for our survival, as in judging the distance of approaching vehicles. This is especially important for young children, who are not proficient at detecting approaching vehicles from their sounds (Pfeffer & Barnecutt, 1998).

We are aided in localizing sounds by having two ears. Sounds that come from points other than those equidistant between our two ears reach one ear slightly before they reach the other. Such sounds are also slightly more intense at the ear closer to the sound source, because the head blocks some of the sound waves as they move from one side of the head to the other. The auditory cortex has cells that respond to these differences in intensity and arrival time, permitting the brain to determine the location of a sound (Jin, Schenkel, & Carlile, 2000). Even sounds that come from points equidistant between our ears can be located, because the irregular shape of the pinna alters sounds differently, depending on the direction from which they enter the ear (Middlebrooks & Green, 1991).

STAYING ON TRACK: *Hearing*

1. What are the major structures of the outer, middle, and inner ear?
2. What is the place theory of pitch perception?
3. What are the basic processes in sound localization?

Answers to Staying on Track start on p. ST-2.

◆ CHEMICAL SENSES

The chemical senses of smell and taste let us identify things on the basis of their chemical content. These senses also provide us with both pleasure and protection.

Smell

olfaction

The sense of smell, which detects molecules carried in the air.

Helen Keller (1880–1968), though deaf and blind from infancy, could identify her friends by their smell and could even tell whether a person had recently been in a kitchen, garden, or hospital room by his or her odor (Ecenbarger, 1987). Though most of us do not rely on smell to that extent, the sense of smell (or **olfaction**) is important to all of us. It warns us of dangers, such as fire, deadly gases, or spoiled food, and lets us enjoy the pleasant odors of food, nature, and other people.

North Americans find odors so important that they spend millions of dollars on perfumes, colognes, and deodorants to make themselves more socially appealing. Workers might also feel more motivated when in the presence of a pleasant fragrance. This was demonstrated in a study in which men wore cologne for 10 days and reported their moods twice daily on those days, as well as on 2 baseline days. The results showed that their moods while wearing cologne were improved over their moods during the 2 baseline days (Schiffman, Suggs, & Sattely-Miller, 1995). This was replicated in a study in which women exposed to pleasant odors had enhanced moods in response to them (Schiffman et al., 1995). The possible influence of fragrances on moods has led some business owners to diffuse scents into their stores to gain a competitive advantage. Nonetheless, few research studies have supported the effectiveness of this technique (Spangenberg, Crowley, & Henderson, 1996). There also are cultural differences in the perceived intensity and pleasantness of particular odors. This appears to be attributable to cultural differences in people's experience with different odors (Ayabe-Kanamura et al., 1998). A study of Mexican, German, and Japanese women found that participants rated familiar odors to be more intense and more pleasant (Distal et al., 1999).

The ability of odors to affect our moods has led to the advent of so-called *aromatherapy,* which attempts to use different fragrances to enhance cognitive abilities or psychological well-being. In one experiment, college students performing a simulated driving test in the

▲ **Helen Keller (1880–1968)**

Because she was deaf and blind, Helen Keller relied on her senses of touch and smell to perceive the world. She used her fingers to read Braille well enough to earn a college degree, and she used her nose to recognize people by their scent.

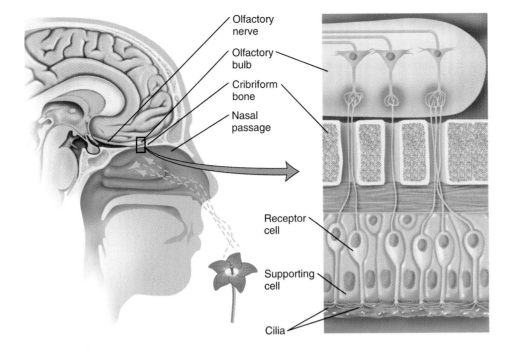

Olfactory nerve

Olfactory bulb

Cribriform bone

Nasal passage

Receptor cell

Supporting cell

Cilia

◀ **Figure 5.26**
The Olfactory Pathway

Inhaled molecules from the flower attach to receptor cells high up in the nasal passages. This stimulates neural activity in the olfactory bulbs, which generates olfactory-nerve impulses that are sent to brain regions that process smell sensations.

presence or absence of a pleasant aroma did better when exposed to the aroma (Baron & Kalsher, 1998). In another experiment, groups of adults were exposed to either an alerting aroma (rosemary) or a relaxing odor (lavender) and were asked to perform mathematical calculations. Those exposed to the rosemary aroma showed heightened alertness, as measured by self-reports and brain waves. Both groups increased their speed of calculations, but only the lavender group showed improved accuracy of calculations (Diego et al., 1998). Despite some positive research findings regarding aromatherapy, consumers should remain skeptical of some of the extreme claims made for its effectiveness by those who stand to profit from aromatherapy products and services.

What accounts for our ability to smell odors? In part because of the practical difficulty of gaining access to the olfactory pathways, we have relatively limited knowledge of how olfactory anatomy affects the detection and recognition of odors. We do know that molecules carried in inhaled air stimulate smell receptor cells on the olfactory epithelium high up in the nasal passages. Figure 5.26 illustrates the major structures of the olfactory system.

Today, research findings indicate that molecules that reach the olfactory epithelium alter the resting potential and firing frequency of receptor cells, stimulating some and inhibiting others. Distinctive patterns in the firing of receptor cells evoke particular odors. Leading olfaction researcher Linda Bartoshuk has found that regardless of the exact mechanisms by which this occurs, olfaction depends on stimulation of different receptors, composed of proteins, on the olfactory epithelium by specific airborne chemicals (Bartoshuk & Beauchamp, 1994).

Neural impulses from the receptor cells travel along the short *olfactory nerves* to the frontal lobes of the brain. Smell is the only sense that is not processed first in the thalamus before being processed in other olfactory centers in the brain. The *limbic system,* a structure of the brain that is important in the experience of emotion discussed in Chapter 3, receives many neural connections from the olfactory nerves. This might account for the powerful emotional effects of certain odors that evoke vivid, emotional memories of important events, places, or persons (Herz & Engen, 1996). In one study, participants were exposed to 20 different odors and were asked to rate odors and report whether they evoked a personal memory. In keeping with popular belief, memories evoked by the odors tended to be rare, vivid, emotional, and relatively old (Herz & Cupchik, 1992).

Our sense of smell has a remarkably low absolute threshold; we can detect minute amounts of chemicals diffused in the air. For example, *National Geographic* needed only 1 ounce of an odorous chemical to include a sample of it with 11 million copies of a smell

The ChemoReception Web
www.mhhe.com/sdorow5

▲ **Linda Bartoshuk**

"Although taste and olfaction have different properties and functions, they can be integrated to determine what does and does not enter the body."

Pheromones
www.mhhe.com/sdorow5

pheromone
An odorous chemical secreted by an animal that affects the behavior of other animals.

gustation
The sense of taste, which detects molecules of substances dissolved in the saliva.

taste buds
Structures lining the grooves of the tongue that contain the taste receptor cells.

Monell Chemical Senses Center
www.mhhe.com/sdorow5

survey (Gibbons, 1986). Our ability to identify familiar odors was highlighted in a study of college students who showered themselves, put on fresh T-shirts, and used no soap, deodorant, or perfume for 24 hours. Participants then sniffed the shirts, one at a time, through an opening in a bag. Of the 29 participants, 22 correctly identified their own shirts (Russell, 1976). In a more recent study, elementary school students were able to recognize their classmates from the smell of their T-shirts (Mallet & Schaal, 1998).

Though smell is important to human beings, it is more important to many other animals. For example, salmon have an amazing ability to travel hundreds of miles to their home streams to spawn, following the familiar odors of the soil and plants on the banks of the waterways that mark the correct route home (Gibbons, 1986). Researchers have been especially interested in the effects of secretions called **pheromones** on the sexual behavior of animals. For example, *aphrodisin,* a vaginal pheromone released by female hamsters stimulates copulation when inhaled by males (Singer & Macrides, 1990). Recent research indicates there might be human pheromones that affect emotions and behavior (Grosser et al., 2000). But beware of companies offering to sell you pheromones they "guarantee" will help your romantic life.

Taste

Our other chemical sense, taste (or **gustation**), protects us from harm by preventing us from ingesting poisons and enhances our enjoyment of life by letting us savor food and beverages. Taste depends on thousands of **taste buds,** which line the grooves between bumps called *papillae* on the surface of the tongue. The taste buds contain receptor cells that send neural impulses when stimulated by molecules dissolved in saliva (Smith & Margolis, 1999). Taste sensitivity varies with the density of taste buds (Zuniga et al., 1993). Taste buds die and are replaced every few days, so the taste buds destroyed when you burn your tongue with hot food or drink are quickly replaced. But because replacement of taste buds slows with age, elderly people might find food less flavorful than they did earlier in life. This means older adults often prefer foods with more intense flavors (deGraaf, Polet, & van Staveren, 1994).

In the 11th century, the Arab scientist Avicenna proposed there were four basic tastes: sweet, sour, salty, and bitter. In 1891 Hjalmar Ohrwall provided support for Avicenna's proposal. Ohrwall tested the sensitivity of the papillae by applying a variety of chemicals, one at a time, to different papillae. Some papillae responded to one taste and some to more than one. But, overall, he found that particular papillae were maximally sensitive to sweet, sour, salty, or bitter substances (Bartoshuk, Cain, & Pfaffman, 1985). Different areas of the tongue are most sensitive to sweet and salty, the sides are most sensitive to sour and salty, and the back is most sensitive to bitter. All other tastes are combinations of these basic tastes and depend on the pattern of stimulation of the taste receptors (Sato & Beidler, 1997).

Gustation depends, in part, on the shape and size of molecules that stimulate the taste receptors. Taste researchers use this knowledge when they develop artificial sweeteners. Taste receptors in different areas of the tongue are maximally sensitive to molecules of particular shapes. Animal research has shown that different clusters of nerve fibers in pathways from the tongue to the brain (so-called labeled lines) serve the senses of sweet, salty, and bitter (Hellekant, Ninomiya, & Danilova, 1998). There also are taste receptors that are sensitive to the presence of particular nutrients, such as fats, and *umami,* the pleasurable taste elicited by monosodium glutamate (Bellisle, 1999). Different regions of the somatosensory cortex respond more to certain tastes than to others (Kobayakawa et al., 1999).

Do not confuse taste with flavor, which is more complex. Taste depends on sensations from the mouth; flavor relies on both taste and smell, as well as on texture, temperature, and even pain—as in chili peppers (Bartoshuk, 1991). If you closed your eyes and held your nose, you would have trouble telling the difference between a piece of apple and a piece of potato placed in your mouth. Because smell is especially important for flavor, you might find that when you have a head cold that interferes with your ability to smell, food lacks flavor. In fact, people who lose their sense of smell because of disease or brain damage (a condition known as *anosmia*) find food less appealing (Ferris & Duffy, 1989).

1. What are pheromones?
2. Why might a head cold affect your ability to enjoy the flavor of food?

Answers to Staying on Track start on p. ST-3.

◆ Skin Senses

We rely on our **skin senses** of touch, temperature, and pain to identify objects, communicate feelings, and protect us from injury. Though there are a variety of receptors that produce skin sensations, there is no simple one-to-one relationship between specific kinds of receptors and specific skin senses. For example, there is only one kind of receptor in the cornea, but it is sensitive to touch, temperature, and pain. The pattern of stimulation of receptors, not the specific kind of receptor, determines skin sensations. Neural impulses from the skin receptors reach the thalamus, which relays them to the **somatosensory cortex** of the brain (see Chapter 3). Now consider what research has discovered about the senses of touch and pain.

skin senses
The senses of touch, temperature, and pain.

somatosensory cortex
The area of the parietal lobes that processes information from sensory receptors in the skin.

Touch

Your sense of *touch* lets you identify objects rapidly and accurately even when you cannot see them, as when you find your house key while fumbling with a key chain in the dark. Touch is important in our social attachments, whether between lovers or between parent and child, and in our well-being, as in helping physicians conduct medical examinations (Thompson & Lambert, 1995). The sense of touch can have therapeutic effects. A study found that massage therapy improved physiological signs of well-being in infants at risk for depression (Jones, Field, & Davalos, 1998). Touch sensitivity depends on the concentration of receptors. The more sensitive the area of skin (such as the lips or fingertips), the larger its representation on the somatosensory cortex. Touch sensitivity declines with age, perhaps because of the loss of touch receptors (Gescheider et al., 1994) or alterations in the somatosensory cortex (Spengler, Godde, & Dinse, 1995).

The sense of touch is so precise that it can be used as a substitute for vision. In 1824 a blind Frenchman named Louis Braille invented the Braille system for reading and writing, which uses patterns of raised dots to represent letters. Blind adults who have used Braille for reading are superior to sighted adults in using their fingers to recognize fine details on objects. This may be the result of a lifetime of using their fingers for reading (Van Boven, 2000). The Braille concept has been extended to provide a substitute for vision, as shown in Figure 5.27. The blind person wears a camera on special eyeglasses and a special computer-controlled electronic vest covered with a grid of tiny Teflon cones. Outlines of images provided by the camera are impressed onto the skin by vibrations of the cones. People who have used the device have been able to identify familiar objects (Hechinger, 1981).

Pain

The sense of *pain* (or *nociception*) protects us from injury or even death. People born without a sense of pain, or who lose it through nerve injuries, may harm themselves without realizing it. Because acute pain can be extremely distressing, and chronic pain is severely depressing (Banks & Kerns, 1996), researchers are studying the factors that cause pain and possible ways of relieving it.

Pain Factors

An injury or intense stimulation of sensory receptors induces pain. So, bright lights, loud noises, hot spices, and excessive pressure, as well as cuts, burns, and bruises, are painful. The main pain receptors (or *nociceptors*) are *free nerve endings* in the skin. Two kinds of neuronal

▲ **Figure 5.27**
Tactile Sensory Replacement

This man is "seeing" with his skin. Images provided by the video camera on his eyeglasses are impressed onto his skin by tiny vibrating Teflon cones. People who have used this device have been able to identify objects with distinctive shapes (Hechinger, 1981).

▲ **Ronald Melzack**

"Research and observation indicate that a gate-control theory of pain is a better way of understanding pain and approaches to blocking pain."

gate-control theory
The theory that pain impulses can be blocked by the closing of a neuronal gate in the spinal cord.

American Academy of Medical Acupuncture
www.mhhe.com/sdorow5

placebo
An inactive substance that might induce some of the effects of the drug for which it has been substituted.

acupuncture
A pain-relieving technique that relies on the insertion of fine needles into various sites on the body.

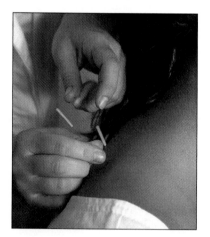

▲ **Acupuncture**

Acupuncture appears to achieve its pain-relieving effects by stimulating the release of endorphins.

fibers transmit pain impulses: *A-delta fibers* carry sharp or pricking pain, and *C fibers* carry dull or burning pain (Mengel et al., 1993). Many pain receptor neurons transmit pain impulses by releasing the neurotransmitter *substance P* from their axons (Honore et al., 1999). For example, the intensity of arthritis pain varies with the amount of substance P released by neurons that convey pain impulses, and analgesics that reduce levels of substance P reduce arthritis pain intensity (Torri et al., 1995). In the brain, a region called the *periaqueductal gray* is an important pain-processing center (Borszcz, 1999), and pathways to the limbic system might affect emotional responses to pain (Giesler, Katter, & Dado, 1994).

The most influential theory of pain is **gate-control theory,** formulated by psychologist Ronald Melzack and biologist Patrick Wall (1965). The theory assumes pain impulses from the limbs or body pass through a part of the spinal cord that provides a "gate" for pain impulses, perhaps involving substance P neurons (Holland, Goldstein, & Aronstam, 1993). Stimulation of neurons that convey touch sensations "closes" the gate, preventing input from neurons that convey pain sensations. This might explain why rubbing a shin that you have banged against a table will relieve the pain. The closing of the pain gate is stimulated by the secretion of *endorphins* (Taddese, Nah, & McCleskey, 1995), which (as described in Chapter 3) are the brain's natural opiates. Endorphins might close the gate by inhibiting the secretion of substance P (Ruda, 1982). In one study, participants who exercised showed a negative correlation between pain and endorphin levels: as endorphin levels increased, pain intensity decreased (Droste et al., 1991).

The pain gate is also affected by neural impulses that originate in the brain (Dubner & Bennett, 1983). This might explain why anxiety, relaxation, and other psychological factors can affect pain perception (Melzack, 1993). For example, it might explain the so-called Anzio effect, in which wounded soldiers returning from the fierce World War II battle for control of Anzio, Italy, needed less morphine than did civilians with similar wounds. Perhaps because the soldiers interpreted their wounds as tickets away from the battlefield, they experienced their pain as less intense (Wallis, 1984). Their pain might have been reduced by neural impulses sent from the brain to the spinal cord, closing the pain gate. The Anzio effect also shows that the *reinterpretation* of pain can reduce its intensity (Devine & Spanos, 1990).

Other social-cutural factors have been found to influence the perception of pain. A meta-analysis of experimental studies found that women reported higher levels of pain sensitivity than did men. Moreover, effect sizes ranged from large to moderate, depending on the type of painful stimulus (Riley et al., 1998). Women and men do appear to respond to painful stimuli and analgesia differently, a difference that is only in part biological (Miaskowski, 1999). Cross-cultural research has found that women find it more socially appropriate to admit to experiencing pain than do men (Nayak et al., 2000). And cultural factors can influence pain perception and responses to pain treatments (Goldberg & Remy-St. Louis, 1998), as in cross-cultural differences in the interpretation and expression of pain (Rollman, 1998) and research on reactions to childbirth of women from different cultures (see the Anatomy of a Research Study feature).

Pain Control

Chronic pain afflicts millions of Americans. The pain of cancer, surgery, injuries, headaches, and backaches makes pain control an important topic of research in both medicine and psychology. The most popular approach to the relief of severe pain relies on drugs such as morphine, which affects endorphin receptors in the brain. Even **placebo** "sugar pills," which are supposedly inactive substances that are substituted for pain-relieving drugs, can relieve pain. One study found that patients with chronic pain who respond to placebos produce higher levels of endorphins than do those who fail to respond (Lipman et al., 1990). But other studies have failed to find a role for endorphins in the placebo effect (Montgomery & Kirsch, 1996).

Other techniques that do not rely on drugs or placebos also relieve pain by stimulating the release of endorphins. For example, the technique of **acupuncture,** popular in China for thousands of years, relies on the insertion of fine needles into various sites on the body. *Naloxone,* a drug that blocks the effects of opiates, inhibits the analgesic effects of acupuncture. This provides evidence for the role of endorphins in acupuncture (Murray, 1995), perhaps by

Anatomy of a Research Study

Are There Cultural Differences in the Painfulness of Childbirth?

Childbirth is both a physiological and cultural event of major importance in many women's lives. Italian researchers Alda Scopesi, Mirella Zanobini, and Paolo Carossino (1997), of the University of Genoa, wondered to what extent cultural factors would affect women's reactions to childbirth, including the degree of pain they experienced during labor and delivery. They decided to study the reactions of women in comparable cities in four different cultures.

Method

The research study was carried out in 18 hospitals in four industrialized cities: Boston in the United States, Genoa in Italy, Cologne in Germany, and Reims in France. Of the 414 women in the study, 93 were from Boston, 109 from Genoa, 107 from Cologne, and 105 from Reims. The women were asked to respond to a questionnaire with 29 questions about the course of their pregnancy and their subjective reactions to childbirth.

Results and Discussion

The results indicated that there was no statistically significant difference between the groups regarding pain during labor. But there was a statistically significant difference in their degree of pain during delivery. Most of the women in each city reported delivery was bearable, but significantly fewer women in Genoa (only 6 percent) reported that delivery was unbearably painful. Boston and Reims had the highest percentage of women (22 percent in each city) reporting that delivery was unbearably painful.

The authors, looking at possible cultural differences for these findings, concluded that women in Genoa were less likely to experience delivery as unbearable because childbirth is more likely to be considered a medical event there, in which pain is expected. This interpretation agrees with research findings that our expectations can affect our responses to pain. If we can predict that we will experience pain, we will experience it as less intense than if severe pain is not considered a part of delivery.

Another potentially important finding was that there was a tendency for women who reported that pain during delivery was unbearable to also report that they experienced a greater degree of joy afterward. This phenomenon, in which a positive emotional experience follows a powerful negative one, is discussed in Chapter 12. This study provided evidence that women in different cultures will respond differently to the pain of delivering a child. But it will take more cross-cultural studies like this one to determine the factors that account for this, including the reasons why women in four different cultures would differ in their subjective level of pain during delivery but not during labor. One possible explanation for these differences is the influence of the medical staff's expectations. Cross-cultural studies indicate that women's responses during labor might, indeed, be affected by the attitudes of their hospital caregivers (Sheiner et al., 1999).

---

blocking impulses at the pain gate in the spinal cord (Lee & Beitz, 1992). Research using functional MRI of the brain (see Chapter 3) found that acupuncture might exert its pain-relieving effects in part by affecting the limbic system (Hui et al., 2000).

A similar, more modern technique for pain relief relies on **transcutaneous electrical nerve stimulation (TENS),** which involves electrical stimulation of sites on the body. TENS has proved effective in relieving many kinds of pain, including back pain (Marchand, Charest, & Chenard, 1993), dental pain (Schwolow, Wilckens, & Roth, 1988), and headache pain (Solomon & Guglielmo, 1985). A survey of chronic-pain patients who used TENS found that they had a significant reduction in their use of pain-killing drugs (Chabal et al., 1998). As in the case of placebos and acupuncture, TENS might relieve pain by stimulating the release of endorphins, because its effects are blocked by naloxone (Wang, Mao, & Han, 1992). TENS might also inhibit activity in the pain gate in the spinal cord (Garrison & Foreman, 1994).

Still another technique, hypnosis, has been useful in relieving pain. For example, it has helped relieve pain experienced by burn victims (Patterson, Adcock, & Bombardier, 1997) and cancer patients (Peter, 1997). But unlike other pain-relieving techniques, hypnosis does not appear to work by stimulating the release of endorphins. A recent study found that hypnosis might exert its effects by sending neural impulses that block pain impulses at the spinal cord pain gate (Kiernan et al., 1995) or by reducing attention to pain sensations (Crawford, Knebel, & Vendemia, 1998).

transcutaneous electrical nerve stimulation (TENS)

The use of electrical stimulation of sites on the body to provide pain relief, apparently by stimulating the release of endorphins.

Pain victims can also control their pain by using distracting thoughts or distracting stimuli (Johnson et al., 1998). In a study of dental patients, participants distracted by music during procedures experienced less pain and distress than did participants in a control group who were not exposed to it (Anderson, Baron, & Logan, 1991). And a meta-analysis found that distraction is effective in reducing children's pain and distress during medical procedures (Kleiber & Harper, 1999).

STAYING ON TRACK: *Skin Senses*

1. How has the sense of touch been used to provide an electronic substitute for vision?
2. What is the gate-control theory of pain?
3. How is naloxone used to determine whether a pain-relieving technique works by stimulating endorphin activity?

Answers to Staying on Track start on p. ST-3.

◆ BODY SENSES

Just as your skin senses let you judge the state of your skin, your body senses tell you the position of your limbs and help you maintain your equilibrium. The body senses—the *kinesthetic sense* and the *vestibular sense*—often are taken for granted and have inspired less research than the other senses. But they are crucial to everyday functioning.

The Kinesthetic Sense

kinesthetic sense
The sense that provides information about the position of the joints, the degree of tension in the muscles, and the movement of the arms and legs.

The **kinesthetic sense** informs you of the position of your joints, the tension in your muscles, and the movement of your arms and legs. This information is provided by special receptors in your joints, muscles, and tendons. Kinesthetic receptors in your muscles let you judge the force as well as the path of your limb movements. Limb movements produce activity in specific regions of the somatosensory cortex (Prud'homme, Cohen, & Kalaska, 1994).

If your leg has ever "fallen asleep" (depriving you of kinesthetic sensations) and collapsed on you when you stood up, you realize that the kinesthetic sense helps you maintain enough tension in your legs to stand erect. Your kinesthetic sense also protects you from injury. If you are holding an object that is too heavy, kinesthetic receptors signal you to put it down to prevent injury to your muscles and tendons. Alcohol intoxication interferes with kinesthetic feedback, impairing movement by disrupting the sense of limb position (Wang et al., 1993).

Imagine losing your kinesthetic sense permanently, as happened to a woman described in a case study by Oliver Sacks (1985). This robust, athletic young woman developed a rare inflammatory condition that affected only her kinesthetic neurons. She lost all feedback from her body, making it impossible for her to sit, stand, or walk. Her body became as floppy as a rag doll, and she reported feeling like a disembodied mind. She was able to compensate only slightly by using her sense of vision to regulate her body posture and movements. Thus, our kinesthetic sense, which we usually take for granted, plays an important role in our everyday motor functioning, such as writing (Teasdale et al., 1993).

As in the case of other senses, kinesthetic perception is subject to "top-down" processes, as in its ability to judge the weight of objects. This was demonstrated in a study that compared the ability of golfers and nongolfers to judge the weights of practice golf balls and real golf balls. Though practice balls are normally heavier than real balls, the balls used in this study were equal in weight. The golfers, whose experience told them practice balls are heavier than real balls, judged the practice balls to be heavier. The nongolfers, who had no experience with golf balls, correctly judged the balls to be equal in weight. Thus, the golfers' experience with golf balls affected their kinesthetic perception of their comparative weights (Ellis & Lederman, 1998).

▲ **The Body Senses**
The kinesthetic sense and the vestibular sense provide gymnasts, as well as dancers, athletes, and other performers, with exquisite control over their body movements.

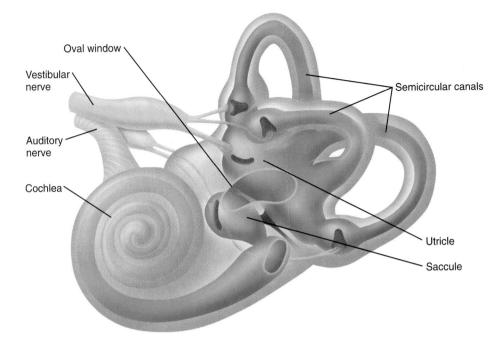

Oval window

Vestibular nerve

Auditory nerve

Cochlea

Semicircular canals

Utricle

Saccule

◀ **Figure 5.28**
The Vestibular Organs
When your head moves, fluid movement in the vestibular organs of the inner ear cause hair cells to bend, generating neural impulses that travel along the vestibular nerve to the brain. The semicircular canals detect tilting or rotation of your head. The otolith organs (the saccule and the utricle) detect linear movements of the head.

The Vestibular Sense

Whereas the kinesthetic sense informs you of the state of your body parts, your **vestibular sense,** which depends on organs in the inner ear, informs you of your head's position in space, helping you maintain your balance and orientation.

The Vestibular Organs

The **otolith organs** detect horizontal or vertical linear movement of the head and help you orient yourself in regard to gravity. The other vestibular organs are the **semicircular canals,** which are three fluid-filled tubes oriented in different planes. Their location is indicated in Figure 5.28. When your head moves in a given direction, the jellylike fluid in the semicircular canal oriented in that direction at first lags behind the movement of the walls of the canal. This makes hair cells protruding into the fluid bend in the direction opposite to the direction of head movement. The bending of hair cells triggers neural impulses that are relayed to your cerebellum, to help you maintain your balance.

Motion Sickness

Though the vestibular sense helps you maintain your equilibrium, it can also induce motion sickness. Fortunately, repeated exposure to situations that induce motion sickness tends to produce tolerance. Experienced sailors will be less prone to seasickness than new sailors are (Hu & Stern, 1999), and a study of paratroopers found that two-thirds had motion sickness on their first jump, but only one-quarter had it on their fifth jump (Antunano & Hernandez, 1989).

The mechanisms that underlie motion sickness are still debated, but an influential view holds that motion sickness is induced by conflict between visual and vestibular sensations. Suppose you are in a windowless cabin aboard a ship in a rough sea. Your eyes tell you that you are stationary in relationship to one aspect of your environment—your cabin. Yet your vestibular sense tells you that you are moving in relationship to another aspect of your environment—the ocean. But this does not explain *why* conflict between visual and vestibular sensations induces nausea. One hypothesis is that the motion-induced disruption of the normal association between visual and vestibular sensations is similar to that produced by toxins, such as those in spoiled food, that induce nausea. As a result, motion induces nausea (Warwick-Evans et al., 1998).

vestibular sense
The sense that provides information about the head's position in space and helps in the maintenance of balance.

otolith organs
The vestibular organs that detect horizontal or vertical linear movement of the head.

semicircular canals
The curved vestibular organs of the inner ear that detect rotary movements of the head in any direction.

 Seasickness: Causes and Prevention
www.mhhe.com/sdorow5

1. What is the kinesthetic sense?
2. What is the role of the vestibular sense in motion sickness?

Answers to Staying on Track start on p. ST-3.

◆ EXTRASENSORY PERCEPTION

extrasensory perception (ESP)
The alleged ability to perceive events without the use of sensory receptors.

parapsychology
The study of extrasensory perception, psychokinesis, and related phenomena.

As you have just read, perception depends on the stimulation of sensory receptors by various kinds of energy. But you have certainly heard claims that support the possibility of perception independent of sensory receptors, so-called **extrasensory perception (ESP).** The field that studies ESP and related phenomena is called **parapsychology** (*para-* means "besides"). The name indicates its failure to gain widespread acceptance within mainstream psychology. Parapsychological abilities are typically called *paranormal.*

Despite scientific skepticism about paranormal abilities, a survey found that more than 99 percent of American college students believed in at least one paranormal ability and that more than 65 percent claimed a personal experience with at least one (Messer & Griggs, 1989). Moreover, mainstream journals in psychology, philosophy, and medicine periodically publish articles on paranormal abilities. Public belief in paranormal abilities was exemplified in a 1986 lawsuit in which a Philadelphia woman who made a living as a psychic sued a hospital, insisting that a CT scan of her head made her lose her ESP abilities. A jury, impressed by the testimony of police officers who claimed she had helped them solve crimes by using ESP, awarded her $988,000 for the loss of her livelihood (Tulsky, 1986). (The jury's decision was later overturned on appeal.) Despite such widespread public acceptance of paranormal abilities, most psychologists are skeptical (Bem & Honorton, 1994). Before learning why they are, consider several of the paranormal abilities studied by parapsychologists.

Alleged Paranormal Abilities

mental telepathy
The alleged ability to perceive the thoughts of others without any sensory contact with them.

About three decades ago, members of the Grateful Dead rock group had their audiences at a series of six concerts in Port Chester, New York, try to transmit mental images of slides to a person asleep in a dream laboratory miles away at Maimonides Hospital in Brooklyn. When the sleeper awoke he described the content of his dreams. Independent judges rated his dream reports as more similar to the content of the slides than were the dream reports of another person who had not been designated to receive the images (Ullman, Krippner, & Vaughan, 1973). It was reported as a successful demonstration of **mental telepathy,** the alleged ability to perceive the thoughts of others. This was part of a series of ESP-dream studies carried out at Maimonides Hospital (Krippner, 1993).

clairvoyance
The alleged ability to perceive objects or events without any sensory contact with them.

Another study of dream telepathy had a "sender" advertise in a national newspaper that he would send a dream telepathy image between midnight and 10 A.M. on a specified night. Different images were sent every 2 hours. More than 500 readers sent dream reports and the times they "received" the images. Judges blind to the target sequence decided whether the reports matched the pictures. Unlike the results of the Grateful Dead demonstration, their assessments provided no support for dream telepathy—the reports did not match the images that were sent (Hearne, 1989). Related to mental telepathy is **clairvoyance,** the alleged ability to perceive objects or events without any sensory contact (Steinkamp, Milton, & Morris, 1998). You might be considered clairvoyant if you could identify all of the objects in your psychology professor's desk drawer without looking in it. Many colleges host "psychic" entertainers, such as "the Amazing Kreskin," who impress their audiences by giving demonstrations such as "reading" the serial number of a dollar bill in an audience member's wallet. Reports that clairvoyant psychics have solved crimes by leading police to bodies or stolen items are exaggerated. A survey of police departments in the fifty largest American cities found not a single report of a clairvoyant who had solved a crime for them (Sweat & Durm, 1993).

Whereas mental telepathy and clairvoyance deal with the present, **precognition** is the alleged ability to perceive events in the future. An example would be predicting the next spin of a roulette wheel, one of the common ways of measuring precognitive ability (Kugel, 1990–1991). Do not confuse precognition with déjà vu, an uncanny feeling that you have experienced a present situation in the past and that you can anticipate what will happen in the next few moments. There is no widely accepted explanation of déjà vu experiences (Sno, Schalken, & de Jonghe, 1992). Parapsychologists who are open to the possibility that precognition does exist are left with the daunting scientific problem of explaining how minds that exist in the present can perceive events that take place in the future (Randall, 1998).

Closely allied with ESP is **psychokinesis (PK),** the alleged ability to control objects with the mind alone. Our use of "body English" to affect the movements of dice, roulette wheels, baseballs, golf balls, or bowling balls reflects a superstitious belief in PK. PK researchers have even assessed people's ability to influence computer games (Broughton & Perlstrom, 1992). Even the military has examined the possibility of PK. But a report by the National Academy of Sciences found no basis for any kind of paranormal ability (Palmer, Honorton, & Utts, 1989).

Problems with Paranormal Research

Parapsychology has attracted many prominent supporters. Mark Twain, William James, and G. Stanley Hall were members of the Society for Psychical Research, with James serving a term as president and Hall a term as vice president. Credit for making parapsychology a legitimate area of scientific research to some scientists goes to J. B. Rhine (1895–1980) of Duke University, who began a program of experimentation on paranormal phenomena in the 1930s (Matlock, 1991). Several leading British universities also have lent credibility to parapsychology by sponsoring paranormal research. Edinburgh University in Scotland even set up the first faculty chair in parapsychology with a $750,000 grant from the estate of author Arthur Koestler (Dickson, 1984).

Despite the popular acceptance of parapsychology, most psychologists remain skeptical (Wesp & Montgomery, 1998). One reason is that many supposed instances of paranormal phenomena turn out to be the result of poorly controlled demonstrations. In a case reported by the magician James "The Amazing" Randi, a woman claimed she could influence fish by PK. Every time she put her hand against one side of an aquarium, the fish swam to the opposite side. Randi responded, "She calls it psychic; I call it frightened fish." He suggested she put dark paper over a side of the aquarium and test her ability on that side. After trying Randi's suggestion and finding that the fish no longer swam to the opposite side, she exclaimed, "It's marvelous! The power doesn't penetrate brown paper!" (Morris, 1980, p. 106). You might recognize this as an example of Piaget's concept of assimilation (see Chapter 4).

Supporters of parapsychology might also too readily accept chance events as evidence of paranormal phenomena (Diaconis, 1978). For example, at some time you probably have decided to call a friend, picked up the phone, and found your friend already on the other end of the line. Does this mean mental telepathy made you call each other at the same time? Not necessarily. Perhaps you and your friend call each other often and at about the same time of the day, so on occasion you might call each other at exactly the same moment by mere coincidence.

Another blow against the credibility of parapsychology is that some impressive demonstrations later have been found to involve fraud. In a widely publicized case, the noted psychic Tamara Rand claimed to have predicted the 1981 assassination attempt on U.S. President Ronald Reagan in a videotape made before the attempt and later shown on the *Today* show. This was considered evidence of precognition—until James Randi discovered that she had made the videotape *after* the assassination attempt ("A Psychic Watergate," 1981).

Magic tricks also are often passed off as paranormal phenomena. James Randi sponsored an elaborate hoax that demonstrated the inability of parapsychology researchers to detect magic tricks. In 1979 James McDonnell, chairman of the board of the McDonnell-Douglas corporation, gave $500,000 to Washington University in St. Louis to establish a parapsychology research laboratory. A respected physics professor took charge of the project and

precognition
The alleged ability to perceive events in the future.

psychokinesis (PK)
The alleged ability to control objects with the mind alone.

James Randi Educational Foundation
www.mhhe.com/sdorow5

▲ **J. B. Rhine (1895–1980)**
"Good evidence of parapsychological ability is not only more difficult to obtain than that of the whole range of sensorimotor exchange; it is also harder to accept. Therefore, it requires more security in the way of test conditions, perhaps the most of any field."

invited alleged psychics to be tested there. Randi sent two magicians, aged 17 and 18, to be tested as "psychics." After demonstrating their PK "abilities" during 120 hours of testing over a 3-year period, the two were proclaimed the only participants with PK ability.

But both had relied on magic—in some instances, beginner's-level magic. For example, they demonstrated PK by moving a clock across a table using an ultrathin thread held between their thumbs. Because of demonstrations like this, Randi has urged parapsychologists to permit magicians to observe their research so that magic tricks are not mistaken for paranormal phenomena ("Psychic Abscam," 1983). Since 1965 Randi has offered a reward—now amounting to $1 million—to anyone who can demonstrate a true paranormal ability under well-controlled conditions. No one has done so.

Parapsychologists defend their research by insisting that critics often reject positive findings by assuming that they are impossible and therefore must be caused by some other factor, such as poor controls, magic tricks, or outright fraud (Child, 1985). Thus, opposition to paranormal research might reflect the current scientific paradigm as much as it does any methodological weaknesses in paranormal research (Krippner, 1995). Moreover, parapsychologists argue, paranormal abilities might be so subtle that they require highly motivated individuals to demonstrate them. For example, believers in paranormal abilities perform better on paranormal tests than do nonbelievers (Schmeidler, 1985). Likewise, experimenters who believe in paranormal abilities are more likely than nonbelievers to conduct research studies that produce positive findings. Gertrude Schmeidler (1997), a leading parapsychologist, notes that experimenter bias might account for the poor performance of some participants in ESP or PK studies. She insists experimenters who are cynical about ESP or PK might inhibit talented people from performing well in research studies.

But even many parapsychologists agree that, from a scientific standpoint, the main weakness of research studies on paranormal abilities is the difficulty in replicating them. As discussed in Chapter 2, scientists discredit events that cannot be replicated under similar conditions. Yet some parapsychologists insist that positive research findings related to paranormal phenomena have been replicated more often than critics of parapsychology will acknowledge (Roig, 1993), that meta-analyses show effects greater than expected by chance alone (Krippner et al., 1993), and that paranormal phenomena are so subtle that they are more likely to occur spontaneously in everyday life than on demand in a laboratory setting (Alvarado, 1996).

A final criticism of parapsychology is that there is no satisfactory explanation of paranormal phenomena (Fassbender, 1997). Their acceptance might require the discovery of new forms of energy. Evidence for the role of some sort of energy force comes from the finding that research studies conducted during periods of low geomagnetic activity have been associated with the most positive ESP research findings (Krippner, Vaughan, & Spottiswoode, 2000). But attempts to detect any unusual form of energy radiating from people with supposed paranormal abilities have failed (Balanovski & Taylor, 1978).

The Status of Parapsychology

Parapsychologists point out, however, that failure to know the cause of something does not mean that the phenomenon does not exist (Rockwell, 1979). They remind psychologists to be skeptical rather than cynical, because many phenomena that are now scientifically acceptable were once considered impossible and unworthy of study. For example, scientists used to ridicule reports of stones falling from the sky and refused to investigate them. In 1807, after hearing of a report by two Yale University professors of a stone shower in Connecticut, President Thomas Jefferson, a scientist himself, said, "Gentlemen, I would rather believe that those two Yankee professors would lie than to believe that stones fell from heaven" (quoted in Diaconis, 1978). Today, even young children know that such stones are meteorites and that they, indeed, fall from the sky. Nonetheless, because alleged paranormal abilities are so unusual, seemingly inexplicable, and difficult to demonstrate reliably, even open-minded psychologists will continue to discount them unless they receive more compelling evidence. The extraordinary claims made by parapsychologists will require extraordinary evidence for mainstream psychologists to accept their validity (Grey, 1994).

STAYING ON TRACK: *Extrasensory Perception*

1. What are the four alleged paranormal abilities?
2. What are the major shortcomings of paranormal research?

Answers to Staying on Track start on p. ST-3.

Chapter Summary

SENSORY PROCESSES

- Sensation is the process that detects stimuli from one's body or environment.
- Perception is the process that organizes sensations into meaningful patterns.
- Psychophysics is the study of the relationship between the physical characteristics of stimuli and the conscious psychological experiences they produce.
- The minimum amount of stimulation that can be detected is called the absolute threshold.
- According to signal-detection theory, the detection of a stimulus depends on both its intensity and the physiological and psychological state of the receiver.
- Research on subliminal perception investigates whether participants can unconsciously perceive stimuli that do not exceed the absolute threshold.
- The minimum amount of change in stimulation that can be detected is called the difference threshold.
- Weber's law states that the amount of change in stimulation needed to produce a just noticeable difference is a constant proportion of the original stimulus.
- The tendency of our sensory receptors to be increasingly less responsive to an unchanging stimulus is called sensory adaptation.

VISUAL SENSATION

- Vision lets us sense objects by the light reflected from them into our eyes.

- The lens focuses light onto the rods and cones of the retina.
- Visual input is transmitted by the optic nerves to the brain, ultimately reaching the visual cortex.
- During dark adaptation the rods and cones become more sensitive to light, with the rods becoming significantly more sensitive than the cones.
- The trichromatic theory of color vision considers the interaction of red, green, and blue cones.
- Opponent-process theory assumes that color vision depends on activity in red-green, blue-yellow, and black-white ganglion cells and cells in the thalamus.
- Color blindness is usually caused by an inherited lack of a cone pigment.

VISUAL PERCEPTION

- Form perception depends on distinguishing figure from ground.
- In studying form perception, Gestalt psychologists identified the principles of proximity, similarity, closure, and continuity.
- Whereas Gestalt psychologists claim that we perceive objects as wholes, other theorists claim that we construct objects from their component parts.
- Depth perception lets us determine how far away objects are from us.
- Binocular cues to depth require the interaction of both eyes.
- Monocular cues to depth require only one eye.
- Experience in viewing objects contributes to size constancy, shape constancy, and brightness constancy.

- The misapplication of depth perception cues and perceptual constancies can contribute to visual illusions.
- Sensory experience and cultural background both affect visual perception.

HEARING
- The sense of hearing (audition) detects sound waves produced by the vibration of objects.
- Sound waves cause the tympanic membrane to vibrate.
- The ossicles of the middle ear convey the vibrations to the oval window of the cochlea, which causes waves to travel through fluid within the cochlea.
- The waves make hair cells on the basilar membrane bend, sending neural impulses along the auditory nerve.
- Sounds are ultimately processed by the auditory cortex of the temporal lobes.
- The frequency of a sound determines its pitch.
- Pitch perception is explained by place theory, frequency theory, and volley theory.
- The intensity of a sound determines its loudness.
- Hearing loss can be associated with conduction deafness or nerve deafness.
- The mixture of sound waves determines a sound's quality, or timbre.
- Sound localization depends on differences in a sound's arrival time and intensity at the two ears.

CHEMICAL SENSES
- The chemical senses of smell and taste detect chemicals in the air we breathe or the substances we ingest.
- The sense of smell (olfaction) depends on receptor cells on the nasal membrane that respond to particular chemicals.
- Odorous secretions called pheromones affect the behavior of animals.
- The sense of taste (gustation) depends on receptor cells on the taste buds of the tongue that respond to particular chemicals.
- The basic tastes are sweet, salty, sour, and bitter.

SKIN SENSES
- Skin senses depend on receptors that send neural impulses to the somatosensory cortex.
- Touch sensitivity depends on the concentration of receptors in the skin.
- Pain depends on both physical and psychological factors.
- According to the gate-control theory of pain, stimulation of touch neurons closes a spinal "gate," which inhibits neural impulses underlying pain from traveling up the spinal cord.
- Pain-relieving techniques such as placebos, acupuncture, and transcutaneous nerve stimulation relieve pain by stimulating the release of endorphins.
- Hypnosis appears to relieve pain by distracting the hypnotized person.

BODY SENSES
- Your body senses make you aware of the position of your limbs and help you maintain your equilibrium.
- The kinesthetic sense informs you of the position of your joints, the tension in your muscles, and the movement of your arms and legs.
- The vestibular sense informs you of your position in space, helping you maintain your equilibrium.
- The vestibular organs comprise the otolith organs and the semicircular canals.
- An influential theory of motion sickness attributes it to conflict between the visual and vestibular senses.

EXTRASENSORY PERCEPTION
- Most members of the lay public accept the existence of paranormal phenomena such as extrasensory perception and psychokinesis; most psychologists do not.
- Psychologists are skeptical because research in parapsychology has been marked by sloppy procedures, acceptance of coincidences as positive evidence, fraudulent reports, use of magic tricks, failure to replicate studies, and inability to explain paranormal phenomena.
- Supporters of parapsychology claim that their research has been subjected to unfair criticism.

Key Concepts

perception 133
prosopagnosia 133
sensation 133
visual agnosia 133

SENSORY PROCESSES
absolute threshold 134
difference threshold 136
just noticeable difference
   (jnd) 136
psychophysics 134
sensory adaptation 138
sensory receptors 134
sensory transduction 134

signal-detection theory 135
subliminal perception 135
Weber's law 138

VISUAL SENSATION
accommodation 140
color afterimage 145
color blindness 146
cones 140
cornea 139
dark adaptation 144
fovea 140
hyperopia 140
iris 139

lens 140
myopia 140
opponent-process theory 145
optic chiasm 142
optic nerve 140
photopigments 144
pupil 139
retina 140
rods 140
sclera 139
sex-linked traits 146
smooth pursuit movements 142
trichromatic theory 144
visible spectrum 138

vision 138
visual cortex 143

VISUAL PERCEPTION
binocular cues 150
brightness constancy 152
depth perception 149
feature-detector theory 148
figure-ground perception 147
monocular cues 150
moon illusion 152
shape constancy 152
size constancy 152
visual illusion 152

Key Contributors

Thought Questions

1. Why is it conceivable that creatures on planets in other solar systems have evolved sensory receptors that detect radio and television waves?
2. How does the opponent-process theory of color vision explain afterimages?

3. Why are both frequency and place theories needed to explain pitch perception?
4. Why do psychologists tend to discount the existence of paranormal abilities?

Possible Answers to Thought Questions start on p. PT-2.

OLC Preview

 For additional quizzing and a variety of interactive resources, visit the book's Online Learning Center at www.mhhe.com/sdorow5.

chapter six

6

Consciousness

HENRI ROUSSEAU
The Sleeping Gypsy, 1897

If you are like many students, you have experienced the dreaded "all-nighter"—staying awake through the night to write a paper or study for an exam. You probably felt exhausted the next night, collapsed into bed, slept a bit longer than usual, and awoke refreshed—none the worse for your experience. But what would happen to you if you stayed awake for several days? Would you suffer mental and physical deterioration? Would any negative effects be long-lasting?

Though research on prolonged sleep deprivation began in the 1890s, the first study to gain widespread attention took place in 1959. On January 21, Peter Tripp, a popular disc jockey in New York City, began a radiothon to raise money for the March of Dimes fight against polio. He decided to proceed despite anecdotal reports about animals and human beings who had died after prolonged sleep deprivation. He chose to believe, instead, other anecdotal reports about explorers and military men who had survived bouts of extended sleep deprivation (Coren, 1996).

During his radiothon, Tripp stayed awake for 200 hours (more than 8 days), each evening broadcasting his 5-to-8 P.M. radio show from an Army recruiting booth in Times Square. He did this for the publicity and to permit passersby to look through the windows of the booth and verify that he was awake. Tripp periodically left the booth to go to the Astor Hotel across the street to wash up, use the toilet, change his clothes, and undergo medical examinations. Physicians and researchers monitored several of his physiological responses for his safety and to obtain scientific data on the effects of sleep deprivation.

As the days passed, Tripp showed signs of psychological deterioration. After 4 days he could not focus his attention well enough to do simple tasks, and he began experiencing hallucinations, such as seeing a rabbit run across the booth and flames shooting out of a drawer in his hotel room. Some accounts of Tripp's radiothon note that after 5 days he began taking a stimulant drug to stay awake (Luce & Segal, 1966). On the eighth and final day, he displayed delusional thinking, insisting his physician was an undertaker coming to prepare him for burial. Tripp became so paranoid that he refused to undergo requested tests and insisted that unknown enemies were trying to force him to fall asleep by putting drugs in his food and drink. After his ordeal Tripp slept 13 hours and quickly returned to his customary level of psychological well-being.

Did Tripp's experience demonstrate that we need to sleep to maintain healthy psychological functioning and that a single night's sleep can overcome any ill effects of sleep deprivation? Possibly—but possibly not. First, Tripp's experiences were those of a single subject. His reactions to sleep deprivation might have been unique and not necessarily true of other people. Second, as you will learn later in this chapter, the delusions Tripp displayed near the end of his ordeal might have been caused by the stimulant drugs he took to stay awake and not by his lack of sleep. Our knowledge of the effects of sleep deprivation and the effects of stimulant drugs comes from research by psychologists and other scientists interested in the study of *consciousness*.

▲ **Two Hundred Hours Without Sleep**
Peter Tripp experienced emotional, perceptual, and cognitive disturbances during his 200-hour radiothon.

◆ THE NATURE OF CONSCIOUSNESS

What is consciousness? In 1690 John Locke wrote, "Consciousness is the perception of what passes in a man's own mind" (Locke, 1690/1959, p. 138). Today psychologists share a similar view of **consciousness,** defining it as the awareness of one's own mental activity, including thoughts, feelings, and sensations.

consciousness
Awareness of one's own mental activity, including thoughts, feelings, and sensations.

 Psyche: An International Journal of Research on Consciousness
www.mhhe.com/sdorow5

The Stream of Consciousness

Two hundred years after Locke offered his definition of consciousness, William James (1890/1981) noted that consciousness is personal, selective, continuous, and changing. Consider your own consciousness. It is *personal* because you feel that it belongs to you—you do not share it with anyone else. Consciousness is *selective* because you can attend to certain things while ignoring other things. Right now you can shift your attention to a nearby voice, the first word in the next sentence, or the feel of this book against your fingers. Consciousness is *continuous* because its contents blend into one another—the mind cannot be broken down into meaningful segments. And consciousness is *changing* because its contents are in a constant state of flux; normally, you cannot focus on one thing more than momentarily without other thoughts, feelings, or sensations drifting through your mind.

Because consciousness is both continuous and changing, James likened it to a stream (Natsoulas, 1999–2000). Your favorite stream remains the same stream even though the water at a particular site is continuously being replaced by new water. Even as you read this paragraph, you might notice irrelevant thoughts, feelings, and sensations passing through your own mind. Some might grab your attention; others might quickly fade away. If you were to write them down as they occurred, a person reading what you had written might think you were confused or even that you were mentally ill. The disjointed nature of stream-of-consciousness writing makes it hard to follow without knowing the context of the story. You can appreciate this by trying to make sense of the opening passage from James Joyce's *A Portrait of the Artist as a Young Man:*

▶ Once upon a time and a very good time it was there was a moocow coming down along the road and this moocow that was coming down along the road met a nicens little boy named baby tuckoo. . . .

His father told him that story: his father looked at him through a glass: he had a hairy face.

He was baby tuckoo. The moocow came down the road where Betty Byrne lived: she sold lemon platt.

O, the wild rose blossoms
On the little green place.

He sang that song. That was his song.

O, the green wothe botheth.

When you wet the bed first it is warm then it gets cold. His mother put on the oilsheet. That had the queer smell.

His mother had a nicer smell than his father. She played on the piano the sailor's hornpipe for him to dance. (Joyce, 1916/1967, p. 171)

As a functionalist, William James believed consciousness is an evolutionary development that enhances our ability to adapt to the environment. James declared, "It seems reasonable to suppose that, unless consciousness served some useful purpose, it would not have been superadded to life" (quoted in Rieber, 1980, p. 205). That is, consciousness helps us function. Consciousness provides us with a mental representation of the world that permits us to try out courses of action in our mind before acting on them. This makes us more reflective and more flexible in adapting to the world, thereby reducing our tendency to engage in aimless, reckless, or impulsive behavior.

Attention

Today researchers are especially interested in an aspect of consciousness identified by James: its *selectivity*. We refer to the selectivity of consciousness as **attention,** which functions like a tuner to make us aware of certain stimuli while blocking out others. This selectivity is adaptive because it prevents our consciousness from becoming a chaotic jumble of thoughts, feelings, and sensations. For example, while you are reading this paragraph, it

Center for Consciousness Studies
www.mhhe.com/sdorow5

attention

The process by which the individual focuses awareness on certain contents of consciousness while ignoring others.

would be maladaptive for you to also be aware of irrelevant stimuli, such as the shoes on your feet or people talking. Of course, it would be adaptive to shift your attention if your shoes are too tight or someone yelled "Fire!" outside your room.

Experimental research, as well as everyday experience, illustrates the selectivity of attention. Consider a study in which participants watched two videotapes superimposed on each other (Neisser & Becklen, 1975). One videotape portrayed two people playing a hand-slapping game, and the other portrayed three people bouncing and throwing a basketball. Participants were told to watch one of the games and to press a response key whenever a particular action occurred. Those watching the hand game had to respond whenever the participants slapped hands with each other. Those watching the ball game had to respond whenever the ball was thrown. The results showed participants made few errors. But when they were asked to watch both games simultaneously, using their right hand to respond to one game and their left hand to respond to the other, their performances deteriorated and they made significantly more errors than when they attended to just one of the games.

What determines whether we will attend to a given stimulus? Among the many stimulus factors that affect attention are whether the stimulus is important, changing, or novel. We tend to notice stimuli that are personally *important*. You have certainly experienced this in regard to the "cocktail party phenomenon" (Wood & Cowan, 1995), in which you might be engrossed in one conversation at a party yet notice that other people have mentioned your name in their conversation. A *change* in stimulation is likely to attract our attention. When watching television, you are more likely to pay attention to a commercial that is much louder or quieter than the program it interrupts. The importance of attention in everyday life is illustrated by the controversy over the use of cellular telephones in motor vehicles. Research indicates that using a cellular telephone while driving distracts drivers from potentially dangerous situations they should notice and react to (McKnight & McKnight, 1993).

An Investigation of the Implications of Wireless Communications in Vehicles
www.mhhe.com/sdorow5

STAYING ON TRACK: *The Nature of Consciousness*

1. What psychological topic did William James and James Joyce share an interest in?
2. What is the "cocktail party" phenomenon?

Answers to Staying on Track start on p. ST-3.

The Unconscious

In the late 19th century, William James (1890/1981), in his classic psychology textbook, included a section entitled "Can States of Mind Be Unconscious?" which presented ten arguments answering yes and ten answering no. Today the extent to which we are affected by unconscious influences still provokes animated debate. But the notion of the unconscious involves any of three different concepts: (1) *perception without awareness,* the unconscious perception of stimuli that exceed our normal absolute threshold (see Chapter 5) but that fall outside our focus of attention; (2) the *Freudian unconscious,* a region of the mind containing thoughts and feelings that motivate us without our awareness; and (3) *subliminal perception,* the unconscious perception of stimuli that are too weak to exceed the absolute threshold for detection. (For a discussion of subliminal perception, see Chapter 5.)

Perception Without Awareness

There is substantial evidence that we can be affected by stimuli that are above the normal absolute threshold but to which we are not attending at the time. At the turn of the century, the existence of such **perception without awareness** (Merikle & Joordens, 1997) led some psychologists to assume that suggestions given to people while they sleep might help children study harder or adults quit smoking (Jones, 1900). But subsequent research has failed to support such sleep learning. Any learning that does take place apparently occurs during brief

perception without awareness
The unconscious perception of stimuli that normally exceed the absolute threshold but fall outside our focus of attention.

In studies of dichotic listening, participants repeat a message presented to one ear while a different message is presented to the other ear.

awakenings (Wood et al., 1992). So, if you decide to study for your next psychology exam by playing an audiotape of class lectures while you are asleep, you will be more likely to disrupt your sleep than to learn significant amounts of material.

Dichotic Listening. Research on attention also has demonstrated the existence of perception without awareness. Consider studies of *dichotic listening,* in which the participant, wearing headphones, repeats—or "shadows"—a message being presented to one ear while another message is being presented to the other ear (Wood, Hiscock, & Widrig, 2000). This is illustrated in Figure 6.1. By shadowing one message, the participant is prevented from consciously attending to the other one. Though participants cannot recall the unattended message, they might recall certain qualities of it, such as whether it was spoken by a male voice or by a female voice. This demonstrates that our brain can process incoming stimuli that exceed the normal absolute threshold even when we do not consciously attend to them (Cherry, 1953).

Blindsight. Perception without awareness is also supported in studies of brain damage. Consider *prosopagnosia,* the inability to recognize faces. The disorder is caused by damage to a particular region of the cerebral cortex (see Chapter 5). In one study, two women with prosopagnosia were shown photographs of strangers, friends, and relatives while their galvanic skin response (a measure of arousal based on changes in the electrical activity of the skin) was recorded. Though the women were unable to recognize their friends and relatives from the photographs, they gave larger galvanic skin responses to those photographs than to the photographs of strangers. This indicated intact visual pathways in the brain had distinguished between the familiar and the unfamiliar faces without the women's conscious awareness of it (Tranel & Damasio, 1985). This phenomenon of *blindsight*—which also can occur for visual stimuli other than faces—indicates that certain unknown retinal pathways process visual information without our conscious awareness (Danckert & Goodale, 2000).

Controlled Versus Automatic Processing. Of course, "awareness" is usually not an all-or-none phenomenon. For example, there is a continuum between controlled processing and automatic processing of information (Walczyk, 2000). At one extreme, when we focus our attention on one target, we use **controlled processing,** which involves more conscious awareness (attention) and mental effort, and interferes with the performance of other activities. At the other extreme, when we do one thing while focusing our attention on another, we use **automatic processing,** which requires less conscious awareness and mental effort and does not interfere with the performance of other activities. As we practice a task, we need to devote less and less attention to it because we move from controlled processing to

Face Blind
www.mhhe.com/sdorow5

controlled processing
Information processing that involves conscious awareness and mental effort, and that interferes with the performance of other ongoing activities.

automatic processing
Information processing that requires less conscious awareness and mental effort, and that does not interfere with the performance of other ongoing activities.

| PINK | RED | BLUE | GREEN | PINK | YELLOW | BLUE | GREEN |
| GREEN | BLUE | YELLOW | BLUE | GREEN | PINK | RED | BLUE |

◀ **Figure 6.2**
The Stroop Effect

You will find it easier to read the words than to name their colors. Evidently, after years of daily reading, reading words has become so automatic that you cannot completely inhibit that tendency even when you try. In contrast, naming colors is a more unusual task that requires controlled processing.

automatic processing. Think back to when you first learned to write in script. You depended on controlled processing, which required you to focus your complete attention on forming each letter. Today, after years of practice in writing, you make use of automatic processing. This lets you write notes in class while focusing your attention on the professor's lecture rather than on the movements of your pen.

Automatic processing can, at times, interfere with controlled processing. Consider the *Stroop effect* (named for its discoverer), illustrated in Figure 6.2. Time how long it takes you to read the words. Then time how long it takes you to name the colors of the words. You probably performed the first task faster, presumably because of your extensive experience in reading. But the automaticity of reading words interfered with your ability to name the colors, a task that you are rarely called upon to do (Lindsay & Jacoby, 1994). Thus, even when you try to name the colors and ignore the words, automatic, unconscious processes make it difficult for you not to read the words.

The Freudian Unconscious

During the 1988 National League baseball playoffs between the New York Mets and the Los Angeles Dodgers, relief pitcher Brian Holton of the Dodgers became so nervous that he could not grip the baseball. Suddenly he found himself singing the lyrics to a folk song, "You take the high road and I'll take the low road." This surprised him, because he believed he had never heard the song. Yet for some reason, singing it relaxed him enough to enable him to grip the baseball. When he told his mother about this mysterious behavior, she informed him his father had comforted him by singing the song to him when he was a young child.

Levels of Consciousness. Psychoanalytic theorists use anecdotal reports like this to support the existence of the Freudian unconscious. Freud divided consciousness into three levels: the *conscious,* the *preconscious,* and the *unconscious* (see Figure 6.3). As had William James, Freud viewed the **conscious mind** as the awareness of fleeting images, feelings, and sensations. The **preconscious mind** contains memories of which we are unaware at the moment, but of which we can become aware at will. And the **unconscious mind** contains repressed feelings, memories, and response tendencies of which we are unaware. Through what Freud called *psychic determinism,* these unconscious factors affect our behavior. Perhaps this explains why we instantly like or dislike someone for no apparent reason, engage in repeated, irrational, self-defeating behavior, or commit a "Freudian slip," in which we replace intended words with sexual or aggressive ones (Reason, 2000).

Subliminal Psychodynamic Activation. Until recently, the Freudian unconscious was considered impossible to study scientifically because evidence of its existence came solely from anecdotal or clinical reports and because it could not be observed directly. But more sophisticated techniques, though they have not necessarily convinced all psychologists of the existence of the Freudian unconscious, make it subject to scientific research (Epstein, 1994). One technique, developed by Lloyd Silverman, is called **subliminal psychodynamic activation.** It is based on the assumption that emotionally charged subliminal messages will alter the recipient's moods and behaviors by stimulating unconscious fantasies (Weinberger & Silverman, 1990).

Silverman claimed unconscious "oneness fantasies" (which express emotional union with one's mother, an important concept from Freud's theory that emphasizes the importance of maternal love and care in early childhood) relieve anxiety and enhance task performance. For example, participants are typically presented with a oneness phrase, such as *Mommy and I are one,* or a neutral phrase, such as *People are walking.* The messages are presented by a device called a *tachistoscope,* which flashes visual stimuli too briefly (for only a fraction of a second) to exceed the absolute threshold.

conscious mind

The level of consciousness that includes the mental experiences that we are aware of at a given moment.

preconscious mind

The level of consciousness that contains feelings and memories that we are unaware of at the moment but can become aware of at will.

unconscious mind

The level of consciousness that contains thoughts, feelings, and memories that influence us without our awareness and that we cannot become aware of at will.

subliminal psychodynamic activation

The use of subliminal messages to stimulate unconscious fantasies.

Levels of Consciousness

According to Sigmund Freud, there are three levels of consciousness. The conscious level contains thoughts, images, and feelings of which we are aware. The preconscious level contains memories that we can retrieve at will. And the unconscious level contains repressed motives and memories that would evoke intense feelings of anxiety if we became aware of them.

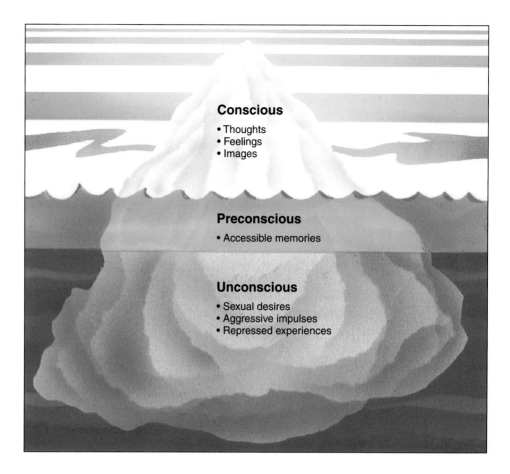

A study of subliminal psychodynamic activation used students who had failed a university mathematics assessment test who then took part in a summer mathematics enrichment program. One group viewed a subliminal oneness message and the other a subliminal neutral message. After 20 weeks of the program, the group exposed to the oneness message performed better on a mathematics test than did the group not exposed to it (Hudesman, Page, & Rautiainen, 1992). But other studies have failed to find any effects of subliminal psychodynamic activation (Fudin, 2000). For example, a study of subliminal psychodynamic activation studied the effect of subliminal messages on anxiety, using heart rate changes to measure the level of anxiety. Participants were 100 college students. They were divided into five groups, depending on which message they were shown: "Mommy and I are one," "Daddy and I are one," "Mommy has left me," "I'm happy and calm," and a neutral stimulus that presumably had no emotional effect. The results showed heart rate changes were unrelated to the kind of message presented. This provided evidence against any special effect of "oneness" messages (Malik et al., 1996). Overall, the results of studies of subliminal psychodynamic activation indicate that at best it has only small effects on moods and behaviors (Hardaway, 1990).

Based on the foregoing discussion of unconscious influences, you should now realize that solid scientific evidence indicates we can be affected by stimuli of which we are unaware. Some of the more extreme claims for unconscious influences on our moods and behaviors, however, have tainted an otherwise legitimate topic for psychological research.

STAYING ON TRACK: *The Unconscious*

1. Why is automatic processing considered to be an example of perception without awareness?
2. How has subliminal psychodynamic activation been used to test Freud's notion of unconscious motivation?

Answers to Staying on Track start on p. ST-3.

◆ SLEEP

Perhaps the most obvious alternative to waking consciousness is *sleep.* The daily sleep-wake cycle is one of our **biological rhythms,** which are cyclical changes in physiological processes. Other examples of biological rhythms are the 28-day menstrual cycle in women and the annual cycle of waking and hibernation in bears. Be sure not to confuse biological rhythms, a legitimate topic of scientific research, with "biorhythms," a topic better left to pop psychology. Those who believe in biorhythms claim that each of us is born with physical, emotional, and intellectual cycles that stay constant in length and govern us for the rest of our lives. No scientifically worthy research supports these claims (Hines, 1998).

Biological Rhythms and the Sleep-Wake Cycle

The daily sleep-wake cycle is the most obvious of our **circadian rhythms,** which are 24-hour cycles of changes in physiological processes. Our circadian rhythm of body temperature parallels our circadian rhythm of brain arousal, with most people beginning the day at low points on both and rising on them through the day. College roommates who are out of phase with each other in their circadian rhythms are more likely to express dissatisfaction with their relationship (Watts, 1982). A student who is a "morning person"—already warmed up and chipper at 7 A.M.—might find it difficult to socialize with a roommate who can barely crawl out of bed at that time. There is some evidence that these individual differences in circadian rhythms are established early in childhood (Cofer et al., 1999).

Factors in Biological Rhythms

What governs our circadian rhythms? A chief factor is an area of the hypothalamus called the *suprachiasmatic nucleus* (Grossman et al., 2000), which regulates the secretion of the hormone *melatonin* by the **pineal gland,** an endocrine gland in the center of the brain. The suprachiasmatic nucleus receives neural input from the eyes, making it sensitive to changes in light levels. As a result, melatonin secretion varies with light levels, decreasing in daylight and increasing in darkness (Caldwell, 2000). As discussed in Chapter 2, because sleepiness increases as levels of melatonin increase, researchers have been studying the possible use of melatonin as a treatment for insomnia.

When people are cut off from cues related to the day-night cycle, perhaps by living in a cave or a windowless room for several weeks, a curious thing happens. For unknown reasons their sleep-wake cycle changes from 24 hours to 25 hours in length. They go to bed slightly later and get up slightly later each successive day (Webb & Agnew, 1974). You may have experienced this during vacations from work and school. Perhaps you find yourself going to bed later and later and, as a result, awakening later and later.

Jet Lag and Shift Work

The natural tendency for the sleep-wake cycle to lengthen might explain why "jet lag" is more severe when we fly west to east than when we fly east to west. The symptoms of jet lag, caused by a disruption of the normal sleep-wake cycle, include fatigue, depressed mood, and poor physical performance. Consider professional baseball players. Eastbound travel shortens the sleep-wake cycle (**phase advance**), countering its natural tendency to lengthen. In contrast, westbound travel lengthens the sleep-wake cycle (**phase delay**), which agrees with its natural tendency to lengthen. So, phase advance requires more adjustment by travelers. Athletes typically take 3 days to overcome jet lag and restore their normal physical and mental functioning (Steenland & Deddens, 1997).

One-quarter of American workers—including airplane pilots, police officers, factory workers, and military personnel—are on rotating shifts and also find their sleep-wake cycles disrupted (Goh et al., 2000). Given the natural tendency of the sleep-wake cycle to increase in length, workers on rotating shifts respond better to phase delay than to phase advance. This was demonstrated in a study of industrial workers. Those on a phase-delay schedule moved from the night shift (12 midnight to 8 A.M.) to the day shift (8 A.M. to 4 P.M.) to the evening shift (4 P.M. to 12 midnight). Those on a phase-advance schedule moved in the

biological rhythms
Repeating cycles of physiological changes.

circadian rhythms
24-hour cycles of physiological changes, most notably the sleep-wake cycle.

 Biological Rhythms Group
www.mhhe.com/sdorow5

pineal gland
An endocrine gland that secretes a hormone that has a general tranquilizing effect on the body and that helps regulate biological rhythms.

phase advance
Shortening the sleep-wake cycle, as occurs when traveling from west to east.

phase delay
Lengthening the sleep-wake cycle, as occurs when traveling from east to west.

opposite direction, from the night shift to the evening shift to the day shift. The results showed workers on a phase-delay schedule had better health, greater satisfaction, higher productivity, and lower turnover (Czeisler, Moore-Ede, & Coleman, 1982).

Patterns of Sleep

In 1960, four leading introductory psychology textbooks made no mention of sleep, and the most extensive coverage in any introductory textbook was two pages (Webb, 1985). Today, in contrast, all introductory psychology textbooks include (usually extensive) coverage of sleep. This reflects the explosion of scientific interest in studying sleep since the 1960s. Two of the main topics of interest regarding sleep patterns are the nightly sleep cycle and the duration of sleep.

A Typical Night's Sleep

Imagine you are participating in a sleep study. You would first sleep a night or two in a sleep laboratory to get accustomed to the novel surroundings. You would then sleep several nights in the laboratory while special devices recorded changes in your brain waves, eye movements, heart rate, blood pressure, body temperature, breathing rate, muscle tension, and respiration rate. Your behavior, including any utterances you made, would be recorded on videotape and audiotape.

The physiological recordings would reveal that you do not simply drift into deep sleep, stay there all night, and suddenly awaken in the morning. Instead, they would show that you pass through repeated sleep cycles, which are biological rhythms marked by variations in the depth of sleep, as defined by particular brain-wave patterns. Figure 6.4 illustrates these patterns, which were first identified in the 1930s through the use of the electroencephalograph, or EEG (Loomis, Harvey, & Hobart, 1937).

Falling Asleep. As you lie in bed with your eyes closed, an EEG recording would show that your brain-wave pattern changes from primarily high-frequency *beta waves* (14 to 30 cycles a second), which mark an alert mental state, to a higher proportion of lower-frequency *alpha waves* (8 to 13 cycles a second), which mark a relaxed, introspective mental state. As you drift off to sleep, you would exhibit slow, rolling eye movements and your brain-wave pattern would show a higher proportion of *theta waves* (4 to 7 cycles a second), which have a lower frequency than alpha waves. You would also exhibit a decrease in other signs of arousal, including heart rate, breathing rate, muscle tension, and respiration rate.

The cessation of the rolling eye movements would signify the onset of sleep. This initial light stage of sleep is called *stage 1*. After 5 to 10 minutes in stage 1, you would enter the slightly deeper *stage 2*, associated with periodic bursts of higher-frequency (12 to 16 cycles

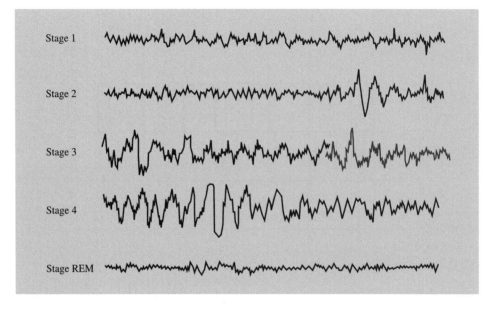

Stage 1	
Stage 2	
Stage 3	
Stage 4	
Stage REM	

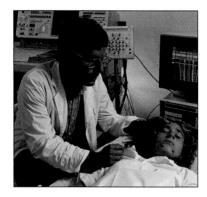

◀ **Figure 6.4**
The Stages of Sleep
Studies of participants in sleep laboratories have found that the stages of sleep are associated with distinctive patterns of brain-wave activity. As we drift into deeper stages of sleep, our brain waves decrease in frequency and increase in amplitude. When we are in REM sleep, our brain-wave patterns are similar to those in the waking state.

REM sleep

The stage of sleep associated with rapid eye movements, an active brain-wave pattern, and vivid dreams.

NREM sleep

The stages of sleep not associated with rapid eye movements and marked by relatively little dreaming.

a second) brain waves known as sleep spindles. After 10 to 20 minutes in stage 2, you would enter *stage 3,* marked by the appearance of extremely low-frequency (½ to 3 cycles a second) *delta waves.* When at least 50 percent of your brain waves are delta waves, you would be in *stage 4,* the deepest stage of sleep. After remaining in stages 3 and 4 for 30 to 40 minutes, you would drift up through stages 3, 2, and 1 until, about 90 minutes after falling asleep, you would reach the *rapid eye movement* stage, better known as **REM sleep.**

The NREM-REM Cycle.   REM sleep gets its name from the darting eye movements that characterize it. You have probably seen these movements under the eyelids of sleeping people—or even a sleeping pet dog or cat. Because stages 1, 2, 3, and 4 are not characterized by these eye movements, they are collectively called *non-REM,* or **NREM sleep.** NREM sleep is characterized by slow brain waves, deep breathing, regular heart rate, and lower blood pressure. After an initial 10-minute period of REM sleep, you would again drift down into NREM sleep, eventually reaching stage 4.

The NREM-REM cycles take an average of 90 minutes, meaning you pass through four or five cycles in a typical night's sleep. Adults normally spend about 25 percent of the night in REM sleep, 5 percent in stage 1, 50 percent in stage 2, and 20 percent in stages 3 and 4. As shown in Figure 6.5, the first half of your night's sleep has relatively more NREM sleep than the second half, whereas the second half has relatively more REM sleep than the first half. You might not even reach stages 3 and 4 during the second half of the night.

While you are in REM sleep, your heart rate, respiration rate, and brain-wave frequency increase, making you appear to be awake. But you also experience flaccid paralysis of your limbs, making it impossible for you to shift your position in bed. Given that you become physiologically aroused, yet immobile and difficult to awaken, REM sleep is also called *paradoxical sleep.* Because we are paralyzed during REM sleep, sleepwalking (or *somnambulism*) occurs only during NREM sleep, specifically stages 3 and 4. A survey of almost 5,000 people aged 15 to 100 years found that 2 percent engaged in sleepwalking. Sleepwalking is more common in children than in adults (Ohayon, Guilleminault, & Priest, 1999). Despite warnings to the contrary, sleepwalkers may be awakened without fear of doing physical or psychological harm to them. Of course, the habitual sleepwalker should be protected from injury by keeping doors and windows locked. Sleepwalking has been used successfully as a legal defense in criminal cases (Thomas, 1997).

Another characteristic of REM sleep is erection of the penis and clitoris. This occurs spontaneously and is not necessarily indicative of a sexual dream. Sleep clinics use REM erections to determine whether men who are unable to have erections while awake are suffering from a physical or a psychological disorder. If a man has erections while in REM sleep, his problem is psychological, not physical (Gordon & Carey, 1995).

► **Figure 6.5**
A Typical Night's Sleep
During a typical night's sleep we pass through cycles that involve stages of NREM sleep and the stage of REM sleep. Note that we obtain our deepest sleep during the first half of the night and that the periods of REM sleep become longer with each successive cycle (Cartwright, 1978).

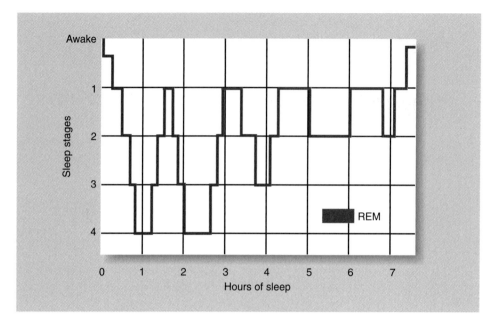

REM sleep is associated with dreaming. We know this because of research conducted in the early 1950s by Eugene Aserinsky and Nathaniel Kleitman (1953) of the University of Chicago. When they awakened sleepers displaying rapid eye movements, the sleepers usually reported they had been dreaming. In contrast, people awakened during NREM sleep rarely reported they had been dreaming. Because the longest REM period occurs during the last sleep cycle of the night, you often find yourself in the middle of a dream when your alarm clock wakes you in the morning. You might be tempted to infer that rapid eye movements reflect the scanning of dream scenes, but Aserinsky and his colleagues (1985) have found they do not—so if you were dreaming about, say, a tennis match, your rapid eye movements would not have been following the ball's flight.

Researchers are learning more and more about the physiological bases of the sleep cycle. Brain structures that help regulate sleep include the pons, thalamus, hypothalamus, and reticular formation. For example, destruction of the suprachiasmatic nucleus of the hypothalamus in animals disrupts the sleep-wake cycle to the extent that they fall asleep and awaken unpredictably. Neurotransmitters that help regulate sleep include serotonin, which plays a role in triggering NREM sleep, and norepinephrine, which plays a role in triggering REM sleep.

Though sleep patterns are similar across cultures, there is some evidence for ethnic and gender differences in some aspects of the sleep cycle. In a recent study, which recruited a large community sample, African Americans showed more stage 1 and stage 2 sleep and less stage 4 sleep than European Americans, Latinos, and Asians (Rao et al., 1999). A study of Israeli elementary school students found that girls slept longer than boys and exhibited more "motionless sleep." However, there were no gender differences in the perceived quality of sleep (Sadeh, Raviv, & Gruber, 2000). As you will read later in this chapter, there are many situational factors that affect sleep patterns, sleep continuity, and sleep disorders. These differences in the sleep-wake cycle might be attributable to stress levels, sleep environments, and other variables that are correlated with ethnicity and gender.

The Duration of Sleep

Sleep not only is cyclical, but varies in duration. Human beings are moderately long sleepers, with young adults averaging 8 hours of sleep a day. In contrast, some animals, such as elephants, sleep as little as 2 hours a day, and other animals, such as bats, sleep as much as 20 hours a day. Efforts to wean human beings from sleep indicate it cannot be reduced much below 4 hours without inducing extreme drowsiness and severe mood alterations (Webb, 1985). Figure 6.6 indicates that our daily need for sleep varies across the life span. At one extreme, infants typically sleep 16 hours a day. At the other extreme, elderly people typically

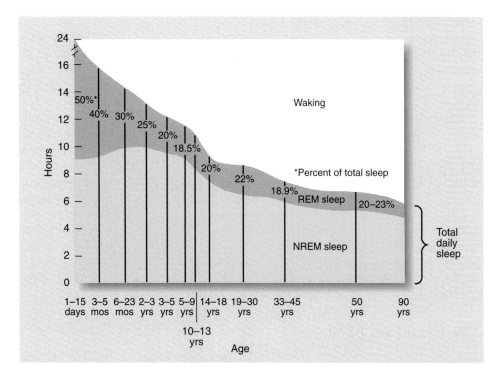

◀ **Figure 6.6**
Sleep Across the Life Span
Our amount of daily sleep declines
across the life span, decreasing rapidly in
infancy and childhood and more gradually
in adulthood. The proportion of time
spent in REM sleep also declines across
the life span. Reprinted with permission
from "Ontogenetic Development of the
Human Sleep-Dream Cycle," by H. P. Rof-
fwarg, et al., *Science,* 152:608, April 1996.

sleep 6 hours a day. Of course, you might need to sleep more or less than your age peers. This variability in normal sleep duration among people of the same age appears to have a hereditary basis (Heath et al., 1990).

Regardless of how much sleep they need, North Americans habitually get less than their ideal quota. They might stay awake to watch television, do schoolwork, or perform other activities. You might go to bed when you want to (perhaps after watching the late movie) and awaken when you have to (perhaps in time for an 8 A.M. class), making you chronically sleep deprived. According to sleep researcher William Dement, "Most Americans no longer know what it feels like to be fully alert" (quoted in Toufexis, 1990, p. 79). His conclusion is supported by the results of a survey of over 4,000 Long Island mass transit commuters. More than 50 percent of the respondents reported experiencing problems with sleep and wakefulness (Walsleben et al., 1999). Cross-cultural research suggests that the proportion of Japanese adults who suffer from inadequate sleep is comparable to that reported in surveys of Western samples (Liu et al., 2000).

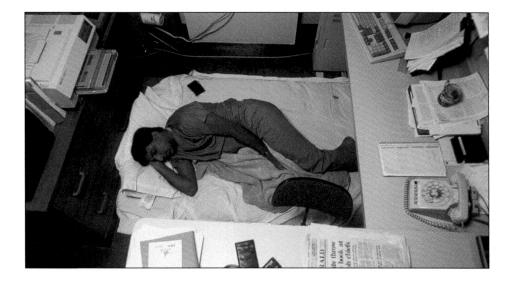

◀ **Sleep Deprivation**
Many workers, especially harried medical residents, must snatch moments of sleep whenever they can. The resulting sleep disruption and deprivation can impair their ability to function well on the job.

Difficulty in getting a good night's sleep has been increasing among college students. In a replication of an earlier study, a survey of college students conducted in 1992 found that they reported sleeping less and being less satisfied with their sleep than college students had reported in a survey conducted in 1978 (Hicks, Johnson, & Pellegrini, 1992). This lack of sleep is associated with daytime sleepiness, mood disturbances, deterioration of performance, and vulnerability to accidents (Carskadon, 1990).

Many people try to overcome the effects of inadequate nighttime sleep by taking daytime naps. Some cultures, typically in hot climates, even incorporate siestas as part of everyday life. Stores and businesses shut down for part of the afternoon so individuals can rest or nap for an hour or two instead of being worn out by working during the hottest time of the day. With the growth of the European Union, though, many corporations in Mediterranean countries are adopting the workday schedules of their European neighbors. One recent survey conducted in Spain found that only 24 percent of the population were regular siesta-takers, and anecdotal reports of chronic fatigue were on the rise (Boudreaux, 2000). However, even students and executives in nonsiesta cultures have come to value their "power naps." They are being wise, because an afternoon nap can increase alertness and improve task performance (Horne & Reyner, 1996). Older adults, who sleep less at night and find it more difficult to stay asleep, appreciate the benefits of napping—they nap more than younger adults do (Beh, 1994).

The Functions of Sleep

Assuming that you live to be 90, you will have spent about 30 years asleep. Are you wasting one-third of your life, or does sleep serve important functions for you? Among the many hypothesized functions of sleep, two are most prominent: *sleep as physically restorative* and *sleep as adaptive inactivity.*

Sleep as Physically Restorative

The most commonsense view of sleep holds that it restores the body and the mind after the wear and tear imposed by waking activities. Perhaps sleep repairs body tissues, removes metabolic waste products, and replenishes neurotransmitters (Inoue, Honda, & Komoda, 1995). Formal, as well as anecdotal, research has provided evidence of the detrimental effects of sleep loss and the restorative effects of sleep. Sleep deprivation is associated with a decline in the ability to perform physical and cognitive tasks (Quigley et al., 2000). A study of performances in a flight simulator after 24 hours of sleep deprivation found that it impaired participants' ability to complete a complex defensive maneuver (Chelette et al., 1998).

The longer we stay awake, the more we crave sleep. In the case of Peter Tripp, sleep deprivation apparently produced hallucinations and delusional thinking, which disappeared after a single night's sleep. In a similar case in 1965, Randy Gardner, a 17-year-old San Diego high school student, stayed awake 264 hours (11 days) as his contribution to a science fair. He hoped to get his name in the *Guinness Book of World Records.* Two of his friends alternated shifts to keep him from falling asleep. Gardner stayed awake by remaining physically active—talking, walking, and playing games. He found it easier to stay awake during the daytime than at night—a finding in keeping with his natural circadian rhythm. At various times during the 11 days, Gardner had trouble focusing his eyes, suffered incoordination, became moody, showed memory deterioration, had difficulty concentrating, thought a street sign was a person, and experienced the delusion that he (though a person of European background) was a famous African American football player who was being oppressed by racism.

During the last 4 days, leading sleep researcher William Dement monitored Gardner's behavioral and physiological reactions to his prolonged sleep deprivation. When the media began covering Gardner near the end of his feat, he seemed to become more motivated. On the last night, he even defeated Dement in 100 consecutive games of pinball. Gardner also performed well at a press conference at the end of the eleventh day. When a reporter asked him how he managed to stay awake so long, he simply replied, "It's just mind over matter" (Dement, 1976, p. 12). Gardner then slept 14 hours, 40 minutes, and awoke practically recovered—recovering completely after a second night's sleep (Gulevich, Dement, & Johnson, 1966). Gardner's remarkable physical performance was attributed to his excellent

Is Sleep Necessary for Good Health?

Your parents may have repeatedly urged you to go to bed at a reasonable hour so you would maintain your health. Is this just another example of a well-intentioned, but erroneous, commonsense belief or one with scientific backing? As mentioned in Chapter 2, commonsense beliefs are sometimes true, but scientists insist they be supported by research findings before accepting them. But what of the effects of sleep deprivation on health? It seems that, in this case, common sense might be right—sleep is necessary for proper functioning of the immune system (Everson, 1997). Many students anecdotally report that after obtaining only a few hours sleep night after night during final exams, they often become ill a few days after their exams are over. And, when we become ill, we tend to sleep more—perhaps because sleep promotes the immunological response to invading microorganisms.

Consider natural killer cell (NKC) activity. NKCs are lymphocytes—white blood cells—that help defend the body against cancer cells. Many studies have found sleep loss is associated with a reduction in NKC activity (Heiser et al., 2000). In one study, 29 persons, aged 40 to 78 years, spent 3 nights in a sleep laboratory. NKC activity was positively correlated with how long they slept (Hall et al., 1998). But additional research is needed to determine whether this reduction in NKC activity makes sleep-deprived people more susceptible to cancer by impairing the ability of NKCs to destroy cancer cells before they can reproduce and form invasive tumors. Moreover, as noted in Chapter 2, scientists caution against confusing causation and correlation. The positive correlation between hours of sleep and NKC activity does not necessarily mean sleep deprivation *causes* a reduction in NKC activity. Other factors might account for the relationship between sleep and NKC activity. In fact, it is conceivable that the presumed direction of causality is just the opposite: immunological activity might promote sleep, thereby accounting for the positive correlation between the two (Karnovsky, 1986).

Because of this, scientists rely on experimental, rather than correlational, research to study possible causal relationships between sleep loss and immune responses. Experiments that have used hours of sleep as the independent variable and immunological activity as the dependent variable have consistently shown that depriving humans and animals of sleep does, in fact, reduce immunological activity. In one experiment laboratory rats were deprived of sleep for 8 hours. They showed a significant reduction in their immunological responses to foreign cells (Brown et al., 1989). Moreover, when animals are purposely subjected to infections, those who obtain more deep sleep are more likely to survive (Toth & Krueger, 1990). In an experiment involving human participants, 23 healthy men, aged 22 to 61 years, were prevented from obtaining a full night's sleep. Eighteen of the men showed a decrease in NKC activity, with a statistically significant reduction to 72 percent of their average baseline levels of NKC activity. After just a single full night's sleep, their NKC activity returned to baseline levels (Irwin et al., 1994).

These findings supporting the role of sleep in immune responses have practical implications. To prevent illness, make sure you get enough sleep. When you are ill, make sure to get more sleep than normal. Moreover, perhaps hospital patients, who especially need their immune systems to function optimally, should not routinely be awakened to give them medicine or to take blood from them.

physical condition, strong motivation, and support from those around him. But some scientists noted he might have gained a boost from so-called microsleep, which is a period of sleep lasting but a few seconds (which you might have experienced when exhausted and fighting to stay awake during a boring lecture—but which are dangerous when they occur while driving). The cumulative effect of these ultra-short "naps" might have helped Gardner combat the effects of sleep deprivation.

▲ Wilse Webb

"Natural sleep is when you go to bed when you're sleepy and wake up when you're rested. But the modern system of sleeping is to go to bed when you want to and get up when you have to."

Another source of evidence for the restorative function of sleep is research on the effects of vigorous physical activity on subsequent sleep patterns. Sleep, especially deep sleep, increases on the nights after vigorous exercise (Vein et al., 1991). This was supported by a study of runners who participated in a 57-mile ultramarathon. They experienced an increase in the duration of sleep, particularly stage 3 and stage 4, on the first two nights after the race (Shapiro et al., 1981). Though we still do not know exactly what, if anything, sleep restores, one explanation for the increase in deep sleep after vigorous exercise concerns the secretion of growth hormone, which increases during deep sleep. Growth hormone promotes the synthesis of proteins needed for the repair of muscles and other body tissues. During the past decade, research studies have indicated that sleep has another important function: the maintenance of physical health through its effects on the immune system (see the Psychology Versus Common Sense feature on p. 189).

Sleep as Adaptive Inactivity

An alternative view on the functions of sleep, championed by Wilse Webb (1992), looks to evolution. Webb believes sleep evolved because it protected the sleeper from harm and prevented the useless expenditure of energy.

Sleep as Protection from Harm. Our prehistoric ancestors who slept at night were less likely to gain the attention of hungry nocturnal predators. The limb paralysis accompanying REM sleep may have evolved because it prevented cave dwellers from acting out their dreams, when they might have bumped into trees, fallen off cliffs, or provided dinner for saber-toothed tigers. Evidence for this protective function of REM sleep comes from studies of cats: Destruction of a portion of the pons that normally induces REM paralysis in cats produces stalking and attacking movements during sleep, as though the cats are acting out their dreams (Morrison, 1983).

Further support for the protective function of sleep comes from studies showing that animals with little to fear while asleep (either because they are predators or because they sleep in safe places) sleep for much of the 24-hour day. In contrast, animals that have much to fear while asleep (either because they are prey or because they sleep in exposed places) sleep for relatively little of the 24-hour day. Thus, cats, which are predators, sleep much longer (15 hours) than rabbits (8 hours), which are prey. Likewise, bats, which sleep in caves, sleep much longer (20 hours) than horses (3 hours), which sleep in the open.

Sleep as a Conserver of Energy. Another reason to believe that sleep might be a period of adaptive inactivity is that it conserves energy (Berger & Phillips, 1995). Evidence supportive of this view comes from studies of the food-finding habits of different species. Because the length of sleep for a given species is negatively correlated with how long it takes members of that species to find their daily food, perhaps animals stay awake only long enough to eat sufficient food to meet their energy needs. Animals might have evolved sleep in part to conserve energy the remainder of the time. Thus, the typical young adult human's need for about 8 hours of nightly sleep might mean that our prehistoric ancestors needed about 16 hours to find their daily food (Cohen, 1979).

According to Wilse Webb (1992), both the restorative theory and the adaptive-inactivity theory must be included in an adequate theory of sleep. The restorative theory explains why sleepiness increases as sleep loss increases. The adaptive-inactivity theory explains why sleep follows a circadian rhythm. You have experienced this if you have done an "all-nighter" while studying for exams. If you fight your sleepiness and force yourself to stay awake all night, you might be surprised to find yourself less sleepy in the morning (when your circadian rhythm would make you more alert). Later, you would find yourself becoming sleepy when your normal bedtime approaches again.

Sleep Disorders

You might take sleep for granted, but many people do not. They suffer from sleep disorders such as *insomnia, sleep apnea,* and *narcolepsy.*

Insomnia

Up to 30 million Americans suffer from **insomnia** (Roth, 1995), chronic difficulty in sleeping. People with *sleep-onset insomnia* tend to lie in bed worrying about personal problems, events of the previous day, and even their inability to fall asleep (Harvey, 2000). If you suffer from sleep-onset insomnia, what should you do? Many people with sleep-onset insomnia resort to sedative drugs, including alcohol and barbiturates, to fall asleep. Though sedatives will, at least initially, help you fall asleep, they do so at a cost. First, they interfere with the normal sleep cycle, most notably by reducing REM sleep or awakening the sleeper early. Second, they eventually lose their effectiveness, leaving you with the same problem you began with. And third, they have harmful side effects, including drug dependence.

Instead of turning to sedatives, sleep-onset insomnia victims can use behavioral techniques to obtain a good night's sleep (Perlis et al., 2000). If you suffer from sleep-onset insomnia, reduce your presleep arousal by avoiding exercise and caffeine products too close to bedtime. It also is advisable to avoid napping. If you nap during the day, you might not feel sleepy enough to fall asleep at your desired bedtime. You might even benefit from *paradoxical intention,* in which you try to stay awake while lying in bed. This can, paradoxically, induce sleep by preventing fruitless, anxiety-inducing efforts to fall asleep (Katz, 1984). Another technique, *stimulus control,* requires arranging your bedtime situation to promote sleep. First, go to bed only when you feel sleepy. Second, to assure that you associate lying in bed with sleep and not with being awake, do not eat, read, watch television, or listen to music while lying in bed. Third, if you toss and turn, get out of bed and return only when you are sleepy.

Sleep Apnea

Imagine that you stopped breathing hundreds of times every night and awakened each time in order to breathe. You would be suffering from **sleep apnea** (*apnea* means the absence of breathing). Victims of sleep apnea have repeated episodes throughout the night in which they fall asleep and then stop breathing for up to a minute or so. This produces a decrease in blood oxygen that stimulates the brain to awaken them, permitting them to start breathing again. People with sleep apnea typically feel chronically sleepy during the day, yet do not recall their repeated nighttime awakenings.

There are two major causes of sleep apnea. One is the failure of the respiratory center of the brain to maintain normal breathing while the person is asleep. Cases with this cause sometimes respond to drug therapy (Mendelson, Maczaj, & Holt, 1991). The second major cause is the collapse of the breathing passage, which is more common in obese people. An effective treatment in these cases uses a device that pumps a steady flow of air through a breathing mask worn by the sleeper, making the breathing passage resist collapsing (Sforza & Lugaresi, 1995).

Narcolepsy

In contrast to victims of sleep apnea who find it impossible to stay asleep at night, victims of **narcolepsy** find it impossible to stay awake all day. If you suffered from narcolepsy, you would experience repeated, irresistible sleep attacks. During these attacks, you would immediately fall into REM sleep for periods lasting from a few minutes to a half hour. Because of its association with REM sleep, narcolepsy is typically accompanied by a loss of muscle tone that causes the victim to collapse. You can imagine how dangerous narcolepsy is for people performing hazardous activities. For example, many people with narcolepsy fall asleep while driving (Aldrich, 1992).

Because narcoleptic attacks can be instigated by strong emotions, victims try to maintain a bland emotional life, avoiding both laughing and crying. Thus, narcolepsy can interfere with victims' sex lives, work performance, and social relationships (Goswami, 1998). The cause of narcolepsy is unknown, but given that it runs in families, it might have a genetic basis (Mignot, 1998). Though there is no cure for narcolepsy, victims might benefit from naps (Mullington & Broughton, 1993) or stimulants (Fry, 1998). Recent animal research indicates that drugs that stimulate the release of thyroid hormones reduce daytime sleep attacks and hold promise as a treatment for human narcolepsy (Riehl et al., 2000).

1. What cycles take place during a typical night's sleep?
2. What evidence supports the view that sleep is a form of adaptive inactivity?
3. What helpful tips would you give to a person suffering from sleep-onset insomnia?

Answers to Staying on Track start on p. ST-3.

◆ DREAMS

dream

A storylike sequence of visual images, usually occurring during REM sleep.

The most dramatic aspect of sleep is the **dream,** a storylike sequence of visual images that commonly evoke strong emotions. Actions that would be impossible in real life may seem perfectly normal in dreams. In a dream, you might find it reasonable to hold a conversation with a dinosaur or to leap across the Grand Canyon. But what are the major characteristics of dreams? This was the question addressed in a classic study conducted more than a century ago by Mary Whiton Calkins (1893).

Though Sigmund Freud is famous for making the analysis of dreams an important part of psychoanalysis, beginning with the publication of *The Interpretation of Dreams* in 1900, he was not the first person to study them formally. An article published by Mary Whiton Calkins (1893) described a dream study she conducted with her colleague Edmund Clark Sanford. The study is noteworthy because Freud referred to it in his book and its findings have held up well. It also shows the transition in late-19th-century psychology from philosophical speculation about psychological topics, such as dreams, to empirical research on them. It is also a landmark study because Sanford presented a paper on it in 1892 at the first meeting of the American Psychological Association.

Calkins recorded her own dreams for 55 nights, and Sanford recorded his for 46 nights. They used alarm clocks to awaken themselves at various times during the night in order to jot down any dreams they were having. Calkins observed dream characteristics that later research has confirmed. One researcher, J. Allan Hobson (1988), credits Calkins with anticipating modern approaches to dream research and pioneering the intensive study of dreams over many nights. Her findings included the following:

- *We dream every night.* On several nights, Calkins believed she had not dreamed—only to find that she had written down several dreams during the night. Calkins hypothesized that we forget our dreams because of a lack of congruity between dreaming and the waking states of consciousness. This finding anticipated interest in *state-dependent memory,* which has inspired research studies in the past few decades and is discussed in Chapter 8.
- *We have about four dreams a night.* Calkins recorded 205 dreams on 55 nights, and Sanford 170 on 46 nights. This agrees with modern research indicating we have four or five REM periods on a typical night.
- *As the night progresses, we are more likely to be dreaming.* Calkins found that most dreams occurred during the second half of the night. This agrees with research findings, obtained with modern physiological recording equipment, that successive REM periods increase in length across the night.
- *Most dreams are mundane and refer to recent life events.* We might not realize that dreams are usually mundane because we tend to recall only the most dramatic ones.
- *Dreams can incorporate external stimuli.* In one of her dreams Calkins found herself struggling to crawl from an elevator through a tiny opening into an eighth-floor apartment. She awoke to find herself in a cramped position with a heavy blanket over her face.
- *What Calkins called "real thinking" occurs during sleep.* This finding anticipated research findings that NREM sleep is marked by ordinary thinking, as opposed to the fantastic images and events common to REM dreaming.
- *We can reason while dreaming and even, to an extent, control our dreams.* This finding anticipated research on lucid dreaming, which became a serious topic of research only in the past two decades and is discussed later in this chapter.

- *Dreams can disguise their true meaning.* Calkins reported a "romance dream" that included disguised sexual material. This finding anticipated Freud's belief that dreams can use symbols to represent their true—often sexual—meaning.

The Content of Dreams

Human beings long have been intrigued by dreams; references to the content of dreams are found on Babylonian clay tablets dating from 5000 B.C. As just described, Mary Whiton Calkins (1893) found that we tend to dream about mundane personal matters, usually involving familiar people and places. This finding was supported by the research of Calvin Hall (1966), who analyzed the content of thousands of dreams reported by his participants. A more recent study likewise found that about half of our dreams include material about waking events of the preceding day (Botman & Crovitz, 1989–1990). But what of recurrent dreams? A study of 52 college students who recorded their dreams over a 14-day period found that recurrent dreamers tended to report more stress in their lives, lower levels of psychological well-being, and more negative topics in their dreams (Zadra, O'Brien, & Donderi, 1998). Research indicates that the dreams of people blind since birth or infancy contain no visual imagery. Their dreams, however, are rich in content related to smell, taste, and touch (Hurovitz et al., 1999).

Dream content is also associated with gender and cultural factors. Though Hall noted several gender-related differences in dreams, these differences have been decreasing. In fact, a recent study of the dreams of 40 male and 40 female college students found that there was greater gender similarity in their dream content than would have been true several decades ago (Bursik, 1998). Another study found that women tend to recall their dreams better than men do (Schredl, 2000). A study of the relationship between culture and dream content examined the dreams of 205 children aged 7 to 12 years from peaceful Finland, from violence-prone regions of Palestine, and from relatively violence-free regions of Palestine. The children recorded their dreams each morning for 7 days. The results showed that the children exposed to violence had more vivid dreams, incorporating more themes of persecution and aggression (Punamacki & Joustie, 1998).

The content of some dreams, which we call **nightmares,** is frightening. Children as young as 4 years old report having nightmares (Muris et al., 2000). Nightmares tend to occur when we feel emotionally distressed. Frequent nightmares have been reported in studies of military personnel who have experienced combat trauma (Esposito et al., 1999), people who have survived traumatic brain injury (Bryant et al., 2000), and children and adults who have survived sexual assault (Krakow et al., 2000). Consider the apparent effect on nightmares of the major earthquake that struck the San Francisco Bay area of California in 1989. After the earthquake, a study of almost 100 San Francisco Bay area college students found they had twice as many nightmares as an equivalent group of participants in Tucson, Arizona. About 40 percent of the San Francisco participants had nightmares about earthquakes; only 5 percent of the Tucson participants had them (Wood et al., 1992).

Do not confuse nightmares, frightening dreams that occur during REM sleep, with **night terrors,** which occur during NREM sleep stages 3 and 4. The person experiencing a night terror will suddenly sit upright in bed, feel intense fear, let out a bloodcurdling scream, exhibit a rapid pulse and breathing rate, and speak incoherently. After a night terror, the person typically falls right back to sleep and does not recall the experience the next morning. As a result, a night terror can be more disturbing to the family members who are rudely awakened by it than to the person who has experienced it. Though night terrors are more common in children, they can afflict adults as well (Llorente et al., 1992). A survey of almost 5,000 people aged 15 to 100 years found that 2 percent experienced night terrors (Ohayon, Guilleminault, & Priest, 1999).

As noted by Mary Whiton Calkins, the content of dreams can be affected by immediate environmental stimuli. Even before Calkins observed this, Herman Melville portrayed it in his novel *Moby Dick* in describing the effect of Captain Ahab's peg leg on the dreams of his ship's sailors. Melville wrote, "To his weary mates, seeking repose within six inches of his ivory heel, such would have been the reverberating crack and din of that bony step that their

nightmare
A frightening dream occurring during REM sleep.

night terror
A frightening NREM experience, common in childhood, in which the individual may suddenly sit up, let out a bloodcurdling scream, speak incoherently, and quickly fall back to sleep, yet usually fails to recall it on awakening.

▲ **The Nightmare**
The Nightmare, painted by Henry Fuseli (1741–1825), depicts the fearsome imagery of the typical nightmare.

dreams would have been of the crunching teeth of sharks." Similarly, you might find your-self dreaming of an ice cream truck ringing its bell, only to awaken suddenly and discover your dream had been stimulated by the ringing of your telephone.

Such anecdotal reports of the incorporation of stimuli into dreams have inspired laboratory experiments. In one of the first of these, researchers sprayed sleepers with a water mist when they were in REM sleep. On being awakened, many of the participants reported dreams with watery themes, such as a leaky roof or being caught in the rain (Dement & Wolpert, 1958). Experiments also have found that sleeping participants who are touched on their bodies (Nielsen, 1993) or rocked in a hammock (Leslie & Ogilvie, 1996) might incorporate that stimulation into their dreams. Despite these positive findings, stimuli that we experience when we are asleep are not always incorporated into our dreams. For example, a study of sleep apnea patients found no increase in dream content related to breathing problems (Gross & Lavie, 1994).

You will recall that Mary Whiton Calkins also noted that we might be able to control our ongoing dreams. This is the basis of **lucid dreaming,** an approach, devised by Stephen LaBerge, in which sleeping individuals learn how to be aware while dreaming and how to direct their dreams (Kahan & LaBerge, 1994). Lucid dreamers report an enhanced sense of well-being (Wolpin et al., 1992), though the reasons for this are unclear. Lucid dreaming has been used to help people with recurrent nightmares alter aspects of the dreams to make them less frightening (Zadra & Pihl, 1997).

The Purpose of Dreaming

REM sleep—dream sleep—is important. Participants who have been deprived of sleep, and then are allowed to sleep as long as they like, show an increase in REM sleep (Dement, 1960). This is known as the *REM rebound effect* and indicates that dream sleep serves certain functions. But what are the functions of dreams? People have pondered this question for thousands of years, and cultures vary in the significance and value they place on dreams (Wax, 1999). Native American cultures tend to make less of a demarcation between waking and dreaming realities and view dreams as messages from another realm that can enlighten the dreamer (Krippner & Thompson, 1996). The ancient Hebrews, Egyptians, and Greeks believed dreams brought prophecies from God or the gods, as in the Pharaoh's dream that was interpreted by Joseph in the Old Testament and in dreams described in Homer's *Iliad* and *Odyssey*. But Aristotle, who at first accepted the divine origin of dreams, later rejected this belief, claiming it is merely coincidental when prophetic dreams come true.

Dreaming as Wish Fulfillment

Sigmund Freud (1900/1990) provided the first formal view of dreaming as wish fulfillment. Freud claimed that dreams function as the "royal road to the unconscious" by serving as safe outlets for unconscious sexual or aggressive impulses that we cannot act on while we are awake because of cultural prohibitions against them. Freud distinguished between a dream's **manifest content,** which is the dream as recalled by the dreamer, and its **latent content,** which is the dream's hidden, underlying meaning. Thus, the manifest content of a dream hides its latent content. But why do we not dream about the latent content directly? If we dreamed directly about emotionally charged sexual or aggressive material, we might repeatedly awaken ourselves from our sleep.

How can we uncover a dream's latent content from its manifest content? According to Freud, a dream's manifest content consists of symbols that disguise its latent sexual or aggressive content. Thus, in our dreams, trees, rifles, or skyscrapers might be phallic symbols representing unconscious sexual impulses. The manifest content of a dream reported by a person is translated into its latent content during the process of psychoanalysis, which is discussed in Chapter 15. Nonetheless, even Freud said that "sometimes a cigar is just a cigar"—meaning that sometimes the manifest content is not symbolic, but instead is the true content of the dream.

lucid dreaming
The ability to be aware that one is dreaming and to direct one's dreams.

The Lucidity Institute
www.mhhe.com/sdorow5

manifest content
Sigmund Freud's term for the verbally reported dream.

latent content
Sigmund Freud's term for the true, though disguised, meaning of a dream.

◀ **The Dream as Prophecy**

Belief in the predictive nature of dreams has been common throughout history. This woodcut from the Lubeck Bible of 1494 illustrates Pharaoh's famous dream, which Joseph interpreted as portending 7 years of abundance, then famine.

Dreaming as Problem Solving

The failure of psychoanalysts to provide convincing research support for dreaming as a form of disguised wish fulfillment (Fisher & Greenberg, 1985) led researchers to study other possible functions of dreams, such as problem solving. Anecdotal reports and clinical studies long have supported the view that dreaming serves the function of problem solving (Fiss, 2000). For example, Elias Howe completed his invention of the sewing machine only after gaining insight from a dream. Rosalind Cartwright, a leading dream researcher, has conducted formal studies of the possible role of dreaming in solving practical and emotional problems (Newell & Cartwright, 2000). According to Cartwright, dreaming provides a more creative approach to problem solving because it is freer and less constrained by the more logical thinking of waking life. In a study of people in the process of divorcing their spouse, Cartwright (1991) found that those who dreamed about their relationship with their spouse while they were going through the divorce were less depressed and better adjusted to single life a year later. This was particularly true of those who had highly emotional dreams. Note, however, that this study revealed a positive *correlation* between dreaming and emotional adjustment. It did not provide evidence that dreaming *caused* better emotional adjustment.

Dreaming as an Aid to Memory

Do you ever stay up all night to study for exams? If so, you might be impairing your ability to memorize the material you have studied. Decades of research indicate that sleep can help you form long-term memories of material you learn during the day. REM sleep appears to be even more beneficial to memory than NREM sleep (Smith, 1996). Consider a study in which undergraduates learned a story during the day and then were awakened periodically to deprive them of equal periods of either REM sleep or stage 4 sleep. The next day they were asked to recall the story they had learned the day before. Participants who had been deprived of REM sleep showed poorer recall than participants who had been deprived of stage 4 sleep (Tilley & Empson, 1978).

Additional evidence for the importance of REM sleep comes from research findings that the more REM sleep we have during a night's sleep, the better our memory will be for material learned during the day before. A study using positron emission tomography showed that waking experiences influence activity in specific brain regions during sleep. Some participants learned to perform a reaction-time test; the remainder did not. Several brain areas activated during the execution of the reaction-time task during wakefulness were significantly more active during REM sleep in those trained on the task than in those who were not trained. These results support the assumption that memory traces are processed during REM sleep (Maquet et al., 2000).

▲ **Rosalind Cartwright**

"The dreams of a night have meaning which is characteristic of the individual and responsive to his or her particular waking situation."

Dreaming as the By-Product of Random Brain Activity

activation-synthesis theory
The theory that dreams are the by-products of the mind's attempt to make sense of the spontaneous changes in physiological activity generated by the brain stem during REM sleep.

The **activation-synthesis theory** of J. Allan Hobson and Robert McCarley (1977) holds that dreams are the by-products of the cerebral cortex's attempt to make sense of activity generated by the brain stem during REM sleep. That is, the cortex interprets brain *activation* and *synthesizes* it into a dream. As an example, consider a dream in which you are being chased but feel that you cannot run away. According to the activation-synthesis theory, this might reflect the cortex's attempt to explain the failure of signals from the motor areas of the brain to stimulate limb movements during the paralysis that accompanies REM sleep—paralysis produced by activity in the brain stem. The inability of the cortex to make logical sense of patterns of random brain stem activity might explain why our REM dreams tend to be bizarre or unrealistic (Williams et al., 1992).

The activation-synthesis theory does not discount the influence of psychological factors on one's dreams. That is, the theory accepts that the cortex's interpretation of random brain stem activity presumably reveals something about the personality and experiences of the dreamer. The theory simply assumes dreams are generated by random brain stem activity, not by unconscious wishes or emotional conflicts. Thus, psychological factors come into play only *after* the onset of brain stem activity (Rittenhouse, Stickgold, & Hobson, 1994).

Despite a century of research, no dream theory has been clearly shown to be superior at explaining the functions of dreams. One of the difficulties in dream research is that the same dream can be explained equally well by different theories.

STAYING ON TRACK: *Dreams*

1. In what ways did Mary Whiton Calkins's 1893 study of dreams anticipate later research findings?
2. What is Freud's theory of dreaming?

Answers to Staying on Track start on p. ST-3.

◆ HYPNOSIS

hypnosis
An induced state of consciousness in which one person responds to suggestions by another person for alterations in perception, thinking, and behavior.

In contrast to sleep, which is a naturally occurring state of consciousness, **hypnosis** is an induced state of consciousness in which one person responds to suggestions by another person to alter perception, thinking, feelings, and behavior. Hypnosis originated in the work of the Viennese physician Anton Mesmer (1734–1815), who claimed he could cure illnesses by transmitting to his patients a form of energy he called *animal magnetism.* This process became known as *mesmerism.* In the late 18th century, Mesmer became the rage of Paris, impressing audiences with his demonstrations of mesmerism (Ellenberger, 1970). Today we still use the word *mesmerized* to describe a person who is engaged in an activity while in a trancelike state and *animal magnetism* to describe people with charismatic personalities.

The Scientific Hypnosis Home Page
www.mhhe.com/sdorow5

Mesmer's flamboyance and extravagant claims, as well as the professional jealousy of other physicians, provoked King Louis XVI to appoint a commission to investigate mesmerism. The commission was headed by Benjamin Franklin and included Antoine Lavoisier (the founder of modern chemistry) and J. I. Guillotin (the inventor of the infamous decapitation device, the guillotine). It completed its investigation in 1784, concluding that there was no evidence of animal magnetism and that the effects of mesmerism were attributable to the power of suggestion and people's active imagination. In 1842 the English surgeon James Braid (1795–1860) used mesmerism in his practice as an anesthetic and concluded it induced a sleeplike state. He renamed mesmerism *hypnotism,* from Hypnos, the Greek god of sleep.

Hypnotic Induction and Susceptibility

How do hypnotists induce a hypnotic state? The process depends less on the skill of the hypnotist than on the susceptibility of the individual. Highly hypnotizable people have more active fantasy lives and the ability to vividly imagine things suggested to them. They have

a capacity for absorption in what they are doing, whether reading a book, playing a sport, listening to music, or holding a conversation (Braffman & Kirsch, 1999).

Psychologists have developed tests of hypnotizability, such as the Stanford Hypnotic Susceptibility Scale (Weitzenhoffer & Hilgard, 1962). These tests determine the extent to which participants will comply with hypnotic suggestions after a brief hypnotic induction. A simple suggestion, to test for some susceptibility, might direct you to hold your hands in front of you and move them apart. A more difficult suggestion, to test for high susceptibility, might direct you to produce handwriting similar to that of a child. Regardless of their susceptibility, people cannot be hypnotized against their will (Lynn, Rhue, & Weekes, 1990).

The aim of hypnotic induction is to create a relaxed, passive, highly focused state of mind. During hypnotic induction the hypnotist might have you focus your eyes on a spot on the ceiling. The hypnotist might then suggest you notice your eyelids closing, feet warming, muscles relaxing, and breathing slowing—events that would take place even without hypnotic suggestions. You would gradually relinquish more and more control of your perceptions, thoughts, and behaviors to the hypnotist.

Effects of Hypnosis

Many extreme claims about remarkable physical effects of hypnosis have been discredited by experimental research. Perhaps you have heard the claim that hypnotized people who are given the suggestion that their hand has touched red-hot metal will develop a blister—a claim first made two centuries ago. Experiments have shown that such hypnotic suggestions can, at best, merely promote warming of the skin by increasing the flow of blood to it (Spanos, McNeil, & Stam, 1982). Nonetheless, research has demonstrated a variety of impressive perceptual, cognitive, and behavioral effects of hypnosis.

Perceptual Effects of Hypnosis

Stage hypnotists commonly use hypnosis to induce alterations in perception, such as convincing participants that a vial of water is actually ammonia. Participants will jerk their heads away after smelling it. But the most important perceptual effect of hypnosis is in pain relief. In the mid 19th century, the Scottish surgeon James Esdaile (1808–1859) used hypnosis to induce anesthesia in more than 300 patients undergoing surgery for the removal of limbs, tumors, or cataracts (Ellenberger, 1970).

A recent meta-analysis found that hyposis has a moderate to large effect in relieving pain in laboratory research studies and in biomedical research studies (Montgomery, DuHamel, & Redd, 2000), including treating cancer pain (Burkhard, 1997) or postoperative pain (Mauer

▶ **Stage Hypnosis**

The "human plank" feat has long been a staple of stage hypnosis. But it can be performed by a motivated nonhypnotized person who places her or his calves on one chair and head and shoulders on the other.

et al., 1999). But how does hypnosis produce its analgesic effects? As discussed in Chapter 5, one way is by using suggestions that help distract sufferers from their pain (Farthing, Venturino, & Brown, 1984). A second way is by sending neural impulses from the brain down the spinal cord, which blocks the transmission of pain impulses from the body to the spinal cord (Holroyd, 1996). This is in keeping with the gate-control theory of pain (see Chapter 5).

Cognitive Effects of Hypnosis

In 1976, 26 elementary school children and their bus driver were kidnapped in Chowchilla, California, and imprisoned in a buried tractor trailer. The bus driver and two of the children dug their way out and got help. The driver, Frank Ray, had seen the license plate number of the kidnappers' van but was unable to recall it. After being hypnotized and told to imagine himself watching the kidnapping unfold on television, he was able to recall all but one of the digits of the number. This enabled the police to track down the kidnappers (M. C. Smith, 1983).

The Chowchilla case was a widely publicized example of one of the chief cognitive applications of hypnosis—**hypermnesia,** the enhancement of memory. Nonetheless, though memories retrieved by hypnosis might be accurate (Ewin, 1994), hypnosis also can create inaccurate memories, or *pseudomemories* (Spanos et al., 1999). In fact, one of the most common misconceptions about hypnosis held by the American public is its role in restoring accurate memories (Johnson & Hauck, 1999). Because of this, the use of hypnosis in legal cases to enhance eyewitness memories is controversial. One problem is that hypnotized eyewitnesses feel more confident about the memories they recall under hypnosis—regardless of their accuracy (Weekes et al., 1992). In one study, 27 participants were hypnotized and then given the suggestion that they had been awakened by a loud noise one night during the preceding week. Later, after leaving the hypnotized state, 13 of the participants claimed the suggested event had actually occurred. Even after being informed of the hypnotic suggestion, 6 participants still insisted they had been awakened by the noise (Laurence & Perry, 1983). This indicates the potential danger of hypnotically enhanced eyewitness testimony, particularly because juries put more trust in confident eyewitnesses (Sheehan & Tilden, 1983) and hypnotized eyewitnesses (Wagstaff, Vella, & Perfect, 1992).

Behavioral Effects of Hypnosis

Hypnosis is effective in treating physical and psychological disorders. For example, hypnosis has helped individuals recuperate after surgery (Blankfield, 1991) and continue to lose weight after treatment for obesity (Kirsch, 1996). Hypnotherapists make use of **posthypnotic suggestions,** which are suggestions for people to carry out certain behaviors in response to particular stimuli after leaving the hypnosis setting. In one study, posthypnotic suggestions helped collegiate fencers reduce their performance anxiety (Wojcikiewicz & Orlick, 1987).

hypermnesia

The hypnotic enhancement of recall.

posthypnotic suggestions

Suggestions directing people to carry out particular behaviors or to have particular experiences after leaving hypnosis.

Though hypnosis can help some people, a century-long debate (Liegois, 1899) has raged about whether hypnosis can be used to induce harmful behavior. Martin Orne and Frederick Evans (1965) demonstrated that hypnotized people could be induced to commit dangerous acts. Their study included a group of hypnotized participants and a group of participants who simulated being hypnotized. When instructed to do so, participants in both groups plunged their hands into what they were told was a nitric acid solution, threw the liquid in another person's face, and tried to handle a poisonous snake. Of course, the experimenters protected the participants (by immediately washing off the liquid, by actually having them throw water instead of acid, and by stopping them from touching the snake). Because both groups engaged in dangerous acts, the research setting, rather than hypnosis, might have accounted for the results. In any case, there is no evidence that hypnotized people become mindless zombies who blindly obey orders to commit harmful acts (Gibson, 1991).

Similarly, some of the effects of stage hypnosis might have less to do with hypnosis than with the setting in which they occur. For example, you might have seen a stage hypnotist direct a hypnotized audience volunteer to remain as rigid as a plank while lying extended between two chairs. But highly motivated, nonhypnotized persons can also perform this "human plank" trick. According to researcher Theodore Barber, even the willingness of hypnotized participants to obey suggestions to engage in bizarre behaviors, such as clucking like a chicken, might be more attributable to the theatrical "anything goes" atmosphere of stage hypnosis than to the effect of hypnosis itself (Meeker & Barber, 1971). You will appreciate this if you have ever watched contestants on television game shows engage in wacky antics—without their being hypnotized.

The Nature of Hypnosis

In the late 19th century, most notably in France, practitioners of hypnosis disagreed whether hypnosis induced an altered, or trance, state of consciousness. One group argued that hypnosis induces a trancelike state called **dissociation,** in which parts of the mind become separated from one another and form independent streams of consciousness. This is similar to the practice of many distance runners, who use dissociation to divorce their conscious minds from possibly distressing bodily sensations while still remaining consciously aware of the racecourse ahead of them (Masters, 1992). Another group of French hypnotists argued that hypnosis does not induce a trance state. Instead, they insisted it just induces a state of heightened suggestibility. This debate lingers on; some researchers view hypnosis as an altered state of consciousness, and others view it as a normal state of waking consciousness.

Hypnosis as a Dissociated State

Today, the main theory of hypnosis as an altered state is the **neodissociation theory.** This theory originated in a classroom demonstration of hypnotically induced deafness by Ernest Hilgard, who directed a hypnotized blind student to raise an index finger if he heard a sound. When blocks were banged near his head, the student did not even flinch. But when asked if some part of his mind had actually heard the noise, his finger rose. Hilgard called this part of the mind the **hidden observer** (Hilgard, 1978). Hilgard helped make hypnosis scientifically legitimate when he founded his laboratory for hypnosis research at Stanford University in 1957 (Bowers, 1994).

Hilgard has used the concept of the hidden observer to explain hypnotically induced pain relief. He relies on the *cold pressor test,* in which participants submerge an arm in ice water and are asked every few seconds to estimate their degree of pain. Though hypnotized participants who are told that they will feel less pain report they feel little or no pain, the hidden observer, when asked, reports it has experienced intense pain (Hilgard, 1973).

Additional evidence in favor of hypnosis as an altered state comes from experiments in which hypnotized participants experience physiological changes in response to hypnotic suggestions. In one study, highly hypnotizable participants learned lists of words and were given posthypnotic suggestions to forget them. Those who reported *posthypnotic amnesia* (their inability to recognize the words they had read) showed changes in components of their brainwave patterns that are related to attention and recognition. This indicates that posthypnotic

dissociation
A state in which the mind is split into two or more independent streams of consciousness.

neodissociation theory
The theory that hypnosis induces a dissociated state of consciousness.

hidden observer
Ernest Hilgard's term for the part of the hypnotized person's consciousness that is not under the control of the hypnotist but is aware of what is taking place.

Anatomy of a Research Study

Is Hypnosis an Altered State of Consciousness?

Rationale

In an experiment conducted by Nicholas Spanos and Erin Hewitt (1980) of Carleton University in Ottawa, the hidden observer was made to give contradictory reports, depending on the hypnotist's suggestions.

Method

The experiment used undergraduate participants who scored high on a hypnotizability scale and were then given suggestions for hypnotic analgesia. Two groups of participants were given contradictory suggestions. One group was told the hypnotized part of their minds would have little awareness of the pain, while a hidden part would be more aware of the actual intensity of the pain. Another group was told the hypnotized part of their minds would have little awareness of the pain, while a hidden part would be even less aware of the pain. Participants were asked to place a forearm in ice water, which induced pain. They were told to have the hypnotized parts of their minds state their level of pain on a scale from 0 to 20 every 5 seconds for 60 seconds. They also were told to hold a forearm in ice water while having their "hidden self" report their level of pain (from 0 to 20) by tapping out a simple code on a response key every 5 seconds for 60 seconds.

Results and Discussion

When asked to report the intensity of the pain, the hidden observer reported what the participants had been led to expect. It experienced more pain than the hypnotized part when told it would be more aware and less pain when told it would be less aware. The results are presented in Figure 6.7. Thus, the hidden observer might simply be a result of the participant's willingness to act as though he or she has experienced suggested hypnotic effects. Spanos has found this is not a case of faking, but probably reflects the well-established ability of people to distract themselves from their pain. Moreover, the hidden observer never appears spontaneously—it appears only when explicitly asked to. This study, as well as others by Spanos, indicates the hidden observer is a product not of the dissociation of consciousness, but, instead, of the participant's willingness to follow the hypnotist's suggestions.

▶ **Figure 6.7**

Pain Reports by the Hidden Observer

These two graphs show that the "hidden observer" might merely be the product of hypnotic suggestion, rather than an objective perceiver of reality. *(a)* When told that it will be more aware, the "hidden observer" reports more pain. *(b)* When told that it will be less aware, the "hidden observer" reports less pain.

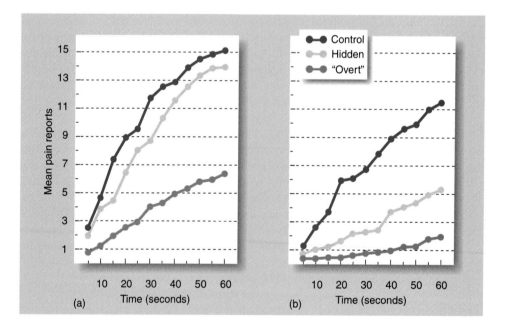

amnesia is more than a state of heightened suggestibility (Allen et al., 1995). Research studies also have found distinctive differences in cerebral blood flow patterns of hypnotized people and nonhypnotized people (Maquet et al., 1999) and the brain-wave patterns of those who are highly susceptible to hypnosis and those who are not (De Pascalis, 1999).

One study provided remarkable evidence that hypnosis can have highly specific effects on brain activity. Hypnotized participants were asked to view a color pattern or a black and white pattern while undergoing a PET scan measuring their brain activity. When they were asked to perceive a colored pattern, a region of their brains that responds to color became more active, regardless of whether they were actually shown the color or the black and white pattern. In contrast, when they were asked to perceive a black and white pattern, the region of their brains that responds to color became less active, regardless of whether they were actually shown the color or black and white pattern (Kosslyn et al., 2000).

Hypnosis as Role Playing

The claim that hypnosis is an altered state of consciousness has not gone unchallenged. Critics insist that hypnotically induced effects are only responses to personal factors, such as the participant's motivation, and situational factors, such as the hypnotist's wording of suggestions. By arranging the right combination of factors, the hypnotist increases the likelihood that the participant will comply with hypnotic suggestions (see the Anatomy of a Research Study feature on p. 200).

Evidence that hypnosis is a state of heightened suggestibility has also come from studies of hypnotic **age regression,** in which hypnotized participants are told to return to childhood. A hypnotized adult might use baby talk or play with an imaginary teddy bear. But a published review of research on hypnotic age regression found that adults do not adopt the true mental, behavioral, and physiological characteristics of children; they just act as though they were children (Nash, 1987). For example, in a classic study, Martin Orne (1951) hypnotized college students and suggested that they regress back to their sixth birthday party. He then asked them to describe the people and activities at the party, which they did in great detail. When Orne asked the participants' parents to describe the same birthday party, he found that many of the participants' "memories" had been fabrications. They reported people and events they presumed would have been at their own sixth birthday party. There was no evidence that they actually reexperienced their sixth birthday party.

Neither side in the debate about the nature of hypnosis has provided sufficient evidence to discount the other side completely. In fact, both sides might be correct: Hypnosis might be a dissociated state of consciousness that can be shaped by the social context and hypnotic suggestions (Kihlstrom & McConkey, 1990). After decades as a leading hypnosis researcher, Theodore Barber (2000) concluded that the all-or-none debate between those who believe hypnosis is an altered state of consciousness and those who do not is fruitless. Instead, he believes researchers should study the three kinds of people he has identified who are susceptible to hypnosis. The first are people who have had active fantasy lives since childhood. The second are people who are prone to dissociation and tend to repress undesirable thoughts, emotions, and memories. The third are people who are motivated to play the role of hypnotized participants.

STAYING ON TRACK: *Hypnosis*

1. How would you induce a state of hypnosis?
2. What are the benefits and risks of using hypnosis in enhancing the recall of memories?
3. Why do some researchers believe that hypnosis is not an altered state of consciousness?

Answers to Staying on Track start on p. ST-3.

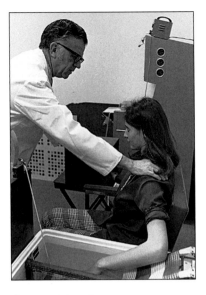

▲ **The Hidden Observer**
Ernest Hilgard uses the cold pressor test to evaluate the ability of hypnosis to prevent the pain that normally accompanies having an arm immersed in ice water. Though the participant might report little or no pain, the "hidden observer" might report severe pain. The results of the study by Spanos and Hewitt (1980) indicate that the "hidden observer" is not an objective observer but, instead, will report whatever it has been told to expect.

age regression
A hypnotic state in which the individual apparently behaves as she or he did as a child.

◆ PSYCHOACTIVE DRUGS

Normal waking consciousness can also be altered by **psychoactive drugs,** which are chemicals that induce changes in mood, thinking, perception, and behavior by affecting neuronal activity. Human beings seem drawn to psychoactive drugs. Many people imbibe beer to reduce social anxiety, take barbiturates to fall asleep, use narcotics to feel euphoric, drink coffee to get going in the morning, or smoke marijuana to enrich their perception of music.

Psychoactive drugs exert their effects by altering synaptic transmission, by either promoting or inhibiting it. But the effects of psychoactive drugs depend on a host of factors. These include their dosage, the user's experience with them, the user's expectations about

psychoactive drugs
Chemicals that induce changes in mood, thinking, perception, and behavior by affecting neuronal activity in the brain.

 National Institute on Drug Abuse
www.mhhe.com/sdorow5

▲ Claude Steele

"Sixty-five percent of murders, 88 percent of knifings, 65 percent of spouse beatings, and 55 percent of physical child abuse involve intoxicated participants."

depressants

Psychoactive drugs that inhibit activity in the central nervous system.

ethyl alcohol

A depressant found in beverages and commonly used to reduce social inhibitions.

their effects, and the setting in which they are taken. Many psychoactive drugs can cause *psychological dependence*—an intense desire to achieve the intoxicated state induced by the drug. Most psychoactive drugs also can cause *physical dependence* (or *addiction*). This means that after people use the drug for a period of time they develop a physiological need for the drug. As people use physically addicting drugs, they develop *tolerance*—a decrease in physiological responsiveness to the drug. As a result, they require increasingly higher doses to achieve the desired effect.

When addicted people stop taking the drug they are addicted to, they experience *withdrawal symptoms.* The pattern and severity of withdrawal symptoms is specific to the kind of drug to which the person is addicted. Common withdrawal symptoms include craving, chills, headache, fatigue, nausea, insomnia, depression, convulsions, and irritability. As shown in Table 6.1, the psychoactive drugs can be divided into four general categories: *depressants, stimulants, hallucinogens,* and *entactogens.* The drugs are categorized based on their effect on the brain.

Depressants

Depressants reduce arousal by inhibiting activity in the central nervous system. This section discusses several kinds of depressants: *alcohol, barbiturates,* and *opiates.*

Alcohol

Ethyl alcohol, an addictive drug, has been used—and abused—for thousands of years. Even the ancient Romans had to pass laws against drunk driving—of chariots (Whitlock, 1987). Drunk drivers are dangerous because they suffer from impaired judgment, perceptual distortions, and motor incoordination. Alcohol is involved in 50 percent of traffic accidents in the United States (Matthews et al., 1996). Alcohol facilitates the actions of the neurotransmitter GABA, which inhibits neuronal transmission in the brain (Loh & Ball, 2000). Given that the typical person metabolizes about one ounce of alcohol an hour, a person who drinks faster than that will become intoxicated. Men metabolize alcohol more efficiently than women do, so a woman might become intoxicated on less alcohol than it would take to intoxicate a man (Mumenthaler et al., 1999).

You probably have seen shy people become the life of the party, proper people become sexually indiscrete, or mild people become verbally or physically aggressive after a few drinks. Intoxicated men are less able to determine when sexual advances are unwelcome, perhaps contributing to the incidence of acquaintance rape (Marx, Gross, & Adams, 1999). And alcohol has been implicated in verbal and physical aggression among female and male heterosexual college students involved in abusive dating relationships (Shook et al., 2000). But the demonstration of an association between drinking alcohol and engaging in violence does not necessarily indicate a causal relationship between the two. Perhaps people who drink alcohol are more likely to be around other people, making aggressive encounters more likely. Or perhaps people who tend to be aggressive prefer to drink more alcohol than people who are not aggressive.

Evidence of a causal relationship between alcohol and aggression comes from experimental, rather than correlational, research. Experiments indicate that participants are, in fact, more likely to be aggressive after drinking alcohol than after drinking a placebo that merely tastes like alcohol (Dougherty, Cherek, & Bennett, 1996). Aside from alcohol's power to make people less inhibited by its direct effects on the brain, psychologists have identified other factors that account for alcohol's ability to weaken our social inhibitions. Alcohol researcher Claude Steele points to "alcohol myopia"—the inability of intoxicated people to foresee the negative consequences of their actions—as one reason they will fail to inhibit undesirable behaviors (Steele & Josephs, 1990). For example, when college men are intoxicated they report a greater willingness to engage in sexual intercourse without wearing condoms (MacDonald et al., 2000). Other researchers have found that because we are aware of alcohol's reputation for removing social inhibitions, we might also use it as an excuse for engaging in socially questionable behaviors (Hull & Bond, 1986). This is known as *self-handicapping.* If we can blame alcohol for our acting too silly, too sexual, or too aggressive, we might feel less guilt and embarrassment for our actions when we sober up.

Table 6.1	Psychoactive Drugs and Their Effects on the Brain

Category	Drugs	Effects on the Brain
Depressants	Alcohol	Removes social inhibitions Relieves anxiety Induces sleep Impairs judgment Causes disorientation
	Barbiturates	Remove social inhibitions Relieve anxiety Induce sleep Impair judgment Cause disorientation
	Inhalants	Create detachment from immediate environment Cause disorientation
	Opiates	Induce feelings of euphoria Relieve pain Induce sleep
Stimulants	Caffeine	Stimulates alertness Promotes wakefulness
	Nicotine	Stimulates alertness Relieves anxiety
	Amphetamines	Stimulate alertness Promote wakefulness and insomnia Create an overblown sense of confidence Induce feelings of elation Can cause symptoms of paranoia
	Cocaine	Induces feelings of euphoria Creates an overblown sense of confidence
Hallucinogens	LSD	Causes visual hallucinations Creates a sense of oneness and timelessness Induces seemingly mystical insights
	Cannabis sativa	Induces relaxation Removes social inhibitions Intensifies sensory experience Interferes with memory formation
Entactogens	MDE	Induces relaxation Induces positive mood Creates a sense of interpersonal closeness
	MDMA	Creates feelings of enhanced well-being Can enhance emotional sensitivity and feelings of interpersonal closeness Alters perceptions of time and physical environment

Barbiturates

Barbiturates are derived from barbituric acid. They produce effects similar to those of alcohol and, likewise, work by facilitating the actions of GABA (Yu & Ho, 1990). Because of this, people who ingest both alcohol and barbiturates risk dying from depression of the respiratory system. The barbiturate Seconal, which acts quickly to induce drowsiness, is

barbiturates
Depressants used to induce sleep or anesthesia.

used as a sleeping pill. The barbiturate Pentothal is used as a general anesthetic in surgery. Because mild doses of Pentothal induce a drunken, uninhibited state in which the intoxicated person is more willing to reveal private thoughts and feelings, it is popularly known as "truth serum," though it does not guarantee that the information revealed will be true.

Opiates

The opium poppy is the source of **opiates,** which include opium, morphine, heroin, and codeine. The opiates have been prized since ancient times for their ability to relieve pain and to induce euphoria. Sumerian clay tablets from about 4000 B.C. refer to the opium poppy as "the plant of joy" (Whitlock, 1987). Some 19th-century artists and writers used opiates to induce altered states of consciousness. Samuel Taylor Coleridge wrote his famous poem "Kubla Khan" under the influence of opium.

In the early 1860s, physicians used *morphine,* the main active ingredient in opium, to ease the pain of wounded soldiers in the American Civil War. Morphine was named after Morpheus, the Greek god of dreams, because it induces a state of blissful oblivion. In 1898 scientists used opium to derive a more potent drug—*heroin.* Heroin was named after the Greek god Hero, because it was welcomed as a powerful painkiller and cure for morphine addiction. But physicians soon found that heroin simply replaced morphine addiction with heroin addiction. Today, morphine, codeine, and the synthetic opiate Demerol routinely are prescribed to relieve severe pain. Morphine, in particular, is one of the most effective means of relieving intense pain in cancer patients (Kumar, Rajagopal, & Naseema, 2000). The euphoric and pain-relieving effects of the opiates are caused by their binding to endorphin receptors, which act to block pain impulses and stimulate the brain's pleasure centers (Levinthal, 1988).

Stimulants

Whereas depressant drugs reduce arousal, stimulant drugs increase it. **Stimulants** include *caffeine, nicotine, amphetamines,* and *cocaine.*

Caffeine

Few North Americans go a day without ingesting the addictive drug **caffeine,** which is found in a variety of products, including coffee, tea, soft drinks, chocolate, cold pills, diet pills, and stimulant tablets. The mind-altering effects of caffeine have made it a popular drug for centuries. Chocolate, for example, was considered a gift from the gods by the Aztecs of Mexico, who drank cocoa during their religious rituals. In the late 19th century, Americans' use of coffee accelerated after the introduction of the first commercial mix of coffee beans at a Nashville hotel called Maxwell House (Ray, 1983).

Today caffeine is popularly used to maintain mental alertness, which it does by stimulating the release of the excitatory neurotransmitter glutamate (Silinsky, 1989). A cup of coffee in the morning might improve alertness enough to reduce the possibility of being involved in early-morning vehicular accidents, which are especially common among young drivers. In one study, participants who had a night of either no sleep or restricted sleep "drove" for 2 hours in an immobile car on a computer-generated dull and monotonous roadway. In a double-blind design, some first received 200 mg of caffeine (the equivalent in two to three cups of coffee) and others received a placebo. Caffeine significantly reduced subjective sleepiness and incidents such as lane drifting for 30 minutes after no sleep and for 2 hours after restricted sleep (Reyner & Horne, 2000).

Unfortunately, caffeine's ability to enhance mental arousal can interfere with nightly sleep, even if the caffeine is ingested only early in the day (Landolt et al., 1995). Because of its ability to increase alertness, caffeine is beneficial to night-shift workers. In one study, workers received either caffeinated or decaffeinated coffee for several nights during a simulated 8.5-hour night shift. The results showed that the caffeine group had decreased sleepiness and enhanced performance on an assembly-line task (Muehlbach & Walsh, 1995). If you are a habitual caffeine user and suddenly stop using it, you will find that caffeine withdrawal is marked by headaches and drowsiness (Hughes et al., 1991).

opiates
Depressants, derived from opium, used to relieve pain or to induce a euphoric state of consciousness.

stimulants
Psychoactive drugs that increase central nervous system activity.

caffeine
A stimulant used to increase mental alertness.

Nicotine

"If you can't send money, send tobacco" read a 1776 appeal from General George Washington (Ray, 1983). Washington's troops actually craved **nicotine,** a powerful addictive drug contained in tobacco. Nicotine works by stimulating certain acetylcholine receptors, which might increase the efficiency of information processing in the brain (Pritchard et al., 1995), a point not lost on students who smoke. And many smokers rely on nicotine to reduce their anxiety (Kassel & Unrod, 2000).

In addictiveness, nicotine is comparable to cocaine, heroin, and alcohol (Stolerman & Jarvis, 1995). But why do some people get quickly addicted to nicotine, others smoke only occasionally, and still others avoid it totally? There seems to be a genetic basis for this variability. The more responsive users are to nicotine, the more quickly they develop tolerance and become dependent on it (Pomerleau, 1995). You can read more about smoking and its negative effects on health in Chapter 16.

Amphetamines

Amphetamines—including Benzedrine, Dexedrine, and Methedrine—are addictive synthetic stimulant drugs that are popularly known as "speed" and are more powerful than caffeine and nicotine. They exert their effects by stimulating the release of dopamine and norepinephrine and inhibiting their reuptake by the neurons that secrete them. In the 1930s, truck drivers discovered that amphetamines would keep them alert during long hauls, letting them drive for many hours without sleeping. For several decades college students have used amphetamines to stay awake while cramming for final exams. Amphetamines even were used during Operation Desert Storm by the U.S. Air Force Tactical Air Command to stay alert during the Persian Gulf War against Iraq (Emonson & Vanderbeek, 1995). Because amphetamines suppress appetite and increase the basal metabolic rate, they are commonly used as diet pills. But chronic users also might experience "amphetamine psychosis," marked by extreme suspiciousness and, sometimes, violent responses to imagined threats (Kokkinidis & Anisman, 1980).

Cocaine

During the 1980s, **cocaine,** an extract from the coca leaf, became the stimulant drug of choice for those who desired the brief but intense feeling of exhilaration and self-confidence that it induces. Cocaine prevents the reuptake of dopamine and norepinephrine by the neurons that secrete them (Gawin, 1991) and by facilitating activity at serotonin synapses (Aronson et al., 1995). Users snort cocaine in powdered form, smoke it in crystal form ("crack"), or inject it in solution form.

People of the Andes have chewed coca leaves for more than a thousand years to induce euphoric feelings and to combat fatigue. In the 19th century, Sir Arthur Conan Doyle made his fictional character Sherlock Holmes a cocaine user. And Robert Louis Stevenson relied on cocaine to stay alert while taking just 6 days to write two drafts of *The Strange Case of Dr. Jekyll and Mr. Hyde.* In 1886 an Atlanta druggist named John Pemberton contributed to cocaine's popularity by introducing a stimulant soft drink that contained both caffeine and cocaine, which he named Coca-Cola.

Unfortunately, cocaine causes harmful side effects, as discovered by Sigmund Freud, who used it himself. In the 1880s, Freud praised cocaine as a wonder drug for combatting depression, inducing local anesthesia, relieving asthmatic symptoms, and curing opiate addiction. But Freud stopped using and prescribing cocaine after discovering its ability to cause addiction, paranoia, and hallucinations (Freud, 1974). Cocaine can stimulate the heart (Foltin, Fischman, & Levin, 1995), which might account for instances of sudden death in users with cardiac dysfunctions.

Hallucinogens

The **hallucinogens** induce extreme alterations in consciousness. Users might experience visual hallucinations, a sense of timelessness, and feelings of depersonalization. It has been difficult to determine whether adverse personality changes associated with hallucinogens

nicotine
A stimulant used to regulate physical and mental arousal.

amphetamines
Stimulants used to maintain alertness and wakefulness.

cocaine
A stimulant used to induce mental alertness and euphoria.

hallucinogens
Psychoactive drugs that induce extreme alterations in consciousness, including visual hallucinations, a sense of timelessness, and feelings of depersonalization.

▲ **Hallucinogens**

The geometric designs in these weavings by the Huichol Indians of Mexico were inspired by visual hallucinations induced by the ingestion of peyote, a cactus that contains the hallucinogen mescaline. LSD and other powerful hallucinogens can induce similar effects.

are caused mainly by the powerful effects of the drugs or by the tendency of people with psychological instability to use them (Strassman, 1984). The hallucinogens can induce psychological dependence, but there is little evidence that they can induce physical dependence. They exert their effects primarily by affecting serotonin neurons, stimulating some and inhibiting others (Glennon, 1990). The most commonly used hallucinogens include *psilocybin,* a chemical present in certain mushrooms, *mescaline,* a chemical in the peyote cactus, and *phencyclidine,* a synthetic drug better known as "PCP" or "angel dust." But perhaps the best known hallucinogens are *LSD* and *cannabis sativa.*

LSD

On April 19, 1943, Albert Hofmann, director of research for the Sandoz drug company in Switzerland, accidentally experienced the effects of a microscopic amount of the chemical lysergic acid diethylamide **(LSD).** He evidently absorbed it through his skin. Hofmann reported he felt as though he was losing his mind: "in a twilight state with my eyes closed . . . I found a continuous stream of fantastic images of extraordinary vividness and intensive kaleidoscopic colours" (Julien, 1981, p. 151). Hofmann found it a horrifying experience. Because many people in the 1960s and 1970s used LSD recklessly, Hofmann (1983) titled his autobiography *LSD: My Problem Child.*

LSD seems to exert its effects by affecting brain receptors for serotonin, most likely by inhibiting their activity (Aghajanian, 1994). A dose of LSD induces a "trip" that lasts up to 12 hours. The trip includes visual hallucinations, such as shifting patterns of colors, changes in the shapes of objects, and distortions in the sizes of body parts. Even **synesthesia** is possible. This phenomenon occurs when stimulation of sensory receptors triggers sensory experiences that characterize another sense (Cytowic, 1989). Thus, someone on an LSD trip while listening to music might report seeing the notes as different colors. Users of LSD also might report a sense of timelessness, a feeling of oneness with the universe, and, at times, mystical insights into the meaning of life. Nonetheless, mystical experiences induced by LSD are different from those induced by nondrug means (Smith & Tart, 1998).

The effects of LSD are so powerful that users can have "bad trips," in which the alteration in their consciousness is so disturbing that it induces feelings of panic. People with unstable personalities, who are not told what to expect, and who are in stressful circumstances, are more likely to have a bad trip (McWilliams & Tuttle, 1973). Hofmann (1983), appalled by the indiscriminate use of LSD and the psychological harm it might do, questioned whether the human mind should be subjected to such extreme alteration. After all, the brain evolved to help us function by letting us perceive reality in a particular way, unaffected by hallucinogens like LSD.

Cannabis Sativa

The most widely used hallucinogenic drug is tetrahydrocannabinol (THC), present in the hemp plant **cannabis sativa.** Hemp fibers traditionally have been used in rope making. Hemp also has been popular for two of its other products: marijuana and the more potent hashish, which many people smoke to induce an altered state of consciousness. Marijuana

LSD

A hallucinogen derived from a fungus that grows on rye grain.

synesthesia

The process in which an individual experiences sensations in one sensory modality that are characteristic of another.

 Synesthesia
www.mhhe.com/sdorow5

cannabis sativa

A hallucinogen derived from the hemp plant and ingested in the form of marijuana or hashish.

is a combination of the crushed stems, leaves, and flowers of the plant, and hashish is its dried resin. Marijuana and hashish exert their effects by stimulating THC receptors in the brain (Herkenhahn et al., 1991).

Marijuana has been used for thousands of years as a painkiller; the earliest reference to that use is in a Chinese herbal medicine book from 2737 B.C. (Julien, 1981). In the 19th century, marijuana was a popular remedy for the pain of headache, toothache, and stomachache. Today most marijuana smokers use it for its mind-altering effects, which are related to its concentration of THC. Moderately potent marijuana makes time seem to pass more slowly and induces rich sensory experiences, in which music seems fuller and colors seem more vivid. Highly potent marijuana induces visual hallucinations, in which objects can appear to change their size and shape.

In 1937, after centuries of unregulated use, marijuana was outlawed in the United States because of claims that it induced bouts of wild sexual and aggressive behavior. Contrary to its popularity as an alleged aphrodisiac, marijuana at best causes disinhibition of the sex drive, which itself might be a placebo effect caused by its reputation as an aphrodisiac (Powell & Fuller, 1983). Moreover, marijuana does not promote aggression and might even inhibit it (Myerscough & Taylor, 1985).

But it would be unwise to drive or to operate machinery while under the influence of marijuana—or any other psychoactive drug. This is because marijuana impairs coordination (Navarro et al., 1993) and the ability to concentrate on tasks without being distracted (Solowij, Michie, & Fox, 1995). And marijuana can disrupt memory formation (Smith, 1995). This finding should be of special concern to students who combine their studies with marijuana smoking. Marijuana smokers also can exhibit amotivational syndrome (Nelson, 1994–1995), in which they prefer doing nothing rather than working or studying. But this raises the issue of causation versus correlation. That is, though marijuana smoking might reduce people's motivation, it is just as logical to assume that unmotivated people are drawn to marijuana.

▲ **Albert Hofmann**

"Now, little by little I could begin to enjoy the unprecedented colors and plays of shapes that persisted behind my closed eyes. Kaleidoscopic, fantastic images surged in on me, alternating, variegated, opening and then closing themselves in circles and spirals, exploding in colored fountains, rearranging and hybridizing themselves in constant flux."

Entactogens

The **entactogens** are a new category of psychoactive drugs that have unique effects intermediate to those associated with hallucinogens and stimulants. Drugs in this category include *methylenedioxyethylamphetamine (MDE,* or "Eve") and *methylenedioxymethamphetamine (MDMA,* or "Ecstasy").

The unique effects of the entactogen substance group were investigated in a study comparing doses of MDE, psilocybin, and methamphetamine in three groups of volunteer participants (Gouzoulis et al., 1999). Participants who ingested MDE reported a sense of contentment, relaxation, peacefulness, and interpersonal closeness. In addition, some stimulant effects and hallucinations were observed—though the hallucinations were weaker than those reported by the participants in the psilocybin group. Similar effects have been reported by participants who receive a single dose of MDMA. These include a feeling of closeness with others, altered perceptions, enhanced mood and well-being, and increased emotional sensitivity (Vollenweider et al., 1998). Both drugs appear to influence the release of the neurotransmitters dopamine and serotonin (Liechti et al., 2000).

The side effects of MDE and MDMA are difficult to assess. The results of animal studies indicate that serotonin levels are disrupted, and there is damage to the hippocampus and areas of the cerebral cortex (Boot, McGregor, & Hall, 2000). Researchers who assess the effects on humans conduct two types of studies: studies of the effects of a single dose upon nonusers and studies of the cumulative effects of the drugs on long-term users. Not surprisingly, studies of long-term use indicate more serious side effects, typically memory impairment (Reneman et al., 2000). These drugs have become known as "club drugs" because they are commonly used by young adults who attend "raves" and other social activities associated with polydrug use. A survey of users in Australia concluded that the side effects reported by users might be due to these factors rather than chronic use of MDE and MDMA (Topp et al., 1999). What is certain, though, is that tolerance to these drugs develops rapidly (Boot, McGregor & Hall, 2000).

entactogens

A new category of psychoactive drugs that have unique effects intermediate to those associated with hallucinogens and stimulants.

STAYING ON TRACK: *Psychoactive Drugs*

1. What are the symptoms of physical dependency on drugs?
2. What are the effects and side effects of cocaine?
3. What are the effects and side effects of marijuana smoking?
4. What are the effects and side effects of entactogens?

Answers to Staying on Track start on p. ST-3.

Chapter Summary

THE NATURE OF CONSCIOUSNESS

- Consciousness is the awareness of one's own mental activity.
- William James noted that consciousness is personal, selective, continuous, and changing.
- The selectivity of consciousness is the basis of research on attention.
- Perception without awareness is the unconscious perception of stimuli that exceed the absolute threshold but fall outside our focus of attention.
- We might experience perception without awareness whenever we use automatic, rather than controlled, processing of information.
- The Freudian unconscious is a portion of the mind containing thoughts and feelings that influence us without our awareness.
- Subliminal psychodynamic activation provides a means of scientifically studying the Freudian unconscious.

SLEEP

- The sleep-wake cycle follows a circadian rhythm.
- The pineal gland and the suprachiasmatic nucleus help regulate circadian rhythms.
- The depth of sleep is defined by characteristic brain-wave patterns.
- REM sleep is associated with dreaming. Our nightly sleep duration and the percentage of time we spend in REM sleep decrease across the life span.
- The functions of sleep still are unclear. One theory views sleep as restorative. A second theory views it as adaptive inactivity, either because it protects us from danger when we are most vulnerable or because it conserves energy.
- The major sleep disorders include insomnia, sleep apnea, and narcolepsy.

DREAMS

- Though we might fail to recall our dreams, everyone dreams.
- Most dreams deal with familiar people and situations.
- REM sleep can be disturbed by nightmares; NREM sleep can be disturbed by night terrors.
- In some cases we might incorporate into our dreams stimuli from the immediate environment.
- The major theories of dreaming view it as wish fulfillment, as problem solving, as an aid to memory, or as a by-product of spontaneous brain activity.

HYPNOSIS

- Hypnosis is a state in which one person responds to suggestions by another person for alterations in perception, thinking, feeling, and behavior.
- Hypnosis had its origin in mesmerism, a technique promoted by Anton Mesmer to restore the balance of what he called animal magnetism.
- Hypnotic induction aims at the creation of a relaxed, passive, highly focused state of mind.
- Hypnosis is useful in treating pain. Though hypnosis can enhance memory, it might also make subjects more confident about inaccurate memories.
- Under certain conditions, hypnotized people—like nonhypnotized people—might obey suggestions to perform dangerous acts.
- The effects of stage hypnosis might result as much from the theatrical atmosphere as from being hypnotized.
- Researchers debate whether hypnosis is an altered state of consciousness or merely roleplaying. Ernest Hilgard has put forth the concept of the "hidden observer" to support his neodissociation theory of hypnosis as an altered state, which has been countered by Nicholas Spanos and his colleagues, who believe that hypnosis is a kind of role playing.

PSYCHOACTIVE DRUGS

- Psychoactive drugs induce changes in mood, thinking, perception, and behavior by affecting neuronal activity.
- Depressants reduce arousal by inhibiting activity in the central nervous system. The main depressants are alcohol, barbiturates, and opiates.
- Stimulants, which increase arousal, include caffeine, nicotine, amphetamines, and cocaine.
- Hallucinogens induce extreme alterations in consciousness, including hallucinations, a sense of timelessness, and feelings of depersonalization. The main hallucinogens are psilocybin, mescaline, phencyclidine, LSD, and cannabis sativa (marijuana and hashish).
- Entactogens induce altered perceptions, a sense of well-being, and closeness with others. Common entactogens include MDE and MDMA.

Key Concepts

Key Contributors

Thought Questions

1. How does research on brain-damaged people support the existence of perception without awareness?
2. Given the nature of our circadian rhythms, why is it easier for people to travel across time zones going from east to west than going from west to east?
3. What evidence is there for the beneficial physical effects of sleep?

4. What would be the difference between Freudian theory and activation-synthesis theory in explaining a sexual dream?
5. How did the experiment by Spanos and Hewitt (1980) demonstrate that hypnosis might be role playing and not an altered state of consciousness?
6. What are the neurotransmitter mechanisms by which cocaine and amphetamines exert their effects?

Possible Answers to Thought Questions start on p. PT-2.

OLC Preview

 For additional quizzing and a variety of interactive resources, visit the book's Online Learning Center at www.mhhe.com/sdorow5.

Learning

HENRY O. TANNER
The Banjo Lesson, 1893

Growing up in Utah, Carl Gustavson learned to love the wolves, coyotes, and other predators that abounded in his home state. Later, after becoming a wildlife psychologist, he sought ways to ensure their survival. Coyotes, in particular, had long drawn the ire—and bullets—of sheep ranchers for their habit of preying on sheep. In 1974 Gustavson began research on psychological methods of fostering the survival of both coyotes and sheep (Gustavson et al., 1974). Taking advantage of the coyote's natural aversion to eating things that make it feel nauseous (Garcia & Gustavson, 1997), Gustavson inserted lithium chloride, a chemical that causes nausea, into sheep carcasses. When coyotes ate the tainted meat, they became nauseous. Gustavson predicted that the coyotes would associate the nausea with eating sheep and would stop killing them. He hoped this method would provide a happy solution for ranchers who want to kill coyotes and conservationists who want to save them.

Gustavson began his research program in zoos, using captured coyotes, wolves, and a cougar. To his delight, the animals refused to eat meat from the kind of prey that had been associated with nausea. More important, the predators also tended to shy away from the live animals themselves. Wolves and coyotes that had eaten tainted lamb and sheep meat avoided live lambs and sheep. Coyotes that had eaten tainted rabbit meat no longer attacked rabbits.

Other researchers successfully replicated this research using other predators, including hawks and ferrets. In one program, researchers scattered sheep meat laced with lithium chloride on a sheep range in Washington. This was followed by a significant reduction in the killing of lambs by predators. Following the introduction of a similar program in southern California's Antelope Valley, the number of sheep kills was reduced to zero. The success of the method led to its adoption as the means of choice for controlling predators in Saskatchewan, Canada.

Despite its success in several field settings, Gustavson's method met with opposition from those with vested interests in killing coyotes. These included trappers who kill coyotes for fees and pelts and pilots who take hunters on flights to shoot coyotes from airplanes. Moreover, many sheep ranchers—more concerned with protecting their sheep than with the survival of coyotes—are reluctant to use the technique, preferring instead to simply eradicate the coyotes (Reese, 1986). Thus, a procedure that is scientifically feasible is not always one that will be practical.

Moreover, as is at times the case in scientific research, some researchers failed to replicate Gustavson's findings. For example, insertion of lithium chloride into meat inhibited some predators from eating, but not killing, their prey (Timberlake & Melcer, 1988). In a recent study, two Alaskan Husky dogs that were given sheep meat laced with lithium chloride shunned sheep meat but still attacked sheep (Hansen, Bakken, & Braastad, 1997).

 Division of Behavior Analysis
www.mhhe.com/sdorow5

Regardless of the extent of its practicality and reliability, Gustavson's method illustrates the importance of **learning,** which is a relatively permanent change in knowledge or behavior that results from experience. What you learn is relatively permanent; it can be changed by future experience. This chapter will answer questions about the role of learning in a variety of areas, including these: How can children learn to stop bedwetting? How can children receiving cancer chemotherapy learn to maintain their appetites? How do animal trainers apply learning principles in their work? How might psychological depression depend on learning?

learning

A relatively permanent change in knowledge or behavior resulting from experience.

▶ **Ivan Pavlov (1849–1936)**
Pavlov is shown here in his laboratory, flanked by his assistants and one of his dogs.

Do not confuse learning with reflexes, instincts, or maturation. A *reflex* is an inborn, involuntary response to a specific kind of stimulus, such as automatically withdrawing your hand when you touch a hot pot. An *instinct* is an inborn complex behavior found in members of a species (such as nest building in birds). And *maturation* is the sequential unfolding of inherited predispositions (such as walking in human infants). Moreover, because learning is more flexible, it enables us to adapt to ever-changing circumstances.

Psychologists began the scientific study of learning in the late 19th century. In keeping with Charles Darwin's theory of evolution, they viewed learning as a means of adapting to the environment. Because Darwin stressed the continuity between animals and human beings, psychologists became interested in studying learning in animals, hoping to identify principles that might also apply to human learning (Purdy, Harriman, & Molitorisz, 1993). As you will read, many of the principles of learning do, indeed, apply to both animals and human beings.

Psychologists have identified three kinds of learning. *Classical conditioning* considers the learning of associations between stimuli and responses. *Operant conditioning* considers the learning of associations between behaviors and their consequences. *Cognitive learning* considers learning to be the acquisition of information.

◆ Classical Conditioning

In the early 20th century, the research of Ivan Pavlov (1849–1936) stimulated worldwide scientific interest in the study of *associative learning,* which involves associating contiguous events (such as lightning and thunder) with each other. Pavlov, a Russian physiologist, won a Nobel Prize in 1904 for his research on digestion in dogs. In his research, Pavlov would place meat powder on a dog's tongue, which stimulated reflexive salivation. He collected the saliva from a tube attached to one of the dog's salivary glands. He found that after repeated presentations of the meat powder, the dog would salivate in response to stimuli (that is, environmental events) associated with the meat powder. A dog would salivate at the sight of its food dish, the sight of the laboratory assistant who brought the food, or the sound of the assistant's footsteps. At first Pavlov was distressed by this phenomenon, which he called "psychic reflexes" or "conditional responses," because he could no longer control the onset of salivation by his dogs. But he eventually became so intrigued by the phenomenon that he devoted the rest of his career to studying it.

Pavlov was not alone in discovering this phenomenon. At the annual meeting of the APA in 1904, the year Pavlov received his Nobel Prize, E. B. Twitmyer, an American graduate student at the University of Pennsylvania, reported the results of a study on the "knee jerk" reflex. As you may know from a past physical examination, when a physician strikes you with a rubber hammer on your patellar tendon just below your bent knee, your lower leg reflexively extends. In his study, Twitmyer rang a bell as a warning that the hammer was about to strike. After repeated trials in which the sound of the bell preceded the hammer strike, the sound of the bell alone caused extension of the lower leg. But, to his disappointment, Twitmyer's presentation was met with indifference. In fact, William James, who chaired Twitmyer's session, was so bored (or hungry) that he adjourned the session for lunch—without providing the customary opportunity for discussion (Coon, 1982). North American psychologists did not begin to take serious note of this kind of learning until John B. Watson described Pavlov's research in his presidential address at the annual meeting of the APA in 1914. Because of Pavlov's extensive early research on "conditional responses," the phenomenon later earned the name of classical conditioning.

Principles of Classical Conditioning

As Pavlov first noted, in **classical conditioning** a stimulus comes to elicit (that is, bring about) a response (either an overt behavior or a physiological change) that it does not normally elicit. But how does this occur?

Acquisition of the Classically Conditioned Response

To demonstrate classical conditioning (see Figure 7.1), you must first identify a stimulus that already elicits a reflexive response. The stimulus is called an **unconditioned stimulus (UCS)** and the response is called an **unconditioned response (UCR).** You then present several trials in which the UCS is preceded by a neutral stimulus—a stimulus that does not normally elicit the UCR. After one or more pairings of the neutral stimulus and the UCS, the neutral stimulus itself elicits the UCR. At that point the neutral stimulus has become a **conditioned stimulus (CS),** and the response to it is called a **conditioned response (CR).** Pavlov used the UCS of meat powder to elicit the UCR of salivation. He then used a tone as the neutral stimulus. After several trials in which the tone preceded the meat powder, the tone itself became a CS that elicited the CR of salivation. But does the CS directly elicit the CR? On the contrary, research indicates that the CS activates a memory trace representing the UCS, which then elicits the CR (Jacobs & Blackburn, 1995).

Higher-Order Conditioning. In **higher-order conditioning,** a neutral stimulus can become a CS after being paired with an existing CS. In this case, the existing CS functions like a UCS. If the neutral stimulus precedes the existing CS, it elicits a CR similar to that elicited by the existing CS. This explains how neutral stimuli that have not been paired with a biological UCS such as food can gain control over our behavior. Higher-order conditioning might explain why music in commercials (such as those advertising fast-food restaurants) can affect our attitudes toward the products presented in the commercials. The classical conditioning of an emotional response to a product is important in enhancing its appeal to consumers (Kim, Lim, & Bhargava, 1998).

Among the most important conditioned stimuli are words. Classical conditioning might account, in part, for the power of words to elicit emotional responses. Perhaps the mere mention of the name of someone with whom you have a romantic relationship makes your heart "flutter." Similarly, if someone repeatedly says something, such as "tickle, tickle," before tickling the sole of your foot, you might eventually learn to jerk away your foot as soon as you hear the words "tickle, tickle" (Newman et al., 1993).

Ivan Pavlov Links
www.mhhe.com/sdorow5

classical conditioning
A form of learning in which a neutral stimulus comes to elicit a response after being associated with a stimulus that already elicits that response.

unconditioned stimulus (UCS)
In classical conditioning, a stimulus that automatically elicits a particular unconditioned response.

unconditioned response (UCR)
In classical conditioning, an unlearned, automatic response to a particular unconditioned stimulus.

conditioned stimulus (CS)
In classical conditioning, a neutral stimulus that comes to elicit a particular conditioned response after being paired with a particular unconditioned stimulus that already elicits that response.

conditioned response (CR)
In classical conditioning, the learned response given to a particular conditioned stimulus.

higher-order conditioning
In classical conditioning, the establishment of a conditioned response to a neutral stimulus that has been paired with an existing conditioned stimulus.

▶ **Figure 7.1**
Classical Conditioning
Before conditioning, the unconditioned stimulus of meat elicits the unconditioned response of salivation, and the neutral stimulus of a tone does not elicit salivation. During conditioning, the tone is repeatedly presented before the meat (UCS), which continues to elicit salivation (UCR). After conditioning, the tone becomes a conditioned stimulus (CS) that elicits salivation as a conditioned response (CR).

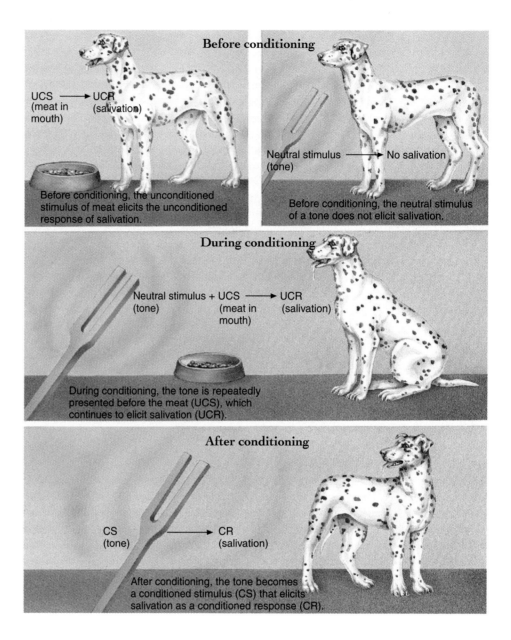

Even bedwetting, or *nocturnal enuresis,* in childhood can be controlled by classical conditioning. An effective technique, devised more than half a century ago (Mowrer & Mowrer, 1938), uses an electrified mattress pad that consists of a cloth sheet sandwiched between two thin metal sheets. The upper metal sheet contains tiny holes. When a drop of urine penetrates that sheet and soaks through the cloth sheet, the moisture completes an electrical circuit between the two metal sheets. This sets off a battery-powered alarm, which wakes the child, who then goes to the toilet. The alarm serves as a UCS, which elicits awakening as a UCR. After repeated trials, bladder tension, which precedes the alarm, becomes a CS, which then elicits awakening as a CR. The child eventually responds to bladder tension by going to the toilet instead of urinating in bed. This technique has become one of the most effective methods of treating nocturnal enuresis (Mellon & McGrath, 2000).

Factors Affecting Classical Conditioning. What factors affect classical conditioning? In general, the greater the intensity of the UCS and the greater the number of pairings of the CS and the UCS, the greater will be the strength of conditioning. The time interval between the CS and the UCS also affects acquisition of the CR. In *delayed conditioning,* the CS is presented first and remains at least until the onset of the UCS. An interval of about 1 second

between the CS and the UCS is often optimal in delayed conditioning (Rescorla & Holland, 1982), though it varies with the kind of CR. In delayed conditioning using Pavlov's procedure, the tone is presented first and remains on at least until the meat powder is placed on the dog's tongue. Thus, the CS and UCS overlap. In *trace conditioning,* the CS is presented first and ends before the onset of the UCS. This requires that a memory trace of the CS be retained until the onset of the UCS. In trace conditioning using Pavlov's procedure, the tone is presented and then turned off just before the meat powder is placed on the dog's tongue. In *simultaneous conditioning,* the CS and UCS begin together. In simultaneous conditioning using Pavlov's procedure, the tone and the meat powder are presented together. And in *backward conditioning,* the onset of the UCS precedes the onset of the CS. In backward conditioning using Pavlov's procedure, the meat powder is presented first, followed immediately by the tone. In general, delayed conditioning produces strong conditioning, trace conditioning produces moderately strong conditioning, and simultaneous conditioning produces weak conditioning. Backward conditioning generally produces no conditioning, though it sometimes is used successfully (McNish et al., 1997).

Stimulus Generalization and Stimulus Discrimination

In classical conditioning, the CR can occur in response to stimuli that are similar to the CS. This is called **stimulus generalization.** A person who learns to fear a particular stimulus might come to fear similar ones (Armory et al., 1997). For example, a child who undergoes a painful dental procedure might develop a fear of all dentists. Likewise, a dog that salivates to a particular bell might eventually salivate to other bells, such as a doorbell. Marketing research has found that, through stimulus generalization, generic brands of products that are similar in name to nationally known products can elicit similar responses from consumers (Till & Priluck, 2000). Thus, a cola soft drink manufactured by a small company might elicit a favorable response from people simply because they are familiar with the more famous national-brand colas.

If a child undergoes painless dentistry with other dentists, she will eventually become afraid only of the dentist she associated with pain. This would be an instance of **stimulus discrimination,** in which the person or animal responds to the CS but not to stimuli that are similar to the CS. Similarly, a dog that has learned to salivate to different bells might eventually salivate only in response to the dinner bell. This would occur if the dog learns that the other bells are not followed by food.

Extinction

In Pavlov's procedure, will a dog conditioned to salivate in response to a dinner bell do so forever? Not necessarily. If a CS is repeatedly presented without the UCS being presented, the CR will diminish and eventually stop occurring. This process is called **extinction.** A dog

stimulus generalization
In classical conditioning, giving a conditioned response to stimuli similar to the conditioned stimulus.

stimulus discrimination
In classical conditioning, giving a conditioned response to the conditioned stimulus but not to stimuli similar to it.

extinction
In classical conditioning, the gradual disappearance of the conditioned response when the conditioned stimulus is repeatedly presented without being paired with the unconditioned stimulus.

▶ **Figure 7.2**

Processes in Classical Conditioning

In classical conditioning, the pairing of the CS and the UCS leads to acquisition of the CR. When the CS is then presented without the UCS, the CR gradually disappears. After extinction and following a rest period, spontaneous recovery of the CR occurs. But extinction takes place again, even more rapidly than the first time.

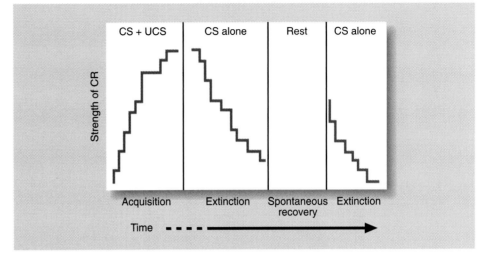

spontaneous recovery

In classical conditioning, the reappearance after a period of time of a conditioned response that has been subjected to extinction.

that has learned to salivate to a dinner bell (the CS) will eventually stop doing so unless presentations of the dinner bell are periodically followed by presentations of food (the UCS).

But extinction only inhibits the CR, it does not eliminate it (Bouton & Swartzentruber, 1991). In fact, after a CR has been subjected to extinction, it can reappear if the CS is reintroduced. For example, suppose you produce extinction of the CR of salivation by no longer presenting the dog with food after ringing the dinner bell. If you rang the dinner bell a few days later, the dog might respond again by salivating. This process, by which a CR that has been subjected to extinction will again be elicited by a CS, is called **spontaneous recovery.** In spontaneous recovery, however, the CR is weaker and extinguishes faster than it did originally. Thus, after spontaneous recovery the dog's salivation to the dinner bell will be weaker and subject to faster extinction than it was originally. Figure 7.2 illustrates the acquisition, extinction, and spontaneous recovery of a classically conditioned response.

Applications of Classical Conditioning

In his 1932 novel *Brave New World,* Aldous Huxley warned of a future in which classical conditioning would be used to mold people into narrow social roles. In the novel, classical conditioning is used to make children who have been assigned to become workers repulsed by any interests other than work. This is achieved by giving them electric shocks (the UCS) in the presence of forbidden objects, such as books or flowers (the CS). Despite such fears of diabolical use, classical conditioning has, in reality, been applied in less ominous, and often beneficial, ways. For example, classical conditioning has been used to explain phobias, drug dependence, and learned taste aversions.

Classical Conditioning and Phobias

Three centuries ago, John Locke (1690/1956) observed that children who had been punished in school for misbehaving became fearful of their books and other stimuli associated with school. Today we would say these children had been classically conditioned to develop school phobias. A phobia is an unrealistic or exaggerated fear, and a phobia was the subject of a classic research study of classical conditioning.

The study was conducted by John B. Watson and his graduate student Rosalie Rayner (Watson & Rayner, 1920). The participant was an 11-month-old boy, Albert B., later known as "Little Albert," who enjoyed playing with animals, including tame white rats. Watson and Rayner hoped to provide scientific evidence that emotional responses could be learned by conditioning. This would provide an alternative to the Freudian idea that phobias are symbolic manifestations of unconscious conflicts that arise from early childhood sexual conflicts (see Chapter 14). On several trials, just as Albert touched a white rat, Watson made a loud noise behind Albert's head by banging a steel bar with a hammer. Albert responded to the

John Broadus Watson
www.mhhe.com/sdorow5

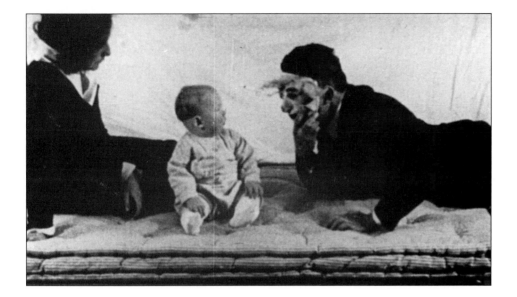

noise (the UCS) with fear (the UCR). He jumped violently, fell forward, and buried his face. After 7 pairings of the rat and the noise (twice on the first day and five times a week later), Albert responded to the rat (the CS) with fear (the CR) by crying and showing distress.

When tested later, Albert showed stimulus generalization. He responded fearfully to other furlike objects, including a dog, a rabbit, cotton wool, and a sealskin fur coat. Two months later he even showed fear of a Santa Claus mask. He had not shown fear of any of these objects at 9 months. Watson and Rayner hypothesized that pleasurable stimulation paired with a feared object would reduce Albert's phobia. But Albert left before they had the opportunity to try that technique. As discussed in Chapter 15, Watson's student Mary Cover Jones (1924), who became a prominent psychologist, used it a few years later to relieve a child's animal phobia.

Current ethical standards of psychological research (see Chapter 2) would prevent the experimental induction of phobias in children. Attempts to locate Little Albert to determine the long-lasting effects of his experience have failed (Harris, 1979). Though this study lacked the experimental control necessary for a convincing demonstration of a classically conditioned phobia, it led to sounder research studies demonstrating that fears and phobias can, indeed, be learned through classical conditioning (McAllister & McAllister, 1994). For example, a study found that breast cancer patients responded with anxiety to a distinctive stimulus that had been presented before each chemotherapy session (Jacobsen et al., 1995).

Classical Conditioning and Drug Dependence

Classical conditioning might even explain dependence on psychoactive drugs. For example, one reason cigarette smokers find it difficult to quit is that their smoking has become a conditioned response to various environmental stimuli (Lazev, Herzog, & Brandon, 1999). Smokers might light up when the telephone rings, when they finish a meal, or under a host of other conditions.

Consider another example of the role of classical conditioning in drug dependence. When a psychoactive drug (the UCS) such as heroin is administered, it produces characteristic physiological effects (the UCR). With continued use, higher and higher doses of the drug are required to produce the same physiological effects. This is known as tolerance (see Chapter 6), which might be, in part, the product of classical conditioning. Stimuli associated with the administration of certain drugs act as conditioned stimuli that elicit conditioned physiological responses opposite to those of the drug. For example, though heroin induces respiratory depression, stimuli associated with its administration induce respiratory excitation. Why would stimuli associated with drug taking elicit effects opposite to those of the drug itself? Perhaps it is an adaptive, compensatory mechanism that prevents the physiological response to the drug from becoming too extreme.

Consider heroin addiction. Tolerance to heroin might occur because stimuli associated with its administration, such as hypodermic needles and particular settings, can act as conditioned stimuli to counter the physiological effects produced by the drug. This might explain why heroin addicts sometimes die of respiratory failure after injecting themselves with their normal dose of heroin in a setting different from that in which they normally administer the drug. By doing so they remove the conditioned stimuli that elicit conditioned physiological responses that normally counter the unconditioned physiological responses elicited by the drug. As a consequence, tolerance is reduced. This means the unconditioned physiological responses, particularly respiratory depression, to a normal dose might be stronger than usual—in some cases strong enough to be fatal (Siegel, Baptista, & Kim, 2000).

Classical Conditioning and Taste Aversions

conditioned taste aversion

A taste aversion induced by pairing a taste with gastrointestinal distress.

Have you ever eaten something, by coincidence contracted a virus several hours later, become nauseated, and later found yourself repulsed by what you had eaten? If so, you have experienced a **conditioned taste aversion**—the classical conditioning of an aversion to a taste that has been associated with a noxious stimulus. The research program of Carl Gustavson described at the beginning of the chapter, in which he used classical conditioning to make coyotes revolted by the taste of sheep meat, was an application of conditioned taste aversion. Research on conditioned taste aversion was prompted by the need to determine the effects of atomic radiation, subsequent to the extensive atomic bomb testing of the 1950s. One of the leading researchers in that effort was John Garcia. Garcia and his colleagues exposed rats to radiation in special cages. He found that the rats failed to drink water in the radiation cages, yet drank normally in their own cages. They continued to refrain from drinking in the radiation cages even when they were no longer exposed to radiation in them. Garcia concluded the plastic water bottles lent a distinctive taste to the water in the radiation cages, which created a conditioned taste aversion after being paired with radiation-induced nausea. Because the water bottles in the rats' own cages were made of glass, the rats did not associate the taste of water from them with nausea (Garcia et al., 1956).

Garcia also found that conditioned taste aversions could occur even when the animal did not become nauseous until hours after being exposed to the taste. In responding to Garcia's finding that a taste aversion could be learned even when the taste preceded feelings of nausea by hours, psychologists were at first shocked by this apparent violation of contiguity in classical conditioning and many of them simply dismissed his findings as impossible (Garcia, 1981). How could the taste of food be associated with nausea that occurs hours later? (Tastes do not linger long enough for that to be an explanation.) Through the persistence of Garcia and his colleagues, who replicated his findings, the conditioning of a taste aversion using a long interval between the CS and the UCS is now an accepted psychological phenomenon. Moreover, there even is evidence that learned taste aversions are more likely to occur when there is a longer interval between the CS and UCS than when there is a shorter interval. For example, a 30-minute interval is superior to a 10-second interval between presentation of a distinctive taste and presentation of a nausea-inducing chemical in the classical conditioning of an aversion to the taste (Schafe, Sollars, & Bernstein, 1995).

Had Garcia been less persistent, we might have been denied a potentially useful tool for combating the nausea-induced loss of appetite experienced by people undergoing cancer chemotherapy. Their loss of appetite makes them eat less and lose weight, weakening them and impairing their ability to fight the disease (see the Anatomy of a Research Study feature).

Biological Constraints on Classical Conditioning

According to Ivan Pavlov (1928, p. 88), "Every imaginable phenomenon of the outer world affecting a specific receptive surface of the body may be converted into a conditioned stimulus." Until the past few decades, learning theorists agreed with Pavlov's proclamation. They assumed that any stimulus paired with an unconditioned stimulus could become a conditioned stimulus. But we now know there are inherited biological constraints, perhaps the product of evolution, on the ease with which particular stimuli can be associated with particular

Anatomy of a Research Study

Can Classical Conditioning Help Maintain the Appetites of Children Undergoing Chemotherapy?

Rationale

Ilene Bernstein (1991), of the University of Washington, has conducted research on taste aversion in chemotherapy patients. In one study, Bernstein (1978) determined whether children receiving chemotherapy would associate a novel taste with the nausea induced by chemotherapy.

Method

Bernstein assigned children receiving chemotherapy to one of three groups. The first group ate "Mapletoff" ice cream, which has a novel maple-walnut flavor, before each chemotherapy session. The second group ate Mapletoff on days when they did not receive chemotherapy. And the third group never ate Mapletoff. From 2 to 4 weeks later the children were given the choice of eating Mapletoff or playing with a game. Later, at an average of 10 weeks after the first session, the children were asked to select Mapletoff or another novel-tasting ice cream.

Results and Discussion

As illustrated in Figure 7.3, when given the option of playing with a game or eating Mapletoff, 67 percent of the children who never ate Mapletoff and 73 percent of the children who ate it only on days when they did not receive chemotherapy chose Mapletoff. In contrast, only 21 percent of the children who ate Mapletoff on days they received chemotherapy chose Mapletoff. When given the option of choosing Mapletoff or another novel ice cream flavor, only 25 percent of those in the Mapletoff-plus-chemotherapy group chose Mapletoff, while 50 percent of the Mapletoff-only group and 66 percent of the no-Mapletoff group chose it. Thus, children exposed to Mapletoff plus chemotherapy developed a taste aversion to Mapletoff.

Based on these findings, and on findings that taste aversion is stronger in response to novel-tasting foods than to familiar-tasting foods (Kimble, 1981), perhaps cancer patients should be given a novel-tasting food before receiving chemotherapy. This might lead them to experience taste aversion in response only to the novel "scapegoat" food instead of to familiar foods, thereby helping them maintain their appetite for familiar, nutritious foods. Bernstein has, in fact, accomplished this with children receiving chemotherapy by using candies with unusual flavors (such as coconut) as "scapegoats" (Broberg & Bernstein, 1987).

▶ **Ilene Bernstein**

"The demonstration of taste aversions in children receiving chemotherapy treatments may prove to be of importance to physicians who administer treatments which induce nausea and vomiting."

▶ **Figure 7.3**
Chemotherapy and Conditioned Taste Aversion

Ilene Bernstein (1978) found that children undergoing cancer chemotherapy developed conditioned taste aversions to a novel flavor of ice cream (Mapletoff) eaten on the same days as they underwent treatment. The children might have developed the aversion to the flavor because it became associated with the nausea induced by the therapy. As the graph shows, when later given the choice of eating Mapletoff or playing a game, children who had eaten Mapletoff on the days when they received therapy were less likely to choose Mapletoff than were children who had never eaten it or who had eaten it on days when they did not receive therapy.

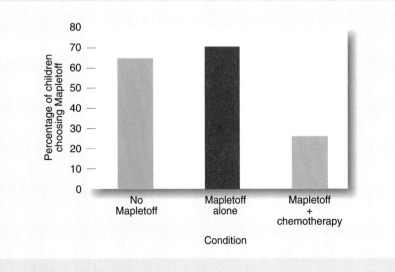

responses. This was demonstrated in an early study that tried to replicate Watson and Rayner's study on conditioned fear by using an opera glass instead of a white rat. The opera glass did not become a fear-inducing conditioned stimulus after being paired with an unconditioned stimulus that induced fear (Valentine, 1930). Nonetheless, as discussed in Chapter 14, some research studies have failed to support the role of biological preparedness in the development of phobias (de Jong & Merckelbech, 1997).

Biological constraints on classical conditioning were more recently demonstrated in a study of classically conditioned taste aversion in which two groups of rats were presented with a CS consisting of three components: saccharin-flavored water, a flash of light, and a clicking sound (Garcia & Koelling, 1966). For one group the CS was followed by a strong electric shock (the UCS) that induced pain (the UCR). For another group the CS was followed by X rays (the UCS) that induced nausea and dizziness (the UCR). The results indicated that the rats that had been hurt by the electric shock developed an aversion to the light and the click but not to the saccharin-flavored water. In contrast, the rats that had been made to feel ill developed an aversion to the saccharin-flavored water but not to the light and the click. This indicates rats have a tendency, apparently inborn, to associate nausea and dizziness with tastes, but not with sights and sounds, and to associate pain with sights and sounds, but not with tastes. Thus, not all stimuli and responses are equally associable (Weiss, Panlilio, & Schindler, 1993).

STAYING ON TRACK: *Classical Conditioning*

1. How would you use classical conditioning to make a pet cat come running at the sound of a can opener?
2. How does Ilene Bernstein suggest using classical conditioning to help chemotherapy patients retain their appetite for nutritious foods by using "scapegoat" foods?
3. In what way did John Garcia demonstrate biological constraints on classical conditioning?

Answers to Staying on Track start on p. ST-3.

◆ OPERANT CONDITIONING

In the late 1890s, while Russian physiologists were studying the relationship between stimuli and responses, an American psychologist named Edward Thorndike (1874–1949) was studying the relationship between actions and their consequences. While pursuing a doctoral degree at Harvard University, Thorndike studied learning in chicks by rewarding them with food for successfully negotiating a maze constructed of books. After his landlady objected to Thorndike's raising the chicks in his bedroom, William James, one of his professors, agreed to raise the chicks in his basement—much to the delight of the James children (Thorndike, 1961).

Thorndike left Harvard and completed his studies at Columbia University. At Columbia he conducted research using cats in so-called puzzle boxes (Hearst, 1999), which were constructed from Heinz wooden shipping crates. In a typical puzzle box study, Thorndike (1898) put a hungry cat in the box and a piece of fish outside of it. A sliding latch kept the door to the box closed. The cat could escape by stepping on a pedal or pulling a string that released the latch. At first the cat performed ineffective actions, such as biting the wooden slats or trying to squeeze between them. Eventually the cat accidentally performed the correct action, thereby releasing the latch, opening the door, and gaining access to the fish. Thorndike repeated this for several trials and found as the trials progressed the cat took less and less time to escape, eventually escaping as soon as it was placed in the box.

The results of his puzzle box studies led Thorndike to develop the **law of effect,** which states that a behavior followed by a "satisfying" state of affairs is strengthened and a behavior followed by an "annoying" state of affairs is weakened. In the puzzle box experiments, behaviors that let the cat reach the fish were strengthened and behaviors that kept it in the

▲ **Edward Thorndike (1874–1949)**

"When a certain connection [between a behavior and a consequence] has been followed by a satisfier the connection lasts longer than it does when it has been followed by an annoyer."

◀ **Puzzle Boxes**
Edward Thorndike, working under a limited budget, used Heinz shipping crates to create puzzle boxes for conditioning his cats. In this example, the cat is prevented from escaping by panes of glass between the slats.

box were weakened. Because Thorndike studied the process by which behaviors are instrumental in producing certain consequences, the process became known as **instrumental conditioning.**

Principles of Operant Conditioning

Thorndike's work inspired B. F. Skinner (1904–1990), perhaps the best-known psychologist during the decades following World War II. In the 1930s Skinner called instrumental conditioning **operant conditioning,** because animals and people learn to "operate" on the environment to produce desired consequences, instead of just responding reflexively to stimuli, as in classical conditioning. Following in Thorndike's footsteps, Skinner used chambers, now known as **Skinner boxes,** to study learning in animals—in particular, rats learning to press levers to obtain food pellets and pigeons learning to peck at lighted disks to obtain grain. Skinner devoted his career to studying the relationships between behaviors and their consequences, which he called **behavioral contingencies:** *positive reinforcement, negative reinforcement, extinction,* and *punishment.*

Positive Reinforcement

Two centuries ago, while leading a fort-building expedition, Benjamin Franklin increased the likelihood of attendance at daily prayer meetings by withholding his men's rations of rum until they had prayed (Knapp & Shodahl, 1974). This showed his appreciation of the power of reinforcement. A reinforcer is a consequence of a behavior that increases the likelihood that the behavior will recur. In **positive reinforcement** a behavior (for example, praying) that is followed by the presentation of a desirable stimulus (for example, rum) becomes more likely to occur in the future. Skinner called the desirable stimulus a positive reinforcer. You certainly are aware of the effect of positive reinforcement in your own life. For example, if you find that helping your parents with household chores earns you their praise, you are more likely to help in the future. Positive reinforcement even has been used to condition bees to make specific antenna movements (Kisch & Erber, 1999) and to make police officers more courteous (Wilson, Boni, & Hogg, 1997).

A handy approach to determining what will be an effective positive reinforcer is provided by the **Premack principle,** named for its discoverer, David Premack. Premack (1965) pointed out a behavior that has a higher probability of occurrence can be used as a positive reinforcer for a behavior that has a lower probability. Parents use the Premack principle with their children when they make television a positive reinforcer for the completion of homework. Even animals are trained using the Premack principle. For example, a study using rats as subjects successfully used wheel-running, a higher-probability behavior, as a positive reinforcement for lever pressing, a lower-probability behavior (Iversen, 1993). Keep in mind that, according to the Premack principle, something that is reinforcing to one individual might be less so to another (Timberlake & Farmer-Dougan, 1991). Parental praise might be a positive reinforcer to you, yet have little effect on your friend's behavior.

positive reinforcement
In operant conditioning, an increase in the probability of a behavior that is followed by a desirable consequence.

Premack principle
The principle that a more probable behavior can be used as a reinforcer for a less probable one.

 Burrhus Frederic Skinner
www.mhhe.com/sdorow5

 Positive Reinforcement: A Self-Instructional Exercise
www.mhhe.com/sdorow5

▲ **The Skinner Box**
The computer-controlled stainless steel and Plexiglas Skinner box is a far cry from Thorndike's puzzle box. Rats learn to obtain food by pressing a bar, and pigeons learn to obtain food by pecking a lighted disk.

primary reinforcer

In operant conditioning, an unlearned reinforcer, which satisfies a biological need such as air, food, or water.

secondary reinforcer

In operant conditioning, a neutral stimulus that becomes reinforcing after being associated with a primary reinforcer.

discriminative stimulus

In operant conditioning, a stimulus that indicates the likelihood that a particular response will be reinforced.

In general, positive reinforcement is strengthened by increasing the magnitude of the reinforcer, decreasing the interval between the behavior and the reinforcer, and increasing the number of pairings of the behavior and the reinforcer. There are two classes of positive reinforcers. A **primary reinforcer** is biological and unlearned, such as oxygen, food, water, and warmth. In contrast, a **secondary reinforcer** (also known as a conditioned reinforcer) is learned and becomes reinforcing by being associated with a primary reinforcer. This was demonstrated in a classic study in which chimpanzees could obtain grapes by inserting tokens into a vending machine (Wolfe, 1936). After using tokens to obtain grapes from the "chimp-o-mat," the chimps would steal tokens and hoard them. The tokens had become secondary reinforcers. Among the most powerful secondary reinforcers to human beings are praise, money, and prestige.

Why do behaviors that have been positively reinforced not occur continually? One reason is that behavior is controlled by discriminative stimuli, a process Skinner called *stimulus control*. A **discriminative stimulus** informs an individual when a behavior is likely to be reinforced. You would be silly to dial a telephone number if you did not first hear a dial tone, which acts as a discriminative stimulus to signal you that dialing might result in positive reinforcement—reaching the person you are calling. Stimulus control even plays a role in drug abuse. Specific stimuli associated with drug use make drug use more likely in their presence (Falk, 1994). This also explains, in part, why drug abusers who have undergone successful treatment often relapse when they return to the people and surroundings associated with their former drug use.

A second reason that reinforced behaviors do not occur continually is the individual's relative degree of satiation in regard to the reinforcer. Reinforcement is more effective when the individual has been deprived of the reinforcer. In contrast, reinforcement is ineffective when the individual has been satiated by having free access to the reinforcer. So, water is more reinforcing to a thirsty person and praise is more reinforcing to a person who is rarely praised.

Shaping and Chaining. Positive reinforcement is useful in increasing the likelihood of behaviors that are already in an individual's repertoire. But how can we use positive reinforcement to promote behaviors that rarely or never occur? Consider the trained dolphins you have seen jump through hoops held high above the water. You cannot reinforce a behavior until it occurs. The trainer who simply waits until a dolphin jumps through a hoop held above the water might wait forever; dolphins do not naturally jump through hoops held above the water.

Animal trainers rely on a technique called **shaping** to train rats, dolphins, and other animals to perform actions they would rarely or never perform naturally. In shaping, the individual is reinforced for successive approximations of the target behavior and eventually reinforced for the target behavior itself. A dolphin trainer might begin by giving a dolphin a fish for turning toward a hoop held underwater and then, successively, for moving toward the hoop, for coming near the hoop, and for swimming through the hoop. The trainer then would gradually raise the hoop and continue to reward the dolphin for swimming through it. Eventually the trainer would reward the dolphin for swimming through the hoop when it was held partly out of the water, then for jumping through the hoop when it was held slightly above the water, and, finally, for jumping through the hoop when it was held several feet above the water. Shaping is also the process by which rats are taught to press levers and pigeons to peck at disks in Skinner boxes.

Shaping occurs naturally in the wild. This might explain why wild rats living next to the Po River in Italy will dive to the river bottom to get shellfish to eat, though similar wild rats living next to other rivers will not. The Po River experiences radical changes in depth. At times the rats can scamper across exposed areas of its bed to get shellfish. As the water rises, the rats wade across the river and submerge their heads to get shellfish. Eventually, when the water becomes deeper, they swim across the river and dive to get shellfish. Thus, the natural changes in the depth of the water shape the rats' behavior by reinforcing the rats for successive approximations of diving (Galef, 1980).

Shaping is not limited to animals. It is also useful in training people to perform novel behaviors. The successful application of what we now call shaping was reported as long

shaping

An operant conditioning procedure that involves the positive reinforcement of successive approximations of an initially improbable behavior to eventually bring about that behavior.

ago as the 7th century, when it was used in England to help a mute person learn to speak (Cliffe, 1991). In a much more recent application, shaping was used to train a child with Down syndrome to jump over a hurdle in preparation for the Special Olympics (Cameron & Cappello, 1993).

What if you wish to teach an individual to perform a series of behaviors, rather than single behaviors? You might use **chaining,** which involves the reinforcement of each behavior in a series of behaviors. For example, in one study chaining was used successfully to train mentally retarded adults to perform the eighteen separate steps required to make a corsage (Hur & Osborne, 1993). In *forward chaining,* a sequence of actions is taught by reinforcing the first action in the chain and then working forward, each time adding a behavioral segment to the chain, until the individual performs all of the segments in sequence. Forward chaining has been successful in areas as diverse as teaching the use of a musical keyboard (Ash & Holding, 1990) and training children with autism to speak more frequently with their siblings (Taylor, Levin, & Jasper, 1999).

In *backward chaining,* a sequence of actions is taught by reinforcing the final action in the chain and then working backward until the individual performs all of the segments in sequence (Hagopian, Farrell, & Amari, 1996). For example, a father could use chaining to teach his child to put on a shirt. The father would begin by putting the shirt on the child, leaving only the top button open. He then would work backward, first reinforcing the child for buttoning the top button, then for buttoning the top two buttons, and so on, until the child could perform the sequence of actions necessary for putting on a shirt. Even flight-training programs for pilots are more successful when they have trainees practice individual segments of a chain of actions they are to learn and combine them together through backward chaining (Wightman & Lintern, 1984). Figure 7.4 shows Barnabus, a rat trained to perform a sequence of actions by backward chaining.

Schedules of Reinforcement. Once an individual has been operantly conditioned to perform a behavior, the performance of the behavior is influenced by its schedule of reinforcement—the pattern of reinforcements given for a desired behavior. In a **continuous schedule of reinforcement,** every instance of a desired behavior is reinforced. A rat in a Skinner box that receives a pellet of food each time it presses a bar is on a continuous schedule of reinforcement. Similarly, candy vending machines put you on a continuous schedule of reinforcement. Each

chaining
An operant conditioning procedure used to establish a desired sequence of behaviors by positively reinforcing each behavior in the sequence.

continuous schedule of reinforcement
A schedule of reinforcement that provides reinforcement for each instance of a desired response.

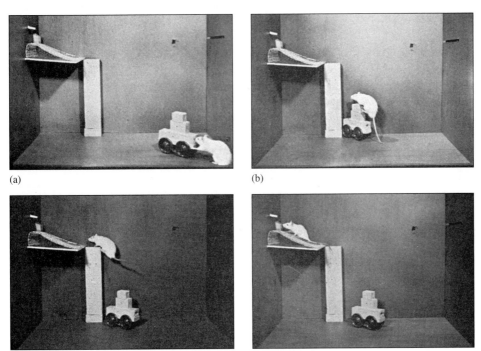

(a)

(b)

(c)

(d)

◀ **Figure 7.4**
The Rat Olympics
Chaining has been used to train animals to perform amazing sequences of actions. Some psychology professors have even instituted so-called Rat Olympics, in which students compete in training rats to perform the longest sequence of actions (Solomon & Morse, 1981). Here, a rat has learned to obtain food by *(a)* pushing a cart to reach a stand, *(b)* climbing onto the cart, *(c)* jumping up to the top of the stand, and *(d)* running up a ramp. Note, however, that the rat learned this chain of behaviors backward, first learning to run up the ramp and finally learning to push the cart.

partial schedule of reinforcement
A schedule of reinforcement that reinforces some, but not all, instances of a desired response.

fixed-ratio schedule of reinforcement
A partial schedule of reinforcement that provides reinforcement after a set number of desired responses.

variable-ratio schedule of reinforcement
A partial schedule of reinforcement that provides reinforcement after varying, unpredictable numbers of desired responses.

time you insert the correct change, you receive a package of candy. If you do not receive the candy, you might pound on the machine, but you would, at best, insert coins only one more time. This illustrates another characteristic of continuous schedules of reinforcement—they are subject to rapid extinction when reinforcement stops. Extinction is the decline in the probability of a behavior and its eventual disappearance as a result of its no longer being followed by a reinforcer.

In **partial schedules of reinforcement** (also known as intermittent schedules), reinforcement is given for only some instances of a desired behavior. Because partial schedules produce less predictable reinforcement, they are more resistant to extinction than are continuous schedules. Skinner (1956) discovered partial schedules by accident when he ran short of food pellets and decided not to reinforce each response but, instead, to reinforce responses only every so often. The rats kept responding and showed resistance to extinction. Partial schedules are further divided into ratio schedules and interval schedules. In a ratio schedule of reinforcement, reinforcement is provided after the individual makes a certain number of desired responses. There are two kinds of ratio schedules: fixed and variable. A **fixed-ratio schedule of reinforcement** provides reinforcement after a specific number of desired responses. A rat in a Skinner box might be reinforced with a pellet of food after every 5 bar presses. Suppose a garment worker is paid with a voucher after every 3 shirts sewn. That person, too, would be on a fixed-ratio schedule. Fixed-ratio schedules produce high, steady response rates, with a pause in responding after each reinforcement.

Unlike a fixed-ratio schedule, a **variable-ratio schedule of reinforcement** provides reinforcement after an unpredictable number of desired responses. The number of responses required will vary around an average. For example, a rat in a Skinner box might be reinforced with a food pellet after an average of 7 bar presses—perhaps 5 presses one time, 10 presses a second time, and 6 presses a third time. People playing slot machines are on a variable-ratio schedule, because they cannot predict how many times they will have to play before they win. Even the archerfish, which hunts insects by spitting water at them as they fly by, continues to hunt that way (despite missing many times) because it is on a variable-ratio schedule of reinforcement (Goldstein & Hall, 1990).

Variable-ratio schedules produce high, steady rates of responding, which are more resistant to extinction than are those produced by any other schedule of reinforcement. In fact, by using a variable-ratio schedule of reinforcement, Skinner conditioned pigeons to peck a lighted disk up to 10,000 times to obtain a single pellet of food. This also explains one reason compulsive gamblers find it so difficult to quit—eventually they will receive positive reinforcement, though their reinforcement history is unpredictable.

Whereas ratio schedules of reinforcement provide reinforcement after a certain number of desired responses, interval schedules of reinforcement provide reinforcement for the first desired response after a period of time. As in the case of ratio schedules, there are two kinds of interval schedules: fixed and variable. A **fixed-interval schedule of reinforcement** reinforces the first desired response after a set period of time. For example, a rat in a Skinner box might be reinforced with a food pellet for its first bar press after intervals of 30 seconds. Bar presses given during the intervals would not be reinforced.

A fixed-interval schedule produces a drop in responses immediately after reinforcement and a gradual increase in responses as the time for the next reinforcement approaches. Suppose that you have a biology exam every 3 weeks. You would study before each exam to obtain a good grade—a positive reinforcer. But you would probably stop studying biology immediately after each exam and not begin studying it again until a few days before the next exam.

A **variable-interval schedule of reinforcement** provides reinforcement for the first desired response made after varying periods of time, which vary around an average. For example, a rat might be reinforced for its first bar press after 19 seconds, then after 37 seconds, then after 4 seconds, and so on, with the interval averaging 20 seconds. When you are fishing, you are on a variable-interval schedule of reinforcement, because you cannot predict how long you will have to wait until a fish bites. Variable-interval schedules produce relatively slow, steady rates of responding, highly resistant to extinction. An individual might continue to fish even if the fish are few and far between. And teachers who give periodic surprise quizzes make use of variable-interval schedules to promote more consistent studying by their students.

Ratio schedules produce faster response rates than do interval schedules, because the number of responses, not the length of time, determines the onset of reinforcement. Variable schedules produce steadier response rates than do fixed schedules, because the pattern of reinforcement is unpredictable. Figure 7.5 illustrates differences in response patterns under different schedules of reinforcement.

Negative Reinforcement

In **negative reinforcement** a behavior that brings about the removal of an aversive stimulus becomes more likely to occur in the future. Note that both positive and negative reinforcement increase the likelihood of a behavior. Consider the boring lecture. Because daydreaming lets you escape from boring lectures, you are likely to daydream whenever you find

▲ **Fixed-Interval Schedule of Reinforcement**

If you receive your mail at the same time every day, say at exactly 11 A.M., you are on a fixed-interval schedule of reinforcement. You would be reinforced the first time you checked your mailbox after 11 A.M., but you would not be reinforced if you checked it before 11 A.M.

fixed-interval schedule of reinforcement

A partial schedule of reinforcement that provides reinforcement for the first desired response made after a set length of time.

variable-interval schedule of reinforcement

A partial schedule of reinforcement that provides reinforcement for the first desired response made after varying, unpredictable lengths of time.

negative reinforcement

In operant conditioning, an increase in the probability of a behavior that is followed by the removal of an aversive stimulus.

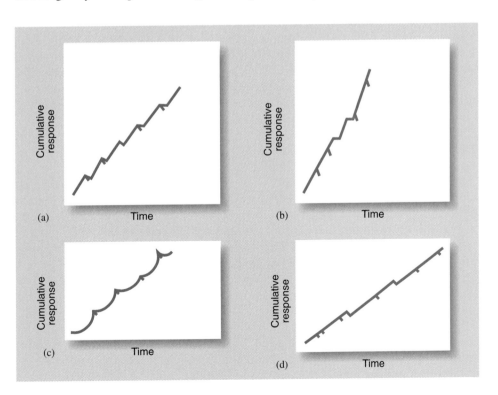

◄ **Figure 7.5**
Schedules of Reinforcement

The hash marks show the delivery of reinforcement. Steeper slopes indicate higher rates of responding. *(a)* Pattern of behavior typically produced by a fixed-ratio schedule of reinforcement. *(b)* Pattern of behavior typically produced by a variable-ratio schedule of reinforcement. *(c)* Pattern of behavior typically produced by a fixed-interval schedule of reinforcement. *(d)* Pattern of behavior typically produced by a variable-interval pattern of reinforcement.

Learning to perform a behavior that terminates an aversive stimulus, as in negative reinforcement.

Learning to prevent the occurrence of an aversive stimulus by giving an appropriate response to a warning stimulus.

yourself listening to one. This form of negative reinforcement is called **escape learning**—learning to end something aversive. For example, you can terminate an irritating warning buzzer by putting on your automobile seat belt.

Of course your class might be so boring that you stop attending it. This is a form of negative reinforcement called **avoidance learning**—learning to prevent something aversive. Thus, you can avoid the sound of a warning buzzer by buckling up before you start your automobile engine. And dormitory students at some schools quickly learn to scamper out of the shower when they hear a toilet being flushed to avoid being scalded when cold water is diverted to the toilet (Reese, 1986).

But if negative reinforcement involves engaging in a behavior that removes an aversive stimulus, how could avoidance learning (which only prevents an aversive stimulus) be a form of negative reinforcement? That is, what is the aversive stimulus that is being removed? Evidently, what is being removed is an internal aversive stimulus—the emotional distress caused by your anticipation of the aversive event, such as a boring class or a scalding shower. Thus, in escape learning the aversive stimulus itself is removed, while in avoidance learning the emotional distress caused by anticipation of that stimulus is removed. Even relatively simple animals engage in avoidance learning. For example, bees that get caught in spider webs—and are fortunate enough to escape—may learn to avoid them in the future (Craig, 1994).

Extinction

In operant conditioning, the gradual disappearance of a response that is no longer followed by a reinforcer.

As in classical conditioning, behaviors learned through operant conditioning are subject to **extinction.** Skinner discovered extinction by accident. In one of his early studies, he conditioned a rat in a Skinner box to press a bar to obtain pellets of food from a dispenser. On one occasion he found that the pellet dispenser had become jammed, preventing the release of pellets. Skinner noted the rat continued to press the bar, though at a diminishing rate, until it finally stopped pressing at all. Extinction might occur when a student who raises her hand is no longer called on to answer questions. Because she is no longer being positively reinforced for raising her hand, she would eventually stop doing so.

When extinction begins, there is typically a burst in the response. This is important in behavior therapy techniques that use extinction, because they might, at first, seem to be ineffective. Experienced therapists realize this and might promote appropriate behavior by reinforcing it while an undesired behavior is undergoing extinction (Lerman & Iwata, 1995).

In operant conditioning, the reappearance after a period of time of a behavior that has been subjected to extinction.

Also, as with classical conditioning, a behavior that has been subjected to extinction can show **spontaneous recovery**—it might reappear after a period of time. This provides a functional advantage. For example, suppose wild animals that visit a certain water hole normally obtain positive reinforcement by finding water. If they visit the water hole on several successive occasions and find it has dried up, their behavior will undergo extinction; they will stop visiting the water hole. But after a period of time, the animals might exhibit spontaneous recovery, again visiting the water hole—in case it had become refilled with water.

Punishment

In operant conditioning, the process by which an aversive stimulus decreases the probability of a response that precedes it.

Still another way of reducing the probability of behaviors is through **punishment,** in which the consequence of a behavior decreases its likelihood. Do not confuse punishment with negative reinforcement. Negative reinforcement is "negative" because it involves the removal of an aversive stimulus; it does not involve punishment. Negative reinforcement increases the probability of a behavior by removing something undesirable as a consequence of that behavior; punishment decreases the probability of a behavior by presenting something undesirable (*positive punishment*) as a consequence of that behavior or by removing something desirable (*negative punishment*) as a consequence of that behavior. For example, a driver who gets a speeding ticket—an example of positive punishment—is less likely to speed in the future. Likewise, a teenager who is not allowed to use the family car because of speeding—an example of negative punishment—will also be less likely to speed again.

Punishment is useful even in animal, as well as human, societies. For example, social animals punish underlings who threaten group well-being. They use punishment to discipline offspring, promote cooperation, and maintain dominance hierarchies (Clutton-Brock & Parker, 1995). Though punishment can be an effective means of reducing undesirable

	Behavioral	Probability of	
Table 7.1	**Behavioral Contingencies**		
Contingency	**Behavioral consequence**	**Probability of behavior**	**Example**
Positive reinforcement	Brings about something desirable	Increases	You study for an exam and receive an A, which makes you more likely to study in the future.
Negative reinforcement	Removes something undesirable	Increases	You go to the dentist to have a cavity filled. This eliminates your toothache, which makes you more likely to visit the dentist in the future when you have a toothache.
Extinction	Fails to bring about something desirable	Decreases	You say hello to a person who repeatedly fails to greet you in return. This leads you to stop saying hello.
Punishment	Brings about something undesirable	Decreases	You overeat at a party and suffer from a severe upset stomach. In the future you become less likely to overeat.

behaviors, it often is ineffective. Consider some effective and ineffective ways of using punishment to discipline children (Walters & Grusec, 1977).

- First, punishment for misbehavior should be immediate so that the child will associate the punishment with the misbehavior. A mother or father should not resort to threats of "wait until your father [mother] gets home," which might separate the misbehavior and punishment by hours.
- Second, punishment should be strong enough to stop the undesirable behavior but not excessive. You might punish a child for throwing clothes about his room by having him clean the room, but you would be using excessive punishment if you had him clean every room in the house. Punishment that is excessive induces resentment aimed at the person who administers the punishment.
- Third, punishment should be consistent. If parents truly want to reduce a child's misbehavior, they must punish the child each time it occurs. Otherwise the child learns only that her parents are unpredictable—that is, the child is on a variable-ratio schedule of reinforcement (which is highly resistant to extinction).
- Fourth, punishment should be aimed at the misbehavior, not at the child. For example, a child who is repeatedly called "stupid" for making mistakes while playing softball might feel incompetent and lose interest in softball and other sports.
- Fifth, punishing undesirable behavior merely suppresses the behavior in response to a specific discriminative stimulus, such as the parent who administers punishment, and only tells the child what not to do. To make sure the child learns what to do, positive reinforcement of desirable behavior should also be used.

One of the main controversies concerning punishment is the use of physical punishment. Children imitate parental models. If they observe that their parents rely on physical punishment, they might rely on it in dealing with their friends, siblings, and, eventually, their own children. A study of over 900 American parents found that 94 percent had used some form of physical punishment—defined as slapping, spanking, pinching, shaking, or hitting with belts or paddles—to control their children (Straus & Stewart, 1999). Though physical punishment of children can suppress misbehavior in the short run, in the long run it is associated with problems such as juvenile delinquency and adult criminality (Straus, 1991). Being physically punished as a child also is associated with subsequent adult depression, suicidal tendencies, alcohol and spousal abuse, and physical brutality against children (Straus & Kantor, 1994). Table 7.1 summarizes the differences among the behavioral contingencies of positive reinforcement, negative reinforcement, extinction, and punishment.

Applications of Operant Conditioning

B. F. Skinner (1986) claimed that many of our everyday problems could be solved by more widespread use of operant conditioning. As one example, consider the problem of injuries and deaths caused by automobile accidents. Operant conditioning has been effectively used to teach children to use seat belts, thereby reducing their risk of injury (Roberts & Fanurik, 1986). Now consider several other ways in which operant conditioning has been applied to everyday life.

Operant Conditioning and Animal Training

Skinner and some of his colleagues have been pioneers in the use of shaping and chaining to train animals to perform novel behaviors (Lukas, Marr, & Maple, 1998). Perhaps Skinner's most noteworthy feat in animal training occurred during World War II in "Project Pigeon." This was a secret project in which Skinner (1960) trained pigeons to guide missiles toward enemy ships by training them to peck at an image of the target ship shown on a display to obtain food pellets. Though this guidance system proved feasible, it was never used in combat.

More recently, pigeons were trained to serve as air-sea rescue spotters in the U.S. Coast Guard's "Project Sea Hunt" (Stark, 1981). The pigeons were reinforced with food pellets for responding to objects colored red, orange, or yellow—the common colors of flotation devices. Three pigeons were placed in a compartment under a search plane so they looked out of windows oriented in different directions. When a pigeon spotted an object floating in the sea, it pecked a key, which sounded a buzzer and flashed a light in the cockpit. Pigeons are superior to human spotters, because they have the ability to focus over a wider area and to scan the sea for longer periods of time without becoming fatigued.

In another beneficial application of operant conditioning, psychologists have trained capuchin monkeys to serve as aides to physically disabled people (Mack, 1981). These monkeys act as extensions of the disabled person—bringing drinks, turning pages in books, changing television channels, and performing a host of other services. The person directs the monkey by using an optical pointer that focuses a beam of light on a desired object.

Operant Conditioning and Child Rearing

In 1945 Skinner shocked the public when he published the article "Baby in a Box," which described how he and his wife had reared an infant daughter in an enclosure called an *air crib*. The air crib filtered and controlled the temperature of the infant's air supply. Instead of diapers, it used a roll of paper that permitted sections to be placed under the baby and discarded when dirty. The parents could even pull down a shade over the front window of the air crib when the baby was ready to go to sleep. Skinner claimed the air crib was a more convenient way to rear infants and allowed more time for social interaction with them. Critics disagreed with Skinner, claiming his treatment of his daughter was dehumanizing. Over the past few decades, rumors have claimed Skinner's daughter's experience with the air crib eventually led her to sue her father, to become insane, or to commit suicide. In reality, she had a happy childhood and has pursued a successful career as an artist (Langone, 1983).

The air crib provoked fears of impersonal child rearing, and it was never widely used. Skinner had tried, unsuccessfully, to market the air crib under the clever brand name *Heir Conditioner* (Benjamin & Neilsen-Gammon, 1999). Nonetheless, operant conditioning has proved useful in child rearing. For example, teachers have promoted toothbrushing by positively reinforcing children for having clean teeth by posting their names on the classroom wall (Swain, Allard, & Holborn, 1982). And parents have used extinction to eliminate their child's tantrums. When parents ignore the tantrums, rather than give in to the child's demand for toys, candy, or attention, the tantrums might at first intensify but eventually will stop (Williams, 1959).

Operant Conditioning and Educational Improvement

Teachers likewise have used positive reinforcement to improve their students' classroom performance. For example, verbal praise has been used to increase participation in classroom discussions (Smith et al., 1982), and positive reinforcement in the form of token

▲ **Monkeys as Aides**

Psychologists have trained capuchin monkeys to serve as aides to physically disabled persons. An organization called Helping Hands, based in Boston, uses operant conditioning to train the monkeys to respond to one-word commands and a laser pointer. They bring drinks, turn on televisions, and scratch itches. The monkeys are rewarded with edibles, such as sips of fruit juice or licks of peanut butter. The monkeys also help relieve the loneliness of their companions.

 Dr. P.'s Dog Training
www.mhhe.com/sdorow5

 Behaviour Analysis
www.mhhe.com/sdorow5

economies has been used to promote desirable classroom behaviors (Swiezy, Matson, & Box, 1992). In a **token economy** teachers use tokens to reward students for proper conduct and academic excellence. The students then use the tokens to purchase items such as toys or privileges such as extra recess time. Token economies have been used to reduce television watching by children (Wolfe, Mendes, & Factor, 1984) and inappropriate social behavior by adults with mental retardation (LeBlanc, Hagopian, & Maglieri, 2000).

Perhaps the most distinctive contribution operant conditioning has made to education has been **programmed instruction,** which had its origin in the invention of the teaching machine by Sidney Pressey of Ohio State University in the 1920s. His machines provided immediate knowledge of results and a piece of candy to reward correct answers (Benjamin, 1988). But credit for developing programmed instruction is generally given to B. F. Skinner for his invention of a teaching machine that takes the student through a series of questions related to a particular subject, gradually moving the student from simple to more complex questions. After the student answers a question, the correct answer is revealed.

The teaching machine failed to catch on in the 1950s and 1960s because of fears that it would be dehumanizing, that it could teach only certain narrow subjects, and that teachers would lose their jobs. Nonetheless, supporters note that programmed instruction has several advantages over traditional approaches to education (Vargas & Vargas, 1991). Programmed instruction provides immediate feedback of results (positive reinforcement for correct answers and only mild punishment for incorrect answers), eliminates the need for anxiety-inducing exams, and permits the student to go at her or his own pace. Skinner (1984) claimed that if schools adopted programmed instruction, students would learn twice as much in the same amount of time.

Today's use of **computer-assisted instruction** (Skinner, 1989) in many schools is a descendant of Skinner's programmed instruction. Computer programs take the student through a graded series of items at the student's own pace. The programs even branch off to provide extra help on items the student finds difficult. Though teaching machines and computers have not replaced teachers, they have added another teaching tool to the classroom. Computer-assisted instruction has proved useful with students, whether teaching academic skills to preschoolers (Hitchcock & Noonan, 2000), industrial plant procedures to

token economy
An operant conditioning procedure that uses tokens as positive reinforcers in programs designed to promote desirable behaviors, with the tokens later used to purchase desired items or privileges.

programmed instruction
A step-by-step approach, based on operant conditioning, in which the learner proceeds at his or her own pace through more and more difficult material and receives immediate knowledge of the results of each response.

computer-assisted instruction
The use of computer programs to provide programmed instruction.

Learning | **229**

► **Computer-Assisted Instruction**
Students may benefit from computer-assisted instruction because it permits them to go at their own pace, receive immediate feedback on their progress, and, in some cases, obtain remedial help in areas of weakness.

learned helplessness
A feeling of futility caused by the belief that one has little or no control over events in one's life, which can make one stop trying and become depressed.

 The Cambridge Center for Behavioral Studies
www.mhhe.com/sdorow5

workers (Ujita et al., 1996), or introductory psychology to college students (Pear & Crone-Todd, 1999). Computer-assisted instruction also is useful with special populations, such as deaf students (Mertens & Rabiu, 1992), illiterate adults (Lavery, Townsend, & Wilton, 1998), and autistic children (Chen & Bernard-Opitz, 1993).

Operant Conditioning and Psychological Disorders

Operant conditioning has enhanced our understanding of psychological disorders, particularly depression. The concept of **learned helplessness** has gained influence as an explanation for depression through the work of Martin Seligman (see Chapter 14). In his original research, Seligman exposed dogs restrained in harnesses to electric shocks. One group of dogs could turn off the shock by pressing a switch with their noses. A second group could not. The dogs then were tested in a shuttle box, which consisted of two compartments separated by an easily hurdled divider. A warning tone was sounded, followed a few seconds later by an electric shock. Dogs in the first group escaped by jumping over the divider into the other compartment. In contrast, dogs in the second group whimpered but did not try to escape (Seligman & Maier, 1967).

Though replications of various versions of this study have produced inconsistent support for learned helplessness in animals (Klosterhalfen & Klosterhalfen, 1983) and human beings (Winefield, 1982), the possibility that learned helplessness is a factor in depression has inspired hundreds of studies (Deuser & Anderson, 1995). Depressed people experience less control over obtaining positive reinforcers and avoiding punishments. As a consequence, they are less likely to try to change their life situations—which further contributes to their feelings of depression. You may have seen this in students who study many hours but still do poorly; they might become depressed, stop studying, and even drop out of school.

Operant conditioning also has been used to change maladaptive behaviors. This is known as *behavior modification.* For example, token economies have been useful in training mental hospital patients to care for themselves (Morisse et al., 1996). Residents are trained to dress themselves, to use toilets, to brush their teeth, and to eat with utensils. They use the tokens to purchase merchandise or special privileges.

Operant Conditioning and Biofeedback

One day, more than three decades ago, the eminent learning researcher Neal Miller stood in front of a mirror trying to teach himself to wiggle one ear. By watching his ear in the mirror, he eventually was able to make it wiggle (Jonas, 1972). The mirror provided Miller with

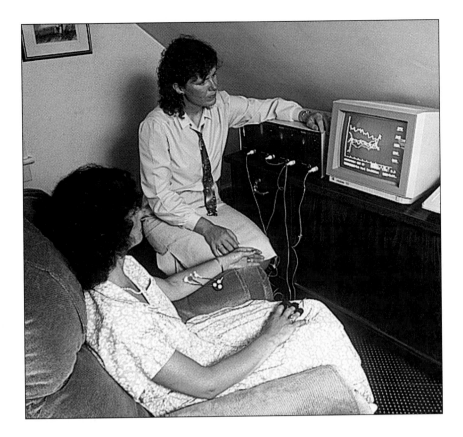

biofeedback

A form of operant conditioning that enables an individual to learn to control a normally involuntary physiological process or to gain better control of a normally voluntary one when provided with visual or auditory information indicating the state of that response.

Association for Applied Psychophysiology and Biofeedback
www.mhhe.com/sdorow5

▲ **Neal Miller**

"The biofeedback and behavioral medicine techniques already available are preventing unnecessary suffering, correcting disabling conditions, and helping people regain control of their lives."

visual *feedback* of his ear's movement. This convinced him that people might learn to control physiological responses that are not normally subject to voluntary control if they were provided with feedback of those responses. Since the 1960s Miller and other psychologists have developed a technique called *biofeedback* to help people learn to control normally involuntary responses such as brain waves, blood pressure, and intestinal contractions.

Biofeedback is a form of operant conditioning that enables an individual to learn to control a normally involuntary physiological response or to gain better control of a normally voluntary one when provided with visual or auditory information indicating the state of that response. The feedback acts as a positive reinforcer for changes in the desired direction. The feedback might be provided by a light that changes in brightness as heart rate changes, a tone that changes in pitch as muscle tension changes, or any of a host of other visual or auditory stimuli that vary with changes in the target physiological response.

Biofeedback was popularized in the late 1960s by reports of participants who learned to control their alpha brain-wave patterns, which are associated with a relaxed state of mind. But biofeedback did not become scientifically credible to many psychologists until Neal Miller reported success in training rats to gain voluntary control over physiological responses normally controlled solely by the autonomic nervous system. In his studies, Miller used electrical stimulation of the brain's reward centers (positive reinforcement) or, in some cases, escape or avoidance of shock (negative reinforcement) to train rats to increase or decrease their heart rate, intestinal contractions, urine formation, or blood pressure. Because Miller was an eminent, hard-nosed researcher, serious scientists became more willing to accept the legitimacy of biofeedback. Ironically, for unknown reasons, attempts at replicating his rat studies generally have failed (Dworkin & Miller, 1986).

Disappointment at the failure to replicate Miller's rat studies and of biofeedback to fulfill early promises to induce mystical states of consciousness led to skepticism about its merits. But even though biofeedback has not proven to be an unqualified success, it has not proven to be a failure. Hundreds of studies have demonstrated the effectiveness of biofeedback in helping people learn to control a variety of physiological responses, such as blood pressure (Nakao et al., 2000). Clinical applications have included reducing hyperactivity by training children to regulate their own brain waves (Boyd & Campbell, 1998), improving balance and mobility among older adults with a history of falling (Rose & Clark, 2000), and even helping people with painfully cold hands to warm them by increasing blood flow (Sedlacek & Taub, 1996).

One of biofeedback's main uses has been in training people to gain better control of their skeletal muscles. For example, biofeedback has been used to train brain-damaged people to maintain their balance (Simmons et al., 1998), typists to prevent carpal tunnel syndrome by warning them when their wrists are in improper positions (Thomas et al., 1993), and headache sufferers to relax their neck muscles (Arena et al., 1995).

Though biofeedback is widely used by psychologists and health professionals, it is not a panacea. In fact, there is controversy about its effectiveness and practicality. To demonstrate the effectiveness of biofeedback, one must show that self-regulation of physiological responses is caused by the feedback and not by extraneous factors (Roberts, 1985). For example, early biofeedback studies showed that feedback of alpha brain waves could increase them and induce a state of relaxation. But replications of those early studies showed that the effects were caused by the participants' sitting quietly with their eyes closed. The brain-wave feedback added nothing (Plotkin, 1979).

Even when the results of a biofeedback study can be attributed to the feedback, the technique still might not be of practical use. Why is this so?

- First, the typical biofeedback device costs hundreds or even thousands of dollars. Thus, clinicians must decide whether the benefits of biofeedback justify its cost, especially when other equally effective, less expensive treatments are available. Yet, overall, treatment programs that include biofeedback have proved cost effective in enhancing the quality of life and in reducing physician visits, medication use, medical care costs, hospital stays, and mortality (Schneider, 1987).
- Second, laboratory experiments on biofeedback can produce results that are statistically significant (a concept discussed in Chapter 2) and merit being reported but that are too small to be of practical use in clinical settings (Steiner & Dince, 1981). For example, biofeedback might produce a *statistically significant* reduction in blood pressure in hypertensive persons that is too small to be *clinically meaningful.*
- Third, biofeedback training in a clinician's office might produce results that do not last much beyond the training sessions. However, a study of women with migraine headaches found that those who continued to practice handwarming at home showed a greater decline in headaches compared to those who did not (Gauthier, Cote, & French, 1994). One way to promote the generalization of benefits from clinical training sessions to everyday life is to use portable biofeedback devices (Harrison, Gavin, & Isaac, 1988).
- Fourth, the results of laboratory studies might not be applicable to the clinical setting. The therapist who uses biofeedback typically achieves success by combining biofeedback with other therapeutic approaches. Thus, biofeedback does not achieve its clinical effects by itself, as an antibiotic might do in curing a bacterial infection (Green & Shellenberger, 1986). That is, though it would be scientifically sound to compare a psychotherapy-plus-biofeedback group to a psychotherapy-alone group, it would be scientifically unsound to compare a psychotherapy-alone group to a biofeedback-alone group.

Biological Constraints on Operant Conditioning

Around the turn of the century, Edward Thorndike put forth the concept of *belongingness* to explain why he found it easier to train cats to escape from his puzzle boxes by stepping on a pedal than by scratching themselves. Thorndike observed that evolution seemed to have endowed animals with inherited tendencies to associate the performance of certain behaviors with certain consequences. Cats are more predisposed to escape by performing actions that affect the environment, such as stepping on a pedal, than by performing actions that affect their bodies, such as scratching themselves.

Thorndike's observation had little influence on his contemporaries, and it was not until the 1950s that psychologists rediscovered what he had observed. Among the first psychologists to make this rediscovery were Keller and Marian Breland, former students of B. F. Skinner who became renowned animal trainers (Bailey & Bailey, 1993). Beginning in 1947, their Animal Behavior Enterprises in Hot Springs, Arkansas, trained animals to perform in zoos, fairs, movies, circuses, museums, amusement parks, department stores, and television commercials.

Despite their success in training animals, the Brelands were distressed by the tendency of some animals to "misbehave" (Breland & Breland, 1961). Their misbehavior was actually a reversion to behaviors characteristic of their species, which the Brelands called **instinctive drift.** For example, they used operant conditioning to train a chicken to hit a baseball by pulling a string to swing a miniature bat and then run to first base for food. Sometimes, instead, the chicken chased after the ball and pecked at it. This "misbehavior" of animals has distressed animal trainers, but it demonstrates that animals sometimes may revert back to species-specific behaviors even when being reinforced for other behaviors.

After considering instinctive drift and related problems in operant conditioning, psychologist Martin Seligman (1970) concluded that there is a continuum of **behavioral preparedness** for certain behaviors. For example, a hamster more easily learns to dig than to wash its face to obtain positive reinforcement (Shettleworth & Juergensen, 1980). The continuum of behavioral preparedness ranges from *prepared* to *unprepared* to *contraprepared.* Behaviors for which members of a species are *prepared* have evolved because they have survival value for them and are easily learned by members of that species. Behaviors for which members of a species are *unprepared* have no survival value for them and are difficult to learn for members of that species. And behaviors for which members of a species are *contraprepared* have no survival value for them and are impossible to learn for members of that species. For example, human beings are prepared, chimpanzees are unprepared, and dogs are contraprepared to use language. Human beings can learn to speak, read, write, and use sign language. Chimpanzees can learn to use sign language. And dogs cannot learn any of these language skills.

instinctive drift
The reversion of animals to behaviors characteristic of their species even when being reinforced for performing other behaviors.

behavioral preparedness
The degree to which members of a species are innately prepared to learn particular behaviors.

STAYING ON TRACK: *Operant Conditioning*

1. In what way was Edward Thorndike's instrumental conditioning the forerunner of B. F. Skinner's operant conditioning?
2. How would you use shaping to train a child to straighten up his room?
3. In what ways are positive reinforcement and negative reinforcement similar and in what ways are they different?

Answers to Staying on Track start on ST-3.

◆ COGNITIVE LEARNING

Both classical conditioning and operant conditioning traditionally have been explained by the principle of contiguity—the mere association of events in time and space. Contiguity has been used to explain the association of a conditioned stimulus and an unconditioned stimulus in classical conditioning and the association of a behavior and its consequence in operant conditioning. Over the past few decades, the associationistic explanation of learning has been criticized for viewing human and animal learners as passive reactors to "external carrots, whips, and the stimuli associated with them" (Boneau, 1974, p. 308). These critics, influenced by the "cognitive revolution" in psychology, favor the study of cognitive factors in classical conditioning and operant conditioning, as well as the study of learning by observation, which had routinely been ignored by learning researchers (Wasserman, 1997).

Cognitive Factors in Associative Learning

As discussed earlier, the traditional view of classical conditioning and operant conditioning is that they are explained by contiguity alone. But evidence has accumulated that mere contiguity of a neutral stimulus and an unconditioned stimulus is insufficient to produce classical conditioning, and mere contiguity of a behavior and a consequence is insufficient to produce operant conditioning. This evidence has led to cognitive interpretations of associative learning, as in the case of operant conditioning. For example, secondary reinforcers have traditionally been thought to gain their reinforcing ability through mere *contiguity* with primary reinforcers. Cognitive theorists believe, instead, that secondary reinforcers gain their reinforcing ability because they have reliably *predicted* the occurrence of primary reinforcers (Rose & Fantino, 1978).

Suppose that you are using dog biscuits as positive reinforcers to train your dog to "shake hands." Just before giving your dog a biscuit, you might offer praise by saying "Good dog!" If you did so every time your dog shook hands, the words "Good dog!" might become a secondary reinforcer. The traditional view of operant conditioning would claim the praise became a secondary reinforcer by its mere *contiguity* with food. In contrast, the cognitive view would claim that the praise became a secondary reinforcer because it had become a good *predictor* of the food reward.

Psychologists also have provided cognitive explanations of classical conditioning that rule out mere contiguity as a sufficient explanation. The most influential of these explanations states that classical conditioning will occur only when the conditioned stimulus permits the individual to predict reliably the occurrence of the unconditioned stimulus (Siegel & Allan, 1996). The better the conditioned stimulus is as a predictor, the stronger the conditioning will be. This means that conditioning involves learning relations, or contingencies, among events in the environment.

This was demonstrated by Robert Rescorla (1968), who favors a cognitive explanation of conditioning. In one experiment, he paired a buzzer (the neutral stimulus) with an electric shock (a UCS), which he administered to rats. All of the rats received the same number of pairings of the buzzer and the electric shock. But some of the rats were given additional shocks not preceded by a buzzer. According to the traditional contiguity-based explanation of classical conditioning, because the buzzer and the electric shock had been paired an equal number of times for all of the rats, the buzzer should have become an equally strong CS, eliciting a CR, for all of them. Yet those for whom the buzzer always preceded the electric shock showed stronger conditioning.

Rescorla would explain this cognitively. The rats that always received an electric shock after the buzzer developed a stronger *expectancy* that an electric shock would follow the buzzer than did the rats that sometimes did and sometimes did not receive an electric shock after the buzzer. Consider this explanation in regard to Pavlov's studies of salivation in dogs. The dog learns a tone is followed by meat powder. The more consistently the tone precedes the meat powder, the more predictable the relationship will be and, as a consequence, the stronger the conditioning will be.

Another source of evidence that supports the cognitive explanation of classical conditioning is the phenomenon of **blocking,** in which a neutral stimulus paired with a CS that already elicits a CR will fail to become a CS itself (Blaisdell, Gunther, & Miller, 1999). Blocking is illustrated in Table 7.2. Suppose that you have conditioned a dog to salivate to the sound of a bell by repeatedly presenting the bell before presenting meat powder. If you then repeatedly paired a light with the bell before presenting the meat powder, the principle of contiguity would make you expect that the light, too, would gain the ability to elicit salivation. But it will not. Instead, the CS (the bell) "blocks" the neutral stimulus (the light) from becoming a conditioned stimulus. According to the cognitive explanation, blocking occurs because the neutral stimulus (the light) adds nothing to the predictability of the UCS (the meat powder). The CS (the bell) already predicts the occurrence of the UCS. Blocking has been demonstrated in animals (Smith, 1997) and human beings (Hinchy, Lovibond, & Ter-Horst, 1995).

Still another source of evidence against a strictly contiguity-based view of classical conditioning comes from research on conditioned taste aversion. As you learned earlier,

▲ **Robert Rescorla**

"Simple contiguity of CS and UCS fails to capture the relation required to produce an association."

blocking

The process by which a neutral stimulus paired with a conditioned stimulus that already elicits a conditioned response fails to become a conditioned stimulus.

Table 7.2   Blocking

In this example, in phase 1, rats in the experimental group are presented with a tone (the CS) immediately followed by an electric shock (the UCS), while rats in the control group receive neither stimulus. In phase 2, both groups are exposed to a tone and a light, followed by a shock. In phase 3, both groups show fear (the CR) in response to the tone, but only the control group shows fear in response to the light. Because the tone already served as a reliable predictor of the shock for the experimental group, the tone blocked the light from becoming a CS for the rats in that group.

	Phase 1	Phase 2	Phase 3
Experimental group	CS (tone) + UCS (shock)	CS (tone + light) + UCS (shock)	CS (tone) →CR (fear) CS (light) →No CR
Control group	No training	CS (tone + light) + UCS (shock)	CS (tone) →CR (fear) CS (light) →CR (fear)

individuals who suffer gastrointestinal illness hours after eating novel food might avoid that food in the future. This contradicts the notion that events must be contiguous for us to learn to associate those events with each other.

Latent Learning

The "cognitive revolution" in psychology also has produced a trend to view learning less in terms of changes in overt behavior, as in classical or operant conditioning, and more in terms of the acquisition of knowledge (Greeno, 1980). This means learning can occur without revealing itself in observable behavior. For example, suppose after studying many hours and mastering the material for a psychology exam, you fail the exam. Should your professor conclude that you had not learned the material? Not necessarily. Perhaps you failed the exam because the questions were ambiguous or because you were so anxious that your mind "went blank." Your performance on the exam did not reflect how well you had learned the material.

But some researchers were interested in cognitive factors in learning decades before the onset of the cognitive revolution, even in regard to animal learning (Dewsbury, 2000). The first psychologist to stress the distinction between learning and performance was Edward Tolman (1932), who pointed out that learning can occur without rewards being given for overt actions, a process that he called **latent learning.** In latent learning, learning is not immediately revealed in performance but is revealed later when a reward is provided for performance. In a classic study, Tolman had three groups of rats run individually through a maze once a day for 10 days. One group received food as a positive reward for reaching the end of the maze, and the other two groups did not. The rewarded rats quickly learned to run through the maze with few wrong turns, while the nonrewarded rats did not. Beginning on the eleventh day, one of the groups of nonrewarded rats was also positively rewarded with food for reaching the end of the maze. The next day that group ran the maze as efficiently as the previously rewarded group did, while the remaining, still nonrewarded group continued to perform poorly. This demonstrated latent learning. The rats that were not rewarded until the eleventh day had learned the route to the end of the maze, but they revealed this learning only when rewarded for doing so (Tolman & Honzik, 1930).

More recent research has provided additional support for latent learning. In one study, rats given an opportunity to observe a water maze before swimming through it for a food reward performed better than did rats who were not given such an opportunity (Keith & McVety, 1988). This provided evidence that rats can form what Tolman called "cognitive maps"—mental representations of physical reality. But they use their cognitive maps only when rewarded for doing so. Nonetheless, some researchers have found in similar experiments that rats might be guided in their swimming not by cognitive maps, but instead by visual cues in their environment (Prados, Chamizo, & MacKintosh, 1999).

latent learning
Learning that occurs without the reinforcement of overt behavior.

Does Television Influence Children's Behavior?

Research on observational learning has contributed to concerns about the effects of the media on people, particularly children. Concern about the effects of television on behavior is not new. It has existed ever since television became a popular medium in the 1950s (Carpenter, 1955). The first congressional report on the effects of television was a 1954 report on its impact on juvenile delinquency. Other reports on the social effects of television appeared in 1972 and 1982. Both reports found that violence on television led to aggressive behavior in children and adolescents and recommended a decrease in televised violence (Walsh, 1983). But critics of these reports claimed, on the one hand, that the results of laboratory experiments on the effects of televised violence might not generalize to real life and, on the other hand, that field studies on the effects of televised violence failed to control all of the other variables that might encourage violence (Fisher, 1983).

In a classic experiment by Albert Bandura (1965) on the potential effect of television viewing on children, three groups of preschool children watched a film of an adult punching and verbally abusing a blow-up Bobo doll. Each group saw a different version of the film. In the first version the model was rewarded with candy, soda, and praise by another adult. In the second version the other adult scolded and spanked the model. And in the third version there were no consequences to the model. The children then played individually in a room with a Bobo doll and other toys (see Figure 7.6). Those who had seen the model being rewarded for being aggressive were more aggressive in their play than were those who had seen the other two versions of the film. This demonstrated that operant conditioning can occur vicariously, simply through observing others receiving positive reinforcement for engaging in the target behavior.

Over the past four decades, research and field studies have presented a complex picture of the effects of televised violence. A recent meta-analysis of research studies found that there is a positive, significant correlation between televised violence and aggressive behavior (Paik & Comstock, 1994). Another meta-analysis found a causal relationship in which viewing televised aggression led to small increases in viewer aggression. This effect was stronger in cultures outside of the United States (Hogben, 1998).

Children who watch television are exposed not only to antisocial models but also to prosocial models. Whereas children who watch violent programs tend to be more aggressive, children who watch altruistic programs such as *Mister Rogers' Neighborhood* tend to engage in more prosocial behaviors (Huston, Watkins, & Kunkel, 1989). In a recent study, Lawrence Rosenkoetter (1999) assessed whether elementary-school-age children understood the moral lessons in two situation comedies, *The Cosby Show* and *Full House*. One-third of the first graders and one-half of the third graders in his sample were able to describe the prosocial theme of each show. Moreover, children's prosocial behavior was positively correlated with the frequency with which they viewed prosocial programs. This relationship was even stronger for the children who understood the underlying moral of the programming. Thus, children who watched such programs *and* understood their underlying messages engaged in more prosocial behavior.

Television is only one of many influences on children's psychosocial development. The time children spend watching television is influenced by school and homework schedules, playing with other children, and other activities. One recent study of an ethnically diverse sample of low- and middle-income children found that participants who lived in more stimulating home environments and who had better educated mothers spent more of their television viewing time watching educational programming (Huston et al., 1999). Thus, many psychologists believe that caregivers can exert considerable influence on children's viewing habits by using TV rating information to regulate television viewing and discussing program content with children (Abelman, 1999).

 Violence on Television
www.mhhe.com/sdorow5

▲ **Figure 7.6**
Observational Learning
Children who observe aggressive behavior being positively reinforced are more likely to engage in it themselves (Bandura, 1965).

Observational Learning

In the 1960s, research on latent learning stimulated interest in **observational learning,** in which an individual learns a behavior by watching others (models) perform it. That is, learning occurs without any overt behavior by the learner. Research on observational learning in animals dates back to at least 1881 (Robert, 1990). Observational learning has been demonstrated in a variety of animals, including cattle (Veissier, 1993), chimpanzees (Lyn & Savage-Rumbaugh, 2000), pigeons (Zentall, Sutton, & Sherburne, 1996), horses (Lindberg, Kelland, & Nicol, 1999), and even octopuses (Fiorito & Scotto, 1992). Consider rats. A rat that observes other rats eating foods will be more likely to eat those foods (Galef, 1993), infant rats that observe older rats opening pine cones will learn to do so themselves (Aisner & Terkel, 1992), and rats that observe other rats pushing a joystick in a particular direction to get food will learn to push it in that direction themselves (Heyes, Dawson, & Nokes, 1992).

There are numerous examples of human observational learning. A few examples include infants learning to perform tasks after observing other infants perform them (Hanna & Meltzoff, 1993), ballet dancers learning to perform dance sequences they have seen (Gray et al., 1991), and students learning to behave properly by observing other students doing so (Hallenbeck & Kauffman, 1995). The Thinking Critically About Psychology and the Media feature on p. 236 discusses the potential effects of television viewing on children's behavior.

Observational learning is central to Albert Bandura's **social learning theory,** which assumes behavior is learned chiefly through observation and the mental processing of information. What accounts for observational learning? Bandura (1986) has identified four factors: First, you must pay *attention* to the model's actions; second, you must *remember* the model's actions; third, you must have the *ability* to produce the actions; and fourth, you must be *motivated* to perform the actions. Consider a gymnast learning to perform a flying dismount from the uneven bars. She might learn to perform this feat by first paying attention to a gymnast who can already perform it. To be able to try the feat later, the learner would have to remember what the model did. But to perform the feat, the learner must have the strength to swing from the bars. Assuming that she paid attention to the model, remembered what the model did, and had the strength to perform the movement, she still might be motivated only to perform the feat in important competitions.

Observational learning can promote undesirable, as well as desirable, behavior. For example, we can develop phobias vicariously through observing people who exhibit them (Rachman, 1991). In fact, a study of people with spider phobia found that 71 percent traced it to observational learning, 57 percent to classical conditioning, and 45 percent to their knowledge of spiders (Merckelbach, Arntz, & de Jong, 1991). Even monkeys can develop fears through observing other monkeys (Mineka & Cook, 1993). For example, in a study that also found support for the concept of preparedness in the development of phobias through

observational learning
Learning a behavior by observing the consequences that others receive for performing it.

social learning theory
A theory of learning that assumes that people learn behaviors mainly through observation and mental processing of information.

▲ **Albert Bandura**
"Most human behavior is learned observationally through modeling."

observation, rhesus monkeys watched videotapes of monkey models showing fear of presumably fear-relevant stimuli (toy snakes or a toy crocodile) or presumably fear-irrelevant stimuli (flowers or a toy rabbit). The monkeys developed fears of the fear-relevant, but not the fear-irrelevant, stimuli (Cook & Mineka, 1989). Perhaps they are prepared by evolution to do so, because such fears have survival value.

STAYING ON TRACK: *Cognitive Learning*

1. How does Robert Rescorla's research support a cognitive interpretation of classical conditioning?
2. In what ways do latent learning and observational learning support a cognitive view of learning?

Answers to Staying on Track start on ST-4.

Chapter Summary

CLASSICAL CONDITIONING

- Learning is a relatively permanent change in knowledge or behavior resulting from experience.
- In the kind of learning called classical conditioning, a stimulus (the conditioned stimulus) comes to elicit a response (the conditioned response) that it would not normally elicit. It does so by being paired with a stimulus (the unconditioned stimulus) that already elicits that response (the unconditioned response).
- In stimulus generalization, the conditioned response occurs in response to stimuli that are similar to the conditioned stimulus.
- In stimulus discrimination, the conditioned response occurs only in response to the conditioned stimulus.
- In extinction, the conditioned stimulus is repeatedly presented without the unconditioned stimulus, causing the conditioned response to diminish and eventually stop.
- In spontaneous recovery, a conditioned response that has been extinguished will reappear after the passage of time.
- Classical conditioning has been applied in many ways, as in explaining phobias, drug dependence, and learned taste aversions.
- Research has shown that in classical conditioning there are biological constraints on the ease with which particular stimuli can be associated with particular responses.

OPERANT CONDITIONING

- Operant conditioning involves learning the relationship between behaviors and consequences.
- There are four behavioral contingencies between behaviors and consequences: positive reinforcement, negative reinforcement, extinction, and punishment.
- In shaping, positive reinforcement involving successive approximations of the desired behavior is used to increase the likelihood of a behavior that is not in an individual's repertoire.
- In chaining, positive reinforcement is used to teach an individual to perform a series of behaviors.
- In operant conditioning, behavior is affected by schedules of reinforcement. In a continuous schedule, every instance of a desired behavior is reinforced.

- In partial schedules, reinforcement is not given for every instance. Partial schedules include ratio schedules, which provide reinforcement after a certain number of responses, and interval schedules, which provide reinforcement for the first desired response after a certain interval of time.
- In negative reinforcement, a behavior followed by the removal of an aversive stimulus becomes more likely to occur in the future. Negative reinforcement is implicated in avoidance learning and escape learning.
- When a behavior is no longer followed by reinforcement, it is subject to extinction. But after a period of time the behavior might reappear, in so-called spontaneous recovery.
- In punishment, an aversive consequence of a behavior decreases the likelihood of the behavior. To be effective, punishment should be immediate, firm, consistent, aimed at the misbehavior rather than the individual, and coupled with reinforcement of desirable behavior.
- Operant conditioning has even more diverse applications than does classical conditioning; these include animal training, child rearing, educational improvement, and understanding and treating psychological disorders.
- Biofeedback is a form of operant conditioning that enables an individual to learn to control a normally involuntary physiological response or to gain better control of a normally voluntary physiological response when provided with visual or auditory feedback of the state of that response.
- Like classical conditioning, operant conditioning is subject to biological constraints, because the process of evolution has selected members of particular species to be more prepared to perform certain behaviors than to perform others.

COGNITIVE LEARNING

- Cognitive psychologists have shown that contiguity might not be sufficient to explain learning. Mere contiguity of a neutral stimulus and an unconditioned stimulus is insufficient to produce classical conditioning, and mere contiguity of a behavior and a consequence is insufficient to produce operant conditioning.

- Instead, for learning to occur, cognitive assessment of the relationship between stimuli or the relationship between behaviors and consequences appears to be essential.
- In latent learning, learning is revealed in overt behavior only when such behavior is reinforced.
- Albert Bandura's social learning theory considers how individuals learn through observing the behavior of others.
- There is a relationship between watching television and aggressive and prosocial behavior. But the extent to which this is a causal relationship is unclear.

Key Concepts

learning 211

CLASSICAL CONDITIONING
classical conditioning 213
conditioned response (CR) 213
conditioned stimulus (CS) 213
conditioned taste aversion 218
extinction 215
higher-order conditioning 213
spontaneous recovery 216
stimulus discrimination 215
stimulus generalization 215
unconditioned response (UCR) 213
unconditioned stimulus (UCS) 213

OPERANT CONDITIONING
avoidance learning 226
behavioral contingencies 221
behavioral preparedness 233
biofeedback 231
chaining 223
computer-assisted instruction 229
continuous schedule of reinforcement 223
discriminative stimulus 222
escape learning 226
extinction 226
fixed-interval schedule of reinforcement 225

fixed-ratio schedule of reinforcement 224
instinctive drift 233
instrumental conditioning 221
law of effect 220
learned helplessness 230
negative reinforcement 225
operant conditioning 221
partial schedule of reinforcement 224
positive reinforcement 221
Premack principle 221
primary reinforcer 222
programmed instruction 229
punishment 226

secondary reinforcer 222
shaping 222
Skinner box 221
spontaneous recovery 226
token economy 229
variable-interval schedule of reinforcement 225
variable-ratio schedule of reinforcement 224

COGNITIVE LEARNING
blocking 234
latent learning 235
observational learning 237
social learning theory 237

Key Contributors

CLASSICAL CONDITIONING
Ilene Bernstein 219
John Garcia 218
Ivan Pavlov 212

John B. Watson 216

OPERANT CONDITIONING
Neal Miller 230

David Premack 221
Martin Seligman 230
B. F. Skinner 221
Edward Thorndike 220

COGNITIVE LEARNING
Albert Bandura 237
Robert Rescorla 234
Edward Tolman 235

Thought Questions

1. What are the shortcomings of research on the use of conditioned taste aversion to prevent predators from killing sheep?
2. How would you use the Premack principle to get a child to clean his room?
3. How would you use shaping to teach a child to ride a tricycle?

Possible Answers to Thought Questions start on p. PT-2.

4. How does the phenomenon of blocking support a cognitive interpretation of classical conditioning?
5. Why do researchers still disagree about the existence of a causal relationship between televised violence and real-life aggression?

OLC Preview

For additional quizzing and a variety of interactive resources, visit the book's Online Learning Center at www.mhhe.com/sdorow5.

chapter eight

8

Memory

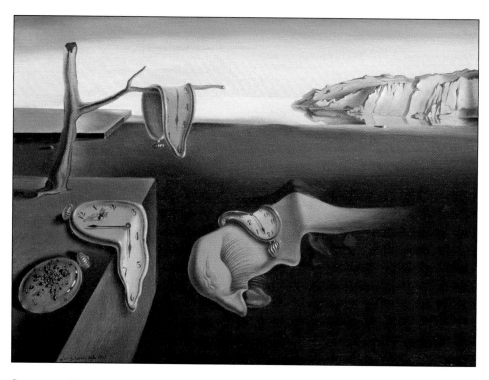

SALVADOR DALI
The Persistence of Memory, 1931

In 1898, a survey of 179 middle-aged and elderly American adults asked, "Do you recall where you were when you heard that Lincoln was shot?" Of those surveyed, 127 claimed they could recall exactly where they were and what they were doing at that moment on April 14, 1865 (Colegrove, 1899). Such vivid, long-lasting memories of important, surprising, emotionally arousing events are called **flashbulb memories** (Brown & Kulik, 1977). People with flashbulb memories of an event might recall who told them about it, where they were, and trivial things that occurred at the time.

Perhaps you have a flashbulb memory of your first kiss or an award you received. Depending on your age, you might have a flashbulb memory of the fall of the Berlin Wall, the death of Princess Diana or John F. Kennedy, Jr., the massacre at Columbine High School in Colorado, or even the reading of the verdict in the O. J. Simpson murder trial (Winningham, Hyman, & Dinnel, 2000). Older adults might have a flashbulb memory from November 22, 1963, when they heard that President John F. Kennedy had been assassinated. A survey of British college students found that 86 percent had formed flashbulb memories of the unexpected resignation of British Prime Minister Margaret Thatcher. In contrast, only 26 percent of students from outside the United Kingdom had flashbulb memories of that event. This supports research indicating that the formation of a flashbulb memory requires that an event be perceived as both important and surprising (Conway et al., 1994).

What accounts for flashbulb memories? The answer is unclear. Some psychologists believe they are the product of a special brain mechanism that evolved because it ensures that we remember important, surprising experiences (Schmidt & Bohannon, 1988). Other psychologists disagree, insisting instead that normal memory processes, such as thinking more often and more elaborately about such experiences, can explain the phenomenon (McCloskey, Wible, & Cohen, 1988).

flashbulb memory
A vivid, long-lasting memory of a surprising, important, emotionally arousing event.

Memory
www.mhhe.com/sdorow5

◀ **Flashbulb Memories**
Memory researchers are searching for explanations of flashbulb memories of momentous events.

One psychology professor took advantage of a coincidence to test the common belief that flashbulb memories are more accurate than normal memories. On January 16, 1991, as part of a demonstration regarding flashbulb memories, he had students try to form a vivid memory of an ordinary event. On the same day, as shown on CNN, warplanes attacked Baghdad, beginning the Persian Gulf War. The professor had the students complete questionnaires about their memories for the classroom event and the beginning of the war. They completed them again in April 1991 and January 1992. The accuracy of the students' memories for the two events did not differ significantly. Their level of confidence in their memories, however, did. They were significantly more confident about their memories of the onset of the Persian Gulf War. These results indicate that flashbulb memories might seem special, not because of a special mechanism, but because of the undue confidence we place in them (Weaver, 1993).

The exact nature of flashbulb memories will be discovered by research on **memory,** the process by which information is acquired, stored in the brain, later retrieved, and eventually possibly forgotten. As William James noted a century ago, memory provides our consciousness with its continuity over time. Later in this chapter you will read about a man called "H. M." who suffers from brain damage that has impaired his ability to maintain this continuity of consciousness. Memory also enables us to adapt to situations by letting us call on skills and information gained from our relevant past experiences. Your abilities to drive a car, to perform well on an exam, and to serve as a witness at a trial all depend on memory. Moreover, memory enriches our emotional lives. Your memory lets you reexperience events from your past, such as an uplifting family gathering.

In studying memory, psychologists consider several major "how" questions: How are memories formed? How are memories stored? How are memories retrieved? How are memories forgotten? How can we improve memory? How are brain anatomy and brain chemistry related to memory? This chapter addresses these questions.

◆ INFORMATION PROCESSING AND MEMORY

During the past three decades, memory research has been driven by the "cognitive revolution" in psychology, which views the mind as an information processor. This is reflected in the most influential model of memory, developed by Richard Shiffrin and Richard Atkinson (1969). Their model assumes that memory involves the processing of information in three successive stages: *sensory memory, short-term memory,* and *long-term memory.* **Sensory memory** stores, in *sensory registers,* exact replicas of stimuli impinging on the senses. Sensory memories last for a brief period—from less than 1 second to several seconds. When you attend to information in sensory memory, it is transferred to **short-term memory,** which stores it for up to about 20 seconds unless you maintain it through mental rehearsal—as when you repeat a phone number to yourself long enough to dial it. Information transferred from short-term memory into **long-term memory** can be stored for up to a lifetime. Your ability to recall old memories indicates that information also passes from long-term memory into short-term memory.

The handling of information at each memory stage has been compared to information processing by a computer, which involves encoding, storage, and retrieval. **Encoding** is the conversion of information into a form that can be stored in memory. When you strike the keys on a computer keyboard, your actions are translated into a code that the computer understands. Similarly, information in your memory is stored in codes that your brain can

memory
The process by which information is acquired, stored in the brain, later retrieved, and eventually possibly forgotten.

sensory memory
The stage of memory that briefly, for at most a few seconds, stores exact replicas of sensations.

short-term memory
The stage of memory that can store a few items of unrehearsed information for up to about 20 seconds.

long-term memory
The stage of memory that can store a virtually unlimited amount of information relatively permanently.

encoding
The conversion of information into a form that can be stored in memory.

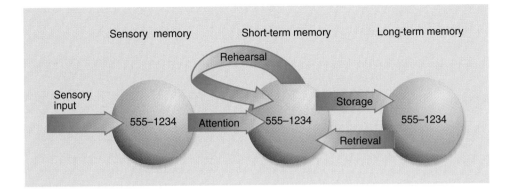

◀ **Figure 8.1**
Memory Processes
The information-processing model of memory assumes that information (such as a phone number) passes from sensory memory to short-term memory to long-term memory. Information might also pass from long-term memory to short-term memory. Each of the stages involves information encoding, storage, and retrieval.

process. **Storage** is the retention of information in memory. Personal computers typically store information on diskettes or hard drives. In human and animal memory, information is stored in the brain. **Retrieval** is the recovery of information from memory. When you strike certain keys, you provide the computer with cues that make it retrieve the information you desire. Similarly, we often rely on cues to retrieve memories that have been stored in the brain. We also are subject to **forgetting**—the failure to retrieve information from memory. This is analogous to the erasing of information on a diskette or hard drive. Figure 8.1 summarizes this **information-processing model** of memory. Though some psychologists question the existence of separate information-processing stages for sensory memory, short-term memory, and long-term memory, there is strong evidence in support of them (Medina, Schroeder, & Izquierdo, 1999).

STAYING ON TRACK: *Information Processing and Memory*

1. What evidence is there that flashbulb memories are not the product of a special brain mechanism?
2. How do sensory memory, short-term memory, and long-term memory differ from one another?

Answers to Staying on Track start on p. ST-4

storage
The retention of information in memory.

retrieval
The recovery of information from memory.

forgetting
The failure to retrieve information from memory.

information-processing model
The view that the processing of memories involves encoding, storage, and retrieval.

◆ SENSORY MEMORY

Think back to the last movie you saw. It actually was a series of frames, each containing a picture slightly different from the one before it. So why did you see smooth motion instead of a rapidly presented series of individual pictures? You did so because of your *visual sensory memory*, which stores images for up to a second. Visual sensory memory is called **iconic memory**; an image stored in it is called an *icon* (from the Greek word for "image"). The movie projector presented the frames at a rate (commonly 24 frames a second) that made each successive frame appear just before the previous one left your iconic memory, making the successive images blend together and create the impression of smooth motion. You can demonstrate iconic memory by rapidly swinging a pen back and forth. Notice how iconic memory lets you see a blurred image of the path taken by the pen. But how much of the information that stimulates our visual receptors is stored in iconic memory? That question inspired the classic experiment described in the Anatomy of a Research Study feature on p. 244.

Auditory sensory memory serves a purpose analogous to that of visual sensory memory, blending together successive pieces of auditory information. Auditory sensory memory is

iconic memory
Visual sensory memory, which lasts up to about a second.

Anatomy of a Research Study

Do We Form Sensory Memories of All the Information That Stimulates Our Sensory Receptors?

Rationale

Though we have a sensory register for each of our senses, most research on sensory memory has been concerned with iconic memory. The classic experiment on this was carried out by a Harvard University doctoral student named George Sperling (1960). Sperling used an ingenious procedure to test the traditional wisdom that sensory memory stores only a small amount of the information that stimulates our sensory receptors.

Method

Sperling's procedure is illustrated in Figure 8.2. Participants, tested individually, stared at a screen as Sperling projected sets of 12 letters, arranged in 3 rows of 4, onto it. Each presentation lasted for only 0.05 second—a mere flash. Sperling then asked the participants to report as many of the letters as possible. He found that participants could accurately report an average of only 4 or 5. Participants claimed, however, that they had briefly retained an image of the 12 letters, but by the time they had reported a few of them the remaining ones had faded away.

Rather than dismiss these claims, Sperling decided to test them experimentally by using a variation of this task. Instead of using whole report (asking participants to report as many of the 12 letters as possible), he used partial report (asking participants to report as many of the 4 letters as possible from a designated row). The task again included displays of 12 letters arranged in 3 rows of 4. But this time, at the instant the visual display was terminated, a tone was sounded.

Results and Discussion

When participants gave partial reports, they accurately reported an average of 3.3 of the 4 letters in a designated row. Because participants did not know which row would be designated until after the display was terminated, the results indicated that, on the average, 9.9 of the 12 letters were stored in iconic memory. Sperling concluded that virtually all of the information from visual receptors is stored as an image in iconic memory, but, as his participants had claimed, the image fades rapidly.

This inspired Sperling to seek the answer to another question: How fast does the information in iconic memory fade? He found the answer by repeating his partial-report procedure, but this time delaying the tone that signaled the participant to give a partial report. He varied the period of delay from 0.1 second to 1.0 second. As the delay lengthened, the participant's ability to recall letters in a designated row declined more and more. Sperling found that when the delay reached 1.0 second, the number of letters that could be recalled was about the same as when whole report was used. Subsequent research has found that the typical duration of iconic memory is closer to 0.3 second than to 1.0 second (Loftus, Duncan, & Gehrig, 1992).

▶ **George Sperling**

"The fact that observers commonly assert that they can *see* more than they can *report* suggests that memory sets a limit on a process that is otherwise rich in available information."

▶ **Figure 8.2**

Testing Sensory Memory

In Sperling's (1960) study of sensory memory, the participant fixated on a cross on a projection screen. A display of letters was then flashed briefly on the screen. This was repeated with many different displays. At varying times after a display had been flashed, a tone signaled the participant to report the letters in a particular row. This enabled Sperling to determine how many of the letters were stored in sensory memory. By delaying the tone for longer and longer intervals, Sperling was also able to determine how quickly images in sensory memory fade.

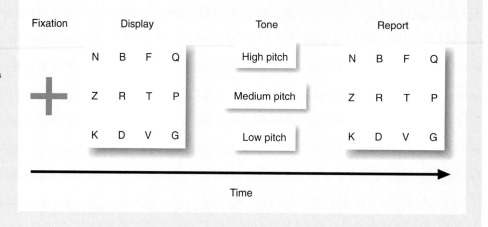

called **echoic memory,** because sounds linger in it. Echoic memory stores information longer than iconic memory does, normally holding sounds for 3 or 4 seconds, but perhaps as long as 10 seconds (Samms et al., 1993). The greater persistence of information in echoic memory lets you perceive speech by blending together successive spoken sounds that you hear (Ardila, Montanes, & Gempeler, 1986). You become aware of your echoic memory when someone says something to you that you do not become aware of until a few seconds after it was said. Suppose that while you are enthralled by a television movie a friend asks, "Where did you put the can opener?" After a brief delay you might say, "What? . . . Oh, it's in the drawer to the left of the sink." Researchers have identified a precise region in the primary auditory cortex that processes echoic memories (Lu, Williamson, & Kaufman, 1992).

Based on Sperling's study, and subsequent research, we know that sensory memory can store virtually all the information provided by our sensory receptors and that this information fades rapidly (though the fade rates vary among the senses). Nonetheless, we can retain information that is in sensory memory by attending to it and transferring it into short-term memory.

STAYING ON TRACK: *Sensory Memory*

1. How did George Sperling demonstrate that iconic memory stores more information than commonly believed?
2. How does the comparatively longer duration of echoic memory help us perceive speech?

Answers to Staying on Track start on p. ST-4.

Answers to Staying on Track start on p. ST-4.

◆ SHORT-TERM MEMORY

When you pay attention to information in your sensory memory or information retrieved from your long-term memory, the information enters your short-term memory, which has a limited capacity and holds information for about 20 seconds. Because you are paying attention to this sentence, it has entered your short-term memory. In contrast, other information in your sensory memory, such as the feeling of this book against your hands, will not enter your short-term memory until your attention is directed to it. And note that you are able to comprehend the words in this sentence because you have retrieved their meanings from your long-term memory. Because we use short-term memory to think about information provided by either sensory memory or long-term memory, it also is called *working memory* (Caplan & Waters, 1999). For example, you use your working memory when you perform mental arithmetic calculations.

Information stored in short-term memory is encoded as sounds or visual images and then manipulated in working memory (Logie, 1999). We typically encode information as sounds—even when the information is visual. This was demonstrated in a study in which participants were shown a series of 6 letters and immediately tried to recall them. Participants' errors showed they more often confused letters that sounded alike (for example, T and C) than letters that looked alike (for example, Q and O). This indicated that the letters, though presented visually, had been encoded according to their sounds (Conrad, 1962).

In comparison to sensory memory or long-term memory, short-term memory has a relatively small storage capacity. You can demonstrate this for yourself by performing this exercise: Read the following numerals one at a time, and then (without looking at them) write them down in order on a sheet of paper: 6, 3, 9, 1, 4, 6, 5. Next, read the following numerals one at a time and write them down from memory: 5, 8, 1, 3, 9, 2, 8, 6, 3, 1, 7. If you have average short-term memory storage capacity, you were probably able to recall the 7 numbers in the first set but not the 11 numbers in the second set.

The normal limit of 7 items in short-term memory was the theme of a famous article by psychologist George Miller (1956) entitled "The Magical Number Seven, Plus or Minus Two." Miller noted that short-term memory has, on the average, a capacity of 7 "chunks" of information, with a range of 5 to 9 chunks. His observation has received support from

echoic memory
Auditory sensory memory, which lasts up to 4 or more seconds.

▶ Figure 8.3

The Duration of Short-Term Memory

Peterson and Peterson (1959) demonstrated that the information in short-term memory lasts no more than 20 seconds. *(a)* A warning light signaled that a trial was to begin. The participant then heard a 3-letter trigram and a 3-digit number. To prevent rehearsal of the trigram, the participant counted backward by threes from the number. After a period of 3 to 18 seconds, a light signaled the participant to recall the trigram. *(b)* The longer the delay between presentation and recall of the trigram, the less likely the participant was to recall it accurately.

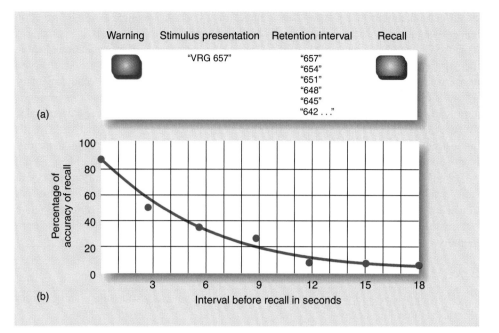

other research studies (Glassman et al., 1994), though some researchers have found the normal range of capacity is greater than 5 to 9 chunks (Smith, 1992). A *chunk* is a meaningful unit of information, such as a date, a word, or an abbreviation. For example, to a college student familiar with American culture, a list that includes the meaningful chunks *CBS, NFL,* and *FBI* would be easier to recall than a list that includes the meaningless combinations of letters *JOL, OBS,* and *CWE.*

Miller also noted that the ability to chunk individual items of information can increase the amount of information stored in short-term memory (Baddeley, 1994). For example, after a 5-second look at the positions of pieces on a chessboard, expert chess players are significantly better than novice chess players at reproducing the positions of the pieces. This reflects experts' greater ability to chunk chess pieces into thousands of familiar configurations (Chase & Simon, 1973). Thus, though chess experts do not store more memory chunks in their short-term memory than novices do, their memory chunks contain more information (Gobet & Simon, 1998).

Given that about 7 chunks is the typical amount of information in short-term memory, how long will it remain stored? Without **maintenance rehearsal** (that is, without repeating the information to ourselves), we can store information in short-term memory for no more than about 20 seconds. But if we use maintenance rehearsal, we can store it in short-term memory indefinitely. You could use maintenance rehearsal to remember the items on a short grocery list long enough to select each of them at the store.

Early evidence that unrehearsed information in short-term memory lasts up to 20 seconds came from a study conducted by Lloyd and Margaret Peterson (1959) in which they orally presented trigrams that consisted of three consonants (for example, VRG) to their participants. Their procedure is presented in Figure 8.3. To distract the participants and prevent them from engaging in maintenance rehearsal of the trigrams, immediately after a trigram was presented a light signaled the participant to count backward from a 3-digit number by threes (for example, "657, 654, 651, . . . "). Following an interval that varied from 3 seconds to 18 seconds, a light signaled that the participant was to recall the trigram. The longer the interval, the less likely the participants were to recall the trigram. And when the interval was 18 seconds, the participants could rarely recall the trigram. Thus, the results indicated that unrehearsed information normally remains in short-term memory for no longer than about 20 seconds.

Information stored in short-term memory is lost primarily by *decay* (the mere fading of information over time) and by *displacement* by new information (Reitman, 1974). The displacement of information from short-term memory was demonstrated in a study in which

maintenance rehearsal

Repeating information to oneself to keep it in short-term memory.

Chapter Eight

participants called a telephone operator for a long-distance number. They showed poorer recall of the number if the operator said, "Have a nice day" after giving them the number than if the operator did not. Evidently the cheery message displaced the phone number from short-term memory (Schilling & Weaver, 1983).

STAYING ON TRACK: *Short-Term Memory*

1. Why do psychologists believe visual information tends to be stored acoustically in short-term memory?
2. How did Lloyd and Margaret Peterson demonstrate that short-term memories last about 20 seconds?

Answers to Staying on Track start on p. ST-4.

◆ LONG-TERM MEMORY

As mentioned earlier, information moves back and forth between short-term memory and long-term memory. Information processing in long-term memory has been compared to the workings of a library. Information in a library is encoded in materials such as books or magazines, stored on shelves in a systematic way, retrieved by using cues given by on-line catalogs, and forgotten when it is misplaced or its computer record is erased. Similarly, information in long-term memory is encoded in several ways, stored in an organized manner, retrieved by using cues, and forgotten due to a failure to store it adequately or to use appropriate retrieval cues.

Encoding

William James (1890/1981, Vol. 1, p. 646) noted, "A curious peculiarity of our memory is that things are impressed better by active than by passive repetition." To appreciate James's claim, try to draw the face side of a United States penny from memory. Next, look at the drawings of pennies in Figure 8.4. Which one is accurate? Even if you have handled thousands of pennies over the years and realize the front of a penny has a date and a profile of Abraham Lincoln, you probably were unable to draw every detail. And even when presented with several drawings to choose from, you might still have chosen the wrong one. If you had difficulty, you are not alone. A study of adult Americans found few could draw a penny from memory, and less than half could recognize the correct drawing of one (Nickerson & Adams, 1979).

◀ Figure 8.4
Can You Identify the Real Penny?

What accounts for our failure to remember an image that is a common part of everyday life? The answer depends in part on the distinction between *maintenance rehearsal* and *elaborative rehearsal.* As noted earlier, in using maintenance rehearsal, we simply hold information in short-term memory without trying to transfer it into long-term memory, as when we remember a phone number just long enough to dial it. In **elaborative rehearsal,** we actively organize information and integrate it with information already stored in long-term memory, as when studying material from this chapter for an exam. Though maintenance rehearsal can encode some information (such as the main features of a penny) into long-term memory (Wixted, 1991), elaborative rehearsal encodes more information (such as the exact arrangement of the features of a penny) into long-term memory (Greene, 1987).

You can experience the benefits of elaborative rehearsal when you are confronted by new concepts in a textbook. If you try to understand a concept by integrating it with information already in your long-term memory, you will be more likely to encode the concept firmly into your long-term memory. For example, when the concept "flashbulb memory" was introduced earlier in this chapter, you would have been more likely to encode it into long-term memory if it provoked you to think about your own flashbulb memories. Elaborative rehearsal also has important practical benefits. In one study, sixth-graders who were taught cardiopulmonary resuscitation showed better retention of what they learned if they used elaborative rehearsal (Rivera-Tovar & Jones, 1990).

The superior encoding of information through elaborative rehearsal supports the **levels of processing theory** of Fergus Craik and Robert Lockhart, which originally was presented as an alternative to the information-processing model of memory. They believe the level, or "depth," at which we process information determines how well it is encoded and, as a result, how well it is encoded in memory (Lockhart & Craik, 1990). When you process information at a shallow level, you attend to its superficial, sensory qualities—as when you use maintenance rehearsal of a telephone number. In contrast, when you process information at a deep level, you attend to its meaning—as when you use elaborative rehearsal of textbook material. Similarly, if you merely listen to the sound of a popular song over and over on the radio—a relatively shallow level of processing—you might recall the melody but not the lyrics. But if you listen to the lyrics and think about their meaning (perhaps even connecting them to personally significant events)—a deeper level of processing—you might recall both the words and the melody.

In a study that supported the levels of processing theory, researchers induced participants to process words at different levels by asking them different kinds of questions about each word just before it was flashed on a screen for a fifth of a second (Craik & Tulving, 1975). Imagine that you are replicating the study, and one of the words is *bread.* You could induce a shallow, *visual* level of encoding by asking how the word *looks*—for instance, "Is the word written in capital letters?" You could induce a somewhat deeper, *acoustic* level of encoding by asking how the word *sounds*—"Does the word rhyme with head?" And you could induce a much deeper, *semantic* level of encoding by asking a question related to what the word *means*—"Does the word fit in the sentence *The boy used the ___ to make a sandwich?"* After repeating this with several words, you would present the participant with a list of words and ask him or her to identify which of the words had been presented before.

Craik and Tulving found that the deeper the level at which a word had been encoded, the more likely it was to be correctly identified (see Figure 8.5). Thus, the deeper the level at which information is encoded, the better it will be remembered (Rhodes & Anastai, 2000). This has been supported by research showing that participants have better recognition of previously presented words when they had attended to their meanings than when they had attended to their sounds (Ferlazzo, Conte, & Gentilomo, 1993).

Storage

There are several major viewpoints on the nature of memory storage. Memory researchers look to *memory systems, semantic networks,* and *cognitive schemas* to explain the storage of memories.

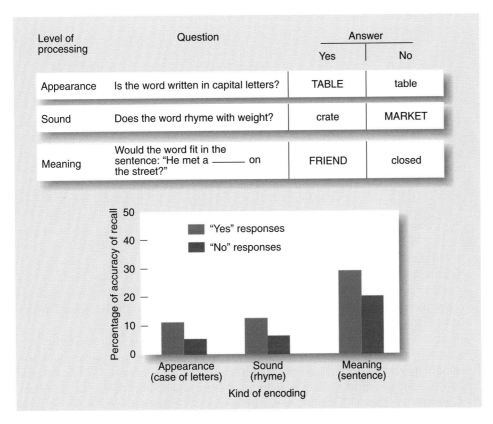

Level of processing	Question	Answer	
		Yes	No
Appearance	Is the word written in capital letters?	TABLE	table
Sound	Does the word rhyme with weight?	crate	MARKET
Meaning	Would the word fit in the sentence: "He met a ——— on the street?"	FRIEND	closed

◀ **Figure 8.5**
Levels of Processing

Craik and Tulving (1975) found that the greater the depth of processing of words, the better will be memory for them. Encoding words according to their meaning produced better recognition of them than did encoding them according to their sound or appearance.

semantic memory

The subsystem of declarative memory that contains general information about the world.

episodic memory

The subsystem of declarative memory that contains memories of personal experiences tied to particular times and places.

Memory Systems

According to influential memory researcher Endel Tulving (1985), we store information in two kinds of long-term memory: **Procedural memory** includes memories of how to perform behaviors, such as making an omelette or using a word processor; **declarative memory** includes memories of facts. Declarative memory and procedural memory also are referred to, respectively, as **explicit memory** and **implicit memory** (Schacter, 1992). Implicit memory for odors can influence human behavior, as in a study of adults who performed creative, counting, and mathematical tasks in unscented rooms or rooms weakly scented with jasmine or lavender. Though none of the participants reported smelling either odor, results showed that jasmine hurt performance and lavender helped performance (Degel & Koester, 1999).

Tulving (1993) subdivides declarative memory into *semantic memory* and *episodic memory*. **Semantic memory** includes memories of general knowledge, such as the definition of an omelette or the components of a word processor. **Episodic memory** includes memories of personal experiences tied to particular times and places, such as the last time you made an omelette or used a word processor.

Some memory researchers believe that the brain evolved different memory systems for storing these different kinds of memory into declarative memory for facts and events and procedural memory for skills, habits, and conditioned responses (Eichenbaum, 1997). There is evidence that brain-wave activity distinguishes different memory systems. Participants in one study were presented with a series of pairs of words and had to judge whether members of the pairs were related in meaning (semantic memory) or whether they had been presented with specific pairs before (episodic memory). The semantic-memory task was associated with an abundance of alpha brain waves and the episodic-memory task was associated with an abundance of slower theta brain waves (Klimesch, Schmke, & Schwaiger, 1994).

The main line of evidence in support of multiple memory systems in human beings comes from studies of people with brain damage. For example, either implicit or explicit memory can be intact while the other is impaired (Gabrieli et al., 1995). In a case study (Schacter, 1983), a victim of Alzheimer's disease, a degenerative brain disorder marked by

 Endel Tulving
www.mhhe.com/sdorow5

▲ **Endel Tulving**

"Semantic memory is concerned with the retention and use of general . . . knowledge independent of personal time and space; episodic memory, with the storage and retrieval of information based on particular . . . experiences located in personal time and space."

► **Figure 8.6**
Memory Systems

Some memory researchers believe there is sufficient behavioral and physiological evidence for the existence of memory systems that store different kinds of information. The declarative memory system stores explicit memories, which involve factual information that can be consciously recalled. Whereas the semantic memory system stores general information, the episodic memory system stores information about personal experiences. The procedural memory system stores implicit memories, which involve behavioral tendencies that can occur without conscious recollection of their origins. These memories include skills, habits, and conditioned responses.

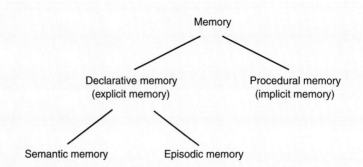

severe memory impairment, was able to play golf (procedural memory) and had good knowledge of the game (semantic memory) but could not find his tee shots (episodic memory). This indicates that though semantic memory and episodic memory are both forms of declarative memory, they might involve different brain systems. This is supported by PET-scan studies that have found that different brain regions are involved in the performance of semantic and episodic memory tasks (Wiggs, Weisberg, & Martin, 1999). Figure 8.6 illustrates how the different memory systems are related.

Nonetheless, some theorists believe that the selective loss of procedural, semantic, or episodic memories does not necessarily mean we have separate memory systems (Horner, 1990). The question that many memory researchers seek to answer is this: Do different brain systems serve the different kinds of memory, or does a single brain system serve all of them? Regardless of how many memory systems we have, long-term memories must be stored in a systematic way. Unlike short-term memory, in which a few unorganized items of information can be stored and retrieved efficiently, long-term memory requires that millions of pieces of information be stored in an organized, rather than arbitrary, manner. Otherwise, you might spend years searching your memory until you retrieved the one you wanted, just as you might spend years searching the Library of Congress for William James's *The Principles of Psychology* if the library's books were shelved randomly. The better we are at organizing our memories, the better our recall is. For example, a study of a waiter who could take twenty complete full-course dinner orders without writing them down found he did so by quickly categorizing the items into meaningful groupings. When he was prevented from doing so, he was unable to recall all of the orders (Ericsson & Polson, 1988).

semantic network theory
The theory that memories are stored as nodes interconnected by links that represent their relationships.

Semantic Networks. A theory that explains how semantic information is meaningfully organized in long-term memory is the **semantic network theory,** which assumes that semantic memories are stored as nodes interconnected by links (see Figure 8.7). A *node* is a concept such as "pencil," "green," "uncle," or "cold," and a *link* is a connection between two concepts. More related nodes have shorter (that is, stronger) links between them. Even young children organize memories into semantic networks. For example, preschool children who enjoy playing with toy dinosaurs and listening to their parents read to them about dinosaurs might organize their knowledge of dinosaurs into semantic networks (Chi & Koeske, 1983). The dinosaurs would be represented as nodes (for example, "Brontosaurus" or "Tyrannosaurus Rex") and their relationships would be represented by links. The retrieval of a dinosaur's name from memory would activate nodes with which it is linked. So, retrieval of *Brontosaurus* would be more likely to activate nodes that contain the names of other plant-eating dinosaurs than nodes that contain the names of meat-eating dinosaurs, such as *Tyrannosaurus Rex.* Deterioration of semantic networks might help account for the memory and language disruption seen in many people with schizophrenia (Granholm, Chock, & Morris, 1998) or Alzheimer's disease (Chan, Butters, & Salmon, 1997).

schema theory
The theory that long-term memories are stored as parts of schemas, which are cognitive structures that organize knowledge about events or objects.

Cognitive Schemas. An alternative to the semantic network theory of memory organization is **schema theory,** which is used to explain both episodic memory and semantic memory. Schema theory was put forth decades ago by the English psychologist Frederick Bartlett

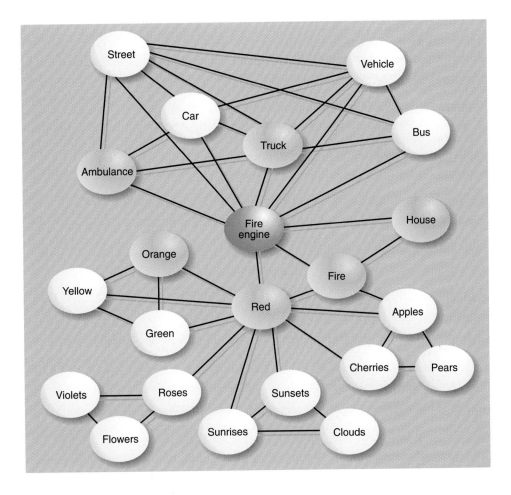

◀ **Figure 8.7**
A Semantic Network
According to Collins and Loftus (1975), our long-term memories are organized into semantic networks in which concepts are interconnected by links. The shorter the link between two concepts, the stronger the association between them. After a retrieval cue has activated a concept, related concepts will also be activated and retrieved from long-term memory.

(1932), who found that long-term memories are stored as parts of schemas. A schema is a cognitive structure that organizes knowledge about an event or an object and that affects the encoding, storage, and retrieval of information related to it (Alba & Hasher, 1983). Examples of schemas include "birthday party," "class clown," and "Caribbean vacation."

In a classic study, Bartlett had British college students read a Native American folktale which told about a warrior fighting ghosts, and later write the story from memory. He found that participants recalled the theme of the story but added, eliminated, or changed details to fit their own story schemas. For example, participants added a moral, left out an event, or altered an aspect (such as changing a canoe to a boat). In a cross-cultural study of memory for stories, American and Mexican college students read brief stories of everyday activities. There were two versions of each story, each consistent with an American cultural schema or a Mexican cultural schema. A week later, when tested on their recognition of information in the stories, both groups of participants recognized the stories from the other culture as being more like their own culture than they actually were (Harris, Schoen, & Hensley, 1992). Thus, participants' schemas of their native cultures influenced their recall.

Schema theory also has been used to explain gender differences in memory. In one study, children were taken to a playroom where they played with toys for 2 minutes. Half of the toys were male-stereotyped (for example, a space shuttle and train) and half were female-stereotyped (for example, a Barbie doll and a tea set). Later, each child was asked to identify the toys from the playroom from a set of picture cards provided by the experimenter. Though there were no gender differences in the number of items identified, both girls and boys recognized more toys that were traditionally associated with their sex (Cherney & Ryalls, 1999). These results are consistent with studies that have reported similar biases in memory of masculine and feminine behaviors and female and male characters in children's literature (Signorella, Bigler, & Liben, 1997). Thus, children's memories appear to be influenced by gender schemas (see Chapter 4).

Other researchers have begun to investigate the influence of gender schemas on autobiographical memory in adults and children. In a series of studies, Penelope Davis (1999) found that women and girls reported more childhood memories—and accessed these memories more rapidly—than did men and boys. This gender difference was observed for events that were associated with both positive and negative emotions. In other words, female participants were more likely to recall incidents when they, or someone else, were happy, sad, or fearful. Moreover, this gender difference also has been observed for everyday life events that are not associated with strong emotions (Seidlitz & Diener, 1998). The results of these studies have been attributed to gender differences in encoding of life events.

Retrieval

Memory researchers not only are interested in how we encode and store memories but also in how we retrieve them. Psychologists who favor the semantic network theory study the role of *spreading activation,* and psychologists who favor schema theory study the role of *constructive recall.*

Spreading Activation

▶ In short, we may search in our memory for forgotten ideas, just as we rummage our house for a lost object. In both cases we visit what seems to us the probable neighborhood of that which we miss. We turn over the things under which, or within which, or alongside which, it may possibly be; and if it lies near them, it soon comes to view. But these matters, in the case of a mental object sought, are nothing but its *associatives.* (James, 1890/1981, Vol. 1, p. 615)

The semantic network theory of memory agrees with William James's statement that the retrieval of memories from long-term memory begins by searching a particular region of memory and then tracing the associations among nodes (memories) in that region, rather than by haphazardly searching through information stored in long-term memory. The retrieval of a node from memory stimulates activation of related nodes, so-called *spreading activation* (Collins & Loftus, 1975). This is analogous to looking for a book in a library. You would use the online catalog to give you a retrieval cue (a book number) to help you locate the book you want. Similarly, when you are given a memory retrieval cue, the relevant stored memories are activated, which in turn activate memories with which they are linked (Anderson, 1983). In keeping with this, advertisers incorporate distinctive retrieval cues in their advertisements for specific products so that the repetition of those cues will evoke recall of those products. For example, a study found the use of a visual cue helped children recall advertised cereal better and made them more likely to ask their parents to buy the cereal (Macklin, 1994).

To illustrate retrieval from a semantic network, suppose you were given the cue "sensory memory." If your semantic network were well organized, the cue might activate nodes for "Sperling," "iconic," and "partial report." But if your semantic network were less well organized, the cue might also activate nodes for "amnesia," "chunks," or "Alzheimer's." And if your semantic network were poorly organized, the cue might activate nodes completely unrelated to sensory memory, such as "hallucination," "sensory deprivation," or "extrasensory perception."

Research findings indicate that spreading activation is important in a variety of contexts. The retrieval of mathematical facts depends on spreading activation within an arithmetic memory network (Niedeggen & Roesler, 1999). Inappropriate spreading activation might account for some of the language disturbances seen in victims of schizophrenia (Moritz et al., 1999). And a study of radiologists found that their ability to make correct diagnoses from X-ray films depended, in part, on how well their relevant semantic networks facilitated spreading activation (Raufaste, Eyrolle, & Marine, 1998).

Constructive Recall

In contrast to semantic network theory, schema theory assumes that when we retrieve memories we might alter them to make them consistent with our schemas. An example of the schematic nature of memory retrieval, taken from testimony about the 1972 Watergate burglary that led to the resignation of President Richard Nixon, was provided by the eminent memory researcher Ulric Neisser (1981). Neisser described how a schema influenced the testimony of John Dean, former legal counsel to President Nixon, before the Senate Watergate Investigating Committee in 1973. Dean began his opening testimony with a 245-page statement in which he recalled the details of dozens of meetings that he had attended over a period of several years. Dean's apparently phenomenal recall of minute details prompted Senator Daniel Inouye of Hawaii to ask skeptically, "Have you always had a facility for recalling the details of conversations which took place many months ago?" (Neisser, 1981, p. 1).

Neisser found that Inouye's skepticism was well founded. In comparing Dean's testimony with tape recordings (secretly made by Nixon) of those conversations, Neisser found that Dean's recall of their themes was accurate, but his recall of many of the details was inaccurate. Neisser took this as evidence for Dean's reliance on a schema to retrieve memories. The schema reflected Dean's knowledge that there had been a cover-up of the Watergate break-in. Neisser (1984) used this to support his conclusion that, in recalling real-life events, we rely on constructive recall more often than literal recall.

What Neisser called **constructive recall** is the distortion of memories by adding or changing details to fit a schema (Schacter, Norman, & Koutstaal, 1998). Schemas in the form of scripts for particular events can even affect eyewitness testimony. For example, the scripts we have for different kinds of robberies can affect our recall of events related to them. We might recall things that did not actually occur during a robbery if they fit our script for that kind of robbery (Holst & Pezdek, 1992). Constructive recall might even explain why honest people have reported being abducted by aliens in UFOs. Their memories might be constructed from nightmares, media attention, hypnotic suggestions during therapy, and support for their claims by alien-abduction groups (Clark & Loftus, 1996). But neither schema theory nor the semantic network theory has yet emerged as the best explanation of the storage and retrieval of long-term memories. Perhaps a complete explanation requires both.

constructive recall

The distortion of memories by adding, dropping, or changing details to fit a schema.

Forgetting

According to William James (1890/1981, Vol. 1, p. 640), "if we remembered everything, we should on most occasions be as ill off as if we remembered nothing." James believed that forgetting is adaptive because it rids us of useless information that might impair our recall of useful information. But as you are sometimes painfully aware of when taking exams, even useful information that has been stored in memory is not always retrievable. The inability to retrieve previously stored information is called *forgetting.*

Measuring Forgetting

The first formal research on forgetting was conducted by the German psychologist Hermann Ebbinghaus (1885/1913). Ebbinghaus (1850–1909) made a purposeful decision to do for the study of memory what Gustav Fechner had done for the study of sensation—subject it to the scientific method (Postman, 1985). Ebbinghaus studied memory by repeating lists of items over and over until he could recall them in order perfectly. The items he used were called *nonsense syllables* (consisting of a vowel between two consonants, such as *VEM*) because they were not real words. He used nonsense syllables instead of words because he wanted a "pure" measure of memory, unaffected by prior associations with real words. Despite this effort, he discovered that even nonsense syllables varied in their meaningfulness, depending on how similar they were to words or parts of words.

Ebbinghaus found that immediate recall is worse for items in the middle of a list than for those at the beginning and end of a list (see Figure 8.8). His finding was replicated in the 1890s by Mary Whiton Calkins (Madigan & O'Hara, 1992). This differential forgetting is called the **serial-position effect.** The better memory for items at the beginning of a list is called the *primacy effect,* and the better memory for items at the end of a list is called the *recency effect.* Thus, in memorizing a list of terms from this chapter you would find it harder to memorize terms from the middle of the list than terms from the beginning or end of the list. The serial-position effect can even influence our memory for television commercials. A study demonstrated that when participants watched blocks of television commercials

serial-position effect

The superiority of immediate recall for items at the beginning and end of a list.

► **Figure 8.8**
The Serial-Position Effect
This is a typical serial-position curve, showing that items in the middle of a list are the most difficult to recall.

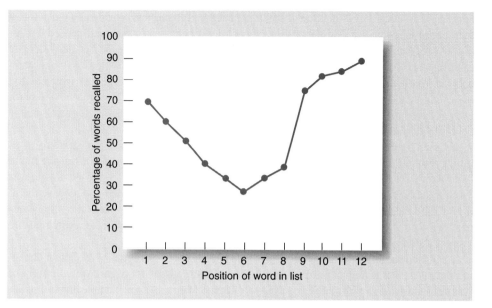

method of savings
The assessment of memory by comparing the time or number of trials needed to memorize a given amount of information and the time or number of trials needed to memorize it again at a later time.

▲ **Hermann Ebbinghaus (1850–1909)**
"Physical states of every kind, sensations, feelings, ideas, which at one time were present and then disappeared from consciousness, have not absolutely ceased to exist. Although an inward glance may not find them, they are not absolutely denied and annulled, but continue to live in a certain way, retained, as one says, in memory."

their recall was worse for commercials in the middle of the blocks than at the beginning (especially) and end of the blocks. This indicates that television advertisers need to consider the relative placement of their advertisements for maximum impact on viewers' memories (Pieters & Bijmolt, 1997).

What accounts for the serial-position effect? The primacy effect seems to occur because the items at the beginning of a list are subjected to more rehearsal as a learner memorizes the list, firmly placing those items in long-term memory. And the recency effect seems to occur because items at the end of the list remain readily accessible in short-term memory. In contrast, items in the middle of the list are neither firmly placed in long-term memory nor readily accessible in short-term memory. Note that this explanation supports Shiffrin and Atkinson's distinction between short-term memory and long-term memory. Before Ebbinghaus's work, knowledge of memory was based on common sense, with little supporting empirical evidence. Ebbinghaus moved memory from the philosophical realm into the psychological realm, making it subject to scientific research.

Ebbinghaus also introduced the **method of savings,** which commonly is called *relearning,* as a way to assess memory. In using the method of savings, Ebbinghaus memorized items in a list until he could recall them perfectly, noting how many trials he needed to achieve perfect recall. After varying intervals, during which he naturally forgot some of the items, Ebbinghaus again memorized the list until he could recall it perfectly. The delay varied from 20 minutes to 31 days. He found it took him fewer trials to relearn a list than to learn it originally. He called the difference between the number of original trials and the number of relearning trials *savings,* because he relearned the material more quickly the second time. The phenomenon of savings demonstrates that even when we cannot recall information, much of it still remains stored in memory. If it were not still stored, we would take just as long to relearn material as we took to learn it originally.

When you study for a cumulative final exam, you experience savings. Suppose your psychology course lasts 15 weeks and you study your notes and readings for 6 hours a week to perform at an A level on exams given during the semester. You will have studied for a total of 90 hours. If you then studied for a cumulative final exam, you would not have to study for 90 hours to memorize the material to your original level of mastery. In fact, you would have to study for only a few hours to master the material again. Savings occurs because relearning improves the retrieval of information stored in memory (MacLeod, 1988).

Relearning is a method of testing implicit memory, because it assesses information that has been retained without necessarily being accessible to conscious awareness prior to relearning. As another example of an implicit-memory test, consider the word-stem-completion test. Suppose you are exposed in passing to a list of words that includes *telegraph.* Later,

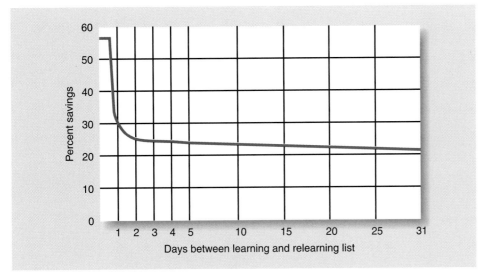

◀ **Figure 8.9**
The Forgetting Curve
The graph presents the results of a study by Ebbinghaus on memory for nonsense syllables. It shows that forgetting is initially rapid and then levels off.

despite having no recollection of having seen the word, you would be more likely to take the word stem *tele-* and form the word *telegraph* than if you had not been exposed to that word earlier.

You are more familiar with tests of explicit memory. A *recognition test* measures your ability to identify information that you have been exposed to previously when it is presented again. Recognition tests you might encounter in college include matching, true/false, and multiple-choice exams. A *recall test* measures your ability to remember information without the information being presented to you. Recall tests you might encounter in college include essay and fill-in-the-blanks exams. Ebbinghaus also found that, once we have mastered a list of items, forgetting is initially rapid and then slows (see Figure 8.9). This phenomenon has been replicated many times (Wixted & Ebbesen, 1991). So, if you memorized a list of terms from this chapter for an exam, you would do most of your forgetting in the first few days after the exam. But in keeping with the concept of levels of processing, meaningless nonsense syllables are initially forgotten more rapidly than is meaningful material, such as psychology terms.

Ebbinghaus's **forgetting curve,** which shows rapid initial forgetting followed by less and less forgetting over time, even holds for material learned decades before, as demonstrated in a cross-sectional study of the retention of Spanish words learned in high school by groups of participants ranging from recent graduates to those who had graduated 50 years earlier. Though some of the participants had not spoken Spanish in 50 years, they showed surprisingly good retention of some words. Their forgetting was rapid during the first 3 years after high school, then remained relatively unchanged. This indicates that after a certain amount of time, memories that have not been forgotten can become permanently held, in a kind of "permastore" (Bahrick, 1984).

forgetting curve
A graph showing that forgetting is initially rapid and then slows.

Explanations of Forgetting

Psychologists have provided several explanations of forgetting. These include *trace decay, interference, motivation,* and *encoding specificity.*

Trace Decay. Plato, anticipating **decay theory,** likened memory to an imprint made on a block of soft wax: Just as soft-wax imprints disappear over time, memories fade over time. But decay theory has received little research support, and a classic study provided evidence against it. John Jenkins and Karl Dallenbach (1924) had participants memorize a list of 10 nonsense syllables and then either stay awake or immediately go to sleep for 1, 2, 4, or 8 hours. At the end of each period, participants tried to recall the nonsense syllables. The researchers wondered whether sleep would prevent waking activities from interfering with the memories.

decay theory
The theory that forgetting occurs because memories naturally fade over time.

Jenkins and Dallenbach (1924) found that when participants learned a list of nonsense syllables and then slept, they forgot less than when they stayed awake.

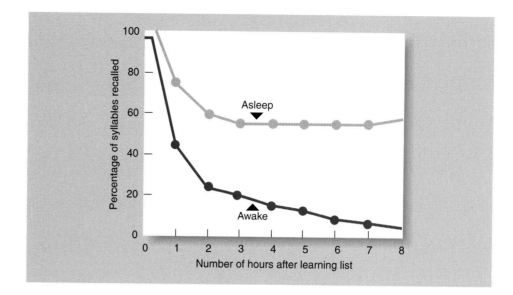

The graph in Figure 8.10 shows that participants had better recall if they slept than if they remained awake. There was some memory loss during sleep, providing modest support for decay theory, but if decay theory were an adequate explanation of forgetting, participants should have shown the same level of recall whether they remained awake or slept. Jenkins and Dallenbach concluded that participants forgot more if they remained awake because experiences they had while awake interfered with their memories of the nonsense syllables. In contrast, participants had forgotten less after sleeping because they had few experiences while asleep that could interfere with their memories for the nonsense syllables. The durability of many childhood memories throughout adulthood, such as high school memories held in "permastore," also provides evidence against decay theory.

interference theory

The theory that forgetting results from some memories interfering with the ability to remember other memories.

proactive interference

The process by which old memories interfere with the ability to remember new memories.

retroactive interference

The process by which new memories interfere with the ability to remember old memories.

Interference. Since Jenkins and Dallenbach's classic study contradicting decay theory, psychologists have come to favor interference as a better explanation of forgetting. **Interference theory** assumes forgetting results from particular memories interfering with the retrieval of other memories. This occurs, for example, when trying to recall advertisements for the myriad of products we are exposed to in everyday life (Kent & Allen, 1994). In **proactive interference,** old memories interfere with new memories (if you move to a new home, for instance, your memory of your old phone number might interfere with your ability to recall your new one). Proactive interference has been used to demonstrate that sign language and spoken language may be stored separately in human memory. A study found that there is less proactive interference in memory when old and new materials are each presented in a different language (that is, sign language and spoken language) than if both are presented in the same language (Hoemann & Keske, 1995). In **retroactive interference,** new memories interfere with old ones (your memory of your new phone number might interfere with your memory of your old one). This explains why names of people we meet today can interfere with our ability to retrieve names we learned before (Chandler, 1993). Figure 8.11 illustrates the difference between proactive interference and retroactive interference.

You certainly have experienced both kinds of interference when taking an exam. Material you have studied for other courses sometimes interferes with your memories of the material on the exam. And interference is stronger when the materials are similar. Thus, biology material will interfere more than computer science material with your recall of psychology material. Because of the great amount of material you learn during a semester, proactive interference might be a particularly strong influence on your later exam performance (Dempster, 1985). So it would be best to study different subjects as far apart as possible rather than studying a bit of each every day. Moreover, be sure to do some of your studying before going to sleep and right before your exam to reduce the effect of retroactive interference on your retrieval of relevant memories during the exam.

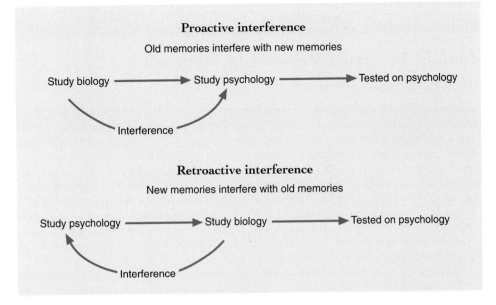

Proactive interference

Old memories interfere with new memories

Study biology → Study psychology → Tested on psychology

Interference

Retroactive interference

New memories interfere with old memories

Study psychology → Study biology → Tested on psychology

Interference

◀ **Figure 8.11**
Proactive and Retroactive Interference

Forgetting takes place, in part, because memories interfere with each other. In proactive interference, old memories interfere with new memories. In retroactive interference, new memories interfere with old memories.

Motivation. Sigmund Freud (1901/1965) claimed we can forget experiences through **repression,** the process by which emotionally threatening experiences, such as witnessing a murder, are banished to the unconscious mind. Though research findings tend to contradict Freudian repression as an explanation of forgetting (Abrams, 1995), some studies suggest we are more motivated to forget emotionally upsetting experiences than other kinds of experiences. Yet, other studies find there is no difference in recall of pleasant or unpleasant experiences (Bradley & Baddeley, 1990).

In an experiment that possibly demonstrated motivated forgetting, participants were shown one of two versions of a training film for bank tellers that depicted a simulated bank robbery. In one version, a shot fired by the robbers at pursuers hit a boy in the face. The boy fell to the ground, bleeding profusely. In the other version, instead of showing the boy being shot, the bank manager was shown talking about the robbery. When asked to recall details of the robbery, participants who had seen the violent version had poorer recall of the details of the crime than did participants who had seen the nonviolent version. One possible explanation is that the content of the violent version motivated participants to forget what they had seen (Loftus & Burns, 1982). However, in some cases memory of traumatic events will be superior to memory of ordinary events (Christianson & Loftus, 1987).

repression

In psychoanalytic theory, the defense mechanism that involves banishing threatening thoughts, feelings, and memories into the unconscious mind.

◀ **Motivated Forgetting**

According to Sigmund Freud, a person (such as the man in this photograph, whose heroic effort to save a friend from a fire was futile) might forget a traumatic event by repressing its memory to the unconscious mind.

Should We Trust Recovered Memories of Childhood Abuse?

False and Repressed Memory Connections
www.mhhe.com/sdorow5

One day in 1989, Eileen Franklin-Lipsker looked into her 7-year-old daughter's eyes and was overcome by a horrible memory. Twenty years earlier, as an 8-year-old child, she had witnessed her father sexually assault and bludgeon to death her best friend, Susan Nason. Eileen recalled her father, George Franklin, had warned her that he would kill her if she told anyone about the murder. Her attorney claimed she had been so emotionally overwhelmed that she repressed the event for two decades—until the look in her daughter's eyes evoked the same feelings she had when looking into the eyes of Susan as she was being attacked. In 1990 George Franklin was convicted of murder (MacLean, 1993). The case was widely publicized by the media and was the basis of a made-for-television movie. In 1996 George Franklin's conviction was overturned on appeal because of a legal technicality.

During the 1990s, the media reported—and often sensationalized—several cases in which adults (usually women undergoing psychotherapy) have suddenly recalled terrible childhood memories, most often of being sexually abused by an adult. Some of the people who have recalled these memories have made emotionally touching appearances on television talk shows to recount their stories of abuse. Many juries have convicted people based on such testimony, sending some defendants to prison and ordering others to make multimillion-dollar payments to their accusers.

Psychologists agree that most people who have survived childhood sexual assault remember all or part of their traumatic experiences. However, in a minority of cases childhood memories of sexual abuse have resurfaced in adulthood. The media have become more skeptical in their treatment of such cases after finding that memory researchers are divided about whether to accept the validity of recovered memories. Researchers who support their validity believe childhood trauma may result in total or partial amnesia and memories may be recovered many years later (Alpert, Brown, & Courtois, 1998). Other researchers warn either that recovered memories are scientific fictions or that even if one accepts that phenomena such as dissociation or repression exists, therapists might purposely or unwittingly manipulate their clients into recalling vivid memories of events that never took place (Walcott, 2000). This becomes even more of an issue when therapists use techniques like hypnosis to help their clients recover past memories. Hypnotized people are especially susceptible to forming memories of events that never took place (Wagstaff & Frost, 1996).

Those who believe there is little or no support for the validity of recovered memories call this phenomenon *false memory syndrome.* There is even a national False Memory Syndrome Foundation that acts as a resource for people who insist they have been falsely accused of crimes based on recovered memories. People who claim they have been accused of crimes based on false recovered memories are suing therapists for implanting and convincing their clients of the reality of those memories. Nonetheless, supporters of the validity of recovered memories note that opposition to their existence comes primarily from memory researchers, rather than from clinicians. Some clinicians insist that even though laboratory research has provided little support for this phenomenon (Zoellner et al., 2000), clinical experience with clients has convinced them that some cases of recovered memory are true. For example, clinicians have reported cases in which World War II veterans have recovered memories of traumatic, independently verified, war-time experiences many years later (Karon & Widener, 1998).

But many memory researchers counter that these clinical reports are not reliable enough to support the validity of recovered memories (Lilienfeld & Loftus, 1998). Supporters of the validity of recovered memories respond by pointing to scientific research indicating that recovered memories of childhood abuse can occur and are just as accurate as memories of abuse that have been recalled continuously from the time the events took place (Brown, Scheflin, & Whitfield, 1999). Memory researchers and clinicians do agree, though, that more research is necessary to identify the psychological processes that affect memory of childhood sexual abuse.

Chapter Eight

Memory researcher Elizabeth Loftus insists that we might hold dearly to memories of events that never took place if we are led to believe they truly occurred. She stresses the need to protect both the accused and the accuser—a delicate balance, indeed. No one wants to see abusers or murderers go free. But no one wants innocent people convicted of acts they did not commit. Aside from concern that innocent people might be falsely accused based on therapist-induced memories, child advocates warn that such cases, when exposed, might undermine support for cases involving survivors of actual childhood sexual abuse (Lindsay, 1994).

Encoding Specificity. Because the retrieval of long-term memories depends on adequate retrieval cues, forgetting can sometimes be explained by the failure to have or to use them. For example, odors that we associate with an event can aid our recall of it (Smith, Standing, & de Man, 1992). This is known as *cue-dependence theory.* At times we might fail to find an adequate cue to activate the relevant portion of a semantic memory network. Consider the **tip-of-the-tongue phenomenon,** in which you cannot quite recall a familiar word—though you feel that you know it (Schwartz et al., 2000). As a demonstration, you might induce a tip-of-the-tongue experience by trying to recall the names of the seven dwarfs. You might fail to recall one or two of them, yet still feel that you know them (Miserandino, 1991). This indicates that when we speak we might retrieve the meaning of a word before we retrieve its sound pattern (Vigliocco et al., 1999). The tip-of-the-tongue phenomenon is universal, increases with age, and occurs about once a week for the typical person (Brown, 1991).

A study of the tip-of-the-tongue phenomenon presented college students with the faces of 50 celebrities and asked them to recall their names. The results indicated that the students searched for the names by using cues associated with the celebrities. The students tried to recall their professions, where they usually performed, and the last time they had seen them. Characteristics of the names also served as cues for recalling them. These cues included the first letters of the names, the first letters of similar-sounding names, and the number of syllables in the names (Yarmey, 1973). This study supports the concept of **encoding specificity,** which states that recall will be best when cues that were associated with the encoding of a memory are also present during attempts at retrieving the memory (Tulving & Thomson, 1973). Researchers interested in the role of encoding specificity in forgetting study *context-dependent memory* and *state-dependent memory.*

Context-Dependent Memory. In an unusual experiment on encoding specificity, scuba divers memorized lists of words while either underwater or on a beach, and then tried to recall the words while either in the same location or in the other location (Godden & Baddeley, 1975). The participants communicated with the experimenter through a special intercom system. The results (see Figure 8.12) indicated that when participants memorized and recalled the words in different locations, they recalled about 30 percent fewer than when they memorized and recalled the words in the same location. This tendency for recall to be best when the environmental context present during the encoding of a memory is also present during attempts at retrieving it is known as **context-dependent memory.** The findings of the study even have practical implications. Instructions given to scuba divers should be given underwater, as well as on dry land, and if divers are making observations about what they see underwater, they should record them there and not wait until they get on dry land (Baddeley, 1982).

When you return to your old school or neighborhood, long-lost memories might come flooding back, evoked by environmental cues that you had not been exposed to for years. This effect of environmental context on recall is not lost on theater directors, who hold dress rehearsals in full costume amid the scenery that will be used during actual performances. Similarly, even your academic performance can be affected by environmental cues, as in a study in which college students read an article in either noisy or silent conditions and then were tested on their comprehension of it in either noisy or silent conditions (Grant et al., 1998). They performed better when they read the article and were tested under the same conditions (noisy-noisy or silent-silent) than when they did so under different conditions (noisy-silent or silent-noisy). Likewise, college students may perform worse when their

tip-of-the-tongue phenomenon
The inability to recall information that one knows has been stored in long-term memory.

encoding specificity
The principle that recall will be best when cues that were associated with the encoding of a memory are also present during attempts at retrieving it.

context-dependent memory
The tendency for recall to be best when the environmental context present during the encoding of a memory is also present during attempts at retrieving it.

► **Figure 8.12**
Context-Dependent Memory
Godden and Baddeley (1975) found
that words learned underwater were
best recalled underwater and that words
learned on land were best recalled on land.

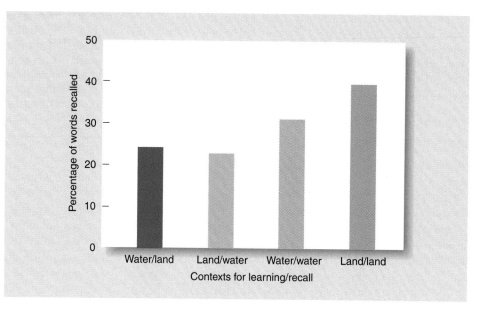

exams are given in classrooms other than their normal ones (Abernethy, 1940). Perhaps you have noticed this when you have taken a final exam in a strange room. If you find yourself in that situation, you might improve your performance by mentally reinstating the environmental context in which you learned the material (Smith, 1984).

There is controversy among memory researchers about whether the environmental context is important when *recall* is required, but not when *recognition* is required. This means that your performance on an essay exam might be impaired if you took an exam in a strange room, but your performance on a multiple-choice test would not. Perhaps tasks that require recognition include enough retrieval cues of their own, making environmental retrieval cues relatively less important (Eich, 1980). But some research indicates that even recognition memory is affected by environmental context. In one study, participants observed a person and were then asked to identify the individual in a photo lineup. Some participants had to identify the individual under the same environmental context and some under different contexts. Recognition was better under the same contexts. In fact, simply imagining being in the original context improved recognition performance (Smith & Vela, 1992).

state-dependent memory
The tendency for recall to be best when one's emotional or physiological state is the same during the recall of a memory as it was during the encoding of that memory.

State-Dependent Memory. Our recall of memories depends not only on cues from the external environment but also on cues from our internal states. The effect on recall of the similarity between a person's internal state during encoding and during retrieval is called **state-dependent memory.** For example, memories encoded while the person is in a psychoactive drug-induced state will be recalled better when the person is in that state. A variety of drugs induce state-dependent memory, a fact first noted in 1835 (Overton, 1991). These drugs include alcohol (Weissenborn & Duka, 2000), nicotine (Peters & McGee, 1982), Valium (Roy-Byrne et al., 1987), barbiturates (Kumar, Ramalingam, & Karanth, 1994), and nitrous oxide (Mewaldt et al., 1988). Likewise, people who learn material while exerting themselves on a bicycle ergometer will recall the material better if they do so while exerting themselves on a bicycle ergometer (Miles & Hardman, 1998). Given this, perhaps people who discuss business deals during aerobic exercise might have some difficulty recalling what they discussed while exercising when they return to their offices.

In a government-sponsored study on the possible state-dependent effects of marijuana (Eich et al., 1975), one group of participants memorized a list of words after smoking marijuana, and a second group memorized the same list after smoking a placebo that tasted like marijuana. Participants were "blind"; that is, they did not know whether they were smoking marijuana or a placebo. Four hours later, half of each group smoked either marijuana or a placebo and then tried to recall the words they had memorized. Recall was better either when participants smoked the placebo on both occasions or when they smoked marijuana on both occasions than when they smoked marijuana on one occasion and the placebo on the other. You should *not* conclude that marijuana smoking improves memory. As noted in Chapter 6, marijuana actually impairs memory. And, indeed, in this study the group that smoked the placebo on both occasions performed *better* than the groups that smoked marijuana on either occasion or both occasions.

Our internal states also involve our moods, which can play a role in a form of state-dependent memory called *mood-dependent memory,* in which our recall of information that has been encoded in a particular mood will be best when we are in that mood again. If you study material while listening to music that evokes a particular mood and then tested on the material later, you might perform better if you are tested while listening to music that evokes a similar mood (Balch, Myers, & Papotto, 1999). Mood appears to act as a cue for the retrieval of memories. Thus victims of crimes might have difficulty recalling details of the crimes because of the radically different moods they are in during the crime and when police or lawyers later question them. Mood-dependent memory also might account for claims by some criminals who have committed violent crimes, but who have since calmed down, that they were so angry while committing the crimes they cannot recall what they did (Swihart, Yuille, & Porter, 1999).

Memory, Forgetting, and Eyewitness Testimony

In August 1979, Father Bernard Pagano went on trial for a series of armed robberies. Eyewitnesses had identified him as the so-called gentleman bandit, a polite man who had robbed several convenience stores in Wilmington, Delaware. Father Pagano was arrested after several people who knew him told the police he resembled published drawings of the bandit. Seven eyewitnesses, who were shown photographs in which Father Pagano wore his clerical collar, identified him as the robber. They might have been influenced by previous police reports that indicated that the perpetrator looked like a clergyman. Fortunately for Father Pagano, while he was on trial, another man, Ronald Clouser, confessed to the crimes (Rodgers, 1982).

There was little resemblance between Father Pagano and Ronald Clouser. The possibility of convicting innocent people or of exonerating guilty people based on inaccurate eyewitness testimony has led psychologists to study the factors that affect eyewitness memories. This concern is not new. Hugo Münsterberg (1908), a pioneer in the study of psychology and the law, warned us to consider the imperfections of human memory when evaluating the accuracy of **eyewitness testimony.** At about the same time, Alfred Binet, who gained fame for developing the first IQ test, championed the scientific study of eyewitness testimony. He introduced the *picture-description test,* which required participants to examine a picture of a scene and, after varying lengths of time, recall as much as possible about the picture or to answer questions about it posed by an interrogator. Binet found that eyewitness testimony usually included inaccuracies and that testimony under questioning was less accurate than spontaneous testimony (Postman, 1985).

Web Page of Professor Gary L. Wells
www.mhhe.com/sdorow5

eyewitness testimony
Witnesses' recollections about events, most notably about criminal activity.

◀ **Eyewitness Testimony**
Eyewitnesses mistakenly identified Father Bernard Pagano *(left)* as the perpetrator of a series of convenience store robberies actually committed by Ronald Clouser *(right)*.

During the past few decades, psychologists have conducted many research studies of the factors that affect the accuracy of eyewitness testimony. Research on eyewitness memories shows they are not like mental tape recordings that record and play back exact representations of events. Instead, eyewitness recollections are reconstructive, somewhat altering the events that they represent. The misidentification of Father Pagano would not surprise psychologists who study eyewitness testimony. They know misidentifications from lineups of suspects are the single leading cause of wrongful criminal convictions (Lindsay & Pozzulo, 1999).

The fragility of eyewitness testimony has been supported cross-culturally. In a study conducted in Japan based on a real-life event, customers (confederates of the researcher) visited stores and bought items from professional sales clerks. Three months later each clerk was asked to identify the customer who had bought the items from a photograph. Half of the sales clerks recalled details of the event and the customer, but only two-thirds of those were accurate. Of the two-thirds who claimed they could identify the customer from a photograph, only 14 percent were accurate (Naka, Itsukushima, & Itoh, 1996). And cross-cultural differences can influence eyewitness testimony. This was demonstrated in a study using 48 Spanish and 48 English undergraduates. Participants were shown two films, one of an event common in Spanish culture and one of an event common in English culture. Later they were asked to recall what they had seen. Perhaps contrary to common sense, recall accuracy was greater for the event that was not from the participants' own culture (Davies & Alonso-Quecuty, 1997).

A number of studies have found that recall is even less accurate when eyewitnesses are asked to recognize persons from other ethnic groups. In one study, European American and African American participants were more accurate when they identified suspects from their own ethnic group (Devine & Malpass, 1985). These findings have been replicated with Latino (Platz & Hosch, 1988) and Asian samples (Ng & Lindsay, 1994). Two of the main topics of interest regarding eyewitness testimony are the accuracy of children's eyewitness testimony and the effects of questioning on eyewitness testimony, the subject of the Psychology Versus Common Sense feature on p. 263.

Children as Eyewitnesses. An issue that has concerned psychologists since the beginning of the 20th century is whether the testimony of children is trustworthy. As first demonstrated by the German psychologist William Stern, children tend to be less accurate than adults in their eyewitness accounts of crimes, in part because they are more suggestible—that is, they are more susceptible to leading questions (Templeton & Wilcox, 2000). Concerns about children as eyewitnesses have been supported by research indicating that misleading information about events can distort children's memories of them. In an experiment that tested this finding, children 3 to 12 years old listened to a story about a girl who had a *stomachache* after eating *eggs* too fast. When asked questions about the story, the children answered correctly almost all of the time. But when asked if they remembered the story of a little girl who got a *headache* because she ate her *cereal* too fast, the children typically responded that they had. The effect of misleading questions was greater on the younger children than on the older ones (Ceci, Ross, & Toglia, 1987).

Still another study revealing the fallibility of young children's testimony involved interviewing children 3 to 7 years old immediately after they had undergone a routine physical examination and several weeks later. Younger children remembered less information spontaneously and provided fewer details, and there was less consistency between their earlier and their later testimony. Though there was no difference in the accuracy of spontaneously recalled information, the younger children were less accurate in response to specific questions, and only 7-year-olds responded correctly at significantly above the level of chance guessing (Gordon & Follmer, 1994).

Children are also more likely to guess when testifying, as in a study in which kindergartners viewed a slide show of a staged theft and then were asked to identify the perpetrator from a lineup. Many identified a person in the lineup even when the perpetrator was not in the lineup. Moreover, some children who had made correct identifications when the perpetrator was present in the lineup later identified a person in a lineup in which the perpetrator was absent. This is an example of the tendency of children to guess or make up answers when they testify repeatedly about the same event (Ackil & Zaragoza, 1998; Beal, Schmitt, & Dekle, 1995).

One of the main factors potentially affecting eyewitness testimony is the wording of questions. If you saw an automobile accident and were asked questions about its speed, color, and direction, you would probably assume your responses would be independent of these questions. Common sense tells you that being asked questions about your memory does not change your memories. In fact, a survey of university students found that they believed their own common sense was their single best source of information about eyewitness testimony (Shaw, Garcia, & McClure, 1999).

But Elizabeth Loftus, a contemporary pioneer in experimental research on eyewitness testimony, would disagree. Many of her research studies on eyewitness testimony have demonstrated that eyewitnesses might be subject not only to normal memory lapses but also to alterations in their memories produced by questioning by lawyers, prosecutors, and police officers. Judges and lawyers are taught to beware of leading questions, which can affect the testimony of eyewitnesses. Nonetheless, clever lawyers use subtle wording to influence testimony. In a dramatic study on the influence of questioning on eyewitness memories, Loftus and John Palmer (1974) examined the effect of leading questions regarding eyewitness accounts of an automobile accident.

Forty-five undergraduates viewed one of seven driver education films of two-car automobile accidents lasting 5 to 30 seconds. Some participants were asked, "About how fast were the cars going when they smashed into each other?" Other participants were asked a similar question, with the word *smashed* replaced by *contacted, hit, bumped,* or *collided.* In a similar version of the experiment, 150 other undergraduates likewise viewed films of two-car automobile accidents. Participants in one group were asked, "About how fast were the cars going when they *smashed* into each other?" and participants in a second group were asked, "About how fast were the cars going when they *hit* each other?" A week later, participants were asked, "Did you see any broken glass?" To avoid sensitizing participants to its purpose, the question was embedded in a list of ten questions. In reality, there was no broken glass at the accident scene.

Participants' estimates of the speed of the cars in the first part of the study were influenced by the word used in the question. The average estimates for *contacted, hit, bumped, collided,* and *smashed* were, respectively, 31.8, 34.0, 38.1, 39.3, and 40.8 miles per hour. In the second part of the study, though there had been no broken glass, participants in both groups recalled seeing some. But participants who had been given the question containing the word *smashed* were significantly more likely to report having seen broken glass than were participants who had been given the question containing the word *hit.*

Loftus's findings have been replicated in other studies. In one study, college students were shown a videotaped mock crime. One week later they read a passage that described the crime. The passage contained leading, misleading, or control (no supplemental) information. When asked to recall the crime they had witnessed, the participants placed more confidence in the biased information presented by the experimenter than in their own memories (Ryan & Geiselman, 1991).

Studies like this one demonstrate that the memories of eyewitnesses can be reconstructions, instead of exact replicas, of the events witnessed. This phenomenon was noted in 1846 in a trial that marked the first admission of hypnotically obtained testimony in an American court. Though the defendant was acquitted because of inadequate evidence, testimony by one expert noted that memory is often a reconstruction of events incorporating fact and fantasy (Gravitz, 1995).

Eyewitness memories can be altered by inaccurate information introduced during questioning. That is, "Under some conditions misleading postevent information can impair the ability to remember what was witnessed and can lead people to believe that they witnessed things that they did not" (Lindsay, 1993, p. 86). This also supports the practice of barring

Can Leading Questions Alter Our Memories of Vivid Events?

▲ **Elizabeth Loftus**

"One reason most of us, as jurors, place so much faith in eyewitness testimony is that we are unaware of how many factors influence its accuracy."

 Web Page of Professor Elizabeth F. Loftus
www.mhhe.com/sdorow5

leading questions in courtroom proceedings. Though leading questions can affect the recall of eyewitnesses, research indicates that eyewitnesses might be less susceptible to them than had been suggested by earlier research (Kohnken & Maass, 1988).

Eyewitness memory can be improved by relatively simple procedures. One procedure, based on the principle of encoding specificity, improves recall by mentally reinstating the physical setting of the event. In one study, store clerks were asked to identify a previously encountered customer from an array of photographs. The original context was reinstated by providing physical cues from the encounter and by instructing the clerk to mentally recall events that led up to the customer's purchase. As discussed earlier, mentally reinstating the context in which you learned something can improve your recall of it. In this study, the reinstatement of the original context led to a significant increase in the accuracy of identifications (Krafka & Penrod, 1985).

We can also prevent misleading information from influencing the memories of eyewitnesses by warning them about that possibility. This was the finding of a study in which participants were warned just prior to the presentation of misleading information about a simulated crime. Participants viewed slides of a wallet being snatched from a woman's purse and then read descriptions of the crime. Participants who had been given warnings showed greater resistance to misleading information in the descriptions (Greene, Flynn, & Loftus, 1982). But some psychologists argue that informing jurors of the unreliability of eyewitness testimony might make already skeptical jurors too skeptical, perhaps leading to the exoneration of guilty persons (McCloskey & Egeth, 1983).

Regardless of the exact extent to which eyewitness testimony can be influenced by misleading information and the reasons for that influence, Elizabeth Loftus believes eyewitness testimony is, in fact, too easily affected by such information. She expressed this in a statement that was a takeoff on John B. Watson's claim (quoted in Chapter 1) regarding his ability to condition infants to become any kind of person one desired. Loftus remarked:

▶ Give us a dozen healthy memories, well-informed, and our own specified world to handle them in. And we'll guarantee to take any at random and train it to become any type of memory that we might select—hammer, screwdriver, wrench, stop sign, yield sign, Indian chief—regardless of its origin or the brain that holds it. (Loftus & Hoffman, 1989, p. 103)

Not only are young children more fallible in their testimony than older children, children tend to be less accurate in their testimony than adults. One study compared adults and children in the accuracy of their memories for an event they experienced 2 years earlier. The children were less accurate in responding to yes/no questions and open-ended questions, and were more likely to fabricate responses to a question about a man's occupation. This tendency might have an effect on court cases that take a long time to reach trial (Poole & White, 1993).

Of course, especially because of the prevalence of child sexual and physical abuse, courts must achieve a delicate balance between believing children's testimony and being skeptical of it (Goodman & Schaaf, 1997). Fortunately, children can give accurate testimony, provided that they are not given leading questions and provided that the questions are worded so that they can understand them (Brooks & Siegel, 1991). To promote accuracy in children's testimony, the questioning of children should be done by neutral parties rather than by individuals who are biased either toward or against believing the children's stories of abuse. Failure to do so might induce children to testify in a manner consistent with the questioner's personal agenda.

Questioning the Eyewitness. Though issues regarding the accuracy of children's eyewitness testimony have important social consequences, there has been even more research on the effects of questioning on adult eyewitness testimony. Because jurors attribute greater accuracy to the testimony of eyewitnesses who display confidence, an important factor in eyewitness testimony is how confident eyewitnesses are about their memories. In the 1972 case of *Neil v. Biggers,* the U.S. Supreme Court even ruled that one of the criteria that juries should use in judging the accuracy of an eyewitness's testimony is the degree of confidence expressed by the eyewitness. But this ruling might be misguided, because even though hypnotized eyewitnesses are more confident in the accuracy of their testimony than nonhypnotized eyewitnesses are (Steblay & Bothwell, 1994), eyewitnesses' level of confidence is generally unrelated to the accuracy of their testimony (Wells & Lindsay, 1985) and hypnotized witnesses can be subject to the formation of inaccurate "pseudomemories" (Green, Lynn, & Malinoski, 1998). As a consequence, it can be unwise for jurors to assume that a confident eyewitness is necessarily an accurate eyewitness.

STAYING ON TRACK: *Long-Term Memory*

1. How does the superiority of elaborative rehearsal, compared to maintenance rehearsal, support the levels of processing theory of long-term memory encoding?
2. What is the difference between procedural memory and declarative memory?
3. What is the difference between proactive interference and retroactive interference?
4. What evidence is there to support the notion of state-dependent memory?
5. What concerns Elizabeth Loftus and other researchers about the accuracy of recovered memories and eyewitness testimony?

Answers to Staying on Track start on p. ST-4.

♦ IMPROVING YOUR MEMORY

More than a century ago William James (1890/1981) criticized those who claimed that memory ability could be improved by practice. To James, memory was a fixed, inherited ability and not subject to improvement. He concluded this after finding that practice in memorizing did not decrease the time it took him and others to memorize poetry or other kinds of literature. Regardless of the extent to which memory ability is inherited, we can certainly make better use of the ability we have by improving our study habits and by using *mnemonic devices.* Professional actors, for example, make good use of various memory techniques to help them recall their parts in plays (Noice et al., 1999).

Websites for College Study Strategies
www.mhhe.com/sdorow5

Using Effective Study Habits

Given two students with equal memory ability, the one with better study habits will probably perform better in school (Sanghvi, 1995). To practice good study habits, you would begin by setting up a schedule in which you would do the bulk of your studying when you are most alert and most motivated—whether in the early morning, in the late afternoon, or at some other time. You should also study in a quiet, comfortable place, free of distractions. If you study in a dormitory lounge with students milling around and holding conversations, you might find yourself distracted from the information being processed in your short-term memory, making it more difficult for you to transfer the information efficiently into your long-term memory. As for particular study techniques, you might consider using the *SQ3R method, overlearning,* and *distributed practice.*

The SQ3R Method

In the **SQ3R method** (Robinson, 1970), SQ3R stands for Survey, Question, Read, Recite, and Review. This method has proved helpful to students in college (Martin, 1985) and elementary school (Darch, Carnine, & Kameenui, 1986). It requires elaborative rehearsal, in which you process information at a relatively deep level. This is distinct from rote memorization, in which you process information at a relatively shallow level. If you have ever found yourself studying for hours, yet doing poorly on exams, it might be the consequence of failing to use elaborative rehearsal. For example, in one study students used either rote

SQ3R method

A study technique in which the student surveys, questions, reads, recites, and reviews course material.

memory, writing down unfamiliar terms and their definitions, or elaborative rehearsal, writing down how the words might or might not describe them. One week later, students who had used elaborative rehearsal recalled significantly more definitions than did students who had used rote memory (Flannagan & Blick, 1989).

Suppose you decide to use the SQ3R method to study the final major section of this chapter. You would follow several steps:

- First, *survey* the main headings and subheadings to create an organized framework in which to fit the information you are studying.
- Second, as you survey the sections, ask yourself *questions* to be answered when you read them. For example, you might ask yourself, What is the physiological basis of memory?
- Third, *read* the material carefully, trying to answer your questions as you move through each section. In memorizing new terms, you might find it especially helpful to say them out loud. A study found that participants who read terms out loud remembered more of them than did participants who read them silently, wrote them down, or heard them spoken by someone else (Gathercole & Conway, 1988).
- Fourth, after reading a section, *recite* information from it to see whether you understand it. Do not proceed to the next section until you understand the one you are studying.
- Fifth, periodically (perhaps every few days) *review* the information in the entire chapter by quizzing yourself on it and then rereading anything you fail to recall. Asking questions of yourself as you read can increase elaborative rehearsal and the depth of processing, thereby improving your memory for the material (Andre, 1979). You will also find yourself experiencing savings; each time you review the material, it will take you less time to reach the same level of mastery.

Overlearning Material

overlearning
Studying material beyond the point of initial mastery.

You might also wish to apply other principles to improve your studying. Take advantage of **overlearning.** That is, study the material until you feel you know all of it—and then go over it several more times. A meta-analysis of research studies found that overlearning significantly improves the retention of material (Driskell, Willis, & Copper, 1992). Overlearning appears to work by making you less likely to forget material you have studied and more confident that you know it (Nelson et al., 1982). This might improve your exam performance by making you less anxious. The power of overlearning is revealed by the amazing ability people show for recognizing the names and faces of their high school classmates decades after graduation. This is attributable to their having overlearned the names and faces during their years together in school (Bahrick, Bahrick, & Wittlinger, 1975).

Distributed Practice

distributed practice
Spreading out the memorization of information or the learning of a motor skill over several sessions.

massed practice
Cramming the memorization of information or the learning of a motor skill into one session.

Use **distributed practice** instead of **massed practice.** The advantage of distributed practice over massed practice is especially important in studying academic material (Zimmer & Hocevar, 1994). If you can devote a total of 5 hours to studying this chapter, you would be better off studying for 1 hour on five different occasions than studying for 5 hours on one occasion. Moreover, longer breaks between practice sessions have been found to facilitate memory in complex tasks more than in simple tasks (Donovan & Radosevich, 1999). You might recognize this as a suggestion to avoid "cramming" for exams. Note how the following explanation by William James for the negative effects of cramming anticipated recent research into the effects of elaborative rehearsal, overlearning, environmental cues, and semantic networks on memory:

▶ The reason why *cramming* is such a bad mode of study is now made clear. . . . Things learned thus in a few hours, on one occasion, for one purpose, cannot possibly have formed many associations with other things in the mind. . . . Speedy oblivion is the almost inevitable fate of all that is committed to memory in this simple way. . . . Whereas on the contrary, the same information taken in gradually, day after day, recurring in different contexts, considered in various relations, associated with other external incidents, and repeatedly reflected on, grow into a fabric, lie open to so many paths of approach, that they remain permanent possessions. (James, 1890/1981, Vol. 1, pp. 623–624)

Even novices who are learning word processing can benefit from distributed practice, as in a study of students in a word-processing seminar. The students were assigned to groups that received either a single 60-minute session or a 60-minute session broken into two segments by a 10-minute break. The students were tested on their speed and accuracy immediately after the training and 1 week later. The group that had received distributed practice performed significantly faster and more accurately on both occasions. The results indicate that those who teach word processing might be wise to divide long sessions into shorter ones (Bouzid & Crawshaw, 1987).

Using Mnemonic Devices

Mnemonic devices are techniques for organizing information and providing memory cues to make it easier to recall, such as learning the names of U.S. presidents (Mastropieri, Scruggs, & Whedon, 1997) or learning to associate painters and their paintings in art history courses (Carney & Levin, 1994). These devices are named after Mnemosyne, the Greek goddess of memory. You are familiar with certain mnemonic devices, such as *acronyms.* An **acronym** is a term formed from the first letters of a series of words. Examples of acronyms include *USA, NFL,* and even *SQ3R.* Many students have used the acronym *Roy G Biv* to help them recall the colors of the rainbow. Acronyms have also proved useful to psychiatrists, helping them recall the diagnostic criteria for psychological disorders (Pinkofsky, 1997).

You are probably familiar with the use of rhymes as mnemonic devices, as in "*I* before *e* except after *c*" and "Thirty days has September. . ." Though rhymes are useful mnemonic devices, they sometimes can impair memory. In one study, children who listened to stories presented in prose had better recall of them than did children who listened to the stories presented in verse. Evidently, the children who listened to verse processed the stories at a shallow level, as sounds, while the children who listened to prose processed the stories at a deeper level, in terms of their meaning (Hayes, Chemelski, & Palmer, 1982). The possible negative effect of using rhyming to help children learn academic material has been replicated in other research studies (Hayes, 1999). The major mnemonic devices include the *method of loci,* the *pegword method,* and the *link method.*

The Method of Loci

About 2,500 years ago the Greek poet Simonides stepped outside of the banquet hall where he was to recite a poem in honor of a nobleman (Bower, 1970). While Simonides was outside, the hall collapsed, killing all the guests and maiming them beyond recognition. Yet, by recalling where each guest had been sitting, Simonides was able to identify all of them. He called this the **method of loci** (*loci* means "place" in Latin). The method of loci is useful for memorizing lists of items. You might memorize concrete terms from this chapter by associating them with places and landmarks on your campus, and then retrieving them while taking a mental walk across it. The method of loci has proved helpful in training older adults to improve their memory for grocery lists (Anschutz et al., 1985). Even the places on a Monopoly board have been used successfully to help students employ the method of loci (Schoen, 1996).

The Pegword Method

A mnemonic device that relies on both imagery and rhyming is the **pegword method,** which begins with memorizing a list of concrete nouns that rhyme with the numbers 1, 2, 3, 4, 5, and so on. For this method to work well, the image of the pegword object and the image of the object to be recalled should interact, rather than just be paired with each other (Wollen, Weber, & Lowry, 1972). Suppose that you wanted to remember the grocery list presented in Figure 8.13. You might imagine, among other things, sugar being poured from a shoe, bees in a hive brushing their teeth, and a hen drinking from a soda bottle. To recall an item, you would simply imagine the pegword that is paired with a particular number, which would act as a cue for retrieving the image of the object that interacted with that pegword. Thus, if you imagined a shoe, you would automatically retrieve an image of sugar being poured from it. The pegword method has proved successful even when used by young

mnemonic devices
Techniques for organizing information to be memorized to make it easier to remember.

acronym
A mnemonic device that involves forming a term from the first letters of a series of words that are to be recalled.

Memory Techniques and Mnemonics
www.mhhe.com/sdorow5

method of loci
A mnemonic device in which items to be recalled are associated with landmarks in a familiar place and then recalled during a mental walk from one landmark to another.

pegword method
A mnemonic device that involves associating items to be recalled with objects that rhyme with the numbers 1, 2, 3, and so on, to make the items easier to recall.

The pegword method can be used to recall a grocery list. Each grocery item is paired with a pegword. Thus, the retrieval of a pegword will cue the retrieval of the associated grocery item.

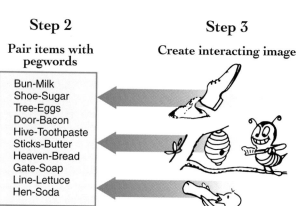

Step 1

Memorize pegwords in order

One is a bun
Two is a shoe
Three is a tree
Four is a door
Five is a hive
Six is sticks
Seven is heaven
Eight is a gate
Nine is a line
Ten is a hen

Step 2

Pair items with pegwords

Bun-Milk
Shoe-Sugar
Tree-Eggs
Door-Bacon
Hive-Toothpaste
Sticks-Butter
Heaven-Bread
Gate-Soap
Line-Lettuce
Hen-Soda

Step 3

Create interacting image

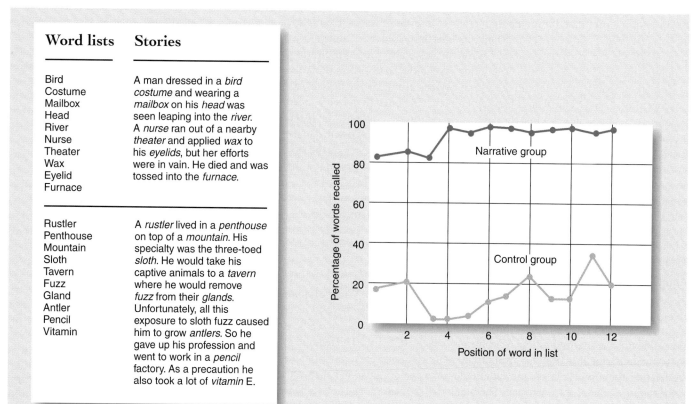

Word lists

Bird
Costume
Mailbox
Head
River
Nurse
Theater
Wax
Eyelid
Furnace

Rustler
Penthouse
Mountain
Sloth
Tavern
Fuzz
Gland
Antler
Pencil
Vitamin

Stories

A man dressed in a *bird costume* and wearing a *mailbox* on his *head* was seen leaping into the *river*. A *nurse* ran out of a nearby *theater* and applied *wax* to his *eyelids*, but her efforts were in vain. He died and was tossed into the *furnace*.

A *rustler* lived in a *penthouse* on top of a *mountain*. His specialty was the three-toed *sloth*. He would take his captive animals to a *tavern* where he would remove *fuzz* from their *glands*. Unfortunately, all this exposure to sloth fuzz caused him to grow *antlers*. So he gave up his profession and went to work in a *pencil* factory. As a precaution he also took a lot of *vitamin* E.

▲ **Figure 8.14**
The Narrative Method

In using the narrative method to recall a list of words, you would create a story using each of the words. The graph shows the superior recall of participants who used the narrative method in a study by Bower and Clark (1969).

link method

A mnemonic device that involves connecting, in sequence, images of items to be memorized, to make them easier to recall.

children to learn nouns (Krinsky & Krinsky, 1996). The effectiveness of the pegword method also was demonstrated in a study in which one group of undergraduates memorized a list of 10 daily tasks using the pegword method and a second group of undergraduates memorized the list without using it. When asked to recall the list 24 hours later, the group that used the pegword method performed significantly better than the other group (Harris & Blaiser, 1997).

The Link Method

Still another mnemonic device that makes use of imagery is the **link method,** which takes images of the items to be memorized and connects them in sequence. One version of the link method is the *narrative method* (see Figure 8.14), in which unrelated items are connected to one another in a story. In a study that showed its effectiveness, two groups of participants memorized 12 lists of 10 nouns. One group used the narrative method to memorize the nouns; the other group used ordinary mental rehearsal. Both groups showed nearly perfect immediate recall. But when later asked to recall all of the lists, the narrative group recalled an average of 93 percent of the words, whereas the mental rehearsal group recalled an average of only 13 percent (Bower & Clark, 1969). More recent research has replicated the effectiveness of this technique (Hill, Allen, & McWhorter, 1991).

Ironically, despite the usefulness of mnemonic devices, a survey of college professors found that memory researchers were no more likely than other professors to use formal mnemonic devices. Instead, memory researchers and other professors alike recommended that memory be improved by writing things down, by organizing material to be learned, or by rehearsing material to be remembered (Park, Smith, & Cavanaugh, 1990). Like physicians who smoke, memory researchers might not always practice what they preach.

STAYING ON TRACK: *Improving Your Memory*

1. What are some suggestions for improving your study habits?
2. How would you use the pegword method to recall lists of objects?

Answers to Staying on Track start on ST-4.

◆ THE BIOPSYCHOLOGY OF MEMORY

Though study habits and mnemonic devices depend on overt behavior and mental processes, they ultimately work by affecting the encoding, storage, and retrieval of memories in the brain. Today, research on the neuroanatomy and neurochemistry of memory is revealing more and more about its biological bases.

The Neuroanatomy of Memory

During the first half of the 20th century, psychologist Karl Lashley (1890–1958) carried out an ambitious program of research aimed at finding the sites where individual memories are stored in the brain. Lashley trained rats to run through mazes to obtain food rewards. He then destroyed small areas of their cerebral cortex and noted whether this made a difference in their maze performance. To Lashley's dismay, no matter what area he destroyed, the rats still negotiated the mazes, showing at most a slight decrement in performance. Lashley concluded he had failed in his lifelong search for the *memory trace* (or **engram**), which he had assumed was the basis of memories (Lashley, 1950).

engram
A memory trace in the brain.

The Engram

But many scientists remained undaunted by Lashley's pessimistic conclusion and continued to search for the engram. This persistence paid off decades later when a team of researchers located the site of a specific engram in studies of the sea snail *Aplysia* (Glanzman, 1995). This creature has relatively few neurons, making it a simpler subject of study than animals with complex brains. Researchers have identified a neuronal engram formed when an Aplysia is classically conditioned to withdraw its gills in response to the movement of water (Kandel & Schwartz, 1982). This (the conditioned response) occurs after several trials in which the movement of the water (the conditioned stimulus) has preceded an electric shock (the unconditioned stimulus) that automatically elicits gill withdrawal (the unconditioned response).

Evidence for the localization of engrams in more complex animals comes from research that has identified engrams in the cerebellum (see Chapter 3), a brain structure that plays a role in both memory and the maintenance of equilibrium. The researchers classically conditioned rabbits to blink in response to a tone. Presentations of the tone (the conditioned stimulus) were followed by puffs of air (the unconditioned stimulus) directed at the rabbit's

▲ **Karl Lashley (1890–1958)**
"I sometimes feel, in reviewing the evidence on the localization of the memory trace, that the necessary conclusion is that learning just is not possible."

eyes, which elicited blinking (the unconditioned response). After several pairings of the tone and puffs of air, the tone itself elicited blinking (the conditioned response). After conditioning, the researchers found that electrical stimulation of a tiny site in the cerebellum of the rabbit elicited the conditioned eye blink, while destruction of the site eliminated it—but not the unconditioned response. Thus, they had succeeded in locating an engram for a classically conditioned memory (Krupa, Thompson, & Thompson, 1993).

The Synapse

As for human memory, in 1894 Sigmund Freud and Santiago Ramón y Cajal independently speculated that learning produces changes in the efficiency of synaptic connections between neurons, and that these changes might be the basis of memory formation. Their speculation has been supported by research findings that the formation of memories is associated with synaptic changes, including increases in the number of dendritic branches and the number of dendritic spines (protuberances on the dendrites) at certain sites (Murphy & Regan, 1998). Recent research indicates that memory might also depend on the facilitation of neural impulses across synapses in the brain. The most widely studied phenomenon related to the facilitation of neural impulses is **long-term potentiation,** in which synaptic transmission of impulses is made more efficient by brief electrical stimulation of specific neural pathways. This is viewed as a possible basis for long-term memory, because long-term potentiation induced by specific experiences might likewise strengthen synaptic connections in specific pathways (Thompson, 2000).

The Hippocampus

Researchers such as Larry Squire who study long-term potentiation are particularly interested in the *hippocampus,* which lies deep within the temporal lobes and helps consolidate memories (Dudchenko & Eichenbaum, 1999). Figure 8.15 illustrates the location of the hippocampus and other brain structures important in memory, including the thalamus (Mumby, Cameli, & Glenn, 1999), the amygdala (Cahill & McGaugh, 1998), and the cerebellum (Green & Woodruff-Pak, 2000). The amygdala is particularly important in the formation of emotional memories (Adolphs, Tranel, & Denburg, 2000).

Long-term potentiation in the hippocampus apparently promotes the storage of new memories but is required for only a limited period of time after a learning experience. Evidence for this comes from animal studies in which the hippocampus is purposely damaged at varying times after learning. The longer the delay before hippocampal damage, the less effect it has on the storage of the new memories (Zola-Morgan & Squire, 1990). More evidence for the importance of the hippocampus in the formation of long-term memories comes from research on Alzheimer's disease, which is marked by degeneration of neural pathways from the hippocampus. Victims of Alzheimer's disease have a progressively more difficult time forming new long-term memories, particularly declarative memories (Salmon, Butters, & Chan, 1999). We know that the hippocampus plays a role in the consolidation of short-term memory into long-term memory, but the exact sites of memory storage are unknown—though research findings indicate that they involve the cerebral cortex (McClelland, McNaughton, & O'Reilly, 1995).

The hippocampus might provide an explanation for *infantile amnesia,* the inability to recall declarative memories from early childhood. A study of college students found that their earliest childhood memories were from age 2 for being hospitalized or the birth of a sibling, and from age 3 for the death of a family member or making a family move to a new home. If these events occurred earlier, the students were unable to recall them (Usher & Neisser, 1993). Perhaps infantile amnesia occurs because the hippocampus is too physically immature during infancy to consolidate short-term declarative memories into long-term ones. Note that we show perfectly good retention of procedural memories from infancy. Such memories, which involve skills, habits, and conditioned responses, do not seem to depend on the hippocampus.

The most celebrated single source of evidence for the role of the hippocampus in memory comes from the case study of a man known as "H. M.," who has been studied since the

▲ **Larry Squire**

"Studies of human amnesia and studies of an animal model of human amnesia in the monkey have identified the anatomical components of the brain system for memory in the medial temporal lobe and . . . this neural system consists of the hippocampus and adjacent anatomically related cortex."

long-term potentiation

A phenomenon related to the facilitation of neural impulses, in which synaptic transmission of impulses is made more efficient by brief electrical stimulation of specific neural pathways.

The Amnesia and Cognition Unit
www.mhhe.com/sdorow5

Chapter Eight

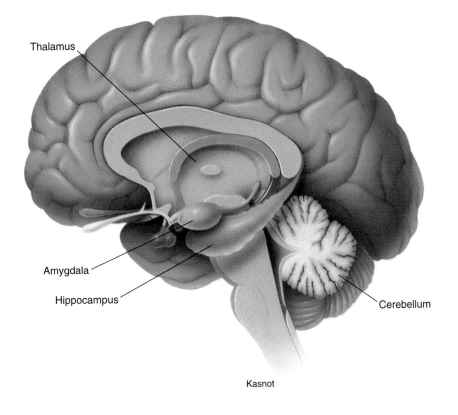

Thalamus

Amygdala

Hippocampus

Cerebellum

Kasnot

◀ **Figure 8.15**
Anatomy of Memory
The brain contains no memory center. Instead, memory depends on the integration of activity in several areas of the brain, including the thalamus, the amygdala, the cerebellum, and, especially, the hippocampus.

1950s by Brenda Milner of the Montreal Neurological Institute (Scoville & Milner, 1957) and more recently by Suzanne Corkin. H. M. has formed few new declarative memories since undergoing brain surgery in 1953, when he was 27 years old. The surgery, performed to relieve uncontrollable epileptic seizures, removed almost all of his hippocampus. As a result, H. M. developed anterograde amnesia, the inability to form new long-term declarative memories. Because he cannot recall events after 1953, he feels that each moment of his life is like waking from a dream, as short-term memories continually enter his consciousness and then fade away.

H. M. can recall memories from before 1953, but because of his inability to convert short-term memories into long-term memories, he will read the same magazine over and over, without realizing he has read it before. He will meet the same person on repeated occasions, yet have to be reintroduced each time. Though H. M. cannot form new declarative memories, he can form new procedural memories. For example, he has learned to play tennis since his surgery and has retained that procedural memory—even though he does not recall having taken lessons (Herbert, 1983). Moreover, after undergoing classical conditioning of an eyeblinking response, he retained this procedural memory for 2 years, yet he could not recall the experimenters, instructions, or methodology that had been used to condition the response—each of which involves declarative memory (Woodruff-Pak, 1993).

A few years ago Corkin used magnetic resonance imaging (MRI) to specify the extent of the damage H. M.'s surgery did to his brain. The MRI found that, in fact, he had lost much of his hippocampus in each temporal lobe, as well as most of his amygdala and portions of other structures (Corkin et al., 1997). Corkin is one of many neuroscientists who are using brain scanning techniques to refine our knowledge of the specific roles of brain structures in memory processes. For example, memory researchers using the PET scan have found that episodic memories are encoded by the front region and retrieved by the rear region of the hippocampus (Lepage, Habib, & Tulving, 1998). Other neuroscientists have found that the hippocampus is, indeed, involved in the formation of declarative, but not procedural, memories (Teng & Squire, 1999). Some neuroscientists also have provided evidence that the hippocampus is more involved in the formation of episodic than semantic memories (Tulving & Markowitsch, 1998).

The Neurochemistry of Memory

In 1959 James McConnell and his colleagues stunned the scientific world by reporting the results of an unusual experiment (McConnell, Jacobson, & Kimble, 1959). They had classically conditioned flatworms to contract their bodies in response to a light by repeatedly pairing presentations of the light with mild electric shocks. They then cut the flatworms in half. Because flatworms can regenerate themselves, both halves grew into whole flatworms. They then were retrained to contract in response to a light. As expected, the flatworms that had regenerated from the head (brain) ends showed memory savings—they took fewer trials to learn to respond to the light than had the original flatworms, which provided evidence that prior learning had been retained by the brain end. But, to the researchers' surprise, the flatworms that had regenerated from the tail ends learned to respond to the light as fast as those that had regenerated from the brain ends. This indicated that the memory of the classically conditioned response might have been encoded chemically and transported to the tail ends.

These findings led to a series of even more unusual experiments by a variety of researchers, which seemed to demonstrate that memories could be transferred from one animal to another (Setlow, 1997). In one study, rats were trained to run to a lighted compartment instead of to a dark compartment (which they would normally favor) by shocking them whenever they entered the dark compartment. When extracts from the brains of these rats were injected into mice, the mice spent less time in the dark compartment than they normally would have. The researchers later isolated the proteinlike substance apparently responsible for this effect, which they called *scotophobin,* meaning "fear of the dark" (Unger, Desiderio, & Parr, 1972).

As you might assume, the results of successful memory transfer studies created controversy, leading 23 researchers to write a letter to the influential journal *Science* in which they reported their failure to produce memory transfer in 18 studies in seven laboratories ("Memory Transfer," 1966). Failure to replicate memory transfer studies became the main reason to reject those that found positive results (Rilling, 1996). But a few years later a published review of the research literature concluded that many studies of flatworms, goldfish, chickens, mice, rats, and hamsters had demonstrated the transfer of memories (Smith, 1974). Yet, because of the failure of other researchers to replicate those studies and to identify a physiological basis for the chemical transfer of memories, interest in the study of memory transfer has waned.

Perhaps interest has declined in part because the very notion of memory transfer seems better suited to science fiction than to science. Scientists in all disciplines, including biology, chemistry, and physics, tend to avoid topics that appear to violate accepted scientific paradigms (see Chapter 2). In contrast with the conflict generated by research on the chemical transfer of memories, there is no controversy about whether certain other neurochemical processes play a role in memory. Neuroscientists have concentrated their efforts on studying the roles of the neurotransmitter *acetylcholine,* receptors for the amino acid *NMDA,* hormones such as *epinephrine,* and levels of blood *glucose* in memory.

Acetylcholine and Memory

The neurotransmitter that is most strongly implicated in memory processes is *acetylcholine* (Shulz et al., 2000). Acetylcholine might be more important in the formation of declarative memories than in the formation of procedural memories. This was implied by the results of a study in which one group of adult participants received a drug that blocked the effects of acetylcholine, while another group received a placebo (Nissen, Knopman, & Schacter, 1987). Those who received the active drug showed a reduced ability to recall and recognize stimuli presented previously (declarative memory) but no reduction in their ability to perform a reaction-time task they had learned previously (procedural memory).

But the most striking evidence of the role of acetylcholine in memory comes from studies of victims of Alzheimer's disease. Autopsies of victims of Alzheimer's disease show degeneration of acetylcholine neurons that connect the hippocampus to other brain areas (Crews, 1994). In fact, when normal participants are given drugs that inhibit the activity of acetylcholine neurons, they show memory losses similar to those seen in victims of Alzheimer's disease (McKinney & Richelson, 1984). Given this, it would seem logical that treatments aimed at elevating brain levels of acetylcholine would improve the ability of

▲ **Alzheimer's Disease**
Because victims of Alzheimer's disease suffer severe memory impairment, they may benefit from a "prosthetic environment." Strategically placed signs enable this woman to locate her personal belongings.

Alzheimer's victims to form new memories. One approach has been to administer *choline*—the dietary substance from which acetylcholine is synthesized and that is found in milk and eggs. Unfortunately, administration of high doses of choline has been only marginally effective in improving the cognitive functioning of Alzheimer's victims (Davidson et al., 1991). Evidently the degeneration of acetylcholine neurons prevents the additional choline from having a beneficial effect, just as adding gasoline to the empty tank of a car with no spark plugs would not make it more likely to start.

The Alzheimer Page
www.mhhe.com/sdorow5

NMDA and Memory

Perhaps the most exciting area of current research on the chemical basis of memory concerns N-methyl-D-aspartate (NMDA) receptors. NMDA is an amino acid that, when injected into an animal, binds to specific receptors in the hippocampus and enhances the efficiency of synaptic transmission along particular neural pathways. Blocking NMDA receptors in the amygdala prevents the formation of fear memories (Lee & Kim, 1998).

Consider a study in which rats learned to respond to a conditioned stimulus that had been paired with an unconditioned stimulus. A drug that blocked NMDA receptors prevented the formation of a conditioned response, but only if it was given during conditioning trials. If it was given after them, it had no effect. This supports the role of NMDA receptors in the acquisition, but not the performance, of a conditioned response (Kim et al., 1991). Additional support for the role of NMDA receptors in long-term memory consolidation comes from research on Alzheimer's disease. In the brains of victims of the disease, neural degeneration occurs in pathways rich in NMDA receptors (Maragos et al., 1987).

Hormones and Memory

Even hormones play a role in memory formation. The adrenal hormone *epinephrine* might have a special function in ensuring that we recall emotionally arousing events. For example, in one study participants were given injections of either an epinephrine blocker or a placebo. An hour later they watched a series of slides accompanied by a neutral or an emotional story. When tested 1 week later, participants who received the epinephrine blocker had poorer recall of the emotional story than of the neutral story (Cahill et al., 1994). Given such findings, perhaps, if flashbulb memories are a real phenomenon, epinephrine plays a role in their formation. The effectiveness of epinephrine in promoting memory formation is independent of its role in stimulating the release of glucose (a memory-enhancing nutrient) from the liver (Gamaro et al., 1997).

Glucose and Memory

Still another topic of research interest regarding the chemical basis of memory is the effect of glucose, simple blood sugar. One way in which glucose enhances memory is by increasing the synthesis of acetylcholine in the hippocampus (Messier et al., 1990). Injections of insulin, which reduces the level of blood glucose, have impaired memory in laboratory animals (Kopf & Baratti, 1996). There is a positive correlation between blood glucose levels and memory performance. For example, studies indicate that college students' performance on memory tasks is significantly improved by having a glucose drink but not by having a placebo drink (Martin & Benton, 1999). Dietary supplements of glucose might also improve memory in the elderly. In one study, adults aged 60 years or older received doses of either glucose or saccharin (a placebo) before or after memorizing a brief prose passage. Their recall of the passage was tested 24 hours later. Those who had ingested glucose, before or after memorizing the passage, showed significantly better recall than those who had ingested saccharin. Evidently, the glucose promoted the storage of the prose passages in memory (Manning, Parsons, & Gold, 1992). Nonetheless, students should not conclude that it would be wise to ingest massive amounts of glucose. On the contrary, moderate doses of glucose produce the greatest positive effect on memory (Parsons & Gold, 1992).

As you can see, research on the biopsychology of memory cannot be divorced from the psychology of memory. And biopsychological research promises to discover ways of improving memory. This would be a boon both to people with intact brains and to people with damaged brains.

1. How did researchers demonstrate the presence of a classically conditioned engram in the cerebellum?
2. How does the case of H. M. support the role of the hippocampus in the consolidation of long-term memories?
3. Why do researchers believe that acetylcholine plays an important role in long-term memory?

Answers to Staying on Track start on p. ST-4.

Chapter Summary

INFORMATION PROCESSING AND MEMORY

- Memory research has been influenced by the cognitive revolution in psychology.
- The most widely accepted model of memory assumes that memory processing involves the stages of sensory memory, short-term memory, and long-term memory.
- At each stage the processing of memories involves encoding, storage, retrieval, and forgetting.

SENSORY MEMORY

- Stimulation of sensory receptors produces sensory memories.
- Visual sensory memory is called iconic memory, and auditory sensory memory is called echoic memory.
- George Sperling found that iconic memory contains more information than had been commonly believed and that almost all of it fades within a second.

SHORT-TERM MEMORY

- Short-term memory is called working memory, because we use it to manipulate information provided by either sensory memory or long-term memory.
- We tend to encode information in short-term memory as sounds.
- We can store an average of seven chunks of information in short-term memory without rehearsal.
- Memories in short-term memory last about 20 seconds without rehearsal.
- Forgetting in short-term memory is caused by decay and displacement of information.

LONG-TERM MEMORY

- Memories stored in long-term memory are relatively permanent.
- Elaborative rehearsal of information in short-term memory is more likely to produce long-term memories than is maintenance rehearsal.
- Levels of processing theory assumes that information processed at deeper levels will be more firmly stored in long-term memory.
- Researchers distinguish between procedural, semantic, and episodic memories.
- Semantic-network theory assumes that memories are stored as nodes interconnected by links.
- Schema theory assumes that cognitive structures affect the encoding, storage, and retrieval of information related to them.

- Hermann Ebbinghaus began the formal study of memory by employing the method of savings.
- Ebbinghaus identified the serial-position effect and the forgetting curve.
- The theories of forgetting include decay theory, interference theory, motivation theory, and encoding-specificity theory.
- Encoding-specificity theory explains the phenomena of context-dependent memory and state-dependent memory.
- Research by Elizabeth Loftus and her colleagues has shown that eyewitness testimony often can be inaccurate.
- An important research finding is that eyewitnesses' confidence in their memories is not a good indicator of their accuracy.
- Another important finding is that leading questions can alter the recall of memories by eyewitnesses.
- Of special concern is the need for care in determining the accuracy of children's eyewitness testimony.

IMPROVING YOUR MEMORY

- You can improve your memory by practicing good study habits and by using mnemonic devices.
- A useful study technique is the SQ3R method, in which you survey, question, read, recite, and review.
- Overlearning and distributed practice are also useful techniques.
- Mnemonic devices are memory aids that organize material to make it easier to recall.
- The main mnemonic devices include acronyms, the method of loci, the pegword method, and the link method.

THE BIOPSYCHOLOGY OF MEMORY

- Though Karl Lashley failed in his search for the engram, researchers have discovered some of the anatomical and chemical bases of memory.
- The hippocampus plays an important role in converting short-term memories into long-term memories.
- Neurotransmitters, particularly acetylcholine, play crucial roles in memory formation.
- Research on NMDA receptors promises to contribute to our understanding of the physiological bases of memory.
- Hormones, especially epinephrine, might have a special function in the formation of emotional memories.
- Even blood glucose can facilitate memory formation.

Key Concepts

flashbulb memory 241
memory 242

INFORMATION PROCESSING AND MEMORY
encoding 242
forgetting 243
information-processing
   model 243
long-term memory 242
retrieval 243
sensory memory 242
short-term memory 242
storage 243

SENSORY MEMORY
echoic memory 245
iconic memory 243

SHORT-TERM MEMORY
maintenance rehearsal 246

LONG-TERM MEMORY
constructive recall 253
context-dependent memory 259
decay theory 255
declarative memory 249
elaborative rehearsal 248
encoding specificity 259
episodic memory 249
explicit memory 249
eyewitness testimony 261
forgetting curve 255
implicit memory 249
interference theory 256
levels of processing theory 248
method of savings 254

proactive interference 256
procedural memory 249
repression 257
retroactive interference 256
schema theory 250
semantic memory 249
semantic network theory 250
serial-position effect 253
state-dependent memory 260
tip-of-the-tongue
   phenomenon 259

IMPROVING YOUR MEMORY
acronym 267
distributed practice 266
link method 268
massed practice 266
method of loci 267

mnemonic devices 267
overlearning 266
pegword method 267
SQ3R method 265

THE BIOPSYCHOLOGY OF MEMORY
engram 269
long-term potentiation 270

Key Contributors

William James 242

INFORMATION PROCESSING AND MEMORY
Richard Atkinson 242
Richard Shiffrin 242

SENSORY MEMORY
George Sperling 244

SHORT-TERM MEMORY
George Miller 245
Lloyd and Margaret
   Peterson 246

LONG-TERM MEMORY
Frederick C. Bartlett 250
Fergus Craik and Robert
   Lockhart 248

Hermann Ebbinghaus 253
Sigmund Freud 257
Elizabeth Loftus 263
Ulric Neisser 253
Endel Tulving 249

THE BIOPSYCHOLOGY OF MEMORY
Suzanne Corkin 271

Karl Lashley 269
Brenda Milner 271
Larry Squire 270

Thought Questions

1. How would you use levels of processing theory to improve your memory for material you learn in your introductory psychology course?
2. How might the notion of state-dependent memory explain the difficulty depressed people often have in getting rid of their depressed mood?

3. Why should we be wary about the accuracy of eyewitness testimony?
4. What does the case of H. M. indicate about the role of the hippocampus in memory?

Possible Answers to Thought Questions start on p. PT-3.

OLC Preview

 For additional quizzing and a variety of interactive resources, visit the book's Online Learning Center at www.mhhe.com/sdorow5.

Thinking and Language

PABLO PICASSO
Buste D'Homme Au Chapeau

In 1800 a boy who appeared to be about 12 years old emerged from a forest near Aveyron, France, apparently having survived for many years without human contact (Hunter, 1993). The boy, named Victor by physician Jared Itard, became known as the "Wild Boy of Aveyron." Victor learned to use gestures and to comprehend speech and read and write on a basic level. Though Itard made an intensive effort to teach him to speak French, the only word Victor learned to say was *lait* ("milk"). Other similar reports also provide evidence of a **critical period** for language acquisition that extends from infancy to adolescence, during which language learning is optimal. If people are not exposed to a language until after childhood, they might never become proficient in speaking it (Grimshaw et al., 1998).

A more recent and well-documented case is that of an American girl named Genie, who had been raised in isolation. In 1970, 13-year-old Genie was discovered by welfare workers in a room in which her father had kept her restrained in a harness and away from social contact—and language—since infancy. He had communicated with her by barking and growling, and beat her whenever she made a sound. Genie was moved from her home and given intensive language training, but by 1981 she had acquired only a limited ability to speak. Like Victor, Genie might have been past her critical period for language acquisition when she was rescued (Pines, 1981).

critical period
A period in childhood when experience with language produces optimal language acquisition.

Secret of the Wild Child
www.mhhe.com/sdorow5

 **The Wild Boy of Aveyron**
Francois Truffaut's movie *The Wild Child* portrayed the case of Victor, the so-called Wild Boy of Aveyron. After living for years in the woods without human contact, Victor failed to develop normal language despite intensive efforts to teach him. This provided evidence that there might be a critical period for language development that ends before adolescence. The photo shows Victor learning to identify common objects.

Though the cases of Victor and Genie, as well as those of other children reared in social isolation (Kenneally et al., 1998), support the view there is a critical period for language acquisition, you may recall from Chapter 2 that it is unwise to generalize too freely from case studies. For example, some children who have lived for years in social isolation (such as Kaspar Hauser, who was discovered in Nuremberg, Germany, in 1828 at age 17) have been able to learn language even after reaching adolescence

(Simon, 1979). Perhaps other factors could account for the findings in the cases of Victor and Genie. For example, suppose Victor and Genie were born with brain disorders that interfered with their ability to acquire language. Even if they had been reared from birth in normal family settings, they still might have failed to acquire mature language.

Language acquisition and other topics related to how the brain processes information fall within the domain of *cognitive psychology*—perhaps the most influential field of psychology in recent years. In fact, the 1950s and 1960s saw a "cognitive revolution" in which strict behaviorism was countered by increased study of both the mind and behavior (Moore, 1996). This was inspired by an explosion of interest in the study of computer science, cognitive processes, and language acquisition.

Cognitive psychology combines William James's concern with mental processes and John B. Watson's concern with observable behavior. Cognitive psychologists accomplish this by using techniques that permit them to infer mental processes from overt behavior (Greenwood, 1999). Cognitive psychologists who are interested in the neurological bases of cognitive processes pursue their research interests in **cognitive neuroscience** (Sarter, Berntson, & Cacioppo, 1996). A cognitive neuroscientist might, for example, use PET scans or functional MRI to assess brain activity during the performance of cognitive tasks such as language, memory, creativity, or decision making.

cognitive psychology
The psychological viewpoint that favors the study of how the mind organizes perceptions, processes information, and interprets experiences.

cognitive neuroscience
The study of the neurological bases of cognitive processes.

◆ THINKING

thinking
The mental manipulation of words and images, as in concept formation, problem solving, and decision making.

Forming concepts. Solving problems. Being creative. Making decisions. Each of these processes depends on **thinking,** which is the purposeful mental manipulation of words and images. One of the basic cognitive processes is concept formation, the next topic in this chapter.

Concept Formation

concept
A category of objects, events, qualities, or relations that share certain features.

If a biology teacher asked you to hold a snake, you would be more willing to hold a nonpoisonous snake than a poisonous snake. Similarly, you might be willing to eat a nonpoisonous mushroom but not a poisonous mushroom. Your actions would show that you understood the concepts "poisonous" and "nonpoisonous." A **concept** represents a category of objects, events, qualities, or relations whose members share certain features; for example, poisonous objects share the ability to make you ill or kill you if you ingest them. Concepts enable us to respond to events appropriately and to store our memories in an organized way (Corter & Gluck, 1992).

Logical Concepts

logical concept
A concept formed by identifying the specific features possessed by all things that the concept applies to.

How do we form concepts? Consider the case of a **logical concept,** which is formed by identifying the specific features possessed by all things that the concept applies to. "Great Lakes state" is a logical concept. Each of its members has the features of being a state and bordering one or more of the Great Lakes. Logical concepts like "Great Lakes state" typically are not studied in the laboratory. Instead, laboratory studies generally use logical concepts created by the researcher. This lets the researcher exert more precise control over the definitions of particular concepts. An experiment on the formation of a logical concept might present participants with a series of symbols varying in size, shape, and color. The participants' task is to discover the features that define the concept. For example, a symbol might have to be large, square, and blue to be considered an example of the particular concept. Participants determine the features of the concept by testing hypotheses about its possible defining features on successive examples that are labeled as either positive or negative instances of it. A positive instance would include the defining features of the concept (in this case, large, square, and blue); a negative instance would lack at least one of the defining features (for example, large, square, and red). Try to identify the concept presented in Figure 9.1.

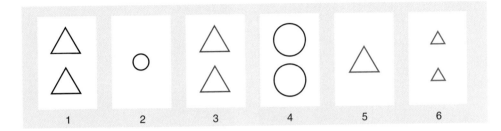

◀ **Figure 9.1**
Concept Formation

Laboratory studies of the formation of logical concepts present participants with a series of examples varying on specific features. The participant's task is to identify the features that compose the concept. The figures in this example can vary in size (small or large), shape (circle or triangle), color (black or magenta), or number (one or two). Given that the odd-numbered cards are members of the concept and the even-numbered cards are not, see how quickly you can identify the concept. (The answer appears at the bottom of this page.)

Natural Concepts

Is baseball a sport? How about table tennis? fishing? shuffleboard? golf? bridge? professional wrestling? You have an intuitive sense of how "sportlike" each of these activities is. "Sport" is an example of a **natural concept,** a concept formed through everyday experience rather than by testing hypotheses about particular features common to all members of the concept. We might be unable to identify the defining features of natural concepts such as "sport." That is, natural concepts have "fuzzy borders." Such concepts include "love" (Regan, Kocan, & Whitlock, 1998), "moral" (Hart, 1998), and "prejudice" (Inman & Baron, 1996).

The difficulty in defining natural concepts led psychologist Eleanor Rosch (1975) to propose that they are related to prototypes. A **prototype** is the best representative of a concept. According to Rosch, the more similarity between an example and a prototype, the more likely we are to consider the example to be a member of the concept represented by the prototype. A robin is a more prototypical bird than a penguin is. Both have wings and feathers and hatch from eggs, but only the robin can fly.

In regard to the concept "sport," baseball is more prototypical than golf, which in turn is more prototypical than bridge. The "fuzziness" of natural concepts can lead to arguments about whether a particular example is a member of a given concept (Medin, 1989). This was evident in 1988 in a series of letters to the editor of *Sporting News* either supporting or opposing its coverage of Wrestlemania, the Indianapolis 500, and the World Chess Championship. Supporters considered these to be examples of the concept "sport"; opponents did not.

Subsequent research has indicated that we do form concepts by creating prototypes of the relevant objects, events, qualities, or relations (Palmieri & Nosofsky, 2001). Influenced by the work of Rosch, psychologists have become more interested in conducting laboratory studies of natural concept formation. Consider the following study of the identification of artistic styles (Hartley & Homa, 1981). Participants who were naive about artistic styles were shown works by the painters Manet, Renoir, and Matisse (see Figure 9.2). Later, participants were shown more paintings by these artists and by other artists, without being told the identity of the artists. After viewing the second set of paintings, participants accurately matched particular paintings with the styles of the artists whose works they had seen in the first set of paintings. Participants used the first set to form concepts representing the styles of the three artists: a "Manet," a "Renoir," and a "Matisse." This could not be explained as an example of logical concept formation, because the participants were unable to identify a set of features that distinguished a Manet from a Renoir from a Matisse. Similar approaches to teaching artistic concepts have been successful in teaching artistically naïve persons how to comprehend works of art (Seifert, 1996).

Problem Solving

One of the most important uses of concepts is in **problem solving,** the thought process that enables us to overcome obstacles to reach goals. Suppose your car will not start. In looking for a solution to your problem, you might follow a series of steps commonly used in solving problems (Kramer & Bayern, 1984). First, you *identify the problem:* My car won't start.

natural concept
A concept, typically formed through everyday experience, whose members possess some, but not all, of a common set of features.

prototype
The best representative of a concept.

problem solving
The thought process by which an individual overcomes obstacles to reach a goal.

Answer to question in Figure 9.1: large triangles.

(a)   (b)   (c)

▲ **Figure 9.2**
Artistic Styles as Natural Concepts
We might be able to recognize an artistic style without necessarily being able to specify the characteristics that distinguish it from other styles. Thus, the concepts *(a)* "a Manet," *(b)* "a Renoir," and *(c)* "a Matisse" are natural concepts rather than logical concepts.

▲ **Wolfgang Köhler (1887–1967)**

"Association theorists know and recognize what one calls insight in man. . . . The only thing that follows for animal behavior is that, where it has an intelligent character, they will treat it in the same way; but not at all that the animal lacks that which is usually called insight in man."

Second, you *gather information* relevant to the problem: Am I out of gas? Is my battery dead? Are my ignition wires wet? Third, you *try a solution:* I'm not out of gas, so I'll dry off the wires. Finally, you *evaluate the result:* The car started, so the wires were, indeed, wet. If the solution fails to work, you might try a different one: Drying off the wires didn't work, so I'll try a jump start.

Approaches to Problem Solving

Problem solving commonly involves one of several strategies. A common strategy for solving problems is **trial and error,** which involves trying one possible solution after another until one works. But psychologists are more interested in studying *insight, algorithms,* and *heuristics.*

Insight. **Insight** is an approach to problem solving that depends on mental manipulation of information rather than on overt trial and error. It is characterized by an "Aha!" experience—the sudden realization of the solution to a problem (Ansburg, 2000)—as found in research by Janet Metcalfe. In a typical experiment, every 10 seconds Metcalfe asks participants working on either insight problems or noninsight problems (such as algebra) how close they feel they are to the correct solution. She has found that those working on insight problems are less accurate, indicating that solutions to noninsight problems are incremental and predictable, whereas solutions to insight problems are sudden and unpredictable (Metcalfe & Wiebe, 1987). Nonetheless, her interpretations of her research findings have been countered by Robert Weisberg (1992), who claims that insight is a fiction—what we call insight might seem sudden and unpredictable, but it is the product of the gradual accumulation of knowledge as one works on a problem.

Assuming that insight does exist, can animals use it to solve problems? The classic study of insight in animals was conducted by Gestalt psychologist Wolfgang Köhler (1887–1967) on the island of Tenerife in the Canary Islands during World War I. Köhler (1925) presented a chimpanzee named Sultan with bananas, hanging them from the top of Sultan's cage, well out of his reach (see Figure 9.3). But his cage also contained several crates. After trying fruitlessly to reach the bananas by jumping, Sultan suddenly hit upon the solution. He piled the crates on top of one another, quickly climbed to the top, and grabbed a banana—just as the shaky structure came tumbling down.

The assumption that Sultan displayed insight was challenged more than a half century later by several behaviorists (Epstein et al., 1984). In a tongue-in-cheek study analogous to the one involving Sultan, they used food rewards to train a pigeon to first perform the separate acts of moving a tiny box, standing on the box, and pecking a plastic, miniature banana. When later confronted with the banana hanging out of reach from the top of its cage, the pigeon at first seemed confused but then suddenly moved the box under the banana, climbed on the box, and pecked at the banana to get a food reward (see Figure 9.4). According to the researchers, if a pigeon can perform supposedly insightful behavior, then perhaps insight in animals—and even in people—is no more than the chaining together of previously rewarded behaviors.

trial and error
An approach to problem solving in which the individual tries one possible solution after another until one works.

insight
An approach to problem solving that depends on mental manipulation of information rather than overt trial and error, and produces sudden solutions to problems.

Wolfgang Köhler
www.mhhe.com/sdorow5

▲ **Figure 9.3**
Insight in Apes
Köhler (1925) demonstrated that chimpanzees can use insight to solve problems. The chimpanzee Sultan found a way to reach bananas hanging out of reach without engaging in mere trial-and-error behavior.

▲ **Figure 9.4**
Insight in a Pigeon?
This pigeon was trained to perform the separate actions of pushing a box to a designated location and climbing on the box to peck a plastic banana. When presented with the box and the banana in separate locations, the pigeon pushed the box under the banana, climbed on the box, and pecked the banana. This showed that an apparent instance of insight might be no more than performing a chain of previously learned behaviors.

algorithm

A problem-solving rule or procedure that, when followed step by step, assures that a correct solution will be found.

heuristic

A general principle that guides problem solving, though it does not guarantee a correct solution.

Algorithms and Heuristics. If you use the formula *length times width,* you will obtain the area of a rectangle. A mathematical formula is an example of a problem-solving strategy called an algorithm. An **algorithm** is a rule that, when followed step by step, assures that a solution to a problem will be found. Many physicians use algorithms to diagnose diseases by noting specific combinations of symptoms and personal characteristics of patients (Hatzichristou, Bertero, & Goldstein, 1994).

Like trial and error, an algorithm can be an inefficient means of finding the solution to a problem. To appreciate this, imagine that you are in the middle of a chess game. An algorithm for finding your best move would require tracing all possible sequences of moves from the current position. Because an average of 35 different moves can be made from any single position in the middle of a chess game, you would need literally millions of years to find the best move by tracing all possible sequences of moves. Even using an algorithm to follow all possible sequences of just the next 3 moves in the middle of a chess game would require the analysis of an average of 1.8 billion moves (Waltz, 1982). Because a formal chess match has a typical time limit of 5 hours, even world chess champions do not rely on algorithms. Instead, they rely on problem-solving strategies called heuristics.

A **heuristic** is a general principle that guides problem solving in everyday life and in scientific fields, such as chemistry (Seroussi, 1995). Unlike an algorithm, a heuristic does not guarantee a solution. But a heuristic can be more efficient, because it rules out many useless alternatives before they are even attempted. A chess player might rely on heuristics, such as trying to control the center of the board or trading weaker pieces for stronger ones. A person putting together a jigsaw puzzle would rely on heuristics by sorting the pieces by color and working on the edges of the puzzle first.

Obstacles to Problem Solving

Researchers who study problem solving are interested in obstacles that interfere with it. Two of the major obstacles are *mental sets* and *functional fixedness.*

Mental Sets. Before reading on, try to solve the six problems presented in Figure 9.5, in which you must use three jars to measure out exact amounts of water. If you are like most research participants, you could easily solve the first five problems but ran into difficulty with the sixth. In an early study using the water-jar problem, participants quickly realized that the solution to the first problem was to fill jar B, pour enough water from it to fill jar A, and then pour enough water from jar B to fill jar C twice. This left the desired amount in jar B. Participants then found that the same strategy worked for each of the next four problems. But when they reached the sixth problem, two-thirds of them were unable to solve it. Those who failed to solve it had developed a strategy that was effective in solving previous examples but made the simple solution to problem 6 difficult to discover. In contrast, of

▶ **Figure 9.5**
Mental Sets

Luchins (1946) asked participants to use jars with the capacities shown in columns A, B, and C to obtain the amounts required in the right-hand column. The first five problems led participants to overlook a simpler solution in the sixth problem.

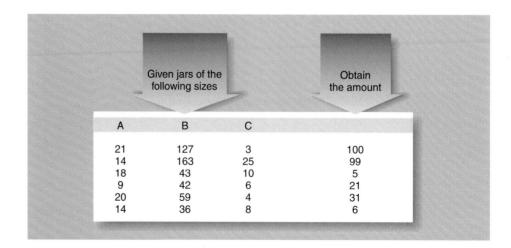

Given jars of the following sizes			Obtain the amount
A	B	C	
21	127	3	100
14	163	25	99
18	43	10	5
9	42	6	21
20	59	4	31
14	36	8	6

Chapter Nine

participants who were asked to solve only the sixth problem, few had difficulty discovering the simple solution: fill jar A and pour enough water from it to fill jar C, leaving the desired amount in jar A (Luchins, 1946).

This study demonstrated that we sometimes are hindered by a **mental set,** a problem-solving strategy that has succeeded in the past but can interfere with solving a problem that requires a new strategy. In one study, expert computer programmers and novice computer programmers were given a programming problem that could be solved by using a simple programming strategy that is more often used by novices. The results showed that novices were more likely to solve the problem, because the experts tried to use a more sophisticated, but ineffective, strategy that they had adopted during their careers as computer programmers. In other words, the experts had developed a mental set that blinded them to the simpler solution (Adelson, 1984). You can overcome a mental set by making assumptions opposite to those you normally make. This approach might have helped the expert computer programmers who were unable to solve the problem that the novices were able to solve.

Functional Fixedness. Another way in which past experience can impede our ability to solve problems is through **functional fixedness,** the inability to realize that a problem can be solved by using a familiar object in an unusual way. The role of functional fixedness in problem solving was demonstrated in a classic study (Maier, 1931) in which each participant was asked to perform the simple task of tying together two long strings hanging from a ceiling. The problem was that the two strings were too far apart for the participant to grasp them both at the same time. The room contained a variety of objects, including a table, a chair, an extension cord, and a pair of pliers.

Participants were given 10 minutes to solve the problem. Each time a participant identified a solution, the experimenter said, "Now do it a different way." One solution was to tie the extension cord to one string, grasp the other string, pull the strings toward one another, and then tie them together. The experimenter was interested in one particular solution. Participants who discovered that solution tied the pliers to one of the strings and started it swinging like a pendulum. They then grabbed the other string, walked toward the swinging pliers, and tied the two strings together. To discover that solution, the participants had to realize that the pliers could be used as a weight and not solely as a tool. Only 39.3 percent of the participants discovered this solution on their own. More participants discovered it when the experimenter provided a hint by subtly setting one of the strings in motion.

As with mental sets, functional fixedness can be overcome. One of the best ways is to change or ignore the names of familiar objects. In a study that used this technique, participants were given a bulb, some wire, a switch, a wrench, and batteries. Participants were told to create a circuit that would light the bulb, even though they had too little wire to complete the circuit. The solution was to use the wrench to complete it. Participants who were told to use nonsense names such as *jod* to refer to the wrench were more likely to solve the problem than were participants who referred to it as a "wrench" (Glucksberg & Danks, 1968). By using nonsense words to refer to the wrench, participants were less likely to think of it as just a mechanical tool.

STAYING ON TRACK: *Concept Formation and Problem Solving*

1. What is the difference between a logical concept and a natural concept?
2. Why might heuristics be both superior and inferior to algorithms?
3. How do mental sets hamper problem solving in everyday life?

Answers to Staying on Track start on ST-4.

Creativity

What is creativity? Like other natural concepts, creativity cannot be defined by a specific set of features—that is, it has "fuzzy borders." Psychologists generally define **creativity** as a form of problem solving characterized by finding solutions that are novel, as well as useful

▲ **A Picasso of Pachydermia?**

This elephant produces original paintings. But are they examples of creativity?

Creativity Web
www.mhhe.com/sdorow5

convergent thinking
The cognitive process that focuses on finding conventional solutions to problems.

divergent thinking
The cognitive process by which an individual freely considers a variety of potential solutions to artistic, literary, scientific, or practical problems.

or socially valued, whether practical, artistic, or scientific. Said the French mathematician Henri Poincaré (1948, p. 16), "To create consists precisely in not making useless combinations and in making those which are useful and which are only a small minority. Invention is discernment, choice." Thus, if you gave a monkey a canvas, a paintbrush, and a pallet of paint, it might produce novel paintings, but they would not be considered examples of creativity.

Characteristics of Creative People

What characteristics are associated with creativity? Though creative people tend to have above-average intelligence, you do not have to be a genius to be highly creative. A study of children found a positive correlation between their intelligence and their creativity up to an IQ of 120 (above average but not in the genius range), but no relationship beyond that level of intelligence (Fuchs-Beauchamp, Karnes, & Johnson, 1993).

Creative people also tend to exhibit certain personality characteristics. Creative children engage in more imaginative pretend play (Russ, Robins, & Christiano, 1999). Creative people also tend to have a wide range of interests, be open to new experiences, and be nonconformists and unconventional (Simonton, 1999). And creative people tend to be more creative when they are engaged in creative behavior for its own sake (Ruscio, Whitney, & Amabile, 1998). To read about this, see the Psychology Versus Common Sense feature.

Creativity and the Social-Cultural Environment

Psychologists also have studied the extent to which socialization and culture influence the development and expression of creativity. For example, cultures differ in the extent to which they encourage the expression of individuality and originality. One study compared musical innovation among dancers in four cultures. In two cultures, Samoan and Balinese, dancers are expected to emphasize their individuality as a form of artistic expression. In two other cultures, Japanese and Omaha Indian, individual expression is discouraged in favor of perfecting traditional form and style. Musical innovation was found to be more common in the Samoan and Balinese cultures (Colligan, 1983). It is important to remember, though, there are cultural differences in how creativity is conceptualized, the extent to which creativity is encouraged, and, as in this instance, the nature of artistic and creative processes (Lubart, 1999).

Gender roles also can influence the expression of creativity. Omar Khaleefa and his colleagues administered a battery of Western tests of individual creativity to a sample of Sudanese women and men. In this study, men outperformed women on two of the four tests. The researchers attributed these results to the fact that women in traditional Sudanese culture have fewer opportunities for freedom and independence than men have (Khaleefa, Erdos, & Ashria, 1996). This interpretation is supported by the results of a subsequent study, which found that Sudanese men and women who attended traditional Islamic schools scored lower on Western measures of creativity than those who attended nontraditional schools (Khaleefa, Erdos, & Ashria, 1997).

Creativity and Divergent Thinking

How many ways can you use a brick? If you could think of only such uses as "to build a house" or "to build a fireplace," you would exhibit convergent thinking. According to Guilford, **convergent thinking** focuses on finding conventional "correct" solutions to problems. If you also thought of less conventional "correct" uses for a brick, such as "to prop open a door" or "to save water by putting it in a toilet tank," you would be engaging in divergent thinking. **Divergent thinking,** a hallmark of creativity (Guilford, 1984), involves freely considering a variety of potential solutions to artistic, literary, scientific, or practical problems. One way of inducing divergent thinking is brainstorming, in which thinkers are encouraged to conjure up as many solutions as possible to a problem, though there is no guarantee that the many solutions produced by brainstorming will be superior to those produced by more focused attempts at problem solving (Simonton, 2000).

To further appreciate the notion of divergent thinking, consider the Remote Associates Test created by Sarnoff Mednick (1962), which presents participants with sets of three apparently unrelated words. For each set, participants are asked to find a fourth word that is related to the other three. To do so, they must use divergent thinking. For example, what word would

Can Rewarding Creative Behavior Inhibit Creativity?

Common sense might make us presume that we can encourage people to become more creative by rewarding them when they engage in creative activities. But this common-sense bit of wisdom has been called into question by scientific research on creativity. According to creativity researcher Teresa Amabile (1989), creative people are more motivated by their intrinsic interest in creative tasks than by extrinsic factors, such as fame, money, or approval. In fact, when people are presented with extrinsic reasons for performing intrinsically interesting creative tasks, they can lose their motivation to perform them. A classic study provided further evidence of this (Amabile, 1985).

Participants were recruited through advertisements asking for writers to participate in a study of people's reasons for writing. Most of the respondents were undergraduate or graduate students in English or creative writing. All of the participants were asked to write two brief poems on designated themes (the first on snow, and the second on laughter). Each participant was assigned to one of three groups. After the participants wrote the first poem, one group completed a questionnaire that focused on intrinsic reasons for writing, such as the opportunity for self-expression, while a second group completed a questionnaire that focused on extrinsic reasons for writing, such as gaining public recognition. The third group served as a control group and was not given a questionnaire.

Twelve experienced poets judged the creativity of the poems on a 40-point scale. When the first poems were judged for their creativity, the three groups did not differ. However, when the second poems were judged for their creativity, the poems written by the group exposed to the questionnaire that focused on extrinsic reasons for writing were judged less creative than those written by the other two groups; the intrinsic-reasons group and the control group showed no change in creativity from the first poem to the second, but the extrinsic-reasons group showed a significant decrease.

Thus, though concentrating on intrinsic reasons for creative writing did not improve creativity, concentrating on extrinsic reasons for creativity impaired it. Even the mere expectation that one's performance will be evaluated will hamper creativity (Joussemet & Koestner, 1999). Perhaps, given students who enjoy writing, teachers should avoid pointing out the extrinsic advantages of it, such as obtaining a better job or getting accepted into graduate school. Chapter 11 discusses theories that explain the negative effects of extrinsic motivation.

◀ **Teresa Amabile**
"Intrinsic motivation is conducive to creativity, while extrinsic motivation is detrimental."

Psychology and the Arts
www.mhhe.com/sdorow5

you choose to associate with the words *piano, record,* and *baseball?* The word *player* would be one possibility. Try testing your ability to find remote associates for the items in Table 9.1. Performance on tests of divergent thinking correlates moderately highly with creative behavior (Runco, 1993). But creative ability in one area, such as writing poetry, might not correlate highly with creativity in another, such as writing stories. That is, divergent thinking might not be a general trait, but might instead be limited to specific creative domains. This was illustrated in a study of seventh-graders in which half were given divergent-thinking training in writing poetry and half were not. The students later were asked to write poems

Table 9.1	The Remote Associates Test

Items like these are included in the Remote Associates Test (Mednick, 1962). For each of the items, find a word that is associated with all three of the given words.

	Given Words			Your Word?
1. Worker	Boiled	Core		_____
2. York	World	Born		_____
3. Base	Foot	Basket		_____
4. Range	Climber	Grown		_____

Possible responses: (1) hard; (2) new; (3) ball; (4) mountain

Source: Data from S. A. Mednick, "The Associative Basis of the Creative Process" in *Psychological Review 69:* 220–232, American Psychological Association, 1962.

and short stories. Experts judged that the students who had received divergent-thinking training wrote more creative poetry than the ones who had not received special training. Moreover, the trained students showed greater creativity in their poems than in their short stories. This indicates that training in divergent thinking might affect performance on targeted tasks without affecting performance on presumably related tasks (Baer, 1996).

Divergent thinking can be cultivated. This idea is not lost on industrial leaders, many of whom have their employees attend seminars so they can learn to think more creatively by engaging in divergent thinking. Divergent thinking also is promoted by positive emotional states (Vosburg, 1998). When you are angry, anxious, or depressed, you are more likely to engage in convergent thinking. Thus, teachers who evoke positive emotions in their students, and managers who evoke positive emotions in their employees, can encourage creative academic or vocational problem solving.

STAYING ON TRACK: *Creativity*

1. What are some personal characteristics associated with creativity?
2. How did Amabile's study demonstrate that extrinsic rewards can impair creativity?

Answers to Staying on Track start on p. ST-4.

Decision Making

Each of our days is filled with decisions. They can be minor, such as deciding whether to take along a raincoat when leaving home, or major, such as deciding which college to attend. **Decision making** is a form of problem solving in which we try to make the best choice from among alternative courses of action to produce a desired outcome. Studies in the 1970s found that decision making also is subject to biases that can keep us from making objective decisions. Biases in decision making have been studied most extensively by cognitive psychologists Amos Tversky and Daniel Kahneman. They have found that our decision making is often biased by our reliance on heuristics (Kahneman, 1991).

decision making

A form of problem solving in which one tries to make the best choice from among alternative judgments or courses of action.

Heuristics in Decision Making

Kahneman and Tversky have identified several kinds of heuristics involved in decision making. Two that have been widely studied are the *representativeness heuristic* and the *availability heuristic.*

The Representativeness Heuristic. In using the **representativeness heuristic,** we assume that a small sample is representative of its population (Kahneman & Tversky, 1973). For example, we use the representativeness heuristic when we eat at a fast-food restaurant and

representativeness heuristic

In decision making, the assumption that a small sample is representative of its population.

assume that other restaurants in the restaurant chain will be that good (or bad). Because a sample might not accurately represent its population, the use of the representativeness heuristic does not guarantee that our decisions will be correct ones.

Consider a study of the effect of the representativeness heuristic in regard to the "hot hand" in basketball, in which a player makes several baskets in a row (Gilovich, Vallone, & Tversky, 1985). The study was prompted by a survey, which found that fans and players tend to believe that during a basketball game the chance of making a basket is greater following a made basket than following a miss. The researchers analyzed shooting records of the Boston Celtics and the Philadelphia 76ers. The results indicated that the chance of making a basket after a made basket was no greater than the chance following a miss. Apparently, fans and players alike incorrectly assume that brief runs of successful shooting are representative of a more general tendency to shoot well.

The Availability Heuristic. To appreciate another kind of heuristic, answer the following question: In English, is the letter *k* more likely to be the first letter or the third letter of a word? Though the letter *k* is more likely to be the third letter, most people decide that it is more likely to be the first. This is explained by what Tversky and Kahneman (1973) call the **availability heuristic,** which is the tendency to estimate the probability of an event by how easily instances of it come to mind. The more easily an instance comes to mind, the more probable we assume the event will be. But the ease with which instances come to mind might not reflect their actual probability. Instead, instances might come to mind because they are vivid, recent, or important. Thus, because it is easier to recall words that begin with *k*, such as *kick* or *kiss,* than words that have *k* as their third letter, such as *make* or *hike,* we conclude that more words have *k* as their first letter than as their third letter.

In a study of the impact of the availability heuristic, undergraduates were given lists containing equal numbers of male and female names of famous people and nonfamous people and then were asked to estimate whether the lists contained more male or female names. The students' estimates depended on whether the male names or the female names were more famous. Apparently, the availability heuristic affected the students' judgment of the relative number of names—even though the number of male and female names was always equal (McKelvie, 1997). A study in which participants estimated the prevalence of cheating by welfare recipients showed the practical effect of the availability heuristic. Participants who first read a vivid case of welfare cheating overestimated its prevalence (Hamill, Decamp Wilson, & Nisbett, 1980). This reflects our tendency to respond to rare but vivid news reports of instances of welfare recipients living in luxurious comfort by overestimating the likelihood of welfare cheating.

Framing Effects in Decision Making

Consider the following statements: "Dr. Jones fails 10 percent of his students" and "Dr. Jones passes 90 percent of his students." Though both statements report the same reality, you might be more inclined to enroll in Dr. Jones's course after hearing the second comment than you would be after hearing the first. This is an example of what Kahneman and Tversky call **framing effects,** biases introduced in the decision-making process by presenting a situation in a particular manner. Judges, lawyers, and prosecutors are aware of framing effects in the form of "leading questions," which can bias jury decisions. Research also indicates that the manner in which television news coverage portrays social protests can create powerful framing effects that influence viewer decisions about the merits of the protesters' causes (McLeod & Detenber, 1999).

Framing effects also influence our everyday decisions. In one study (Levin, Schnittjer, & Thee, 1988), undergraduates rated the incidence of cheating at their school higher when told that "65 percent of students had cheated at some time in their college career" than when told that "35 percent of the students had never cheated." The undergraduates were also more likely to rate a medical treatment as more effective, and were more apt to recommend it to others, when they were told it had a "50 percent success rate" than when told it had a "50 percent failure rate." A similar study found that undergraduates rated meat more highly when it was labeled "75 percent lean" than when it was labeled "25 percent fat" (Donovan & Jalleh,

▲ **Amos Tversky and Daniel Kahneman**

"Most people are . . . very sensitive to the difference between certainty and high probability and relatively insensitive to intermediate gradations of probability."

availability heuristic
In decision making, the tendency to estimate the probability of an event by how easily relevant instances of it come to mind.

framing effects
In decision making, biases introduced into the decision-making process by presenting an issue or situation in a certain manner.

1999). Note that in each study both statements present the same fact and differ only in how they frame the information. A recent meta-analysis of 136 studies found that the overall effect size of framing on decision making to be small to moderate (Kuehberger, 1998).

Artificial Intelligence

Almost 200 years ago a Hungarian inventor named Wolfgang von Kempelen toured Europe with the Maezel Chess Automaton, a chess-playing machine. The Automaton defeated almost all the people who dared play against it. One of its admirers was the noted American author Edgar Allen Poe, who wrote an essay speculating—incorrectly—on how it worked. After years of defeating one challenger after another, the Automaton's mechanism was finally revealed. Inside it was a legless Polish army officer named Worouski, who was a master chess player ("Program Power," 1981).

During the past five decades, computer scientists have developed computer programs that actually can play chess. Computer chess programs are the offshoot of studies in **artificial intelligence (AI),** a field founded by Nobel Prize winner Herbert Simon, which integrates computer science and cognitive psychology. Those who study AI try to simulate or improve on human thinking by using computer programs. For example, computer scientists have developed a program that answers political questions as though it were either a politically liberal or a politically conservative person (Abelson, 1981) and a program that combines vast amounts of data to help officials make decisions on how to protect the environment (Cortes et al., 2000).

Not long ago, AI authorities noted that computer chess programs would be unable to defeat human world chess champions until AI researchers were able to develop advanced chess programs that used both serial and parallel information processing (Kurzweil, 1985). This finally took place in 1997 when the computer program *Deep Blue* defeated world chess champion Gary Kasparov in a formal chess match. *Deep Blue* used 500 processors working in parallel and combining their outputs to select the best moves.

STAYING ON TRACK: *Decision Making and Artificial Intelligence*

1. What is the availability heuristic?
2. How does the framing of "leading questions" influence decision making?
3. How do studies in artificial intelligence apply computer programming to human thinking?

Answers to Staying on Track start on p. ST-4.

◆ LANGUAGE

Arguing about politics. Reading a newspaper. Using sign language. Each of these is made possible by **language,** a formal system of communication involving symbols—whether spoken, written, or gestured—and rules for combining them. In using language, we rely on spoken symbols to communicate through speech, written symbols to communicate through writing, and gestured symbols to communicate through sign language. We use language to communicate with other people, to store and retrieve memories, and to plan for the future.

But what makes a form of communication "language"? The world's several thousand languages share three characteristics: *semanticity, generativity,* and *displacement.* **Semanticity** is the conveying of the thoughts of the communicator in a meaningful way to those who understand the language. For example, you know that *anti-* at the beginning of a word means being against something and *-ed* at the end of a word means past action.

Generativity is the combining of language symbols in novel ways, without being limited to a fixed number of combinations. In fact, each day you probably say or write things that have never been said or written by anyone before. This generativity of language accounts for baby talk, rap music, Brooklynese, and the works of Shakespeare.

artificial intelligence (AI)
The field that integrates computer science and cognitive psychology in studying information processing through the design of computer programs that appear to exhibit intelligence.

language
A formal system of communication involving symbols—whether spoken, written, or gestured—and rules for combining them.

semanticity
The characteristic of language marked by the use of symbols to convey thoughts in a meaningful way.

generativity
The characteristic of language marked by the ability to combine words in novel, meaningful ways.

▲ **A Computer Chess Champion**
The human world chess champion Gary Kasparov is shown with *Deep Blue,* a computer that, because of its powerful chess program, allows it to consider 400 million possible moves each second. In 1997, Deep Blue defeated Kasparov in a formal six-game match and became the first computer chess player to overcome a human world champion.

Displacement is the use of language to refer to objects and events that are not present. The objects and events can be in another place or in the past or future. Thus, you can talk about someone in China, your fifth birthday party, or who will win the World Series next year.

Language is only one form of communication. Many animals, ourselves included, can communicate without using language. For instance, a pet dog can indicate when it is hungry by pacing around its food dish, or indicate when it wants to go out by scratching at the door. But is the dog using language? No, because the only characteristic of language that the dog is displaying is semanticity. Dogs do not exhibit generativity or displacement in their communications.

Consider also how monkeys use different alarm calls to signal the presence of particular kinds of predators. In one study, researchers presented Vervet monkeys with tape recordings of alarm calls that signified the presence of an eagle, a boa constrictor, or a leopard. The monkeys responded to eagle alarms by looking up, to boa constrictor alarms by looking down, and to leopard alarms by climbing up into trees (Seyfarth, Cheney, & Marler, 1980). Though monkeys use alarm calls to communicate, they do not use true language. Their calls have semanticity because they communicate the presence of a particular kind of predator, but they lack generativity and displacement. Monkeys neither combine their calls in novel ways nor use them to refer to animals that are not present. In contrast to dogs and monkeys, human beings use true language.

The Structure of Language

English and all other languages have structures governed by rules known as **grammar.** The components of grammar include *phonology, syntax,* and *semantics.*

Phonology

All spoken languages are composed of **phonemes**—the basic sounds of a language. The study of phonemes is called **phonology.** Languages use as few as 20 and as many as 80 phonemes. English contains about 40—the number varies with the dialect. Each phoneme is represented by either a letter (such as the *o* sound in *go*) or a combination of letters (such as the *sh* sound in *should*). Words are combinations of phonemes, and each language permits only certain combinations. A native speaker of English would realize the combination of phonemes in *cogerite* forms an acceptable word in English even though there is no such word. That person would also realize the combination of phonemes in *klputng* does not form an acceptable word in English.

One language might not include all the phonemes found in another language, and people learning to speak a foreign language might have more difficulty pronouncing the phonemes in the foreign language that are not in their native language. This could be due to differences in how phonemes are processed by the brain and early childhood experience with language. Catherine Best and Robert Avery investigated American and African adults' perception of *click consonants*—sounds produced by creating suction in the mouth and then releasing with the tongue, producing a sound that is similar to a "tsk" with an abrupt stop. English speakers process clicks acoustically, that is as nonspeech sounds. In some African languages clicks have linguistic significance, and are perceived as consonants. Participants in their study were native speakers of English and Zulu and Xhosa, two African tone languages with click consonants. The experimental task involved identifying and matching click consonants and nonsense syllables. Results indicated that native Zulu and Xhosa speakers demonstrated more accurate performance on the experimental task, a finding the researchers attributed to the fact that African tone language speakers processed the clicks linguistically rather than acoustically (Best & Avery, 2000).

Individual phonemes and combinations of phonemes form **morphemes,** the smallest meaningful units of language. Words are composed of one or more morphemes. For example, the word *book* is composed of a single morpheme. In contrast, the word *books* is composed of two morphemes: *book,* which refers to an object, and *-s,* which indicates the plural of a word. One of the common morphemes that affect the meaning of words is the *-ing* suffix,

grammar
The set of rules that governs the proper use and combination of language symbols.

phoneme
The smallest unit of sound in a language.

phonology
The study of the sounds that compose languages.

morpheme
The smallest meaningful unit of language.

▲ **Language**
The ability of human beings to use language makes us much more flexible than any other animal in communicating with one another. We can communicate complex thoughts through written language or sign language, as well as spoken language.

syntax

The rules that govern the acceptable arrangement of words in phrases and sentences.

semantics

The study of how language conveys meaning.

deep structure

The underlying meaning of a statement.

surface structure

The word arrangements used to express thoughts.

transformational grammar

The rules by which languages generate surface structures from deep structures, and deep structures from surface structures.

pragmatics

The relationship between language and its social context.

which indicates ongoing action. Note that the 40 or so phonemes in English build more than 100,000 morphemes, which in turn build almost 500,000 words. Using these words, we can create a virtually infinite number of sentences. This shows that one of the outstanding characteristics of language is, indeed, its generativity.

Syntax

In addition to rules that govern the acceptable combinations of sounds in words, languages have **syntax**—rules that govern the acceptable arrangement of words in phrases and sentences. Poor readers commonly have difficulty comprehending sentences with complex syntax (Nation & Snowling, 2000).

Because you know English syntax, you would say "She ate the ice cream" but not "She the ice cream ate" (though poets do have a "license" to violate normal syntax). And syntax varies from one language to another. The English sentence *John hit Bill* would be translated into its Japanese equivalent as *John Bill hit.* This is because the normal order of the verb and the object in Japanese is the opposite of their normal order in English (Gliedman, 1983). As for adjectives, in English they usually precede the nouns they modify, whereas in Spanish, adjectives usually follow the nouns they modify. The English phrase *the red book* would be *el libro rojo* in Spanish. Therefore, a Spanish-speaking person learning English might say "the book red," while an English-speaking person learning Spanish might say "el rojo libro."

Semantics

Not only must words be arranged appropriately in phrases and sentences, they must be meaningful. The study of how language conveys meaning is called **semantics.** Psycholinguist Noam Chomsky has been intrigued by our ability to convey the same meaning through different phrases and sentences. Consider the sentences *The boy fed the horse* and *The horse was fed by the boy.* Both express the same meaning, but they use different syntax. Moreover, the meaning expressed by these sentences can be expressed in French, Chinese, Swahili, and so on, though the sentences used to express it in those languages would be different from the English sentences.

To explain this ability to express the same meaning using different phrases or different languages, Chomsky distinguishes between a language's deep structure and its surface structure. The **deep structure** is the underlying meaning of a statement; the **surface structure** is the word arrangements that express the underlying meaning. Chomsky calls the rules by which languages generate surface structures from deep structures, and deep structures from surface structures, **transformational grammar.** In terms of transformational grammar, language comprehension involves transforming the surface structure, which is the verbal message, into its deep structure, which is its meaning. Thus, the sentences *The boy fed the horse* and *The horse was fed by the boy* are transformed into the same deep structure, or meaning. Our ability to discern the deep structure of literary works, for example, lets us appreciate the motives of the main characters (Carroll, 1999).

The meaning of a statement depends not only on its words and their arrangement but on the social context in which the statement is made (Paradis, 1998). The branch of semantics that is concerned with the relationship between language and its social context is called **pragmatics.**

To appreciate the relationship between language and its social context, consider the following embarrassing incident recounted by Elisabeth Kübler-Ross, the prominent death-and-dying researcher (see Chapter 4). She was reared in Switzerland but lived most of her adult life in the United States. "Last evening I spent 10 minutes trying to understand what a nurse was talking about when she invited me to attend a baby shower!" she said. "Why should I want to look at a bathroom constructed for infants?" (Gill, 1980, p. 201). The incident is an example of the importance of a fund of cultural knowledge as a basis for language pragmatics. Cross-cultural differences in the pragmatics that characterize Western and Asian languages include turn-taking (Lerner & Takagi, 1999) and directness of speech (Holtgraves, 1997).

1. What roles do semanticity, generativity, and displacement play in language?
2. What is the relationship between transformational grammar and the deep structure and surface structure of language?

Answers to Staying on Track start on p. ST-4.

The Acquisition of Language

What accounts for a child's ability to progress from a crying, gurgling infant to a talkative 3-year-old? The process of language acquisition seems to be universal, with infants in all cultures acquiring language in similar ways as they pass through distinct stages (Rice, 1989). Though the timing of the stages can vary among infants, the order does not.

Language Milestones

For the first few months after birth, infants are limited to communicating vocally through cooing, gurgling, and crying, which they use to indicate that they are content, happy, distressed, hungry, or in pain. Between 4 and 6 months of age, infants enter the babbling stage. When infants babble, they repeat sequences of phonemes, such as *ba-ba-ba*. Infants in all cultures begin babbling at about the same age and produce the same range of phonemes, including some that are not part of their parents' language (Roug et al., 1989). This might account for the prevalence of the words *mama, papa,* and *dada* to refer to parents in a variety of cultures. Even deaf infants begin babbling at the same age as infants who can hear, though their babbling is different from that of hearing infants (Oller & Eilers, 1988). The universality of the onset and initial content of babbling indicates that it is a product of the maturation of an inborn predisposition, rather than a product of experience. Nonetheless, by the age of 9 months, infants begin to show the influence of experience, as they limit their babbling to the phonemes of their family's language.

When infants are about 1 year old, they begin to say their first words. Their earliest words typically refer to objects that interest them. Thus, common early words include milk and doggie. In using words, older infants exhibit **overextension,** applying words too broadly (Behrend, 1988). Consider an infant who refers to her cat as "kitty." If she also refers to dogs, cows, horses, and other four-legged animals as "kitty," she would be exhibiting overextension. In contrast, if she refers to her cat, but to no other cats, as "kitty," she would be exhibiting **underextension**—applying words too narrowly (Caplan & Barr, 1989). As infants gain experience with objects and language, they rapidly learn to apply their words to the correct objects.

After learning to say single words, infants begin using them in **holophrastic speech,** which is the use of single words to represent whole phrases or sentences. For example, an infant might say "car" on one occasion to indicate the family car has pulled into the driveway, and on another occasion to indicate he would like to go for a ride. Between the ages of 18 and 24 months, infants go beyond holophrastic speech by speaking two-word phrases, typically including a noun and a verb in a consistent order. The infant now is showing a rudimentary appreciation of proper syntax, as in "Baby drink" or "Mommy go." Because, in the two-word stage, infants rely on nouns and verbs and leave out other parts of speech (such as articles and prepositions), their utterances are called **telegraphic speech.** To save time and money, telegrams leave out connecting parts of speech yet still communicate meaningful messages.

Until they are about 2 years old, infants use words to refer only to objects that are located in their immediate environment. At about age 2, children begin speaking sentences that include other parts of speech in addition to nouns and verbs. They also begin to exhibit displacement, as when a 2-year-old asks, "Grandma come tomorrow?" After age 2, children show a rapid increase in their vocabulary and in the length and complexity of their sentences.

overextension
The tendency to apply a word to more objects or actions than it actually represents.

underextension
The tendency to apply a word to fewer objects or actions than it actually represents.

holophrastic speech
The use of single words to represent whole phrases or sentences.

telegraphic speech
Speech marked by reliance on nouns and verbs, while omitting other parts of speech, including articles and prepositions.

▲ Jean Berko Gleason

"Theorists of language have been at odds with one another for the last quarter century over questions having to do with the nature of language and the possible prerequisites of its development."

overregularization

The application of a grammatical rule without making necessary exceptions to it.

 Center for Second-Language Research

www.mhhe.com/sdorow5

▲ Modeling Language

The modeling of language by parents is an important factor in the acquisition of a particular language by the child.

The language rules children in European American cultures learn are strongly influenced by their parents' speech—especially mothers' (Leaper, Anderson, & Sanders, 1998). In most non-Western cultures, however, children acquire language through interacting with a number of adults and other children (Mohanty & Perregaux, 1997). Many languages, like English, have many exceptions to grammatical rules. This might explain the phenomenon of **overregularization**—the application of grammatical rules without making necessary exceptions (Maratsos, 2000). For example, at first children using the past tense will, correctly, say words such as *did, went,* and *brought,* which violate the *-ed* rule for forming the past tense. They learn these words by hearing the speech of older children and adults. But as children learn the *-ed* rule, they say words such as *doed, goed,* or *bringed.* Later, when they realize grammatical rules have exceptions, they learn not to apply the *-ed* rule to irregular verbs, and again say *did, went,* and *brought* (Kolata, 1987). Thus, children tend at first to use correct wording, then begin to overregularize, and finally realize when to follow grammatical rules and when to break them (Marcus, 1995).

How do we know that infants learn rules, rather than a series of specific instances of correct grammar? One source of evidence is a study by Jean Berko (1958), who reasoned if children use correct grammar when confronted with words they have never heard, then they must be relying on rules, not rote memory. To test her assumption, Berko developed the "Wugs test," which included drawings of imaginary creatures called "wugs." Berko found that children would, indeed, apply grammatical rules to novel words. For example, when shown a picture identified as a "wug" and then a picture with two of them, children completed the statement "There are two _____" with the word *wugs.* This indicates that they have learned to use the *-s* ending to indicate the plural.

Is There a Critical Period for Language Acquisition?

As described at the beginning of the chapter, many language researchers believe that there is a *critical period* for the acquisition of language during childhood. Children who are kept isolated from contact with language and are not intensively exposed to language until adolescence—typically because they live in an abusive household—usually have great difficulty becoming proficient in their use of language. But such case studies do not permit us to know for certain whether these children would have shown normal language development had they been exposed to language beginning in infancy.

Another, perhaps stronger, line of research on critical periods is concerned with adults who learn second languages. Second languages become progressively more difficult to learn as we get older (Guion et al., 2000). Support for this came from a study in which older Korean and Chinese immigrants to the United States found it more difficult to learn English than did their younger fellow immigrants—even though the groups were intellectually equal (Johnson & Newport, 1989). Nonetheless, this finding must be viewed with caution in light of the many other factors that could account for differences in the ease with which younger and older immigrants learn a new language.

Theories of Language Acquisition

Language researchers debate this question: Is language acquired solely through learning, or is it strongly influenced by the maturation of an inherited predisposition to develop language? Those who favor the learning position assume that if it were possible to raise two infants together with no exposure to language, they would not develop true language. In contrast, those who favor the view that language emerges from an inherited predisposition assume the two infants might develop a rudimentary form of language marked by semanticity, generativity, and displacement. According to this position, learning normally determines only which language an infant will speak, whether English, French, or Navajo.

Language as the Product of Learning. B. F. Skinner (1957) claimed that language is acquired solely through learning, chiefly through the positive reinforcement of appropriate speech. For example, a 1-year-old child might learn to say "milk" because her parents give her milk and praise her when she says "milk." Similarly, a 2-year-old child named Jane might be given a cookie and praise for saying "Give Jane cookie" but not for saying "Jane cookie give." In a study supportive of Skinner's position, two groups of infants between 2 and 7 months old were positively reinforced for producing different phonemes. The infants were reinforced by smiles, *tsk* sounds, and light stroking of the abdomen. One group was reinforced for making vowel sounds, while the other group was reinforced for making consonant sounds. The infants responded by increasing their production of the phonemes that were reinforced. This study showed that positive reinforcement can affect language acquisition (Routh, 1969). Of course, it does not indicate that language is acquired *solely* through learning.

Albert Bandura (1977), the influential cognitive-behavioral psychologist, stresses the role of observational learning in language acquisition. He assumes that children develop language primarily by imitating the vocabulary and grammatical constructions used by their parents and others in their everyday lives. In a study that supported his position, adults replied to statements made by 2-year-old children by purposely using slightly more complex syntax than they normally would. After 2 months, the children had developed more complex syntax than did children who had not been exposed to the adult models (Nelson, 1977). Additional support for the effect of modeling comes from findings that 2-year-olds whose parents read to them acquire language more rapidly than do 2-year-olds whose parents do not (Whitehurst et al., 1988). Yet we cannot discount the possibility that other differences between the two groups of parents produced this effect.

Language as an Inherited Predisposition. The assumption that language is acquired solely through learning has been challenged by Noam Chomsky and his followers (Rondall, 1994). Chomsky insists that infants are born with the predisposition to develop language. He believes they inherit a *language acquisition device*—a brain mechanism that makes them sensitive to phonemes, syntax, and semantics. In analyzing parent-child interactions, Chomsky has found that children in different cultures progress through similar stages and learn their native languages without formal parental instruction. Children say things that adults never say, and their parents do not positively reinforce proper grammar (or correct improper grammar) in any consistent manner. Modeling, too, cannot explain all language learning, because observations of children show they vary greatly in the extent to which they imitate what their parents say (Snow, 1981).

What evidence is there to support Chomsky's position? One source of evidence is the universality in the basic features of language and the stages of language acquisition (Miller, 1990), which indicates that the tendency to develop language is inborn. Studies of deaf children support Chomsky's position. One study observed deaf children who were neither rewarded for using sign language nor exposed to a model who used it. Nonetheless, the children spontaneously developed their own gestural system, in which they communicated by using signs with the characteristics of true language (Goldin-Meadow & Mylander, 1998).

Despite the evidence favoring language as innate and contradicting learning as an explanation for language acquisition, research has provided some support for the learning position (Messer, 2000). One study tested the claim made by those who favor Chomsky's position that adults typically ignore children's speech errors and fail to correct their ungrammatical statements. The study found that language acquisition does depend in part on feedback provided by adults who correct specific instances of improper grammar. Adults do so by repeating a child's grammatically incorrect statements in grammatically correct form or by asking the child to clarify his or her statements (Bohannon & Stanowicz, 1988).

It seems that the positions of Chomsky, Skinner, and Bandura must be integrated to explain how language is acquired. We appear to be born with a predisposition to develop language, which provides us with an innate sensitivity to grammar. But we might learn our specific language, including its grammar, mainly through operant conditioning and observational learning.

▲ **Noam Chomsky**

"We should expect heredity to play a major role in language because there is really no other way to account for the fact that children learn to speak in the first place."

STAYING ON TRACK: *The Acquisition of Language*

1. What are the main characteristics of the stages of language development during infancy?
2. How do the theories of Skinner and Chomsky differ in regard to language development?

Answers to Staying on Track start on p. ST-4.

The Relationship Between Language and Thinking

In his novel *1984,* George Orwell (1949) envisioned a totalitarian government that controlled its citizen's thoughts by regulating their language. By adding, removing, or redefining words, the government used *Newspeak* to ensure citizens would not think rebellious thoughts against their leader, "Big Brother." For example, in Newspeak the word *joycamp* referred to a forced labor camp. And the word *free* was redefined to refer only to physical reality, as in *The dog is free from lice,* rather than to political freedom.

The Linguistic Relativity Hypothesis

Orwell's view of the influence of language on thought was shared by the linguist-anthropologist Benjamin Lee Whorf (1897–1941), who expressed it in his **linguistic relativity hypothesis,** which assumes that our perception of the world is determined by the particular language we speak (Smith, 1996). Whorf (1956) noted that Eskimo languages have several words for snow (such as words that distinguish between falling snow and fallen snow), whereas English has only one. According to the linguistic relativity hypothesis, the variety of words for snow in an Eskimo language causes people who speak it to perceive differences in snow that people who speak English do not.

Critics argue, on the contrary, thinking determines language. Perhaps the greater importance of snow in their culture led Eskimos to coin several words for snow, each referring to a different kind. Moreover, English-speaking people to whom snow is important, such as avid skiers, use different adjectives to describe different kinds of snow. Their ability to distinguish between crusty, powdery, and granular snow indicates that even English-speaking people can perceive wide variations in the quality of snow. And the number of words for snow in Eskimo languages might have been exaggerated in the early reports that influenced Whorf and other linguistic relativity theorists (Pullum, 1991).

What does formal research have to say about the linguistic relativity hypothesis? In an early study bearing on Whorf's hypothesis (Carmichael, Hogan, & Walter, 1932), participants were presented with ambiguous drawings of objects that were given either of two labels (see Figure 9.6). When later asked to draw the objects, participants drew pictures that

▶ **The Linguistic Relativity Hypothesis**
According to Whorf's linguistic relativity hypothesis, a forest ranger who has learned the names of many kinds of trees would, as a consequence, perceive more differences between trees than would people who know the names of few trees.

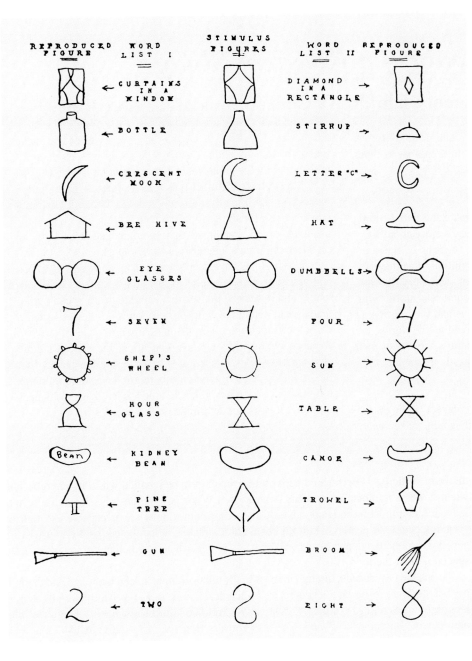

Participants were shown the pictures in the middle column with one of two different labels. When later asked to draw what they had seen, the participants drew pictures that were consistent with the labels, not with the pictures (Carmichael, Hogan, & Walter, 1932). This indicates that language can affect how we think about the world, even though it might not affect how we perceive the world.

looked more like the object that had been named than like the object they had seen. This supported Whorf's hypothesis, at least in that language appeared to influence the participants' recall of objects.

Eleanor Rosch (1975) conducted a classic study to test whether language influences the perception of colors. Rosch found that the language of the Dani people of New Guinea has two basic color words: *mili* for dark, cool colors, and *mola* for light, warm colors. In contrast, English has eleven basic color words: *black, white, red, green, yellow, blue, brown, purple, pink, orange,* and *gray.* To describe these colors, the Dani use relatively long phrases. Rosch wondered whether these differences in language would be associated with differences in the perception of colors. She decided to test this by using "focal" colors, which are considered the best representatives of each of the colors (for example, "fire-engine red" for red), and nonfocal colors.

Dani and American participants were given a series of trials on which they were first shown a colored plastic chip for 5 seconds. After another 30 seconds, they were asked to select the chip from among 160 colored chips. Both the English-speaking participants and

Anatomy of a Research Study

Does Language Influence Children's Conceptions of Gender Roles?

Rationale

Janet Shibley Hyde (1984) conducted a classic study to test the effects of gendered pronouns on children's stereotypes about women and men.

Method

Participants in Hyde's study were 132 male and female third- and fifth-grade children. All children read a story about a fictitious occupation, *wudgemaker*. Four versions of the story were prepared. In each version the description of wudgemakers was identical. The pronouns used in each story differed. One group read stories with *he,* the second read stories with *they,* the third read stories with *he or she,* and the fourth read stories with *she* for the pronoun. After reading the stories, the children were asked to provide two ratings: how well men could do the job and how well women could do the job.

Results and Discussion

Children's ratings of the male wudgemakers' competence were not affected by the pronouns. Male wudgemakers were seen as equally competent regardless of the pronouns used in the stories. However, pronouns did have an effect on mean ratings of female wudgemakers. The group who read stories with *he* as the pronoun rated female wudgemakers as "just O.K." In contrast, the other three groups rated female wudgemakers as significantly more competent. The highest rating was obtained for the group who read stories with *she* as the pronoun. Hyde concluded that pronoun use does have an effect on children's gender-role stereotypes.

These findings have been supported by more recent empirical research. For example, in one study students read sentences and described images that came to mind; when participants read sentences with the pronoun *he,* they reported a disproportionate number of male images (Gastil, 1990). Because our use of language can affect the way we think about gender roles, as well as other aspects of everyday life, the linguistic relativity hypothesis might have some merit, as long as it is used to recognize that though language influences thinking, it does not determine it (Davies, 1998).

---

the Dani participants performed better when the chip to be recalled was a focal color than when it was a nonfocal color. This contradicted Whorf's hypothesis, because the results indicated that though the Dani use only two color names, they are as capable as English-speaking people of perceiving all the focal colors in the English language. Perhaps we are genetically prepared to perceive these focal colors, regardless of whether our language takes special note of them.

During the past decade, though, interest in the relationship between language and thought has been spurred by research in cognitive linguistics. For example, one study investigated 39 languages spoken in 71 cultures. Cultures with "pronoun drop languages"—languages that omit personal pronouns ("I" and "you") in conversation—are less individualistic than cultures with languages that include personal pronouns (Kashima & Kashima, 1998).

Linguistic Relativity and Sexist Language

Though language does not *determine* how we think about the world, it might *influence* how we think about the world. This is the basis of concern about the traditional use of male pronouns, such as *his* and *him,* to refer to all persons. Perhaps repeated exposure to such use of the male pronoun to refer to both women and men promotes the belief that certain activities are more suitable for men than for women, the topic of the study discussed in the Anatomy of a Research Study feature.

STAYING ON TRACK: *The Relationship Between Language and Thinking*

1. How does Orwell's concept of Newspeak embody the belief that language affects thought?
2. How are concerns about sexist language related to the linguistic relativity hypothesis?

Answers to Staying on Track start on p. ST-5.

Language in Apes

In the early 17th century, the philosopher René Descartes argued that language is the critical feature that distinguishes human beings from other animals. Interest in teaching animals cognitive skills, such as language, that normally are associated with human beings was stimulated by the case of "Clever Hans," a horse who impressed onlookers by solving arithmetic problems in Germany in the early 20th century. Hans was trained to count out the answers to arithmetic problems by tapping one of his hooves until he reached the correct answer. He counted anything present, including persons, hats, or umbrellas. Oskar Pfungst showed that Hans stopped counting when he noticed tiny movements of his questioner's head, which cued the initiation and termination of counting. When the questioner knew the answer, Hans was correct almost all of the time. But when the questioner did not know the answer, Hans was wrong all of the time. So, Hans might have been clever, but he had no idea how to perform arithmetic (Davis & Memmott, 1982).

As interest in teaching animals to perform arithmetic waned, interest in teaching them language grew. As you read at the beginning of this chapter, some animals such as monkeys, can communicate in limited, stereotyped ways. But they do not use true language, which is characterized by semanticity, generativity, and displacement. Research on language learning in dolphins (Herman & Uyeyama, 1999) and sea lions (Gisiner & Schusterman, 1992) is promising but has yet to provide conclusive findings. A much larger body of research indicates that at least one kind of nonhuman animal might be capable of acquiring true language—the ape (Williams, Brakke, & Savage-Rumbaugh, 1997).

Teaching Chimpanzees to Use Language

More than 50 years ago, Winthrop and Luella Kellogg (1933) published a book about their experiences raising a chimpanzee named Gua with their infant son, Donald. Even after being exposed to speech as a member of the family, Gua could not speak a single word. Another couple, Cathy and Keith Hayes (Hayes, 1951), had only slightly better results with Viki, a chimpanzee they, too, raised as a member of their family. Despite their intensive efforts over a period of several years, Viki learned to say only four words: *mama, papa, cup,* and *up.* The Hayeses concluded that the vocal anatomy of apes is not designed for producing speech.

In 1925, primatologist Robert Yerkes, wondering whether apes have lots to say but no way of saying it, suggested teaching them to use sign language instead of speech. His suggestion was not carried out until 1966, when Allen and Beatrix Gardner (Gardner, Gardner, & Van Cantfort, 1969) of the University of Nevada began teaching American Sign Language (ASL) to a 1-year-old chimpanzee named Washoe. To encourage her to use ASL, they never spoke in her presence; instead, they signed to each other and Washoe using simple words about various objects and everyday events (Dewsbury, 1996). They also asked Washoe simple questions, praised her correct utterances, and tried to comply with her requests, just as parents do with young children. After 4 years of training, Washoe had a repertoire of 132 signs, which she used to name objects and to describe qualities of objects.

Washoe also seemed to show an important characteristic of true language—generativity. On seeing a swan for the first time, Washoe made the sign for *water bird*. And, in a chimpanzee colony in Washington State, Washoe taught ASL to a young chimpanzee named Loulis. After 5 years, Loulis had acquired a vocabulary of more than 50 ASL signs, which he could have learned only from Washoe and other chimpanzees, since all human signing was forbidden when Loulis was present (Gardner, Gardner, & Van Cantfort, 1989).

During the past few decades several other apes have been taught to use sign language or other forms of language. For example, Duane Rumbaugh taught a chimpanzee named Lana to use a computer to create sentences by pressing large keys marked by lexigrams—geometric shapes representing particular words (Rumbaugh, Gill, & von Glasersfeld, 1973). Lana formed sentences by pressing keys in a particular order. Lana's language was called "Yerkish," in honor of Robert Yerkes. When Lana made grammatically correct requests, she was rewarded with food, toys, music, or other things she enjoyed.

Controversy About Ape-Language Research

Did Washoe, Sarah, and Lana learn to use true language? Did they exhibit semanticity, generativity, and displacement? Columbia University psychologist Herbert Terrace, who once believed apes can use language, says no (Terrace et al., 1979). Terrace taught a chimpanzee named Nim Chimpsky to use sign language. (Nim was named after Noam Chomsky, who believes apes cannot learn true language.) After 5 years of training, Nim had mastered 125 signs. At first, Terrace assumed that Nim had learned true language. But after analyzing videotapes of conversations with Nim and videotapes of other apes that had been taught sign language, he concluded that Nim and the other apes did not display true language.

On what did Terrace base his conclusion? He found that apes merely learned to make signs, arrange forms, or press computer keys in a certain order to obtain rewards. In other words, their use of language was no different from that of a pigeon that learns to peck a sequence of keys to get food rewards. So, the ability of an ape to produce a string of words does not indicate that the ape has learned to produce a sentence. Terrace also claims that the apparent generativity of ape language might be a misinterpretation of their actions. For example, Washoe's apparent reference to a swan as a "water bird" might have been a reference to two separate things—a body of water and a bird.

As additional evidence against ape language, Terrace claims that many instances of allegedly spontaneous signing by chimpanzees are actually responses to subtle cues from trainers. Terrace found that Nim communicated primarily in response to prompting by his trainer or by imitating signs recently made by his trainer. Thus, he did not use language in an original or spontaneous way, and his signs were simply gestures prompted by cues from his trainer that produced consequences he desired—a kind of operant conditioning (Terrace, 1985).

Terrace's attack has not gone unchallenged. Francine Patterson taught a gorilla named Koko to use more than 300 signs ("Ape Language," 1981). Koko even displays generativity, as in spontaneously referring to a zebra as a "white tiger." Patterson criticized Terrace for basing his conclusions on his work with Nim and on isolated frames he has examined from films of other apes using ASL. She claimed that Nim's inadequate use of language might stem from his being confused by having sixty different trainers. In contrast, Patterson reported, Koko had only one primary trainer and used signs more spontaneously than Nim did. For example, Koko responded to a velvet hat by signing "that soft" (Patterson, Patterson, & Brentari, 1987).

The Washoe Project
www.mhhe.com/sdorow5

Koko.org
www.mhhe.com/sdorow5

▲ **Nim Chimpsky**
According to Herbert Terrace, even his own chimpanzee, Nim Chimpsky, uses sign language only in response to cues from his trainers. The photo shows Nim learning the sign for "drink."

Koko

Whereas most ape-language researchers have used chimpanzees as subjects, Francine Patterson has taught sign language to the gorilla Koko. Here Koko is signing "smoke" in response to her pet kitten, Smoky.

▲ Duane Rumbaugh and Sue Savage-Rumbaugh

"Pygmy chimpanzees may employ a sort of primitive language in the wild."

In recent years, the strongest evidence in support of ape language comes from studies by Duane Rumbaugh and Sue Savage-Rumbaugh. They trained two chimpanzees, Austin and Sherman, to communicate through Yerkish, the language used earlier by Lana. In one study, Austin, Sherman, and Lana were taught to categorize three objects (an orange, a beancake, and a slice of bread) as "edible" and three objects (a key, a stick, and a pile of coins) as "inedible." When given other objects, Austin and Sherman, but not Lana, were able to categorize them as edible or inedible. Perhaps Lana could not learn this task because she had been trained to use language to associate labels with specific objects rather than to understand the concepts to which the labels referred (Savage-Rumbaugh et al., 1980).

Moreover, Sue Savage-Rumbaugh and her colleagues (1986) described their work with two pygmy chimpanzees, Kanzi and Mulika, who achieved language ability superior to that of previous apes. According to Savage-Rumbaugh, an important factor in achieving this was exposing the chimpanzees to human language during everyday activities rather than as part of an artificial training program (Brakke & Savage-Rumbaugh, 1996). Kanzi learned Yerkish spontaneously by observing people and other chimpanzees pressing appropriate lexigrams on a keyboard (Savage-Rumbaugh, 1990). He also can identify symbols referred to in human speech. Previous apes depended on their own particular language system to comprehend human communications. Kanzi can even form requests in which other individuals are either the agent or the recipient of action—which reflects his appreciation of syntax (Savage-Rumbaugh et al., 1993). Before, apes such as Nim made spontaneous requests only in which they were the targets of a suggested action. Moreover, Kanzi shows displacement, using lexigrams to refer to things that are not present (Lyn & Savage-Rumbaugh, 2000).

Nonetheless, some critics insist even Kanzi does not display all of the characteristics of true language (Kako, 1999). Savage-Rumbaugh has responded to this by asking critics to stress the important language skills that Kanzi has exhibited, rather than continually seeking to identify the relatively minor aspects of language he has failed to exhibit (Shanker, Savage-Rumbaugh, & Taylor, 1999).

Perhaps future studies using pygmy chimpanzees will succeed where others have failed in demonstrating convincingly that apes are capable of using true language. But even if apes can use true language, no ape has gone beyond the language level of a 3-year-old child. Is that the upper limit of ape language ability, or is it just the upper limit using current training methods? Research might soon provide the answer. In any case, we do know apes are capable of more complex communication than simply grunting to convey crude emotional states.

STAYING ON TRACK: *Language in Apes*

1. What evidence is there that apes such as Washoe demonstrate the characteristics of true language?
2. Why do critics doubt that these apes have acquired true language?

Answers to Staying on Track start on p. ST-5.

▲ Kanzi

Kanzi is one of the apes who have shown the most sophisticated use of language. Here he is using Yerkish, a language consisting of geometric symbols.

Thinking and Language | 299

Chapter Summary

THINKING

- The past few decades have seen a cognitive revolution in psychology, with increased interest in the study of thinking.
- Thinking is the purposeful mental manipulation of words and images.

CONCEPT FORMATION

- Thinking depends on concepts, which are categories of objects, events, qualities, or relations whose members share certain features.
- A logical concept is formed by identifying specific features possessed by all members of the concept.
- A natural concept is formed through everyday experiences and has "fuzzy borders."
- The best representative of a concept is called a prototype.

PROBLEM SOLVING

- One of the most important uses of concepts is in problem solving, the thought process that enables us to overcome obstacles to reach goals.
- The problem-solving strategy called insight depends on the mental manipulation of information.
- An algorithm is a rule that, when followed step by step, assures that a solution to a problem will be found.
- A heuristic is a general principle that guides problem solving but does not guarantee the discovery of a solution.
- A mental set is a problem-solving strategy that has succeeded in the past but that can interfere with solving a problem that requires a new strategy.
- Our past experience can also impede problem solving through functional fixedness, the inability to realize that a problem can be solved by using a familiar object in an unusual way.

CREATIVITY

- Creativity is a form of problem solving characterized by novel solutions that are also useful or socially valued.
- Creative people tend to have above-average intelligence and are able to integrate different kinds of thinking.
- Creative people are more motivated by their intrinsic interest in creative tasks than by extrinsic factors.
- Social-cultural factors also influence the development and expression of creativity.
- Creativity also depends on divergent thinking, in which a person freely considers a variety of potential solutions to a problem.

DECISION MAKING

- In decision making we try to make the best choice from among alternative courses of action.
- In using the representativeness heuristic, we assume that a small sample is representative of its population.
- In using the availability heuristic, we estimate the probability of an event by how easily relevant instances of it come to mind.
- We are subject to framing effects, which are biases introduced in the decision-making process by presenting a situation in a certain manner.

ARTIFICIAL INTELLIGENCE

- Artificial intelligence is a field that integrates computer science and cognitive psychology to try to simulate or improve on human thinking by using computer programs.
- Computer scientists are trying to develop programs that use parallel information processing, as well as serial information processing.

LANGUAGE

- In using language, we rely on spoken symbols to communicate through speech, written symbols to communicate through writing, and gestured symbols to communicate through sign language.
- We use language to communicate with other people, to store and retrieve memories, and to plan for the future.

THE STRUCTURE OF LANGUAGE

- True language is characterized by semanticity, generativity, and displacement.
- The rules of a language are its grammar.
- Phonemes are the basic sounds of a language, and morphemes are its smallest meaningful units.
- A language's syntax includes rules governing the acceptable arrangement of words and phrases.
- Semantics is the study of how language conveys meaning.
- Noam Chomsky calls the underlying meaning of a statement its deep structure and the words themselves its surface structure.
- We translate between deep and surface structures by using transformational grammar.
- The branch of semantics concerned with the relationship between language and its social context is called pragmatics.

THE ACQUISITION OF LANGUAGE

- Infants in all cultures progress through similar stages of language development.
- Infants begin babbling between 4 and 6 months of age and say their first words when they are about 1 year old.
- At first infants use holophrastic speech, in which single words represent whole phrases or sentences.
- Between the ages of 18 and 24 months, infants begin speaking two-word sentences and use telegraphic speech.
- As infants learn their language's grammar, they tend to engage in overregularization, in which they apply grammatical rules without making necessary exceptions.
- There might be a critical period for language acquisition, extending from infancy to adolescence.
- B. F. Skinner and Albert Bandura believe that language is acquired solely through learning, whereas Chomsky believes that we have an innate predisposition to develop language.

THE RELATIONSHIP BETWEEN LANGUAGE AND THINKING

- Benjamin Lee Whorf's linguistic relativity hypothesis assumes that our view of the world is determined by the particular language we speak.
- But research has shown that though language can influence thinking, it does not determine it.

LANGUAGE IN APES

- Researchers have taught apes to communicate by using sign language, form boards, and computers.
- The best known of these apes include the gorilla Koko and the chimpanzees Washoe and Lana.
- Herbert Terrace, the trainer of Nim Chimpsky, claims that apes have not learned true language; instead, they have learned to give responses that lead to rewards, just as pigeons learn to peck at keys to obtain food.
- Francine Patterson, Duane Rumbaugh, and Sue Savage-Rumbaugh have countered by providing evidence that the apes have, indeed, learned true language characterized by semanticity, generativity, and displacement.

Key Concepts

Key Contributors

Thought Questions

1. Why might people be more likely to argue whether "bowling" is a true sport than whether "tennis" is a true sport?
2. How might heuristics contribute to ethnic prejudice?
3. How might the notion of "politically correct" speech (e.g., calling people "senior citizens" rather than "elderly" and calling people "mentally challenged" as opposed to "mentally retarded") be related to the linguistic relativity hypothesis?
4. What issues must be confronted by researchers who wish to demonstrate the acquisition of true language in apes?

Possible Answers to Thought Questions start on p. PT-3.

OLC Preview

 For additional quizzing and a variety of interactive resources, visit the book's Online Learning Center at www.mhhe.com/sdorow5.

Intelligence

MICHELLE PULEO
Shakespeare in his Study

In the 1988 movie *Rain Man,* Dustin Hoffman portrays Raymond Babitt, an autistic man who could perform amazing mental feats, such as memorizing restaurant menus, recalling the telephone number of anyone in the telephone book, and rapidly calculating complicated mathematical problems in his head. Raymond refuses to fly, basing his decision on the many airplane crashes he can recall, including the dates and fatalities of each one.

The film depicts a cross-country journey of self-discovery for Raymond's younger brother, Charlie, a self-centered young man whose father dies and leaves his $3 million estate to Raymond—a brother Charlie never knew he had and whom he "kidnaps" from an institution, hoping to ransom him for half the money. Along the way, Raymond uses his unusual memory ability to help Charlie win almost $100,000 playing blackjack in Las Vegas. Charlie learns to be less self-centered and to accept—and even love—someone who is different from him.

The film is likewise a journey of discovery for viewers, who come to understand some aspects of **autism.** For example, as is typical in autism, Raymond follows a strict routine—even insisting that pancake syrup always be put on the table before the pancakes arrive. He also shows the compulsive repetition of phrases and the difficulty in connecting emotionally to other people that is common in autism.

Raymond is not only autistic, but also exhibits **savant syndrome.** A person with savant syndrome is a person with below-average general intelligence but who has a talent—typically in art (Hermelin & Pring, 1998), music (Heaton, Hermelin, & Pring, 1998), or calculating (Kelly, Macaruso, & Sokol, 1997)—developed beyond the person's level of functioning in other areas.

The savant syndrome was first noted in a 1751 German magazine article that described the case of an uneducated farmhand with an extraordinary memory (Foerstl, 1989). In a much more recent case, an autistic savant could give the day of the week for any date in the 20th century (Hurst & Mulhall, 1988); he had spent many hours memorizing the day of the week of each date, just as Dustin Hoffman's character spent many hours memorizing the telephone book. Because autistic savants tend to be socially aloof and persistent at tasks, they can spend the many hours needed to memorize large amounts of material (Heavey, Pring, & Hermelin, 1999).

Not all savants function at the level of Dustin Hoffman's character in *Rain Man.* There are many autistic savants, but fewer than a hundred *prodigious savants*—the kind portrayed by the media—have been identified. A prodigious savant is a person who has a talent so highly developed that it would be remarkable even in a person of normal intellectual ability. Though there is no single accepted cause of savant syndrome, research findings implicate prenatal damage to the left cerebral hemisphere of the brain compensated for by the overdevelopment of certain structures of the right cerebral hemisphere that govern particular talents. The talents exhibited by autistic savants seem to be processed by implicit, rather than the explicit, memory. As discussed in Chapter 8, the implicit memory system deals with memories that are processed without the conscious intention to do so. Moreover, the outstanding talents of prodigious savants, are probably strongly affected by heredity, because these individuals' remarkable knowledge of the rules of art, music, or mathematics does not appear to be the product of practice alone (Treffert, 1989).

An autistic savant who memorizes enormous amounts of material is displaying *intelligence.* You certainly recognize intelligent behavior when you see it, such as someone writing a great symphony or discovering a cure for a disease. Recognizing intelligent behavior, though, is easier than defining intelligence

autism
An often severe developmental disorder that includes deficiencies in social relationships, disordered communication, and repetitive and restricted patterns of behavior.

savant syndrome
The presence, in a person with below-average general intelligence, of a talent—typically in art, music, or calculating—developed beyond the person's level of functioning in other areas.

The Savant Syndrome: Islands of Genius
www.mhhe.com/sdorow5

▲ **Savant Syndrome**
Tom Cruise and Dustin Hoffman are shown in a scene from *Rain Man,* in which Hoffman portrays an autistic savant.

itself. The word *intelligence* comes from the Latin word meaning "to understand," but the concept of intelligence is broader than that. David Wechsler (1958), a leading intelligence researcher, put forth an influential definition of intelligence. He called **intelligence** the global capacity to act purposefully, to think rationally, and to deal effectively with the environment. In other words, intelligence reflects how well we *function.*

◆ INTELLIGENCE TESTING

Modern interest in the study of intelligence began with the development of tests of mental abilities, which include achievement tests, aptitude tests, and intelligence tests. An **achievement test** assesses knowledge of a particular subject, such as English, history, or mathematics. An **aptitude test** predicts your potential to benefit from instruction in a particular academic or vocational setting. Aptitude tests are commonly used to screen job applicants and college applicants. In applying to colleges, you may have submitted the results of your performance on either the Scholastic Assessment Test (SAT) or the American College Test (ACT). An **intelligence test** is a kind of aptitude test that assesses overall mental ability, which influences our functioning in a variety of areas of life, including school and work (Brody, 1999).

The History of Intelligence Testing

The use of tests of mental abilities has been traced back to 2200 B.C., when the Chinese appear to have used them to select talented individuals to serve as civil servants (Fox, 1981). But ability testing did not become the subject of scientific study until the late 19th century, when the English scientist Francis Galton (1822–1911) set up his Anthropometric Laboratory at the 1884 International Health Exhibition in London.

Francis Galton and Anthropometry

The word *anthropometric* means "human measurement." More than 9,000 visitors to Galton's laboratory paid to be measured on a variety of physical characteristics, including head size, grip strength, visual acuity, and reaction time to sounds (Morse, 1999). Galton was

▲ **David Wechsler (1896–1981)**
"Intelligence, operationally defined, is the aggregate or global capacity of the individual to act purposefully, to think rationally, and to deal effectively with his environment."

History of the Influences in the Development of Intelligence Theory and Testing
www.mhhe.com/sdorow5

intelligence
The global capacity to act purposefully, to think rationally, and to deal effectively with the environment.

achievement test
A test that measures knowledge of a particular subject.

aptitude test
A test designed to predict a person's potential to benefit from instruction in a particular academic or vocational setting.

intelligence test
A test that assesses overall mental ability.

▶ **Galton's Anthropometric Laboratory**
Francis Galton measured the physical traits of more than 9,000 persons in his Anthropometric Laboratory in London.

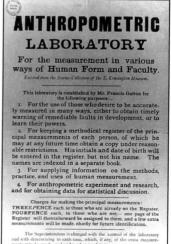

inspired by his cousin Charles Darwin's theory of evolution. Galton assumed that people with superior physical abilities, especially sensory and motor abilities, are better adapted for survival. Thus, he viewed such people as more intelligent than those with average or inferior physical abilities.

Galton's research on individual differences established the field of **differential psychology,** which is concerned with the study of cognitive and behavioral differences among individuals. Galton's anthropometric method was introduced to the United States by James McKeen Cattell (1860–1944), who administered Galton's tests—which Cattell called *mental tests*—to American students (Cattell, 1890). But anthropometry proved fruitless as a way of measuring general intelligence, because many anthropometric measurements, such as grip strength, proved to have little or no relationship to mental measures of intelligence, such as reasoning ability.

Alfred Binet, Theodore Simon, and the IQ Test

The first formal test of general intelligence—the *Binet-Simon scale*—appeared in 1905. It grew out of an 1881 French law that required all children to attend school even if they could not profit from a standard curriculum (Levine, 1976). This led the French minister of public education to ask psychologist Alfred Binet (1857–1911) to develop a test to identify children who required special classes for slow learners. Binet collaborated with psychiatrist Theodore Simon (1873–1961) to develop a test that could assess children's ability to perform in school. Binet and Simon began by administering many questions related to language, reasoning, and arithmetic to elementary school children of all ages. Binet and Simon eliminated questions that tended to be answered the same by children of all ages. Questions that were answered correctly by more and more children at each successive age were retained and became the Binet-Simon scale.

Each student was assigned a *mental age,* based on the number of test items she or he passed—the greater the number of items passed, the higher the mental age. A student with a mental age significantly below his or her chronological age was considered a candidate for placement in a class for slow learners. Binet urged that his test be used solely for class placement. He disagreed with those who claimed the test measured a child's inherited level of intelligence or that a child's level of intelligence could not be improved by education.

The Binet-Simon scale proved useful, but the measure of mental age occasionally proved misleading. Suppose that a 10-year-old child had a mental age of 8 and a 6-year-old child had a mental age of 4. Both would be 2 years below their chronological ages, but the 6-year-old would be proportionately farther behind her or his age peers than the 10-year-old would be. This problem was solved by German psychologist William Stern (1871–1938), who recommended using the ratio of mental age to chronological age to determine a child's level of intelligence (Kreppner, 1992). A 10-year-old with a mental age of 8 has a ratio of 8/10 = 0.80, and a 6-year-old with a mental age of 4 has a ratio of 4/6 = 0.67. This indicates that the 6-year-old is relatively farther behind his or her age peers. Stanford University psychologist Lewis Terman eliminated the decimal point by multiplying the ratio by 100. Thus, 0.80 becomes 80, and 0.67 becomes 67. The formula *(mental age/chronological age) X 100* became known as the **intelligence quotient (IQ).** As you can see, a child whose mental and chronological ages are the same has an IQ of 100, and a child who has a higher mental than chronological age has an IQ above 100.

Lewis Terman and American Intelligence Testing

The Binet-Simon scale was translated into English and first used in the United States by the American psychologist Henry Goddard (1866–1957). In 1916 Lewis Terman (1877–1956) published a revised version of the Binet-Simon scale, more suitable for children reared in American culture. The American version became known as the *Stanford-Binet Intelligence Scale* and is still used today. Terman also redesigned the Stanford-Binet to make it suitable for testing both children and adults. (The test has been revised repeatedly since 1916.)

▲ **Francis Galton (1822–1911)**

"Social hindrances cannot impede men of high ability from being eminent . . . [and] social advantages are incompetent to give that status to a man of moderate ability."

differential psychology
The field of psychology that studies individual differences in physical, personality, and intellectual characteristics.

▲ **Alfred Binet (1857–1911)**

"It will be seen that a profound knowledge of the normal intellectual development of the child would not only be of great interest but useful in formulating a course of instruction really adapted to their aptitudes."

intelligence quotient (IQ)
1. Originally, the ratio of mental age to chronological age; that is, MA/CA $\times$ 100.
2. Today, the score on an intelligence test, calculated by comparing a person's performance to norms for her or his age group.

Because the Stanford-Binet is given individually and can take an hour or more to administer, it is not suitable for testing large groups of people in a brief period of time. This became a problem during World War I, when the U.S. Army sought a way to assess the intelligence of large groups of recruits. The army wanted to reject recruits who did not have the intelligence to perform well and to identify recruits who would be good officer candidates. Terman and several other prominent psychologists provided the solution to this problem. They developed two group tests of intelligence—the *Army Alpha Test* and the *Army Beta Test*. The Army Alpha Test was given in writing to those who could read English, and the Army Beta Test was given orally to those who could not read English. The tests, reflecting their functionalist heritage, viewed intelligence as the ability to adapt to the environment (von Mayrhauser, 1989). Descendants of these group intelligence tests include the *Otis-Lennon Mental Abilities Tests* and the *Armed Forces Qualification Test*.

David Wechsler and the Deviation IQ

After World War I the Stanford-Binet became the most widely used intelligence test. But the ratio IQ devised by Stern, which was adequate for representing the intelligence of children, proved inadequate for representing the intelligence of adults. Because growth in mental age slows markedly after childhood, the use of the ratio IQ led to the absurdity of people with average or above-average intelligence becoming below average simply because their chronological age increased. This inadequacy of the ratio IQ was overcome by David Wechsler (1896–1981). He replaced Stern's ratio IQ with a *deviation IQ,* which compares a person's intelligence test score with the mean score of his or her age peers. Those who perform at exactly the mean of their age peers receive an IQ of 100; those who perform above the mean of their age peers receive an IQ above 100; and those who perform below the mean of their age peers receive an IQ below 100.

In 1939 Wechsler developed his own intelligence test. While working as chief psychologist at Bellevue Hospital in New York City, he sought a way to assess the intelligence of adult psychiatric patients with low verbal ability. Because the Stanford-Binet stressed verbal ability and was geared toward testing children, it was not suitable for that purpose. This led Wechsler to develop an adult intelligence test that tested nonverbal, as well as verbal, ability, which he called the *Wechsler-Bellevue Intelligence Scale.*

Wechsler later developed versions of his test for use with different age groups, beginning with the *Wechsler Intelligence Scale for Children (WISC),* for ages 6 to 16; followed by the *Wechsler Adult Intelligence Scale (WAIS),* for older adolescents and adults; and concluding with the *Wechsler Preschool and Primary Scale of Intelligence (WPPSI),* for ages 4 to 6½. The Wechsler scales have been revised periodically. Each of the Wechsler intelligence scales contains subtests that measure different aspects of verbal and nonverbal intelligence. The test taker receives a verbal IQ, a performance (nonverbal) IQ, and an overall IQ.

Issues in Intelligence Testing

Psychological tests must be standardized, reliable, and valid (see Chapter 2). *Standardization* refers to both the establishment of performance norms on a test and uniformity in how the test is administered and scored. When an intelligence test is standardized, the mean performance of the standardization group for each age range is given a score of 100, with a standard deviation of 15. Figure 10.1 shows that IQ scores fall along a *normal curve.* For the Wechsler scales, this means that about 68 percent of test takers will score between 85 and 115, and about 95 percent will score between 70 and 130. Average intelligence falls between 85 and 115. IQs below 70 fall in the mentally retarded range, and IQs above 130 fall in the mentally gifted range.

The Reliability of Intelligence Tests

You would have confidence in an intelligence test only if it were reliable. The *reliability* of a test is the degree to which it gives consistent results. Suppose you took an IQ test and scored 102 (average) one month, 53 (mentally retarded) the next month, and 146 (mentally gifted) the third month. Because your level of intelligence normally would not fluctuate that

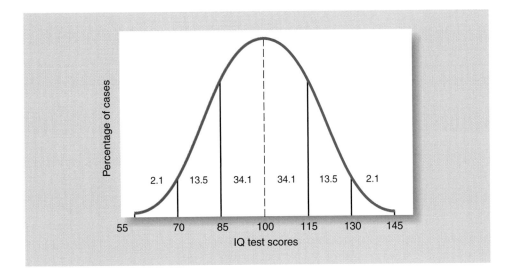

much in 3 months, you would argue that the test is unreliable. Because the test-retest reliability correlations for the Stanford-Binet and Wechsler scales are at least .90 (out of a maximum of 1.00), the tests are reliable.

Though standardized IQ tests are reliable, an individual's IQ score can change over a period of years. The Berkeley Growth Study, conducted at the University of California at Berkeley, contradicted the once-popular belief that intelligence does not change during childhood. The study found that mental ability increases through adolescence and then levels off at about the age of 20 (Bayley, 1955). The nature of intellectual change later in life is discussed in Chapter 4 and later in this chapter.

The Validity of Intelligence Tests

A reliable test is not necessarily a valid one. A test's *validity* depends on whether the test measures what it is supposed to measure. The validity of IQ tests can be assessed by comparing their results to each other. A study of 40 children aged 6 to 16 years found a high correlation between their scores on the Stanford-Binet Intelligence Scale and on the Wechsler Intelligence Scale for Children (Lavin, 1996). This indicates the two tests are indeed measuring the same thing.

College Admissions Tests. *Predictive validity* is especially important. Consider the SAT's ability to predict school performance. A review of research on the SAT reported that the SAT correlated .41 with first-year college grade-point average. This means that the SAT is a moderately good predictor. But high school grade-point average, which correlated .52 with first-year college grade-point average, is an even better predictor. Moreover, the combination of the SAT and high school grade-point average was a still better predictor, correlating .58 with first-year college grade-point average (Linn, 1982).

Bias in Testing. The Stanford-Binet and Wechsler scales correlate between .40 and .75 with school performance, depending on the aspect of school performance being measured (Aiken, 1982). These correlations indicate that the tests are good, but far from perfect, predictors of school performance. Because the correlations are less than a perfect 1.00, factors other than those measured by the SAT or IQ tests also contribute to school performance. This has made the fairness of intelligence tests one of the most controversial issues in contemporary psychology.

Critics argue that IQ tests and other tests of mental ability might be unfair to minority groups in the United States—most notably African Americans (Bender et al., 1995), who score an average of 10 to 15 points lower than European Americans. A review of research on ethnic differences in intelligence found no adequate explanation—whether genetic or environmental—for this (Neisser et al., 1996). There also has been a similar long-standing difference in scores on achievement tests between African Americans and European Americans. But this gap has been declining slowly in recent decades (Hedges & Nowell, 1999). Critics of IQ testing allege that because African Americans are less likely to have the same cultural and educational experiences as European Americans, they tend, on the average, to perform more poorly on IQ tests that assume both groups share common cultural and educational experiences (Brooks-Gunn, Klebanov, & Duncan, 1996).

But others assert that IQ tests are not biased against African Americans, because the tests have good predictive validity—they accurately predict the performance of both African American children and European American children in elementary school classes (Elder, 1997). The differences in IQ scores between the two groups of children might reflect the fact that African American children might be more likely to be reared in socially disadvantaged circumstances that do not provide them with the opportunity to gain experiences that are important in doing well on IQ tests and in school (Lambert, 1981). A committee of scholars from several academic fields reported to the National Academy of Science that standardized tests are accurate predictors of school and job performance for all groups and therefore are not biased against any particular group ("NAS Calls Tests Fair but Limited," 1982). This conclusion was supported by a study of Native American high school students, which showed that their performance on the American College Testing (ACT) Program accurately predicted their college performance (House, 1998). Thus, the consensus appears to be that tests of intellectual ability are not biased (Brown, Reynolds, & Whitaker, 1999).

Culturally Unbiased Tests. One possible solution to this controversy presents a compromise: Use tests that are not affected by the test taker's cultural background. The desirability of culturally unbiased tests has inspired research in a variety of cultures, including India (Misra, Sahoo, & Puhan, 1997) and South Africa (Claassen, 1997). But efforts to develop "culture-free" tests, beginning in the 1940s (Cattell, 1940), and "culture-fair" tests, beginning in the 1950s (Davis & Eels, 1953), produced disappointing results. These tests presented test takers with items that emphasized perceptual and spatial abilities, rather than verbal abilities, and avoided the use of items that would presume an extensive background in a particular culture. Figure 10.2 presents an example of the Raven Progressive Matrices, a nonverbal intelligence test that some have favored over the Stanford-Binet or Wechsler scales. But, just like on traditional intelligence tests, people of higher socioeconomic status perform better on these nonverbal tests than do people of lower socioeconomic status (Jensen, 1980). And European Americans typically perform better than African Americans on tests of cognitive ability, even when the tests are reworded to make them more comfortable to African American test takers (DeShon et al., 1998).

Moreover, members of one culture might even perform the same on intelligence tests developed in another culture as they do on ones developed in their own culture. This was demonstrated in a study in which more than 600 grade-school children from India and more than 1,000 grade-school children from Holland were given two IQ tests, one developed in each country. The tests were slightly modified when given to students from the other country. The results showed the students' performances were comparable on the two tests, indicating that cultural biases did not affect their IQ test performances (Bleichrodt, Hoksbergen, & Khire, 1999).

Stereotype Threat and IQ Test Performance. According to Claude Steele, self-fulfilling prophecy might account for the poorer performance of African Americans on intelligence tests because of what he calls *stereotype threat*. As discussed in Chapter 2, research has found that teachers' expectancies can help or hinder student's academic performance. Steele's twist is that in certain situations you become aware of others' expectations about your own stereotyped group—in turn, this affects your performance. Because African Americans are aware of stereotypes some people hold of their academic abilities, they might become anxious and not perform as well on intelligence tests. In one study, Steele (Steele & Aronson, 1995) administered a verbal ability test to African American and European American college students approximately equal in their intellectual ability. Half of each

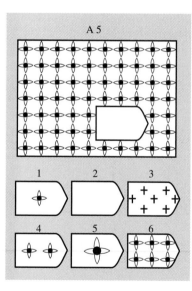

▲ **Figure 10.2**
Raven Progressive Matrices Test

In this "culture-fair" test, the person is presented with a series of matrices and must complete each by selecting the appropriate symbol from an accompanying group of symbols. Item A5 from Raven's Standard Progressive Matrices. Copyright J. C. Raven Ltd. Reprinted with permission of Campbell, Thomson & McLaughlin Ltd.

Chapter Ten

group was told the test simply served to assess how people solve problems. The other half was told the test measured verbal reasoning ability. The performance of the two groups did not differ under the first condition, but African American participants performed worse than European American participants under the second condition. Steele concluded that under the second condition African American participants succumbed to stereotype threat, became anxious, and thus performed more poorly.

Imagine how Alfred Binet would have reacted to the controversy that has arisen over the use of standardized tests, considering that he saw testing as an unbiased means of assessing students' abilities. In fact, despite the shortcomings of standardized tests, no alternative is as unbiased in assessing individuals without regard to irrelevant characteristics such as sex or ethnic background (Reilly & Chao, 1982).

STAYING ON TRACK: *Intelligence Testing*

1. What is savant syndrome?
2. How was Galton's view of intelligence influenced by his cousin Charles Darwin's theory of evolution?

Answers to Staying on Track start on ST-5.

◆ EXTREMES OF INTELLIGENCE

Another controversial issue regarding intelligence is the classification and education of people who fall at either extreme of the range of intelligence. As you learned earlier, 95 percent of the population score between 70 and 130 on IQ tests. Of the remaining 5 percent, half score below 70 and half score above 130. Those who score below 70 are considered to have mental retardation, and those who score above 130 fall in the mentally gifted range—though the classification of a person as having mental retardation or being mentally gifted is not based on IQ scores alone.

Mental Retardation

Adaptive behavior, and not just level of intelligence, needs to be assessed before a person is classified as having **mental retardation.** In fact, the current trend in classification is to rely more on the person's everyday functioning and less on his or her IQ score (Haywood, Meyers, & Switzky, 1982).

Classification of Mental Retardation

To be classified as having mental retardation, a person must have an IQ below 70 and, beginning in childhood, difficulties performing in everyday life (Landesman & Ramey, 1989)—including difficulties in self-care (such as eating and dressing), schoolwork (such as reading and arithmetic), and social relationships (such as conversing and developing friendships). Moreover, before a person can be classified as having mental retardation, alternative causes of the person's low IQ score and performance difficulties must be ruled out. These alternative causes include physical illness, impaired vision or hearing, and coming from a family of people who are not native speakers of the language in which the IQ test was administered.

People with mental retardation suffer from varying degrees of cognitive deficits (Detterman, 1999). One of the most common deficits they exhibit is inadequate use of language, in part related to difficulty with pragmatics (see Chapter 9). That is, people with mental retardation often interpret speech too literally, making them miss some of the subtleties of what is being said.

Today, there are four categories of mental retardation (American Psychiatric Association, 1994):

mental retardation
Intellectual deficiency marked by an IQ below 70 and difficulties performing in everyday life.

The ARC of the United States
www.mhhe.com/sdorow5

- Those with IQs of 50 to 70 have *mild retardation* and constitute 85 percent of persons with mental retardation. They are able to care for themselves, reach a sixth-grade level of education, hold responsible jobs, be married, and serve as adequate parents.
- Those with IQs of 35 to 49 have *moderate retardation* and constitute 10 percent of persons with mental retardation. They might be trained to care for themselves, reach a second-grade level of education, and hold menial jobs, often in sheltered workshops, but they have difficulty maintaining social relationships and they rarely marry.
- Those with IQs between 20 and 34 have *severe retardation* and constitute 3 to 4 percent of persons with mental retardation. They can learn rudimentary language and work skills but might be unable to care for themselves, benefit from schooling, hold jobs, or maintain social relationships.
- Those with IQs below 20 have *profound retardation* and constitute 1 to 2 percent of persons with mental retardation. They have so few skills that they might spend their lives in institutions that provide them with no more than custodial care.

Causes of Mental Retardation

Though some cases of mental retardation might be linked to genetic factors (Higgins et al., 2000), about 75 percent of cases of mental retardation are caused by social-cultural deprivation, so-called **cultural-familial retardation.** In fact, almost all persons with mild retardation come from such backgrounds. Their families might not provide them with adequate intellectual stimulation, such as encouraging them to read, helping them with homework, and taking them on educational outings. They also are more likely to attend inferior schools, to suffer from malnutrition, and to lack adequate medical care—each of which can impair intellectual growth.

Some cases of mental retardation are caused by brain damage, which we can now identify by using modern brain-scanning techniques (Schaefer & Bodensteiner, 1999). Brain damage in mentally retarded persons is often seen in the hippocampus, a structure associated with memory processes, and the cerebellum, a structure associated with motor coordination (Pulsifer, 1996). The brain damage that in some cases produces mental retardation is commonly caused by harmful environmental factors, sometimes related to parental health habits (Bryant & Maxwell, 1999). For example, pregnant women who ingest drugs or alcohol can cause brain damage in their offspring.

Women who suffer from severe *malnutrition* while pregnant can produce infants who have mental retardation because of a reduction in the number of their brain cells (Read, 1982). Prenatal exposure to X rays can impair the normal migration of brain cells, increasing the possibility of mental retardation (Schull, Norton, & Jensh, 1990). And a newborn infant who fails to breathe for several minutes after birth will experience *hypoxia,* a lack of oxygen to the brain. Hypoxia can cause the brain damage that characterizes **cerebral palsy** (Hoon & Johnston, 1998), a motor disorder often—but not always—accompanied by mental retardation.

Mental retardation also is caused by genetic factors (Simonoff, Bolton, & Rutter, 1996), as in the case of **phenylketonuria (PKU).** PKU is caused by an inherited lack of the enzyme required to metabolize the amino acid *phenylalanine,* which is found in milk and other common foods. This produces chemical changes that block the ability of brain cells to produce myelin (see Chapter 3), which leads to brain dysfunction and, as a result, mental retardation (Dyer, 1999). Fortunately, routine screening of newborns in the United States and other countries can detect PKU early enough to protect infants from brain damage by putting them on a diet that eliminates almost all of their intake of phenylalanine.

Some cases of mental retardation are produced by genetic defects that cause abnormal development during gestation, as in the case of **Down syndrome.** Human beings normally have 23 pairs of chromosomes. A person with Down syndrome has an extra, third chromosome on the 21st pair (Capone, 2001). The extra chromosome can come from either the mother or the father. Down syndrome usually is characterized by moderate retardation and distinctive physical characteristics. These include small ears and hands; short necks, feet, and fingers; protruding tongues; and a fold over the eyes, giving them an almond-shaped appearance. The chances of having a child with Down syndrome increase with age, being more common in middle-aged parents than in younger ones.

cultural-familial retardation
Mental retardation apparently caused by social or cultural deprivation.

cerebral palsy
A movement disorder caused by brain damage and that is sometimes accompanied by mental retardation.

phenylketonuria (PKU)
A hereditary enzyme deficiency that, if left untreated in the infant, causes mental retardation.

Down syndrome
A form of mental retardation, associated with certain physical deformities, that is caused by an extra, third chromosome on the 21st pair.

▲ **A Group Home**
People with mental retardation might live in supervised group homes, instead of in large institutions. They learn to develop self-care skills, including preparing their own meals.

Chapter Ten

Education of Persons with Mental Retardation

Today persons with mild retardation are called "educable," and persons with moderate retardation are called "trainable." From the 1950s to the 1970s, persons categorized as being educable mentally retarded were placed in special classes in which they received teaching tailored to their level of ability. But in the 1970s, dissatisfaction with the results of this approach led to *mainstreaming,* which places children with mental retardation in as many normal classes as possible and encourages them to participate in activities with children who do not have retardation. To promote mainstreaming in America, the Education for All Handicapped Children Act of 1975 mandated that children with mental retardation be given instruction in the most normal academic setting that is feasible for them (Sussan, 1990).

The educational needs of individuals with mental retardation are not limited to academic subjects. They also might need training in self-care skills (including eating, toileting, hygiene, dressing, and grooming); home management skills (including home maintenance, clothing care, food preparation, and home safety); consumer skills (including telephone use, money management, and shopping); and community mobility skills (including pedestrian safety and use of public transportation). Behavior modification has been especially useful in teaching self-care to persons with mental retardation (Huang & Cuvo, 1997).

A movement that has paralleled mainstreaming is *normalization,* the transfer of individuals with mental retardation from large institutional settings into community settings so they can live more normal lives. Given adequate support services, even people with severe and profound retardation can progress in settings other than large, custodial institutions, with the greatest benefit shown in their ability to care for themselves (Lynch, Kellow, & Willson, 1997).

Mental Giftedness

The study of mental retardation has been accompanied by interest in the study of **mental giftedness.** Francis Galton (1869) began the study of the mentally gifted in the 19th century. The mentally gifted are considered those with IQs above 130 and with exceptionally high scores on achievement tests in specific subjects, such as mathematics (Fox, 1981). The special needs of the mentally gifted have traditionally received less attention than those of persons with mental retardation. Because of this, many gifted children feel isolated and unchallenged in their classes (Winner, 1997). In the United States there has been a decline in funding for research on the gifted and a lack of funding for the education of gifted children (Sternberg, 1996). One positive trend has been a greater attempt to identify gifted ethnic minority children (Scott et al., 1996). Perhaps the best-known organization dedicated to meeting the needs of the mentally gifted is Mensa (Serebriakoff, 1985), which limits its membership to those who score in the top 2 percent on a standardized intelligence test.

One of the reasons for the traditional lack of interest in the mentally gifted was the belief in "early ripe, early rot"—that children who are intellectually precocious are doomed to become academic, vocational, and social failures. The classic case study in support of this viewpoint was that of William James Sidis (1898–1944). He was named in honor of William James, a colleague of his father, Boris, at Harvard University. Sidis was a mathematically gifted boy who enrolled at Harvard in 1909 at the age of 11 and received national publicity a year later when he gave a talk on higher mathematics to the Harvard Mathematical Club. But constant pressure from his father to excel and the glare of publicity eventually led Sidis to retreat from the world. In his early twenties, Sidis left the faculty position he had taken at Rice Institute in Houston and spent the rest of his life working at menial jobs. Years later, in 1937, James Thurber, writing under a pen name in the *New Yorker,* published a sarcastic article about Sidis entitled "April Fool" (Sidis was born on April 1). Thurber wrote that Sidis was a failure, living in a single room in a rundown section of Boston, which Thurber took to be evidence of the dire consequences of being too intelligent at too young an age. Sidis sued the *New Yorker* for libel and won a modest settlement shortly before dying—in obscurity—in 1944 (Wallace, 1986).

mental giftedness
Intellectual superiority marked by an IQ above 130 and exceptionally high scores on achievement tests in specific subjects, such as mathematics.

 Mensa International
www.mhhe.com/sdorow5

 The Archives of William James Sidis
www.mhhe.com/sdorow5

▲ **William James Sidis (1898–1944)**
"He died alone, obscure, and destitute, and he left a troublesome legacy best termed the 'Sidis Fallacy'—that talent like his rarely matures or becomes productive" (Montour, 1977, p. 265).

Contrary to the case of William James Sidis, mentally gifted children do not tend to become failures. This was demonstrated in perhaps the most famous longitudinal study ever conducted, Lewis Terman's Genetic Studies of Genius, which still inspires interest today—more than 80 years after it began.

Anatomy of a Research Study

What Is the Fate of Childhood Geniuses?

Rationale
Terman began his study in 1921, and it has continued ever since. He hoped to counter the commonsense belief that being too intelligent too early led to later failure.

Method
Terman used the Stanford-Binet Intelligence Scale to identify California children between the ages of 8 and 12 with IQs above 135. He found 1,528 such children. Their average IQ was 150. Reports on Terman's gifted children have appeared every decade or two since 1921. After Terman's death in 1956, Robert Sears (who was a member of the original sample) and Pauline Sears of Stanford University continued the study.

Results and Discussion
The Terman Genetic Studies of Genius has shown that mentally gifted children tend to become socially, physically, vocationally, and academically superior adults. They are healthier and more likely to attend college, to have professional careers, and to have happy marriages. Recent follow-up studies found that participants who reported having lived up to their intellectual potential at age 49 were more satisfied with their work and family lives than those who felt they had not realized their potential (Holahan, Holahan, & Wonacott, 1999).

Of course, Terman's study is not without certain weaknesses. Perhaps participants' awareness of being in such an important study affected how they performed in life—a kind of self-fulfilling prophecy. Also, could socioeconomic status, and not solely intelligence, have been a contributing factor? A follow-up study of samples of men from the original study found that men who maintained better health, had more stable marriages, and pursued more lucrative careers were less likely to come from families in which there was divorce, alcoholism, or other major family problems (Oden, 1968). Evidently, even for geniuses, the family environment is related to their success in life.

Opportunities for educational and occupational achievement also differed for the men and women who participated in the Terman study. Though two-thirds of the Terman women graduated from college, an astounding proportion considering they reached college age during the Great Depression of the 1930s—approximately half of the sample were employed outside the home at some point in their adult lives (Tomlinson-Keasey, 1990). It is important to remember, though, that women of their generation were expected to devote themselves to their spouses and family, and there were fewer professional opportunities for women than for men. Most (63 percent) of the Terman women expected to be wives and mothers, and many of them contributed to their spouse's career, worked in traditionally feminine occupations (typically teaching) after their children were grown, or dedicated themselves to volunteer organizations or the arts. Educational and employment opportunities for gifted women have improved over the last 50 years, however, and later studies find that the majority of gifted women—single or married—are employed in professional occupations. Nevertheless, a comparison of the Terman women and a younger sample, born in 1940, revealed no differences in life satisfaction (Schuster, 1990).

Other studies have added to our understanding of mentally gifted people. Despite their high level of intelligence, mentally gifted people—as in Terman's study—rarely become recognized for extraordinarily creative achievements. This indicates that outstanding creativity involves skills and personality traits different from those of the typical mentally gifted person (Winner, 2000).

◄ **Lewis Terman (1877–1956)**
"Children of IQ 140 or higher are, in general, appreciably superior to unselected children in physique, health, and social adjustment; markedly superior in moral attitudes as measured either by character tests or trait ratings; and vastly superior in their mastery of school subjects."

◀ **The Mentally Gifted**
Children who are mentally gifted, like those who are mentally retarded, benefit from special educational programs to help them develop their abilities.

STAYING ON TRACK: *Extremes of Intelligence*

1. What are some possible causes of mental retardation?
2. In what way has Terman's Genetic Studies of Genius countered the notion of "early ripe, early rot"?

Answers to Staying on Track start on ST-5.

 Terman Life Cycle Study of Children with High Ability
www.mhhe.com/sdorow5

 The Hollingworth Center for Highly Gifted Children
www.mhhe.com/sdorow5

◆ THEORIES OF INTELLIGENCE

Is intelligence a general characteristic that affects all facets of behavior, or are there different kinds of intelligence, each affecting a specific facet of behavior? Today intelligence researchers tend to assume there are several kinds of intelligence (Sternberg & Wagner, 1993). The notion that intelligence is positively correlated with faster brains is explored in the Psychology Versus Common Sense feature.

Factor-Analytic Theories of Intelligence

At about the same time as Alfred Binet was developing his intelligence test, British psychologist Charles Spearman (1863–1945) was developing a theory of intelligence. He considered intelligence a general ability that underlies a variety of behaviors.

Spearman's Theory of General Intelligence

In 1927, after more than two decades of research, Spearman published his conclusions about the nature of intelligence. He had developed a statistical technique called **factor analysis,** which determines the degree of correlation between performances on various tasks. If performances on certain tasks have a high positive correlation, then they are presumed to reflect the influence of a particular underlying factor. For example, if performances on a vocabulary test, a reading test, and a writing test correlate highly, they might reveal the influence of a "verbal ability" factor.

In using factor analysis, Spearman first gave a large group of people a variety of mental tasks. He found that scores on the tasks had high positive correlations with one another. This meant that participants tended to score high *or* moderate *or* low on all the tests. This led Spearman to conclude that performance on all of the tasks depended on the operation of a single underlying factor. He called this "*g*"—a general intelligence factor.

factor analysis
A statistical technique that determines the degree of correlation between performances on various tasks to determine the extent to which they reflect particular underlying characteristics, which are known as factors.

Are Faster Brains More Intelligent Brains?

Psychology Versus Common Sense

We sometimes refer to people as being "quick-witted," "fast thinkers," or mentally swift in some other way. Common sense presumes that the faster our brains process information, the more intelligent we will be. Many research studies have, indeed, found that people who score high on intelligence tests tend to be relatively faster in cognitive processing (Baumeister, 1998; Nettelback, 1998). For example, studies consistently have found a negative correlation between intelligence and reaction time (Neubauer et al., 1997). That is, shorter reaction times are associated with higher intelligence and longer reaction times are associated with lower intelligence. One explanation for this relationship is that intelligence might partly depend on the speed of neural impulse conduction (Barrett, Daum, & Eysenck, 1990). Perhaps one can, indeed, be "quick-witted."

A major criticism of the research on the relationship between intelligence and information-processing speed is that researchers who claim that there is a strong relationship between intelligence and the speed of information processing have exaggerated the implications of generally modest correlations between the two. A second criticism is that researchers have failed to explain the meaning of significant correlations between intelligence and the speed of information processing (Stankov & Roberts, 1997). In addition, the strength of the relationship between intelligence and reaction time varies across cultures. One study found, for example, that the size of the relationship between intelligence test scores and reaction time is smaller and, in fact, relatively weaker in rural Guatemalans than in residents from more urbanized environments (Choudhury & Gorman, 1999). This means that it might be unwise to make sweeping statements about the importance of information-processing speed in intelligent behavior.

Still another, somewhat humorous, source of criticism comes from research comparing the information-processing speed of animals and human beings. In one study, rhesus monkeys demonstrated faster reaction times on an information-processing task than human participants did (Washburn & Rumbaugh, 1997). But few human beings would use this finding to jump to the conclusion that monkeys are more intelligent than they are. At this time, the commonsense belief that people who are faster at information processing tend to be more intelligent than other people has some research backing, but the extent to which intelligence depends on information-processing speed remains to be determined.

But because the correlations between the tasks were less than a perfect 1.00, Spearman concluded that performance on each task also depended, to a lesser extent, on its own specific factor, which he called "*s*." For example, Spearman explained that scores on vocabulary tests and arithmetic tests tended to have a high positive correlation with each other because vocabulary ability and arithmetic ability are both influenced by a general intelligence factor. But because scores on vocabulary tests and arithmetic tests are not perfectly correlated, each ability must also depend on its own intelligence factor. Nonetheless, Spearman believed that the general intelligence factor was more important than any specific intelligence factor in governing a given ability. The existence of the factor *g* has received some research support. It appears to be associated mainly with activity in the frontal lobes (Duncan et al., 2000).

Thurstone's Theory of Primary Mental Abilities

Like Spearman, Louis Thurstone (1887–1955) used factor analysis to determine the nature of intelligence. But unlike Spearman, Thurstone (1938) concluded that there is no general intelligence factor. Instead, based on a battery of tests that he gave to college students, he identified seven factors, which he called *primary mental abilities:* reasoning, word fluency, perceptual speed, verbal comprehension, spatial visualization, numerical calculation, and associative memory.

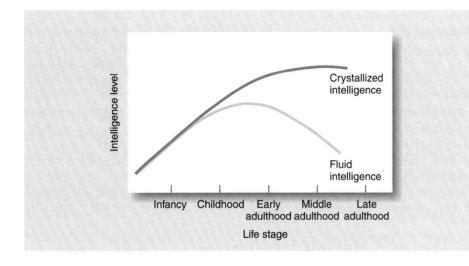

◀ **Figure 10.3**
Life-Span Changes in Intelligence
Whereas fluid intelligence tends to decline
in old age, crystallized intelligence tends to
increase (Horn & Donaldson, 1976).

Though scores on tests measuring these abilities had moderately high positive correlations with one another, they did not correlate highly enough for Thurstone to assume the existence of a general underlying intelligence factor. Suppose that you took tests to assess your abilities in reasoning, verbal comprehension, and numerical calculation. Thurstone would insist that your performance on any single test would reflect, not the influence of a general intelligence factor, but instead the influence of a specific intelligence factor related to the particular ability assessed by that test.

Horn and Cattell's Two-Factor Theory of Intelligence

Another theory of intelligence based on factor analysis was developed by John Horn and Raymond Cattell (1966), who identified two intelligence factors. **Fluid intelligence** reflects thinking ability, memory capacity, and speed of information processing. Whereas the ability to apply learned solutions to new problems depends on *crystallized intelligence,* the ability to find novel solutions to problems depends on fluid intelligence (Hunt, 1997). Horn and Cattell believe that fluid intelligence is largely inherited, is affected little by training, and declines in late adulthood. Recent research studies indicate that fluid intelligence does, in fact, decline across late adulthood (Schretlen et al., 2000).

Crystallized intelligence reflects the acquisition of skills and knowledge through schooling and everyday experience. Horn and Cattell have found that crystallized intelligence increases or remains the same in late adulthood. Changes in fluid intelligence and crystallized intelligence across the life span are illustrated in Figure 10.3.

It remains for psychologists to determine which, if any, of the factor-analytic theories of intelligence is the best. Perhaps a more telling criticism of factor-analytic theories of intelligence is that they assume that intelligence primarily reflects those cognitive abilities related to academic performance. A more encompassing theory of intelligence would consider a broader range of abilities. Theories proposed by Robert Sternberg and Howard Gardner have done so.

The Triarchic Theory of Intelligence

During the past two decades, Robert Sternberg (2000) has developed a **triarchic theory of intelligence,** which claims intelligence comprises three kinds of abilities. He based his theory on his observations of how people process information. *Componential intelligence* is similar to the kind of intelligence considered by traditional theories of intelligence. It primarily reflects our information-processing ability, which helps in academic performance. *Experiential intelligence* is the ability to combine different experiences in insightful ways to solve novel problems based on past experience. In part it reflects creativity, as exhibited by an artist, composer, or scientist. *Contextual intelligence* is the ability to function in practical,

fluid intelligence
The form of intelligence that reflects reasoning ability, memory capacity, and speed of information processing.

crystallized intelligence
The form of intelligence that reflects knowledge acquired through schooling and in everyday life.

triarchic theory of intelligence
Robert Sternberg's theory of intelligence, which assumes that there are three main kinds of intelligence: componential, experiential, and contextual.

everyday social situations. It reflects "street smarts," as in negotiating the price of a new car. Though many situations require the use of all three kinds of intelligence, some people are better at using one kind than at using the other two (Sternberg & Clinkenbeard, 1995).

The triarchic theory recognizes that we must be able to function in settings other than school. According to Sternberg (1999) this makes the triarchic theory of intelligence a better basis for developing intelligence tests that take into consideration cultural factors more than conventional intelligence tests do. Though Sternberg's theory goes beyond traditional theories by considering creative intelligence and practical intelligence, as well as academic intelligence, more research is needed to determine its merits. In one of the few experimental studies of the triarchic theory, classroom instructional methods based on that theory (which involved analytical, creative, and practical instruction) produced better student performance among third-graders and eighth-graders on a variety of tests than was produced by traditional instructional methods (Sternberg, Torff, & Grigorenko, 1998).

The Theory of Multiple Intelligences

theory of multiple intelligences
Howard Gardner's theory of intelligence, which assumes that the brain has evolved separate systems for seven kinds of intelligence.

Whereas Sternberg bases his theory on his study of information processing, Howard Gardner (1983) bases his **theory of multiple intelligences** on his belief that the brain has evolved separate systems for different adaptive abilities that he calls "intelligences." According to Gardner, there are seven types of intelligence, each of which is developed to a different extent in each of us: linguistic, logical-mathematical, spatial, musical, bodily-kinesthetic, intrapersonal, and interpersonal. Gardner assumes that certain brain structures and pathways underly these intelligences and that brain damage interferes with one or more of the intelligences. For example, damage to speech centers interferes with linguistic intelligence, and damage to the cerebellum interferes with bodily-kinesthetic intelligence.

Several of Gardner's kinds of intelligence are assessed by traditional intelligence tests. *Linguistic intelligence* is the ability to communicate through language. If you are good at reading textbooks, writing term papers, and presenting oral reports, you would be high in linguistic intelligence. A person with high *logical-mathematical intelligence* would be good at analyzing arguments and solving mathematical problems. And a person with high *spatial intelligence,* such as a skilled architect or carpenter, would be good at perceiving and arranging objects in the environment.

The remaining kinds of intelligence are assessed little, if at all, by traditional intelligence tests. *Musical intelligence* is the ability to analyze, compose, or perform music. A person with good *bodily-kinesthetic intelligence* would be able to move effectively, as in dancing or playing sports, or to manipulate objects effectively, as in using tools or driving a car. If you have high *intrapersonal intelligence,* you know yourself well and understand what motivates your behavior. And if you have high *interpersonal intelligence,* you function well in social situations because you are able to understand the needs of other people and to predict their behavior. People high in interpersonal intelligence are better at judging, for example, whether other people are trustworthy (Yamagishi, Kikuchi, & Kosugi, 1999).

According to Gardner, our ability to succeed in life depends on the degree to which we develop the kinds of intelligence needed to function well in our culture. For example, for most people in the United States, success depends more on linguistic intelligence than on musical intelligence. Success in a culture that relies on hunting skills would put a greater premium on spatial intelligence and bodily-kinesthetic intelligence. Gardner's theory is so new that it has yet to generate sufficient research to determine its merits, particularly research demonstrating valid means of assessing multiple intelligences (Plucker, Callahan, & Tomchin, 1996). But it is potentially superior to traditional theories of intelligence in its attention to the kinds of abilities needed to function in both academic and nonacademic settings. The theory has been used to determine the relationship between multiple intelligences and academic performance among high school students (Snyder, 2000). Unfortunately, the theory sometimes has been used to develop academic programs in schools simply based on the assumption that programs that seem logically related to the theory will be effective—with little research evidence to support that belief (Mettetal, Jordan, & Harper, 1997).

(a) (b) (c) (d)

▲ **The Theory of Multiple Intelligences**

Howard Gardner believes that we have evolved seven kinds of intelligence, which are developed to different extents in each of us. *(a)* The late Texas Congress person Barbara Jordan's excellent speaking ability exemplified linguistic intelligence. *(b)* Basketball star Michael Jordan's superb athletic ability exemplifies bodily-kinesthetic intelligence. *(c)* Rock musicians Eddie Vedder *(left)* and Neil Young *(right)*, who are both proficient in singing, playing, and composing music, exemplify musical intelligence. *(d)* And physicist Stephen Hawking has used his outstanding logical-mathematical intelligence to contribute to our knowledge of the cosmos—despite being disabled by amyotrophic lateral sclerosis (Lou Gehrig's disease).

A recent area of interest to researchers who are interested in identifying different kinds of intelligence has been the concept of *emotional intelligence,* which overlaps intrapersonal intelligence and interpersonal intelligence. People who are high in emotional intelligence are more empathetic (Davies, Stankov, & Roberts, 1998) and better able to manage their emotional states (Ciarocchi, Chan, & Caputi, 2000).

Consortium for Research on Emotional Intelligence in Organizations
www.mhhe.com/sdorow5

STAYING ON TRACK: *Theories of Intelligence*

1. What is the difference between Spearman's and Thurstone's factor-analytic theories of intelligence?
2. According to Gardner's theory of multiple intelligences, what kinds of intelligence are there?

Answers to Staying on Track start on ST-5.

eugenics

The practice of encouraging supposedly superior people to reproduce, while preventing supposedly inferior people from reproducing.

◆ NATURE, NURTURE, AND INTELLIGENCE

In the 1870s Francis Galton popularized the phrase *nature versus nurture* (Fancher, 1984). As a follower of his cousin Charles Darwin, Galton (1869) concluded that intelligence is inherited after finding that eminent men had a higher proportion of eminent relatives than other men did. This led Galton to champion **eugenics** (Rabinowitz, 1984), the practice of encouraging supposedly superior people to reproduce, while preventing supposedly inferior people from reproducing. Even at the turn of the 21st century, many people still believed in the controversial practice of eugenics (Ouimet & De Man, 1998).

Early Studies of Women

Gender differences in mental abilities were studied as early as 1900 when Helen Bradford Thompson (1874–1947)—later known by her married name, Helen Thompson Woolley—compared 25 men and 25 women on measures of motor and sensory abilities, intellect, and emotion. She concluded that the gender differences she observed were due to socialization rather than to biological differences between women and men (Milar, 2000). In a later review of the psychological research on gender differences she concluded, "There is perhaps no field aspiring to be scientific where flagrant personal bias, logic martyred in the cause of supporting a prejudice, unfounded assertions, and even sentimental rot and drivel, have run riot to such an extent as here" (Woolley, 1910, p. 340).

▲ **Helen Thompson Woolley (1874–1947)**

"There seems to be a general trend toward the opinion that mind is probably not a secondary sexual character—in other words that there are probably few if any psychological differences of sex which are of biological origin."

▲ **Leta Stetter Hollingworth (1886–1939)**

"In view of the facts that in many of the cases the conclusions are based on a small number of subjects and that the evidence is conflicting, it seems necessary to conclude that the comparative variability of the sexes in mental traits has not been determined experimentally."

variability hypothesis

The prediction that men, as a group, are more variable than women.

Despite this empirical evidence—and the fact that women were entering higher education in record numbers—belief in the superiority of the male intellect was unshaken. Differential psychologists turned to the *variability hypothesis* (Shields, 1982). The **variability hypothesis,** derived from evolutionary theory, stated that men, as a group, are more variable than women. Thus, whereas groups of women and men might be equivalent *on average*—as Helen Thompson Wooley's review reported—only men will be found at the extremes of human attributes. The variability hypothesis was used to explain why there were more men with extraordinary intellects—and more men with intellectual deficits—than women.

The variability hypothesis was tested in a series of studies by Leta Stetter Hollingworth (1886–1939). In 1912 and 1913, she studied 1,000 female and male residents of the Clearing-House for Mental Defectives. She found that men and boys were admitted more frequently, but these data were biased. Male residents were admitted at an earlier age than female residents, which she attributed to the fact that women were identified as "mentally deficient" less often. In contrast, boys' deficits in intellectual abilities and functioning were more readily apparent. She concluded that many women escaped institutionalization because they could perform menial domestic tasks (Hollingworth, 1914).

Leta Stetter Hollingworth's empirical research and her conclusion that social factors played an important role in the observed differences between women's and men's lives strongly influenced her contemporaries. By the 1920s the variability hypothesis was discredited and prominent psychologists such as Lewis Terman began to consider the role of social discrimination in women's intellectual achievement (Benjamin & Shields, 1990).

Early Studies of Immigrants

In 1912 Henry Goddard became director of the program for testing the intelligence of immigrants arriving at Ellis Island in New York Harbor. Goddard (1917) made the astonishing claim that 79 percent of Italians, 80 percent of Hungarians, 83 percent of Jews, and 87 percent of Russians scored in the "feebleminded" range on the Binet-Simon scale, which today we would call the mildly retarded range. After later reevaluating his data, he claimed that an average of "only" 40 percent of these groups were feebleminded (Gelb, 1986). Goddard, following in the footsteps of Galton, concluded that these ethnic groups were, by nature, intellectually inferior.

You probably realize that Goddard discounted possible environmental causes for the poor test performance of immigrants. He failed to consider a lack of education, a long ocean voyage below deck, and anxiety created by the testing situation as causes of their poor performance. Moreover, even though the tests were translated into the immigrants' native languages, the translations were often inadequate. Despite the shortcomings of the tests, low test scores were used as the basis for having many supposedly "feebleminded" immigrants deported. This was ironic, because at the 1915 meeting of the APA in Chicago a critic of Goddard's program of intelligence testing reported that the native-born mayor of Chicago had taken an IQ test and had scored in the feebleminded range (Gould, 1981).

Further support for Goddard's position was provided by the army's intelligence testing program during World War I, headed by Robert Yerkes (1876–1956). One of Yerkes's colleagues, Carl Brigham (1923), published the results of the testing program. He found that immigrants scored lower on the IQ tests than their American-born counterparts did. Brigham attributed these differences in IQ scores to differences in heredity. The U.S. Congress passed the Immigration Act of 1924, which restricted immigration from eastern and southern Europe. There is disagreement between those who believe that Brigham's findings influenced passage of the act (McPherson, 1985) and those who believe that they did not (Snyderman & Herrnstein, 1983).

Regardless, in 1930 Brigham stated he had been wrong in assuming that the poorer performance of immigrants was attributable to heredity. He noted that in their everyday lives, immigrants—living in their original cultures—might not have had the opportunity to encounter much of the material in the army IQ tests. To appreciate this, consider the following multiple-choice items from the Army Alpha Test: "Crisco is a: patent medicine, disinfectant, toothpaste, food product [the correct answer]"; and "Christy Mathewson is famous as a(n): writer, artist, baseball player [the correct answer], comedian" (Gould, 1981). Similarly, the poorer performance of African Americans on IQ tests was attributed to social-cultural deprivation caused by segregation (Rury, 1988). Contemporary controversy surrounding the heritability of intelligence is described in the Thinking Critically About Psychology and the Media feature.

The Influence of Heredity and Environment on Intelligence

After three decades of relative indifference to it, the issue of nature versus nurture reemerged in the 1960s when President Lyndon Johnson began *Project Head Start,* which provides preschool children from deprived socioeconomic backgrounds with enrichment programs to promote their intellectual development. Head Start was stimulated in part by the finding that African Americans scored lower than European Americans on IQ tests. Those who supported Head Start attributed this difference to the poorer socioeconomic conditions in which African American children were more likely to be reared.

But in 1969 an article by psychologist Arthur Jensen questioned whether programs such as Head Start could significantly boost the intellectual level of deprived children. Jensen's doubts were based on the notion of **heritability,** the extent to which the variability in a characteristic within a group can be attributed to heredity. Jensen claimed that intelligence has a heritability of .80, which would mean that 80 percent of the variability in intelligence among the members of a group can be explained by heredity. This led him to conclude that the IQ gap between European American and African American children was mainly attributable to heredity. But he was accused of making an unwarranted inference. Just because intelligence might have high heritability *within* a group does not mean that IQ differences between groups, such as African Americans and European Americans, are caused by heredity. Moreover, research has found that the heritability of intelligence is closer to .50 than to .80 (Casto, DeFries, & Fulker, 1995). Jensen's article led to accusations that he was a racist and to demonstrations against him when he spoke on college campuses, illustrating the tension between academic freedom and social sensitivity.

A vigorous response to those who claimed that intelligence is chiefly the product of heredity came from Leon Kamin (1974). Kamin had discovered that important data supporting the hereditary basis of intelligence had been falsified. Cyril Burt (1883–1971), a British psychologist, had reported findings from three studies showing that the positive correlation in IQ scores between identical twins reared apart was higher than the correlation in IQ of fraternal twins reared together. Because identical twins reared apart have the same genes but different environments, yet had a higher correlation in intelligence than did fraternal twins reared together, the data supported the greater influence of heredity on intelligence.

In each of his studies, supposedly using different sets of twins, Burt reported that the correlation in intelligence between identical twins reared apart was .771. But, as Kamin observed, the odds against finding the same correlation to three decimal places in three different studies are so high as to defy belief. Even Burt's official biographer, who began as an admirer and who believed Burt had not falsified his data, grudgingly concluded that the data

heritability
The proportion of variability in a trait across a population attributable to genetic differences among members of the population.

(a)

(b)

◀ **The Nurturing of Intelligence**
Children from *(a)* higher socioeconomic backgrounds will be more likely than children from *(b)* lower socioeconomic backgrounds to receive the intellectual enrichment they need to reach their intellectual potential.

How Should We Respond to *The Bell Curve?*

Few books have provoked, in both professional journals and the popular media, the kind of controversy provoked by *The Bell Curve: Intelligence and Class Structure in American Life* (Herrnstein & Murray, 1994). For a while it was impossible to go a day without being confronted by media coverage of the controversy surrounding the book, which spent 15 weeks on the *New York Times* best seller list and sold more than 500,000 copies within a few months of its publication. The controversy made the cover of *Newsweek* and the *New York Times Magazine.* And radio and television programs, including *Nightline*, *Charlie Rose,* and the *McNeil-Lehrer News Hour,* pitted the book's supporters and detractors against each other. But what was it about *The Bell Curve*— a book about intelligence—that created this furor?

The furor was created primarily by a conclusion implied by psychologist Richard Herrnstein and political scientist Charles Murray, the authors of *The Bell Curve.* They implied, without formally stating it, that research studies had convincingly demonstrated that there are significant ethnic differences in intelligence, with people of European descent being intellectually superior to those of African descent. They also concluded that because intelligence is largely inherited, efforts to improve the intellectual abilities of poor children, such as Project Head Start, will have little effect. The authors urged that, instead of fruitless efforts to improve the status of people who cannot improve, we should simply place people in the social positions they are genetically well suited for.

Many academics who opposed the book's premise accused its authors of basing their conclusions on flawed statistical analyses (Darlington, 1996) and weak scientific evidence (Poston & Winebarger, 1996). Some critics accused Herrnstein and Murray of using poor science to support their own unadmitted racist social and political agendas. The APA even established a task force on intelligence to assess the claims made in *The Bell Curve* (Neisser et al., 1996).

Other scholars noted that the authors, in tracing the history of attempts to examine the hereditary basis of intelligence, left out any instances in which claims of ethnic differences in intelligence were based on scientific fraud or biased interpretations of data (Samelson, 1997). Moreover, there is evidence that the consistent 10-15-point difference, on average, between European Americans and African Americans is the product of the environment, not heredity. A study by psychologist Jeanne Brooks-Gunn found that factors related to socioeconomic status explained the difference in intelligence test scores between European American and African American children. She found no evidence that the difference was attributable to heredity (Brooks-Gunn, Klebanov, & Duncan, 1996).

Though *The Bell Curve* received more criticism than support, some scholars have praised its scientific merits (Weidman, 1997). Supporters accused the book's critics of ignoring strong evidence favoring its claims in order to support their own sociopolitical agendas (Rushton, 1997). In response to the widespread criticism of *The Bell Curve,* 52 international scholars in the field of intelligence signed a statement entitled "Mainstream Science on Intelligence," supporting a number of the book's scientific conclusions, that was published in the *Wall Street Journal* (December 13, 1994). Few of the signees had ever been accused of letting racism guide their scientific practices. They refrained from endorsing some of the more inflammatory claims made in the book. Though supporting the reality of a genetic basis for IQ differences, they made no claims about the contribution of heredity to IQ differences between ethnic groups.

Of all the arguments put forth by psychologists in favor of the book's premise, perhaps the most astounding—to those who oppose it—is that many of the book's critics, especially college professors, are genetically predisposed to express moral outrage at it! According to this view, those who are genetically programmed to be more altruistic are drawn to helping occupations, such as education. This, according to the argument, inclines them toward more liberal sociopolitical positions—such as opposing any evidence of a genetic basis for social status in favor of insisting that environmental manipulations can have profound effects on people's upward mobility (Ellis, 1998).

 Testing and Intelligence
www.mhhe.com/sdorow5

| Chapter Ten

In his highly critical article, Stephen Jay Gould (1994), concludes that, given what he believes to be the scientific impossibility of determining whether there are hereditary ethnic differences in intelligence, the best position to take is one of intellectual agnosticism toward the issue—though he believes intellectuals should be free to study that and virtually any other topic. But another critic of *The Bell Curve,* Andrew Barrett, went even further, arguing that the topic of ethnic differences in intelligence should not be studied at all because, regardless of what research studies find, the harm that such research would do would not be worth the knowledge it might provide.

were indeed fraudulent (Hearnshaw, 1979). This has not prevented others from coming to Burt's defense, trying to explain away his apparent falsification of data as merely the product of careless data recording (Samelson, 1992). Whatever the explanation, his data are not trustworthy (Butler & Petrulis, 1999). Ironically, less than a decade after Kamin's critique of Burt's research, the Minnesota Study of Twins Reared Apart found that the correlation in intelligence of identical twins reared apart was .710—not very different from what Burt had reported (Lykken, 1982).

Family Studies of Intelligence

Though the publicity generated by the discovery of Cyril Burt's deception struck a blow against the hereditary view of intelligence, other researchers have conducted legitimate family studies of intelligence. As shown in Figure 10.4, the closer the genetic relationship between relatives, the more similar they are in intelligence (Bouchard & McGue, 1981). But the closer the genetic relationship between relatives, the more likely they also are to share similar environments. Consequently, the size of the correlation in intelligence between relatives of varying degrees of genetic similarity is, by itself, inadequate to determine whether this similarity is caused primarily by hereditary factors or by environmental factors.

Twin Studies. Perhaps the higher correlation in intelligence between identical twins reared together than between fraternal twins reared together might be attributable to the more similar treatment received by identical twins. But research findings have provided strong evidence against this interpretation. When identical twins are mistakenly reared as fraternal twins, they become as similar in intelligence as identical twins who are reared as identical twins. Moreover, fraternal twins who are mistakenly reared as identical twins become no more similar in intelligence than do fraternal twins reared as fraternal twins (Scarr & Carter-Saltzman, 1979). These findings indicate that the similarity in intelligence between twins is determined more by their genetic similarity than by their environmental similarity.

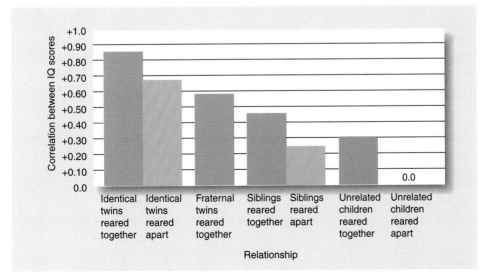

◄ **Figure 10.4**
Heredity Versus Environment

The correlation in IQ between relatives increases as their hereditary or environmental similarity increases.

▲ **Sandra Scarr**

"Behavioral differences among individuals . . . can arise in any population from genetic differences, from variations among their environments, or both."

 Head Start
www.mhhe.com/sdorow5

Adoption Studies. To separate the effects of heredity and environment, researchers have turned to adoption studies. Some of these studies compare the correlation in intelligence between adopted children and their adoptive parents to the correlation in intelligence between adopted children and their biological parents. A review of adoption studies found that the positive correlation in intelligence between adoptees and their biological parents is larger than the positive correlation between adoptees and their adoptive parents (Loehlin, Horn, & Willerman, 1994). This supports a genetic basis of intelligence; the genes inherited from the natural parents appear to exert a stronger influence on adoptees than does the environment provided by their adoptive parents (Bouchard & McGue, 1981).

In addition to their support for the influence of heredity on intelligence, adoption studies have provided support for the effect of the environment on intelligence. If nature dominates nurture, then poor children who are adopted by parents from higher socioeconomic classes should show little or no gain in IQ when compared to equivalent children who remain with their biological parents. This possibility was tested by Sandra Scarr and Richard Weinberg (1976) in the Minnesota Adoption Study. The study included African American children who had been adopted by European American couples of higher socioeconomic status than the children's biological parents. The study found that the children who had been adopted had an average IQ of 110. This indicated that the environment had a strong effect on their intelligence, because the adoptees scored about 20 points higher than the average IQ of African American children of the same socioeconomic status reared by their biological parents. These findings indicate that nurture, as well as nature, is important in intellectual development, because children adopted into families of higher socioeconomic status have IQs that are higher than those of their biological parents, though lower than those of their adoptive parents (Weinberg, Scarr, & Waldman, 1992). Based on their review of adoption studies, Scarr and Weinberg (1983) concluded that intelligence is influenced by both heredity and environment, with neither dominating the other.

Intellectual Enrichment Programs

Further support for the influence of the environment on intelligence comes from the finding that the difference between European American and African American performance on the SAT narrowed between 1976 and 1983 (Jones, 1984). Moreover, the difference between African American and European American children in IQ test scores is declining, possibly because more African American children have gained access to better educational and economic resources (Vincent, 1991). Access to enrichment programs such as Project Head Start also might play a role. Head Start ensures that poor children get medical care, helps their families gain access to social services, finds employment for parents, serves nutritious meals, provides intellectual stimulation, and helps children develop the social competence necessary to succeed in school (Zigler, 1999).

Poor children who attend Project Head Start show an average gain of 10 points in their IQ scores (Zigler et al., 1982) and greater improvement in their cognitive abilities, compared to those not in such programs. This contradicts Jensen's (1969) prediction that Head Start would have no significant effect on intellectual growth. Unfortunately, the gains achieved by children in preschool enrichment programs often decline during grade school (Locurto, 1991), perhaps in part because these children typically attend inferior schools (Lee & Loeb, 1995). This might indicate the need to continue enrichment programs beyond the preschool years.

Preschool enrichment programs other than Head Start also can have beneficial effects, as shown in a study of disadvantaged African American children who attended Head Start, other preschool, or no preschool programs. Those in the Head Start and preschool programs showed greater improvement in several intellectual abilities than did those who did not attend either kind of program. This could not be attributed to initial differences in intellectual abilities, because the children were statistically matched on various relevant characteristics (Lee et al., 1990).

Even more evidence of the influence of the environment on intelligence comes from the finding that IQ scores have increased from 5 to 25 points in fourteen nations during the past few decades, apparently because of better nutrition, education, and health care (Flynn, 1987). And both Galton and Goddard would be surprised to find that today the Japanese,

Chapter Ten

◀ **Project Head Start**

Intellectual enrichment programs, such as Project Head Start, provide a stimulating preschool environment that better prepares children for success in elementary school.

whom they considered intellectually inferior, score significantly higher than Americans on IQ tests that have been standardized on Americans. Japanese children score about 10 points higher than American children (Lynn, 1982). The Japanese increase in IQ scores parallels that country's increased emphasis on education, with children going to school more hours, attending school more days, and studying more hours than American children do. It is difficult to attribute this increase in IQ scores to accelerated evolution of Japanese brains.

Some psychologists have suggested that it might not be in our best interest to study the relative importance of nature and nurture in intellectual development (Sarason, 1984). To do so might discover little of scientific import, while providing apparent scientific support for discrimination against ethnic minorities. Instead of examining the relative importance of nature versus nurture, it might be better to do what Anne Anastasi (1958), an authority on psychological testing, suggested more than four decades ago: determine *how* both achieve their effects (Turkheimer, 1991).

STAYING ON TRACK: *Nature, Nurture, and Intelligence*

1. What have adoption studies (especially studies of identical twins reared apart) discovered about the role of nature and nurture in intelligence?
2. What effects do programs such as Head Start have on deprived children's intellectual abilities?

Answers to Staying on Track start on ST-5.

Chapter Summary

INTELLIGENCE TESTING
- Intelligence is the global capacity to act purposefully, to think rationally, and to deal effectively with the environment.
- An achievement test assesses knowledge of a particular subject; an aptitude test predicts the potential to benefit from instruction in a particular academic or vocational setting; and an intelligence test is a kind of aptitude test that assesses overall mental ability.

- Francis Galton began the study of mental abilities in the late 19th century and founded the field of differential psychology.
- The first formal test of general intelligence was the Binet-Simon scale, which was developed to help place children in school classes.
- The American version of the test became known as the Stanford-Binet Intelligence Scale. Today that test and the Wechsler Intelligence Scales are the most commonly used intelligence tests.

- Tests must be standardized so that they are administered in a uniform manner and so that test scores can be compared with norms.
- A test must also be reliable, giving consistent results over time.
- And a test must be valid, meaning that it measures what it is supposed to measure.
- Controversy has arisen over whether intelligence testing is fair to ethnic minority groups, particularly African Americans.
- Those who oppose intelligence testing claim that because African Americans, on the average, score lower than European Americans do, the tests are biased against African Americans.
- Those who support their use claim that the tests accurately predict the academic performance of both African Americans and European Americans, and typically attribute the differences in performance to the deprived backgrounds that are more common among African American children.

EXTREMES OF INTELLIGENCE
- To be classified as mentally retarded, a person must have an IQ below 70 and, beginning in childhood, difficulties performing in everyday life.
- The four categories of mental retardation are mild retardation, moderate retardation, severe retardation, and profound retardation.
- Though most cases of mental retardation are caused by cultural-familial factors, some are caused by brain damage.
- Most people with mental retardation can benefit from education and training programs.
- To be classified as mentally gifted, a person must have an IQ above 130 and demonstrate unusual ability in at least one area, such as art, music, or mathematics.
- Lewis Terman's Genetic Studies of Genius have demonstrated that mentally gifted children tend to become successful in their academic, social, physical, and vocational lives.
- Social change and increased occupational opportunity for women are reflected in generational differences in gifted women's achievement.

THEORIES OF INTELLIGENCE
- Theories of intelligence have traditionally depended on factor analysis, a statistical technique for determining the abilities that underlie intelligence.

- The theories differ in the extent to which they view intelligence as a general factor or a combination of different factors.
- The most recent factor-analytic theory distinguishes between fluid intelligence and crystallized intelligence.
- Robert Sternberg's triarchic theory of intelligence is based on his research on information processing. The theory distinguishes between componential (academic) intelligence, experiential (creative) intelligence, and contextual (practical) intelligence.
- Howard Gardner's theory of multiple intelligences is a biopsychological theory, which assumes that the brain has evolved separate systems for different adaptive abilities that he calls "intelligences": linguistic, logical-mathematical, spatial, musical, bodily-kinesthetic, intrapersonal, and interpersonal intelligences.
- We all vary in the degree to which we have developed each of these kinds of intelligence.

NATURE, NURTURE, AND INTELLIGENCE
- One of the most controversial issues in psychology has been the extent to which intelligence is a product of heredity or of environment.
- Early studies of women addressed gender differences and variability in physical and mental attributes. Few gender differences were observed, and the variability hypothesis was not supported.
- Early studies of immigrants concluded that many were "feeble-minded." The examiners attributed this to hereditary factors rather than to a host of cultural and environmental factors that actually accounted for that finding.
- Arthur Jensen created a stir by claiming that heredity is a much more powerful determinant of intelligence than is environment.
- Studies of twins, adopted children, and enrichment programs indicate that neither heredity nor environment is a significantly more important determinant of intelligence.
- Though intelligence might be highly heritable, there is no widely accepted evidence that differences in intelligence between particular ethnic groups are caused by heredity.

Key Concepts

Thought Questions

1. Why do some psychologists believe that Gardner's theory of multiple intelligences might lead to intelligence tests that are superior to traditional ones?

2. How did Terman's longitudinal study of geniuses revise people's thinking about extremely intelligent people?

3. In what ways have science, politics, and social-cultural factors become part of the debate on the relative roles of nature and nurture in intelligence?

Possible Answers to Thought Questions start on p. PT-3.

OLC Preview

 For additional quizzing and a variety of interactive resources, visit the book's Online Learning Center at www.mhhe.com/sdorow5.

Motivation

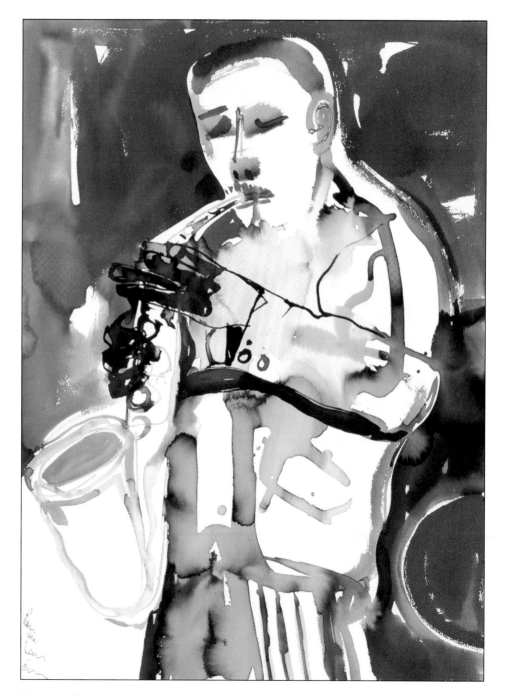

ROMARE BEARDON
Saxaphone Solo, 1987

On a beautiful spring day in 2000, hundreds of residents of the popular arts community comprising New Hope, Pennsylvania, and Lambertville, New Jersey, attended the funeral of a man who had been known as "Mother" since his arrival in 1949. Mother, born Joseph Cavellucci in New York City in 1925, "came out of the closet" regarding his homosexuality as a teenager growing up in Philadelphia.

Mother was so beloved and well known that the *Philadelphia Inquirer* published a major obituary for him, calling him an icon of the gay community. His local daily newspaper called him "larger than life" and said, "Cavellucci achieved something many of us aspire to—he lived life on his own terms" (Duffy, 2000, p. A-1). Mother often behaved like a curmudgeon with a sense of humor. On one occasion, while working as a server (his longtime profession) at a canal-side restaurant in New Hope, Mother responded to a woman who complained that her companion had one more shrimp than she had by simply tossing one of her partner's shrimps into the canal. He added, "Now you both have the same number." Yet, Mother was also kind-hearted. As noted by New Hope Mayor Larry Keller in his eulogy for Mother, "She'd never decline to perform at any event to raise money for someone in need."

As one of Mother's "family" remarked after his death, "She was truly the town's mother. She embraced everyone no matter what" (Duffy, 2000, p. A-4). Mother's "children," gay, lesbian, and straight, repaid his kindness by holding several fundraisers to pay for his long battle against cancer. In his last days, Mother lived at Buckingham Valley Nursing Home, which he naturally renamed "Buckingham Palace," with himself as both king and queen. "I am the reigning man and woman," he announced. The nurses took turns putting on Mother's makeup and nail polish and teasing his hair.

▲ **Joseph "Mother" Cavellucci**
"Mother" was an early supporter of gay rights and a well-known and beloved leader of the gay community in the Philadelphia area.

motivation
The psychological process that arouses, directs, and maintains behavior toward a goal.

After reading this brief passage on the life of Joseph "Mother" Cavellucci, you might ask, Why would a person born male be sexually attracted to other men? Possible answers to this question are presented in this chapter's section on human sexuality. This chapter also discusses other kinds of human *motivation*, including hunger, arousal, and achievement.

◆ THE NATURE OF MOTIVATION

Motivation is the psychological process that arouses, directs, and maintains behavior toward a goal. The hunger motive, for example, normally arouses us to take action, directs us to find food, and makes us eat until our hunger subsides. Because we cannot directly observe people's motivation, we must infer it from their behavior. We might infer that a person who drinks a quart of water is motivated by a strong thirst and that a person who becomes dictator of a country is motivated by a strong need for power. The concept of motivation also is useful in explaining fluctuations in behavior over time (Atkinson, 1981). If yesterday morning you ate three stacks of pancakes but this morning you ate only a piece of toast, your friends would not attribute your change in behavior to a change in your personality. Instead, they would attribute it to a change in your degree of hunger—your motivation.

Sources of Motivation

What are the main sources of motivation? In seeking answers to this question, psychologists have implicated *genes*, *drives*, and *incentives*.

▲ **Motivation**
Why did Bill Irwin, a blind man, risk hiking the entire Appalachian Trail, which extends from Maine to Georgia? Psychologists rely on the concept of motivation to explain this and other behavior.

▲ **William McDougall (1871–1938)**

"The human mind has certain innate or inherited tendencies which are the essential springs or motive powers of all thought and action."

Sociobiology
www.mhhe.com/sdorow5

instinct

A complex, inherited behavior pattern characteristic of a species.

sociobiology

The study of the hereditary basis of human and animal social behavior.

drive-reduction theory

The theory that behavior is motivated by the need to reduce drives such as sex or hunger.

need

A motivated state caused by physiological deprivation, such as a lack of food or water.

drive

A state of psychological tension induced by a need.

homeostasis

A steady state of physiological equilibrium.

Genes and Motivation

In the early 20th century, many psychologists, influenced by Charles Darwin's theory of evolution and led by William McDougall (1871–1938), attributed human and animal motivation to *instincts*. An **instinct** is a complex, inherited (that is, unlearned) behavior pattern characteristic of a species. Instincts are at work when birds build nests, spiders weave webs, and salmon swim upstream to their spawning grounds. But what of human instincts? McDougall (1908) claimed that human beings are guided by a variety of instincts, including instincts for "pugnacity," "curiosity," and "gregariousness." As discussed in Chapter 13, McDougall's contemporary, Sigmund Freud, based his theory of personality on instincts that motivate sex and aggression. And William James (1890/1981) claimed that human beings are motivated by more instincts than any other animal.

In the 1920s, psychologists, influenced by behaviorist John B. Watson, rejected instincts as factors in human motivation. Watson believed that human behavior depends on learning, not heredity. One reason instinct theorists lost scientific credibility was that they had attempted to explain almost all human behavior as instinctive, in some cases compiling lists of thousands of alleged human instincts (Cofer, 1985). An instinct theorist might say, for example, that people paint because of an "aesthetic instinct" or play sports because of a "competitive instinct." A second reason instinct theorists fell out of favor was their failure to explain the behaviors they labeled as instinctive. Consider the following hypothetical dialogue about an alleged "parenting instinct":

Why do parents take care of their children?
Because they have a parenting instinct.
But how do you know parents have a parenting instinct?
Because they take care of their children.

Such circular reasoning neither explains why parents take care of their children nor provides evidence of a parenting instinct. Each assertion is simply used to support the other.

Though instinct theory, as applied to human beings, has fallen into disfavor, some contemporary psychologists who stress the importance of evolution see a role for the instinct concept in the study of personality (De Raad & Doddema-Winsemius, 1999). Today, psychologists who stress the role of heredity in human behavior might work in the field of **sociobiology**, founded by Edward O. Wilson in the 1970s (Wilson, 1975). But sociobiology has been criticized for overestimating the role of heredity in human social behavior (Hood, 1995). Critics fear that acceptance of sociobiology would lend support to the status quo, making us less inclined to change what many people believe has been "ordained by God or nature," such as differences in the social status of men and women, African Americans and European Americans, and rich and poor. Nonetheless sociobiology has contributed to the emergence of the evolutionary psychology perspective (see Chapter 1) and influenced research on personality and other topics (Heckhausen, 2000).

Drives and Motivation

Following the decline of the instinct theory of human motivation, the **drive-reduction theory** of Clark Hull (1884–1952) dominated psychology in the 1940s and 1950s (Webster & Coleman, 1992). According to Hull (1943), a **need** caused by physiological deprivation, such as a lack of food or water, induces a state of tension called a **drive**, which motivates the individual to reduce it.

Drive reduction aims at the restoration of **homeostasis**, a steady state of physiological equilibrium. Consider your thirst drive. When your body loses water, as when you perspire, receptor cells in your *hypothalamus* (see Chapter 3) respond and make you feel thirsty. Thirst arouses you, signaling you that your body lacks water, and directs you to drink. By drinking, you reduce your thirst and restore homeostasis by restoring your body's normal water level. Undoubtedly we are motivated to reduce drives such as thirst, hunger, and sex, but drive reduction cannot explain all human motivation. In some cases we perform behaviors that do not reduce physiological drives, as in athletes' performance in sports. This shows we are sometimes motivated by *incentives*.

Incentives and Motivation

Whereas a drive is an internal state of tension that "pushes" you toward a goal, an **incentive** is an external stimulus that "pulls" you toward a goal. Through experience, we learn that certain stimuli (such as a puppy) are desirable and should be approached, making them *positive* incentives. We also learn that other stimuli (such as elevator music) are undesirable and should be avoided, making them *negative* incentives. Thus, we are pulled toward positive incentives and away from negative ones. Incentives often are used by teachers and employers to motivate students (Kastner et al., 1995) and employees (Loeser, Henderlite, & Conrad, 1995).

Incentives may be associated with drives. For example, your thirst drive motivates you to replenish your body's water, but incentives determine what you choose to drink. Your thirst would push you to drink, but your favorite flavor would pull you toward a particular beverage. As with all incentives, your favorite flavor would partly depend on learning, which in this case would depend on your past experience with a variety of flavors. In the case of airline passengers who survived a crash in the Andes years ago and cannibalized the bodies of passengers who had died, a strong hunger drive made them respond to a weak incentive, human flesh. The opposite can occur in your everyday life. Despite not feeling hungry, you might be motivated to eat in response to a strong incentive, such as an ice cream sundae.

Maslow's Hierarchy of Needs

If forced to make a choice, would you prefer to get enough food to eat or straight A's in school? Would you prefer to have a home or close friends? In each case, though both options are appealing, you would probably choose the first; this shows that some motives have priority over others. The fact that we have such preferences led the humanistic psychologist Abraham Maslow (1970) to develop a **hierarchy of needs** (see Figure 11.1), which ranks important needs by their priority. Maslow used the term *need* to refer to both physiological and psychological motives. According to Maslow you must first satisfy your basic *physiological* needs, such as your needs for food and water, before you will be motivated to meet your higher needs for *safety* and *security,* and so on up the hierarchy from

▲ **Edward O. Wilson**
"The hypothalamus and the limbic system are engineered to perpetuate DNA."

Abraham H. Maslow Publications
www.mhhe.com/sdorow5

incentive
An external stimulus that pulls an individual toward a goal.

hierarchy of needs
Abraham Maslow's arrangement of needs in the order of their motivational priority, ranging from physiological needs to the needs for self-actualization and transcendence.

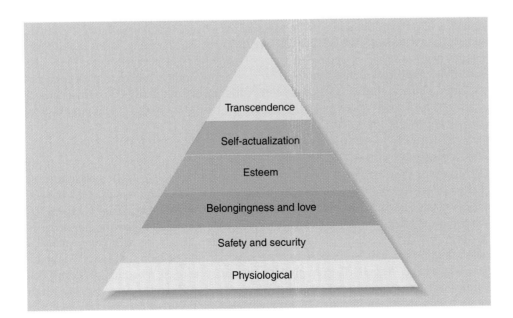

◀ **Figure 11.1**
Maslow's Hierarchy of Needs
Abraham Maslow assumed that our needs are arranged in a hierarchy, with our most powerful needs at the bottom. We will be weakly motivated by higher needs until our lower needs are met.

the need for *belongingness and love,* through the need for *esteem,* and ultimately to the needs for *self-actualization* (achievement of all your potentials) and *transcendence* (spiritual fulfillment).

Maslow believed that because few people satisfy all their lower needs, few reach the two highest levels. Nonetheless, success in meeting lower-level needs in the hierarchy is positively correlated with psychological well-being (Lester, 1990). Though Maslow died before conducting much research on people who had reached transcendence, he did study the lives of people he considered self-actualized, including Abraham Lincoln and Eleanor Roosevelt.

Though some research on Maslow's hierarchy of needs—such as a study of the satisfaction of needs in 88 countries from 1960 to 1994 (Hagerty, 1999)—has supported his sequence of need achievement, we do not always place a higher priority on lower-level needs (Goebel & Brown, 1981). This was supported by a survey of 150 college students that asked them to identify which of the needs in Maslow's hierarchy was most important to them. Both male and female undergraduates chose being in love as more important than any other need (Pettijohn, 1996). Moreover, martyrs such as Mahatma Gandhi will starve themselves for the sake of others. Now consider the biological motives of *hunger, sex,* and *arousal,* and the social motive of *achievement.*

STAYING ON TRACK: *The Nature of Motivation*

1. Why do some scientists criticize sociobiological explanations of human behavior?
2. What are the different levels in Maslow's hierarchy of needs?

Answers to Staying on Track start on p. ST-5.

◆ THE HUNGER MOTIVE

The *hunger* motive impels you to eat to satisfy your body's need for nutrients. If you have just eaten, food might be the last thing on your mind. But if you have not eaten for a few days—or even for a few hours—food might be the only thing on your mind.

Factors That Regulate Eating

Research on hunger and eating has grown in recent decades, largely because of concerns about the health risks associated with the increase in obesity and eating disorders in industrialized countries. One factor involved in body weight is heredity, which plays a role in the regulation of eating (De Castro, 1999). Much of the evidence for this has come from twin studies. The Minnesota Study of Twins Reared Apart compared identical twins reared apart, fraternal twins reared apart, and nontwins in regard to their dietary preferences. The results showed that participants' dietary preferences were more strongly related to their degree of hereditary similarity than to their degree of environmental similarity (Hur, Bouchard, & Eckert, 1998). Though some researchers study the hereditary basis of eating regulation, most study bodily, brain, or environmental factors.

Bodily Factors and Eating

The main bodily mechanisms that regulate hunger involve the mouth, the stomach, the small intestine, the liver, and the pancreas. Though sensations from your mouth affect hunger, they are not its sole source. The stomach also plays a role. In 1912, physiologist Walter Cannon had his assistant Arthur Washburn swallow a balloon, which inflated in his stomach. The balloon was connected by a tube to a device that recorded stomach contractions by measuring changes they caused in the air pressure inside the balloon. Whenever Washburn felt a hunger pang, he pressed a key, producing a mark next to the recording of his stomach contractions. The recordings revealed that Washburn's hunger pangs were associated with stomach contractions, prompting Cannon and Washburn (1912) to conclude that stomach

▲ **Insulin and Hunger**
The mere sight of rich, delicious food can stimulate your pancreas to secrete insulin, making you more hungry and, as a consequence, more likely to eat the food.

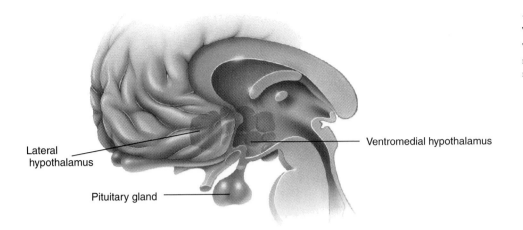

◀ **Figure 11.2**
The Hypothalamus and Hunger
The lateral hypothalamus and ventromedial hypothalamus play important
roles in regulating hunger.

Lateral
hypothalamus

Ventromedial hypothalamus

Pituitary gland

contractions cause hunger. Later research revealed that hunger sensations are not entirely dependent on the stomach; even people whose stomachs have been removed because of cancer or severe ulcers can experience hunger (Ingelfinger, 1944).

Though the stomach is not necessary for the regulation of hunger, it normally plays an important role. Receptor cells in the stomach detect the amount of food it contains. After gorging yourself on a Thanksgiving dinner, you might become all too aware of the stretch receptors in your stomach that respond to the presence of food (Stricker & McCann, 1985). These receptors inform the brain of the amount of food in the stomach by way of neural impulses sent along the vagus nerve, reducing your level of hunger.

Food stored in the stomach eventually reaches the small intestine, the main site of digestion, where it stimulates the secretion of the hormone cholecystokinin, which in turn affects the hypothalamus and reduces your level of hunger (Blevins, Stanley, & Reidelberger, 2000). In a study demonstrating the inhibitory effect of cholecystokinin on hunger, men received doses of either cholecystokinin or a saline placebo. Those who received doses of cholecystokinin reported less hunger than those who received the placebo (Greenough et al., 1998). Of special importance in the regulation of hunger is the hormone *insulin,* which is secreted by the pancreas in response to increases in blood sugar. Insulin helps blood sugar enter body cells for use in metabolism, promotes the storage of fat, and induces feelings of hunger.

Brain Factors and Eating

Signals from the body regulate hunger by their effects on the brain, particularly the hypothalamus (see Figure 11.2). Electrical stimulation of the *ventromedial hypothalamus (VMH),* an area at the lower middle of the hypothalamus, inhibits eating, and its destruction induces eating. Rats whose VMH has been destroyed will eat until they become grossly obese (Hetherington & Ranson, 1942). The *lateral hypothalamus (LH),* comprising areas on both sides of the hypothalamus, has been implicated in increasing hunger. One way in which cholecystokinin inhibits hunger is by enhancing neuronal activity in the LH and suppressing it in the VMH (Shiraishi, 1990). Electrical stimulation of the LH promotes eating; its destruction inhibits eating (Anand & Brobeck, 1951). Though early experiments led to the conclusion that the LH acts as our "hunger center" and the VMH acts as our "satiety center," later experiments have shown these sites are merely important components in the brain's complex system for regulating hunger and eating (Stricker & Verbalis, 1987). There is no simple "on/off" switch for eating.

But how does damage to the hypothalamus affect hunger? It does so in part by altering the body's **set point**—that is, its normal weight (Michel & Cabanac, 1999). Damage to the LH lowers the set point, reducing hunger and making the animal eat less to maintain a lower body weight. In contrast, damage to the VMH raises the set point, increasing hunger and making the animal eat more to maintain a higher body weight (Keesey & Powley, 1986). Whereas signals from the body regulate changes in hunger from meal to meal, the set point regulates changes in hunger over months or years. Nonetheless, some researchers insist there is relatively weak evidence for the role of a set point in hunger and eating (Assanand, Pinel, & Lehman, 1998).

set point
A specific body weight that the brain tries to maintain through the regulation of diet, activity, and metabolism.

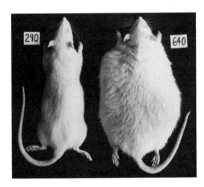

▲ **The VMH Rat**

Destruction of the ventromedial hypothalamus induces overeating and gross obesity. A rat whose ventromedial hypothalamus has been destroyed might eat until it becomes three times its normal weight.

Motivation | **331**

Environmental Factors and Eating

Hunger, especially in human beings, is regulated by external, as well as internal, factors. Food can act as an incentive to make you feel hungry. The taste, smell, sight, sound, and texture of food can pull you toward it. But how can the mere sight of food induce feelings of hunger? One way is by increasing the level of insulin in your blood. In fact, even daydreaming about food can stimulate your pancreas to release insulin, making you hungry and possibly sending you on a hunt for cake, candy, or ice cream (Rodin, 1985).

Obesity

Obesity is defined as a body weight more than 20 percent above the norm for one's height and build. Obesity is associated with health risks—notably cancer, diabetes, and heart disease—and costs Americans $70 billion a year in medical costs and lost productivity (Wickelgren, 1998). Obesity has been increasing in the United States. Obesity also has been increasing in other countries, particularly industrialized countries—though less than in the United States. There has been a marked increase in the obesity in Brazil, Canada, Thailand, Australia, and Scandinavia (Taubes, 1998). Obesity depends on the interaction of biopsychological and behavioral factors.

Biopsychological Factors in Obesity

Research studies are providing more and more evidence that obesity is prompted by several biopsychological factors. They include heredity, set point, and basal metabolic rate.

Heredity and Obesity. Thinness runs in families; research findings support a genetic basis for this tendency (deCastro, 1993). Heredity influences our caloric intake (Faith et al., 1999) and our degree of preference for fatty foods and sweet-tasting carbohydrates, each of which promotes obesity (Reed et al., 1997). Twin, adoption, and family studies show that obesity risk is higher for persons who have obese relatives. The heritability of fat mass and basal metabolic rate is about 40 percent (Comuzzie & Allison, 1998).

The role of heredity in obesity has been supported by studies of identical twins. Identical twins who have been reared together show a correlation of .75 in their amount of body fat. Even when identical twins have been reared apart, they show only a slightly lower correlation in their amount of body fat (Price & Gottesman, 1991). Evidence that heredity helps determine body weight also was provided by archival research on Danish adoption records. The results (see Figure 11.3) revealed a strong positive correlation between the weights of

▶ **Figure 11.3**
Heredity and Obesity

Data from Danish adoption records indicate that there is a positive relationship between the weight of adopted children and that of their biological parents, but no relationship between the weight of adopted children and that of their adoptive parents. The graph illustrates the relationship between adoptees and their biological and adoptive mothers. The relationship also holds true for adoptees and their biological and adoptive fathers (Stunkard, Stinnett, & Smoller, 1986).

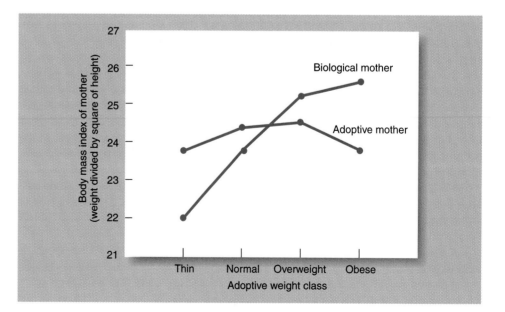

Chapter Eleven

adoptees and the weights of their biological parents, but little relationship between the weights of adoptees and those of their adoptive parents. This indicates that heredity plays a more important role in obesity than do habits learned from the family in which one is reared (Stunkard, Stinnett, & Smoller, 1986).

Set Point and Obesity. An important factor in obesity is the body's set point, which reflects the amount of fat stored in the body. Though fat cells can increase in number and can increase or decrease in size, they cannot decrease in number. This means obese people can lose weight only by shrinking the size of their fat cells. Because this induces constant hunger, it is difficult to maintain weight loss for an extended period of time (Kolata, 1985).

The set point seems to be affected by early nutrition, as shown by the results of an archival study of 300,000 men who, years earlier, had been exposed to a famine in Holland during World War II. Men who had been exposed to the famine during a critical period of development, which encompassed the third trimester of gestation and the first month after birth, were less likely to become obese than were men who had been exposed to the famine at other times during their early development (Ravelli, Stein, & Susser, 1976). The men exposed to the famine during this critical period might have developed lower set points than the other men. Even the results of the study of weight in Danish adoptees (Stunkard, Stinnett, & Smoller, 1986) might be explained by prenatal nutrition rather than by heredity. Perhaps adopted offspring are more similar in body weight to their biological mothers, not because they share their genes, but because they spent their prenatal period in their wombs, where they were subject to environmental influences, such as nutrients provided by their mothers. These prenatal influences might affect their later body weight (Bonds & Crosby, 1986).

Basal Metabolic Rate and Obesity. Another important factor in obesity is the **basal metabolic rate,** the rate at which the body burns calories just to keep itself alive. The basal metabolic rate typically accounts for 65 to 75 percent of the calories that you ingest (Shah & Jeffery, 1991). One way aerobic exercise promotes weight loss is by elevating the basal metabolic rate (Davis et al., 1992).

basal metabolic rate
The rate at which the body burns calories just to keep itself alive.

Behavioral Factors in Obesity

The chief behavioral factors in promoting obesity are having easy access to food, eating large portions, eating foods high in fat, and failing to engage in regular physical activity (Hill & Peters, 1998). Scientists interested in the role of behavioral factors in obesity are particularly interested in studying the effects of physical inactivity, responsiveness to external food cues, and stress-related eating patterns.

Inactivity and Obesity. Though Americans are eating less fat, obesity continues to increase. One possible cause is physical inactivity (Bar-Or et al., 1998). Sedentary children are more likely to become obese (Epstein et al., 1997). Moreover, girls are less physically active than boys throughout childhood, thus increasing their risk of obesity (Lindquist, Reynolds, & Goran, 1999). But the commonsense assumption that lack of exercise causes obesity is not necessarily correct. People who are obese might, as a result of being obese, engage in less physical activity. Moreover, some studies have found that health risks associated with obesity might be related more to a lack of physical activity than to excess body fat (Wickelgren, 1998). And the tendency to be physically inactive appears to have a hereditary basis (Hewitt, 1997).

Eating Cues and Obesity. Some researchers also have linked obesity to differences in responsiveness to external food cues. Because a series of studies in the 1960s indicated that obese people feel hungrier and eat more in the presence of external food cues, Stanley Schachter (1971) concluded that obese people are more responsive to those cues. Subsequent studies have provided some support for this belief. In one naturalistic observation study, researchers observed people eating in a diner. Obese people were more likely to order a dessert when the server provided an appetizing description of it than when she did not. Nonobese people were unaffected by her description of the dessert (Herman, Olmsted, & Polivy, 1983).

Many obese people are constantly dieting, so they might be in a chronic state of hunger—making them more responsive to food cues (Polivy, 1998). Moreover, obesity researcher Judith Rodin (1981) has found that obese people can have chronically high levels of insulin, making them hungrier and, as a result, more responsive to food cues. More recent research findings indicate that even when obese people are less hungry than lean people, obese people will tend to eat more than lean people when presented with appealing food (Spiegel, 1999).

Stress and Obesity. Another external factor—stressful situations—can induce hunger and overeating (Epel et al., 2001). But how does stress induce overeating? One possibility is that stress stimulates the brain to secrete *endorphins*. As discussed in Chapters 3 and 5, endorphins are neurotransmitters that relieve pain. They also stimulate eating. In one study, pigs that were given doses of endorphins began to eat more. When the pigs were given naloxone, a drug that blocks the effect of endorphins, they ate less—even when they had been deprived of food (Baldwin et al., 1990). Because endorphin levels increase when we are under stress, endorphins might contribute to stress-related overeating (Morley & Levine, 1980).

Eating Disorders

Are you pleased with the appearance of your body? As revealed in the Anatomy of a Research Study feature, your answer might depend, in part, on whether you are a woman or a man. Your satisfaction with your body might also influence the likelihood that you will develop an eating disorder.

A review of research conducted during the second half of the 20th century found that gender differences in body image had increased, with women showing progressively more negative body images over that time period (Feingold & Mazzella, 1998). Though about 3 percent of American women will have an eating disorder during their lifetimes, gender interacts with other social-cultural variables such that some groups of women are more at risk of eating disorders than others. For example, African American women are less likely to develop eating disorders than European American women. This could be due to the fact that African American women are more satisfied with their bodies (Miller et al., 2000). Also, lesbian women report greater satisfaction with their bodies and fewer eating disorders than heterosexual women (Lakkis, Ricciardelli, & Williams, 1999). This might be attributable to lesbians being less likely to have internalized cultural norms for thinness than heterosexual women (Bergeron & Senn, 1998).

Men also experience pressure to conform to cultural ideals, though these norms tend to emphasize muscularity rather than thinness (Edwards & Launder, 2000). Sexual orientation also influences the incidence of dissatisfaction with one's body and eating disorders among men. Whereas eating disorders are *more* prevalent among heterosexual women, they are *less* prevalent among heterosexual men. Gay men express more dissatisfaction with their bodies and are more likely to engage in disordered eating than heterosexual men (Lakkis, Ricciardelli, & Williams, 1999). The comparatively high rate of eating disorders among both gay men and heterosexual women may be due to a shared desire to attract men. One study found that heterosexual and gay men place a higher priority on physical appearance when judging a potential romantic partner than heterosexual or lesbian women do (Siever, 1994).

Though eating disorders are associated with social-cultural differences, they are influenced by many other factors. One factor is heredity. Though the heritability of many eating disorders has yet to be firmly established (Fairburn, Cowen, & Harrison, 1999), there is convincing evidence that some people have a genetic predisposition to develop an eating disorder if they have certain life experiences (Wade et al., 1999). Moreover, women who are under high psychological stress are more prone to eating disorders than are women who are under low psychological stress (Ball, Lee, & Brown, 1999). Experiencing physical, sexual, or emotional abuse in childhood also is associated with the development of eating disorders (Wiederman, Sansone, & Sansone, 1998).

▲ **Judith Rodin**
"Almost any overweight person can lose weight; few can keep it off."

The National Eating Disorder Information Centre
www.mhhe.com/sdorow5

Anatomy of a Research Study

How Satisfied Are Men and Women with Their Bodies?

Rationale

Some researchers believe eating disorders can be promoted by distorted body images. This inspired researchers April Fallon and Paul Rozin (1985) to examine the issue empirically.

Method

College students were presented with a set of 9 drawings of figures that ranged from very thin to very heavy. Participants were asked to indicate which figures were closest to their current physique, their ideal physique, and the physique they felt was most attractive to the other sex.

Results and Discussion

As shown in Figure 11.4, for men the current, the ideal, and the most attractive physiques were almost identical. For women, the current physique was heavier than the most attractive, and the most attractive was heavier than the ideal. The women also thought men liked women thinner than the men actually reported. Moreover, women tended to be less satisfied with their own physiques than men were with their own physiques.

This tendency to have a distorted body image might contribute to women's greater tendency to develop eating disorders marked by excessive concern with weight control, most notably anorexia nervosa and bulimia nervosa. But it is unclear whether a distorted body image causes eating disorders or whether both a distorted body image and eating disorders are the result of concerns about meeting perceived cultural standards of thinness (Wiederman & Pryor, 2000).

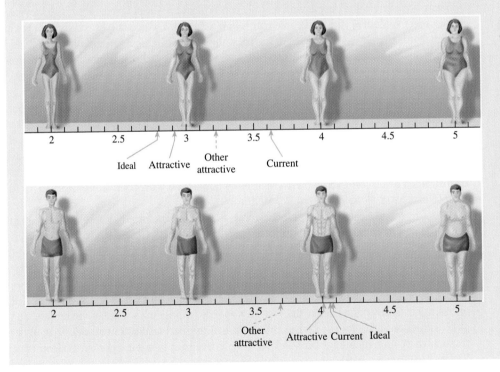

◀ **Figure 11.4**
Gender Differences in Body Images
Fallon and Rozin (1985) found that for men (lower illustration) their self-perceived physique ("Current"), the physique they believed was ideal ("Ideal"), and the physique they believed was most attractive to women ("Attractive"), were almost identical. The physique they believed women preferred ("Attractive") was heavier than the one women actually preferred ("Other Attractive"). In contrast, for women (upper illustration), their self-perceived physique ("Current") was heavier than the physique they believed was ideal ("Ideal") and the physique they believed was most attractive to men ("Attractive"). Moreover, the physique they believed men preferred ("Attractive") was thinner than the one men actually preferred ("Other Attractive").

Anorexia Nervosa

In 1983 the popular singer Karen Carpenter died of heart failure caused by starvation—despite having access to all the food she could have wanted. She suffered from **anorexia nervosa,** a sometimes fatal disorder in which the victim is so desperate to lose weight that she or he goes on a starvation diet and becomes emaciated. People with anorexia nervosa view themselves as fat, even when they are objectively thin, and they are preoccupied with food—talking about it, cooking it, and urging others to eat it. Anorexia nervosa is more

anorexia nervosa
An eating disorder marked by self-starvation.

American Anorexia-Bulimia Association
www.mhhe.com/sdorow5

bulimia nervosa

An eating disorder marked by binging and purging.

Binge-Eating Disorders
www.mhhe.com/sdorow5

common in young women; perhaps 5 to 10 percent of cases occur in men (Frasciello & Willard, 1995). Some women and men who participate in sports or activities that stress weight control are more prone to develop eating disorders (Pierce & Daleng, 1998). Moreover, a recent meta-analysis of the relationship of athletic participation to eating disorders among women concluded that elite athletes were most at risk (Smolak et al., 2000).

Possible causes of anorexia nervosa include heredity (Wade et al., 2000), a malfunctioning hypothalamus (Stoving et al., 1999), excessive secretion of cholecystokinin (Philipp et al., 1991), an emotionally enmeshed family (Wallin & Hansson, 1999), and an excessive desire for self-control of eating (Fairburn, Cowen, & Harrison, 1999). Anorexia nervosa also is associated with perfectionism (Ghizzani & Montomoli, 2000) and excessive exercising, such as distance running (Davis et al., 1994).

Bulimia Nervosa

Persons with the related, more common, disorder called **bulimia nervosa,** go on repeated eating binges in which they might ingest thousands of calories at a time but they maintain normal weight by then ridding themselves of the food by self-induced vomiting. People with bulimia nervosa think obsessively about food but fear becoming obese. One reason is social disapproval. For example, adolescent girls who become bulimic report they have been subjected to excessive teasing for being overweight (Thompson et al., 1995). As in the case of anorexia nervosa, most victims of bulimia nervosa are young women; about 10 to 15 percent of victims are men (Carlat & Camargo, 1991). The repeated bouts of vomiting can lead to medical problems, such as dehydration, tooth decay, or ulceration of the esophagus. Though the core features of bulimia seem to be consistent across cultures, there is research evidence that some features might vary from one culture to another (Mangweth et al., 1996).

There is evidence that people with bulimia nervosa have a genetic predisposition to develop the disorder (Wade et al., 2000). People with bulimia also secrete less cholecystokinin than normal eaters do, thereby reducing one of the main inhibitors of hunger (Brambilla et al., 1995). Another possible cause of bulimia nervosa is a low level of the neurotransmitter serotonin, which is associated with depression (Goldbloom & Garfinkel, 1990). Bingeing on carbohydrates might elevate mood, because certain carbohydrates increase serotonin levels in the brain.

Factors other than brain chemistry also play a role in bulimia nervosa. People who pursue activities that emphasize weight control are more likely to develop the disorder. For example, men with bulimia nervosa often are dancers or collegiate wrestlers (Striegel-Moore, Silberstein, & Rodin, 1986). Women who develop bulimia are more likely to have been sexually abused as children (Bulik et al., 1997). And victims of bulimia nervosa may be restrained eaters, people who are continually concerned with controlling their desire for food (Heatherton, Polivy, & Herman, 1990).

When restrained eaters eat a "taboo" food, such as ice cream, they might say to themselves, "I've blown my diet, so I might as well keep eating." In one study, restrained and unrestrained eaters were given a placebo they were told was a vitamin pill. Participants were told either nothing about how the "vitamin" would affect them or that it would make them feel hungry or full. The results indicated that restrained eaters followed the placebo message. They ate more when given the "hungry" instructions and less when given the "full" instructions. Unrestrained eaters did just the opposite, eating less ice cream under the "hungry" instructions and more under the "full" instructions. Perhaps restrained eaters are underresponsive to internal hunger cues and overresponsive to external hunger cues (Heatherton, Polivy, & Herman, 1989).

STAYING ON TRACK: *The Hunger Motive*

1. What is the role of the hypothalamus in hunger?
2. What evidence is there for a hereditary basis of obesity?
3. What are some possible explanations for the greater incidence of eating disorders among heterosexual women and gay men?

Answers to Staying on Track start on p. ST-5.

◆ THE SEX MOTIVE

Though some individuals, such as religious celibates, can live long lives without engaging in sexual intercourse, the survival of the species requires that many individuals engage in it. Had sexual intercourse not evolved into an extremely pleasurable behavior, we would have no inclination to seek it. But what factors account for the power of the sex motive?

Biopsychological Factors in Sexual Behavior

Sexual behavior is influenced by biopsychological factors. Many sex researchers study the physiological factors that affect human and animal sexual behavior. Some of these researchers focus on the physiology of the human sexual response cycle.

Physiological Factors and Sex

Important physiological factors in sexual motivation are sex hormones secreted by the **gonads,** the sex glands. Hormones secreted by the pituitary gland, which in turn is controlled by the hypothalamus, control the secretion of sex hormones. Sex hormones direct sexual development as well as sexual behavior (see Chapter 4). Research indicates that testosterone motivates both male and female sexual behavior (Exton et al., 1999), though women secrete less of it than men do.

gonads
The male and female sex glands.

The Sexual Response Cycle

Many Americans were shocked in the 1960s by reports of research conducted by William Masters and Virginia Johnson. They studied sexual behavior in the laboratory and recorded physiological changes that accompanied it in hundreds of men and women. Based on their study of more than 10,000 orgasms experienced by more than 300 men and 300 women, Masters and Johnson (1966) identified four phases in the **sexual response cycle** (see Figure 11.5): excitement, plateau, orgasm, and resolution. During the *excitement phase,* mental or physical stimulation causes sexual arousal. In men the penis becomes erect as it becomes engorged with blood. In women the nipples become erect, the vagina becomes lubricated, and the clitoris protrudes as it, too, becomes engorged with blood in response to both direct and vaginal stimulation (Lavoisier et al., 1995).

sexual response cycle
During sexual activity, the phases of excitement, plateau, orgasm, and resolution.

Masters and Johnson
www.mhhe.com/sdorow5

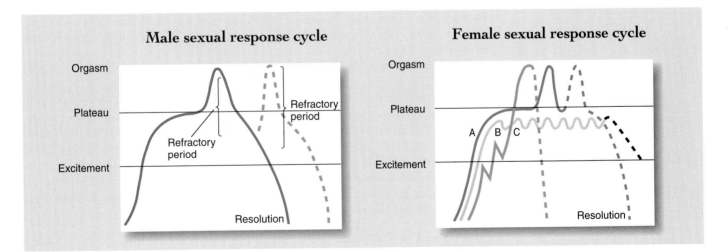

▲ **Figure 11.5**
The Human Sexual Response Cycle

Masters and Johnson found that men and women have sexual response cycles comprising four phases: excitement, plateau, orgasm, and resolution. After reaching orgasm, men cannot achieve another orgasm until they have passed through a refractory period. In contrast, pattern A shows that women might experience more than one orgasm during a single cycle. Pattern B shows a cycle during which a woman has reached the plateau stage without proceeding to orgasm. Pattern C shows a cycle during which a woman has reached orgasm quickly. Men, too, may experience pattern B and pattern C.

▲ **Masters and Johnson**

"Aside from obvious anatomic variants, men and women are homogenous in their physiological responses to sexual stimuli."

During the *plateau phase,* heart rate, blood pressure, muscle tension, and breathing rate increase. In men the erection becomes firmer and the testes are drawn closer to the body to prepare for ejaculation. Drops of seminal fluid, often containing sperm, may appear at the tip of the penis. In women the body flushes, lubrication increases, the clitoris retracts, and the breasts swell around the nipples (making the nipples seem to shrink). During the *orgasm phase,* heart rate and breathing rate reach their peak, men ejaculate, and both men and women experience intensely pleasurable sensations induced by rhythmic muscle contractions. When women and men are asked to write subjective descriptions of their orgasms, readers cannot distinguish between male and female descriptions (Vance & Wagner, 1976). This suggests women's and men's experiences of orgasm are similar.

Following the orgasm phase, the person enters the *resolution phase,* as blood leaves the genitals and sexual arousal lessens. This is associated with a *refractory period,* lasting from minutes to hours, during which the person cannot achieve orgasm. For many women, however, continued sexual stimulation can induce multiple orgasms (Darling, 1991).

Masters and Johnson's research has made a remarkable contribution to our understanding of human sexuality. However, critics have pointed to the selective nature of their sample—primarily sexually experienced married men and women who were willing to engage in sexual intercourse in the laboratory. Perhaps more important, they failed to study individuals who had difficulty in experiencing orgasm and failed to consider individual differences in sexual responses (Tiefer, 1995).

Psychosocial Factors in Sexual Behavior

Human sexuality also is strongly influenced by psychosocial factors. Researchers who study psychosocial factors in sexuality are particularly interested in the role of culture in sexual behavior. We know much about sexual behavior in American culture from surveys that have been carried out since the mid 20th century.

Culture and Sexual Behavior

Sex hormones are the main motivators of animal sexual behavior, but human sexual behavior depends more on social-cultural factors. As a result, we vary greatly in our sexual behavior. For example, breast caressing is a prelude to sexual intercourse among the Marquesan islanders of the Pacific but not among the Sirionian Indians of Bolivia (Klein, 1982; Seligman & Hardenburg, 2000). In Western cultures, acceptable sexual behavior has varied over time. The ancient Greeks viewed bisexuality as normal and masturbation as a desirable way for youths to relieve their sexual tensions. In contrast, most Americans and Europeans of the Victorian era in the 19th century believed that all sexual activity should be avoided except when aimed at procreation.

The liberalization of attitudes toward sexual behavior in Western industrialized countries during the 20th century was shown in 1983 when the *Journal of the American Medical Association* published an article on human sexuality. This would not be noteworthy except that the article had been submitted for publication in 1899, near the end of the Victorian era. The article, based on a paper presented by gynecologist Denslow Lewis (1899/1983) at the annual meeting of the American Medical Association, concerned female sexuality. Lewis even made the radical (for his time) suggestion that wives be encouraged to enjoy sex as much as their husbands did. At the time, the editor of the journal refused to publish the paper, which a prominent physician called "filth" and another editor feared would bring charges of sending obscene material through the mail (Hollender, 1983).

Surveys of Human Sexual Behavior

Denslow Lewis's critics would have been even more upset by research in human sexuality that has taken place in the past few decades. Shortly after World War II Alfred Kinsey (1894–1956), a biologist at Indiana University, found that he was unable to answer his students' questions about human sexual behavior because of a lack of relevant information. This inspired him to conduct surveys to gather information on the sexual behavior of American men (Kinsey, Pomeroy, & Martin, 1948) and women (Kinsey et al., 1953).

The Kinsey Institute
www.mhhe.com/sdorow5

Chapter Eleven

Kinsey's Findings. Kinsey obtained his data from interviews with thousands of men and women and published his findings in two best-selling books. Kinsey's books (which contained statistics but no pictures) shocked the public, because Kinsey reported that masturbation, oral sex, premarital sex, extramarital sex, homosexuality, and other sexual behaviors were more prevalent than commonly believed.

Among Kinsey's many findings were that most of the men and almost half of the women engaged in premarital sexual intercourse and many of the women and almost all of the men masturbated. The public was particularly startled to learn that about one-third of men had engaged in at least one sexual act with another man to orgasm and that about 10 percent had more than casual same-sex relations. Kinsey concluded that most people were not either homosexual or heterosexual but, instead, fit along a continuum from exclusively homosexual to exclusively heterosexual. Kinsey's survey of women was noteworthy because it challenged the widely held belief that women were uninterested in sex (Bullough, 1998).

Sex Surveys Since Kinsey. Scientists warned that care should be taken in generalizing Kinsey's findings to all Americans, because his sample was not representative of the American population; the sample included primarily European American, well-educated easterners and midwesterners who were willing to be interviewed about their sexual behavior. Moreover, what is true of people in one generation might not be true of those in another. Changes in sexual behavior since Kinsey's day indicate that sexual norms do, indeed, depend on the time period when they are studied. However, some gender differences in human sexual behavior appear to be unchanged. Mary Beth Oliver and Janet Shibley Hyde (1993) conducted a meta-analysis of 177 studies of sexual attitudes and behavior published between 1966 and 1990. Two large gender differences emerged: women were less likely than men to have masturbated, and men were more likely to approve of casual sex. Moreover, these effect sizes held steady, regardless of the year of publication. Most other gender differences were small to moderate, and became smaller over time. For example, men report more permissive attitudes toward extramarital sex and tend to have more permissive attitudes about sex overall. And men report having had more sex partners than women do, but this effect size is small. Gender similarities were the rule for many variables, including sexual satisfaction and incidence of sexual behaviors other than sexual intercourse.

Sexual Orientation

Considerable psychological research has addressed the factors influencing people's **sexual orientation,** or pattern of erotic attraction. *Homosexuals*—gay men or lesbians—are attracted to persons of the same sex; *heterosexuals* are attracted to persons of the opposite sex. And *bisexuals* have erotic feelings toward persons of both sexes. Today, attitudes toward homosexuality and bisexuality vary both among and within cultures. Moreover, there is considerable cross-cultural variation in same-sex behaviors and the expression of sexual orientations (Dykes, 2000).

Biopsychological Factors in Sexual Orientation

Given that our evolutionary history, reproductive anatomy, and contemporary cultural norms favor heterosexuality, why are an estimated 1 percent of women and 3 percent of men self-identified as homosexual (Lauman et al., 1994)? Theories of sexual orientation abound, and none has gained universal acceptance. Biopsychological theories of sexual orientation implicate hereditary and physiological factors.

Heredity and Sexual Orientation. Homosexuality runs in families (Bailey, Dunne, & Martin, 2000). For example, lesbians are more likely than nonlesbians to have lesbians among their sisters, daughters, and nieces (Pattatucci & Hamer, 1995). Likewise, identical twins are more likely to both be homosexual than are fraternal twins, but the extent to which these findings are due to shared genetic or shared environmental influences is unclear. Moreover, the strength of sexual attraction and concordance rates differ for men and women (Bailey, Dunne, & Martin, 2000).

▲ **Alfred Kinsey (1894–1956)**
"The present study was undertaken because the senior author's students were bringing him, as a college teacher of biology, questions on matters of sex. . . . They had found it more difficult to obtain strictly factual information which was not biased by moral, philosophic, or social interpretations."

sexual orientation
A person's pattern of erotic attraction to persons of the same sex, opposite sex, or both sexes.

 The Society for the Psychological Study of Lesbian, Gay, and Bisexual Issues
www.mhhe.com/sdorow5

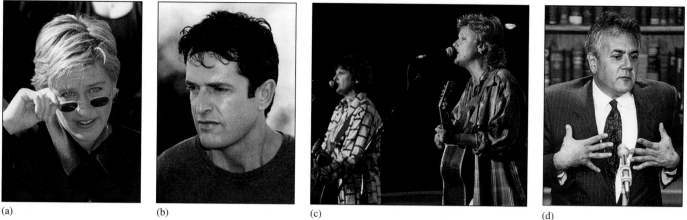

(a) (b) (c) (d)

 Sexual Orientation

Research indicates that your sexual orientation is the outcome of the interaction of biological, psychological, and social factors. Whereas this interaction leads most people to develop a heterosexual orientation, many persons—such as *(a)* comic Ellen DeGeneres, *(b)* actor Rupert Everett, *(c)* singer-musicians Amy Ray *(left)* and Emily Saliers *(right)*, and *(d)* U.S. Representative Barney Frank—develop a homosexual orientation.

Stronger support for the hereditary basis of homosexuality comes from research showing the following regarding identical twins (who have the same genes) who have been adopted as infants by different families: If one of the twins is homosexual, the other twin has a higher likelihood of also being homosexual than does a nontwin sibling reared together in the same family with a homosexual sibling (Eckert et al., 1986). But, if homosexuality were completely genetically determined, then when one identical twin is homosexual, the other would always be homosexual.

Hormones and Sexual Orientation. Additional support for the physiological basis of homosexuality comes from research on prenatal hormonal influences—though some researchers warn against concluding a correlation between prenatal hormonal exposure and sexual orientation necessarily indicates a causal relationship between the two (Doell, 1995). An unusual piece of evidence of a possible hormonal influence on sexual orientation comes from a sample of almost 1,000 gay men and more than 4,000 heterosexual men interviewed by the Kinsey Institute between 1938 and 1963. The survey found that gay men, on average, had larger penises than heterosexual men. This supports the possibility that differences in prenatal hormonal levels or other factors affecting the development of reproductive organs might affect sexual orientation (Bogaert & Hershberger, 1999). Also, a recent meta-analysis of 20 studies reported that gay men and lesbians had a 39 percent greater likelihood of being non-right-handed than heterosexual women and men, a difference also attributed to prenatal development (Lalumiere, Blanchard, & Zucker, 2000). However, it is important to be cautious in interpreting the results of studies that report physiological or behavioral differences that vary by sexual orientation. Many researchers have studied a number of physical correlates of sexual orientation, most recently structure and function of the cochlea (McFadden & Pasanen, 1999) and finger length patterns (Williams et al., 2000). Not only is it difficult to ascertain the direction of causality, but critics assert that studies that report findings consistent with stereotypes about gender and sexual orientation might be more easily accepted by the scientific and lay communities than studies that do not (Carroll, 1998). Research investigating the genetic determinants of sexual orientation is discussed in the Thinking Critically About Psychology and the Media feature.

Psychosocial Factors in Sexual Orientation

Traditional psychosocial explanations of sexual orientation have been influenced by psychoanalytic views of child development. They emphasize early childhood experience and the family environment.

Is There a Gay Brain?

In 1991, Simon LeVay, a neuroanatomist at the Salk Institute in La Jolla, California, published research findings indicating that there are specific structural differences between the brains of gay and heterosexual men. As part of his study, LeVay examined hypothalamic tissue from 19 gay men (all of whom had died of AIDS), 16 heterosexual men (6 of whom had died of AIDS), and 6 heterosexual women (1 of whom had died of AIDS). LeVay (1991) found that a region of the anterior hypothalamus was significantly larger in heterosexual men than in gay men.

Because LeVay's report provided evidence that men's sexual orientation might be determined by localized brain differences—perhaps genetically based—it created a media sensation. For several years after the publication of LeVay's report, there was a flood of television stories and magazine and newspaper articles about the possible genetic basis of sexual orientation. The excitement generated by his research is reflected in the titles of some of these articles, which included "Hypothalamus Study Stirs Social Questions" in the *APA Monitor* (Adler, 1991), "Does DNA Make Some Men Gay?" in *Newsweek* (Begley & Hager, 1993), and "Search for the Gay Gene" in *Time* (Thompson, 1995).

LeVay's report also attracted a mountain of commentary on its scientific weaknesses and social implications. Scientists criticized LeVay's study on several grounds. Isn't it possible, critics noted, that the direction of causality might be opposite to what common sense would presume? That is, perhaps brain differences do not cause differences in sexual orientation but, instead, perhaps a lifetime of being homosexual, bisexual, or heterosexual produces the differences in hypothalamic structures that LeVay found. Moreover, LeVay's research failed to account for lesbians' sexual orientation.

Scientific critics also noted that the differences in the brains of gay and heterosexual men in LeVay's study might have been the product of AIDS, which afflicted all of the gay men in his sample but only a minority of the heterosexual men. Neuroanatomist William Byne reported that many men with AIDS suffer testicular atrophy before death, and animal research shows that certain gonadal hormones affect the size of hypothalamic structures. Because of this, he wondered whether LeVay's research would have produced the same findings if he had compared the brains of gay and heterosexual men who had not died of AIDS (Byne, 1997). LeVay responded to this criticism by pointing out that the hypothalamic structure of interest was larger in the heterosexual men who had died of AIDS than in the gay men who had died of AIDS. If testicular atrophy related to AIDS in turn caused atrophy of that structure, it should have done so in both gay and heterosexual men.

Many gay men and lesbians were overjoyed by LeVay's research, because it indicated that sexual orientation is not the product of a freely chosen lifestyle, but, instead, is determined by brain differences—perhaps as the result of heredity. If so, this would counter the contention of many conservative religious leaders and their followers that homosexuality is a matter of free choice and a sin. But other homosexual activists warned that LeVay's contention that sexual orientation is produced by brain differences might provide fuel to those who would use it to support their belief that homosexuality is the product of a genetic defect. They fear that this might lead to demands that scientists seek ways to "cure" gay men and lesbians of their brain disorder, perhaps by tinkering with a "gay gene" that might be identified. They also fear that many parents would choose to abort fetuses that they were told had a "gay gene." LeVay responded to these fears by noting that public opinion polls have found that people who believe that sexual orientation is the product of free choice are more likely to be biased against lesbians and gay men than are people who believe that sexual orientation is biologically determined.

Childhood Upbringing and Sexual Orientation. The traditional view favored the Freudian notion that sexual orientation is caused by mothers' and fathers' relations with their pre-school-aged children. However, there is no evidence that any particular pattern of childhood experiences alone determines one's sexual orientation (Bell, Weinberg, & Hammersmith, 1981). In addition, the importance of the family environment in determining sexual orientation is contradicted by research findings that the great majority of children who are raised in lesbian families develop a heterosexual orientation (Golombok & Tasker, 1996).

Gender and Sexual Orientation. The patterns and development of sexual orientation among women appear to differ from those of men. Lisa Diamond has conducted a longitudinal study investigating the determinants of sexual orientation, sexual attraction, and sexual behavior among lesbian, bisexual, and "unlabeled" adolescents and young women. Her research counters the notion that sexual orientation is stable and established in childhood—at least among women. A majority of her respondents reported that their sexual attractions varied over time and across situations, and they failed to consider themselves to be exclusively attracted to other women (Diamond, 1998). In a follow-up study 2 years later, she found that the vast majority of the 80 participants had changed their self-described sexual orientation at least once. Changes were more likely to be reported by bisexual and unlabeled women. Sexual behaviors also varied, with one-quarter of the lesbians reporting having sex with men (Diamond, 2000).

The results of research investigating gender differences in women's and men's sexuality has prompted psychologist Roy Baumeister (2000) to suggest that women's sexuality is more flexible than men's. He suggests that women—lesbian, bisexual, or heterosexual—exhibit more variability in sexual behaviors and attractions, and are more strongly influenced by situational and cultural influences than men. Perhaps most controversial is his assertion that women's sex drive might be weaker than men's. His theory has met with criticisms—perhaps most notably that he neglects to consider the extent to which gender differences in sexual behavior and attitudes are far outweighed by gender similarities (Andersen, Cyranowski, & Aarestad, 2000) and that gender roles have a profound influence on women's sexual experiences (Hyde & Durik, 2000)—but it provides intriguing hypotheses for future research on the social-cultural determinants of women's sexuality.

The Current Status of Theories of Sexual Orientation

Despite numerous studies on the origins of sexual orientation, none has identified any physiological or psychosocial factor that, by itself, explains why one person develops a heterosexual orientation and another develops a homosexual orientation. As suggested by Alfred Kinsey 50 years ago, it might be a mistake to view homosexuality and heterosexuality as mutually exclusive categories (Haslam, 1997). This was the finding of a study in which gay men and heterosexual men rated their degree of homosexuality/heterosexuality and the size of their penile erections was measured while they watched brief video clips of nude men and nude women. The men's self-ratings and penile responses where positively correlated. As you might expect, the more homosexual their rating, the greater their penile response to nude men; and the more heterosexual their rating, the greater their penile response to nude women. Yet both the gay men and the heterosexual men tended to respond at least somewhat to nude men *and* to nude women (McConaghy & Blaszcynski, 1991). A complete explanation of human sexual orientation will probably have to include biological, psychological, and sociocultural factors (Friedman & Downey, 1993).

STAYING ON TRACK: *The Sex Motive*

1. According to Masters and Johnson, what are the four phases of the human sexual response cycle?
2. Why were Kinsey's sex surveys controversial, and what are the best-established gender differences in sexual behavior and attitudes?
3. What biopsychological factors have been implicated in the development of sexual orientation?

Answers to Staying on Track start on p. ST-5.

Chapter Eleven

◆ THE AROUSAL MOTIVE

Though the hunger motive and the sex motive seem to dominate North American culture, human beings also are influenced by another biological motive, the **arousal motive.** *Arousal* is the general level of physiological activation of the brain and body. Three of the main areas of research interest regarding the arousal motive are *optimal arousal, sensory deprivation,* and *sensation seeking.*

Optimal Arousal

In 1908 researchers reported that mice learned tasks best at moderate levels of external stimulation, and that the more complex the task, the lower the level of optimal stimulation (Yerkes & Dodson, 1908). Later researchers, led by Donald Hebb (1955) of McGill University in Montreal, showed that people perform best at a moderate level of arousal, with performance deteriorating under excessively high or low arousal levels. This relationship between arousal and performance, represented by an inverted U-shaped curve (see Figure 11.6), became known as the **Yerkes-Dodson law,** after the researchers who had conducted the earlier animal study—even though that study dealt with the level of external stimulation rather than with the level of arousal (Teigen, 1994).

Hebb found that optimal arousal is higher for simple tasks than for complex tasks. For example, the optimal level of arousal for doing a simple addition problem would be higher than for doing a complex geometry problem. Hebb also found that optimal arousal is higher for well-learned tasks than for novel tasks. Perhaps, when studying bores you, you find that playing music in the background helps you raise your level of brain arousal enough for you to maintain your concentration (Patton, Routh, & Stinard, 1986).

Maintaining an optimal level of arousal is particularly important in sport performance. If you have ever played a competitive sport, you know what it is to "choke"—to be so anxious that you perform below your normal level of ability. Choking occurs when your anxiety makes you attend to the normally automatic movements involved in playing a sport. If you consciously attend to those movements, they will be disrupted (Baumeister, 1984). Consider foul shooting in basketball. If you attend to each movement of your arm and hand as you shoot foul shots, you will disrupt the smooth sequence of movements that foul shooting requires. Athletes at an optimal level of arousal are less likely to be undermotivated or to choke, as shown in a study of female collegiate basketball players. Those with a moderate level of pregame anxiety performed better than did those with a low or high level (Sonstroem & Bernardo, 1982).

arousal motive

The motive to maintain an optimal level of physiological activation.

Yerkes-Dodson law

The principle that the relationship between arousal and performance is best represented by an inverted U-shaped curve.

 Exercise and Sport Psychology
www.mhhe.com/sdorow5

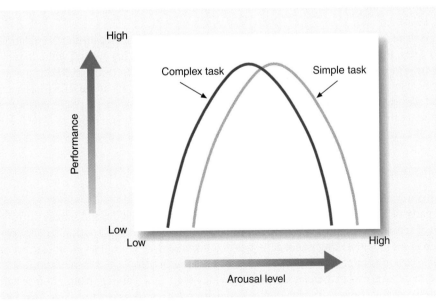

◀ **Figure 11.6**
The Yerkes-Dodson Law

The graph depicts the relationship between arousal level and task performance. Note that the best performance occurs at a moderate level of arousal. Performance declines when arousal is below or above that level. Note that the optimal level of arousal is lower for complex tasks than for simple tasks.

Though some research studies based on the Yerkes-Dodson law have been methodologically flawed and inconsistent in their findings (Baumler, 1994), many studies have supported the notion of an optimal level of arousal for task performance (Robazza, Bortoli, & Nougier 1998). But research findings have been inconsistent in supporting the belief that the optimal level of arousal will be lower for more difficult tasks than for easier tasks (Watters, Martin, & Schreter, 1997). Moreover, for any given task there is no single optimal level of arousal; the optimal level varies from person to person (Ebbeck & Weiss, 1988). So an outstanding math student would have a higher optimal level of arousal for performing arithmetic than would a poor math student. As a consequence, the outstanding math student might have to "psych up" before an exam, and the poor math student might have to relax—each in an effort to reach an optimal arousal level.

Sensory Deprivation

Though people differ in the amount of arousal they prefer, we require at least a minimal amount for our brains to function properly. Anecdotal reports from Arctic explorers, shipwrecked sailors, and prisoners in solitary confinement made early psychologists aware that human beings require sensory stimulation for proper perceptual, cognitive, and emotional functioning. Sensory deprivation is the prolonged withdrawal of normal levels of external stimulation. When people are subjected to sensory deprivation, they might experience delusions, hallucinations, and emotional arousal caused by the brain's attempt to restore its optimal level of arousal. The experimental study of sensory deprivation began in the early 1950s when the Defense Research Board of Canada asked Donald Hebb to find ways of countering the "brainwashing" techniques the Chinese communists used on prisoners during the Korean War. During brainwashing, prisoners were deprived of social and physical stimulation. This became so unpleasant that they cooperated with their captors just to receive more stimulation (Hebb, 1958).

Hebb and his colleagues conducted studies of sensory deprivation in which each participant was confined to a bed in a soundproof room with only the monotonous hum of a fan and an air conditioner. The participants wore translucent goggles to reduce visual sensations and cotton gloves and cardboard tubes over their arms to reduce touch sensations. They were permitted to leave the bed only to eat or to use the toilet. They stayed in the room for as many days as they could tolerate.

After many hours of sensory deprivation, some participants experienced hallucinations, emotional instability, and intellectual deterioration. Though the students who served as volunteers for the study were paid $20 a day (a tidy sum at the time) for participating, most quit within 48 hours. They found the lack of sensory stimulation so aversive that they preferred to forego the monetary incentive in favor of sensory stimulation (Bexton, Heron, & Scott, 1954).

A form of sensory deprivation called flotation restricted environmental stimulation (REST), developed by Peter Suedfeld, has been effective in reducing arousal without causing distress or cognitive impairment (Suedfeld & Borrie, 1999). In flotation REST, participants float in a dark, soundproof tank filled with warm salt water. Flotation REST has been applied successfully in a variety of other ways, particularly in situations that call for a reduction in arousal. These applications include the reduction of high blood pressure (McGrady et al., 1987) and the relief of chronic tension headache (Wallabaum et al., 1991).

Sensation Seeking

Would you prefer to ride a roller coaster or lie on a beach? Would you prefer to attend a lively party or have a quiet conversation? Your preferences would depend in part on your degree of **sensation seeking,** which is your motivation to pursue sensory stimulation. People high in sensation seeking prefer activities that increase their arousal levels; those low in sensation seeking prefer activities that decrease their arousal. People high in sensation seeking are more likely to participate in risky activities such as skydiving, hang gliding, and automobile racing (Jack & Ronan, 1998). A study of music preferences in college students

Flotation REST in Applied Psychophysiology
www.mhhe.com/sdorow5

sensation seeking
The extent to which an individual seeks sensory stimulation.

▲ **Sensation Seeking**

People low in sensation seeking prefer activities that decrease their arousal levels; people high in sensation seeking prefer activities that increase their arousal levels.

found that those who scored higher in sensation seeking preferred more arousing music than did those who scored lower in sensation seeking (McNamara & Ballard, 1999).

Sensation seeking also is related to dangerous habits. Those who score high in sensation seeking are more likely to engage in binge drinking and drinking games (Johnson & Cropsey, 2000), to have risky sex (Donohew et al., 2000), and to associate with friends who introduce them to the use of illegal drugs (Donohew et al., 1999).

There is evidence that many people who are high in sensation seeking pursue activities like these because of a desire to counteract a chronic inability to experience pleasure in their daily lives (Pierson et al., 1999). As discussed in Chapter 2, correlation does not necessarily imply causation. In this case, the association between sensation seeking and risky behaviors does not necessarily mean that sensation seeking, in itself, causes those behaviors.

STAYING ON TRACK: *The Arousal Motive*

1. How would the Yerkes-Dodson law explain poor exam performance by students who are either too relaxed or too anxious?
2. What evidence is there to support the effectiveness of flotation REST?

Answers to Staying on Track start on p. ST-5.

◆ THE ACHIEVEMENT MOTIVE

Human beings are motivated by social, as well as physiological, needs. Interest in studying social motivation was stimulated in the 1930s and 1940s by the work of Henry Murray (1938), who identified a variety of important social motives, including achievement and affiliation. Since Murray's pioneering research, psychologists, led by John Atkinson and David McClelland, have been especially interested in studying the **achievement motive,** which is the desire for mastery, excellence, and accomplishment.

In the context of Maslow's hierarchy of needs, the need for achievement would be associated with one of the higher levels, the need for esteem. This means the need for achievement would be stronger in cultures, such as Canada and the United States, in which most people have satisfied their lower needs. But even in the United States the relative importance of the need for achievement has changed over time. Consider an archival study of children's readers published between 1810 and 1950; the results showed that the number of achievement themes in the readers increased until about 1890 and then decreased through 1950. This was accompanied by a parallel change in the number of patents issued, indicating that changes in a country's achievement motivation can be related to its practical achievements (DeCharms & Moeller, 1962). Nonetheless, it is not certain from the data

achievement motive

The desire for mastery, excellence, and accomplishment.

▲ **Figure 11.7**
The Thematic Apperception Test
What is happening in this picture? What led up to it? How does the person feel? How will it turn out? Your responses to several ambiguous pictures like this might contain themes revealing the strength of your need for achievement.

that changes in achievement motivation caused changes in practical achievements. You will recall a positive correlation between two variables does not necessarily mean that changes in one cause changes in the other. Of course, it does not preclude the possibility of a causal relationship, either.

Changes in the achievement motive over time also differ for men and women. From the late 1950s to the late 1970s, American men showed no change in their achievement motivation, whereas American women showed a marked increase. This has been attributed to the contemporary feminist movement of the past few decades, which made it more acceptable for women to pursue personal achievement outside of traditional women's domains, such as homemaking (Veroff et al., 1980).

Need for Achievement

Henry Murray (1938) referred to the achievement motive as the *need for achievement,* which reveals itself in efforts to meet high standards of performance or to compete successfully against other people. How do psychologists measure the need for achievement? The most common means has been the *Thematic Apperception Test* (*TAT*), developed by Murray and his colleague Christiana Morgan (Morgan & Murray, 1935). The TAT is based on the assumption that our fantasies reveal our motives. The test consists of a series of drawings of people in ambiguous situations (see Figure 11.7). Participants are asked to tell what is happening in the picture, what led up to it, how the people feel, and how the situation turns out. The responses are scored for any consistent themes. Individuals with a high need for achievement will tell stories in which people overcome obstacles, work hard to reach goals, and accomplish great things.

Research shows that people who score high on the need for achievement persist at tasks in the face of difficulties, delay gratification in the pursuit of long-term goals, and are more successful than people with a low need for achievement. They also select moderately difficult challenges, neither so easy that they guarantee success nor so difficult that they guarantee failure (McClelland, 1985). Athletes with a high need for achievement are motivated to seek competition that provides a fair test of their abilities. Early evidence for this came from a study in which college students played a game of ringtoss. Those with a high need for achievement were more likely to stand at an intermediate distance from the peg, while those with a low need for achievement were more likely to stand either close to the peg or far from it (Atkinson & Litwin, 1960).

(a)　　　　(b)　　　　(c)　　　　(d)

▲ **Achievement Motivation**
The need for achievement is demonstrated in the lives of persons who reach the top of their fields, including *(a)* the late Andy Warhol, who championed Pop art; *(b)* Toni Morrison, who won a Nobel Prize for her writing; *(c)* Julia Child, who became a famous television chef; and *(d)* Secretary of State Colin Powell, who served as head of the U.S. army.

Intrinsic motivation is the desire to perform a task for its own sake. In contrast, **extrinsic motivation** is the desire to perform a task to gain external rewards, such as praise, grades, or money. For example, you might take a psychology course because you find it interesting (an intrinsic reason) or because it is a graduation requirement (an extrinsic reason). Until the 1970s, most psychologists agreed with B. F. Skinner's commonsense belief that rewards will increase the probability of behavior. But then research began to show otherwise. In one of the first experiments on intrinsic motivation, children were given a period of time during which they could draw. Some of them were were given a certificate as a reward for having drawn. When given a subsequent chance to draw, students who had been rewarded for drawing spent less time at it than did students who had not been rewarded (Lepper, Greene, & Nisbett, 1973). A meta-analysis of 128 studies concluded that extrinsic rewards undermined children's intrinsic motivation (Deci, Koestner, & Ryan, 1999).

Keep in mind that, despite consistent research findings showing the negative effect of external rewards on motivation, research findings on intrinsic versus extrinsic motivation have been based almost solely on studies in Western, individualistic cultures. Cross-cultural research indicates that the effects of extrinsic motivation might be culturally dependent. A study on the effect of free choice on intrinsic motivation in task performance found that European American students showed greater intrinsic motivation after making their own choices than after the choices were made for them by trusted others. In contrast, Asian American students—from more interdependent cultures—showed greater intrinsic motivation after the choices were made for them by trusted others than after making their own choices (Iyengar & Lepper, 1999).

Given the everyday observation that extrinsic rewards can increase achievement motivation, especially in people who initially have little or no motivation in a particular area, why do extrinsic rewards sometimes decrease achievement motivation? Two theories provide possible answers: *overjustification theory* and *cognitive-evaluation theory.*

Overjustification theory assumes that an extrinsic reward decreases intrinsic motivation when a person attributes his or her performance to the extrinsic reward. The children who were rewarded for drawing might have attributed their behavior to the reward rather than to their interest in drawing. Overjustification occurs when there is high intrinsic interest and the reward is perceived as more than adequate justification for performing the act. In a study of first- and second-graders, children played with an interesting or uninteresting toy and were rewarded or not rewarded. Rewards reduced the motivation to play with the interesting, but not the uninteresting, toy (Newman & Layton, 1984). A meta-analysis found strong support for overjustification theory (Tang & Hall, 1995), though some research studies indicate that it has limitations as an explanation for decreases in intrinsic motivation (Pittenger, 1996).

An alternative theory, **cognitive-evaluation theory,** holds that a reward perceived as providing *information* about a person's competence in an activity will increase her or his intrinsic motivation to perform that activity (Deci, Nezlek, & Sheinman, 1981). For example, intrinsic motivation was higher among Division I athletes who perceived that their coach's feedback focused on positive and informational feedback (Amorose & Horn, 2000). But a reward perceived as an attempt to *control* a person's behavior will decrease his or her intrinsic motivation to perform that activity. The more controlling and less informative that students perceive a teacher to be, for example, the lower will be the students' intrinsic motivation (Noels, Clement, & Pelletier, 1999). Consider a student whose teacher rewards her for doing well in drawing. If the student believes that the reward is being used to provide information about her competence, her intrinsic motivation to perform that activity may increase. But if she believes that the reward is being used to control her behavior (perhaps to make her spend more time drawing), her intrinsic motivation to perform can decrease. Though there is strong research support for this theory (Rummel & Feinberg, 1988), some research findings have contradicted it (Carton, 1996).

Will Rewarding a Behavior Always Increase Our Desire to Perform It?

intrinsic motivation

The desire to perform a behavior for its own sake.

extrinsic motivation

The desire to perform a behavior in order to obtain an external reward, such as praise, grades, or money.

overjustification theory

The theory that an extrinsic reward will decrease intrinsic motivation when a person attributes her or his performance to that reward.

cognitive-evaluation theory

The theory that a person's intrinsic motivation will increase when a reward is perceived as a source of information but will decrease when a reward is perceived as an attempt to exert control.

Though the importance of achievement motivation in situations such as academic courses has been demonstrated in different cultures (Jegede, Jegede, & Ugodulunwa, 1997), the achievement motive appears to be multidimensional and culture specific. In individualistic cultures, the achievement motive primarily is expressed in terms of individual achievement. In collectivist cultures, which value interdependence, achievement primarily is expressed through the family and other groups (Niles, 1998). Moreover, bicultural individuals might express both motives. Angela Lew and her colleagues (1998) found that acculturation among Asian American college students was positively correlated with the achievement motive. However, students who endorsed both American and Asian values also had higher scores in individual-oriented and, to a lesser extent, social-oriented achievement.

Intrinsic Motivation

If you have ever written a term paper just to obtain a grade, you can appreciate William James's distress at having to complete his now-classic 1890 textbook, *Principles of Psychology,* for an extrinsic reason. According to Edward Thorndike (1961, p. 267), "James wrote the *Principles* with wailing and gnashing of teeth to fulfill a contract with a publishing firm." Though James enjoyed writing, he did not enjoy writing for money. He was not unusual, because research has shown receiving extrinsic rewards for performing intrinsically rewarding activities can reduce the motivation to perform them. Athletes, for example, are more strongly motivated by intrinsic rewards than by extrinsic rewards (Vallerand & Losier, 1999). The effects of extrinsic rewards are explored in the Psychology Versus Common Sense feature on page 347.

STAYING ON TRACK: *The Achievement Motive*

1. What are the characteristics of people high in need for achievement?
2. What is the difference between overjustification theory and cognitive-evaluation theory in explaining the negative effects of extrinsic motivation?

Answers to Staying on Track start on p. ST-5.

Chapter Summary

THE NATURE OF MOTIVATION

- Motivation is the psychological process that arouses, directs, and maintains behavior.
- The main sources of motivation include genes, drives, and incentives.
- Though William McDougall's instinct theory failed to achieve scientific credibility, interest in the hereditary basis of social behavior remains alive today in the field of sociobiology.
- Instinct theories gave way to the drive-reduction theory of Clark Hull, which assumes that physiological deprivation causes a need, which induces a state of tension called a drive.
- Drive reduction aims at restoring a steady state of physiological equilibrium called homeostasis.
- A drive "pushes" you toward a goal, whereas an incentive is an external stimulus that "pulls" you toward a goal.
- Abraham Maslow categorized human needs in a hierarchy, with the pursuit of higher needs contingent on the satisfaction of lower ones.

THE HUNGER MOTIVE

- Hunger is regulated by bodily, brain, and environmental factors.
- Areas of the hypothalamus regulate hunger by responding to signals from the blood and internal organs.

- External food-related cues also influence hunger and eating.
- The most common eating problem is obesity, which is defined as a body weight more than 20 percent above normal for one's height and body build.
- Obesity depends on one's set point, basal metabolic rate, responsiveness to external cues, chronic level of blood insulin, and reactions to stress.
- Two of the most prevalent eating disorders are anorexia nervosa, which involves self-starvation, and bulimia nervosa, which typically involves bingeing and purging.

THE SEX MOTIVE

- Sex serves as both a drive and an incentive.
- Sex hormones direct sexual development and sexual behavior.
- Unlike in other animals, adult human sexual behavior is controlled more by social-cultural factors than by sex hormones.
- Formal research on human sexuality began with surveys on men's and women's sexual behavior conducted by Alfred Kinsey and his colleagues.
- Later research by William Masters and Virginia Johnson showed that women and men have similar sexual response cycles.
- Sexual orientation is influenced by biological, psychological, and sociocultural factors.

THE AROUSAL MOTIVE

- The Yerkes-Dodson law holds that there is an optimal level of arousal for the performance of a given task, with the optimal level becoming lower as the task becomes more complex.
- Studies of sensory deprivation by Donald Hebb and his colleagues show that we are motivated to maintain at least a minimal level of sensory stimulation.
- Flotation REST has been successful in improving human physical and psychological functioning.
- People differ in their degree of sensation seeking, which is the motivation to seek high or low levels of sensory stimulation.

THE ACHIEVEMENT MOTIVE

- The achievement motive is the desire for mastery, excellence, and accomplishment.

- Henry Murray and Christiana Morgan introduced the Thematic Apperception Test as a means of assessing the need for achievement.
- People with a high need for achievement persist at tasks in the face of difficulties, delay gratification in the pursuit of long-term goals, and achieve greater success than do people with a low need for achievement. They also prefer moderately difficult challenges.
- The intrinsic motivation to engage in an activity can be reduced by extrinsic rewards.
- Overjustification theory and cognitive-evaluation theory provide different explanations for the detrimental effects of extrinsic rewards.

Key Concepts

THE NATURE OF
MOTIVATION
drive 328
drive-reduction theory 328
hierarchy of needs 329
homeostasis 328
incentive 329
instinct 328
motivation 327

need 328
sociobiology 328

THE HUNGER MOTIVE
anorexia nervosa 335
basal metabolic rate 333
bulimia nervosa 336
obesity 332
set point 331

THE SEX MOTIVE
gonads 337
sexual orientation 339
sexual response cycle 337

THE AROUSAL MOTIVE
arousal motive 343
sensation seeking 344
Yerkes-Dodson law 343

THE ACHIEVEMENT MOTIVE
achievement motive 345
cognitive-evaluation theory 347
extrinsic motivation 347
intrinsic motivation 347
overjustification theory 347

Key Contributors

THE NATURE OF
MOTIVATION
Sigmund Freud 328
Clark Hull 328
Abraham Maslow 329
William McDougall 328
Edward O. Wilson 328

THE HUNGER MOTIVE
Walter Cannon 330
Judith Rodin 334
Stanley Schachter 333

THE SEX MOTIVE
Alfred Kinsey 338

William Masters and Virginia
   Johnson 337

THE AROUSAL MOTIVE
Donald Hebb 343
Peter Suedfeld 344

THE ACHIEVEMENT MOTIVE
John Atkinson 345
David McClelland 345
Christiana Morgan 346
Henry Murray 345

Thought Questions

1. Given the factors that regulate hunger and eating, what are some ways to maintain a healthy body weight?
2. How would the concept of optimal arousal explain your performance on an English exam?

Possible Answers to Thought Questions start on p. PT-3.

3. How might research findings on the roles of intrinsic and extrinsic motivation explain why professional athletes can lose their desire to play when they are paid millions of dollars to play games that children enjoy playing for free?

OLC Preview

 For additional quizzing and a variety of interactive resources, visit the book's Online Learning Center at www.mhhe.com/sdorow5.

chapter twelve

12 *Emotion*

PAUL GAUGUIN
Tahitian Idyll

On September 16, 1999, CNN reported that U.S. Energy Secretary Bill Richardson had taken a polygraph test—popularly known as a "lie detector"—during which he was asked if he had ever been a spy or met with foreign espionage agents. Richardson took the test not because he was suspected of being a spy but to demonstrate to scientists that they had nothing to fear from mandatory polygraph testing. Following evidence of Chinese spying at weapons laboratories, Richardson urged that 5,000 scientists with access to top secret information working for the Department of Energy submit to polygraph tests about security matters. If they failed even one question, they would be subject to an FBI investigation.

Richardson's proposal was met by outrage from scientists, who claimed that it threatened their sense of honor and violated their right to privacy. Scientists at Lawrence Livermore National Laboratory in California argued that polygraph testing is neither valid nor reliable. Scientists at Los Alamos National Laboratory in New Mexico threatened to form a union to oppose the testing program. In response, Richardson said, "I took the test. It was administered effectively, efficiently. It's easy and I believe scientifically sound I respect the views of some of the lab scientists. But I think they have nothing to worry about." The U.S. Congress, backing Richardson and disregarding the scientists, passed a law permitting polygraph testing of employees with access to top-secret information. Directors of national laboratories insisted that the threat of this practice was hurting their efforts to recruit top scientists.

Did scientists have good reason to fear the polygraph test? This question will be addressed later in this chapter. But to understand the nature and effectiveness of polygraph testing it would be helpful to first learn about the nature of emotion.

◀ **Polygraph Testing**
Scientists at Los Alamos National Laboratory in New Mexico organized in protest of a Federal polygraph testing program.

*T*he word *emotion* comes from a Latin word meaning "to set in motion," and, like motives (such as sex and hunger), emotions (such as love and anger) have evolved to motivate behavior that helps us adapt to different situations (Lang, Bradley, & Cuthbert, 1998). An **emotion** is a motivated state, varying in its intensity and pleasantness, marked by physiological arousal, expressive behavior, and cognitive experience. Consider an angry man. His heart might pound (a sign of physiological arousal), he might grit his teeth (an expressive behavior), and he might feel enraged (an intense, unpleasant cognitive experience).

emotion
A motivated state marked by physiological arousal, expressive behavior, and cognitive experience.

◆ THE BIOPSYCHOLOGY OF EMOTION

What are the physiological bases of emotion? To answer this question, psychologists study the autonomic nervous system, the brain, and neurochemicals.

The Autonomic Nervous System and Emotion

Both your emotional expression and your emotional experience depend on physiological arousal, which reflects activity in your *autonomic nervous system.* Figure 12.1 illustrates the functions of the two branches of the autonomic nervous system: the *sympathetic nervous system* and the *parasympathetic nervous system.* The interplay of these two systems contributes to the ebb and flow of emotions. The sympathetic nervous system relies on the neurotransmitter *norepinephrine* to regulate its target organs; the parasympathetic nervous system relies on the neurotransmitter *acetylcholine* to regulate its target organs.

Activation of the sympathetic nervous system can stimulate the **fight-or-flight response,** which evolved because it enabled our prehistoric ancestors to meet sudden physical threats (whether from nature, animals, or human beings) by either confronting them or running away. After a threat has been met or avoided, the sympathetic nervous system becomes less active and the parasympathetic nervous system becomes more active, calming the body. Yet because the sympathetic nervous system stimulates the secretion of epinephrine and norepinephrine from the adrenal glands into the bloodstream, physiological arousal can last for a while after the threat has disappeared.

The fight-or-flight response is triggered not only by physical threats but also by psychological threats. To appreciate the role of the autonomic nervous system in the emotional response to a psychological threat, imagine you are about to give a classroom speech that you did not prepare adequately. As you walk to your class, you experience anxiety associated with physiological arousal induced by your sympathetic nervous system.

As you enter the classroom, you become more alert and energetic as your circulatory system diverts blood rich in oxygen and other nutrients normally destined for your stomach and intestines to your brain and skeletal muscles. Your heart pounds rapidly and strongly in response to epinephrine secreted by your adrenal glands. And you might notice your mouth becoming dry, goose bumps appearing on your arms, and beads of perspiration forming on your forehead.

Suppose that as you sit in class in this anxious, aroused state, your teacher announces that a surprise guest speaker will lecture for the entire class period. You immediately feel relieved at not having to give your speech; your arousal subsides partly because of activity in your parasympathetic nervous system. The measurement of changes in autonomic nervous system activity is the basis of the polygraph test.

How Do We Study Emotion?
www.mhhe.com/sdorow5

fight-or-flight response
A state of physiological arousal that enables us to meet sudden threats by either confronting them or running away from them.

The American Polygraph Association
www.mhhe.com/sdorow5

Thinking Critically About Psychology and the Media

Do Lie Detectors Tell the Truth?

Hardly a week goes by without the media reporting a controversy about the use of the polygraph test. This chapter opened with a summary of a 1999 controversy about U.S. Department of Energy Secretary Bill Richardson's proposal to subject nuclear scientists to polygraph testing. The media also reported on the role of polygraph testing in several high-profile legal cases, including the O. J. Simpson murder trial and the Bill Clinton-Monica Lewinsky sex scandal. But the media tend to report disagreements about the use of polygraph testing without reporting what scientific research says about its validity. Let's consider what research studies, as opposed to media reports, say about the polygraph as a means of identifying liars and truth-tellers.

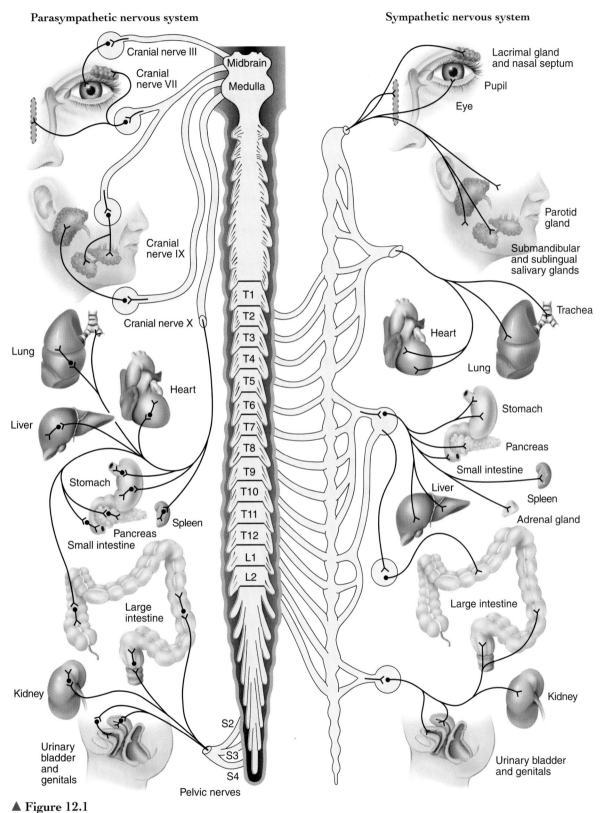

Parasympathetic nervous system

Cranial nerve III
Cranial nerve VII
Midbrain
Medulla
Cranial nerve IX
Cranial nerve X
Lung
Liver
Heart
Stomach
Spleen
Pancreas
Small intestine
Large intestine
Kidney
Urinary bladder and genitals
Pelvic nerves

T1
T2
T3
T4
T5
T6
T7
T8
T9
T10
T11
T12
L1
L2
S2
S3
S4

Sympathetic nervous system

Lacrimal gland and nasal septum
Pupil
Eye
Parotid gland
Submandibular and sublingual salivary glands
Trachea
Heart
Lung
Stomach
Pancreas
Small intestine
Spleen
Liver
Adrenal gland
Large intestine
Kidney
Urinary bladder and genitals

▲ **Figure 12.1**
The Autonomic Nervous System

Emotional responses involve the interplay of the two branches of the autonomic nervous system: the sympathetic nervous system, which tends to arouse us, and the parasympathetic nervous system, which tends to return us to a calmer state.

Modern lie detection began in the 1890s with the work of Cesare Lombroso, an Italian criminologist who questioned suspects while recording their heart rate and blood pressure. He assumed that if they showed marked fluctuations in heart rate and blood pressure while responding to questions, they were lying (Kleinmuntz & Szucko, 1984b). But the current polygraph test is the direct descendant of research conducted in the 1920s by William Marston, better known as the creator of the comic book character Wonder Woman (Bunn, 1997).

The Polygraph Test

Today the lie detector, or **polygraph test,** typically measures breathing patterns, heart rate, blood pressure, and electrodermal activity. Electrodermal activity reflects the amount of sweating; greater emotionality is associated with more sweating. Though the polygraph test is used to detect lying, no pattern of physiological responses by itself indicates lying. Instead, the test detects physiological arousal produced by activation of the sympathetic nervous system. As David Lykken, an expert on lie detection, has said, "The polygraph pens do no special dance when we are lying" (Lykken, 1981, p. 10).

Given that there is no pattern of physiological responses that indicates lying, how is the recording of physiological arousal used to detect lies? The typical polygraph test begins with an explanation of the test and the kinds of questions to be asked. The suspect is then asked *control questions,* which are designed to provoke lying about minor transgressions common to almost everyone. For example, the suspect might be asked, "Have you ever stolen anything from an employer?" It is a rare person who has not stolen at least an inexpensive item, yet many people would answer no, creating an increase in physiological arousal; and even suspects who answer yes to a control question would probably experience some increase in physiological arousal in response to that question.

The suspect's physiological response to control questions is compared to her or his physiological response to *relevant questions,* which are concerned with facts about the crime, such as "Did you steal money from the bank safe?" Polygraphers assume that a guilty person will show greater physiological arousal in response to relevant questions and that an innocent person will show greater physiological arousal in response to control questions. Figure 12.2 shows a polygraph printout of differences in arousal in response to the different questions. The typical polygraph test asks about twelve relevant questions, which are repeated three or four times.

Issues in Lie Detection

Polygraph testing has provoked controversy because it is far from being a perfect measure of lying (Saxe & Ben-Shakhar, 1999). One difficulty is that the accuracy of the polygraph depends, in part, on the suspect's physiological reactivity. People with low

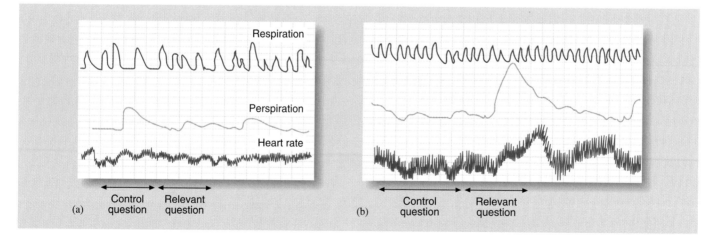

▲ **Figure 12.2**
Relevant Questions Versus Control Questions

The polygraph test compares physiological responses to relevant and control questions. *(a)* This is the record of a person who responded less strongly to a question relevant to a crime than to an emotionally arousing control question not relevant to the crime. Such responses indicate to the examiner that the person is telling the truth. *(b)* This is the record of a person who responded more strongly to a question relevant to a crime than to an emotionally arousing control question not relevant to the crime. Responses such as this indicate to the examiner that the person is lying.

Chapter Twelve

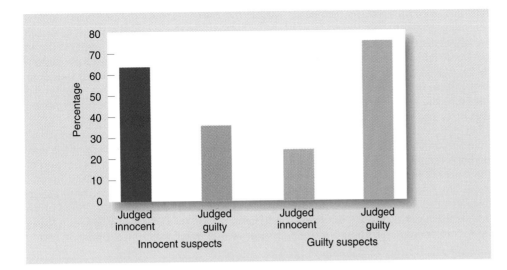

◀ **Figure 12.3**
The Validity of Polygraph Testing
A study by Kleinmuntz and Szucko (1984a) found that the polygraph test is far from foolproof in determining guilt or innocence. About one-third of innocent suspects were judged guilty and about one-quarter of guilty suspects were judged innocent.

reactivity exhibit a smaller difference between their responses to control questions and their responses to relevant questions than do people with high reactivity. This might cause an unemotional criminal to be declared innocent and an emotional innocent person to be declared guilty (Waid, Wilson, & Orne, 1981). Moreover, antianxiety drugs can reduce the detectability of lying by reducing physiological arousal (Waid & Orne, 1982). Another technique that can fool the polygraph uses the properly timed induction of pain. For example, suppose that during control questions a guilty man bites his tongue or steps on a tack hidden in his shoe. This would increase his level of physiological arousal in response to control questions, perhaps reducing the difference between his physiological responses to control questions and relevant questions (Honts, Hodes, & Raskin, 1985).

Though aware that some criminals might use techniques like these to fool the polygraph, critics of the test are more concerned with the possibility that the polygraph will find innocent people guilty. What evidence led to the widespread opposition to the unrestricted use of the polygraph? Though supporters of the polygraph test claim accuracy rates of 90 percent or better (Raskin & Podlesny, 1979), research findings indicate that it is much less accurate than that, as revealed, for example, by the following study (Kleinmuntz & Szucko, 1984a). The polygraph printouts of 50 thieves and 50 innocent people were presented to 6 professional polygraphers. The results showed that the polygraphers correctly identified 76 percent of the guilty persons and 63 percent of the innocent persons (see Figure 12.3). Though their performance was better than chance, this also meant that they incorrectly identified 24 percent of the guilty persons as innocent and 37 percent of the innocent persons as guilty. The tendency of the polygraph test to produce unacceptably high rates of false positives (that is, identifying innocent persons as guilty) has been replicated in other studies (Horowitz et al., 1997). The polygraph test's high rate of false positives can have tragic consequences for those who are unjustly denied employment, fired from jobs, or prosecuted for crimes.

The Guilty Knowledge Test

A possible improvement over the polygraph test is the **Guilty Knowledge Test,** developed by David Lykken (1974). In contrast to the polygraph test, Lykken's test assesses knowledge about a transgression rather than alleged anxiety about it. The Guilty Knowledge Test is useful only when details of the transgression are known to the transgressor but not to others who take the test. Consider its use in interrogating suspects in a bank robbery. A suspect would be asked questions about the victim, the site of the crime, and the commission of the crime. Instead of being asked, "Did you steal money from the bank safe?" the suspect would be asked, "Was the money stolen from the _____?" This question would be asked several times, each time with different words completing the statement. In this case, the words might include *teller's drawer* and *armored car.*

The Guilty Knowledge Test assumes that a guilty person (who knows details of the crime), but not an innocent person, will show more physiological reactivity to the

Guilty Knowledge Test
A method that assesses lying by measuring physiological arousal in response to information that is relevant to a transgression and physiological arousal in response to information that is irrelevant to that transgression.

relevant words than to the irrelevant words. If a person shows greater physiological reactivity to the relevant words in a *series* of statements (a single positive instance would be insufficient), that person would be considered guilty. Of course, examiners should not know any details of the crime; otherwise, they might affect the suspect's physiological response to relevant words (Elaad, 1997), perhaps by saying those words louder or softer. Researchers are developing a version of the Guilty Knowledge Test that would measure changes in brain-wave patterns to determine when a person has information that he or she is trying to conceal (Seymour et al., 2000).

In its first use in a study of real criminals, the Guilty Knowledge Test was given to 50 innocent and 48 guilty participants. The results supported the effectiveness of the test, particularly its ability to avoid false positives. Judges correctly classified 94 percent of the innocent and 65 percent of the guilty (Elaad, 1990). Research findings indicate that the Guilty Knowledge Test is biased toward false negatives, whereas control-question tests are biased toward false positives (McCauley & Forman, 1988). So, those more interested in protecting the innocent would favor the Guilty Knowledge Test, and those more interested in ferreting out transgressors would favor the control-question test.

The Brain and Emotion

Though bodily arousal plays a role in emotionality, the brain is ultimately in control of emotional responses. Emotion researchers are especially interested in the roles of the limbic system and cerebral hemispheres.

The Limbic System and Emotion

The main limbic system structures are illustrated in Figure 12.4. As discussed in Chapter 3, autonomic nervous system arousal is regulated by the *hypothalamus,* a component of the *limbic system,* which also includes the *septum* and the *amygdala.* Among other things, the hypothalamus helps control changes in breathing and heart output during the fight-or-flight response. The septum suppresses aversive emotional states. For example, electrical stimulation of the septum in rats reduces their tendency to avoid fear-inducing stimuli (Thomas, 1988).

But researchers are particularly interested in the amygdala. The amygdala prompts us to react emotionally to different environmental circumstances (Killcross, 2000). The amygdala plays more of a role in recognizing stimuli evoking negative emotions than in recognizing stimuli evoking positive emotions. One study of 9 patients with amygdala damage found that all had difficulty recognizing facial expressions of negative emotions, such as fear, but none had difficulty recognizing facial expressions of positive emotions, such as happiness (Adolphs, Russell, & Tranel, 1999). This indicates the crucial role of the amygdala in processing information about environmental threats.

▲ **David Lykken**

"Since, in the field, most subjects tend to 'fail' the lie test whether they are truthful or deceptive, the method more often detects lying than it does truthful responding."

Neurobiology of Brain Systems Mediating Memory, Emotion, and Social Behavior
www.mhhe.com/sdorow5

▶ **Figure 12.4**
The Limbic System

Our emotional responses are regulated by activity in the limbic system.

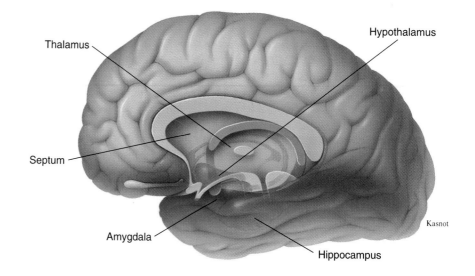

| **Chapter Twelve**

The frontal lobes of the cerebral cortex (see Chapter 3) can inhibit emotional responses produced by the amygdala so they do not become excessive. The interaction of the amygdala and the frontal lobes in regulating the intensity of emotional responses was demonstrated in a study that used functional magnetic resonance imaging (see Chapter 3). Participants either matched the emotional expression of 2 angry or frightened faces (a perceptual task, presumably involving little frontal lobe activity) or identified the angry or frightened emotional expression of a face by choosing an emotional label for it (a cognitive task, presumably dependent on frontal lobe activity). Matching angry or frightened expressions was associated with increased activity in the amygdala. But identifying the angry or frightened expressions was associated with decreased activity in the amygdala and increased activity in the right frontal lobe of the cerebral cortex. The results of this study lend additional support to the inhibitory effect of the frontal lobes on negative emotionality associated with amygdala activity (Hariri, Bookheimer, & Mazziotta, 2000).

Hemispheric Specialization and Emotion

Research findings indicate that the cerebral hemispheres play different roles in emotion. PET scans indicate, for example, that the right hemisphere is more active than the left when we try to assess emotional states from facial expressions (Anderson & Phelps, 2000). And the right hemisphere plays a greater role than the left hemisphere in regulating facial expressions of emotion (Borod, Haywood, & Koff, 1997). Research findings also suggest that each cerebral hemisphere is specialized to process different emotions, with the left hemisphere more involved in positive emotions and the right hemisphere more involved in negative emotions (Bartolic et al., 1999). But keep in mind that both cerebral hemispheres play a role in all emotional experience (Buchanan et al., 2000).

Much of our knowledge about the role of each hemisphere in emotional experience comes from studies, particularly those conducted by Richard Davidson and his colleagues, that have measured the relative degree of activity in each hemisphere during emotional arousal. One study measured electrical activity while participants watched emotionally positive or negative film clips. Those who watched positive clips had higher left-hemisphere activity; those who watched negative clips had higher right-hemisphere activity (Wheeler, Davidson, & Tomarken, 1993). A study that recorded electrical activity from the brains of 10-month-old infants found that hemispheric differences in the processing of emotion appear early in life. Greater activation of the left hemisphere was associated with a pleasant facial expression and a tendency to approach people. In contrast, greater activation of the right hemisphere was associated with an unpleasant facial expression and a tendency to withdraw from people (Fox & Davidson, 1988).

The *Wada test,* which involves selective anesthesia of one cerebral hemisphere to determine hemispheric functions (particularly the site of the speech center), also has provided evidence of the lateralization of emotionality. In the Wada test, the anesthetic sodium amobarbital is injected into the left or right carotid artery of patients who are about to undergo brain surgery. Because the carotid arteries supply blood to the brain, injection of sodium amobarbital into one of them will anesthetize the associated hemisphere. Research using the Wada test shows that laughter and elation (positive emotionality) are more frequent after right-hemisphere anesthesia, whereas crying (negative emotionality) is more frequent after left-hemisphere anesthesia (Lee et al., 1990).

The Chemistry of Emotion

When we say that there is "good chemistry" or "bad chemistry" between people, we mean that they experience positive or negative emotions in response to each other. Research has shown that our emotional responses do, indeed, depend on chemistry—hormones and neurotransmitters that convey emotion-related impulses from one neuron to another or between neurons and body organs (Baum, Grunberg, & Singer, 1992).

Hormones and Emotion

As noted earlier, stressful situations cause the secretion of the hormones epinephrine and norepinephrine, which also serve as neutrotransmitters. In a study of psychologists and physicians, levels of these hormones were measured on a day when participants gave a public speech and

▲ **Richard Davidson**

"In adults and infants, the experimental arousal of positive, approach-related emotions is associated with selective activation of the left frontal region, while arousal of negative, withdrawal-related emotions is associated with selective activation of the right frontal region."

on a day when they did not. Public speaking was associated with an increase in the level of both epinephrine and norepinephrine. Moreover, there was a rise in blood cholesterol on days when participants gave speeches relative to days when they did not. Perhaps stress hormones, by stimulating an increase in low-density lipoproteins (which are implicated in cardiovascular disease), provide one of the mechanisms by which emotional responses to stressful situations contribute to the development of cardiovascular disease (Bolm-Audorff et al., 1989).

Endorphins and Emotion

Endorphins, a class of neurotransmitters discussed in Chapters 3 and 5, contribute to emotional experiences by providing pain relief and evoking feelings of pleasure. For example, blood levels of endorphins rise markedly after bungee jumping and correlate positively with resulting feelings of euphoria (Hennig, Laschefski, & Opper, 1994). Even the emotional thrill we experience from a music concert or a dance performance can depend on endorphin activity. This was demonstrated in a double-blind study of college students who listened to a musical passage and then received an injection of either naloxone (a drug that blocks the effects of endorphins) or a placebo (in this case, a saline solution that does not block the effects of endorphins). After receiving the injection, participants again listened to the musical passage. When asked to estimate the intensity of their emotional thrill in response to the music, participants who had received naloxone reported a significant decrease in intensity. Participants who had received a placebo reported no such decrease. Because naloxone blocks the effects of endorphins, but a placebo does not, the findings support the role of endorphins in positive emotional experiences (Goldstein, 1980).

STAYING ON TRACK: *The Biopsychology of Emotion*

1. What evidence is there that positive and negative emotions are processed primarily in different cerebral hemispheres?
2. What evidence is there that endorphins are involved in feelings of euphoria?

Answers to Staying on Track start on p. ST-5.

◆ THE EXPRESSION OF EMOTION

Because our emotional experiences are private, they cannot be directly observed by others. Instead, emotions are typically inferred from expressive behaviors, including vocal qualities, body movements, and facial expressions. Psychologists are particularly interested in the role of facial expressions in conveying emotions.

Philip D. Chesterfield, an 18th-century British statesman, noted that our faces give away our emotions: "Look in the face of the person to whom you are speaking if you wish to know his real sentiments, for he can command his words more easily than his countenance." Chesterfield's observation might explain, in part, how teachers' expectations create the Pygmalion effect (see Chapter 2). Though teachers might believe they are unbiased when speaking to their students, their facial expressions can communicate their true feelings, whether positive or negative, about particular students (Babad, Bernieri, & Rosenthal, 1989).

The facial expressions of television network news anchors might even unintentionally affect our preferences for political candidates. A study conducted during the 1984 presidential campaign found that NBC's Tom Brokaw, CBS's Dan Rather, and ABC's Peter Jennings did not show biases in what they said about Republican candidate Ronald Reagan and Democratic candidate Walter Mondale. But unlike Brokaw and Rather, Jennings displayed significantly more positive facial expressions when speaking about Reagan than when speaking about Mondale. A telephone survey found that voters who regularly watched Jennings were significantly more likely to vote for Reagan than were those who watched Brokaw or Rather. The researchers concluded that Jennings's biased facial expressions might have made some viewers more favorable toward Reagan. Of course we must be careful to avoid making hasty inferences about causation (see Chapter 2). The researchers cautioned that, instead, those who already favored Reagan might have preferred to watch Jennings's newscast because he smiled more when talking about Reagan (Mullen et al., 1986).

Women are superior to men in recognizing emotions from facial expressions—a gender difference that emerges as early as infancy (McClure, 2000). Moreover, though men and women tend to respond empathetically by mimicking facial expressions, women do so more demonstratively (Lundqvist, 1995). Does women's greater nonverbal expressivity reflect greater emotionality? Two studies tested the relationship between gender-role stereotypes and the interpretation of emotional expression in women (Plant et al., 2000). A sample of 117 female and male undergraduates completed a questionnaire assessing their estimates of the frequency with which men and women experienced 19 emotions. Participants believed that most of these emotions (awe, embarrassment, fear, distress, happiness, guilt, sympathy, sadness, love, surprise, shame, and shyness) were experienced more frequently by women than by men. Men were thought to experience only 2 emotions more frequently—pride and anger.

Another sample of over 150 male and female undergraduates then was asked to rate slides of 2 men and 2 women trained to pose facial expressions of 4 emotions. Two of the slides posed unambiguous emotions—pure expressions of anger and sadness. Two of the slides posed ambiguous emotions—facial expressions that were a blend of anger and sadness. Participants rated women expressing ambiguous emotions as both sadder and less angry than men. This effect also was observed for the 2 slides depicting women posing unambiguous facial expressions of anger—participants rated these stimuli as a blend of anger and sadness. Thus, it appears that observers' interpretations of men's and women's emotional expression can be influenced by gender-role stereotypes. Women were perceived to be expressing greater sadness, a female-stereotyped emotion, whereas men were perceived to be expressing more anger, a male-stereotyped emotion.

Actors who actually feel the emotions that they are portraying facially produce performances that are more emotionally convincing to audiences (Gosselin, Kirovac, & Dore, 1995). And knowledge of the relationship between facial expressions and emotions has enabled researchers to distinguish honest emotional expressions from fake ones. For example, sincere smiles include muscular activity around the eyes, causing the skin to wrinkle, and around the mouth, causing the corners of the lips to rise (Messinger, Fogel, & Dickson, 1999). This natural smile is called the *Duchenne smile*. In contrast, when people display insincere smiles, perhaps to hide their negative emotional state, the corners of their lips are drawn downward and their upper lip curls up. In one experiment, participants were more likely to display the Duchenne smile when they watched a pleasant film than when they watched an unpleasant film. They also reported more positive emotions when they exhibited the Duchenne smile, verifying it as a sign of a pleasant emotional state (Ekman, Davidson, & Friesen, 1990).

Center for Nonverbal Studies
www.mhhe.com/sdorow5

Nonverbal Behaviour, Nonverbal Communication Links
www.mhhe.com/sdorow5

Facial Analysis
www.mhhe.com/sdorow5

▲ **Can a Smile Influence Voters?**
During the 1984 presidential campaign, Peter Jennings showed more positive facial expressions when speaking about Ronald Reagan than when speaking about Walter Mondale. Tom Brokaw and Dan Rather showed no such bias. People who watched Jennings were more likely to vote for Reagan than were people who watched Brokaw or Rather (Mullen et al., 1986). Could those voters have been influenced by Jennings's smiles? What other reasons can you think of that might explain this correlation?

Heredity and Facial Expressions

Charles Darwin (1872/1965) believed that facial expressions evolved because they promoted survival. Darwin's belief was supported in an experiment that measured how quickly participants could detect an angry face or a happy face in a crowd (Hansen & Hansen, 1988). Participants reported that a single angry face seemed to pop out of the crowd faster than a single happy face. A more recent study also found that angry faces are detected faster than others, though they might not always seem to pop out immediately (Fox et al., 2000). Why might we have evolved the ability to detect angry faces more quickly than other faces? A possible reason is that it promotes our survival by motivating us to take more immediate action to confront or to escape from a person displaying an angry face.

Research by Carroll Izard (1990) and his colleagues supports Darwin's view that facial expressions for basic emotions are inborn and universal. One line of research support for the inborn, universal nature of facial expressions comes from studies showing that young infants produce facial expressions for the basic emotions. In one study, newborn infants were given solutions of sugar or quinine (which tastes bitter). Despite having no prior experience with those tastes, their facial expressions showed pleasure or displeasure, depending on which solution they had tasted. And the intensity of their facial expressions varied with the strength of the solutions (Ganchrow, Steiner, & Deher, 1983). Though infants can produce facial expressions for the basic emotions, their degree of expressiveness varies across cultures. For example, Chinese infants are less facially expressive in smiling and crying than Japanese or European American infants (Camras et al., 1998). Another line of research has found that even people who are blind from birth exhibit facial expressions for the basic emotions, including joy, fear, anger, disgust, sadness, and surprise. Nonetheless, blind infants exhibit a more limited repertoire of facial expressions than do sighted infants, indicating that visual experience might contribute to even the early development of facial expressions (Troster & Brambring, 1992).

Culture and Facial Expressions

Further support for Darwin's evolutionary view of facial expressions comes from studies showing that facial expressions for the basic emotions are universal across cultures. Research participants in one study were members of the Fore tribe of New Guinea, who had had almost no contact with Westerners (Ekman & Friesen, 1971). The tribe members listened to descriptions of a series of emotion-arousing situations representing joy, fear, anger, disgust, sadness, or surprise. After each description, the tribe members viewed a set of 3 photographs of Western faces expressing different emotions, from which they selected the face portraying the emotion of the person in the description they had just heard.

The tribe members correctly identified expressions portraying joy, anger, sadness, and disgust but failed to distinguish between expressions portraying fear and surprise. Perhaps the tribe members' expressions for fear and surprise did not differ because similar situations (such as an enemy or a wild animal suddenly appearing from out of the jungle) evoke both fear and surprise in their culture. This study was replicated, with similar results, in a more recent study of people in 10 different cultures from around the world (Ekman et al., 1987).

▶ **The Universality of Facial Expressions**

Support for the inborn, universal nature of facial expressions representing the basic emotions comes from studies showing similar facial expressions in people from different cultures, such as these smiling people from Rwanda, Thailand, and the United States.

Nonetheless, some researchers have found that cross-cultural differences in the detection of universal facial expressions of emotion depend on the methodology used in the studies (Haidt, & Keltner 1999).

STAYING ON TRACK: *The Expression of Emotion*

1. What gender differences have been found in nonverbal expressivity?
2. What evidence is there that certain emotional facial expressions are universal?

Answers to Staying on Track start on p. ST-5.

▲ **Robert Plutchik**

"The history of psychology is so marked with differences as to the meaning of emotion that some psychologists have suggested that the term be eliminated from psychological writings."

◆ THE EXPERIENCE OF EMOTION

Though we have hundreds of words for emotions, there seem to be only a few basic emotions, from which all others are derived. One model of emotion, devised by Robert Plutchik (1980), considers joy, fear, anger, disgust, sadness, surprise, acceptance, and anticipation to be the basic emotions. More complex emotions arise from mixtures of these basic ones.

The experience of emotion varies in both its intensity and its pleasantness. People who tend to experience intensely pleasant emotions (such as elation) also tend to experience intensely unpleasant emotions (such as despair). People who tend to experience mildly pleasant emotions (such as gladness) also tend to experience mildly unpleasant emotions (such as disappointment) (Diener et al., 1991).

There is evidence, however, that the experience of pleasant and unpleasant emotions is influenced by culture. One study compared self-reported emotional experiences in a number of situations in samples of American and Chinese undergraduates. Positive and negative emotions were negatively correlated in the American sample. Thus, in situations that American participants experienced as very joyful and loving, they reported experiencing less sadness and fear. In contrast, ratings of positive and negative emotions were positively correlated in the Chinese sample. In situations that Chinese participants experienced as very joyful and loving, they reported experiencing more sadness and fear. Though gender differences were observed across cultures—the correlation for women in both samples was stronger than that for men—the researchers attributed these findings to cultural differences in the interpretation of positive and negative events. Westerners appear to adopt an optimistic *or* pessimistic perspective, depending on the circumstances. In Chinese culture, successes are not celebrated with elation, as things might not turn out so well in the future. And the blow of failure might be softened by the thought that things might turn out better next time (Bagozzi, Wong, & Yi, 1999).

People tend to view pleasant emotions, such as happiness, as normal and unpleasant emotions, such as depression, as abnormal (Sommers, 1984). Yet, until the past three decades, psychologists had conducted many more studies of unpleasant emotions. To counter the traditional overemphasis placed on unpleasant emotions, and because unpleasant emotions such as anxiety and depression are discussed in later chapters, this chapter discusses two positive topics: happiness and humor. This also reflects increased recognition by psychologists that we should conduct more research on positive emotions, particularly because they promote our physical and psychological well-being (Lyubomirsky, 2000).

Happiness

Many philosophers have considered happiness, what researchers in the field now call *subjective well-being* (Diener, 2000), the highest good. Most people—regardless of age, nationality, or gender—report being at least moderately happy (Myers, 2000). In fact, most people believe that they are happier than the average person, apparently because we attend more to our own level of contentment than to other people's (Klar & Giladi, 1999).

Factors that correlate with happiness in cultures around the world include political systems that promote human rights and societal equality (Diener, Diener, & Diener, 1995). Financial

World Database of Happiness
www.mhhe.com/sdorow5

satisfaction is positively correlated with life satisfaction—but only in poorer countries (Oishi et al., 1999). Happiness is positively correlated with religiosity (French & Joseph, 1999) and with intelligence, social skills, and family support (Diener & Fujita, 1995). Physical attractiveness is positively correlated with happiness. But this relationship does not necessarily mean that physical attractiveness causes happiness. Perhaps happy people make themselves more physically attractive. For example, happy people are more likely to wear attractive clothing, jewelry, and hairstyles (Diener, Wolsic, & Fujita, 1995).

Happiness also is related to marital status. A cross-cultural study found that married people were, on average, consistently happier than unmarried people (Diener et al., 2000). This held equally true for men and women. Happiness was more weakly associated with simply living together unmarried. The role of marriage in promoting happiness was linked to improved health and financial security (Stack & Eshleman, 1998). Personality factors that correlate highly with happiness are trust, extraversion, agreeableness, self-esteem, emotional stability, and a sense of control (DeNeve & Cooper, 1998). Happiness is especially related to what has been called *stable extraversion*—that is, being outgoing but not out of control (Francis, 1999). The association between extraversion and happiness has gained support from studies not only in Western cultures but also in non-Western cultures, such as China (Lu & Shih, 1997).

Cultural differences are found, though, in what makes people feel good. One research study investigated the correlates of positive emotions in a sample of 283 American and 630 Japanese male and female undergraduates. Results indicated that among Japanese participants—who live in a culture that values interdependence—positive emotions were correlated with social emotions (such as feeling friendly toward others). In contrast, among American participants—who live in a culture that values independence—positive emotions were correlated with personal emotions (such as feeling pride in personal accomplishments) (Kitayama, Markus, & Kurokawa, 2000).

Social-Comparison Theory

Our happiness depends on comparisons we make between ourselves and others and between our current circumstances and our past circumstances (Smith, Diener, & Wedell, 1989). Charles Montesquieu, an 18th-century French philosopher, noted: "If one only wished to be happy, this could be easily accomplished; but we wish to be happier than other people, and this is always difficult, for we believe others to be happier than they are." One of the most influential theories of happiness—**social-comparison theory**—considers happiness to be the result of believing that one's life circumstances are more favorable than those of others (VanderZee, Buunk, & Sanderman, 1996), as when you discover that your grade is one of the highest in the class. In one study, college students felt happier when in the presence of a person who was relatively worse off (Strack et al., 1990). Thus, you can make yourself happier with your own life by purposely comparing it with the lives of those who are less fortunate.

A factor in social comparison that is less important than commonly believed is wealth. Though there is an association between economic well-being and happiness (Schyns, 1998), wealth does not necessarily bring greater happiness. According to happiness researcher Edward Diener (1984), wealthy Americans are no happier than nonwealthy Americans, provided that the nonwealthy people have at least the basic necessities of life, such as a job, home, and family. Though this finding holds true in the United States, it does not hold true in all cultures. For example, a study of people in 39 other countries found a stronger relationship between high income and happiness than in the United States (Diener et al., 1993).

Adaptation-Level Theory

Adaptation-level theory holds that your current happiness depends not on comparing yourself with other people but on comparing yourself with yourself. Thus, your current happiness depends in part on comparing your present circumstances and your past circumstances. Your present state of happiness is governed more by the most recent events in your life than by the more distant events (Suh, Diener, & Fujita, 1996). But as your circumstances improve, your standard of happiness becomes higher. This can have surprising emotional consequences for people who gain sudden financial success. Life's small pleasures might no longer make them happy—their standards of happiness might have become too high.

social-comparison theory
The theory that happiness is the result of estimating that one's life circumstances are more favorable than those of others.

adaptation-level theory
The theory that happiness depends on comparing one's present circumstances with one's past circumstances.

▲ Edward Diener

"Cross-national data suggest that there is a positive level of subjective well-being throughout the world, with the possible exception of very poor societies."

This was illustrated in a study of Illinois state lottery winners (Brickman, Coates, & Janoff-Bulman, 1978). Despite winning from $50,000 to $1 million, these winners were no happier than they had been in the past. In fact, they found less pleasure in formerly enjoyable everyday activities, such as watching television, or talking with a friend. So, though comparing our circumstances with those of less-fortunate people can make us happier, improvements in our own circumstances might make us adopt increasingly higher standards of happiness—making happiness more and more elusive. Recognizing this, the 19th-century clergyman Henry Van Dyke remarked, "It is better to desire the things we have than to have the things we desire."

Humor

Happiness is enhanced by humor, whether offered by friends, funny movies, or stand-up comedians in nightclubs. Research findings support the importance of humor in our everyday lives. Humor promotes romance (Lundy, Tan, & Cunningham, 1998), defuses interpersonal conflicts (Brown & Keegan, 1999), contributes to effective teaching (Wanzer & Frymier, 1999), reduces the emotional effects of stress (Cann, Holt, & Calhoun, 1999), and strengthens the immune response (Harrison et al., 2000).

What makes humor amusing? The brain, particularly the right hemisphere, plays an important role. For example, damage to the right frontal lobe disrupts humor appreciation, including diminished smiling and laughing, more than damage to other parts of the brain (Shammi & Stuss, 1999). Though the brain is important in humor appreciation, we know more about psychological factors that affect our reactions to humor. One factor is the social contexts, such as night clubs, in which humor is expressed. To people who are inebriated, comedians who use blunt, simple humor will seem funnier than comedians who use subtle, complex humor (Weaver et al., 1985). Thus, if you drank a few beers, you would probably find a Three Stooges comedy more amusing and a Dennis Miller monologue less amusing.

Other factors that influence the perceived funniness of humor are gender and culture. A recent study, for example, found that women liked sexual humor with a male target as much as men did, but they disliked sexual humor when the target was a woman. These findings differed from research conducted a decade earlier, which found that men enjoyed sexual humor more than women did regardless of the gender of the humor's target. The researchers who conducted the more recent study attributed this to changes in women's attitudes toward humor as a result of the women's movement (Herzog, 1999). There also are cross-cultural commonalties and differences in what people view as humorous, as demonstrated in a study of German and Italian adults' reactions to jokes and cartoons. Participants gave similar rankings for the quality of the jokes and cartoons, but Germans, compared to Italians, rated nonsense humor as funnier and sexual humor as less funny (Ruch & Forabosco, 1996).

But what other factors account for our responses to humor? Major theories include *disparagement theory, incongruity theory,* and *release theory* (Berger, 1987).

Disparagement Theory

According to C. L. Edson, a 20th-century American newspaper editor, "We love a joke that hands us a pat on the back while it kicks the other fellow down the stairs." Edson's comment indicates that he favored the **disparagement theory** of humor, first put forth by 17th-century English philosopher Thomas Hobbes. Hobbes claimed we feel amused when humor makes us feel superior to other people (Nevo, 1985). One study found that humor in which the target is disparaged is perceived as funnier than humor in which the target is uplifted (Mio & Graesser, 1991). Research supporting Hobbes's position has found that we are especially amused when we dislike those to whom we are made to feel superior (Wicker, Barron, & Willis, 1980). Satirists and television commentators take this approach by disparaging certain commonly disliked groups, such as greedy lawyers, crooked politicians, and phony evangelists. We also enjoy disparaging humor more when we like the person doing the disparaging (Oppliger & Sherblom, 1992).

▲ **Money Does Not Necessarily Buy Happiness**
If you buy lottery tickets because you believe that winning the jackpot would make you happy, you might be in for a disappointment should you someday win. Lottery winners often are no happier after they win than they were before. In fact, they might no longer gain satisfaction from life's little pleasures.

 The Laughter Remedy
www.mhhe.com/sdorow5

disparagement theory
The theory that humor is amusing when it makes one feel superior to other people.

 Humor Research
www.mhhe.com/sdorow5

(a)   (b)   (c)

▲ **Theories of Humor**

Humor researchers have found that humor is based on disparagement, incongruity, or release. *(a)* If you have seen Sandra Bernhard make critical remarks about prominent people, you have observed a performance that supports the disparagement theory of humor. *(b)* The incongruity theory of humor gains support from comedians such as David Letterman, who play on our sense of the absurd to make us laugh. *(c)* Comedians such as Chris Rock, who base their humor on racism and social injustice, exemplify the release theory of humor, which assumes that the sudden release of sexual or aggressive tension induces a feeling of amusement.

incongruity theory

The theory that humor is amusing when it brings together incompatible ideas in a surprising outcome that violates one's expectations.

release theory

The theory that humor relieves anxiety caused by sexual or aggressive energy.

Incongruity Theory

In the 18th century, German philosopher Immanuel Kant put forth an alternative theory of humor—**incongruity theory.** Incongruous humor brings together incompatible ideas in a surprising outcome that violates our expectations (Attardo, 1997). Incongruous jokes tend to be perceived as more humorous than other jokes (Hillson & Martin, 1994), and incongruity is one of the most important factors in the perceived humorousness of television commercials (Alden, Mukherjee, & Hoyer, 2000). Incongruity theory explains why many jokes require timing and can lose something on the second hearing—bad timing or repetition can destroy the incongruity (Kuhlman, 1985). The appreciation of incongruous humor varies with age and conservatism. A study of more than 4,000 participants aged 14 to 66 found that older people and conservative people preferred incongruous humor more, and nonsense humor less, than did younger people and liberal people (Ruch, McGhee, & Hehl, 1990).

Release Theory

Another theory of humor, **release theory,** is based on Sigmund Freud's claim that humor is a cathartic outlet for anxiety caused by repressed sexual or aggressive energy (Freud, 1905). Humor can raise your level of anxiety—and then suddenly lower it, providing you relief so pleasurable that it can make you laugh (McCauley et al., 1983). In a study bearing on the release theory of humor in regard to aggression, high school students were given a frustrating exam. Afterward, they were more likely to respond aggressively to a subsequent frustrating situation. But students who were exposed after the exam to a humorous situation that provoked laughter were less likely to respond aggressively to the later frustration. According to release theory, the students' laughter provided a cathartic experience, which released energy that would have provoked later aggression (Ziv, 1987).

A recent study tested another prediction from Freud's theory—that hostility toward women might underlie sexist humor. A sample of college undergraduates completed a series of attitude and personality inventories and rated 10 sexist cartoons on perceived funniness. Enjoyment of the cartoons was positively correlated with rape-related beliefs and psychological, physical, and sexual aggression in men, but not in women. That is, men who were more tolerant of rape and were more aggressive also found the sexist cartoons to be more enjoyable. Women found the cartoons to be less acceptable and less enjoyable and funny than men—though they were not less likely to retell them (Ryan & Kanjorski, 1998).

The field of humor research is relatively young, and more research is needed to uncover the factors that make people find amusement in one kind of humor but not in another. Such research might explain, for example, why some people (most notably, the French) find Jerry Lewis amusing, while others do not.

STAYING ON TRACK: *The Experience of Emotion*

1. What factors are associated with personal happiness?
2. What are the disparagement, incongruity, and release theories of humor?

Answers to Staying on Track start on p. ST-5.

◆ THEORIES OF EMOTION

How do we explain emotional experience? Theories of emotion vary in their attention to physiological, expressive, and cognitive factors. Figure 12.5 illustrates several major theories.

Biopsychological Theories of Emotion

Though most theories of emotion recognize the importance of physiological factors, certain theories stress them. These include the *James-Lange theory,* the *Cannon-Bard theory,* and *opponent-process theory.*

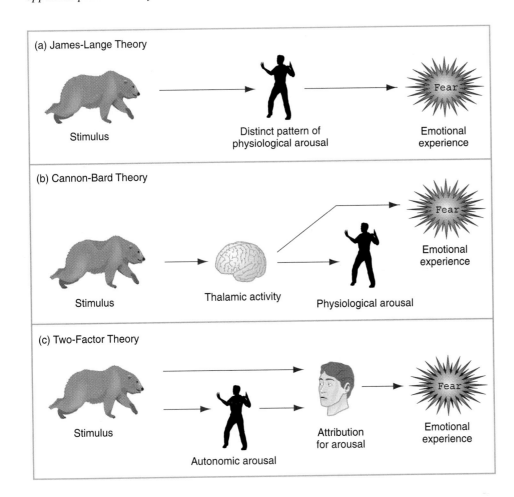

◀ **Figure 12.5**
Theories of Emotion
(a) According to the James-Lange theory, specific patterns of physiological changes evoke specific emotional experiences. *(b)* According to the Cannon-Bard theory, activity in the thalamus precedes both arousal and emotional experience. *(c)* And according to Schachter and Singer's two-factor theory, physiological arousal and a cognitive label that explains it combine to produce emotional experiences.

The James-Lange Theory of Emotion

In the late 19th century, American psychologist William James (1884) claimed that physiological changes precede emotional experiences. Because a Danish physiologist named Carl Lange (1834–1900) made the same claim at about the same time, it became known as the **James-Lange theory** (see Figure 12.5). Note that the theory violates the commonsense belief that physiological changes *follow* emotional experiences.

Psychology Versus Common Sense

Do Emotional Experiences Depend on Physical Responses to Emotional Situations?

The main implication of the James-Lange theory is that particular emotional events stimulate specific patterns of physiological changes, each evoking a specific emotional experience (Lang, 1994). According to James (1890/1981, Vol. 2, p. 1065):

Common-sense says, we lose our fortune, are sorry and weep; we meet a bear, are frightened and run; we are insulted by a rival, are angry and strike . . . the more rational statement is that we feel sorry because we cry, angry because we strike, afraid because we tremble.

The James-Lange theory provoked criticism from American physiologist Walter Cannon (1927). One of his criticisms was based on his assumption that individuals have poor ability to perceive many of the subtle physiological changes induced by the sympathetic nervous system. How could the perception of physiological changes be the basis of emotional experiences when we cannot perceive many of those changes? Cannon also believed that different emotions are associated with the same pattern of physiological arousal. How could different emotions be evoked by the same pattern of arousal? In part because of Cannon's criticisms, the James-Lange theory fell into disfavor for several decades.

But recent research has lent some support to the James-Lange theory (Barbalet, 1999). One line of support for the theory comes from research studies showing that fear can be evoked by threatening situations before we are consciously aware of them. This process might have evolved because it is an adaptive, potentially life-saving, process that permits us to react more quickly to confront or flee from a threat than we would if we had to first become consciously aware of it (Robinson, 1998).

In a study that supported the basic assumptions of the James-Lange theory, participants were directed to adopt facial expressions representing fear, anger, disgust, sadness, surprise, and happiness (Ekman, Levenson, & Friesen, 1983). Participants were told which muscles to contract or relax but were not told which emotions they were expressing. Recordings of heart rate and skin temperature were taken as they maintained the facial expressions. The results supported the assumption that the physiological changes underlying emotional responses to situations can occur before we consciously experience an emotion.

The results also supported the assumption that, contrary to Cannon's belief, different behavioral reactions can induce different patterns of physiological activity. The facial expression of fear induced a large increase in heart rate and a slight decrease in finger temperature, whereas the facial expression of anger induced a large increase in both heart rate and finger temperature. Finger temperature varies with the amount of blood flow: a decrease in blood flow causes a decrease in temperature, and an increase in blood flow causes an increase in temperature. The presence of different patterns of autonomic activity for different emotions has been replicated in non-Western cultures, such as West Sumatra (Levenson et al., 1992).

The difference in the patterns of physiological arousal between fear and anger thus supports the James-Lange theory. More recent studies have lent further support to the specificity of autonomic nervous system responses in different emotions. In one study, children watched *E.T., The Extraterrestrial*, while being monitored physiologically. Scenes that evoked sadness were associated with greater variability in heart rate and blood oxygenation than were scenes that evoked happiness (Miller & Wood, 1997).

The Cannon-Bard Theory of Emotion

After rejecting the James-Lange theory of emotion, Walter Cannon (1927) and Philip Bard (1934) put forth their own theory, giving equal weight to physiological changes and cognitive processes. The **Cannon-Bard theory** (see Figure 12.5) claims that an emotion is produced when an event or object is perceived by the thalamus, the brain structure that conveys this information simultaneously to the cerebral cortex and to the skeletal muscles and sympathetic nervous system. The cerebral cortex then uses memories of past experiences to determine the nature of the perceived event or object, providing the subjective experience of emotion. Meanwhile, the muscles and sympathetic nervous system provide the physiological arousal that prepares the individual to take action to adjust to the situation that evoked the emotion.

Unlike the James-Lange theory, the Cannon-Bard theory assumes that different emotions are associated with the same state of physiological arousal. The Cannon-Bard theory has failed to gain extensive research support, because the thalamus does not appear to play the role the researchers envisioned. But if the theory is recast in terms of the limbic system, it is supported by research findings. For example, though the thalamus might not directly cause emotional responses, it does relay sensory information to the amygdala, which then processes the information.

Research on victims of spinal cord damage has provided support for the Cannon-Bard theory, while contradicting the James-Lange theory. Studies have found that even people with spinal cord injuries that prevent them from perceiving their bodily arousal experience distinct emotions, often more intensely than before their spinal cord injury (Bermond et al., 1991). This violates the James-Lange theory's assumption that emotional experience depends on the perception of bodily arousal, while supporting the Cannon-Bard theory's assumption that emotional experience depends on the brain's perception of ongoing events.

The Opponent-Process Theory of Emotion

In an anticipation of another theory of emotion, Plato, in the *Phaedo*, states:

▶ How strange would appear to be this thing that we call pleasure! And how curiously it is related to what is thought to be its opposite, pain! The two will never be found together in a man, and yet if you seek the one and obtain it, you are almost bound always to get the other as well, just as though they were both attached to one and the same head. . . . Wherever the one is found, the other follows up behind. So, in my case, since I had pain in my leg as a result of the fetters, pleasure seems to have come to follow it up.

If Plato were alive today, he might favor the **opponent-process theory** of emotion (see Figure 12.6), which holds that the mammalian brain has evolved mechanisms that counteract strong positive or negative emotions by evoking an opposite emotional response to maintain

Cannon-Bard theory
The theory that an emotion is produced when an event or object is perceived by the thalamus, which conveys this information simultaneously to the cerebral cortex and the skeletal muscles and autonomic nervous system.

opponent-process theory
The theory that the brain counteracts a strong positive or negative emotion by evoking an opposite emotional response.

▼ **Figure 12.6**
Opponent-Process Theory of Emotion
According to opponent-process theory, when we experience an emotion (A), an opposing emotion (B) will counter the first emotion, dampening the experience of that emotion (as indicated by the steady level of A being lower than the peak of A). As we experience the first emotion (A') on repeated occasions, the opposing emotion (B') becomes stronger and the first emotion weaker, which leads to an even weaker experience of the first emotion (as indicated by the steady level of A' being lower than the peak of A'). For example, the first time you drove on a highway you might have experienced fear, followed by a feeling of relief. As you drove on highways on repeated occasions, your feeling of fear eventually gave way to a feeling of mild arousal (Solomon, 1980).

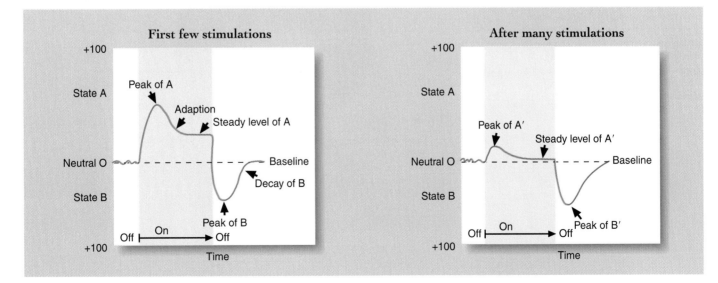

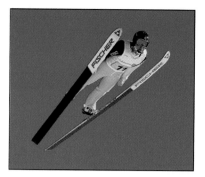

▲ Fear and Euphoria

According to the opponent-process theory of emotion, the fear this ski jumper experienced when he first learned to jump eventually gave way to a feeling of euphoria.

facial-feedback theory

The theory that particular facial expressions induce particular emotional experiences.

homeostasis. According to Richard Solomon (1980), who first put forth the theory, the opposing emotion begins sometime after the onset of the first emotion and lasts longer than the first emotion. If we experience the first emotion on repeated occasions, the opposing emotion grows stronger and the emotion that is experienced becomes a compromise between the two opposing emotional states.

Suppose that you took up skydiving. The first time you parachuted from an airplane you would probably feel terror. After surviving the jump, your feeling of terror would be replaced by a feeling of relief. As you jumped again and again, you would feel anticipation instead of terror as you prepared to jump. And your initial postjump feeling of relief might intensify into a feeling of exhilaration.

Opponent-process theory also might explain the euphoria that often follows the anxiety of final-exams week. It might even explain why some blood donors become seemingly "addicted" to donating blood. When a person first donates blood, she might experience fear—but afterward might experience a pleasant feeling known as the "warm glow" effect. If she repeatedly donates blood, the "warm glow" strengthens, leading her to donate blood in order to induce that feeling (Piliavin, Callero, & Evans, 1982).

The Facial-Feedback Theory of Emotion

Benjamin Franklin claimed, "A cheerful face is nearly as good for an invalid as healthy weather." Have you ever received the advice "Put on a happy face" or "Keep a stiff upper lip" from people trying to help you overcome adversity? Both of these bits of advice are commonsense versions of the **facial-feedback theory** of emotion (see Figure 12.7), which holds that our facial expressions affect our emotional experiences. As you learned in the discussion of the James-Lange theory, adopting a facial expression characteristic of a particular emotion can induce that emotion. But unlike the James-Lange theory, which is primarily concerned with the effects of autonomic nervous system activity on emotion, facial-feedback theory is limited to the effects of facial expressions. Facial-feedback theory was put forth in 1907 by French physician Israel Waynbaum. Waynbaum assumed that particular facial expressions alter the flow of blood to particular regions of the brain, thereby evoking particular emotional experiences. For example, smiling might increase the flow of blood to regions of the brain

▶ Figure 12.7

The Facial-Feedback Theory of Emotion

According to the facial-feedback theory of emotion, particular patterns of sensory feedback from facial expressions evoke particular emotions. Thus, sensory feedback from the corrugator muscles, which are active when we frown, might contribute to unpleasant emotional experiences. Similarly, sensory feedback from the zygomatic muscles, which are active when we smile, might contribute to pleasant emotional experiences.

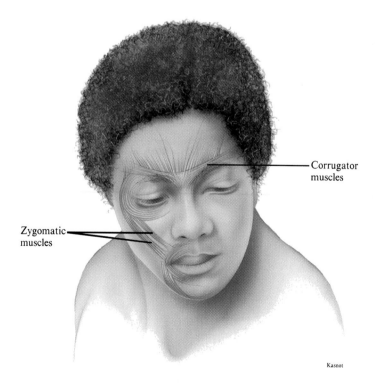

Corrugator muscles

Zygomatic muscles

Kasnot

that elevate mood. Most contemporary facial-feedback theorists, led by Paul Ekman (1992), assume that evolution has endowed us with facial expressions that provide different patterns of sensory feedback of muscle tension levels to the brain, thereby evoking different emotions. Support for the theory has come from studies that have found that emotional experiences follow facial expressions rather than precede them, and that sensory neurons convey information from facial muscles directly to the hypothalamus, which plays an important role in emotional arousal (Zajonc, 1985).

But facial-feedback theory has not received unqualified support. Though there is a positive association between particular facial expressions and particular emotional experiences (Adelmann & Zajonc, 1989), the effect of facial feedback on emotional experience tends to be small (Matsumoto, 1987). Though facial expressions might not be the sole cause of emotions, they can affect the intensity of ongoing emotions and induce emotions, with positive facial expressions inducing positive moods and negative facial expressions inducing negative moods (Kleinke, Peterson, & Rutledge, 1998). Try smiling and then frowning, and note the subtle differences they induce in your mood. For example, adopting a hostile or friendly facial expression can move one's mood in that direction (Ohira & Kurono, 1993).

Cognitive Theories of Emotion

More recent theories of emotion—*two-factor theory* and *cognitive appraisal theory*—emphasize the importance of cognition (thinking). They assume that our emotional experiences depend on our subjective interpretation of situations in which we find ourselves.

The Two-Factor Theory of Emotion

Stanley Schachter and Jerome Singer's **two-factor theory** (see Figure 12.5) views emotional experience as the outcome of two factors: Physiological arousal and the attribution of a cause for it. According to Schachter and Singer, when you experience physiological arousal, you search for its source. Your attribution of a cause for your arousal determines the emotion that you experience. For example, if you experience intense physiological arousal in the presence of an appealing person, you might attribute your arousal to that person, and, as a result, feel that you are attracted to him or her. You can read a discussion of Schachter and Singer's classic study inspired by their two-factor theory in the Anatomy of a Research Study feature.

The Cognitive-Appraisal Theory of Emotion

Though two-factor theory has failed to gain strong support, it has stimulated interest in the cognitive basis of emotion. The purest cognitive theory of emotion is the **cognitive-appraisal theory** of Richard Lazarus (1993a). Unlike two-factor theory, cognitive-appraisal theory downplays the role of physiological arousal. Like two-factor theory, cognitive-appraisal theory assumes that our emotion at a given time depends on our interpretation of the situation we are in at that time. The cognitive appraisal of specific kinds of situations tends to be consistent across different cultures. This conclusion was supported by a study of almost 3,000 people in 37 countries who had been asked to recall their cognitive appraisal of recent events associated with feelings of joy, fear, shame, guilt, anger, disgust, and sadness (Scherer, 1997).

An early study by Lazarus and his colleagues supported the cognitive-appraisal theory of emotion (Speisman et al., 1964). Participants watched a film about a tribal ritual in which incisions were made in adolescents' penises. Participants' emotional arousal was measured by recording their heart rate and skin conductance (an increase in the electrical conductivity of the skin, caused by sweating). Participants all watched the same film but heard different sound tracks. Those in the *silent group* saw the film without a sound track. Those in the *trauma group* were told that the procedure was extremely painful and emotionally distressing. Those in the *intellectualization group* were told about the procedure in a detached, matter-of-fact way, with no mention of feelings. And those in the *denial group* were told that the procedure was not painful and that the boys were overjoyed because it signified their

two-factor theory

The theory that emotional experience is the outcome of physiological arousal and the attribution of a cause for that arousal.

cognitive-appraisal theory

The theory that one's emotion at a given time depends on one's interpretation of the situation one is in.

▲ **The Cognitive-Appraisal Theory of Emotion**

According to cognitive-appraisal theory, our interpretation of events, rather than the events themselves, determines our emotional experiences. Thus, the same event might evoke different emotions in different people, as in this exhilarated boy and his terrified mother riding on a Ferris wheel.

Anatomy of a Research Study

Do Emotions Depend on the Attribution of a Cause for Our Physiological Arousal?

Rationale

Two-factor theory resembles the James-Lange theory in assuming that emotional experience follows physiological arousal (Winton, 1990). But it is different from the James-Lange theory in holding, as does the Cannon-Bard theory, that all emotions involve similar patterns of physiological arousal. But the Cannon-Bard theory assumes that emotional experience and physiological arousal occur simultaneously; two-factor theory assumes instead that emotion follows the attribution of a cause for one's physiological arousal.

Method

The original experiment on two-factor theory provided evidence that when we experience physiological arousal, we seek to identify its source, and that what we identify as the source in turn determines our emotional experience (Schachter & Singer, 1962). Male college student volunteers participated one at a time and were told that they were getting an injection of a new vitamin called "Suproxin" to assess its effect on vision. In reality, they received an injection of the hormone epinephrine, which activates the sympathetic nervous system. The epinephrine caused hand tremors, a flushed face, a pounding heart, and rapid breathing. Some participants (the informed group) were told to expect these changes. Other participants (the misinformed group) were told to expect itching, numb feet, and headache, and some (the uninformed group) were told nothing about the effects. Still other participants received a placebo injection of a saline solution instead of an injection of epinephrine and were told nothing about its physiological effects.

The participant then waited in a room with the experimenter's accomplice, a man who acted either happy or angry. When acting happy, the accomplice was cheerful and threw paper airplanes, played with a Hula Hoop, and shot wads of paper into a wastebasket. When acting angry, the accomplice acted upset, stomped around, and complained about a questionnaire given by the experimenter, which included questions about the bathing habits of the respondent's family and the sex life of his mother. The participant's emotional response to the accomplice was assessed by observing him through a one-way mirror and by having him complete a questionnaire about his feelings.

Results and Discussion

The results showed that the informed participants were unaffected by the accomplice, whereas the misinformed participants and uninformed participants expressed and experienced emotions similar to those of the accomplice. But the placebo group also expressed and experienced situation-appropriate emotions, despite the lack of drug-induced physiological arousal. Schachter concluded that the informed participants attributed their arousal to the injection and did not exhibit situation-appropriate emotions. In contrast, the misinformed participants and the uninformed participants attributed their physiological arousal to the situation they were in, responding positively when the accomplice acted happy and responding negatively when the accomplice acted angry. Schachter and Singer assumed that the placebo participants became physiologically aroused in response to the emotional display of the accomplice and interpreted their own feelings as congruent with those of the accomplice.

Since the original studies of two-factor theory in the early 1960s, research has produced inconsistent findings regarding it. Consider the theory's assumption that unexplained physiological arousal can just as well provoke feelings of joy as provoke feelings of sadness, depending on the person's interpretation of the source of the arousal. This was contradicted by a study in which participants received injections of epinephrine without being informed of its true effects. The participants tended to experience negative emotions, regardless of their immediate social environment. Even those in the presence of a happy person tended to experience unpleasant emotions (Marshall & Zimbardo, 1979). A review of research on Schachter and Singer's two-factor theory concluded that the only assumption of the theory that has been consistently supported is that physiological arousal misattributed to an outside source will *intensify* an emotional experience. There is little evidence that such a misattribution will *cause* an emotional experience (Reisenzein, 1983). More recent research has likewise provided mixed support for two-factor theory (Mezzacappa, Katkin, & Palmer, 1999).

▶ **Stanley Schachter**

"Given a state of physiological arousal for which an individual has no immediate explanation, he will label this state and describe his feelings in terms of the cognitions available to him."

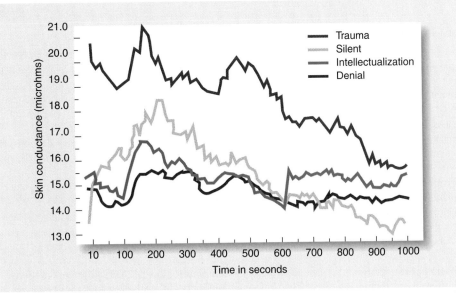

Cognitive Appraisal and Emotion
The graph shows that the emotional responses of participants who viewed a film of a ritual in which incisions were made in adolescents' penises depended on the nature of the sound track. Those who heard a sound track that described the procedure as traumatic experienced the greatest emotional arousal (Speisman et al., 1964).

entrance into manhood. Results showed that the trauma group experienced greater arousal than the silent group, which in turn experienced greater arousal than the denial and intellectualization groups (see Figure 12.8). These findings indicate that subjective appraisal of the situation, rather than the objective situation itself, accounted for participants' emotional arousal.

More recent studies provide additional support for the assumption that your interpretation of a situation affects your emotional state (Rotenberg, Kim, & Herman-Stahl, 1998). Consider a situation that is all too familiar to people who fly frequently: lost luggage. A study of more than 100 airline passengers who had reported that their luggage was lost found that their emotional response to the loss depended on their cognitive appraisal of it (Scherer & Ceschi, 1997). But cognitive-appraisal theory has been challenged by Robert Zajonc (1984) and others, who insist that cognitive appraisal is not essential to the experience of emotion. For example, you have probably taken an instant liking or disliking to a person without knowing why. And, as noted in Chapters 5 and 6, research findings show that we can respond emotionally to stimuli we are unaware of (Dimberg, Thunberg, & Elmehed, 2000).

This and other evidence indicates that emotional experience can take place without conscious cognitive appraisal (Izard, 1993). There even is physiological evidence for this, because of the direct pathways from the thalamus (which relays sensory input to other brain regions) to the limbic system (which plays an important role in emotional processing). These pathways bypass the cerebral cortex, the involvement of which seems required for conscious cognitive appraisal. Thus, we can have emotional reactions to stimuli of which we are unaware (LeDoux, 1986).

What can we conclude from the variety of contradictory theories of emotion? The best we can do is to realize that none of them is sufficient to explain emotion, though each describes a process that contributes to it. Moreover, the theories illustrate the importance of the physiological, expressive, and experiential components of emotion.

STAYING ON TRACK: *Theories of Emotion*

1. What evidence is there for and against the James-Lange theory of emotion?
2. How has research supported the facial-feedback theory of emotion?
3. What does research conducted since Schachter and Singer's classic study say about the two-factor theory of emotion?

Answers to Staying on Track start on p. ST-6.

Chapter Summary

THE BIOPSYCHOLOGY OF EMOTION

- Emotion is a motivated state marked by physiological arousal, expressive behavior, and cognitive experience.
- Emotional arousal depends on activity in the autonomic nervous system and the limbic system.
- The polygraph test assumes that differences in physiological arousal in response to control questions and relevant questions can be used to determine whether a person is lying.
- Critics point out that the polygraph can be fooled and that it has poor validity because it finds a large proportion of guilty people innocent and an even larger proportion of innocent people guilty.
- A promising alternative to the traditional polygraph test is the Guilty Knowledge Test, which depends on the guilty person's physiological arousal to important facts about his or her transgression.
- The limbic system plays a role in the activation of the fight-or-flight response and emotional reactions to different environment stimuli.
- The left cerebral hemisphere plays a greater role in positive emotions; the right cerebral hemisphere plays a greater role in negative emotions.
- Hormones and neurotransmitters, including endorphins, alter our moods by affecting neuronal activity.

THE EXPRESSION OF EMOTION

- Psychologists are particularly interested in how we express our emotions through facial expressions.
- Charles Darwin believed that facial expressions evolved because they promoted survival.
- The hereditary basis of facial expressions is supported by research showing cross-cultural consistency in the positive association between particular facial expressions and particular emotions.

THE EXPERIENCE OF EMOTION

- Robert Plutchik considers the basic emotions to be joy, fear, anger, disgust, sadness, surprise, acceptance, and anticipation.

- Emotions vary in their intensity and pleasantness; people who tend to experience intensely pleasant emotions are also likely to experience intensely unpleasant emotions.
- According to social-comparison theory, happiness is the result of estimating that one's life circumstances are more favorable than those of others.
- According to adaptation-level theory, happiness depends on estimating that one's current life circumstances are more favorable than one's past life circumstances.
- Humor is explained by disparagement theory, incongruity theory, and release theory.

THEORIES OF EMOTION

- The James-Lange theory assumes that physiological changes precede emotional experiences and that different patterns of physiological arousal are associated with different emotions.
- The Cannon-Bard theory claims that the thalamus perceives an event and communicates this information to the cerebral cortex (which provides the subjective experience of emotion) and stimulates the physiological arousal characteristic of emotion.
- According to opponent-process theory, the brain has evolved mechanisms that counteract strong positive or negative emotions by evoking an opposite emotional response. If the first emotion is repeated, the opposing emotion gradually strengthens and the first emotion gradually weakens, until a more moderate response becomes habitual.
- According to facial-feedback theory, different emotions are caused by sensory feedback from different facial expressions.
- Two-factor theory views emotional experience as the consequence of attributing physiological arousal to a particular aspect of one's immediate environment.
- Cognitive-appraisal theory ignores the role of physiological arousal and considers emotional experience to be solely the result of a person's interpretation of her or his current circumstances.

Key Concepts

emotion 351

THE BIOPSYCHOLOGY OF EMOTION
fight-or-flight response 352
Guilty Knowledge Test 355

polygraph test 354

THE EXPERIENCE OF EMOTION
adaptation-level theory 362
disparagement theory 363

incongruity theory 364
release theory 364
social-comparison theory 362

THEORIES OF EMOTION
Cannon-Bard theory 367

cognitive-appraisal theory 369
facial-feedback theory 368
James-Lange theory 366
opponent-process theory 367
two-factor theory 369

Key Contributors

Thought Questions

1. Why is it technically incorrect to refer to the polygraph test as a "lie detector"?
2. What are the main sources of evidence supporting hemispheric lateralization in emotion?
3. How does research on the nonverbal expression of emotion support the James-Lange theory?

Possible Answers to Thought Questions start on p. PT-4.

OLC Preview

For additional quizzing and a variety of interactive resources, visit the book's Online Learning Center at www.mhhe.com/sdorow5.

13 *Personality*

PABLO PICASSO
Girl Before a Mirror, 1932

Years ago a researcher placed a newspaper advertisement that offered a free, personalized astrological profile. Of the 150 persons who responded 141 (94 percent) later said they had recognized their own personalities in the "personalized" profiles. Each of the respondents had actually received the same personality profile—the profile of a mass murderer who had terrorized France (Waldrop, 1984). Take a moment to see if you recognize yourself in the following personality description:

▶ You have a strong need for other people to like and admire you. You have a tendency to be critical of yourself. You have a great deal of unused capacity, which you have not turned to your advantage. . . . Disciplined and controlled on the outside, you tend to be worrisome and insecure inside. . . . At times you are extraverted, affable, and sociable; at other times, you are introverted, wary, and reserved. (Ulrich, Stachnik, & Stainton, 1963, p. 831)

Study after study has shown that when people are given personality tests and then presented with a mock personality description like this one, they tend to accept the description as accurate. They do so because the description *is* accurate. But such descriptions are accurate because they list traits that are shared by almost everyone; they say nothing that distinguishes one person from another. The acceptance of personality descriptions that are true of almost everyone is known as the "Barnum effect" (Davies, 1997). This reflects P. T. Barnum's saying, "There's a sucker born every minute." The Barnum effect demonstrates that useful personality descriptions must distinguish one person from another. You should no more accept a personality profile that fails to recognize your distinctive combination of personality traits than you would accept a physical description that merely states that you have a head, a torso, two eyes, ten toes, and other common physical characteristics.

▲ **Personality**
Actor-comedian Jim Carrey exemplifies the notion that one's personality involves a unique pattern of thinking, feeling, and behaving.

The Personality Project
www.mhhe.com/sdorow5

Great Ideas in Personality
www.mhhe.com/sdorow5

Personality: What Makes Us Who We Are?
www.mhhe.com/sdorow5

personality
An individual's unique, relatively consistent pattern of thinking, feeling, and behaving.

The word *personality* comes from the Latin word *persona,* meaning "mask." Just as masks distinguished one character from another in ancient Greek and Roman plays, your personality distinguishes you from other people. Your **personality** is your unique, relatively consistent pattern of thinking, feeling, and behaving. Given that each of us has a unique personality, how do we explain our distinctive patterns of thinking, feeling, and behaving? Personality theorists favor several approaches to this question. In reading about them, you will see that theorists' own life experiences often color their personality theories. The approaches to the study of personality differ on several dimensions, including the influence of unconscious motivation, the extent to which we are molded by learning, the role of cognitive processes, the importance of subjective experience, and the effects of biological factors.

◆ THE PSYCHOANALYTIC APPROACH

The *psychoanalytic approach* to personality is rooted in medicine and biology. Sigmund Freud, the founder of psychoanalysis, was a physician who hoped to find the biological basis of the psychological processes described in his psychosexual theory.

repression

In psychoanalytic theory, the defense mechanism that involves banishing threatening thoughts, feelings, and memories into the unconscious mind.

id

In Freud's theory, the part of the personality that contains inborn biological drives and that seeks immediate gratification.

pleasure principle

The process by which the id seeks immediate gratification of its impulses.

ego

In Freud's theory, the part of the personality that helps the individual adapt to external reality by making compromises between the id, the superego, and the environment.

reality principle

The process by which the ego directs the individual to express sexual and aggressive impulses in socially acceptable ways.

superego

In Freud's theory, the part of the personality that acts as a moral guide telling us what we should and should not do.

▲ **Sigmund Freud (1856–1939) and Anna Freud (1895–1982)**

After Sigmund Freud's death, his theory was championed by his daughter Anna, who pursued a career as a psychoanalyst.

Freud's Psychosexual Theory

Freud (1856–1939) was born in Moravia to Jewish parents, who moved with him to Vienna when he was 4 years old. Though Freud desired a career as a physiology professor, anti-Semitism limited his choice of professions to law, business, or medicine. He eventually practiced as a neurologist. Freud remained in Vienna until the Nazis threatened his safety. In 1938 he emigrated to England, where he died the following year after suffering for many years from mouth cancer.

Early in his career, Freud studied with French neurologist Jean Charcot, who demonstrated the power of hypnosis in treating *conversion hysteria,* a disorder characterized by physical symptoms such as deafness, blindness, or paralysis without any physical cause. Freud also was intrigued by a report that psychiatrist Josef Breuer had successfully used a "talking cure" to treat conversion hysteria. Breuer found that by encouraging his patients to talk freely about whatever came to mind, they became aware of the psychological causes of their physical symptoms and, as a result, experienced emotional release, or *catharsis.* This led to the disappearance of the symptoms.

Freud's personality theory reflected his time—the Victorian era of the late 19th century, which valued rationality and self-control of physical drives. Freud attributed the symptoms of conversion hysteria to unconscious sexual conflicts, which were symbolized in the symptoms. For example, paralyzed legs might represent a sexual conflict. Freud's claim that sexuality was an important determinant of human behavior shocked and disgusted many of his contemporaries (Rapp, 1988).

Levels of Consciousness

As described in Chapter 6, Freud divided the mind into three levels. The *conscious mind* is merely the "tip of the iceberg," representing a tiny region of the mind. Just below the conscious mind lies the *preconscious mind,* which includes accessible memories—that is, memories we can recall at will. The *unconscious mind,* the bulk of the mind, lies below both the conscious mind and the preconscious mind. It contains material we cannot recall at will.

Freud claimed that threatening thoughts or feelings are subject to **repression,** the banishment of conscious material into the unconscious. Because Freud assumed unconscious thoughts and feelings are the most important influences on our behavior, he proclaimed: "The theory of repression is the cornerstone on which the whole structure of psychoanalysis rests" (Freud, 1914/1957, p. 16). The notion of repressed thoughts and feelings led to the concept of *psychic determinism,* which holds that all behavior is influenced by unconscious motives. Psychic determinism is exhibited in *Freudian slips,* unintentional statements that might reveal our repressed feelings (Reason, 2000). For example, the slip "I loathe you . . . I mean I love you" might reveal repressed hostility.

The Structure of Personality

As illustrated in Figure 13.1, Freud distinguished three structures of personality: the *id,* the *ego,* and the *superego.* The **id** (Latin for "it") is unconscious and consists of our inborn biological drives. In demanding immediate gratification of drives, most notably sex and aggression, the id obeys the **pleasure principle.**

Through life experiences we learn that acting on every sexual or aggressive impulse is socially maladaptive. As a consequence, each of us develops an **ego,** Latin for "I." The ego obeys the **reality principle,** directing us to express sexual and aggressive impulses in socially acceptable ways. Suppose a teacher refuses to change your grade on an exam that was graded with an incorrect answer key. Your ego would encourage you to argue with the teacher instead of punching him or her.

The **superego** (Latin for "over the I") counteracts the id, which is concerned only with immediate gratification, and the ego, which is concerned only with adapting to reality. The

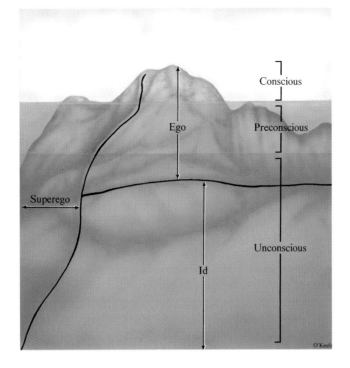

◀ **Figure 13.1**
The Structure of Personality
Freud divided personality into the id, ego, and superego. The id is entirely unconscious and demands immediate gratification of its desires. The ego is partly conscious and partly unconscious. This permits it to balance the id's demands with the external demands of reality and the moralistic demands of the superego, which is also partly conscious and partly unconscious.

superego acts as our moral guide. To Freud, your personality is the outcome of the continual battle for dominance among the id, the ego, and the superego.

Defense Mechanisms

The ego might resort to **defense mechanisms,** which distort reality, to protect itself from the anxiety caused by id impulses. The ego also might use defense mechanisms to relieve the anxiety caused by unacceptable personal characteristics and unpleasant or even traumatic personal experiences (Bluhm, 1999). Each of us uses defense mechanisms to varying extents, which contributes to the distinctiveness of our personalities. Because all defense mechanisms involve repression, we are not aware when we are using them. Researchers studying the role of unconscious processes in coping with stress have renewed scientific interest in defense mechanisms (Cramer, 2000).

We sometimes rely on immature kinds of defense mechanisms. In resorting to the defense mechanism of **regression,** the individual displays immature behaviors that have relieved anxiety in the past. An adult might respond to job frustrations by crying or throwing temper tantrums.

Other defense mechanisms rely on changing our perception of reality. When we resort to **rationalization,** we provide socially acceptable reasons for our inappropriate behavior. For example, a student whose semester grades include one D and four F's might blame the four F's on studying too much for the course in which he received a D.

In some cases, defense mechanisms direct sexual or aggressive drives in safer directions. A person who fears the consequences of expressing his feelings toward a particular person might express them toward someone less threatening. This is known as **displacement.** For example, a worker who hates his boss, but fears criticizing him, might instead abuse his children (Brennan & Andrews, 1990). If we cannot accept our own undesirable feelings, we might resort to **projection,** attributing our undesirable feelings to others. Paranoid people, who are unreasonably suspicious of others, might use projection to justify their own hostile feelings (Berman & McCann, 1995).

defense mechanism
In Freud's theory, a process that distorts reality to prevent the individual from being overwhelmed by anxiety.

regression
In psychoanalytic theory, the defense mechanism that involves reverting to immature behaviors that have relieved anxiety in the past.

rationalization
Giving socially acceptable reasons for one's inappropriate behavior.

displacement
In psychoanalytic theory, the defense mechanism that involves expressing feelings toward a person who is less threatening than the person who is the true target of those feelings.

projection
In psychoanalytic theory, the defense mechanism that involves attributing one's own undesirable feelings to other people.

reaction formation

In psychoanalytic theory, the defense mechanism that involves a tendency to act in a manner opposite to one's true feelings.

sublimation

In psychoanalytic theory, the defense mechanism that involves expressing sexual or aggressive impulses through indirect, socially acceptable outlets.

libido

Freud's term for the sexual energy of the id.

fixation

In Freud's theory, the failure to mature beyond a particular stage of psychosexual development.

oral stage

In Freud's theory, the stage of personality development, between birth and age 1 year, during which the infant gains pleasure from oral activities and faces a conflict over weaning.

anal stage

In Freud's theory, the stage of personality development, between ages 1 and 3, during which the child gains pleasure from defecation and faces a conflict over toilet training.

phallic stage

In Freud's theory, the stage of personality development, between ages 3 and 5, during which the child gains pleasure from the genitals and must resolve the Oedipus complex.

Oedipus complex

In Freud's theory, a conflict, during the phallic stage, between the child's sexual desire for the parent of the opposite sex and fear of punishment from the same-sex parent.

Electra complex

A term used by some psychoanalysts, but not by Freud, to refer to the Oedipus complex in girls.

latency stage

In Freud's theory, the stage, between age 5 and puberty, during which there is little psychosexual development.

Reaction formation involves countering undesirable feelings by acting in a manner opposite to them. Samuel Johnson, the 18th-century writer and dictionary editor, reported a classic example of reaction formation. A pair of proper ladies who met him at a literary tea commented, "We see, Dr. Johnson, that you do not have those naughty words in your dictionary." Johnson replied, "And I see, dear ladies, that you have been looking for them" (Morris & Morris, 1985, p. 101).

According to Freud, the most successful defense mechanism is **sublimation,** the expression of sexual or aggressive impulses through indirect, socially acceptable outlets. The sex drive can be sublimated through creative activities, such as painting, ballet dancing, or composing music. And the aggressive drive can be sublimated through sports such as football, lacrosse, or field hockey.

Psychosexual Development

Freud assumed that personality development depends on changes in the distribution of sexual energy, which he called **libido,** in regions of the body he called *erogenous zones.* Stimulation of these regions produces pleasure. Thus, he was concerned with stages of *psychosexual development.* Failure to progress smoothly through a particular stage can cause **fixation,** a tendency to continue to engage in behaviors associated with that stage. Freud called the first year of infancy the **oral stage** of development, because the infant gains pleasure from activities such as biting, sucking, and chewing. The most important social conflict of this stage is *weaning.* An infant inadequately weaned, because of too much or too little oral gratification, might become fixated at the oral stage. Fixation might lead to an *oral-dependent* personality, marked by passivity, dependency, and gullibility. The person will "swallow anything" and might become a "sucker." Or fixation might lead to an *oral-aggressive* personality, marked by cruelty and sarcastic, "biting" remarks.

At the age of 1 year, children enter the **anal stage.** They now obtain pleasure from defecation and experience an important conflict regarding toilet training. Freud claimed that inadequate toilet training, either premature or delayed, can lead to fixation at the anal stage. The main characters in the play, movie, and television series *The Odd Couple* represent two kinds of anal fixation. Felix represents the *anal-retentive* personality, marked by compulsive cleanliness, orderliness, and fussiness. Oscar represents the *anal-expulsive* personality, marked by sloppiness, carelessness, and informality.

Freud claimed that between the ages of 3 and 5, the child passes through the **phallic stage,** in which pleasure is gained from the genitals. This stage is associated with the **Oedipus complex,** in which the child sexually desires the parent of the opposite sex while fearing punishment from the parent of the same sex. Freud noted this conflict in Sophocles' play *Oedipus Rex,* in which Oedipus, abandoned as an infant, later kills his father and marries his mother—without knowing they are his parents.

Freud believed that the Oedipus story reflected a universal truth—the sexual attraction of each child to the opposite-sex parent. Resolution of the conflict leads to identification with the same-sex parent. The boy gives up his desire for his mother because of *castration anxiety*—his fear that his father will punish him by removing his genitals. The girl, because of *penis envy,* becomes angry at her mother, whom she believes caused her to be born without a penis, and becomes attracted to her father. This is now known as the **Electra complex,** named by Carl Jung after a Greek character who had her mother killed (Kilmartin & Dervin, 1997). But, fearing the loss of maternal love, the girl identifies with her mother, hoping to still attract her father. Through the process of *identification,* boys and girls establish their gender identity and sexual orientation, and form their superego.

Freud called the period between age 5 and puberty the **latency stage.** He was relatively uninterested in this stage because he believed that this was a time of little psychosexual development. Instead, the child develops social skills and friendships. Finally, during adolescence, the child reaches the **genital stage** and becomes sexually attracted to other people. To Freud, the first three stages are the most important determinants of personality development. He assumed that personality is essentially fixed by the age of 5. Figure 13.2 summarizes the stages of psychosexual development.

Chapter Thirteen

Stage	Age	Characteristics
Oral	Birth to 1	Gratification from oral behaviors, such as sucking, biting, and chewing. Conflict over weaning.
Anal	1 to 3	Gratification from defecation. Conflict over toilet training.
Phallic	3 to 5	Gratification from genital stimulation. Resolution of the Oedipus complex.
Latency	5 to puberty	Sexual impulses repressed. Development of friendships.
Genital	Puberty on	Gratification from genital stimulation. Development of intimate relationships.

genital stage
In Freud's theory, the last stage of personality development, associated with puberty, during which the individual develops erotic attachments to others.

▲ **Alfred Adler (1870–1937)**
"I began to see clearly in every psychological phenomenon the striving for superiority."

Adler's Individual Psychology

Because Freud's intellectual descendants altered his theory, they became known as *neo-Freudians*. Three of the most renowned neo-Freudians are Alfred Adler, Carl Jung, and Karen Horney. Alfred Adler (1870–1937) was one of Freud's most inluential followers. But in 1911 Adler broke with Freud, downplaying the importance of sexual motivation and the unconscious mind. Adler (1927) developed his own theory, which he called *individual psychology.*

personal unconscious

In Jung's theory, the individual's own unconscious mind, which contains repressed memories.

collective unconscious

In Jung's theory, the unconscious mind that is shared by all human beings and that contains archetypal images passed down from our prehistoric ancestors.

archetypes

In Jung's theory, inherited images that are passed down from our prehistoric ancestors and that reveal themselves as universal symbols in art, dreams, and religion.

extravert

A person who is socially outgoing and prefers to pay attention to the external environment.

introvert

A person who is socially reserved and prefers to pay attention to his or her private mental experiences.

▲ Carl Jung (1875–1961)

"While the personal unconscious is made up essentially of contents which have at one time been conscious but which have disappeared from consciousness through having been forgotten or repressed, the contents of the collective unconscious have never been in consciousness, and therefore have never been individually acquired, but owe their existence exclusively to heredity."

Adler's childhood experiences inspired his theory of personality. He was a sickly child, and felt inferior to his stronger and healthier older brother. Adler assumed that because children feel small, weak, and dependent on others, they develop an *inferiority complex.* This motivates them to compensate by *striving for superiority*—that is, developing certain abilities to their maximum. Perhaps Adler compensated for his childhood frailty by becoming an eminent psychoanalyst.

Adler believed striving for superiority is healthiest when it promotes active concern for the welfare of oneself and others, which he called *social interest* (Adler, 1994). For example, both a physician and a criminal strive for superiority, but the physician expresses this motive in a socially beneficial way. This is the basis of programs aimed at increasing grade school children's social interest by encouraging them to help younger students (Brigman & Molina, 1999).

Jung's Analytical Psychology

Freud's favorite disciple was Carl Jung (1875–1961). Though Jung, a native of Switzerland, came from a family in which the men traditionally pursued careers as Protestant pastors, he was inspired to become a psychoanalyst after reading Freud's *The Interpretation of Dreams* (1900/1990). Beginning in 1906, Freud and Jung carried on a lively correspondence, and Freud hoped Jung would become his successor as head of the psychoanalytic movement. But in 1914 they parted over revisions Jung made in Freud's theory, especially Jung's deemphasis of the sex motive. Jung called his version of psychoanalysis *analytical psychology.*

Though Jung agreed with Freud that we each have our own unconscious mind (the **personal unconscious**), he claimed that we also share a common unconscious mind—the **collective unconscious.** Jung held that the collective unconscious contains inherited memories passed down from generation to generation. He called these memories **archetypes,** which are images that represent important aspects of the accumulated experience of humanity (Maloney, 1999). Jung claimed that archetypes influence our dreams, religious symbols, and artistic creations.

Jung (1959/1969) even connected the archetype of God to reports of flying saucers. Widespread accounts of flying saucer sightings began in the late 1940s, following the horrors of World War II and the advent of the atomic bomb. According to Jung, these sightings stemmed from the desire of people, inspired by the archetype of God, to have a more powerful force than themselves save humanity from self-destruction. Even the round shape of the flying saucer represented the archetypal image of godlike unity and perfection of the archetype of the *self.*

Jung even contributed to our everyday language by distinguishing between two personality types. **Extraverts** are socially outgoing and pay more attention to the surrounding environment; **introverts** are socially reserved and pay more attention to their private mental experiences. Jung applied this concept in his own life, viewing Freud as an extravert and Adler as an introvert (Monte, 1980).

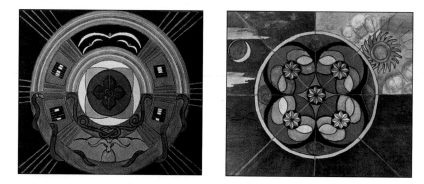

▲ The Mandala

Balanced, circular paintings such as these have been found in cultures throughout history and throughout the world. Jung claimed that this showed the influence of the archetype of the self, which symbolizes unity and wholeness.

Chapter Thirteen

Horney's Feminine Psychology

Though Karen Horney (1885–1952) never studied with Freud, she was a prominent neo-Freudian. She challenged many of his theoretical assumptions, beginning with a ground-breaking paper she presented at the Seventh International Psychoanalytic Congress in 1922—at a session chaired by Freud—that ultimately formed the basis of her theory of feminine psychology. Most important, she believed that Freudian psychoanalytic theory neglected the role of social and cultural factors in personality development. She was an early advocate of a cross-cultural approach to psychology, and in her later years she worked on integrating psychoanalysis and concepts from Zen Buddhism (Morvay, 1999).

Horney believed that psychoanalytic theory was *androcentric,* using male personality development as the norm by which to explain women's personalities. In particular, she critiqued his emphasis on penis envy, noting that men were just as likely to experience *womb envy* (Horney, 1926/1967). She also believed that Freud overemphasized sexuality in the phallic stage. Horney asserted that girls were envious not of boys' genitalia but rather of men's holding superior—and more powerful—positions in society (O'Connell, 1990). In her later work, she continued to emphasize the importance of gender roles, interpersonal power, and social and cultural factors influencing women's personality.

Like Adler, Horney's childhood experiences are reflected in many aspects of her theory. She was an anxious child who felt unwanted and struggled to gain her parents' love. Later, in self-analysis, she realized she felt hostile toward her parents, especially her authoritarian father. Horney theorized that children develop *basic anxiety* due to their emotional and physical dependency on adults—who have the power to give or withhold love. Basic anxiety leads to *basic hostility,* an emotional response that children must suppress to gain love and security from their parents. To combat these intense feelings of anxiety and hostility and gain a sense of security, children develop coping styles that become part of their personality. Horney identified three major coping styles: moving *toward* others, moving *against* others, and moving *away from* others. Neurotic people rigidly rely upon one style; mentally healthy people are flexible and use different styles when appropriate (Horney, 1950).

Psychoanalytic Assessment of Personality

Psychoanalytic assessment relies on **projective tests.** They are based on the assumption that we will "project" our repressed feelings and conflicts onto ambiguous stimuli. Because of this, it is especially important that those interpreting responses to projective tests do not let their own preconceptions about the test takers affect their interpretations (Wiederman, 1999). Today the most popular projective tests are the *Rorschach test* and the *Thematic Apperception Test.*

The Rorschach Test

Have you ever argued about images in abstract paintings? If so, you will have some appreciation for the *Rorschach test,* which asks participants to report what they see in inkblots. The Rorschach test was introduced in 1921 by Swiss psychiatrist Hermann Rorschach (1884–1922), who died before he was able to conduct much research with it. The test consists of ten bilaterally symmetrical inkblots. Some of the inkblots are in black and white, and the others include colors.

In responding to the inkblots, the person tells what she sees in each one and then reports the features of the inkblot that prompted the response. After scoring each response, based on formal criteria, the examiner uses clinical judgment and one of several available scoring systems to write a profile of the person's motives and conflicts. Such profiles have been used for diverse purposes, such as distinguishing between the personalities of murderers and nonviolent criminals (Coram, 1995).

The Thematic Apperception Test

The Thematic Apperception Test (TAT) (Morgan & Murray, 1935) was created by the American psychoanalyst Henry Murray and his associate Christiana Morgan (Morgan, 1995). The TAT (described in Chapter 11) consists of one blank card and nineteen cards containing

▲ **Karen Horney (1885–1952)**
"It remains one of Freud's great achievements to have seen the role of rivalry in the family, as expressed in his concept of the Oedipus complex and in other hypotheses. It must be added, however, that this rivalry itself is not biologically conditioned but is a result of given cultural conditions."

Rorschach Inkblot Test
www.mhhe.com/sdorow5

projective test
A Freudian personality test based on the assumption that individuals project their unconscious feelings when responding to ambiguous stimuli.

▲ **Hermann Rorschach (1884–1922)**
"The [ink-blot] test often indicates the presence of latent schizophrenia, neuroses which are barely perceptible clinically, and constitutional mood trends."

black-and-white pictures of people in ambiguous situations. Murray and Morgan assumed that people's responses would reveal their most important needs, such as the need for sex, power, achievement, or affiliation. The TAT is a moderately good predictor of real-life achievement, such as career success (Spangler, 1992). The TAT also has been used to measure changes in the use of defense mechanisms as a result of psychotherapy (Cramer, 1999).

The Status of the Psychoanalytic Approach

Of all the psychoanalytic theories of personality, Freud's has been the most influential, but it has received limited support for its concepts. As described in Chapter 6, there is substantial evidence that unconscious processes affect human behavior (Dixon & Henley, 1991). There also is support for the Freudian view of repression from research showing that people are less likely to recall emotionally unpleasant personal experiences (Sparks, Pellechia, & Irvine 1999), though the notion of total repression of traumatic emotional experiences has received only weak support (Bowers & Farvolden, 1996). Recent research has supported the existence of several defense mechanisms, including projection and reaction formation. However, there is little support for certain other defense mechanisms, including displacement and sublimation (Baumeister, Dale, & Sommer, 1998).

There also has been little support for some of Freud's other concepts, such as Freud's idea that resolution of the Oedipus and Electra complexes is essential for gender identity, sexual orientation, and superego development (Schrut, 1994). Perhaps the greatest weakness of Freudian theory is that many of its terms refer to processes that are neither observable nor measurable. As noted in Chapter 2, we cannot conduct experiments on concepts that are not operationally defined.

Despite the limited support for certain psychoanalytic concepts, the psychoanalytic approach has contributed to our understanding of personality. It has revealed that much of our behavior is governed by motives of which we are unaware. It has demonstrated the importance of early childhood experiences, such as infant attachment; it has contributed to the emergence of formal psychological therapies; and it has inspired research into the effects of psychological factors on illness. It also has influenced the works of artists, writers, and filmmakers (Highet, 1998).

Though Adler's individual psychology has influenced humanistic—as well as cognitive (Watts & Critelli, 1997)—approaches to personality and psychotherapy, interest in individual psychology itself has declined in recent years (Freeman, 1999). And what of Jung's theory? Jung's concept of personality types has received research support. One study compared the styles of extraverted painters and introverted painters. Extraverted painters tended to use realistic styles, reflecting their greater attention to the external environment. In contrast, introverted painters tended to use abstract styles, reflecting their greater attention to private mental experience (Loomis & Saltz, 1984).

Jung's concept of the archetype has been criticized because it violates known mechanisms of inheritance in its assumption that memories can be inherited. Nonetheless, hereditary tendencies akin to archetypes might affect human behavior (Neher, 1996). Evidence for this comes from research, explained in Chapter 14, showing that we might have an inborn predisposition to develop phobias about snakes, heights, and other situations that were dangerous to our prehistoric ancestors.

Horney influenced other psychological theorists. For example, her idea of basic anxiety is similar to Erikson's concept of basic trust-mistrust explained in Chapter 4. Moreover, her emphasis on social-cultural determinants of women's personality has been carried forward in the work of contemporary feminist psychoanalytic theorists, such as Nancy Chodorow (1978), who explore the relation of gender roles, family relationships, and power to women's personality development.

As for projective tests of personality, a meta-analysis of validity studies found that they are better predictors of certain behaviors, such as interpersonal dependency (Bornstein, 1999), than are objective tests (discussed later in the chapter). Another review of the research literature found that objective tests tend to be better predictors of short-term behavior and that projective tests tend to be better predictors of long-term behavior (Masling, 1997).

The North American Society of Adlerian Psychology
www.mhhe.com/sdorow5

The C. G. Jung Page
www.mhhe.com/sdorow5

Horney
www.mhhe.com/sdorow5

1. What is the relationship between the three structures of personality in Freud's theory?
2. What are the basic tenets of Adler's theory?
3. According to Jung, how do the collective unconscious and its archetypes affect our lives?
4. How did Horney broaden psychoanalytic theory to include social and cultural forces?

Answers to Staying on Track start on p. ST-6.

◆ THE DISPOSITIONAL APPROACH

In his book *Characters,* Greek philosopher Theophrastus (ca. 372–ca. 287 B.C.) wondered why Greeks differed in personality despite sharing the same culture and geography. He concluded that personality differences arise from inborn predispositions to develop particular personality *types* dominated by a single characteristic. Like Theophrastus, we rely on personality typing when we call someone a "morning person" or an "evening person" (Mecacci & Rocchetti, 1998).

Trait Theories

Instead of describing personality in terms of single types, trait theorists (who favor a *dispositional approach* to personality) describe personality in terms of distinctive combinations of personal dispositions. A **trait** is a relatively enduring, cross-situationally consistent personality characteristic that is inferred from a person's behavior. The first influential trait theory is that of Gordon Allport (1897–1967), who was a leader in making personality an important area of psychological research in the 1920s and 1930s (Nicholson, 1998).

Allport's Trait Theory

Early in his career, Allport had a brief meeting in Vienna with Sigmund Freud that convinced him that psychoanalysis was not the best approach to the study of personality. Confronted with a silent Freud, Allport broke the silence by describing a boy he had met on a train who had complained of dirty people and whose mother had acted annoyed at his behavior. Freud responded, "And was that little boy you?" Based on this meeting, Allport concluded that Freud was too concerned with finding hidden motives for even the most mundane behaviors (Allport, 1967).

Allport distinguished three kinds of traits. *Cardinal traits* are similar to personality types, in that they affect every aspect of the person's life. For example, altruism was a cardinal trait in the personality of Mother Teresa. Because cardinal traits are rare, you probably know few

▲ **Cardinal Traits**
Gordon Allport would have noted that Mother Teresa, who had spent her life helping the poor, exemplified the cardinal trait of altruism.

trait
A relatively enduring, cross-situationally consistent personality characteristic that is inferred from a person's behavior.

(a)   (b)   (c)

◀ **Personality Types**
Many movie and television comedies have portrayed the stereotypical personality type known as the "nerd." These include *(a)* Jerry Lewis in several movies, *(b)* Gilda Radner and Bill Murray on the old *Saturday Night Live,* and *(c)* Jaleel White, who played Urkel on *Family Matters.*

▲ **Gordon Allport (1897–1967)**

"Important—indeed central—to my theoretical position is my own particular conception of 'trait.'"

people whose lives are governed by them. *Central traits* affect many aspects of our lives but do not have the pervasive influence of cardinal traits. When you refer to someone as kind, humorous, or conceited, you are usually referring to a central trait. The least important traits are *secondary traits,* because they affect relatively narrow aspects of our lives. Preferences for wearing cuffed pants or eating chocolate ice cream reflect secondary traits.

Eysenck's Three-Factor Theory

Today one of the most influential trait theories of personality is Hans Eysenck's *three-factor theory* (Eysenck, 1990). Eysenck (1916–1997), a German psychologist, fled to England after refusing to become a member of Hitler's secret police. By the time of his death Eysenck had become the most cited psychologist in the world (Farley, 2000). Eysenck used the statistical technique of factor analysis (see Chapter 10) in identifying three trait dimensions of personality. The dimension of *neuroticism* measures a person's level of stability/instability. Stable people are calm, even-tempered, and reliable; unstable people are moody, anxious, and unreliable. A study of students who began an on-campus exercise program found that a year later those who dropped out had scored higher in neuroticism than those who remained in the program (Potgieter & Venter, 1995). The dimension of *psychoticism* measures a person's level of tough-mindedness/tender-mindedness. Tough-minded people are hostile, ruthless, and insensitive, whereas tender-minded people are friendly, empathetic, and cooperative. Juvenile delinquents score high in psychoticism (Furnham & Thompson, 1991). The dimension of *extraversion* measures a person's level of introversion/extraversion. This dimension, first identified by Jung, has stimulated the most research interest. For example, studies have shown that there are proportionately more introverts among expert chess players than in the general population (Olmo & Stevens, 1984). Figure 13.3 illustrates the interaction of the dimensions of introversion/extraversion and stability/instability.

There is evidence that the dimensions in Eysenck's theory have a biological basis (Matthews & Gilliland, 1999). For example, research on twins indicates that neuroticism, psychoticism, and extraversion have genetic bases. Heredity might explain why introverts are more physiologically reactive than extraverts are (Stelmack, 1990). The greater physiological reactivity of introverts might explain why extroverts can work better than introverts under distracting conditions. Consider students who, perhaps like yourself, study while music is playing in the background. The best kind of background music will depend on whether the student is introverted or extraverted. A study comparing the effect of background music on a word-comprehension task found that extraverts performed better while listening to more complex (that is, more distracting) music and introverts performed better while listening to simpler (that is, less distracting) music (Furnham & Allass, 1999).

The Five-Factor Model

The most influential personality research of the past few decades indicates that there are five basic personality traits (McCrae & Costa, 1995). These are commonly known as "The Big Five." *Extraversion* resembles Eysenck's factor of introversion/extraversion, and *neuroticism* resembles his factor of stability/instability. *Agreeableness* indicates whether a person is warm, good-natured, and cooperative. *Conscientiousness* indicates whether a person is ethical, reliable, and responsible. And *openness to experience* indicates whether a person is curious, imaginative, and interested in intellectual pursuits.

The five-factor model of personality has been used successfully in predicting procrastination (Watson, 2001), eating disorders (Ghaderi & Scott, 2000), and marital adjustment (Nemechek & Olson, 1999). Though the five-factor model has been applied to a wide range of behaviors, it has been especially popular in studies of work-related behaviors. A review of research studies that included a total of almost 24,000 participants found that the factor of conscientiousness was positively correlated with all aspects of job performance and the factor of extraversion was positively correlated with success in sales and management positions (Mount & Barrick, 1998). The five-factor model also has cross-cultural validity, as demonstrated in a study that involved participants from Spain, Italy, Germany, and the United States (Vittorio Caprara et al., 2000).

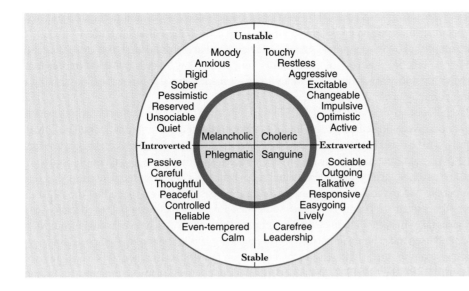

Dispositional Assessment of Personality

The dispositional assessment of personality relies on tests of personality types or traits. These are called *objective tests* or *inventories,* because they present participants with straightforward statements rather than with ambiguous stimuli, as in projective tests.

Tests of Personality Types

One of the most popular objective tests is the *Myers-Briggs Type Indicator* (Briggs & Myers, 1943). The test assesses various personality characteristics, including personality types derived from Jung's analytical theory of personality. The participant is presented with pairs of statements and selects the statement in each pair that is closest to how she or he usually acts or feels. A typical item would be "At parties, do you (a) sometimes get bored or (b) always have fun?" An introvert would be more likely to select (a) and an extravert (b). The test has satisfactory validity (J. B. Murray, 1990) and has been used in a variety of research studies, including one that assessed personality differences between physicians who choose particular medical specialties (Stilwell et al., 2000).

Tests of Personality Traits

Researchers recently have developed personality tests based on the five-factor model of personality. These include the Five-Factor Personality Inventory (Hendriks, Hofstee, & De Raad, 1999) and the NEO Personality Inventory, which has been used to study relationships between personality traits and attitudes or behaviors, such as musical preferences (Rawlings & Ciancarelli, 1997). But the most widely used of all personality tests is the *Minnesota Multiphasic Personality Inventory (MMPI),* which measures personality traits.

The MMPI was developed at the University of Minnesota by psychologist Starke R. Hathaway and psychiatrist John C. McKinley (1943) to diagnose psychological disorders. Hathaway and McKinley used the *empirical method* of test construction, which retains only those questions that discriminate between people who differ on the characteristics of interest. Hathaway and McKinley collected 1,000 statements, which they administered to 700 people, including nonpatients, medical patients, and psychiatric patients. Participants responded "True," "False," or "Cannot Say" to each statement, depending on whether it was true of them. Hathaway and McKinley kept those statements that tended to be answered the same way by people with particular psychiatric disorders. For example, they included the statement "Nothing in the newspaper interests me except the comics" solely because significantly more depressed people than nondepressed people responded "True" to that statement (Holden, 1986).

The MMPI has ten clinical scales that measure important personality traits. For example, *hypochondriasis* measures concern with bodily functions and symptoms, and *paranoia* measures suspiciousness and delusions of persecution. The MMPI also has four *validity scales* that test for evasiveness, defensiveness, lying to look good, and faking to look bad. For example, the Lie scale contains statements that describe common human failings to which almost all people respond "True." So, a person who responded "False" to statements such as "I sometimes have violent thoughts" might be lying to create a good impression. The MMPI validity scales can even detect when a mental health professional is feigning a disorder (Bagby et al., 2000).

Psychologists commonly use the MMPI to screen applicants for positions in which people with serious psychological disorders might be dangerous, such as police officers. The MMPI has proved to be a valid means of diagnosing psychological disorders (Parker, Hanson, & Hunsley, 1988). But researchers found that by the 1980s it was diagnosing a higher proportion of people as psychologically disordered than it did when it was first adopted. Did this mean that more people had psychological disorders than in the past? Or did it mean that the MMPI's norms were outdated? The latter seemed to be the case. As one critic noted two decades ago, "Whoever takes the MMPI today is being compared with the way a man or woman from Minnesota endorsed those items in the late 1930s and early 1940s" (Herbert, 1983, p. 228).

Because of this, the MMPI was restandardized in the 1980s (Butcher, 2000). The revised 567-item MMPI (the MMPI-2) has added, deleted, or changed many statements. It also has new norms based on a more representative sample of Americans in regard to age, sex, ethnic background, educational level, and region of the country.

Uses of the MMPI-2 have included, identifying potential child molesters (Ridenour et al., 1997) and determining the effect of parental divorce on adolescents (Borkhuis & Patalano, 1997). Research findings indicate that the MMPI-2 is valid across many ethnic groups and cultures, including African American (Hall, Bansal, & Lopez, 1999) and Latino (Fantoni-Salvador & Rogers, 1997). A recent study found that acculturation appears to influence Asian Americans' MMPI profiles. That is, the more acculturated the participants, the more similar their personality profiles were to European American profiles (Tsai & Pike, 2000).

The Status of the Dispositional Approach

Though the dispositional approach to personality has been useful in *describing* personality differences, it is less successful in *explaining* those differences. One of the few dispositional theories that tries to explain personality is Eysenck's three-factor theory. Other researchers have verified the existence of the three personality factors identified by Eysenck (Zuckerman et al., 1999). The introversion/extraversion dimension has received especially strong research support. One of Eysenck's assumptions is that a person's degree of introversion/extraversion depends on his or her customary level of physiological reactivity. This might explain why introverts avoid stimulation and extraverts seek it. For example, introverted students prefer to work in quieter conditions than extraverted students do (Geen, 1984). The validity of the Eysenck Personality Questionnaire has been demonstrated across different cultures (Barrett et al., 1998).

There also is support for the possible universality of the five-factor model of personality (McCrae et al., 1998). One study found that the model, developed in the United States, holds up even when applied to personality profiles of people from China, Korea, Japan, Israel, Portugal, and Germany (McCrae & Costa, 1997). Nonetheless, psychologists who agree there are five basic personality factors often fail to agree on their nature. Some researchers, for example, have failed to find support for the openness-to-experience factor (McKenzie, 1998). The nature of personality consistency is addressed in the Psychology Versus Common Sense feature.

STAYING ON TRACK: *The Dispositional Approach*

1. What are the basic characteristics of Allport's trait theory of personality?
2. In what way is the MMPI based on an empirical approach to personality test construction?
3. What evidence is there that personality is more consistent across situations than Mischel believed?

Answers to Staying on Track start on p. ST-6.

Is Personality Consistent from One Situation to Another?

You might recall that the definition of personality includes the word *consistent*. But do people really behave consistently from one situation to another? Professors who write letters of recommendation for students assume that they do, when they refer to their students as "mature," "friendly," and "conscientious." But will a student who has been mature, friendly, and conscientious in college necessarily exhibit those traits in a job or in graduate school? The degree of cross-situational consistency in personality has been one of the most controversial issues in personality research. Until the late 1960s, commonsense belief among psychologists and nonpsychologists alike held that personality is consistent across different situations, with few researchers questioning that belief. But then some psychologists began reporting research findings indicating that personality might not be as cross-situationally consistent as was commonly believed.

Personality as Inconsistent

The debate over the consistency of personality began in 1968 with the publication of a book by the personality theorist Walter Mischel. Mischel found that the correlation between any two behaviors presumed to represent the same underlying personality trait rarely exceeded a relatively modest .30. This means that you could not predict with confidence whether a person who scored high on the trait of generosity would behave in a generous manner in a given situation. For example, a person might donate to the Salvation Army but might not pick up the check in a restaurant—though both behaviors would presumably reflect the trait of generosity. Based on his review of research findings, Mischel concluded that our behavior is influenced more by the situations in which we find ourselves than by our personality.

If personality is inconsistent across situations, why do we perceive it to be consistent in our everyday lives?

- First, we might confuse the consistency of behavior in a given situation over time with the consistency of that behavior across different situations (Mischel & Peake, 1982). If a fellow student is consistently humorous in your psychology class, you might mistakenly infer that she is humorous at home, at parties, and in the dormitory.
- Second, we tend to avoid situations that are inconsistent with our personalities (Snyder, 1983). If you view yourself as "even-tempered," you might avoid situations that might make you lose your temper.
- Third, our first impression of a person can make us discount later behavior that is inconsistent with it (Hayden & Mischel, 1976). If someone is friendly to you the first time you meet but is rude to you the next time you meet, you might say that he was "not himself" today.
- Fourth, our perception of cross-situational consistency in others might reflect a powerful situational factor—our presence in their environment (Lord, 1982). If others adapt their behavior to our presence, we might erroneously infer that they are consistent across situations.

▲ **Walter Mischel**

"If human behavior is determined by many interacting variables—both in the person and in the environment—then a focus on any one of them is likely to lead to limited predictions and generalizations."

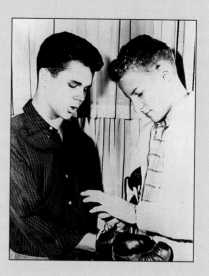

► **Personality Consistency**

Perhaps the most controversial issue in personality research during the past few decades has been the extent to which personality is consistent from one situation to another. If you have watched reruns of *Leave It to Beaver,* you know that Eddie Haskell is unbearably polite in the presence of Mr. and Mrs. Cleaver, but a wise guy in the presence of Wally and Beaver. Research findings have convinced some personality researchers that our behavior is influenced more by the situation we are in than by the personality characteristics we possess.

Personality as Consistent

These attacks on cross-situational consistency provoked responses from those who claim there is more cross-situational consistency than Mischel and his allies believed (Kenrick & Funder, 1988).

• First, individuals do show consistency on certain traits. But how do we know *which* traits? One way to find out is to ask. In one study, students were asked to judge how consistent they were on the trait of friendliness. Those who claimed to be friendly across situations were, in fact, more consistently friendly than were students who did not claim to be—as verified by their peers, parents, and other observers (Bem & Allen, 1974).

• Second, cross-situational consistency in behavior depends on whether a person is a *high self-monitor* or a *low self-monitor.* High self-monitors are concerned about how people perceive them and adapt their behaviors to fit specific situations; low self-monitors are less concerned about how people perceive them and do not adapt their behaviors as much to fit specific situations. This means that low self-monitors show greater cross-situational consistency in their behaviors than do high self-monitors (Gangestad & Snyder, 1985).

• Third, many of the studies that Mischel reviewed were guaranteed to find low cross-situational consistency, because they either correlated trait test scores with single instances of behaviors or correlated single instances of behaviors with each other. This would be like trying to predict your exact score on your next psychology test from your score on the SAT or from your score on a biology test. The prediction would most likely be wrong, because many factors influence your performance on any given academic test. Similarly, many factors other than a given personality trait influence your behavior in a given situation.

Psychologists have achieved greater success in demonstrating cross-situational consistency by using *behavioral aggregation.* In aggregating behaviors, you would observe a person's behavior across several situations. You then would determine how the person *typically,* but not necessarily *always,* behaves—much in the same way that you would find your average on several exams to determine your typical performance in a course. A "humorous" person would be humorous in many, but not all, situations. When we predict how a person will typically behave, instead of how that person will behave in a specific situation, the correlation between traits and behaviors becomes a robust correlation of .60 or more (Epstein & O'Brien, 1985).

◆ THE COGNITIVE-BEHAVIORAL APPROACH

Those who favor the *cognitive-behavioral approach* to personality discount biological factors, unconscious influences, and dispositional traits. Instead, they stress the importance of cognitive and situational factors. The cognitive-behavioral approach was influenced by B. F. Skinner, whose *operant conditioning theory* is described in Chapter 7. What we call *personality,* in Skinner's view, is simply a person's unique pattern of behavior, tied to specific situations (Skinner, 1974). You might say a fellow student has a "gregarious" personality because you have observed the student engage in behaviors such as initiating conversations or going to parties every weekend. According to Skinner, we tend to engage in behaviors that have been positively or negatively reinforced and to avoid engaging in behaviors that have been punished or extinguished. Thus, Skinner might assume a gregarious person has a history of receiving attention or anxiety relief for being socially outgoing in a variety of situations. In contrast, a shy person might have a history of being criticized or ignored in a variety of situations for being socially outgoing.

Social-Cognitive Theory

Social-cognitive theory builds a bridge between Skinner's strict behavioral approach and a more cognitive approach to personality. Social-cognitive theory is similar to traditional behavioral theories in stressing the role of reinforcement and punishment in the development of personality. But it is different from traditional behavioral theories in arguing that cognitive processes affect behavior. That is, our interpretation of our own personal characteristics and environmental circumstances affects our behavior (Bandura, 1989).

Social-cognitive theory was developed by Albert Bandura, who was reared in Canada but became a professor in the United States and served as president of the APA in 1974. Other social-cognitive theories have been developed by Julian Rotter and Walter Mischel. Bandura's theory of personality grew out of his research on observational learning (see Chapter 7). Bandura's (1986) theory of personality also stresses the concept of **reciprocal determinism,** which reflects his belief that neither personal dispositions nor environmental factors can by themselves explain behavior. As illustrated in Figure 13.4, Bandura assumes cognitive factors, environmental factors, and overt behavior affect one another.

Research studies have found that reciprocal determinism can explain many kinds of behaviors, such as why depression is so difficult to overcome (Teichman & Teichman, 1990). A depressed person's negative thoughts and emotions might induce gloomy statements, sad facial expressions, and aloof social behavior. This might make other people avoid or respond negatively toward the depressed person. This social response would promote continued negative thoughts and emotions in the depressed person, thereby completing a vicious cycle that is difficult to break.

According to Bandura, one of the most important cognitive factors in reciprocal determinism is **self-efficacy.** This is the extent to which a person believes that she can perform behaviors that are necessary to bring about a desired outcome. Self-efficacy determines our choice of activities, our intensity of effort, and our persistence in the face of obstacles and

reciprocal determinism
Bandura's belief that personality traits, environmental factors, and overt behavior affect each other.

self-efficacy
In Bandura's theory, a person's belief that she or he can perform behaviors that are necessary to bring about a desired outcome.

Information on Self-Efficacy
www.mhhe.com/sdorow5

◄ **Figure 13.4**
Reciprocal Determinism

Bandura's concept of reciprocal determinism considers the mutual influence of the person's characteristics, behavior, and situation. Each of the three factors can affect the other two.

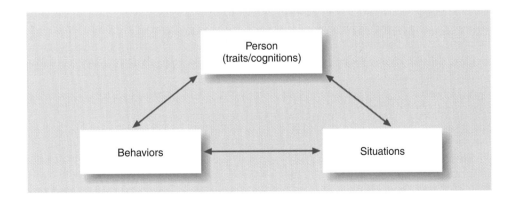

▲ Julian Rotter

"Internal versus external control refers to the degree to which persons expect that a reinforcement or an outcome of their behavior is contingent on their own behavior or personal characteristics versus the degree to which persons expect that the reinforcement or outcome is a function of chance, luck, or fate, is under the control of powerful others, or is simply unpredictable."

collective efficacy
People's perception that with collaborative effort the group will obtain its desired outcome.

unpleasant experiences, in part by reducing the anxiety that might interfere with engaging in the activity (Bandura, Reese, & Adams, 1982). Self-efficacy promotes parenting effectiveness (Coleman & Karraker, 1998), performance in academic courses (Shell, Colvin, & Bruning, 1995) and adherence to HIV medication regimens (Catz et al., 2000).

Bandura (1997) has continued to develop the concept of self-efficacy, noting that with increased interdependence between people, communities, and nations individuals often have to work together toward shared goals. **Collective efficacy** refers to people's perception that with collaborative effort the group will obtain its desired outcome. Thus, whereas self-efficacy refers to the perception that "I think *I* can do it," collective efficacy refers to the perception that "I think *we* can do it." Collective efficacy has been found, for example, to be higher among cohesive rugby teams (Kozub & McDonnell, 2000). Collective efficacy and self-efficacy might be relatively more or less important depending on the culture. A study of white-collar workers' ability to face job stress showed that self-efficacy was more beneficial to American workers and collective efficacy was more beneficial to Hong Kong workers (Schaubroeck, Lam, & Xie, 2000).

Cognitive-Behavioral Assessment of Personality

There are several cognitive-behavioral approaches to the assessment of personality. Two of the most widely used are the *experience-sampling method* and the *Locus of Control Scale*.

The Experience-Sampling Method

In a typical study using the *experience-sampling method*, a participant carries a beeper that is programmed to sound at random times, and on hearing the beep the participant reports his experiences and behaviors at that time. This reveals relationships between specific situations and the person's thoughts, feelings, and behaviors. Several studies have demonstrated the practical usefulness of experience sampling, such as studying sex offenders (Hillbrand & Waite, 1994) and assessing the relationship between mood changes and alcohol consumption (Swendsen et al., 2000).

The Locus of Control Scale

The *Internal-External Locus of Control Scale* was developed by Julian Rotter (1966) to measure what he calls the locus of control. Your *locus of control* is the degree to which you expect either that you are in control of the outcomes of your behavior or that those outcomes are controlled by factors such as fate, luck, or chance. In the former case you would have an internal locus of control, and in the latter case you would have an external locus of control. Rotter's concept of the locus of control has been so influential that his original study has been one of the most frequently cited studies in the recent history of psychology (Sechrest, 1984).

The scale contains 29 pairs of statements, including 6 that serve to disguise the purpose of the test. A typical relevant pair would be similar to the following: "The more effort you expend, the more likely you are to succeed" and "Luck is more important than hard work in job advancement." Just as your sense of self-efficacy might affect your behavior in everyday life, your locus of control might determine whether you try to exert control over real-life situations. People with a strong internal locus of control are more likely to take protective action when warned of an impending natural disaster, such as an earthquake (McClure, Walkey, & Allen, 1999). And people reared in individualistic societies, such as the United States, tend to have a more internal locus of control than people from collectivist societies (Rawdon, Willis, & Ficken, 1995).

The Status of the Cognitive-Behavioral Approach

The cognitive-behavioral approach has inspired numerous studies of its merits. The importance of self-efficacy has been supported by research findings in a variety of areas in addition to those mentioned earlier. A meta-analysis of more than 100 studies involving more than 21,000 participants found that self-efficacy is positively correlated with performance

How Effective Is Psychological Profiling in Identifying Criminals?

Over the years you probably have read books or articles or seen television shows about FBI profilers, who provide descriptions of wanted criminals—typically serial killers or terrorists—with the hope of tracking them down more easily by helping investigators narrow the range of potential suspects. But how accurate are psychological profilers? Though the media might publicize individual cases in which psychological profiles apparently have helped to solve crimes, there are other cases in which profilers have been inaccurate, sometimes even identifying the wrong person as a suspect. In December 1996, for example, security guard Richard Jewell won a settlement of more than $500,000 from NBC. Nightly news anchor Tom Brokaw had mentioned that Jewell was a suspect in the widely publicized bombing incident at the 1996 Summer Olympic Games in Atlanta that killed one person and injured more than a hundred others. Brokaw noted that investigators believed that Jewell fit the psychological profile of other bombers. Nonetheless, investigators eventually cleared Jewell of any responsibility for the bombing.

In a widely publicized case in late 1999, nuclear scientist Wen Ho Lee accused the government of racism for imprisoning him after charging him with spying for China and stealing military secrets while working at Los Alamos Laboratory in New Mexico. Lee claimed that he was the victim of overzealous psychological profiling. Though not truly the same as psychological profiling, the use of racial profiling by law enforcement in making stops and searches on highways and in airports has come under fire for being disproportionately applied to African Americans and Latinos (Holly, 2000).

Given psychological profiling's popularity, researchers are conducting research and publishing articles on it in professional journals. One reason for supporting psychological profiling is that some courts let prosecutors and defense attorneys consider the psychological state of the defendant (Cochran, 1999). Though personality profiling in criminal cases has gained media attention, its validity remains to be established (Wilson, Lincoln, & Kocsis, 1997). Nonetheless, there is evidence that specially trained profilers do produce more accurate profiles than other professionals do (Kocsis et al., 2000). But even those who support the usefulness of psychological profiling insist that it should be used to generate leads and direct investigations and that it should not be used by itself to identify particular suspects (Homant & Kennedy, 1998). Researchers are trying to provide a more scientific grounding for psychological profiling. In one study, profilers successfully developed psychological profiles that were useful in distinguishing between distinctly different kinds of arsonists (Kocsis, Irwin, & Hayes, 1998). The media probably will continue to celebrate psychological profiling, but it will be up to science to determine whether psychological profiling is a valid technique.

on work-related tasks (Stajkovic & Luthans, 1998). An area of interest to some cognitive-behaviorally oriented personality researchers that has received attention from the media in recent years is the psychological profiling of criminals, the topic of the Thinking Critically About Psychology and the Media feature.

STAYING ON TRACK: *The Cognitive-Behavioral Approach*

1. How does the social-cognitive theory of personality differ from the operant conditioning theory?
2. What is reciprocal determinism?
3. How do psychologists use experience sampling in the assessment of personality?

Answers to Staying on Track start on p. ST-6.

◆ THE HUMANISTIC APPROACH

The *humanistic approach* to personality, which emerged in the 1950s, holds that human beings are naturally good. This contrasts with psychoanalytic theorists, who believe that human beings are predisposed to be selfish and aggressive, and behavioral theorists, who believe that human beings are neither naturally good nor naturally evil. The humanistic approach also contrasts with the psychoanalytic and behavioral approaches in accepting subjective mental experience (*phenomenological experience*) as its subject matter. This makes the humanistic approach similar to the social-cognitive theory, though more concerned with emotional experience. Moreover, the humanistic approach assumes that we have free will, meaning that our actions are not compelled by id impulses or environmental stimuli.

Self-Actualization Theory

The first humanistic theory of personality was that of Abraham Maslow (1970). Maslow, reared in Brooklyn, was urged by his parents to attend law school. One day he found himself in a course in which he had no interest, and he bolted from the classroom. Maslow never returned to law school. Instead, against his parents' wishes, he decided to pursue a career in psychology. This willingness to fulfill one's own needs, rather than trying to please other people, became a hallmark of humanistic theories of personality. As discussed in Chapter 11, Maslow believed we have a need for **self-actualization,** the predisposition to try to reach our potentials.

But who is self-actualized? Maslow presented several candidates, including President Abraham Lincoln, psychologist William James, and humanitarian Eleanor Roosevelt. Self-actualized people have a realistic orientation, accept themselves as well as others, enjoy strong, intimate relationships, and are autonomous, creative, and philosophical. Maslow decided on these characteristics after testing, interviewing, or reading the works of individuals he considered self-actualized. Our psychological well-being is related, in part, to the extent to which we are self-actualized. For example, it seems that parents who score high on measures of self-actualization tend to practice authoritative parenting (Dominguez & Carton, 1997), a parenting style that is superior to permissive parenting and authoritarian parenting. These parenting styles are discussed in Chapter 4.

Self Theory

Carl Rogers (1902–1987) was born near Chicago to a devoutly religious family. His upbringing led him to enter Union Theological Seminary in New York City. But Rogers left the seminary to pursue a career in psychology, eventually serving as president of the APA in 1946.

The Self

Rogers pointed out that self-actualization requires acceptance of one's *self* or *self-concept.* But each of us experiences some incongruence between the self and personal experience. We might learn to deny our feelings, perhaps claiming that we are not angry or embarrassed even when we are. This might make us feel phony or, as Rogers would say, not genuine. This incongruence between our self and our experience causes us anxiety, which in turn motivates us to reduce the incongruence by altering the self or reinterpreting the experience. People who have a great incongruence between the self and experience can develop psychological disorders (see Chapter 14).

According to Rogers, children who do not receive *unconditional positive regard*—that is, complete acceptance—from their parents will develop incongruence by denying aspects of their experience. For example, a boy whose parents insist "boys don't cry" might learn to deny his own painful experiences in order to gain parental approval. Such *conditions of worth* lead children to become rigid and anxious. Instead of self-actualizing, such children might adopt a lifestyle of conformity and ingratiation (Baumeister, 1982). Rogers, like other personality theorists, reveals his own life experiences in his theory. He recalled that as a child he felt that his parents did not love him for himself apart from his accomplishments (Dolliver, 1995).

self-actualization

In Maslow's theory, the individual's predisposition to try to fulfill her or his potentials.

▲ **Carl Rogers (1902–1987)**

"It has been my experience that persons have a basically positive direction."

Psychologically healthy people have greater congruence between the *actual self* (Rogers's *self*) and the *ideal self* (the person they would like to be). The more self-actualized the person, the less the incongruence between the person's actual self and ideal self and, as a result, the greater the person's self-esteem (Moretti & Higgins, 1990). A study of undergraduates found that as the congruence between their actual and their ideal selves increased, their feelings of happiness increased (Mikulincer & Peer-Goldin, 1991).

Self-Esteem

Childhood experiences have marked effects on self-esteem. Children with warm, nurturant parents are higher in self-esteem (Pawlak & Klein, 1997). Children who have been verbally abused by their parents have lower self-esteem (Solomon & Serres, 1999).

Self-esteem also has important implications for adults. A longitudinal study found that adolescents who had positive relationships with their parents during their transition into adulthood had higher self-esteem then and 20 years later (Roberts & Bengtson, 1996). Moreover, the quality of interpersonal relationships—between friends and between spouses—is positively related to self-esteem (Voss, Markiewicz, & Doyle, 1999).

Self-Schema Theory

schema
A cognitive structure that guides people's perception and information processing that incorporates the characteristics of particular persons, objects, events, procedures, or situations.

Contemporary theories of personality have moved toward an information-processing model, based on the concept of **schemas.** Schemas are cognitive structures that guide people's perception, organization, and processing of social information (see Chapters 4 and 9). Individual differences in personality are related to the different schemas people use to process information—in this case, about the self. According to Hazel Markus, self-schemas are specialized cognitive structures about the self. Your self-schema consists of aspects of your life and behavior that are important to you. Because each of us has different experiences and interests, not everything we do becomes part of our self-schema (Markus, 1983).

For example, two college students might be avid cyclists and fans of foreign cinema. But these activities might not both be part of their self-schemas. If one student is training for a triathlon and describes herself as a serious recreational athlete, then cycling might be a part of her self-schema. If the other student has career aspirations to become an accomplished film director, then studying cinematography and attending foreign films might be part of his self-schema. Thus, activities, interests, and behaviors that are relevant to the self might become part of the self-schema.

Schema theory has provided a glimpse into the cultural determinants of personality, especially the dimension of individualism versus collectivism. Hazel Markus and Shinobu Kitayama (1991) have proposed that there are differences in the construal of self-schema. People in Western cultures strive to be unique, engage in self-expression, and promote individual goals. In contrast, people in Asian cultures value interdependent aspects of the self. People in Asian cultures value being part of a group, cooperation, and pursuing group goals. In this way, cultural values and social experiences become integrated into the self-schema. Schema theory has been tested in research investigating the relationship between children's self-schemas and their willingness to share with and help others (Froming, Nasby, & McManus, 1998) and American and Chinese consumers' self-schemas and their response to advertising (Wang et al., 2000).

▲ Hazel Markus and Shinobu Kitayama
"People in different cultures have strikingly different construals of the self, of others, and of the interdependence of the two."

Humanistic Assessment of Personality

How do humanistic psychologists assess personality? Two of the main techniques are the *Personal Orientation Inventory* and the *Q-sort*.

The Personal Orientation Inventory

Psychologists who wish to assess self-actualization commonly use the *Personal Orientation Inventory (POI)* (Shostrom, 1962). The POI determines the degree to which a person's values and attitudes agree with Maslow's description of self-actualized people. The inventory contains items that force the person to choose between options, such as (a) "Impressing others is most important" and (b) "Expressing myself is most important." A study of students in a university preparatory course found that they became more self-actualized, as assessed by the POI, by the end of the course (Fogarty, 1994).

The Q-Sort

The *Q-sort,* derived from Rogers's self theory, is used to measure the degree of congruence between a person's actual self and ideal self. If you took a Q-sort test, you would be given a pile of cards with a self-descriptive statement on each. A typical statement might be "I feel comfortable with strangers." You would put the statements in several piles, ranging from a pile containing statements that are most characteristic of your actual self to a pile containing statements that are least characteristic of your actual self. You would then follow the same procedure for your ideal self, creating a second set of piles. The greater the degree of overlap between the two sets of piles, the greater the congruence between your actual self and your ideal self. Psychotherapists have used the Q-sort method to determine whether therapy has increased the congruence between a client's actual self and ideal self (Leaf et al., 1992). The Q-sort also has been used to assess the quality of children's attachment to their mothers (DeMulder et al., 2000).

The Status of the Humanistic Approach

Research has produced mixed support for Maslow's concept of self-actualization. There have been inconsistent findings regarding the assumption that self-actualization increases with age. A cross-sectional study of women aged 19 to 55 found that older participants were more motivated by their own feelings than by the influence of other people—a characteristic of self-actualized people (Hyman, 1988). Yet, another cross-sectional study of faculty members aged 30 to 68 found that self-actualization did not increase with age (Hawkins, Hawkins, & Ryan, 1989). Researchers are working on cross-cultural approaches to identify the universal characteristics of self-actualization and to develop a valid measure (LeClerc et al., 1998).

There has been relatively more research on the self, per se, than on self-actualization. In fact, there has been a sprouting of a variety of "selves." A view of the self put forth by E. Tory Higgins (1987), *self-discrepancy theory,* considers the relationship between three selves: the *actual self,* the *ideal self,* and the *ought self.* Discrepancy between the actual self and the ideal self will make a person feel depressed (Bruch, Rivet, & Laurenti, 2000). Discrepancy between the actual self and the ought self will make a person feel anxious. We are motivated to alleviate personal distress by reducing the discrepancy between these selves (Higgins, 1990).

The humanistic approach has been praised for countering psychologists' tendency to study the negative aspects of human experience by encouraging them to study love, creativity, and other positive aspects of human experience. The humanistic approach also has renewed interest in studying conscious mental experience, which was the original subject matter of psychology a century ago (Singer & Kolligian, 1987). The humanistic approach also has contributed to the recent interest in self-development. But critics accuse the humanistic approach of divorcing the person from both the environment and the unconscious mind and for failing to operationally define and experimentally test concepts such as self-actualization (Daniels, 1982). Moreover, cross-cultural psychologists question whether positive self-regard is a universal human need. For example, a self-critical focus is more characteristic of Japanese society (Heine et al., 1999), whereas self-enhancement is more characteristic of American culture (Taylor & Brown, 1988).

Other researchers have questioned the importance and benefits of self-esteem. Whereas self-esteem is positively correlated with many measures of mental health and negatively correlated with depression (Taylor & Brown, 1988), the direction of causality is unclear. Though the humanistic approach to personality has received its share of criticism, Rogers has been widely praised for his contributions to the advancement of psychotherapy, which is discussed in Chapter 15.

1. What are the principal characteristics of humanistic theories of personality?
2. What are some of the topics in research on the "self"?
3. How would you use the Q-sort to assess someone's personality?

Answers to Staying on Track start on p. ST-6.

◆ THE BIOPSYCHOLOGICAL APPROACH

Personality researchers who favor the *biopsychological approach* warn that "any theory that ignores the evidence for the biological underpinnings of human behavior is bound to be an incomplete one" (Kenrick & Dantchik, 1983, p. 302). Ancient and modern thinkers alike have recognized the biological basis of personality. Greek physician-philosopher Hippocrates (460–377 B.C.) presented an early biological view of personality, which was elaborated on by Greek physician Galen (A.D. 130–200). Hippocrates and Galen claimed that **temperament,** a person's predominant emotional state, reflects the relative levels of body fluids they called *humors.* They associated blood with a cheerful, or *sanguine,* temperament; phlegm with a calm, or *phlegmatic,* temperament; black bile with a depressed, or *melancholic,* temperament; and yellow bile with an irritable, or *choleric,* temperament. Research has failed to find a humoral basis for personality, though personality traits show some relationship to patterns of hormonal secretion (Adler et al., 1997). But as discussed earlier in the chapter, Hans Eysenck's research supports the existence of these four basic temperaments (Stelmack & Stalikas, 1991).

The humoral theory of personality was dominant until the late 18th century, when it was joined by *phrenology* and *physiognomy.* As described in Chapter 3, phrenologists assumed that specific areas of the brain controlled specific personality characteristics and that the bumps and depressions of the skull indicated the size of those brain areas. Those who believed in physiognomy, the study of physical appearance, held that the features of one's face revealed one's personality. Research failed to support phrenology and physiognomy. Phrenologists did, however, spark interest in the study of the biological bases of personality. And some psychologists still study the effects of facial features on perceptions of personality (Hassin & Trope, 2000). The early 20th century saw biologically inclined personality researchers begin to study the relationship between heredity and personality.

temperament

A person's characteristic emotional state, first apparent in early infancy and possibly inborn.

◀ **Separated at birth, the Mallifert twins meet accidentally.**
Drawing by Chas. Addams; © 1981
The New Yorker Magazine, Inc.

Heredity and Personality

More than a century ago Francis Galton insisted that "nature prevails enormously over nurture" (Holden, 1987, p. 598). Today those who, like Galton, believe that heredity molds personality assume that evolution has provided us with inborn behavioral tendencies that differ from person to person (MacDonald, 1998). The field that studies the relationship between heredity and behavior is called *behavioral genetics* (see Chapters 3 and 4). Research in behavioral genetics has shown that even newborn infants differ in temperament—some are emotionally placid, others are emotionally reactive (Braungart et al., 1992).

How might these initial differences in temperament contribute to the development of differences in personality? They might affect how infants respond to other people and, in turn, how other people respond to them. For example, a placid infant would be less responsive to other people. As a consequence, others would be less responsive to the infant. This might predispose the infant to become less sociable later in childhood, laying the groundwork for an introverted personality. Inherited differences in temperament contribute to the development of differences in specific personality traits, such as self-esteem (Kendler, Gardner, & Prescott, 1998).

Biopsychological Assessment of Personality

One of the newer biopsychological approaches to personality assessment involves the measurement of brain activity. Much of the research has involved correlating brain activity with introversion and extraversion. Studies have found differences in the electrical activity of the brain between introverts and extraverts (Tran, Craig, & McIsaac, 2001). Studies that have used the PET scan likewise have found differences in patterns of brain activity between introverts and extraverts (Johnson et al., 1999).

But more researchers are interested in the genetic asssessment of personality. In general, the closer the genetic relationship between two persons, the more alike they will be in personality characteristics. But this relationship might reflect common life experiences rather than common genetic inheritance. Because of the difficulty in separating genetic effects and environmental effects in studies of relatives who share similar environments, researchers have resorted to adoption studies. The Texas Adoption Project found that, in regard to personality, adopted children tend to resemble their biological parents more than their adoptive parents (Loehlin, Horn, & Willerman, 1990). Findings such as these indicate that parent-child personality similarity is influenced more by common heredity than by common life experiences. A powerful means of assessing the role of heredity in personality is the study of identical twins reared apart, the topic of the Anatomy of a Research Study feature.

The Status of the Biopsychological Approach

How heritable is personality? Research has been consistent in finding that the heritability of personality is about .30 to .60 (Plomin et al., 1998). Moreover, there is cross-cultural support for these estimates (Jang et al., 1998). As for environmental influences on personality, research findings have contradicted the commonsense belief that shared environmental experiences (such as living with one's siblings) play a major role in personality similarity between close relatives. Research findings have consistently demonstrated that nonshared environmental experiences (such as interacting with one's friends) outweigh the effects of shared environmental experiences in affecting personality development (Hur, McGue, & Iacono, 1998). Nonetheless, some personality traits, such as religious orthodoxy, do show substantial relationships to shared environmental experiences (Beer, Arnold, & Loehlin, 1998).

And what of Bouchard's research on identical twins reared apart? Care must be taken in drawing conclusions from the amazing behavioral similarities in some of the twins he has studied. Imagine that you and a fellow student were both asked thousands of questions (as Bouchard asks his participants). You would undoubtedly find some surprising similarities between the two of you, even though you were not genetically related. This was demonstrated in a study that found many similarities between pairs of strangers. For example, one

Behavior Genetics and Personality Theory
www.mhhe.com/sdorow5

▲ **Thomas Bouchard**

"On multiple measures of personality and temperament, occupational and leisure-time interests, and social attitudes, monozygotic twins reared apart seem to be about as similar as monozygotic twins reared together."

Anatomy of a Research Study

How Similar Are the Personalities of Identical Twins Reared Apart?

Rationale

Since 1979, psychologist Thomas Bouchard of the University of Minnesota has conducted the most comprehensive study of identical twins reared apart and then reunited later in life. He has found amazing behavioral similarities between some of the twins. Consider the case of Oskar Stohr and Jack Yufe, who were born in Trinidad to a Jewish father and a Catholic mother. The twins were separated shortly after birth and reared in vastly different life circumstances. Oskar was reared in Germany as a Nazi by his maternal grandmother; Jack was reared in Trinidad as a Jew by his father. Decades later, when they arrived at the airport in Minneapolis to take part in Bouchard's study, both Jack and Oskar sported mustaches, wire-rimmed glasses, and two-pocket shirts with epaulets. Bouchard found that they both preferred sweet liqueurs, stored rubber bands on their wrists, flushed the toilet before using it, read magazines from back to front, and dipped buttered toast in their coffee (Holden, 1980). Though there are probably no "flush toilet before using" genes, the men's identical genetic inheritance might have provided them with similar temperaments that predisposed them to develop certain behavioral similarities. In fact, Bouchard and his colleagues have found that the rearing environment has relatively little influence on the development of personality (Bouchard & McGue, 1990).

Studies of identical twins reared apart provide the strongest support for the hereditary basis of personality. Identical twins have 100 percent of their genes in common, whereas fraternal twins are no more alike genetically than nontwin siblings. This might explain why identical twins who are adopted and reared by different families are more similar in personality than fraternal twins who are reared by their biological parents—even three decades after adoption (Tellegen et al., 1988).

Method

Participants were volunteers in the Minnesota Twin Study between 1970 and 1984. There were 217 identical twin pairs reared together and 114 fraternal twin pairs reared together. There were 44 identical twin pairs reared apart and 27 fraternal twin pairs reared apart. The twins who had been reared apart had been separated, on the average, for more than 30 years. Participants were given the Multidimensional Personality Questionnaire, which measures basic personality traits.

Results and Discussion

The results indicated that identical twins reared together and identical twins reared apart were highly similar in personality. Identical twins reared apart also were more similar than fraternal twins reared together. Overall, the heritability of personality was .48. (The heritability of personality is the proportion of the variability in personality within a population that is caused by heredity.) Thus, the participants' personalities were strongly, though not solely, influenced by heredity.

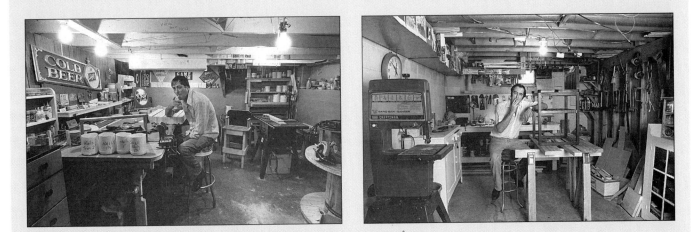

▲ **Identical Twins Reunited**

When reunited at the age of 39 as part of Thomas Bouchard's study, identical twins Jim Lewis and Jim Springer revealed remarkable similarities even though they had been adopted into different homes at 4 weeks of age. Both liked arithmetic but not spelling, drove Chevrolets, had dogs named Toy, chewed their fingernails to the nub, served as deputy sheriffs, enjoyed vacationing in Florida, married women named Linda, and got divorced and then married women named Betty. Both also enjoyed mechanical drawing and carpentry. The photos show them in their basement workshops, where both had built white benches that encircle trees in their backyards.

pair of women were both Baptists, nursing students, active in tennis and volleyball, fond of English and mathematics, not fond of shorthand, and partial to vacations at historic places (Wyatt et al., 1984). Of course, by comparing twins' performances on formal personality tests, Bouchard does more than simply report selected instances of amazing similarities between certain ones. Given the evidence for both genetic and environmental influences, the best bet is to accept that they both strongly—apparently about equally—affect the development of personality.

STAYING ON TRACK: *The Biopsychological Approach*

1. What is the relationship between temperament and individual differences in personality?
2. How do studies of identical twins who have been reunited provide evidence supporting the role of heredity in personality development?

Answers to Staying on Track start on p. ST-6.

Chapter Summary

THE PSYCHOANALYTIC APPROACH

- Your personality is your unique, relatively consistent pattern of thoughts, feelings, and behaviors.
- Freud's psychosexual theory emphasizes the conflict between biological drives and social-cultural prohibitions in the development of personality.
- Freud divided the mind into conscious, preconscious, and unconscious levels.
- Freud distinguished between the personality structures called the id, the ego, and the superego.
- According to Freud, we progress through oral, anal, phallic, latency, and genital stages of development.
- We might use defense mechanisms to protect us from being overwhelmed by anxiety.
- Freud's intellectual descendants altered his theory, generally downplaying the importance of sexuality and emphasizing the importance of social relationships.
- Alfred Adler's theory of individual psychology assumes that personality develops from our attempts to overcome early feelings of inferiority.
- Carl Jung's theory of analytical psychology assumes that we are influenced by both a personal unconscious and the archetypes in a collective unconscious.
- Karen Horney's theory emphasized the role of social and cultural factors in personality development.
- The Rorschach test and the Thematic Apperception Test are projective tests used to assess unconscious motives and conflicts.

THE DISPOSITIONAL APPROACH

- The dispositional approach to personality attributes the consistency we see in personality to relatively enduring personality attributes.
- In his trait theory of personality, Gordon Allport distinguished three kinds of traits: cardinal traits, central traits, and secondary traits.

- Hans Eysenck's three-factor theory sees personality as dependent on the interaction of three dimensions: stability/instability, tough-minded/tender-minded, and introversion/extraversion.
- Personality types are measured by tests such as the Myers-Briggs Type Indicator, and personality traits are measured by tests such as the MMPI.
- Research indicates that personality is neither as inconsistent as Walter Mischel originally claimed nor as consistent as personality theorists had previously claimed.

THE COGNITIVE-BEHAVIORAL APPROACH

- B. F. Skinner's operant conditioning theory assumes that what we call personality is simply a person's unique pattern of behavior.
- Albert Bandura's social-cognitive theory argues that cognitive processes influence behavior.
- Bandura's concept of reciprocal determinism points out the mutual influence of personality characteristics, overt behaviors, and environmental factors.
- One of the most important personality characteristics is self-efficacy, the extent to which a person believes that she or he can perform behaviors that are necessary to bring about a desired outcome.
- Cognitive-behavioral assessment is accomplished through the experience-sampling method and the Internal-External Locus of Control Scale.

THE HUMANISTIC APPROACH

- Abraham Maslow's self-actualization theory is based on his hierarchy of needs.
- Maslow assumed that we have a need to develop all of our potentials, a process he called self-actualization.
- Maslow identified the characteristics of eminent people who he believed were self-actualized.
- Carl Rogers's self theory holds that psychological well-being depends on the congruence between the actual self and the ideal self.

- Other researchers point to the importance of congruence between the actual self, the ideal self, and the ought self.
- Self-schemas are cognitive structures about the self and might reflect cross-cultural differences in the construal of the self.
- Self-actualization is measured by the Personal Orientation Inventory.
- Actual self and ideal self congruence is measured by the Q-sort.

THE BIOPSYCHOLOGICAL APPROACH
- Closely related to personality is temperament, a person's most characteristic emotional state.
- Research in behavioral genetics has found evidence of hereditary basis of temperament and other aspects of personality.

Key Concepts

personality 375

THE PSYCHOANALYTIC APPROACH
anal stage 378
archetypes 380
collective unconscious 380
defense mechanism 377
displacement 377
ego 376
Electra complex 378
extravert 380

fixation 378
genital stage 378
id 376
introvert 380
latency stage 378
libido 378
Oedipus complex 378
oral stage 378
personal unconscious 380
phallic stage 378
pleasure principle 376
projection 377

projective test 381
rationalization 377
reaction formation 378
reality principle 376
regression 377
repression 376
sublimation 378
superego 376

THE DISPOSITIONAL APPROACH
trait 383

THE COGNITIVE-BEHAVIORAL APPROACH
collective efficacy 390
reciprocal determinism 389
self-efficacy 389

THE HUMANISTIC APPROACH
schemas 393
self-actualization 392

THE BIOPSYCHOLOGICAL APPROACH
temperament 395

Key Contributors

THE PSYCHOANALYTIC APPROACH
Alfred Adler 379
Sigmund Freud 376
Karen Horney 381
Carl Jung 380
Hermann Rorschach 381

THE DISPOSITIONAL APPROACH
Gordon Allport 383
Hans Eysenck 384
Walter Mischel 387

THE COGNITIVE-BEHAVIORAL APPROACH
Albert Bandura 389

Julian Rotter 390
B. F. Skinner 389

THE HUMANISTIC APPROACH
Hazel Markus and Shinobu Kitayama 393
Abraham Maslow 392
Carl Rogers 392

THE BIOPSYCHOLOGICAL APPROACH
Thomas Bouchard 396

Thought Questions

1. How might Karen Horney's concept of basic anxiety explain the three coping styles she observed in how people relate to one another?
2. What are the arguments in favor of the cross-situational consistency of personality traits?

3. How are cross-cultural differences in the way people construe the self related to self-schemas?

Possible Answers to Thought Questions start on p. PT-4.

OLC Preview

 For additional quizzing and a variety of interactive resources, visit the book's Online Learning Center at www.mhhe.com/sdorow5.

Psychological Disorders

VINCENT VAN GOGH
Self-Portrait Dedicated to Paul Gauguin, 1888

You might be surprised to learn that the United States once had an emperor, Emperor Norton I. He began his life as Joshua Norton, a respected San Francisco merchant. But after going bankrupt, in 1859 he deteriorated psychologically and placed an advertisement in the *San Francisco Bulletin* proclaiming himself Norton I, Emperor of the United States and Protector of Mexico.

Emperor Norton (as he was affectionately known to his subjects) also declared streetcars to be free and issued bonds and collected taxes, which were actually donations to support him given by friendly bankers and shopkeepers. Norton became a renowned figure in the San Francisco–Oakland region. And he did his best to protect his subjects. On one occasion he prevented a frenzied crowd from attacking Chinese residents by reciting the Lord's Prayer—shaming them into silence and freezing them in their places. He was so popular that when he was arrested for vagrancy, newspapers published editorials criticizing the police for their treatment of San Francisco's first citizen.

Though Norton was talkative, many of his speeches were virtually incomprehensible—consisting of his delusional thinking about the state of the country. Yet some of his ideas were farsighted. In 1869 he placed an announcement in the *Oakland Daily News* ordering the construction of a bridge across the bay. He was ridiculed for proposing such a "foolish" venture, an endeavor that was considered impossible at the time.

At the time of his death in 1880, Emperor Norton had become the most famous and beloved person in San Francisco. But he died a pauper, his meager financial resources comprising $5.50 in coins and several Bonds of the Empire. The day after Norton's death, the *San Francisco Chronicle* carried the headline, "Le Roi Est Mort"—"The King is Dead." Well-to-do friends paid for an elaborate funeral—fit for an emperor—attended by many thousands of Norton's subjects (McDonald, 1980). At Norton's final resting place, his friends erected a marble tombstone, that read:

Norton I
Emperor of the United States and Protector of Mexico
Joshua A. Norton, 1819–1880

▲ **Emperor Norton I**
The life story of Joshua Norton illustrates that even people with serious mental illness can live full lives.

 Emperor Norton's Archives
www.mhhe.com/sdorow5

 National Institute of Mental Health
www.mhhe.com/sdorow5

Aside from demonstrating that San Francisco has long been hospitable to people with alternative lifestyles, the story of Joshua Norton is an example of a person with the psychological disorder called *schizophrenia*, which often is marked by language problems, unusual behavior, and delusions of grandeur—such as believing that one is a rich, famous, or powerful person. It also demonstrates that a person with schizophrenia might be able to live a fulfilling life.

◆ THE NATURE OF PSYCHOLOGICAL DISORDERS

How do psychologists determine whether a person has a psychological disorder? What are the causes of psychological disorders? And how are psychological disorders classified? Answers to these questions are provided by professionals with expertise in **psychopathology**—the study of psychological disorders.

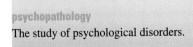

psychopathology
The study of psychological disorders.

Criteria for Psychological Disorders

From 1990 to 1992, an ambitious study called the National Comorbidity Survey examined the prevalence of psychological disorders in the United States. This survey of more than 8,000 persons aged 15 to 54 years found that 29 percent had had at least one psychological disorder within the past year and 48 percent had had at least one during their lifetime (Kessler, 1994). But what are the criteria for determining that a person has a disorder? The main criteria are *abnormality, maladaptiveness,* and *personal distress.*

The Criterion of Abnormality

Abnormal behavior deviates from the behavior of the "typical" person—the *norm.* A norm can be qualitative or quantitative. *Qualitatively* abnormal behavior deviates from culturally accepted standards, perhaps even seeming bizarre. A railroad conductor who announces train stops would be normal. But a passenger who announces train stops would be abnormal. *Quantitatively* abnormal behavior deviates from the statistical average. A woman who washes her hands three times a day would be normal. But a woman who washes her hands thirty times a day would be abnormal.

By itself abnormality is not a sufficient criterion for determining the presence of a psychological disorder. If qualitative abnormality were sufficient, then people who achieve rare accomplishments, such as a Nobel Prize winner, would be considered psychologically disordered. And if quantitative abnormality were sufficient, then even a physician who washes her hands thirty times a day in the course of seeing patients would be considered psychologically disordered. Thus, the social-cultural context in which "abnormal" behavior occurs must be considered before deciding that it is symptomatic of a psychological disorder.

The Criterion of Maladaptiveness

According to the criterion of *maladaptiveness,* you would have a psychological disorder if your behavior seriously disrupted your life. As an example, a person who uses drugs or alcohol excessively would be considered psychologically disordered, because such behavior would interfere with everyday functioning. But maladaptive behavior is not always a sign of a psychological disorder. Though cramming for exams and driving 90 miles an hour on a busy highway are maladaptive behaviors, they would not necessarily be symptomatic of a psychological disorder.

The Criterion of Personal Distress

The criterion of *personal distress* assumes that our subjective feeling of anxiety, depression, or another unpleasant emotion determines whether we have a psychological disorder. Nonetheless, personal distress might not be a sufficient criterion for determining the presence of a psychological disorder (Widiger & Trull, 1991). Some people, like the notorious John Wayne Gacy—a Chicago man who killed 33 boys and young men in the 1970s but expressed no guilt—might have a psychological disorder without feeling any distress.

Behavior that is abnormal, maladaptive, or personally distressing might indicate that a person has a psychological disorder. However, there is a degree of subjectivity in even the best answers to the question of how abnormal, maladaptive, or personally distressing a person's behavior must be before we determine that he or she has a psychological disorder. Note that beginning diagnosed as having a serious psychological disorder does not necessarily mean that a person is *insane.* The Thinking Critically About Psychology and the Media feature considers the use of the insanity defense in criminal cases.

Viewpoints on Psychological Disorders

Even when psychologists agree on the presence of a particular psychological disorder, they can disagree on its causes. Since ancient times, people have tried to explain the unusual or distressing behavior patterns that we now call psychological disorders. Many ancient

Does the Insanity Defense Let Many Violent Criminals Escape Punishment?

Spurred by the media's coverage of the successful insanity plea of John Hinckley, Jr., following his attempted assassination of President Ronald Reagan in 1981, many people have criticized the insanity defense as a miscarriage of justice. But do the Hinckley case and other cases portrayed in the media indicate that many people have gotten away with murder by using the insanity defense?

◀ **The Insanity Defense**

John Hinckley, Jr., was found not guilty (by reason of insanity) of his attempted assassination of President Reagan.

The Nature of the Insanity Defense

Insanity is a legal, not a psychological or psychiatric, term attesting that a person is not responsible for his or her own actions. The insanity defense was formalized in 1843 in the case of Daniel M'Naghten, a paranoid schizophrenic man who had tried to murder the English prime minister Robert Peel. But M'Naghten killed Peel's secretary Edward Drummond by mistake. After a controversial trial, M'Naghten was ruled not guilty by reason of insanity and was committed to a mental hospital. *The M'Naghten rule* became a guiding principle in English law. The rule states that a person is not guilty if, at the time of a crime, the person did not know what she or he was doing or did not know that it was wrong.

Today the most widely used standard for determining insanity in the United States comprises two rules. First, the *cognitive rule,* similar to the M'Naghten rule, says that a person was insane at the time of a crime if the person did not know what he or she had done or did not know that it was wrong. Based on this rule, some defendants who have killed a person while sleepwalking have been acquitted of murder charges (Thomas, 1997).

Second, the *volitional rule* says that a person was insane at the time of a crime if the person was not in voluntary control of her or his behavior. In 1857, in an early use of the volitional rule, Abraham Lincoln—then an attorney in Illinois—prosecuted a case in which defense attorneys claimed a defendant was insane at the time he committed a murder because he was under the influence of chloroform, a drug that can induce anesthesia (Spiegel & Suskind, 1998).

Controversy Concerning the Insanity Defense

In 1979, in a widely publicized case, former San Francisco city supervisor Dan White murdered mayor George Moscone and city supervisor Harvey Milk. White's attorney claimed that White had been insane at the time of the killings because eating junk food had made him lose voluntary control over his behavior. This became known as the "Twinkie defense." White's use of the insanity defense was considered an injustice by critics of the "not guilty by reason of insanity" plea (Szasz, 1980). Despite media-driven

insanity

A legal term attesting that a person is not responsible for his or her own actions, including criminal behavior.

concern about alleged abuses of the insanity defense, it rarely is used in felony crimes and generally is successful only with the most obviously disturbed persons. Even when the insanity defense is successful, the person usually is confined for an extended period (Lymburner & Roesch, 1999).

Guilty but Mentally Ill

Some states have abandoned the insanity defense entirely; others have adopted a rule of *guilty but mentally ill* (Palmer & Hazelrigg, 2000). This requires that an insane person convicted of a crime be placed in a mental hospital until she or he is no longer mentally ill, at which time the person would serve the remainder of the sentence in prison. The American Psychiatric Association believes that the insanity defense is a legal and moral question, not a psychiatric one, and that psychiatrists should testify only about a defendant's mental status—not about a defendant's responsibility for a crime (Herbert, 1983). The American Psychological Association takes a more cautious approach, calling for research on the effects of the insanity defense before deciding to eliminate it or replace it with a plea of guilty but mentally ill (Mervis, 1984). The past two decades have, in fact, seen a series of studies on the insanity defense. In one experiment, undergraduates participated as jurors in a mock trial. They then answered questions about the case. When participants were given the option of finding the defendant guilty but mentally ill, verdicts of either guilty or not guilty by reason of insanity were reduced by two-thirds compared to participants not given that option (Poulson, 1990).

Greeks assumed that the gods inflicted psychological disorders on people to punish them for their misdeeds. But the Greek physician Hippocrates (ca. 460–ca. 377 B.C.) argued, instead, that psychological disorders had natural causes.

Despite the efforts of Hippocrates and his followers, supernatural explanations existed alongside naturalistic ones until the 19th century. The 16th-century Swiss physician Paracelsus (1493–1541) rejected the supernatural viewpoint. Instead of attributing unusual behavior to demons, he attributed it to the moon. Paracelsus called the condition *lunacy* and the people who exhibited it *lunatics*. These terms were derived from the Latin word for "moon." Yet, contrary to popular belief, the moon does not affect the incidence of crime, mental illness, or other abnormal behavior (Rotton & Kelly, 1985).

Current viewpoints on psychological disorders attribute them to natural factors. As shown in Table 14.1, the viewpoints differ in the extent to which they attribute psychological disorders to biological, mental, or environmental factors. But no single viewpoint provides an adequate explanation of psychological disorders. This has led to the emergence of **the diathesis-stress model,** the view that people differ in their biological predispositions to develop psychological disorders (Cabib et al., 1997). Such a predisposition is called a *diathesis*. A person with a strong predisposition to develop a psychological disorder might succumb to even relatively low levels of psychological stress. In contrast, a person with a weak predisposition to develop a psychological disorder might resist even extremely high levels of psychological stress. Research findings indicate that social stress interacts with biological predispositions to cause some psychological disorders, including schizophrenia (Siris, 2000) and major depression (Hammen, Risha, & Daley, 2000).

The Biopsychological Viewpoint

A century ago Sigmund Freud remarked, "In view of the intimate connection between things physical and mental, we may look forward to a day when paths of knowledge will be opened up leading from organic biology and chemistry to the field of neurotic phenomena" (Taulbee, 1983, p. 45). As a physician and biologist, Freud might have approved of the *biopsychological viewpoint,* which favors the study of the biological causes of psychological disorders. Modern interest in the biological causes of psychological disorders was stimulated in the late 19th century when researchers discovered that a disorder called *general paresis,* marked by severe mental deterioration, was caused by syphilis. Today biopsychological researchers are interested in the role of heredity, brain structure, brain activity, and brain chemistry in the development of psychological disorders. Research on the role of

diathesis-stress model
The assumption that psychological disorders are consequences of the interaction of a biological, inherited predisposition (diathesis) and exposure to stressful life experiences.

Table 14.1   The Major Viewpoints on Psychological Disorders

Viewpoint	Causes of Psychological Disorders
Biopsychological	Inherited or acquired brain disorders involving imbalances in neurotransmitters or damage to brain structures
Psychoanalytic	Unconscious conflicts over impulses such as sex and aggression, originating in childhood
Behavioral	Reinforcement of inappropriate behaviors and punishment or extinction of appropriate behaviors
Cognitive	Irrational or maladaptive thinking about one's self, life events, and the world in general
Humanistic	Incongruence between one's actual self and public self as a consequence of trying to live up to the demands of others
Social-Cultural	Social-cultural factors influence psychological symptoms and the prevalence of psychological disorders.
Diathesis-Stress	A biological predisposition interacting with stressful life experiences

heredity in the development of psychological disorders has found that correlations in traits that indicate psychopathology are higher among identical twins reared apart than among nontwin siblings reared together (DiLalla et al., 1996).

The Psychoanalytic Viewpoint

The *psychoanalytic viewpoint,* which originated in medicine, grew out of the biopsychological viewpoint. But instead of looking for underlying biological causes of psychological disorders, the psychoanalytic viewpoint looks for unconscious causes. As discussed in Chapter 13, Sigmund Freud stressed the continual conflict between inborn biological drives, particularly sex, which demand expression, and the norms of society that inhibit their expression. According to Freud, conflicts about sex and aggression can be repressed into the unconscious mind. This can lead to feelings of anxiety caused by pent-up sexual or aggressive energy.

Freud also stressed the importance of anxiety-provoking childhood experiences in promoting the development of psychological disorders. A major government survey on psychological disorders among Americans found that adult disorders are, in fact, often associated with adverse experiences during childhood (Kessler, Davis, & Kendler, 1997).

The Behavioral Viewpoint

The *behavioral viewpoint* arose in opposition to psychological viewpoints that looked for mental causes of behavior. In the tradition of B. F. Skinner, those who favor the behavioral viewpoint look to the environment and to the learning of maladaptive behaviors as the causes of psychological disorders. Social-cognitive behaviorists, such as Albert Bandura, would add that we might develop a psychological disorder by observing other people's behavior. For example, a person might develop a phobia (an unrealistic fear) of dogs after either being bitten by a dog or observing someone else being bitten by a dog.

The Cognitive Viewpoint

The Greek Stoic philosopher Epictetus (A.D. ca. 60–ca. 120) taught that "men are disturbed not by things, but by the views which they take of things." This is the central assumption of the *cognitive viewpoint,* which holds that psychological disorders arise from maladaptive ways of thinking about oneself and the world. Yet, studies indicate that people with moderate levels of depression might think *more* rationally and objectively than other people about themselves and the world (Taylor & Brown, 1988). That is, if you are mentally healthy, you might be unrealistically optimistic and view the world through "rose-colored glasses."

The Humanistic Viewpoint

As described in Chapter 13, psychologists who favor the *humanistic viewpoint,* most notably Carl Rogers and Abraham Maslow, stress the importance of self-actualization, which is the fulfillment of one's potential. According to Rogers and Maslow, psychological disorders occur when people fail to reach their potential, perhaps because others, especially their parents, discourage them from expressing their true desires, thoughts, and interests. The distress caused by the failure to behave in accordance with one's own desires, thoughts, and interests can lead to the development of a psychological disorder.

The Social-Cultural Viewpoint

Psychologists who stress the importance of cultural influences on psychological disorders favor the *social-cultural viewpoint.* Instead of presuming that psychological disorders are identical in their prevalence and symptoms across cultures, they note that though some disorders are universal, others are unique to particular cultures (Thakker, Ward, & Strongman, 1999). There is some cross-cultural universality in the symptoms of certain disorders, such as depression and schizophrenia, but less universality in others. Most psychological disorders show the influence of social-cultural factors (Draguns, 1995). For example, hunger, low-paid work under dangerous conditions, and chronic domestic violence are the social root of many mental health problems experienced by women worldwide. Similarly, the social disruption, unemployment, and culture shock experienced by young male immigrants are risk factors for substance abuse (López & Guarnaccia, 2000).

Classification of Psychological Disorders

In 1883 German psychiatrist Emil Kraepelin (1856–1926) devised the first modern classification system for psychological disorders (Weber & Engstrom, 1997). Today, the most widely used system of classification of psychological disorders is the fourth edition of the *Diagnostic and Statistical Manual of Mental Disorders (DSM-IV),* published by the American Psychiatric Association.

The *DSM-IV*

The *DSM-IV,* published in 1994, is a revised version of the *DSM-III,* which was published in 1980 (and revised in 1987 as the *DSM-III-R*). They were preceded by the *DSM-II* in 1968 and the *DSM-I* in 1952. The *DSM-IV* provides a means of communication among mental health practitioners, offers a framework for research on the causes of disorders, and helps practitioners diagnose and choose the best treatment for particular disorders (Clark, Watson, & Reynolds, 1995).

There is a growing body of research on the reliability and validity of the *DSM-IV.* The *reliability* of a diagnosis refers to the extent to which different evaluators make the same diagnosis. The *validity* of a diagnosis refers to the extent to which a diagnosis is accurate. Though some critics accuse the *DSM-IV* of having poor reliability and unknown validity (Sarbin, 1997), research indicates that the *DSM-IV* has good to excellent reliability and improved validity over the *DSM-III* (Nathan & Langenbucher, 1999).

▶ **Figure 14.1**
Prevalence of Some Major Psychological Disorders in the United States

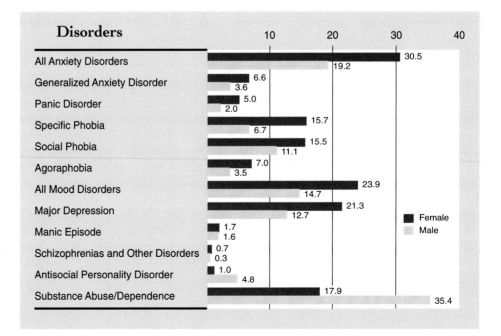

| **Chapter Fourteen**

Can Normal People Be Recognized in a Mental Hospital?

Psychologist David Rosenhan (1973) wondered whether we should accept the commonsense belief that normal people, complaining of symptoms of schizophrenia, could gain admission to a mental hospital and, once admitted, be discovered to be normal by the staff. Rosenhan had 8 apparently normal persons, including himself, gain admission to mental hospitals by calling the hospitals for appointments and then complaining of hearing voices that said "empty, hollow, thud." Hearing imaginary voices is a symptom of schizophrenia.

The 8 "pseudopatients" were admitted to 12 hospitals in 5 states; their stays ranged from 7 to 52 days. During their stays, they behaved normally, did not complain of hearing voices, and sometimes wrote hundreds of pages of notes about their experiences in the hospitals. Rosenhan concluded that the diagnosis of psychological disorders is influenced more by preconceptions and by the setting in which we find a person than by any objective characteristics of the person. According to his findings, the commonsense belief that professionals can easily determine whether someone has a psychological disorder is mistaken.

But Rosenhan's study provoked psychiatrist Robert Spitzer, who helped revise the *DSM,* to insist that Rosenhan had misinterpreted the results (Spitzer, 1975). First, the admission of the pseudopatients to the mental hospitals was justified, because people who report hearing imaginary voices might have schizophrenia. Second, people with schizophrenia can go long periods of time without displaying obvious symptoms of the disorder. Thus, the staff members who observed the pseudopatients during their stays had no reason to conclude they were faking. Nonetheless, the power of the label *mentally ill* to color our judgment of a person was supported by another study. When participants observed people labeled as mental patients (who actually were not) or similar people not given that label, they were more likely to rate the alleged mental patients as being "unusual" (Piner & Kahle, 1984).

The diagnosis of psychological disorders also can be influenced by social-class and gender-role stereotypes. In two studies (Landrine, 1987, 1989), clinicians and undergraduate psychology students read case study descriptions and were asked to assign diagnoses to each. Participants were cautioned that the descriptions might be of normal cases. Patterns of diagnosis varied by gender and social class. For example, descriptions of lower-class men were more likely to be labeled antisocial and descriptions of married middle-class women were more likely to be labeled dependent. Thus, both clinicians' and undergraduate psychology judgments of psychopathology were influenced by cultural stereotypes.

The leading critic of diagnostic labels is psychiatrist Thomas Szasz, who has gone so far as to call mental illness, including schizophrenia, a "myth" (Dammann, 1997). He believes that the behaviors that earn the label of mental illness are "problems in living." According to Szasz, labeling people as mentally ill wrongly blames their maladaptive functioning on an illness. He believes the notion of "mental illness" is a two-edged sword—it might excuse heinous behavior committed by those labeled "mentally ill," and it might enable governments to oppress nonconformists by labeling them "mentally ill." Szasz's claim that mental illness is a myth has provoked critical responses from other mental-health practitioners (Bentall & Pilgram, 1993)

The many mental-health professionals who helped create the *DSM-IV* do not view the psychological disorders it describes as myths. Among the most important categories of psychological disorders are *anxiety disorders, dissociative disorders, mood disorders, schizophrenic disorders,* and *personality disorders.* Figure 14.1 indicates the prevalence of several important psychological disorders in the United States.

▲ Thomas Szasz

"Mental illness is a myth, whose function it is to disguise and thus render more palatable the bitter pill of moral conflicts in human relations."

Criticisms of the Diagnosis of Psychological Disorders

Though the *DSM-IV* has been praised for increasing attention to cultural factors that might influence the diagnoses of psychological disorders (Smart & Smart, 1997), it also has been criticized for not going far enough in doing so (Thakker & Ward, 1998). And though some critics have argued that the *DSM-IV* makes it easier to diagnose certain disorders in women than in men (Hartung & Widiger, 1998), most research studies have failed to support this claim (Funtowicz & Widiger, 1999).

Despite the widespread reliance on the *DSM,* some professionals criticize the potential negative effects of the diagnosis of psychological disorders. This critical attitude was inspired, in part, by a classic study on the effects of diagnosis (see the Psychology Versus Common Sense feature on p. 407).

STAYING ON TRACK: *The Nature of Psychological Disorders*

1. How do the various viewpoints regarding the causes of psychological disorders differ from one another?
2. What is the difference between the cognitive rule and the volitional rule in regard to the insanity defense?
3. What is the main implication of Rosenhahn's study on the diagnosis of psychological disorders?

Answers to Staying on Track start on p. ST-6.

◆ ANXIETY DISORDERS

Anxiety is a feeling of apprehension accompanied by sympathetic nervous system arousal, which produces increases in sweating, heart rate, breathing rate, and other physiological responses. Though anxiety is a normal and beneficial part of everyday life, warning us about potential threats, in **anxiety disorders** it becomes intense, chronic, and disruptive of everyday functioning. About 10 to 15 percent of adult Americans suffer from anxiety disorders (Robins et al., 1984), which include *generalized anxiety disorder, obsessive-compulsive disorder, panic disorder,* and *phobias.*

Generalized Anxiety Disorder

Though we normally experience anxiety in response to stressful situations, the person with a **generalized anxiety disorder** is in a continual state of anxiety that exists independent of any particular stressful situation.

The Nature of Generalized Anxiety Disorder

The central feature of generalized anxiety disorder is worry. About 5 percent of the population suffers from generalized anxiety disorder sometime during their lifetime (Wittchen et al., 1994), and it is more common in women than in men. This gender difference emerges as early as age 6, with girls being twice as likely as boys to experience an anxiety disorder (Lewinsohn et al., 1998). The experience of anxiety appears to be universal, though there are cross-cultural differences in symptoms and their meaning. For example, a common expression of anxiety among Latinos is *nervio*s, characterized by fear, trembling, and bodily symptoms. These symptoms usually are related to disrupted family relationships and are socially acceptable manifestations of feeling "out of control" (Al-Issa & Oudji, 1998).

Causes of Generalized Anxiety Disorder

What accounts for the development of a generalized anxiety disorder? Biopsychological researchers look to heredity, neurochemistry, and brain arousal for answers. The children of victims of anxiety disorders are seven times more likely to develop them than are children whose parents are not victims. Anxiety researcher Samuel Turner notes that though this

anxiety disorder
A psychological disorder marked by persistent anxiety that disrupts everyday functioning.

generalized anxiety disorder
An anxiety disorder marked by a persistent state of anxiety that exists independently of any particular stressful situation.

hints at a possible genetic basis for anxiety disorders, it does not permit us to conclude that anxiety disorders are affected more by heredity than by life experiences (Turner, Beidel, & Costello, 1987). Whether it is affected by heredity or not, generalized anxiety is associated with an unusually large amygdala. Because the amygdala is important in governing our response to threats (De Bellis et al., 2000), this might account in part for the chronically high level of anxiety in generalized anxiety disorder.

Psychoanalytic theorists view anxiety as the consequence of id impulses that threaten to overwhelm ego controls. Cognitive-behavioral theorists find that people with generalized anxiety disorder are more prone than other people to worry (Breitholtz, Johansson, & Ost, 1999). This places the person in a constant "fight-or-flight" state of arousal, worrying continually. Humanistic psychologists believe that anxiety arises from an incongruence between the actual self and the ideal self (Strauman & Higgins, 1988), which are described in Chapter 13. This means that we might develop generalized anxiety disorder when we feel we have failed to live up to standards of behavior.

Obsessive-Compulsive Disorder

Have you ever been unable to keep an advertising jingle from continually running through your mind? If so, you have experienced a mild *obsession,* which is a persistent, recurring thought. If you have ever repeatedly checked to make sure you set your alarm clock the night before an early-morning exam, you have experienced a mild *compulsion,* which is a repetitive action that you feel compelled to perform.

The Nature of Obsessive-Compulsive Disorder

People whose obsessions and compulsions interfere with their daily functioning suffer from **obsessive-compulsive disorder (OCD).** OCD is found in about 3 percent of the population and is more common among women than men (Samuels & Nestadt, 1997). Cross-cultural research indicates a similar prevalence of OCD in Western and non-Western cultures (Horwath & Weissman, 2000). The most common compulsive symptoms include hoarding, checking, washing, cleanliness, and the desire for excessive symmetry and order (Leckman et al., 1997).

Causes of Obsessive-Compulsive Disorder

Some people appear to have a hereditary predisposition to develop OCD, based in part on research findings that OCD is more common in twin pairs than in other pairs of relatives (Wolff, Alsobrook, & Pauls, 2000). Heredity might predispose certain people to OCD because of its effects on the brain. OCD is associated with low levels of the neurotransmitter serotonin. Drugs that treat OCD raise serotonin levels (Stein, 2000). PET scans have found that people with OCD have abnormally high activity in the frontal lobes (Saxena & Rauch, 2000). This might mean that compulsive behavior serves to prevent anxiety from rising to uncomfortable levels. You might have experienced this, in a milder form, when you felt anxious about schoolwork, spent an hour rearranging your room, and, as a result, felt less anxious.

According to psychoanalysts, OCD is caused by fixation at the anal stage. This causes repressed anger directed at the parents. The child defends against the guilt generated by these feelings of anger and later transgressions by repeating certain thoughts and actions. A study found that people with OCD do, in fact, feel more guilt than people without OCD (Safran, Watkins, & Charman, 1996).

Behavioral theorists view obsessions and compulsions as ways of avoiding anxiety-inducing situations. So you might compulsively write and rewrite to-do lists instead of studying for an upcoming final exam. Cognitive theorists note that OCD symptoms might be responses to imagined threats. In one study, for example, people with handwashing compulsions washed their hands more often when they felt they were in danger than when they felt relatively safe (Jones & Menzies, 1997). Humanistic theorists, like psychoanalytic theorists, note the relationship between guilt and OCD—but they stress the importance of the conscious, rather than the unconscious, experience, of guilt.

▲ **Samuel Turner**

"Emerging human and nonhuman primate data suggest that some individuals are likely to be more vulnerable to anxiety than others, and hence are at a greater risk for developing an anxiety disorder."

obsessive-compulsive disorder (OCD)
An anxiety disorder in which the person has recurrent, intrusive thoughts (obsessions) and recurrent urges to perform ritualistic actions (compulsions).

▲ **"But that's what you said yesterday— 'Just one more cord'!"**

Copyright; © The New Yorker Collection 1986, Bill Woodman from cartoonbank.com. All rights reserved.

▲ Panic

Edvard Munch's painting *The Scream* (1893) conveys the intense anxiety and terror characteristic of a panic attack.

panic disorder

An anxiety disorder marked by sudden, unexpected attacks of overwhelming anxiety, often associated with the fear of dying or "losing one's mind."

phobia

An anxiety disorder marked by excessive or inappropriate fear.

specific phobia

An anxiety disorder marked by an intense, irrational fear of a specific object or situation.

Panic Disorder

In describing the motivation for his painting *The Scream,* Norwegian artist Edvard Munch (1863–1944) remarked, "I was walking . . . and I felt a loud, unending scream piercing nature" (Blakemore, 1977, p. 155). Both the painting and the statement indicate that Munch might have suffered a *panic attack,* which is a symptom of **panic disorder.**

The Nature of Panic Disorder

Panic disorder is marked by sudden attacks of overwhelming anxiety, accompanied by dizziness, trembling, cold sweats, heart palpitations, shortness of breath, fear of dying, and fear of going crazy. Symptoms of panic disorder differ from one culture to another. Japanese with panic disorder, for example, show different patterns of symptoms than Americans with panic disorder (Shioiri et al., 1996). Though panic attacks usually last only a few minutes, they are so distressing that more people seek therapy for panic disorder than for any other psychological disorder (Boyd, 1986). About 3 percent of Americans experience panic disorder sometime in their lives (Kessler et al., 1998), and women are more likely than men to develop the disorder (Rouillon, 1997).

Causes of Panic Disorder

Biopsychological theorists note that the concordance rate for panic disorder is higher for identical twins than for fraternal twins (Stein, Jang, & Livesley, 1999). Again, these findings hint at, but do not guarantee, a genetic predisposition for panic disorder. The biopsychological factor that has gained substantial support is that people with panic disorder are hypersensitive to carbon dioxide levels in their blood. Instead of responding by breathing normally to reduce their carbon dioxide levels, they might at times respond as though they are being suffocated—and experience a panic attack (van Beek & Griez, 2000).

Psychoanalytic theorists look to early childhood experiences as influences on the development of panic disorders (Vuksic-Mihaljevic et al., 1998). Adults with panic disorder, for example, tend to have experienced early separation anxiety in childhood (Silove et al., 1996) and to recall parents who were overly protective of them, yet showed little emotional caring toward them (Wilborg & Dahl, 1997). Research studies by behavioral psychologists implicate the classical conditioning of panic as a response to physiological and environmental cues (Bouton, Mineka, & Barlow, 2001). According to cognitive theorists, panic disorder results from faulty thinking. People prone to panic disorders tend to misattribute physical symptoms of arousal caused by factors such as caffeine, exercise, mild stress, or emotional memories, to a serious mental or physical disorder (Schmidt, Lerew, & Jackson, 1999).

Phobias

The word **phobia** comes from the name of the Greek god of fear, *Phobos,* and refers to the experience of excessive or inappropriate fear. The phobic person realizes that the fear is irrational but cannot prevent it.

The Nature of Phobias

Phobias are among the most common psychological disorders, afflicting about 6 percent of Americans (Boyd et al., 1990). The major classes of phobias are *specific phobias, social phobias,* and *agoraphobia.*

Specific Phobias. A **specific phobia** is an intense, irrational fear of a specific object or situation, such as a spider or height. People with specific phobias might go to great lengths to avoid the object or situation they fear. Specific phobias are more common in women than in men, and there are gender differences in the prevalence of specific phobias (Fredrikson et al., 1996). Some specific phobias are closely connected to particular cultures. Fear of ocean storms, for example, is more common among the people of the Faroe Islands in the North Atlantic (Wang, 2000).

◄ **Acrophobia**

An acrophobic person might feel anxiety just looking at this photograph of workers constructing the world's longest cable bridge over an estuary where the Seine River meets the sea in Normandy, France.

Social Phobia. People with a **social phobia,** which affects about 13 percent of Americans (Magee et al., 1996), fear public scrutiny. This can lead them to avoid activities like playing sports, making telephone calls, or performing music in public. The most common social phobia is public-speaking phobia (Kessler, Stein, & Berglund, 1998). Women are more likely than men to have social phobias; women also have more severe symptoms (Turk et al., 1998). A large proportion of the social phobias reported by East Asians constitute a culture-specific category: offensive social phobias. One type of offensive social phobia common among Koreans, for example, is a fear of being with others due to a pervasive sense that one's body odors are offensive (Lee & Oh, 1999). *Taijin Kyofusho* is a Japanese form of social phobia that reflects an unreasonable fear of offending others with inappropriate behavior or an offensive physical appearance (Kleinknecht et al., 1997). These cultural differences have been attributed to the collectivist orientation of Asian cultures.

social phobia
A phobia of situations that involve public scrutiny.

Social Phobia/Social Anxiety Association
www.mhhe.com/sdorow5

Agoraphobia. **Agoraphobia,** which affects up to 11 percent of Americans (Magee et al., 1996), is the fear of being in public. The word *agoraphobia,* from the Greek term for "fear of the marketplace," was coined in 1871 to describe the cases of four men who feared being in a city plaza (Boyd & Crump, 1991). Agoraphobic people typically have a history of panic attacks. They tend to avoid public places because they fear the embarrassment of having witnesses to their panic attacks (Amering et al., 1997). In extreme cases the person can become a prisoner in her or his own home—terrified to leave for any reason. African Americans and European Americans with agoraphobia tend to differ in their symptom patterns. African Americans tend to have more intense symptoms; European Americans tend to have an earlier onset of the disorder (Smith, Friedman, & Nevid, 1999). Because agoraphobia disrupts every aspect of the victim's life, and potentially can destroy intimate relationships (McCarthy & Shean, 1996), it is the phobia most commonly seen by psychotherapists.

agoraphobia
A fear of being in public, usually because the person fears the embarrassment of a panic attack.

Causes of Phobias

Phobias have been the target of much scientific research into their causes. Many researchers search for biopsychological factors, and many others look to possible psychological factors.

Biopsychological Factors. Some people have a biological, possibly hereditary, predisposition to develop phobias. One bit of evidence for this is that identical twins have a higher concordance rate than do fraternal twins (Lichtenstein & Annas, 2000). According to Martin Seligman, evolution has biologically prepared us to develop phobias toward potentially dangerous natural objects or situations, such as fire, snakes, and heights. This might explain why phobias that involve potentially dangerous natural objects, such as snakes, are more persistent than phobias that involve usually safe natural objects, such as flowers (McNally, 1987). Though some researchers question the existence of inherited preparedness to fear specific objects or situations (de Jong & Merckelbach, 1997), there is experimental research supporting it. For example, when fear is induced by pairing snakes or houses with electric shocks, fear of snakes lasts longer than fear of houses (Ohman, Erixon, & Lofberg, 1975).

Phobias are also associated with relatively greater right-hemisphere activity, as was found in a study of people with social phobia whose brain-wave patterns were recorded while they waited to make a public speech (Davidson et al., 2000). Moreover, there is evidence that serotonin might play a role in phobias, because drugs that increase serotonin levels in the brain are useful in treating phobias, such as social phobia (van der Linden, Stein, & van Balkom, 2000).

Psychological Factors. Psychoanalytic theorists trace the origin of phobias to early childhood experiences. School phobia, for example, is associated with separation anxiety related to one's parents (Flakierska-Praquin, Lindstroem, & Gillberg, 1997). The psychoanalytic viewpoint holds that phobias might be caused by anxiety displaced from a feared object or situation onto another object or situation. By displacing the anxiety, the person keeps the true source unconscious. Behavioral psychologists view phobias as learned responses to life situations. Phobias develop because of learning, either through personal experience, observation of phobic people, or exposure to information about fearful situations. One study found that children's dog phobias arose, as predicted, from personal experience with dogs, observation of other people's experiences with dogs, or exposure to information about the dangerousness of dogs (King, Clowes-Hollins, & Ollendick, 1997). And cognitive explanations of phobias stress the importance of exaggerated beliefs about the harmfulness of the fear-inducing object or situation. A study of people with social phobia found that they felt that their anticipated social experiences would more likely be negative than positive (Gilboa-Schechtman, Franklin, & Foa, 2000).

STAYING ON TRACK: *Anxiety Disorders*

1. How have psychologists connected the fear of suffocation and panic disorder?
2. Why does agoraphobia prompt people to seek therapy more than any other phobia does?

Answers to Staying on Track start on p. ST-6.

◆ DISSOCIATIVE DISORDERS

International Society for the Study of Dissociation
www.mhhe.com/sdorow5

dissociative disorder
A psychological disorder in which thoughts, feelings, and memories become separated from conscious awareness.

dissociative amnesia
The inability to recall personally significant memories.

In a **dissociative disorder,** the person's conscious mind loses access to certain thoughts, feelings, and memories. The dissociative disorders include *dissociative amnesia, dissociative fugue,* and *dissociative identity disorder.* About 3 percent of North Americans show symptoms of dissociative disorders (Waller & Ross, 1997). Though dissociative symptoms appear in all cultures, they are not always considered signs of a psychological disorder. This means that diagnosing dissociative disorders should be done within the individual's cultural context (Lewis-Fernandez, 1998).

Dissociative Amnesia and Fugue

While being interrogated about his assassination of Robert F. Kennedy in 1968, Sirhan Sirhan was unable to recall the incident. He apparently suffered from **dissociative amnesia,** the inability to recall personally significant memories. In September 1980, a young woman was found wandering in Birch State Park, in Florida. She could not recall who she was or where she was from. After a nationally televised appearance on a morning television show, she was reunited with her family in Illinois. She suffered from **dissociative fugue,** which is marked by the memory loss characteristic of dissociative amnesia as well as the loss of one's identity and fleeing from one's prior life. (The word *fugue* comes from the Latin word meaning "to flee.")

dissociative fugue

Memory loss characteristic of dissociative amnesia as well as the loss of one's identity and fleeing from one's prior life.

The Nature of Dissociative Amnesia and Fugue

In dissociative amnesia, the lost memories are usually related to a traumatic event, such as witnessing a catastrophe, but the lost memories typically return within hours or days. In dissociative fugue, the person might adopt a new identity, only to emerge from the fugue state days, months, or years later, recalling nothing that happened during the intervening period (Kopelman et al., 1994).

Causes of Dissociative Amnesia and Fugue

The psychoanalytic viewpoint assumes that repression of painful memories causes dissociative amnesia. The most common factors implicated in dissociative amnesia are combat, adult rape, criminal acts, attempted suicide, disasters and accidents, and experiencing the violent death of a parent during childhood (Arrigo & Pezdek, 1997). Childhood abuse also is associated with later development of dissociative amnesia (Chu, 2000). Nonetheless, as discussed in Chapter 8, the existence of repressed memories of childhood abuse is controversial (Powell, 2000).

There is emerging evidence that biopsychological processes can contribute to dissociative amnesia. Researchers investigating the role of sexual trauma on memory loss point to the role of chronic elevations of stress hormones in impaired memory functioning. The relationship of stress hormones to disrupted memory of traumatic events is complex, however; some traumatized people display *hypermnesia*—stronger than normal recall of the traumatic event—and others display dissociative amnesia (Nadel & Jacobs, 1998).

Dissociative Identity Disorder

In 1812 Benjamin Rush, the founder of American psychiatry, reported the following case involving a minister's wife:

> ▶ In her paroxysms of madness she resumed her gay habits, spoke French, and ridiculed the tenets and practices of the sect to which she belonged. In the intervals of her fits she renounced her gay habits, became zealously devoted to the religious principles and ceremonies of the Methodists, and forgot everything she did and said during the fits of her insanity. (Carlson, 1981, p. 668)

This was one of the first well-documented cases of *multiple personality disorder* (now called **dissociative identity disorder**), in which a person has two or more distinct personalities that alternate with one another.

dissociative identity disorder

A dissociative disorder, more commonly known as multiple personality disorder, in which the person has two or more distinct personalities that alternate with one another.

The Nature of Dissociative Identity Disorder

An individual's alternate personalities might include men, women, and children. Each personality might have its own way of walking, writing, and speaking. You are probably familiar with two cases of dissociative identity disorder that were made into popular movies: the story of Chris Sizemore, portrayed by Joanne Woodward in *The Three Faces of Eve,* and the story of Sybil Dorsett, portrayed by Sally Field in *Sybil.*

Causes of Dissociative Identity Disorder

People who develop dissociative identity disorder almost always have had traumatic experiences in early childhood, typically including sexual, physical, and emotional abuse, leading them to escape into their alternate personalities. A study of 71 patients with dissociative identity disorder in the Netherlands found that 94.4 percent had a history of childhood sexual and physical abuse (Boon & Draijer, 1993). Psychoanalytic theorists believe that multiple personalities arise from the child's impossible predicament—the need to escape intolerable abuse while maintaining emotional attachment to the abusive parent (Blizard, 1997).

▶ **Dissociative Identity Disorder**
In the 1957 film *The Three Faces of Eve*, Joanne Woodward portrayed a woman with 3 different personalities. *(a)* The personality named Eve White was prim and proper; *(b)* the personality named Eve Black was sexually promiscuous; and *(c)* the personality named Jane was a balanced compromise between the other two. *(d)* More than two decades later, a woman named Chris Sizemore revealed that she was the woman portrayed by Joanne Woodward. After years of therapy she was finally able to maintain a single, integrated personality—instead of the 22 she displayed at one point in her life.

(a)

(b)

(c)

(d)

Because of a marked increase in reported cases of dissociative identity disorder since the 1980s, some cognitive theorists believe multiple personalities are being overdiagnosed and are simply the product of role playing (Lilienfeld et al., 1999). This possibility was demonstrated in a study in which students were hypnotized and asked to reveal the hidden personality of an accused multiple murderer called Harry Hodgins or Betty Hodgins. Eighty percent did so. This indicates that at least some reputed cases of dissociative identity disorder could be no more than role playing, whether intentional or not (Spanos, Weekes, & Bertrand, 1985).

Despite this, a review of the research evidence found little support for the view that alternate personalities are induced by suggestions during psychotherapy (Gleaves, 1996). Even biopsychological evidence supports this view. In one study, functional MRI of the brain found that when a middle-aged woman with dissociative identity disorder was switching from one personality to another, there was a distinctive pattern of changes in her hippocampus—the brain structure most important in memory for personal experiences and general information (Tsai et al., 1999). Given the conflicting evidence regarding the reality of dissociative identity disorder, the existence of the disorder promises to remain a controversial issue for years to come.

STAYING ON TRACK: *Dissociative Disorders*

1. What kind of life experiences are common among people who develop dissociative disorders?
2. Why do some psychologists doubt the existence of dissociative identity disorder?

Answers to Staying on Track start on p. ST-6.

◆ MOOD DISORDERS

People with **mood disorders** experience prolonged periods of extreme depression or elation, often unrelated to their current circumstances, that disrupt their everyday functioning. The mood disorders include *major depression* and *bipolar disorder*. Some researchers have identified still another mood disorder: **seasonal affective disorder (SAD).** People with this disorder suffer from severe depression during certain seasons, usually in the winter. SAD has been linked to disruption of serotonin regulation (Sher et al., 1999) and often responds to phototherapy—daily exposure to artificial bright light (Lee & Chan, 1999).

Major Depression

We normally feel depressed after personal losses or failures; the frequency and intensity of depressive episodes varies from person to person. Since World War II, depression has become ten times more prevalent among Americans (Seligman, 1989) and is considered the common cold of psychological disorders.

The Nature of Major Depression

People with **major depression** experience extreme distress that disrupts their lives for weeks or months at a time. They commonly express despondency, helplessness, and low self-esteem. They might also suffer from an inability to fall asleep or to stay asleep, lose their appetite or overeat, abandon good grooming habits, withdraw from social relations, lose interest in sex, find it difficult to concentrate, and fail to perform up to their normal standards. About 2 to 3 percent of men and about 5 to 9 percent of women suffer from major depression (American Psychiatric Association, 1994).

Causes of Major Depression

What accounts for major depression? Each of the viewpoints offers its own explanation.

The Biopsychological Viewpoint. Mood disorders have a biological basis, apparently influenced by heredity. Identical twins have higher concordance rates for major depression (Lyons et al., 1998) than fraternal twins do. But it is important to note that our sensitivity to stressful events and our choice of stressful environments to expose ourselves to are affected by genetic factors (Kendler, 1998). The hereditary predisposition to develop mood disorders might manifest itself by its effect on neurotransmitters. Major depression is related to abnormally low levels of *serotonin* or *norepinephrine.* Antidepressant drugs, act by increasing levels of serotonin or norepinephrine (Delgado & Morenc, 2000).

The Psychoanalytic Viewpoint. The classic psychoanalytic view holds that the loss of a parent or rejection by a parent early in childhood predisposes the person to experience depression whenever she or he suffers a personal loss later in life. Because these children feel that it

Seasonal Affective Disorder
www.mhhe.com/sdorow5

mood disorder
A psychological disorder marked by prolonged periods of extreme depression or elation, often unrelated to the person's current situation.

seasonal affective disorder (SAD)
A mood disorder in which severe depression arises during a particular season, usually the winter.

major depression
A mood disorder marked by depression so intense and prolonged that the person may be unable to function in everyday life.

(a)   (b)   (c)

◀ **Mood Disorders**
Celebrities, as well as everyday people, might face lives dominated by a mood disorder. Among the best known have been *(a)* actor Patty Duke, *(b)* former talk-show host Dick Cavett, and *(c) 60 Minutes* reporter Mike Wallace.

is unacceptable to express anger at the lost or rejecting parent, they turn their anger on themselves, creating feelings of guilt and self-loathing. But research studies have found that this cannot explain all cases of depression. For example, both depressed and nondepressed adults are equally likely to have suffered the loss of a parent in childhood (Crook & Eliot, 1980).

The Behavioral Viewpoint. One of the most influential behavioral explanations is Peter Lewinsohn's *reinforcement theory,* which assumes that depressed people lack the social skills needed to gain social reinforcement from others and might instead provoke negative reactions from them. For example, depressed people stimulate less smiling, fewer statements of support, more unpleasant facial expressions, and more negative remarks from others than do nondepressed people (Gotlib & Robinson, 1982). Lewinsohn points out that the depressed person is caught in a vicious cycle in which reduced social reinforcement leads to depression and depressed behavior further reduces social reinforcement (Youngren & Lewinsohn, 1980). This might account in part for the association between depression and conflict in intimate relationships (Zlotnick et al., 2000).

An influential cognitive-behavioral theory of depression is based on Martin Seligman's attributional theory of depression. Depressed people attribute negative events in their lives to internal, stable, and global factors. An *internal factor* is a characteristic of one's self rather than of the environment. A *stable factor* is unlikely to change. And a *global factor* affects almost all areas of one's life. Research on depression has tended to find that, as predicted, depressed people make internal, stable, and global attributions for negative events in their lives (Sweeney, Anderson, & Bailey, 1986). For example, first-year college students who attribute their poor academic performance to internal, stable, and global factors—such as intelligence—become more depressed than do those who attribute their poor academic performance to external, unstable, and specific factors—such as being assigned difficult teachers (Peterson & Barrett, 1987). It seems depressed people blame themselves for problems in their lives more than nondepressed people do (Wall & Hayes, 2000).

Seligman's attributional theory has also been supported in other cultures, such as Turkey (Aydin & Aydin, 1992). But there are cultural differences in the relationship of attributions and depression. A study of American and Chinese students found that Chinese students tended to be more depressed than American students. Most notably, the Chinese students tended to blame themselves more for social failures and to credit themselves less for social successes than did the American students. This might reflect the relatively greater interdependence of people in Chinese culture (Anderson, 1999).

The Cognitive Viewpoint. The most influential cognitive view of depression is Aaron Beck's *cognitive theory.* Beck has found that depressed people exhibit what he calls a *cognitive triad:* They have a negative view of themselves, of their current circumstances, and of their future possibilities (Anderson & Skidmore, 1995). The cognitive triad is maintained by the tendency of depressed people to overgeneralize from negative events. For example, depressed people tend to assume that a single failure means they are incompetent (Carver & Ganellen, 1983).

As mentioned earlier in the chapter, people with psychological disorders might have more objective beliefs about themselves and the world than do people without such disorders. Depression researcher Lauren Alloy and her colleagues have found that this is especially true of depressed people. Nondepressed people overestimate the likelihood that positive events, and underestimate the likelihood that negative events, will happen to them (Crocker, Alloy, & Kayne, 1988). This leads to the surprising conclusion that if you are not depressed, it might mean that you might have an unrealistically positive view of reality, and that depressed people are more accurate in their view of their reality—so-called *depressive realism* (Haaga & Beck, 1995). Nonetheless, some researchers have found that this difference between depressed and nondepressed people holds more in laboratory studies than in real-life emotional situations (Pacini, Muir, & Epstein, 1998).

Another cognitive view of depression, put forth by Susan Nolen-Hoeksema, implicates continual *rumination* about one's plight. People who constantly think about the sad state of their lives experience more severe and more chronic depression than do people who take action to improve their lives or who distract themselves by pursuing enjoyable activities

▲ Susan Nolen-Hoeksema

"People who use ruminative coping do not tend to use structured problem solving to cope. Instead, they simply think about or talk about how unmotivated, sad, or lethargic they feel without doing anything to relieve their symptoms."

Anatomy of a Research Study

Are People Who Ruminate About Their Problems More Likely to Become Depressed?

Rationale

Finding an association between rumination and depression does not guarantee there is a causal relationship between them. This prompted Susan Nolen-Hoeksema (Nolen-Hoeksema & Morrow, 1993) to conduct an experiment to determine whether rumination does, in fact, affect depression.

Method

Nolen-Hoeksema randomly assigned 24 nondepressed and 24 mildly to moderately depressed undergraduates to spend 8 minutes focusing their attention on their current feelings and personal characteristics (the *rumination condition*) or on descriptions of geographic locations and objects (the *distraction condition*).

Results and Discussion

Nolen-Hoeksema found that depressed participants in the rumination condition became significantly more depressed. In contrast, depressed participants in the distraction condition became significantly less depressed. Moreover, rumination and distraction did not affect the moods of nondepressed participants. Thus, the results support her contention that depressed people who ruminate are prone to more intense depression, making them take longer to return to a normal mood. The results also support her contention that depressed people who try to distract themselves become less depressed, enabling them to return to normal moods faster.

(Nolen-Hoeksema, 2000). Nolen-Hoeksema believes that this could explain why, after age 15, women are about twice as likely as men to be depressed (Nolen-Hoeksema & Girgus, 1994): depressed women tend to ruminate about their depression, and depressed men tend to distract themselves from it (Trask & Sigmon, 1999). In fact, Nolen-Hoeksema found that among college undergraduates, rumination was the single most important predictor of how long depression would last. Because female undergraduates tended to ruminate more than male undergraduates, depressed women tended to have longer-lasting bouts of depression (Butler & Nolen-Hoeksema, 1994). Nolen-Hoeksema's *rumination theory* was tested in the study described in the Anatomy of a Research Study feature.

The Humanistic Viewpoint. Psychologists who favor the humanistic viewpoint attribute depression to the frustration of self-actualization. More specifically, depressed people suffer from incongruence between their actual self and their ideal self (Strauman & Higgins, 1988).

The Social-Cultural Viewpoint. There are some cross-cultural commonalities in the manifestation of depression, but also differences in depressive symptoms. The symptoms of depression are the result of the interaction of universal tendencies and cultural factors (Draguns, 1995). Many of these factors might be related to ethnic differences in the prevalence of depression. A survey of more than 2,000 Americans found that African Americans were more likely to be depressed than European Americans. But when socioeconomic status was factored in, there were no differences. That is, African Americans and European Americans of the same socioeconomic class had equal rates of depression. Thus, because African Americans, on average, are more likely to be poor, it is poverty, not ethnicity, that probably accounts for the ethnic difference in depression rates (Biafora, 1995).

Bipolar Disorder

According to a biblical story, King Saul stripped off his clothes in public, exhibited alternating bouts of elation and severe depression, and eventually committed suicide. Though the story attributes his behavior to evil spirits, psychologists might attribute it to bipolar disorder.

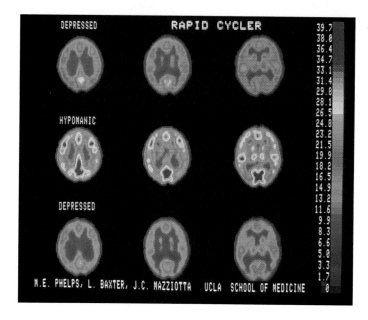

► **Figure 14.2**

Brain Activity in Bipolar Disorder

These PET scans show the brain activity of a rapid-cycling bipolar patient. The patient cycled between mania and depression every 24 to 48 hours. The top and bottom sets of scans were obtained during periods when the patient was depressed. The middle set of scans was obtained during a manic period. Note that the red areas indicate significantly higher brain activity during the manic period (Phelps & Mazziotta, 1985).

American Foundation for Suicide Prevention
www.mhhe.com/sdorow5

The Nature of Bipolar Disorder

Bipolar disorder, formerly called *manic depression,* is characterized by days or weeks of mania alternating with longer periods of major depression. **Mania** (from the Greek term for "madness") involves euphoria, hyperactivity, grandiose ideas, incoherent talkativeness, wild optimism, and inflated self-esteem. Manic people are sexually, physically, and financially reckless. At some time in their lives, about 1 percent of adults have bipolar disorder, which is equally common in men and women (American Psychiatric Association, 1994).

Causes of Bipolar Disorder

Heredity plays a role in bipolar disorder (McMahon et al., 2000), though initially promising attempts to isolate particular chromosomal abnormalities have provided unreliable research findings (Kelsoe et al., 1993). Whereas depression is associated with a combination of low levels of both serotonin and norepinephrine, mania is associated with a combination of low levels of serotonin and high levels of norepinephrine. Figure 14.2 shows that mania also is associated with unusually high levels of brain arousal, perhaps related to these neurotransmitter levels. Despite its biological roots, the course of bipolar disorder also is affected by life experiences, with stressful life events interacting with a biological vulnerability (Johnson & Roberts, 1995). This is in keeping with the diathesis-stress model of psychological disorders.

Suicide and Mood Disorders

Though some suicides are done for honor, as in the Japanese ritual of hara-kiri, or to escape intolerable pain, as in some cases of terminal illnesses, most are associated with major depression. Suicide accounts for 1 to 2 percent of deaths in industrially developed countries (Gunnell, 2000).

Who commits suicide? People who suffer from mood disorders are more susceptible. Roy Baumeister (1990) believes that people commit suicide when their self-image becomes so negative that it is too painful to bear. For example, a study of Australian university students found that perfectionism might predispose people to suicide. Students high in perfectionism were more likely to view suicide as a potential solution to their problems, which they see as a sign that they cannot meet their unreasonably high standards (Hamilton & Schweitzer, 2000). Gender, ethnicity, and age are also factors. In most countries, women are much more likely than men to attempt suicide, yet many more men than women succeed (Schmidtke et al., 1999)—partly because men tend to use more lethal means, such as gunshots to the head, whereas women tend to use less lethal means, such as overdoses of depressant drugs. This gender difference holds both in Western and Asian countries (He & Lester, 1998).

Widowed and divorced people are more likely to commit suicide than are single or married people (Canetto & Lester, 1995). There is some evidence that marriage protects men against suicide more than it protects women (Kposowa, 2000). Though suicide rates are lower for high school and college students than for older people, suicide is one of the most common causes of death for the 15- to 24-year-old age group. Adolescent suicide often is associated with dysfunctional family relations (Husain, 1990) and drug or alcohol abuse (Rivinus, 1990). Because even young children commit suicide (Lester, 1995), parents and school personnel should be aware of the possibility in depressed, withdrawn children.

According to Edwin Shneidman (1994), a leading authority, at least 90 percent of people who attempt suicide give verbal or behavioral warnings before their attempts. People who have tried suicide in the past are at especially high risk of trying again. A study of almost 400 youth suicides in Paris found that one-third of them had made earlier attempts (Lecomte & Fornes, 1998). This makes it important to take threats seriously and to take appropriate actions to prevent suicide attempts. Major warning signs include changes in moods and habits associated with severe depression, such as emotional apathy, social withdrawal, poor grooming habits, and loss of interest in recreational activities; giving away cherished belongings; tying up loose ends in their lives; and outright suicide threats (Shaughnessy & Nystul, 1985).

One of the obvious ways to prevent suicide is to restrict access to means of suicide, such as guns or drugs (Lester, 1997). But interpersonal action also is important. Shneidman suggests that because suicide attempts are usually cries for help, the simple act of providing an empathetic response might reduce the immediate likelihood of an actual attempt. An immediate goal should be to relieve the person's psychological pain by intervening, if possible, with those who might be contributing to the pain, whether friends, lovers, teachers, or family members. You should also encourage the person to seek professional help, even if you have to make the appointment for the person and accompany him or her to it.

STAYING ON TRACK: *Mood Disorders*

1. How does Seligman's attributional theory explain depression?
2. How does rumination affect depression?
3. What are Edwin Shneidman's suggestions for preventing someone from committing suicide?

Answers to Staying on Track start on p. ST-6.

◆ SCHIZOPHRENIA

In middle age, Edvard Munch, the founder of modern expressionist painting, began acting oddly. He became a social recluse, believed that his paintings were his children, and claimed that they were too jealous to be exhibited with other paintings. Munch's actions were symptoms of **schizophrenia,** a severe psychological disorder characterized by impaired social, emotional, cognitive, and perceptual functioning.

The Nature of Schizophrenia

In 1911 the Swiss psychiatrist Eugen Bleuler (1857–1939) coined the term *schizophrenia* (from the Greek terms for "split mind"). About 1 percent of the world's population are victims of schizophrenia. Schizophrenic patients occupy half of the beds in American mental hospitals and cost the American economy billions of dollars each year. There is some evidence that the course of schizophrenia is more favorable in developing countries, possibly due to a higher interdependence of the individual within the community and the role of the family in providing care and interpersonal support to mentally ill relatives (López & Guarnaccia, 2000).

▲ **Kurt Cobain**
Even fame, youth, wealth, and talent might not be enough to prevent suicide, as in the case of Kurt Cobain, lead singer and guitarist of Nirvana. Cobain committed suicide after a long battle with depression and drug abuse.

schizophrenia
A class of psychological disorders characterized by grossly impaired social, emotional, cognitive, and perceptual functioning.

 Schizophrenia and Mental Health
www.mhhe.com/sdorow5

▲ **The Paintings of Louis Wain**
Wain (1860–1939) was a British artist who gained acclaim for his paintings of cats in human situations. But, after developing schizophrenia, he no longer painted with a sense of humor. Instead, his paintings revealed his mental deterioration, becoming progressively more fragmented and bizarre.

Characteristics of Schizophrenia

Schizophrenia is associated with sensory-perceptual, cognitive, social-emotional, and motor symptoms. Men and women are equally likely to develop schizophrenia, though men across all cultures tend to develop it 3 to 4 years earlier than women (Raesaenen et al., 2000).

Sensory-Perceptual Symptoms. People with schizophrenia typically experience *hallucinations,* which are sensory experiences in the absence of sensory stimulation. Schizophrenic hallucinations usually are auditory, typically voices that ridicule the person or order the person to commit harmful, perhaps violent, acts (Zisook et al., 1995). Researchers using functional magnetic resonance imaging have demonstrated that schizophrenic hallucinations are associated with increased activity in the region of the cerebral cortex that normally processes the relevant sensory information. People with auditory hallucinations, for example, have increased activity in their temporal lobes (Shergill et al., 2000).

Cognitive Symptoms. Chief among the cognitive symptoms of schizophrenia is difficulty with attention. People with schizophrenia are easily distracted by irrelevant stimuli (Mirsky et al., 1995) and have difficulty voluntarily switching their attention from one stimulus to another (Smith et al., 1998). This inability to control attention might account for the cognitive fragmentation that is a hallmark of schizophrenia.

Among the most distinctive cognitive disturbances in schizophrenia are delusions. A *delusion* is a belief that is held despite compelling evidence to the contrary. The most common delusions are delusions of influence, such as the belief that one's thoughts are being beamed to all parts of the universe (*thought broadcasting*). Less common are *delusions of grandeur,* in which the person believes that she or he is a famous or powerful person. The fascinating book *The Three Christs of Ypsilanti* (Rokeach, 1964/1981) describes the cases of three men in a mental hospital who had the same delusion of grandeur—each claimed to be Jesus Christ. The workings of the schizophrenic mind are vividly illustrated when they meet and each man tries to explain why he is Jesus and the others merely impostors. Delusions vary from culture to culture, as in a large-scale study of German and Japanese schizophrenic patients. The study found that Germans were more likely to have delusions of direct persecution, such as poisoning. The Japanese were more likely to have delusions of reference, such as delusions of being slandered (Tateyama et al., 1993).

Social-Emotional Symptoms. Schizophrenia is characterized by flat or inappropriate emotionality. For example, people with schizophrenia are less facially responsive to emotional films than other people are (Blanchard, Kring, & Neale, 1995). Emotional inappropriateness is shown by bizarre outbursts, such as laughing when someone is seriously injured. People with schizophrenia also have difficulty recognizing emotions from voices and facial expressions (Poole, Tobias, & Vinodogrov, 2000). People with schizophrenia tend to be socially withdrawn, with few, if any, friends. This usually first appears in childhood.

Motor Symptoms. Schizophrenia is also associated with unusual motor behavior. The person might rock incessantly, make bizarre faces, pace back and forth, hold poses for hours, or trace patterns in the air. Moreover, people with schizophrenia often exhibit unusual eye movements (Wolff & O'Driscoll, 1999).

Kinds of Schizophrenia

Diagnosticians distinguish several kinds of schizophrenic disorders. Cases that do not fall neatly into any one of the major categories of schizophrenia are commonly lumped into a category called *undifferentiated schizophrenia.* The major kinds of schizophrenia are *disorganized schizophrenia, catatonic schizophrenia,* and *paranoid schizophrenia.*

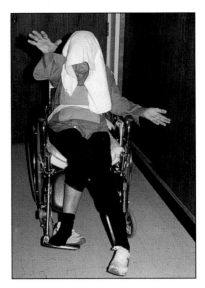

▲ **Catatonic Schizophrenia**
A person with catatonic schizophrenia might maintain bizarre postures.

- People with **disorganized schizophrenia** show personality deterioration, speak gibberish, dress outlandishly, perform ritualized movements, and engage in obscene behavior. Odd, inappropriate laughter is a hallmark of the disorder. Their bizarre behavior and incoherent speech can make it impossible for them to maintain normal social relationships.
- **Catatonic schizophrenia** is characterized by unusual motor behavior, often alternating between catatonic excitement and catatonic stupor. In *catatonic excitement* the person paces frantically, speaks incoherently, and engages in stereotyped movements. In *catatonic stupor* the person might become mute and barely move, possibly freezing in positions for hours or days. People with catatonic schizophrenia might even exhibit "waxy flexibility," in which they can be moved from one frozen pose to another. Nonetheless, even when in a catatonic stupor, the individual typically remains aware of what is happening in the immediate environment
- **Paranoid schizophrenia** is marked by hallucinations, delusions, suspiciousness, and argumentativeness. In more extreme cases, people with paranoid schizophrenia might feel so threatened that they become violent.

The diagnosis of schizophrenia is affected by cultural factors. In one study, 58 Japanese and 61 European psychiatrists with equal experience made diagnoses of the same 10 clinical case studies of schizophrenia. The Japanese psychiatrists tended to make diagnoses of disorganized schizophrenia. In contrast, the European psychiatrists tended to make diagnoses of paranoid schizophrenia (Tateyama et al., 1999). Another study found that clinicians' diagnoses of the symptoms of schizophrenia differed for African American inpatients compared to non-African Americans (Trierweiler et al., 2000).

disorganized schizophrenia
A type of schizophrenia marked by severe personality deterioration and extremely bizarre behavior.

catatonic schizophrenia
A type of schizophrenia marked by unusual motor behavior, such as bizarre actions, extreme agitation, or immobile stupor.

paranoid schizophrenia
A type of schizophrenia marked by hallucinations, delusions, suspiciousness, and argumentativeness.

Causes of Schizophrenia

The variety, complexity, and diversity of schizophrenic symptoms make the discovery of the causes of schizophrenia one of the most challenging of all tasks facing those who study the disorder (Andreasen, 1997). No single viewpoint can explain all cases of schizophrenia or why some people with certain risk factors develop schizophrenia and others do not.

The Biopsychological Viewpoint

Biopsychological theories of schizophrenia consider genetic, biochemical, and neurological factors.

Hereditary Factors. Figure 14.3 shows that the concordance rates for schizophrenia appear to have a strong hereditary basis. Yet the higher concordance rate for identical twins than for fraternal twins might be caused by the more similar treatment that identical twins receive, rather than by their identical genetic endowment. To assess the relative contributions of heredity and experience, researchers have turned to adoption studies. These studies support the genetic basis of schizophrenia. For example, schizophrenia is more common in the biological relatives of schizophrenic adoptees than in their adoptive relatives; children adopted from schizophrenic parents have a greater risk of schizophrenia than do children adopted from normal parents; and children of normal parents adopted by schizophrenic parents do not show an increased risk of schizophrenia (Buchsbaum & Haier, 1983).

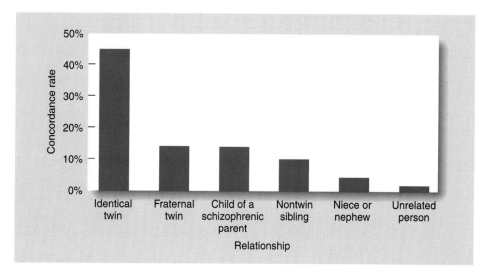

Though there is a hereditary basis for schizophrenia, it seems that schizophrenia is best explained by the diathesis-stress model (Tsuang, 2000). A review of research found that schizophrenic patients are predisposed to be more vulnerable to stressors, so stress that would hardly affect other people might cause them to develop symptoms of schizophrenia (Norman & Malla, 1993). For example, children who have both a genetic predisposition to become schizophrenic and the stress of losing their father are more likely to develop schizophrenia than are children with only one of those factors (Walker et al., 1981).

Neurochemical Factors. Given the apparent hereditary basis of schizophrenia, what biological differences might exist between people who develop schizophrenia and those who do not? One factor is the effect of genetic influences on the activity of the neurotransmitter dopamine (Amin et al., 1999). Studies have found a relationship between schizophrenia and high levels of activity at synapses sensitive to dopamine. Because hallucinogens such as LSD, which induce hallucinations, affect serotonin neurons, researchers are also looking at the possible role of serotonin in schizophrenia—with some initially positive findings (Aghajanian & Marek, 2000).

What evidence is there of a dopamine basis for schizophrenia?

- First, drugs that are used to treat schizophrenia work by blocking dopamine receptors (Kapur et al., 2000).
- Second, drugs such as amphetamines, which increase dopamine levels, can induce schizophrenic symptoms in normal people (Laruelle et al., 1999).
- Third, *L-dopa*, a drug used to treat Parkinson's disease because it increases dopamine levels, can induce schizophrenic symptoms in Parkinson's victims (Nicol & Gottesman, 1983).
- Fourth, brain-imaging studies have found that people with schizophrenia have overactive dopamine neurons (Farde, 1997).

Season-of-Birth Factors. In seeking other factors in schizophrenia, biopsychological researchers are struck by one of the most well-replicated findings regarding schizophrenia: a disproportionate number of victims are born in the winter or early spring (Torrey et al., 1997). This has been confirmed in countries throughout the Northern hemisphere, including Taiwan (Tam & Sewell, 1995), Denmark (Mortensen et al., 1999), and Switzerland (Modestin, Ammann, & Wurmle, 1995). But studies in the Southern hemisphere have found that people with schizophrenia are born disproportionately in the Southern hemisphere's spring and early summer (November, December, and January). This indicates that schizophrenia might be associated with certain months, not certain seasons (Berk et al., 1996).

The observation that people are more likely to develop schizophrenia if they are born during certain months has inspired a search for a possible connection to influenza viruses prevalent during the preceding months. These viruses might have infected the brains of schizophrenic people prenatally, particularly during the second trimester, when brain development accelerates. Many studies have investigated the relationship between a worldwide influenza epidemic in 1957 and the development of schizophrenia in people born shortly afterward. Unfortunately, findings have been inconsistent. Some studies have found that people exposed to influenza prenatally, especially during the second trimester, have higher rates of schizophrenia (Brown et al., 2000). But other studies have found that they do not (Selten, Slaets, & Kahn, 1998). Moreover, efforts to find viruses in the brains of schizophrenics have had little success (Taller et al., 1996), though this does not mean they do not exist. Perhaps they are viruses that do their damage before ultimately being destroyed by the immune system (Sierra-Honigmann, Carbone, & Yolken, 1995).

Neurological Factors. If viral infections play a role in schizophrenia, they would do so by affecting the brain. Brain-imaging studies have shown that schizophrenia is often associated with unusual brain activity. Schizophrenia is marked by greater abnormalities in activity in the left cerebral hemisphere than in the right cerebral hemisphere (Gur & Chin, 1999). Schizophrenic people also tend to have lower frontal-lobe activity than other people when performing cognitive tasks (Parellada et al., 1998).

As illustrated in Figure 14.4, some schizophrenics show atrophy of brain tissue, reducing the size of the amygdala and the hippocampus, as well as creating enlargement of the cerebral ventricles, the fluid-filled chambers inside the brain (Lawrie & Abukmeil, 1998). A meta-analysis of MRI studies found that the largest difference between the brains of schizophrenic patients and healthy controls was in the lateral ventricles (Wright et al., 2000).

Particular kinds of brain dysfunctions might be associated with particular sets of schizophrenic symptoms. According to schizophrenia researcher Nancy Andreasen, there are two kinds of schizophrenic syndromes, characterized by either positive symptoms or negative symptoms (Purnine et al., 2000). *Positive symptoms* are active symptoms that include hallucinations, delusions, thought disorders, and bizarre behaviors. People with positive symptoms experience acute episodes, show progressively worsening symptoms, respond well to drug treatment, have increased numbers of dopamine receptors, and reveal no brain structure pathology. In contrast, *negative symptoms* are passive symptoms that include mutism, apathy, flat affect, social withdrawal, intellectual impairment, poverty of speech, and inability to experience pleasure. People with negative symptoms typically respond poorly to traditional drug treatment (Rubin, 1994).

But Andreasen and her associates have reported that negative symptoms are not consistently associated with ventricular enlargement (Andreasen et al., 1990). In fact, ventricular enlargement appears in most schizophrenia patients, regardless of their pattern of symptoms (Vita et al., 2000). Moreover, it might be premature to divide schizophrenia into just two categories with either positive or negative symptoms. There is more evidence for a syndrome of negative symptoms than for a syndrome of positive symptoms (Andreasen et al., 1995).

The Psychoanalytic Viewpoint

According to the psychoanalytic viewpoint, people who become schizophrenic fail to overcome their dependence on their mothers and, as a result, become fixated at the oral stage. This gives them a weak ego. They cope with anxiety by resorting to behaviors characteristic of the oral stage, including fantasy, silly actions, incoherent speech, and irrational thinking.

Research in the spirit of the psychoanalytic viewpoint has found that parents high in what is known as *expressed emotion* can contribute to the maintenance or relapse of schizophrenia in their child. Parents who are high in expressed emotion criticize their child and become emotionally overprotective. Because of the impact of expressed emotion, schizophrenic children from families high in expressed emotion are more prone to relapse than children from families lower in expressed emotion (Cutting & Docherty, 2000). Though the notion of expressed emotion was developed first in England and then in other Western countries, it has gained support from research studies in non-Western countries (Hashemi & Cochrane, 1999), including Japan (Mino et al., 1997).

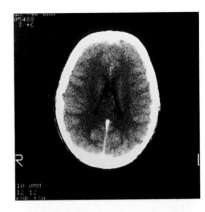

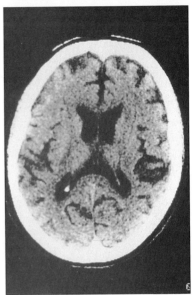

▲ Figure 14.4
Schizophrenia and Neurological Dysfunctions
CAT scans of the brains of people with schizophrenia often show atrophy and enlarged ventricles. Notice that the ventricles (the dark areas) in the schizophrenic brain *(below)* are much larger than those in the normal brain *(above)*.

The Behavioral Viewpoint

Behavioral theories of schizophrenia, which stress the role of learning, assume that schizophrenics are rewarded for behaving in bizarre ways (Ullmann & Krasner, 1975). Behavioral theorists also assume that a person who engages in bizarre behavior provokes social rejection from others, which in turn contributes to the suspiciousness and social withdrawal displayed by some people with schizophrenia.

The Cognitive Viewpoint

Proponents of the cognitive viewpoint point to disturbances of attention and thinking as the main factors in schizophrenia. As the leading schizophrenia researcher Eugen Bleuler observed earlier in this century, people with schizophrenia seem "incapable of holding the train of thought in the proper channel" (Baribeau-Braun, Picton, & Gosselin, 1983). Children exposed to parents who communicate in confusing, irrational ways are predisposed to develop the disturbed cognitive activity of schizophrenia (Doane et al., 1981).

The Humanistic Viewpoint

According to the humanistic viewpoint, schizophrenia is caused by extreme incongruence between the public self and the actual self. R. D. Laing claimed that schizophrenia results when a person develops a false public self to confront an intolerable life situation. This retreat from reality permits the person to experience her or his actual self. The schizophrenic person's bizarre thinking, language, and behavior are indicative of this retreat from reality. In contrast to other humanistic psychologists, Laing recommended that family, friends, and professionals permit the schizophrenic person to go on what he called a "voyage of self-discovery," rather than interfere with that process through the administration of drugs or commitment to a mental hospital. According to Laing, traditional psychiatry and psychology unfairly try to force the person to conform to unfulfilling circumstances (Redler, 2000).

The Social-Cultural Viewpoint

Cultural factors can affect the precise pattern of symptoms in schizophrenia (Draguns, 1995), but there is some cross-cultural universality in schizophrenic symptoms. A study of French and North African people with schizophrenia, for example, found little difference in their symptoms (Taleb et al., 1996). Though the *DSM-IV* considers cultural factors in schizophrenia more than prior editions did, critics insist that the *DSM* should pay even greater attention to them (Jenkins, 1998).

The Unofficial R. D. Laing Website
www.mhhe.com/sdorow5

STAYING ON TRACK: *Schizophrenia*

1. What are the major symptoms of schizophrenia?
2. What evidence is there supporting the role of dopamine in schizophrenia?
3. How do positive symptoms and negative symptoms of schizophrenia differ?

Answers to Staying on Track start on p. ST-7.

◆ PERSONALITY DISORDERS

Personality disorders are long-standing, inflexible, maladaptive patterns of behavior. Personality disorders are influenced by social-cultural factors (Paris, 1998), but some critics assert that the *DSM-IV* does not adequately represent the role of social-cultural factors in personality disorders (Alarcon, 1996).

Borderline Personality Disorder

A personality disorder of growing interest to psychologists is **borderline personality disorder (BPD).** This is because BPD has become more prevalent, devastates the lives of its victims and their loved ones, and presents one of the greatest challenges to therapists. Though BPD occurs in all cultures, it is more prevalent in developed ones. This has been attributed in part to the breakdown of family ties in those cultures (Millon, 2000).

personality disorder
A psychological disorder characterized by enduring, inflexible, maladaptive patterns of behavior.

borderline personality disorder (BPD)
A personality disorder marked by impulsivity, unstable moods, an inconsistent sense of identity, and difficulty maintaining intimate relationships.

The Nature of Borderline Personality Disorder

The hallmark symptoms of people with BPD include impulsivity, unstable moods, an inconsistent sense of identity, and difficulty maintaining fulfilling intimate relationships. Their impulsivity leads them into unwise behavior regarding sex, eating, driving, gambling, and spending (Links, Heslegrave, & van Reekum, 1999). They can be in a friendly, lighthearted mood and suddenly become angry and vindictive for no apparent reason. Their sense of identity can be grandiose one moment and marked by suicidal self-loathing the next.

People with BPD will desperately seek intimacy, only to run away when they find it. In romance, they can be charming and ingratiating at first contact only to become hostile and manipulative when true intimacy beckons. The chief reason for this is that people with BPD desire love but are terrified at being engulfed by an intimate relationship. So they vacillate between clinging to their romantic partner and pushing their lover away. This often leads to a romantic life marked by stormy, short-term relationships. Because of their inability to maintain healthy intimate relationships, people with BPD tend to feel painfully alone (Pazzagli & Monti, 2000).

Causes of Borderline Personality Disorder

BPD affects 2 percent of the population. Many studies have found that BPD is more common among women, but these findings are controversial. The higher incidence of the disorder in women might reflect the greater incidence of sexual abuse of female infants and girls, because there is a strong relationship between BPD and sexual abuse (Zanarini et al., 2000). The child who has been sexually, physically, or emotionally abused develops a powerful conflict between her or his normal need for closeness and attachment and fear of the pain that it might bring (Sable, 1997). There also is evidence of a biological basis for BPD. For example, people with BPD tend to have smaller (Lyoo, Han, & Cho, 1998) and less active (De La Fuente, 1997) frontal lobes. Whether this contributes to BPD is unknown.

Antisocial Personality Disorder

Until the recent surge of interest in BPD, the personality disorder of greatest interest to the general public was **antisocial personality disorder,** perhaps because it has been implicated in many notorious criminal cases. Between 1972 and 1978, John Wayne Gacy murdered 33 boys and young men and buried them under his house. After his capture, Gacy expressed no remorse and, instead, reported that the cold-blooded murders had given him pleasure. Gacy's personal history indicated he had antisocial personality disorder.

The Nature of Antisocial Personality Disorder

Antisocial personality disorder is found in about 3 percent of American men and less than 1 percent of American women. The disorder is characterized by maladaptive behavior beginning in childhood. This includes lying, stealing, truancy, vandalism, fighting, drug abuse, and physical cruelty. Adults with an antisocial personality do not conform to social norms. They might fail to hold a job, to honor financial obligations, or to fulfill parental responsibilities.

Two hallmarks of the antisocial personality are impulsive behavior, such as reckless driving or promiscuous sexual relations, and a remarkable lack of guilt for the pain and suffering they inflict on others (Rogers et al., 1994). In extreme cases, people with an antisocial personality engage in criminal activities, yet fail to change their behavior even after being punished for it. Robert Hare, a noted researcher on antisocial personality disorder, has found that, fortunately for society, criminals with an antisocial personality tend to "burn out" after age 40 and commit fewer crimes than do other criminals (Hare, McPherson, & Forth, 1988).

Causes of Antisocial Personality Disorder

Antisocial personality disorder has been subjected to more research than other personality disorders. Thomas Bouchard's University of Minnesota study of identical twins who were separated in infancy and then reunited years later (see Chapter 13) indicates that the antisocial personality has a genetic basis (Grove et al., 1990). Heredity seems to provide people who develop an antisocial personality with an unusually low level of physiological reactivity to

Personality Disorders
www.mhhe.com/sdorow5

antisocial personality disorder
A personality disorder marked by impulsive, manipulative, often criminal behavior, without any feelings of guilt in the perpetrator.

sources of stress, most notably physical punishment (Arnett et al., 1993). A recent MRI study found that men with antisocial personality disorder showed an 11 percent reduction in prefrontal gray matter compared to controls. The researchers believe that this deficit in the frontal lobe might underlie the low arousal, lack of conscience, and poor decision making that characterizes antisocial personality disorder (Raine et al., 2000).

But what makes one person with a low level of physiological arousal seek thrills through auto racing and another seek thrills through robbing banks? In explaining antisocial personality disorder, psychoanalysts stress the influence of abusive parents or physically absent parents, who make the child feel rejected. Because such children have no emotional ties to their parents, they fail to develop an adequate superego, including a conscience. Behaviorists believe that antisocial personality disorder is caused by parents who reward, or fail to punish, their children for engaging in antisocial behaviors such as lying, stealing, or aggression.

STAYING ON TRACK: *Personality Disorders*

1. What would be some signs that the person you are dating has borderline personality disorder?
2. Why do you think antisocial personality disorder at one time was called "moral insanity"?

Answers to Staying on Track start on p. ST-7.

Chapter Summary

THE NATURE OF PSYCHOLOGICAL DISORDERS

- Researchers in the field of psychopathology study psychological disorders.
- The criteria for determining the presence of a psychological disorder include abnormality, maladaptiveness, and personal distress.
- Though the insanity defense is rarely used and even more rarely successful in criminal cases, it has sparked controversy over concern that people guilty of violent crimes might escape punishment.
- The major viewpoints on the causes of psychological disorders include the biopsychological, psychoanalytic, behavioral, cognitive, humanistic, and social-cultural viewpoints.
- The more recent diathesis-stress viewpoint sees psychological disorders as products of the interaction between a biological predisposition and stressful life experiences.
- The *Diagnostic and Statistical Manual of Mental Disorders*, fourth edition (*DSM-IV*), published by the American Psychiatric Association, is the standard for classifying psychological disorders.
- Some psychologists and psychiatrists have questioned the reliability and validity of the *DSM-IV*.
- Psychologist David Rosenhan and psychiatrist Thomas Szasz have noted certain dangers involved in diagnosing psychological disorders.

ANXIETY DISORDERS

- Anxiety disorders are associated with anxiety that is intense and disruptive of everyday functioning.
- A generalized anxiety disorder is marked by a constant state of anxiety that exists independently of any particular stressful situation.
- People with obsessions and compulsions that interfere with their daily functioning suffer from obsessive-compulsive disorder.

- An obsession is a persistent, recurring thought, and a compulsion is a repetitive action that one feels compelled to perform.
- A panic disorder is marked by sudden attacks of overwhelming anxiety, accompanied by dizziness, trembling, cold sweats, heart palpitations, shortness of breath, fear of dying, and fear of going crazy.
- Phobias are excessive or inappropriate fears.
- A specific phobia involves a specific object or situation; a social phobia involves fear of public scrutiny; and agoraphobia involves fear of being in public places.

DISSOCIATIVE DISORDERS

- In a dissociative disorder, the person's conscious awareness becomes separated from certain aspects of her or his thoughts, feelings, and memories.
- A person with dissociative amnesia is unable to recall personally significant memories.
- A person with dissociative fugue suffers from dissociative amnesia and loss of identity and flees from home.
- A person with a dissociative identity disorder has two or more distinct personalities that might vie for dominance.

MOOD DISORDERS

- Mood disorders involve prolonged periods of extreme depression or elation, often unrelated to objective circumstances.
- People with major depression experience depression that is so intense and prolonged that it causes severe distress and disrupts their lives.
- In cases of major depression, suicide is always a concern.
- People who attempt suicide usually give warnings, so suicidal threats should be taken seriously.

- In bipolar disorder, the person alternates between periods of mania and major depression.
- Mania is characterized by euphoria, hyperactivity, grandiose ideas, annoying talkativeness, wild optimism, and inflated self-esteem.

SCHIZOPHRENIA
- Schizophrenia is characterized by a severe disruption of perception, cognition, emotionality, behavior, and social relationships.
- The most serious kind of schizophrenia is disorganized schizophrenia, marked by a complete collapse of the personality and the intellect.
- Catatonic schizophrenia is marked by unusual motor behavior.

- Paranoid schizophrenia is marked by hallucinations, delusions, suspiciousness, and argumentativeness.

PERSONALITY DISORDERS
- Personality disorders are long-standing, inflexible, maladaptive patterns of behavior.
- Of growing concern is the prevalence of borderline personality disorder, marked by emotional instability and severely maladaptive social relationships.
- Of greatest concern is antisocial personality disorder, associated with lying, stealing, fighting, drug abuse, physical cruelty, and lack of responsibility.

Key Concepts

Key Contributors

Thought Questions

1. How would the three criteria for diagnosing psychological disorders be applied to agoraphobia?
2. Why might public concern about the use of the insanity defense in criminal cases be overblown?

3. A student becomes overwhelmed with anxiety when he is faced with major exams. How might the different viewpoints on psychological disorders explain this reaction?

Possible Answers to Thought Questions start on p. PT-4

OLC Preview

 For additional quizzing and a variety of interactive resources, visit the book's Online Learning Center at www.mhhe.com/sdorow5.

Therapy

GAYLE RAY
The Armour

From 1880 to 1882, Austrian physician Josef Breuer (1842–1925) treated a wealthy, intelligent, young woman he called Anna O. who suffered from *conversion hysteria*—that is, physical symptoms without any evident physical cause (van der Kolk, 2000). Her symptoms apparently were triggered by her difficulty in dealing with her father's terminal illness. She displayed a variety of symptoms that came and went, including eye squinting, loss of speaking ability, and paralyzed arms and legs.

Breuer found that when Anna O. spoke freely about her condition—at times under hypnosis—her symptoms disappeared. She called this her "talking cure" or "chimney sweeping." As she spoke, she often recalled distressing childhood experiences that had been repressed, sometimes violently reexperiencing the emotions she had felt in childhood. By talking about her feelings and experiences, she obtained emotional release, typically followed by the disappearance of her physical symptoms. Breuer called this process of emotional release **catharsis.** His treatment of Anna O. marked the beginning of modern psychotherapy. Breuer related the story of Anna O. to his young friend Sigmund Freud, who was so impressed by Breur's approach that he began to use it himself. This led to the founding of psychoanalysis, which Freud always attributed to his mentor, Breuer.

As for Anna O., she led a rich, productive life under her real name, Bertha Pappenheim (1859–1936). She became a founder of the social work profession (Swenson, 1994) and championed the rights of the poor. Pappenheim also was an early feminist and wrote *A Woman's Right,* a play that denounced the exploitation of women (Kimball, 2000). Bertha Pappenheim's life is testimony to the power of psychotherapy to help individuals overcome psychological disorders and live full lives. At some time in your life you might develop a psychological disorder that leads you to seek professional help. If this happens, you will be in good company. Since the 1950s the percentage of Americans who seek psychotherapy during their lifetime has doubled (VandenBos, 1996).

▲ Bertha Pappenheim (1859–1936)

catharsis
In psychoanalysis, the release of repressed emotional energy as a consequence of insight into the unconscious causes of one's psychological problems.

◆ THE HISTORY OF THERAPY

The treatment of psychological disorders has come a long way since its ancient origins. Treatment practices have been influenced by their cultural, religious, and scientific contexts. If you visit the Smithsonian Institution in Washington, D.C., you will encounter a display of Stone Age skulls with holes that were cut into them with stones—in the ancient practice of **trephining.** Some authorities assume that these ancient trephiners believed that they were releasing demons that caused abnormal behavior. Of course, without written records there is no way to know if this was the true reason. Perhaps, instead, trephining was performed for some unknown medical purpose.

Greek philosopher Hippocrates (460–377 B.C.) turned away from supernatural explanations of psychological disorders in favor of naturalistic explanations. Hippocrates believed that many psychological disorders were caused by imbalances in fluids that he called humors, which included blood, phlegm, black bile, and yellow bile, and he recommended treatments aimed at restoring their balance. For example, because Hippocrates believed that an excess of blood caused the agitated state of mania, he treated mania with bloodletting. As you would expect, people weakened by the loss of blood became less agitated.

During the early Christian era, such naturalistic treatments existed side by side with supernatural ones. But by the late Middle Ages, treatments increasingly involved physical punishment. This inhumane treatment continued into the Renaissance, which also saw the advent of *insane asylums.* Though some of these institutions were pleasant communities in which residents received humane treatment, most were no better than prisons in which

Pre-Columbian Trephination
www.mhhe.com/sdorow5

trephining
An ancient technique in which sharp stones were used to chip holes in the skull, possibly to let out evil spirits that supposedly caused abnormal behavior.

▲ Trephining

These skulls show the effect of trephining, in which sharp rocks were used to chip holes in the skull. Some authorities believe this was to let out evil spirits that supposedly caused bizarre thinking and behavior. The growth of new bone around the holes in some trephined skulls indicates that many people survived the surgery.

moral therapy

An approach to therapy, developed by Philippe Pinel, that provided mental patients with humane treatment.

psychotherapy

The treatment of psychological disorders through psychological means generally involving verbal interaction with a professional therapist.

inmates lived under deplorable conditions. The most humane asylum was the town of Geel in Belgium, where people with mental disorders lived in the homes of townspeople, moved about freely, and worked to support themselves. In the 1990s, Geel continued to provide humane care for 800 individuals living with 600 families (Godemont, 1992).

Few Renaissance asylums were as pleasant as Geel. The most notorious was St. Mary's of Bethlehem in London. This was a nightmarish place where inmates were treated like animals in a zoo. On weekends, families would go on outings to the asylum, pay a small admission fee, and be entertained by the antics of the inmates. Visitors called the male inmates of St. Mary's "Tom Fools," contributing the word *tomfoolery* to our language. And the asylum became known as "Bedlam" (Hattori, 1995), reflecting the cockney pronunciation of Bethlehem.

In 1792, inhumane conditions in French insane asylums and the positive model of Geel spurred physician Philippe Pinel (1745–1826) to institute what he called **moral therapy** at the Bicêtre asylum in Paris (Weiner, 1992). Moral therapy was based on the premise that humane treatment, honest work, and pleasant recreation would promote mental well-being. Pinel had the inmates unchained, provided with good food, and treated with kindness. He even instituted the revolutionary technique of speaking with them about their problems. The first inmate released was a giant, powerful man who had been chained in a dark cell for 40 years after killing a cruel guard with a blow from his manacles. Onlookers were surprised (and relieved) when he simply strolled outside, gazed up at the sky, and exclaimed, "Ah, how beautiful" (Bromberg, 1954, p. 83).

Pinel's moral therapy spread throughout Europe. It was introduced to the United States by Benjamin Rush (1745–1813), the founder of American psychiatry. As part of moral therapy, Rush prescribed work, music, and travel (Farr, 1994). He also prescribed physical treatments that with hindsight we might view as barbaric, but he believed had therapeutic value (see Figure 15.1). For example, because Rush assumed depressed people had too little blood in their brains, he whirled them around in special chairs to force blood from their bodies into their heads. One can imagine that, much as an amusement park ride can do today, this induced a temporary feeling of elation.

In the 1840s Dorothea Dix (1802–1887), a Massachusetts schoolteacher, shocked the U.S. Congress with reports of the brutal treatment of the inmates confined to insane asylums. Due to her efforts, many state mental hospitals were built throughout the United States, usually in rural settings, that provided good food, social activities, and employment on farms. Though Canadian asylums were influenced more by Britain and France (Sussman, 1998), Dix's efforts also prompted Canadian reforms, including the establishment of the first mental hospital in Nova Scotia (Goldman, 1990). Unfortunately, over time many of these mental hospitals became human warehouses, providing little more than custodial care. This contradicted the humane treatment Dix had envisioned for asylum residents.

Today, specially trained professionals offer therapy for psychological disorders. Psychological therapy, or **psychotherapy,** involves the therapeutic interaction of a professional therapist with one or more persons suffering from a psychological disorder. Though there are many approaches to psychotherapy, most psychotherapists favor an *eclectic orientation,* in which they select techniques from different kinds of therapy they believe will help particular clients.

▶ Figure 15.1
19th-Century Treatment Devices

Benjamin Rush invented *(a)* the "tranquilizing chair" to calm manic patients. Other devices that were popular in the 19th century included *(b)* the "crib," which was used to restrain violent patients, and *(c)* the "circulating swing," which was used to restore balance to allegedly out-of-balance body fluids.

(a)

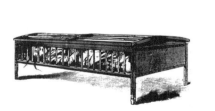

(b)

(c)

A recent trend in psychotherapy is increased attention to social-cultural factors that might influence the course of therapy. For example, the 1999 National Multicultural Conference and Summit was a collaborative attempt by psychologists to address social-cultural variables relevant to the practice of psychology—culture, ethnicity, gender, and sexual orientation. The focus of the conference was the implementation of *cultural competence* in psychological training, research, and clinical practice (Sue et al., 1999). According to Stanley Sue, cultural competence is the "belief that people should not only appreciate and recognize other cultural groups but also be able to effectively work with them" (Sue, 1998, p. 440). Thus, cultural competence consists of cultural knowledge and the interpersonal skills to effectively use this knowledge.

In part, the need for cultural competence is driven by changing demographics—by the year 2050, about 50 percent of Americans will be members of ethnic minority groups. Therapists need to be aware of cultural differences in beliefs and behaviors they may encounter in therapy. For example, members of Western cultures disclose intimate details more readily than do members of Asian cultures (Toukmanian & Brouwers, 1998). Failure to understand this could affect assessment, the development of an empathetic relationship, and the effective provision of treatment. The University of South Dakota's clinical psychology training program for Native Americans, The Four Winds, is an example of how cultural competence can be incorporated into the psychological curriculum and clinical practice. The program aims to increase the number of Native American psychotherapists and the availability of culturally sensitive psychotherapists to serve that ethnic group (Yutrzenka, Todd-Bazemore, & Caraway, 1999).

STAYING ON TRACK: *The History of Therapy*

1. Does the existence of trephined skulls necessarily mean that trephining was performed to release evil spirits?
2. What were some of the basic techniques used in moral therapy?

Answers to Staying on Track start on p. ST-7.

◆ THE PSYCHOANALYTIC ORIENTATION

As you read at the beginning of this chapter, psychoanalysis grew out of Josef Breuer's case study of Anna O. Though Breuer was the first to describe this "talking cure," it was Sigmund Freud who elaborated it into a system of psychotherapy.

The Nature of Psychoanalysis

Freud found that childhood emotional conflicts repressed into the unconscious mind cause the symptoms of psychological disorders, including conversion hysteria. Freud's aim was to make the person gain insight into his or her repressed conflicts, thereby inducing catharsis and relieving the underlying conflict. This led Freud to develop the form of therapy known as **psychoanalysis.** Traditional Freudian psychoanalysis takes place with the client reclining on a couch and the therapist sitting nearby, just out of sight. Freud claimed that this arrangement relaxes the client, thereby reducing the client's inhibitions about discussing emotional topics. Traditional Freudian psychoanalysts might see clients three to five times a week for years.

Techniques in Psychoanalysis

An important goal of psychoanalytic techniques is to make the client's unconscious conflicts conscious. To accomplish this, the therapist actively *interprets* the significance of what the client says. The therapist's interpretations are based on the analysis of *free associations, resistances, dreams,* and *transference.*

▲ **Dorothea Dix (1802–1887)**
"Were I to recount the one hundreth part of the shocking scenes of sorrow, suffering, abuse, and degradation to which I have been witness—searched out in jails, in poorhouses, in pens and block-houses, in caves, in cages and cells, in dungeons and cellars; men and women in chains, frantic, bruised, lacerated, and debased, your souls would grow sick at the horrid recital."

psychoanalysis

A type of psychotherapy, developed by Sigmund Freud, aimed at uncovering the unconscious causes of psychological disorders.

 Psychoanalysis
www.mhhe.com/sdorow5

▲ **Josef Breuer (1842–1925)**
"In 1880 I had observed a patient suffering from a severe hysteria, who in the course of her illness displayed such peculiar symptoms as to convince me that here a glimpse was being offered into deeper layers of psychopathological processes."

Analysis of Free Associations

The main technique of psychoanalysis is the **analysis of free associations,** which has much in common with Anna O.'s "talking cure." In free association, the client is urged to report any thoughts or feelings that come to mind—no matter how trivial or embarrassing they seem. Freud assumed, based on the principle of psychic determinism (see Chapter 1), that free association would unlock meaningful information related to the client's psychological disorder (Busch, 1994).

analysis of free associations
In psychoanalysis, the process by which the therapist interprets the underlying meaning of the client's uncensored reports of anything that comes to mind.

Analysis of Resistances

In the **analysis of resistances,** the psychoanalyst notes behaviors that interfere with therapeutic progress. Signs of resistance include arriving late, missing sessions, abruptly changing topics, and talking about insignificant things. The client holds on dearly to resistances to block awareness of painful memories or conflicts. By interpreting the meaning of the client's resistances, the therapist helps the client uncover these unconscious memories and conflicts. Suppose a client changes the topic whenever the therapist asks him about his father. The therapist might interpret this as a sign that the client has unconscious emotional conflicts regarding his father. But resistances might also indicate that the client simply does not trust the therapist's approach to therapy (Rennie, 1994).

analysis of resistances
In psychoanalysis, the process by which the therapist interprets client behaviors that interfere with therapeutic progress toward uncovering unconscious conflicts.

Analysis of Dreams

Freud believed that the **analysis of dreams** was the "royal road to the unconscious" (see Chapter 6). He claimed that dreams symbolize unconscious sexual and aggressive conflicts. Having the client free-associate about the content of a series of dreams allows the psychoanalyst to interpret the symbolic, or *manifest,* content of the client's dreams to reveal the true, or *latent,* content—their true meaning.

analysis of dreams
In psychoanalysis, the process by which the therapist interprets the symbolic, manifest content of dreams to reveal their true, latent content to the client.

Analysis of Transference

The key to a psychoanalytic cure is the **analysis of transference.** Transference is the client's tendency to act toward the therapist in the way she or he acts toward important people in everyday life, such as a boss, lover, parent, or teacher. Transference can be positive or negative. In *positive transference* the client expresses feelings of approval and affection toward the therapist. In *negative transference* the client expresses feelings of disapproval and rejection toward the therapist—such as criticizing the therapist's skill. By interpreting transference, the therapist helps the client gain insight into the earlier interpersonal origins of her or his current emotional problems.

analysis of transference
In psychoanalysis, the process by which the therapist interprets the feelings expressed by the client toward the therapist as being indicative of the feelings typically expressed by the client toward important people in his or her personal life.

Offshoots of Psychoanalysis

Traditional Freudian psychoanalysis inspired many offshoots. Nonetheless, psychoanalysis, in its various forms, went from being the choice of most therapists in the 1950s to being the choice of about 15 percent in the 1980s (Smith, 1982). One of the main reasons for this declining trend is that other, less costly and less lengthy, therapies are at least as effective as psychoanalysis (Fisher & Greenberg, 1985).

Today few therapists are strict Freudians. Instead, many practice what is called *psychodynamic therapy*, which employs aspects of psychoanalysis in face-to-face, once-a-week therapy lasting months instead of years. Psychodynamic therapists also rely more on discussions of past and present social relationships than on trying to uncover unconscious emotional conflicts. Psychodynamic therapy has proved effective in the treatment of a variety of psychological disorders (Goldfried, Greenberg, & Marmar, 1990).

STAYING ON TRACK: *The Psychoanalytic Orientation*

1. How do psychoanalysts employ the analysis of free associations?
2. How do psychoanalysts employ the analysis of resistances?

Answers to Staying on Track start on p. ST-7.

◆ THE BEHAVIORAL ORIENTATION

In 1952 British psychologist Hans Eysenck coined the term **behavior therapy** to refer to treatments that favor changing maladaptive behaviors rather than providing insight into unconscious conflicts. Unlike traditional psychoanalysts, behavior therapists ignore unconscious conflicts, emphasize present behavior, and assume that therapy can be accomplished in weeks or months. To behavior therapists, abnormal behavior—like normal behavior—is learned and therefore can be unlearned. Behavior therapists change maladaptive behaviors by applying the principles of classical conditioning, operant conditioning, and social-learning theory (see Chapter 7). In practice, behavior therapists often combine various behavioral techniques in their practices.

behavior therapy
The therapeutic application of the principles of learning to change maladaptive behaviors.

 Association for the Advancement of Behavior Therapy: For the General Public
www.mhhe.com/sdorow5

Classical-Conditioning Therapies

Several kinds of behavior therapy have been derived from Ivan Pavlov's work on classical conditioning. In classical conditioning, a stimulus associated with another stimulus that elicits a response might itself come to elicit that response (see Chapter 7). Therapies based on classical conditioning stress the importance of stimuli in controlling behavior. The goal of these therapies is the removal of the stimuli that control maladaptive behaviors or the promotion of more adaptive responses to those stimuli.

Counterconditioning

The classical-conditioning technique of **counterconditioning** replaces unpleasant emotional responses to stimuli with pleasant ones, or vice versa (Paunovic, 1999). The procedure is based on the assumption that we cannot simultaneously experience an unpleasant feeling, such as anxiety, and a pleasant feeling, such as relaxation. Therapeutic counterconditioning was introduced by John B. Watson's student Mary Cover Jones (1896–1987). Watson had conditioned a boy he called Little Albert to fear a white rat by pairing the rat with a loud sound (see Chapter 7). Watson proposed that the fear could be eliminated by pairing the rat with a pleasant stimulus, such as pleasurable stroking. Jones (1924) took Watson's suggestion and, under his advisement, tried to rid a 3-year-old boy named Peter of a rabbit phobia. Jones used what is now known as counterconditioning. Jones presented Peter with candy and then brought a caged rabbit closer and closer to him. This was done twice a day for 2 months.

counterconditioning
A behavior therapy technique that applies the principles of classical conditioning to replace unpleasant emotional responses to stimuli with more pleasant ones.

systematic desensitization

A form of counterconditioning that trains the client to maintain a state of relaxation in the presence of imagined anxiety-inducing stimuli.

in vivo desensitization

A form of counterconditioning that trains the client to maintain a state of relaxation in the presence of anxiety-inducing stimuli.

aversion therapy

A form of behavior therapy that inhibits maladaptive behavior by pairing a stimulus that normally elicits a maladaptive response with an unpleasant stimulus.

▲ In Vivo Desensitization

A phobia sufferer might gain relief through in vivo desensitization, which involves gradual exposure to more and more anxiety-inducing situations related to the phobia. This man, suffering from a fear of heights (acrophobia), might have begun therapy by simply looking out of a first-floor window. He has progressed to the point that he is able to walk onto the roof of a tall building. But note that he still holds tightly to the ledge. He should eventually be able to peer over the ledge without having to grasp it.

At first Peter cried when the rabbit was within 20 feet of him. Over the course of the two months, he became less and less fearful of it. On the last day he asked for the rabbit, petted it, tried to pick it up, and finally played with it. Evidently, the pleasant feelings Peter experienced in response to the candy gradually became associated with the rabbit. This reduced his fear of the rabbit. Jones cautioned, however, that this was a delicate procedure. If performed too rapidly, it could produce the opposite effect—fear of the candy.

Systematic Desensitization

Today the most widely used form of counterconditioning is **systematic desensitization,** developed by Joseph Wolpe (1958) for treating phobias. Systematic desensitization involves three steps. The first step is for the client to practice *progressive relaxation,* a technique developed in the 1930s by Edmund Jacobson to relieve anxiety. To learn progressive relaxation, clients sit in a comfortable chair and practice successively tensing and relaxing each of the major muscle groups until they gain the ability to relax their entire body.

The second step is the construction of an *anxiety hierarchy,* consisting of a series of anxiety-inducing scenes related to the person's phobia. The client lists 10 to 20 scenes, rating them on a 100-point scale from least to most anxiety inducing. A rating of zero would mean that the scene induces no anxiety; a rating of 100 would mean that the scene induces abject terror. Suppose that you have *arachnophobia*—spider phobia. You might rate a photo of a spider a 5, a spider on your arm a 60, and a spider on your face an 85.

The third step involves imagining each of the anxiety-inducing stimuli in the anxiety hierarchy while relaxing. The therapist would start with the scene with the lowest rating, moving along the hierarchy from least to most threatening. For example, you first would learn to relax while imagining holding a photo of a spider. Once the relaxation response had been reliably conditioned to this stimulus, the therapist would move to the next scene on the anxiety hierarchy. In this way the new response, relaxation, would become conditioned to each of the anxiety-inducing stimuli.

Systematic desensitization has been successful in treating a wide variety of phobias. These include fear of flying (Rothbaum et al., 1996), dentists (Klepac, 1986), and public speaking (Rossi & Seiler, 1989–1990). Given the success of systematic desensitization in treating phobias, what accounts for its effectiveness? For one possible answer, read the Anatomy of a Research Study feature.

Of course, the ultimate test of systematic desensitization is the ability to face the actual source of your phobia. One way to ensure such success is to use **in vivo desensitization,** which physically exposes the client to successive situations on the client's anxiety hierarchy. In vivo desensitization has been successful in treating claustrophobia (Edinger & Radtke, 1993), school phobia (Houlihan & Jones, 1989), and many other kinds of phobias.

Aversion Therapy

The goal of **aversion therapy** is to make a formerly pleasurable, but maladaptive, behavior unpleasant. In aversion therapy, a stimulus that normally elicits a maladaptive response is paired with an unpleasant stimulus, leading to a reduction in the maladaptive response. Aversion therapy has been used to treat a variety of behavioral problems, including smoking, bedwetting, and overeating.

Anatomy of a Research Study

Do Endorphins Mediate the Effect of Systematic Desensitization on Phobias?

Rationale

Might systematic desensitization exert its effects through the actions of endorphins? Perhaps pleasurable feelings induced by endorphins can counter phobic anxiety. This was the rationale behind a study conducted by Kelly Egan, John Carr, Daniel Hunt, and Richard Adamson of the University of Washington (Egan et al., 1988).

Method

Participants all suffered from specific phobias (see Chapter 14), such as fear of heights, fear of dogs, and fear of elevators. Using a double-blind procedure, participants were randomly assigned into 2 groups. Prior to sessions of systematic desensitization, participants in the experimental group received intravenous infusions of naloxone, a drug that blocks the effect of endorphins, and participants in the control group received intravenous infusions of a placebo, a saline solution with no specific effects. Participants received 8 sessions over a period of 4 weeks.

Results and Discussion

The results indicated that participants who received the placebo experienced a significant decrease in the severity of their phobias, whereas those who received naloxone did not. Because naloxone blocks the effects of the endorphins, the results support the possible role of endorphins in the effects of systematic desensitization. The pleasant feelings produced by the endorphins might become conditioned to the formerly fear-inducing stimuli.

But aversion therapy was originally introduced in the 1930s to treat alcoholism by administering painful electric shocks to alcoholic patients in the presence of the sight, smell, and taste of alcohol. Today aversion therapy for alcoholism uses drugs that make the individual feel deathly ill after drinking alcohol. The drugs interfere with the metabolism of alcohol, leading to the buildup of a toxic chemical that induces nausea and dizziness. A study of more than 400 alcoholic patients who underwent a treatment program that included aversion therapy found that 60 percent were abstinent a year later (Smith & Frawley, 1993).

Operant-Conditioning Therapies

Treatments based on operant conditioning modify maladaptive behaviors by controlling their consequences. This is based on the work of learning theorist B. F. Skinner. Popular forms of behavior modification rely on the behavioral contingencies of positive reinforcement, punishment, and extinction.

Positive Reinforcement

One of the most important uses of positive reinforcement has been in treating patients in mental hospitals. Residents of mental hospitals have traditionally relied on the staff to take care of all their needs. This often leads to passivity, a decrease in self-care, and a general decline in dignified behavior.

The development of the *token economy* provided a way to overcome this problem. The **token economy** provides tokens (often plastic poker chips) as positive reinforcement for desirable behaviors, such as making beds, taking showers, or wearing appropriate clothing. The patients use the tokens to purchase items such as books or candy and privileges such as television or passes to leave the hospital grounds. The use of token economies has proved successful, for example, in reducing injurious actions and unauthorized absences of young adult residents of a mental hospital (LePage, 1999). Token economies also are employed in grade-school classes and in programs for the mentally retarded. In one study, a token economy motivated a mentally retarded man to behave in a more socially appropriate manner (LeBlanc, Hagopian, & Maglieri, 2000).

token economy
An operant conditioning procedure that uses tokens as positive reinforcers in programs designed to promote desirable behaviors, with the tokens later used to purchase desired items or privileges.

► Figure 15.2
Modeling and Phobias

People might learn to overcome their phobias by observing other people either handle objects they are afraid to handle or perform in situations in which they are afraid to perform. The graph shows the results of a study comparing the effectiveness of three kinds of therapy for snake phobia. The control group received no therapy. As you can see, all three therapies produced more approaches to the snakes than did the control condition. But participant modeling produced more improvement than did symbolic modeling (in which participants watched models on film) or systematic desensitization (Bandura, Blanchard, & Ritter, 1969).

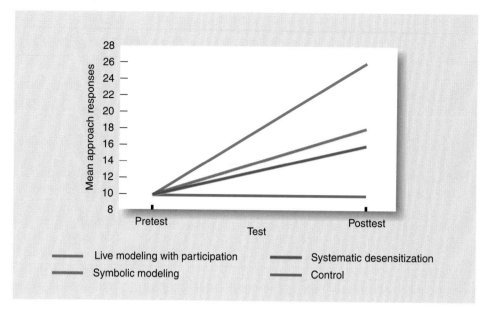

flooding

An extinction procedure in which a phobic client is exposed to a stimulus that evokes intense anxiety.

Punishment

Though less desirable than positive reinforcement, punishment can be effective in changing maladaptive behaviors. In fact, sometimes it is the only way to prevent inappropriate, or even dangerous, behavior. In using punishment, the therapist provides aversive consequences for maladaptive behavior. A controversial application of punishment has been the use of mild electric shocks to reduce self-biting, head banging, and other self-destructive behaviors in autistic children, who do not respond to talk therapy. *Autism* is a disorder marked by social withdrawal and language difficulties. Before using punishments such as mild electric shocks, therapists must first present their rationale and gain approval from parents and fellow professionals. Once the self-injurious behavior has stopped, the therapist uses positive reinforcement to promote more appropriate behaviors. The combination of punishment and positive reinforcement has been effective in improving the behavior of autistic children (Lovass, 1987).

Extinction

If a behavior is not reinforced, whether adaptive or maladaptive, it will become extinguished. The technique of *flooding* takes advantage of this in the elimination of intense fears and phobias. Unlike systematic desensitization, which trains the client to relax and experience a graded series of anxiety-inducing situations, **flooding** exposes the client to a situation that evokes intense anxiety. In *imaginal flooding,* the client is asked to hold in mind an image of the feared situation; in *in vivo flooding,* the client is placed in the actual feared situation. As clients experience the situation mentally or in reality, their anxiety diminishes because they are prevented from escaping and thereby negatively reinforcing their flight behavior through fear reduction. Of course, care must be taken to protect the client from being overwhelmed by fear. Flooding has helped clients overcome anxiety disorders such as noise phobia (Houlihan et al., 1993), panic disorder (Fava et al., 1991), and posttraumatic stress disorder (Foa et al., 1999).

Social-Learning Therapies

In treating Peter's rabbit phobia, Mary Cover Jones (1924) sometimes let Peter observe children playing with a rabbit. By doing so, Jones made use of social learning (see Chapter 7). Therapists who use social learning have their clients watch other people model adaptive behaviors either in person or on videotape. Clients learn better social skills or to overcome phobias by performing the modeled behavior (see Figure 15.2). Therapists also might use

participant modeling, in which the therapist models the desired behavior while the client watches. The client then tries to perform the behavior. Participant modeling has been successful in helping individuals overcome their fears, including fears of spiders (Mineka et al., 1999) and hypodermic injections (Trijsburg et al., 1996).

STAYING ON TRACK: *The Behavioral Orientation*

1. How would you use systematic desensitization to treat a student who is terrified of making oral presentations in class?
2. How would you use a token economy to improve spelling and arithmetic performance by third-graders?

Answers to Staying on Track start on p. ST-7.

participant modeling

A form of social-learning therapy in which the client learns to perform more adaptive behaviors by first observing the therapist model the desired behaviors.

◆ THE COGNITIVE ORIENTATION

Cognitive therapists believe that events in themselves do not cause maladaptive emotions and behaviors. Instead, these arise from our interpretation of events. Given this assumption, cognitive therapists believe that changes in thinking can produce changes in maladaptive emotions or behaviors. Because cognitive therapies can include aspects of behavior therapy, they are commonly called *cognitive-behavior therapies.* They have been effective in treating many kinds of disorders, including social phobia (Cottraux et al., 2000) and panic disorder (Stuart, Treat, & Wade, 2000).

Rational-Emotive Behavior Therapy

Albert Ellis (1962) developed the first cognitive therapy, which he called *rational-emotive therapy (R-E-T).* He more recently renamed it **rational-emotive behavior therapy (R-E-B-T)** to emphasize the interaction of thinking, feeling, and behaving in psychological well-being (Ellis, 1999). A survey of therapists found that Ellis has been second only to Carl Rogers in his influence on the field of psychotherapy (Smith, 1982). Ellis's therapy is based on his *A-B-C theory* of emotion, in which *A* is an activating event, *B* is an irrational belief, and *C* is an emotional consequence. Ellis points out that most of us believe that *A* causes *C*, when in fact *B* causes *C*.

Imagine that you fail an exam (*A*) and become depressed (*C*). Ellis would attribute your depression not to your failure but to an irrational belief, such as the belief (*B*) that you must be perfect. Thus, your irrational belief, not your failure, causes your depression—and the behaviors it produces. Ellis has pointed out similarities between the Western practice of R-E-B-T and the Eastern practice of Zen Buddhism and urged that the two practices be integrated into an effective means of improving psychological well-being (Kwee & Ellis, 1998).

Though therapists who use R-E-B-T can develop warm, empathetic relationships with their clients, Ellis himself is more interested in demolishing, sometimes harshly, the irrational ideas of his clients. After identifying a client's irrational beliefs, Ellis challenges the client to provide evidence supporting them. Ellis then contradicts any irrational evidence, almost demanding that the client agree with him. Table 15.1 presents a verbatim transcript illustrating the use of R-E-B-T. A meta-analysis of research studies found that R-E-B-T is more effective than placebo treatment and as effective as other therapies (Engels, Garnefski, & Diekstra, 1993). It has helped people overcome depression (Macaskill & Macaskill, 1996), extreme jealousy (Ellis, 1996), and childhood sexual abuse (Rieckert & Moeller, 2000).

Cognitive Therapy

Psychiatrist Aaron Beck has found that depression is caused by negative beliefs about oneself, the world, and the future (Beck, 1997). Thus, depressed people tend to blame themselves rather than their circumstances for their misfortunes, attend more to negative events

rational-emotive behavior therapy (R-E-B-T)

A type of cognitive therapy, developed by Albert Ellis, that treats psychological disorders by forcing the client to give up irrational beliefs.

 Albert Ellis Institute
www.mhhe.com/sdorow5

Table 15.1	Rational-Emotive Therapy

This transcript illustrates how the rational-emotive therapist (T) challenges the client (C) to change irrational beliefs. The client is a 23-year-old young woman experiencing intense feelings of guilt for not living up to her parents' strict standards.

C: Well, this is the way it was in school, if I didn't do well in one particular thing, or even on a particular test—and little crises that came up—if I didn't do as well as I had wanted to do.

T: Right. You beat yourself over the head.

C: Yes.

T: But why? What's the point? Are you supposed to be perfect? Why the hell shouldn't human beings make mistakes, be imperfect?

C: Maybe you always expect yourself to be perfect.

T: Yes. But is that *sane?*

C: No.

T: Why do it? Why not give up that unrealistic expectation?

C: But then I can't accept myself.

T: But you're saying, "It's shameful to make mistakes." Why is it shameful? Why can't you go to somebody else when you make a mistake and say, "Yes, I made a mistake"? Why is that so awful? . . .

C: It might all go back to, as you said, the need for approval. If I don't make mistakes, then people will look up to me. If I do it all perfectly—

T: Yes, that's part of it. That, is the erroneous belief; that if you never make mistakes everybody will love you and that it is necessary they do. That's right. That's a big part of it. But is it true, incidentally? Suppose you never did make mistakes—*would* people love you? They'd sometimes hate your guts, wouldn't they?

Source: From Science & Behavior Books, Inc., Palo Alto, California, 1971. Reprinted by permission.

cognitive therapy

A type of therapy, developed by Aaron Beck, that aims at eliminating exaggerated negative beliefs about oneself, the world, or the future.

▲ Aaron Beck

"The depressed person has a global negative view of himself, the outside world, and the future."

than to positive events, and have a pessimistic view of the future (see Chapter 14). Depressed people also overgeneralize from rare or minor negative events in their lives. The goal of Beck's **cognitive therapy** is to change such exaggerated beliefs in treating psychological disorders, most notably depression.

Beck is less directive in his approach than Ellis is. Beck employs a Socratic technique, in which he asks clients questions that lead them to recognize their irrational beliefs. Beck has clients keep a daily record of their thoughts and urges them to note irrational beliefs and replace them with rational ones. A client who claims, "I am an awful student and will never amount to anything," might be encouraged to think, instead, "I am doing poorly in school because I do not study enough. If I change my study habits, I will graduate and pursue a desirable career." To promote positive experiences, Beck might begin by giving the client homework assignments that guarantee success, such as having a client who feels socially incompetent speak to a close friend on the telephone. Cognitive therapy has been especially successful in treating depression (Reinecke, Ryan, & DuBois, 1998). It also is effective in treating other problems, such as panic disorder (Clark et al., 1999), chronic anger (Dahlen & Deffenbacher, 2000), and obsessive-compulsive disorder (O'Connor et al., 1999).

STAYING ON TRACK: *The Cognitive Orientation*

1. What are the basic assumptions and techniques of Ellis's rational-emotive behavior therapy?
2. What are the basic assumptions and techniques of Beck's cognitive therapy?

Answers to Staying on Track start on p. ST-7.

◆ THE HUMANISTIC ORIENTATION

Unlike the psychoanalytic orientation, the *humanistic orientation* stresses the present rather than the past, and conscious, rather than unconscious, experience. Unlike the behavioral orientation, the humanistic orientation stresses the importance of subjective mental experience rather than objective environmental circumstances. And, unlike the cognitive orientation, the humanistic orientation encourages the expression of emotion rather than its control.

Person-Centered Therapy

The most popular kind of humanistic therapy is **person-centered therapy,** originally called *client-centered therapy.* It was developed in the 1950s by Carl Rogers (1902–1987) as one of the first alternatives to psychoanalysis. As noted earlier, Rogers has been the most influential of all contemporary psychotherapists (Smith, 1982). Unlike the rational-emotive behavior therapist, who is *directive* in challenging the irrational beliefs of clients, the person-centered therapist is *nondirective* in encouraging clients to find their own answers to their problems (Bozarth & Brodley, 1991). Japanese psychologists have noted the similarity between person-centered therapy and the nondirective aspects of Taoist philosophy (Hayashi et al., 1998).

Given that person-centered therapists offer no advice, how do they help their clients? Their goal is to facilitate the pursuit of self-actualization, not by offering expertise but by providing a climate in which clients feel comfortable being themselves. Person-centered therapists do so by promoting self-acceptance. Humanistic psychologists assume that psychological disorders arise from an incongruence between a person's ideal self and her or his actual self (see Chapter 14). This makes the person distort reality or deny feelings, trying to avoid the anxiety caused by failing to act in accordance with those feelings. The goal of person-centered therapy is to help individuals reduce this discrepancy by expressing and accepting their true feelings. The person-centered therapist promotes self-actualization through reflection of feelings, genuineness, accurate empathy, and unconditional positive regard (Rogers, 1957). Note that a close friend or relative whom you consider a "good listener" and valued counselor probably exhibits these characteristics, too.

Reflection of feelings is the main technique of person-centered therapy. The therapist is an active listener who serves as a therapeutic mirror, attending to the emotional content of what the client says and restating it to the client. This helps clients recognize their true feelings. By being *genuine,* the therapist acts in a concerned, open, and sincere manner rather than in a detached, closed, and phony manner. This makes clients more willing to disclose their true feelings. During his career, Rogers increasingly stressed the importance of therapist genuineness (Bozarth, 1990). The client also becomes more willing to share feelings when the therapist shows *accurate empathy,* which means that the therapist's words and actions indicate a true understanding of how the client feels (Meissner, 1996).

Perhaps the most difficult task for the person-centered therapist is the maintenance of *unconditional positive regard*—acting in a personally warm and accepting manner. The therapist must remain nonjudgmental no matter how distasteful she or he finds the client's thoughts, feelings, and actions to be. This encourages clients to freely express and deal with even the most distressing aspects of themselves. Table 15.2 presents a verbatim transcript that illustrates the use of person-centered therapy.

Gestalt Therapy

Fritz Perls (1893–1970), a former psychoanalytic psychotherapist and the founder of **Gestalt therapy,** claimed, "The idea of Gestalt therapy is to change paper people to real people" (Perls, 1973, p. 120). To Perls, paper people are out of touch with their true feelings and therefore live "inauthentic lives." Like psychoanalysis, Gestalt therapy seeks to bring unconscious feelings into conscious awareness. Like person-centered therapy, Gestalt therapy tries to increase the client's emotional expressiveness. And like rational-emotive behavior therapy, Gestalt therapy can be confrontational in forcing clients to change maladaptive ways of thinking and behaving.

Despite its name, Gestalt therapy is not derived from Gestalt psychology, which is discussed in Chapter 1, except in stressing the need to achieve wholeness of the personality—meaning

person-centered therapy
A type of humanistic therapy, developed by Carl Rogers, that helps clients find their own answers to their problems.

Gestalt therapy
A type of humanistic therapy, developed by Fritz Perls, that encourages clients to become aware of their true feelings and to take responsibility for their own actions.

Table 15.2 Person-Centered Therapy

This transcript illustrates how the person-centered therapist (T) acts as a psychological mirror, reflecting back the feelings expressed in statements by the client (C). The client feels anxious about taking responsibility for her life. Notice how the therapist is less directive than the one in the transcript of rational-emotive therapy in Table 15.1.

C: Um-hum. That's why I say . . . *(slowly and very thoughtfully)* well, with that sort of foundation, well, it's really up to me. I mean, it seems to be really apparent to me that I can't depend on someone else giving me an education. *(very softly)* I'll really have to get it myself.

T: It really begins to come home—there's only one person that can educate you— a realization that perhaps nobody else can give you an education.

C: Um-hum. *(long pause—while she sits thinking)* I have all the symptoms of fright *(laughs softly)*.

T: Fright: That this is a scary thing, is that what you mean?

C: Um-hum. *(very long pause—obviously struggling with feelings in herself)*

T: Do you want to say any more about what you mean by that? That it really does give you the symptoms of fright?

C: *(laughs)* I, uh . . . I don't know whether I quite know. I mean . . . Well, it really seems like I'm cut loose *(pause)*, and it seems that I'm very—I don't know—in a vulnerable position, but I, uh, I brought this up and it, uh, somehow it almost came out without saying it. It seems to be . . . it's something I let out.

T: Hardly a part of you.

C: Well, I felt surprised.

T: As though, "Well for goodness sake, did I say that?" *(both chuckle)*.

Source: Rogers, Carl R., *On Becoming a Person.* Copyright © 1961 by Houghton Mifflin Company. Reprinted by permission.

▲ **Fritz Perls (1893–1970)**
Fritz Perls, the founder of Gestalt therapy, was a refugee from Nazi Germany. Loyal followers were attracted to his center at Esalen Institute in Big Sur, California, in the 1960s in the hope of becoming "authentic people." Perls was a charismatic person who thought as highly of himself as did his followers, claiming, "I believe I am the best therapist for any type of neurosis in the States, maybe in the world" (Prochaska, 1984, p. 128).

that one's emotions, language, and actions should be consistent with one another (Polster & Polster, 1993). Gestalt therapists insist that clients take responsibility for their own behavior, rather than blame other people or events for their problems, and that clients live in the here and now, rather than be concerned about events occurring at other places and times. Gestalt therapists also assume that people who are aware of their feelings can exert greater control over their reactions to events. The Gestalt therapist notes any signs that the client is not being brutally honest about his or her feelings, at times by observing the client's non-verbal communication, posture, gestures, facial expressions, and tone of voice. For example, a client who denies feeling anxious while tightly clenching his fists would be accused of lying about his emotions.

STAYING ON TRACK: *The Humanistic Orientation*

1. What are the basic characteristics of person-centered therapy?
2. What are the basic characteristics of Gestalt therapy?

Answers to Staying on Track start on p. ST-7.

◆ THE SOCIAL-RELATIONS ORIENTATION

The therapeutic orientations that have been discussed so far involve a therapist and a client. In contrast, the *social-relations orientation* assumes that, because many psychological problems involve interpersonal relationships, additional people must be brought into the therapy process. Many psychotherapists insist that differences in ethnicity (Maiello, 1999), social class (Storck, 1997), and religion (Gopaul-McNicol, 1997) must be considered in any group approach to psychotherapy.

Group Therapy

In 1905 Joseph Pratt, a Boston physician, found that his tuberculosis patients gained relief from emotional distress by meeting in groups to discuss their feelings. This marked the beginning of group therapy (Allen, 1990). Because group therapy allows a therapist to see more people (typically six to twelve in a group) in less time, more people can receive help at less cost per person. Group therapy provides participants with a range of role models, encouragement from others with similar problems, feedback about their own behavior, assurance that their problems are not unique, and the opportunity to try out new behaviors. Group therapy has been used to improve the emotional well-being of cancer patients (Harman, 1991) and depression sufferers (Levkovitz et al., 2000). The procedures used in group therapy depend on the theoretical orientation of the therapist.

Transactional Analysis

Group therapies derived from psychoanalysis emphasize insight and emotional catharsis. A form of group therapy inspired by psychoanalysis is **transactional analysis (TA),** popularized in the 1960s by psychiatrist Eric Berne (1910–1970) in his best-selling book *Games People Play* (1964). Berne claimed that we act according to three roles: child, parent, or adult. These resemble the Freudian personality structures of id, superego, and ego, respectively. The *child,* like the id, acts impulsively and demands immediate gratification. The *parent,* like the superego, is authoritarian and guides moral behavior. And the *adult,* like the ego, promotes rational and responsible behavior.

Each role is adaptive in certain situations and maladaptive in others. For example, acting childish might be appropriate at parties but not at job interviews. According to Berne, our relationships involve *transactions*—social interactions between these roles. *Complementary transactions,* in which both individuals act according to the same role, are usually best. *Crossed transactions,* as when one person acts as a child and the other acts as an adult, are maladaptive. The goal of TA is to analyze transactions between group members. For example, a person might engage in transactions that support her or his feelings of worthlessness and continually provoke responses from others that support those feelings. TA has been used to treat various problems, including personality disorders (Haimowitz, 2000).

Social-Skills Training

Psychologists who favor behavioral group therapies assume that changes in overt behavior will bring relief from emotional distress. A popular form of behavioral group therapy, also used in individual therapy, is **social-skills training.** Its goal is to improve social relationships by enhancing social skills, such as cultivating friendships or carrying on conversations. Participants are encouraged to rehearse new behaviors in the group setting. Members of the group might model more effective behaviors. Social-skills training has been used to help mentally retarded people improve their social competence (Soresi & Nota, 2000) and in the treatment of social phobia (van Dam-Baggen & Kraaimaat, 2000).

A form of social-skills training called **assertiveness training** helps people learn to express their feelings constructively in social situations. Many people experience poor social relations because they are unassertive. They are unable to ask for favors, to say no to requests, or to complain about poor service. By learning to express their feelings, formerly unassertive people relieve their anxiety and have more rewarding social relations. Members of assertiveness-training groups try out assertive behaviors in the group situation. Assertiveness training has improved the communication skills and self-esteem of Taiwanese nurses (Lee & Crockett, 1994) and physically disabled adults (Glueckauf & Quittner, 1992). It also has been used to reduce risky sexual behavior in gay and bisexual men (Peterson et al., 1996).

Self-Help Groups

In the 1950s Carl Rogers introduced the encounter group, which comprised strangers who met to honestly assess their emotional and behavioral issues. The encounter group movement died out but led to the emergence of *self-help groups* for drug abusers and others with specific shared problems. For example, a recent survey of directors of substance-abuse programs

transactional analysis (TA)
A form of psychoanalytic group therapy, developed by Eric Berne, that helps clients change their immature or inappropriate ways of relating to other people.

 International Transactional Analysis Association
www.mhhe.com/sdorow5

social-skills training
A form of behavioral group therapy that improves the client's social relationships by enhancing her or his interpersonal skills.

assertiveness training
A form of social-skills training that teaches clients to express their feelings constructively.

▲ **Virginia Satir (1916–1988)**

"Any individual's behavior is a response to the complex set of regular and predictable 'rules' governing his family group, though these rules may not be consciously known to him or the family."

family therapy

A form of group therapy that encourages the constructive expression of feelings and the establishment of rules that family members agree to follow.

affiliated with the U.S. Department of Veterans Affairs found that 79 percent of their patients were referred to Alcoholics Anonymous (Humphreys, 1997). Self-help groups are conducted by people who have experienced those problems. For example, self-help groups for the elderly are often run by older adults (Gottlieb, 2000).

Family Therapy

Group therapy usually brings together unrelated people; **family therapy** brings together members of the same family. The basic assumption of family therapy is that a family member cannot be treated apart from the family. The main goals of family therapy are the constructive expression of feelings and the establishment of rules that family members agree to follow. The therapist helps family members establish an atmosphere in which no individual is blamed for all of the family's problems. As in the case of other kinds of group therapy, family therapy is paying greater attention to social-cultural factors, including ethnicity, sexual orientation, and religion (Wieling & Marshall, 1999).

Family therapists, such as the late Virginia Satir, who favor a *systems approach* might have family members draw diagrams of their relationships and discuss how certain of the relationships are maladaptive (Satir, Bitter, & Krestensen, 1988). Perhaps the family is too child-oriented, or perhaps a parent and child are allied against the other parent. The goal of the therapist is to have the family replace these maladaptive relationships with more effective ones.

STAYING ON TRACK: *The Social-Relations Orientation*

1. What are the basic assumptions and techniques of transactional analysis?
2. What are the basic characteristics of assertiveness training?

Answers to Staying on Track start on p. ST-7.

◆ THE BIOPSYCHOLOGICAL ORIENTATION

Though Sigmund Freud practiced psychoanalysis, he predicted that, as science progressed, therapies for psychological disorders would become more and more biological (Trotter, 1981). During the past few decades, the *biopsychological orientation* has, indeed, become an important approach to therapy. It is based on the assumption that psychological disorders are associated with brain dysfunctions and consequently will respond to treatments that alter brain activity. Biopsychological treatments, because they involve medical procedures, can be offered only by psychiatrists and other physicians. Biopsychological treatments include *psychosurgery, electroconvulsive therapy,* and *drug therapy.*

Psychosurgery

psychosurgery

The treatment of psychological disorders by destroying brain tissue.

The History of Psychosurgery
www.mhhe.com/sdorow5

While attending a professional meeting in 1935, Portuguese neurologist Egas Moniz was impressed by a report that agitated chimpanzees became calmer after undergoing brain surgery that separated their frontal lobes from the rest of their brain. Moniz wondered whether such **psychosurgery** might benefit agitated mental patients. Moniz convinced neurosurgeon Almeida Lima to perform a *prefrontal leucotomy* (also known as a *prefrontal lobotomy*) on anesthetized patients. Lima drilled holes in the patients' temples, inserted a scalpel through the holes, and cut away portions of the frontal lobes. Moniz reported many successes in calming agitated patients (Moniz, 1937/1994). As a result, he won a Nobel Prize in 1949 for inventing psychosurgery, which was considered a humane alternative to the common practice of locking patients in padded rooms or restraining them in straitjackets.

By 1979, psychosurgery had been performed on about 35,000 mental patients in the United States. But the use of psychosurgery declined markedly. One reason was its unpredictable effects (Swayze, 1995). A second reason for its decline was the advent of drug therapies in the 1950s and 1960s, which provided safer, more effective, and more humane treatment (Tierney, 2000). And a third reason was public opposition to what seemed to be a barbaric means of behavior control.

Today, psychosurgery is rarely used in the United States; when it is used, it more often involves the use of electrodes inserted into the limbic system. A direct current is sent through the electrodes, destroying small amounts of tissue in precise areas of that brain region. This technique has achieved some success in treating cases of obsessive-compulsive disorder that have not responded to other treatments (Baer et al., 1995).

Electroconvulsive Therapy

In 1938, on a visit to a slaughterhouse, Italian psychiatrist Ugo Cerletti watched pigs being rendered unconscious by electric shocks. Cerletti reasoned that electric shock might be a safe way to calm agitated schizophrenic patients. This inspired Cerletti to introduce **electroconvulsive therapy (ECT)**. ECT uses a brief electrical current to induce brain seizures. Though ECT was originally used for treating agitated patients, it proved more successful in elevating the mood of severely depressed patients who had failed to respond to drug therapy.

As shown in Figure 15.3, a psychiatrist administers ECT by attaching electrodes to one or both temples of a patient who is under general anesthesia and who has been given a muscle relaxant. The muscle relaxant prevents injuries that might otherwise be caused by violent contractions of the muscles. A burst of electricity is passed through the brain for about half a second. This induces a brain seizure, which is followed by a period of unconsciousness lasting up to 30 minutes. The patient typically receives three treatments a week for several weeks.

A major review of the research literature found that it is unclear whether ECT or antidepressant drugs is best in the treatment of major depression (Piper, 1993). But because ECT produces more rapid improvement than antidepressant drugs, which can take several weeks, it is the treatment of choice for depressed people in imminent danger of committing suicide (Persad, 1990). But ECT's mechanism of action is unclear. For example, its antidepressant effect is unrelated to its induction of seizures (Sackeim, 1994). Because depression is associated with low levels of norepinephrine, one explanation is that ECT stimulates an increase in the level of norepinephrine (Andrade & Sudha, 2000).

electroconvulsive therapy (ECT)
A biopsychological therapy that uses brief electric currents to induce brain seizures in victims of major depression.

 Electroconvulsive Therapy
www.mhhe.com/sdorow5

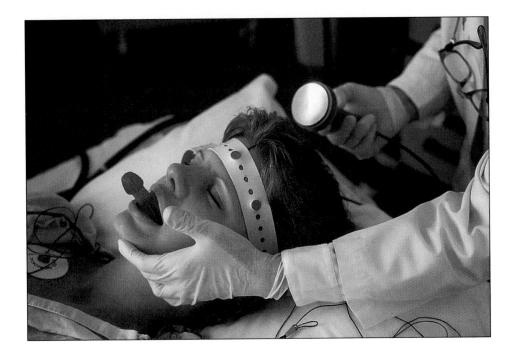

◀ **Figure 15.3**
Electroconvulsive Therapy

In electroconvulsive therapy, the patient receives a series of treatments in which a brief electric current is passed through the brain, inducing a brain seizure that relieves the person's depression through mechanisms that are still unclear.

Despite its effectiveness in relieving major depression, there has been controversy about ECT's safety and effectiveness. In the past, the violence of the convulsions induced by ECT often broke bones and tore muscles. Today, muscle relaxants prevent such injury. But ECT still causes *retrograde amnesia*—the forgetting of events that occurred from minutes to days prior to the treatment (Weiner, 2000). The debate about the desirability of using ECT remains as much emotional as scientific.

Drug Therapy

Since its introduction in the 1950s, drug therapy has become the most widely used form of biopsychological therapy. Because many psychological disorders are associated with abnormal levels of neurotransmitters (see Chapter 14), drug therapies generally work by restoring neurotransmitter activity to more normal levels. But a common criticism of drug therapies is that they might relieve symptoms without changing the person's ability to cope with stress. This means that concurrent psychotherapy is desirable to help clients learn more adaptive ways of thinking and behaving. The following discussion uses brand names for drugs, with their generic names in parentheses.

Antianxiety Drugs

antianxiety drugs
Psychoactive drugs that are used to treat anxiety disorders.

Because of their calming effect, the **antianxiety drugs** were originally called *tranquilizers.* Today the most widely prescribed are the *benzodiazepines,* such as Xanax (alprazolam) and Valium (diazepam). In fact, the prevalence of anxiety disorders has made the antianxiety drugs the most widely prescribed psychoactive drugs (Sand et al., 2000). The benzodiazepines act almost immediately and work by stimulating receptors in the brain that enhance the effects of the neurotransmitter GABA, which inhibits brain activity. The benzodiazepines can also produce side effects, including drowsiness, depression, and dependence. A new drug, Buspar (buspirone), is effective in relieving anxiety without the side effects of the benzodiazepines, but it takes up to several weeks to have an effect. Buspar works by increasing serotonin levels in the brain (Haller, Halasz, & Makara, 2000).

Antidepressant Drugs

antidepressant drugs
Psychoactive drugs that are used to treat major depression.

The first **antidepressant drugs** were the *MAO inhibitors,* such as Nardil. Originally used to treat tuberculosis, they were prescribed as antidepressants after physicians noted they induced euphoria in tuberculosis patients. The MAO inhibitors work by blocking enzymes that normally break down the neurotransmitters serotonin and norepinephrine. This increases the levels of those neurotransmitters in the brain, elevating the patient's mood. But the MAO inhibitors fell into disfavor because they can cause dangerously high blood pressure.

The MAO inhibitors gave way to the *tricyclic antidepressants,* such as Elavil (amitriptyline), Tofranil (imipramine), and Anafranil (clomipramine). The tricyclics increase serotonin and norepinephrine levels by preventing their reuptake by neurons that release them. Though the tricyclics are effective in treating depression (Task Force on the Use of Laboratory Tests in Psychiatry, 1985), they take 2 to 4 weeks to have an effect. This means that suicidal patients given antidepressants must be watched carefully during that period.

More recently, drugs known as *selective serotonin reuptake inhibitors* (SSRIs) have been added to the arsenal of antidepressants. These drugs elevate serotonin levels by preventing its reuptake by neurons that release it. Among the most popular of these drugs are Zoloft (sertraline), Paxil (paroxetine), and Prozac (fluoxetine). A meta-analysis of studies with 10,706 participants found that SSRIs and tricyclic antidepressants are equally effective in the relief of depression, with fewer patients discontinuing SSRIs due to side effects (Anderson, 2000).

But what is the relative effectiveness of drug therapy and psychotherapy for depression? A meta-analysis compared the results of six studies evaluating the treatment outcomes of almost 600 depressed clients—some of whom received psychotherapy and some of whom received combined drug therapy and psychotherapy. In less severe cases of depression, recovery rates for psychotherapy and combined therapy were not significantly different. However, in more severe cases, recovery rates for clients who received psychotherapy combined with drug therapy were higher (Thase et al., 1997).

Antimania Drugs

In the 1940s, Australian physician John Cade observed the chemical lithium calmed agitated guinea pigs. Cade then tried lithium on patients and found that it calmed those suffering from mania—apparently that because of its ability to reduce abnormal firing patterns of brain neurons (Lenox & Hahn, 2000). Psychiatrists now prescribe the **antimania drug** *lithium carbonate* to prevent the extreme mood swings of bipolar disorder (Compton & Nemeroff, 2000). It is important to stay on the drug because, of those who discontinue its use, 50 percent relapse within 3 months (Baker, 1994). Psychiatrists must vigilantly monitor patients taking lithium because it can produce dangerous side effects, including seizures, brain damage, and irregular heart rhythms.

antimania drugs
Psychoactive drugs, most notably lithium carbonate, that are used to treat bipolar disorder.

Antipsychotic Drugs

For centuries, physicians in India prescribed the snakeroot plant for calming agitated patients. Beginning in the 1940s, a chemical derivative of the plant, *reserpine,* was used to reduce symptoms of mania and schizophrenia. But reserpine fell into disfavor because of its tendency to cause depression and low blood pressure. The 1950s saw the development of safer **antipsychotic drugs** called *phenothiazines,* such as Thorazine (chlorpromazine), for treating people with schizophrenia.

antipsychotic drugs
Psychoactive drugs that are used to treat schizophrenia.

The phenothiazines work by blocking brain receptor sites for the neurotransmitter dopamine (Schwartz et al., 2000). Unfortunately, long-term use of antipsychotic drugs can cause the bizarre motor side effects that characterize *tardive dyskinesia,* which include grimacing, lip smacking, and limb flailing. A newer antipsychotic drug, Clozaril (clozapine), produces fewer symptoms of tardive dyskinesia while effectively treating many cases of schizophrenia that have not responded well to the phenothiazines (Sachdev, 2000).

Staying on Track: *The Biopsychological Orientation*

1. Why has the use of ECT been controversial?
2. How do the tricyclic antidepressants produce their results?

Answers to Staying on Track start on p. ST-7.

◆ COMMUNITY MENTAL HEALTH

Since the 1960s, psychologists have played a role in the community mental-health movement. Psychologists involved in *community psychology* have been involved in deinstitutionalization and the prevention of psychological disorders.

 Community Psychology Network
www.mhhe.com/sdorow5

Deinstitutionalization

As discussed earlier, for most of the 19th and 20th centuries, state mental hospitals were the primary sites of treatment for people with serious psychological disorders. But since the 1950s there has been a movement toward **deinstitutionalization,** which promotes the treatment of people in community settings. Since the 1950s the number of occupied beds in state mental hospitals has decreased from 339 to just 29 per 100,000 members of the population (Lamb, 1998). What accounts for this trend?

deinstitutionalization
The movement toward treating people with psychological disorders in community settings instead of mental hospitals.

- First, the introduction of drug treatments made it more feasible for mental patients to function in the outside world.
- Second, mental hospitals had become underfunded, understaffed, and overcrowded. Community-based treatment seemed to be a cheaper, superior alternative.
- Third, increasing concern for the legal rights of mental patients made it more difficult to have people committed to mental hospitals and to keep them there.

• Fourth, the Community Mental Health Centers Act of 1963, sponsored by President John F. Kennedy, mandated the establishment of federally funded centers in every community in the United States. These centers were to provide services to prevent and treat psychological disorders, further reducing the need for mental hospitals.

Despite its noble intentions and the fact that many people have benefited from it (Goldman, 1998), deinstitutionalization has worked better in theory than in practice. Even when funding is available for treatment facilities, such as halfway houses, homeowners often oppose the placement of such facilities in their neighborhoods (Piat, 2000). As a consequence, former mental-hospital patients who lack family support might have little choice but to live on the street. Others languish in prisons.

The potential benefits of adequately supported deinstitutionalization are evident in the results of a study that compared community care for former mental-hospital patients in the comparable cities of Portland, Oregon, and Vancouver, British Columbia. At the time of the study, Portland provided few community mental-health services, while Vancouver provided many private and public services. One year after their discharge, formerly hospitalized patients with schizophrenia in Vancouver were less likely than those in Portland to have been readmitted and more likely to be employed and to report a greater sense of psychological well-being. Because the two groups were initially equivalent, the greater progress of the Vancouver group was attributed to community mental-health services rather than to preexisting differences between the groups (Beiser et al., 1985). A more recent study assessed the effectiveness of a brief intervention focusing on psychosocial skills and continuity of care for men with schizophrenia living in a homeless shelter. Symptoms were assessed at the study's onset and 6 months after participants moved into the community. Men in the intervention group exhibited a significant decrease in some symptoms of schizophrenia compared to men in the control group (Herman et al., 2000). Thus, the provision of support services can ease the transition of mental-health patients into the community.

▲ **The Crisis Intervention Center**
The community mental-health system is aided by crisis intervention centers. These centers handle emergencies such as rape cases, physical abuse, suicide threats, or other problems that require immediate help. This photograph shows an emergency telephone for use by those who contemplate jumping from a bridge that has been the site of many suicides.

Prevention of Psychological Disorders

Community mental-health centers have three main goals in the prevention of psychological disorders: primary prevention, secondary prevention, and tertiary prevention.

Primary prevention helps prevent psychological disorders by fostering social support systems, eliminating sources of stress, and strengthening individuals' ability to deal with stressors. This might be promoted, for example, by reducing unemployment and making available low-cost housing. Canada has instituted a community-based primary prevention program called Better Beginnings, Better Futures to prevent physical, cognitive, emotional, and behavioral problems in children from economically disadvantaged families (Peters, 1994). Primary prevention programs have been effective in preventing social and behavioral problems in children and adolescents (Durlak & Wells, 1997).

Secondary prevention provides early treatment for people at immediate risk of developing psychological disorders, sometimes through *crisis intervention,* as in the case of survivors of violence, natural disasters, or political terrorism (Everly, 2000). Secondary prevention has been used, for example, to prevent eating disorders in college women with symptoms predisposing them to eating disorders (Franko, 1998). A review of 130 secondary prevention programs for children and adolescents with early signs of maladjustment found that the programs were successful in preventing the development of full-blown psychological disorders (Durlak & Wells, 1998).

Tertiary prevention helps keep people who have full-blown psychological disorders from getting worse or having relapses after successful treatment for a disorder, such as drug dependence (Carroll, Tanneberger, & Monti, 1998). Tertiary prevention has been used in a Canadian program to prevent abusive parents from continuing to abuse their children. The program involves home visits by specially trained nurses who provide emotional support, education in proper child-rearing practices, and assistance in helping parents obtain help from other human services (MacMillan & Thomas, 1993). Among the main community approaches to tertiary prevention are community residences, that provide homelike, structured environments in which former mental-hospital patients readjust to independent living.

STAYING ON TRACK: *Community Mental Health*

1. What brought about the deinstitutionalization movement, and why has it failed to achieve its original promise?
2. How do community mental-health centers provide primary, secondary, and tertiary prevention?

Answers to Staying on Track start on p. ST-7.

◆ FINDING THE PROPER THERAPY

At times in your life, you or someone you know might face psychological problems that require more than friendly advice. When personal problems disrupt your social, academic, or vocational life, or when you experience severe and prolonged emotional distress, you might be wise to seek the help of a therapist. You could receive therapy from a psychologist, a psychiatrist, or a variety of other kinds of therapists. You might even choose to read one of the many self-help books for specific psychological problems—an approach called *bibliotherapy*.

Selecting the Right Therapist

Just as there is no single way to find a physician, there is no single way to find a therapist. As explained later in the chapter, in general the personal qualities of the therapist matter more than the kind of therapy she or he practices. How might you find a therapist? Your college counseling center would be a good place to start. You might have a friend, relative, or professor who can recommend a therapist or counseling center to you. Other potential sources of help or referral include community mental-health centers, psychological associations, and mental-health associations.

After finding a therapist, try to assess her or his credentials, reputation, therapeutic approach, and interpersonal manner as best you can. For example, is the therapist licensed or certified? Do you know anyone who will vouch for the therapist's competence? Does the therapist's approach make sense for your problem? The therapist should be warm, open, concerned, and empathetic. Clients prefer therapists who are helpful and likeable (Alexander et al., 1993).

Bibliotherapy as an Alternative

You can't visit a typical bookstore without noting the large section devoted to self-help books. Some traditional psychotherapists even have their clients read books relevant to their central problem. The use of books as a form of psychotherapy is called *bibliotherapy*. Many self-help books are written by people who make unrealistic claims about what they can offer you. Nonetheless, if you choose high-quality books written by credible authors, bibliotherapy can be helpful. Bibliotherapy has been used to treat disorders such as insomnia (Mimeault & Morin, 1999), panic disorder (Wright et al., 2000), and sexual dysfunctions (van Lankveld, 1998). Bibliotherapy also has been used by psychotherapists as part of cognitive-behavioral therapy (Broder, 2000). And bibliotherapy has been widely used in treating depression. A review of research on bibliotherapy for depression found that it can be effective (Cuijpers, 1997).

◆ THE EFFECTIVENESS OF PSYCHOTHERAPY

In 1952 Hans Eysenck published an article that sparked a debate on the effectiveness of psychotherapy that has continued to this day. Based on his review of 24 studies of psychotherapy with neurotics (people suffering from disorders involving moderate anxiety or depression),

The improvement of some persons with psychological disorders without their undergoing formal therapy.

Eysenck concluded that about two-thirds of those who received psychotherapy improved. This would have provided strong evidence in support of the effectiveness of psychoanalysis (then the dominant kind of psychotherapy), had Eysenck not also found that about two-thirds of control participants who had received *no* therapy also improved. He called improvement without therapy **spontaneous remission** and attributed it to beneficial factors that occurred in the person's everyday life. Because those who received no therapy were as likely to improve as those who received therapy, Eysenck concluded that psychotherapy is ineffective.

Eysenck's article provoked criticisms of its methodological shortcomings. One shortcoming was that many members of the control groups were under the care of physicians who prescribed drugs for them and provided informal counseling. Another shortcoming was that the psychotherapy groups and control groups were not equivalent, differing in educational level, socioeconomic status, and motivation to improve. This meant that the control groups might have had a better initial prognosis than the treatment groups had. Still another shortcoming was that Eysenck overestimated the rate of spontaneous remission, which other researchers have found is closer to 40 percent than to 65 percent (Bergin & Lambert, 1978). Many years later, Eysenck (1994) still insisted that psychotherapy does not produce improvement beyond that of spontaneous remission.

Evaluation of Psychotherapy

During the decades since Eysenck's article, hundreds of studies have assessed the effectiveness of psychotherapy. This is a difficult scientific endeavor. One of the basic issues concerns what criteria to use in evaluating the success of psychotherapy.

Criteria of Success

The definition of *effective* varies with the orientation to therapy. Thus, the criteria of therapeutic success must consider the theoretical orientation of the therapy being evaluated. Changing a specific target behavior, for example, might be a goal of behavioral therapy but not of humanistic therapy (Bohart, O'Hara, & Leitner, 1998).

Moreover, who is to judge whether desired changes have occurred? A survey of client satisfaction with psychotherapy found that most of those who responded said they were pleased with their experience (Hollon, 1996). But clients, as well as therapists, can be biased in favor of reporting improvement. To avoid bias, friends, family members, teachers, or employers might also be asked for their assessment of the client. This provides cross-validation of client and therapist reports of improvement.

What has the admittedly imperfect research on the effectiveness of psychotherapy found? The general conclusion drawn from research conducted since Eysenck issued his challenge is that, overall, psychotherapy is more effective than placebo treatment, which, in turn, is more effective than no-treatment control conditions (Grissom, 1996). Placebo effects in psychotherapy are caused by factors such as the client's faith in the therapist's ability and the client's expectation of success.

Major Research Studies

Mary Lee Smith and her colleagues published a comprehensive meta-analysis of 475 studies on the effectiveness of psychotherapy (Smith, Glass, & Miller, 1980). They found that, on the average, the typical psychotherapy client is better off than 80 percent of untreated persons—and that there is little overall difference in the effectiveness of the various approaches to therapy (see Figure 15.4). So, psychotherapy does work, but no single kind stands out as being clearly more effective than the others.

More recently, results of an ambitious $10 million U.S. government study—the National Institute of Mental Health Treatment of Depression Collaborative Research Program—in the 1980s have lent further support to the effectiveness of psychotherapy. The study randomly assigned 239 severely depressed adult participants into 4 groups. One group received Beck's cognitive therapy. A second group received interpersonal psychotherapy (a form of

▲ **Lester Luborsky**

"Researchers have reached the consensus opinion that the evidence strongly supports the positive conclusion that most patients will benefit from psychotherapy."

 The Effectiveness of Psychotherapy: The *Consumer Reports* Study
www.mhhe.com/sdorow5

Chapter Fifteen

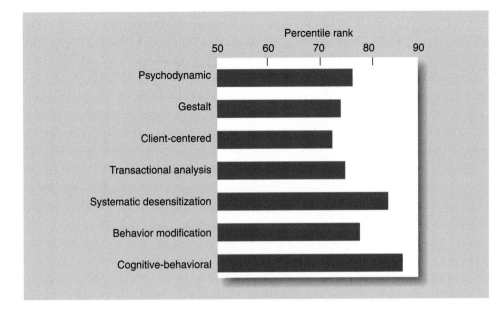

◀ **Figure 15.4**
The Effectiveness of Psychotherapy
Research has found that psychotherapy is effective, but that no approach is consistently better than any other approach. This graph shows the effectiveness of different kinds of therapy relative to no treatment. Overall, people given psychotherapy show, on the average, significantly greater improvement than about 80 percent of untreated people (Smith, Glass, & Miller, 1980).

psychoanalytic therapy). A third group received the antidepressant drug imipramine (Tofranil) plus a minimal amount of social support from a therapist. And a fourth group received a placebo treatment, involving an inactive pill plus a minimal amount of social support from a therapist (Stewart et al., 1998).

The participants were assessed after 16 weeks of therapy and again at a follow-up 18 months later. As expected, all of the groups had improved by the end of the 16 weeks; the three forms of active therapy eliminated depression in more than 50 percent of the participants, and the placebo therapy eliminated depression in 29 percent of the participants. There were no differences in effectiveness between the three active forms of therapy. Though drug therapy relieved symptoms more quickly, the two psychotherapies eventually caught up in their effectiveness (Mervis, 1986). But a follow-up study found that many of the participants relapsed, indicating that 16 weeks of therapy might be insufficient to produce lasting relief from depression (Shea et al., 1992).

Factors in the Effectiveness of Psychotherapy

Given the consensus that psychotherapy is usually effective and that no approach is significantly more effective than any other approach, researchers are faced with the question, What factors account for the effectiveness of psychotherapy? In trying to answer this question, researchers study the characteristics of therapies, clients, and therapists.

Therapy Characteristics

One of the first comprehensive reviews of therapy, client, and therapist factors, carried out by Lester Luborsky and his colleagues (1971), found that the poorest predictor of success in therapy was the nature of the therapy itself. More recent research studies have likewise found that the major kinds of psychotherapy are equally effective (Shapiro, 1995). Moreover, group therapy and individual psychotherapy are equally effective (McRoberts, Burlingame, & Hoag, 1998).

The inability to establish a reliable difference between psychotherapies in clinical outcomes has led some researchers to consider the *therapeutic alliance* to be a more important predictor of successful treatment. The therapeutic alliance involves three aspects of the therapeutic context: the degree of collaboration, the quality of the emotional bond, and the ability of the client and the therapist to agree upon the goals and means of treatment. A review of 79 studies found that the quality of the therapeutic alliance was positively correlated with therapeutic outcomes; therapeutic alliance is a consistent predictor of therapeutic success,

As the number of therapy sessions increases, the percentage of clients who improve increases. But after the 26th session, additional sessions help relatively few clients. Note the slight difference between objective ratings of improvement given by therapists and subjective ratings given by the clients themselves, though the general trend is similar for both (Howard et al., 1986).

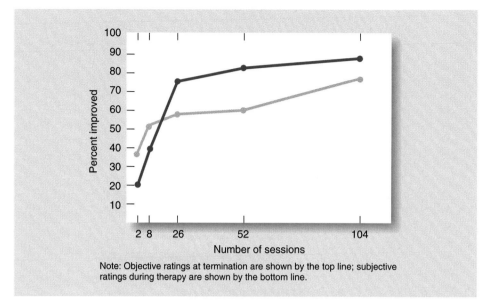

Note: Objective ratings at termination are shown by the top line; subjective ratings during therapy are shown by the bottom line.

regardless of the type of therapy (Martin, Garske, & Davis, 2000). Findings such as these have led some researchers to argue that therapeutic alliance is a common factor that underlies psychotherapeutic approaches—regardless of theoretical orientation.

The only important characteristic of therapy itself seems to be the number of therapy sessions—the more sessions, the greater the improvement. A review of 15 studies of psychotherapy using more than 2,400 clients found that 50 percent of clients improved by the end of 8 weekly sessions and 75 percent improved by the end of 26 weekly sessions (Howard et al., 1986; see Figure 15.5). A recent meta-analysis of over 100 studies of clinical patients found that the effectiveness of psychotherapy continued to increase over time, with benefits leveling off at approximately 1 year (Shadish et al., 2000). Nonetheless, certain kinds of psychotherapy, particularly psychoanalytic therapy (Doidge, 1997), might require more sessions to produce positive effects.

Client Characteristics

The classic review by Luborsky and his colleagues (1971) found that therapeutic success was related to client characteristics. Clients were more likely to improve if they were higher in education, intelligence, and socioeconomic status. Improvement also was greatest in those with less severe disorders and disorders of recent onset. Other factors that promoted therapeutic success were a more adequate personality and greater motivation to change.

Unfortunately, no client characteristics have been documented that can serve as a basis for the selection of a particular treatment (Dance & Neufeld, 1988). And studies have tended to use European American clients to the exclusion of African Americans and members of other ethnic minority groups (Matt & Navarro, 1997). This makes it difficult to generalize research findings from the participants in psychotherapy studies to the population in general.

Therapist Characteristics

Therapy is an intense, intimate, vulnerable relationship between human beings. Though it might be logical to assume that therapy would be best when the client and therapist are similar, there is little evidence that similarity in their sex (Zlotnick, Elkin, & Shea, 1998) or personality (Rinaldi, 1987) is a crucial factor in therapeutic outcomes. But research investigating ethnic similarity of clients and therapists has found that therapists' ratings of client functioning are higher when both are of the same ethnicity (Russell et al., 1996). And, ethnic minority clients are less likely to drop out of therapy when they use mental health services designed to meet the needs of ethnic minority clients (Takeuchi, Sue, & Yee, 1995).

Just what therapist characteristics *are* important, then? The client's perception of therapist empathy has been consistently identified as an important factor in the effectiveness of psychotherapy (Keijsers, Schaap, & Hoogduin, 2000). In fact, one of the main factors in negative effects of pychotherapy is a lack of empathy by the therapist (Mohr, 1995). But empathy is not enough. Personal warmth has been found to be a factor that differentiates successful and unsuccessful therapists (Wilkins, 2000). And professional training also is important. A meta-analysis found that highly trained therapists are more successful than less well-trained therapists, particularly in having fewer clients drop out of therapy (Stein & Lambert, 1995).

Researchers, particularly those who favor an eclectic approach (Beutler & Consoli, 1993), are refining their methods to study the more precise question: What kind of therapy, offered by what kind of therapist, is helpful for what kind of client, experiencing what kind of problem, in what kind of circumstances? Currently, the best we can do is determine the effectiveness of two of these factors at a time, such as the kind of therapy and the kind of problem. For example, cognitive therapy is superior to other therapies in the treatment of depression (Gaffan, Tsaousis, & Kemp-Wheeler, 1995), and behavior therapy is usually superior to other therapies in the treatment of phobias (Goisman, 1983) and for treating children and adolescents (Weisz et al., 1995).

STAYING ON TRACK: *Finding the Proper Therapy and*
the Effectiveness of Psychotherapy

1. How would you advise a friend to go about seeking a psychotherapist?
2. Why did Eysenck claim that psychotherapy produces no better results than spontaneous remission?
3. What therapist factors are important in the effectiveness of psychotherapy?

Answers to Staying on Track start on p. ST-7.

Chapter Summary

THE HISTORY OF THERAPY

- In trephining, holes were cut in the skull, possibly to release evil spirits that were believed to cause abnormal behavior.
- Hippocrates introduced a more naturalistic form of treatment, including procedures to restore the balance of body humors.
- The Renaissance saw the appearance of insane asylums; some, such as Bedlam, were awful places, but some towns, such as Geel, provided humane treatment.
- Near the end of the 18th century, Philippe Pinel released asylum inmates and championed moral therapy.
- Moral therapy was introduced to America by Benjamin Rush, who also used unusual devices for treating certain disorders.
- Through the efforts of Dorothea Dix, state mental hospitals were built throughout the United States. But they became crowded and deteriorated into mere human warehouses.
- Increasing cultural diversity in the United States has prompted interest in developing cultural competence in psychological training and practice.

THE PSYCHOANALYTIC ORIENTATION

- After hearing Josef Breuer's report of the benefits of catharsis in the case of Anna O., Sigmund Freud developed psychoanalysis.
- Psychoanalysis principally involves the analysis of free associations, dreams, resistances, and transference.

- The goal of these analyses is to have the client gain insight into unconscious conflicts and experience catharsis.

THE BEHAVIORAL ORIENTATION

- The behavioral orientation emphasizes the importance of learning and environmental influences.
- Two of the main kinds of behavioral therapy based on classical conditioning are systematic desensitization, which is useful in treating phobias, and aversion therapy, which makes formerly pleasurable, but maladaptive, behavior unpleasant.
- One of the main applications of the operant conditioning principle of positive reinforcement is the use of a token economy in institutional settings.
- The operant conditioning principle of punishment is useful in eliminating behaviors, such as self-injurious behavior in autistic children.
- Social-learning theory has contributed participant modeling as a way to overcome phobias.

THE COGNITIVE ORIENTATION

- The cognitive orientation assumes that thoughts about events, rather than events themselves, cause psychological disorders.
- In Albert Ellis's rational-emotive behavior therapy, the client learns to change irrational thinking.

- Aaron Beck developed cognitive therapy to help depressed people think less negatively about themselves, the world, and the future.

The Humanistic Orientation
- The humanistic orientation emphasizes the importance of being aware of one's emotions and feeling free to express them.
- Carl Rogers's person-centered therapy, a form of nondirective therapy, helps clients find their own solutions to their problems.
- In contrast, Fritz Perls's Gestalt therapy is more directive in making clients face their true feelings and act on them.

The Social-Relations Orientation
- The social-relations orientation assumes that people cannot be treated as isolated individuals.
- In group therapy, people, usually strangers, meet together for therapy.
- Group therapies derived from the psychoanalytic approach include transactional analysis.
- Group therapies derived from the behavioral approach include social-skills training and assertiveness training.
- In family therapy, family members gain insight into their unhealthy patterns of interaction and learn to change them.

The Biopsychological Orientation
- The biopsychological orientation uses medical procedures to treat psychological disorders.
- The main procedures include psychosurgery (rarely used today), electroconvulsive therapy for depression, and drug therapy.

- Psychiatrists may prescribe antianxiety drugs, antidepressant drugs, antimania drugs, and antipsychotic drugs.

Community Mental Health
- The community mental-health movement was stimulated by deinstitutionalization, the treatment of people in community settings instead of in mental hospitals.
- The failure to provide adequate housing and services for former mental-hospital patients has contributed to the growing number of homeless people.
- Community mental-health centers take a preventive approach to psychological disorders.

Finding the Proper Therapy
- Most professional therapists are eclectic.
- You should be as careful in selecting a therapist as you are in selecting a physician.

The Effectiveness of Psychotherapy
- In 1952 Hans Eysenck challenged psychotherapists by claiming that people who received psychotherapy improved no more than did people who received no therapy.
- Subsequent research has shown that psychotherapy is better than no therapy and better than placebo therapy.
- No single kind of therapy stands out as clearly superior to the rest.
- More sophisticated research is required to determine the ideal combinations of therapy, therapist, and client factors for treating specific disorders.

Key Concepts

Key Contributors

Thought Questions

1. If a friend of yours had acrophobia (fear of heights), how would you use systematic desensitization to treat it?
2. Why has deinstitutionalization not produced all of the beneficial effects that were envisioned for it?

3. What criteria would you use to determine whether an approach to psychotherapy is effective?

Possible Answers to Thought Questions start on p. PT-4

OLC Preview

For additional quizzing and a variety of interactive resources, visit the book's Online Learning Center at www.mhhe.com/sdorow5.

Psychology and Health

ERIC ISENBURGER
Summer

In 1991, Earvin "Magic" Johnson, one of the greatest of all basketball players, announced that he had contracted human immunodeficiency virus (HIV), which causes acquired immune deficiency syndrome (AIDS), by engaging in unprotected, nonmonogamous heterosexual sex. Johnson's statement contradicted the common belief that AIDS was a disease restricted to gay men. The case of actor Rock Hudson further dramatized the fact that no one—not even a wealthy, talented, popular movie and television star—is immune to HIV infection. These cases, and the millions of other cases of HIV infection that have occurred worldwide since AIDS was first identified in the early 1980s, show that we are not always passive victims of disease. In many cases we inflict illness or injury on ourselves—and others—through our own behavior, whether through ignorance or carelessness.

D o you overeat, smoke cigarettes, drive recklessly, exercise rarely, drink excessive amounts of alcohol, or respond ineffectively to stressful situations? If you engage in any of these maladaptive behaviors, which are among the leading causes of death in the United States, you might be reducing your life span. According to the National Academy of Sciences, half of the mortality from the 10 leading causes of death in the United States is strongly influenced by lifestyle (Hamburg, 1982).

This statement would not have been true at the beginning of the 20th century, when most North Americans died from infectious diseases such as influenza, pneumonia, or tuberculosis. But the development of vaccines and antibiotics, as well as improved hygiene led to a decline in illness and mortality due to infectious diseases. This was accompanied by a surge in the prevalence of noninfectious diseases, especially those caused by dangerous or unhealthy behaviors. A century ago, cancer and cardiovascular disease, which are promoted by unhealthy lifestyles pursued over a span of decades, were relatively uncommon causes of death among Americans. Today they are the two most common causes. One of the main problems studied by psychologists who do research in *health psychology* is the role of psychological factors in the onset and prevention of cancer, cardiovascular disease, and other illnesses that are affected by lifestyle and social-cultural variables associated with gender, ethnicity, and poverty.

Health psychology is the field that studies the role of biopsychological and social-cultural factors in the promotion of health and the prevention of illness. Health psychologists favor a *biopsychosocial model* of health and illness, which emphasizes the interaction of biological, psychological, and social factors (Huyse et al., 2001). In contrast, the traditional

Health Web
www.mhhe.com/sdorow5

Health Psychology on the Net
www.mhhe.com/sdorow5

health psychology
The field that applies psychological principles to the prevention and treatment of physical illness.

◀ **Behavioral Causes of Illness and Death**
Half of the mortality from the leading causes of death in the United States is influenced by unhealthy or dangerous behaviors, such as overeating, physical inactivity, and overexposure to the sun.

biomedical model emphasizes biological factors and neglects psychological and social ones. The chief topics of interest to health psychologists are the relationship between stress and illness and how to change health-impairing habits.

◆ PSYCHOLOGICAL STRESS AND STRESSORS

In the 1960s, undergraduates at Penn State University, recognizing their isolation in rural, peaceful State College, Pennsylvania, dubbed the town and its surroundings "Happy Valley." The students were vindicated in 1988, when California psychologist Robert Levine reported the results of his survey of living conditions in the United States—conferring on State College the distinction of being the least stressful place to live in America (Rossi, 1988).

But what is *stress?* According to Canadian endocrinologist Hans Selye (1907–1982), the founder of modern stress research, **stress** is the physiological response of the body to physical and psychological demands. Such demands are known as **stressors.** Though stress has been implicated as a factor in illness, some degree of stress is normal, necessary, and unavoidable. Stress motivates us to adjust our behavior to meet changing demands, as when we study for an upcoming exam or seek companionship when lonely. Stress can even be pleasurable, as when we attend a party or shoot river rapids on a raft. Selye called unpleasant stress *distress* and pleasant stress *eustress* (from the Greek for "good stress"). The major sources of stress include *life changes* and *daily hassles.*

Life Changes

Throughout life each of us must adjust to life changes, both pleasant ones (such as moving into a new home) and unpleasant ones (such as the death of a loved one). Health psychologists who study the effects of life changes are mainly concerned with *life events* and *posttraumatic stress disorder.*

Life Events

Interest in the relationship between life changes and illness began when Thomas Holmes and Richard Rahe (1967) developed the *Social Readjustment Rating Scale.* Holmes and Rahe asked medical patients to report positive and negative life changes they had experienced during the months before they became ill. This generated the list of 43 life changes in Table 16.1. Members of another sample were then asked to rate, on a 100-point scale, the degree of *adjustment* required by each of the 43 life changes. Note that the scale includes both negative events, such as the foreclosure of a mortgage or loan, and positive events, such as Christmas. Your *life-change score* is the sum of the scores for your life changes that occurred in a given period of time, generally the past year. Holmes and Rahe found that people who had a total life-change score of more than 300 points in the preceding year were more than twice as likely to become ill as people who had a total of less than 300 points. Similarly, a survey of adults found that the more life changes they had experienced, the more stress-related symptoms they had reported (Scully, Tosi, & Banning, 2000).

An important weakness of the Social Readjustment Rating Scale is that its very content might make researchers overestimate the relationship between life changes and illness. The scale contains some life changes that can be either causes *or* effects of illness (Zimmerman, 1983). The most obvious examples are "change in eating habits" and "personal injury or illness." Thus, a positive correlation between life changes and illness indicates only that there *might* be a causal relationship between the two. But some experiments have provided evidence supporting the causal effect of life events on illness. One of these studies exposed 17 volunteers to a rhinovirus (which causes the common cold) and then isolated them individually for 5 days. The 12 participants who developed colds had experienced significantly more life changes in the previous year than had the 5 participants who did not (Stone et al.,

stress

The physiological response of the body to physical and psychological demands.

stressor

A physical or psychological demand that induces physiological adjustment.

Table 16.1 Social Readjustment Rating Scale

Life Event	Mean Value	Life Event	Mean Value
Death of spouse	100	Son or daughter leaving home	29
Divorce	73	Trouble with in-laws	29
Marital separation	65	Outstanding personal achievement	28
Jail term	63	Spouse begins or stops work	26
Death of close family member	63	Begin or end school	26
Personal injury or illness	53	Change in living conditions	25
Marriage	50	Revision of personal habits	24
Fired at work	47	Trouble with boss	23
Marital reconciliation	45	Change in work hours or conditions	20
Retirement	45	Change in residence	20
Change in health of family member	44	Change in schools	20
Pregnancy	40	Change in recreation	19
Sex difficulties	39	Change in church activities	19
Gain of new family member	39	Change in social activities	18
Business readjustment	39	Mortgage or loan for lesser purchase (car, TV, etc.)	17
Change in financial state	38	Change in sleeping habits	16
Death of close friend	37	Change in number of family get-togethers	15
Change to different line of work	36	Change in eating habits	15
Change in number of arguments with spouse	35	Vacation	13
Mortgage or loan for major purchase (home, etc.)	31	Christmas	12
Foreclosure on mortgage or loan	30	Minor violations of the law	11
Change in responsibilities at work	29		

Source: Reprinted with permission from *Journal of Psychosomatic Research,* 11: 213–218, T. H. Holmes and R. H. Rahe, "The Social Readjustment Rating Scale," 1967, Elsevier Science Ltd., Pergamon Imprint, Oxford, England.

1992). An explanation for this finding is provided by research studies showing that the greater the number of life changes one has experienced in the past year, the weaker one's immune response is (Birmaher et al., 1994).

Though Holmes and Rahe assumed that adjustment to life changes induces stress, subsequent research has shown that it is the nature of the change, rather than change itself, that induces stress. Negative life changes induce more stress than neutral or positive life changes do (Monroe, 1982). One study of adolescent boys found that those with more positive changes in their lives had lower blood pressure than other adolescent boys (Caputo, Rudolph, & Morgan, 1998). Moreover, there are gender and ethnic differences in the type of life events experienced by individuals. One study of children and adolescents found that girls reported more interpersonal stressors—such as parent-child conflicts—than did boys (Rudolph & Hammen, 1999). And African Americans—especially men—are more likely to experience negative life events related to racism and discrimination (Klonoff & Landrine, 1999). These findings support Selye's distinction between distress and eustress.

Posttraumatic Stress Disorder

Traumatic events, such as wars or disasters, are particularly stressful and can lead to **posttraumatic stress disorder,** which can appear months or years after the event. Emotional symptoms include anxiety, emotional apathy, and survivor guilt. Cognitive symptoms include hypervigilance, difficulty concentrating, and flashbacks of the event. Behavioral symptoms include insomnia and social detachment. Posttraumatic stress disorder is especially common among rape survivors; those who were sexually abused as children are particularly vulnerable (Nishith, Mechanic, & Resick, 2000). Rape survivors initially experience intense anxiety and depression, which tend to diminish gradually over the first year.

posttraumatic stress disorder
A syndrome of physical and psychological symptoms that appears as a delayed response after exposure to an extremely emotionally distressing event.

▶ **Posttraumatic Stress Disorder**
The bombing of the federal building in Oklahoma City in 1995 shocked Americans throughout the country, and left survivors with physical and psychological damage that they might never overcome completely. Survivors of disasters like this often experience posttraumatic stress disorder.

 National Center for PTSD
www.mhhe.com/sdorow5

Nonetheless, 20 percent of rape survivors have severe, long-lasting emotional scars (Hanson, 1990). Posttraumatic stress disorder has been linked to the amygdala, a brain structure that maintains our vigilance against potential threats (see Chapter 3). A study that used functional magnetic resonance imaging found that combat veterans with posttramatic stress disorder had greater amygdala activity in response to threatening stimuli than combat veterans without posttraumatic stress disorder (Rauch et al., 2000).

Posttraumatic stress disorder also is associated with an increased risk of physical illness. For example, in 1980 the state of Washington was struck by a natural disaster—the eruption of the Mount Saint Helens volcano in the Cascade Mountains. Though more than 100 miles from the volcano, the town of Othello was covered by volcanic ash. Residents of that farming community suffered distress over their fields being covered with ash, fear of the effects of the ash on their health, and dread that the volcano would erupt again. During the 6 months that followed the disaster, a local medical clinic reported an almost 200 percent increase in stress-related illnesses among the residents of Othello. There also was an almost 20 percent increase in the local death rate (Adams & Adams, 1984).

Daily Hassles

Though major life changes are important stress-inducing events, they are not the sole ones. Richard Lazarus and his colleagues have found other important, though less dramatic, stress-inducing events: the *hassles* of everyday life. A typical day can be filled with dozens of hassles, such as forgetting one's keys, being stuck in traffic, or dealing with a rude salesclerk. People who experience the cumulative effect of many daily hassles are more likely to suffer from health problems, including headaches, sore throats, and influenza (DeLongis, Folkman, & Lazarus, 1988).

Life Changes and Daily Hassles

Life changes can promote illness indirectly by increasing daily hassles. Some studies have even found that there is a stronger association between hassles and illness than between life changes and illness (Ruffin, 1993). For example, a study that examined 930 victims of a devastating hurricane found that the stress they experienced was due less to the hurricane itself than to the chronic physical, family, and financial hassles it created for them (Norris & Uhl, 1993).

Our adrenal glands might respond to hassles by increasing their secretion of the hormones cortisol, epinephrine, and norepinephrine. Though these hormones help us adapt to stressors, they also impair the immune system's ability to protect us from illness (Cacioppo, 1994). And increases in daily hassles are, indeed, associated with impairment of the immune response (Delahanty et al., 2000). Daily hassles also can indirectly impair health by triggering unhealthy behaviors, including smoking more, exercising less, and eating fattier foods (Twisk et al., 1999).

Prospective Studies of Daily Hassles

Most research on the relationship between daily hassles and illnesses makes it difficult to determine whether they are just correlated with each other or whether hassles actually promote illness. This is because few *prospective* studies have been conducted on the relationship between hassles and health. A prospective study would investigate whether a person's current level of hassles is predictive of his or her future health. This contrasts with *retrospective* studies, which simply find that people who are ill report more hassles in their recent past.

One of the few prospective studies of the effects of daily hassles found that hassles do, in fact, promote illness. On two occasions, adolescent girls who participated in the study were asked to indicate, for each of 20 commonly experienced circumstances, whether it had occurred in their lives and whether they rated its occurrence as positive or negative. They also completed an illness symptoms checklist and a measure of depression. The results indicated that negative circumstances were associated with depression and poor health. But this was true only when the girls also reported low levels of positive circumstances, or *uplifts*. Apparently, uplifts can buffer the effects of hassles, reducing their negative effects (Siegel & Brown, 1988). This, again, is in keeping with Selye's distinction between distress (such as hassles) and eustress (such as uplifts). In fact, the immune system response can be stronger during periods of eustress than during periods of distress (Snyder, Roghmann, & Sigal, 1993).

STAYING ON TRACK: *Psychological Stress and Stressors*

1. Why are cancer and cardiovascular disease the most common causes of death today but not a century ago?
2. What are the characteristics of posttraumatic stress disorder?
3. Why do some researchers believe that life changes create stress through their effects on daily hassles?

Answers to Staying on Track start on p. ST-8.

◆ THE BIOPSYCHOLOGY OF STRESS AND ILLNESS

Whether it is caused by life changes or daily hassles, stress is marked by physiological arousal and, in some cases, diminished resistance to disease. As explained in Chapter 12, physical and psychological stressors evoke the *fight-or-flight response,* first described by physiologist Walter Cannon (1915/1989). The fight-or-flight response involves activation of the sympathetic nervous system and secretion of stress hormones (cortisol, epinephrine, and norepinephrine) by the adrenal glands.

The hormonal response to stress does not vary significantly between the sexes. Recently, though, researchers have begun to investigate the role of one hormone, oxytocin, that might be related to gender differences in stress and coping. Both men and women under stress release oxytocin. However, oxytocin release is greater in women than in men. Androgens (male hormones) appear to inhibit the release of oxytocin, and estrogens (female hormones) also modulate the effect of oxytocin, increasing its effect in women's stress response.

The differential effects of oxytocin in female and male stress responses have led Shelley Taylor and her colleagues (Taylor et al., 2000b) to question whether the fight-or-flight response is more descriptive of the male stress response. According to this model, men are

▲ Hans Selye (1907–1982)

"Even prehistoric man must have recognized a common element in the sense of exhaustion that overcame him in conjunction with hard labor, agonizing fear, lengthy exposure to cold or heat, starvation, loss of blood, or any kind of disease."

general adaptation syndrome

As first identified by Hans Selye, the body's stress response, which includes the stages of alarm, resistance, and exhaustion.

atherosclerosis

The narrowing of arteries caused by the accumulation of cholesterol deposits.

▲ Multiphasic Activity

The Type A behavior pattern is associated with multiphasic activity, in which the person engages in several activities at once as part of a continual effort to do more and more in less and less time.

likely to respond to stress with hostile and aggressive behaviors, but women are more likely to respond to stress with a *tend-and-befriend* response. The results of animal and human studies suggest that the release of oxytocin in the female stress response is associated with three biopsychosocial outcomes: reduced anxiety, increased affiliative behaviors, and increased nurturing behaviors. As described in Chapter 4, gender-role socialization and family responsibilities have a profound influence on women's lives—particularly in the domains of caregiving and interpersonal relationships. However, this research points to a biological factor that might contribute to gender differences in stress and coping.

General Adaptation Syndrome

Cannon's work influenced that of Hans Selye. Selye (1936) had hoped to discover a new sex hormone. As part of his research, he injected rats with extracts of ovarian tissue. He found that the rats developed stomach ulcerations, enlarged adrenal glands, and atrophied spleens, lymph nodes, and thymus glands. Selye later observed that rats displayed these same responses to a variety of stressors. This indicated that his initial findings were not necessarily caused by a sex hormone.

Selye also found that animals and people, in reacting to stressors, go through three stages, which he called the **general adaptation syndrome.** During the first stage, the *alarm reaction,* the body prepares to cope with the stressor by increasing activity in the sympathetic nervous system and adrenal glands (the fight-or-flight response). For example, medical students experiencing the stress of a series of academic exams respond with increased cortisol secretion (Malarkey et al., 1995). Selye noted that during the alarm stage, different stressors produced similar symptoms, including fatigue, fever, headache, and loss of appetite.

If the body continues to be exposed to the stressor, it enters the *stage of resistance,* during which it becomes more resistant to the stressor. Yet, during the stage of resistance, your resistance to disease can decline. If you succumb to disease, though, you might have entered the *stage of exhaustion.* At this point, the person's resistance to disease collapses; in extreme cases, the person might die.

Stress and Noninfectious Diseases

The fight-or-flight response evolved because it helped animals and human beings cope with periodic stressors, such as wildfires or animal attacks. Unfortunately, in modern industrialized countries we are subjected to continual, rather than periodic, stressors. The infrequent saber-toothed-tiger attack has been replaced by three exams on one day and threats of muggers on city streets. The repeated activation of the fight-or-flight response takes its toll on the body, possibly causing or aggravating diseases. Stress-affected noninfectious diseases include asthma (Moran, 1991), diabetes (Fisher et al., 1982), gastric ulcers (Young et al., 1987), and essential hypertension (Mellors, Boyle, & Roberts, 1994). Such diseases have traditionally been called *psychosomatic,* based on the assumption that they are caused or worsened by emotional factors.

Stress and Cardiovascular Disease

Of all the diseases that might be affected by stress, coronary heart disease has received the most attention from health psychologists. More recently, health psychologists have begun studying the role of stress in the promotion of cancer.

Cardiovascular Effects of Stress. Coronary heart disease is caused by **atherosclerosis,** which is promoted by cholesterol deposits in the coronary arteries (see Figure 16.1). Even the stress of everyday college life can affect the level of cholesterol in your blood. College students who merely anticipate an upcoming exam show significant increases in their levels of blood cholesterol (Van Doornen & van Blokland, 1987). Stress also can promote coronary heart disease by elevating heart rate and blood pressure, as well as by stimulating the release of stress hormones. This can damage the walls of the coronary arteries, making them more susceptible to the buildup of cholesterol plaques (Krantz & Manuck, 1984).

Type A Behavior and Cardiovascular Disease. On November 2, 1988, "Iron Mike" Ditka, the tough head coach of the Chicago Bears football team, was hospitalized with a mild heart attack. In a televised interview on ESPN, Ditka's physician reported that Ditka had none of the common physical risk factors for coronary heart disease. His only risk factor was a psychological one: *Type A behavior.* A review of research on Type A behavior in middle-aged men (such as Mike Ditka) found that Type A behavior was present in 70 percent of those with coronary heart disease, and in only 46 percent of those who were healthy (Miller et al., 1991). And, in men Type A behavior is associated with an increased risk of coronary heart disease, including strokes (Kim et al., 1998)—though its presence does not guarantee coronary heart disease and its absence does not guarantee freedom from it.

Characteristics of Type A Behavior. In the late 1950s, San Francisco cardiologist Meyer Friedman noticed that his patients were easily angered, highly competitive, and driven to do more and more in less and less time. Friedman, with his colleague Ray Rosenman, called this syndrome of behaviors **Type A behavior.** In contrast, *Type B behavior* is characterized by patience, an even temper, and willingness to do a limited number of things in a reasonable amount of time. The Type A person might also show time urgency by changing lanes to advance a single car length, chronic activation by staying busy most of every day, and *multiphasic activity* by reading, eating, and watching television at the same time. This lifestyle means that the Type A person is in a constant state of fight or flight. Would this lifestyle be associated with a greater risk of heart disease?

Friedman and Rosenman asked managers and supervisors of large companies to identify colleagues who fit the description of the Type A and Type B behavior patterns. They identified 83 men, including many executives, who fit each pattern. No women were included because at the time there were relatively few women in executive positions. Participants were interviewed about their medical history and behavioral tendencies, such as being driven to succeed, feeling highly competitive, and feeling under chronic time pressure. They were observed for body movements, tone of voice, teeth clenching, and any observable signs of impatience. Based on the interview, 69 of the men were labeled pure Type A and 58 of the men were labeled pure Type B.

Friedman and Rosenman found that the Type A participants had significantly higher levels of blood cholesterol than did the Type B participants. More important, 28 percent of the Type A participants had symptoms of coronary heart disease, but only 4 percent of the Type B participants had such symptoms. Before leaping to the conclusion that the study definitely demonstrated that Type A behavior promotes heart disease, note two other findings. First, the Type A participants smoked much more than Type B did. Today we know that smoking is a major risk factor in heart disease. Second, the Type A participants' parents had a higher incidence of coronary heart disease than did the Type B participants' parents. Perhaps the Type A participants inherited a genetic tendency to develop heart disease (Vogler et al., 1997). Of course, there could just as well be a genetic tendency toward Type A behavior, which in turn might promote heart disease. In any case, Friedman and Rosenman contributed one of the first formal studies demonstrating a possible link between behavior and heart disease. Later, based on subsequent research findings, Friedman and Rosenman boldly concluded:

▶ In the absence of Type A Behavior Pattern, coronary heart disease almost never occurs before 70 years of age, regardless of the fatty foods eaten, the cigarettes smoked or the lack of exercise. But when this behavior pattern is present, coronary heart disease can easily erupt in one's thirties or forties. (Friedman & Rosenman, 1974, p. xi)

The pattern of behavior shown by Type A's indicates that they are overconcerned with control of their environment. This leads to repeated physiological arousal when other people, time constraints, or personal responsibilities threaten their sense of control. Type A behavior is not just a style of responding to the environment; it can induce the very environmental circumstances that evoke it. This was illustrated in a study that compared Type A and Type B police radio dispatchers during work shifts. Type A's generated more job pressures by initiating extra work for themselves and attending to multiple tasks at the same

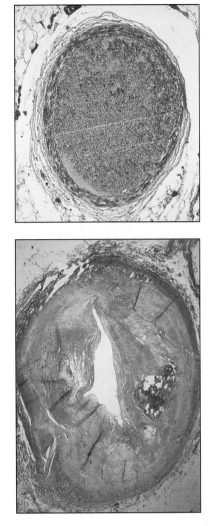

▲ **Figure 16.1**
Atherosclerosis

Diets high in cholesterol contribute to atherosclerosis, which narrows coronary arteries and predisposes the person to heart attacks. The top photograph shows a cross section of a healthy artery, and the bottom photograph shows a cross section of an atherosclerotic artery.

Type A behavior

A syndrome—marked by impatience, hostility, and extreme competitiveness—that is associated with the development of coronary heart disease.

▲ **Redford Williams**

"Research evaluating the relationship between hostility and coronary heart disease suggests that higher levels of anger toward others coupled with difficulty in expressing that anger form a key neurotic conflict in the predisposition to coronary heart disease."

time. Moreover their coworkers and supervisors looked to them when there were additional tasks to be performed. So, Type A people can help create work conditions that help maintain their driven, time-urgent, impatient behavioral style (Kirmeyer & Biggers, 1988).

But the role of Type A behavior in coronary heart disease was brought into question by the results of a 22-year follow-up of participants in a large-scale study of Type A behavior and heart disease (Ragland & Brand, 1988). In fact, Type A's who had suffered a heart attack had a somewhat *lower* risk of a second heart attack. Of course, this might have been a result of other factors, such as greater medical attention given to Type A than to Type B heart-attack victims. Though this study indicated that the *overall* pattern of Type A behavior is unrelated to coronary heart disease, research findings have been converging on a specific component of the Type A behavior pattern, *cynical hostility,* as the factor most related to coronary heart disease. Cynical hostility, marked by antagonistic and manipulative behavior, is an independent risk factor for cardiovascular disease (Miller et al., 1996).

Effects of Type A Behavior. Regardless of whether cynical hostility or some other aspect of Type A behavior does promote coronary heart disease, how might it do so? One way might be by inducing a chronic stress response. In fact, people who display cynical hostility are more physiologically reactive to physical and emotional stressors (Smith, Cranford, & Mann, 2000). One study investigated the relationship between hostility and cardiovascular reactivity during social interactions in male and female undergraduates. The participants wore blood-pressure monitors and kept diaries of their daily activities. Men who were more hostile had greater increases in systolic blood pressure during social interaction than did men who were less hostile. Women did not show any relationship between their hostility level and their blood-pressure level. This might account, in part, for men's greater risk of cardiovascular disease (Guyll & Contrada, 1998).

High physiological reactivity also might unleash harmful effects through the actions of stress hormones. This was confirmed in a study in which Redford Williams and his colleagues (1982) had Type A and Type B male college students compete in a stressful laboratory task. The results indicated that the Type A's displayed a significantly greater increase in levels of the adrenal gland stress hormones cortisol, epinephrine, and norepinephrine. These stress hormones promote the buildup of cholesterol plaques on the walls of arteries, and increase the risk of heart attack.

Type A behavior might also indirectly contribute to cardiovascular disease by promoting the eating of fast foods, which have higher levels of fat, salt, and sugar (Barker, Thompson, & McClean, 1996). Another possible factor mediating the effect of Type A behavior on coronary heart disease is the tendency of Type A people to ignore symptoms of illness. Before being hospitalized with his heart attack, Mike Ditka had ignored pain earlier in the week until his assistant coaches forced him to seek medical attention. This tendency of Type A's to discount illness first appears in childhood. Type A children are less likely to complain of symptoms of illness, and Type A children who have surgery miss fewer days of school than do Type B's (Leikin, Firestone, & McGrath, 1988).

Development of Type A Behavior. Though there is only weak evidence of a hereditary basis for Type A behavior, there is strong evidence that the pattern runs in families. Karen Matthews, a leading researcher on Type A behavior, points to child-rearing practices as the primary origin of Type A behavior. Parents of Type A children encourage them to try harder even when they do well and offer them few spontaneous positive comments. Type A children might be given no standards except "Do better," which makes it difficult for them to develop internal standards of achievement. They might then seek to compare their academic performance with the best in their class. This might contribute to the development of the hard-driving component of the Type A behavior pattern (Matthews & Woodall, 1988).

There are also social-cultural differences in Type A behavior tendencies. One study found that low socioeconomic status was associated with increased cardiovascular reactivity in response to stress among African American and European American children (Gump, Matthews, & Raeikkoenen, 1999). In fact, the term *John Henryism* has been coined to describe the psychological effects of trying to actively cope with chronic stress in the face of insurmountable odds—as many poor and ethnic-minority individuals must do. John Henryism appears to be particularly lethal for African American men (Dressler, Bindon, & Neggers, 1998).

Modification of Type A Behavior. Because of the possible association between Type A behavior and coronary heart disease, its modification might be wise. But a paradox of Type A behavior is that Type A persons are not necessarily disturbed by their behavior. Why change a behavior pattern that is rewarded in competitive Western society? Programs to modify the Type A behavior of those who are willing to participate try to alter specific components of the Type A behavior pattern, particularly impatience, hostility, and competitiveness. One hostility-reduction program reduced diastolic blood pressure in participants compared to nonparticipants (Gidron, Davidson, & Bata, 1999). And a Swedish intervention study reduced both hostility and time pressure in Type A participants (Karlberg, Krakau, & Unden, 1998).

Stress and Cancer

In the 2nd century A.D., Greek physician Galen noted that depressed women were more likely than happy women to develop cancer. This relationship between emotionality and cancer has received support from modern research. Consider a study of medical students who had been given personality tests in medical school and were assessed 30 years later. Of those who had been emotionally expressive, less than 1 percent had developed cancer. Those who had been loners, and presumably more emotionally controlled, were 16 times more likely to develop cancer than were those who were emotionally expressive (Shaffer et al., 1987). Other studies have supported the relationship between the tendency to suppress emotions and the development of cancer (Anderson, Kiecolt-Glaser, & Glaser, 1994), apparently because suppression of emotions is associated with suppression of the immune response (Eysenck, 1994). A recent meta-analysis has found that psychosocial variables such as personality, emotionality, and coping have a modest, but consistent, relationship to the development of cancer (McKenna et al., 1999).

Assuming that our emotions can affect the progress of cancer, what mechanisms might account for this? Stress might indirectly promote cancer by affecting health behaviors, such as smoking tobacco, eating high-fat foods, and drinking too much alcohol. Stress also might directly interfere with the immune system's ability to defend against cancer. In fact, during periods when they are under intense academic pressure, medical students exhibit a reduction in the activity of *natural killer cells,* the lymphocytes responsible for detecting and destroying cancer cells (Glaser et al., 1986). A review of research studies found that depression is consistently associated with large decreases in natural killer cell activity (Herbert & Cohen, 1993). Simply being diagnosed with cancer or being treated for cancer can induce stress-related suppression of the very immune responses that are needed to combat the cancer (van der Pompe, Antoni, & Heijnen, 1998). Note that though stress can *impair* the immune system's ability to destroy cancerous cells, there is little evidence that stress can directly *cause* normal cells to become cancerous (Levenson & Bemis, 1991).

Stress and Infectious Diseases

In 1884 a physician reported in a British medical journal that the depression experienced by mourners at funerals predisposed them to develop illnesses (Baker, 1987). A century later, a research study provided a scientific basis for this observation. The study found that men whose wives had died of breast cancer showed impaired functioning of their immune systems during the first 2 months of their bereavement (Schleifer et al., 1983). This agrees with research showing that depression is associated with suppression of the immune system (Zisook et al., 1994).

Psychoneuroimmunology

The realization that stressful events, such as the death of a loved one, can impair the immune system led to the emergence of **psychoneuroimmunology,** the interdisciplinary field that studies the relationship between psychological factors and illness, especially the effects of stress on the immune system. Though many of the mechanisms by which stress suppresses the

▲ **Karen Matthews**
"Type A children's awareness of high standards . . . may maintain their struggle to strive after everescalating goals."

National Cancer Institute
www.mhhe.com/sdorow5

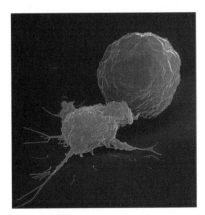

▲ **Natural Killer Cell**
A natural killer cell *(left)* as it begins to engulf a cancer cell *(right).* Research has shown that stress can impair the ability of natural killer cells to destroy cancer cells.

psychoneuroimmunology
The interdisciplinary field that studies the relationship between psychological factors and physical illness.

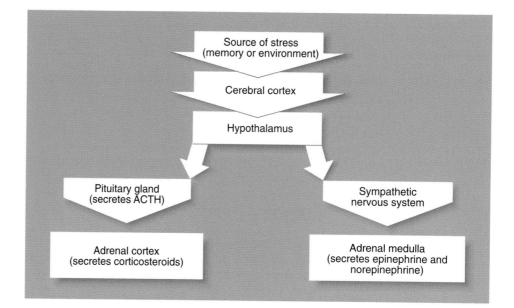

► Figure 16.2

Stress Pathways

When the cerebral cortex processes stressful memories or stressful input from the immediate environment, it stimulates a physiological response by way of the endocrine system and the sympathetic nervous system. Both pathways involve the hypothalamus. The hypothalamus signals the pituitary gland, which secretes adrenocorticotropic hormone (ACTH). ACTH, in turn, stimulates the adrenal cortex to secrete corticosteroid hormones, which mobilize the body's energy stores, reduce tissue inflammation, and inhibit the immune response. The hypothalamus also sends signals through the sympathetic nervous system to the adrenal medulla, which in turn stimulates the release of epinephrine and norepinephrine. These hormones contribute to the physiological arousal characteristic of the "fight-or-flight" response.

immune system remain to be determined, one mechanism is well established (see Figure 16.2). Stress prompts the hypothalamus to secrete a hormone that stimulates the pituitary gland to secrete adrenocorticotropic hormone (ACTH), which then stimulates the adrenal cortex to secrete corticosteroids. The hypothalamus also increases activity in the sympathetic nervous system, which stimulates the adrenal medulla to secrete the hormones epinephrine and norepinephrine. As noted earlier, though adrenal hormones might make us more resistant to stressors, they also can impair our immune systems (Kiecolt-Glaser & Glaser, 1995).

The cells chiefly responsible for the immunological response to infections are white blood cells called B-lymphocytes and T-lymphocytes. *B-lymphocytes* attack invading bacteria, and *T-lymphocytes* attack viruses, cancer cells, and foreign tissues. The immunosuppressive effects of stress hormones might explain why Apollo astronauts, after returning to Earth from stressful trips to the moon, had impaired immune responses (Jemmott & Locke, 1984). But you do not have to go to the moon to experience stress-induced suppression of your immune response, as revealed in a study of college students. After the students had given speeches that were evaluated for their merit, they showed impairment of their immune response (Marsland et al., 1995). And the chronic stress experienced by women who care for husbands suffering from Alzheimer's disease is associated with impaired immune functioning (Wu et al., 1999).

Conditioning the Immune Response

Given that the immune system is affected by stressful life experiences, is it conceivable that learning could alter the immune response? This question inspired the experiment on classical conditioning of the immune response described in the Anatomy of a Research Study feature. Perhaps classical conditioning will one day be applied clinically to enhance immune responses in people who have low resistance to infection, such as people who are HIV positive or living with AIDS. People with AIDS experience stress induced by both their illness and hostile social reactions to them. Such stress might further impair the functioning of their immune systems, making them even more vulnerable to infections that often prove fatal (Ironson et al., 1994).

Staying on Track: *The Biopsychology of Stress and Illness*

1. What is the relationship between stress and cancer?
2. How might stress impair immune system functioning?
3. What evidence is there that the immune response can be classically conditioned?

Answers to Staying on Track start on p. ST-8.

Anatomy of a Research Study

Can the Immune Response Be Altered by Classical Conditioning?

Rationale

Certain chemicals can enhance or suppress the immune response. Researcher Robert Ader wondered whether such a chemical could be used as the basis for classically conditioning the immune response. He reasoned that a neutral stimulus paired with the chemical might come to have the same effect on the immune response. This possibility inspired him to test his hypothesis experimentally.

Method

Ader and his colleague Nicholas Cohen (1982) used the drug cyclophosphamide, which suppresses the immune system, as the unconditioned stimulus. When mice were injected with the drug, they experienced both nausea and immunosuppression—dual effects of the drug. Ader and Cohen used saccharin-flavored water as the neutral stimulus. They hoped that if the mice drank it before being injected with the drug, the taste of sweet water would suppress their immune response to an antigen.

Results and Discussion

As Ader and Cohen expected, the mice developed an aversion to sweet-tasting water, because they associated it with nausea caused by the drug. But when some of them were later forced to drink sweet-tasting water, several developed illnesses and died. Ader and Cohen attributed this to conditioned suppression of the mice's immune response, with the sweet-tasting water having become a conditioned stimulus after being paired with the drug (see Figure 16.3). Many subsequent studies have provided additional evidence that the immune response is subject to classical conditioning (Exton et al., 2000). Animal research indicates that epinephrine and norepinephrine mediate conditioned immunosuppression (Lysle, Cunnick, & Maslonek, 1991).

▶ **Figure 16.3**
Conditioned Immunosuppression
When Ader and Cohen (1982) paired saccharin-sweetened water with cyclophosphamide, a drug that suppresses the immune response, they found that the sweet-tasting water itself came to elicit immunosuppression. (See Chapter 7 for a discussion of the relationship between the UCS, UCR, CS, and CR.)

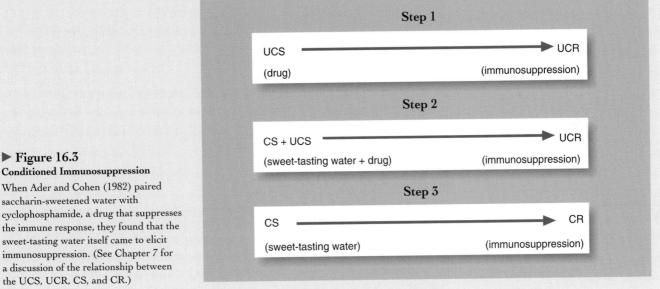

◆ FACTORS THAT MODERATE THE STRESS RESPONSE

More than 2,000 years ago, Hippocrates recognized the relationship between individual factors and physiological responses when he observed that it is more important to know what sort of person has a disease than to know what sort of disease a person has. Because of variability among individuals, a given stressor will not evoke the same response in every person. Our reactions to stress are moderated by a variety of factors. These include *physiological reactivity, cognitive appraisal, explanatory style, perceived control, psychological hardiness,* and *social support.*

Physiological Reactivity

physiological reactivity
The extent to which a person displays increases in heart rate, blood pressure, stress hormone secretion, and other physiological activity in response to stressors.

People differ in their pattern of physiological responses to stressors (Walsh, Wilding, & Eysenck, 1994). **Physiological reactivity** refers to increased heart rate, blood pressure, stress hormone secretion, and other physiological activity in response to stressors. People with slower cardiovascular recovery after exposure to stress are more prone to develop high blood pressure (Hocking-Schuler & O'Brien, 1997). In one study, men with mild hypertension played a video game while their heart rate and blood pressure were measured. Those who displayed greater increases in heart rate and blood pressure also had higher levels of blood cholesterol (Jorgensen et al., 1988). This might help explain why people with greater physiological reactivity have a higher risk of atherosclerosis (Aheneku, Nwosu, & Ahaneku, 2000). And men show greater increases than women in both cardiovascular activity and secretion of stress hormones, such as cortisol, in response to stressors. This might contribute to the greater vulnerability of men to coronary heart disease (Earle, Linden, & Weinberg, 1999).

Cognitive Appraisal

cognitive appraisal
The subjective interpretation of the severity of a stressor.

Though Hans Selye believed that all stressors produce similar patterns of physiological responses, more recent research indicates that different stressors might produce different patterns (Krantz & Manuck, 1984). Richard Lazarus, whose work on daily hassles was discussed earlier in the chapter, believes that one of the reasons different stressors can produce different responses in the same person is that the person interprets the two stressors differently. Such interpretation is known as **cognitive appraisal** (Lazarus, 1993), which Lazarus also uses as the basis of his theory of emotion (see Chapter 12).

Cognitive appraisal involves two stages: primary appraisal and secondary appraisal. In *primary appraisal* you judge whether a situation requires a coping response. If you judge that a situation requires a coping response, you would then engage in *secondary appraisal* by determining whether you have the ability to cope with the situation. The greater the perceived controllability of a stressful situation, the lower its perceived stressfulness (Peeters, Buunk, & Schaufeli, 1995). Consider final exams. Students who perceive their exams to be highly demanding and who lack confidence in their ability to perform well on them will experience more stress than students who perceive their upcoming exams as moderately demanding and are confident of their ability to perform well. This view has been supported by research that has found more positive emotion and better coping among people who appraise stressors as challenging (Folkman & Moskowitz, 2000).

Explanatory Style

explanatory style
The tendency to explain events optimistically or pessimistically.

Depressed people tend to have a pessimistic **explanatory style** (see Chapter 14). They attribute unpleasant events to *internal, stable,* and *global* factors. In other words, depressed people attribute unpleasant events to their own unchanging, pervasive, personal characteristics—such as a lack of intelligence. The possible role of a pessimistic explanatory style in the promotion of illness was supported by a retrospective study of 99 graduates of the Harvard University classes of 1942 to 1944. Graduates who had used a pessimistic explanatory style at the age of 25 (based on questionnaires they had completed at that time) became less healthy between the ages of 45 and 60 than graduates who did not use a pessimistic explanatory style. All of the graduates had been healthy at age 25 (Peterson, Seligman, & Vaillant, 1988).

The researchers hypothesized that pessimism might make people less likely to take actions to counter the effects of negative life events, leading to more severe stress in their lives. A pessimistic explanatory style might increase susceptibility to illness by leading to poor health habits, suppression of the immune system, and withdrawal from sources of social support. Each of these factors can promote illness. Moreover, explanatory style has been found to be related to premature mortality. In particular, catastrophizing (operationally defined as making global attributions) has been found to predict mortality, especially among men (Peterson et al., 1998). Fortunately for many people, as demonstrated by health psychologist Shelley Taylor (Taylor et al., 2000a), people with a more optimistic outlook on life—even a somewhat unrealistically positive one—are less susceptible to illness.

Perceived Control

In a best-selling book describing his recovery from a massive heart attack, Norman Cousins, former editor of the *Saturday Review,* claimed that his insistence on taking personal responsibility for his recovery—including devising his own rehabilitation program—helped him regain his health. In contrast, as Cousins noted in his book, "good patients" (patients who remain passive) discover that "a weak body becomes weaker in a mood of total surrender" (Cousins, 1983, p. 223). Research findings have supported his anecdotal report by converging on **perceived control** over stressors as one of the most important factors moderating the relationship between stress and illness. Perceived control over stressors reduces stress (Shirom, Melamed, & Nir-Dotan, 2000). People who work at demanding jobs and feel they have little control over job stressors are more likely to develop coronary heart disease (Krantz et al., 1988). And consider the person whom Cousins called the "good patient" in the hospital, who adopts a passive, compliant role—leaving his or her recovery up to nurses and physicians. The poorer recuperative powers of such patients are associated with **learned helplessness**—the feeling that one has little control over events in one's life.

People in all walks of life benefit from a sense of control over the stressors that affect them. One study found that residents of retirement homes who are given greater responsibility for self-care and everyday activities live longer and healthier lives than residents whose lives are controlled by staff members (Langer & Rodin, 1976), possibly in part because residents who feel greater control over their daily lives maintain stronger immune responses. People who feel a lack of control tend to secrete more adrenal hormones in response to stress (Peeters et al., 1998), which in turn can impair their immune systems. In fact, people who lack a sense of control over their lives show reduced T helper cell (Brosschot et al., 1998) and natural killer cell activity (Reynaert et al., 1995) in response to stressors. This would impair their immunological defense against cancer.

Psychological Hardiness

Psychologist Suzanne Kobasa Ouelette was puzzled by the fact that whereas some people can work under chronic, intense pressure and remain healthy, others cannot. She wondered whether this might be related to personality differences. To test this possibility scientifically, she gave a group of business executives a battery of personality tests and then conducted a 5-year prospective study during which she periodically recorded their health. She found that those who were illness-resistant tended to share a set of personality characteristics that those who were illness-prone did not (Kobasa, Maddi, & Kahn, 1982).

Kobasa called this set of personality characteristics *psychological hardiness.* She has found that people high in **psychological hardiness** are more resistant to stressors and, possibly as a result, are less susceptible to stress-related illness. Other researchers have supported this, as well. For example, a study of college undergraduates found that participants high in hardiness reported lower levels of stress and depression (Pengilly & Dowd, 2000). A 10-week study of college students found a negative correlation between hardiness and visits to the college health center. That is, psychologically hardier students tended to be physically healthier than less hardy students were (Mathis & Lecci, 1999).

What characteristics are shared by people high in hardiness? Kobasa found that hardy people face stressors with a sense of commitment, challenge, and control. People with a sense of *commitment* are wholeheartedly involved in everyday activities and social relationships, rather than being alienated from them. People with a sense of *challenge* view life's stressors as opportunities for personal growth rather than as burdens to be endured. And people with a sense of *control* believe that they have the personal resources to cope with stressors, rather than feeling helpless in the face of them.

▲ **Shelley Taylor**
"Mentally healthy people exhibit positive illusions."

The Learned Helplessness Home Page
www.mhhe.com/sdorow5

perceived control
The degree to which a person feels in control over life's stressors.

learned helplessness
A feeling of futility caused by the belief that one has little or no control over events in one's life, which can make one stop trying and become depressed.

The Hardiness Institute
www.mhhe.com/sdorow5

psychological hardiness
A personality characteristic marked by feelings of commitment, challenge, and control that promotes resistance to stress.

But how does hardiness reduce susceptibility to illness? One way is by making hardy individuals less physiologically reactive to stressors, as demonstrated in a study of patients who were awaiting dental surgery (Solcova & Sykora, 1995). Another way is by affecting health habits. People high in psychological hardiness, compared to people low in it, are more likely to maintain good health habits in the face of stress (Wiebe & McCallum, 1986). Thus, hardy students might be more resistant to illness because they are more likely to eat well, take vitamins, exercise more, and seek medical attention for minor ailments even when under stress.

Social Support

social support
The availability of support from other people, whether tangible or intangible.

People who have **social support** are less likely to become ill. For example, a lack of social support is a key factor in the "broken-heart phenomenon": the tendency of some bereaved spouses to die sooner than others. Those who die sooner tend not to remarry, to live by themselves, to feel lonelier, and to have no one to talk to (Stroebe, 1994). Social support can be tangible, in the form of money or practical help, or intangible, in the form of advice or encouragement about how to eliminate or cope with stress. Social support promotes health by reducing the effects of stressful life events, promoting recovery from illness, and increasing adherence to medical regimens (Heitzmann & Kaplan, 1988).

We show lower cardiovascular reactivity in the face of a stressful situation when someone else accompanies us (Kamarck, Peterman, & Raynor, 1998). Social support can retard the progress of atherosclerosis by reducing stress-related increases in heart rate, blood pressure, and stress hormones (Knox & Uvnaes-Moberg, 1998). Social support is associated with a stronger immune response in AIDS patients (Theorell et al., 1995). This is important, because HIV-positive individuals show reductions in the activity of natural killer cells and certain other lymphocytes when facing stressful live events (Evans et al., 1995).

But what experimental evidence is there that social support boosts the immune response? In one study, samples of saliva were taken from healthy college students 5 days before their first final exam, during the final-exams period, and 14 days after their last final exam. The samples were analyzed for the level of immunoglobulin A, an antibody that provides immunity against infections of the upper respiratory tract, gastrointestinal tract, and urogenital system. Salivary concentrations of immunoglobulin A after the final-exams period were lower than before it. But students who reported more adequate social support during the pre-exam period had consistently higher immunoglobulin A concentrations than did their peers who reported less adequate social support (Jemmott & Magloire, 1988). This indicates that social support may promote health by directly strengthening the immune response.

There are social-cultural differences in the expressed need for social support in coping with illness. A study of European American, Chinese American, and Japanese American breast cancer patients found that European Americans desired more social support than the other two groups (Wellisch et al., 1999). Social support groups are more likely to be sought out by people suffering from stigmatizing illnesses—such as AIDS, substance abuse, and cancer—than equally serious, but less embarrassing, disorders such as heart disease (Davison, Pennebaker, & Dickerson, 2000). There also are gender differences in the effects of social support. In one study of 2,348 married or cohabiting heterosexual adults, social support from one's partner and family predicted psychological well-being among both women and men. However, women's psychological and physical health were more likely to suffer when their family was under stress. Moreover, whereas social support reduced stress among men and women in this sample, friends and family were more common sources of social support for women than for men (Walen & Lachman, 2000).

STAYING ON TRACK: *Factors That Moderate the Stress Response*

1. What are the components of psychological hardiness?
2. How does social support moderate the stress response?

Answers to Staying on Track start on p. ST-8.

◆ COPING WITH STRESS

Given that stress is unavoidable and often harmful, coping with stress is an important part of everyday life. One approach to coping divides it into task-oriented, emotion-oriented, and avoidance-oriented coping (Higgins & Endler, 1995). For example, suppose you find it distressing to make oral presentations. You might engage in task-oriented coping by preparing carefully for them, emotion-oriented coping by cognitively reappraising the possible negative consequences of peer responses to your presentations, or avoidance-oriented coping by not enrolling in courses that require oral presentations.

Of course, some people pursue more formal ways of coping with stress. Among the most common of these are stress-management programs, which have been effective in reducing high blood pressure (Garcia-Vera, Labrador, & Sanz, 1997) and angina pectoris (Gallacher et al., 1997). And a 10-week stress-management program produced long-term improvements in immune functioning in HIV-positive gay men (Antoni et al., 2000).

Emotional Expression and Stress Management

Psychologist James Pennebaker and his colleagues have found that writing about our emotions is a stress-relieving practice with both physical and psychological benefits (Esterling et al., 1999). Writing about stressful life experiences relieved symptoms in asthma and arthritis patients when compared with patients who did not participate in writing (Stone et al., 2000), and undergraduates who wrote about traumatic experiences—the trauma itself as well as how they grew or benefited from the experience—made fewer visits to the university health center compared to participants who did not write about their experiences (King & Miner, 2000). Other approaches to coping with stress are aerobic exercise and relaxation training.

Exercise and Stress Management

Four decades ago, President John F. Kennedy, a physical fitness proponent, observed, "The Greeks knew that intelligence and skill can only function at the peak of their capacity when the body is healthy and strong—that hearty spirits and tough minds usually inhabit sound bodies" (Silva & Weinberg, 1984, p. 416). Kennedy would approve of the recent trend toward greater concern with personal fitness among adults. The only way to achieve cardiovascular fitness is to maintain a program that includes regular aerobic exercise (exercise that markedly raises heart rate for at least 20 minutes). The possible beneficial effect of aerobic exercise was demonstrated in a longitudinal study (Brown & Siegel, 1988) that found that adolescents under high levels of stress who exercised regularly had a significantly lower incidence of illness than did adolescents who exercised little (see Figure 16.4).

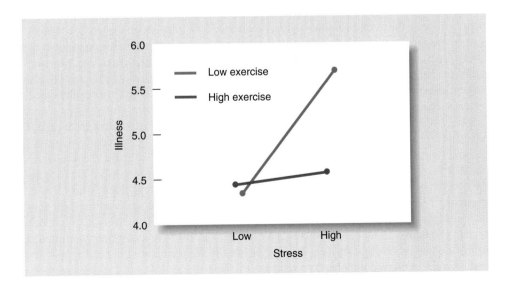

◀ Figure 16.4
Exercise and Illness

A study of the relationship between exercise and illness found that adolescents who exercised little and adolescents who exercised regularly did not differ in their incidence of illness when under low levels of stress. In contrast, when under high levels of stress, those who exercised regularly had a significantly lower incidence of illness than did those who exercised little (Brown & Siegel, 1988).

▲ Janice Kiecolt-Glaser

"The possible enhancement of immune function by behavioral strategies has generated considerable interest."

progressive relaxation

A stress-management procedure that involves the successive tensing and relaxing of each of the major muscle groups of the body.

 Stress Management
www.mhhe.com/sdorow5

Experimental research likewise shows that aerobic exercise programs improve both cardiovascular fitness and psychological well-being (DiLorenzo et al., 1999). People who exercise become less physiologically reactive to stressors (Throne et al., 2000) and more confident in their ability to cope (Steptoe et al., 1993). There also is evidence that exercise can enhance the functioning of the immune system (Hong, 2000).

Relaxation and Stress Management

Because stress is associated with physiological arousal, health psychologists emphasize the importance of relaxation training. Several techniques have proved effective in reducing psychological or physiological arousal. These include hypnosis (Leung, 1994), biofeedback (Tyson & Sobschak, 1994), and restricted environmental stimulation, or REST (Schulz & Kaspar, 1994). Hypnosis is discussed in Chapter 6, biofeedback in Chapter 7, and REST in Chapter 11.

The most basic relaxation technique is **progressive relaxation** (see Chapter 15). Progressive relaxation has been effective in reducing high blood pressure (Hoelscher, 1987). And heart-attack patients who receive training in breathing and relaxation develop a slower breathing rate and more normal heart rate (van Dixhoorn, 1998). Progressive relaxation can even enhance the immune response (Lekander et al., 1997). Consider the following experiment that involved medical students, conducted by Janice Kiecolt-Glaser, a leading researcher on psychoneuroimmunology. Blood samples were taken from students 1 month before midterm exams and then on the day of the exams. Half of the students were randomly assigned to participate in relaxation practice during the month between the two measurement days. The students who were not assigned to practice relaxation, compared to the students who were, displayed a significantly greater decrease in natural killer cell activity between the first and second measurements (Kiecolt-Glaser et al., 1986). You will recall that natural killer cells are one of the body's main defenses against cancer cells.

STAYING ON TRACK: *Coping with Stress*

1. What did the study of adolescents by Brown and Siegel (1988) conclude about the relationship between exercise and health?
2. What did the study by Kiecolt-Glaser et al. (1986) find about the relationship between relaxation and the immune response?

Answers to Staying on Track start on p. ST-8.

◆ HEALTH-PROMOTING HABITS

Habits as varied as smoking, overeating, avoiding exercise, and failing to wear seat belts sharply increase the chances of illness, injury, or death. Yet a study found that college students underestimated the actual probability that their own risky behaviors would lead to illness or injury. Because many people underestimate the true riskiness of their behaviors, programs aimed at changing health-impairing habits must not only point out risky behaviors but also make participants realize that those habits make them more susceptible to unhealthy consequences than they might believe (Weinstein, 1984).

One of the most important factors influencing whether people are motivated to engage in health-promoting behavior is their feeling of self-efficacy (Kelly, Zyzanski, & Alemagno, 1991). People high in self-efficacy feel that their actions will be effective. People with a high sense of self-efficacy in regard to health-promoting behaviors are more likely to see the benefits of such behaviors and to downplay barriers to performing them (Alexy, 1991). Feelings of self-efficacy are positively related to important health-promoting behaviors, including maintenance of smoking cessation, control of diet and body weight, and adherence to preventive health behaviors (O'Leary, 1985). The most important health-promoting habits include practicing safe sex, keeping physically fit, maintaining a healthy diet and body weight, and avoiding tobacco products.

(a)

(b)

Practicing Safe Sex

Today many health psychologists have turned their attention to unsafe sexual practices that contribute to the spread of sexually transmitted diseases, including AIDS, syphilis, gonorrhea, chlamydia, and genital herpes. But, because it is almost inevitably fatal, AIDS has become of greatest interest to them.

HIV and AIDS

AIDS kills its victims by impairing their immune systems, making them eventually succumb to cancer or opportunistic infections—that is, infections that rarely occur in people with healthy immune systems. Since 1981, when it was first identified, AIDS has spread through much of the world with alarming rapidity. AIDS afflicts people of all ages, sexes, ethnicities, and sexual orientations.

HIV is spread by infected protein-rich body fluids, such as blood or semen (Catania et al., 1990). Drug addicts can contract HIV by sharing hypodermic needles with infected addicts. The virus can also be transmitted through sexual activity, including anal sex and vaginal sex. Even infants born to HIV-positive mothers are at high risk of infection, especially if they are breast fed. There is no evidence that kissing, simple touching, food handling, or other casual kinds of contact spread the virus.

Promoting Safe Sex

One of the primary means of AIDS prevention is educating people to avoid risky behaviors. Foremost among the suggestions has been to practice "safe sex" (or at least "safer sex"). In regard to AIDS, the safest sex is abstinence or limiting oneself to one uninfected partner. Many people do not abstain, however, and might have many sexual partners, so the next best suggestions are to use latex condoms and limit the number of one's sex partners.

Efforts to reduce risky behaviors have achieved some success. Though elsewhere in the world AIDS is more prevalent among heterosexuals, especially women, in North America it has been more prevalent among gay men. This has been attributed to the common practice of unprotected anal sex among gay men. The 10 percent of heterosexuals who practice anal sex also are at increased risk of infection (Voeller, 1991). Because it has so ravaged the North American gay community, the earliest anti-AIDS programs in the United States were aimed at gay men. Cities with large homosexual populations have instituted workshops on AIDS prevention for gay and bisexual men. For example, a survey of gay men in San Francisco, where there is a high level of AIDS education, found a significant increase in their use of condoms (Catania et al., 1991).

A review of research on the use of HIV-AIDS prevention videotapes found that they increase knowledge of HIV and AIDS and improve attitudes regarding risky sexual behavior. But it is unclear whether these changes translate into actual reductions in risky behavior (Kalichman, 1996). The National Institute of Mental Health conducted a program in 37 clinics across the United States with high-risk populations. The participants, compared to controls, showed a reduction in risky sexual behavior. They showed fewer acts of unprotected sex and increased condom use over a 12-month follow-up period (NIMH, 1998).

Keeping Physically Fit

People who exercise regularly are healthier and live longer than those who do not. Exercise promotes health and longevity, in part by boosting the immune system. A study found that HIV-positive people showed enhanced immunological responses after participating in an aerobic exercise program (Antoni et al., 1991).

Beneficial Effects of Exercise

There is especially strong evidence for the effectiveness of exercise in preventing obesity and cardiovascular disease. Aerobic exercise combats obesity by burning calories, raising the basal metabolic rate, and inhibiting the appetite. Aerobic exercise also reduces the cardiovascular risk factors of elevated cholesterol and high blood pressure.

The health risks of physical inactivity and the health benefits of exercise have led many sedentary people to start exercising. Unfortunately, of those who begin formal exercise programs, about 50 percent will drop out within 6 months. According to Rod Dishman, an authority on exercise adherence, people who are obese or who have symptoms of cardiovascular disease—the very people who might benefit most from exercise—are the least likely to exercise (Dishman & Gettman, 1980). Physical inactivity is a greater health problem among African Americans and Latinos, who engage in less physical activity during leisure time than do European Americans. Moreover, this difference appears to be unrelated to social class (Crespo et al., 2000).

Adhering to an Exercise Program

Exercise Adherence
www.mhhe.com/sdorow5

Though exercise programs are beneficial, many people find it difficult to adhere to them. One study assessed barriers to physical activity in a multiethnic sample of 2,912 middle-aged and elderly women. Regardless of ethnicity, lack of energy and the demands of caregiving duties were cited as two of the top four most frequent barriers to exercising. The vast majority of the sample (62 percent) preferred to exercise at home with appropriate instruction rather than attend an instructor-led class (King et al., 2000). Because of this, home training might promote adherence relative to group training at an exercise facility (Perri et al., 1997).

Other factors influence exercise adherence. Intrinsic motivation (see Chapter 11) promotes exercise adherence. People who exercise for enjoyment, competence, and social interaction show greater adherence than those who exercise just to improve their fitness or appearance (Ryan et al., 1997). And people who fail to adhere to exercise programs might have low self-efficacy—that is, a lack of confidence in their ability to meet the demands of the program. One study measured the self-efficacy of participants in a step-aerobics exercise class who participated in an 8-week program. There was a positive relationship between their self-efficacy levels and their attendance (Fontaine & Shaw, 1995).

The failure of people to maintain exercise programs has prompted health psychologists to study ways of increasing exercise adherence (Godin et al., 1995). One of the best ways is to make exercising enjoyable (Wankel, 1993). Perhaps this explains the popularity of kickboxing classes and similar approaches to exercise. But some programs aimed at increasing adherence are more formal. In one study, groups of people engaged in jogging, aerobic dancing, or conditioning for skiing for 10 weeks. Some of the participants in each of the 3 groups also took part in a special program to increase their motivation to exercise. The program made participants more aware of obstacles to exercise and taught them how to cope with periodic exercise lapses, instead of having an all-or-none attitude. Exercisers were urged to return immediately to their exercise programs, instead of giving up after exercise lapses. The results showed that those who participated in the adherence program, compared to those who did not, were indeed more likely to adhere to their exercise programs (Belisle, Roskies, & Levesque, 1987).

▲ **Exercise**
People who exercise are more stress resistant and disease resistant than people who do not. The well-publicized benefits of exercise account for the popularity of exercise "gurus" such as Jane Fonda, Karen Voight, and Billy Blanks.

◀ **Figure 16.5**
The Ideal Female Figure

In Western cultures the ideal female figure has changed over time. The ideal has at times been represented by the plump Rubenesque nude of the early 17th century, the voluptuous actress Marilyn Monroe of the 1950s, and the muscular athlete Venus Williams of the 21st century.

Maintaining a Healthy Diet and Body Weight

Health psychologists recognize the importance of maintaining a healthy diet and body weight. A high-fat diet is one of the main risk factors in cardiovascular disease. High-fat diets contribute to high blood pressure and high levels of cholesterol in the blood, which promote atherosclerosis. The narrowing of cerebral arteries and coronary arteries reduces blood flow, promoting strokes and heart attacks. Health psychologists have developed programs that combine nutritional education and behavior modification to help people reduce their risks of cardiovascular disease by adopting healthier eating habits. For example, programs that reduce fat intake produce significant reductions in blood pressure in participants with elevated blood pressure (Jacob, Wing, & Shapiro, 1987).

Cultural Influences on Desirable Physiques

A high-fat diet also contributes to obesity—an important risk factor in illness for both men and women. Yet, in Western cultures, a leaner figure has been stylish for women only since the early 20th century, and a toned, muscular figure only in the past few decades. For the preceding 600 years, cultural standards favored a more rounded figure (Bennett & Gurin, 1982). Figure 16.5 depicts changes in cultural views concerning the ideal female figure. Thus, what we consider an ideal body weight is regulated by cultural, as well as biological and behavioral, factors (Brownell & Wadden, 1991). Today, cultures differ in what they view as ideal physiques. For example, one study found that Singaporeans rated muscular physiques as more attractive than British participants did. All participants rated muscular physiques as more attractive in men than in women. There was no difference in ratings given by male and female raters (Furnham & Lim, 1997).

But current Western standards of beauty, and concern with the health-impairing effects of obesity, make weight loss a major North American preoccupation. Losing weight seems deceptively easy: You simply make sure that you burn more calories than you ingest. Yet, as noted by obesity researcher Kelly Brownell (1982), less than 5 percent of obese people maintain their weight loss long enough to be considered "cured." Some obesity researchers argue that this pessimistic figure represents only people who have been in formal weight-loss programs. Perhaps the people who seek treatment for obesity are the ones who are the least likely to succeed (Schachter, 1982). In fact, negative results typically come from university-based treatment programs. A small percentage of participants in these programs lose weight—but they differ from the general population of obese people. They tend to be more overweight, more likely to engage in binge eating, and more prone to psychological disorders (Brownell, 1993).

Approaches to Weight Control

Though many people do, in fact, desire to lose weight for health reasons, others wish to do so for social or aesthetic reasons. But how can people control their weight? A common but ineffective approach is dieting. Unfortunately, as dieters lose weight, their basal metabolic rate decreases (Foreyt, 1987), forcing them to diet indefinitely to maintain their lower level of weight—an impossible feat. Because dieting cannot last for a lifetime, dieters eventually return to the same eating habits that contributed to their obesity. Moreover, dieting is unhealthy; 25 percent of weight lost solely through dieting consists of lean body tissue, including skeletal muscle (Brownell, 1982).

Formal psychological approaches to weight loss rely on cognitive-behavior modification in conjunction with aerobic exercise. In cognitive-behavior modification programs, participants monitor their eating behaviors, change their maladaptive eating habits, and correct their misconceptions about eating. Aerobic exercise promotes weight loss not only by burning calories during exercise but also by raising the basal metabolic rate for hours afterward. Weight loss through aerobic exercise also is healthier than weight loss through dieting alone, because only 5 percent of lost weight will be lean tissue (Brownell, 1982). Despite the effectiveness of aerobic exercise in weight control, most people who are trying to lose weight do not increase their physical activity or engage in regular exercise (Gordon et al., 2000). Moreover, it is difficult for many obese people to maintain the intensity of exercise necessary to produce significant weight loss (Blix & Blix, 1995). And, though the past three decades have demonstrated the short-term effectiveness of behavior modification in helping mildly or moderately obese people lose weight, relapse rates are high. The typical 15-week weight-loss program of dieting or dieting plus exercise, for example, produces a loss of about 22 pounds, with 60 to 80 percent of participants maintaining weight loss for 1 year. But few participants maintain their weight loss after 3 to 5 years (Miller, 1999). Longer treatment programs that emphasize the importance of physical activity are more successful in promoting long-term weight loss (Jeffery et al., 2000).

Avoiding Tobacco Products

During the 1996 presidential campaign, Senator Robert Dole provoked controversy when he declared that smoking was not addictive. Dole's proclamation went against an enormous amount of evidence that smoking tobacco is addictive and perhaps the single worst health-impairing habit. Despite the harmful effects of smoking, governments permit it—and even profit from it. In 1565 King James I of England, though viewing smoking as a despicable habit, chose to tax cigarettes rather than ban them, a practice governments still follow today.

The Effects of Smoking

Contrary to Dole's claim, smokers can become addicted to the nicotine in tobacco—though a small minority of smokers remain "chippers" who are able to smoke intermittently without becoming addicted (Shiffman et al., 1995). Though many addicted smokers insist that they smoke to relieve anxiety or to make them more alert, they actually smoke to avoid the unpleasant symptoms of nicotine withdrawal, which include irritability, hand tremors, heart palpitations, and impaired concentration. Thus, smoking regulates the level of nicotine in their bodies (Parrott, 1995) and reduces craving (Gilbert & Warburton, 2000). Smoking is especially difficult to stop because it can become a conditioned response to many everyday situations; you probably know smokers who light a cigarette when answering the telephone, after eating a meal, or upon leaving a class.

Smoking produces harmful side effects through the actions of tars and other substances in cigarette smoke. Smoking causes fatigue by reducing the blood's ability to carry oxygen, making smoking an especially bad habit for athletes. But, more important, smoking contributes to the deaths of more than 300,000 Americans each year from stroke, cancer, emphysema, and heart disease. Thus, prevention of smoking is of paramount importance.

The Prevention of Smoking

The ill effects of smoking make it imperative to devise programs to prevent the onset of smoking. Children are more likely to start smoking if their parents and peers smoke. Many smoking-prevention programs are based in schools and provide information about the immediate and long-term social and physical consequences of smoking. But simply providing children with information about the ill effects of smoking is not enough to prevent them from starting. Smoking-prevention programs must also teach students how to resist peer pressure and advertisements that encourage them to begin smoking. Overall, smoking-prevention programs have been effective, reducing the number of new smokers among participants by 50 percent (Flay, 1985).

The Treatment of Smoking

Though programs to prevent the onset of smoking are important, techniques to help people stop smoking are also essential. But quitting is difficult. A major University of Minnesota study followed 802 smokers for 2 years. Of those, 62 percent tried to quit, but only 16 percent succeeded and 9 percent became "chippers" (Hennrikus, Jeffery, & Lando, 1995). Smokers who do quit find it difficult to resist relapsing. The problem of relapse is so great that the U.S. Public Health Service considers dependence on tobacco to be a chronic condition (Fiore, 2000). Moreover, relapse rates are higher among women. As yet, researchers are unable to account for this gender difference, as women's relapse rates are not influenced by gender-related factors such as weight gain or weight concerns (Wetter, et al., 1999).

Health psychologists use a variety of techniques to help those who cannot quit on their own. Participants are taught to expect the symptoms of nicotine withdrawal, which begin 6 to 12 hours after smoking cessation, peak in 1 to 3 days, and last 3 to 4 weeks (Hughes, Higgins, & Bickel, 1994). Certain consequences of quitting, including hunger, weight gain, and nicotine craving, can persist for 6 months or more (Hughes et al., 1991).

Because tars and other chemicals in tobacco—not nicotine—cause the harmful effects of smoking, some treatments aim at preventing smoking by providing participants with safer ways of obtaining nicotine. These nicotine-replacement techniques prevent some of the relapse caused by the desire to avoid weight gain (Nides et al., 1994) or withdrawal symptoms (Levin et al., 1994). Nicotine replacement therapy has proved successful. The two most common techniques use *nicotine chewing gum* or a *nicotine patch,* which provides nicotine through the skin. A meta-analysis of well-controlled experiments found that of participants who used a nicotine patch, 22 percent abstained from smoking after 6 months. Moreover, those who used a nicotine patch smoked less than those who used a placebo patch—that is, a patch without nicotine (Fiore et al., 1994). Higher-dose nicotine patches produce greater long-term abstinence than lower-dose nicotine patches do (Daughton et al., 1999).

Of course, though replacement therapy reduces the health risks of smoking, it does not help smokers overcome their *addiction* to nicotine. Those who wish to overcome their addiction do better if they are high in two of the factors that appear repeatedly as health promoters: a feeling of self-efficacy (Ockene et al., 2000) and the presence of social support (Nides et al., 1995). And for those who are motivated to overcome their addiction, *nicotine fading* is useful. This technique gradually weans smokers off nicotine by having them smoke cigarettes with lower and lower nicotine content until it has been reduced to virtually zero (Becona & Garcia, 1993).

STAYING ON TRACK: *Health-Promoting Habits*

1. What behaviors can transmit HIV from one person to another?
2. What are the beneficial effects of regular aerobic exercise?
3. Why is it unwise to try to lose weight strictly by dieting?

Answers to Staying on Track start on p. ST-8.

Chapter Summary

PSYCHOLOGICAL STRESS AND STRESSORS

- Health psychology is the field that studies the role of psychological factors in the promotion of health and the prevention of illness and injury.
- One of the main topics of interest to health psychologists is stress, the physiological response of the body to physical and psychological demands.
- The chief psychological stressors are often categorized as either life changes or daily hassles.

THE BIOPSYCHOLOGY OF STRESS AND ILLNESS

- Hans Selye identified a pattern of physiological response to stress that he called general adaptation syndrome, which includes the alarm reaction, the stage of resistance, and the stage of exhaustion.
- Stress has been linked to infectious and noninfectious diseases.
- The field that studies the relationship between psychological factors and illness is called psychoneuroimmunology.
- There is evidence that the immune response can be altered by classical conditioning.
- The main noninfectious diseases linked to stress are cardiovascular disease and cancer.

FACTORS THAT MODERATE THE STRESS RESPONSE

- The relationship between stress and illness is mediated by the interaction of a variety of factors.
- The major factors include physiological reactivity, cognitive appraisal, explanatory style, perceived control, personal hardiness, and social support.

COPING WITH STRESS

- Health psychologists use stress-management programs to help people learn to cope with stress.
- Two of the main ways of reducing stress are exercise and relaxation.

HEALTH-PROMOTING HABITS

- Most deaths in the United States are associated with unhealthy habits, including risky sexual practices, lack of exercise, poor nutrition, and smoking tobacco.
- Programs aimed at changing these habits hold promise for reducing the incidence of illness and premature death.

Key Concepts

health psychology 455

PSYCHOLOGICAL STRESS AND STRESSORS
posttraumatic stress disorder 457
stress 456
stressor 456

THE BIOPSYCHOLOGY OF STRESS AND ILLNESS
atherosclerosis 460
general adaptation syndrome 460
psychoneuroimmunology 463
Type A behavior 461

FACTORS THAT MODERATE THE STRESS RESPONSE
cognitive appraisal 466
explanatory style 466
learned helplessness 467
perceived control 467
physiological reactivity 466

psychological hardiness 467
social support 468

COPING WITH STRESS
progressive relaxation 470

Key Contributors

PSYCHOLOGICAL STRESS AND STRESSORS
Thomas Holmes and Richard Rahe 456
Hans Selye 456

THE BIOPSYCHOLOGY OF STRESS AND ILLNESS
Robert Ader and Nicholas Cohen 465
Walter Cannon 459
Meyer Friedman and Ray Rosenman 461
Karen Matthews 462

Shelley Taylor 459
Redford Williams 462

FACTORS THAT MODERATE THE STRESS RESPONSE
Richard Lazarus 466
Suzanne Kobasa Ouellette 467

COPING WITH STRESS
Janice Kiecolt-Glaser 470
James Pennebaker 469

HEALTH-PROMOTING HABITS
Kelly Brownell 473
Rod Dishman 472

1. Some researchers believe that major life events exert their harmful health effects through the daily hassles and related problems they create. How might getting divorced induce stress by this route?

2. Imagine that a friend of yours exhibits a pattern of Type A behavior. Which aspects of this pattern might it be best for her to alter?

Possible Answers to Thought Questions start on p. PT-5

3. Students commonly experience intense stress during the final weeks of the academic semester due to factors such as research papers, final exams, and lack of money. What physiological pathway might explain how these stressors could impair your immune system and make you more susceptible to illness immediately after the end of the semester?

4. What five risky or unhealthy behaviors would you be wisest to avoid?

OLC Preview

For additional quizzing and a variety of interactive resources, visit the book's Online Learning Center at www.mhhe.com/sdorow5.

chapter seventeen

17

Social Psychology

CLAUDE MONET
Boulevard des Capucines, 1873

On March 26,1997, millions around the world were shocked by the mass suicide of 39 members of the Heaven's Gate cult in a wealthy San Diego suburb. Cult members ingested lethal doses of phenobarbital, put plastic bags over their heads, and suffocated themselves. The scene was made even more chilling by its being meticulously neat and tidy, with people identically clad (down to their black Nike sneakers) lying peacefully on their backs, in purple shrouds, with their belongings (including lip balm and spiral notebooks) packed neatly in overnight bags.

Cult members even left videotaped messages explaining why they took their lives. They committed suicide because their leader, Marshall Applewhite, had promised that they would be resurrected into a better life aboard a space ship allegedly hidden behind the comet Hale-Bopp. Applewhite, seeking more members to accompany the cult on its journey to Hale-Bopp, had taken out an advertisement in *USA Today* reading "UFO Cult Resurfaces with Final Offer." The advertisement warned that it would be "the last chance to advance beyond human."

How could Applewhite, an outgoing former music teacher at the University of Alabama, transform himself into a charismatic cult leader? How could normal, intelligent adults be convinced to forsake their families, abandon successful careers, and flee their "bodily containers" with a mere promise of a better life at the "Next Level"? The answers to these questions are sought by social psychologists, who study human social interaction.

Social psychology is the study of behavior in its interpersonal context—that is, how the actual, imagined, or implied presence of other people affects one another's thoughts, feelings, and behaviors. The major topics of interest to social psychologists include *social cognition, interpersonal attraction, attitudes, group dynamics, prosocial behavior,* and *aggression.*

social psychology
The field that studies how the actual, imagined, or implied presence of other people affects one another's thoughts, feelings, and behaviors.

◄ **Heaven's Gate Cult**
The mass suicide of 39 members of the Heaven's Gate cult is a tragic example of the powerful influence charismatic leaders can exert over their followers.

 Social Psychology Network
www.mhhe.com/sdorow5

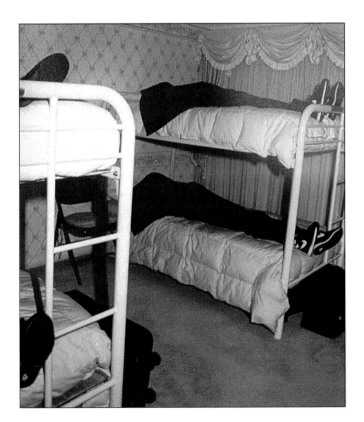

◆ SOCIAL COGNITION

social cognition

The process of perceiving, interpreting, and predicting social behavior.

causal attribution

The cognitive process by which we infer the causes of both our own and other people's social behavior.

Psychologists who study **social cognition** are concerned with how we perceive, interpret, and predict social behavior. As you will read, though social cognition is usually accurate, biases and subjectivity can distort it. Two of the main topics in social cognition are *causal attribution* and *person perception.*

Causal Attribution

As first noted in the 1940s by social psychologist Fritz Heider (1944), when we engage in **causal attribution** we judge the extent to which behavior is caused by the person or by the situation. One of the most influential attribution theorists is Harold Kelley; he identified factors that determine when we make either dispositional attributions or situational attributions.

When you decide that someone is responsible for his or her behavior, you are making a *dispositional attribution.* That is, you would be attributing the behavior to personal qualities, such as emotions, abilities, or personality traits. When you decide that circumstances are primarily responsible for a person's behavior, you are making a *situational attribution.* Consider explanations given for poverty. Two research studies (Zucker & Weiner, 1993), one using university students and one using nonstudents, found that political liberals tended to make situational attributions for poverty (blaming it on factors such as discrimination and lack of opportunities) and political conservatives tended to make dispositional attributions (blaming it on factors such as a lack of effort or ability). Moreover, there is evidence that there are cultural differences in people's tendencies to make dispositional or situational attributions. One study compared Korean and American undergraduates' explanations for criminal behavior. Korean undergraduates made more external attributions for crime than did American undergraduates (Na & Loftus, 1998). As you will read later in this chapter, social-cultural factors influence many aspects of social cognition and social behavior.

Dimensions of Causal Attribution

Kelley's theory of attribution was soon joined by one devised by Bernard Weiner (1985). Whereas Kelley's has been used primarily to explain the behavior of others, Weiner's has been used primarily to explain how we make causal attributions for our own behavior (Martinko & Thomson, 1998). Weiner identified three dimensions that govern the attribution process. The *internal-external dimension* is akin to Kelley's distinction between dispositional and situational attributions. The *stable-unstable dimension* refers to the degree to which we attribute a behavior to a factor that is stable or unstable. And the *controllable-uncontrollable dimension* indicates the extent to which we attribute a behavior to a factor that is controllable or uncontrollable. Weiner has found that people in a variety of cultures around the world use these dimensions in making attributions for their successes and failures (Schuster, Forsterling, & Weiner, 1989).

Weiner's three attributional dimensions are commonly used by students in explaining their academic performance (Anazonwu, 1995). In fact, students might use these dimensions in making excuses that both maintain their self-esteem and prevent professors from becoming angry at them (Weiner, Figueroa-Munoz, & Kakihara, 1991). Suppose you wanted to make an excuse for submitting a term paper late. Your excuse would be more effective if you attributed your behavior to external, unstable, and uncontrollable factors, such as a family emergency, than if you attributed it to internal, stable, and controllable factors, such as chronic problems with budgeting your time.

Biases in Causal Attribution

Because human beings are somewhat irrational and subjective, we exhibit biases in the causal attributions we make. These include the *fundamental attribution error* and *self-serving bias.*

▲ **Bernard Weiner**

"A variety of sources of information are used to reach causal inferences in achievement-related contexts. The primary perceived causes of success and failure are ability and effort."

The Fundamental Attribution Error. One bias is the tendency to attribute other people's behavior to dispositional factors. This is known as the **fundamental attribution error.** In one study, college undergraduates read descriptions of an expectant mother or father who was anticipating staying at home with the baby or returning to work after its birth. Participants rated the parents who expected to remain at home to care for their child as being more nurturing than parents who expected to return to work. Moreover, these ratings were unaffected by information about whether parents' employment was a matter of choice or necessity (Riggs, 1998). Thus, in explaining why parents work outside the home, we might commit the fundamental attribution error by overemphasizing the role of individual preference or personality (dispositional attributions) rather than situational factors.

Cross-cultural research finds that the fundamental attribution error is more common in Western cultures. Studies indicate that Asian participants are *less* likely to attribute people's behavior to dispositional factors. These cultural differences are attributable to East Asians' tendency to see people—and their behavior—as being constrained by social situations or circumstances (Choi, Nisbett, & Norenzayan, 1999).

Self-Serving Bias. We are also subject to the **self-serving bias,** which is the tendency to make dispositional attributions for our own positive behaviors and situational attributions for our own negative behaviors, especially when our self-esteem is threatened (Campbell & Sedikides, 1999). For example, a study of college students found that those who received high grades (A's or B's) tended to make dispositional attributions, attributing their high grades to their own efforts and abilities. In contrast, students who received lower grades (C's, D's, or F's) tended to make situational attributions, attributing their lower grades to bad luck and difficult tests (Bernstein, Stephan, & Davis, 1979). And the self-serving bias even holds when we make causal attributions for our favorite sport team's performance. Fans tend to make internal attributions for their teams' victories and external attributions for their losses (Wann & Schrader, 2000). The self-serving bias is in keeping with evidence (see Chapter 14) that psychological well-being is associated with the maintenance of a somewhat unrealistically positive view of oneself (Taylor & Brown, 1988).

But is psychological well-being achieved only by focusing on oneself? People also can derive a sense of well-being from their group identity or collective achievements. In collectivist cultures, attributions might follow a self-effacing, rather than self-enhancing, pattern. In one study, Japanese participants were more likely to make dispositional attributions following failure and less likely to make dispositional attributions following success on some achievement tasks (Kashima & Triandis, 1986). Moreover, Japanese students have been found to attribute the successes of others to dispositional factors and the failures of others to situational factors (Yamaguchi, 1988). Hazel Markus and Shinobu Kitayama (1991) have coined the term *modesty bias* for this apparent reversal of the self-serving bias in collectivist cultures.

Person Perception

In addition to making causal attributions, we spend a great deal of our time making judgments about other people. This is known as **person perception.** Researchers interested in person perception study topics such as *stereotypes, first impressions*, and *self-fulfilling prophecy.*

Stereotypes

College professor. Rock concert. Bill Cosby. Eskimo. Each of these concepts involves a **social schema,** which comprises the presumed characteristics of a role, event, person, or group. Social schemas can have powerful effects on our social perception. Consider *stereotypes*. A **stereotype** is a social schema that includes characteristics that are ascribed to almost

fundamental attribution error
The bias to attribute other people's behavior to dispositional factors.

self-serving bias
The tendency to make dispositional attributions for one's successes and situational attributions for one's failures.

person perception
The process of making judgments about the personal characteristics of others.

social schema
A cognitive structure comprising the presumed characteristics of a role, an event, a person, or a group.

stereotype
A social schema that incorporates characteristics, which can be positive or negative, supposedly shared by almost all members of a group.

▲ First Impressions

Do these women bring different thoughts and feelings to mind? Your first impressions of them might determine how you initially act toward them.

self-fulfilling prophecy
The tendency for one person's expectations to influence another person to behave in accordance with them.

all members of a group. Note that stereotypes, though usually negative, can be positive. American television commercials portray Asian Americans as a "model minority" consisting of people with a high work ethic. A study that analyzed more than 1,300 television commercials found that the commercials supported the stereotype of the hardworking Asian American by frequently showing them in business situations and rarely at social functions or in family settings (Taylor & Stern, 1997).

Stereotypes are reinforced, in part, by our tendency to view members of our own group (our *in-group*) as more variable than members of another group (an *out-group*). For example, a study compared views of South Africans and European Americans about their own group and the other group. The results showed that both groups held relatively complex views of their own group but a relatively simplistic view of the other group (Bartsch et al., 1997).

Stereotypes have a strong influence when we have little information about people other than their group membership. Of course, few people assume that *all* members of an out-group share the same characteristics. Thus, when confronted with someone who violates a stereotype, they simply assimilate that person into their out-group schema as an exception to the rule (Wilder, Simon, & Faith, 1996).

First Impressions

When we first meet a person, we might have little information about the individual other than her or his sex, ethnicity, and physical appearance. Each of these might activate a particular social schema, which in turn will create a first impression of that person. A first impression functions as a social schema to guide our predictions of a person's behavior and our desire to interact with that person. One clever study of first impressions had trained coders evaluate the firmness of undergraduates' handshakes. Participants with firm handshakes received more positive first-impression ratings than participants with weaker handshakes—especially female participants (Chaplin et al., 2000). And even criminal defendants might be judged more or less severely based on what they wear into court. An experiment found that college students who dressed in black clothing in a mock criminal proceeding were judged more harshly than those who wore light clothing (Vrij, 1997).

Self-Fulfilling Prophecy

One of the important effects of first impressions is **self-fulfilling prophecy,** which is the tendency for one person's expectations to make another person behave in accordance with them. This occurs because the social schema we have of the other person will make us act a certain way toward that person, which in turn will make the person respond in accordance with our expectations (Darley & Fazio, 1980). Thus, if you expect a person to be unfriendly and, as a result, act cold and aloof, you might elicit unfriendly behavior from that person—even if he or she would normally be inclined to be friendly. In fact, research shows that dating partners who expect to be rejected tend to behave in ways that provoke their partner to eventually reject them (Downey et al., 1998). But in contrast, a study conducted across a year found that dating partners who idealized each other at the beginning tended to create a self-fulfilling prophecy that produced the very relationship they sought (Murray, Holmes, & Griffin, 1996).

Stereotypes also can contribute to self-fulfilling prophecies. People perform better when they are unaware of negative stereotypes that others might hold of them. But what of positive stereotypes? Consider Asian American women, who are members of two stereotyped groups. As Asians they are stereotyped as being good in mathematics. As women they are stereotyped as being poor in mathematics. In one study, Asian women who completed a questionnaire including items about their ethnicity then performed better on a mathematics test than did Asian women who did not fill out the questionnaire. But Asian women who completed a questionnaire including items about their gender then performed worse on a mathematics test than Asian women who did not fill out the questionnaire. Evidently, the women's performances depended on whether ethnic or gender stereotypes had been made salient to them (Shih, Pittinsky, & Ambady, 1999). And a replication study addressed the social costs of being a "model minority." In this study, Asians' *extremely* high performance in mathematics was made salient to Asian women. Under these conditions, participants found it difficult to concentrate and performed more poorly. Hence, people's awareness of positive stereotypes that others might hold can lead to "choking" under pressure (Cheryan & Bodenhausen, 2000).

STAYING ON TRACK: *Social Cognition*

1. What are the three dimensions in Weiner's attribution model?
2. What is the self-serving bias?
3. How can a first impression create a self-fulfilling prophecy?

Answers to Staying on Track start on p. ST-8.

◆ INTERPERSONAL ATTRACTION

While forming impressions of other people, we also might develop *interpersonal attraction* toward some of them. Social psychologists seek answers to questions like these: Why do we like certain people more than others? What is the nature of romantic love?

Liking

Think of the students you have met this semester. Which ones do you like? Which ones do you not like? Among the factors that determine which ones you like are *proximity, familiarity, physical attractiveness,* and *similarity.*

Proximity

You are more likely to like someone who lives near you, works with you, or attends the same classes as you. Research has consistently supported the importance of *proximity* in the development of friendships, as in a classic study of the residents of a married student housing complex at the Massachusetts Institute of Technology. The closer students lived to one another, the more likely they were to become friends. In fact, 41 percent of the students reported that their best friends lived next door. Because the students had been randomly assigned to apartments, their initial degree of liking for one another could not explain the findings (Festinger, Schachter, & Back, 1950). Proximity is important in dating relationships, too. A study of college students across a 3-month period found that those engaged in long-distance relationships were as emotionally close to their partners as students with partners who were nearby. But partners involved in long-distance relationships felt less satisfied with their relationships than the others did (Van Horn et al., 1997).

Familiarity

Proximity makes us more familiar with certain people. But contrary to the popular saying, familiarity tends to breed liking, not contempt. As explained in Chapter 6, the more familiar we become with a stimulus—whether a car, a painting, or a professor—the more we will like it. So, in general, the more we interact with particular people, the more we tend to like them (Moreland & Zajonc, 1982). Of course, this tendency, called the *mere exposure effect,* holds only when the people do not behave in negative ways.

The mere exposure effect was supported by a clever experiment that used female college students as participants. Two photographs of each participant were presented to the participant and to a friend. One photograph was a direct image of the participant; the second was a mirror image—what the participant would see when looking at herself in a mirror. Mirror images and normal photographic images differ because our faces are not perfectly symmetrical—the left and right sides look different. Participants and friends were asked to choose which of the two photographs they preferred. Friends were more likely to choose the direct image. In contrast, participants were more likely to choose the mirror image. This was evidence for the mere exposure effect, because the friends were more familiar with the direct image, whereas the participants were more familiar with their own mirror image (Mita, Dermer, & Knight, 1977).

▲ Ellen Berscheid *(above)* and Elaine Hatfield

"The evidence suggests that most individuals docilely accept the prescription that beauty and sexual and romantic passion are inexorably linked."

passionate love

Love characterized by intense emotional arousal and sexual feelings.

companionate love

Love characterized by feelings of affection and commitment to a relationship with another person.

Physical Attractiveness

Proximity not only lets us become familiar with people, it also lets us note their appearance. We tend to like physically attractive people more than physically unattractive ones. Attractive adults and children are judged more positively and treated more positively by others. In turn—consistent with self-fulfilling prophecy—attractive adults and children also exhibit more positive behaviors and personality traits (Langlois et al., 2000). Physically attractive people are more likely to be hired for jobs than other applicants with equivalent qualifications (Marlowe, Schneider, & Nelson, 1996). Physically attractive defendants are less likely to be convicted of crimes and, if convicted, less likely to receive severe punishment (Mazzella & Feingold, 1994). Physically attractive college students are less likely to be asked for proof of age by bartenders (McCall, 1997). And physical attractiveness is an important factor in dating relationships. Both men and women value character and physical attractiveness in dating relationships. But men put a higher premium on youth and physical attractiveness and women put a higher premium on character, social status, and personality traits (Ben-Hamida, Mineka, & Bailey, 1998; Shaffer & Bazzini, 1997).

Judgments of facial attractiveness have strong cross-cultural consistency (Langlois et al., 2000). In one study, native-born European Americans and newly arrived Asian and Latino students rated the attractiveness of photographs of African American, European American, Asian, and Latina women. The correlation in ratings, .93, was almost perfect. In a companion study, African American and European American men rated the attractiveness of photos of African American women. Ratings of facial attractiveness correlated .94, but there were ethnic differences in ratings of body attractiveness (Cunningham et al., 1995).

Similarity

Do opposites attract? Or do birds of a feather flock together? You might recall the experiment discussed in Chapter 2 that showed that we are more attracted to people whose attitudes are similar to our own (Byrne, Ervin, & Lamberth, 1970). The findings of that classic study have been replicated in many research studies (Lancaster, Royal, & Whiteside, 1995). But this interpretation has been challenged by research showing that we are likely to associate with people who hold similar attitudes simply by default, because we are *repulsed* by those who have dissimilar ones (Singh & Ho, 2000). Life's circumstances simply put us in settings where we are likely to associate with people who share our attitudes.

But the results of research studies indicate that attitude similarity plays a more important role in interpersonal attraction than attitude dissimilarity does in preventing it (Drigotas, 1993). And other research indicates that we like people who share our activity preferences even more than we like people who share our attitudes (Lydon, Jamieson, & Zanna, 1988). Thus, you might enjoy playing sports or going to music concerts with someone whose sexual, religious, and political values differ from yours. And in certain cases we are attracted to people who are not similar to us if we find that their personal characteristics are fulfilling. This might occur, for example, when one person is dominant and the other is submissive. These partners are more satisfied with their relationship than partners who are similar in those personality characteristics (Dryer & Horowitz, 1997).

Romantic Love

Love might make the world go round, but there were few scientific studies of romantic love until the 1970s. What have researchers discovered since then about the nature of romantic love?

Theories of Love

Researchers Elaine Hatfield and Ellen Berscheid distinguish between passionate love and companionate love (Hatfield, 1988). **Passionate love** involves intense emotional arousal, including sexual feelings. **Companionate love** involves feelings of affection and commitment to the relationship. Over time, romantic relationships tend to decline in passionate love and increase in companionate love.

◀ **The Two-Factor Theory of Romantic Love**
This couple (accompanied by their attendants) was married on the Montu roller coaster at Busch Gardens in Florida. According to two-factor theory, the physiological arousal from the roller coaster ride might have heightened the couple's emotional experience of the romantic moment.

More research has been conducted on passionate love than on companionate love. According to Berscheid and Hatfield, passionate love depends on three factors. First, the culture must promote the notion of passionate love. Passionate love has been important in Western cultures only for a few centuries, and even today some cultures have no concept of it. Second, the person must experience a state of intense emotional arousal. Third, the emotional arousal must be associated with a romantic partner (Berscheid & Walster, 1974).

Berscheid and Hatfield's theory of romantic love incorporates aspects of Schachter and Singer's two-factor theory of emotion (see Chapter 12). Two-factor theory assumes that romantic love is the result of being physiologically aroused in a situation that promotes the labeling of that arousal as romantic love. The two-factor theory of romantic love was supported by a clever experiment that took place on two bridges in Vancouver, British Columbia (Dutton & Aron, 1974). One, the Capilano River Bridge, was 5 feet wide, 450 feet long, and suspended 230 feet above rocky rapids. It had low handrails and was constructed of wooden boards attached to wire cables, making it prone to wobble back and forth, inducing fear-related physiological arousal in those who walked across it. The other bridge, over a tiny tributary of the Capilano River, was wide, solid, immobile, and only 10 feet above the water. These characteristics made that bridge less likely to induce arousal in those who walked across it.

Whenever a man walked across one of the bridges, he was met by an attractive woman who was the experimenter's accomplice. The woman asked each man to participate in a psychology course project about the effects of scenic attractions on creativity. Each man was shown a picture of a man and a woman in an ambiguous situation and was asked to write a brief dramatic story about the picture. The woman then gave the man her telephone number in case he wanted to ask her any questions about the study. Compared with the men on the other bridge, the men who were on the bridge that induced physiological arousal wrote stories with more sexual content and were more likely to call the woman later.

According to the two-factor theory of romantic love, the men on the bridge that induced arousal had attributed their arousal to the presence of the attractive woman, leading them to experience romantic feelings toward her. But this interpretation of the results has been rejected by some researchers, who offer an alternative interpretation that assumes that the presence of the woman reduced the men's fear of the bridge, which, as a consequence, conditioned them to find her more attractive (Riordan & Tedeschi, 1983). Nonetheless, results of other studies have supported the two-factor theory of romantic love. In one such study, men who were physiologically aroused by exercise while in the presence of an attractive woman were more attracted to that woman than were men who were not physiologically aroused (White, Fishbein, & Rutstein, 1981). A recent meta-analysis also found consistent effects of arousal on attraction, with effect sizes ranging from small to moderate across a number of conditions (Foster et al., 1998).

▲ Companionate Love

For romantic love to last after passionate love has waned somewhat, romantic partners must maintain the deep affection that characterizes companionate love.

There also are culture-related differences in the definition of romantic love (Landis & O'Shea, 2000). One study compared love songs in the United States and Hong Kong and mainland China. In Chinese songs, love was expected to come to an unhappy end and involved intense suffering. Though songs from both cultures depicted similar levels of desire, Chinese songs depicted love as being less individualistic and more influenced by family relationships and even the environment—a reflection of the Taoist principle of harmony with nature and society (Rothbaum & Tsang, 1998).

Promoting Romantic Love

What factors promote romantic love? As in the case of personal liking, similarity is an important factor. We tend to form romantic relationships with people who are similar to us in attractiveness (Murstein, 1972), as well as in religion, ethnic background, and educational level (Buss, 1985). One factor is an exception to the similarity rule—age. Gay and heterosexual men prefer younger partners than do heterosexual and lesbian women (Silverthorne & Quinsey, 2000). Another important factor in romantic relationships is a sense of humor. A recent survey of heterosexual college students found that both men and women viewed humorous people as more appealing for serious relationships, including marriage, but only when they perceived them as physically attractive (Lundy, Tan, & Cunningham, 1998).

Still another important factor in romantic relationships is equity, the belief that each partner is contributing equally to the relationship, which promotes contentment and commitment (Winn, Crawford, & Fischer, 1991). An archival study of 800 advertisements placed by individuals seeking romantic partners found that the advertisers tended to seek equitable relationships. But women and men differed in the rewards they sought and offered. Men tended to seek attractive women, while offering financial security in return. In contrast, women tended to seek financially secure men, while offering physical attractiveness in return (Harrison, 1977). These findings have been replicated in a laboratory experiment (Sprecher, 1989) and in more recent archival research studies (Cicerello & Sheehan, 1995).

These findings hold across cultures, as in a study of the marital preferences of more than 1,500 heterosexual college students in Japan, Russia, and the United States (Hatfield & Sprecher, 1995). But personal advertisements placed by heterosexuals, lesbians, and gay men differ. Two studies found, for example, that heterosexuals mentioned financial security more frequently than did gay men or lesbians. Physical characteristics were mentioned the most by gay men and the least by lesbians (Gonzales & Meyers, 1993). And gay men mentioned sex most often; heterosexual men offered financial security most often; and heterosexual women offered personality qualities and physical attractiveness most often (Child et al., 1996).

Evolutionary psychologists would claim that these findings are not surprising because they reflect millions of years of evolution. According to this interpretation, men prefer younger, physically attractive women because they would be more likely to be fertile, bear children and, as a result, pass on the men's genes. Similarly, women prefer men of higher financial status—especially those who are kind, caring, and loyal—because they would probably be more able and willing to care for them and their offspring (Greenlees & McGrew, 1994). Of course, the evolutionary psychology viewpoint provides an after-the-fact explanation for behaviors that might be explained just as well by cultural differences in gender roles. This interpretation is supported by the results of a recent study of almost 10,000 heterosexual women and men in 37 cultures. Women (but not men) preferred mates with greater financial resources in cultures that limited reproductive freedom and educational equality for women (Kasser & Sharma, 1999).

STAYING ON TRACK: *Interpersonal Attraction*

1. What evidence is there that the mere exposure effect contributes to liking?
2. How does two-factor theory explain romantic love?
3. How do personal advertisements for romantic partners support equity as a factor in romantic relationships?

Answers to Staying on Track start on p. ST-8.

◆ ATTITUDES

What are your opinions about the insanity defense? surprise parties? abstract art? sorority members? Your answers to these questions would reveal your attitudes. **Attitudes** are evaluations of ideas (such as the insanity defense), events (such as surprise parties), objects (such as abstract art), or people (such as sorority members).Thus, attitudes have emotional, cognitive, and behavioral components (Breckler, 1984). To appreciate this, imagine that you have been asked to participate in a market research survey of attitudes toward a new low-cholesterol, fast-food hamburger called "Burger-Lo." The market researcher would determine your attitude toward Burger-Lo by measuring one or more of the three components of your attitude. Your *emotional* response might be measured by a questionnaire asking you to rate your feelings about Burger-Lo's taste, aroma, texture, and appearance. Your *cognitive* response might be measured by asking you to describe the thoughts that Burger-Lo brings to mind, such as "It's better than a Big Mac." And your *behavioral* response might be measured by observing whether you choose Burger-Lo over several other fast-food hamburgers in a blind taste test.

attitude
An evaluation, containing cognitive, emotional, and behavioral components, of an idea, event, object, or person.

Attitudes and Behavior

Common sense tells us that if we know a person's attitudes, we can accurately predict her or his behavior. But the relationship is not that simple. For one thing, our behavior might not always agree with our attitudes. Perhaps more surprisingly, our behavior can sometimes affect our attitudes.

Links on Attitudes, Persuasion, and Influence
www.mhhe.com/sdorow5

The Influence of Attitudes on Behavior

Until the late 1960s, most social psychologists accepted the commonsense notion that our behavior is consistent with our attitudes. But since then researchers have found that attitudes are not as consistent with behavior as previously believed. What determines whether our attitudes and behaviors will be consistent? Attitudes that are strongly held (Kraus, 1995) or personally important (Crano & Prislin, 1995) are better predictors of behavior. Attitude-behavior consistency also is affected by the specificity of the attitude and the behavior. Your attitudes and behaviors are more consistent with one another when they are at similar levels of specificity (Weigel, Vernon, & Tognacci, 1974). For example, your attitude toward safe driving might not predict whether you will obey the speed limit tomorrow morning, but it will predict your general tendency, over time, to engage in safe driving behaviors, such as checking your tire pressure, using turn signals, and obeying the speed limit.

The Influence of Behavior on Attitudes

In the mid 1950s, Leon Festinger (1919–1989) and his colleagues were intrigued by a sect whose members believed they would be saved by aliens in flying saucers at midnight prior to the day of a prophesized worldwide flood (Festinger, Riecken, & Schachter, 1956). But neither the aliens nor the flood arrived. Did the members lose their faith? Some did, but many reported that their faith was strengthened. They simply concluded that the aliens had rewarded their faith by saving the world from the flood. These members simply changed their belief in order to justify their action.

The ability of the sect's members to relieve the emotional distress they experienced when the prophecy failed to come true stimulated Festinger's interest in attitude change and his development of **cognitive dissonance theory.** Cognitive dissonance is an unpleasant state of tension associated with increased physiological (Harmon-Jones et al., 1996) and psychological (Harmon-Jones, 2000) arousal, caused by the realization that one has beliefs that are inconsistent with each other or a belief that is inconsistent with one's behavior. We are motivated to reduce the unpleasant arousal associated with cognitive dissonance by making our cognitions consistent. Consider a person who drinks alcohol despite believing drinking is wrong. A study of drinkers found that those who had negative attitudes toward drinking were more likely than those with a positive attitude to claim that other people drank more than they did, apparently to reduce their cognitive dissonance in response to performing a behavior they believed was inappropriate (Maekelae, 1997).

cognitive dissonance theory
Leon Festinger's theory that attitude change is motivated by the desire to relieve the unpleasant state of arousal caused when one holds cognitions and/or behaviors that are inconsistent with each other.

The more we feel responsible for the inconsistencies between our cognitions, the stronger will be our feelings of cognitive dissonance and the more motivated we will be to change them. This was the finding of the first experimental study of cognitive dissonance (Festinger & Carlsmith, 1959). Students were asked to perform boring tasks, one of which was to arrange small spools on a tray, dump the tray, and arrange the spools again and again for half an hour. Each student was paid either $1 or $20 to tell the next student that the task was enjoyable. After the experiment was over, the students were asked to express their attitude toward the task. Their responses violated what common sense predicted. Those who were paid less ($1) tended to rate the task as interesting, while those who were paid more ($20) tended to rate the task as boring.

What could account for this finding? According to the theory of cognitive dissonance, the students experienced unpleasant arousal because their claim that the task was interesting did not agree with their belief that the task was boring. But those who were paid $20 to lie about the task experienced weaker cognitive dissonance because they could justify their lies by attributing them to the large payment they received. In contrast, those who were paid only $1 to lie experienced stronger cognitive dissonance because they could not attribute their lies to such a paltry sum. Consequently, those who were paid only $1 reduced the dissonance between their cognitions by changing their attitudes toward the task, rating it as more interesting than it actually was.

The cognitive dissonance interpretation of attitude change has been challenged by a theory put forth by Daryl Bem (1967). According to his **self-perception theory,** attitude change is not motivated by our need to reduce cognitive dissonance. Instead, we infer our attitudes from our behavior in the same way that we infer other people's attitudes from their behavior. When we observe people behaving under no apparent external constraints, we use their behavior to make inferences about their attitudes. Likewise, when the situation we are in does not place strong constraints on our behavior, we might infer our attitudes from our behavior.

But how does self-perception theory explain why students who were paid $1 for lying showed greater attitude change than students who were paid $20? According to Bem, the students did not experience cognitive dissonance. Instead, they determined whether their behavior was attributable to themselves or to the situation. The students who were paid $20 attributed their behavior to being paid a relatively large sum of money. They had no reason to attribute their behavior to their attitude. In contrast, the students who were paid $1 could not attribute their behavior to such a small sum of money. Consequently, those students attributed their behavior to their attitude, perhaps saying to themselves, "If I told another student that the task was interesting and I was not induced to do so by a large amount of money, then the task must have been interesting to me."

Neither cognitive dissonance theory nor self-perception theory has emerged as the superior explanation of the effect of behavior on attitudes. But each seems to be superior in certain circumstances. Whereas cognitive dissonance theory seems to be better at explaining the effect of behavior on well-defined attitudes, self-perception theory seems to be better at explaining the effect of behavior on poorly defined attitudes (Chaiken & Baldwin, 1981).

The Art of Persuasion

In 1956, Edward Schein published an article that described the results of his interviews with U.S. soldiers who, as prisoners during the Korean War, had been subjected to so-called brainwashing, which in some cases made them express sympathy for the North Koreans and antipathy toward the United States. Publicity about brainwashing, and fears that it could be used by totalitarian governments to control citizens, stimulated further interest in studying factors that affect persuasion and resistance to it. **Persuasion** is the attempt to influence the attitudes of other people.

According to the **elaboration likelihood model** of Richard Petty and John Cacioppo (1981), persuasive messages can take a *central route* or a *peripheral route.* A message that takes a central route relies on clear, explicit arguments about the issue at hand. In contrast, a message that takes a peripheral route relies on factors other than the merits of the arguments, such as characteristics of the source or the situational context. The more elaborately

---

self-perception theory
The theory that we infer our attitudes from our behavior in the same way that we infer other people's attitudes from their behavior.

persuasion
The attempt to influence the attitudes of other people.

elaboration likelihood model
A theory of persuasion that considers the extent to which messages take a central route or a peripheral route.

▲ **The Power of Persuasion**

Attempts at persuasion pervade our everyday lives, as in this confrontation between abortion activists.

we think about the merits of an argument, the more lasting will be any attitude change that occurs. The central and peripheral routes are related to the main factors in persuasion: the *source,* the *message,* and the *audience.*

The Source and Persuasion

One of the important peripheral factors in persuasion is the source of the message. The greater the *credibility* of the source, the more persuasive the message is. Politicians realize this and gain votes by having credible supporters praise their merits and criticize their opponents' faults (Calantone & Warshaw, 1985). But what determines a source's credibility? Perhaps the most important factor is the source's *expertise.* A meta-analysis of 114 studies of the effects of source characteristics on persuasion found that expertise was the single most credibility-enhancing source characteristic (Wilson & Sherrell, 1993). For example, people who read stories about UFOs that include supportive statements from a scientific authority become more likely to express beliefs in UFOs than people who read stories that do not include such statements (Sparks & Pellechia, 1997).

Another important factor in promoting source credibility is *trustworthiness.* When we perceive a source as trustworthy, we are less likely to critically scrutinize her or his message. This makes us more likely to be persuaded by the message (Priester & Petty, 1995). We perceive sources as especially trustworthy when their message is not an obvious attempt at persuasion, particularly when the message is contrary to the source's expected position (Wood & Eagly, 1981). For example, as noted in Chapter 10, Sir Cyril Burt's biographer concluded that Burt had fabricated data supporting a strong genetic basis for intelligence. The author of an article that discussed Burt's biography claimed, "The conclusion carries more weight because the author of the biography, Professor Leslie Hearnshaw, began his task as an admirer" (Hawkes, 1979, p. 673). If Hearnshaw had been a critic of Burt's work, his conclusion would have been less credible.

Sources that are *attractive,* because they are likable or physically appealing, also are more persuasive. Advertisers take advantage of this by having attractive actors appear in their commercials (Shavitt et al., 1994). Even the appeal of politicians is affected by their attractiveness. Richard Nixon's unattractive appearance during a debate with John F. Kennedy might have cost him the 1960 presidential election. Nixon's five-o'clock shadow and tendency to perspire made him less attractive to voters who watched the debate on television. Surveys found that those who watched the debate on television rated Kennedy the winner, while those who listened to it on the radio rated Nixon the winner (Weisman, 1988). Having learned from Nixon's mistake, today's politicians make sure that they appear as attractive as possible on television.

The Message and Persuasion

It might surprise you to learn that it is not always desirable to present arguments that support only your position. Simply acknowledging the other side of an issue, while strongly supporting your own, is at times more effective. A meta-analysis found that two-sided messages are generally more effective than one-sided messages in changing attitudes (Allen, 1993). This was discovered by social psychologist Carl Hovland and his colleagues in the waning days of World War II, following the surrender of Germany (Hovland, Lumsdaine, & Sheffield, 1949). The military asked Hovland for advice on how to convince soldiers that the war against Japan would take a long time to win. The researchers presented soldiers with a 15-minute talk that presented either one-sided or two-sided arguments. In the one-sided argument, they presented only arguments about why the war would not be over soon, such as the fighting spirit of the Japanese. In the two-sided argument, they presented both that argument *and* arguments explaining why the war might end earlier, such as Allied air superiority. Before and after the message, participants were given surveys that included questions about how long they believed the war would last.

The results showed that those who originally believed the war would take a long time to win were more influenced by the one-sided argument. But those who originally believed there would be an early end to the war were more influenced by the two-sided argument. As you can see, if the listener already favors your position or has no counterarguments

▲ **Credibility and Persuasion**
Roger Ebert has become a persuasive movie reviewer. His credibility is based on his perceived expertise and trustworthiness.

Influence at Work: The Psychology of Persuasion
www.mhhe.com/sdorow5

Media Psychology
www.mhhe.com/sdorow5

▲ The Appeal to Fear

Persuasive appeals that rely on fear can be effective if the supposed threat is severe, its likelihood is high, and we can do something to prevent or eliminate it. For example, a study of public service announcements about AIDS found that fear-evoking messages were especially effective in convincing sexually active people that they should use condoms (Struckman-Johnson, Struckman-Johnson, & Gilliland, 1994).

handy, arguments that favor your position alone will be more persuasive. But if the listener opposes your position, arguments that acknowledge both sides of the issue will be more persuasive. Two-sided arguments are effective, in part, because they enhance the credibility of the source and decrease counterarguing by the listener (Kamins & Assael, 1987).

The Audience and Persuasion

Persuasion depends on the audience, as well as the message and its source. An important audience factor is intelligence, because it determines whether a message will be more effective using the central or the peripheral route. People of relatively high intelligence are more likely to be influenced by messages supported by rational arguments—the central route. People of relatively low intelligence are more likely to be influenced by messages supported by factors other than rational arguments—the peripheral route (Eagly & Warren, 1976). Overall, people of lower intelligence are more easily influenced than people of higher intelligence (Rhodes & Wood, 1992).

Another important audience factor is whether the audience finds the message personally important (Zuwerink & Devine, 1996). A message's importance for a particular audience determines whether the central route or the peripheral route will be more effective (Petty & Cacioppo, 1990). When a message has high importance to an audience, the central route will be more effective. When a message has low importance, the peripheral route will be more effective. This was the finding of a study that measured student attitudes toward recommended policy changes at a university. The changes would be instituted either the following year (high importance) or in 10 years (low importance). Students who were asked to respond to arguments about policy changes of high importance were influenced more by the quality of the arguments (central route) than by the expertise of the source (peripheral route). In contrast, students who were asked to respond to arguments about policy changes of low importance were influenced more by the expertise of the source than by the quality of the arguments (Petty, Cacioppo, & Goldman, 1981).

Prejudice

Years ago, third-grade teacher Jane Elliott of Riceville, Iowa, gained national attention for her demonstration of the devastating psychological effects of a particular kind of attitude: prejudice. She divided her students, who all were European American, into a blue-eyed group and a brown-eyed group. On the first day of the demonstration, Elliott declared that blue-eyed people were superior to brown-eyed people. The next day, she declared that brown-eyed people were superior to blue-eyed people.

Members of the superior group were given privileges, such as sitting where they wanted to in class, going to lunch early, and staying late at recess. Members of the inferior group were made to wear identification collars and were not permitted to play with members of the superior group. Elliott reported that during the two-day demonstration, students who were made to feel inferior became depressed and performed poorly on classwork (Leonard, 1970). If prejudice could have this effect in an artificial, temporary situation, imagine the effect that prejudice has on children who are its targets in everyday life.

Fortunately, some forms of prejudice appear to be declining in North America. Surveys of European American adults have found that those born after World War II are less prejudiced than those born before the war toward people with Jewish, Asian, African, or Latino backgrounds (Wilson, 1996). Canadians have become more accepting of immigrant groups and multicultural diversity (Berry & Kalin, 1995). And sexual prejudice is declining as Americans have become more tolerant of gay men and lesbians. However, a majority of adult Americans still believe homosexual behavior is "wrong" (Yang, 1997). This lack of tolerance also is reflected in a high rate of violence. More than 1,100 hate crimes against lesbians, bisexuals, and gay men were reported to American law enforcement agencies in 1997 (Herek, 2000).

Prejudice is a positive or negative attitude toward a person based on her or his membership in a particular group. People vary in their awareness of their own prejudiced attitudes. Some people are well aware of their prejudices; others might act in a prejudiced manner

prejudice
A positive or negative attitude toward a person based on her or his membership in a particular group.

without even realizing they are *implicitly* prejudiced (Dovidio et al., 1997). For example, a survey of four Western European countries found that respondents who scored high on a measure of blatant prejudice were more likely to endorse harsh exclusionary policies reducing immigration. In contrast, respondents who scored high on a measure of implicit prejudice shared exclusionary attitudes toward immigrants—however, they supported methods that were ostensibly nondiscriminatory (Meertens & Pettigrew, 1997). This *modern racism* could develop from social norms that discourage the expression of overt prejudice (McConahay, 1986).

The behavioral component of prejudice is *discrimination,* which involves treating persons differently, whether positively or negatively, based only on their group membership. For example, a study found that students who evaluated the applications of men and women favored women for jobs that required warmth and submission and men for jobs that required shrewdness and leadership. The jobs for which men were favored also were those for which high-achieving applicants were favored. This suggests that female applicants are more apt to be discriminated against when applying for higher-status jobs (Zebrowitz, Tenenbaum, & Goldstein, 1991). Researchers who have applied the concept of modern racism to contemporary sexism believe that similar beliefs underlie negative attitudes toward affirmative action programs for women (Masser & Abrams, 1999). Moreover, this form of sexism is not unique to the United States. A cross-cultural study of 15,000 women and men found similar sexist beliefs in 19 countries (Glick et al., 2000).

Implicit Association Test
www.mhhe.com/sdorow5

Factors That Promote Prejudice

What factors account for the origin and maintenance of prejudice? As with all attitudes, learning plays an important role. Parents, peers, and the media all provide input, informing us of the supposed characteristics of particular groups. For example, an analysis of 1,699 television commercials found that they stereotyped European American men as powerful, European American women as sex objects, African American men as aggressive, and African American women as unimportant (Coltrane & Messineo, 2000). Even humor can promote prejudice. A Canadian study found that college students who were exposed to disparaging humor about an ethnic minority group became more prejudiced against that group than were students exposed to nondisparaging humor (Maio, Olson, & Bush, 1997).

People also exhibit favoritism to their own kind. In a series of experiments, Henri Tajfel and colleagues demonstrated that the social experience of becoming a member of a group can produce an *in-group bias,* or a tendency to exhibit favoritism toward members of one's group (Tajfel, 1981; Tajfel & Billig, 1974). Moreover, perceived threats to the in-group appear to increase this tendency. One study assessed the relationship between perceived threats to the in-group, intergroup anxiety, and negative stereotypes of Cuban, Mexican, and Asian immigrants in Florida, New Mexico, and Hawaii. Each of these factors was positively correlated with prejudice toward immigrants (Stephan, Ybarra, & Bachman, 1999). Similar results were found in a study of Moroccan, Russian, and Ethiopian immigrants in Spain and Israel (Stephan et al., 1998).

▲ **Mamie Phipps Clark and Kenneth Clark**

Mamie and Kenneth Clark were among the first researchers to study African American children.

Factors That Reduce Prejudice

Social psychologists also are concerned with finding ways to reduce prejudice. But this is difficult, because stereotypes are resistant to change. We modify the stereotypes we hold only gradually through individual experiences and by creating subtypes to accommodate instances that we cannot easily assimilate. As mentioned earlier, we do not necessarily revise our stereotypes after experiencing a few dramatic exceptions to them (Weber & Crocker, 1983). Nonetheless, exceptions to stereotypes do make the out-group seem more variable, which tends to weaken the stereotypes somewhat (Hamburger, 1994).

In the 1950s, Gordon Allport (1954) insisted that increasing social contact between members of different social groups could reduce prejudice. At about the same time, in 1954, in the landmark case *Brown v. Board of Education of Topeka,* the U.S. Supreme Court ruled that "separate but equal" schools did not provide African American children with the same benefits as European American children received. The Court's decision was influenced by research showing that segregated schools hurt the self-esteem of African American children and increased racial prejudice. For example, a study by Kenneth Clark and Mamie Phipps Clark found that African American children believed European American dolls were better than African American ones and preferred to play with European American ones (Clark & Clark, 1947). A review of studies of African American children's self-esteem revealed that research findings differ according to whether the research was conducted before or after the civil rights movement of the 1960s. Earlier studies reported that African Americans had lower self-esteem than European Americans; more recent studies conducted after the civil rights movement have found that this is no longer true (Gray-Little & Hafdahl, 2000).

Events during the past century have shown that social contact alone might not produce the effects predicted by Allport and the Supreme Court. For contact between groups to reduce prejudice, the contact must be between group members of equal status (Spangenberg & Nel, 1983). The effectiveness of equal-status contact in reducing racial prejudice was supported by a study of African American children and European American children who spent a week at a summer camp. The children were between 8 and 12 years old and were of equally low socioeconomic status. At the end of the week, children of both ethnic groups had more positive attitudes toward children of the other ethnic group (Clore et al., 1978). Contact with members of an out-group can weaken stereotypes by increasing the perceived heterogeneity of that group (Lee & Ottati, 1993).

STAYING ON TRACK: *Attitudes*

1. What factors influence the consistency between attitudes and behaviors?
2. What factors determine whether the central route or the peripheral route will be more effective in persuasion?
3. What does research say about the effect of contact between in-group members and out-group members on prejudice?

Answers to Staying on Track start on p. ST-8.

Group Dynamics
www.mhhe.com/sdorow5

group

A collection of two or more persons who interact and have mutual influence on each other.

◆ GROUP DYNAMICS

In everyday life we refer to any collection of people as a "group." But social psychologists favor a narrower definition of a **group** as a collection of two or more persons who interact and have mutual influence on each other. In the late 1940s, hoping to understand the social factors that contributed to the Great Depression, the rise of European dictatorships, and World War II, social psychologists became more interested in studying the factors that affect relationships between members of groups. This remains an important area of research in social psychology, and includes the topics of *groupthink in decision making, group effects on performance,* and *social influence.*

Groupthink in Decision Making

On January 28, 1986, the space shuttle *Challenger* exploded shortly after taking off from Cape Canaveral, Florida, killing all of the crew members and shocking the millions of television viewers excited by the presence of the first teacher-astronaut, Christa McAuliffe. The investigative committee reported that the explosion was caused by a faulty joint seal in one of the rocket boosters. The decision to launch the shuttle had been made despite warnings from engineers that the joint might fail in cold weather. This ill-fated decision has been attributed to *groupthink* (Moorhead, Ference, & Neck, 1991).

The term **groupthink,** coined by psychologist Irving Janis (1918–1990), refers to a decision-making process in small, cohesive groups that places unanimity ahead of critical thinking and aims at premature consensus. Groupthink is promoted by several factors: a charismatic leader, feelings of invulnerability, discrediting of contrary evidence, fear of criticism for disagreeing, the desire to maintain group harmony, isolation from outside influences, and disparaging outsiders as incompetent. A central factor in groupthink is a shared overestimate of the group's capabilities (Whyte, 1998). In criticizing the decision to launch the *Challenger*, Senator John Glenn of Ohio, the first American to orbit Earth, referred to feelings of invulnerability among the officials who made the decision: "The mindset of a few people in key positions at NASA had changed from an optimistic and supersafety conscious 'can do' attitude, when I was in the program, to an arrogant 'can't fail' attitude" (Zaldivar, 1986, p. 12-A). This was unfortunate, because having a devil's advocate in a group promotes consideration of alternatives (Valacich & Schwenk, 1995).

Janis's concept of groupthink has received support from experimental studies on group decision making. Groups with directive leaders consider fewer alternatives than do groups with leaders who encourage member participation, especially if the leader expresses her or his opinion early in deliberation (Ahlfinger & Esser, 2001). Group cohesiveness also has an effect. A meta-analysis found that if other conditions conducive to groupthink are present, group cohesiveness will promote groupthink; if those conditions are not present, cohesiveness actually will improve decision making (Mullen et al., 1994). Of course, the groupthink phenomenon does not always occur during group decision making and, when it does occur, it does not always produce negative outcomes (Choi & Kim, 1999). Though the concept of groupthink seems convincing, evidence for it has come primarily from after-the-fact interpretations of well-known, misguided group decisions. In fact, there has been relatively little support for the groupthink phenomenon from experimental research (Park, 2000). More experimental research is needed to determine whether groupthink is a robust phenomenon and, if it does exist, to identify the factors that account for it.

Group Effects on Performance

One of the first topics to be studied by social psychologists was the influence of groups on the task performances of their members. Social psychologists have been especially interested in studying the effects of *social facilitation* and *social loafing* on performance.

Social Facilitation

More than a century ago Norman Triplett (1898) observed that bicyclists who raced against other bicyclists rode faster than those who raced against the clock. He studied this phenomenon experimentally by having boys spin fishing reels while competing either against time or against another boy. He found that those who competed against another boy performed faster. Two decades later psychologist Floyd Allport (1920) found that people performed a variety of tasks better when working in the same room than when working in separate rooms. Allport called the improvement in performance caused by the presence of other people **social facilitation.**

But later studies found that the presence of others sometimes *impairs* performance. A review of 241 studies involving almost 24,000 participants found that the presence of other people improves performance on simple or well-learned tasks and impairs performance on complex or poorly learned tasks (Bond & Titus, 1983). For example, in one study, children

▲ **Irving Janis (1918–1990)**
"I use the term *groupthink* as a quick and easy way to refer to a mode of thinking that people engage in when they are deeply involved in a cohesive in-group, when the members' strivings for unanimity override their motivation to realistically appraise alternative courses of action."

groupthink
The tendency of small, cohesive groups to place unanimity ahead of critical thinking in making decisions.

social facilitation
The improvement in a person's task performance when in the presence of other people.

▲ **Social Facilitation**

Cyclists, such as Tour de France winner Lance Armstrong, ride faster when they are competing with others than when they are competing against the clock.

social loafing

A decrease in the individual effort exerted by group members when working together on a task.

▲ **Social Loafing**

Because of social loafing, these children will probably exert less individual effort than they would if they pulled by themselves.

tried to balance on a teeterboard for as long as possible. Children who were highly skilled performed better in the presence of others; children who were poorly skilled performed better when alone (MacCracken & Stadulis, 1985). Even college students learning to use computers might perform better when working alone than when working in the presence of an instructor (Schneider & Shugar, 1990).

What would account for these findings? The most influential explanation for both social facilitation and social inhibition is the *drive theory* of Robert Zajonc (1965). According to Zajonc the presence of other people increases physiological arousal, which energizes the performer's most likely responses to a task. For those who are good at a task, the most likely responses will be effective ones. Consequently, those people will perform *better* in the presence of others. In contrast, for those who are not good at a task, the most well-learned responses will be ineffective ones. Consequently, those people will perform *worse* in the presence of others.

People's arousal levels also might increase in the presence of others because of *evaluation apprehension.* Consider a field study in which male and female runners were timed (without their being aware of it) as they ran along a 90-yard segment of a footpath. One-third of the participants ran alone, one-third encountered a woman facing them at the halfway point, and one-third encountered a woman seated with her back to them at the halfway point. Only the group that encountered a woman facing them (putting her in position to evaluate them) showed a significant acceleration between the first and second halves of the segment (Worringham & Messick, 1983).

Social Loafing

Social facilitation is concerned with the effects of others on individual performance. But what of the effect of working in a group that has a common goal? In the 1880s, a French agricultural engineer named Max Ringelmann found that people exerted less effort when working in groups than when working alone. He had men pull on a rope attached to a meter that measured the strength of their pull. As the number of men pulling increased from one to eight, the average strength of each man's pull decreased. Ringelmann attributed this to a loss of coordination when working with other people, a phenomenon known as the *Ringelmann effect* (Kravitz & Martin, 1986). His study has been replicated in other countries, including Japan (Kugihara, 1999) and Canada (Lichacz & Partington, 1996), but the effect diminishes markedly beyond a group size of three (Ingham et al., 1974).

More recently, the Ringelmann effect has been attributed to a decrease in the effort exerted by individuals when working together, a phenomenon known as **social loafing.** This supports the old saying "Many hands make light the work." In one experiment, high school cheerleaders cheered either alone or in pairs. Sound-level recordings found that individual cheerleaders cheered louder when alone than when cheering with a partner (Hardy & Latané, 1988). Social loafing also has been demonstrated in sports, such as elite rowing (Anshel, 1995) and high school swimming (Miles & Greenberg, 1993). A meta-analysis of 78 studies found that social loafing has been demonstrated across cultures, though it is more common in individualistic cultures, such as Canada and the United States (Karau & Williams, 1993).

According to the concept of *diffusion of responsibility,* social loafing occurs when group members feel anonymous; believing that their individual performance is not evaluated, they are less motivated to exert their maximum effort. Ways to reduce social loafing include convincing group members that they will be held accountable (Weldon & Gargano, 1988), their individual effort will be evaluated (Hoeksema-Van Order, Gaillard, & Buunk, 1998), or their individual effort will matter to the group's performance (Shepperd & Taylor, 1999).

Social Influence

The groups we belong to influence our behavior in ways that range from subtle prodding to direct demands. Group influence is sometimes negative but often is positive, as, for example, in the case of exercise adherence. The influence of others tends to make us more likely to maintain a program of regular exercise (Carron, Hausenblas, & Mack, 1996). The most important kinds of social influence include *conformity* and *obedience.*

Conformity

Do you dress the way you do because your friends dress that way? Do you hold certain religious beliefs because your parents hold them? If you answered yes to these questions, you would be exhibiting **conformity,** which means behaving in accordance with real or imagined group pressure. For example, a study of more than 100 men and 100 women found that people eating in a cafeteria were more likely to select a dessert if a dining companion did so (Guarino, Fridrich, & Sitton, 1994). And, of greater importance, we are more likely to refuse to enter a vehicle with a drunk driver if a companion refuses than if the companion enters the vehicle (Powell & Drucker, 1997).

The power of conformity was demonstrated in a classic series of experiments conducted by psychologist Solomon Asch (1907–1996) in the 1950s. These experiments showed that even visual perception, something we take for granted, can be influenced by the social context (Gleitman, Rozin, & Sabini, 1997). In a typical experiment, a male college student who had volunteered to be a research participant was told that he would be taking part in a study of visual perception. He was seated at a table with six other "participants," who were actually the experimenter's confederates. As illustrated in Figure 17.1, the experimenter presented a series of trials in which he displayed two large white cards. One card contained three vertical lines of different lengths. The second card contained a single vertical line clearly equal in length to one of the three lines on the first card. On each of 18 trials, the participants were asked, one person at a time, to choose the line on the first card that was the same length as the line on the second card. The lengths of the lines varied from trial to trial. On the first 2 trials each confederate chose the correct line. But on the third trial, and on 11 of the succeeding trials, the confederates chose a line that was clearly *not* the same length as the single line.

conformity

Behaving in accordance with group expectations with little or no overt pressure to do so.

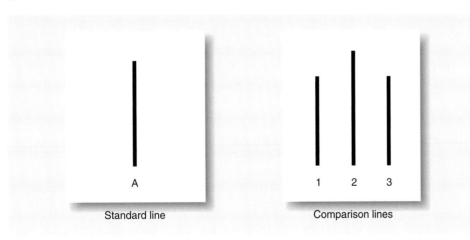

(a)

(b)

A

Standard line

1   2   3

Comparison lines

(c)

◀ **Figure 17.1**
The Asch Study

Participants *(a)* in one of Solomon Asch's studies *(c)* had to decide which of three lines was equal in length to another line. The photograph *(b)* shows the confusion of participant number 6 when other participants chose the wrong line.

▲ **Solomon Asch (1907–1996)**

"How, and to what extent, do social forces constrain people's opinions and attitudes?"

Solomon Asch Center for Study of Ethnopolitical Conflict
www.mhhe.com/sdorow5

obedience
Following orders given by an authority.

foot-in-the-door technique
Increasing the likelihood that someone will comply with a request by first getting him or her to comply with a smaller one.

The Stanley Milgram Website
www.mhhe.com/sdorow5

On the first few trials, the participant appeared uncomfortable but usually chose the correct line. Yet, over the course of the 12 trials, the participant sometimes conformed to the erroneous choices made by the confederates. The results indicated that, overall, participants conformed on 37 percent of the trials. Three-quarters of the participants conformed on at least one trial. In other versions of the experiment, Asch varied the number of confederates from 1 to 15 persons. He found that the conformity increased dramatically until there were 3 confederates, with additional confederates inducing smaller increases in conformity (Asch, 1955).

Though some attempts to replicate Asch's study have failed (Lalancette & Standing, 1990), his research has been successfully replicated in different cultures, including studies using American (Larsen, 1990), Dutch (Vlaander & Van Rooijen, 1985), Kuwaiti (Amir, 1984), British (Nicholson, Cole, & Rocklin, 1985), or Australian (Walker & Andrade, 1996) participants. But a meta-analysis of 133 studies from 17 countries found that conformity has declined since the 1950s. And collectivist countries tended to show greater conformity than individualistic countries (Bond & Smith, 1996). For example, Chinese college students tend to be more conforming than American college students (Zhang & Thomas, 1994).

These differences may be attributable to cultural values related to uniqueness. In a series of experiments, East Asian and European American participants' preferences were assessed in a number of domains. In one version of the experiment, for example, participants were asked to select a ballpoint pen as a gift from a collection of five pens. At least one of the five pens was a different color from the rest of the group. Participants' choices were coded for uniqueness if they chose one of the pens that was different from the rest of the pens in the group. Participants' choices were coded for conformity if they chose one of the pens that did not differ from the group. European Americans were more likely to choose the unique pen, whereas East Asians were more likely to choose a pen that did not differ from the group (Kim & Markus, 1999).

In Asch's study, why did the participants conform to the obviously erroneous judgments of strangers? A few claimed they really saw the lines as equal, and others assumed that the confederates knew something they did not. But their main reason for conforming was that they feared social rejection. Participants found, as do many people, that it is difficult to be the lone dissenter in a group. In variations of the experiment in which one of the confederates joined the participant in dissenting, participants conformed on less than one-tenth, rather than on one-third, of the trials (Asch, 1955). Thus, dissent is more likely when we have fellow dissenters.

Obedience

Would you assist in the cold-blooded murder of innocent people if your superior ordered you to? This question deals with the limits of **obedience**—the following of orders from an authority. The limits of obedience were at the heart of the Nuremberg war crimes trials held after World War II. The defendants were Nazis accused of crimes against humanity for their complicity in the executions of millions of innocent people during World War II, most notably the genocide of 6 million Jews. The defendants claimed that they were only following orders. In his journal Adolf Eichmann, who personally oversaw the deportation and murder of millions of Jews as a high-ranking Nazi official, described his role in the genocide as "the same as millions of others who had to obey" (Trounson, 2000, p. A1). The extent to which people will obey others is surprising. To read about this, see the Anatomy of a Research Study feature.

STAYING ON TRACK: *Group Dynamics*

1. How would you prevent groupthink in decision making?
2. How does social facilitation both enhance and impair performance?
3. How would you prevent social loafing during group performance?
4. How might the foot-in-the-door technique have contributed to the high rates of obedience in Milgram's experiments?

Answers to Staying on Track start on p. ST-8.

Anatomy of a Research Study

Would You Harm Someone Just Because an Authority Figure Ordered You To?

Rationale

Are people who obey orders to hurt innocent people unusually cruel, or are most human beings susceptible to obeying such orders? This question led psychologist Stanley Milgram (1933–1984) of Yale University to conduct perhaps the most famous—and controversial—of all psychology experiments (Milgram, 1963).

Method

Milgram's participants were adult men who had responded to an advertisement for volunteers to participate in a study of the effects of punishment on learning. On arriving at the laboratory, each participant was introduced to a pleasant man who also would participate in the experiment. In reality, the man was a confederate of the experimenter. The experimenter asked both men to draw a slip of paper out of a hat to determine who would be the "teacher" and who would be the "learner." The drawing was rigged so that the participant was always the teacher.

As shown in Figure 17.2, the teacher communicated with the learner over an intercom as the learner performed a memory task while strapped to an electrified apparatus in another room. The teacher sat at a control panel with a series of switches with labels ranging from "Slight Shock" (15 volts) to "Danger: Severe Shock" (450 volts) in 15-volt increments. The experimenter instructed the participant to administer an increasingly strong electric shock to the learner's hand whenever he made an error. At higher shock levels, the learner cried out in pain or begged the teacher to stop. Many participants responded to the learner's distress with sweating, trembling, and stuttering. If the participant hesitated to administer a shock, the experimenter might say, "You have no other choice, you must go on," and remind the teacher that he, the experimenter, was responsible for any ill effects. This incremental approach has much in common with the **foot-in-the-door technique,** which is a well-known sales technique, that is even used by professional torturers and "brainwashers" (Gibson, 1991). The foot-in-the-door technique is based on findings that people who comply with small requests will then become more likely to comply with larger requests. For example, if you agree to test drive a car, you become more likely to buy the car.

Results and Discussion

How far do you think you would have gone as the teacher in Milgram's study? Surveys of psychiatrists and Yale students

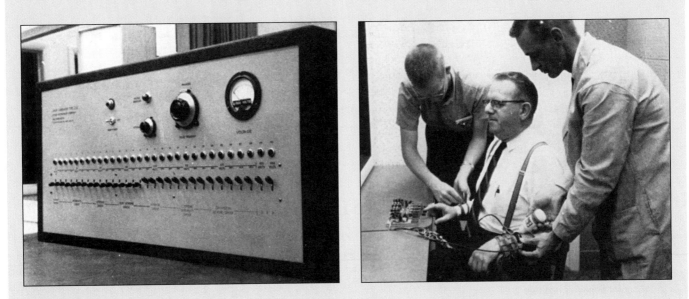

▲ **Figure 17.2**
Milgram's Study of Obedience
Stanley Milgram advertised for people who would be willing to take part in a study of memory. The photographs show the "shock generator" that he used and a participant helping the experimenter attach electrodes to the learner's arm.

had predicted that less than 2 percent of the participants would reach the maximum level. To Milgram's surprise, two-thirds of the participants reached the maximum level of shock, and none stopped before reaching 300 volts—the point at which the learner frantically banged on the wall and stopped answering questions. (By the way, the learner never received a shock. In fact, his "responses" were played on a tape recorder.)

Could the prestige of Yale University and the apparent legitimacy of a laboratory study have affected the participants? Milgram replicated the study in a rundown office building in Bridgeport, Connecticut. He did not wear a laboratory coat, and he made no reference to Yale. He obtained impressive results nonetheless. Of those who participated, 48 percent reached the maximum level of shock. Would physically separating the teacher and the learner have an effect? Somewhat. When the participant sat near the learner, 40 percent reached the maximum. Even when the participant had to force the learner's hand onto a shock grid, 30 percent still reached the maximum (Milgram, 1974). Replication studies have found no gender differences in obedience, and no change in obedience over the past 35 years (Blass, 1999). Milgram's original experiment also has been successfully replicated in other countries, which indicates that obedience to authority is common across cultures (Shanab & Yahya, 1977).

Milgram's research has disturbing implications. The line that separates us from Nazi war criminals might be thinner than we would like to believe. Many of us, given orders by someone we consider to be a legitimate authority who we assume will be responsible for our actions, might be willing to harm an innocent person. Despite the insight it provided into the nature of obedience, Milgram's research provoked criticism, most notably from Diana Baumrind (1964). She claimed that Milgram's use of deception increased distrust of psychological researchers and that his participants' self-esteem was damaged by the realization that they might harm an innocent person simply because an authority figure ordered them to.

In response to these criticisms, Milgram reported that 84 percent of the participants in his studies reported that they were glad they had participated, that there was no evidence that any of them developed long-term emotional distress, and that the importance of the findings made the use of deception worthwhile (Milgram, 1964). Given today's increased concern with the rights of research participants, partly in response to studies like Milgram's, it is unlikely that his studies would be replicated. Milgram's research still sparks interest today, particularly in regard to those who disobey despite threats to their life and well-being—such as those who smuggled slaves out of southern states via the underground railroad in the mid 19th century. One lesson is that those who resist early are more likely to maintain their defiance. For example, a reanalysis of audio recordings of participants in one of Milgram's replications of his original study found that the sooner participants resisted, the more likely they were to become defiant and refuse to give any more shocks (Modigliani & Rochat, 1995).

▲ **Stanley Milgram (1933–1984)**
"A substantial proportion of people do what they are told to do, irrespective of the content of the act and without limitations of conscience, so long as they perceive that the command comes from a legitimate authority."

The Altruistic Personality and Prosocial Behavior Institute
www.mhhe.com/sdorow5

◆ PROSOCIAL BEHAVIOR

On a spring day in 1986, 1-year-old Jennifer Kroll, of West Chicago, Illinois, fell into her family's swimming pool. Jennifer's mother, after pulling Jennifer out of the pool and discovering that she was not breathing, ran outside and began screaming for help. Her screams were heard by James Patridge, who had been confined to a wheelchair since losing his legs in a land-mine explosion during the Vietnam War. Patridge rolled his wheelchair toward the pool, until he encountered heavy brush, then crawled the final 20 yards. Patridge revived Jennifer by using cardiopulmonary resuscitation ("God's Hand," 1986). Patridge's heroic act led to offers of financial rewards, which he declined to accept, saying that saving Jennifer's life was reward enough.

Altruism

Patridge's act is an example of **prosocial behavior**—helping others in need. His behavior also is an example of **altruism**—helping others without the expectation of a reward in return. But are altruistic acts ever truly selfless? Social psychologists who study altruism have been especially concerned with *empathy,* the ability to feel the emotions that someone else is feeling. Some researchers have found that prosocial behavior associated with feelings of empathy is truly altruistic (Batson et al., 1999), whereas prosocial behavior associated with the desire to relieve one's own distress is not (Cialdini et al., 1997). Research studies on the role of empathy in prosocial behavior have provided contradictory findings. In one study, participants completed a questionnaire that measured their level of sadness and their level of empathy for a person in need. Participants then were given the opportunity to help the person. The results indicated that the participants' willingness to help was related more to their sadness score than to their empathy score, indicating that they acted more out of a desire to reduce their own distress than out of a desire to reduce the distress of the other person. In fact, when the participants were given a "mood fixing" placebo that allegedly (but not actually) made it impossible for them to alter their moods, fewer participants were willing to help, even those with high empathy scores (Cialdini et al., 1987). This study provided support for Robert Cialdini's **negative state relief theory** of prosocial behavior (Schaller & Cialdini, 1988).

But what of people whose prosocial behavior is associated with helpers' feelings of both distress and empathy? In an experiment, participants were empathetically aroused and led to anticipate an imminent mood-enhancing experience. The experimenters reasoned that if the motivation to help were directed toward the goal of negative-state relief, then empathetically aroused individuals who anticipate mood-enhancement should help less than those who do not. The rate of helping among high-empathy participants was no lower when they anticipated mood enhancement than when they did not. Regardless of anticipated mood enhancement, high-empathy participants helped more than low-empathy participants did. The results supported the *empathy-altruism hypothesis* (Batson et al., 1989). Reviews of relevant research report inconsistent findings in regard to the existence of altruistic helping (Carlson & Miller, 1987; Cialdini & Fultz, 1990). So it is still unclear whether prosocial behavior is motivated more by empathy for others or by the desire to relieve one's own negative emotional state.

Bystander Intervention

Regardless of his motivation, James Patridge's rescue of Jennifer was an example of **bystander intervention,** the act of helping someone who is in immediate need. Interest in the study of bystander intervention was stimulated by a widely publicized tragedy. At 3:20 A.M. on March 13, 1964, Kitty Genovese was returning home from her job as a bar manager. As she walked to her apartment building in the New York City borough of Queens, she was attacked by a mugger who repeatedly stabbed her. Thirty-eight of her neighbors reported that they had been awakened by her screams and had rushed to look out their windows, but had not seen the attack. The assailant left twice, returning each time to continue his attack until, 30 minutes after her ordeal had begun, Kitty Genovese died.

How would you have responded had you been one of her neighbors? At no time during these three separate attacks did any of the 38 persons try to help Kitty Genovese or even call the police. When questioned by police and reporters, the witnesses gave a variety of explanations for why they had not called the police. Their reasons included feeling tired, assuming it was a lovers' quarrel, and believing that "it can't happen here" (Gansberg, 1964). The murder of Kitty Genovese gained national attention, and the apparent apathy of her neighbors was taken as a sign of the callous, impersonal nature of the residents of big cities.

But social psychologists John Darley and Bibb Latané rejected this commonsense explanation as too simplistic. Instead, they conducted a program of research studies to determine the factors that affect the willingness of bystanders to intervene in emergencies. This is important today, as it was when Kitty Genovese was murdered. In fact, a survey of more than 500 undergraduates and faculty members found that only 25 percent of those who had

▲ Robert Cialdini

"An observer's heightened empathy for a sufferer brings with it increased personal sadness in the observer and . . . it is the egoistic desire to relieve the sadness, rather than the selfless desire to relieve the sufferer, that motivates helping."

prosocial behavior
Behavior that helps others in need.

altruism
The helping of others without the expectation of a reward.

negative state relief theory
The theory that we engage in prosocial behavior to relieve our own state of emotional distress at another's plight.

bystander intervention
The act of helping someone who is in immediate need of aid.

▲ Bibb Latané

"Even when bystanders to an emergency cannot see or be influenced by each other, the more bystanders who are present, the less likely any one bystander will be to intervene and provide aid."

witnessed children being abused in public had ever intervened (Christy & Voight, 1994). Darley and Latané found that bystander intervention involves a series of steps. The intervention process might continue through each of these steps or be halted at any one.

Noticing the Victim

To intervene in an emergency, you must first notice the event or the victim. James Patridge heard the screams of Jennifer Kroll's mother, and neighbors heard the screams of Kitty Genovese.

Interpreting the Situation as an Emergency

The same event might be interpreted as an emergency or as a nonemergency. James Patridge was confronted by an unambiguous situation. He interpreted the screams of Jennifer's mother as a sign that there was an emergency. In contrast, there was some ambiguity in Kitty Genovese's situation. In fact, when there is an apparent confrontation between a man and a woman, bystanders tend to assume that it is a lovers' quarrel rather than an emergency (Shotland & Straw, 1976). Because almost all of Kitty Genovese's neighbors interpreted the situation as a nonemergency, at that point there was little likelihood that any would help.

Taking Personal Responsibility

After interpreting the situation as an emergency, Patridge took responsibility for intervening. But not even those who might have interpreted Kitty Genovese's situation as an emergency took responsibility for helping her. Darley and Latané discovered a surprising reason for this. Contrary to what you might expect, as the number of bystanders *increases,* the likelihood of a bystander's intervening *decreases.* Note that this is true only in situations involving strangers. In emergencies involving highly cohesive groups of people, such as friends or relatives, the probability of intervention will increase as the number of bystanders increases (Rutkowski, Gruder, & Romer, 1983).

The influence of the number of bystanders on bystander intervention was demonstrated in an early study by Darley and Latané (1968). They had college students meet to discuss the problems they faced in attending school in New York City. Each student was led to a room and told to communicate with other students over an intercom. The students were told that there were 2, 3, or 6 students taking part in the discussion, but all of the other students were the experimenter's confederates; in fact, the remarks of the other students were tape recordings. Early in the session the participant (the nonconfederate) heard another student apparently having an epileptic seizure and crying out for help. Figure 17.3 shows that of those participants who believed they were a lone bystander, 85 percent sought help for the

▶ Figure 17.3
Diffusion of Responsibility
Darley and Latané (1968) found that as the number of bystanders increased, the likelihood of any of them going to the aid of a woman apparently having an epileptic seizure decreased.

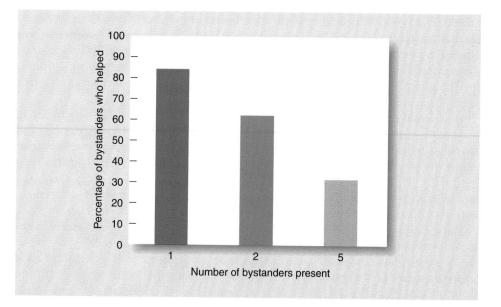

Chapter Seventeen

◀ Expertise and Bystander Intervention
In dangerous situations, bystanders will
be more likely to intervene when they feel
competent to do so. A person specially
trained to rescue people trapped by flood-
water, such as this park ranger, will be
more likely to intervene than will someone
who is not.

stricken person. Of those who believed they were 1 of 2 bystanders, 62 percent sought help. And of those who believed they were 1 of 5 bystanders, only 31 percent sought help. One reason for this is diffusion of responsibility: as the number of bystanders increases, individual responsibility decreases. So, the students who were exposed to a mock epileptic seizure felt less responsibility for helping the victim when they believed other bystanders were present. In contrast to Kitty Genovese's neighbors, who assumed that other neighbors likewise had been awakened, Patridge might have assumed that no one else could intervene, leaving him with the sole responsibility.

Deciding on a Course of Action

The decision to intervene depends, in part, on whether the bystander feels competent to meet the demands of the situation (Clark & Word, 1974). Because Patridge had training in cardiopulmonary resuscitation, he felt competent to try to revive Jennifer. A study that interviewed people who had intervened in violent crimes, such as muggings and armed robberies, found that they were usually larger and stronger than those who did not. Moreover, they typically were better trained to cope with crimes and emergencies, having had more police training or emergency medical training. Thus, they felt more competent to help (Huston et al., 1981).

Taking Action

Patridge believed that the potential benefits of intervention outweighed the potential costs. In one study, undergraduates reported the likelihood that they would help in a series of scenarios. The majority (76 percent) of their decisions reflected an assessment of the costs and benefits of each intervention (Fritzsche, Finkelstein, & Penner, 2000). This "bystander calculus" might explain why bystanders who believe that intervening in an emergency would place them in danger (as some might have believed in the case of Kitty Genovese) are less likely to intervene.

As you can now appreciate, bystander intervention is not simply the product of a particular personality type. Instead, it is a complex process that depends on the interaction between characteristics of the victim, the bystander, and the situation. For example, a recent study found that women reported that they would be more likely to intervene when a child is being hit than when a dog or a woman is being hit. In contrast, men reported that they would be more likely to intervene when a woman is being hit than when a dog or a child is being hit (Laner, Benin, & Ventrone, 2001). These findings are consistent with the gender-role analysis of altruism discussed in Chapter 2.

▲ Catharsis and Violence

According to Freud, both the participants and the spectators at this wrestling match should show a decrease in their tendencies toward violence as the result of catharsis. But research has found that, on the contrary, watching or taking part in violence will increase one's tendency to engage in it.

aggression

Verbal or physical behavior aimed at harming another person.

International Society for Research on Aggression
www.mhhe.com/sdorow5

Answers to Staying on Track start on p. ST-8.

1. What research evidence is there to support the negative state relief theory of seemingly altruistic behavior?
2. What is the role of the diffusion of responsibility in bystander intervention?

◆ AGGRESSION

As much as human beings are capable of prosocial behavior, they are, unfortunately, just as capable of antisocial behavior. The most extreme form of antisocial behavior is **aggression,** which is verbal or physical behavior aimed at causing harm to another person. What accounts for the prevalence of aggression?

Theories of Aggression

One class of theories views aggression as the product of physiology. A second class of theories views aggression as the product of experience. Obviously, both are important, as is their interaction.

Aggression as the Product of Physiology

The earliest theories of aggression claimed that it was instinctive. After observing the extraordinary violence of World War I, Sigmund Freud concluded that human aggression is caused by an instinct that he called *Thanatos* (Greek for "death"). According to Freud, Thanatos causes a buildup of aggressive energy, which must be released periodically through a process called *catharsis*. This would prevent outbursts of extreme violence. You might experience catharsis by playing football, field hockey, or another aggressive sport. But research has failed to support the belief that aggression can be reduced through catharsis. In fact, people who engage in aggression usually become *more* likely to engage in it (Geen, Stonner, & Shope, 1975). Nobel Prize–winning ethologist Konrad Lorenz (1966) agreed with Freud that we have an instinct for aggression. He claimed that all animals have a powerful aggressive drive that, like the sex drive, promotes the survival of their species.

The relatively new field of *evolutionary psychology* (see Chapter 13) assumes that there is a hereditary basis for aggression and other social behaviors (Buss, 1999). Psychologists who study twins have compared the aggressiveness of identical twins reared together to the aggressiveness of fraternal twins reared together. These researchers assume that if heredity plays a role in aggression, identical twins will be more similar in aggressiveness than will fraternal twins. Twin studies have, indeed, found this, providing evidence for the hereditary basis of aggressiveness (Rushton et al., 1986). Of course, this does not rule out the possibility that identical twins are more similar in aggressiveness because they are treated more alike than fraternal twins are.

What might be the physiological means by which heredity affects aggression? Several brain structures play important roles, particularly structures in the limbic system, including the amygdala and the hypothalamus (Potegal et al., 1996). A review of brain-imaging studies found a relationship between frontal lobe abnormalities and aggressiveness (Mills & Raine, 1994). Another factor is testosterone. Violent criminals have higher levels of testosterone than do nonviolent criminals (Harris, 1999). And athletes who use anabolic steroids, which are synthetic derivatives of testosterone, become more aggressive (Gregg & Rejeski, 1990).

But some research has failed to find a relationship between testosterone levels and aggressiveness. One study found no relationship between increased testosterone levels in male adolescents during puberty and increased likelihood of aggression (Halpern et al., 1993). Other studies have found that men who receive testosterone injections might become more aggressive because of an expectancy effect—they act more aggressively simply because they believe that they have received testosterone (Bjorkqvist et al., 1994).

Aggression as the Product of Experience

Whereas some researchers look to physiological factors, most look to life experiences as the main determinants of aggression. In the late 1930s, a team of behaviorists concluded that aggression is caused by frustration (Dollard et al., 1939). This became known as the **frustration-aggression hypothesis.** We experience frustration when we are blocked from reaching a goal. But the frustration-aggression hypothesis is an inadequate explanation of aggression, because experiences other than frustration can cause aggression, and frustration does not always lead to it.

These inadequacies inspired psychologist Leonard Berkowitz to develop the *revised frustration-aggression hypothesis.* According to Berkowitz (1974), frustration does not directly provoke aggression. Instead, it directly provokes anger. Anger, in turn, will provoke aggression—particularly when aggressive stimuli (such as guns) are present. Berkowitz demonstrated this in a study in which male college students gave electric shocks to other students to induce feelings of anger in the shock recipients. When students who had received shocks were given the opportunity to give shocks to those who had shocked them, they gave more shocks when an aggressive stimulus such as a revolver, rather than a neutral stimulus such as a badminton racket, was left on the table (Berkowitz & LePage, 1967). Though some studies have failed to support the revised frustration-aggression hypothesis (Buss, Booker, & Buss, 1972), many have found that anger in the presence of aggressive stimuli does tend to provoke aggression (Rule & Nesdale, 1976). Moreover, unexpected frustrations, because they evoke stronger unpleasant emotions, are more likely to provoke aggression than are expected frustrations (Berkowitz, 1989).

As described in Chapter 7, much of our behavior is the product of social learning. Aggression is no exception to this. We might learn to be aggressive by observing people who act aggressively. For example, women who as children observed their parents being aggressive are more likely to become aggressive themselves (White & Humphrey, 1994). And one explanation for the gender difference in aggression is gender-role socialization (see Chapter 4). Moreover, many of the laboratory studies of aggression have relied upon male samples and operational definitions of aggression that rely upon physical aggression—like the application of electric shock to a stranger. When other measures of aggression are studied, levels of aggression observed among women and girls rise dramatically.

In an extensive review of the literature, Jacquelyn White and Robin Kowalski (1994) found that gender differences in aggression reflect the social structure of women's and men's lives. For example, women are more likely to be verbally aggressive or sexually coercive within intimate relationships. In contrast, men are far more likely to be physically aggressive—and assault strangers in public places. Moreover, this gender difference is evident in childhood. A cross-cultural study of over 2,000 European children aged 8 to 15 years found that girls were more likely to engage in indirect aggression and less likely to engage in direct aggression. In contrast, boys were more likely to engage in direct aggression and less likely to engage in indirect aggression (Oesterman et al., 1998).

Group Violence

In the year A.D. 59, opposing fans rioted at the Pompeii amphitheater during a gladiatorial contest, prompting the Roman Senate to ban such contests in Pompeii for 10 years. The past few decades likewise have seen their share of riots at athletic events. In June 2000, hundreds of basketball fans spilled into the streets the night the Los Angeles Lakers won the NBA playoffs, torching or destroying more than half a dozen vehicles—including police cars and a public bus. Within an hour, the crowd had grown to more than 6,000 (Hall & Briggs, 2000).

What makes normally peaceful individuals become violent when they are in groups? We usually are aware of our own thoughts, feelings, and perceptions and are concerned about being evaluated. But when in groups, we may become less aware of ourselves and less concerned about being evaluated, the process of **deindividuation** (Festinger, Pepitone, & Newcomb, 1952). As the result of deindividuation, our behavior might no longer be governed by social norms, which in turn can lead to the loss of normal restraints against behavior, making us more likely to participate in group violence. Moreover, the anonymity provided by group

▲ **Leonard Berkowitz**

"Frustrations generate aggressive inclinations to the degree that they arouse negative affect."

frustration-aggression hypothesis
The assumption that frustration causes aggression.

deindividuation
The process by which group members become less aware of themselves as individuals and less concerned about being socially evaluated.

Deindividuation might lead to violence when people in large groups experience anonymity, reduced self-awareness, and emotional arousal.

membership can make us less concerned with the impression we make on other people, because we feel less accountable for our own actions (Prentice-Dunn & Rogers, 1982).

Deindividuation is most likely in large groups and when group members feel anonymous, have reduced self-awareness, and are emotionally aroused. This means that large groups of people, wearing masks, uniforms, or disguises and aroused by drugs, dancing, chanting, or oratory, will be more likely to engage in violence. Despite theoretical support for deindividuation, research findings are far from convincing in supporting the existence of such a state of consciousness (Postmes & Spears, 1998).

STAYING ON TRACK: *Aggression*

1. What evidence is there for the role of testosterone in aggression?
2. What is the role of deindividuation in aggression?

Answers to Staying on Track start on p. ST-8.

Chapter Summary

SOCIAL COGNITION

- Social psychology is the field that studies behavior in its interpersonal context.
- The process by which we try to explain social behavior is called causal attribution.
- When you decide that a person is responsible for her or his own behavior, you are making a dispositional attribution. And when

you decide that circumstances are responsible for a person's behavior, you are making a situational attribution.
- Bernard Weiner's theory of attribution looks at the interaction of the internal-external, stable-unstable, and controllable-uncontrollable dimensions.
- Major biases in causal attribution include the fundamental attribution error and the self-serving bias.

- Person perception is the process by which we make judgments about the personal characteristics of people.
- Social schemas that are applied to almost all members of a group are called stereotypes.
- Our first impressions play an important role in person perception, in some cases creating a self-fulfilling prophecy.

INTERPERSONAL ATTRACTION

- Psychologists interested in studying interpersonal attraction are concerned with the factors that make us like or love other people.
- Liking depends on the factors of proximity, familiarity, physical attractiveness, and similarity.
- Researchers who study love distinguish between passionate love and companionate love.
- According to Ellen Bersheid and Elaine Hatfield, romantic love depends on cultural support for the concept of romantic love, a state of physiological arousal, and the presence of an appropriate person to love.
- Two of the most important factors in promoting love are similarity and equity.

ATTITUDES

- Attitudes are evaluations of ideas, events, objects, or people.
- Attitudes have emotional, cognitive, and behavioral components.
- Our attitudes might not always accurately predict our behavior.
- Our behavior can sometimes affect our attitudes, a phenomenon that is explained by cognitive dissonance theory and self-perception theory.
- We are often subjected to persuasive messages aimed at getting us to change our attitudes.
- Persuasive messages can take a central route or a peripheral route.
- Persuasiveness depends on the message, the source, and the audience.
- Sources that are more credible and attractive are more persuasive.
- Under certain circumstances, two-sided messages will be more effective than one-sided messages.
- The intelligence level of the audience and the relevance of the message also determine the effectiveness of persuasive messages.
- Prejudice is a positive or negative attitude toward others based on their membership in particular groups.
- The behavioral component of prejudice is discrimination.
- Prejudice can be reduced when there is equal-status contact.

GROUP DYNAMICS

- Psychologists interested in group dynamics study the effects of social relationships on thinking, feeling, and behaving.
- Group decisions are sometimes characterized by groupthink, in which group members place greater emphasis on unanimity than on critical thinking.
- Groups can affect task performance through social facilitation, which is the improvement of performance caused by the presence of other people.

- Our performance can also be affected by social loafing, which is the tendency of individuals to exert less effort when performing in groups.
- Human relations are characterized by conformity and obedience.
- Conformity is behaving in accordance with group norms with little or no overt pressure to do so.
- Obedience is following orders given by an authority.
- Stanley Milgram found that most people are all too willing to harm other people when ordered to do so by a legitimate authority figure.

PROSOCIAL BEHAVIOR

- Prosocial behavior involves helping others in need.
- Altruism is helping others without the expectation of a reward in return.
- Some researchers have found that true altruism occurs only when prosocial behavior is done out of empathy, rather than out of a desire to reduce one's own distress at the plight of another person.
- Other researchers have found, instead, that prosocial behavior is never truly altruistic—it always depends on the desire to reduce our own distress.
- Psychologists who study prosocial behavior are especially concerned with bystander intervention, the act of helping someone who is in immediate need of aid.
- Bystander intervention depends on noticing the victim, interpreting the situation as an emergency, taking personal responsibility, deciding on a course of action, and taking action to help.

AGGRESSION

- Aggression is verbal or physical behavior aimed at causing harm to someone else.
- Some theories view aggression as biologically based, perhaps inborn.
- Sigmund Freud and Konrad Lorenz believed that aggression is instinctive, meaning that we have no choice but to engage in it periodically.
- Today most researchers reject the instinct theory of aggression but still study hormonal and hereditary influences on it.
- Most researchers look to life experiences as the main determinants of aggression.
- According to the frustration-aggression hypothesis, aggression becomes more likely after we have been blocked from reaching a goal.
- According to social-learning theory, we may learn to be aggressive by observing people who act aggressively.
- Group violence is promoted by deindividuation, which is the loss of self-awareness and the feeling of anonymity that comes from being part of a group.

Key Concepts

social psychology 479

SOCIAL COGNITION

causal attribution 480
fundamental attribution
  error 481
person perception 481
self-fulfilling prophecy 482
self-serving bias 481
social cognition 480
social schema 481
stereotype 481

INTERPERSONAL ATTRACTION

companionate love 484
passionate love 484

ATTITUDES

attitude 487
cognitive dissonance theory 487
elaboration likelihood
  model 488
persuasion 488

prejudice 490
self-perception theory 488

GROUP DYNAMICS

conformity 495
foot-in-the-door technique 497
group 492
groupthink 493
obedience 496
social facilitation 493
social loafing 494

PROSOCIAL BEHAVIOR

altruism 499
bystander intervention 499
negative state relief theory 499
prosocial behavior 499

AGGRESSION

aggression 502
deindividuation 503
frustration-aggression
  hypothesis 503

Key Contributors

SOCIAL COGNITION

Harold Kelley 480
Bernard Weiner 480

INTERPERSONAL ATTRACTION

Ellen Berscheid 484
Elaine Hatfield 484

ATTITUDES

Kenneth Clark and Mamie
  Phipps Clark 492
Leon Festinger 487
Richard Petty and John
  Cacioppo 488

GROUP DYNAMICS

Solomon Asch 495
Irving Janis 493
Stanley Milgram 497
Robert Zajonc 494

PROSOCIAL BEHAVIOR

Robert Cialdini 499

John Darley and Bibb
  Latané 499

AGGRESSION

Leonard Berkowitz 503
Sigmund Freud 502

Thought Questions

1. How might the attributions you make about a failed romantic relationship make you feel better about yourself?
2. In trying to persuade other students that your school's core curriculum should be made more rigorous, how might you use research findings on the role of the source, the message, and the audience to be more persuasive?
3. How might you keep your family from succumbing to groupthink in making a decision on whether to buy a particular house?
4. If you were asked to coordinate a group of students in running a special lecture series, how might you prevent social loafing?

Possible Answers to Thought Questions start on p. PT-5.

OLC Preview

For additional quizzing and a variety of interactive resources, visit the book's Online Learning Center at www.mhhe.com/sdorow5.

Appendix A

Statistics

▶ To understand God's thoughts we must study statistics; for these are the measure of his purpose. (Florence Nightingale, 1820–1910)

Most psychological research involves measurement, whether from a *naturalistic observational study* of chimpanzee parental behavior in the wild, a *correlational study* of the relationship between aerobic exercise and well-being, or an *experimental study* of the effects of mood on memory. In each case, measurement yields a set of numbers, which are the research findings, or *data*. Though a simple perusal of a set of data might provide an appreciation of the gist of the research findings, such an approach to data analysis is too imprecise for science. The use of *statistics* provides a more precise approach. As discussed in Chapter 2, psychologists and other scientists use statistics to summarize data, find relationships between sets of data, and determine whether experimental manipulations have had a statistically significant effect.

The word **statistics** has two meanings: (1) the field that applies mathematical techniques to the organizing, summarizing, and interpreting of data, and (2) the actual mathematical techniques themselves. Knowledge of statistics has many practical benefits. Even a rudimentary knowledge of statistics will make you better able to evaluate statistical claims made by science reporters, weather forecasters, government officials, and other persons who use statistics in the information or arguments they present.

statistics
Mathematical techniques used to summarize research data or to determine whether the data support the researcher's hypothesis.

◆ REPRESENTATION OF DATA

Because a list of raw data can be difficult to interpret, psychologists prefer to represent their data in an organized way. Two of the most common ways are frequency distributions and graphs.

Frequency Distributions

Suppose that you had a set of 20 scores from a 100-point psychology exam. You might arrange them in a frequency distribution, which lists the frequency of each score or group of scores in a set of scores. Using the set of scores in Table A.1, you would set up a column that included the highest and lowest scores, as well as the possible scores in between. In this

Table A.1	Frequency Distributions of Exam Scores

Exam Scores

83	81	90	82	83
89	81	80	90	80
88	90	88	92	88
90	93	89	84	94

Ungrouped Data		Grouped Data	
Score	Frequency	Score	Frequency
94	1	90–94	7
93	1	85–89	5
92	1	80–84	8
91	0		$N = 20$
90	4		
89	2		
88	3		
87	0		
86	0		
85	0		
84	1		
83	2		
82	1		
81	2		
80	2		
$N = 20$			

case, the highest score is 94 and the lowest is 80. You would then count the frequency of each score and list it in a separate column. The total of the frequencies in the distribution is symbolized by the letter N.

The frequency distribution might show a pattern in the set of scores that is not apparent when simply examining the individual scores. In this example (presented in Table A.1), the exam scores do not bunch up toward the lower, middle, or upper portions of the distribution. In some cases, when you have a relatively large number of scores, you might prefer to use a *grouped* frequency distribution. The scores would be grouped into intervals, and the frequency of scores in each internal would be listed in a separate column. A grouped frequency distribution provides less precise information than does an ungrouped one, because the individual scores are lost.

Graphs

If a picture is worth a thousand words, then a graph is worth several paragraphs in a research report. Because it provides a pictorial representation of the distribution of scores, a graph can be an even more effective representation of data than is a frequency distribution. Among the most common kinds of graphs are *pie graphs, frequency histograms, frequency polygons,* and *line graphs.*

Pie Graph

pie graph
A graph that represents data as percentages of a pie.

A simple, but visually effective, way of representing data is the **pie graph.** It represents data as percentages of a pie. The total of the slices of the pie must add up to 100 percent. Note that a pie graph is used in Figure 1.1 in Chapter 1 to represent the percentage of psychologists working in major fields of psychology.

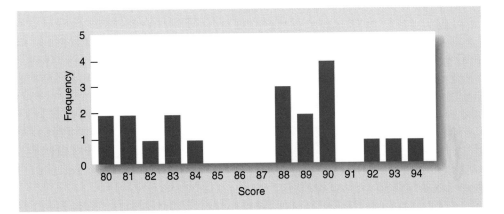

◀ **Figure A.1**
Frequency Histogram of Exam Scores

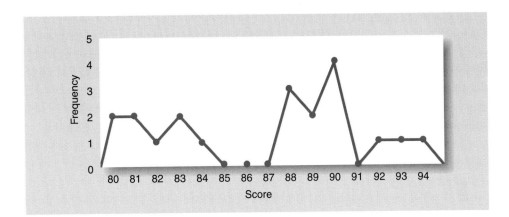

◀ **Figure A.2**
Frequency Polygon of Exam Scores

Frequency Histogram

Another approach to representing frequency data is the **frequency histogram,** which graphs frequencies as bars. In general, the scores are plotted on the horizontal axis and the frequencies on the vertical axis. The width of the bars represents the intervals, and the height of the bars represents the frequency of scores in each interval. Figure A.1 is a frequency histogram of the exam scores in the ungrouped frequency distribution presented in Table A.1.

Frequency Polygon

A **frequency polygon** serves the same purpose as a frequency histogram. As shown in Figure A.2, the frequency polygon is drawn by connecting the points, representing frequencies, located above the scores. Note that the polygon is completed by extending it to the horizontal axis one score below the lowest score and one score above the highest score in the distribution.

An advantage of the frequency polygon over the frequency histogram is that it permits the plotting of more than one distribution on the same set of axes. If more than one frequency polygon is plotted on a set of axes, they should be distinguished from one another. This can be done by drawing a different kind of line for each polygon (perhaps a solid line for one and a broken line for the other), drawing the lines in different colors (perhaps red for one polygon and blue for the other), or representing the points above the scores with geometric shapes (perhaps a circle for one polygon and a triangle for the other).

A graph in which scores bunch up toward either end of the horizontal axis (as shown in Figure A.3) is *skewed.* The skewness of a graph is in the direction of its "tail." If the scores bunch up toward the high end, the graph has a **negative skew.** This might occur on an unusually easy exam. If the scores bunch up toward the low end, the graph has a **positive skew.** This might occur on an unusually difficult exam.

frequency histogram
A graph that displays the frequency of scores as bars.

frequency polygon
A graph that displays the frequency of scores by connecting points representing them above each score.

negative skew
A graph that has scores bunching up toward the positive end of the horizontal axis.

positive skew
A graph that has scores bunching up toward the negative end of the horizontal axis.

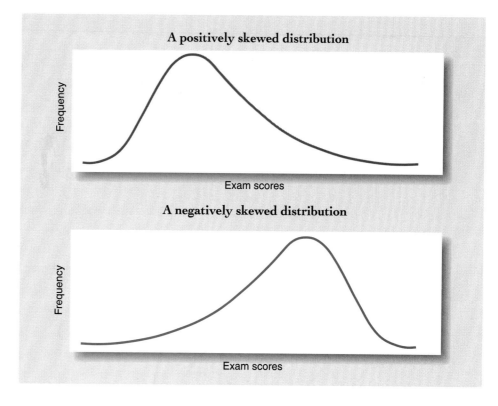

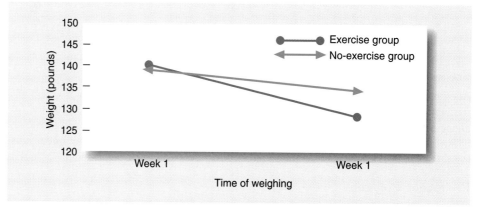

line graph

A graph used to plot data showing the relationship between independent and dependent variables in an experiment.

Line Graph

Whereas pie graphs, frequency histograms, and frequency polygons are useful for plotting frequency data, a **line graph** is useful for plotting data generated by experiments. It uses lines to represent the relationship between independent and dependent variables. If you skim through this textbook, you will see several examples of line graphs. The graph shown in Figure A.4 represents the data from a hypothetical experiment on exercise and weight loss

◆ DESCRIPTIVE STATISTICS

Suppose you gained access to the hundreds, or thousands, of high school grade point averages of all of the first-year students at your college or university. What is the most typical score? How similar are the scores? Simply scanning the scores would provide, at best, gross approximations of the answers to these questions. To obtain precise answers, psychologists use **descriptive statistics**, which include *measures of central tendency* and *measures of variability*.

descriptive statistics
Statistics that summarize research data.

Measures of Central Tendency

A measure of central tendency is a score that best represents a distribution of scores. The measures of central tendency include the *mode,* the *median,* and the *mean.*

Mode

The **mode** is the most frequently occurring score in a set of scores. The winner of a presidential primary election in which there are several candidates would represent the mode—the person selected by more voters than any other. In the frequency distribution of exam scores discussed earlier, the mode is 90. If two scores occur equally often, the distribution is *bimodal.* Any distribution that has two or more scores that occur equally often is called *multimodal.*

mode
The score that occurs most frequently in a set of scores.

Median

The **median** is the middle score in a distribution of scores that have been ranked in numerical order. If the median is located between two scores, it is assigned the value of the midpoint between them (for example, the median of 23, 34, 55, and 68 would be 44.5). The median is the best measure of central tendency for skewed distributions, because it is unaffected by extreme scores. Note that in the example below the median is the same in both sets of exam scores, even though the second set contains an extreme score.

median
The middle score in a set of scores that have been ordered from lowest to highest.

| **Exam A** | 23, | 25, | **63,** | 64, | 67 |
| **Exam B** | 23, | 25, | **63,** | 64, | 98 |

Mean

The **mean** is the arithmetic average of a set of scores. You are probably more familiar with it than with the mode or the median. You encounter the mean in everyday life whenever you calculate your exam average, batting average, or a host of other averages.

The mean of a sample is calculated by adding all the scores and dividing by the number of scores. Unlike the median, the mean is affected by extreme scores. As shown below, one extreme score will pull the mean in its direction—especially if there are few scores in the set of scores. Thus, the mean can be a misleading statistic when used with a skewed distribution. For example, whereas the mean of the five exam scores below is 79, the median would be 93—a more satisfying estimate of the student's typical performance.

mean
The arithmetic average of a set of scores.

Exam Scores: 19, 92, 93, 94, 97

$$\overline{X} = \frac{\Sigma X}{N} \quad \frac{19 + 92 + 93 + 94 + 97}{5} = 79$$

When Disraeli pointed out the ease of lying with statistics, he might have been referring, in particular, to measures of central tendency. Suppose a baseball general manager is negotiating with an agent about a salary for a baseball catcher of average ability. Both might use a measure of central tendency to prove his own point, perhaps based on the salaries of the top seven catchers, as shown in Table A.2. The general manager might claim that a salary of $340,000 (the median) would provide the player with what he deserves—an average salary. The agent might counter that a salary of $900,000 (the mean) would provide the player with what he deserves—an average salary. Note that neither would technically be lying—they would simply be using statistics that favored their position. As Scottish writer Andrew Lang (1844–1912) warned, beware of anyone who "uses statistics as a drunken man uses lampposts—for support rather than for illumination."

Table A.2	Baseball Salaries for Catchers
Player	**Salary**
A	$ 200,000
B	$ 250,000
C	$ 290,000
D	$ 340,000
E	$ 550,000
F	$ 670,000
G	$4,000,000

Measures of Variability

A distribution of identical scores would have no variability. This is rare. Almost all distributions have variability; that is, they contain scores that differ from one another. Consider the members of your psychology class. They would vary on a host of measures, including height, weight, and grade point average. Measures of variability include the *range,* the *variance,* and the *standard deviation.*

Range

range

A statistic representing the difference between the highest and lowest scores in a set of scores.

The **range** is the difference between the highest and lowest scores in a distribution. This provides limited information, because distributions in which scores bunch up toward the beginning, middle, or end of the distribution might have the same range. Of course the range is useful as a rough estimate of how a score compares with the highest and lowest in a distribution. For example, a student might find it useful to know whether his or her score was near the best or the worst on an exam. The range of scores in the distribution of 20 grades in the earlier example in Table A.1 would be the difference between 94 and 80, or 14.

Variance

variance

A measure based on the average deviation of a set of scores from their group mean.

A more informative measure of variability is the **variance,** which represents the variability of scores around their group mean. Unlike the range, the variance takes into account every score in the distribution. Technically, the variance is the average of the squared deviations from the mean.

Suppose you wanted to calculate the variance for the sets of 10-point quiz scores in Quiz A and Quiz B.

- First, find the group mean.
- Second, find the deviation of each score from the group mean. Note that deviation scores will be negative for scores that are below the mean. As a check on your calculations, the sum of the deviation scores should equal zero.
- Third, square the deviation scores. By squaring the scores, negative scores are made positive and extreme scores are given relatively more weight.
- Fourth, find the sum of the squared deviation scores.
- Fifth, divide the sum by the number of scores. This yields the variance. Note that the variance for Quiz A is larger than that for Quiz B, indicating that the students' performances varied more on Quiz A.

Quiz A

1, 2, 6, 8, 9

Quiz B

4, 5, 6, 7, 8

$$\bar{X} = \frac{\Sigma X}{N} = \frac{1 + 2 + 6 + 8 + 9}{5} = \frac{26}{5} = 5.2 \qquad \bar{Y} = \frac{\Sigma Y}{N} = \frac{4 + 5 + 6 + 7 + 8}{5} = \frac{30}{5} = 6$$

Score	Deviation	Deviation^2	Score	Deviation	Deviation^2
1	−4.2	17.64	4	−2	4
2	−3.2	10.24	5	−1	1
6	.8	.64	6	0	0
8	2.8	7.84	7	1	1
9	3.8	14.44	8	2	4
		ΣDeviation^2 = 50.80			ΣDeviation^2 = 10

$$\text{Variance} = \frac{\Sigma\text{Deviation}^2}{N} = \frac{50.80}{5} = 10.16 \qquad \text{Variance} = \frac{\Sigma\text{Deviation}^2}{N} = \frac{10}{5} = 2$$

Standard Deviation

The **standard deviation,** or S, is the square root of the variance. The standard deviation of Quiz A would be

$$S = \sqrt{S^2} = \sqrt{10.16} = 3.19.$$

The standard deviation of Quiz B would be

$$S = \sqrt{S^2} = \sqrt{2} = 1.41.$$

Why not simply use the variance? One reason is that, unlike the variance, the standard deviation is in the same units as the raw scores. This makes the standard deviation more meaningful. Thus, it would make more sense to discuss the variability of a set of IQ scores in IQ points than in squared IQ points. The standard deviation is used in the calculation of many other statistics.

The Normal Curve

As illustrated in Figure A.5, the **normal curve** is a bell-shaped graph that represents a hypothetical frequency distribution in which the frequency of scores is greatest near the mean and progressively decreases toward the extremes. In essence, the normal curve is a smooth frequency polygon based on an infinite number of scores. The mean, median, and mode of a normal curve are the same. Many physical or psychological characteristics, such as height, weight, and intelligence, fall on a normal curve.

One useful characteristic of a normal curve is that certain percentages of scores fall at certain distances (measured in standard deviations) from its mean. A special statistical table makes it a simple matter to determine the percentage of scores that fall above or below a particular score or between two scores on the curve. For example, about 68 percent of scores fall between plus and minus one standard deviation from the mean; about 95 percent fall between plus and minus two standard deviations from the mean; and about 99 percent fall between plus and minus three standard deviations from the mean.

standard deviation

A statistic representing the degree of dispersion of a set of scores around their mean.

normal curve

A bell-shaped graph representing a hypothetical frequency distribution for a given characteristic.

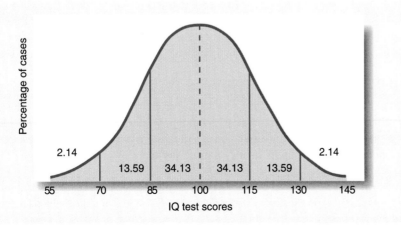

◀ **Figure A.5**
Normal Distribution, or Bell-Shaped Curve

This graph shows the normal distribution of IQ scores as measured by the Wechsler Adult Intelligence Scale. The normal distribution is a type of bell-shaped frequency polygon in which most of the scores are clustered around the mean. The scores become less frequent the farther they appear above or below the mean.

For example, consider an IQ test, with a mean of 100 and a standard deviation of 15. What percentage of people score above 130? Because intelligence scores fall on a normal curve, about 95 percent of the scores fall within two standard deviations of the mean. Thus, about 5 percent fall more than two standard deviations from the mean. Because the normal curve is symmetrical, about 2.5 percent of the people would score above 130 (mentally gifted) and about 2.5 percent below 70 (mentally retarded). The precise percentages would be 2.14 percent above 130 and 2.14 percent below 70.

◆ CORRELATIONAL STATISTICS

correlational statistics
Statistics that determine the relationship between two variables.

So far, you have been reading about statistics that describe sets of data. In many research studies, psychologists rely on **correlational statistics,** which determine the relationship between two variables. The nature of correlation is discussed in Chapter 2.

Scatter Plots

scatter plot
A graph of a correlational relationship.

Correlational data is graphed using a **scatter plot,** also known as a *scattergram* or *scatter diagram.* In a scatter plot, one variable is plotted on the horizontal axis and the other on the vertical axis. Each participant's scores on both variables are indicated by a dot placed at the junction between those scores on the graph. This produces one dot for each participant. The pattern of the dots gives a rough impression of the size and direction of the correlation. In fact, a line drawn through the dots, or *line of best fit,* helps estimate this. The closer the dots lie to a straight line, the stronger the correlation. Figure A.6 illustrates several kinds of correlation.

Pearson's Product-Moment Correlation

Pearson's product-moment correlation (Pearson's *r*)
Perhaps the most commonly used correlational statistic.

The most commonly used correlational statistic is the **Pearson's product-moment correlation (Pearson's *r*),** named for English statistician Karl Pearson. One formula for calculating it is presented in Figure A.7. The example assesses the relationship between home runs and stolen bases by 5 baseball players during 1 month of a season.

◆ INFERENTIAL STATISTICS

inferential statistics
Statistics used to determine whether changes in a dependent variable are caused by an independent variable.

Inferential statistics help psychologists determine whether the difference they find between the experimental and control groups is caused by the manipulation of the independent variable or by chance variation in the performances of the groups. If the difference has a low probability of being caused by chance variation, they can feel confident in the inferences they make from the samples to the populations they represent. When psychologists test the difference between the means of two sets of scores, they often use a technique called the *t test.* When they wish to test the differences between the means of three or more such groups, they often use *analysis of variance.*

Major Inferential Statistics.

***t* test**
A statistical technique used to determine whether the difference between two sets of scores is statistically significant.

One of the main inferential statistics, the *t* **test,** is used to determine whether there is a significant difference between the scores of two groups. The *t* test would be used to determine whether there was a significant difference in nightly sleep duration between the experimental group and the control group in the melatonin experiment described in Chapter 2. The *t* test was invented by statistician and brewmaster William Sealy Gosset (1876–1937) to maintain quality control in the brewing and storage of Guinness Stout, the popular dark, bitter beer. The beverage is still produced by Arthur Guinness, Son and Company, which shows its continued interest in statistics by publishing the *Guinness Book of World Records.*

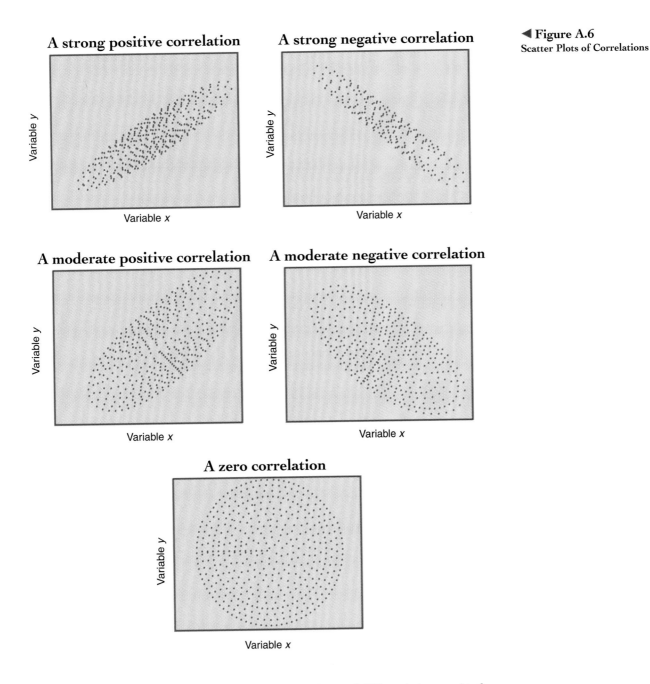

A strong positive correlation

Variable *y*

Variable *x*

A strong negative correlation

Variable *y*

Variable *x*

A moderate positive correlation

Variable *y*

Variable *x*

A moderate negative correlation

Variable *y*

Variable *x*

A zero correlation

Variable *y*

Variable *x*

Gosset compared pairs of batches of stout that he had treated differently in regard to factors such as ingredients, brewing temperature, or storage temperature. He analyzed the data using what became known as Student's *t* test. It was given this name because the brewery refused to permit its employees to publish anything that might reflect poorly on the company, leading Gosset to take the pseudonym *Student.* The first use of the *t* test in psychological research was in a paper published by Gosset in 1925, which found that one sleep medication was better than another in the treatment of insomnia.

Another important inferential statistic, the **analysis of variance,** enables researchers to compare three or more groups. The analysis of variance is also called the *F* test, after Ronald Fisher, who devised it in his research aimed at the improvement of agricultural productivity through the varying of a number of factors, including manure. In fact, the first use of the analysis of variance in a published study was in a 1923 article entitled "The Manuarial Response of Different Potato Varieties." The analysis of variance would be useful in the melatonin experiment if we used three groups: perhaps a melatonin group, a placebo group, and a no-drug group.

analysis of variance
A statistical technique used to determine whether the difference between three or more sets of scores is statistically significant.

► **Figure A.7**

Pearson's Product-Moment Correlation

This is a small negative correlation. It indicates that there is a slight tendency for stolen bases to decrease as home runs increase; that is, home-run hitters are somewhat less likely to steal bases.

Player	Home Runs *(X)*	Stolen Bases *(Y)*
A	8	3
B	2	6
C	1	2
D	5	1
E	6	3
	$\Sigma X = 22$	$\Sigma Y = 15$

$$r = \frac{\Sigma(\text{deviation from } \bar{X})(\text{deviation from } \bar{Y})}{N(S_X)(S_Y)}$$

Step 1: Calculate the means ($\bar{X}$ and $\bar{Y}$, respectively) of the two groups

$$\bar{X} = \frac{\Sigma X}{N} = \frac{22}{5} = 4.4 \qquad \bar{Y} = \frac{\Sigma Y}{N} = \frac{15}{5} = 3$$

Step 2: Find the deviation of each score from its mean

Deviation from $\bar{X}$	Deviation from $\bar{Y}$
$8 - 4.4 = 3.6$	$3 - 3 = 0$
$2 - 4.4 = -2.4$	$6 - 3 = 3$
$1 - 4.4 = -3.4$	$2 - 3 = -1$
$5 - 4.4 = 0.6$	$1 - 3 = -2$
$6 - 4.4 = 1.6$	$3 - 3 = 0$

Step 3: Multiply the paired deviation scores

(Deviation from $\bar{X}$)(Deviation from $\bar{Y}$)

$$
\begin{aligned}
(3.6)(0) &= 0.0 \\
(-2.4)(3) &= -7.2 \\
(-3.4)(-1) &= 3.4 \\
(0.6)(-2) &= -1.2 \\
(1.6)(0) &= 0.0 \\
\hline
\Sigma &= -5.0
\end{aligned}
$$

Step 4: Calculate the standard deviations for both groups

$$S_X = \sqrt{\frac{\Sigma \text{ Deviation}^2}{N}} \qquad S_Y = \sqrt{\frac{\Sigma \text{ Deviation}^2}{N}}$$

1) Square the deviation scores

(Deviation from $\bar{X}$)^2	(Deviation from $\bar{Y}$)^2
$(3.6)^2 = 12.96$	$0^2 = 0$
$(-2.4)^2 = 5.76$	$3^2 = 9$
$(-3.4)^2 = 11.56$	$-1^2 = 1$
$(0.6)^2 = 0.36$	$-2^2 = 4$
$(1.6)^2 = 2.56$	$0^2 = 0$
$\Sigma(\text{Deviation from } \bar{X})^2 = 33.20$	$\Sigma(\text{Deviation from } \bar{Y})^2 = 14$

2) Substitute in the formula and calculate

$$S_X = \sqrt{\frac{33.20}{5}} \qquad S_Y = \sqrt{\frac{14}{5}}$$

$$S_X = 2.58 \qquad S_Y = 1.67$$

Step 5: Substitute in the correlation formula and calculate

$$r = \frac{-5}{5(2.58)(1.67)}$$

$$r = -0.23$$

Hypothesis Testing

null hypothesis

The prediction that the independent variable will have no effect on the dependent variable in an experiment.

In experiments, psychologists use inferential statistics to test the **null hypothesis.** This hypothesis states that the independent variable has no effect on the dependent variable. Consider an experimental study of the effect of overlearning on memory in college students. As discussed in Chapter 8, when students use overlearning, they study material until they know it perfectly—

and then continue to study it some more. At the beginning of the experiment, participants would be selected from the same population (college students) and randomly assigned to either the experimental group (overlearning) or the control group (normal studying). Thus, the independent variable would be the method of studying (overlearning versus normal studying). The dependent variable might be performance on a 100-point exam on the material studied.

If the experimental manipulation has no effect, the experimental and control groups would not differ significantly in their performance on the exam. In that case, we would fail to reject the null hypothesis. If the experimental manipulation has an effect, the two groups would differ significantly in their performance on the exam. In that case, we would reject the null hypothesis. This would indirectly support the *research hypothesis,* which would predict that overlearning improves exam performance. But how large must a difference be between groups for it to be significant? To determine whether the difference between groups is large enough to minimize chance variation as an alternative explanation of the results, we must determine the *statistical significance* of the difference between them.

Statistical Significance

The characteristics of samples drawn from the population they represent will almost always vary somewhat from those of the true population. This is known as sampling error. Thus, a sample of 5 students taken from your psychology class (the population) would vary somewhat from the class means in age, height, weight, intelligence, grade point average, and other characteristics.

If a psychologist repeatedly took random samples of 5 students, she or he would continue to find that they differ from the population means. But what of the difference between the means of two samples, presumably representing different populations, such as a population of students who practice overlearning and a population of students who practice normal study habits? How large would the differences have to be before the psychologist attributed them to the independent variable rather than to chance? In this example, how much difference in the performance of the experimental group and the control group would be needed before the psychologist could confidently attribute the difference to the practice of overlearning?

The larger the difference between the means of two samples, the less likely it would be attributable to chance. Psychologists typically accept a difference between sample means as statistically significant if it has a probability of less than 5 percent of occurring by chance. This is known as the .05 level of statistical significance. In regard to the example, if the difference between the experimental group and the control group has less than a 5 percent probability of occurring by chance, the psychologist would reject the null hypothesis. The research hypothesis would be supported: overlearning is effective; the sample means of the experimental and control groups represent different populations (that is, the population that would be exposed to overlearning and the population that would not be exposed to it). Scientists who wish to use a stricter standard employ the .01 level of statistical significance. This means that a difference would be statistically significant if it had a probability of less than 1 percent of being obtained by chance alone.

The difference between the means of two groups will more likely be statistically significant when

- the samples are large,
- the difference between the means is large, and
- the variability within the groups is small.

Note that **statistical significance** is a statement of probability. Psychologists can never be certain that what is true of their samples is true of the population they represent. This is one of the reasons why, as stressed in Chapter 2, all scientific findings are tentative. Moreover, a statistically significant effect may be too small or be produced at too great a cost of time or money to be useful. What if those who practice overlearning must study an extra hour each day to improve their exam performance by a statistically significant, yet relatively small, 3 points. Knowing this, students might choose to spend their time in another way. As the American statesman Henry Clay (1777–1852) noted, in determining the importance of research findings, by themselves "statistics are no substitute for judgment."

statistical significance
A low probability (usually less than 5 percent) that the results of a research study are due to chance factors rather than to the independent variable.

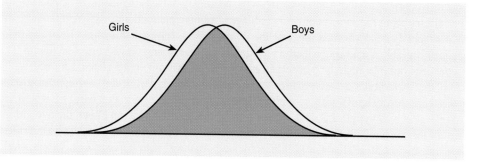

▶ **Figure A.8**
Statistically Significant Gender Differences
These overlapping curves represent frequency distributions of a sample of girls and boys. Though these curves represent a statistically significant gender difference, note that many of the boys and girls did not differ in their aggressiveness (the shaded area of the overlapping curves).

Group Differences and Individual Differences

When psychologists report gender, ethnic, or cross-cultural differences in research studies, they are describing group differences. For example, one study might conclude that boys are more aggressive than girls. This conclusion is based on tests of inferential statistics—the mean for the sample of boys was greater than the mean for the sample of girls. And the difference between these two means was statistically significant. Thus, *on average* boys were more aggressive than girls.

A statement about group differences—as in this case of gender differences in aggression—does not mean that the behavior of all of the male participants differed from all of the female participants. When frequency distributions of gender, ethnic, or other group scores are plotted there usually is considerable overlap between the two curves. It is extremely unlikely that *each* participant in one group scored higher or lower than *each* participant in the other group.

A statistically significant gender difference in aggression also might be smaller than individual differences in aggression. In this example, it is important to consider within-group variability. As you can see in Figure A.8, many of the boys and girls in these two samples did not differ in their aggressiveness. The areas shared by the overlapping curves represent this similarity. Moreover, some boys were not very aggressive at all whereas some girls were very aggressive. As you can see, the variability of the girls' and boys' scores—the spread of each curve—is greater than the distance between the two group means.

It is important, then, to understand that though there might be average group differences, it is likely that there are considerable individual differences. And when individual differences are greater in magnitude than group differences, it is difficult to predict a particular person's behavior. Suppose a researcher reports significant differences in parenting behaviors between European American and Asian American participants. It would be a mistake to conclude from these findings that *all* European American parents treat their children differently than *all* Asian American parents. And the difference between two European American parents is likely to be greater than the average cross-cultural difference.

Key Concepts

statistics 507

REPRESENTATION OF DATA
frequency histogram 509
frequency polygon 509
line graph 510
negative skew 509
pie graph 508
positive skew 509

DESCRIPTIVE STATISTICS
descriptive statistics 511
mean 511
median 511
mode 511
normal curve 513
range 512
standard deviation 513
variance 512

CORRELATIONAL STATISTICS
correlational statistics 514
Pearson's product-moment
  correlation (Pearson's *r*) 514
scatter plot 514

INFERENTIAL STATISTICS
analysis of variance 515
inferential statistics 514
null hypothesis 516
statistical significance 517
t test 514

Industrial/Organizational Psychology

Industrial/organizational (I/O) psychology applies psychological principles to the workplace. I/O psychologists study, among other things, the structure of organizations and organizational policies, individual and organizational performance, and the match between people and jobs. Traditionally, industrial psychology and organizational psychology have been distinguished from one another by their content areas. Industrial psychology (sometimes called personnel psychology) has long been associated with job analysis, training, selection, and performance measurement and appraisal. Organizational psychology deals with motivation, work attitudes, and leadership, as well as organizational development, structure, and culture.

This dichotomy, however, is in some sense a false one because the two areas largely overlap. In addition, most I/O psychologists are trained as exactly that—I/O psychologists—not as industrial psychologists only or organizational psychologists only. Finally, there is no broad line that divides workplace problems into organizational ones and industrial ones. For example, a performance problem (a subject of industrial psychology) might very likely be motivationally based (a subject of organizational psychology). *I* and *O* are put together into *I/O* for good reason—they are interdependent, related areas that form one subspecialty of psychology.

◆ ONE HUNDRED YEARS OF HISTORY

Though the field of I/O psychology is relatively young compared to other areas of psychology, its history is rich and interesting. (See Katzell & Austin, 1992, for a thorough review.)

Pre–World War I

The initial phase spans the period from the turn of the 20th century to World War I. In 1901, Walter Dill Scott, a professor at Northwestern University and former student of Wilhelm Wundt, was invited to give a talk at the Agate Club in Chicago on the psychological aspects of advertising. Many refer to this as the beginning of business and industrial psychology. Two contemporaries of Scott, Frank and Lillian Gilbreth, were pioneers in time and motion studies that assessed efficiency and employee productivity (Koppes, 1997). In 1915 the Division of Applied Psychology was established at Carnegie Tech (now Carnegie Mellon University), and in 1916 Scott became its first Professor of Applied Psychology. At about this same time Hugo Münsterberg (another Wundt student) moved to the United States and continued doing the applied work he had begun in Germany.

The World War I Years

The second period in the history of I/O psychology spans the World War I years through the 1920s. This is when I/O psychology came of age. Walter Dill Scott and Walter VanDyke Bingham (who was the director of the program at Carnegie Tech) established a program under the U.S. army's personnel office. Their staff was responsible for such things as the development of personnel files for military personnel and performance rating forms. As described in Chapter 10, Robert Yerkes (at that time the president of the APA) worked for the government doing selection and placement of military personnel using their newly developed tools—the Army Alpha and Army Beta mental ability tests.

In 1921, Bruce V. Moore received from Carnegie Tech what is believed to be the first Ph.D. in industrial psychology. At this time I/O psychology began to expand beyond the academic and military realms into government and private industry. I/O psychologists started consulting firms—such as the Scott Company (founded by Walter Dill Scott) and the Psychological Corporation (founded by James Cattell), which still exists today, specializing in testing. Historians estimate that prior to 1917 there were fewer than ten I/O psychologists and that by 1929 there were about fifty, a large increase in a little over 10 years.

The 1930s to World War II

The defining event of this next stage is what are collectively referred to as the Hawthorne Studies. These studies examined the impact of illumination on productivity at Western Electric's Hawthorne plant. After observing employees, researchers realized that social and

▶ **The Hawthorne Studies**

Five women, shown here with their supervisor, assemble telephone relays in the late 1920s at Western Electric's Hawthorne plant. Their production is being monitored to determine how various factors, such as changes in the intensity of the lighting, affect their work.

| **Appendix B**

psychological conditions of work were often more important than physical conditions (Roethlisberger & Dickson, 1939). Many view this time period, and the Hawthorne Studies in particular, as the birth of organizational psychology.

World War II to the Mid 1960s

The World War II years were an important and dynamic time for the development of I/O psychology. Bingham and Scott were brought back to the military to help match recruits to jobs. Organizational psychology became a more equal partner with industrial psychology and emphasized areas like organizational dynamics, work groups, and employee morale. As in the preceding period, there was more extension into industry and a great rise of consulting firms hired by industry for various purposes, as well as rapid growth in the number and diversity of graduate programs training I/O psychologists.

The Mid 1960s to the Present

One strong indication of the increasing role of organizational psychology is the fact that in 1970 Division 14 of the APA changed its name from "Division of Business and Industrial Psychology" to "Division of Industrial and Organizational Psychology." Organizational psychology had truly arrived. During the past few decades, the field of I/O has grown rapidly, with more work in the traditional areas that we have already discussed as well as branching into new domains—such as the fairness of employment tests and personnel and labor law. Cognitive processes have become an important area of research, as have motivation, organizational structure, and organizational systems. It is estimated that by 1939 there were fewer than 100 I/O psychologists (Katzell & Austin, 1992) in the world—and that their numbers grew to 760 by 1960, 2,000 by 1980, and 3,000 in the United States alone by 1990. And in 1998, Division 14 of the APA, renamed the Society for Industrial-Organizational Psychology, reported more than 3,250 professional and 2,000 student members (Muchinsky, 2000).

Cultural trends have generated interest in cross-cultural factors that affect the workplace. These trends include the increasing ethnic diversity of the U.S. labor force, the establishment of the European Community, the dissolution of the Soviet Union, and changing immigration patterns. The number of international and multinational corporations is increasing. Moreover, technological change is rapidly altering the nature of work and increasing the frequency of global communications. As a result, workers who are relocated through corporate transfers to jobs overseas might experience culture shock or other work-related problems. Difficulties in cultural adaptation can be related to job dissatisfaction, low morale, and increased employee turnover (Hui & Luk, 1997). Thus, cross-cultural differences in the meaning and value of work must be considered in the practice of I/O psychology (Erez, 1994).

◆ INDUSTRIAL PSYCHOLOGY

Industrial psychology is the older element of I/O and deals with the traditional personnel functions such as job analysis, testing, selection, and performance appraisal.

Job Analysis

The foundation for most of what is done in I/O psychology is the **job analysis**—the process of defining a job in terms of its component tasks or duties and then determining the requirements to perform them. A major element that emerges from a job analysis is the job description.

The **job description** is a written statement of what the jobholder does, how she does it, and why she does it (McCormick, 1979). These are often called the *task requirements.* This task information is used to determine the *person requirements,* or KSAs (i.e., knowledge,

job analysis
Defining a job in terms of the tasks and duties involved and the requirements needed to perform it.

job description
A written statement of what a job entails and how and why it is done.

skills, and abilities), deemed necessary to do the job. These KSAs often serve as the standards for recruitment, selection, and placement. A job description for a professor might resemble the following:

> ▶ A college professor teaches and mentors students, serves on various university and professional committees, and demonstrates research scholarship through a program of published research in his or her chosen field. College professors usually work independently, in that a direct supervisor is not usually available to monitor their performance.

KSAs that are identified by a job analysis as instrumental to performing the job might include an ability to read and write at an advanced level (postcollege), an advanced degree (usually a Ph.D.), and an ability to relate to groups of people as well as to individuals on a one-to-one basis. The KSAs, or person requirements, constitute the *job specifications.*

There are many methods for gathering job analysis data. Job-oriented approaches usually involve a questionnaire, checklist, or some other standardized measure and are best suited for jobs that involve manual labor or a clearly specified set of tasks. Worker-oriented approaches are often less standardized and emphasize the behaviors of an individual in a particular job. Jobs that involve judgment and decision making are best suited to this approach. Job analysis data are usually provided by employees who currently hold the job, or by supervisors, or by trained job analysts. Supervisors and current jobholders—together termed *subject matter experts* (SME)—generally do the job analysis through questionnaires or interviews.

Selection

The area of selection and placement should be of interest to everyone because most people, at one time or another, have been selected or rejected for a job, a school, or a team. For example, at the undergraduate level, college admissions committees consider an applicant's SAT or ACT scores and high school GPA, the quality of the high school, and perhaps the applicant's extracurricular activities. These are called tests or **predictors.** Experience and education are two of the most common predictors used to select and place job applicants, but many other predictors are often used.

Validation

You might recall the concept of *validity,* which was discussed in Chapter 2. **Validation** is the process that I/O psychologists use to demonstrate that tests are accurate predictors of job success. For example, it makes sense to use tests of physical abilities to select people for the job of firefighter only if those measures predict success as a firefighter.

When I/O psychologists talk about the validity of employment selection tests, they are referring to how well the tests predict success on the job. Certainly, they would not want to use tests of physical abilities like strength and running speed to select data entry clerks, but such tests might be valid for selecting firefighters. There are many different possible approaches to validation (Cascio, 1991), but the basic idea is to examine the relationship between individuals' scores on the predictors and job success, or the *criterion.* The strength of this relationship is called the validity coefficient and is indexed by a correlation. It provides information about the strength of the relationship between the predictor and the criterion. These coefficients seldom exceed .50. Common categories of predictors include ability tests, personality tests, work sample tests, application forms and biodata, and interviews.

Ability Tests. Tests of cognitive abilities include measures of general intellectual functioning such as the Wonderlic Personnel Test (Wonderlic, 1983), which assesses basic verbal and numerical abilities. Motor and physical abilities tests are often used for selecting individuals into jobs, like machine operator or assembler, that require a certain amount of physical dexterity. Validity coefficients for these types of tests are good and range from about .40 to .55 (Hunter & Hunter, 1984), indicating that ability tests predict the criterion—job success—fairly well.

Personality Tests. Measures of individual attributes include tests that measure personality characteristics, such as sociability, conscientiousness, and openness, as well as interest inventories, which tap individuals' likes and dislikes regarding hobbies, recreational activities, and

predictors

Tests that measure the attributes an employee needs in order to be successful at a job.

validation

A process that determines whether tests are accurate predictors of job success.

tasks. The notion here is that individuals who have particular personalities or interests might be best suited for a particular job or for all jobs. For example, the five-factor model of personality (described in Chapter 13) has been used as a predictor of job performance. Conscientiousness and emotional stability tend to be the best predictors across all jobs and occupational categories for North American and European samples (Salgado, 1997). Moreover, personality tests appear to be better predictors of job performance when workers and their supervisors are from the same cultural background. They are less useful in predicting job performance of workers who are transferred to other countries. This is attributable to the fact that supervisors in other cultures might have different standards of satisfactory job performance (Dalton & Wilson, 2000).

Work Sample Tests. Work sample tests measure the applicant's ability to perform brief examples of the critical tasks required on the job (Riggio, 1999). Assessment centers use a standardized series of work sample tests and have become popular ways of selecting managers and promoting employees into managerial positions, especially in the public sector (Lowry, 1997). For example, a prospective manager might be given an "in-basket" exercise in which he or she is presented with many and varied memoranda, letters, requests from supervisors and subordinates, and customer complaints. The prospect's job is to deal with these however she or he sees fit. The in-basket exercise seems to be a valid way of predicting managerial success, with validity coefficients among the best of all predictors, .54 (Hunter & Hunter, 1984).

Application Forms and Biodata. Many application forms ask applicants about their work history, education, and work or school accomplishments. Some research suggests that this type of information is among the best predictors of future job performance (Hough & Oswald, 2000). Biodata instruments are like application forms, but might also include more personal items related to the applicant's attitudes and values (Owens, 1976). Of course, the biodata items must be validated against a performance criterion. In other words, if employers are going to ask individuals about their hobbies and use that information in hiring decisions, they must ensure that responses to those items are related to job performance. And there is some evidence that cultural values can be reflected in biodata items that might contribute to ethnic differences in respondents' choices (Whitney & Schmitt, 1997). A recent meta-analysis reported a validity coefficient of .33 for biodata (Rothstein et al., 1990).

Interviews. Interviews are among the most popular selection devices and are used across all job levels. In fact, it is estimated that over 80 percent of U.S. organizations use some type of interview process; estimates range as high as 99 percent (McDaniel et al., 1994). An interview is designed to predict future performance based on an applicant's oral responses to a series of oral questions. The rationale is that interviewers can gather information about applicants that is an accurate predictor of job performance. The validity of interviews for employee selection has been hotly debated for more than 30 years. A recent review of the literature uncovered a validity coefficient of .37 overall (McDaniel et al., 1994). Moreover, structuring the interviewing situation, using standardized interviews, and carefully training the interviewers can improve the reliability and validity of interviews (Campion, Palmer, & Campion, 1998).

Legal Implications

Legal issues have become important in personnel selection as well as other areas in which I/O psychologists work. In 1964, the U.S. Congress passed the Civil Rights Act, which included Title VII to protect individuals from discrimination in the arena of work. In particular, this act was intended to protect individuals from being discriminated against based on their ethnicity, sex, national origin, or religion (Riggio, 1999). Other laws have helped prevent discrimination against those over 40 years of age and people with mental or physical disabilities; the Civil Rights Act of 1991 has reaffirmed the major points of the earlier act and expanded some others. This legislation has led to more careful selection processes as well as the creation of the **EEOC** (Equal Employment Opportunity Commission) to ensure fair employment practices. Finally, as American society becomes more multicultural and diverse, the area of I/O psychology will continue to interface with the legal arena to ensure that no one's rights are trampled. Terms like *protected groups, adverse impact,* and *affirmative action* are as much a part of our language as they are a part of the political and legal lexicons.

Performance Appraisal

Performance appraisal is the systematic review, evaluation, and feedback of an employee's job performance. Performance measures often are categorized as *judgmental* or *nonjudgmental.* Nonjudgmental performance criteria are largely objective, such as the number of units produced and the number of absences. In contrast, judgmental performance criteria include measures such as supervisor ratings of employee performance. The job analysis identifies the important criteria for the job, which are then used as standards by which employees' performance can be judged.

Rating Errors

Evaluating another individual's performance accurately and fairly is not an easy thing to do. Many biases, both intentional and unintentional, can come into play. For example, you might believe that you are fairly evaluating a co-worker and not realize that you are allowing your close friendship to interfere with your objectivity. On the other hand, you might give a co-worker a more favorable evaluation than you believe he deserves just because, like Jack Nicholson in *A Few Good Men,* you do not think he can handle the truth.

I/O psychologists have examined the biases and errors that might influence the performance appraisal process. For example, one error that has received a great deal of attention is the **halo effect.** Halo effects are evaluations of employees based on the rater's general feelings toward an employee. Generally, raters who like their employees rate all dimensions of employee performance positively (Lefkowitz, 2000).

Leniency is another common error in the appraisal process. The lenient rater tends to routinely give all workers very positive appraisals. This is the teacher who gives everyone A's or the boss who rates all of her subordinates at the top of the rating scale. The rater who makes the **central tendency error** rates everyone in the middle. In this situation there appear to be no differences between employees' performances. Both leniency and the central tendency error can result in organizational problems; because raters are not discriminating among employees, the appraisal data are useless in making decisions about such things as raises or layoffs.

New-Wave Performance Appraisal

In an influential paper, Landy and Farr (1980) suggested a *cognitive process model* to direct future performance appraisal research. As a result, focus shifted from rating errors to the cognitive processing (for example, encoding, storage, retrieval, and judgment) of raters. Many organizations require supervisors to conduct formal performance appraisals of all subordinates once or twice each year. This means that the rater is required to recall and integrate information from a period of 6 to 12 months for a number of people and then objectively evaluate the performance of each. Research has indicated that this is difficult to do and is influenced by many of the errors and biases mentioned earlier. There is some evidence, though, that training raters in techniques such as structured diary keeping and structured recall reduces errors and bias, and increases raters' satisfaction with the performance appraisal process (DeNisi & Peters, 1996).

Other I/O psychologists suggest that we pay more attention to other, noncognitive elements of the appraisal process (Ilgen, Barnes-Farrell, & MeKellin, 1993). Many experts have begun to heed this advice by examining the context (social, legal, organizational, and political) in which appraisal takes place (Levy & Steelman, 1997). For example, a recent meta-analysis found that employee participation in the performance appraisal process was strongly related to employee satisfaction with the process (Cawley, Keeping, & Levy, 1998).

Training

The third major content area of industrial psychology is employee training. In fact, surveys routinely report that over 90 percent of all private companies use some formal training. Employees selected into a particular job might still need training to learn the job, and current employees often require training as their jobs change. The job analysis identifies what KSAs they must have to be able to perform the job, and this information can be used to determine which of these behaviors employees need to be trained in and how much training is required.

Needs Analysis

The first phase in any training program is to identify training needs through the use of a needs analysis. Typically, this is done at three levels. First, *organization analysis,* which involves looking at the whole organization and perhaps breaking it down into departments or functional units. Second, *task analysis,* which looks at each job (separate from the person performing the job) to determine what the employee must do to adequately perform the job. Finally, *person analysis,* which identifies employees who need training. This often involves evaluating the individual's performance.

Training Methods

There are many training programs and approaches available to organizations. First, *on-the-job training* is something that almost all trainees are exposed to at some point in their careers (Goldstein, 1993). Informally, this is often called "hands-on" training and involves new employees' learning how to do their job while actually working with an experienced employee. A second common approach to training is the *lecture method,* in which employees are taught about the job through lectures.

Programmed instruction (PI) is a self-instructional approach to training based on the work of learning theorist B. F. Skinner (see Chapter 7). Typically, the material to be learned is broken down into small steps arranged in a logical sequence. Trainees work through these steps at their own pace; they are tested for knowledge after each step is completed, and provided with feedback on their performance. *Computer-assisted instruction* is a similar process, but the trainee interacts with a computer. In this way, employees who are grasping the new material well can move on to more challenging material, whereas those who are not can continue to focus on the areas where they are having problems.

Evaluation

The third phase of any training program is an evaluation of program effectiveness. Kirkpatrick (1959) suggested four levels of criteria to consider in training evaluations. First, measures at the *reaction* level include what the trainees think or feel about the training program. Certainly, the organization wants to conduct a training program that the trainees like. The next level, *learning,* evaluates how much has been learned in the training program. This might involve a multiple-choice exam after the trainees have completed the program.

Kirkpatrick suggested that the *behavioral* level of criteria includes measures of actual changes in performance once the trainee is back on the job. The issue here is **transfer—**bringing what was learned during the training program back to the actual job environment. The last level of criteria is commonly referred to as *results* and has to do with the utility of the training program for the organization. At the results level, effectiveness means that the expense of the training program was more than offset by benefits, such as improved performance, productivity, and profits.

transfer
Bringing back to the job environment what was learned in training.

◆ ORGANIZATIONAL PSYCHOLOGY

Organizational psychology focuses on individual behavior and improving the well-being of employees.

▲ Edwin Locke

"Goals affect performance by affecting effort, persistence, and direction of attention, and by motivating strategy development."

valence

The value an individual places on a particular outcome.

instrumentality

The extent to which an individual believes that attaining a particular outcome will lead to other positively valued outcomes.

expectancy

The strength of the individual's beliefs about whether a particular outcome is attainable.

goal-setting theory

The theory that performance is improved by setting specific goals.

Motivation

Work motivation has been defined in many ways, but Steers and Porter (1991) suggest that when we speak of work motivation we are concerned with (1) what energizes human behavior, (2) what directs it, and (3) how it is maintained or sustained. For example, researchers have studied cross-cultural differences in work-related values and norms (Hui & Luk, 1997). Kanfer (1990) presents a useful framework for organizing motivational theories.

The Need-Motive-Value Perspective

Approaches to motivation from the need-motive-value perspective argue that individuals are motivated as a result of their personalities, dispositions, and values. Examples of theories that fall into this class are Maslow's hierarchy of needs (described in Chapter 11) and Alderfer's existence-relatedness-growth theory (ERG). Both of these theories hypothesize that unmet needs drive behavior. However, there has not been a great deal of research supporting the validity or usefulness of these theories. Other examples of this category include intrinsic motivation and achievement motivation (also described in Chapter 11). These theories focus on a more narrowly defined set of psychological motives such as mastery and competence (Kanfer, 1990).

Cognitive Choice Theories

The most famous cognitive choice theory is Vroom's expectancy-value theory (Vroom, 1964). According to Vroom, our behavior results from conscious choices among alternatives that are evaluated with respect to three key concepts. First, **valence** is how much an individual values a particular outcome. Second, **instrumentality** is the extent to which an individual believes that attaining a particular outcome will lead to other positively valued outcomes. Finally, **expectancy** is the strength of an individual's belief about whether a particular outcome is attainable. Putting all of this together, Vroom suggests that people's beliefs about valances, instrumentalities, and expectancies interact psychologically to create a motivational force to act. For example, if I think that performing a certain task will lead to a *valued* outcome, and I believe that completing the task is *instrumental* in that it is likely to lead to other desired outcomes, but I *expect* that I cannot complete the task, I will not be motivated to attempt the task. On the other hand, if expectancy, valence, and instrumentality are high, this will be reflected in a strong motivational force to perform the task.

A meta-analysis of 77 studies testing Vroom's theory found that the three components, valence, instrumentality, and expectancy, predicted a number of work-related criteria as well as the complete model. Thus, each of the theory's concepts appears to be a valid predictor of work motivation, but the complete model does little to enhance our understanding of work motivation (Van Eerde & Thierry, 1996).

Self-Regulation/Metacognition Theories

Self-regulation/metacognition theories differ from the other two paradigms because the notion here is that motivation is directly linked to self-regulation and translated into behavior and performance as a result of cognition (Kanfer, 1990). Note the distinction between cognitive choice theories, which focus on making the choice to pursue an activity or goal, and self-regulation/metacognition theories, which describe the behaviors involved in attaining that goal. In other words, cognitive choice theories deal with intentions or choices, whereas the latter deal with volition or will (Lord & Levy, 1994).

The most researched theory of this type is **goal-setting theory.** Edwin Locke has spent nearly 40 years examining the effect of goals on performance (Locke & Latham, 1990). The most important conclusion from this huge literature is that individuals who (1) are assigned (or choose) difficult, specific goals, (2) accept them, and (3) receive feedback about their performance, outperform those who are aspiring to a "do your best" goal (Tubbs, 1986). This effect is consistently found in the laboratory setting and likewise has been shown to be robust in real-world settings (Latham & Lee, 1986).

In sum, motivation is a complex topic. Our thinking on the topic has evolved from a rather narrow focus on human needs to an emphasis on individual goals and the effect of

Appendix B

self-regulation on cognitive processing of information as well as subsequent task behavior (Kanfer, 1990). In addition, recent I/O work on motivation seems to have recognized the need to move beyond choice processes and to focus on the implementation of those choices (Lord & Levy, 1994).

Work Attitudes

Employees' attitudes, beliefs, and values have received a great deal of research attention from I/O psychologists, for several reasons. As discussed in Chapter 17, there is a widespread assumption that attitudes lead to behaviors. We will see shortly that it is not so simple. Because of the complexities of human behavior, no one attitude is going to be strongly related to any one behavior.

Job Satisfaction

The most frequently studied job-related attitude is job satisfaction. Locke (1976) defined job satisfaction as a pleasurable, positive emotional state resulting from the appraisal of one's job or job experiences. There are certainly individual differences with respect to job satisfaction—some people tend to be more satisfied than others with their jobs (Staw & Ross, 1985)—but situational factors such as the work environment also seem to play a role (Gerhart, 1987; Newton & Keenan, 1991).

One study investigated the relationship of personality and situational factors in workers coping with reorganization of their workplace. Employees who had higher levels of self-esteem, optimism, and personal control and who received information about the changes and participated in the decision-making process were more open to change and had higher levels of job satisfaction (Wanberg & Banas, 2000). In addition, the conceptualization of job satisfaction has been broadened to include multiple dimensions of job satisfaction. For example, important dimensions of job satisfaction include satisfaction with (1) the work itself, (2) the supervisor, (3) co-workers, (4) pay, and (5) growth opportunities.

Certainly, businesses need to turn a profit to survive, so they are almost always interested in the relationship between satisfaction and work outcomes. Research has examined the relationships among satisfaction and three work outcomes in particular: (1) performance, (2) absenteeism, and (3) turnover. Research findings on the relationship between satisfaction and performance are mixed. Generally there is a small positive relationship ($r = .17$) between satisfaction and performance (Iaffaldano & Muchinsky, 1985).

Though satisfaction is certainly an important part of the puzzle, satisfaction does not have a strong direct effect on absenteeism, because of the other variables involved. For example, a recent meta-analysis found that a flexible workweek—that is, providing workers with "flextime" that enables them to modify their work hours—significantly reduced absenteeism (Baltes et al., 1999). Despite the complexities involved, Johns's (1997) quantitative review of the literature in this area reports a small negative correlation ($r = -.25$) between the two, indicating that more satisfied employees tend to be absent less often.

Finally, there is some support for the notion that job dissatisfaction leads to **turnover.** Carsten and Spector (1987) report a small negative correlation (average $r = -.20$ to $-.30$), suggesting that dissatisfaction is associated with turnover. Of course, turnover is much more complicated than this. Usually the best predictor of *involuntary* turnover is employee performance that results in being fired or laid off. Many researchers have put forth models of the *voluntary* turnover process, and most include job dissatisfaction as an important variable (Lee & Mitchell, 1994).

turnover
The ratio of new employees to established employees.

Organizational Commitment

The second most examined work-related attitude is organizational commitment (OC). This has traditionally been defined as the relative strength of an individual's identification with and involvement in a particular organization (Mowday, Steers, & Porter, 1979). As in the case of work-related attitudes, there are cross-cultural differences in organizational commitment related to organizational structure, norms, and management-employee relations (Hui & Luk, 1997).

A recent meta-analysis found that organizational commitment predicted a number of work-related outcome measures (Brown, 1996). Organizational commitment was positively correlated with job satisfaction (average $r = .53$), job involvement (average $r = .50$), and job performance (average $r = .11$). Organizational commitment was negatively correlated with turnover (average $r = -.28$). Thus, organizational attitudes appear to be strongly correlated. However, the relationship between organizational attitudes and behavior is substantially weaker, probably due to the fact that job performance and turnover may be influenced by a number of factors other than employee attitudes.

A meta-analysis of organizational commitment by Mathieu and Zajac (1990) reported only a small relationship between organizational commitment and absenteeism ($r = .10$). This is not surprising, though, given what we know about the complexities involved in absenteeism (Hackett, Bycio, & Guion, 1989; Steers & Rhodes, 1978). Based on the limited research to date, it appears that organizational commitment is not a very important predictor of absenteeism.

◆ WHERE I/O PSYCHOLOGY IS GOING

The 21st century promises to be fast, frenzied, competitive, and turbulent. Dramatic changes are taking place in the world of work.

global competition

Business competition among countries worldwide.

First, **global competition** is increasing. Global competition will continue to make it absolutely necessary that countries have well-trained, competent workforce to compete favorably with the many countries that now workforces are competitors. Second, new technology has significantly affected workers' jobs and organizational structure. I/O psychology is important for helping the laid-off worker to be competitive for other jobs and helping those left behind to handle more diverse jobs (Cascio, 1995; Methot & Phillips-Grant, 1998). And the very nature of work is changing, posing challenges for personnel selection and retention (Hough & Oswald, 2000).

Third, the latest trend in organizations is flatter organizational structures and empowered workers. No longer is it typical for organizations to have a manager for every 10 employees; rather, an upper-level manager might supervise 50 employees in teams of 10. Employees, or team members, are given greater responsibility for their performance as well as for setting objectives and decision making. Employees and teams manage themselves. I/O psychologists need to prepare current and future employees for this very different approach to organizational functioning (Cascio, 1995).

Finally, the workplace is becoming more diverse in terms of sex, age, ethnicity, and culture. This diversity requires increased sensitivity to differences on the part of management and employees. Education and training in the world of work has become an important area for I/O psychologists and will continue to grow in importance in the 21st century (Hough & Oswald, 2000).

Key Concepts

INDUSTRIAL PSYCHOLOGY
central tendency error 524
EEOC 524
halo effect 524
job analysis 521
job description 521

leniency 524
performance appraisal 524
predictors 522
transfer 525
validation 522

ORGANIZATIONAL PSYCHOLOGY
expectancy 526
global competition 528
goal-setting theory 526

instrumentality 526
turnover 527
valence 526

Answers to Staying on Track

Chapter 1: The Nature of Psychology

Staying on Track: The History of Psychology

1. Kant believed that the mind could not be studied scientifically, partly because it could not be measured.
2. Functionalism stressed the importance of how the mind helps us adapt to reality, and it expanded the kinds of methods, subjects, and settings used in psychological research.
3. Psychic determinism is the belief that all behavior is influenced by psychological motives, often unconscious ones.
4. The Experimentalists' original bylaws excluded women; thus women did not have the opportunity to "network" and make the same professional connections as men.

Staying on Track: Contemporary Psychological Perspectives

1. The humanistic perspective is called "the third force" because it was the first major alternative to the behavioral and psychoanalytic perspectives.
2. Like Gestalt psychologists, cognitive psychologists stress the active role of the mind in organizing perceptions, processing information, and interpreting experiences. Like behavioral psychologists, cognitive psychologists stress the need for objective, well-controlled laboratory studies.
3. The social-cultural perspective is a reaction against the tendency to presume that psychological research findings in Western cultures are automatically generalizable to other cultures.

Staying on Track: Psychology as a Profession

1. Basic research aims at contributing to knowledge, and applied research aims at solving practical problems.
2. A psychiatrist is a physician who has served a residency in psychiatry, which takes a medical approach to the treatment of psychological disorders.

Chapter 2: Psychology as a Science

Staying on Track: Sources of Knowledge

1. The basic assumptions of science are that the universe is orderly, determinism is the best approach to explaining events, and skepticism is the proper scientific attitude.
2. Critical thinking is the systematic evaluation of claims by identifying the claim being made, examining evidence in support of the claim, and considering alternative explanations of the claim.
3. The steps in the scientific method include providing a rationale, conducting the study, analyzing the data, communicating the research findings, and replicating the study.

Staying on Track: Goals of Scientific Research

1. Scientists use operational definitions to provide precise, concrete definitions of events or characteristics in their research.
2. Science involves probabilistic prediction because so many variables are at work at any given time that it is usually impossible to be certain about the accuracy of one's predictions.
3. Scientific explanation in psychology involves the discovery of the causes of overt behaviors, mental experiences, and physiological changes.

Staying on Track: Methods of Psychological Research

1. A random sample permits generalization of survey findings from the sample to the population.
2. The validity of a test is the extent to which a test measures what it is supposed to measure.
3. The independent variable is manipulated by the experimenter, who determines its values before the experiment begins.
4. Internal validity is the extent to which changes in the dependent variable are attributable to the independent variable.

Staying on Track: Statistical Analysis of Research Data

1. Measures of central tendency, which are used to represent a set of scores, include the mode, median, and mean.
2. Measures of variability, which are used to describe the degree of dispersion of a set of scores, include the range, the variance, and the standard deviation.
3. Statistical significance involves deciding whether the difference between group performances is of sufficiently low probability that it can be attributed to the independent variable.
4. Meta-analysis combines the results of a large number of published and unpublished studies. After collecting the studies, the research computes the average size of the effect of the independent variable on the dependent variable.

Staying on Track: The Ethics of Psychological Research

1. Critics argue that the methodological benefits of deception do not outweigh the mistrust of psychological research it might create and the distress it might cause in deceived participants.
2. Debriefing involves informing participants of the purpose of the research study in which they participated and any unusual aspects, such as the use of deception.
3. Animal rights advocates oppose all laboratory research using animals, regardless of its scientific merit or practical benefits. Animal welfare advocates would permit laboratory research on animals as long as the animals are given humane care and the potential benefits of the research outweigh any pain and distress caused to the animals.

Chapter 3: Behavioral Neuroscience

Staying on Track: Heredity and Behavior

1. Behavioral neuroscience studies the psychological bases of human and animal behavior and mental processes.
2. The closer two persons are related biologically, the more genetically similar they will be, but also, in general, the closer their biological relation, the more similar they will be in life experiences. Thus, we have no more right to attribute personal similarities between two closely related people solely to heredity than we do to attribute them solely to common life experiences.

Staying on Track: Communication Systems

1. The nervous system is divided into the central nervous system (including the brain and spinal cord) and the peripheral nervous system (including the somatic nervous system and the autonomic nervous system).
2. Endocrine glands secrete hormones into the bloodstream; exocrine glands secrete their chemicals into the body surface

or into the body cavities. More-over, endocrine secretions have many behavioral effects, but exocrine secretions have few.

3. Adrenal hormones contribute to proper neural functioning and play a role in responses to stress.

Staying on Track: The Neuron

1. The major structures of the neuron are the cell body, dendrites, and axon.

2. Neural impulses depend on the flow of positively charged ions into the neuron, which produces an action potential.

Staying on Track: The Brain

1. The brain stem regulates breathing, heart rate, motor coordination, brain arousal, attention, and other important life functions. The limbic system regulates processes related to emotion, motivation, and memory. And the cerebral cortex contains motor areas that control body movements, sensory areas that process sensory input, association areas that permit the integration of information from different brain areas, and, in human beings, language areas that permit the production and comprehension of speech.

2. Broca's area selects the muscle movements necessary for the expression of words and communicates them to the motor cortex. Wernicke's area selects words that convey meaning and communicates them to Broca's area.

3. Split-brain research involves special testing procedures in which the left and right hemispheres can no longer communicate with each other. Results of split-brain research indicate, for example, that the right hemisphere is superior at perceiving spatial relationships and the left hemisphere is superior at producing and comprehending speech.

Chapter 4: Human Development

Staying on Track: Research Methods in Developmental Psychology

1. Maturation is the sequential unfolding of inherited abilities, such as an infant's progression from crawling to walking to standing.

2. Cross-sectional research designs assess age differences at one point in time. However, it might not be possible to generalize the results of cross-sectional research to other cohorts. Longitudinal research designs assess how individuals change over time. However, longitudinal designs require considerable financial support, and participants often drop out. If the participants who drop out differ from the remaining participants, the results of such studies might not be generalizable to the population of interest.

Staying on Track: Prenatal Development

1. Cell-adhesion molecules direct the movement of cells and determine which cells will adhere to one another, thereby determining the size, shape, and location of organs in the embryo.

2. The hallmarks of fetal alcohol syndrome are facial deformities and mental retardation.

Staying on Track: Infant and Child Development

1. Depth perception is present in human infants by 6 months of age, and generally it develops in animals about the time that they can move about on their own.

2. Piaget assumed that the child proceeds through qualitatively different stages of cognitive development during which cognitive schemas are altered by the processes of assimilation and accommodation.

3. Securely attached infants have more successful peer relationships and more secure romantic attachments later in life.

4. Permissive parents set few rules and rarely punish misbehavior; authoritarian parents set strict rules and rely on punishment; and authoritative parents tend to be warm and loving, yet insist that their children behave appropriately. Authoritative parenting is the most successful, and the preferred, style of parenting.

Staying on Track: Adolescent Development

1. Cultural and historical factors that are unique to particular cohorts can make those cohorts somewhat different from cohorts that precede or succeed them.

2. The person who has reached the formal operational stage can apply abstract principles and make predictions about hypothetical situations.

3. The adolescent develops a sense of identity by adopting his or her own set of values and social behaviors. This is a normal part of finding answers to questions such as these: What do I believe is important? What are my goals in life?

Staying on Track: Gender Differences and Human Development

1. The best-established psychological gender difference is that the average male score is higher than the average female score on standardized tests in mathematics.

2. Some psychologists argue that gender differences are too small to have any practical meaning and that publicizing them might promote sex discrimination. Others insist that scientists are obliged to study topics even when their research findings might be disapproved of. And others caution that differences should not be interpreted as deficiencies and attributed to inherited biological factors.

Staying on Track: Adult Development

1. A reduction in caloric intake is associated with increased longevity.

2. Research indicates that fluid intelligence declines in old age but that crystallized intelligence does not.

3. Adults who achieve generativity become less self-absorbed and more concerned about being a productive worker, spouse, or parent.

Chapter 5: Sensation and Perception

Staying on Track: Sensory Processes

1. Sensation is the process that detects stimuli from one's body or environment. Perception is the process that organizes sensations into meaningful patterns.

2. Psychophysics is the study of the relationships between the physical characteristics of stimuli and the corresponding psychological responses to them.

3. Sensory adaptation is the tendency of sensory receptors to respond less and less to an unchanging stimulus.

Staying on Track: Visual Sensation and Perception

1. Light waves pass through the cornea, pupil, lens, and photoreceptors.

2. Trichromatic theory assumes that the retina has three kinds of receptors, each of which is maximally sensitive to red, green, or blue light.

3. These are the principles of proximity, closure, similarity, and continuity.

4. Two binocular cues are retinal disparity and convergence.

Staying on Track: Hearing

1. The major structures are the pinna, auditory canal, tympanic membrane, eustachian tube, ossicles, oval window, cochlea, basilar membrane, hair cells, and auditory nerve.

2. Place theory assumes that particular points on the basilar membrane vibrate maximally in response to sound waves of particular frequencies.

3. Sound localization depends on sounds reaching one ear slightly before reaching the other, on sounds being slightly more intense at the closer ear, and on the irregular shape of the pinna altering sounds differently depending on their location.

Staying on Track: Chemical Senses

1. Pheromones are odorous chemicals that affect animals' behavior. Recent research suggests that pheromones may have some effect on humans' behavior and emotions.

2. The enjoyment of flavors depends on not only the sense of taste but also the sense of smell, which is diminished by a head cold.

Staying on Track: Skin Senses

1. The blind person wears a camera on special eyeglasses and a computer-controlled electronic vest covered with a grid of tiny Teflon cones. Outlines of images provided by the camera are impressed onto the skin by vibrations of the cones.

2. The gate-control theory of pain assumes that pain impulses from the limbs or body pass through a part of the spinal cord that provides a "gate" for pain impulses, perhaps involving substance P neurons. When neurons that convey touch sensations are stimulated, this "closes" the gate, preventing input from neurons that convey pain sensations.

3. If human participants or animal subjects are given naloxone and the pain-relieving technique becomes less effective, it is assumed that the technique depends on the release of endorphins, because naloxone blocks the effects of endorphins.

Staying on Track: Body Senses

1. The kinesthetic sense informs you of the position of your joints, the tension in your muscles, and the movement of your arms and legs.

2. One of the major theories of motion sickness holds that it is produced by a conflict between sensory input to the eyes and sensory input to the vestibular organs.

Staying on Track: Extrasensory Perception

1. The four paranormal abilities are mental telepathy, clairvoyance, precognition, and psychokinesis.

2. The major shortcomings of paranormal research are that it might involve poorly controlled demonstrations, chance events, fraud, or magic. Moreover, paranormal events cannot be explained by any known physical processes.

Chapter 6: Consciousness

Staying on Track: The Nature of Consciousness

1. Both William James and James Joyce were interested in studying the stream of consciousness.

2. The "cocktail party phenomenon" involves being engrossed in one conversation at a noisy party yet noticing when your name is mentioned in another conversation.

Staying on Track: The Unconscious

1. Automatic processing involves less conscious awareness and mental effort than controlled processing. As a result, it does not interfere with our performance of other activities.

2. Subliminal psychodynamic activation presents emotionally charged subliminal messages to alter the recipient's moods and behaviors by stimulating unconscious fantasies.

Staying on Track: Sleep

1. The night typically involves four or five cycles in which the sleeper descends into the depths of NREM sleep, ascends to lighter stages of NREM sleep, and ends each cycle in REM sleep. During the second half of the night, the sleeper might not reach sleep deeper than stage 2 and will have longer REM periods.

2. The length of sleep varies negatively with how long it takes animals to find their daily food and positively with how secure they are from attack while asleep.

3. Persons with sleep-onset insomnia should avoid ingesting caffeine or exercising too close to bedtime. They should also avoid napping during the day; go to bed only when they feel sleepy; refrain from eating, reading, watching television, or listening to music while in bed; and get out of bed instead of tossing and turning.

Staying on Track: Dreams

1. Among Calkins's findings were that we dream every night, that we have several dream periods each night, that we are more likely to dream during the second half of the night, that most dreams are mundane, that we can incorporate external stimuli into our dreams, that we can engage in "real thinking" while asleep, that we can control our dreams, and that dreams can disguise their true meanings.

2. Freud believed that dreams are often disguised forms of wish fulfillment in which the manifest content of the dream symbolically represents its true meaning (its latent content).

Staying on Track: Hypnosis

1. During hypnotic induction you might have the person focus on a spot on the ceiling. You might then suggest that the person's eyelids are closing, feet are warming, muscles are relaxing, and breathing is slowing. You would gradually induce the person to relinquish more and more control of his or her perceptions, thoughts, and behaviors to you.

2. Hypnosis can help people recall memories but might make them overly confident in their recall of inaccurate "memories."

3. Some researchers believe that hypnosis is merely a state of heightened suggestibility in which people are willing to act out the suggestions given by the hypnotist. They also note that motivated nonhypnotized people can often perform the same feats as hypnotized people.

Staying on Track: Psychoactive Drugs

1. Physical drug dependency is marked by tolerance and withdrawal symptoms.

2. Cocaine is a stimulant drug that induces a relatively brief state of euphoria. It can cause addiction, paranoia, hallucinations, and sudden death from cardiac arrest.

3. Marijuana alters sensory experiences and in higher doses can induce hallucinations. It impairs coordination, disrupts memory formation, and has been linked to amotivational syndrome.

4. Entactogens are a category of psychoactive drugs that induce altered perceptions and feelings of well-being and interpersonal closeness; they have been linked to memory impairment in chronic users.

Chapter 7: Learning

Staying on Track: Classical Conditioning

1. You would repeatedly turn on the can opener just before presenting the cat with food. Eventually the cat will come running at the sound of the can opener.

2. Bernstein suggests offering patients unusual, strange-tasting food before they have chemotherapy so that they will associate their resulting nausea with that food instead of with more common, nutritious foods.

3. Garcia found that rats have a tendency, apparently inborn, to associate nausea and dizziness with tastes, but not with sights and sounds, and to associate pain with sights and sounds, but not with tastes.

Staying on Track: Operant Conditioning

1. Thorndike, like Skinner, found that behavior can be changed by altering its consequences.

2. You might train him by giving him a piece of cookie for looking at toys strewn on the floor, then for taking a step toward them, then for approaching them, then for touching one of them, then for picking it up, and finally for placing it in the toy box.

3. Both produce an increase in behavior, but whereas positive reinforcement involves the presentation of something appealing, negative reinforcement involves the removal of something unappealing.

Staying on Track: Cognitive Learning

1. Rescorla's research suggests that the conditioned stimulus allows individuals to predict the occurrences of the uncondtioned stimulus.

2. Latent learning and observational learning show that learning can take place without performing the relevant overt behavior.

Chapter 8: Memory

Staying on Track: Information Processing and Memory

1. Some psychologists note that normal memory processes, such as thinking more often and more elaborately about certain experiences, can explain so-called flashbulb memories. Moreover, there is evidence that people are more confident in their flashbulb memories, even though those might be no more accurate than normal memories.

2. Sensory memory stores exact replicas of stimuli impinging on the senses for a brief period—from a fraction of second to several seconds. Short-term memory stores a limited amount of information in conscious awareness for about 20 seconds. And long-term memory stores a virtually unlimited amount of information for up to a lifetime.

Staying on Track: Sensory Memory

1. By using partial report, Sperling demonstrated that iconic memory stores virtually all the information that strikes the photoreceptors, though the information fades so quickly that it seems that we store only a fraction of it.

2. Echoic memory helps us store speech sounds long enough to blend them with subsequent speech sounds, thereby letting us perceive a meaningful sequence of sounds.

Staying on Track: Short-Term Memory

1. Research indicates that even when participants are tested on their short-term memory for letters presented visually, their errors indicate that they confuse letters based on their sounds more than on their appearance.

2. When they presented participants with trigrams to recall and prevented rehearsal of them, they found that after about 20 seconds participants could not recall any trigrams.

Staying on Track: Long-Term Memory

1. Elaborative rehearsal involves processing the meaning of information instead of (as in maintenance rehearsal) its superficial qualities.

2. Procedural memory includes memories of how to perform behaviors, whereas declarative memory includes memories of facts.

3. In proactive interference, old memories interfere with new memories. In retroactive interference, new memories interfere with old ones.

4. Memories encoded while a person is in a specific state (such as a psychoactive drug-induced state) will be recalled better when the person is again in that state. There is also research showing that our recall of information that has been encoded in a particular mood will be best when we are in that mood again.

5. Loftus believes that biased or leading questions can alter people's memory of past events. This becomes even more of an issue when hypnosis is used to recreate memories.

Staying on Track: Improving Your Memory

1. You should set up a study schedule in a comfortable, nondistracting environment. You might also use the SQ3R method of studying. Other suggestions would be to use overlearning, distributed practice, and mnemonic devices.

2. You would memorize a list of concrete nouns that rhyme with numbers 1, 2, 3, 4, and so on. You would then imagine the objects to be recalled interacting with the objects represented by the concrete nouns. Then simply recall the concrete nouns associated with each number. This should automatically make you recall the interacting object.

Staying on Track: The Biopsychology of Memory

1. After classically conditioning an eyeblink response in a rabbit, researchers found that electrical simulation of a tiny site in the cerebellum of the rabbit elicited the conditioned eye blink and that destruction of the site eliminated it.

2. Since his hippocampus was removed decades ago, H. M. has been unable to form new long-term memories.

3. When participants are given a drug that blocks the effects of acetylcholine, they have trouble forming new long-term declarative memories. Other evidence comes from the loss of memory in victims of Alzheimer's disease, which is associated with the destruction of acetylcholine neurons in the brain.

Chapter 9: Thinking and Language

Staying on Track: Concept Formation and Problem Solving

1. A logical concept is formed by identifying the specific features possessed by all things that the concept applies to. A natural concept is formed through everyday experience rather than by testing hypotheses about particular features that are common to all members of the concept.

2. A heuristic can be more efficient, because it rules out many useless alternatives before they are even attempted. But unlike an algorithm, a heuristic does not guarantee a correct solution.

3. We sometimes are hindered by mental sets, which are commitments to problem-solving strategies that have succeeded in the past but that interfere with solving a problem that requires a new strategy.

Staying on Track: Creativity

1. Creative people tend to be above average in intelligence, to have a wide range of interests, and to be imaginative, open to new experiences, unconventional, and nonconforming.

2. Amabile found that when students were given extrinsic reasons for writing poetry, they wrote less creative poems—though there was no decline in the creativity in poems by students who wrote for intrinsic reasons.

Staying on Track: Decision Making and Artificial Intelligence

1. The availability heuristic is the tendency to estimate the probability of an event by how easily relevant instances of it come to mind.

2. Leading questions affect people's decision making by the way in which they present the facts of a case, often as subtle as describing a 50 percent success rate versus a 50 percent failure rate.

3. Psychologists who study artificial intelligence use computer programs to simulate human thought processes or improve human thinking and decision making.

Staying on Track: The Structure of Language

1. Semanticity is the conveying of thoughts in a meaningful way to those who understand the language. Generativity is the combining of language symbols in novel ways, without being limited to a fixed number of combinations. Displacement is the use of language to refer to objects and events that are not present.

2. In terms of transformational grammar, language comprehension involves transforming the surface structure, which is the verbal message, into its deep structure, which is its meaning.

Staying on Track: The Acquisition of Language

1. Between 4 and 6 months of age, infants enter the babbling stage. When infants are about 1 year old, they begin to say their first words. Infants then begin using holophrastic speech, which is the use of single words to represent whole phrases or sentences. Next, in the two-word stage, infants use telegraphic speech.

2. Skinner believes that all aspects of language are learned. Chomsky believes that we have an inborn language mechanism that makes us sensitive to the rules of grammar.

Staying on Track: The Relationship Between Language and Thinking

1. In *1984* Orwell portrays a society in which the government changes the meaning of words or invents words to limit citizens' ability to think rebellious thoughts.

2. Research indicates that when male pronouns are used to represent people generically, those who read or hear them tend to take them to refer to males rather than to both males and females.

Staying on Track: Language in Apes

1. Some apes have been able to use words meaningfully, use words in novel ways, and use words to refer to things that are not physically present.

2. Some researchers believe that apes do not use language spontaneously but instead use it to get things they want or simply as responses to prompting by their trainers.

Chapter 10: Intelligence

Staying on Track: Intelligence Testing

1. Savant syndrome is characterized by below-average intelligence but an outstanding ability, typically in art, music, memory, or calculating.

2. Galton similarly assumed that people with superior physical abilities, especially sensory and motor abilities, are better adapted for survival and, therefore, more intelligent.

Staying on Track: Extremes of Intelligence

1. The possible causes of mental retardation include hereditary defects, social-cultural deprivation, and brain damage.

2. The Studies of Genius have shown that mentally gifted children tend to become socially, physically, vocationally, and academically superior adults.

Staying on Track: Theories of Intelligence

1. Spearman found that intelligence depends on a general intelligence factor more than on separate kinds of intelligence. In contrast, Thurstone found that intelligence depends more on separate kinds of intelligence than on a general intelligence factor.

2. The seven types of intelligence are linguistic, logical-mathematical, spatial, musical, bodily-kinesthetic, intrapersonal, and interpersonal.

Staying on Track: Nature, Nurture, and Intelligence

1. In intelligence, adopted children are more like their biological parents than like their adoptive parents. Moreover, identical twins reared apart are more alike in intelligence than nontwin siblings reared together are.

2. The beneficial effects of intellectual enrichment programs include gains in IQ scores and improved cognitive skills.

Chapter 11: Motivation

Staying on Track: The Nature of Motivation

1. Critics fear that acceptance of sociobiology would lend support to the status quo, making us less inclined to change what many people believe has been "ordained by God or nature," such as differences in the social status of women and men, African Americans and European Americans, rich and poor.

2. According to Maslow, you must first satisfy your basic physiological needs before you will be motivated to meet your higher needs for safety and security, and so on up the hierarchy from the need for belongingness and love, through the need for esteem, and ultimately to the needs for self-actualization and transcendence.

Staying on Track: The Hunger Motive

1. Stimulation of the lateral hypothalamus provokes eating, and stimulation of the ventromedial hypothalamus inhibits eating.

2. The role of heredity in obesity has been supported by studies showing that the correlation in the amount of body fat between identical twins stays roughly the same whether they are reared together or apart. Moreover, adopted children are more similar in weight to their biological parents than to their adoptive parents.

3. Factors might include cultural emphasis on thinness, dissatisfaction with their bodies, and concerns about physical attractiveness.

Staying on Track: The Sex Motive

1. The four phases of the human sexual response cycle are excitement, plateau, orgasm, and resolution.

2. Kinsey's surveys found that people engaged in more sex and a greater variety of sexual activities than was popularly believed. Women are less likely than men to have masturbated, and men are more likely to approve of casual sex.

3. Biopsychological factors influencing sexual orientation include genetics and prenatal exposure to sex hormones.

Staying on Track: The Arousal Motive

1. According to the Yerkes-Dodson law, performance will be best at a moderate level of arousal.

2. Flotation REST has proved useful in reducing tension headache and high blood pressure.

Staying on Track: The Achievement Motive

1. People high in need for achievement are persistent, able to delay gratification in the short term in order to meet long-term goals, and successful. They also tend to choose challenges that are neither too easy nor too difficult.

2. Overjustification theory assumes that an extrinsic reward decreases intrinsic motivation when a person attributes her or his performance to the extrinsic reward. Cognitive-evaluation theory holds that a reward perceived as providing information about a person's competence in an activity will increase her or his intrinsic motivation to perform that activity. But a reward perceived as an attempt to control a person's behavior will decrease that person's intrinsic motivation to perform that activity.

Chapter 12: Emotion

Staying on Track: The Biopsychology of Emotion

1. Studies measuring brain activity have found that increased activity in the left hemisphere is associated with positive emotions and increased activity in the right hemisphere is associated with negative emotions.

2. Endorphin levels rise markedly after activities that induce euphoria.

Staying on Track: The Expression of Emotion

1. Studies have found that people perceive women and men to experience emotions with different frequency. And people perceive women to be expressing more sadness and men to be expressing more anger.

2. One line of research has found that even people who are blind from birth exhibit facial expressions for the basic emotions. A second line of research shows that young infants produce facial expressions for the basic emotions. Some studies also show that facial expressions for the basic emotions are universal across cultures.

Staying on Track: The Experience of Emotion

1. Happiness is positively correlated with physical health, an outgoing and agreeable personality, a sense of personal control, intelligence, social skills, and family support. Physical attractiveness has a low to moderate correlation with happiness. Our happiness also depends on comparisons we make between ourselves and others and between our current circumstances and our past circumstances.

2. According to disparagement theory, we feel amused when humor makes us feel superior to other people. According to incongruity theory, incongruous humor brings together incompatible ideas in a surprising outcome that violates our expectations. And according to release theory, humor is a cathartic outlet for anxiety caused by repressed sexual or aggressive energy.

Staying on Track: Theories of Emotion

1. Evidence for the theory comes from studies finding different patterns of physiological responses for different emotions. Evidence against the theory includes the findings that we have poor ability to perceive many of the subtle physiological changes induced by the sympathetic nervous system, that different emotions are associated with the same pattern of physiological arousal, and that physiological changes dependent on the secretion of hormones by the adrenal glands are too slow to be the basis of all emotions.

2. When participants alter their facial expressions, they report changes in their subjective emotional experience.

3. Participants who experience unexplained arousal will experience negative emotions, regardless of their social context, thereby contradicting the theory. The only consistent finding in favor of the theory is that misattribution of physiological arousal to an outside source will intensify an emotional experience.

Chapter 13: Personality

Staying on Track: The Psychoanalytic Approach

1. The id is unconscious, consists of our inborn biological drives, and demands immediate gratification. The ego directs us to express sexual and aggressive impulses in socially acceptable ways. The superego, our moral guide, counteracts the id, which is concerned only with immediate gratification, and the ego, which is concerned only with adapting to reality.

2. Adler assumed that because children feel small, weak, and dependent on others, they develop an inferiority complex. This motivates them to compensate by striving for superiority.

3. Jung claimed that archetypes influence our dreams, religious symbols, and artistic creations.

4. Horney emphasized the role of gender roles, interpersonal power, and social-cultural factors in personality development, especially women's. She also was a proponent of cross-cultural research.

Staying on Track: The Dispositional Approach

1. Allport believed we are guided by the interaction among our cardinal traits, central traits, and secondary traits.

2. The MMPI was constructed by retaining only those questions that discriminate between people who differ on the characteristics of interest.

3. First, individuals do show consistency on certain traits. Second, cross-situational consistency in behavior depends on whether a person is a high self-monitor or a low self-monitor. Third, many of the studies that Mischel reviewed were guaranteed to find low cross-situational consistency, because they either correlated trait test scores with single instances of behaviors or correlated single instances of behaviors with each other. Psychologists have achieved greater success in demonstrating cross-situational consistency by using behavioral aggregation.

Staying on Track: The Cognitive-Behavioral Approach

1. It is different from operant conditioning theory in arguing that behavior is affected by cognitive processes.

2. Reciprocal determinism reflects Bandura's belief that neither personal dispositions nor environmental factors can by themselves explain behavior. Instead, Bandura assumes that personality traits, environmental factors, and overt behavior affect one another.

3. In experience sampling, participants carry a beeper that sounds at random times, and on hearing the beep the person reports her or his experiences and behaviors at that time.

Staying on Track: The Humanistic Approach

1. The humanistic approach tends to have a positive view of human nature, studies subjective mental experience, and assumes we have free will.

2. Some of the research topics include self-actualization, self-schema, self-concept, and self-esteem.

3. You would have the person sort the cards twice, first into piles of statements that are or are not characteristic of the actual self and then into piles of statements that are or are not characteristic of the ideal self.

Staying on Track: The Biopsychological Approach

1. Temperament is marked by differences in emotional reactivity, which might affect social interaction. These differences, which are apparent as early as infancy, contribute to the development of personality traits.

2. Researchers have found amazing similarities in the personalities of identical twins reared apart and reunited later in life.

Chapter 14: Psychological Disorders

Staying on Track: The Nature of Psychological Disorders

1. The biopsychological viewpoint emphasizes the role of genetic and biological factors. The psychoanalytic perspective emphasizes the role of the unconscious mind. The behavioral perspective emphasizes the role of the environment and learning in the development of maladaptive behaviors. The cognitive viewpoint emphasizes maladaptive thoughts. The humanistic perspective emphasizes failure in reaching one's human potential. And the social-cultural viewpoint emphasizes the role of cultural factors.

2. The cognitive rule says that a person was insane at the time of a crime if the person did not know what he or she had done or did not know that it was wrong. The volitional rule says that the person was insane at the time of the crime if the person was not in voluntary control of his or her actions.

3. Rosenhan's findings indicate that the diagnosis of psychological disorder is influenced more by the label provided by the diagnosis and the treatment setting than behavioral or psychological attributes of the person.

Staying on Track: Anxiety Disorders

1. Some people with panic disorder are hypersensitive to carbon dioxide levels in their blood. Instead of breathing normally to reduce carbon dioxide levels, they might respond as if they are being suffocated and experience a panic attack.

2. Agoraphobia prompts so many people to seek therapy because it disrupts every aspect of the sufferer's life, including intimate relationships.

Staying on Track: Dissociative Disorders

1. Most of them have suffered physical and sexual abuse as young children.

2. Some psychologists believe that people suffering from dissociative identity disorder are doing little more than role playing and do not, in fact, have more than one personality.

Staying on Track: Mood Disorders

1. The theory explains depression in terms of the attributions we make for events in our lives.

According to this theory, depressed people attribute negative events in their lives to stable, global, internal factors.

2. People who constantly think about the sad state of their lives experience more severe and more chronic depression than people who take action to improve their lives or who distract themselves by pursuing enjoyable activities.

3. Shneidman suggests that because suicide attempts are usually cries for help, the simple act of providing empathetic response can reduce the immediate likelihood of an actual attempt. Just talking about a problem might reduce its apparent dreadfulness and help the person realize that solutions other than suicide are possible and that his or her options include more than a choice between death and a hopeless, helpless life. An immediate goal should be to relieve the person's psychological pain by intervening, if possible, with those who might be contributing to the pain, whether friends, lovers, teachers, or family members. You should also encourage the person to seek professional help, even if you have to make the appointment for the person and accompany her or him to it.

Staying on Track: Schizophrenia

1. The major symptoms of schizophrenia are hallucinations, problems maintaining attention, language disturbances, delusions, flat or inappropriate emotionality, unusual motor behavior, and social withdrawal.

2. First, drugs that are used to treat schizophrenia work by blocking dopamine receptors. Second, drugs such as amphetamines, which increase dopamine levels in the brain, can induce schizophrenic symptoms in normal people. Third, L-dopa, a drug used to treat Parkinson's disease because it increases dopamine levels in the brain, can induce schizophrenic symptoms in Parkinson's victims. Fourth, brain-imaging studies have found that schizophrenic

people have overactive dopamine neurons.

3. Positive symptoms are active symptoms, including hallucinations, delusions, thought disorders, and bizarre behaviors. Negative symptoms are passive symptoms, including mutism, apathy, flat affect, social withdrawal, intellectual impairment, poverty of speech, and inability to experience pleasure.

Staying on Track: Personality Disorders

1. People with borderline personality disorder are impulsive, have unstable moods, and exhibit problems in establishing interpersonal relationships. At first, the person you are dating might seem to be pleasant and charming. As the relationship continues, though, she or he becomes hostile and manipulative—especially if the relationship is becoming more intimate.

2. People with antisocial personality disorder show an appalling lack of conscience and have no qualms about harming other people.

Chapter 15: Therapy

Staying on Track: The History of Therapy

1. No, it might have been done for other purposes, perhaps medical, religious, or punitive.

2. Moral therapy used humane treatment, honest work, and pleasant recreation to promote mental well-being.

Staying on Track: The Psychoanalytic Orientation

1. In free association, the client is urged to report any thoughts or feelings that come to mind—no matter how trivial or embarrassing they seem. This is supposed to reveal important information that can help the client gain self-knowledge.

2. In the analysis of resistances, the psychoanalyst notes behaviors that interfere with therapeutic progress toward self-awareness. These resistances are interpreted in order to uncover the unconscious conflicts that underlie them.

Staying on Track: The Behavioral Orientation

1. You would first use progressive relaxation to train the person to relax. You would then set up a hierarchy of scenes related to oral presentation. Finally, you would have the person relax while first imagining low-anxiety scenes and gradually progressing to higher-anxiety scenes.

2. You would give the students tokens for doing well in spelling and arithmetic and let them trade in the tokens for things or activities they enjoy.

Staying on Track: The Cognitive Orientation

1. Ellis assumes that maladaptive emotions and behaviors are caused by irrational thinking. Therefore, his therapeutic techniques are aimed at making his clients think more rationally.

2. Beck assumes that depression is caused by negative beliefs about oneself, the world, and the future. Beck's cognitive therapy teaches clients to recognize their negative beliefs and replace them with positive beliefs.

Staying on Track: The Humanistic Orientation

1. Person-centered therapy strives to create greater congruence between the client's actual self and the client's ideal self by encouraging clients to express and accept their true feelings. The person-centered therapist promotes self-actualization through reflection of feelings, genuineness, accurate empathy, and unconditional positive regard.

2. Gestalt therapy attempts to help clients become aware of their unconscious feelings, increase their emotional expressiveness, and change their maladaptive thoughts and behaviors.

Staying on Track: The Social-Relations Orientation

1. TA assumes that there are basic roles we all play and that these are sometimes adaptive, sometimes maladaptive. TA teaches group members to recognize the roles they play in

their interactions (their transactions, or the "games" they play) and to use this understanding to improve their social relations.

2. Assertiveness training is a form of social-skills training that teaches people to express their feelings constructively in social situations.

Staying on Track: The Biopsychological Orientation

1. Critics believe that ECT is dangerous because it can cause brain damage, memory loss, and other problems. Others say its dangers are outweighed by its ability to relieve depression and prevent suicide.

2. Tricyclics increase the levels of serotonin and norepinephrine in the brain by preventing their reuptake by brain neurons that release them.

Staying on Track: Community Mental Health

1. Four factors brought this movement about: (1) new drug treatments, (2) the underfunding and overcrowding of mental hospitals, (3) an increased concern for the legal rights of mental patients, and (4) the Community Mental Health Centers Act of 1963, which mandated the establishment of federally funded mental health centers in every community in the United States.

2. Primary prevention helps prevent psychological disorders by fostering social support systems, eliminating sources of stress, and strengthening individuals' ability to deal with stressors. Secondary prevention provides early treatment for people at immediate risk of developing psychological disorders. Tertiary prevention helps people with psychological disorders from getting worse or relapsing after successful treatment.

Staying on Track: Finding the Proper Therapy and the Effectiveness of Psychotherapy

1. The college counseling center might be a good place to start. A friend, relative, or professor might be able to recommend a therapist or counseling center to you. Other potential sources of help or referral include community mental health associations. Many of these organizations, as well as private practitioners, are listed in the Yellow Pages.

2. He found that about two-thirds of people with psychological disorders improve, with or without psychotherapy.

3. The client's perception of therapist empathy has been consistently identified as an important factor in the effectiveness of psychotherapy. Personal warmth has also been found to be a factor that differentiates successful and unsuccessful therapists.

Chapter 16: Psychology and Health

Staying on Track: Psychological Stress and Stressors

1. A century ago most people died young from infectious diseases. Today, with infectious diseases under control, people live longer and tend to succumb to behavior-related diseases, including cancer and cardiovascular disease.

2. This is a disorder that appears months or years after a person experiences a traumatic event. It includes emotional, cognitive, and behavioral symptoms.

3. Some studies have found that there is a stronger association between hassles and illness than between life changes and illness. Moreover, life changes might produce their negative effects by increasing daily hassles.

Staying on Track: The Biopsychology of Stress and Illness

1. Stress can suppress the immune response, most notably natural killer cell activity.

2. Stress stimulates the secretion of adrenal hormones and increases sympathetic nervous system activity.

3. In animal studies, when a neutral stimulus is paired with a drug that alters the immune response,

the neutral stimulus will come to also alter the immune response.

Staying on Track: Factors That Moderate the Stress Response

1. Hardiness involves a sense of commitment, challenge, and control.

2. Social support promotes health by reducing the effects of stressful life events, promoting recovery from illness, and increasing adherence to medical regimens.

Staying on Track: Coping with Stress

1. The study found that adolescents under high levels of stress who exercised regularly had a significantly lower incidence of illness than did adolescents who exercised little.

2. The study found that the students who were not assigned to practice relaxation, compared to the students who were, displayed a significantly greater decrease in natural killer cell activity at final-exams time.

Staying on Track: Health-Promoting Habits

1. HIV is most commonly transmitted by breast-feeding, the sharing of hypodermic needles by drug users, and unprotected anal and vaginal sex.

2. Aerobic exercise boosts the basal metabolic rate, promotes weight control, and reduces the risk of cardiovascular disease.

3. Dieting by itself slows the basal metabolic rate, cannot last a lifetime, promotes the loss of lean body tissue, and tends to result in greater weight gain from rebound eating when the diet ends.

Chapter 17: Social Psychology

Staying on Track: Social Cognition

1. The three dimensions in Weiner's attribution model are internal-external, stable-unstable, and controllable-uncontrollable.

2. Self-serving bias is the tendency to make dispositional attributions for our own positive behaviors and situational attributions for our negative behaviors.

3. This occurs because the social schema we have of the other person will make us act a certain way toward that person, which in turn can make the person respond in accordance with our expectations.

Staying on Track: Interpersonal Attraction

1. Evidence includes the fact that we like people more, the more we are exposed to them. We even like the view of our own face that we see in a mirror more than the view of our face as seen by other people.

2. According to two-factor theory, the experience of physiological arousal in a situation that promotes the labeling of this arousal as love results in the development of romantic love.

3. Men offer financial status and seek physical attractiveness. Women seek financially well-off men and note their own physical attractiveness.

Staying on Track: Attitudes

1. Attitudes that are strongly held or personally important are better predictors of behavior. Attitude-behavior consistency is also affected by the specificity of the attitude and the behavior.

2. A message that takes a central route relies on clear, explicit arguments about the issue at hand. A message that takes a peripheral route relies on factors other than the merits of the arguments, such as characteristics of the source or the situational context.

3. For such contact to reduce prejudice, it must be between people of equal status.

Staying on Track: Group Dynamics

1. Groupthink can be prevented by not assigning a group leader and encouraging group members to consider as many alternatives as possible.

2. Social facilitation enhances performance on easy or well-learned tasks. Social facilitation impairs performance on difficult tasks or tasks that are not well learned.

3. A good way to reduce social loafing is to convince group members that their individual efforts will be evaluated or that they will be held accountable. Social loafing can also be overcome when a task is important to an individual and that person believes other group members lack the ability to perform better.

4. Participants in Milgram's experiments were asked to increase shock gradually, in 15-volt increments. Their initial compliance in administering mild shock might have contributed to their obedience to the experimenter's instructions to administer higher levels of shock.

Staying on Track: Prosocial Behavior

1. Some research indicates that people will be more likely to help other people if they believe it will relieve their own negative feelings, such as guilt.

2. When strangers notice someone in trouble, as their number increases, their probability of helping decreases, apparently because each feels less responsible for helping.

Staying on Track: Aggression

1. Violent criminals have higher levels of testosterone than nonviolent criminals do. Athletes who use anabolic steroids become more aggressive.

2. When people feel anonymous, are emotionally aroused, and experience reduced self-awareness, they are more likely to take part in group aggression.

Possible Answers to Thought Questions

Chapter 1: The Nature of Psychology

1. Nativists, who insist abilities are largely the product of heredity, would have less faith in the effectiveness of such programs in improving the abilities of children. In contrast, empiricists, who insist that abilities are largely the product of life experiences, would have more faith in such programs.

2. At the time, women's roles were centered in the family; they were to be first and foremost dutiful daughters, wives, and mothers. Women who contemplated entering the young field of psychology often were faced with a dilemma. Establishing oneself as a psychologist, especially in higher education, meant choosing between family and career. Whereas men could combine work and family, women often had to delay or postpone marriage and parenthood. The few women who became pioneers in psychology typically received support from their families, husbands, or male mentors.

3. A behavioral psychologist might assume that your professor is happy because she or he has received positive reinforcement, which might include students who remain alert and interested during lectures. A psychoanalytic psychologist might assume that your professor is happy because she or he has successfully expressed unconscious aggressive urges in socially acceptable ways, perhaps by playing racquetball or creating extremely difficult exams. A humanistic psychologist might assume that your professor is happy because she or he has a sense of self-actualization, having reached his or her potential as a friend, spouse, parent, artist, athlete, and psychology professor. A cognitive psychologist might assume that your professor is happy because she or he has an optimistic outlook on life, marked by positive thoughts about herself or himself, the world, and the future. A biological psychologist might assume that your professor is happy because she or he has unusually high levels of brain chemicals associated with positive moods. And a social-cultural psychologist might assume that the factors that make this professor happy in her or his culture might not have the same effect on persons in others.

Chapter 2: Psychology as a Science

1. Topics such as the possible existence of ESP and UFOs are controversial. A cynical person would insist that their existence is impossible and would, therefore, discount all evidence in their favor. A gullible person would accept their existence based on the flimsiest of evidence. In contrast, a skeptical person would not entirely rule out the possibility of their existence, but would require strong scientific evidence before concluding that they do exist.

2. The four goals of science are description, prediction, control, and explanation. Consider, for example, research on the effects of violent child-rearing practices. In pursuing the goal of description, researchers might record the number of incidents of violence involving the parents and children they are studying. In pursuing the goal of prediction, the researchers might predict, for example, that children who are the victims of parental violence will be more likely to be violent toward their own children later in life. In pursing the goal of control, the researchers might assess the effectiveness of particular means of reducing violent parenting, such as stress-management training. And in pursuing the goal of explanation, the researchers would try to determine the causes of parental violence toward children, such as poor parenting skills, frustration in the parents' own lives, or other possible factors.

3. Scientific predictions are probabilistic. That is, they involve predicting the likelihood of particular events based on knowledge of the relationship between specific variables. Thus, available data is used to predict the likelihood that a particular medical treatment will work, a particular weather pattern will occur, a particular horse will win a race, a particular student will succeed in college, and a particular child-rearing practice will be effective.

4. The experimental method manipulates one (or more) independent variables to assess the effect on one or more dependent variables. By controlling other (confounding) variables, the experimenter presumes that changes in the dependent variable(s) are caused by the independent variable(s). In nonexperimental methods, in contrast, the researcher records data but does not exert control over any variables. Thus, changes in the dependent variable might be caused by a host of different variables. As a result, there is no way to determine with confidence cause-and-effect relationships between any of the variables.

5. Many psychologists believe that animal research in psychology has been the disproportionate target of activists because relatively few psychologists conduct animal research, APA has a stringent code of ethics regarding animal research, and few animal studies in psychology involve inflicting pain or suffering. Moreover animal research, particularly research that inflicts pain or suffering, is much more common in medical, biological, and cosmetic research. And abuse of pets and farm animals is much more prevalent than their abuse in psychological research.

Chapter 3: Behavioral Neuroscience

1. Researchers at universities such as the University of Minnesota study identical twins who have been separated early in life and reunited years later. Because identical twins share identical genes and even when separated for many years show remarkable similarity in intelligence, personality, and other characteristics, researchers conclude that heredity plays an important role in those aspects of human development.

2. One way of determining whether feelings of joy are related to endorphins would be to administer an endorphin antagonist, such as naloxone, or a placebo (randomly determined) to 4.00 students just before they receive their semester grade reports. If the level of joy experienced by 4.00 students is less under the naloxone condition than under the placebo condition, then the level of joy would most likely be attributable to endorphin activity. In contrast, if there was no difference in the level of joy experienced by 4.00 students under the naloxone condition and under the placebo condition, then the level of joy would probably not be related to endorphin levels.

3. Phrenology was important because it was the first systematic attempt to localize functions in the brain, which eventually led to more sophisticated—and more successful—approaches. Phrenology was misguided because it made erroneous assumptions about the location of specific functions and the relationship of skull shape to underlying brain structures.

4. Split-brain research shows that the left hemisphere predominates in speech because split-brain patients can respond orally only when information is presented the left hemisphere. Likewise, we know the right hemisphere predominates in spatial relations because split-brain patients perform better on tests of spatial relations using the left hand than using the right hand.

Chapter 4: Human Development

1. You might use a longitudinal research design by assessing the attitudes of first-year students toward ethnic groups and reassessing the same students as seniors to determine if their attitudes had become more positive. You might use a cross-sectional research design by assessing the attitudes of current first-year students and seniors and determining if seniors had more positive attitudes.

2. An authoritarian parent might yell at or strike the child and demand that he do his homework immediately and perhaps even punish the child by not letting him go out to play for a week. A permissive parent might weakly request that the child do his homework and then stand by passively as the child leaves to go play. An authoritative parent might insist—without verbal or

physical abuse—that the child do his homework first, explaining why the child should do so and let the child go out to play once the homework has been completed.

3. Our evolutionary history might contribute to gender differences. Evolutionary psychologists believe that contemporary gender differences reflect the evolution of women's and men's roles and, thus, differences in our prehistoric ancestors' social arrangements and behaviors. Exposure to prenatal hormones, especially testosterone, influences men's and women's physical and cognitive development. There also is some evidence that exposure to prenatal hormones might contribute to differences in brain organization. Social-cultural factors are reflected in the opportunities, expectations, and reinforcement that women and men experience through the life-long process of socialization. Thus, the social-cultural environment also might contribute to gender differences in cognition and social behavior.

4. An adult might resolve the crisis of intimacy vs. isolation by building social relationships, including friendships, romance, and marriage. An adult might resolve the crisis of generativity vs. stagnation by rearing children, coaching youth sports, and volunteering with organizations that serve children. An adult might resolve the crisis of integrity vs. despair by living a rich and fulfilling life regarding work and social relations.

Chapter 5: Sensation and Perception

1. Though human beings and many other animals on earth have receptors that are limited to detecting energy from the region of the electromagnetic spectrum that we call the visible spectrum, some animals have receptors that can detect ultraviolet or infrared energy as well. Thus, there is no reason to rule out the possibility that creatures elsewhere in the universe have evolved receptors

that can detect energy from the regions of the electromagnetic spectrum devoted to radio and television waves.

2. Afterimages occur when a person stares at a patch of red, blue, green, or yellow and then looks at a white surface. The person will see an afterimage that is the complementary color of the original patch of color. The opponent-process theory assumes that there are red-green, blue-yellow, and black-white opponent processes. Stimulation of one process inhibits its opponent. When stimulation stops, the inhibition is removed and the complementary color is seen as a brief afterimage of the complementary color.

3. According to place theory, pitch perception depends on sounds of different frequencies making the basilar membrane vibrate maximally at different points. According to frequency theory, pitch perception depends on sounds making the basilar membrane vibrate in proportion to their frequencies. Because the basilar membrane does not vibrate maximally at any particular point for sounds below 1,000 Hz and neurons can fire only up to 1,000 Hz, place theory explains pitch perception above 1,000 Hz and frequency theory explains pitch perception below 1,000 Hz.

4. Psychologists typically discount paranormal abilities because alleged examples of such abilities might be the product of chance, fraud, magic, or misinterpretation. Moreover, there is no demonstrated explanation of how paranormal abilities can occur and difficulty in replicating seemingly convincing demonstrations of paranormal abilities. As scientists often remark, extraordinary claims require extraordinary evidence. To date, relatively few psychologists believe that such evidence exists in support of the paranormal.

Chapter 6: Consciousness

1. People with brain damage might be unable to consciously perceive objects or people, yet

respond as though they had. For example, people who are unable to consciously discriminate between familiar and unfamiliar faces might have different physiological responses to the faces of people they know and the faces of strangers.

2. It is easier to travel from the east to west because it is in keeping with our daily sleep-wake cycle's tendency to increase from 24 hours to 25 hours. In contrast, traveling from west to east runs counter to this tendency.

3. Sleep appears to be physically beneficial because it increases after vigorous exercise, is associated with levels of growth hormone, and strengthens the immunological response.

4. A Freudian explanation would look at the dream as symbolizing an unconscious conflict about sex. In contrast, an activation-synthesis explanation would look at the dream as a by-product of the brain's attempt to make sense of spontaneous sexual arousal that occurred while the dreamer was asleep.

5. The responses of the "hidden observer" were contradictory, differing according to the instructions given by the hypnotist. This indicates that the hypnotized people were simply playing a role suggested by the hypnotist.

6. Both cocaine and amphetamines exert their effects by increasing levels of dopamine and norepinephrine. Both of the drugs prevent the neuronal reuptake of those neurotransmitters, and amphetamines stimulate their release by neurons.

Chapter 7: Learning

1. Research findings are inconsistent about whether predators that have a conditioned taste aversion to the taste of sheep meat will also refrain from attacking them. Thus, just because a predator can be conditioned not to eat sheep does not necessarily mean that it will also stop killing them.

2. You would look for a behavior that the child has a higher probability of performing than cleaning his room. Perhaps the behavior is

Possible Answers to Thought Questions

playing a video game. You would then make playing the video game (the higher-probability behavior) contingent on the child's cleaning his room (the lower-probability behavior).

3. First you would determine the target behavior, perhaps having the child sit on the tricycle and pedal it along a path. Second, you would find a positive reinforcer, perhaps pieces of cookies. Third, you would reinforce successive approximations of the target behavior with pieces of cookie. You might reinforce the child for, in turn, looking at the tricycle, moving closer and closer to the tricycle, touching the tricyle, sitting on the tricycle, pedaling the tricycle, and following a path. You might also pair the pieces of cookie with verbal praise, so that the child comes to be motivated by praise as a reinforcer instead. This might eventually be less messy and better for the child's appetite.

4. Blocking demonstrates that mere contiguity of a neutral stimulus and an unconditioned stimulus will not convert the neutral stimulus into a conditioned stimulus. Instead, blocking indicates that the neutral stimulus will become a conditioned stimulus when it reliably predicts the unconditioned stimulus.

5. Research has consistently demonstrated a positive correlation between watching televised violence and aggressiveness in viewers. But this does not necessarily indicate a causal relationship between the two. Many laboratory experiments do indicate a causal relationship between the two, but they have been criticized for not necessarily being generalizable to "real life."

Chapter 8: Memory

1. According to levels of processing theory, the deeper the level at which you process information in memory, the better will be your memory for it. In studying material from this course you would be wise to use more than rote memory. Instead, you should try to connect the concepts you learn to aspects of your own life. This will make the concepts more meaningful and, as a result, easier to recall.

2. According to the concept of state-dependent memory, people will be more likely to recall memories that are congruent with their current psychological state. If you are depressed, you will be more likely to recall depressing memories. This, in turn, will make it difficult to overcome being depressed.

3. Even honest eyewitnesses can have faulty memories for events they have witnessed, can be influenced by leading questions, and can be highly confident without necessarily being accurate. Moreover, children tend to be less accurate then adults.

4. As a young man in the 1950s, H. M. had brain surgery to relieve his uncontrollable epilespy. The surgery removed large portions of his hippocampus. Ever since then he has been unable to form new declarative memories but has been able to form new procedural memories. This indicates that the hippocampus is important in creating declarative, but not procedural, memories.

Chapter 9: Thinking and Language

1. Bowling would be less likely to be considered a sport because it is less prototypically "sport-like" than tennis. But the argument might rage on because sport is a "natural concept," not a "logical concept." Thus, it would be difficult to state the precise criteria that would make one activity a sport and another activity a non-sport.

2. Heuristics might contribute to ethnic prejudice by making certain characteristics seem to be more prevalent among members of a particular ethnic group than they really are. If members of that ethnic group are portrayed by the media as exhibiting certain undesirable characteristics, such as being boisterous, then the representativeness heuristic might make people believe other members of the group are likely to be boisterous. Likewise, if it is easy to think of members of a particular ethnic group who exhibit certain undesirable characteristics, such as being boisterous, the availability heuristic might likewise make people believe that boisterous behavior is common among most members of that ethnic group.

3. People argue about the desirability of "politically correct" speech because some people believe the terms we use to refer to people can influence how we think of them (which is akin to the linguistic-relativity hypothesis). For example, perhaps we would feel less respect for people called "elderly" or "mentally retarded." In contrast, one reason some people oppose "politically correct" speech is that they don't believe replacing one descriptive term with another would have much effect on how we think about people. This kind of argument rages in regard to emotionally arousing issues, such as abortion. One side is commonly called "pro-life" and the other side is called "pro-choice." Would you perceive either side differently if we called its members "anti-abortion" or "pro-abortion?"

4. To demonstrate that an ape has learned true language, researchers must demonstrate that the ape must exhibit semanticity, displacement, and generativity. Merely using sign language to make requests or to respond to stock questions would not be enough. The latter would demonstrate semanticity but not displacement or generativity.

Chapter 10: Intelligence

1. Traditional IQ tests are descendants of the original Binet-Simon IQ test, which was designed to assess the abilities needed to function well in school. Though these abilities also help us function in other areas of life, they are not the only abilities we rely on. Tests based on the theory of multiple intelligences might provide a means of assessing all of these abilities, rather than just those— primarily verbal abilities—that are needed for success in school.

2. Prior to the publicizing of the results of Terman's study, popular belief held that extremely intelligent people were more likely to be physically frail, socially incompetent, and emotionally disturbed. Terman's study contradicted this by finding that people with higher intelligence tend to have greater physical, social, and emotional well-being than other people.

3. Science is an approach to gaining knowledge and ultimately explaining phenomena. But when psychologists and other scientists study the relative role of nature and nurture in intelligence they risk offending members of particular groups if they find any evidence that supports inherited intellectual differences between one group and another. Moreover, bigoted scientists have used science to provide flawed evidence to support their own biases against particular groups. But members of particular groups and those sympathetic to them might refuse to accept any evidence of innate intellectual differences that are unflattering to those groups. On the one hand are those who believe scientists should be free to study any topic that interests them, regardless of what they might discover. On the other hand are those who believe that scientists should not study topics that might provide ammunition for those who are prone to prejudice against members of particular groups.

Chapter 11: Motivation

1. Because body weight depends on the relative balance between caloric intake and caloric expenditure, keeping them about equal will help maintain a steady body weight. One way of doing this is to eat regular meals but avoid eating high-calorie foods or large portions of moderate-calorie foods. A second approach to this would be to maintain a regular schedule of exercise to burn calories directly and, perhaps, to increase the basal metabolic rate for a number of hours after exercising. Dieting should be avoided because it might lead to hunger-induced overeating and even binge eating. Because stretch receptors in the stomach help regulate eating, make sure to eat slowly enough to allow this mechanism to work. Given that some people are affected by visual food cues, keep all foods out of sight and make sure that you have just eaten when you go shopping, so you will be less likely to buy high-calorie foods. In addition, because stress and depression may instigate eating, you might need to practice stress control and find ways to relieve your depression other than eating.

2. To perform well on an exam requires that you be at your optimal level of arousal. If you are too relaxed when you take the exam you will lack concentration and might make "stupid" mistakes, such as writing down the wrong letter on a multiple-choice question, even if you know the correct answer. If you are too anxious when you take an exam you might be unable to recall answers that you could easily recall before or after the exam.

3. When children play sports they typically do it out of sheer joy and competitive zeal. When professionals are paid reasonable salaries for their talents they are more likely to retain their intrinsic motivation to play than when they make large salaries. According to overjustification theory, athletes who make huge sums of money might attribute their interest in playing to an extrinsic factor—money. In contrast, when professional athletes were paid more reasonable salaries, they attributed their interest in playing to an intrinsic factor—love of the sport. This might make high-paid athletes less motivated to play their sports.

Chapter 12: Emotion
1. The polygraph test typically measures changes in breathing, heart rate, blood pressure, and skin conductivity associated with emotionality. No specific pattern of these responses by itself has been found to indicate

lying. Comparison of physiological changes to relevant and control questions is what polygraphers use to determine whether a person is lying. But this is far from foolproof, producing false negatives and, more commonly, false positives. Thus, the polygraph test might measure emotionality, but it does not directly measure lying—or truth telling.

2. The two general research findings concerning emotional laterality are that the right hemisphere plays a greater role than the left hemisphere in emotionality and that left-hemisphere activity promotes positive emotions while right-hemisphere activity promotes negative emotions. Evidence supporting these findings comes primarily from studies that record lateralized brain activity using the EEG or brain scans during the expressing or experiencing of emotions and studies that assess the effects of lateralized brain damage on the expressing or experiencing of emotions.

3. Research indicates that when people are instructed to contract the facial muscles involved in the expression of emotions they experience changes in physiological arousal. Moreover, different facial expressions induce different patterns of physiological arousal. This supports the James-Lange theory because it explains how we can respond behaviorally and physiologically to a situation before we have a conscious emotional experience in response to it.

Chapter 13: Personality
1. Horney believed that personality arises out of the infant's response to basic anxiety, which is produced by their dependence on adults to have their physical and emotional needs satisfied. Basic anxiety evokes basic hostility. Personality development depends on how the child deals with these feelings. Much of this has to do with the nurturing they receive from parents. Some children learn to move toward others, becoming agreeable and seeking intimacy and affection. Other children

learn to move against other people, becoming angry and aggressive. And still other children learn to move away from others, fleeing the hurt they experience in interpersonal relations by becoming socially aloof and emotionally cool.

2. Walter Mischel's observation that personality is more consistent over time than across situations was met by several arguments supporting the cross-situational consistency of traits. First, when we employ behavioral aggregation cross-situational consistency increases. Second, though we are cross-situationally inconsistent on certain traits, we tend to be consistent on others. Third, people who are low self-monitors show stronger cross-situational consistency than people who are high self-monitors. Thus, the degree to which people are cross-situationally consistent in exhibiting personality traits depends in part on how we study the issue.

3. Individualistic and collectivistic cultures differ on the dimension of independence and interdependence. In collectivistic cultures interdependent aspects of the self are valued. People in these cultures value being part of an extended family or a community and collaborating toward mutual goals. In individualistic cultures independent aspects of the self are valued. People in individualistic cultures value individuality and pursuing individual goals. According to schema theory, these cultural differences in values and social experiences become part of the self-schema.

Chapter 14: Psychological Disorders
1. Agoraphobia fits each of the three criteria for diagnosing a psychological disorder. The tendency to stay at home and avoid going to school, to work, or to social events is abnormal. Not going to school, to work, or to social events is maladaptive. It makes it impossible to function well and be successful in life. And agoraphobia is personally distressing to the person who has it.

2. Public concern about the use of the insanity defense in criminal cases has been fueled by a few widely publicized cases, most notably that of John Hinckley. In reality, the insanity defense is rarely used and, when it is used, it is rarely successful. In cases where it is used successfully, the defendant is typically so psychologically disordered that both the prosecution and the defense agree that the person is legally insane.

3. In explaining a student's test anxiety, a biopsychologist might look for imbalances in stress hormones or neurotransmitters. A psychoanalytic psychologist might look to fear of losing parental approval stemming from early childhood interactions with them. A behavioral psychologist might look to the student's history of poor performance on exams. A cognitive psychologist might look to the student's negative thinking about his academic ability. A humanistic psychologist might look to the student's feeling that he has a conflict between social pressure to be an excellent student and his desire to leave school and get a job. A social-cultural psychologist might look to the student's cultural heritage to see if it puts extra pressure on him to excel academically. And a psychologist who favors the diathesis-stress viewpoint might look to the interaction between the student's inherited temperament and his life experiences.

Chapter 15: Therapy
1. Systematic desensitization involves training the client in progressive relaxation and creating a hierarchy of scenes about the feared object or situation. After training the acrophobic client in progressive relaxation, you would help the client create a hierarchy of scenes related to heights from the least anxiety producing to the most anxiety producing. You would then have her relax while imaging the least anxiety-producing scene and progressively do this for each of the scenes, making sure that her subjective level of anxiety in

response to a scene had decreased before moving to the next scene.

2. Deinstitutionalization, which began in earnest in the 1950s has had mixed effects. It has freed many people from being restrained in little more than human warehouses, permitting them to receive treatment and pursue rewarding lives on the outside. But many other people are so psychologically disordered that they might benefit from custodial care. Moreover, many communities actively resist residences for the mentally ill and few legislators put a top priority on providing funds for services to the mentally ill. This has increased the number of homeless people and has left other people without adequate access to treatment.

3. The criteria for assessing the effectiveness of psychotherapy vary. Based on the three criteria for diagnosing psychological disorders (see Chapter 14), you might determine whether the therapy clients have become less abnormal in their behavior, more adaptive in their behavior, and less personally distressed. You might, instead, base your criteria on the theoretical orientation of the therapeutic approach you are evaluating. For example, if you were using a psychodynamic approach, you might assess whether the clients are using defense mechanisms in a healthier way. And if you were using a cognitive approach, you might assess whether the clients are thinking more rationally.

Chapter 16: Psychology and Health

1. Getting divorced, a major life event, brings with it numerous hassles. These include doing all household chores; relying solely on one's own income for general overhead expenses; not having someone to encourage one to eat a good diet, maintain a regular exercise schedule, and take care of minor ailments before they become serious; and losing the social support of the former spouse and associated friends and relatives.

2. The aspect of the Type A behavior pattern that has been implicated most strongly in the development of cardiovascular disease is cynical hostility. A program aimed at managing this emotion might be most beneficial. Other aspects of Type A behavior that might be best to alter include failing to delegate responsibilities, working under constant time pressure, doing more than one thing at a time, and setting perfectionist goals that are impossible to reach.

3. Your cerebral cortex and limbic system interact to determine the perceived stressfulness of your papers and exams. The more stressful they seem, the more likely your hypothalamus is to stimulate your adrenal glands to secrete stress hormones. Whereas neural connections from the hypothalamus stimulate the adrenal medulla, ACTH secreted by the hypothalamus stimulates the adrenal cortex. The adrenal medulla secretes hormones such as epinephrine and the adrenal cortex secretes hormones such as cortisol. These hormones might impair the functioning of cells in your immune system, leaving you more susceptible to viral or bacterial infections.

4. The poor health habits that are most dangerous to your health include smoking, eating a high-fat diet, failing to exercise, driving in a risky manner, and failing to practice safe sex. Thus, to maintain good health you would be wise to quit or never start smoking, eat a low-fat diet, exercise regularly, drive safely, and practice safe sex.

Chapter 17: Social Psychology

1. You might attribute your failed relationship to external, unstable, and uncontrollable factors such as distance, a lack of compatibility, a failure to share priorities, or simply fate. Moreover, consistent with the self-serving bias, you might attribute your failed relationship to situational factors while attributing your successful friendships to dispositional factors.

2. In regard to the source of the message, you might include people who are similar to the audience (such as fellow students), people who are personally and physically appealing, and people who are credible because of their expertise regarding curriculum (perhaps a professor) and trustworthiness (perhaps an administrator known to the students). In regard to the message, you might weakly acknowledge the other side of the argument (for example, the new curriculum might reduce the number of electives students may take) and present strong arguments in favor of our side. In regard to the audience, you might use the central route rather than the peripheral route by using arguments that are more rational than emotional. You might even use rhetorical questioning, such as, "Do you want to graduate from a school with high academic standards or one that students can breeze through?" to provoke cognitive dissonance, which might make some students become more favorable to your viewpoint.

3. To avoid groupthink in house hunting, your family members might try to avoid ridiculing one another for having different opinions, seek outside opinions about the houses you're considering, and encourage at least one family member to be a "devil's advocate" who would try to contradict each of the arguments that are presented. Moreover, you might try to avoid having your parents—the final decision makers—give their opinions too early in the process.

4. To avoid social loafing, you might avoid assigning any responsibilities to groups of students. Instead, make one person responsible for accomplishing specific tasks. Otherwise, diffusion of responsibility might make each student expend less effort and wrongly presume that others will take up the slack. Moreover, you might let the students know that there will be meetings at which each of them will have to discuss the progress they have made in their area of responsibility.

Glossary

A

absolute threshold The minimum amount of stimulation that an individual can detect through a given sense. 134

accommodation 1. The cognitive process that revises existing schemas to incorporate new information. 103 2. The process by which the lens of the eye increases its curvature to focus light from close objects or decreases its curvature to focus light from more distant objects. 140

achievement motive The desire for mastery, excellence, and accomplishment. 345

achievement test A test that measures knowledge of a particular subject. 303

acronym A mnemonic device that involves forming a term from the first letters of a series of words that are to be recalled. 267

action potential A series of changes in the electrical charge across the axonal membrane that occurs after the axon has reached its firing threshold. 69

activation-synthesis theory The theory that dreams are the by-products of the mind's attempt to make sense of the spontaneous changes in physiological activity generated by the brain stem during REM sleep. 196

acupuncture A pain-relieving technique that relies on the insertion of fine needles into various sites on the body. 166

adaptation-level theory The theory that happiness depends on comparing one's present circumstances with one's past circumstances. 362

adolescence The transition period lasting from the onset of puberty to the beginning of adulthood. 115

adrenal glands Endocrine glands that secrete hormones that regulate the excretion of minerals and the body's response to stress. 66

adulthood The period beginning when the individual assumes responsibility for her or his own life. 123

age regression A hypnotic state in which the individual apparently behaves as she or he did as a child. 201

aggression Verbal or physical behavior aimed at harming another person. 502

agoraphobia A fear of being in public, usually because the person fears the embarrassment of a panic attack. 411

algorithm A problem-solving rule or procedure that, when followed step by step, assures that a correct solution will be found. 281

all-or-none law The principle that once a neuron reaches its firing threshold, a neural impulse travels at full strength along the entire length of its axon. 69

altruism The helping of others without the expectation of a reward. 499

Alzheimer's disease A brain disorder characterized by difficulty in forming new memories and by general mental deterioration. 72

amphetamines Stimulants used to maintain alertness and wakefulness. 205

amygdala A limbic system structure that evaluates information from the immediate environment, contributing to feelings of fear, anger, or relief. 81

anal stage In Freud's theory, the stage of personality development, between ages 1 and 3, during which the child gains pleasure from defecation and faces a conflict over toilet training. 378

analysis of dreams In psychoanalysis, the process by which the therapist interprets the symbolic, manifest content of dreams to reveal their true, latent content to the client. 432

analysis of free associations In psychoanalysis, the process by which the therapist interprets the underlying meaning of the client's uncensored reports of anything that comes to mind. 432

analysis of resistances In psychoanalysis, the process by which the therapist interprets client behaviors that interfere with therapeutic progress toward uncovering unconscious conflicts. 432

analysis of transference In psychoanalysis, the process by which the therapist interprets the feelings expressed by the client toward the therapist as being indicative of the feelings typically expressed by the client toward important people in his or her personal life. 432

analysis of variance A statistical technique used to determine whether the difference between three or more sets of scores is statistically significant. 515

analytic introspection A research method in which highly trained participants report the contents of their conscious mental experiences. 8

anorexia nervosa An eating disorder marked by self-starvation. 335

antianxiety drugs Psychoactive drugs that are used to treat anxiety disorders. 444

antidepressant drugs Psychoactive drugs that are used to treat major depression. 444

antimania drugs Psychoactive drugs, most notably lithium carbonate, that are used to treat bipolar disorder. 445

antipsychotic drugs Psychoactive drugs that are used to treat schizophrenia. 445

antisocial personality disorder A personality disorder marked by impulsive, manipulative, often criminal behavior, without any feelings of guilt in the perpetrator. 425

anxiety disorder A psychological disorder marked by persistent anxiety that disrupts everyday functioning. 408

applied research Research aimed at improving the quality of life and solving practical problems. 21

aptitude test A test designed to predict a person's potential to benefit from instruction in a particular academic or vocational setting. 303

archetypes In Jung's theory, inherited images that are passed down from our prehistoric ancestors and that reveal themselves as universal symbols in art, dreams, and religion. 380

archival research The systematic examination of collections of letters, manuscripts, tape recordings, video recordings, or other records. 39

arousal motive The motive to maintain an optimal level of physiological activation. 343

artificial intelligence (AI) The field that integrates computer science and cognitive psychology in studying information processing through the design of computer programs that appear to exhibit intelligence. 288

assertiveness training A form of social-skills training that teaches clients to express their feelings constructively. 441

assimilation The cognitive process that interprets new information in light of existing schemas. 103

association areas Regions of the cerebral cortex that integrate information from the primary cortical areas and other brain areas. 82

atherosclerosis The narrowing of arteries caused by the accumulation of cholesterol deposits. 460

attention The process by which the individual focuses awareness on certain contents of consciousness while ignoring others. 178

attitude An evaluation, containing cognitive, emotional, and behavioral components, of an idea, event, object, or person. 487

audition The sense of hearing. 156

auditory cortex The area of the temporal lobes that processes sounds. 84

auditory nerve The nerve that conducts impulses from the cochlea to the brain. 158

authoritative parenting An effective style of parenting, in which the parent is warm and loving, yet sets well-defined limits that he or she enforces in an appropriate manner. 108

autism An often severe developmental disorder that includes deficiencies in social relationships, disordered communication, and repetitive and restricted patterns of behavior. 303

automatic processing Information processing that requires less conscious awareness and mental effort, and that does not interfere with the performance of other ongoing activities. 180

autonomic nervous system The division of the peripheral nervous system that controls automatic, involuntary physiological processes. 63

autonomy versus shame and doubt Erikson's developmental stage in which success is achieved by gaining a degree of independence from one's parents. 107

availability heuristic In decision making, the tendency to estimate the probability of an event by how easily relevant instances of it come to mind. 287

aversion therapy A form of behavior therapy that inhibits maladaptive behavior by pairing a stimulus that normally elicits a maladaptive response with an unpleasant stimulus. 434

avoidance learning Learning to prevent the occurrence of an aversive stimulus by giving an appropriate response to a warning stimulus. 226

axon The part of the neuron that conducts neural impulses to glands, muscles, or other neurons. 67

axonal conduction The transmission of a neural impulse along the length of an axon. 68

B

barbiturates Depressants used to induce sleep or anesthesia. 203

basal metabolic rate The rate at which the body burns calories just to keep itself alive. 333

basic research Research aimed at finding answers to questions out of theoretical interest or intellectual curiosity. 21

basilar membrane A membrane running the length of the cochlea that contains the auditory receptor (hair) cells. 157

behavior therapy The therapeutic application of the principles of learning to change maladaptive behaviors. 433

behavioral contingencies Relationships between behaviors and their consequences, such as positive reinforcement, negative reinforcement, extinction, and punishment. 220

behavioral genetics The study of the effects of heredity and life experiences on behavior. 60

behavioral neuroscience The field that studies the physiological bases of human and animal behavior and mental processes. 22, 57

behavioral perspective The psychological viewpoint, descended from behaviorism, that stresses the importance of studying the effects of learning and environmental factors on overt behavior. 16

behavioral preparedness The degree to which members of a species are innately prepared to learn particular behaviors. 233

behaviorism The early school of psychology that rejected the study of mental processes in favor of the study of overt behavior. 10

binocular cues Depth perception cues that require input from the two eyes. 150

biofeedback A form of operant conditioning that enables an individual to learn to control a normally involuntary physiological process or to gain better control of a normally voluntary one when provided with visual or auditory information indicating the state of that response. 231

biological rhythms Repeating cycles of physiological changes. 183

biopsychological perspective The psychological viewpoint that stresses the relationship of physiological factors to behavior and mental processes. 18

bipolar disorder A mood disorder marked by periods of mania alternating with longer periods of major depression. 418

blocking The process by which a neutral stimulus paired with a conditioned stimulus that already elicits a conditioned response fails to become a conditioned stimulus. 234

borderline personality disorder (BPD) A personality disorder marked by impulsivity, unstable moods, an inconsistent sense of identity, and difficulty maintaining intimate relationships. 425

brain The structure of the central nervous system that is located in the skull and plays important roles in sensation, movement, and information processing. 63

brightness constancy The perceptual process that makes an object maintain a particular level of brightness despite changes in the amount of light reflected from it. 152

Broca's area The region of the frontal lobe responsible for the production of speech. 85

bulimia nervosa An eating disorder marked by binging and purging. 336

bystander intervention The act of helping someone who is in immediate need of aid. 499

C

caffeine A stimulant used to increase mental alertness. 204

cannabis sativa A hallucinogen derived from the hemp plant and ingested in the form of marijuana or hashish. 206

Cannon-Bard theory The theory that an emotion is produced when an event or object is perceived by the thalamus, which conveys this information simultaneously to the cerebral cortex and the skeletal muscles and autonomic nervous system. 367

case study An in-depth study of an individual. 36

catatonic schizophrenia A type of schizophrenia marked by unusual motor behavior, such as bizarre actions, extreme agitation, or immobile stupor. 421

catharsis In psychoanalysis, the release of repressed emotional energy as a consequence of insight into the unconscious causes of one's psychological problems. 429

causal attribution The cognitive process by which we infer the causes of both our own and other people's social behavior. 480

causation An effect of one or more variables on another variable. 39

central nervous system The division of the nervous system consisting of the brain and the spinal cord. 63

central tendency error The tendency to rate everyone in the middle. 524

cerebellum A brain-stem structure that controls the timing of well-learned movements. 80

cerebral cortex The outer covering of the brain. 82

cerebral hemispheres The left and right halves of the cerebrum. 82

cerebral palsy A movement disorder caused by brain damage and that is sometimes accompanied by mental retardation. 310

chaining An operant conditioning procedure used to establish a desired sequence of behaviors by positively reinforcing each behavior in the sequence. 223

childhood The period that extends from birth until the onset of puberty. 99

circadian rhythms 24-hour cycles of physiological changes, most notably the sleep-wake cycle. 183

clairvoyance The alleged ability to perceive objects or events without any sensory contact with them. 170

classical conditioning A form of learning in which a neutral stimulus comes to elicit a response after being associated with a stimulus that already elicits that response. 213

clinical psychology The field that applies psychological principles to the prevention, diagnosis, and treatment of psychological disorders. 22

cocaine A stimulant used to induce mental alertness and euphoria. 205

cochlea The spiral, fluid-filled structure of the inner ear that contains the receptor cells for hearing. 157

coefficient of correlation A statistic that assesses the degree of association between two or more variables. 46

cognitive appraisal The subjective interpretation of the severity of a stressor. 466

cognitive dissonance theory Leon Festinger's theory that attitude change is motivated by the desire to relieve the unpleasant state of arousal caused when one holds cognitions and/or behaviors that are inconsistent with each other. 487

cognitive neuroscience The study of the neurological bases of cognitive processes. 278

cognitive perspective The psychological viewpoint that favors the study of how the mind organizes perceptions, processes information, and interprets experiences. 19

cognitive psychology The psychological viewpoint that favors the study of how the mind organizes perceptions, processes information, and interprets experiences. 278

cognitive therapy A type of therapy, developed by Aaron Beck, that aims at eliminating exaggerated negative beliefs about oneself, the world, or the future. 438

cognitive-appraisal theory The theory that one's emotion at a given time depends on one's interpretation of the situation one is in. 369

cognitive-evaluation theory The theory that a person's intrinsic motivation will increase when a reward is perceived as a source of information but will decrease when a reward is perceived as an attempt to exert control. 347

cohort A group of people of the same age group. 96

collective efficacy People's perception that with collaborative effort the group will obtain its desired outcome. 390

collective unconscious In Jung's theory, the unconscious mind that is shared by all human beings and that contains archetypal images passed down from our prehistoric ancestors. 379

color afterimage A visual image that persists after the removal of a visual stimulus. 145

color blindness The inability to distinguish between certain colors, most often red and green. 146

companionate love Love characterized by feelings of affection and commitment to a relationship with another person. 484

comparative psychology The field that studies similarities and differences in the physiology, behaviors, and abilities of different species of animals, including human beings. 22

computed tomography (CT) A brain-scanning technique that relies on X rays to construct computer-generated images of the brain or body. 79

computer-assisted instruction The use of computer programs to provide programmed instruction. 229

concept A category of objects, events, qualities, or relations that share certain features. 278

concrete operational stage The Piagetian stage, extending from 7 to 11 years of age, during which the child learns to reason logically about objects that are physically present. 104

conditioned response (CR) In classical conditioning, the learned response given to a particular conditioned stimulus. 213

conditioned stimulus (CS) In classical conditioning, a neutral stimulus that comes to elicit a particular conditioned response after being paired with a particular unconditioned stimulus that already elicits that response. 213

conditioned taste aversion A taste aversion induced by pairing a taste with gastrointestinal distress. 218

conduction deafness Hearing loss usually caused by blockage of the auditory canal, damage to the eardrum, or deterioration of the ossicles of the middle ear. 160

cones Receptor cells of the retina that play an important role in daylight vision and color vision. 140

conformity Behaving in accordance with group expectations with little or no overt pressure to do so. 495

confounding variable A variable whose unwanted effect on the dependent variable might be confused with that of the independent variable. 41

conscious mind The level of consciousness that includes the mental experiences that we are aware of at a given moment. 181

consciousness Awareness of one's own mental activity, including thoughts, feelings, and sensations. 177

conservation The realization that changing the form of a substance does not change its amount. 104

constructive recall The distortion of memories by adding, dropping, or changing details to fit a schema. 253

context-dependent memory The tendency for recall to be best when the environmental context present during the encoding of a memory is also present during attempts at retrieving it. 259

continuous schedule of reinforcement A schedule of reinforcement that provides reinforcement for each instance of a desired response. 223

control group The participants in an experiment who are not exposed to the experimental condition of interest. 40

controlled processing Information processing that involves conscious awareness and mental effort, and that interferes with the performance of other ongoing activities. 180

conventional level In Kohlberg's theory, the level of moral reasoning characterized by concern with upholding laws and conventional values and by favoring obedience to authority. 112

convergent thinking The cognitive process that focuses on finding conventional solutions to problems. 284

cornea The round, transparent area in the front of the sclera that allows light to enter the eye. 139

corpus callosum A thick bundle of axons that provides a means of communication between the cerebral hemispheres, which is severed in so-called split-brain surgery. 91

correlation The degree of relationship between two or more variables. 39

correlational research Research that studies the degree of relationship between two or more variables. 39

correlational statistics Statistics that determine the relationship between two variables. 514

counseling psychology The field that applies psychological principles to help individuals deal with problems of daily living, generally less serious ones than those treated by clinical psychologists. 22

counterconditioning A behavior therapy technique that applies the principles of classical conditioning to replace unpleasant emotional responses to stimuli with more pleasant ones. 433

creativity A form of problem solving that generates novel, socially valued solutions to problems. 284

critical period A period in childhood when experience with language produces optimal language acquisition. 277

cross-cultural psychology An approach that tries to determine the extent to which research findings about human psychology hold true across cultures. 19

cross-sectional research A research design in which groups of participants of different ages are compared at the same point in time. 96

crystallized intelligence The form of intelligence that reflects knowledge acquired through schooling and in everyday life. 124, 315

cultural psychology An approach that studies how cultural factors affect human behavior and mental experience. 19

cultural-familial retardation Mental retardation apparently caused by social or cultural deprivation. 310

D

dark adaptation The process by which the eyes become more sensitive to light when under low illumination. 144

debriefing A procedure, after the completion of a research study, that informs participants of the purpose of the study and aims to remove any physical or psychological distress caused by participation. 51

decay theory The theory that forgetting occurs because memories naturally fade over time. 256

decision making A form of problem solving in which one tries to make the best choice from among alternative judgments or courses of action. 286

declarative memory The long-term memory system that contains memories of facts. 249

deep structure The underlying meaning of a statement. 290

defense mechanism In Freud's theory, a process that distorts reality to prevent the individual from being overwhelmed by anxiety. 377

deindividuation The process by which group members become less aware of themselves as individuals and less concerned about being socially evaluated. 503

deinstitutionalization The movement toward treating people with psychological disorders in community settings instead of mental hospitals. 445

dendrites The branchlike structures of the neuron that receive neural impulses. 67

dependent variable A variable showing the effect of the independent variable. 40

depressants Psychoactive drugs that inhibit activity in the central nervous system. 202

depth perception The perception of the relative distance of objects. 149

descriptive research Research that involves the recording of behaviors that have been observed systematically. 34

descriptive statistics Statistics that summarize research data. 45, 511

determinism The assumption that every event has physical, potentially measurable, causes. 29

developmental psychology The field that studies physical, perceptual, cognitive, and psychosocial changes across the life span. 95

diathesis-stress viewpoint The assumption that psychological disorders are consequences of the interaction of a biological, inherited predisposition (diathesis) and exposure to stressful life experiences. 404

difference threshold The minimum amount of change in stimulation that can be detected. 136

differential psychology The field of psychology that studies individual differences in physical, personality, and intellectual characteristics. 7

discriminative stimulus In operant conditioning, a stimulus that indicates the likelihood that a particular response will be reinforced. 222

disorganized schizophrenia A type of schizophrenia marked by severe personality deterioration and extremely bizarre behavior. 421

disparagement theory The theory that humor is amusing when it makes one feel superior to other people. 363

displacement 1. In psychoanalytic theory, the defense mechanism that involves expressing feelings toward a person who is less threatening than the person who is the true target of those feelings. 377
2. The characteristic of language marked by the ability to refer to objects and events that are not present. 289

dissociation A state in which the mind is split into two or more independent streams of consciousness. 199

dissociative amnesia The inability to recall personally significant memories. 412

dissociative disorder A psychological disorder in which thoughts, feelings, and memories become separated from conscious awareness. 412

dissociative fugue Memory loss characteristic of dissociative amnesia as well as the loss of one's identity and fleeing from one's prior life. 413

dissociative identity disorder A dissociative disorder, more commonly known as multiple personality disorder, in which the person has two or more distinct personalities that alternate with one another. 413

distributed practice Spreading out the memorization of information or the learning of a motor skill over several sessions. 266

divergent thinking The cognitive process by which an individual freely considers a variety of potential solutions to artistic, literary, scientific, or practical problems. 285

double-blind technique A procedure that controls experimenter bias and participant bias by preventing experimenters and participants from knowing which participants have been assigned to particular conditions. 44

Down syndrome A form of mental retardation, associated with certain physical deformities, that is caused by an extra, third chromosome on the 21st pair. 310

dream A storylike sequence of visual images, usually occurring during REM sleep. 192

drive A state of psychological tension induced by a need. 328

drive-reduction theory The theory that behavior is motivated by the need to reduce drives such as sex or hunger. 328

E

echoic memory Auditory sensory memory, which lasts up to 4 or more seconds. 245

educational psychology The field that applies psychological principles to help improve curriculum, teaching methods, and administrative procedures. 22

EEOC Equal Employment Opportunity Commission. 524

ego In Freud's theory, the part of the personality that helps the individual adapt to external reality by making compromises between the id, the superego, and the environment. 376

egocentrism The inability to perceive reality from the perspective of another person. 104

elaboration likelihood model A theory of persuasion that considers the extent to which messages take a central route or a peripheral route. 488

elaborative rehearsal Actively organizing new information to make it more meaningful, and integrating it with information already stored in long-term memory. 248

Electra complex A term used by some psychoanalysts, but not by Freud, to refer to the Oedipus complex in girls. 378

electroconvulsive therapy (ECT) A biopsychological therapy that uses brief electric currents to induce brain seizures in victims of major depression. 443

electroencephalograph (EEG) A device used to record patterns of electrical activity produced by neuronal activity in the brain. 77

embryonic stage The prenatal period that lasts from the end of the second week through the eighth week. 97

emotion A motivated state marked by physiological arousal, expressive behavior, and cognitive experience. 351

empiricism The philosophical position that true knowledge comes through the senses. 5

encoding The conversion of information into a form that can be stored in memory. 242

encoding specificity The principle that recall will be best when cues that were associated with the encoding of a memory are also present during attempts at retrieving it. 259

endocrine system Glands that secrete hormones into the bloodstream. 65

endorphins Neurotransmitters that play a role in pleasure, pain relief, and other functions. 73

engineering psychology The field that applies psychological principles to the design of equipment and instruments. 22

engram A memory trace in the brain. 269

entactogens A new category of psychoactive drugs that have unique effects intermediate to those associated with hallucinogens and stimulants. 207

environmental psychology The field that applies psychological principles to help improve the physical environment, including the design of buildings and the reduction of noise. 22

episodic memory The subsystem of declarative memory that contains memories of personal experiences tied to particular times and places. 249

escape learning Learning to perform a behavior that terminates an aversive stimulus, as in negative reinforcement. 226

ethnic psychology The field that employs culturally appropriate methods to describe the experience of members of groups that historically have been underrepresented in psychology. 19

ethology The study of animal behavior in the natural environment. 35

ethyl alcohol A depressant found in beverages and com-

monly used to reduce social inhibitions. 202

eugenics The practice of encouraging supposedly superior people to reproduce, while preventing supposedly inferior people from reproducing. 317

evolutionary psychology The study of the evolution of behavior through natural selection. 19, 59

existential psychology A branch of humanistic psychology that studies how individuals respond to the basic philosophical issues of life, such as death, meaning, freedom, and isolation. 17

expectancy The strength of the individual's beliefs about whether a particular outcome is attainable. 526

experimental group The participants in an experiment who are exposed to the experimental condition of interest. 40

experimental method Research that manipulates one or more variables, while controlling other factors, to determine the effects on one or more other variables. 40

experimental psychology The field primarily concerned with laboratory research on basic psychological processes, including perception, learning, memory, thinking, language, motivation, and emotion. 21

experimenter bias effect The tendency of experimenters to let their expectancies alter the way they treat their participants. 42

explanatory style The tendency to explain events optimistically or pessimistically. 466

explicit memory Conscious recollection of general information or personal experiences. 249

external validity The extent to which the results of a research study can be generalized to other people, animals, or settings. 44

extinction 1. In classical conditioning, the gradual disappearance of the conditioned response when the conditioned stimulus is repeatedly presented

without being paired with the unconditioned stimulus. 215 2. In operant conditioning, the gradual disappearance of a response that is no longer followed by a reinforcer. 226

extrasensory perception (ESP) The alleged ability to perceive events without the use of sensory receptors. 170

extravert A person who is socially outgoing and prefers to pay attention to the external environment. 380

extrinsic motivation The desire to perform a behavior in order to obtain an external reward, such as praise, grades, or money. 347

eyewitness testimony Witnesses' recollections about events, most notably about criminal activity. 261

F

facial-feedback theory The theory that particular facial expressions induce particular emotional experiences. 368

factor analysis A statistical technique that determines the degree of correlation between performances on various tasks to determine the extent to which they reflect particular underlying characteristics, which are known as factors. 313

family therapy A form of group therapy that encourages the constructive expression of feelings and the establishment of rules that family members agree to follow. 442

feature-detector theory The theory that we construct perceptions of stimuli from activity in neurons of the brain that are sensitive to specific features of those stimuli. 148

fetal alcohol syndrome A disorder, marked by physical defects and mental retardation, that can afflict the offspring of women who drink alcohol during pregnancy. 99

fetal stage The prenatal period that lasts from the end of the eighth week through birth. 98

fight-or-flight response A state of physiological arousal that

enables us to meet sudden threats by either confronting them or running away from them. 352

figure-ground perception The distinguishing of an object (the figure) from its surroundings (the ground). 147

fixation In Freud's theory, the failure to mature beyond a particular stage of psychosexual development. 378

fixed-interval schedule of reinforcement A partial schedule of reinforcement that provides reinforcement for the first desired response made after a set length of time. 225

fixed-ratio schedule of reinforcement A partial schedule of reinforcement that provides reinforcement after a set number of desired responses. 224

flashbulb memory A vivid, long-lasting memory of a surprising, important, emotionally arousing event. 241

flooding An extinction procedure in which a phobic client is exposed to a stimulus that evokes intense anxiety. 436

fluid intelligence The form of intelligence that reflects reasoning ability, memory capacity, and speed of information processing. 124, 315

foot-in-the-door technique Increasing the likelihood that someone will comply with a request by first getting him or her to comply with a smaller one. 496

forensic psychology The field that applies psychological principles to improve the legal system, including the work of police and juries. 22

forgetting The failure to retrieve information from memory. 255

forgetting curve A graph showing that forgetting is initially rapid and then slows. 243

formal operational stage The Piagetian stage, beginning at about age 11, marked by the ability to use abstract reasoning and to solve problems by testing hypotheses. 116

fovea A small area at the center of the retina that contains only cones and provides the most acute vision. 140

framing effects In decision making, biases introduced into the decision-making process by presenting an issue or situation in a certain manner. 287

frequency histogram A graph that displays the frequency of scores as bars. 509

frequency polygon A graph that displays the frequency of scores by connecting points representing them above each score. 509

frequency theory The theory of pitch perception that assumes that the basilar membrane vibrates as a whole in direct proportion to the frequency of the sound waves striking the eardrum. 159

frontal lobe A lobe of the cerebral cortex responsible for motor control and higher mental processes. 82

frustration-aggression hypothesis The assumption that frustration causes aggression. 502

functional fixedness The inability to realize that a problem can be solved by using a familiar object in an unusual way. 283

functionalism The early school of psychology that studied how the conscious mind helps the individual adapt to the environment. 9

fundamental attribution error The bias to attribute other people's behavior to dispositional factors. 481

G

gate-control theory The theory that pain impulses can be blocked by the closing of a neuronal gate in the spinal cord. 166

gender roles The behaviors that are considered appropriate for females or males in a given culture. 110

gender schema theory A theory of gender-role development that combines aspects of social learning theory and the cognitive perspective. 111

general adaptation syndrome As first identified by Hans Selye,

the body's stress response, which includes the stages of alarm, resistance, and exhaustion. 460

generalized anxiety disorder An anxiety disorder marked by a persistent state of anxiety that exists independently of any particular stressful situation. 408

generativity The characteristic of language marked by the ability to combine words in novel, meaningful ways. 289

generativity versus stagnation Erikson's developmental stage in which success is achieved by becoming less self-absorbed and more concerned with the well-being of others. 128

genital stage In Freud's theory, the last stage of personality development, associated with puberty, during which the individual develops erotic attachments to others. 378

genotype An individual's genetic inheritance. 60

germinal stage The prenatal period that lasts from conception through the second week. 97

Gestalt psychology The early school of psychology that claimed that we perceive and think about wholes rather than simply combinations of separate elements. 11

Gestalt therapy A type of humanistic therapy, developed by Fritz Perls, that encourages clients to become aware of their true feelings and to take responsibility for their own actions. 439

glial cell A kind of cell that provides a physical support structure for the neurons, supplies them with nutrition, removes neuronal metabolic waste materials, facilitates the transmission of messages by neurons, and helps regenerate damaged neurons in the peripheral nervous system. 67

global competition Business competition among countries worldwide. 528

goal-setting theory The theory that performance is improved by setting specific goals. 526

gonads The male and female sex glands. 66, 337

grammar The set of rules that governs the proper use and combination of language symbols. 289

group A collection of two or more persons who interact and have mutual influence on each other. 492

groupthink The tendency of small, cohesive groups to place unanimity ahead of critical thinking in making decisions. 493

Guilty Knowledge Test A method that assesses lying by measuring physiological arousal in response to information that is relevant to a transgression and physiological arousal in response to information that is irrelevant to that transgression. 355

gustation The sense of taste, which detects molecules of substances dissolved in the saliva. 164

H

hallucinogens Psychoactive drugs that induce extreme alterations in consciousness, including visual hallucinations, a sense of timelessness, and feelings of depersonalization. 205

halo effect A type of rating bias in which the overall evaluation of an individual and other specific ratings are based on the rater's general feeling about an employee. 524

health psychology The field that applies psychological principles to the prevention and treatment of physical illness. 22, 455

heritability The proportion of variability in a trait across a population attributable to genetic differences among members of the population. 61, 319

heuristic A general principle that guides problem solving, though it does not guarantee a correct solution. 282

hidden observer Ernest Hilgard's term for the part of the hypnotized person's consciousness that is not under the control of the hypnotist but is aware of what is taking place. 199

hierarchy of needs Abraham Maslow's arrangement of needs

in the order of their motivational priority, ranging from physiological needs to the needs for self-actualization and transcendence. 329

higher-order conditioning In classical conditioning, the establishment of a conditioned response to a neutral stimulus that has been paired with an existing conditioned stimulus. 213

hippocampus A limbic system structure that contributes to the formation of memories. 81

holophrastic speech The use of single words to represent whole phrases or sentences. 290

homeostasis A steady state of physiological equilibrium. 328

hormones Chemicals, secreted by endocrine glands, that play a role in a variety of functions, including synaptic transmission. 65

humanistic perspective The psychological viewpoint that holds that the proper subject matter of psychology is the individual's subjective mental experience of the world. 17

hypermnesia The hypnotic enhancement of recall. 198

hyperopia Visual farsightedness, which is caused by a shortened eyeball. 140

hypnosis An induced state of consciousness in which one person responds to suggestions by another person for alterations in perception, thinking, and behavior. 196

hypothalamus A limbic system structure that, through its effects on the pituitary gland and the autonomic nervous system, helps to regulate aspects of motivation and emotion, including eating, drinking, sexual behavior, body temperature, and stress responses. 81

hypothesis A testable prediction about the relationship between two or more events or characteristics. 30

I

iconic memory Visual sensory memory, which lasts up to about a second. 243

id In Freud's theory, the part of the personality that contains inborn biological drives and that seeks immediate gratification. 376

identity versus role confusion Erikson's developmental stage in which success is achieved by establishing a sense of personal identity. 117

implicit memory Recollection of previous experiences demonstrated through behavior, rather than through conscious, intentional remembering. 249

in vivo desensitization A form of counterconditioning that trains the client to maintain a state of relaxation in the presence of anxiety-inducing stimuli. 434

incentive An external stimulus that pulls an individual toward a goal. 329

incongruity theory The theory that humor is amusing when it brings together incompatible ideas in a surprising outcome that violates one's expectations. 364

independent variable A variable manipulated by the experimenter to determine its effect on another, dependent, variable. 40

industrial/organizational psychology The field that applies psychological principles to improve productivity in businesses, industries, and government agencies. 22

industry versus inferiority Erikson's developmental stage in which success is achieved by developing a sense of competency. 107

infancy The period that extends from birth through 2 years of age. 99

inferential statistics Statistics used to determine whether changes in a dependent variable are caused by an independent variable. 48, 524

information-processing model The view that the processing of memories involves encoding, storage, and retrieval. 243

initiative versus guilt Erikson's developmental stage in which success is achieved by behaving in a spontaneous but socially appropriate way. 107

insanity A legal term attesting that a person is not responsible for his or her own actions, including criminal behavior. 403

insight An approach to problem solving that depends on mental manipulation of information rather than overt trial and error, and produces sudden solutions to problems. 280

insomnia Chronic difficulty in either falling asleep or staying asleep. 191

instinct A complex, inherited behavior pattern characteristic of a species. 328

instinctive drift The reversion of animals to behaviors characteristic of their species even when being reinforced for performing other behaviors. 233

instrumental conditioning A form of learning in which a behavior becomes more or less probable, depending on its consequences. 220

instrumentality The extent to which an individual believes that attaining a particular outcome will lead to other positively valued outcomes. 526

integrity versus despair Erikson's developmental stage in which success is achieved by reflecting back on one's life and finding that it has been meaningful. 128

intelligence The global capacity to act purposefully, to think rationally, and to deal effectively with the environment. 303

intelligence quotient (IQ) 1. Originally, the ratio of mental age to chronological age; that is, MA/CA × 100. 2. Today, the score on an intelligence test, calculated by comparing a person's performance to norms for her or his age group. 306

intelligence test A test that assesses overall mental ability. 303

interference theory The theory that forgetting results from some memories interfering with the ability to remember other memories. 257

internal validity The extent to which changes in a dependent variable can be attributed to one or more independent variables rather than to a confounding variable. 41

interneuron A neuron that conveys messages between neurons in the brain or spinal cord. 67

intimacy versus isolation Erikson's developmental stage in which success is achieved by establishing a relationship with a strong sense of emotional attachment and personal commitment. 125

intrinsic motivation The desire to perform a behavior for its own sake. 347

introvert A person who is socially reserved and prefers to pay attention to his or her private mental experiences. 380

iris The donut-shaped band of muscles behind the cornea that gives the eye its color and controls the size of the pupil. 139

J

James-Lange theory The theory that specific patterns of physiological changes evoke specific emotional experiences. 366

job analysis Defining a job in terms of the tasks and duties involved and the requirements needed to perform it. 521

job description A written statement of what a job entails and how and why it is done. 521

just noticeable difference (jnd) Weber and Fechner's term for the difference threshold. 136

K

kinesthetic sense The sense that provides information about the position of the joints, the degree of tension in the muscles, and the movement of the arms and legs. 168

L

language A formal system of communication involving symbols—whether spoken, written, or gestured—and rules for combining them. 289

latency stage In Freud's theory, the stage, between age 5 and puberty, during which there is little psychosexual development. 378

latent content Sigmund Freud's term for the true, though disguised, meaning of a dream. 194

latent learning Learning that occurs without the reinforcement of overt behavior. 235

law of effect Edward Thorndike's principle that a behavior followed by a satisfying state of affairs is strengthened and a behavior followed by an annoying state of affairs is weakened. 220

learned helplessness A feeling of futility caused by the belief that one has little or no control over events in one's life, which can make one stop trying and become depressed. 230, 467

learning A relatively permanent change in knowledge or behavior resulting from experience. 211

leniency The tendency to rate too positively. 524

lens The transparent structure behind the pupil that focuses light onto the retina. 140

levels of processing theory The theory that the "depth" at which we process information determines how well it is encoded, stored, and retrieved. 248

libido Freud's term for the sexual energy of the id. 378

limbic system A group of brain structures that, through their influence on emotion, motivation, and memory, promote the survival of the individual and, as a result, the continuation of the species. 81

line graph A graph used to plot data showing the relationship between independent and dependent variables in an experiment. 510

linguistic relativity hypothesis Whorf's hypothesis that one's perception of the world is molded by one's language. 294

link method A mnemonic device that involves connecting, in sequence, images of items to be memorized, to make them easier to recall. 268

logical concept A concept formed by identifying the

specific features possessed by all things that the concept applies to. 278

long-term memory The stage of memory that can store a virtually unlimited amount of information relatively permanently. 242

long-term potentiation A phenomenon related to the facilitation of neural impulses, in which synaptic transmission of impulses is made more efficient by brief electrical stimulation of specific neural pathways. 270

longitudinal research A research design in which the same group of participants is tested or observed repeatedly over a period of time. 96

loudness perception The subjective experience of the intensity of a sound, which corresponds most closely to the amplitude of the sound waves composing it. 159

LSD A hallucinogen derived from a fungus that grows on rye grain. 206

lucid dreaming The ability to be aware that one is dreaming and to direct one's dreams. 194

M

magnetic resonance imaging (MRI) A brain-scanning technique that relies on strong magnetic fields to construct computer-generated images of the brain or body. 79

maintenance rehearsal Repeating information to oneself to keep it in short-term memory. 246

major depression A mood disorder marked by depression so intense and prolonged that the person may be unable to function in everyday life. 415

mania A mood disorder marked by euphoria, hyperactivity, grandiose ideas, annoying talkativeness, unrealistic optimism, and inflated self-esteem. 418

manifest content Sigmund Freud's term for the verbally reported dream. 194

massed practice Cramming the memorization of information or

the learning of a motor skill into one session. 266

maturation The sequential unfolding of inherited predispositions in physical and motor development. 95

mean The arithmetic average of a set of scores. 46, 511

measure of central tendency A statistic that represents the "typical" score in a set of scores. 45

measure of variability A statistic describing the degree of dispersion in a set of scores. 46

measurement The use of numbers to represent events or characteristics. 32

median The middle score in a set of scores that have been ordered from lowest to highest. 45, 511

medulla A brain-stem structure that regulates breathing, heart rate, blood pressure, and other life functions. 79

memory The process by which information is acquired, stored in the brain, later retrieved, and eventually possibly forgotten. 242

menarche The beginning of menstruation, usually occurring between the ages of 11 and 13. 116

mental giftedness Intellectual superiority marked by an IQ above 130 and exceptionally high scores on achievement tests in specific subjects, such as mathematics. 311

mental retardation Intellectual deficiency marked by an IQ below 70 and difficulties performing in everyday life. 309

mental set A tendency to use a particular problem-solving strategy that has succeeded in the past but that may interfere with solving a problem requiring a new strategy. 283

mental telepathy The alleged ability to perceive the thoughts of others without any sensory contact with them. 170

meta-analysis A technique that combines the results of many similar studies to determine the effect size of a particular kind of independent variable. 49

method of loci A mnemonic device in which items to be recalled are associated with landmarks in a familiar place and then recalled during a mental walk from one landmark to another. 267

method of savings The assessment of memory by comparing the time or number of trials needed to memorize a given amount of information and the time or number of trials needed to memorize it again at a later time. 254

mnemonic devices Techniques for organizing information to be memorized to make it easier to remember. 267

mode The score that occurs most frequently in a set of scores. 45, 511

monocular cues Depth perception cues that require input from only one eye. 150

mood disorder A psychological disorder marked by prolonged periods of extreme depression or elation, often unrelated to the person's current situation. 415

moon illusion The misperception that the moon is larger when it is at the horizon than when it is overhead. 152

moral therapy An approach to therapy, developed by Philippe Pinel, that provided mental patients with humane treatment. 429

morphemes The smallest meaningful units of language. 290

motivation The psychological process that arouses, directs, and maintains behavior toward a goal. 327

motor cortex The area of the frontal lobes that controls specific voluntary body movements. 82

motor neuron A neuron that sends messages from the central nervous system to smooth muscles, cardiac muscle, or skeletal muscles. 67

myelin A white fatty substance that forms sheaths around certain axons and increases the speed of neural impulses. 69

myopia Visual nearsightedness, which is caused by an elongated eyeball. 140

N

narcolepsy A condition in which an awake person suffers from repeated, sudden, and irresistible REM sleep attacks. 191

nativism The philosophical position that heredity provides individuals with inborn knowledge and abilities. 4

natural concept A concept, typically formed through everyday experience, whose members possess some, but not all, of a common set of features. 279

naturalistic observation The recording of the behavior of people or animals in their natural environments, with little or no intervention by the researcher. 34

need A motivated state caused by physiological deprivation, such as a lack of food or water. 328

negative correlation A correlation in which variables tend to change values in opposite directions. 39

negative reinforcement In operant conditioning, an increase in the probability of a behavior that is followed by the removal of an aversive stimulus. 225

negative skew A graph that has scores bunching up toward the positive end of the horizontal axis. 510

negative state relief theory The theory that we engage in prosocial behavior to relieve our own state of emotional distress at another's plight. 499

neodissociation theory The theory that hypnosis induces a dissociated state of consciousness. 199

nerve A bundle of axons that conveys information to or from the central nervous system. 64

nerve deafness Hearing loss caused by damage to the hair cells of the basilar membrane, the axons of the auditory nerve, or the neurons of the auditory cortex. 160

nervous system The chief means of communication in the body. 63

neuron A cell specialized for the transmission of information in the nervous system. 63

neurotransmitters Chemicals secreted by neurons that provide the means of synaptic transmission. 71

nicotine A stimulant used to regulate physical and mental arousal. 205

night terror A frightening NREM experience, common in childhood, in which the individual may suddenly sit up, let out a bloodcurdling scream, speak incoherently, and quickly fall back to sleep, yet usually fails to recall it on awakening. 193

nightmare A frightening dream occurring during REM sleep. 193

norm A score, based on the test performances of large numbers of participants, that is used as a standard for assessing the performances of test takers. 38

normal curve A bell-shaped graph representing a hypothetical frequency distribution for a given characteristic. 513

NREM sleep The stages of sleep not associated with rapid eye movements and marked by relatively little dreaming. 185

null hypothesis The prediction that the independent variable will have no effect on the dependent variable in an experiment. 517

O

obedience Following orders given by an authority. 496

obesity A body weight more than 20 percent above the norm for one's height and build. 332

object permanence The realization that objects exist even when they are no longer visible. 103

observational learning Learning a behavior by observing the consequences that others receive for performing it. 237

obsessive-compulsive disorder (OCD) An anxiety disorder in which the person has recurrent, intrusive thoughts (obsessions) and recurrent urges to perform ritualistic actions (compulsions). 409

occipital lobe A lobe of the cerebral cortex responsible for processing vision. 84

Oedipus complex In Freud's theory, a conflict, during the phallic stage, between the child's sexual desire for the parent of the opposite sex and fear of punishment from the same-sex parent. 378

olfaction The sense of smell, which detects molecules carried in the air. 162

operant conditioning B. F. Skinner's term for instrumental conditioning, a form of learning in which a behavior becomes more or less probable, depending on its consequences. 220

operational definition The definition of behaviors or qualities in terms of the procedures used to measure or produce them. 33

opiates Depressants, derived from opium, used to relieve pain or to induce a euphoric state of consciousness. 204

opponent-process theory 1. The theory that color vision depends on red-green, blue-yellow, and black-white opponent processes in the brain. 145 2. The theory that the brain counteracts a strong positive or negative emotion by evoking an opposite emotional response. 367

optic chiasm The point under the frontal lobes at which some axons from each of the optic nerves cross over to the opposite side of the brain. 142

optic nerve The nerve, formed from the axons of ganglion cells, that carries visual impulses from the retina to the brain. 140

oral stage In Freud's theory, the stage of personality development, between birth and age 1 year, during which the infant gains pleasure from oral activities and faces a conflict over weaning. 378

otolith organs The vestibular organs that detect horizontal or vertical linear movement of the head. 169

ovaries The female gonads, which secrete hormones that regulate the development of the female reproductive system and secondary sex characteristics. 66

overextension The tendency to apply a word to more objects or actions than it actually represents. 290

overjustification theory The theory that an extrinsic reward will decrease intrinsic motivation when a person attributes her or his performance to that reward. 347

overlearning Studying material beyond the point of initial mastery. 266

overregularization The application of a grammatical rule without making necessary exceptions to it. 290

P

panic disorder An anxiety disorder marked by sudden, unexpected attacks of overwhelming anxiety, often associated with the fear of dying or "losing one's mind." 410

paranoid schizophrenia A type of schizophrenia marked by hallucinations, delusions, suspiciousness, and argumentativeness. 421

parapsychology The study of extrasensory perception, psychokinesis, and related phenomena. 170

parasympathetic nervous system The division of the autonomic nervous system that calms the body and performs maintenance functions. 63

parietal lobe A lobe of the cerebral cortex responsible for processing bodily sensations and perceiving spatial relations. 84

Parkinson's disease A degenerative disease of the dopamine pathway, which causes marked disturbances in motor behavior. 72

partial schedule of reinforcement A schedule of reinforcement that reinforces some, but not all, instances of a desired response. 224

participant bias The tendency of people who know they are participants in a study to behave differently than they normally would. 42

participant modeling A form of social-learning therapy in which the client learns to perform more adaptive behaviors by first observing the therapist model the desired behaviors. 432

passionate love Love characterized by intense emotional arousal and sexual feelings. 484

Pearson's product-moment correlation (Pearson's r) Perhaps the most commonly used correlational statistic. 514

pegword method A mnemonic device that involves associating items to be recalled with objects that rhyme with the numbers 1, 2, 3, and so on, to make the items easier to recall. 267

perceived control The degree to which a person feels in control over life's stressors. 467

perception The process that organizes sensations into meaningful patterns. 133

perception without awareness The unconscious perception of stimuli that normally exceed the absolute threshold but fall outside our focus of attention. 179

performance appraisal Systematic review, evaluation, and feedback regarding an employee's job performance. 524

peripheral nervous system The division of the nervous system that conveys sensory information to the central nervous system and motor commands from the central nervous system to the skeletal muscles and internal organs. 64

person perception The process of making judgments about the personal characteristics of others. 481

person-centered therapy A type of humanistic therapy, developed by Carl Rogers, that helps clients find their own answers to their problems. 439

personal unconscious In Jung's theory, the individual's own unconscious mind, which contains repressed memories. 380

personality An individual's unique, relatively consistent pattern of thinking, feeling, and behaving. 375

personality disorder A psychological disorder characterized by enduring, inflexible, maladaptive patterns of behavior. 424

personality psychology The field that focuses on factors accounting for the differences in behavior and enduring personal characteristics among individuals. 22

persuasion The attempt to influence the attitudes of other people. 488

phallic stage In Freud's theory, the stage of personality development, between ages 3 and 5, during which the child gains pleasure from the genitals and must resolve the Oedipus complex. 378

phase advance Shortening the sleep-wake cycle, as occurs when traveling from west to east. 183

phase delay Lengthening the sleep-wake cycle, as occurs when traveling from east to west. 183

phenomenological psychology A branch of humanistic psychology primarily concerned with the study of subjective mental experience. 17

phenotype The overt expression of an individual's genotype (genetic inheritance) in their appearance or behavior. 60

phenylketonuria (PKU) A hereditary enzyme deficiency that, if left untreated in the infant, causes mental retardation. 310

pheromone An odorous chemical secreted by an animal that affects the behavior of other animals. 164

phi phenomenon Apparent motion caused by the presentation of different visual stimuli in rapid succession. 11

phobia An anxiety disorder marked by excessive or inappropriate fear. 410

phoneme The smallest unit of sound in a language. 289

phonology The study of the sounds that compose languages. 289

photopigments Chemicals, including rhodopsin and iodopsin, that enable the rods and cones to generate neural impulses. 144

phrenology A discredited technique for determining intellectual abilities and personality traits by examining the bumps and depressions of the skull. 75

physiological reactivity The extent to which a person displays increases in heart rate, blood pressure, stress hormone secretion, and other physiological activity in response to stressors. 466

pie graph A graph that represents data as percentages of a pie. 509

pineal gland An endocrine gland that secretes a hormone that has a general tranquilizing effect on the body and that helps regulate biological rhythms. 183

pitch perception The subjective experience of the highness or lowness of a sound, which corresponds most closely to the frequency of the sound waves that compose it. 159

pituitary gland An endocrine gland that regulates many of the other endocrine glands by secreting hormones that affect the secretion of their hormones. 65

place theory The theory of pitch perception that assumes that hair cells at particular points on the basilar membrane are maximally responsive to sound waves of particular frequencies. 159

placebo An inactive substance that might induce some of the effects of the drug for which it has been substituted. 44, 166

pleasure principle The process by which the id seeks immediate gratification of its impulses. 376

polygraph test The "lie detector" test, which assesses lying by measuring changing patterns of physiological arousal in response to particular questions. 352

pons A brain-stem structure that regulates the sleep-wake cycle. 80

population A group of individuals who share certain characteristics. 37

positive correlation A correlation in which variables tend to change values in the same direction. 39

positive reinforcement In operant conditioning, an increase in the probability of a behavior that is followed by a desirable consequence. 221

positive skew A graph that has scores bunching up toward the negative end of the horizontal axis. 510

positron-emission tomography (PET) A brain-scanning technique that produces color-coded pictures showing the relative activity of different brain areas. 78

postconventional level In Kohlberg's theory, the level of moral reasoning characterized by concern with obeying mutually agreed upon laws and by the need to uphold human dignity. 112

posthypnotic suggestions Suggestions directing people to carry out particular behaviors or to have particular experiences after leaving hypnosis. 198

posttraumatic stress disorder A syndrome of physical and psychological symptoms that appears as a delayed response after exposure to an extremely emotionally distressing event. 457

pragmatics The relationship between language and its social context. 290

precognition The alleged ability to perceive events in the future. 171

preconscious mind The level of consciousness that contains feelings and memories that we are unaware of at the moment but can become aware of at will. 181

preconventional level In Kohlberg's theory, the level of moral reasoning characterized by concern with the consequences that behavior has for oneself. 112

predictors Tests that measure the attributes an employee needs in order to be successful at a job. 522

prejudice A positive or negative attitude toward a person based on her or his membership in a particular group. 490

Premack principle The principle that a more probable behavior can be used as a reinforcer for a less probable one. 221

preoperational stage The Piagetian stage, extending from 2 to 7 years of age, during which the child's use of language becomes more sophisticated but the child has difficulty with the logical mental manipulation of information. 104

primary cortical areas Regions of the cerebral cortex that serve motor or sensory functions. 82

primary reinforcer In operant conditioning, an unlearned reinforcer, which satisfies a biological need such as air, food, or water. 222

proactive interference The process by which old memories interfere with the ability to remember new memories. 257

problem solving The thought process by which an individual overcomes obstacles to reach a goal. 280

procedural memory The long-term memory system that contains memories of how to perform particular actions. 249

programmed instruction A step-by-step approach, based on operant conditioning, in which the learner proceeds at his or her own pace through more and more difficult material and receives immediate knowledge of the results of each response. 229

progressive relaxation A stress-management procedure that involves the successive tensing and relaxing of each of the major muscle groups of the body. 470

projection In psychoanalytic theory, the defense mechanism that involves attributing one's own undesirable feelings to other people. 377

projective test A Freudian personality test based on the assumption that individuals project their unconscious feelings when responding to ambiguous stimuli. 381

prosocial behavior Behavior that helps others in need. 499

prosopagnosia A form of visual agnosia in which an individual can identify details of faces but cannot recognize faces as wholes. 133

prototype The best representative of a concept. 279

psychiatry The field of medicine that diagnoses and treats psychological disorders by using medical or psychological forms of therapy. 22

psychic determinism The Freudian assumption that all human behavior is influenced by unconscious motives. 12

psychoactive drugs Chemicals that induce changes in mood, thinking, perception, and behavior by affecting neuronal activity in the brain. 201

psychoanalysis 1. The early school of psychology that emphasized the importance of unconscious causes of behavior. 11 2. A type of psychotherapy, developed by Sigmund Freud, aimed at uncovering the unconscious causes of psychological disorders. 431

psychoanalytic perspective The psychological viewpoint that is descended from psychoanalysis but places less emphasis on biological motives and more emphasis on the importance of interpersonal relationships. 17

psychokinesis (PK) The alleged ability to control objects with the mind alone. 171

psychological hardiness A personality characteristic marked by feelings of commitment, challenge, and control that promotes resistance to stress. 467

psychological test A formal sample of a person's behavior, whether written or performed. 38

psychology The science of behavior and mental processes. 4

psychoneuroimmunology The interdisciplinary field that studies the relationship between psychological factors and physical illness. 463

psychopathology The study of psychological disorders. 401

psychophysics The study of the relationship between the physical characteristics of stimuli and the conscious psychological experiences that are associated with them. 6

psychosurgery The treatment of psychological disorders by destroying brain tissue. 442

psychotherapy The treatment of psychological disorders through psychological means generally involving verbal interaction with a professional therapist. 430

puberty The period of rapid physical change that occurs during adolescence, including the development of the ability to reproduce sexually. 115

punishment In operant conditioning, the process by which an aversive stimulus decreases the probability of a response that precedes it. 226

pupil The opening at the center of the iris that controls how much light enters the eye. 139

R

random assignment The assignment of participants to experimental and control conditions so that each participant is as likely to be assigned to one condition as to another. 42

random sampling The selection of a sample from a population so that each member of the population has an equal chance of being included. 37

range A statistic representing the difference between the highest and lowest scores in a set of scores. 46, 512

rational-emotive behavior therapy (R-E-B-T) A type of cognitive therapy, developed by Albert Ellis, that treats psychological disorders by forcing the client to give up irrational beliefs. 434

rationalism The philosophical position that true knowledge comes through correct reasoning. 4

rationalization Giving socially acceptable reasons for one's inappropriate behavior. 377

reaction formation In psychoanalytic theory, the defense mechanism that involves a tendency to act in a manner opposite to one's true feelings. 378

reality principle The process by which the ego directs the

individual to express sexual and aggressive impulses in socially acceptable ways. 376

reciprocal determinism Bandura's belief that personality traits, environmental factors, and overt behavior affect each other. 389

reflex An automatic, involuntary motor response to sensory stimulation. 64

regression In psychoanalytic theory, the defense mechanism that involves reverting to immature behaviors that have relieved anxiety in the past. 377

release theory The theory that humor relieves anxiety caused by sexual or aggressive energy. 364

reliability The extent to which a test gives consistent results. 38

REM sleep The stage of sleep associated with rapid eye movements, an active brain-wave pattern, and vivid dreams. 185

replication The repetition of a research study, usually with some alterations in its methods or setting, to determine whether the principles derived from that study hold up under similar circumstances. 30

representativeness heuristic In decision making, the assumption that a small sample is representative of its population. 287

repression In psychoanalytic theory, the defense mechanism that involves banishing threatening thoughts, feelings, and memories into the unconscious mind. 257, 376

resting potential The electrical charge of a neuron when it is not firing a neural impulse. 68

reticular formation A diffuse network of neurons, extending through the brain stem, that helps maintain vigilance and an optimal level of brain arousal. 80

retina The light-sensitive inner membrane of the eye that contains the receptor cells for vision. 140

retrieval The recovery of information from memory. 243

retroactive interference The process by which new memories interfere with the ability to remember old memories. 257

rods Receptor cells of the retina that play an important role in night vision and peripheral vision. 140

S

sample A group of participants selected from a population. 37

savant syndrome The presence, in person with below-average general intelligence, of a talent—typically in art, music, or calculating—developed beyond the person's level of functioning in other areas. 303

scatter plot A graph of a correlational relationship. 511

schema A cognitive structure that guides people's perception and information processing that incorporates the characteristics of particular persons, objects, events, procedures, or situations. 103, 399

schema theory The theory that long-term memories are stored as parts of schemas, which are cognitive structures that organize knowledge about events or objects. 249

schizophrenia A class of psychological disorders characterized by grossly impaired social, emotional, cognitive, and perceptual functioning. 419

school psychology The field that applies psychological principles to help improve the academic performance and social behavior of students in elementary, middle, and high schools. 22

scientific method A source of knowledge based on the assumption that knowledge comes from the objective, systematic observation and measurement of particular variables and the events they affect. 30

scientific paradigm A model that determines the appropriate goals, methods, and subject matter of a science. 16

sclera The tough, white outer membrane of the eye. 139

seasonal affective disorder (SAD) A mood disorder in which severe depression arises during a particular season, usually the winter. 415

secondary reinforcer In operant conditioning, a neutral stimulus that becomes reinforcing after being associated with a primary reinforcer. 222

self-actualization In Maslow's theory, the individual's predisposition to try to fulfill her or his potentials. 392

self-efficacy In Bandura's theory, a person's belief that she or he can perform behaviors that are necessary to bring about a desired outcome. 389

self-fulfilling prophecy The tendency for one person's expectations to influence another person to behave in accordance with them. 482

self-perception theory The theory that we infer our attitudes from our behavior in the same way that we infer other people's attitudes from their behavior. 488

self-serving bias The tendency to make dispositional attributions for one's successes and situational attributions for one's failures. 481

semantic memory The subsystem of declarative memory that contains general information about the world. 249

semantic network theory The theory that memories are stored as nodes interconnected by links that represent their relationships. 249

semanticity The characteristic of language marked by the use of symbols to convey thoughts in a meaningful way. 289

semantics The study of how language conveys meaning. 290

semicircular canals The curved vestibular organs of the inner ear that detect rotary movements of the head in any direction. 169

sensation The process that detects stimuli from the body or surroundings. 344

sensation seeking The extent to which an individual seeks sensory stimulation. 133

sensorimotor stage The Piagetian stage, from birth through the second year, during which the infant learns to coordinate sensory experiences and motor behaviors. 103

sensory adaptation The tendency of the sensory receptors to respond less and less to a constant stimulus. 138

sensory memory The stage of memory that briefly, for at most a few seconds, stores exact replicas of sensations. 242

sensory neuron A neuron that sends messages from sensory receptors to the central nervous system. 67

sensory receptors Specialized cells that detect stimuli and convert their energy into neural impulses. 134

sensory transduction The process by which sensory receptors convert stimuli into neural impulses. 134

serial-position effect The superiority of immediate recall for items at the beginning and end of a list. 253

set point A specific body weight that the brain tries to maintain through the regulation of diet, activity, and metabolism. 331

sex-linked traits Traits controlled by genes located on the sex chromosomes. 146

sexual orientation A person's pattern of erotic attraction to persons of the same sex, opposite sex, or both sexes. 339

sexual response cycle During sexual activity, the phases of excitement, plateau, orgasm, and resolution. 337

shape constancy The perceptual process that makes an object appear to maintain its normal shape regardless of the angle from which it is viewed. 152

shaping An operant conditioning procedure that involves the positive reinforcement of successive approximations of an initially improbable behavior to eventually bring about that behavior. 222

short-term memory The stage of memory that can store a few items of unrehearsed information for up to about 20 seconds. 242

signal-detection theory The theory holding that the detection of a stimulus depends on both the intensity of the stimulus and the physical and psychological state of the individual. 135

single photon emission computed tomography (SPECT) A brain-imaging technique that creates images of cerebral blood flow. 79

size constancy The perceptual process that makes an object appear to remain the same size despite changes in the size of the image it casts on the retina. 152

skepticism An attitude that doubts all claims not supported by solid research evidence. 29

skin senses The senses of touch, temperature, and pain. 165

Skinner box An enclosure that contains a bar or key that can be pressed to obtain food or water, and that is used to study operant conditioning in rats, pigeons, or other small animals. 220

sleep apnea A condition in which a person awakens repeatedly in order to breathe. 191

smooth pursuit movements Eye movements that track objects. 142

social attachment A strong emotional relationship between an infant and a caregiver. 106

social clock The typical or expected timing of major life events in a given culture. 115

social cognition The process of perceiving, interpreting, and predicting social behavior. 480

social facilitation The improvement in a person's task performance when in the presence of other people. 493

social learning theory A theory of learning that assumes that people learn behaviors mainly through observation and mental processing of information. 237

social loafing A decrease in the individual effort exerted by group members when working together on a task. 494

social phobia A phobia of situations that involve public scrutiny. 410

social psychology The field that studies how the actual, imagined, or implied presence of other people affects one another's thoughts, feelings, and behaviors. 479

social schema A cognitive structure comprising the presumed characteristics of a role, an event, a person, or a group. 481

social support The availability of support from other people, whether tangible or intangible. 468

social-comparison theory The theory that happiness is the result of estimating that one's life circumstances are more favorable than those of others. 362

social-cultural perspective The psychological viewpoint that favors the scientific study of human behavior in its social-cultural context. 19

social-skills training A form of behavioral group therapy that improves the client's social relationships by enhancing her or his interpersonal skills. 441

sociobiology The study of the hereditary basis of human and animal social behavior. 328

soma The cell body, the neuron's control center. 67

somatic nervous system The division of the peripheral nervous system that sends messages from the sensory organs to the central nervous system and messages from the central nervous system to the skeletal muscles. 64

somatosensory cortex The area of the parietal lobes that processes information from sensory receptors in the skin. 84, 175

sound localization The process by which the individual determines the location of a sound. 161

specific phobia An anxiety disorder marked by an intense, irrational fear of a specific object or situation. 410

spermarche The first ejaculation, usually occurring between the ages of 13 and 15. 116

spinal cord The structure of the central nervous system that is located in the spine and plays a role in bodily reflexes and in communicating information between the brain and the peripheral nervous system. 63

split-brain research Research on hemispheric specialization that studies individuals in whom the corpus callosum has been severed. 90

spontaneous recovery 1. In classical conditioning, the reappearance after a period of time of a conditioned response that has been subjected to extinction. 216 2. In operant conditioning, the reappearance after a period of time of a behavior that has been subjected to extinction. 226

spontaneous remission The improvement of some persons with psychological disorders without their undergoing formal therapy. 448

sport psychology The field that applies psychological principles to help amateur and professional athletes improve their performance. 22

SQ3R method A study technique in which the student surveys, questions, reads, recites, and reviews course material. 265

standard deviation A statistic representing the degree of dispersion of a set of scores around their mean. 46, 513

standardization 1. A procedure assuring that a test is administered and scored in a consistent manner. 2. A procedure for establishing test norms by giving a test to large samples of people who are representative of those for whom the test is designed. 38

state-dependent memory The tendency for recall to be best when one's emotional or physiological state is the same during the recall of a memory as it was during the encoding of that memory. 260

statistical significance A low probability (usually less than 5 percent) that the results of a research study are due to chance factors rather than to the independent variable. 48, 512

statistics Mathematical techniques used to summarize research data or to determine whether the data support the researcher's hypothesis. 30, 518

stereotype A social schema that incorporates characteristics, which can be positive or negative, supposedly shared by almost all members of a group. 481

stimulants Psychoactive drugs that increase central nervous system activity. 204

stimulus discrimination In classical conditioning, giving a conditioned response to the conditioned stimulus but not to stimuli similar to it. 215

stimulus generalization In classical conditioning, giving a conditioned response to stimuli similar to the conditioned stimulus. 215

storage The retention of information in memory. 243

stress The physiological response of the body to physical and psychological demands. 456

stressor A physical or psychological demand that induces physiological adjustment. 456

structuralism The early school of psychology that sought to identify the components of the conscious mind. 8

sublimation In psychoanalytic theory, the defense mechanism that involves expressing sexual or aggressive impulses through indirect, socially acceptable outlets. 378

subliminal perception The unconscious perception of stimuli that are too weak to exceed the absolute threshold for detection. 135

subliminal psychodynamic activation The use of subliminal messages to stimulate unconscious fantasies. 181

superconducting quantum interference device (SQUID) A brain-imaging technique that uses changes in magnetic fields to trace pathways of brain activity associated with processes such as hearing or movement. 79

superego In Freud's theory, the part of the personality that acts as a moral guide telling us what we should and should not do. 376

surface structure The word arrangements used to express thoughts. 290

survey A set of questions related to a particular topic of interest administered to a sample of people through an interview or questionnaire. 36

sympathetic nervous system The division of the autonomic nervous system that arouses the body to prepare it for action. 63

synapse The junction between a neuron and a gland, muscle, sensory organ, or another neuron. 70

synaptic transmission The conveying of a neural impulse between a neuron and a gland, muscle, sensory organ, or another neuron. 70

synesthesia The process in which an individual experiences sensations in one sensory modality that are characteristic of another. 206

syntax The rules that govern the acceptable arrangement of words in phrases and sentences. 290

systematic desensitization A form of counterconditioning that trains the client to maintain a state of relaxation in the presence of imagined anxiety-inducing stimuli. 434

T

t test A statistical technique used to determine whether the difference between two sets of scores is statistically significant. 514

taste buds Structures lining the grooves of the tongue that contain the taste receptor cells. 164

telegraphic speech Speech marked by reliance on nouns and verbs, while omitting other parts of speech, including articles and prepositions. 290

temperament A person's characteristic emotional state, first apparent in early infancy and possibly inborn. 395

temporal lobe A lobe of the cerebral cortex responsible for processing hearing. 84

teratogen A noxious substance, such as a virus or drug, that can cause prenatal defects. 99

testes The male gonads, which secrete hormones that regulate the development of the male

reproductive system and secondary sex characteristics. 66

thalamus A brain-stem structure that acts as a sensory relay station for taste, body, visual, and auditory sensations. 81

theory An integrated set of statements that summarizes and explains research findings, and from which research hypotheses can be derived. 33

theory of multiple intelligences Howard Gardner's theory of intelligence, which assumes that the brain has evolved separate systems for seven kinds of intelligence. 316

thinking The mental manipulation of words and images, as in concept formation, problem solving, and decision making. 278

timbre The subjective experience that identifies a particular sound and corresponds most closely to the mixture of sound waves composing it. 160

tip-of-the-tongue phenomenon The inability to recall information that one knows has been stored in long-term memory. 259

token economy An operant conditioning procedure that uses tokens as positive reinforcers in programs designed to promote desirable behaviors, with the tokens later used to purchase desired items or privileges. 229

trait A relatively enduring, cross-situationally consistent personality characteristic that is inferred from a person's behavior. 383

transactional analysis (TA) A form of psychoanalytic group therapy, developed by Eric Berne, that helps clients change their immature or inappropriate ways of relating to other people. 441

transcutaneous electrical nerve stimulation (TENS) The use of electrical stimulation of sites on the body to provide pain relief, apparently by stimulating the release of endorphins. 167

transfer Bringing back to the job environment what was learned in training. 525

transformational grammar The rules by which languages generate surface structures from deep structures, and deep structures from surface structures. 290

transitive inference The application of previously learned relationships to infer new relationships. 104

trephining An ancient technique in which sharp stones were used to chip holes in the skull, possibly to let out evil spirits that supposedly caused abnormal behavior. 429

trial and error An approach to problem solving in which the individual tries one possible solution after another until one works. 280

triarchic theory of intelligence Robert Sternberg's theory of intelligence, which assumes that there are three main kinds of intelligence: componential, experiential, and contextual. 315

trichromatic theory The theory that color vision depends on the relative degree of stimulation of red, green, and blue receptors. 144

trust versus mistrust Erikson's developmental stage in which success is achieved by having a secure social attachment with a caregiver. 106

turnover The ratio of new employees to established employees. 527

two-factor theory The theory that emotional experience is the outcome of physiological arousal and the attribution of a cause for that arousal. 369

tympanic membrane The eardrum; a membrane separating the outer from the middle ear that vibrates in response to sound waves that strike it.157

Type A behavior A syndrome—marked by impatience, hostility, and extreme competitiveness—that is associated with the development of coronary heart disease. 461

U

unconditioned response (UCR) In classical conditioning, an unlearned, automatic response to a particular unconditioned stimulus. 213

unconditioned stimulus (UCS) In classical conditioning, a stimulus that automatically elicits a particular unconditioned response. 213

unconscious mind The level of consciousness that contains thoughts, feelings, and memories that influence us without our awareness and that we cannot become aware of at will. 181

underextension The tendency to apply a word to fewer objects or actions than it actually represents. 290

unilateral neglect A disorder, caused by damage to a parietal lobe, in which the individual acts as though the side of her or his world opposite to the damaged lobe does not exist. 57

V

valence The value an individual places on a particular outcome. 526

validation A process that determines whether tests are accurate predictors of job success. 526

validity The extent to which a test measures what it is supposed to measure. 38

variability hypothesis The prediction that men, as a group, are more variable than women. 318

variable An event, behavior, condition, or characteristic that has two or more values. 39

variable-interval schedule of reinforcement A partial schedule of reinforcement that provides reinforcement for the first desired response made after varying, unpredictable lengths of time. 225

variable-ratio schedule of reinforcement A partial schedule of reinforcement that provides reinforcement after varying, unpredictable numbers of desired responses. 224

variance A measure based on the average deviation of a set of scores from their group mean. 46, 512

vestibular sense The sense that provides information about the head's position in space and helps in the maintenance of balance. 169

visible spectrum The portion of the electromagnetic spectrum that we commonly call light. 138

vision The sense that detects objects by the light reflected from them into the eyes. 138

visual agnosia A condition in which an individual can see objects and identify their features but cannot recognize the objects. 133

visual cortex The area of the occipital lobes that processes visual input. 84, 143

visual illusion A misperception of physical reality usually caused by the misapplication of visual cues. 152

volley theory The theory of pitch perception that assumes that sound waves of particular frequencies induce auditory neurons to fire in volleys, with one volley following another. 159

W

Wada test A technique in which a cerebral hemisphere is anesthetized to assess hemispheric specialization. 89

Weber's law The principle that the amount of change in stimulation needed to produce a just noticeable difference is a constant proportion of the original stimulus. 138

Wernicke's area The region of the temporal lobe that controls the meaningfulness of speech. 86

Y

Yerkes-Dodson law The principle that the relationship between arousal and performance is best represented by an inverted U-shaped curve. 343

References

"A psychic Watergate." (1981, June). *Discover,* p. 8.

Abelman, R. (1999). Preaching to the choir: Profiling TV advisory ratings users. *Journal of Broadcasting and Electronic Media, 43,* 529–550.

Abelson, R. P. (1981). Psychological status of the script concept. *American Psychologist, 36,* 715–729.

Abernethy, E. M. (1940). The effect of changed environmental conditions upon the results of college examinations. *Journal of Psychology, 10,* 293–301.

Abrams, S. (1995). False memory syndrome versus total repression. *Journal of Psychiatry and the Law, 23,* 283–293.

Ackil, J. K., & Zaragoza, M. S. (1998). Memorial consequences of forced confabulation; Age differences in susceptibility to false memories. *Developmental Psychology, 34,* 1358–1372.

Adams, P. R., & Adams, G. R. (1984). Mount Saint Helen's ashfall: Evidence for a disaster stress reaction. *American Psychologist, 39,* 252–260.

Adelmann, P. K., & Zajonc, R. B. (1989). Facial efference and the experience of emotion. *Annual Review of Psychology, 40,* 249–289.

Adelson, B. (1984). When novices surpass experts: The difficulty of a task may increase with expertise. *Journal of Experimental Psychology: Learning, Memory, and Cognition, 10,* 483–495.

Ader, R., & Cohen, N. (1982). Behaviorally conditioned immunosuppression and murine systemic lupus erythematosus. *Science, 215,* 1534–1536.

Adler, A. (1927). *Understanding human nature.* New York: Greenberg.

Adler, K. A. (1994). Socialist influences on Alderian psychology. *Individual Psychology, 50,* 131–141.

Adler, L., Wedekind, D., Pilz, J., Weniger, G., & Huether, G. (1997). Endocrine correlates of personality traits: A comparison between emotionally stable and emotionally labile healthy young men. *Neuropsychobiology, 35,* 205–210.

Adler, T. (1991, November). Hypothalamus study stirs social questions. *APA Monitor,* pp. 8–9.

Adolphs, R., Russell, J. A., & Tranel, D. (1999). A role for the human amygdala in recognizing emotional arousal from unpleasant stimuli. *Psychological Science, 10,* 167–171.

Adolphs, R., Tranel, D., & Denburg, N. (2000). Impaired emotional declarative memory following unilateral amygdala damage. *Learning and Memory, 7,* 180–186.

Aggleton, J. P., Kentridge, R. W., & Neave, N. J. (1993) Evidence for longevity differences between left handed and right handed men: An archival study of cricketers. *Journal of Epidemiology and Community Health, 47,* 206–209.

Aghajanian, G. K. (1994). Serotonin and the action of LSD in the brain. *Psychiatric Annals, 24,* 137–141.

Aghajanian, G. K., & Marek, G. J. (2000). Serotonin model of schizophrenia: Emerging role of glutamate mechanisms. *Brain Research Reviews, 31,* 302–312.

Aheneku, J. E., Nwosu, C. M., & Ahaneku, G. I. (2000). Academic stress and cardiovascular health. *Academic Medicine, 75,* 567–568.

Ahlfinger, N. R., & Esser, J. K. (2001). Testing the groupthink model: Effects of promotional leadership and conformity predisposition. *Social Behavior and Personality, 29,* 31–41.

Aiken, L. R. (1982). *Psychological testing and assessment.* Boston: Allyn & Bacon.

Aisner, R., & Terkel, J. (1992). Ontogeny of pine cone opening behavior in the black rat, *Rattus rattus. Animal Behaviour, 44,* 327–336.

Al-Issa, I., & Oudji, S. (1998). Culture and anxiety disorders. In S. S. Kazarian & D. R. Evans (Eds.), *Cultural clinical psychology: Theory, research, and practice* (pp. 8–9). New York: Oxford University Press.

Alais, D., & Blake, R. (1999). Grouping visual features during binocular rivalry. *Vision Research, 39,* 4341–4353.

Alarcon, R. D. (1996). Personality disorders and culture in DSM-IV: A critique. *Journal of Personality Disorders, 10,* 260–270.

Alba, J. W., & Hasher, L. (1983). Is memory schematic? *Psychological Bulletin, 93,* 203–231.

Albert, M. S., & Drachman, D. A. (2000). Alzheimer's disease: What is it, how many people have it, and why do we need to know? *Neurology, 55,* 166–168.

Alden, D. L., Mukherjee, A., & Hoyer, W. D. (2000). Extending a contrast resolution model of humor in television advertising: The role of surprise. *Humor, 13,* 193–217.

Aldrich, M. S. (1992). Narcolepsy. *Neurology, 42,* 34–43.

Alexander, L. B., Barber, J. P., Luborsky, L., & Crits-Christoph, P. (1993). On what bases do patients choose their therapists? *Journal of Psychotherapy Practice and Research, 2,* 135–146.

Alexy, B. B. (1991). Factors associated with participation or nonparticipation in a workplace wellness center. *Research in Nursing and Health, 14,* 33–40.

Allen, J. J., Iacono, W. G., Laravuso, J. J., & Dunn, L. A. (1995). An event-related potential investigation of posthypnotic recognition amnesia. *Journal of Abnormal Psychology, 104,* 421–430.

Allen, M. (1993). Determining the persuasiveness of message sidedness: A prudent note about utilizing research summaries. *Western Journal of Communication, 57,* 98–103.

Allen, M. G. (1990). Group psychotherapy: Past, present, and future. *Psychiatric Annals, 20,* 358–361.

Allport, F. H. (1920). The influence of the group upon association and thought. *Journal of Experimental Psychology, 3,* 159–182.

Allport, G. W. (1967). Autobiography. In E. G. Boring & G. Lindzey (Eds.), *A history of psychology in autobiography* (Vol. 5, pp. 1–25). New York: Appleton-Century-Crofts.

Alpert, J. L., Brown, L. S., & Courtois, C. A. (1998). Symptomatic clients and memories of childhood abuse: What the abuse literature tells us. *Psychology, Public Policy, and Law, 4,* 941–995.

Alvarado, C. S. (1996). The place of spontaneous cases in parapsychology. *Journal of Broadcasting and Electronic Media, 41,* 345–359.

Alvarado, K. A., Templer, D. I., Bresler, C., & Thomas-Dobson, S. (1995). The relationship of religious variables to death depression and death anxiety. *Journal of Clinical Psychology, 51,* 202–204.

Amabile, T. M. (1985). Motivation and creativity effects of motivational orientation on creative writers. *Journal of Personality and Social Psychology, 48,* 393–399.

Amabile, T. M. (1989). *Growing up creative.* New York: Random House.

Amato, P. R., & Keith, B. (1991). Parental divorce and the well-being of children: A meta-analysis. *Psychological Bulletin, 110,* 26–46.

American Psychiatric Association. (1994). *Diagnostic and statistical manual of mental disorders* (4th ed.). Washington, DC: Author.

American Psychological Association. (1999). *APA directory survey.* [On-line]. Available: *http://research.apa.org/ 1999profiles.pdf.*

Amering, M., Katschnig, H., Berger, P., Windhaber, J., Baischer, W., & Dantendorfer, K. (1997). Embarrassment about the first panic attack predicts agoraphobia in disorder patients. *Behaviour Research and Therapy, 35,* 517–521.

Amin, F., Silverman, J. M., Siever, L. J., Smith, C. J., Knott, P. J., & Davis, K. L. (1999). Genetic antecedents of dopamine dysfunction in schizophrenia. *Biological Psychiatry, 45,* 1143–1150.

Amir, T. (1984). The Asch conformity effect: A study in Kuwait. *Social Behavior and Personality, 12,* 187–190.

Amorose, A. J., & Horn, T. S. (2000). Intrinsic motivation: Relationships with collegiate athletes' gender, scholarship status, and perceptions of their coaches' behavior. *Journal of Sport and Exercise Psychology, 22,* 63–84.

Anand, A., & Charney, D. S. (2000). Norepinephrine dysfunction in depression. *Journal of Clinical Psychiatry, 61,*16–24.

Anastasi, A. (1958). Heredity, environment, and the question "How?" *American Psychologist, 65,* 197–208.

Anastasi, A. (1972). The cultivation of diversity. *American Psychologist, 27,* 1091–1099.

Anastasi, A. (1985). Psychological testing: Basic concepts and common misconceptions. In A. M. Rogers & C. J. Scheirer (Eds.), *The G. Stanley Hall Lecture Series* (Vol. 5, pp. 87–120). Washington, DC: American Psychological Association.

Anazonwu, C. O. (1995). Locus of control, academic self-concept, and attribution of responsibility for performance in statistics. *Psychological Reports, 77,* 367–370.

Andersen, B. L., Cyranowski, J. M., & Aarestad, S. (2000). Beyond artificial, sex-linked distinctions to conceptualize female sexuality: Comment on Baumeister (2000). *Psychological Bulletin, 126,* 380–384.

Andersen, B. L., Kiecolt-Glaser, J. K., & Glaser, R. A (1994). A biobehavioral model of cancer stress and disease course. *American Psychologist, 49,* 389–404.

Anderson, A. K., & Phelps, E. A. (2000). Perceiving emotion: There's more than meets the eye. *Current Biology, 10,* R551–R554.

Anderson, C. A. (1999). Attributional style, depression, and loneliness: A cross-cultural comparison of American and Chinese students. *Personality and Social Psychology Bulletin, 25,* 482–499.

Anderson, I. M. (2000). Selective serotonin reuptake inhibitors versus tricyclic antidepressants: A meta-analysis of efficacy and tolerability. *Journal of Affective Disorders, 58,* 19–36.

Anderson, J. R. (1983). Retrieval of information from long-term memory. *Science, 220,* 25–30.

Anderson, K. W., & Skidmore, J. R. (1995). Empirical analysis of factors in depressive cognition: The Cognitive Triad Inventory. *Journal of Clinical Psychology, 51,* 603–609.

Anderson, R. A., Baron, R. S., & Logan, H. (1991). Distraction, control, and dental stress. *Journal of Applied Social Psychology, 21,* 156–171.

Anderson, S. W., & Rizzo, M. (1994). Hallucinations following occipital lobe damage: The pathological activation of visual representations. *Journal of Clinical and Experimental Neuropsychology, 16,* 651–663.

Andrade, C., & Sudha, S. (2000). Electroconvulsive therapy and the alpha-2–noradrenergic receptor: Implications of treatment schedule effects. *Journal of ECT, 16,* 268–278.

Andre, T. (1979). Does answering higher-level questions while reading facilitate productive learning? *Review of Educational Research, 49,* 280–318.

Andreasen, N. C. (1997). The evolving concept of schizophrenia: From Kraepelin to the present and future. *Schizophrenia Research, 28,* 105–109.

Andreasen, N. C., Arndt, S., Alliger, R., & Miller, D. (1995). Symptoms of schizophrenia: Methods, meanings, and mechanisms. *Archives of General Psychiatry, 52,* 341–351.

Andreasen, N. C., Flaum, M., Swayze, V. W., & Tyrrell, G. (1990). Positive and negative symptoms in schizophrenia: A critical reappraisal. *Archives of General Psychiatry, 47,* 615–621.

Andreasen, O A., Dedeoglu, A, Kilvenyi, P., Beal, M. F., & Bush, A. I. (2000). N-acetyl-L-cysteine improves survival and preserves motor performance in an animal model of familial amyotrophic lateral sclerosis. *Neuroreport, 11,* 2491–2493.

Anisfeld, M. (1996). Only tongue protrusion modeling is matched by neonates. *Developmental Review, 16,* 149–161.

Ansburg, P. I. (2000). Individual differences in problem solving via insight. *Current Psychology: Developmental, Learning, Personality, Social, 19,* 143–146.

Anschutz, L., Camp, C. J., Markley, R. P., & Kramer, J. J. (1985). Maintenance and generalization of mnemonics for grocery shopping by older adults. *Experimental Aging Research, 11,* 157–160.

Anshel, M. H. (1995). Examining social loafing among elite female rowers as a function of task duration and mood. *Journal of Sport Behavior, 18,* 39–49.

Antoni, M. H., Cruess, D. G., Cruess, S., Lutgendorf, S., et al. (2000). Cognitive-behavioral stress management intervention effects on anxiety, 24–hr urinary norepinephrine output, and T-cytotoxic/suppressor cells over time among symptomatic HIV-infected gay men. *Journal of Consulting and Clinical Psychology, 68,* 31–45.

Antunano, M. J., & Hernandez, J. M. (1989). Incidence of airsickness among military parachutists. *Aviation, Space, and Environmental Medicine, 60,* 792–797.

Ape language. (1981). *Science, 211,* 86–88.

Ardila, A., Montanes, P., & Gempeler, J. (1986). Echoic memory and language perception. *Brain and Language, 29,* 134–140.

Arena, J. G., Bruno, G. M., Hannah, S. L., & Meador, K. J. (1995). A comparison of frontal electromyographic feedback training, and progressive muscle relaxation therapy in the treatment of tension headache. *Headache, 35,* 411–419.

Armory, J. L., Servan-Schreiber, D., Romanski, L. M., Cohen, J. D., & Le Doux, J. E. (1997). Stimulus generalization of fear responses: Effects of auditory cortex lesions in a computational model and in rats. *Cerebral Cortex, 7,* 157–165.

Arnett, J. J. (1999). Adolescent storm and stress, reconsidered. *American Psychologist, 54,* 317–326.

Arnett, P. A., Howland, E. W., Smith, S. S., & Newman, J. P. (1993). Autonomic responsivity during passive avoidance in incarcerated psychopaths. *Personality and Individual Differences, 14,* 173–184.

Aronson, S. C., Black, J. E., McDougle, C. J., & Scanley, B. E. (1995). Serotonergic mechanisms of cocaine effects in humans. *Psychopharmacology, 119,* 179–185.

Arrigo, J. M., & Pezdek, K. (1997). Lessons from the study of psychogenic amnesia. *Current Directions in Psychological Science, 6,* 148–152.

Arterberry, M., Yonas, A., & Benson, A. S. (1989). Self-produced locomotion and the development of responsiveness to linear perspective and texture gradients. *Developmental Psychology, 25,* 976–982.

Asch, S. E. (1955, November). Opinions and social pressure. *Scientific American,* pp. 31–35.

Aseltine, R. H., Jr. (1996). Pathways linking parental divorce with adolescent depression. *Journal of Health and Social Behavior, 37,* 133–148.

Aserinsky, E., & Kleitman, N. (1953). Regularly occurring periods of eye motility and concomitant phenomena during sleep. *Science, 118,* 273–274.

Aserinsky, E., Lynch, J. A., Mack, M. E., Tzankoff, S. P., & Hurn, E. (1985). Comparison of eye motion in wakefulness and REM sleep. *Psychophysiology, 22,* 1–10.

Ash, D. W., & Holding, D. H. (1990). Backward versus forward chaining in the acquisition of a keyboard skill. *Human Factors, 32,* 139–146.

Aslin, R. N., & Smith, L. B. (1988). Perceptual development. *Annual Review of Psychology, 39,* 435–474.

Assanand, S., Pinel, J. P. J., & Lehman, D. R. (1998). Personal theories of hunger and eating. *Journal of Applied Social Psychology, 28,* 998–1015.

Atkinson, J. W., & Litwin, G. H. (1960). Achievement motive and test anxiety concerned as motive to approach success and motive to avoid failure. *Journal of Abnormal and Social Psychology, 60,* 52–63.

Attardo, S. (1997). The semantic foundations of cognitive theories of humor. *Humor, 10,* 395–420.

Ayabe-Kanamura, S., Schicker, I., Laska, M., Hudson, R., Distel, H., Kobayakawa, T., & Saito, S. (1998). Differences in perception of everyday odors: A Japanese-German cross-cultural study. *Chemical Senses, 23,* 31–38.

Aydin, G., & Aydin, O. (1992). Learned helplessness and explanatory style in Turkish samples. *Journal of Social Psychology, 132,* 117–119.

Babad, E., Bernieri, F., & Rosenthal, R. (1989). When less information is more informative: Diagnosing teacher expectations from brief samples of behavior. *British Journal of Educational Psychology, 59,* 281–295.

Baddeley, A. D. (1982). Domains of recollection. *Psychological Review, 89,* 708–729.

Baddeley, A. D. (1994). The magical number seven: Still magic after all these years? *Psychological Review, 101,* 353–356.

Baer, J. (1996). The effects of task-specific divergent-thinking training. *Journal of Creative Behavior, 30,* 183–187.

Baer, L., Rauch, S. L., Ballantine, T., & Martuza, R. (1995). Cingulotomy for intractable obsessive-compulsive disorder: Prospective long-term follow-up of 18 patients. *Archives of General Psychiatry, 52,* 384–392.

Bagby, R. M., Nicholson, R. A., Buis, T., & Bacchiochi, J. R. (2000). Can the MMPI-2 validity scales detect depression feigned by experts? *Assessment, 7,* 55–62.

Bagozzi, R. P., Wong, N., & Yi, Y. (1999). The role of culture and gender in the relationship between positive and negative affect. *Cognition and Emotion, 13,* 641–672.

Bagwell, C. L., Newcomb, A. F., & Bukowski, W. M. (1998). Preadolescent friendship and peer rejection as predictors of adult adjustment. *Child Development, 69,* 140–153.

Bahill, A. T., & Karnavas, W. J. (1993). The perceptual illusion of baseball's rising fastball and breaking curveball. *Journal of Experimental Psychology: Human Perception and Performance, 19,* 3–14.

Bahill, A. T., & LaRitz, T. (1984). Why can't batters keep their eyes on the ball? *American Scientist, 72,* 249–253.

Bahrick, H. P. (1984). Semantic memory content in permastore: Fifty years of memory for Spanish learned in school. *Journal of Experimental Psychology: General, 113,* 1–29.

Bahrick, H. P., Bahrick, P. O., & Wittlinger, R. P. (1975). Fifty years of memory for names and faces: A cross-sectional approach. *Journal of Experimental Psychology: General, 104,* 54–75.

Bailey, J. M., Dunne, M. P., & Martin, N. G. (2000). Genetic and environmental influences on sexual orientation and its correlates in an Australian twin sample. *Journal of Personality and Social Psychology, 78,* 524–536.

Bailey, M. B., & Bailey, R. E. (1993). "Misbehavior": A case history. *American Psychologist, 48,* 1157–1158.

Baillargeon, R., & DeVos, J. (1991). Object permanence in young infants: Further evidence. *Child Development, 62,* 1227–1246.

Baird, J. C., & Wagner, M. (1982). The moon illusion: I. How high is the sky? *Journal of Experimental Psychology: General, 111,* 296–303.

Baird, J. C., Wagner, M., & Fuld, K. (1990). A simple but powerful theory of the moon illusion. *Journal of Experimental Psychology: Human Perception and Performance, 16,* 675–677.

Baker, G. H. B. (1987). Psychological factors and immunity. *Journal of Psychosomatic Research, 31,* 1–10.

Baker, J. P. (1994). Outcomes of lithium discontinuation: A meta-analysis. *Lithium, 5,* 187–192.

Baker, R. (1996, September). [Review of the movie *Phenomenon*]. Available on the World Wide Web at: http://www.reversespeech.com/globe.shtml.

Balanovski, E., & Taylor, J. G. (1978). Can electromagnetism account for extra sensory phenomena? *Nature, 276,* 64–67.

Balch, W. R., Myers, D. M., & Papotto, C. (1999). Dimensions of mood in mood-dependent memory. *Journal of Experimental Psychology: Learning, Memory, and Cognition, 25,* 70–83.

Baldwin, B. A., de la Riva, C., & Ebenezer, I. S. (1990). Effects of intracerebroventricular injection of dynorphin, leumorphin, and a neoendorphin on operant feeding in pigs. *Physiology and Behavior, 48,* 821–824.

Baldwin, E. (1993). The case for animal research in psychology. *Journal of Social Issues, 49,* 121–131.

Baldwin, M. W. (1954). Subjective measurements in television. *American Psychologist, 9,* 231–234.

Ball, K., Lee, C., & Brown, W. (1999). Psychological stress and disordered eating: An exploratory study with young Australian women. *Women and Health, 29,* 1–15.

Baltes, B. B., Briggs, T. E., Huff, J. W., Wright, J. A., & Neuman, G. A. (1999). Flexible and compressed workweek schedules. A meta-analysis of their effects on work-related criteria. *Journal of Applied Psychology, 84,* 496–513.

Bandura, A. (1965). Influence of model's reinforcement contingencies on the acquisition of imitative responses. *Journal of Personality and Social Psychology, 1,* 589–595.

Bandura, A. (1977). *Social learning theory.* Englewood Cliffs, NJ: Prentice Hall.

Bandura, A. (1982). The psychology of chance encounters and life paths. *American Psychologist, 37,* 747–755.

Bandura, A. (1986). *Social foundations of thought and action: A social-cognitive theory.* Englewood Cliffs, NJ: Prentice Hall.

Bandura, A. (1989). Human agency in social cognitive theory. *American Psychologist, 44,* 1175–1184.

Bandura, A. (1997). *Self-efficacy: The exercise of control.* New York: Freeman.

Bandura, A., Blanchard, E. B., & Ritter, B. (1969). The relative efficacy of desensitization and modeling approaches for inducing behavioral, affective, and attitudinal changes. *Journal of Personality and Social Psychology, 13,* 173–199.

Bandura, A., Reese, L., & Adams, N. E. (1982). Microanalysis of action and fear arousal as a function of differential levels of perceived self-efficacy. *Journal of Personality and Social Psychology, 43,* 5–21.

Banks, S. M., & Kerns, R. D. (1996). Explaining high rates of depression in chronic pain: A diathesis-stress framework. *Psychological Bulletin, 119,* 95–110.

Bar-Or, O., Foreyt, J., Bouchard, C., Brownell, K. D., Dietz, W. H., et al. (1998). Physical activity, genetic, and nutritional considerations in childhood weight management. *Medicine and Science in Sports and Exercise, 30,* 2–10.

Barbalet, J. M. (1999). William James' theory of emotions: Filling in the picture. *Journal for the Theory of Social Behaviour, 29,* 251–266.

Barber, T. X. (2000). A deeper understanding of hypnosis: Its secrets, its nature, its essence. *American Journal of Clinical Hypnosis, 42,* 208–272.

Bard, P. (1934). On emotional experience after decortication with some remarks on theoretical views. *Psychological Review, 41,* 309–329.

Baribeau-Braun, J., Picton, T. W., & Gosselin, J. Y. (1983). Schizophrenia: A neuropsychological evaluation of abnormal information processing. *Science, 219,* 874–876.

Barker, M. E., Thompson, K. A., & McClean, S. I. (1996). Do Type As eat differently? A comparison of men and women. *Appetite, 26,* 277–286.

Barker, R. A., & Dunnett, S. B. (1999). Functional integration of neural grafts in Parkinson's disease. *Nature Neuroscience, 2,* 1047–1048.

Barnes, M. L., & Rosenthal, R. (1985). Interpersonal effects of experimenter attractiveness, attire, and gender. *Journal of Personality and Social Psychology, 48,* 435–446.

Barnett, M. A., Quackenbush, W. W., & Sinisi, C. S. (1995). The role of critical experiences in moral development: Implications for justice and care orientations. *Basic and Applied Social Psychology, 17,* 137–152.

Barnett, S. K. (1984). The mentor role: A task of generativity. *Journal of Human Behavior and Learning, 1,* 15–18.

Baron, R. A., & Kalsher, M. J. (1998). Effects of a pleasant ambient fragrance on simulated driving performance: The sweet smell of. . . safety? *Environment and Behavior, 30,* 535–552.

Barrett, P. T., Daum, I., & Eysenck, H. J. (1990). Sensory nerve conduction and intelligence: A methodological study. *Journal of Psychophysiology, 4,* 1–13.

Barrett, P. T., Petrides, K. V., Eysenck, S. B. G., & Eysenck, H. J. (1998). The Eysenck Personality Questionnaire: An examination of the factorial similarity of P, E, N, and L across 34 countries. *Personality and Individual Differences, 25,* 805–819.

Bartlett, F. C. (1932). *Remembering: A study in experimental and social psychology.* Cambridge, England: Cambridge University Press.

Bartolic, E. I., Basso, M. R., Schefft, B. K., Glauser, T., & Titanic-Schefft, M. (1999). Effects of experimentally-induced emotional states on frontal lobe cognitive task performance. *Neuropsychologia, 37,* 677–683.

Bartoshuk, L. M. (1991). Sensory factors in eating behavior. *Bulletin of the Psychonomic Society, 29,* 250–255.

Bartoshuk, L. M., & Beauchamp, G. K. (1994). Chemical senses. *Annual Review of Psychology, 45,* 419–449.

Bartoshuk, L. M., Cain, W. S., & Pfaffmann, C. (1985). Taste and

olfaction. In G. A. Kimble & K. Schlesinger (Eds.), *Topics in the history of psychology* (Vol. 1, pp. 221–260). Hillsdale, NJ: Erlbaum.

Bartsch, R. A., Judd, C. M., Louw, D. A., Park, B., & Ryan, C. S. (1997). Cross-national outgroup homogeneity: United States and South African stereotypes. *South African Journal of Psychology, 27,* 166–170.

Bartussek, D., Becker, G., Diedrich, O., & Naumann, E. (1996). Extraversion, neuroticism, and event-related brain potentials in response to emotional stimuli. *Personality and Individual Differences, 20,* 301–312.

Baskett, L. M. (1984). Ordinal position differences in children's family interactions. *Developmental Psychology, 20,* 1026–1031.

Batson, C. D., Ahmad, N., Yin, J., Bedell, S. J., et al. (1999). Two threats to the common good: Self-interested egoism and empathy and empathy-induced altruism. *Personality and Social Psychology Bulletin, 25,* 3–16.

Batson, C. D., Batson, J. G., Griffitt, C. A., Barrientos, S., et al. (1989). Negative-state relief and the empathy-altruism hypothesis. *Journal of Personality and Social Psychology, 56,* 922–933.

Baum, A., Grunberg, N. E., & Singer, J. E. (1992). Biochemical measurements in the study of emotion. *Psychological Science, 3,* 56–60.

Baumeister, A. A. (1998). Intelligence and the "personal equation." *Intelligence, 26,* 255–265.

Baumeister, R. F. (1982). A self-presentational view of social phenomena. *Psychological Bulletin, 91,* 3–26.

Baumeister, R. F. (1984). Choking under pressure: Self-consciousness and paradoxical effects of incentives on skillful performance. *Journal of Personality and Social Psychology, 46,* 610–620.

Baumeister, R. F. (1988). Should we stop studying sex differences altogether? *American Psychologist, 43,* 1092–1095.

Baumeister, R. F. (1990). Suicide as escape from self. *Psychological Review, 97,* 90–113.

Baumeister, R. F. (2000). Gender differences in erotic plasticity: The female sex drive as socially flexible and responsive. *Psychological Bulletin, 126,* 347–374.

Baumeister, R. F., Dale, K., & Sommer, K. L. (1998). Freudian defense mechanisms and empirical findings in modern social psychology: Reaction formation, projection, displacement, undoing, isolation, sublimation, and denial. *Journal of Personality, 66,* 1081–1124.

Baumler, G. (1994). On the validity of the Yerkes-Dodson law. *Studia Psychologica, 36,* 205–209.

Baumrind, D. (1964). Some thoughts on ethics of research: After reading Milgram's "Behavioral Study of Obedience." *American Psychologist, 19,* 421–423.

Baumrind, D. (1983). Rejoinder to Lewis's reinterpretation of parental firm control effects: Are authoritative families really harmonious? *Psychological Bulletin, 94,* 132–142.

Baumrind, D. (1985) Research using intentional deception: Ethical issues revisited. *American Psychologist, 40,* 165–174.

Bavelier, D., Corina, D., Jezzard, P., et al. (1998). Hemispheric specialization for English and ASL: Left invariance-right variability. *Neuroreport, 9,* 1537–1542.

Bayley, N. (1955). On the growth of intelligence. *American Psychologist, 10,* 805–818.

Bayton, J. A. (1975). Francis Sumner, Max Meenes, and the training of black psychologists. *American Psychologist, 30,* 185–186.

Beal, C. R., Schmitt, K. L., & Dekle, D. J. (1995). Eyewitness identification of children: Effects of absolute judgments, nonverbal response options, and event encoding. *Law and Human Behavior, 19,* 197–216.

Beatty, W. W. (1984). Discriminating drunkenness: A replication. *Bulletin of the Psychonomic Society, 22,* 431–432.

Beck, A. T. (1997). The past and future of cognitive therapy. *Journal of Psychotherapy Practice and Research, 6,* 276–284.

Becona, E., & Garcia, M. P. (1993). Nicotine fading and smokeholding methods to smoking cessation. *Psychological Reports, 73,* 779–786.

Beer, J. M., Arnold, R. D., & Loehlin, J. C. (1998). Genetic and environmental influences on MMPI factor scales: Joint model fitting to twin and adoption data. *Journal of Personality and Social Psychology, 74,* 818–827.

Begley, S., & Hager, M. (1993, July 26). Does DNA make some men gay? *Newsweek,* p. 59.

Beh, H. C. (1994). A survey of daytime napping in an elderly Australian population. *Australian Journal of Psychology, 46,* 100–106.

Behrend, D. A. (1988). Overextensions in early language comprehension: Evidence from a signal detection approach. *Journal of Child Language, 15,* 63–75.

Beiser, M., Shore, J. H., Peters, R., & Tatum, W. (1985). Does community care for the mentally ill make a difference? A tale of two cities. *American Journal of Psychiatry, 142,* 1047–1052.

Békésy, G. von (1957, August). The ear. *Scientific American,* pp. 66–78.

Bekoff, M., Gruen, L., Townsend, S. E., & Rollin, B. E. (1992). Animals in science: Some areas revisited. *Animal Behaviour, 44,* 473–484.

Belisle, M., Roskies, E., & Levesque, J. M. (1987). Improving adherence to physical activity. *Health Psychology, 6,* 159–172.

Bell, A. P., Weinberg, M. S., & Hammersmith, S. J. (1981). *Sexual preference: Its development in men and women.* Bloomington: Indiana University Press.

Bell, J. E., & Eisenberg, N. (1985). Life satisfaction in midlife childless and empty-nest men and women. *Lifestyles, 7,* 146–155.

Bellisle, F. (1999). Glutamate and the Umami taste: Sensory, metabolic, nutritional and behavioural considerations. A review of the literature published in the last 10 years. *Neuroscience and Biobehavioral Reviews, 23,* 423–438.

Belsky, J. (1988). The "effects" of infant day care reconsidered. *Early Childhood Research Quarterly, 3,* 235–272.

Belsky, J., & Hsieh, K. H. (1998). Patterns of marital change during the early childhood years: Parent personality, coparenting, and division-of-labor correlates. *Journal of Family Psychology, 12,* 511–528.

Bem, D. J. (1967). Self-perception: An alternative interpretation of cognitive dissonance phenomena. *Psychological Review, 74,* 183–200.

Bem, D. J., & Allen, A. (1974). On predicting some of the people some of the time: The search for cross-situational consistencies in behavior. *Psychological Review, 81,* 506–520.

Bem, D. J., & Honorton, C. (1994). Does psi exist? Replicable evidence for an anomalous process of information transfer. *Psychological Bulletin, 115,* 4–18.

Bem, S. L. (1981). Gender schema theory: A cognitive account of sex typing. *Psychological Review, 88,* 354–364.

Ben-Hamida, S., Mineka, S., & Bailey, J. M. (1998). Sex differences in perceived controllability of mate value: An evolutionary perspective. *Journal of Personality and Social Psychology, 75,* 953–966.

Ben-Shlomo, Y., Smith, G. D., Shipley, M., & Marmot, M. G. (1993). Magnitude and causes of mortality differences between married and unmarried men. *Journal of Epidemiology and Community Health, 47,* 200–205.

Benbow, C. P. (1988). Sex differences in mathematical reasoning ability in intellectually talented preadolescents: Their nature, effect, and possible causes. *Behavioral and Brain Sciences, 11,* 169–232.

Benbow, C. P., & Stanley, J. C. (1983). Sex differences in mathematical reasoning ability: More facts. *Science, 222,* 1029–1031.

Bender, S. L., Ponton, L. E., Crittenden, M. R., & Word, C. O. (1995). For underprivileged children, standardized intelligence testing can do more harm than good: Reply. *Journal of Developmental and Behavioral Pediatrics, 16,* 428–430.

Benjamin, L. T., Durkin, M., Link, M., Vestal, M., & Acord, J. (1992). Wundt's American doctoral students. *American Psychologist, 47,* 123–131.

Benjamin, L. T., Jr. (1988). A history of teaching machines. *American Psychologist, 43,* 703–712.

Benjamin, L. T., Jr., & Nielsen-Gammon, E. (1999). B. F. Skinner and psychotechnology: The case of the heir conditioner. *Review of General Psychology, 3,* 155–167.

Benjamin, L. T., Jr., & Shields, S. A. (1990). Leta Stetter Hollingworth (1886–1939). In A. N. O'Connell & N. F. Russo (Eds.), *Women in psychology: A bio-bibliographic sourcebook* (pp. 173–183). New York: Greenwood Press.

Bennett, A. T. D., Cuthill, I. C., Partridge, J. C., & Maier, E. J. (1996). Ultraviolet vision and mate choice in zebra finches. *Nature, 380,* 433–435.

Bennett, W., & Gurin, J. (1982). *The dieter's dilemma.* New York: Basic Books.

Bentall, R. P., & Pilgrim, D. (1993). Thomas Szasz, crazy talk and the myth of mental illness. *British Journal of Medical Psychology, 66,* 69–76.

Berenbaum, S. A., & Hines, M. (1992). Early androgens are related to childhood sex-typed toy preferences. *Psychological Science, 3,* 203–206.

Berenbaum, S. A., & Snyder, E. (1995). Early hormonal influences on childhood sex-typed activity and playmate preferences: Implications for the development of sexual orientation. *Developmental Psychology, 31,* 31–42.

Berger, A. A. (1987). Humor: An introduction. *American Behavioral Scientist, 30,* 6–15.

Berger, R. J., & Phillips, N. H. (1995). Energy conservation and sleep. *Behavioural Brain Research, 69,* 65–73.

Bergeron, S. M., & Senn, C. Y. (1998). Body image and sociocultural norms: A comparison of heterosexual and lesbian women. *Psychology of Women Quarterly, 22,* 385–401.

Bergin, A. E., & Lambert, E. (1978). The evaluation of therapeutic outcome. In S. L. Garfield & A. E. Bergin (Eds.), *Handbook of psychotherapy and behavior change* (pp. 139–189). New York: Wiley.

Berk, M., Terre-Blanche, M. J., Maude, C., & Lucas, M. D. (1996). Season of birth and schizophrenia: Southern hemisphere data. *Australian and New Zealand Journal of Psychiatry, 30,* 220–222.

Berko, J. (1958). The child's learning of English morphology. *Word, 14,* 150–177.

Berkowitz, L. (1974). Some determinants of impulsive aggression. *Psychological Review, 81,* 165–176.

Berkowitz, L. (1989). Frustration-aggression hypothesis: Examination and reformulation. *Psychological Bulletin, 106,* 59–73.

Berkowitz, L., & LePage, A. (1967). Weapons as aggression-eliciting stimuli. *Journal of Personality and Social Psychology, 7,* 202–207.

Berkowitz, M. W., Mueller, C. W., Schnell, S. V., & Padberg, U. (1986). Moral reasoning and judgments of aggression. *Journal of Personality and Social Psychology, 51,* 885–891.

Berman, S. M. W., & McCann, J. T. (1995). Defense mechanisms and personality disorders: An empirical test of Millon's theory. *Journal of Personality Assessment, 64,* 132–144.

Bermond, B., Fasotti, L., Nieuwenhuyse, B., & Schuerman, J. (1991). Spinal cord lesions, peripheral feedback, and intensities of emotional feelings. *Cognition and Emotion, 5,* 201–220.

Berndt, T. J., & Hoyle, S. G. (1985). Stability and change in childhood and adolescent friendships. *Developmental Psychology, 21,* 1007–1015.

Berne, E. (1964). *Games people play.* New York: Grove Press.

Berninger, V. W. (1988). Development of operational thought without a normal sensorimotor stage. *Intelligence, 12,* 219–230.

Bernstein, I. L. (1978). Learned taste aversions in children receiving chemotherapy. *Science, 200,* 1302–1303.

Bernstein, I. L. (1991). Aversion conditioning in response to cancer and cancer treatment. *Clinical Psychology Review, 11,* 185–191.

Bernstein, W. M., Stephan, W. G., & Davis, M. H. (1979). Explaining attributions for achievement: A path-analytic approach. *Journal of Personality and Social Psychology, 37,* 1810–1821.

Berry, J. W., & Kalin, R. (1995). Multicultural and ethnic attitudes in Canada: An overview of the 1991 national survey. *Canadian Journal of Behavioural Science, 27,* 301–320.

Berscheid, E., & Walster, E. (1974). A little bit about love. In T. L. Houston (Ed.), *Foundations of interpersonal attraction.* New York: Academic Press.

Bertenthal, B. I., Campos, J. J., & Kermoian, R. (1994). An epigenetic perspective on the development of self-produced locomotion and its consequences. *Current Directions in Psychological Science, 3,* 140–145.

Best, C. T., & Avery, R. A. (2000). Left-hemisphere advantage for click consonants is determined by linguistic significance and experience. *Psychological Science, 10,* 65–70.

Best, D. L., House, A. S., Barnard, A. E., & Spicker, B. S. (1994). Parent-child interactions in France, Germany, and Italy: The effects of gender and culture. *Journal of Cross Cultural Psychology, 25,* 181–193.

Beutler, L. E., & Consoli, A. J. (1993). Matching the therapist's interpersonal stance to clients' characteristics: Contributions from systematic eclectic psychotherapy. *Psychotherapy, 30,* 417–422.

Bexton, W. H., Heron, W., & Scott, T. H. (1954). Effects of decreased variation in the sensory environment. *Canadian Journal of Psychology, 8,* 70–76.

Biafora, F. (1995). Cross-cultural perspective on illness and wellness: Implications for depression. *Journal of Social Distress and the Homeless, 4,* 105–129.

Bianchi, S. M. (1995). The changing demographic and socioeconomic characteristics of single parent families. *Marriage and Family Review, 20,* 71–97.

Binder, J. R., Frost, J. A., Hammeke, T. A., et al. (2000). Human temporal lobe activation by speech and nonspeech sounds. *Cerebral Cortex, 10,* 512–528.

Binsted, G., & Elliott, D. (1999). The Mueller-Lyer illusion as a perturbation to the saccadic system. *Human Movement Science, 18,* 103–117.

Birch, J. (1997). Efficiency of the Ishihara test for identifying red-green colour deficiency. *Ophthalmic and Physiological Optics, 17,* 403–408

Birmaher, B., Rabin, B. S., Garcia, M. R., & Jain, U. (1994). Cellular immunity in depressed, conduct disorder, and normal adolescents: Role of adverse life events. *Journal of the American Academy of Child and Adolescent Psychiatry, 33,* 671–678.

Bishop, D. V. M. (1990). *Handedness and developmental disorder.* Oxford, England: Mac Keith Press.

Bitsch, A., Schuchardt, J., Bunkowski, S., Kuhlmann, T., & Brueck, W. (2000). Acute axonal injury in multiple sclerosis: Correlation with demyelination and inflammation. *Brain, 123,* 1174–1183.

Bjarnason, T., & Adalbjarnardottir, S. (2000). Anonymity and confidentiality in school surveys on alcohol, tobacco, and cannabis use. *Journal of Drug Issues, 30,* 335–343.

Bjork, D. W. (1988). *William James: The center of his vision.* New York: Columbia University Press.

Bjork, E. L., & Cummings, E. M. (1984). Infant search errors: Stage of concept development or stage of memory development. *Memory and Cognition, 12,* 1–19.

Bjorkqvist, K., Nygren, T., Bjorklund, A.-C., & Bjorkqvist, S.-E. (1994). Testosterone intake and aggressiveness: Real effect or anticipation? *Aggressive Behavior, 20,* 17–26.

Blaisdell, A. P., Gunther, L. M., & Miller, R. R. (1999). Recovery from blocking achieved by extinguishing the blocking CS. *Animal Learning and Behavior, 27,* 63–76.

Blakemore, C. (1977). *Mechanics of the mind.* New York: Cambridge University Press.

Blakemore, C., & Cooper, G. F. (1970). Development of the brain depends on the visual environment. *Nature, 228,* 477–478.

Blanchard, J. J., Kring, A. M., & Neale, J. M. (1994). Flat affect in schizophrenia: A test of neuropsychological models. *Schizophrenia Bulletin, 20,* 311–325.

Blankfield, R. P. (1991). Suggestion, relaxation, and hypnosis as adjuncts in the care of surgery patients: A review of the literature. *American Journal of Clinical Hypnosis, 33,* 172–186.

Blasi, A. (1980). Bridging moral cognition and moral action: A critical review of the literature. *Psychological Bulletin, 88,* 1–45.

Blass, T. (1999). The Milgram Paradigm after 35 years: Some things we now know about obedience to authority. *Journal of Applied Social Psychology, 29,* 955–978.

Blechman, E. A., Tinsley, B., Carella, E. T., & McEnroe, M. J. (1985). Childhood competence and behavior problems. *Journal of Abnormal Psychology, 94,* 70–77.

Bleichrodt, N., Hoksbergen, R. A. C., & Khire, U. (1999). Cross-cultural testing of intelligence. *Cross-Cultural Research, 33,* 3–25.

Blevins, J. E., Stanley, B. G., & Reidelberger, R. D. (2000). Brain regions where cholecystokinin suppresses feeding in rats. *Brain Research, 860,* 1–10.

Blix, G. G., & Blix, A. G. (1995). The role of exercise in weight loss. *Behavioral Medicine, 21,* 31–39.

Blizard, R. A. (1997). The origins of dissociative identity disorder from an object relations and attachment theory perspective. *Dissociation: Progress in the Dissociative Disorders, 10,* 223–229.

Bluhm, H. O. (1999). How did they survive? Mechanisms of defense in Nazi concentration camps. *American Journal of Psychotherapy, 53,* 96–122.

Boddington, S. J. A., & Lavender, A. (1995). Treatment models for couples therapy: A review of the outcome literature and the Dodo's verdict. *Sexual and Marital Therapy, 10,* 69–81.

Bogaert, A. F., & Hershberger, S. (1999). The relation between sexual orientation and penile size. *Archives of Sexual Behavior, 28,* 213–221.

Bohan, J. S. (1993). Women at center stage: A course about the women of psychology. *Teaching of Psychology, 20,* 74–79.

Bohannon, J. N., III, & Stanowicz, L. (1988). The issue of negative evidence: Adult responses to children's language errors. *Developmental Psychology, 24,* 684–689.

Bohart, A. C., O'Hara, M., & Leitner, L. M. (1998). Empirically violated treatments: Disenfranchisement of humanistic and other psychotherapies. *Psychotherapy Research, 8,* 141–157.

Bolm-Audorff, U., Schwammle, J., Ehlenz, K., & Kaffarnik, H. (1989). Plasma level of catecholamines and lipids when speaking before an audience. *Work and Stress, 3,* 249–253.

Bond, C. F., Jr., & Titus, L. J. (1983). Social facilitation: A meta-analysis of 241 studies. *Psychological Bulletin, 94,* 265–292.

Bond, R., & Smith, P. B. (1996). Culture and conformity: A meta-analysis of studies using Asch's (1952b, 1956) line judgment task. *Psychological Bulletin, 119,* 111–137.

Bonds, D. R., & Crosby, L. O. (1986). "An adoption study of human obesity": Comment. *New England Journal of Medicine, 315,* 128.

Boneau, C. A. (1974). Paradigm regained? Cognitive behaviorism revisited. *American Psychologist, 29,* 297–309.

Boon, S., & Draijer, N. (1993). Multiple personality disorder in the Netherlands: A clinical investigation of 71 patients. *American Journal of Psychiatry, 150,* 489–494.

Bordages, J. W. (1989). Self-actualization and personal autonomy. *Psychological Reports, 64,* 1263–1266.

Bordi, F., & Quartaroli, M. (2000). Modulation of nociceptive transmission by NMDA/glycine site receptor in the ventroposterolateral nucleus of the thalamus. *Pain, 84,* 213–224.

Boring, E. G. (1950). *A history of experimental psychology.* New York: Appleton-Century-Crofts.

Borkhuis, G. W., & Patalano, F. (1997). MMPI personality differences between adolescents from divorced and nondivorced families. *Psychology, 34,* 37–41.

Bornstein, R. F. (1999). Criterion validity of objective and projective dependency tests: A meta-analytic assessment of behavioral prediction. *Psychological Assessment, 11,* 48–57

Borod, J. C., Haywood, C. S., & Koff, E. (1997). Neuropsychological aspects of facial asymmetry during emotional expression: A review of the normal adult literature. *Neuropsychology Review, 7,* 41–60.

Borszcz, G. S. (1999). Differential contributions of medullary, thalamic, and amygdaloid serotonin to the antinociceptive action of morphine administered into the periaqueductal gray: A model of morphine analgesia. *Behavioral Neuroscience, 113,* 612–631.

Botman, H. I., & Crovitz, H. F. (1989–1990). Dream reports and autobiographical memory. *Imagination, Cognition, and Personality, 9,* 213–224.

Bouchard, T. J., Jr., & McGue, M. (1981). Familial studies of intelligence: A review. *Science, 212,* 1055–1059.

Bouchard, T. J., Jr., & McGue, M. (1990). Genetic and rearing environmental influences on adult personality: An analysis of adopted twins reared apart. *Journal of Personality, 58,* 263–292.

Bouchard, T. J., Jr., Lykken, D. T., McGue, M., Segal, N. L., & Tellegen, A. (1990). Sources of human psychological differences: The Minnesota Study of Twins Reared Apart. *Science, 250,* 223–228.

Bouchard, T. J., Jr., McGue, M., Hur, Y.-M., & Horn, J. M. (1998). A genetic and environmental analysis of the California Psychological Inventory using adult twins reared apart and together. *European Journal of Personality, 12,* 307–320.

Boudreaux, R. (2000, March 28). Spaniards are missing their naps. *Los Angeles Times,* p. A1.

Bouton, M. E., & Swartzentruber, D. (1991). Sources of relapse after extinction in Pavlovian and instrumental learning. *Clinical Psychology Review, 11,* 123–140.

Bouton, M. E., Mineka, S., & Barlow, D. H. (2001). A modern learning theory perspective on the etiology of panic disorder. *Psychological Review, 108,* 4–32.

Bouzid, N., & Crawshaw, C. M. (1987). Massed versus distributed word processor training. *Applied Ergonomics, 18,* 220–222.

Bowd, A. D. (1990). A decade of debate on animal research on research in psychology: Room for consensus? *Canadian Psychologist, 31,* 74–82.

Bower, G. H. (1970). Analysis of a mnemonic device. *American Scientist, 58,* 496–510.

Bower, G. H., & Clark, M. C. (1969). Narrative stories as mediators for serial learning. *Psychonomic Science, 14,* 181–182.

Bowers, K. S. (1994). A review of Ernest R. Hilgard's books on hypnosis, in commemoration of his 90th birthday. *Psychological Science, 5,* 186–189.

Bowers, K. S., & Farvolden, P. (1996). Revisiting a century-old Freudian slip— From suggestion disavowed to the truth repressed. *Psychological Bulletin, 119,* 355–380.

Bowers, L. B. (1990). Traumas precipitating female delinquency: Implications for assessment, practice, and policy. *Child and Adolescent Social Work Journal, 7,* 389–402.

Bowlby, J. (1988). *A secure base: Parent-child attachment and healthy human development.* New York: Basic Books.

Boyd, J. H. (1986). Use of mental health services for the treatment of panic disorder. *American Journal of Psychiatry, 143,* 1569–1574.

Boyd, J. H., & Crump, T. (1991). Westphal's agoraphobia. *Journal of Anxiety Disorders, 5,* 77–86.

Boyd, J. H., Rae, D. S., Thompson, J. W., & Burns, B. J. (1990). Phobia: Prevalence and risk factors. *Social Psychiatry and Psychiatric Epidemiology, 25,* 314–323.

Boyd, W. D., & Campbell, S. E. (1998). EEG biofeedback in the schools: The use of EEG biofeedback to treat ADHD in a school setting. *Journal of Neurotherapy, 2,* 65–71.

Boynton, R. M. (1988). Color vision. *Annual Review of Psychology, 39,* 69–100.

Bozarth, J. D. (1990). The evolution of Carl Rogers as a therapist. *Person-Centered Review, 5,* 387–393.

Bozarth, J. D, & Brodley, B. T. (1991). Actualization: A functional concept in client-centered therapy. *Journal of Social Behavior and Personality, 6,* 45–59.

Bradley, B. P., & Baddeley, A. D. (1990). Emotional factors in forgetting. *Psychological Medicine, 20,* 351–355.

Braffman, W. & Kirsch, I. (1999). Imaginative suggestibility and hypnotizability: An empirical analysis. *Journal of Personality and Social Psychology, 77,* 578–587.

Brakke, K. E., & Savage-Rumbaugh, E. S. (1996). The development of language skills in *Pan*: II. Production. *Language and Communication, 16,* 361–380.

Brambilla, F., Brunetta, M., Draisci, A., & Peirone, A. (1995). T-lymphocyte concentrations of cholecystokinin-8 and beta-endorphin in eating disorders: II. Bulimia nervosa. *Psychiatry Research, 59,* 51–56.

Braungart, J. M., Plomin, R., DeFries, J. C., & Fulker, D. W. (1992). Genetic influence on tester-rated infant temperament as assessed by Bayley's Infant Behavior Record: Nonadoptive and adoptive siblings and twins. *Developmental Psychology, 28,* 40–47.

Breathnach, C. S. (1989). Validation of language localization by computer-assisted tomographic and topographic techniques. *Irish Journal of Psychological Medicine, 6,* 11–18.

Breathnach, C. S. (1992). Eduard Hitzig, neurophysiologist and psychiatrist. *History of Psychiatry, 3,* 329–338.

Breckler, S. J. (1984). Empirical validation of affect, behavior, and cognition as distinct components of attitude. *Journal of Personality and Social Psychology, 47,* 1191–1205.

Breitholtz, E., Johansson, B., & Ost, L.-G. (1999). Cognitions in generalized anxiety disorder and panic disorder patients: A prospective approach. *Behaviour Research & Therapy, 37,* 533–544.

Breland, K., & Breland, M. (1961). The misbehavior of organisms. *American Psychologist, 16,* 681–684.

Brennan, J. L., & Andrews, G. (1990). An examination of defense style in parents who abuse children. *Journal of Nervous and Mental Disease, 178,* 592–595.

Bretherton, I., & Main, M. (2000). Mary Dinsmore Saltworthy Ainsworth (1913–1999): Obituary. *American Psychologist, 55,* 1148–1149.

Brickman, P., Coates, D., & Janoff-Bulman, R. (1978). Lottery winners and accident victims: Is happiness relative? *Journal of Personality and Social Psychology, 36,* 917–927.

Briggs, K. C., & Myers, I. B. (1943). *Myers-Briggs type indicator.* Palo Alto, CA: Consulting Psychologists Press.

Brigham, C. C. (1923). *A study of American intelligence.* Princeton, NJ: Princeton University Press.

Brigman, G. M., & Molina, B. (1999). Developing social interest and enhancing school success skills: A service learning approach. *Journal of Individual Psychology, 55,* 342–354.

Broberg, A. G., Wessels, H., Lamb, M. E., & Hwang, C. P. (1997). Effects of day care on the development of cognitive abilities in 8-year-olds: A longitudinal study. *Developmental Psychology, 33,* 62–69.

Broberg, D. J., & Bernstein, I. L. (1987). Candy as a scapegoat in the prevention of food aversions in children receiving chemotherapy. *Cancer, 60,* 2344–2347.

Broder, M. S. (2000). Making optimal use of homework to enhance your therapeutic effectiveness. *Journal of Rational and Cognitive Behavior Therapy, 18,* 3–18.

Brody, N. (1999). What is intelligence? *International Review of Psychiatry, 11,* 19–25.

Bromberg, W. (1954). *Man above humanity: A history of psychotherapy.* Philadelphia: Lippincott.

Brooks, K., & Siegel, M. (1991). Children as eyewitnesses: Memory, suggestibility, and credibility. *Australian Psychologist, 26,* 84–88.

Brooks-Gunn, J., & Furstenberg, F. F., Jr. (1989). Adolescent sexual behavior. *American Psychologist, 44,* 249–257.

Brooks-Gunn, J., & Warren, M. P. (1989). Biological and social contributions to negative affect in young adolescent girls. *Child Development, 60,* 40–55.

Brooks-Gunn, J., Klebanov, P. K., & Duncan, G. J. (1996). Ethnic differences in children's intelligence test scores: Role of economic deprivation, home environment, and maternal characteristics. *Child Development, 67,* 396–408.

Brosschot, J. F., Godaert, G. L. R., Benschop, R. J., et al. (1998). Experimental stress and immunological reactivity: A closer look at perceived uncontrollability. *Psychosomatic Medicine, 60,* 359–361.

Broughton, R. S., & Perlstrom, J. R. (1992). PK in a competitive computer game: A replication. *Journal of Parapsychology, 56,* 291–305.

Brown, A. S. (1991). A review of the tip-of-the-tongue experience. *Psychological Bulletin, 109,* 204–223.

Brown, A. S., Schaefer, C. A., Wyatt, R. J., Goetz, R., Begg, M. D., Gorman, J. M., & Susser, E. S. (2000). Maternal exposure to respiratory infections and adult schizophrenia spectrum disorders: A prospective birth cohort study. *Schizophrenia Bulletin, 26,* 287–295.

Brown, D., Scheflin, A. W., & Whitfield, C. L. (1999). Recovered memories: The current weight of the evidence in science and the courts. *Journal of Psychiatry and Law, 27,* 5–156.

Brown, J. D., & Siegel, J. M. (1988). Exercise as a buffer of life stress: A prospective study of adolescent health. *Health Psychology, 7,* 341–353.

Brown, R., & Kulik, J. (1977). Flashbulb memories. *Cognition, 5,* 73–99.

Brown, R., Price, R. J., King, M. G., & Husband, A. J. (1989). Interleukin-1B and muramyl depeptide can prevent decreased antibody response associated with sleep deprivation. *Brain, Behavior, and Immunity, 3,* 320–330.

Brown, R. B., & Keegan, D. (1999). Humor in the hotel kitchen. *Humor, 12,* 47–70.

Brown, R. T., Reynolds, C. R., & Whitaker, J. S. (1999). Bias in mental testing since *Bias in Mental Testing. School Psychology Quarterly, 14,* 208–238.

Brownell, K. D. (1982). Obesity: Understanding and treating a serious, prevalent and refractory disorder. *Journal of Consulting and Clinical Psychology, 50,* 820–840.

Brownell, K. D. (1993). Whether obesity should be treated. *Health Psychology, 12,* 339–341.

Brownell, K. D., & Wadden, T. A. (1991). The heterogeneity of obesity: Fitting treatments to individuals. *Behavior Therapy, 22,* 153–177.

Bruch, M. A., Rivet, K. M., & Laurenti, H. J. (2000). Type of self-discrepancy and relationships to components of the tripartite model of emotional distress. *Personality and Individual Differences, 29,* 37–44.

Bruner, J. S. (1956). Freud and the image of man. *American Psychologist, 11,* 463–466.

Bryant, D. M., & Maxwell, K. L. (1999). The environment and mental retardation. *International Review of Psychiatry, 11,* 56–67.

Bryant, R. A., Marosszeky, J. E., Crooks, J., & Gurka, J. A. (2000). Posttraumatic stress disorder after severe traumatic brain injury. *American Journal of Psychiatry, 157,* 629–631.

Bryden, M. P. (1993). Perhaps not so sinister [Review of *The left-hander syndrome*]. *Contemporary Psychology, 38,* 71–72.

Bryden, M. P., Ardila, A., & Ardila, O. (1993). Handedness in native Amazonians. *Neuropsychologia, 31,* 301–308.

Buchanan, T. W., Lutz, K., Mirzazade, S., Specht, K., Shah, N. J., Zilles, K., & Jaencke, L. (2000). Recognition of emotional prosody and verbal components of spoken language: An MRI study. *Cognitive Brain Research, 9,* 227–238.

Buchsbaum, M. S., & Haier, R. J. (1983). Psychopathology: Biological approaches. *Annual Review of Psychology, 34,* 401–430.

Buechel, C., Price, C., Frackowiak, R. S. J., & Friston, K. (1998). Different activation patterns in the visual cortex of late and congenitally blind subjects. *Brain, 121,* 409–419.

Bulik, C. M., Sullivan, P. F., Fear, J., & Pickering, A. (1997). Predictors of the development of bulimia nervosa in women with anorexia nervosa. *Journal of Nervous and Mental Disease, 185,* 704–707.

Bullough, V. L. (1998). Alfred Kinsey and the Kinsey Report: Historical overview and lasting contributions. *Journal of Sex Research, 35,* 127–131.

Bunge, M. (1992). The scientist's skepticism. *Skeptical Inquirer, 16,* 377–380.

Bunn, G. C. (1997). The lie detector, *Wonder Woman,* and liberty: The life and work of William Moulton Marston. *History of the Human Sciences, 10,* 9–119.

Burchinal, M. R., Bryant, D. M., Lee, M. W., & Ramey, C. T. (1992). Early day care, infant-mother attachment, and maternal responsiveness in the infant's first year. *Early Childhood Research Quarterly, 3,* 383–396.

Burkhard, P. (1997). Hypnosis in the treatment of cancer pain. *Australian Journal of Clinical and Experimental Hypnosis, 25,* 40–52.

Burman, B., & Margolin, G. (1992). Analysis of the association between marital relationships and health problems: An interactional perspective. *Psychological Bulletin, 112,* 39–63.

Bursik, K. (1998). Moving beyond gender differences: Gender-role comparisons of manifest dream content. *Sex Roles, 38,* 203–214.

Busch, F. (1994). Some ambiguities in the method of free association and their implications for technique. *Journal of the American Psychoanalytic Association, 42,* 363–384.

Buss, A., Booker, A., & Buss, E. (1972). Firing a weapon and aggression. *Journal of Personality and Social Psychology, 22,* 296–302.

Buss, D. M. (1985). Human mate selection. *American Scientist, 73,* 47–51.

Buss, D. M. (1995). Psychological sex differences: Origins through sexual selection. *American Psychologist, 50,* 164–168.

Buss, D. M. (1999). *Evolutionary psychology: The new science of the mind.* Boston: Allyn & Bacon.

Buss, D. M., Abbott, M., Angleitner, A., & Asherian, A. (1990). International preferences in selecting mates: A study of 37 cultures. *Journal of Cross-Cultural Psychology, 21,* 5–47.

Buss, D. M., Sarsen, R. J., Westen, D., & Semmelroth, J. (1992). Sex differences in jealousy: Evolution, physiology, and psychology. *Psychological Science, 3,* 251–255.

Bussey, K., & Bandura, A. (1999). Social cognitive theory of gender development and differentiation. *Psychological Review, 106,* 676–713.

Butcher, J. N. (2000). Revising psychological tests: Lessons learned from the revision of the MMPI. *Psychological Assessment, 12,* 263–271.

Butler, B. E., & Petrulis, J. (1999). Some further observations concerning Sir Cyril Burt. *British Journal of Psychology, 90,* 155–160.

Butler, L. D., & Nolen-Hoeksema, S. (1994). Gender differences in responses to depressed mood in a college sample. *Sex Roles, 30,* 331–346.

Buunk, B. P., Angleitner, A., Oubaid, V., & Buss, D. M. (1996). Sex differences in jealousy in evolutionary and cultural perspective: Tests from the Netherlands, Germany, and the United States. *Psychological Science, 7,* 359–363.

Byne, W. (1997). Why we cannot conclude that sexual orientation is primarily a biological phenomenon. *Journal of Homosexuality, 34,* 73–80.

Byrne, D., Ervin, C. R., & Lamberth, J. (1970). Continuity between the experimental study of attraction and real-life computer dating. *Journal of Personality and Social Psychology, 16,* 157–165.

Cabib, S., Oliverio, A., Ventura, R., Lucchese, F., & Puglisi-Allegra, S. (1997). Brain dopamine receptor plasticity: Testing a diathesis-stress hypothesis in an animal model. *Psychopharmacology, 132,* 153–160.

Cacioppo, J. T. (1994). Social neuroscience: Autonomic, neuroendocrine, and immune responses to stress. *Psychophysiology, 31,* 113–128.

Cadoret, R. J., Yates, W. R., Troughton, E., & Woodworth, G. (1995). Adoption study demonstrating two genetic pathways to drug abuse. *Archives of General Psychiatry, 52,* 42–52.

Cahan, E. D., & White, S. H. (1992). Proposals for a second psychology. *American Psychologist, 47,* 224–235.

Cahill, L., & McGaugh, J. L. (1998). Mechanisms of emotional arousal and lasting declarative memory. *Trends in Neurosciences, 21,* 294–299.

Cahill, L., Prins, B., Weber, M., & McGaugh, J. L. (1994). b-Adrenergic activation and memory for emotional events. *Nature, 371,* 702–704.

Calantone, R. J., & Warshaw, P. R. (1985). Negating the effects of fear appraisals in election campaigns. *Journal of Applied Psychology, 70,* 627–633.

Caldwell, J. L. (2000). The use of melatonin: An information paper. *Aviation, Space, and Environmental Medicine, 71,* 238–244.

Calkins, M. W. (1893). Statistics of dreams. *American Journal of Psychology, 5,* 311–343.

Calkins, M. W. (1901). *An introduction to psychology.* New York: Macmillan.

Calkins, M. W. (1906). A reconciliation between structural and functional psychology. *Psychological Review, 13,* 61–81.

Calkins, M. W. (1913). Psychology and the behaviorist. *Psychological Bulletin, 10,* 288–291.

Calkins, M. W. (1930). Mary Whiton Calkins. In C. Murchison (Ed.), *A history of psychology in autobiography* (Vol. 1, pp. 31–62). New York: Russell & Russell.

Camel, J. E., Withers, G. S., & Greenough, W. T. (1986). Persistence of visual cortex dendritic alterations induced by postweaning exposure to a "superenriched" environment in rats. *Behavioral Neuroscience, 100,* 810–813.

Cameron, M. J., & Cappello, M. J. (1993). "We'll cross that hurdle when we get to it": Teaching athletic performance within adaptive physical education. *Behavior Modification, 17,* 136–147.

Campbell, W. K., & Sedikides, C. (1999). Self-threat magnifies the self-serving bias: A meta-analytic integration. *Review of General Psychology, 3,* 23–43.

Campion, M. A., Palmer, D. K., & Campion, J. E. (1998). Structuring employment interviews to improve reliability, validity and users' reactions. *Current Directions in Psychological Science, 7,* 77–82.

Camras, L. A., Oster, H., Campos, J., Campos, R., Ujiie, T., et al. (1998). Production of emotional facial expressions in European American, Japanese, and Chinese infants. *Developmental Psychology, 34,* 616–628.

Canetto, S. S., & Lester, D. (1995). Gender and the primary prevention of suicide mortality. *Suicide and Life-Threatening Behavior, 25,* 58–69.

Cann, A., Holt, K., & Calhoun, L. G. (1999). The roles of humor and sense of humor in responses to stressors. *Humor, 12,* 177–193.

Cannon, M., Jones, P., Huttunen, M. O., et al. (1999). School performance in Finnish children and later development of schizophrenia. *Archives of General Psychiatry, 56,* 457–463.

Cannon, W. B. (1915/1989). *Bodily changes in pain, hunger, fear, and rage.* Birmingham, AL: Gryphon.

Cannon, W. B. (1927). The James-Lange theory of emotions: A critical examination and an alternative. *American Journal of Psychology, 39,* 106–124.

Cannon, W. B., & Washburn, A. L. (1912). An explanation of hunger. *American Journal of Physiology, 29,* 444–454.

Caplan, D., & Waters, G. S. (1999). Verbal working memory and sentence comprehension. *Behavioral and Brain Sciences, 22,* 77–126.

Caplan, L. J., & Barr, R. A. (1989). On the relationship between category intensions and extensions in children. *Journal of Experimental Child Psychology, 47,* 413–429.

Capone, G. T. (2001). Down syndrome: Advances in molecular biology and the neurosciences. *Journal of Developmental and Behavioral Pediatrics, 22,* 40–59.

Caputo, J. L., Rudolph, D. L., & Morgan, D. W. (1998). Influence of positive life events on blood pressure in adolescents. *Journal of Behavioral Medicine, 21,* 115–129.

Carlat, D. J., & Camargo, C. A. (1991). Review of bulimia nervosa in males. *American Journal of Psychiatry, 148,* 831–843.

Carlson, E. R. (1995). Evaluating the credibility of sources: A missing link in the teaching of critical thinking. *Teaching of Psychology, 22,* 39–41.

Carlson, E. T. (1981). The history of multiple personality in the United States: I. The beginnings. *American Journal of Psychiatry, 138,* 666–668.

Carlson, M., & Miller, N. (1987). Explanation of the relation between negative mood and helping. *Psychological Bulletin, 102,* 91–108.

Carmichael, L., Hogan, H. P., & Walter, A. (1932). An experimental study of the effect of language on the reproduction of visually perceived form. *Journal of Experimental Psychology, 15,* 73–86.

Carney, R. N., & Levin, J. R. (1994). Combining mnemonic strategies to remember who painted what when. *Contemporary Educational Psychology, 19,* 323–339.

Carpendale, J. I. M. (2000). Kohlberg and Piaget on stages and moral reasoning. *Developmental Review, 20,*181–205.

Carpenter, C. R. (1955). Psychological research using television. *American Psychologist, 10,* 606–610.

Carroll, J. (1999). The deep structure of literary representations. *Evolution and Human Behavior, 20,* 159–173.

Carroll, J. B. (1997). Psychometrics, intelligence, and public perception. *Intelligence, 24,* 25–52.

Carroll, J. F. X., Tanneberger, M. A., & Monti, T. C. (1998). A tertiary prevention strategy for drug-dependent clients completing residential treatment. *Alcoholism Treatment Quarterly, 16,* 51–61.

Carroll, M. (1998). But fingerprints don't lie, eh? Prevailing gender ideologies and scientific knowledge. *Psychology of Women Quarterly, 22,* 739–749.

Carron, A. V., Hausenblas, H. A., & Mack, D. (1996). Social influence and exercise: A meta-analysis. *Journal of Sport and Exercise Psychology, 18,* 1–16.

Carskadon, M. A. (1990). Patterns of sleep and sleepiness in adolescents. *Pediatrician, 17,* 5–12.

Carsten, J. M., & Spector, P. E. (1987). Unemployment, job satisfaction, and employee turnover: A meta-analytic test of the Muchinsky Model. *Journal of Applied Psychology, 72,* 374–381.

Carta, G., Nava, F., & Gessa, G. L. (1998). Inhibition of hippocampal acetylcholine release after acute and repeated delta-sup-9-tetrahydrocannabinol in rats. *Brain Research, 809,* 1–4.

Carton, J. S. (1996). The differential effects of tangible rewards and praise on intrinsic motivation: A comparison of cognitive evaluation theory and operant theory. *Behavior Analyst, 19,* 237–255.

Cartwright, R. D. (1978). *A primer on sleep and dreaming.* Reading, MA: Addison-Wesley.

Cartwright, R. D. (1991). Dreams that work: The relation of dream incorporation to adaptation to stressful events. *Dreaming, 1,* 3–9.

Carver, C. S., & Ganellen, R. J. (1983). Depression and components of self-punitiveness: High standards, self-criticism, and overgeneralization. *Journal of Abnormal Psychology, 92,* 330–337.

Cascio, W. F. (1991). *Applied psychology in personnel management* (4th ed.). Englewood Cliffs, NJ: Prentice Hall.

Cascio, W. F. (1995). Whither industrial and organizational psychology in a changing work of work? *American Psychologist, 50,* 928–939.

Caspi, A., & Moffitt, T. E. (1991). Individual differences are accentuated during periods of social change: The sample case of girls at puberty. *Journal of Personality and Social Psychology, 61,* 157–168.

Cassidy, J., & Berlin, L. J. (1994). The insecure/ambivalent pattern of attachment: Theory and research. *Child Development, 65,* 971–981.

Cassidy, K. W., Chu, J. Y., & Dahlsgaard, K. K. (1997). Preschoolers' ability to adopt justice and care orientations to moral dilemmas. *Early Education and Development, 8,* 419–434.

Castner, S. A., & Goldman-Rakic, P. S. (1999). Long-lasting psychotomimetic consequences of repeated low-dose amphetamine exposure in rhesus monkeys. *Neuropsychopharmacology, 20,* 10–28.

Casto, S. D., DeFries, J. C., & Fulker, D. W. (1995). Multivariate genetic analysis of Wechsler Intelligence Scale for Children–Revised (WISC-R) factors. *Behavior Genetics, 25,* 25–32.

Catania, J. A., Coates, T. J., Stall, R., & Bye, L. (1991). Changes in condom use among homosexual men in San Francisco. *Health Psychology, 10,* 190–199.

Catania, J. A., Gibson, D. R., Chitwood, D. D., & Coates, T. J. (1990). Methodological problems in AIDS behavioral research: Influences on measurement error and participation bias in studies of sexual behavior. *Psychological Bulletin, 108,* 339–362.

Catherwood, D. (1993). The haptic processing of texture and shape by 7– to 9–month-old infants. *British Journal of Developmental Psychology, 11,* 299–306.

Cattell, J. M. (1890). Mental tests and measurements. *Mind, 15,* 373–381.

Cattell, R. B. (1940). A culture free intelligence test: I. *Journal of Educational Psychology, 31,* 161–179.

Catz, S. L., Kelly, J. A., Bogart, L. M., Benotsch, E. G., & McAuliffe, T. L. (2000). Patterns, correlates and barriers to medication adherence among persons prescribed new treatments for HIV disease. *Health Psychology, 19,* 124–133.

Cawley, B. D., Keeping, L. M., & Levy, P. E. (1998). Participation in the performance appraisal process and employee reactions: A meta-analytic review of field investigations. *Journal of Applied Psychology, 83,* 615–633.

Ceci, S. J., Ross, D. F., & Toglia, M. P. (1987). Suggestibility of children's memory: Psychological implications. *Journal of Experimental Psychology: General, 116,* 38–49.

Cha, K., Horch, K. W., & Normann, R. A. (1992). Mobility performance with a pixelized vision system. *Vision Research, 32,* 1367–1372.

Chabal, C., Fishbain, D. A., Weaver, M., & Heine, L. W. (1998). Long-term transcutaneous electrical nerve stimulation (TENS) use: Impact on medication utilization and physical therapy costs. *Clinical Journal of Pain, 14,* 66–73.

Chaiken, S., & Baldwin, M. W. (1981). Affective-cognitive consistency and the effect of salient behavioral information on the self-perception of attitudes. *Journal of Personality and Social Psychology, 41,* 1–12.

Chamberlin, J. (2000, February). The student union. *Monitor on Psychology,* pp. 32–34.

Chan, A. S., Butters, N., & Salmon, D. P. (1997). The deterioration of semantic networks in patients with Alzheimer's disease: A cross-sectional study. *Neuropsychologia, 35,* 241–248.

Chandler, C. C. (1993). Accessing related events increases retroactive interference in a matching recognition test. *Journal of Experimental Psychology: Learning, Memory, and Cognition, 19,* 967–974.

Chao, R. K. (1994). Beyond parental control and authoritarian parenting style: Understanding Chinese parenting through the cultural notion of training. *Child Development, 65,* 1111–1119.

Chaplin, W. F., Phillips, J. B., Brown, J. D., Clanton, N. R., & Stein, J. L. (2000). Handshaking, gender, personality, and first impressions. *Journal of Personality and Social Psychology, 79,* 110–117.

Chapman, C. R., Oka, S., Bradshaw, D. H., Jacobson, R. C., & Donaldson, G. W. (1999). Phasic pupil dilation response to noxious stimulation in normal volunteers: Relationship to brain evoked potential and pain report. *Psychophysiology, 36,* 44–52.

Chase, W. G., & Simon, H. A. (1973). Perception in chess. *Cognitive Psychology, 4,* 55–81.

Chelette, T. L., Albery, W. B., Esken, R. L., & Tripp, L. D. (1998). Female exposure to high G: Performance of simulated flight after 24 hours of sleep deprivation. *Aviation, Space and Environmental Medicine, 69,* 862–868.

Chen, C., Lee, S.-Y., & Stevenson, H. W. (1995). Response style and cross-cultural comparisons of rating scales among East Asian and North American students. *Psychological Science, 6,* 170–175.

Chen, R. Y. L., & Ho, W. Y. (2000). A five-year longitudinal study of the regional cerebral metabolic changes of a schizophrenic patient from the first episode using Tc-99m HMPAO SPECT. *European Archives of Psychiatry and Clinical Neuroscience, 250,* 69–72.

Chen, S. H. A., & Bernard-Opitz, V. (1993). Comparison of personal and computer-assisted instruction for children with autism. *Mental Retardation, 31,* 368–376.

Cherney, I. D., & Ryalls, B. O. (1999). Gender-linked differences in the incidental memory of children and adults. *Journal of Experimental Child Psychology, 72,* 305–328.

Cherry, E. C. (1953). Some experiments on the recognition of speech with one and two ears. *Journal of the Acoustical Society of America, 25,* 975–979.

Cheryan, S., & Bodenhausen, G. V. (2000). When positive stereotypes threaten intellectual performance: The psychological hazards of "model minority" status. *Psychological Science, 11,* 399–402.

Chi, M. T. H., & Koeske, R. D. (1983). Network representation of a child's dinosaur knowledge. *Developmental Psychology, 19,* 29–39.

Chichilnisky, E. J., & Wandell, B. A. (1999). Trichromatic opponent color classification. *Vision Research, 39,* 3444–3458.

Child, I. L. (1985). Psychology and anomalous observations: The question of ESP in dreams. *American Psychologist, 40,* 1219–1230.

Child, M., Low, K. G., McCormick, C. M., & Cocciarella, A. (1996). Personal advertisements of male-to-female transsexuals, homosexual men, and heterosexuals. *Sex Roles, 34,* 447–455.

Chipuer, H. M., Rovine, M. J., & Plomin, R. (1990). LISREL modeling: Genetic and environmental influences on IQ revisited. *Intelligence, 14,* 11–29.

Chodorow, N. (1978). *The reproduction of mothering.* Berkeley: University of California Press.

Choi, I., Nisbett, R. E., & Norenzayan, A. (1999). Causal attribution across cultures: Variation and universality. *Psychological Bulletin, 125,* 47–63.

Choi, J. N., & Kim, M. U. (1999). The organizational application of groupthink and its limitations in organizations. *Journal of Applied Psychology, 84,* 297–306.

Choi, P. Y. L., & Pope, H. G. (1994). Violence toward women and illicit androgenic-anabolic steroid use. *Annals of Clinical Psychiatry, 6,* 21–25.

Choudhury, N., & Gorman, K. S. (1999). The relationship between reaction time and psychometric intelligence in a rural Guatemalan adolescent population. *International Journal of Psychology, 34,* 209–217.

Christensen, L. (1988). Deception in psychological research: When is its use justified? *Personality and Social Psychology Bulletin, 14,* 664–675.

Christianson, S. A., & Loftus, E. F. (1987). Memory for traumatic events. *Applied Cognitive Psychology, 1,* 225–239.

Christy, C. A., & Voigt, H. (1994). Bystander responses to public episodes of child abuse. *Journal of Applied Social Psychology, 24,* 824–847.

Chu, J. A. (2000). "Memories of childhood abuse: Dissociation, amnesia, and corroboration": Reply. *American Journal of Psychiatry, 157,* 1348–1349.

Cialdini, R. B., & Fultz, J. (1990). Interpreting the negative mood-helping literature via "mega"-analysis: A contrary view. *Psychological Bulletin, 107,* 210–214.

Cialdini, R. B., Brown, S. L., Lewis, B., P. Luce, C., & Neuberg, S. L. (1997). Reinterpreting the empathy-altruism relationship: When one into one equals oneness. *Journal of Personality and Social Psychology, 73,* 481–494.

Cialdini, R. B., Schaller, M., Houlihan, D., Arps, K., Fultz, J., & Beaman, A. L. (1987). Empathy-based helping: Is it selflessly motivated? *Journal of Personality and Social Psychology, 52,* 749–758.

Ciarrochi, J. V., Chan, A. Y.-C., & Caputi, P. (2000). A critical evaluation of the emotional intelligence construct. *Personality and Individual Differences, 28,* 539–561.

Cicerello, A., & Sheehan, E. P. (1995). Personal advertisements: A content analysis. *Journal of Social Behavior and Personality, 10,* 751–756.

Cicerone, C. M., & Hayhoe, M. M. (1990). The size of the pool for bleaching in human rod vision. *Vision Research, 30,* 693–697.

Claassen, N. C. W. (1997). Cultural differences, politics and test bias in South Africa. *European Review of Applied Psychology, 47,* 297–308.

Clark, D. M., Salkovskis, P. M., Hackmann, A., Wells, A., Ludgate, J., & Gelder, M. (1999). Brief cognitive therapy for panic disorder: A randomized controlled trial. *Journal of Consulting and Clinical Psychology, 67,* 583–589.

Clark, K. B., & Clark, M. P. (1947). Racial identification and preference in Negro children. In T. M. Newcomb & E. L. Hartley (Eds.), *Readings in social psychology* (pp. 169–178). New York: Holt.

Clark, L. A., Watson, D., & Reynolds, S. (1995). Diagnosis and classification of psychopathology: Challenges to the current system and future directions. *Annual Review of Psychology, 46,* 121–153.

Clark, R. D., & Word, L. E. (1974). Where is the apathetic bystander? Situational characteristics of the emergency. *Journal of Personality and Social Psychology, 29,* 279–287.

Clark, S. E., & Loftus, E. F. (1996). The construction of space alien abduction memories. *Psychological Inquiry, 7,* 140–143.

Cliffe, M. J. (1991). Behaviour modification by successive approximation: Saxon age examples from Bede. *British Journal of Clinical Psychology, 30,* 367–369.

Clore, G. L., Bray, R. M., Itkin, S. M., & Murphy, P. (1978). Interracial attitudes and behavior at a summer camp. *Journal of Personality and Social Psychology, 36,* 107–116.

Clutton-Brock, T. H., & Parker, G. A. (1995). Punishment in animal societies. *Nature, 373,* 209–216.

Cochran, D. Q. (1999). *Alabama v. Clarence Simmons: FBI "profiler" testimony to establish an essential element of capital murder. Law and Psychology Review, 23,* 69–89.

Cofer, C. N. (1985). Drives and motives. In G. A. Kimble & K. Schlesinger (Eds.), *Topics in the history of psychology* (Vol. 2, pp. 151–190). Hillsdale, NJ: Erlbaum.

Cofer, L. F., Grice, J. W., Sethre-Hofstad, L., Radi, C. J., Zimmerman, L. K., Palmer, Seal, & Santa Maria, G. (1999). Developmental perspectives on morningness-eveningness and social interactions. *Human Development, 42,* 169–198.

Cohen, D. B. (1979). *Sleep and dreaming: Origins, nature and functions.* New York: Pergamon Press.

Cohen, H. H., & Cohen, D. M. (1994). Psychophysical assessment of the perceived slipperiness of floor tile surfaces in a laboratory setting. *Journal of Safety Research, 25,* 19–26.

Coile, D. C., & Miller, N. E. (1984). How radical animal activists try to mislead humane people. *American Psychologist, 39,* 700–701.

Coke-Pepsi slugfest. (1976, July 26). *Time,* pp. 64–65.

Colegrove, F. W. (1899). Individual memories. *American Journal of Psychology, 10,* 228–255.

Coleman, P. K., & Karraker, K. H. (1998). Self-efficacy and parenting quality: Findings and future applications. *Developmental Review, 18,* 47–85.

Collaer, M. L., & Hines, M. (1995). Human behavioral sex differences: A role for gonadal hormones during early development? *Psychological Bulletin, 118,* 55–107.

Colligan, J. (1983). Musical creativity and social rules in four cultures. *Creative Child and Adult Quarterly, 8,* 39–44.

Collins, A. M., & Loftus, E. F. (1975). A spreading-activation theory of semantic processing. *Psychological Review, 82,* 407–428.

Collins, W. A., Maccoby, E. E., Steinberg, L., Hetherington, E. M., & Bornstein, M. H. (2000). Contemporary research on parenting: The case for nature and nurture. *American Psychologist, 55,* 218–232.

Coltraine, S., & Messineo, M. (2000). The perpetuation of subtle prejudice: Race and gender imagery in 1990s television advertising. *Sex Roles, 42,* 363–389.

Colvin, C. R., Block, J., & Funder, D. C. (1995). Overly positive evaluations and personality: Negative implications for mental health. *Journal of Personality and Social Psychology, 68,* 1152–1162.

Compton, M. T., & Nemeroff, C. B. (2000). The treatment of bipolar depression. *Journal of Clinical Psychiatry, 61,* 57–67.

Comuzzie, A. G., & Allison, D. B. (1998). The search for human obesity genes. *Science, 280,* 1374–1377.

Connors, A. (1988, February 5). At 91, she's stepping up in class. *Los Angeles Times,* p. 3.

Conrad, R. (1962). An association between memory errors and errors due to acoustic masking of speech. *Nature, 193,* 1314–1315.

Conway, M. A., Anderson, S. J., Larsen, S. F., & Donnelly, C. M. (1994). The formation of flashbulb memories. *Memory and Cognition, 22,* 326–343.

Cook, M., & Mineka, S. (1989). Observational conditioning of fear to fear-relevant versus fear-irrelevant stimuli in rhesus monkeys. *Journal of Abnormal Psychology, 98,* 448–459.

Coon, D. J. (1982). Eponymy, obscurity, Twitmyer, and Pavlov. *Journal of the History of the Behavioral Sciences, 18,* 255–262.

Coon, D. J. (2000). Salvaging the self in a world without soul: William James's *The principles of psychology. History of Psychology, 3,* 83–103.

Coram, G. J. (1995). A Rorschach analysis of violent murderers and nonviolent offenders. *European Journal of Psychological Assessment, 11,* 81–88.

Coren, S. (1996). *Sleep thieves: An eye-opening exploration into the science and mysteries of sleep.* New York: Free Press.

Coren, S., & Halpern, D. F. (1991). Left-handedness: A marker for decreased survival fitness. *Psychological Bulletin, 109,* 90–106.

Corkin, S., Amaral, D. G., Gonzalez, R. G., Johnson, K. A., & Hyman, B. T. (1997). H. M.'s medial temporal lobe lesion: Findings from magnetic resonance imaging. *Journal of Neuroscience, 17,* 3964–3979.

Corr, C. A. (1993). Coping with dying: Lessons that we should and should not learn from the work of Elisabeth Kübler-Ross. *Death Studies, 17,* 69–83.

Corter, J. E., & Gluck, M. A. (1992). Explaining basic categories: Feature predictability and information. *Psychological Bulletin, 111,* 291–303.

Cortes, U., Sanchez-Marre, M., Ceccaroni, L., R-Roda, I., & Poch, M. (2000). Artificial intelligence and environmental decision support systems. *Applied Intelligence,13,* 77–91.

Costa, E. (1998). From GABA-sub(A) receptor diversity emerges a unified vision of GABAergic inhibition. *Annual Review of Pharmacology and Toxicology, 38,* 321–350.

Cottraux, J., Note, I., Albuisson, E., Yao, S. N., et al. (2000). Cognitive behavior therapy versus supportive therapy in social phobia: A randomized controlled trial. *Psychotherapy and Psychosomatics, 69,* 137–146.

Cousins, N. (1983). *The healing heart: Antidotes to panic and helplessness.* New York: W. W. Norton.

Cowles, M. (1989). *Statistics in psychology: An historical perspective.* Hillsdale, NJ: Erlbaum.

Cowley, G. (1995, November 6). Melatonin mania. *Newsweek,* pp. 60–63.

Coyle, J. T., & Schwarcz, R. (2000). Mind glue: Implications of glial cell biology for psychiatry. *Archives of General Psychiatry, 57,* 90–93.

Craig, C. L. (1994). Limits to learning: Effects of predator pattern and colour on perception and avoidance-learning by prey. *Animal Behaviour, 47,* 1087–1099.

Craik, F. I. M., & Tulving, E. (1975). Depth of processing and the retention of words in episodic memory. *Journal of Experimental Psychology: General, 104,* 268–294.

Cramer, P. (1999). Future directions for the Thematic Apperception Test. *Journal of Personality Assessment, 72,* 74–92.

Cramer, P. (2000). Defense mechanisms in psychology today: Further processes for adaptation. *American Psychologist, 55,* 637–646.

Cramer, P. (2000). Development of identity: Gender makes a difference. *Journal of Research in Personality, 34,* 42–72.

Crano, W. D., & Prislin, R. (1995). Components of vested interest and attitude-behavior consistency. *Basic and Applied Social Psychology, 17,* 1–21.

Crawford, H. J., Knebel, T., & Vendemia, J. M. C. (1998). The nature of hypnotic analgesia: Neurophysiological foundation and evidence. *Contemporary Hypnosis, 15,* 22–33.

Crespo, C. J., Smit, E., Andersen, R. E., Carter-Pokras, O., & Ainsworth, B. E. (2000). Race/ethnicity, social class and their relation to physical inactivity during leisure time: Results from the Third National Health and Nutrition Examination Survey, 1988–1994. *American Journal of Preventive Medicine, 18,* 46–53.

Crestani, F., Lorez, M., Baer, K., et al. (1999). Decreased GABA-sub(A)-receptor clustering results in enhanced anxiety and a bias for threat cues. *Nature Neuroscience, 2,* 833–839.

Crews, F. T. (1994). Amyloid b protein disruption of cholinergic and growth factor phospholipase C signals could underlie cognitive and neurodegenerative aspects of Alzheimer's disease. *Neurobiology of Aging, 15,* S95–S96.

Crocker, J., Alloy, L. B., & Kayne, N. T. (1988). Attributional style, depression, and perceptions of consensus for events. *Journal of Personality and Social Psychology, 54,* 840–846.

Crohan, S. E. (1992). Marital happiness and spousal consensus on beliefs about marital conflict: A longitudinal investigation. *Journal of Social and Personal Relationships, 9,* 89–102.

Crook, T., & Eliot, J. (1980). Parental death during childhood and adult depression: A critical review of the literature. *Psychological Bulletin, 87,* 252–259.

Crozier, J. B. (1997). Absolute pitch: Practice makes perfect, the earlier the better. *Psychology of Music, 25,* 110–119.

Cuellar, I., Roberts, R. E., Nyberg, B., & Maldonado, R. E. (1997). Ethnic identity and acculturation in a young adult Mexican-origin population. *Journal of Community Psychology, 25,* 535–549.

Cuijpers, P. (1997). Bibliotherapy in unipolar depression: A meta-analysis. *Journal of Behavior Therapy and Experimental Psychiatry, 28,* 139–14.

Cunningham, M. R., Roberts, A. R., Barbee, A. P., & Druen, P. B. (1995). "Their ideas of beauty are, on the whole, the same as ours": Consistency and variability in the cross-cultural perception of female physical attractiveness. *Journal of Personality and Social Psychology, 68,* 261–279.

Curcio, C. A., Sloan, K. R., Jr., Packer, O., Hendrickson, A. E., & Kalina, R. E. (1987). Distribution of cones in human and monkey retina: Individual variability and radial asymmetry. *Science, 236,* 579–582.

Curran, W., & Johnston, A. (1994). Integration of shading and texture cues: Testing the linear model. *Vision Research, 34,* 1863–1874.

Cutting, J. E. (1987). Perception and information. *Annual Review of Psychology, 38,* 61–90.

Cutting, L. P., & Docherty, N. M. (2000). Schizophrenia outpatients' perceptions of their parents: Is expressed emotion a factor? *Journal of Abnormal Psychology, 109,* 266–272.

Cytowic, R. E. (1989). Synesthesia and mapping of subjective sensory dimensions. *Neurology, 39,* 849–850.

Czeisler, C. A., Moore-Ede, M. C., & Coleman, R. M. (1982). Rotating shift work schedules that disrupt sleep are improved by applying circadian principles. *Science, 217,* 460–463.

D'Esposito, M., Aguirre, G. K., Zarahn, E., et al. (1998). Functional MRI studies of spatial and nonspatial working memory. *Cognitive Brain Research, 7,* 1–13.

Dahlen, E. R., & Deffenbacher, J. L. (2000). A partial component analysis of Beck's cognitive therapy for the treatment of general anger. *Journal of Cognitive Psychotherapy, 14,* 77–95.

Dahlstrom, W. G. (1993). Tests: Small samples, large consequences. *American Psychologist, 48,* 393–399.

Dalton, M., & Wilson, M. (2000). The relationship of the five-factor model of personality to job performance for a group of Middle Eastern expatriate managers. *Journal of Cross-Cultural Psychology, 31,* 250–258.

Dammann, E. J. (1997). "The myth of mental illness": Continuing controversies and their implications for mental health professionals. *Clinical Psychology Review, 17,* 733–756.

Dance, K. A., & Neufeld, R. W. J. (1988). Aptitude-treatment interaction research in the clinical setting: A review of attempts to dispel the "patient uniformity" myth. *Psychological Bulletin, 104,* 192–213.

Danckert, J., & Goodale, M. A. (2000). Blindsight: A conscious route to unconscious vision. *Current Biology, 10,* R64–R67.

Daniels, M. (1982). The development of the concept of self-actualization in the writings of Abraham Maslow. *Current Psychological Reviews, 2,* 61–75.

Danziger, K. (1994). Does the history of psychology have a future? *Theory and Psychology, 4,* 467–484.

Darch, C. B., Carnine, D. W., & Kameenui, E. J. (1986). The role of graphic organizers and social structure in content area instruction. *Journal of Reading Behavior, 18,* 275–295.

Darley, J. M., & Fazio, R. H. (1980). Expectancy confirmation processes arising in the social interaction sequence. *American Psychologist, 35,* 867–881.

Darley, J. M., & Latané, B. (1968). Bystander intervention in emergencies: Diffusion of responsibilities. *Journal of Personality and Social Psychology, 8,* 377–383.

Darling, N., & Steinberg, L. (1993). Parenting style as context: An integrative model. *Psychological Bulletin, 113,* 487–496.

Darlington, R. B. (1996). On race and intelligence: A commentary on affirmative action, the evolution of intelligence, the regression analyses in *The Bell Curve,* and Jensen's two-level theory. *Psychology, Public Policy, and Law, 2,* 635–645.

Darwin, C. (1859/1975). *On the origin of species.* New York: W. W. Norton.

Darwin, C. (1872/1965). *The expression of the emotions in man and animals.* Chicago: University of Chicago Press.

Daughton, D. M., Fortmann, S. P., Glover, E. D., Hatsukami, D. K., et al. (1999). The smoking cessation efficacy of varying doses of nicotine patch delivery systems 4 to 5 years post-quit day. *Preventive Medicine: An International Devoted to Practice and Theory, 28,* 113–118.

David, A. S., Woodruff, P. W. R., Howard, R., & Mellers, J. D. C. (1996). Auditory hallucinations inhibit exogenous activation of auditory association cortex. *Neuroreport, 7,* 932–936.

Davidson, M., Stern, R. G., Bierer, L. M., & Horvath, T. B. (1991). Cholinergic strategies in the treatment of Alzheimer's disease. *Acta Psychiatrica Scandinavia, 83,* 47–50.

Davidson, R. J., Marshall, J. R., Tomarken, A. J., & Henriques, J. B. (2000). While a phobic waits: Regional brain electrical and autonomic activity in social phobics during anticipation of public speaking. *Biological Psychiatry, 47,* 85–95.

Davies, G., & Alonso-Quecuty, M. (1997). Cultural factors in the recall of a witnessed event. *Memory, 5,* 601–614.

Davies, I. R. L. (1998). A study of colour grouping in three languages: A test of linguistic relativity hypothesis. *British Journal of Psychology, 89,* 433–452.

Davies, M. F. (1997). Private self-consciousness and the acceptance of personality feedback: Confirmatory processing in the evaluation of general vs. specific self-information. *Journal of Research in Personality, 31,* 78–92.

Davies, M., Stankov, L., & Roberts, R. D. (1998). Emotional intelligence: In search of an elusive construct. *Journal of Personality and Social Psychology, 75,* 989–1015.

Davies, P. T., & Cummings, E. M. (1994). Marital conflict and child adjustment: An emotional security hypothesis. *Psychological Bulletin, 116,* 387–411.

Davis, A., & Eels, K. (1953). *Davis-Eels games.* Yonkers, NY: World Book.

Davis, C., Kennedy, S. H., Ravelski, E., & Dionne, M. (1994). The role of physical activity in the development and maintenance of eating disorders. *Psychological Medicine, 24,* 957–967.

Davis, H., & Memmott, J. (1982). Counting behavior in animals: A critical evaluation. *Psychological Bulletin, 92,* 547–571.

Davis, J. M., Sargent, R. G., Brayboy, T. D., & Bartoli, W. P. (1992). Thermogenic effects of pre-prandial and post-prandial exercise in obese females. *Addictive Behaviors, 17,* 185–190.

Davis, K. D., Lozano, A. M., Manduch, M., et al. (1999). Thalamic relay site for cold perception in humans. *Journal of Neurophysiology, 81,* 1970–1973.

Davis, P. J. (1999). Gender differences in autobiographical memory for childhood emotional experiences. *Journal of Personality and Social Psychology, 76,* 498–510.

Davis, S. F., Thomas, R. L., & Weaver, M. S. (1982). Psychology's contemporary and all-time notables: Student, faculty, and chairperson viewpoints. *Bulletin of the Psychonomic Society, 20,* 3–6.

Davison, K. P., Pennebaker, J. W., & Dickerson, S. S. (2000). Who talks? The social psychology of illness support groups. *American Psychologist, 55,* 205–217.

Day, N. L., & Richardson, G. A. (1994). Comparative teratogenicity of alcohol and other drugs. *Alcohol Health and Research World, 18,* 42–48.

De Bellis, M. D., Casey, B. J., Dahl, R. E., Birmaher, B., et al. (2000). A pilot study of amygdala volumes in pediatric generalized anxiety disorder. *Biological Psychiatry, 48,* 51–57.

de Castro, J. M. (1999). Heritability of hunger relationships with food intake in free-living humans. *Physiology and Behavior, 67,* 249–258.

de Castro, J. M. (1993). Genetic influences on daily intake and meal patterns of humans. *Physiology and Behavior, 53,* 777–782.

de Gelder, B., & Rouw, R. (2000). Structural encoding precludes recognition of face parts in prosopagnosia. *Cognitive Neuropsychology, 17,* 89–102.

de Graaf, C., Polet, P., & van Staveren, W. A. (1994). Sensory perception and pleasantness of food flavors in elderly subjects. *Journals of Gerontology, 49,* P93–P99.

de Jong, P. J., & Merckelbach, H. (1997). No convincing evidence for a biological preparedness explanation of phobias. *Behavioral and Brain Sciences, 20,* 362–363.

De la Fuente, J. M., Goldman, S., Stanus, E., Vizuete, C., Morlan, I., Bobes, J., & Mendlewicz, J. (1997). Brain glucose metabolism in borderline personality disorder. *Journal of Psychiatric Research, 31,* 531–541.

De Nil, L. F., Kroll, R. M., Kapur, S., & Houle, S. (2000). A positron-emission tomography study of silent and oral single-word reading in stuttering and nonstuttering adults. *Journal of Speech, Language, and Hearing Research, 43,* 1038–1053.

De Pascalis, V. (1999). Psychophysiological correlates of hypnosis and hypnotic susceptibility. *International Journal of Clinical and Experimental Hypnosis, 47,* 117–143.

De Raad, B., & Doddema-Winsemius, M. (1999). Instincts and personality. *Personality and Individual Differences, 27,* 293–305.

de Valois, R. L., Abramov, I., & Jacobs, G. H. (1966). Analysis of response patterns of LGN cells. *Journal of the Optical Society of America, 56,* 966–977.

De Wolff, M., & van IJzendoorn, M. H. (1997). Sensitivity and attachment: A meta-analysis on parental antecedents of infant attachment. *Child Development, 68,* 571–591.

Deahl, M. (1991). Cannabis and memory loss. *Bristish Journal of Addiction, 86,* 249–252.

Deaux, K. (1985). Sex and gender. *Annual Review of Psychology. 36,* 49–81.

DeCarvalho, R. J. (1992). The institutionalization of humanistic psychology. *Humanistic Psychology, 20,* 124–135.

DeCharms, R., & Moeller, G. H. (1962). Values expressed in American children's readers: 1800–1950. *Journal of Abnormal and Social Psychology, 64,* 136–142.

Deci, E. L., Koestner, R., & Ryan, R. M. (1999). A meta-analytic review of experiments determining the effects of extrinsic rewards on intrinsic motivation. *Psychological Bulletin, 125,* 627–668.

Degel, J., & Koester, E. P. (1999). Odors: Implicit memory and performance effects. *Chemical Senses, 24,* 317–325.

Dehaene, S., Spelke, E., Pinel, P., Stanescu, R., & Tsivkin, S. (1999). Sources of mathematical thinking: Behavioral and brain-imaging evidence. *Science, 284,* 970–974.

Dehue, T. (2000). From deception trials to control reagents: The introduction of the control group about a century ago. *American Psychologist, 55,* 264–268.

Delahanty, D. L., Liegey Dougall, A., Hayward, M., et al. (2000). Gender differences in cardiovascular and natural killer cell reactivity to acute stress following a hassling task. *International Journal of Behavioral Medicine, 7,* 19–27.

Delgado, P. L., & Moreno, F. A. (2000). Role of norepinephrine in depression. *Journal of Clinical Psychiatry, 61,* 5–12.

DeLongis, A., Folkman, S., & Lazarus, R. S. (1988). The impact of daily stress on health and mood: Psychological and social resources as mediators. *Journal of Personality and Social Psychology, 54,* 486–495.

Dember, W. N., & Bagwell, M. (1985). A history of perception. In G. A. Kimble & K. Schlesinger (Eds.), *Topics in the history of psychology* (Vol. 1, pp. 261–304). Hillsdale, NJ: Erlbaum.

Dement, W. C. (1960). The effect of dream deprivation. *Science, 131,* 1705–1707.

Dement, W. C., & Wolpert, E. (1958). The relation of eye movements, body motility, and external stimuli to dream content. *Journal of Experimental Psychology, 53,* 543–553.

Dempster, F. N. (1985). Proactive interference in sentence recall: Topic similarity effects and individual differences. *Memory and Cognition, 13,* 81–89.

DeMulder, E. K., Denham, S., Schmidt, M., & Mitchell, J. (2000). Q-sort assessment of attachment security during the preschool years: Links from home to school. *Developmental Psychology, 36,* 274–282.

DeNeve, K. M., & Cooper, H. (1998). The happy personality: A meta-analysis of 137 personality traits and subjective well-being. *Psychological Bulletin, 124,* 197–229.

DeNisi, A. S., & Peters, L. H. (1996). Organization of information in memory and the performance appraisal process: Evidence from the field. *Journal of Applied Psychology, 81,* 717–737.

Denmark, F. L. (1980). Psyche: From rocking the cradle to rocking the boat. *American Psychologist, 35,* 1057–1065.

Denmark, F. L. (1998). Women and psychology: An international perspective. *American Psychologist, 53*(4), 465–473.

Deouell, L. Y., Haemaelaeinen, H., & Bentin, S. (2000). Unilateral neglect after right-hemisphere damage: Contributions from event-related potentials. *Audiology and Neuro-Otology, 5,* 225–234.

DeShon, R. P., Smith, M. R., Chan, D., & Schmitt, N. (1998). Can racial differences in cognitive test performance be reduced by presenting problems in a social context? *Journal of Applied Psychology, 83,* 438–451.

Detterman, D. K. (1999). The psychology of mental retardation. *International Review of Psychiatry, 11,* 26–33.

Deuser, W. E., & Anderson, C. A. (1995). Controllability attributions and learned helplessness: Some methodological and conceptual problems. *Basic and Applied Social Psychology, 16,* 297–318.

Devine, D., & Forehand, R. (1996). Cascading toward divorce: The roles of marital and child factors. *Journal of Consulting and Clinical Psychology, 64,* 424–427.

Devine, D. P., & Spanos, N. P. (1990). Effectiveness of maximally different cognitive strategies and expectancy in attenuation of reported pain. *Journal of Personality and Social Psychology, 58,* 672–678.

Devine, P. G., & Malpass, R. S. (1985). Orienting strategies in differential face recognition. *Personality and Social Psychology Bulletin, 11,* 33–40.

Dewsbury, D. A. (1990). Early interactions between animal psychologists and animal activists and the founding of the APA Committee on Precautions in Animal Experimentation. *American Psychologist, 45,* 315–327.

Dewsbury, D. A. (1996). Beatrix Tugendhat Gardner (1933–1995). *American Psychologist, 51,* 1332.

Dewsbury, D. A. (2000). Comparative cognition in the 1930s. *Psychonomic Bulletin and Review, 7,* 267–283.

Diaconis, P. (1978). Statistical problems in ESP research. *Science, 201,* 131–136.

Diamond, L. M. (1998). Development of sexual orientation among adolescent and young adult women. *Developmental Psychology, 34,* 1085–1095.

Diamond, L. M. (2000). Sexual identity, attractions, and behavior among young sexual-minority women over a 2–year period. *Developmental Psychology, 36,* 241–250.

Diamond, M. (1993). Homosexuality and bisexuality in different populations. *Archives of Sexual Behavior, 22,* 291–310.

Diamond, M. C. (1988). *Enriching heredity: The impact of the environment on the anatomy of the brain.* New York: Free Press.

Dickson, D. (1984). Edinburgh sets up parapsychology chair. *Science, 223,* 1274.

Diego, M. A., Jones, N. A., Field, T., Hernandez-Reif, M., Schanberg, S., Kuhn, C., McAdam, V., Galamaga, R., &

Galamaga, M. (1998). Aromatherapy positively affects mood, EEG patterns of alertness and math computations. *International Journal of Neuroscience, 96,* 217–224.

Diener, E. (1984). Subjective well-being. *Psychological Bulletin, 95,* 542–575.

Diener, E. (2000). Subjective well-being: The science of happiness and a proposal for a national index. *American Psychologist, 55,* 34–43.

Diener, E., Colvin, C. R., Pavot, W. G., & Allman, A. (1991). The psychic costs of intense positive affect. *Journal of Personality and Social Psychology, 61,* 492–503.

Diener, E., Diener, M., & Diener, C. (1995). Factors predicting the subjective well-being of nations. *Journal of Personality and Social Psychology, 69,* 851–864.

Diener, E., & Fujita, F. (1995). Resources, personal strivings, and subjective well-being: A nomothetic and idiographic approach. *Journal of Personality and Social Psychology, 68,* 926–935.

Diener, E., Gohm, C. L., Suh, E., & Oishi, S. (2000). Similarity of the relations between marital status and subjective well-being across cultures. *Journal of Cross-Cultural Psychology, 31,* 419–436.

Diener, E., Sandvik, E., Seidlitz, L., & Diener, M. (1993). The relationship between income and subjective well-being: Relative or absolute? *Social Indicators Research, 28,* 195–223.

Diener, E., Wolsic, B., & Fujita, F. (1995). Physical attractiveness and subjective well-being. *Journal of Personality and Social Psychology, 69,* 120–129.

DiLalla, D. L., Carey, G., Gottesman, I. I., & Bouchard, T. J., Jr. (1996). Heritability of MMPI personality indicators of psychopathology in twins reared apart. *Journal of Abnormal Psychology, 105,* 491–499.

DiLorenzo, T. M., Bargman, E. P., Stucky-Ropp, R., et al. (1999). Long-term effects of aerobic exercise on psychological outcomes. *Preventive Medicine, 28,* 75–85.

Dimberg, U., Thunberg, M., & Elmehed, K. (2000). Unconscious facial reactions to emotional facial expressions. *Psychological Science, 11,* 86–89.

Dimitrov, M., Phipps, M., Zahn, T. P., & Grafman, J. (1999). A thoroughly modern Gage. *Neurocase, 5,* 345–354.

Dindia, K., & Allen, M. (1992). Sex differences in self-disclosure: A meta-analysis. *Psychological Bulletin, 112,* 106–124.

Dishman, R. J., & Gettman, L. R. (1980). Psychobiologic influences on exercise adherence. *Journal of Sport Psychology, 2,* 295–310.

Distal, H., Ayabe-Kanamura, S., Martinez-Gomez, M., Schicker, I., Kobayakawa, T., Saito, S., & Hudson, R. (1999). Perception of everyday odors: Correlations between intensity, familiarity and strength of hedonic judgement. *Chemical Senses, 24,* 191–199.

Dixon, N. F., & Henley, S. H. (1991). Unconscious perception: Possible implications of data from academic research for clinical practice. *Journal of Nervous and Mental Disease, 179,* 243–252.

Doane, J. A., West, K. L., Goldstein, M. J., Rodnick, E. H., & Jones, J. E. (1981). Parental communication deviance and affective style: Predictors of subsequent schizophrenia spectrum disorders in vulnerable adolescents. *Archives of General Psychiatry, 38,* 679–685.

Dobbins, A. C., Jeo, R. M., Fiser, J., & Allman, J. M. (1998). Distance modulation of neural activity in the visual cortex. *Science, 281,* 552–555.

Docherty, N. M., Hall, M. J., Gordinier, S. W., & Cutting, L. P. (2000). Conceptual sequencing and disordered speech in schizophrenia. *Schizophrenia Bulletin, 26,* 723–735.

Doell, R. G. (1995). Sexuality in the brain. *Journal of Homosexuality, 28,* 345–354.

Doidge, N. (1997). Empirical evidence for the efficacy of psychoanalytic psychotherapies and psychoanalysis: An overview. *Psychoanalytic Inquiry* [Suppl.], 102–150.

Dollard, J., Doob, I. W., Miller, N. E., Mowrer, O. H., & Sears, R. R. (1939). *Frustration and aggression.* New York: McGraw-Hill.

Dolliver, R. H. (1995). Carl Rogers's personality theory and psychotherapy as a reflection of his life and personality. *Journal of Humanistic Psychology, 35,* 111–128.

Dominguez, M. M., & Carton, J. S. (1997). The relationship between self-actualization and parenting style. *Journal of Social Behavior and Personality, 12,* 1093–1100.

Domino, G. (1992). Cooperation and competition in Chinese and American children. *Journal of Cross Cultural Psychology, 23,* 456–467.

Donderi, D. C. (1994). Visual acuity, color vision, and visual search performance at sea. *Human Factors, 36,* 129–144.

Donohew, L., Zimmerman, R., Cupp, P. S., Novak, S., Colon, S., & Abell, R. (2000). Sensation seeking, impulsive decision-making, and risky sex: Implications for risk-taking and design of interventions. *Personality and Individual Differences, 28,* 1079–1091.

Donovan, J. J., & Radosevich, D. J. (1999). A meta-analytic review of the distribution of practice effect: Now you see it, now you don't. *Journal of Applied Psychology, 84,* 795–805.

Donovan, R. J., & Jalleh, G. (1999). Positively versus negatively framed product attributes: The influence of involvement. *Psychology and Marketing, 16,* 613–630.

Donovan, W. L., Leavitt, L. A., & Walsh, R. O. (1997). Cognitive set and coping strategy affect mother's sensitivity to infant cries. *Child Development, 68,* 760–772.

Dorward, F. M. C., & Day, R. H. (1997). Loss of 3–D shape constancy in interior spaces: The basis of the Ames-room illusion. *Perception, 26,* 707–718.

Dougherty, D. M., Cherek, D. R., & Bennett, R. H. (1996). The effects of alcohol on the aggressive responding of women. *Journal of Studies on Alcohol, 57,* 178–186.

Dovidio, J. F., Kawakami, K., Johnson, C., Johnson, B., & Howard, A. (1997). On the nature of prejudice: Automatic and controlled processes. *Journal of Experimental Social Psychology, 33,* 510–540.

Downey, G., Freitas, A. L., Michaelis, B., & Khouri, H. (1998). The self-fulfilling prophecy in close relationships: Rejection sensitivity and rejection by romantic partners. *Journal of Personality and Social Psychology, 75,* 545–560.

Doyle, A. C. (1930). *The complete Sherlock Holmes.* Garden City, NY: Doubleday.

Draguns, J. G. (1995). Cultural influences upon psychopathology: Clinical and practical implications. *Journal of Social Distress and the Homeless, 4,* 79–103.

Dressler, W. W., Bindon, J. R., & Neggers, Y. H. (1998). John Henryism, gender, and arterial blood pressure in an African American community. *Psychosomatic Medicine, 60,* 620–624.

Drevets, W. C., Burton, H., Videen, T. O., & Snyder, A. Z. (1995). Blood flow changes in human somatosensory cortex during anticipated stimulation. *Nature, 373,* 249–251.

Drigotas, S. M. (1993). Similarity revisited: A comparison of similarity-attraction versus dissimilarity-repulsion. *British Journal of Social Psychology, 32,* 365–377.

Driskell, J. E., Willis, R. P., & Copper, C. (1992). Effect of overlearning on retention. *Journal of Applied Psychology, 77,* 615–622.

Droesler, J. (2000). An *n*-dimensional Weber law and the corresponding Fechner law. *Journal of Mathematical Psychology, 44,* 330–335.

Droste, C., Greenlee, M. W., Schreck, M., & Roskamm, H. (1991). Experimental pain thresholds and plasma beta-endorphin levels during exercise. *Medicine and Science in Sports and Exercise, 23,* 334–342.

Dryer, D. C., & Horowitz, L. M. (1997). When do opposites attract? Interpersonal complementarity versus similarity. *Journal of Personality and Social Psychology, 72,* 592–603.

Dubner, R., & Bennett, G. J. (1983). Spinal and trigeminal mechanisms of nociception. *Annual Review of Neuroscience, 6,* 381–418.

Dudchenko, P. A., & Eichenbaum, H. (1999). The global record of memory in hippocampal neuronal activity. *Nature, 397,* 613–616.

Duffy, J. F. (2000, May 9). New Hope bids farewell to "Mother." *Intelligencer Record,* pp. A1, A4.

Duncan, J., Seitz, R. J., Kolodny, J., Bor, D., Herzog, H., Ahmed, A., Newell, F. N., & Emslie, H. (2000). A neural basis for general intelligence. *Science, 289,* 457–460.

Dunn, J. (1993). Psychic conflict and the external world in Freud's light of his adherence to Darwin. *International Journal of Psychoanalysis, 74,* 231–240.

Durbin, D. L., Darling, N., Steinberg, L., & Brown, B. B. (1993). Parenting style and peer group membership among European-American adolescents. *Journal of Research on Adolescence, 3,* 87–100.

Durlak, J. A., & Wells, A. M. (1997). Primary prevention mental health programs for children and adolescents: A meta-analytic review. *American Journal of Community Psychology, 25,* 115–152.

Durlak, J. A., & Wells, A. M. (1998). Evaluation of indicated preventive intervention (secondary prevention) mental health programs for children and adolescents. *American Journal of Community Psychology, 26,* 775–802.

Dutton, D. G., & Aron, A. P. (1974). Some evidence for heightened sexual attraction under conditions of high anxiety. *Journal of Personality and Social Psychology, 30,* 510–517.

Dworkin, B. R., & Miller, N. E. (1986). Failure to replicate visceral learning in the acute curarized rat preparation. *Behavioral Neuroscience, 100,* 299–314.

Dyer, C. A. (1999). Pathophysiology of phenylketonuria. *Mental Retardation and Developmental Disabilities Research Reviews, 5,* 104–112.

Dykes, B. (2000). Problems in defining cross-cultural "kinds of homosexuality"— and a solution. *Journal of Homosexuality, 38,* 1–18.

Eagle, M. (1997). Contributions of Erik Erikson. *Psychoanalytic Review, 84,* 337–347.

Eagly, A. H. (1983). Gender and social influence: A social psychological analysis. *American Psychologist, 38,* 971–981.

Eagly, A. H. (1995). The science and politics of comparing women and men. *American Psychologist, 50,* 145–158.

Eagly, A. H., & Crowley, M. (1986). Gender and helping behavior: A meta-analytic review of the social psychology literature. *Psychological Bulletin, 100,* 283–308.

Eagly, A. H., & Steffen, V. J. (1986). Gender and aggressive behavior: A meta-analytic review of the social psychological literature. *Psychological Bulletin, 100,* 309–330.

Eagly, A. H., & Warren, R. (1976). Intelligence, comprehension, and opinion change. *Journal of Personality and Social Psychology, 44,* 226–242.

Earle, T. L., Linden, W., & Weinberg, J. (1999). Differential effects of harassment on cardiovascular and salivary cortisol stress reactivity and recovery in women and men. *Journal of Psychosomatic Research, 46,* 125–141.

Eaves, L. J., Silberg, J. L., Maes, H. H., Simonoff, E., et al. (1997). Genetics and developmental psychopathology: 2. The main effects of genes and environment on behavioral problems in the Virginia Twin Study of Adolescent Behavioral Development. *Journal of Child Psychology and Psychiatry and Allied Disciplines, 38,* 965–980.

Ebbeck, V., & Weiss, M. R. (1988). The arousal-performance relationship: Task characteristics and performance measures in track and field athletics. *Sport Psychologist, 2,* 13–27.

Ebbinghaus, H. (1885/1913). *Memory: A contribution to experimental psychology.* New York: Columbia University Press.

Ecenbarger, W. (1987, June 4). The forgotten sense. *Philadelphia Inquirer Magazine,* pp. 24–26, 34–35.

Eckerman, C. O., Davis, C. C., & Didow, S. M. (1989). Toddlers' emerging ways of achieving social coordinations with a peer. *Child Development, 60,* 440–453.

Eckert, E. D., Bouchard, T. J., Bohlen, J., & Heston, L. L. (1986). Homosexuality in monozygotic twins reared apart. *British Journal of Psychiatry, 148,* 421–425.

Edeline, J. M., & Weinberger, N. M. (1991). Subcortical adaptive filtering in the auditory system: Associative receptive field plasticity in the dorsal medial geniculate body. *Behavioral Neuroscience, 105,* 154–175.

Edelmann, R. J., & Golombok, S. (1989). Stress and reproductive failure. *Journal of Reproductive and Infant Psychology, 7,* 79–86.

Edinger, J. D., & Radtke, R. A. (1993). Use of in vivo desensitization to treat a patient's claustrophobic response to nasal CPAP. *Sleep, 16,* 678–680.

Edwards, S., & Launder, C. (2000). Investigating muscularity concerns in male body image: Development of the Swansea Muscularity Attitudes Questionnaire. *International Journal of Eating Disorders, 28,* 120–124.

Egan, K. J., Carr, J. E., Hunt, D. D., & Adamson, R. (1988). Endogenous opiate system and systematic desensitization. *Journal of Consulting and Clinical Psychology, 56,* 287–291.

Eich, J. E. (1980). The cue-dependent nature of state-dependent retrieval. *Memory and Cognition, 8,* 157–173.

Eich, J. E., Weingartner, H., Stillman, R. C., & Gillin, J. C. (1975). State-dependent accessibility of retrieval cues in the retention of a categorized list. *Journal of Verbal Learning and Verbal Behavior, 14,* 408–417.

Eichenbaum, H. (1997). Declarative memory: Insights from cognitive neurobiology. *Annual Review of Psychology, 48,* 547–572.

Eisdorfer, C. (1983). Conceptual models of aging: The challenge of a new frontier. *American Psychologist, 38,* 197–202.

Eisenberg, N., & Lennon, R. (1983). Sex differences in empathy and related capacities. *Psychological Bulletin, 94,* 100–131.

Ekman, P. (1992). Facial expressions of emotion: New findings, new questions. *Psychological Science, 3,* 34–38.

Ekman, P., & Friesen, W. V. (1971). Constants across cultures in the face and emotion. *Journal of Personality and Social Psychology, 17,* 124–129.

Ekman, P., Davidson, R. J., & Friesen, W. V. (1990). The Duchenne smile: Emotional expression and brain physiology: 2. *Journal of Personality and Social Psychology, 58,* 342–353.

Ekman, P., Friesen, W. V., & Bear, J. (1984, May). The international language of gestures. *Psychology Today,* pp. 64–69.

Ekman, P., Friesen, W. V., O'Sullivan, M., Chan, A., et al. (1987). Universals and cultural differences in the judgments of facial expressions of emotion. *Journal of Personality and Social Psychology, 53,* 712–717.

Ekman, P., Levenson, R. W., & Friesen, W. V. (1983). Autonomic nervous system activity distinguishes among emotions. *Science, 221,* 1208–1210.

Elaad, E. (1990). Detection of guilty knowledge in real-life criminal investigations. *Journal of Applied Psychology, 75,* 521–529.

Elaad, E. (1997). Polygraph examiner awareness of crime-relevant information and the Guilty Knowledge Test. *Law and Human Behavior, 21,* 107–120.

Elder, C. (1997). What does test bias have to do with fairness? *Language Testing, 14,* 261–277.

Elkind, D. (1996). Inhelder and Piaget on adolescence and adulthood: A postmodern appraisal. *Psychological Science, 7,* 216–220.

Elkins, R. L. (1987). An experimenter effect on place avoidance learning of selectively-bred taste-aversion prone and resistant rats. *Medical Science Research: Psychology and Psychiatry, 15,* 1181–1182.

Ellenberger, H. F. (1970). *The discovery of the unconscious: The history and evolution of dynamic psychiatry.* New York: Basic Books.

Ellis, A. (1962). *Reason and emotion in psychotherapy.* New York: Lyle Stuart.

Ellis, A. (1996). The treatment of morbid jealousy: A rational emotive behavior therapy approach. *Journal of Cognitive Psychotherapy, 10,* 23–33.

Ellis, A. (1997). Using rational emotive behavior therapy techniques to cope with disability. *Professional Psychology: Research and Practice, 28,* 17–22.

Ellis, A. (1999). Why rational-emotive therapy to rational emotive behavior therapy? *Psychotherapy, 36,* 154–159.

Ellis, L. (1998). The evolution of attitudes about social stratification: Why many people (including social scientists) are morally outraged by *The Bell Curve. Personality and Individual Differences, 24,* 207–216.

Ellis, R. R., & Lederman, S. J. (1998). The golf-ball illusion: Evidence for top-down processing in weight perception. *Perception, 27,* 193–201.

Ellison, W. J. (1987). State execution of juveniles: Defining "youth" as a mitigating factor for imposing a sentence of less than death. *Law and Psychology Review, 11,* 1–38.

Emonson, D. L., & Vanderbeek, R. D. (1995). The use of amphetamines in U.S. Air Force tactical operations during Desert Shield and Storm. *Aviation, Space, and Environmental Medicine, 66,* 260–263.

Engel, S. A. (1999). Using neuroimaging to measure mental representations: Finding color-opponent neurons in visual cortex. *Current Directions in Psychological Science, 8,* 23–27.

Engels, G. I., Garnefski, N., & Diekstra, R. F. W. (1993). Efficacy of rational-emotive therapy: A quantitative analysis. *Journal of Consulting and Clinical Psychology, 61,* 1083–1090.

Epel, E., Lapidus, R., McEwen, B., & Brownell, K. (2001). Stress may add bite to appetite in women: A laboratory study of stress-induced cortisol and eating behavior. *Psychoneuroendocrinology, 26,* 37–49.

Epstein, L. H., Saelens, B. E., Myers, M. D., & Vito, D. (1997). Effects of decreasing sedentary behaviors on activity choice in obese children. *Health Psychology, 16,* 107–113.

Epstein, R., Kirshnit, C. E., Lanza, R. P., & Rubin, L. C. (1984). "Insight" in the pigeon: Antecedents and determinants of an intelligent performance. *Nature, 308,* 61–62.

Epstein, S. (1994). Integration of the cognitive and the psychodynamic unconscious. *American Psychologist, 49,* 709–724.

Epstein, S., & O'Brien, E. J. (1985). The person-situation debate in historical and current perspective. *Psychological Bulletin, 98,* 513–537.

Epstein, W., & Hatfield, G. (1994). Gestalt psychology and the philosophy of mind. *Philosophical Psychology, 7,* 163–181.

Erel, O., & Burman, B. (1995). Interrelatedness of marital relations and parent-child relations: A meta-analytic review. *Psychological Bulletin, 118,* 108–132.

Erez, M. (1994). Toward a model of cross-cultural industrial and organizational psychology. In H. C. Triandis, M. D. Dunnette, & L. M. Hough (Eds.), *Handbook of industrial/organizational psychology* (pp. 193–242). San Francisco: New Lexington Press.

Ericsson, K. A., & Polson, P. G. (1988). An experimental analysis of the mechanisms of a memory skill. *Journal of Experimental Psychology: Learning, Memory, and Cognition, 14,* 305–316.

Erikson, E. (1963). *Childhood and society.* New York: W. W. Norton.

Esposito, K., Benitez, A., Barza, L., & Mellman, T. (1999). Evaluation of dream content in combat-related PTSD. *Journal of Traumatic Stress, 12,* 681–687.

Esterling, B. A., L'Abate, L., Murray, E. J., & Pennebaker, J. W. (1999). Empirical foundations for writing in prevention and psychotherapy: Mental and physical health outcomes. *Clinical Psychology Review, 19,* 79–96.

Evans, D. L., Leserman, J., Perkins, D. O., & Stern, R. A. (1995). Stress-associated reductions of cytotoxic T lymphocytes and natural killer cells in asymptomatic HIV infection. *American Journal of Psychiatry, 152,* 543–550.

Everly, G. S., Jr. (2000). Crisis management briefings (CMB): Large group crisis intervention in response to terrorism, disasters, and violence. *International Journal of Emergency Mental Health, 2,* 53–57.

Everson, C. A. (1997). Sleep deprivation and the immune system. In M. R. Pressman et al. (Eds.), *Understanding sleep: The evaluation and treatment of sleep disorders* (pp. 401–424). Washington, DC: American Psychological Association.

Ewin, D. M. (1994). Many memories retrieved with hypnosis are accurate. *American Journal of Clinical Hypnosis, 36,* 174–176.

Exton, M. S., Bindert, A., Krueger, T., Scheller, F., Hartman, U., & Schedlowski, M. (1999). Cardiovascular and endocrine alterations after masturbation-induced orgasm in women. *Psychosomatic Medicine, 61,* 280–289.

Exton, M. S., von Auer, A. K., Buske-Kirschbaum, A., et al. (2000). Pavlovian conditioning of immune function: Animal investigation and the challenge of human application. *Behavioural Brain Research, 110,* 129–141.

Eysenck, H. J. (1952). The effects of psychotherapy: An evaluation. *Journal of Consulting Psychology, 16,* 319–324.

Eysenck, H. J. (1990). Genetic and environmental contributions to individual differences: The three major dimensions of personality. *Journal of Personality, 58,* 245–261.

Eysenck, H. J. (1994). Cancer, personality and stress: Prediction and prevention. *Advances in Behaviour Research and Therapy, 16,* 167–215.

Eysenck, H. J. (1994). The outcome problem in psychotherapy: What have we learned? *Behaviour Research and Therapy, 32,* 477–495.

Fabbro, F. (2000). Introduction to language and cerebellum. *Journal of Neurolinguistics, 13,* 83–94.

Fagot, B. I., & Leinbach, M. D. (1995). Gender knowledge in egalitarian and traditional families. *Sex Roles, 32,* 513–526.

Fairburn, C. G., Cowen, P. J., & Harrison, P. J. (1999). Twin studies and the etiology of eating disorders. *International Journal of Eating Disorders, 26,* 349–358.

Faith, M. S., Rha, S. S., Neale, M. C., & Allison, D. B. (1999). Evidence for genetic influences on human energy intake: Results from a twin study using measured observations. *Behavior Genetics, 29,* 145–154.

Falbo, T., & Polit, D. F. (1986). Quantitative review of the only-child literature: Research evidence and theory development. *Psychological Bulletin, 100,* 176–189.

Falk, J. L. (1994). The discriminative stimulus and its reputation: Role in the instigation of drug abuse. *Experimental and Clinical Psychopharmacology, 2,* 43–52.

Falk, R. (1998). Replication: A step in the right direction: Commentary on Sohn. *Theory and Psychology, 8,* 313–321.

Fallon, A. E., & Rozin, P. (1985). Sex differences in perceptions of desirable body shape. *Journal of Abnormal Psychology, 94,* 102–105.

Fancher, R. E. (1984). Not Conley, but Burt and others: A reply. *Journal of the History of the Behavioral Sciences, 20,* 186.

Fantoni-Salvador, P., & Rogers, R. (1997). Spanish versions of the MMPI-2 and PAI: An investigation of concurrent validity with Hispanic patients. *Assessment, 4,* 29–39.

Farde, L. (1997). Brain imaging of schizophrenia: The dopamine hypothesis. *Schizophrenia Research, 28,* 157–162.

Farley, F. (2000). Obituary: Hans J. Eysenck (1916–1997). *American Psychologist, 55,* 674–675.

Farr, C. B. (1994). Benjamin Rush and American psychiatry. *American Journal of Psychiatry, 151,* 65–73.

Farrell, A. D., & White, K. S. (1998). Peer influences and drug use among urban adolescents: Family structure and parent-adolescent relationship as protective factors. *Journal of Consulting and Clinical Psychology, 66,* 248–258.

Farrimond, T. (1990). Effect of alcohol on visual constancy values and possible relation to driving performance. *Perceptual and Motor Skills, 70,* 291–295.

Farthing, G. W., Venturino, M., & Brown, S. W. (1984). Suggestion and distraction in the control of pain: Test of two hypotheses. *Journal of Abnormal Psychology, 93,* 266–276.

Fassbender, P. (1997). Parapsychology and the neurosciences: A computer-based content analysis of abstracts in the database "Medline" from 1975 to 1995. *Perceptual and Motor Skills, 84,* 452–454.

Fava, G. A., Grandi, S., Canestrari, R., & Grasso, P. (1991). Mechanisms of change of panic attacks with exposure treatment of agoraphobia. *Journal of Affective Disorders, 22,* 65–71.

Favreau, O. E. (1997). Sex and gender comparisons: Does null hypothesis testing create a false dichotomy? *Feminism and Psychology, 7,* 63–81.

Fein, D. (1990). Cerebral lateralization: A dominant question in developmental research. *Contemporary Psychology, 35,* 676–677.

Feingold, A. (1994). Gender differences in personality: A meta-analysis. *Psychological Bulletin, 116,* 429–456.

Feingold, A., & Mazzella, R. (1998). Gender differences in body image are increasing. *Psychological Science, 9,* 190–195.

Ferlazzo, F., Conte, S., & Gentilomo, A. (1993). Event-related potentials and recognition memory within the "levels of processing" framework. *Neuroreport, 4,* 667–670.

Ferris, A. M., & Duffy, V. B. (1989). Effect of olfactory deficits on nutritional status: Does age predict persons at risk? *Annals of the New York Academy of Sciences, 561,* 113–123.

Festinger, L., & Carlsmith, J. M. (1959). Cognitive consequences of forced compliance. *Journal of Abnormal and Social Psychology, 58,* 203–210.

Festinger, L., Pepitone, A., & Newcomb, T. (1952). Some consequences of deindividuation in a group. *Journal of Abnormal and Social Psychology, 47,* 382–389.

Festinger, L., Riecken, H. W., & Schachter, S. (1956). *When prophecy fails.* New York: Harper & Row.

Festinger, L., Schachter, S., & Back, K. (1950). *Social pressures in informal groups: A study of a housing community.* Stanford, CA: Stanford University Press.

Fieckenstein, L. (1996, May 20). Trailblazing Hulda Crooks, 100: Loma Linda resident publishes memoirs. *The Press-Enterprise,* p. B03.

Field, T. M. (1991). Quality infant day-care and grade school behavior and performance. *Child Development, 62,* 863–870.

Field, T. M. (1996). Attachment and separation in young children. *Annual Review of Psychology, 47,* 541–561.

Field, T. M., Woodson, R., Greenberg, R., & Cohen, D. (1982). Discrimination and imitation of facial expressions by neonates. *Science, 218,* 179–181.

Fillingim, R. B., Maddux, V., & Shackelford, J. A. M. (1999). Sex differences in heat pain thresholds as a function of assessment method and rate of rise. *Somatosensory and Motor Research, 16,* 57–62.

Fiore, M. C. (2000). A clinical practice guideline for treating tobacco use and dependence: A U.S. Public Health Service Report. *Journal of the American Medical Assocation, 283,* 3244–3254.

Fiore, M. C., Smith, S. S., Jorenby, D. E., & Baker, T. B. (1994). The effectiveness of the nicotine patch for smoking cessation: A meta-analysis. *Journal of the American Medical Association, 271,* 1940–1947.

Fiorito, G., & Scotto, P. (1992). Observational learning in *Octopus vulgaris. Science, 256,* 545–547.

Fischer, K. W., & Silvern, L. (1985). Stages and individual differences in cognitive development. *Annual Review of Psychology, 36,* 613–648.

Fisher, E. B., Delamater, A. M., Bertelson, A. D., & Kirkley, B. G. (1982). Psychological factors in diabetes and its treatment. *Journal of Consulting and Clinical Psychology, 50,* 993–1003.

Fisher, K. (1983, February). TV violence. *APA Monitor,* pp. 7, 9.

Fisher, K. (1986, March). Animal research: Few alternatives seen for behavioral studies. *APA Monitor,* pp. 16–17.

Fisher, S., & Greenberg, R. P. (1985). *The scientific credibility of Freud's theories and therapy.* New York: Columbia University Press.

Fiske, D. W., Conley, J. J., & Goldberg, L. R. (1987). E. Lowell Kelly (1905–1986). *American Psychologist, 42,* 511–512.

Fiss, H. (2000). A 21st century look at Freud's dream theory. *Journal of the American Academy of Psychoanalysis, 28,* 321–340.

Flakierska-Praquin, N., Lindstroem, M., & Gillberg, C. (1997). School phobia with separation anxiety disorder: A comparative 20– to 29–year follow-up study of 35 school refusers. *Comprehensive Psychiatry, 38,* 17–22.

Flannagan, D. A., & Blick, K. A. (1989). Levels of processing and the retention of word meanings. *Perceptual and Motor Skills, 68,* 1123–1128.

Flay, B. R. (1985). Psychosocial approaches to smoking prevention: A review of findings. *Health Psychology, 4,* 449–488.

Flynn, J. R. (1987). Massive IQ gains in 14 nations: What IQ tests really measure. *Psychological Bulletin, 101,* 171–191.

Foa, E. B., Dancu, C. V., Hembree, E. A., Jaycox, L. H., Meadows, E. A., & Street, G. P. (1999). A comparison of exposure therapy, stress inoculation training, and their combination for reducing posttraumatic stress disorder in female assault victims. *Journal of Consulting and Clinical Psychology, 67,* 194–200.

Foerstl, J. (1989). Early interest in the idiot savant. *American Journal of Psychiatry, 146,* 566.

Fogarty, G. J. (1994). Using the Personal Orientation Inventory to measure change in student self-actualization. *Personality and Individual Differences, 17,* 435–439.

Folkman, S., & Moskowitz, J. T. (2000). Stress, positive emotion, and coping. *Current Directions in Psychological Science, 9,* 115–118.

Foltin, R. W., Fischman, M. W., & Levin, F. R. (1995). Cardiovascular effects of cocaine in humans: Laboratory studies. *Drug and Alcohol Dependence, 37,* 193–210.

Fontaine, K. R., & Shaw, D. F. (1995). Effects of self-efficacy and dispositional optimism on adherence to step aerobic exercise classes. *Perceptual and Motor Skill, 81,* 251–255.

Ford, B. D. (1993). Emergenesis: An alternative and a confound, *American Psychologist, 48,* 1294.

Forehand, R., Miller, K. S., Dutra, R., & Chance, M. W. (1997). Role of parenting in adolescent deviant behavior: Replication across and within two ethnic groups. *Journal of Consulting and Clinical Psychology, 65,* 1036–1041.

Foreyt, J. P. (1987). Issues in the assessment and treatment of obesity. *Journal of Consulting and Clinical Psychology, 55,* 677–684.

Foster, C. A., Witcher, B. S., Campbell, W. K., & Green, J. D. (1998). Arousal and attraction: Evidence for automatic and controlled processes. *Journal of Personality and Social Psychology, 74,* 86–101.

Fox, E., Lester, V., Russo, R., Bowles, R. J., Pichler, A., & Dutton, K. (2000). Facial expressions of emotion: Are angry faces detected more efficiently? *Cognition and Emotion, 14,* 61–92.

Fox, L. H. (1981). Identification of the academically gifted. *American Psychologist, 36,* 1103–1111.

Fox, N. A., & Davidson, R. J. (1988). Patterns of brain electrical activity during facial signs of emotion in 10–month-old infants. *Developmental Psychology, 24,* 230–236.

Fox, S. E., & Burns, D. J. (1993). The mere exposure effect for stimuli presented below recognition threshold: A failure to replicate. *Perceptual and Motor Skills, 76,* 391–396.

Francis, L. J. (1999). Happiness is a thing called stable extraversion: A further examination of the relationship between the Oxford Happiness inventory and Eysenck's dimensional model of personality and gender. *Personality and Individual Differences, 26,* 5–11.

Francis, P. T., Palmer, A. M., Snape, M., & Wilcock, G. K. (1999). The cholinergic hypothesis of Alzheimer's disease: A review of progress. *Journal of Neurology, Neurosurgery and Psychiatry, 66,* 137–147.

Franko, D. L. (1998). Secondary prevention of eating disorders in college women at risk. *Eating Disorders, 6,* 29–40.

Frasciello, L. M., & Willard, S. G. (1995). Anorexia nervosa in males: A case report and review of the literature. *Clinical Social Work Journal, 23,* 47–58.

Frederiksen, N. (1986). Toward a broader conception of human intelligence. *American Psychologist, 41,* 445–452.

Fredrikson, M., Annas, P., Fischer, H., & Wik, G. (1996). Gender and age differences in the prevalence of specific fears and phobias. *Behaviour Research and Therapy, 34,* 33–39.

Freedman, J. L. (1984). Effect of television violence on aggressiveness. *Psychological Bulletin, 96,* 227–246.

Freeman, A. (1999). Will increasing our social interest bring about a loss of our innocence? *Journal of Individual Psychology, 55,* 130–145.

Freivalds, A., & Horii, K. (1994). An oculomotor test to measure alcohol impairment. *Perceptual and Motor Skills, 78,* 603–610.

French, S., & Joseph, S. (1999). Religiosity and its association with happiness, purpose in life, and self-actualization. *Mental Health, Religion and Culture, 2,* 117–120.

Freud, S. (1900/1990). *The interpretation of dreams.* New York: Basic Books.

Freud, S. (1901/1965). *Psychopathology of everyday life.* New York: W. W. Norton.

Freud, S. (1901/1990). *Psychopathology of everyday life.* New York: Gryphon.

Freud, S. (1905). *Jokes and their relationship to the unconscious.* London: Hogarth Press.

Freud, S. (1914/1957). On the history of the psychoanalytic movement. In J. Strachey (Ed.), *The standard edition of the complete psychological works of Sigmund Freud* (Vol. 14, pp. 7–66). London: Hogarth Press.

Freud, S. (1974). *Cocaine papers* (Ed., R. Byck). New York: Stonehill.

Freund, A. M., & Baltes, P. B. (1998). Selection, optimization, and compensation as strategies of life management: Correlations with subjective indicators of successful aging. *Psychology of Aging, 13,* 531–543.

Frick, W. B. (2000). Remembering Maslow: Reflections on a 1968 interview. *Journal of Humanistic Psychology, 40,* 128–147.

Friedman, M., & Rosenman, R. H. (1959). Association of specific overt behavior pattern with blood and cardiovascular findings. *Journal of the American Medical Association, 169,* 1286–1296.

Friedman, M., & Rosenman, R. H. (1974). *Type A behavior and your heart.* New York: Knopf.

Friedman, R. C., & Downey, J. (1993). Neurobiology and sexual orientation: Current relationships. *Journal of Neuropsychiatry and Clinical Neurosciences, 5,* 131–153.

Fritsch, G., & Hitzig, E. (1870/1960). *On the electrical excitability of the cerebrum.* Springfield, IL: Thomas.

Fritzsche, B. A., Finkelstein, M. A., & Penner, L. A. (2000). To help or not to help: Capturing individuals' decision policies. *Social Behavior and Personality, 28,* 561–578.

Froming, W. J., Nasby, W., & McManus, J. (1998). Prosocial self-schemas, self-awareness, and children's prosocial behavior. *Journal of Personality and Social Psychology, 75,* 766–777.

Frost, J. A., Binder, J. R., Springer, J. A., & Hammeke, T. A. (1999). Language processing is strongly left lateralized in both sexes. Evidence from functional MRI. *Brain, 122,* 199–208.

Fry, J. M. (1998). Treatment modalities for narcolepsy. *Neurology, 50,* S43–S48.

Fuchs-Beauchamp, K. D., Karnes, M. B., & Johnson, L. J. (1993). Creativity and intelligence in preschoolers. *Gifted Child Quarterly, 37,* 113–117.

Fudin, R. (2000). Comment on Birgegard and Sohlberg's (1999) suggestions for research in subliminal psychodynamic activation. *Perceptual and Motor Skills, 90,* 740–746.

Fujita, K. (1996). Linear perspective and the Ponzo illusion: A comparison between rhesus monkeys and humans. *Japanese Psychological Research, 38,* 136–145.

Fujita, K., Blough, D. S., & Blough, P. M. (1993). Effects of the inclination of context lines on perception of the Ponzo illusion by pigeons. *Animal Learning and Behavior, 21,* 29–34.

Funtowicz, M. N., & Widiger, T. A. (1999). Sex bias in the diagnosis of personality disorders: An evaluation of DSM-IV criteria. *Journal of Abnormal Psychology, 108,* 195–201.

Furnham, A., & Allass, K. (1999). The influence of musical distraction of varying complexity on the cognitive performance of extroverts and introverts. *European Journal of Personality, 13,* 27–38.

Furnham, A., & Lim, A.-N. (1997). Cross-cultural differences in the perception of male and female body shapes as a function of exercise. *Journal of Social Behavior and Personality, 12,* 1037–1053.

Furnham, A., & Thompson, J. (1991). Personality and self-reported delinquency. *Personality and Individual Differences, 12,* 585–593.

Furnham, A., Gunter, B., & Walsh, D. (1998). Effects of programme context on memory of humorous television commercials. *Applied Cognitive Psychology, 12,* 555–567.

Furstenberg, F. F., & Teitler, J. O. (1994). Reconsidering the effects of marital disruption: What happens to children of divorce in early adulthood? *Journal of Family Issues, 15,* 173–190.

Furumoto, L. (1980). Mary Whiton Calkins (1863–1930). *Psychology of Women Quarterly, 5,* 55–68.

Furumoto, L. (1988). Shared knowledge: The experimentalists, 1904–1929. In J. G. Morawski (Ed.), *The rise of experimentation in American psychology* (pp. 94–113). New Haven, CT: Yale University Press.

Furumoto, L. (1992). Joining separate spheres: Christine Ladd-Franklin, woman-scientist (1847–1930). *American Psychologist, 47,* 175–182.

Gabrieli, J. D. E., Fleischman, D. A., Keane, M. M., & Reminger, S. L. (1995). Double dissociation between memory systems underlying explicit and implicit memory in the human brain. *Psychological Science, 6,* 76–82.

Gaffan, E. A., Tsaousis, J., & Kemp-Wheeler, S. M. (1995). Researcher allegiance and meta-analysis: The case of cognitive therapy for depression. *Journal of Consulting and Clinical Psychology, 63,* 966–980.

Galanter, E. (1962). *New directions in psychology.* New York: Holt, Rinehart & Winston.

Galef, B. G. (1993). Functions of social learning about food: A causal analysis of effects of diet novelty on preference transmission. *Animal Behaviour, 46,* 257–265.

Galef, B. G., Jr. (1980). Diving for food: Analysis of a possible case of social learning in wild rats (*Rattus norvegicus*). *Journal of Comparative and Physiological Psychology, 94,* 416–425.

Gallacher, J. E. J., Hopkinson, C. A., Bennett, P., Burr, M. L., & Elwood, P. C. (1997). Effect of stress management on angina. *Psychology and Health, 12,* 523–532.

Gallup, G. G., Jr., & Suarez, S. D. (1985). Alternatives to the use of animals in psychological research. *American Psychologist, 40,* 1104–1111.

Galton, F. (1869). *Hereditary genius.* London: Macmillan.

Gamaro, G. D., Denardin, J. D., Michalowski, M. B., Catelli, D., Correa, J. B., Xavier, M. H., & Dalmaz, C. (1997). Epinephrine effects on memory are not dependent on hepatic glucose release. *Neurobiology of Learning and Memory, 68,* 221–229.

Ganchrow, J. R., Steiner, J. E., & Daher, M. (1983). Neonatal facial expressions in response to different qualities and intensities of gustatory stimuli. *Infant Behavior and Development, 6,* 189–200.

Gangestad, S., & Snyder, M. (1985). "To carve nature at its joints": On the existence of discrete classes in personality. *Psychological Review, 92,* 317–349.

Gannon, L., Luchetta, T., Rhodes, K., Pardie, L., & Segrist, D. (1992). Sex bias in psychological research: Progress or complacency? *American Psychologist, 47,* 389–396.

Gansberg, M. (1964, March 27). Thirty-seven who saw murder didn't call the police. *New York Times,* pp. 1, 38.

Garcia, J. (1981). Tilting at the paper mills of academe. *American Psychologist, 36,* 149–158.

Garcia, J., & Gustavson, A. R. (1997, January). Carl R. Gustavson (1946–1996): Pioneering wildlife psychologist. *APS Observer,* pp. 34–35.

Garcia, J., & Koelling, R. A. (1966). The relation of cue to consequence in avoidance learning. *Psychonomic Science, 4,* 123–124.

Garcia, J., Kimeldorf, D. J., Hunt, E. L., & Davies, B. P. (1956). Food and water consumption of rats during exposure to gamma radiation. *Radiation Research, 4,* 33–41.

Garcia-Vera, M. P., Labrador, F. J., & Sanz, J. (1997). Stress-management training for essential hypertension: A controlled study. *Applied Psychophysiology and Biofeedback, 22,* 261–283.

Gardner, H. (1983). *Frames of mind: The theory of multiple intelligences.* New York: Basic Books.

Gardner, H. (1985). *The mind's new science: A history of the cognitive revolution.* New York: Basic Books.

Gardner, R. A., Gardner, B. T., & Van Cantfort, T. E. (1969). Teaching sign language to a chimpanzee. *Science, 165,* 664–672.

Gardner, R. A., Gardner, B. T., & Van Cantfort, T. E. (Eds.). (1989). *Teaching sign language to chimpanzees.* Albany: State University of New York Press.

Garmon, L. C., Basinger, K. S., Gregg, V. R., & Gibbs, J. C. (1996). Gender differences in stage and expression of moral judgment. *Merrill-Palmer Quarterly, 42,* 418–437.

Garonzik, R. (1989). Hand dominance and implications for left-handed operation of controls. *Ergonomics, 32,* 1185–1192.

Garrison, D. W., & Foreman, R. D. (1994). Decreased activity of spontaneous and noxiously evoked dorsal horn cells during transcutaneous electrical nerve stimulation (TENS). *Pain, 58,* 309–315.

Gastil, J. (1990). Generic pronouns and sexist language: The oxymoronic character of masculine generics. *Sex Roles, 23,* 629–643.

Gathercole, S. E., & Conway, M. A. (1988). Exploring long-term modality effects: Vocalization leads to best retention. *Memory and Cognition, 16,* 110–119.

Gauthier, J., Cote, G., & French, D. (1994). The role of home practice in the thermal biofeedback treatment of migraine headache. *Journal of Consulting and Clinical Psychology, 62,* 180–184.

Gawin, F. H. (1991). Cocaine addiction: Psychology and neurophysiology. *Science, 251,* 1580–1586.

Gay, P. (1988). *Freud: A life for our time.* New York: W. W. Norton.

Gay, V. (1986). Augustine: The reader as self-object. *Journal for the Scientific Study of Religion, 25,* 64–76.

Gazzaniga, M. S. (1967, August). The split brain in man. *Scientific American,* pp. 24–29.

Gazzaniga, M. S. (1983). Right hemisphere language following brain bisection: A 20-year perspective. *American Psychologist, 38,* 525–537.

Gazzaniga, M. S. (2000). Cerebral specialization and interhemispheric communication: Does the corpus callosum enable the human condition? *Brain, 123,* 1293–1326.

Geen, R. G. (1984). Preferred stimulation levels in introverts and extraverts: Effects on arousal and performance. *Journal of Personality and Social Psychology, 46,* 1303–1312.

Geen, R. G., Stonner, D., & Shope, G. L. (1975). The facilitation of aggression by aggression: Evidence against the catharsis hypothesis. *Journal of Personality and Social Psychology, 31,* 721–726.

Gelb, S. A. (1986). Henry H. Goddard and the immigrants, 1910–1917: The studies and their social context. *Journal of the History of the Behavioral Sciences, 22,* 324–332.

Gerhart, B. (1987). How important are dispositional factors as determinants of job satisfaction? Implications for job design and other personnel programs. *Journal of Applied Psychology, 72,* 366–373.

Gescheider, G. A., Beiles, E. J., Checkosky, C. M., & Bolanowski, S. J. (1994). The effects of aging on information-processing channels in the sense of touch: II. Temporal summation in the P channel. *Somatosensory and Motor Research, 11,* 359–365.

Geschwind, N. (1979, September). Specializations of the human brain. *Scientific American,* pp. 180–199.

Gfellner, B. M., & Hundleby, J. D. (1994). Developmental and gender differences in drug use and problem behaviour during adolescence. *Journal of Child and Adolescent Substance Abuse, 3,* 59–74.

Ghaderi, A., & Scott, B. (2000). The Big Five and eating disorders: A prospective study in the general population. *European Journal of Personality, 14,* 311–323.

Ghizzani, A., & Montomoli, M. (2000). Anorexia nervosa and sexuality in women: A review. *Journal of Sex Education and Therapy, 25,* 80–88.

Gibbons, B. (1986). The intimate sense of smell. *National Geographic, 170,* 324–361.

Gibson, E. J., & Walk, R. D. (1960, April). The visual cliff. *Scientific American,* pp. 67–71.

Gibson, H. B. (1991). Can hypnosis compel people to commit harmful, immoral and criminal acts? A review of the literature. *Contemporary Hypnosis, 8,* 129–140.

Gibson, J. J. (1979). *The ecological approach to visual perception.* Boston: Houghton Mifflin.

Gibson, J. T. (1991). Training people to inflict pain: State terror and social learning. *Journal of Humanistic Psychology, 31,* 72–87.

Gidron, Y., Davidson, K., & Bata, I. (1999). The short-term effects of a hostility-reduction intervention on male coronary heart disease patients. *Health Psychology, 18,* 416–420.

Giesler, G. J., Katter, J. T., & Dado, R. J. (1994). Direct spinal pathways to the limbic system for nociceptive information. *Trends in Neurosciences, 17,* 244–250.

Gilbert, H. M., & Warburton, D. M. (2000). Craving: A problematic concept in smoking research. *Addiction Research, 8,* 381–397.

Gilboa-Schechtman, E., Franklin, M. E., & Foa, E. B. (2000). Anticipated reactions to social events: Differences among individuals with generalized social phobia, obsessive compulsive disorder, and nonanxious controls. *Cognitive Therapy and Research, 24,* 731–746.

Gill, D. (1980). *Quest: The life of Elisabeth Kübler-Ross.* New York: Harper & Row.

Gillam, B. (1980, January). Geometrical illusions. *Scientific American,* pp. 102–111.

Gillam, B. (1992). The status of perceptual grouping 70 years after Wertheimer. *Australian Journal of Psychology, 44,* 157–162.

Gilligan, C. (1982). *In a different voice: Psychological theory and women's development.* Cambridge, MA: Harvard University Press.

Gilovich, T., Vallone, R., & Tversky, A. (1985). The hot hand in basketball: On misperception of random sequences. *Cognitive Psychology, 17,* 295–314.

Gisiner, R., & Schusterman, R. J. (1992). Sequence, syntax, and semantics: Responses of a language-trained sea lion (*Zalophus californianus*) to novel sign combinations. *Journal of Comparative Psychology, 106,* 78–91.

Glanz, J. (1998). Magnetic brain imaging traces a stairway to memory. *Science, 280,* 37.

Glanzman, D. L. (1995). The cellular basis of classical conditioning in *Aplysia californica*: It's less simple than you think. *Trends in Neurosciences, 18,* 30–35.

Glassman, R. B., Garvey, K. J., Elkins, K. M., & Kasal, K. L. (1994). Spatial working memory score of humans in a large radial maze, similar to published score of rats, implies capacity close to the magical number 7±2. *Brain Research Bulletin, 34,* 151–159.

Gleaves, D. H. (1996). The sociocognitive model of dissociative identity disorder: A reexamination of the evidence. *Psychological Bulletin, 120,* 42–59.

Gleitman, H., Rozin, P., & Sabini, J. (1997). Solomon E. Asch (1907–1996): Obituary. *American Psychologist, 52,* 984–985.

Glennon, R. A. (1990). Do classical hallucinogens act as 5–HT-sub-2 agonists or antagonists? *Neuropsychopharmacology, 3,* 509–517.

Glick, P., et al. (2000). Beyond prejudice as simple antipathy: Hostile and benevolent sexism across cultures. *Journal of Personality and Social Psychology, 79,* 763–775.

Gliedman, J. (1983, November). Interview with Noam Chomsky. *Omni,* pp. 112–118, 171–174.

Gloor, P. (1994). Is Berger's dream coming true? *Electroencephalography and Clinical Neurophysiology, 90,* 253–266.

Glucksberg, S., & Danks, J. H. (1968). Effects of discriminative labels and of nonsense labels upon availability of novel functions. *Journal of Verbal Learning and Verbal Behavior, 7,* 72–76.

Glueckauf, R. L., & Quittner, A. L. (1992). Assertiveness training for disabled adults in wheelchairs: Self-report,

role-play, and activity pattern outcomes. *Journal of Consulting and Clinical Psychology, 60,* 419–425.

Gobet, F., & Simon, H. A. (1998). Expert chess memory: Revisiting the chunking hypothesis. *Memory, 6,* 225–255.

"God's hand": Legless veteran crawls to save life of a baby. (1986, June 6). *Philadelphia Inquirer,* pp. 1A, 24A.

Goddard, H. H. (1917). Mental tests and the immigrant. *Journal of Delinquency, 2,* 243–277.

Godden, D. R., & Baddeley, A. D. (1975). Context-dependent memory in two natural environments: On land and under water. *British Journal of Psychology, 66,* 325–331.

Godemont, M. (1992). Six hundred years of family care in Geel, Belgium: 600 years of familiarity with madness in town life. *Community Alternatives: International Journal of Family Care, 4,* 155–168.

Godin, G., Desharnais, R., Valois, P., & Bradet, R. (1995). Combining behavioral and motivational dimensions to identify and characterize the stages in the process of adherence to exercise. *Psychology and Health, 10,* 333–344.

Goebel, B. L., & Boeck, B. E. (1987). Ego integrity and fear of death: A comparison of institutionalized and independently living older adults. *Death Studies, 11,* 193–204.

Goh, V. H. H., Tong, T. Y. Y., Lim, C. L., Low, E. C. T., & Lee, L. K. H. (2000). Circadian disturbances after night-shift work onboard a naval ship. *Military Medicine, 165,* 101–105.

Goisman, R. M. (1983). Therapeutic approaches to phobia: A comparison. *American Journal of Psychotherapy, 37,* 227–234.

Goldberg, M. A., & Remy-St. Louis, G. (1998). Understanding and treating pain in ethnically diverse patients. *Journal of Clinical Psychology in Medical Settings, 5,* 343–356.

Goldbloom, D. S., & Garfinkel, P. E. (1990). The serotonin hypothesis of bulimia nervosa: Theory and evidence. *Canadian Journal of Psychiatry, 35,* 741–744.

Goldfried, M. R., Greenberg, L. S., & Marmar, C. (1990). Individual psychotherapy: Process and outcome. *Annual Review of Psychology, 41,* 659–688.

Goldin-Meadow, S., & Mylander, C. (1998). Spontaneous sign systems created by deaf children in two cultures. *Nature, 391,* 279–281.

Goldman, D. L. (1990). Dorothea Dix and her two missions of mercy in Nova Scotia. *Canadian Journal of Psychiatry, 35,* 139–143.

Goldman, H. H. (1998). Deinstitutionalization and community care: Social welfare policy as mental health policy. *Harvard Review of Psychiatry, 6,* 219–222.

Goldschmidt, L., Day, N. L., & Richardson, G. A. (2000). Effects of prenatal marijuana exposure on child behavior problems at age 10. *Neurotoxicology and Teratology, 22,* 325–336.

Goldstein, A. (1980). Thrills in response to music and other stimuli. *Physiological Psychology, 8,* 126–129.

Goldstein, I. L. (1993). *Training in organizations* (3rd ed.). Pacific Grove, CA: Brooks/Cole.

Goldstein, S. R., & Hall, D. (1990). Variable ratio control of the spitting response in the archer fish (*Toxotes jaculator*). *Journal of Comparative Psychology, 104,* 373–376.

Golombok, S., & Tasker, F. (1996). Do parents influence the sexual orientation of their children? Findings from a longitudinal study of lesbian families. *Developmental Psychology, 32,* 3–11.

Gonzales, M. H., & Meyers, S. A. (1993). "Your mother would like me": Self-presentation in the personals ads of heterosexual and homosexual men and women. *Personality and Social Psychology Bulletin, 19,* 131–142.

Good, R. H., III, Simmons, D. C., & Smith, S. B. (1998). Effective academic intervention in the United States: Evaluating and enhancing the acquisition of early reading skills. *School Psychology Review, 27,* 45–56.

Goodall, J. (1990). *Through a window: My thirty years with the chimpanzees of Gombe.* Boston: Houghton Mifflin.

Goodman, G. S., & Schaaf, J. M. (1997). Over a decade of research on children's eyewitness testimony: What have we learned? Where do we go from here? *Applied Cognitive Psychology, 11,* S5–S20.

Gopaul-McNicol, S. (1997). The role of religion in psychotherapy: A cross-cultural examination. *Journal of Contemporary Psychotherapy, 27,* 37–48.

Gorczynski, R. M. (1990). Conditioned enhancement of skin allografts in mice. *Brain, Behavior and Immunity, 4,* 85–92.

Gordon, B. N., & Follmer, A. (1994). Developmental issues in judging the credibility of children's testimony. *Journal of Clinical Child Psychology, 23,* 283–294.

Gordon, C. M., & Carey, M. P. (1995). Penile tumescence monitoring during morning naps to assess male erectile functioning: An initial study of healthy men of varied ages. *Archives of Sexual Behavior, 24,* 291–307.

Gordon, E. (1999). Brain imaging technologies: How, what, when, and why? *Australian and New Zealand Journal of Psychiatry, 33,* 187–196.

Gordon, I. E., & Earle, D. C. (1992). Visual illusions: A short review. *Australian Journal of Psychology, 44,* 153–156.

Gordon, P. M., Heath, G. W., Holmes, A., & Christy, D. (2000). The quantity and quality of physical activity among those trying to lose weight. *American Journal of Preventive Medicine, 18,* 83–86.

Gorey, K. M., & Leslie, D. R. (1997). The prevalence of child sexual abuse: Integrative review for potential response and measurement biases. *Child Abuse and Neglect, 21,* 391–398.

Gosselin, P., Kirouac, G., & Dore, F. Y. (1995). Components and recognition of

facial expression in the communication of emotion by actors. *Journal of Personality and Social Psychology, 68,* 83–96.

Goswami, M. (1998). The influence of clinical symptoms on quality of life in patients with narolepsy. *Neurology, 50,* S31–S36.

Gotlib, I. H., & Robinson, L. A. (1982). Responses to depressed individuals: Discrepancies between self-report and observer-rated behavior. *Journal of Abnormal Psychology, 91,* 231–240.

Gottesman, I. I., & Shields, J. (1982). *Schizophrenia: The epigenetic puzzle.* Cambridge, MA: Cambridge University Press.

Gottlieb, B. H. (2000). Self-help, mutual aid, and support groups among older adults. *Canadian Journal on Aging, 19,* 58–74.

Gould, S. J. (1981). *The mismeasure of man.* New York: W. W. Norton.

Gould, S. J. (1994, November 28). Curveball. *The New Yorker,* pp. 139–149.

Gouzoulis, M. E., Thelen, B., Habermeyer, E., Kunert, H. J., Kovar, K. A., et al. (1999). Psychopathological, neuroendocrine and autonomic effects of 3,4–methylenedioxyethylamphetamine (MDE), psilocybin, and d-methamphetamine in healthy volunteers. *Psychopharmacology, 142,* 41–50.

Graham, M. J., Larsen, U., & Xu, X. (1999). Secular trend in age at menarche in China: A case study of two rural counties in Anhui province. *Journal of Biosocial Science, 31,* 257–267.

Granholm, E., Chock, D., & Morris, S. (1998). Pupillary responses evoked during verbal fluency tasks indicate semantic network dysfunction in schizophrenia. *Journal of Clinical and Experimental Neuropsychology, 20,* 856–872.

Grant, H. M., Bredahl, L. C., Clay, J., Ferrie, J., Groves, J. E., McDorman, T. A., & Dark, V. J. (1998). Context-dependent memory for meaningful material: Information for students. *Applied Cognitive Psychology, 12,* 617–623.

Gravitz, M. A. (1995). First admission (1846) of hypnotic testimony in court. *American Journal of Clinical Hypnosis, 37,* 326–330.

Gray, J. T., Neisser, U., Shapiro, B. A., & Kouns, S. (1991). Observational learning of ballet sequences: The role of kinematic information. *Ecological Psychology, 3,* 121–134.

Gray-Little, B., & Hafdahl, A. R. (2000). Factors influencing racial comparisons of self-esteem: A quantitative review. *Psychological Bulletin, 126,* 26–54.

Green, J. A., & Shellenberger, R. D. (1986). Biofeedback research and the ghost in the box: A reply to Roberts. *American Psychologist, 41,* 1003–1005.

Green, J. P., Lynn, S. J., & Malinoski, P. (1998). Hypnotic pseudomemories, prehypnotic warnings, and malleability of suggested memories. *Applied Cognitive Psychology, 12,* 431–444.

Green, J. T., & Woodruff-Pak, D. S. (2000). Eyeblink classical conditioning: Hippocampal formation is for neutral stimulus associations as cerebellum is for association-response. *Psychological Bulletin, 126,* 138–158.

Greene, E., Flynn, M. S., & Loftus, E. F. (1982). Inducing resistance to misleading information. *Journal of Verbal Learning and Verbal Behavior, 21,* 207–219.

Greene, R. L. (1987). Effects of maintenance rehearsal on human memory. *Psychological Bulletin, 102,* 403–413.

Greenlees, I. A., & McGrew, W. C. (1994). Sex and age differences in preferences and tactics of mate attraction: Analysis of published advertisements. *Ethology and Sociobiology, 15,* 59–72.

Greeno, J. G. (1980). Psychology of learning, 1960–1980: One participant's observations. *American Psychologist, 35,* 713–728.

Greenough, A., Cole, G., Lewis, J., Lockton, A., & Blundell, J. (1998). Untangling the effects of hunger, anxiety, and nausea on energy intake during intravenous cholecystokinin octapeptide (CCK-8) infusion. *Physiology and Behavior, 65,* 303–310.

Greenwald, A. G., Spangenberg, E. R., Pratkanis, A. R., & Eskenazi, J. (1991). Double-blind tests of subliminal self-help audiotapes. *Psychological Science, 2,* 119–122.

Greenwood, J. D. (1999). Understanding the "cognitive revolution" in psychology. *Journal of the History of the Behavioral Sciences, 35,* 1–22.

Gregg, E., & Rejeski, W. J. (1990). Social psychobiologic dysfunction associated with anabolic steroid abuse: A review. *Sport Psychologist, 4,* 275–284.

Grey, W. (1994). Philosophy and the paranormal. Part 1: The problem of "psi." *Skeptical Inquirer, 18,* 142–149.

Grimshaw, G. M., Adelstein, A., Bryden, M. P., & MacKinnon, G. E. (1998). First-language acquisition in adolescence: Evidence for a critical period for verbal language development. *Brain and Language, 63,* 237–255.

Grissom, R. J. (1996). The magical number .7±2: Meta-meta-analysis of the probability of superior outcome in comparisons involving therapy, placebo, and control. *Journal of Consulting and Clinical Psychology, 64,* 973–982.

Grosser, B. I., Monti-Bloch, L., Jennings-White, C., & Berliner, D. L. (2000). Behavioral and electrophysiological effects of androstadienone, a human pheromone. *Psychoneuroendocrinology, 25,* 289–300.

Grouios, G., Tsorbatzoudis, H., Alexandris, K., & Barkoukis, V. (2000). Do left-handed competitors have an innate superiority in sports? *Perceptual and Motor Skills, 90,* 1273–1282.

Grove, W. M., Eckert, E. D., Heston, L., & Bouchard, T. J. (1990). Heritability of substance abuse and antisocial behavior: A study of monozygotic twins reared apart. *Biological Psychiatry, 27,* 1293–1304.

Grunewald, A., & Grossberg, S. (1998). Self organization of binocular disparity tuning by reciprocal corticogeniculate interactions. *Journal of Cognitive Neuroscience, 10,* 199–215.

Guarino, M., Fridrich, P., & Sitton, S. (1994). Male and female conformity in eating behavior. *Psychological Reports, 75,* 603–609.

Guilford, J. P. (1984). Varieties of divergent production. *Journal of Creative Behavior, 18,* 1–10.

Guion, S. G., Flege, J. E., Liu, S. H., & Yeni-Komshian, G. H. (2000). Age of learning effects on the duration of sentences produced in a second language. *Applied Psycholinguistics, 21,* 205–228.

Gulevich, G., Dement, W., & Johnson, L. (1966). Psychiatric and EEG observations on a case of prolonged (264 hours) wakefulness. *Archives of General Psychiatry, 15,* 29–35.

Gump, B. B., Matthews, K. A., & Raeikkoenen, K. (1999). Modeling relationships among socioeconomic status, hostility, cardiovascular reactivity, and left ventricular mass in African American and White children. *Health Psychology, 18,* 140–150.

Gunderson, V. M., Yonas, A., Sargent, P. L., & Grant-Webster, K. S. (1993). Infant macaque monkeys respond to pictorial depth. *Psychological Science, 4,* 93–98.

Gunnell, D. J. (2000). The epidemiology of suicide. *International Review of Psychiatry, 12,* 21–26.

Gur, R. E., & Chin, S. (1999). Laterality in functional brain imaging studies of schizophrenia. *Schizophrenia Bulletin, 25,* 141–156.

Gustavson, C. R., Garcia, J., Hankins, W. D., & Rusiniak, K. W. (1974). Coyote predation control by aversive conditioning. *Science, 184,* 581–583.

Guyll, M., & Contrada, R. J. (1998). Hostility and adrenergic receptor responsiveness: Evidence of reduced beta-receptor responsiveness in high hostile men. *Health Psychology, 17,* 30–39.

Haaga, D. A. F., & Beck, A. T. (1995). Perspectives on depressive realism: Implications for cognitive theory of depression. *Behaviour Research and Therapy, 33,* 41–48.

Haber, R. N. (1980). How we perceive depth from flat pictures. *American Scientist, 68,* 370–380.

Hackett, R. D., Bycio, P., & Guion, R. M. (1989). Absenteeism among hospital nurses: An idiographic-longitudinal analysis. *Academy of Management Journal, 32,* 424–453.

Hadjikhani, N., & Tootell, R. B. H. (2000). Projection of rods and cones within human visual cortex. *Human Brain Mapping, 9,* 55–63.

Hagopian, L. P., Farrell, D. A., & Amari, A. (1996). Treating total liquid refusal with backward chaining and fading. *Journal of Applied Behavior Analysis, 29,* 573–575.

Haidt, J., & Keltner, D. (1999). Culture and facial expression: Open-ended methods find more expressions and a gradient of recognition. *Cognition and Emotion, 13,* 225–266.

Haight, B. K., Michel, Y., & Hendrix, S. (2000). The extended effects of the life review in nursing home residents. *International Journal of Aging and Human Development, 50,* 151–168.

Haimowitz, C. (2000). Maybe it's not "kick me" after all: Transactional analysis and schizoid personality disorder. *Transactional Analysis Journal, 30,* 84–90.

Hall, C., & Briggs, J. (2000, June 20). NBA Championship: Lakers 116–Pacers 111: Vandalism mars L.A.'s euphoria. *Los Angeles Times,* (pp. A1 et seq.).

Hall, C. S. (1966). *The meaning of dreams.* New York: McGraw-Hill.

Hall, G. C. N., Bansal, A., & Lopez, I. R. (1999). Ethnicity and psychopathology: A meta-analytic review of 31 years of comparative MMPI/MMPI-2 research. *Psychological Assessment, 11,* 186–197.

Hall, M., Baum, A., Buysse, D. J., Prigerson, H. G., Kupfer, D., & Reynolds, C. F. III. (1998). Sleep as a mediator of the stress-immune relationship. *Psychosomatic Medicine, 60,* 48–56.

Hallenbeck, B. A., & Kauffman, J. M. (1995). How does observational learning affect the behavior of students with emotional or behavioral disorders? A review of research. *Journal of Special Education, 29,* 45–71.

Haller, J., Halasz, J., & Makara, G. B. (2000). Housing conditions and the anxiolytic efficacy of buspirone: The relationship between main and side effects. *Behavioural Pharmacology, 11,* 403–412.

Halpern, C. T., Udry, J. R., Campbell, B., & Suchindran, C. (1993). Relationships between aggression and pubertal increases in testosterone: A panel analysis of adolescent males. *Social Biology, 40,* 8–24.

Halpern, D. F. (1994). Stereotypes, science, censorship, and the study of sex differences. *Feminism and Psychology, 4,* 523–530.

Halpern, D. F. (1995). Cognitive gender differences: Why diversity is a critical research issue. In H. Landrine (Ed.), *Bringing cultural diversity to feminist psychology* (pp. 77–92). Washington, DC: American Psychological Association.

Halpern, D. F. (2000a). Mapping cognitive processes onto the brain: Mind the gap. *Brain and Cognition, 42,* 128–130.

Halpern, D. F. (2000b). *Sex differences in cognitive abilities* (3rd ed.). Mahwah, NJ: Erlbaum.

Halpern, D. F., & Coren, S. (1988). Do right-handers live longer? *Nature, 333,* 213.

Halpern, D. F., & Coren, S. (1993). Left-handedness and life span: A reply to Harris. *Psychological Bulletin, 114,* 235–241.

Halpern, D. F., & LeMay, M. L. (2000). The smarter sex: A critical review of sex differences in intelligence. *Educational Psychology Review, 12,* 229–246.

Halpern, L., Blake, R., & Hillerbrand, J. (1986). Psychoacoustics of a chilling sound. *Perception and Psychophysics, 39,* 77–80.

Hamburg, D. A. (1982). Health and behavior. *Science, 217,* 399.

Hamburger, Y. (1994). The contact hypothesis reconsidered: Effects of the atypical outgroup member on the outgroup stereotype. *Basic and Applied Social Psychology, 15,* 339–358.

Hamill, R., Decamp Wilson, T., & Nisbett, R. E. (1980). Insensitivity to sample bias: Generalizing from atypical cases. *Journal of Personality and Social Psychology, 39,* 578–589.

Hamilton, C. E. (2000). Continuity and discontinuity of attachment from infancy through adolescence. *Child Development, 71,* 690–694.

Hamilton, T. K., & Schweitzer, R. D. (2000). The cost of being perfect: Perfectionism and suicide ideation in university students. *Australian and New Zealand Journal of Psychiatry, 34,* 829–835.

Hammen, C., Risha, H., & Daley, S. E. (2000). Depression and sensitization to stressors among young women as a function of childhood adversity. *Journal of Consulting and Clinical Psychology, 68,* 782–787.

Han, S., Humphreys, G. W., & Chen, L. (1999). Uniform connectedness and classical Gestalt principles of perceptual grouping. *Perception and Psychophysics, 61,* 661–674.

Hanna, E., & Meltzoff, A. N. (1993). Peer imitation by toddlers in laboratory, home, and day-care contexts: Implications for social learning and memory. *Developmental Psychology, 29,* 701–710.

Hanna, G., Kundiger, E., & Larouche, C. (1990). Mathematical achievement of grade 12 girls in fifteen countries. In L. Burton (Ed.), *Gender and mathematics: An international perspective* (pp. 87–98). New York: Cassell.

Hansen, C. H., & Hansen, R. D. (1988). Finding the face in the crowd: An anger superiority effect. *Journal of Personality and Social Psychology, 54,* 917–924.

Hansen, I., Bakken, M., & Braastad, B. O. (1997). Failure of LiCl-conditioned taste aversion to prevent dogs from attacking sheep. *Applied Animal Behaviour Science, 54,* 251–256.

Hanson, R. K. (1990). The psychological impact of sexual assault on women and children: A review. *Annals of Sex Research, 3,* 187–232.

Harbach, H., Hell, K., Gramsch, C., Katz, N., Hempelmann, G., & Teschemacher, H. (2000). Beta-endorphin (1–31) in the plasma of male volunteers undergoing physical exercise. *Psychoneuroendocrinology, 25,* 551–562.

Harbin, G., Durst, L., & Harbin, D. (1989). Evaluation of oculomotor response in relationship to sports performance. *Medicine and Science in Sports and Exercise, 21,* 258–262.

Hardaway, R. A. (1990). Subliminally activated symbiotic fantasies: Fact and artifacts. *Psychological Bulletin, 107,* 177–195.

Hardy, C. J., & Latané, B. (1988). Social loafing in cheerleaders: Effects of team membership and competition. *Journal of Sport and Exercise Psychology, 10,* 109–114.

Hare, R. D., McPherson, L. M., & Forth, A. E. (1988). Male psychopaths and their criminal careers. *Journal of Consulting and Clinical Psychology, 56,* 710–714.

Hargadon, R., Bowers, K. S., & Woody, E. Z. (1995). Does counterpain imagery mediate hypnotic analgesia? *Journal of Abnormal Psychology, 104,* 508–516.

Hariri, A. R., Bookheimer, S. Y., & Mazziotta, J. C. (2000). Modulating emotional responses: Effects of a neocortical network on the limbic system. *Neuroreport, 11,* 43–48.

Harlow, H. F., & Zimmerman, R. R. (1959). Affectional responses in the infant monkey. *Science, 130,* 421–432.

Harlow, J. M. (1993). Recovery from the passage of an iron bar through the head. *History of Psychiatry, 4,* 271–281.

Harman, M. J. (1991). The use of group psychotherapy with cancer patients: A review of recent literature. *Journal for Specialists in Group Work, 16,* 56–61.

Harmon-Jones, E. (2000). Cognitive dissonance and experienced negative affect: Evidence that dissonance increases experienced negative affect even in the absence of aversive consequences. *Personality and Social Psychology Bulletin, 26,* 1490–1501.

Harmon-Jones, E., Brehm, J. W., Greenberg, J., & Simon, L. (1996). Evidence that the production of aversive consequences is not necessary to create cognitive dissonance. *Journal of Personality and Social Psychology, 70,* 5–16.

Harris, B. (1979). Whatever happened to Little Albert? *American Psychologist, 34,* 151–160.

Harris, J. A. (1999). Review and methodological considerations in research on testosterone and aggression. *Aggression & Violent Behavior, 4,* 273–291.

Harris, L. J. (1993). Do left-handers die sooner than right-handers? Commentary on Coren and Halpern's (1991) "Left-handedness: A marker for decreased survival fitness." *Psychological Bulletin, 114,* 203–234.

Harris, L. J. (1999). Early theory and research on hemispheric specialization. *Schizophrenia Bulletin, 25,* 11–39.

Harris, L. J., & Blaiser, M. J. (1997). Effects of a mnemonic peg system on the recall of daily tasks. *Perceptual and Motor Skills, 84,* 721–722.

Harris, M. J. (1994). Self-fulfilling prophecies in the clinical context: Review and implications for clinical practice. *Applied and Preventive Psychology, 3,* 145–158.

Harris, M. J., & Rosenthal, R. (1985). Mediation of interpersonal expectancy effects: Thirty-one meta-analyses. *Psychological Bulletin, 97,* 363–386.

Harris, R. J., Schoen, L. M., & Hensley, D. L. (1992). A cross-cultural study of story memory. *Journal of Cross Cultural Psychology, 23,* 133–147.

Harris, R. L., Ellicott, A. M., & Holmes, D. S. (1986). The timing of psychosocial transitions and changes in women's lives: An examination of women aged 45 to 60. *Journal of Personality and Social Psychology, 51,* 409–416.

Harrison, A. A. (1977). Let's make a deal: An analysis of revelations and stipulations in lonely hearts advertisements. *Journal of Personality and Social Psychology, 35,* 257–264.

Harrison, D. W., Gavin, M. R., & Isaac, W. (1988). A portable biofeedback device for autonomic responses. *Journal of Psychopathology and Behavioral Assessment, 10,* 217–224.

Harrison, L. K., Carroll, D., Burns, V. E., Corkill, A. R., Harrison, C. M., Ring, C., & Drayson, M. (2000). Cardiovascular and secretory immunoglobin A reactions to humorous, exciting, and didactic film presentations. *Biological Psychology, 52,* 113–126.

Hart, D. (1998). Can prototypes inform moral developmental theory? *Developmental Psychology, 34,* 420–423.

Hartley, J., & Homa, D. (1981). Abstraction of stylistic concepts. *Journal of Experimental Psychology: Human Learning and Memory, 7,* 33–46.

Hartung, C. M., & Widiger, T. A. (1998). Gender differences in the diagnosis of mental disorders: Conclusions and controversies of the *DSM-IV. Psychological Bulletin, 123,* 260–278.

Hartup, W. W. (1989). Social relationships and their developmental significance. *American Psychologist, 44,* 120–126.

Harvey, A. G. (2000). Pre-sleep cognitive activity: A comparison of sleep-onset insomniacs and good sleepers. *British Journal of Clinical Psychology, 39,* 275–286.

Harvey, M., & Milner, A. D. (1999). Residual perceptual distortion in "recovered" hemispatial neglect. *Neuropsychologia, 37,* 745–750.

Hashemi, A. H., & Cochrane, R. (1999). Expressed emotion and schizophrenia: A review of studies across cultures. *International Review of Psychiatry, 11,* 219–224.

Haslam, N. (1997). Evidence that male sexual orientation is a matter of degree. *Journal of Personality and Social Psychology, 73,* 862–870.

Hassett, J. (1978). *A primer of psychophysiology.* San Francisco: Freeman.

Hassin, R., & Trope, Y. (2000). Facing faces: Studies on the cognitive aspects of physiognomy. *Journal of Personality and Social Psychology, 78,* 837–852.

Hatfield, E. (1988). Passionate and companionate love. In R. J. Sternberg & M. L. Barnes (Eds.), *The psychology of love.* New Haven, CT: Yale University Press.

Hatfield, E., & Sprecher, S. (1995). Men's and women's preferences in marital partners in the United States, Russia, and Japan. *Journal of Cross-Cultural Psychology, 26,* 728–750.

Hathaway, S. R., & McKinley, J. C. (1943). *Minnesota Multiphasic Personality Inventory.* New York: Psychological Corporation.

Hattori, N. (1995). "The pleasure of your Bedlam": The theatre of madness in the Renaissance. *History of Psychiatry, 6,* 283–308.

Hatzichristou, D. G., Bertero, E. B., & Goldstein, I. (1994). Decision making in the evaluation of impotence: The patient profile-oriented algorithm. *Sexuality and Disability, 12,* 29–37.

Hawkes, N. (1979). Tracing Burt's descent to scientific fraud. *Science, 205,* 673–675.

Hawkins, M. J., Hawkins, W. E., & Ryan, E. R. (1989). Self-actualization as related to age of faculty members at a large midwestern university. *Psychological Reports, 65,* 1120–1122.

Hayashi, S., Kuno, T., Morotomi, Y., et al. (1998). Client-centered therapy in Japan: Fujio Tomoda and taoism. *Journal of Humanistic Psychology, 38,* 103–124.

Hayden, T., & Mischel, W. (1976). Maintaining trait consistency in the resolution of behavioral inconsistency: The wolf in sheep's clothing? *Journal of Personality, 44,* 109–132.

Hayes, C. (1951). *The ape in our house.* New York: Harper & Row.

Hayes, D. S. (1999). Young children's exposure to rhyming and nonrhyming stories: A structural analysis of recall. *Journal of Genetic Psychology, 160,* 280–293.

Hayes, D. S., Chemelski, B. E., & Palmer, M. (1982). Nursery rhymes and prose passages: Preschoolers' liking and short-term retention of story events. *Developmental Psychology, 18,* 49–56.

Hayes, R. L., Pechura, C. M., Katayama, Y., Povlishock, J. T., Giebel, M. L., & Becker, D. P. (1984). Activation of pontine cholinergic sites implicated in unconsciousness following cerebral concussions in the cat. *Science, 223,* 301–303.

Hayflick, L. (1980, January). The cell biology of human aging. *Scientific American,* pp. 58–65.

Hayman, L. A., Rexer, J. L., Pavol, M. A., et al. (1998). Klueuer-Bucy syndrome after bilateral selective damage of amygdala and its cortical connections. *Journal of Neuropsychiatry and Clinical Neurosciences, 10,* 354–358.

Haywood, H. C., Meyers, C. E., & Switzky, H. N. (1982). Mental retardation. *Annual Review of Psychology, 33,* 309–342.

Hazelrigg, P. J., Cooper, H., & Strathman, A. J. (1991). Personality moderators of the experimenter expectancy effect: A reexamination of five hypotheses. *Personality and Social Psychology Bulletin, 17,* 569–579.

He, Z.-X., & Lester, D. (1998). Methods for suicide in mainland China. *Death Studies, 22,* 571–579.

Hearne, K. M. (1989). A nationwide mass dream-telepathy experiment. *Journal of the Society for Psychical Research, 55,* 271–274.

Hearnshaw, L. S. (1979). *Cyril Burt: Psychologist.* Ithaca: Cornell University Press.

Hearnshaw, L. S. (1985). Francis Bacon: Harbinger of scientific psychology. *Revista de Historia de la Psicologia, 6,* 5–14.

Hearst, E. (1999). After the puzzle boxes: Thorndike in the 20th century. *Journal of the Experimental Analysis of Behavior, 72,* 441–446.

Heath, A. C., Kendler, K. S., Eaves, L. J., & Martin, N. G. (1990). Evidence for genetic influences on sleep disturbance and sleep pattern in twins. *Sleep, 13,* 318–335.

Heath, D. T., & Orthner, D. K. (1999). Stress and adaptation among male and female single parents. *Journal of Family Issues, 20,* 557–587.

Heatherton, T. F., Polivy, J., & Herman, C. P. (1989). Restraint and internal responsiveness: Effects of placebo manipulation of hunger state on eating. *Journal of Abnormal Psychology, 98,* 89–92.

Heatherton, T. F., Polivy, J., & Herman, C. P. (1990). Dietary restraint: Some current findings and speculations. *Psychology of Addictive Behaviors, 4,* 100–106.

Heaton, P., Hermelin, B., & Pring, L. (1998). Autism and pitch processing: A precursor for savant musical ability. *Music Perception, 15,* 291–305.

Heavey, L., Pring, L., & Hermelin, B. (1999). A date to remember: The nature of memory in savant calendrical calculators. *Psychological Medicine, 29,* 145–160.

Hebb, D. O. (1955). Drives and the C.N.S. (conceptual nervous system). *Psychological Review, 62,* 243–254.

Hebb, D. O. (1958). The motivating effects of exteroceptive stimulation. *American Psychologist, 13,* 109–113.

Hechinger, N. (1981, March). Seeing without eyes. *Science, 81,* pp. 38–43.

Heckhausen, J. (2000). Evolutionary perspectives on human motivation. *American Behavioral Scientist, 43,* 1015–1029.

Hedges, L. V. (1987). How hard is hard science, how soft is soft science? The empirical cumulativeness of research. *American Psychologist, 42,* 443–455.

Hedges, L. V., & Nowell, A. (1999). Changes in the Black-White gap in achievement test scores. *Sociology of Education, 72,* 111–135.

Heffner, H. E. (1983). Hearing in large and small dogs: Absolute thresholds and size of the tympanic membrane. *Behavioral Neuroscience, 97,* 310–318.

Heider, B. (2000). Visual form agnosia: Neural mechanisms and anatomical foundations. *Neurocase, 6,* 1–12.

Heider, F. (1944). Social perception and phenomenal causality. *Psychological Review, 51,* 358–374.

Heine, S. H., Lehman, D. R., Markus, H. R., & Kitayama, S. (1999). Is there a universal need for positive self-regard? *Psychological Review, 106,* 766–794.

Heiser, J. F., & Wilcox, C. S. (1998). Serotonin 5–HT-sub(1A) receptor agonists as antidepressants. *CNS Drugs, 10,* 343–353.

Heiser, P., Dickhaus, B., Schreiber, W., Clement, H. W., Hasse, C., et al. (2000). White blood cells and cortisol after sleep deprivation and recovery sleep in humans. *European Archives of Psychiatry and Clinical Neuroscience, 250,* 16–23.

Heitzmann, C. A., & Kaplan, M. (1988). Assessment of methods for measuring social support. *Health Psychology, 7,* 75–109.

Hellekant, G., Ninomiya, Y., & Danilova, V. (1998). Taste in chimpanzees. I: Labeled-line coding in sweet taste. *Physiology and Behavior, 65,* 191–200.

Helmes, E., & Reddon, J. R. (1993). A perspective on developments in assessing psychopathology: A critical review of the MMPI and MMPI-2. *Psychological Bulletin, 113*, 453–471.

Hendrick, C. (1990). Replications, strict replications, and conceptual replications: Are they important? *Journal of Social Behavior and Personality, 5*, 41–49.

Henle, M. (1993). Man's place in nature in the thinking of Wolfgang Kohler. *Journal of the History of the Behavioral Sciences, 29*, 3–7.

Hennessey, B. A., & Zbikowski, S. M. (1993). Immunizing children against the negative effects of reward: A further examination of intrinsic motivation training techniques. *Creativity Research Journal, 6*, 297–307.

Hennig, J., Laschefski, U., & Opper, C. (1994). Biopsychological changes after bungee jumping: b-Endorphin immunoreactivity as a mediator of euphoria? *Neuropsychobiology, 29*, 28–32.

Hennrikus, D. J., Jeffery, R. W., & Lando, H. A. (1995). The smoking cessation process: Longitudinal observations in a working population. *Preventive Medicine, 24*, 235–244.

Hepper, P. G., Shahidulla, S., & White, R. (1991). Handedness in the human fetus. *Neuropsychologia, 29*, 1107–1111.

Herbert, T. B., & Cohen, S. (1993). Depression and immunity: A meta-analytic review. *Psychological Bulletin, 113*, 472–486.

Herbert, W. (1983). MMPI: Redefining normality for modern times. *Science News, 134*, 228.

Herbert, W. (1983). Remembrance of things partly. *Science News, 124*, 378–381.

Herek, G. M. (2000). The psychology of sexual prejudice. *Current Directions in Psychological Science, 9*, 19–22

Herkenhahn, M., Lynn, A. B., deCosta, B. R., & Richfield, E. K. (1991). Neuronal localization of cannabinoid receptors in the basal ganglia of the rat. *Brain Research, 547*, 267–274.

Herman, C. P., Olmsted, M. P., & Polivy, J. (1983). Obesity, externality, and susceptibility to social influence: An integrated analysis. *Journal of Personality and Social Psychology, 45*, 926–934.

Herman, D., Opler, L., Felix, A., et al. (2000). A critical time intervention with mentally ill homeless men: Impact on psychiatric symptoms. *Journal of Nervous and Mental Disease, 188*, 135–140.

Herman, L. M., & Uyeyama, R. K. (1999). The dolphin's grammatical competency: Comments on Kako (1999). *Animal Learning and Behavior, 27*, 18–23.

Hermelin, B., & Pring, L. (1998). The pictorial context dependency of savant artists: A research note. *Perceptual and Motor Skills, 87*, 995–1001.

Herning, R. I. (1985). Cocaine increases EEG beta: A replication of Hans Berger's historic experiments. *Electroencephalography and Clinical Neurophysiology, 60*, 470–477.

Herrnstein, R. J., & Murray, C. (1994). *The bell curve: Intelligence and class structure in American life.* New York: Free Press.

Herz, R. S., & Cupchik, G. C. (1992). An experimental characterization of odor-evoked memories in humans. *Chemical Senses, 17*, 519–528.

Herz, R. S., & Engen, T. (1996). Odor memory: Review and analysis. *Psychonomic Bulletin and Review, 3*, 300–313.

Herzog, H. A., Jr. (1995). Has public interest in animal rights peaked? *American Psychologist, 50*, 945–947.

Herzog, T. R. (1999). Gender differences in humor appreciation revisited. *Humor, 12*, 411–423.

Hetherington, A. W., & Ranson, S. W. (1942). The spontaneous activity and food intake of rats with hypothalamic lesions. *American Journal of Physiology, 136*, 609–617.

Hewitt, J. K. (1997). The genetics of obesity: What have genetic studies told us about the environment? *Behavior Genetics, 27*, 353–358.

Hewlett, B. S., Lamb, M. E., Shannon, D., Leyendecker, B., & Schoelmerich, A. (1998). Culture and early infancy among central African foragers and farmers. *Developmental Psychology, 34*, 653–661.

Hewson-Bower, B., & Drummond, P. D. (1998). Secretory immunoglobulin A increases during relaxation in children with and without recurrent upper respiratory tract infections. *Journal of Developmental and Behavioral Pediatrics, 17*, 311–316.

Heyes, C. M., Dawson, G. R., & Nokes, T. (1992). Imitation in rats: Initial responding and transfer evidence. *Quarterly Journal of Experimental Psychology Comparative and Physiological Psychology, 45B*, 229–240.

Hicks, R. A., Johnson, C., & Pellegrini, R. J. (1992). Changes in the self-reported consistency of normal habitual sleep duration of college students (1978 and 1992). *Perceptual and Motor Skills, 75*, 1168–1170.

Hicks, R. A., Johnson, C., Cuevas, T., & Debaro, D. (1994). Do right-handers live longer? An updated assessment of baseball player data. *Perceptual and Motor Skills, 78*, 1243–1247.

Higashiyama, A., & Kitano, S. (1991). Perceived size and distance of persons in natural outdoor settings: The effects of familiar size. *Psychologia: An International Journal of Psychology in the Orient, 34*, 188–199.

Higgins, E. T. (1987). Self-discrepancy: A theory relating self and affect. *Psychological Review, 94*, 319–340.

Higgins, E. T. (1990). Self-state representations: Patterns of interconnected beliefs with specific holistic meanings and importance. *Bulletin of the Psychonomic Society, 28*, 248–253.

Higgins, J. E., & Endler, N. S. (1995). Coping, life stress, and psychological and somatic distress. *European Journal of Personality, 9*, 253–270.

Higgins, J. J., Rosen, D. R., Loveless, J. M., Clyman, J. C., & Grau, M. J. (2000). A gene for nonsyndromic mental retardation maps to chromosome 3p25-pter. *Neurology, 55*, 335–340.

Highet, A. (1998). Casablanca, Humphrey Bogart, the Oedipus complex, and the American male. *Psychoanalytic Review, 85*, 761–774.

Hilgard, E. R. (1973). A neodissociative interpretation of pain reduction in hypnosis. *Psychological Review, 80*, 403–419.

Hilgard, E. R. (1978, January). Hypnosis and consciousness. *Human Nature,* pp. 42–49.

Hilgard, E. R. (1987). *Psychology in America: A historical survey.* San Diego: Harcourt Brace Jovanovich.

Hilgard, E. R. (1993). Which psychologists prominent in the second half of this century made lasting contributions to psychological theory? *Psychological Science, 4*, 70–80.

Hill, J. O., & Peters, J. C. (1998). Environmental contributions to the obesity epidemic. *Science, 280*, 1371–1374.

Hill, R. D., Allen, A. C., & McWhorter, P. (1991). Stories as a mnemonic aid for older learners. *Psychology and Aging, 6*, 484–486.

Hillbrand, M., & Waite, B. M. (1994). The everyday experience of an institutionalized sex offender: An idiographic application of the experience sampling method. *Archives of Sexual Behavior, 23*, 453–463.

Hillson, T. R., & Martin, R. A. (1994). What's so funny about that? The domains-interaction approach as a model of incongruity and resolution in humor. *Motivation and Emotion, 18*, 1–29.

Hilsenroth, M. J., Hibbard, S. R., Nash, M. R., & Handler, L. (1993). A Rorschach study of narcissism, defense, and aggression in borderline, narcissistic, and Cluster C personality disorders. *Journal of Personality Assessment, 60*, 346–361.

Hinchy, J., Lovibond, P. F., & Ter-Horst, K. M. (1995). Blocking in human electrodermal conditioning. *Quarterly Journal of Experimental Psychology Comparative and Physiological Psychology, 48*, 2–12.

Hines, T. M. (1998). Comprehensive review of biorhythm theory. *Psychological Reports, 83*, 19–64.

Hirata, Y., Kuriki, S., & Pantev, C. (1999). Musicians with absolute pitch show distinct neural activities in the auditory cortex. *Neuroreport, 10*, 999–1002.

Hirsch, H. V. B., & Spinelli, D. N. (1970). Visual experience modifies distribution of horizontally and vertically oriented receptive fields in cats. *Science, 168*, 869–871.

Hiscock, M., Israelian, M., Inch, R., Jacek, C., & Hiscock-Kalil, C. (1995). Is there a sex difference in human laterality? II. An exhaustive survey of visual laterality studies from six neuropsychology journals. *Journal of Clinical and Experimental Neuropsychology, 17*, 590–610.

Hitchcock, C. H., & Noonan, M. J. (2000). Computer-assisted instruction of early academic skills. *Topics in Early Childhood Special Education, 20*, 145–158.

Hobson, J. A. (1988). *The dreaming brain.* New York: Basic Books.

Hobson, J. A., & McCarley, R. W. (1977). The brain as a dream state generator: An activation-synthesis hypothesis of the dream process. *American Journal of Psychiatry, 134*, 1335–1348.

Hocking-Schuler, J. L., & O'Brien, W. H. (1997). Cardiovascular recovery from stress and hypertension risk factors: A meta-analytic review. *Psychophysiology, 34*, 649–659.

Hoeksema-van Orden, C. Y .D., Gaillard, A. W. K., & Buunk, B. P. (1998). Social loafing under fatigue. *Journal of Personality and Social Psychology, 75*, 1179–1190.

Hoelscher, T. J. (1987). Maintenance of relaxation-induced blood pressure reductions: The importance of continued relaxation practice. *Biofeedback and Self-Regulation, 12*, 3–12.

Hoemann, H. W., & Keske, C. M. (1995). Proactive interference and language change in hearing adult students of American Sign Language. *Sign Language Studies, 86*, 45–61.

Hofmann, A. (1983). *LSD: My problem child.* Los Angeles: Tarcher.

Hofsten, C. (1983). Eye-hand coordination in the newborn. *Developmental Psychology, 18*, 450–461.

Hogben, M. (1998). Factors moderating the effect of televised aggression on viewer behavior. *Communication Research, 25*, 220–247.

Holahan, C. K., Holahan, C. J., & Wonacott, N. L. (1999). Self-appraisal, life satisfaction, and retrospective life choices across one and three decades. *Psychology and Aging, 14*, 238–244.

Holden, C. (1980, November). Twins reunited: More than the faces are familiar. *Science 80*, 55–59.

Holden, C. (1986). Depression research advances, treatment lags. *Science, 233*, 723–726.

Holden, C. (1986). Researchers grapple with problems of updating classic psychological test. *Science, 233*, 1249–1251.

Holden, C. (1987). Animal regulations: So far, so good. *Science, 237*, 598–601.

Holden, C. (1987). The genetics of personality. *Science, 237*, 598–601.

Holland, L. N., Goldstein, B. D., & Aronstam, R. S. (1993). Substance P receptor desensitization in the dorsal horn: Possible involvement of receptor-G protein complexes. *Brain Research, 600*, 89–96.

Hollender, M. H. (1983). The 51st landmark article. *Journal of the American Medical Association, 250*, 228–229.

Hollingworth, L. S. (1914). Variability as related to sex differences in achievement. *American Journal of Sociology, 19*, 510–530.

Hollins, M., Delemos, K. A., & Goble, A. K. (1991). Vibrotactile adaptation on the face. *Perception and Psychophysics, 49*, 21–30.

Hollon, S. D. (1996). The efficacy and effectiveness of psychotherapy relative to medications. *American Psychologist, 51*, 1025–1030.

Holly, D. (2000, January 14). County discourages racial profiling. *Associated Press.*

Holmes, D. S. (1984). Meditation and somatic arousal reduction: A review of the experimental evidence. *American Psychologist, 39*, 1–10.

Holmes, M. (1986, August 3). 20 years ago, the Texas tower massacre. *Philadelphia Inquirer,* p. 3E.

Holmes, T. H., & Rahe, R. H. (1967). The Social Readjustment Rating Scale. *Journal of Psychosomatic Research, 11,* 213–218.

Holroyd, J. (1996). Hypnosis treatment of chronic pain: Understanding why hypnosis is useful. *International Journal of Clinical and Experimental Hypnosis, 44,* 33–51.

Holst, V. F., & Pezdek, K. (1992). Scripts for typical crimes and their effects on memory for eyewitness testimony. *Applied Cognitive Psychology, 6,* 573–587.

Holtgraves, T. (1997). Styles of language use: Individual and cultural variability in conversational indirectness. *Journal of Personality and Social Psychology, 73,* 624–637.

Homant, R. J., & Kennedy, D. B. (1998). Psychological aspects of crime scene profiling: Validity research. *Criminal Justice and Behavior, 25,* 319–343.

Hong, S. (2000). Exercise and psychoneuroimmunology. *International Journal of Sport Psychology, 31,* 204–227.

Honore, P., Menning, P. M., Rogers, S. D., Nichols, M. L., Basbaum, A. I., et al. (1999). Spinal substance P receptor expression and internalization in acute, short-term, and long-term inflammatory pain states. *Journal of Neuroscience, 19,* 7670–7678.

Honts, C. R., Hodes, R. L., & Raskin, D. C. (1985). Effects of physical countermeasures on the physiological detection of deception. *Journal of Applied Psychology, 70,* 177–187.

Hood, K. (1995). Social psychology and sociobiology: Which is the metatheory? *Psychological Inquiry, 6,* 54–56.

Hoon, A. H., Jr., & Johnston, M. V. (1998). "What constitutes cerebral palsy?" Comment. *Developmental Medicine and Child Neurology, 40,* 847.

Hopkins, J. R. (1995). Erik Homburger Erikson (1902–1994). *American Psychologist, 50,* 796–797.

Horn, J. L., & Cattell, R. C. (1966). Refinement and test of the theory of fluid and crystallized general intelligences. *Journal of Educational Psychology, 57,* 253–270.

Horn, J. L., & Donaldson, G. (1976). On the myth of individual decline in adulthood. *American Psychologist, 31,* 701–719.

Horne, J. A., & Reyner, L. A. (1996). Counteracting driver sleepiness: Effects of napping, caffeine, and placebo. *Psychophysiology, 33,* 306–309.

Horner, M. D. (1990). Psychobiological evidence for the distinction between episodic and semantic memory. *Neuropsychology Review, 1,* 281–321.

Horney, K. (1926/1967). The flight from womanhood. In K. Horney, *Feminine psychology* (H. Kelman, Ed., pp. 54–70). New York: W. W. Norton.

Horney, K. (1937). *The neurotic personality of our time.* New York: W. W. Norton.

Horney, K. (1950). *Neurosis and human growth.* New York: W. W. Norton.

Hornstein, G. A. (1992). The return of the repressed: Psychology's problematic relations with psychoanalysis, 1909–1960. *American Psychologist, 47,* 254–263.

Horowitz, F. D. (1992). John B. Watson's legacy: Learning and environment. *Developmental Psychology, 28,* 360–367.

Horowitz, S. W., Kircher, J. C., Honts, C. R., & Raskin, D. C. (1997). The role of comparison questions in physiological detection of deception. *Psychophysiology, 34,* 108–115.

Horwath, E., & Weissman, M. M. (2000). The epidemiology and cross-national presentation of obsessive-compulsive disorder. *Psychiatric Clinics of North America, 23,* 493–507.

Hough, L. M., & Oswald, F. L. (2000). Personnel selection: Looking toward the future—Remembering the past. *Annual Review of Psychology, 51,* 631–664.

Houlihan, D., & Jones, R. N. (1989). Treatment of a boy's school phobia with in vivo systematic desensitization. *Professional School Psychology, 4,* 285–293.

Houlihan, D., Schwartz, C., Miltenberger, R., & Heuton, D. (1993). The rapid treatment of a young man's balloon (noise) phobia using in vivo flooding. *Journal of Behavior Therapy and Experimental Psychiatry, 24,* 233–240.

House, J. D. (1998). High school achievement and admissions test scores as predictors of course performance of American Indian and Alaska Native students. *Journal of Psychology, 132,* 680–682.

Hovland, C. I., Lumsdaine, A., & Sheffield, F. (1949). *Experiments on mass communication.* Princeton, NJ: Princeton University Press.

Howard, K. I., Kopta, S. M., Krausse, M. S., & Orlinsky, D. E. (1986). The dose-effect relationship in psychotherapy. *American Psychologist, 41,* 159–164.

Hu, S., & Stern, R. M. (1999). The retention of adaptation to motion sickness eliciting stimulation. *Aviation, Space, and Environmental Medicine, 70,* 766–768.

Huang, W., & Cuvo, A. J. (1997). Social skills training for adults with mental retardation in job-related settings. *Behavior Modification, 21,* 3–44.

Hubel, D. H., & Wiesel, T. N. (1979, September). Brain mechanisms of vision. *Scientific American,* pp. 130–144.

Hudesman, J., Page, W., & Rautiainen, J. (1992). Use of subliminal stimulation to enhance learning mathematics. *Perceptual and Motor Skills, 74,* 1219–1224.

Hugdahl, K., Satz, P., Mitrushina, M., & Miller, E. N. (1993). Left-handedness and old age: Do left-handers die earlier? *Neuropsychologia, 31,* 325–333.

Hughes, J. R., Gust, S. W., Skoog, K., & Keenan, R. (1991). Symptoms of tobacco withdrawal: A replication and extension. *Archives of General Psychiatry, 48,* 52–59.

Hughes, J. R., Higgins, S. T., & Bickel, W. K. (1994). Nicotine withdrawal versus other drug withdrawal syndromes: Similarities and dissimilarities. *Addiction, 89,* 1461–1470.

Hughes, J. R., Higgins, S. T., Bickel, W. K., Hunt, W. K., Fenwick, J. W., Gulliver, S. B., & Mireault, G. C. (1991). Caffeine self-administration, withdrawal, and adverse effects among coffee drinkers. *Archives of General Psychiatry, 48,* 611–617.

Hughes, J., Smith, T. W., Kosterlitz, H. W., Fothergill, L. A., Morgan, B. A., & Morris, H. R. (1975). Identification of two related pentapeptides from the brain with potent opiate agonistic activity. *Nature, 258,* 577–579.

Hui, H., & Luk, C. L. (1997). Industrial/organizational psychology. In J. W. Berry, M. H. Segall, & C. Kagitçibasi (Eds.), *Handbook of cross-cultural psychology: Vol. 3. Social behavior and applications* (pp. 371–411). Boston: Allyn & Bacon.

Hui, K. K. S., Liu, J., Makris, N., Gollub, R. L., Chen, A. J. W., et al. (2000). Acupuncture modulates the limbic system and subcortical gray structures of the human brain: Evidence from fMRI studies in normal subjects. *Human Brain Mapping, 9,* 13–25.

Hull, C. L. (1943). *Principles of behavior.* New York: Appleton-Century-Crofts.

Hull, J. G., & Bond, C. F., Jr. (1986). Social and behavioral consequences of alcohol consumption and expectancy: A meta-analysis. *Psychological Bulletin, 99,* 347–360.

Humphreys, K. (1997). Clinicians' referral and matching of substance abuse patients to self-help groups after treatment. *Psychiatric Services, 48,* 1445–1449.

Hunt, E. (1997). The status of the concept of intelligence. *Japanese Psychological Research, 39,* 1–11.

Hunt, J. M. (1979). Psychological development: Early experience. *Annual Review of Psychology, 30,* 103–143.

Hunter, I. M. L. (1993). Heritage from the wild boy of Aveyron. *Early Child Development and Care, 95,* 143–155.

Hunter, J. E., & Hunter, R. F. (1984). Validity and utility of alternative predictors of job performance. *Psychological Bulletin, 96,* 72–98.

Hur, J., & Osborne, S. (1993). A comparison of forward and backward chaining methods used in teaching corsage making skills to mentally retarded adults. *British Journal of Developmental Disabilities, 39,* 108–117.

Hur, Y.-M., Bouchard, T. J., Jr., & Eckert, E. (1998). Genetic and environmental influences on self-reported diet: A reared-apart twin study. *Physiology and Behavior, 64,* 629–636.

Hur, Y.-M., McGue, M., & Iacono, W. G. (1998). The structure of self-concept in female preadolescent twins: A behavioral genetic approach. *Journal of Personality and Social Psychology, 74,* 1069–1077.

Hurovitz, C. S., Dunn, S., Domhoff, G. W., & Fiss, H. (1999). The dreams of blind men and women: A replication and extension of previous findings. *Dreaming. 9,* 183–193.

Hurst, L. C., & Mulhall, D. J. (1988). Another calendar savant. *British Journal of Psychiatry, 152,* 274–277.

Husain, S. A. (1990). Current perspective on the role of psychosocial factors in adolescent suicide. *Psychiatric Annals, 20,* 122–127.

Huston, A. C., Watkins, B. A., & Kunkel, E. (1989). Public policy and children's television. *American Psychologist, 44,* 424–433.

Huston, A. C., Wright, J. C., Marquis, J., & Green, S. B. (1999). How young children spend their time: Television and other activities. *Developmental Psychology, 35,* 912–925.

Huston, T. L., Ruggiero, M., Conner, R., & Geis, G. (1981). Bystander intervention into crime: A study based on naturally-occurring episodes. *Social Psychology Quarterly, 44,* 14–23.

Hutchins, C. M. (1981, October). The acoustics of violin plates. *Scientific American,* pp. 170–174, 177–180, 182–186.

Huyse, F. J., Lyons, J. S., Stiefel, F., et al. (2001). Operationalizing the biopsychosocial model: The INTERMED. *Psychosomatics, 42,* 5–13.

Hyde, J. S. (1984). Children's understanding of sexist language. *Developmental Psychology, 20,* 697–706.

Hyde, J. S. (1994). Can meta-analysis make feminist transformations in psychology? *Psychology of Women Quarterly, 18,* 451–462.

Hyde, J. S., & Durik, A. M. (2000). Gender differences in erotic plasticity— Evolutionary or sociocultural forces? Comment on Baumeister (2000). *Psychological Bulletin, 126,* 375–379.

Hyde, J. S., & Linn, M. C. (1988). Gender differences in verbal ability: A meta-analysis. *Psychological Bulletin, 104,* 53–69.

Hyde, J. S., & Plant, E. A. (1995). Magnitude of psychological gender differences: Another side of the story. *American Psychologist, 50,* 159–161.

Hyde, J. S., Fennema, E., & Lamon, S. J. (1990). Gender differences in mathematics performance: A meta-analysis. *Psychological Bulletin, 107,* 139–155. .

Hyland, B. (1998). Neural activity related to reaching and grasping in rostral and caudal regions of rat motor cortex. *Behavioural Brain Research, 94,* 255–269.

Hyman, R. B. (1988). Four stages of adulthood: An exploratory study of growth patterns of inner-direction and time-competence in women. *Journal of Research in Personality, 22,* 117–127.

Iaffaldano, M. T., & Muchinsky, P. M. (1985). Job satisfaction and performance: A meta-analysis. *Psychological Bulletin, 97,* 251–273.

Ickes, W., Gesn, P. R., & Graham, T. (2000). Gender differences in empathic accuracy: Differential ability or differential motivation? *Personal Relationships, 7,* 95–109.

Ilgen, D. R., Barnes-Farrell, J. L., & McKellin, D. B. (1993). Peformance appraisal process research in the 1980s: What has it contributed to appraisals in use? *Organizational Behavior and Human Decision Processes, 54,* 321–368.

Immergluck, L. (1964). Determinism-freedom in contemporary psychology: An ancient problem revisited. *American Psychologist, 19,* 270–281.

Ingelfinger, F. J. (1944). The late effects of total and subtotal gastrectomy. *New England Journal of Medicine, 231,* 321–327.

Ingham, A. G., Levinger, G., Graves, J., & Peckham, V. (1974). The Ringelmann effect: Studies of group size and group performance. *Journal of Experimental Social Psychology, 10,* 371–384.

Inglis, A., & Greenglass, E. R. (1989). Motivation for marriage among women and men. *Psychological Reports, 65,* 1035–1042.

Inkson, K., & Paterson, J. (1993). Organizational behavior in New Zealand, 1987–1992: A review. *New Zealand Journal of Psychology, 22,* 54–66.

Inman, M. L., & Baron, R. S. (1996). Influence of prototypes on perceptions of prejudice. *Journal of Personality and Social Psychology, 70,* 727–739.

Inoue, S., Honda, K., & Komoda, Y. (1995). Sleep as neuronal detoxification and restitution. *Behavioural Brain Research, 69,* 91–96.

Iqbal, H. M., & Shayer, M. (2000). Accelerating the development of formal thinking in Pakistan secondary school students: Achievement effects and professional development issues. *Journal of Research in Science Teaching, 37,* 259–274.

Ironson, G., Schneiderman, H., Kumar, M., & Antoni, M. H. (1994). Psychosocial stress, endocrine and immune response in HIV-1 disease. *Homeostasis in Health and Disease, 35,* 137–148.

Irwin, M., Mascovich, A., Gillin, J. C., & Willoughby, R. (1994). Partial sleep deprivation reduced natural killer cell activity in humans. *Psychosomatic Medicine, 56,* 493–498.

Ishizawa, Y., Ma, H.-C., Dohi, S., & Shimonaka, H. (2000). Effects of cholinomimetic injection into the brain stem reticular formation on halothane anesthesia and antinociception in rats. *Journal of Pharmacology and Experimental Therapeutics, 293,* 845–851.

Ispa, J. M., Thornburg, K. R., & Gray, M. M. (1990). Relations between early childhood care arrangements and college students' psychosocial development and academic performance. *Adolescence, 25,* 529–542.

Iversen, I. H. (1993). Techniques for establishing schedules with wheel running as reinforcement in rats. *Journal of the Experimental Analysis of Behavior, 60,* 219–238.

Iyengar, S. S., & Lepper, M. R. (1999). Rethinking the value of choice: A cultural perspective on intrinsic motivation. *Journal of Personality and Social Psychology, 76,* 349–366.

Izac, S. M., & Banoczi, W. (1999). The Wada test. *American Journal of Electroneurodiagnostic Technology, 39,* 23–33.

Izard, C. E. (1990). Facial expressions and the regulation of emotions. *Journal of Personality and Social Psychology, 58,* 487–498.

Izard, C. E. (1993). Four systems for emotion activation: Cognitive and noncognitive processes. *Psychological Review, 100,* 68–90.

Jack, S. J., & Ronan, K. R. (1998). Sensation seeking among high- and low-risk sports participants. *Personality and Individual Differences, 25,* 1063–1083.

Jacklin, C. N. (1989). Female and male: Issues of gender. *American Psychologist, 44,* 127–133.

Jackson, C., Bee-Gates, D. J., & Henriksen, L. (1994). Authoritative parenting, child competencies, and initiation of cigarette smoking. *Health Education Quarterly, 21,* 103–116.

Jackson, G. R., Owsley, C., & McGwin, G., Jr. (1999). Aging and dark adaptation. *Vision Research, 39,* 3975–3982.

Jacob, R. G., Wing, R. R., & Shapiro, A. P. (1987). The behavioral treatment of hypertension: Long-term effects. *Behavior Therapy, 18,* 325–352.

Jacobs, G. H., Neitz, M., Deegan, J. F., & Neitz, J. (1996). Trichromatic colour vision in New World monkeys. *Nature, 382,* 156–158.

Jacobs, W. J., & Blackburn, J. R. (1995). A model of Pavlovian conditioning: Variations in representations of the unconditional stimulus. *Integrative Physiological and Behavioral Science, 30,* 12–33.

Jacobsen, P. B., Bovbjerg, D. H., Schwartz, M. D., & Hudis, C. A. (1995). Conditioned emotional distress in women receiving chemotherapy for breast cancer. *Journal of Consulting and Clinical Psychology, 63,* 108–114.

Jaeger, J. J., Lockwood, A. H., Van Valin, R. D., Jr., et al. (1998). Sex differences in brain regions activated by grammatical and reading tasks. *Neuroreport, 9,* 2803–2807.

James, W. (1884). What is an emotion? *Mind, 9,* 188–205.

James, W. (1890/1981). *The principles of psychology* (2 vols.). Cambridge, MA: Harvard University Press.

Jang, K. L., Livesley, W. J., & Vernon, P. A. (1996). The genetic basis of personality at different ages: A cross-sectional twin study. *Personality and Individual Differences, 21,* 299–301.

Jang, K. L., McCrae, R. R., Angleitner, A., Riemann, R., & Livesley, W. J. (1998). Heritability of facet-level traits in a cross-cultural twin sample: Support for a hierarchical model of personality. *Journal of Personality and Social Psychology, 74,* 1556–1565.

Jeffery, R. W., Epstein, L. H., Wilson, G. T., et al. (2000). Long-term maintenance of weight loss: Current status. *Health Psychology, 19,* 5–16.

Jegede, J. O., Jegede, R. T., & Ugodulunwa, C. A. (1997). Effects of achievement motivation and study habits on Nigerian secondary school students' academic performance. *Journal of Psychology, 131,* 523–529.

Jemmott, J. B., & Locke, S. E. (1984). Psychosocial factors, immunologic mediation, and human susceptibility to infectious diseases: How much do we know? *Psychological Bulletin, 95,* 78–108.

Jemmott, J. B., & Magloire, K. (1988). Academic stress, social support, and secretory immunoglobulin A. *Journal of Personality and Social Psychology, 55,* 803–810.

Jenkins, J. G., & Dallenbach, K. M. (1924). Oblivescence during sleep and waking. *American Journal of Psychology, 35,* 605–612.

Jenkins, J. H. (1998). Diagnostic criteria for schizophrenia and related psychotic disorders: Integration and suppression of cultural evidence in *DSM-IV. Transcultural Psychiatry, 35,* 357–376.

Jensen, A. R. (1969). How much can we boost IQ and scholastic achievement? *Harvard Educational Review, 39,* 1–123.

Jensen, A. R. (1980). *Bias in mental testing.* New York: Free Press.

Jin, C., Schenkel, M., & Carlile, S. (2000). Neural system identification model of human sound localization. *Journal of the Acoustical Society of America, 108,* 1215–1235.

Jocklin, V., McGue, M., & Lykken, D. T. (1996). Personality and divorce: A genetic analysis. *Journal of Personality and Social Psychology, 71,* 288–299.

Johns, G. (1997). Contemporary research on absence from work: Correlates, causes and consequences. In C. L. Cooper & I. T. Robertson (Eds.), *International review of industrial and organizational psychology* (Vol. 12, pp. 115–173). Chichester: Wiley.

Johnson, D. L., Wiebe, J. S., Gold, S. M., Andreasen, N. C., Hichwa, R. D., et al. (1999). Cerebral blood flow and personality: A positron emission tomography study. *American Journal of Psychiatry, 156,* 252–257.

Johnson, J. S., & Newport, E. L. (1989). Critical period effects in second language learning: The influence of maturational state on the acquisition of English as a second language. *Cognitive Psychology, 21,* 60–99.

Johnson, M. E., & Hauck, C. (1999). Beliefs and opinions about hypnosis held by the general public. *American Journal of Clinical Hypnosis, 42,* 10–20.

Johnson, M. H., Breakwell, G., Douglas, W., & Humphries, S. (1998). The effects of imagery and sensory detection distractors on different measures of pain: How does distraction work? *British Journal of Clinical Psychology, 37,* 141–154.

Johnson, S. L., & Roberts, J. E. (1995). Life events and bipolar disorder: Implications from biological theories. *Psychological Bulletin, 117,* 434–449.

Johnson, T. J., & Cropsey, K. L. (2000). Sensation seeking and drinking game participation in heavy-drinking college students. *Addictive Behaviors, 25,* 109–116.

Jonas, G. (1972). *Visceral learning: Toward a science of self-control.* New York: Viking.

Jones, L. (1900). Education during sleep. *Suggestive Therapeutics, 8,* 283–285.

Jones, L. V. (1984). White-black achievement differences: The narrowing gap. *American Psychologist, 39,* 1207–1213.

Jones, M. C. (1924). The elimination of children's fears. *Journal of Experimental Psychology, 7,* 383–390.

Jones, M. C. (1965). Psychological correlates of somatic development. *Child Development, 36,* 899–911.

Jones, N. A., Field, T., & Davalos, M. (1998). Massage therapy attenuates right frontal EEG asymmetry in one-month-old infants of depressed mothers. *Infant Behavior and Development, 21,* 527–530.

Jorgensen, R. S., Nash, J. K., Lasser, N. L., Hymowitz, N., & Langer, A. W. (1988). Heart rate acceleration and its relationship to total serum cholesterol, triglycerides, and blood pressure. *Psychophysiology, 25,* 39–44.

Joussemet, M., & Koestner, R. (1999). Effect of expected rewards on children's creativity. *Creativity Research Journal, 12,* 231–239.

Joyce, J. (1916/1967). *A portrait of the artist as a young man.* New York: Viking.

Judge, S. J., & Cumming, B. G. (1986). Neurons in the monkey mibrain with activity related to vergence eye movement and accommodation. *Journal of Neurophysiology, 55,* 915–930.

Julien, R. M. (1981). *A primer of drug action.* San Francisco: Freeman.

Jung, C. G. (1959/1969). *Flying saucers: A modern myth of things seen in the sky.* New York: Signet.

Kaemingk, K., & Paquette, A. (1999). Effects of prenatal alcohol exposure on neuropsychological functioning. *Developmental Neuropsychology, 15,* 111–140.

Kahan, T. L., & LaBerge, S. (1994). Lucid dreaming as metacognition: Implications for cognitive science. *Consciousness and Cognition, 3,* 246–264.

Kahneman, D. (1991). Judgment and decision making: A personal view. *Psychological Science, 2,* 142–145.

Kahneman, D., & Tversky, A. (1973). On the psychology of prediction. *Psychological Review, 80,* 237–251.

Kako, E. (1999). Elements of syntax in the systems of three language-trained animals. *Animal Learning and Behavior, 27,* 1–14.

Kalichman, S. C. (1996). HIV-AIDS prevention videotapes: A review of empirical findings. *Journal of Primary Prevention, 17,* 259–280.

Kamarck, T. W., Peterman, A. H., & Raynor, D. A. (1998). The effects of the social environment on stress-related cardiovascular activation: Current findings, prospects, and implications. *Annals of Behavioral Medicine, 20,* 247–256.

Kamin, L. J. (1974). *The science and politics of IQ.* New York: Wiley.

Kamins, M. A., & Assael, H. (1987). Two-sided versus one-sided appeals: A cognitive perspective on argumentation, source derogation, and the effect of disconfirming trial on belief change. *Journal of Marketing Research, 24,* 29–39.

Kandel, E. R., & Schwartz, J. H. (1982). Molecular biology of learning: Modulation of transmitter release. *Science, 218,* 433–443.

Kanfer, R. (1990). Motivation theory and industrial organizational psychology. In M. E. Dunnette & L. M. Hough (Eds.), *Handbook of industrial and organizational psychology* (2nd ed., pp. 75–124). Palo Alto: Consulting Psychologists Press.

Kapur, S., Zipursky, R., Jones, C., Remington, G., & Houle, S. (2000). Relationship between dopamine D-sub-2 occupancy, clinical response, and side effects: A double-blind PET study of first-episode schizophrenia. *American Journal of Psychiatry, 157,* 514–520.

Karau, S. J., & Williams, K. D. (1993). Social loafing: A meta-analytic review and theoretical integration. *Journal of Personality and Social Psychology, 65,* 681–706.

Karlberg, L., Krakau, I., & Unden, A.-L. (1998). Type A behavior intervention in primary health care reduces hostility and time pressure: A study in Sweden. *Social Science and Medicine, 46,* 397–402.

Karney, B. R., & Bradbury, T. N. (1995). The longitudinal course of marital quality and stability: A review of theory, methods, and research. *Psychological Bulletin, 118,* 3–34.

Karney, B. R., & Bradbury, T. N. (2000). Attributions in marriage: State or trait? A growth curve analysis. *Journal of Personality and Social Psychology, 78,* 295–309.

Karnovsky, M. L. (1986). Progress in sleep. *New England Journal of Medicine, 315,* 1026–1028.

Karon, B. P., & Widener, A. (1998). Repressed memories: The real story. *Professional Psychology: Research and Practice, 29,* 482–487.

Kashima, E. S., & Kashima, Y. (1998). Culture and language: The case of cultural dimensions and personal pronoun use. *Journal of Cross-Cultural Psychology, 29,* 461–486.

Kashima, Y., & Triandis, H. C. (1986). The self-serving bias in attributions as a coping strategy: *Journal of Cross-Cultural Psychology, 17,* 83–97.

Kassel, J. D., & Unrod, M. (2000). Smoking, anxiety, and attention: Support for the role of nicotine in attentionally mediated anxiolysis. *Journal of Abnormal Psychology, 109,* 161–166.

Kasser, T., & Sharma, Y. S. (1999). Reproductive freedom, educational equality, and females' preference for resource-acquisition characteristics in mates. *Psychological Science, 10,* 374–377.

Kastner, J., Gottlieb, B. W., Gottlieb, J., & Kastner, S. (1995). Use of incentive structure in mainstream classes. *Journal of Educational Research, 89,* 52–57.

Katz, J. (1984). Symptom prescription: A review of the clinical outcome literature. *Clinical Psychology Review, 4,* 703–717.

Katzell, R. A., & Austin, J. T. (1992). From then to now: The development of industrial-organizational psychology in the United States. *Journal of Applied Psychology, 77,* 803–835.

Kaufman, J., & Cicchetti, D. (1989). Effects of maltreatment on school-age children's socioemotional development: Assessments in a day-camp setting. *Developmental Psychology, 25,* 516–524.

Kaufman, J., & Zigler, E. (1987). Do abused children become abusive parents? *American Journal of Orthopsychiatry, 57,* 186–192.

Kaufman, L., & Rock, I. (1962, July). The moon illusion. *Scientific American,* pp. 120–130.

Kawashima, R., Okuda, J., Umetsu, A., Sugiura, M., et al. (2000). Human cerebellum plays an important role in memory-timed finger movement: An fMRI study. *Journal of Neurophysiology, 83,* 1079–1087.

Kazdin, A. E. (1982). Symptom substitution, generalization, and response covariation: Implications for psychotherapy outcome. *Psychological Bulletin, 91,* 349–365.

Keesey, R. E., & Powley, T. L. (1986). The regulation of body weight. *Annual Review of Psychology, 37,* 109–133.

Keijsers, G. P. J., Schaap, C. P. D. R., & Hoogduin, C. A. L. (2000). The impact of interpersonal patient and therapist behavior on outcome in cognitive-behavioral therapy: A review of empirical studies. *Behavior Modification, 24,* 264–297.

Keith, J. R., & McVety, K. M. (1988). Latent place learning in a novel environment and the influences of prior training in rats. *Psychobiology, 16,* 146–151.

Keller, F. S. (1991). Burrhus Frederic Skinner (1904–1990). *Journal of the History of the Behavioral Sciences, 27,* 3–6.

Kelley, H. H. (1992). Common-sense psychology and scientific discovery. *Annual Review of Psychology, 43,* 1–23.

Kellog, W. N., & Kellogg, L. A. (1933). *The ape and the child.* New York: McGraw-Hill.

Kelly, J. A. (1986). Psychological research and the rights of animals: Disagreement with Miller. *American Psychologist, 41,* 839–841.

Kelly, R. B., Zyzanski, S. J., & Alemagno, S. A. (1991). Prediction of motivation and behavior change following health promotion: Role of health beliefs, social support, and self-efficacy. *Social Science and Medicine, 32,* 311–320.

Kelly, S. J., Macaruso, P., & Sokol, S. M. (1997). Mental calculation in an autistic savant: A case study. *Journal of Clinical and Experimental Neuropsychology, 19,* 172–184.

Kelsoe, J. R., Kristbjanarson, H., Bergesch, P., & Shilling, P. (1993). A genetic linkage study of bipolar disorder and 13 markers on chromosome 11 including the D-sub-2 dopamine receptor. *Neuropsychopharmacology, 9,* 293–301.

Kemp, B., Krause, J. S., & Adkins, R. (1999). Depression among African Americans, Latinos, and Caucasians with spinal cord injury: A exploratory study. *Rehabilitation Psychology, 44,* 235–247.

Kendler, K. S. (1998). Major depression and the environment. A psychiatric genetic perspective. *Pharmacopsychiatry, 31,* 5–9.

Kendler, K. S., Gardner, C. O., & Prescott, C. A. (1998). A population-based twin study of self-esteem and gender. *Psychological Medicine, 28,* 1403–1409.

Kenneally, S. M., Bruck, G. E., Frank, E. M., & Nalty, L. (1998). Language intervention after thirty years of isolation: A case study of a feral child. *Education and Training in Mental Retardation and Developmental Disabilities, 33,* 13–23.

Kenrick, D. T., & Dantchik, A. (1983). Interactionism, idiographics, and the social psychological invasion of personality. *Journal of Personality, 51,* 286–307.

Kenrick, D. T., & Funder, D. C. (1988). Profiting from controversy: Lessons from the person-situation debate. *American Psychologist, 43,* 23–34.

Kent, R. J., & Allen, C. T. (1994). Competitive interference effects in consumer memory for advertising: The role of brand familiarity. *Journal of Marketing, 58,* 97–105.

Kessler, R. C. (1994). The National Comorbidity Survey of the United States. *International Review of Psychiatry, 6,* 365–376.

Kessler, R. C., Davis, C. G., & Kendler, K. S. (1997). Childhood adversity and adult psychiatric disorder in the US National Comorbidity Survey. *Psychological Medicine, 27,* 1101–1119.

Kessler, R. C., Stang, P. E., Wittchen, H.-U., Ustun, T. B., Roy-Burne, P. P., & Walters, E. E. (1998). Lifetime panic-depression comorbidity in the National Comorbidity Survey. *Archives of General Psychiatry, 55,* 801–808.

Kessler, R. C., Stein, M. B., & Berglund, P. (1998). Social phobia subtypes in the National Comorbidity Survey. *American Journal of Psychiatry, 155,* 613–619.

Khaleefa, O. H., Erdos, G., & Ashria, I. H. (1996). Gender and creativity in an Afro-Arab Islamic culture: The case of Sudan. *Journal of Creative Behavior, 30,* 52–60.

Khaleefa, O. H., Erdos, G., & Ashria, I. H. (1997). Traditional education and creativity in Afro-Arab Islamic culture. *Journal of Creative Behavior, 31,* 201–211.

Kiecolt-Glaser, J. K., & Glaser, R. (1995). Psychoneuroimmunology and health consequences: Data and shared mechanisms. *Psychosomatic Medicine, 57,* 269–274.

Kiecolt-Glaser, J. K., Glaser, R., Strain, E. C., et al. (1986). Modulation of cellular immunity in medical students. *Journal of Behavioral Medicine, 9,* 5–21.

Kiecolt-Glaser, J. K., Newton, T., Cacioppo, J. T., et al. (1996). Marital conflict and endocrine function: Are men really more physiologically affected than women? *Journal of Consulting & Clinical Psychology, 64,* 324–332.

Kiernan, B. D., Dane, J. R., Phillips, L. H., & Price, D. D. (1995). Hypnotic analgesia reduces R-III nociceptive reflex: Further evidence concerning the multifactorial nature of hypnotic analgesia. *Pain, 60,* 39–47.

Kihlstrom, J. F., & McConkey, K. M. (1990). William James and hypnosis: A centennial reflection. *Psychological Science, 1,* 174–178.

Killcross, S. (2000). The amygdala, emotion and learning. *Psychologist, 13,* 502–507.

Kilmartin, C. T., & Dervin, D. (1997). Inaccurate representation of the Electra complex in psychology textbooks. *Teaching of Psychology, 24,* 269–271.

Kim, D., Adipudi, V., Shibayama, M., Giszter, S., Tessler, A., Murray, M., & Simansky, K. J. (1999). Direct agonists for serotonin receptors enhance locomotor function in rats that received neural transplants after neonatal spinal transection. *Journal of Neuroscience, 19,* 6213–6224.

Kim, H., & Markus, H. R. (1999). Deviance or uniqueness, harmony or conformity? A cultural analysis. *Journal of Personality and Social Psychology, 77,* 785–800.

Kim, J. J., DeCola, J. P., Landeira-Fernandez, J., & Fanselow, M. S. (1991). N-methyl-D-aspartate receptor antagonist APV blocks acquisition but not expression of fear conditioning. *Behavioral Neuroscience, 105,* 126–133.

Kim, J. S., Yoon, S. S., Lee, S. I., et al. (1998). Type A behavior and stroke: High tenseness dimension may be a risk factor for cerebral infarction. *European Neurology, 39,* 168–173.

Kim, J., Lim, J.-S., & Bhargava, M. (1998). The role of affect in attitude formation: A classical conditioning application. *Journal of the Academy of Marketing Science, 26,* 143–152.

Kimball, M. M. (1995). *Gender and math: What makes a difference? Feminist visions of gender similarities and differences.* New York: Harrington Park Press.

Kimball, M. M. (2000). From "Anna O." to Bertha Pappenheim: Transforming private pain into public action. *History of Psychology, 3,* 20–43.

Kimble, G. A. (1981). Biological and cognitive constraints on learning. In L. T. Benjamin, Jr. (Ed.), *The G. Stanley Hall Lecture Series* (Vol. 1, pp. 11–60). Washington, DC: American Psychological Association.

Kimura, D. (1987). Are men's and women's brains really different? *Canadian Psychology, 28,* 133–147.

Kimura, D., & Hampson, E. (1994). Cognitive pattern in men and women is influenced by fluctuations in sex hormones. *Current Directions in Psychological Science, 3,* 57–61.

King, A. C., Castro, C., Wilcox, S., et al. (2000). Personal and environmental factors associated with physical inactivity among different racial-ethnic groups of U.S. middle-aged and older-aged women. *Health Psychology, 19,* 354–364.

King, D. B., & Viney, W. (1992). Modern history of pragmatic and sentimental attitudes toward animals and the selling of comparative psychology. *Journal of Comparative Psychology, 106,* 190–195.

King, L. A., & Miner, K. N. (2000). Writing about the perceived benefits of traumatic events: Implications for physical health. *Personality and Social Psychology Bulletin, 26,* 220–230.

King, N. J., Clowes-Hollins, V., & Ollendick, T. H. (1997). The etiology of childhood dog phobia. *Behaviour Research and Therapy, 35,* 77.

Kinsey, A. C., Pomeroy, W. D., & Martin, C. E. (1948). *Sexual behavior in the human male.* Philadelphia: Saunders.

Kinsey, A. C., Pomeroy, W. D., Martin, C. E., & Gebhard, T. H. (1953). *Sexual behavior in the human female.* Philadelphia: Saunders.

Kirkpatrick, D. L. (1959). Techniques for evaluating training programs. I. *Journal of the American Society of Training Directors, 13,* 3–9, 21–26.

Kirmeyer, S. L., & Biggers, K. (1988). Environmental demand and demand engineering behavior: An observational analysis of the Type A patterns. *Journal of Personality and Social Psychology, 54,* 997–1005.

Kirsch, I. (1996). Hypnotic enhancement of cognitive-behavioral weight loss treatments: Another meta-reanalysis. *Journal of Consulting and Clinical Psychology, 64,* 517–519.

Kisch, J., & Erber, J. (1999). Operant conditioning of antennal movements in the honey bee. *Behavioural Brain Research, 99,* 93–102.

Kitayama, S., Markus, H. R., & Kurokawa, M. (2000). Culture, emotion, and well-being: Good feelings in Japan and the United States. *Cognition and Emotion, 14,* 93–124.

Kittrell, D. (1998). A comparison of the evolution of men's and women's dreams in Daniel Levinson's theory of adult development. *Journal of Adult Development, 5,* 105–115.

Klar, Y., & Giladi, E. E. (1999). Are most people happier than their peers, or are they just happy? *Personality and Social Psychology Bulletin, 25,* 585–594.

Kleiber, C., & Harper, D. C. (1999). Effects of distraction on children's pain and distress during medical procedures: A meta-analysis. *Nursing Research, 48,* 44–49.

Klein, S. B. (1982). *Motivation: Biosocial approaches.* New York: McGraw-Hill.

Kleinke, C. L., Peterson, T. R., & Rutledge, T. R. (1998). Effects of self-generated facial expressions on mood. *Journal of Personality and Social Psychology, 74,* 272–279.

Kleinknecht, R. A., Dinnell, D. L., Kleinknecht, E. E., & Hiruma, N. (1997). Cultural factors in social anxiety. *Journal of Anxiety Disorders, 11,* 157–177.

Kleinmuntz, B., & Szucko, J. J. (1984a). A field study of the fallibility of polygraph lie detection. *Nature, 308,* 449–450.

Kleinmuntz, B., & Szucko, J. J. (1984b). Lie detection in ancient and modern times: A call for contemporary scientific study. *American Psychologist, 39,* 766–776.

Klepac, R. K. (1986). Fear and avoidance of dental treatment in adults. *Annals of Behavioral Medicine, 8,* 17–22.

Klimesch, W., Schimke, H., & Schwaiger, J. (1994). Episodic and semantic memory: An analysis in the EEG theta and alpha band. *Electroencephalography and Clinical Neurophysiology, 91,* 428–441.

Kling, K. C., Hyde, J. S., Showers, C. J., & Buswell, B. N. (1999). Gender differences in self-esteem: A meta-analysis. *Psychological Bulletin, 125,* 470–500.

Klonoff, E. A., & Landrine, H. (1999). Cross-validation of the Schedule of Racist Events. *Journal of Black Psychology, 25,* 231–254.

Klosterhalfen, W., & Klosterhalfen, S. (1983). A critical analysis of the animal experiments cited in support of learned helplessness. *Psychologische Beitrage, 25,* 436–458.

Klüver, H., & Bucy, P. C. (1937). "Psychic blindness" and other symptoms following bilateral temporal lobectomy in rhesus monkeys. *American Journal of Physiology, 119,* 352–353.

Knapp, T. J., & Shodahl, S. A. (1974). Ben Franklin as a behavior modifier: A note. *Behavior Therapy, 5,* 656–660.

Knox, S. S., & Uvnaes-Moberg, K. (1998). Social isolation and cardiovascular disease: An atherosclerotic pathway? *Psychoneuroendocrinology, 23,* 877–890.

Knudsen, E. I. (1981, December). The hearing of the barn owl. *Scientific American,* pp. 112–113, 115–116, 118–125.

Kobasa, S. C., Maddi, S. R., & Kahn, S. (1982). Hardiness and health: A prospective study. *Journal of Personality and Social Psychology, 42,* 168–177.

Kobayakawa, T., Ogawa, H., Kaneda, H., Ayabe-Kanamura, S., Endo, H., & Saito, S. (1999). Spatio-temporal analysis of cortical activity evoked by gustatory stimulation in humans. *Chemical Senses, 24,* 201–209.

Kocsis, R. N., Irwin, H. J., & Hayes, A. F. (1998). Organised and disorganised criminal behaviour syndromes in arsonists: A validation study of a psychological profiling concept. *Psychiatry, Psychology and Law, 5,* 117–131.

Kocsis, R. N., Irwin, H. J., Hayes, A. F., & Nunn, R. (2000). Expertise in psychological profiling: A comparative assessment. *Journal of Interpersonal Violence, 15,* 311–331.

Kohlberg, L. (1981). *Essays on moral development.* New York: Harper & Row.

Köhler, W. (1959). Gestalt psychology today. *American Psychologist, 14,* 727–734.

Köhler, W. (1925). *The mentality of apes.* New York: Harcourt Brace Jovanovich.

Kohnken, G., & Maass, A. (1988). Eyewitness testimony: False alarms on biased instructions. *Journal of Applied Psychology, 73,* 363–370.

Kokkinidis, L., & Anisman, H. (1980). Amphetamine models of paranoid schizophrenia: An overview and elaboration of animal experimentation. *Psychological Bulletin, 88,* 551–579.

Kolata, G. (1985). Why do people get fat? *Science, 227,* 1327–1328.

Kolata, G. (1987). Associations or rules in learning language? *Science, 237,* 133–134.

Kopelman, M. D., Christensen, H., Puffett, A., & Stanhope, N. (1994). The great escape: A neuropsychological study of psychogenic amnesia. *Neuropsychologia, 32,* 675–691.

Kopf, S. R., & Baratti, C. M. (1996). Memory modulation by post-training glucose or insulin remains evident at long retention intervals. *Neurobiology of Learning and Memory, 65,* 189–191.

Koppe, S. (1983). The psychology of the neuron: Freud, Cajal, and Golgi. *Scandinavian Journal of Psychology, 24,* 1–12.

Koppes, L. L. (1997). American female pioneers of industrial and organizational psychology during the early years. *Journal of Applied Psychology, 82,* 510–515.

Korn, J. H., Davis, R., & Davis, S. F. (1991). Historians' and chairpersons' judgments of eminence among psychologists. *American Psychologist, 46,* 789–792.

Korpi, E. R. (1994). Role of GABA-sub (A) receptors in the actions of alcohol and in alcoholism: recent advances. *Alcohol and Alcoholism, 29,* 115–129.

Kosslyn, S. M., Thompson, W. L., Costantini-Ferrando, M. F., Alpert, N. M., & Spiegel, D. (2000). Hypnotic visual illusion alters color processing in the brain. *American Journal of Psychiatry, 157,* 1279–1284.

Kozar, B., Whitfield, K. E., Lord, R. H., & Mechikoff, R. A. (1993). Timeouts before free-throws: Do the statistics support the strategy? *Perceptual and Motor Skills, 76,* 47–50.

Kozub, S. A., & McDonnell, J. F. (2000). Exploring the relationship between cohesion and collective efficacy in rugby teams. *Journal of Sport Behavior, 23,* 120–129.

Kposowa, A. J. (2000). Marital status and suicide in the National Longitudinal Mortality Study. *Journal of Epidemiology and Community Health, 54,* 254–261.

Krafka, C., & Penrod, S. (1985). Reinstatement of context in a field experiment on eyewitness identification. *Journal of Personality and Social Psychology, 49,* 58–69.

Krakow, B., Germain, A., Tandberg, D., Koss, M., Schrader, R., et al. (2000). Sleep breathing and sleep movement disorders masquerading as insomnia in sexual-assault survivors. *Comprehensive Psychiatry, 41,* 49–56.

Kramer, D. E., & Bayern, C. D. (1984). The effects of behavioral strategies on creativity training. *Journal of Creative Behavior, 18,* 23–24.

Krantz, D. S., & Manuck, S. B. (1984). Acute psychophysiologic reactivity and risk of cardiovascular disease: A review and methodologic critique. *Psychological Bulletin, 96,* 435–464.

Krantz, D. S., Contrada, R. J., Hill, D. R., & Friedler, E. (1988). Environmental stress and biobehavioral antecedents of coronary heart disease. *Journal of Consulting and Clinical Psychology, 56,* 333–341.

Kraus, S. J. (1995). Attitudes and the prediction of behavior: A meta-analysis of the empirical literature. *Personality and Social Psychology Bulletin, 21,* 58–75.

Krause, J. S. (1998). Subjective well-being after spinal cord injury: Relationship to gender, race-ethnicity, and chronologic age. *Rehabilitation Psychology, 43,* 282–296.

Kravitz, D. A., & Martin, B. (1986). Ringelmann rediscovered: The original article. *Journal of Personality and Social Psychology, 50,* 936–941.

Kreppner, K. (1992). William L. Stern, 1871–1938: A neglected founder of developmental psychology. *Developmental Psychology, 28,* 539–547.

Krinsky, R., & Krinsky, S. G. (1996). Pegword mnemonic instruction: Retrieval times and long-term memory performance among fifth-grade children. *Contemporary Educational Psychology, 21,* 193–207.

Krippner, S. (1993). The Maimonides ESP-dream studies. *Journal of Parapsychology, 57,* 39–54.

Krippner, S. (1995). Psychical research in the postmodern world. *Journal of the American Society for Psychical Research, 89,* 1–18.

Krippner, S., & Thompson, A. (1996). A 10-factor model of dreaming applied to dream practices of 16 Native-American cultural groups. *Dreaming, 6,* 71–96.

Krippner, S., Braud, W., Child, I. L., & Palmer, J. (1993). Demonstration research and meta-analysis in parapsychology. *Journal of Parapsychology, 57,* 275–286.

Krippner, S., Vaughan, A., & Spottiswoode, S. J. P. (2000). Geomagnetic factors in subjective precognitive dream experiences. *Journal of the Society for Psychical Research, 64,* 109–117.

Krupa, D. J., Thompson, J. K., & Thompson, R. F. (1993). Localization of a memory trace in the mammalian brain. *Science, 260,* 989–991.

Kübler-Ross, E. (1969). *On death and dying.* New York: Macmillan.

Kübler-Ross, E. (1974). *Questions and answers on death and dying.* New York: Macmillan.

Kuebelbeck, A. (1991, August 23). A real high point. *Los Angeles Times,* p. E1.

Kuehberger, A. (1998). The influence of framing on risky decisions: A meta-analysis. *Organizational Behavior and Human Decision Processes, 75,* 23–55.

Kugel, W. (1990–1991). Amplifying precognition: Two experiments with roulette. *European Journal of Parapsychology, 8,* 85–97.

Kugihara, N. (1999). Gender and social loafing in Japan. *Journal of Social Psychology, 139,* 516–526.

Kuhlman, T. L. (1985). A study of salience and motivational theories of humor. *Journal of Personality and Social Psychology, 49,* 281–286.

Kuhn, T. S. (1970). *The structure of scientific revolutions.* Chicago: University of Chicago Press.

Kukla, A. (1989). Nonempirical issues in psychology. *American Psychologist, 44,* 785–794.

Kumar, K. B., Ramalingam, S., & Karanth, K. S. (1994). Phenytoin and phenobarbital: A comparison of their state-dependent effects. *Pharmacology, Biochemistry, and Behavior, 47,* 951–956.

Kumar, K. S., Rajagopal, M. R., & Naseema, A. M. (2000). Intravenous morphine for emergency treatment of cancer pain. *Palliative Medicine, 14,* 183–188.

Kumari, V., Hemsley, D. R., Cotter, P. A., Checkley, S. A., & Gray, J. A. (1998). Haloperidol-induced mood and retrieval of happy and unhappy memories. *Cognition and Emotion, 12,* 437–508.

Kurdek, L. A. (1998). Relationship outcomes and their predictors: Longitudinal evidence from heterosexual married, gay cohabiting, and lesbian cohabiting couples. *Journal of Marriage and the Family, 60,* 553–568.

Kurdek, L. A. (1999). The nature and predictors of the trajectory of change in marital quality for husbands and wives over the first 10 years of marriage. *Developmental Psychology, 35,* 1283–1296.

Kurtz, L. (1995). Coping processes and behavioral outcomes in children of divorce. *Canadian Journal of School Psychology, 11,* 52–64.

Kurzweil, R. (1985). What is artificial intelligence anyway? *American Scientist, 73,* 258–264.

Kwee, M., & Ellis, A. (1998). The interface between rational emotive behavior therapy (REBT) and Zen. *Journal of Rational-Emotive and Cognitive Behavior Therapy, 16,* 5–43.

La Pointe, F. H. (1970). Origin and evolution of the term "psychology." *American Psychologist, 25,* 640–646.

La Vaque, T. J. (1999). History of EEG Hans Berger: Psychophysiologist. A historical vignette. *Journal of Neurotherapy, 3,* 1–9.

Laakso, M. P., Lehtovirta, M., Partanen, K., Riekkinen, P. J., Sr., & Soininen, H. (2000). Hippocampus in Alzheimer's disease: A 3-year follow-up MRI study. *Biological Psychiatry, 47,* 557–561.

Lakkis, J., Ricciardelli, L. A., & Williams, R. J. (1999). Role of sexual orientation and gender-related traits in disordered eating. *Sex Roles, 41,* 1–16.

Lalancette, M. F., & Standing, L. G. (1990). Asch fails again. *Social Behavior and Personality, 18,* 7–12.

Lalumiere, M. L., Blanchard, R., & Zucker, K. J. (2000). Sexual orientation and handedness in men and women: A meta-analysis. *Psychological Bulletin, 126,* 575–592.

Lamb, M. E. (1996). Effects of nonparental child care on child development: An update. *Canadian Journal of Psychiatry, 41,* 330–342.

Lamb, R. H. (1998). Deinstitutionalization at the beginning of the new millennium. *Harvard Review of Psychiatry, 6,* 1–10.

Lamb, T. (1999). Obituary: Alan Hodgkin (1914–98). *Nature, 397,* 112.

Lamme, V. A. F. (1995). The neurophysiology of figure-ground segregation in primary visual cortex. *Journal of Neuroscience, 15,* 1605–1615.

Lancaster, L., Royal, K. E., & Whiteside, H. D. (1995). Attitude similarity and evaluation of a women's athletic team. *Journal of Social Behavior and Personality, 10,* 885–890.

Landesman, S., & Ramey, C. (1989). Developmental psychology and mental retardation: Integrating scientific princi-

ples with treatment practices. *American Psychologist, 44,* 409–415.

Landis, D., & O'Shea III, W. A. (2000). Cross-cultural aspects of passionate love: An individual differences analysis. *Journal of Cross-Cultural Psychology, 31,* 752–777.

Landolt, H. P., Werth, E., Borbely, A. A., & Dijk, D. J. (1995). Caffeine intake (200 mg) in the morning affects human sleep and EEG power spectra at night. *Brain Research, 675,* 67–74.

Landrine, H. (1987). On the politics of madness: A preliminary analysis of the relationship between social roles and psychopathology. *Psychology Monographs, 113,* 341–406.

Landrine, H. (1989). The politics of personality disorder. *Psychology of Women Quarterly, 13,* 325–339.

Landy, F. J. (1997). Early influences on the development of industrial and organizational psychology. *Journal of Applied Psychology, 86,* 467–477.

Landy, F. J., & Farr, J. L. (1980). Performance rating. *Psychological Bulletin, 87,* 72–107.

Laner, M. R., Benin, M. H., & Ventrone, N. A. (2001). Bystander attitudes toward victims of violence: Who's worth helping? *Deviant Behavior, 22,* 23–42.

Lang, P. J. (1994). The varieties of emotional experience: A meditation on James-Lange theory. *Psychological Review, 101,* 211–221.

Lang, P. J., Bradley, M. M., & Cuthbert, B. N. (1998). Emotion, motivation, and anxiety: Brain mechanisms and psychophysiology. *Biological Psychiatry, 44,* 1248–1263.

Langenbucher, J. W., & Nathan, P. E. (1983). Psychology, public policy, and the evidence for alcohol intoxication. *American Psychologist, 38,* 1070–1077.

Langer, E. J., & Rodin, J. (1976). The effects of choice and enhanced personal responsibility for the aged: A field experiment in an institutional setting. *Journal of Personality and Social Psychology, 34,* 191–198.

Langlois, J. H., Kalakanis, L., Rubenstein, A. J., et al. (2000). Maxims or myths of beauty? A meta-analytic and theoretical review. *Psychological Bulletin, 126,* 390–423.

Langone, J. (1983, September). B. F. Skinner: Beyond reward and punishment. *Discover,* pp. 38–46.

Larsen, K. S. (1990). The Asch conformity experiment: Replication and transhistorical comparisons. *Journal of Social Behavior and Personality, 5,* 163–168.

Laruelle, M., Abi-Dargham, A., Gil, R., Kegeles, L., & Innis, R. (1999). Increased dopamine transmission in schizophrenia: Relationship to illness phases. *Biological Psychiatry, 46,* 56–72.

Lashley, K. S. (1950). In search of the engram. In *Symposium of the Society for Experimental Biology* (Vol. 4, pp. 454–482). New York: Cambridge University Press.

Laska, M., Scheuber, H.-P., Sanchez, E. C., & Luna, E. R. (1999). Taste difference thresholds for sucrose in two

species of nonhuman primates. *American Journal of Primatology, 48,* 153–160.

Latham, G. P., & Lee, T. W. (1986). Goal setting. In E. A. Locke (Ed.), *Generalizing from laboratory to field settings* (pp. 101–117). Lexington, MA: Health.

Laumann, E. O., Gagnon, J. H., Michael, R. T., & Michaels, S. (1994). *The social organization of sexuality.* Chicago: University of Chicago Press.

Laurence, J. R., & Perry, C. (1983). Hypnotically created memory among highly hypnotizable subjects. *Science, 222,* 523–524.

Laursen, B., Coy, K. C., & Collins, W. A. (1998). Reconsidering changes in parent-child conflict across adolescence: A meta-analysis. *Child Development, 69,* 817–832.

Laver, A. B. (1972). Precursors of psychology in ancient Egypt. *Journal of the History of the Behavioral Sciences, 8,* 181–195.

Lavery, L., Townsend, M., & Wilton, K. (1998). Computer-assisted instruction in teaching literacy skills to adults not in paid employment. *New Zealand Journal of Educational Studies, 33,* 181–192.

Lavin, C. (1996). The Wechsler Intelligence Scale for Children, third edition, and the Stanford-Binet Intelligence Scale, fourth edition: A preliminary study of validity. *Psychological Reports, 78,* 491–496.

Lavoisier, P., Aloui, R., Schmidt, M. H., & Watrelot, A. (1995). Clitoral blood flow increases following vaginal pressure stimulation. *Archives of Sexual Behavior, 24,* 37–45.

Lawrie, S. M., & Abukmeil, S. S. (1998). Brain abnormality in schizophrenia: A systematic and quantitative review of volumetric magnetic resonance imaging studies. *British Journal of Psychiatry, 172,* 110–120.

Lazarus, R. S. (1993). Coping theory and research: Past, present, and future. *Psychosomatic Medicine, 55,* 234–247.

Lazarus, R. S. (1993). From psychological stress to the emotions: A history of changing outlooks. *Annual Review of Psychology, 44,* 1–21.

Lazev, A. B., Herzog, T. A., & Brandon, T. H. (1999). Classical conditioning of environmental cues to cigarette smoking. *Experimental and Clinical Psychopharmacology, 7,* 56–63.

Leaf, R. C., Krauss, D. H., Dantzig, S. A., & Alington, D. E. (1992). Educational equivalents of psychotherapy: Positive and negative mental health benefits after group therapy exercises by college students. *Journal of Rational Emotive and Cognitive Behavior Therapy, 10,* 189–206.

Leana, C. R. (1985). A partial test of Janis' groupthink model: Effects of group cohesiveness and leader behavior on defective decision making. *Journal of Management, 11,* 5–17.

Leaper, C., Anderson, K. J., & Sanders, P. (1998). Moderators of gender effects on parents' talk to their children: A meta-analysis. *Developmental Psychology, 34,* 3–27.

LeBlanc, L. A., Hagopian, L. P., & Maglieri, K. A. (2000). Use of a token economy to eliminate excessive inappropriate social behavior in an adult with developmental disabilities. *Behavioral Interventions, 15,* 135–143.

Leckman, J. F., Grice, D. E., Boardman, J., & Zhang, H. (1997). Symptoms of obsessive-compulsive disorder. *American Journal of Psychiatry, 154,* 911–917.

Leclerc, G., Lefrancois, R., Dube, M., Hebert, R., & Gaulin, P. (1998). The self-actualization concept: A content validation. *Journal of Social Behavior and Personality, 13,* 69–84.

Lecomte, D., & Fornes, P. (1998). Suicide among youth and young adults, 15 through 24 years of age: A report of 392 cases from Paris, 1989–1996. *Journal of Forensic Sciences, 43,* 964–968.

LeDoux, J. E. (1986). Sensory systems and emotion: A model of affective processing. *Integrative Psychiatry, 4,* 237–243.

Lee, G. P., Loring, D. W., Meador, K. J., & Brooks, B. B. (1990). Hemispheric specialization for emotional expression: A reexamination of results from intracarotid administration of sodium amobarbital. *Brain and Cognition, 12,* 267–280.

Lee, H., & Kim, J. J. (1998). Amygdalar NMDA receptors are critical for new fear learning in previously fear-conditioned rats. *Journal of Neuroscience, 18,* 8444–8454.

Lee, J.-H., & Beitz, A. J. (1992). Electroacupuncture modifies the expression of c-fos in the spinal cord induced by noxious stimulation. *Brain Research, 577,* 80–91.

Lee, S. H., & Oh, K. S. (1999). Offensive type of social phobia: Cross-cultural perspectives. *International Medical Journal, 6,* 271–279.

Lee, S., & Crockett, M. S. (1994). Effect of assertiveness training on levels of stress and assertiveness experienced by nurses in Taiwan, Republic of China. *Issues in Mental Health Nursing, 15,* 419–432.

Lee, V. E., & Loeb, S. (1995). Where do head start attendees end up? One reason why preschool effects fade out. *Educational Evaluation and Policy Analysis, 17,* 62–82.

Lee, V. E., Brooks-Gunn, J., Schnur, E., & Liaw, F.-R. (1990). Are Head Start effects sustained? A longitudinal follow-up comparison of disadvantaged children attending Head Start, no preschool, and other preschool programs. *Child Development, 61,* 495–507.

Lee, Y. T., & Ottati, V. (1993). Determinants of in-group and out-group perceptions of heterogeneity: An investigation of Sino-American stereotypes. *Journal of Cross-Cultural Psychology, 24,* 298–318.

Lefkowitz, J. (2000). The role of interpersonal affective regard in supervisory performance ratings: A literature review and proposed causal model. *Journal of Occupational and Organizational Psychology, 73,* 67–85.

Lei, T. (1994). Being and becoming moral in a Chinese culture: Unique or universal? *Cross-Cultural Research: The*

Journal of Comparative Social Science, 28, 58–91.

Leibowitz, H. W., & Pick, H. A., Jr. (1972). Cross-cultural and educational aspects of the Ponzo perspective illusion. *Perception and Psychophysics, 12,* 430–432.

Leigh, P. N., & Ray-Chaudhuri, K. (1994). Motor neuron disease. *Journal of Neurosurgery and Psychiatry, 57,* 886–896.

Leikin, L., Firestone, P., & McGrath, P. (1988). Physical symptom reporting in Type A and Type B children. *Journal of Consulting and Clinical Psychology, 56,* 721–726.

Lekander, M., Fuerst, C. J., Rostein, S., Hursti, T. J., & Fredrikson, M. (1997). Immune effects of relaxation during chemotherapy for ovarian cancer. *Psychotherapy and Psychosomatics, 66,* 185–191.

Lenox, R. H., & Hahn, C. G. (2000). Overview of the mechanism of action of lithium in the brain: Fifty-year update. *Journal of Clinical Psychiatry, 61,* 5–15.

Leonard, J. (1970, May 8). Ghetto for blue eyes in the classroom. *Life,* p. 16.

LePage, J. P. (1999). The impact of a token economy on injuries and negative events on an acute psychiatric unit. *Psychiatric Services, 50,* 941–944.

Lepage, M., Habib, R., & Tulving, E. (1998). Hippocampal PET activations of memory encoding and retrieval: The HIPER model. *Hippocampus, 8,* 313–322.

Lepper, M. R., Greene, D., & Nisbett, R. E. (1973). Undermining children's intrinsic interest with extrinsic reward: A test of the "overjustification" hypothesis. *Journal of Personality and Social Psychology, 28,* 129–137.

Lerman, D. C., & Iwata, B. A. (1995). Prevalence of the extinction burst and its attenuation during treatment. *Journal of Applied Behavior Analysis, 28,* 93–94.

Lerner, G. H., & Takagi, T. (1999). On the place of linguistic resources in the organization of talk-in-interaction: A co-investigation of English and Japanese grammatical practices. *Journal of Pragmatics, 31,* 49–75.

Leslie, K., & Ogilvie, R. (1996). Vestibular dreams: The effect of rocking on dream mentation. *Dreaming 6,* 1–16.

Lester, D. (1990). Maslow's hierarchy of needs and personality. *Personality and Individual Differences, 11,* 1187–1188.

Lester, D. (1995). Myths about childhood suicide. *Psychological Reports, 77,* 330.

Lester, D. (1997). Determinants of choice of method for suicide and the person/situation debate in psychology. *Perceptual and Motor Skills, 85,* 497–498.

Leung, J. (1994). Treatment of post-traumatic stress disorder with hypnosis. *Australian Journal of Clinical and Experimental Hypnosis, 22,* 87–96.

LeVay, S. (1991). A difference in hypothalamic structure between heterosexual and homosexual men. *Science, 253,* 1034–1037.

Levenson, J. L., & Bemis, C. (1991). The role of psychological factors in cancer onset and progression. *Psychosomatics, 32,* 124–132.

Levenson, R. W., Ekman, P., Heider, K., & Friesen, W. V. (1992). Emotion and autonomic nervous system activity in the Minangkabau of West Sumatra. *Journal of Personality and Social Psychology, 62,* 972–988.

Levin, E. D., & Simon, B. B. (1998). Nicotinic acetylcholine involvement in cognitive function in animals. *Psychopharmacology, 138,* 217–230.

Levin, E. D., Westman, E. C., Stein, R. M., & Carnahan, E. (1994). Nicotine skin patch treatment increases abstinence, decreases withdrawal symptoms, and attenuates rewarding effects of smoking. *Journal of Clinical Psychopharmacology, 14,* 41–49.

Levin, I. P., Schnittjer, S. K., & Thee, S. L. (1988). Information framing effects in social and personal decisions. *Journal of Experimental Social Psychology, 24,* 520–529.

Levine, J. S., & MacNichol, E. F., Jr. (1982, February). Color vision in fishes. *Scientific American,* pp. 140–149.

Levine, M. (1976). The academic achievement test: Its historical context and social functions. *American Psychologist, 31,* 228–238.

Levine, S. C., Huttenlocher, J., Taylor, A., & Langrock, A. (1999). Early sex differences in spatial skill. *Developmental Psychology, 35,* 940–949.

Levinson, D. J. (1978). *The seasons of a man's life.* New York: Knopf.

Levinson, D. J. (1986). A conception of adult development. *American Psychologist, 41,* 3–13.

Levinthal, C. F. (1988). *Messengers of paradise.* New York: Anchor/Doubleday.

Levkovitz, Y., Shahar, G., Native, G., et al. (2000). Group interpersonal psychotherapy for patients with major depression disorder: Pilot study. *Journal of Affective Disorders, 60,* 191–195.

Levy, G. D. (1999). Gender-typed and non-gender-typed category awareness in toddlers. *Sex Roles, 41,* 851–873.

Levy, J. (1983). Language, cognition, and the right hemisphere: A response to Gazzaniga. *American Psychologist, 38,* 538–541.

Levy, P. E., & Steelman, L. A. (1997). Performance appraisal for team-based organizations: A prototypical multiple rater system. In M. M. Beyerlein, D. A. Johnson, & S. T. Beyerlein (Eds.), *Advances in interdisciplinary studies of work teams,* (Vol. 4, pp. 141–165). Greenwich, CT: Jai Press.

Lew, A. S., Allen, R., Papouchis, N., & Ritzler, B. (1998). Achievement orientation and fear of success in Asian American college students. *Journal of Clinical Psychology, 54,* 97–108.

Lewinsohn, P. M., Gotlib, I. H., Lewinsohn, M., Seeley, J. R., & Allen, N. B. (1998). Gender differences in anxiety disorders and anxiety symptoms in adolescents. *Journal of Abnormal Psychology, 107,* 109–117.

Lewis, D. (1899/1983). The gynecologic consideration of the sexual act. *Journal of the American Medical Association, 250,* 222–227.

Lewis-Fernandez, R. (1998). A cultural critique of the *DSM-IV* dissociative disorders section. *Transcultural Psychiatry, 35,* 387–400.

Li, A. K. F. (1994). A response to Janzen, Paterson, and Paterson: "School psychology and violence prevention in schools." *Canadian Journal of School Psychology, 10,* 105–107.

Lichacz, F. M., & Partington, J. T. (1996). Collective efficacy and true group performance. *International Journal of Sport Psychology, 27,* 146–158.

Lichtenstein, P., & Annas, P. (2000). Heritability and prevalence of specific fears and phobias in childhood. *Journal of Child Psychology and Psychiatry and Allied Disciplines, 41,* 927–937.

Lieberman, D. A. (1979). Behaviorism and the mind: A (limited) call for a return to introspection. *American Psychologist, 34,* 319–333.

Liechti, M. E., Baumann, C., Gamma, A., & Vollenweider, F. X. (2000). Acute psychological effects of 3, 4–methylenedioxymethamphetamine (MDMA, "Ecstasy") are attenuated by the serotonin uptake inhibitor citalopram. *Neuropsychopharmacology, 22,* 513–521.

Liegois, M. J. (1899). The relation of hypnotism to crime. *Suggestive Therapeutics, 6,* 18–21.

Lightdale, J. R., & Prentice, D. A. (1994). Rethinking sex differences in aggression: Aggressive behavior in the absence of social roles. *Personality and Social Psychology Bulletin, 20,* 34–44.

Lilienfeld, S. O., & Loftus, E. F. (1998). Repressed memories and World War II: Some cautionary notes. *Professional Psychology: Research and Practice, 29,* 471–475.

Lilienfeld, S. O., Kirsch, I., Sarbin, T. R., Lynn, S. J., et al. (1999). Dissociative identity disorder and the sociocognitive model: Recalling the lessons of the past. *Psychological Bulletin, 125,* 507–523.

Lindberg, A. C., Kelland, A., & Nicol, C. J. (1999). Effects of observational learning on acquisition of an operant response in horses. *Applied Animal Behaviour Science, 61,* 187–199.

Lindquist, C. H., Reynolds, K. D., & Goran, M. I. (1999). Sociocultural determinants of physical activity among children. *Preventive Medicine, 29,* 305–312.

Lindsay, D. S. (1993). Eyewitness suggestibility. *Current Directions in Psychological Science, 2,* 86–89.

Lindsay, D. S. (1994). Contextualizing and clarifying criticisms of memory work. *Consciousness and Cognition, 3,* 426–437.

Lindsay, D. S., & Jacoby, L. I. (1994). Stroop process dissociations: The relationship between facilitation and interference. *Journal of Experimental Psychology: Human Perception and Performance, 20,* 219–234.

Lindsay, R. C. L., & Pozzulo, J. D. (1999). Sources of eyewitness identification error. *International Journal of Law and Psychiatry, 22,* 347–360.

Links, P. S., Heslegrave, R., & van Reekum, R. (1999). Impulsivity: Core aspect of borderline personality disorder. *Journal of Personality Disorders, 13,* 1–9.

Linn, R. L. (1982). Admissions testing on trial. *American Psychologist, 37,* 279–291.

Lipman, J. J., Miller, B. E., Mays, K. S., & Miller, M. N. (1990). Peak B endorphin concentration in cerebrospinal fluid: Reduced in chronic pain patients and increased during the placebo response. *Psychopharmacology, 102,* 112–116.

Liu, X., Uchiyama, M., Kim, K., Okawa, M., Shibui, K., et al. (2000). Sleep loss and daytime sleepiness in the general adult population of Japan. *Psychiatry Research, 93,* 1–11.

Liu, Y., Gao, J.-H., Liu, H.-L., & Fox, P. T. (2000). The temporal response of the brain after eating revealed by functional MRI. *Nature, 405,* 1058–1062.

Llorente, M. D., Currier, M. B., Norman, S. E., & Mellman, T. A. (1992). Night terrors in adults: Phenomenology and relationship to psychopathology. *Journal of Clinical Psychiatry, 53,* 392–394.

Locke, E. A. (1976). The nature and causes of job satisfaction. In M. Dunnette (Ed.), *Handbook of industrial and organizational psychology* (pp. 1297–1349). Chicago: Rand McNally.

Locke, E. A., & Latham, G. P. (1990). *A theory of goal setting and task performance.* Englewood Cliffs, NJ: Prentice Hall.

Locke, J. (1690/1956). *An essay concerning human understanding.* New York: Dover.

Lockhart, R. S., & Craik, F. I. (1990). Levels of processing: A retrospective commentary on a framework for memory research. *Canadian Journal of Psychology, 44,* 87–112.

Locurto, C. (1991). Beyond IQ in preschool programs? *Intelligence, 15,* 295–312.

Loeb, G. E. (1985, February). The functional replacement of the ear. *Scientific American,* pp. 104–111.

Loehlin, J. C., Horn, J. M., & Willerman, L. (1990). Heredity, environment, and personality change: Evidence from the Texas Adoption Project. *Journal of Personality, 58,* 221–243.

Loehlin, J. C., Horn, J. M., & Willerman, L. (1994). Differential inheritance of mental abilities in the Texas Adoption Project. *Intelligence, 19,* 325–336.

Loeser, J. D., Henderlite, S. E., & Conrad, D. A. (1995). Incentive effects of workers' compensation benefits: A literature synthesis. *Medical Care Research and Review, 52,* 34–59.

Loftus, E. F., & Burns, T. E. (1982). Mental shock can produce retrograde amnesia. *Memory and Learning, 10,* 318–323.

Loftus, E. F., & Hoffman, H. G. (1989). Misinformation and memory: The creation of new memories. *Journal of Experimental Psychology: General, 118,* 100–104.

Loftus, E. F., & Palmer, J. C. (1974). Reconstruction of automobile destruction: An example of the interaction between language and memory. *Journal of Verbal Learning and Verbal Behavior, 13,* 585–589.

Loftus, E., Joslyn, S., & Polage, D. (1998). Repression: A mistaken impression? *Development and Psychopathology, 10,* 781–792.

Loftus, G. R., Duncan, J., & Gehrig, P. (1992). On the time course of perceptual information that results from a brief visual presentation. *Journal of Experimental Psychology: Human Perception and Performance, 18,* 530–549.

Logie, R. H. (1999). Working memory. *Psychologist, 12,* 174–178.

Lonner, W. J., & Malpass, R. S. (Eds.). (1994). *Psychology and culture.* Boston: Allyn & Bacon.

Loomis, A. L., Harvey, E. N., & Hobart, G. A. (1937). Electrical potentials of the human brain. *Journal of Experimental Psychology, 21,* 127–144.

Loomis, M., & Saltz, E. (1984). Cognitive styles as predictors of artistic styles. *Journal of Personality, 52,* 22–35.

López, S. R., & Guarnaccia, P. J. J. (2000). Cultural psychopathology: Uncovering the social world of mental illness. *Annual Review of Psychology, 51,* 571–598.

Lord, C. G. (1982). Predicting behavioral consistency from an individual's perception of situational similarities. *Journal of Personality and Social Psychology, 42,* 1076–1088.

Lord, R. G., & Levy, P. E. (1994). Control theory: Moving from cognition to action. *Applied Psychology, 43,* 335–367.

Lorenz, K. Z. (1966). *On aggression.* New York: Harcourt Brace Jovanovich.

Loring, D. W., & Sheer, D. E. (1984). Laterality of 40 Hz EEG and EMG during cognitive performance. *Psychophysiology, 21,* 34–38.

Lovass, O. I. (1987). Behavioral treatment and normal educational and intellectual functioning in young autistic children. *Journal of Consulting and Clinical Psychology, 55,* 3–9.

Lowry, P. E. (1997). The assessment center process: New directions. *Journal of Social Behavior and Personality, 12,* 53–62.

Lozano, D. I., Crites, S. L., Jr., & Aikman, S. N. (1999). Changes in food attitudes as a function of hunger. *Appetite, 32,* 207–218.

Lu, L., & Shih, J. B. (1997). Personality and happiness: Is mental health a mediator? *Personality and Individual Differences, 22,* 249–256.

Lu, Z. L., Williamson, S. J., & Kaufman, L. (1992). Behavioral lifetime of human auditory sensory memory predicted by physiological measures. *Science, 258,* 1668–1670.

Lubart, T. I. (1999). Creativity across cultures. In R. J. Sternberg (Ed.), *Handbook of creativity* (pp. 339–350). New York: Cambridge University Press.

Lubek, I., Innis, N. K., Kroger, R. O., McGuire, G. R., Stam, H. J., & Herrmann, T. (1995). Faculty genealogies in five Canadian universities: Historiographical and pedagogical concerns. *Journal of the History of the Behavioral Sciences, 31,* 52–72.

Luborsky, L., Chandler, M., Auerbach, A. H., Cohen, J., & Bachrach, H. M. (1971). Factors influencing the outcome of psychotherapy: A review of quantitative research. *Psychological Bulletin, 75,* 145–185.

Luce, G. G., & Segal, J. (1966). *Sleep.* New York: Coward-McCann.

Luchins, A. (1946). Classroom experiments on mental sets. *American Journal of Psychology, 59,* 295–298.

Lukas, K. E., Marr, M. J., & Maple, T. L. (1998). Teaching operant conditioning at the zoo. *Teaching of Psychology, 25,* 112–116.

Lundqvist, L.-O. (1995). Facial EMG reactions to facial expressions: A case of facial emotional contagion? *Scandinavian Journal of Psychology, 36,* 130–141.

Lundy, D. E., Tan, J., & Cunningham, M. R. (1998). Heterosexual romantic preferences: The importance of humor and physical attractiveness for different types of relationships. *Personal Relationships, 5,* 311–325.

Lutz, J., Means, L. W., & Long, T. E. (1994). Where did I park? A naturalistic study of spatial memory. *Applied Cognitive Psychology, 8,* 439–451.

Luu, P., Collins, P., & Tucker, D. M. (2000). Mood, personality, and self-monitoring: Negative affect and emotionality in relation to frontal lobe mechanisms of error monitoring. *Journal of Experimental Psychology: General, 129,* 43–60.

Lydon, J. E., Jamieson, D., & Zanna, M. P. (1988). Interpersonal similarity and the social and intellectual dimensions of first impressions. *Social Cognition, 6,* 269–286.

Lykken, D. T. (1974). Psychology and the lie detector industry. *American Psychologist, 29,* 725–739.

Lykken, D. T. (1981). *A tremor in the blood: Uses and abuses of the lie detector.* New York: McGraw-Hill.

Lykken, D. T. (1982). Research with twins: The concept of emergenesis. *Psychophysiology, 19,* 361–373.

Lykken, D. T., Bouchard, T. J., Jr., McGue, M., & Tellegen, A. (1993). Heritability of interests: A twin study. *Journal of Appiled Psychology, 73,* 303–304.

Lykken, D. T., McGue, M., Tellegen, A., & Bouchard, T. J., Jr. (1992). Emergenesis: Genetic traits that may not run in families. *American Psychologist, 47,* 1565–1577.

Lymburner, J. A., & Roesch, R. (1999). The insanity defense: Five years of research (1993–1997). *International Journal of Law and Psychiatry, 22,* 213–240.

Lyn, H., & Savage-Rumbaugh, E. S. (2000). Observational word learning in two bonobos (*Pan paniscus*): Ostensive and non-ostensive contexts. *Language and Communication, 20,* 255–273.

Lynch, P. S., Kellow, J. T., & Willson, V. L. (1997). The impact of deinstitutionalization on the adaptive behavior of adults with mental retardation: A meta-analysis. *Education and Training in Mental Retardation and Developmental Disabilities, 32,* 255–261.

Lynn, R. (1982). IQ in Japan and the United States shows a growing disparity. *Nature, 297,* 222–223.

Lynn, S. J., Rhue, J. W., & Weekes, J. R. (1990). Hypnotic involuntariness: A social-cognitive analysis. *Psychological Review, 97,* 169–184.

Lyons, M. J., Eisen, S. A., Goldberg, J., True, W., et al. (1998). A registry-based twin study of depression in men. *Archives of General Psychiatry, 55,* 468–472.

Lyoo, I. K., Han, M. H., & Cho, D. Y. (1998). A brain MRI study in subjects with borderline personality disorder. *Journal of Affective Disorders, 50,* 235–243.

Lysle, D. T., Cunnick, J. E., & Maslonek, K. A. (1991). Pharmacological manipulation of immune alterations induced by an aversive conditioned stimulus: Evidence for a-adrenergic receptor-mediated Pavlovian conditioning process. *Behavioral Neuroscience, 105,* 443–449.

Lytton, H., & Romney, D. M. (1991). Parents' differential socialization of boys and girls: A meta-analysis. *Psychological Bulletin, 109,* 267–296.

Lyubomirsky, S. (2000). On studying positive emotions. *Prevention and Treatment, 3.*

Ma, H. K., Shek, D. T. L., Cheung, P. C., & Oi Bun Lam, C. (2000). Parental, peer, and teacher influences on the social behavior of Hong Kong Chinese adolescents. *Journal of Genetic Psychology, 161,* 65–78.

Maag, U., Vanasse, C., Dionne, G., & Laberge-Nadeau, C. (1997). Taxi drivers' accidents: How binocular vision problems are related to their rate and severity in terms of the number of victims. *Accident Analysis and Prevention, 29,* 217–224.

Macaskill, N. D., & Macaskill, A. (1996). Rational-emotive therapy plus pharmacotherapy versus pharmacotherapy alone in the treatment of high cognitive dysfunction depression. *Cognitive Therapy and Research, 20,* 575–592.

Maccoby, E. E., & Jacklin, C. N. (1974). *The psychology of sex differences* (2 vols.). Stanford, CA: Stanford University Press.

MacCracken, M. J., & Stadulis, R. E. (1985). Social facilitation of young children's dynamic balance performance. *Journal of Sport Psychology, 7,* 150–165.

MacDonald, K. (1998). Evolution, culture, and the five-factor model. *Journal of Cross-Cultural Psychology, 29,* 119–149.

MacDonald, T. K., MacDonald, G., Zanna, M. P., & Fong, G. (2000). Alcohol, sexual arousal, and intentions to use condoms in young men: Applying alcohol myopia theory to risky sexual behavior. *Health Psychology, 19,* 290–298.

MacFarlane, J. G., Cleghorn, J. M., Brown, G. M., & Streiner, D. L. (1991). The effects of exogenous melatonin on the total sleep time and daytime alertness of chronic insomniacs: A preliminary study. *Biological Psychiatry, 30,* 371–376.

Mack, A., Heuer, F., Villardi, K., & Chambers, D. (1985). The dissociation of position and extent in Müller-Lyer figures. *Perception and Psychophysics, 37,* 335–344.

Mack, S. (1981). Novel help for the handicapped. *Science, 212,* 26–27.

Macklin, M. C. (1994). The effects of an advertising retrieval cue on young children's memory and brand evaluations. *Psychology and Marketing, 11,* 291–311.

MacLean, H. N. (1993). *Once upon a time: A true story of memory, murder, and the law.* New York: HarperCollins.

MacLeod, C. M. (1988). Forgotten but not gone: Savings for pictures and words in long-term memory. *Journal of Experimental Psychology: Learning, Memory, and Cognition, 14,* 195–212.

MacMillan, H. L., & Thomas, B. H. (1993). Public health nurse home visitation for the tertiary prevention of child maltreatment: Results of a pilot study. *Canadian Journal of Psychiatry, 38,* 436–442.

Macmillan, M. (2000). Nineteenth-century inhibitory theories of thinking: Bain, Ferrier, Freud (and Phineas Gage). *History of Psychology, 3,* 187–217.

MacNiven, E. (1994). Increased prevalence of left-handedness in victims of head trauma. *Brain Injury, 8,* 457–462.

Madigan, M. W., & O'Hara, R. (1992). Short-term memory at the turn of the century: Mary Whiton Calkins's memory research. *American Psychologist, 47,* 170–174.

Maekelae, K. (1997). Drinking, the majority fallacy, cognitive dissonance and social pressure. *Addiction, 92,* 729–736.

Maganaris, C. N., Collins, D., & Sharp, M. (2000). Expectancy effects and strength training: Do steroids make a difference? *Sport Psychologist, 14,* 272–278.

Magee, W. J., Eaton, W. W., Wittchen, H.-U., McGonagle, K. A., & Kessler, R. C. (1996). Agoraphobia, specific phobia, and social phobia in the national comorbidity survey. *Archives of General Psychiatry, 53,* 159–168.

Maiello, S. (1999). Encounter with an African healer: Thinking about the possibilities and limits of cross-cultural psychotherapy. *Journal of Child Psychotherapy, 25,* 217–238.

Maier, N. R. (1931). Reasoning in humans. *Journal of Comparative Psychology, 12,* 181–194.

Main, M., & George, C. (1985). Responses of abused and disadvantaged toddlers to distress in age mates: A study in the day-care setting. *Developmental Psychology, 21,* 407–412.

Maio, G. R., Olson, J. M., & Bush, J. E. (1997). Telling jokes that disparage social groups: Effects on the joke teller's stereotypes. *Journal of Applied Social Psychology, 27,* 1986–2000.

Malarkey, W. B., Pearl, D. K., Demers, L. M., & Kiecolt-Glaser, J. K. (1995). Influence of academic stress and season on 24-hour mean concentrations of ACTH, cortisol, and b-endorphin. *Psychoneuroendocrinology, 20,* 499–508.

Malik, R., Paraherakis, A., Joseph, S., & Ladd, H. (1996). The method of subliminal psychodynamic activation: Do individual thresholds make a difference? *Perceptual and Motor Skills, 83,* 1235–1242.

Malinowski, C. I., & Smith, C. P. (1985). Moral reasoning and moral conduct: An investigation prompted by Kohlberg's theory. *Journal of Personality and Social Psychology, 49*, 1016–1027.

Mallet, P., & Schaal, B. (1998). Rating and recognition of peers' personal odors by 9–year-old children: An exploratory study. *Journal of General Psychology, 125*, 47–64.

Malmberg, A. B., & Basbaum, A. I. (1998). Partial sciatic nerve injury in the mouse as a model of neuropathic pain: Behavioral and neuroanatomical correlates. *Pain, 76*, 215–222.

Mandel, D. R., Jusczyk, P. W., & Pisoni, D. B. (1995). Infants' recognition of the sound patterns of their own names. *Psychological Science, 6*, 314–317.

Mandl, G. (1985). Responses of visual cells in cat superior colliculus to relative pattern movement. *Vision Research, 25*, 267–281.

Mangweth, B., Pope, H. G., Hudson, J. I., & Biebl, W. (1996). Bulimia nervosa in Austria and the United States: A controlled cross-cultural study. *International Journal of Eating Disorders, 20*, 263–270.

Mann, J. J., Huang, Y. Y., Underwood, M. D., et al. (2000). A serotonin transporter gene promoter polymorphism (5–HTTLPR) and prefrontal cortical binding in major depression and suicide. *Archives of General Psychiatry, 57*, 729–738.

Manning, C. A., Parsons, M. W., & Gold, P. E. (1992). Anterograde and retrograde enhancement of 24–hour memory by glucose in elderly humans. *Behavioral and Neural Biology, 58*, 125–130.

Mansfield, N. J., & Griffin, M. J. (2000). Difference thresholds for automobile seat vibration. *Applied Ergonomics, 31*, 255–261.

Maqsud, M. (1998). Moral orientation of Batswana high school pupils in South Africa. *Journal of Social Psychology, 138*, 255–257.

Maquet, P., Faymonville, E., Degueldre, C., Delfiore, G., Franck, G., et al. (1999). Functional neuroanatomy of hypnotic state. *Biological Psychiatry, 45*, 327–333.

Maquet, P., Laureys, S., Peigneux, P., Fuchs, S., Petiau, C., et al. (2000). Experience-dependent changes in cerebral activation during human REM sleep. *Nature Neuroscience, 3*, 831–836.

Maragos, W. F., Greenamyre, J. T., Penney, J. B., & Young, A. B. (1987). Glutamate dysfunction in Alzheimer's disease: A hypothesis. *Trends in Neuroscience, 10*, 65–68.

Maranto, G. (1984, December). Aging: Can we slow the inevitable? *Discover,* pp. 17–21.

Maratsos, M. (2000). More overregularizations after all: New data and discussion on Marcus, Pinker, Ullman, H., and Rosen and Xu. *Journal of Child Language, 27*, 183–212.

Marchand, S., Charest, J., Li, J., & Chenard, J. R. (1993). Is TENS purely a placebo effect? A controlled study on chronic low back pain. *Pain, 54*, 99–106.

Marcus, G. F. (1995). Children's overregularization of English plurals: A quantita-

tive analysis. *Journal of Child Language, 22*, 447–459.

Markus, H. (1983). Self-knowledge: An expanded view. *Journal of Personality, 51*, 543–565.

Markus, H. R., & Kitayama, S. (1991). Culture and the self: Implications for cognition, emotion and motivation. *Psychological Review, 98*, 224–253.

Marlowe, C. M., Schneider, S. L., & Nelson, C. E. (1996). Gender and attractiveness biases in hiring decisions: Are more experienced managers less biased? *Journal of Applied Psychology, 81*, 11–21.

Marshall, G. D., & Zimbardo, P. G. (1979). Affective consequences of inadequately explained physiological arousal. *Journal of Personality and Social Psychology, 37*, 970–988.

Marsland, A. L., Manuck, S. B., Fazzari, T. V., & Stewart, C. J. (1995). Stability of individual differences in cellular immune responses to acute psychological stress. *Psychosomatic Medicine, 57*, 295–298.

Martin, D. J., Garske, J. P., & Davis, M. K. (2000). Relation of the therapeutic alliance with outcome and other variables: A meta-analytic review. *Journal of Consulting and Clinical Psychology, 68*, 438–450.

Martin, M. A. (1985). Students' applications of self-questioning study techniques: An investigation of their efficacy. *Reading Psychology, 6*, 69–83.

Martin, P. Y., & Benton, D. (1999). The influence of a glucose drink on a demanding working memory task. *Physiology and Behavior, 67*, 69–74.

Marx, B., Gross, A. M., & Adams, H. E. (1999). The effect of alcohol on the responses of sexually coercive andnoncoercive men to an experimental rape analog. *Sexual Abuse: Journal of Research and Treatment, 11*, 131–145.

Masling, J. M. (1997). On the nature and utility of projective tests and objective tests. *Journal of Personality Assessment, 69*, 257–270.

Maslow, A. H. (1970). *Motivation and personality.* New York: Harper & Row.

Masoro, E. J., Shimokawa, I., Higami, Y., & McMahan, C. A. (1995). Temporal pattern of food intake not a factor in the retardation of aging processes by dietary restriction. *Journals of Gerontology: Series A: Biological Sciences and Medical Sciences, 50A*, B48–B53.

Masser, B., & Abrams, D. (1999). Contemporary sexism: The relationships among hostility, benevolence, and neosexism. *Psychology of Women Quarterly, 23*, 503–517.

Masters, K. S. (1992). Hypnotic susceptibility, cognitive dissociation, and runner's high in a sample of marathon runners. *American Journal of Clinical Hypnosis, 34*, 193–201.

Masters, W. H., & Johnson, V. E. (1966). *Human sexual response.* Boston: Little, Brown.

Mastropieri, M. A., Scruggs, T. E., & Whedon, C. (1997). Using mnemonic strategies to teach information about U.S. Presidents: A classroom-based investiga-

tion. *Learning Disability Quarterly, 20*, 13–21.

Mathieu, J. E., & Zajac, D. M. (1990). A review and meta-analysis of the antecedents, correlates, and consequences of organizational commitment. *Psychological Bulletin, 108*, 171–194.

Mathis, M., & Lecci, L. (1999). Hardiness and college adjustment: Identifying students in need of services. *Journal of College Student Development, 40*, 305–309.

Matlock, J. G. (1991). Records of the Parapsychology Laboratory: An inventory of the collection in the Duke University library. *Journal of Parapsychology, 55*, 301–314.

Matsumoto, D. (1987). The role of facial response in the experience of emotion: More methodological problems and a meta-analysis. *Journal of Personality and Social Psychology, 52*, 769–774.

Matsumoto, D., Kasri, F., & Kooken, K. (1999). American-Japanese cultural differences in judgements of expression intensity and subjective experience. *Cognition and Emotion, 13*, 201–218.

Matt, G. E., & Navarro, A. M. (1997). What meta-analyses have and have not taught us about psychotherapy effects: A review and future directions. *Clinical Psychology Review, 17*, 1–32.

Matthews, D. B., Best, P. J., White, A. M., Vandergriff, J. L., & Simon, P. E. (1996). Ethanol impairs spatial cognitive processing: New behavioral and electrophysiological findings. *Current Directions in Psychological Science, 5*, 111–115.

Matthews, G., & Gilliland, K. (1999). The personality theories of H. J. Eysenck and J. A. Gray: A comparative review. *Personality and Individual Differences, 26*, 583–626.

Matthews, K. A., & Woodall, K. L. (1988). Childhood origins of overt Type A behaviors and cardiovascular reactivity to behavioral stressors. *Annals of Behavioral Medicine, 10*, 71–77.

Mauer, M. H., Burnett, K. F., Oulette, E. A., Ironson, G. H., & Dandes, H. M. (1999). Medical hypnosis and orthopedic hand surgery: Pain perception, postoperative recovery, and therapeutic comfort. *International Journal of Clinical and Experimental Hypnosis, 47*, 144–161.

Maurino, D. E. (1994). Cross-cultural perspectives in human factors training: Lessons from the ICAO human factors program. *International Journal of Aviation Psychology, 4*, 173–181.

Mazzella, R., & Feingold, A. (1994). The effects of physical attractiveness, race, socioeconomic status, and gender of defendants and victims on judgments of mock jurors: A meta-analysis. *Journal of Applied Social Psychology, 24*, 1315–1344.

McAdams, D. P., de St. Aubin, E., & Logan, R. L. (1993). Generativity among youth, midlife, and older adults. *Psychology and Aging, 8*, 221–230.

McAllister, D. E., & McAllister, W. R. (1994). Extinction and reconditioning of classically conditioned fear before and after instrumental learning: Effects of depth of fear extinction. *Learning and Motivation, 25*, 339–367.

McCall, M. (1997). The effects of physical attractiveness on gaining access to alcohol: When social policy meets social decision making. *Addiction, 92*, 597–600.

McCarthy, L., & Shean, G. (1996). Agoraphobia and interpersonal relationships. *Journal of Anxiety Disorders, 10*, 477–487.

McCauley, C., & Forman, R. F. (1988). A review of the Office of Technology Assessment report on polygraph validity. *Basic and Applied Social Psychology, 9*, 73–84.

McCauley, C., Woods, K., Coolidge, C., & Kulick W. (1983). More-aggressive cartoons are funnier. *Journal of Personality and Social Psychology, 44*, 817–823.

McClelland, D. C. (1985). How motives, skills, and values determine what people do. *American Psychologist, 40*, 812–825.

McClelland, J. L., McNaughton, B. L., & O'Reilly, R. C. (1995). Why there are complementary learning systems in the hippocampus and neocortex: Insights from the successes and failures of connectionist models of learning and memory. *Psychological Review, 102*, 419–437.

McCloskey, M., & Egeth, H. E. (1983). Eyewitness identification: What can a psychologist tell a jury? *American Psychologist, 38*, 550–563.

McCloskey, M., Wible, C. G., & Cohen, N. J. (1988). Is there a special flashbulb-memory mechanism? *Journal of Experimental Psychology: General, 117*, 171–181.

McClure, E. B. (2000). A meta-analytic review of sex differences in facial expression processing and their development in infants, children, and adolescents. *Psychological Bulletin, 126*, 424–453.

McClure, J., Walkey, F., & Allen, M. (1999). When earthquake damage is seen as preventable: Attributions, locus of control and attitudes to risk. *Applied Psychology, 48*, 239–256.

McConaghy, N., & Blaszcynski, A. (1991). Initial stages of validation by penile volume assessment that sexual orientation is distributed dimensionally. *Comprehensive Psychiatry, 32*, 52–58.

McConahay, J. B. (1986). Modern racism, ambivalence and the Modern Racism Scale. In J. F. Dovidio & S. L. Gaertner (Eds.), *Prejudice, discrimination and racism* (pp. 91–125). London: Academic Press.

McConnell, J. V., Cutler, R. L., & McNeil, E. B. (1958). Subliminal stimulation: An overview. *American Psychologist, 13*, 229–242.

McConnell, J. V., Jacobson, A. L., & Kimble, D. P. (1959). The effects of regeneration upon retention of a conditioned response in the planarian. *Journal of Comparative and Physiological Psychology, 52*, 1–5.

McCormick, E. J. (1979). *Job analysis: Methods and applications.* New York: AMACON.

McCormick, N. B., & Jones, A. J. (1989). Gender differences in flirtation. *Journal of Sex Education and Therapy, 15*, 271–282.

McCrae, R. R., & Costa, P. T. (1995). Trait explanations in personality psychology. *European Journal of Personality, 9,* 231–252.

McCrae, R. R., & Costa, P. T., Jr. (1997). Personality trait structure as a human universal. *American Psychologist, 52,* 509–516.

McCrae, R. R., Costa, P. T., Jr., Del Pilar, G. H., Rolland, J.-P., & Parker, W. D. (1998). Cross-cultural assessment of the five-factor model: The Revised NEO Personality Inventory. *Journal of Cross-Cultural Psychology, 29,* 171–188.

McDaniel, M. A., Whetzel, D. L., Schmidt, F. L., & Maurer, S. D. (1994). The validity of employment interviews: A comprehensive review and meta-analysis. *Journal of Applied Psychology, 79,* 599–616.

McDougall, W. (1908). *Social psychology.* New York: Putnam & Sons.

McFadden, D. (1998). Sex differences in the auditory system. *Developmental Neuropsychology, 14,* 261–298.

McFadden, D., & Pasanen, E. G. (1999). Spontaneous otoacoustic emissions in heterosexuals, homosexuals, and bisexuals. *Journal of the Acoustical Society of America, 105,* 2403–2413.

McGaha, A. C., & Korn, J. H. (1995). The emergence of interest in the ethics of psychological research with humans. *Ethics and Behavior, 5,* 147–159.

McGrady, A., Turner, J. W., Fine, T. H., & Higgins, J. T. (1987). Effects of biobehaviorally assisted relaxation training on blood pressure, plasma renin, cortisol, and aldosterone levels in borderline essential hypertension. *Clinical Biofeedback and Health, 10,* 16–25.

McGue, M., Bacon, S., & Lykken, D. T. (1993). Personality stability and change in early adulthood: A behavioral genetic analysis. *Developmental psychology, 29,* 96–109.

McKelvie, S. J. (1997). The availability heuristic: Effects of fame and gender on the estimated frequency of male and female names. *Journal of Social Psychology, 137,* 63–78.

McKenna, M. C., Zevon, M. A., Corn, B., & Rounds, J. (1999). Psychosocial factors and the development of breast cancer: A meta-analysis. *Health Psychology, 18,* 520–531.

McKenzie, J. (1998). Fundamental flaws in the Five Factor Model: A re-analysis of the seminal correlation matrix from which the "openness-to-experience" factor was extracted. *Personality and Individual Differences, 24,* 475–480.

McKinney, M., & Richelson, E. (1984). The coupling of the neuronal muscarinic receptor to responses. *Annual Review of Pharmacology and Toxicology, 24,* 121–146.

McKnight, A. J., & McKnight, A. S. (1993). The effect of cellular phone use upon driver attention. *Accident Analysis and Prevention, 25,* 259–265.

McLeod, D. M., & Detenber, B. H. (1999). Framing effects of television news coverage of social protest. *Journal of Communication, 49,* 3–23.

McMackin, D., Jones-Gotman, M., Dubeau, F., et al. (1998). Regional cerebral blood flow and language dominance: SPECT during intracarotid amobarbital testing. *Neurology, 50,* 943–950.

McMahon, F. J., Chen, Y. S., Patel, S., Kokoszka, J., et al. (2000). Mitochondrial DNA sequence diversity in bipolar affective disorder. *American Journal of Psychiatry, 157,* 1058–1064.

McNally, R. J. (1987). Preparedness and phobia: A review. *Psychological Bulletin, 101,* 283–303.

McNamara, L., & Ballard, M. E. (1999). Resting arousal, sensation seeking, and music preference. *Genetic, Social, and General Psychology Monographs, 125,* 229–250.

McNatt, D. B. (2000). Ancient Pygmalion joins contemporary management: A meta-analysis of the result. *Journal of Applied Psychology, 85,* 314–322.

McNelles, L. R., & Connolly, J. A. (1999). Intimacy between adolescent friends: Age and gender differences in intimate affect and intimate behaviors. *Journal of Research on Adolescence, 9,* 143–159.

McNish, K. A., Betts, S. L., Brandon, S. E., & Wagner, A. R. (1997). Divergence of conditioned eyeblink and conditioned fear in backward Pavlovian training. *Animal Learning and Behavior, 25,* 43–52.

McPherson, K. S. (1985). On intelligence testing and immigration legislation. *American Psychologist, 40,* 242–243.

McRoberts, C., Burlingame, G. M., & Hoag, M. J. (1998). Comparative efficacy of individual and group psychotherapy: A meta-analytic perspective. *Group Dynamics, 2,* 101–117.

McWilliams, S. A., & Tuttle, R. J. (1973). Long-term psychological effects of LSD. *Psychological Bulletin, 79,* 341–351.

Mecacci, L., & Rocchetti, G. (1998). Morning and evening types: Stress-related personality aspects. *Personality and Individual Differences, 25,* 537–542.

Medina, J. H., Schroeder, N., & Izquierdo, I. (1999). Two different properties of short- and long-term memory. *Behavioural Brain Research, 103,* 119–121.

Mednick, S. A. (1962). The associative basis of the creative process. *Psychological Review, 69,* 220–232.

Meeker, W. B., & Barber, T. X. (1971). Toward an explanation of stage hypnosis. *Journal of Abnormal Psychology, 77,* 61–70.

Meertens, R. W., & Pettigrew, T. F. (1997). Is subtle prejudice really prejudice? *Public Opinion Quarterly, 61,* 54–71.

Meichenbaum, D. H., Bowers, K. S., & Ross, R. R. (1969). A behavioral analysis of teacher expectancy effect. *Journal of Personality and Social Psychology, 13,* 306–316.

Meissner, W. W. (1996). Empathy in the therapeutic alliance. *Psychoanalytic Inquiry, 16,* 39–53.

Melanoma risk and socio-economic class. (1983). *Science News, 124,* 232.

Mellon, M. W., & McGrath, M. L. (2000). Empirically supported treatments in pediatric psychology: Nocturnal enuresis. *Journal of Pediatric Psychology, 25,* 193–214.

Mellors, V., Boyle, G. J., & Roberts, L. (1994). Effects of personality, stress and lifestyle on hypertension: An Australian twin study. *Personality and Individual Differences, 16,* 967–974.

Melzack, R. (1993). Pain: Past, present and future. *Canadian Journal of Experimental Psychology, 47,* 615–629.

Melzack, R., & Wall, P. D. (1965). Pain mechanisms: A new theory. *Science, 150,* 971–979.

Memory transfer. (1966). *Science, 153,* 658–659.

Mendelson, W. B., Maczaj, M., & Holt, J. (1991). Buspirone administration to sleep apnea patients. *Journal of Clinical Psychopharmacology, 11,* 71–72.

Mengel, M. K. C., Stiefenhofer, A. E., Jyvasjarvi, E., & Kniffki, K. D. (1993). Pain sensation during cold stimulation of the teeth: Differential reflection of Ad and C fibre activity? *Pain, 55,* 159–169.

Merckelbach, H., Arntz, A., & de Jong, P. (1991). Conditioning experiences in spider phobics. *Behaviour Research and Therapy, 29,* 333–335.

Merckelbach, H., Muris, P., & Kop, W. J. (1994). Handedness, symptom reporting, and accident susceptibility. *Journal of Clinical Psychology, 50,* 389–392.

Merikle, P. M., & Joordens, S. (1997). Parallels between perception without attention and perception without awareness. *Consciousness and Cognition, 6,* 219–236.

Mertens, D. M., & Rabiu, J. (1992). Combining cognitive learning theory and computer assisted instruction for deaf learners. *American Annals of the Deaf, 137,* 399–403.

Mervis, J. (1984, March). Council ends forums trial, opens way for new divisions. *APA Monitor,* pp. 10–11.

Mervis, J. (1986, July). NIMH data point way to effective treatment. *APA Monitor,* pp. 1, 13.

Messer, D. (2000). State of the art: Language acquisition. *Psychologist, 13,* 138–143.

Messer, W. S., & Griggs, R. A. (1989). Student belief and involvement in the paranormal and performance in introductory psychology. *Teaching of Psychology, 16,* 187–191.

Messier, C., Durkin, T., Mrabet, O., & Destrade, C. (1990). Memory-improving action of glucose: Indirect evidence for a facilitation of hippocampal acetylcholine synthesis. *Behavioural Brain Research, 39,* 135–143.

Messinger, D. S., Fogel, A., & Dickson, K. L. (1999). What's in a smile? *Developmental Psychology, 35,* 701–708.

Metcalfe, J., & Wiebe, D. (1987). Intuition in insight and noninsight problem solving. *Memory and Cognition, 15,* 238–246.

Methot, L. L., & Phillips-Grant, K. (1998). Technological advances in the Canadian workplace: An I-O perspective. *Canadian Psychology, 39,* 133–141.

Mettetal, G., Jordan, C., & Harper, S. (1997). Attitudes toward a multiple intelligences curriculum. *Journal of Educational Research, 91,* 115–122.

Mewaldt, S. P., Ghoneim, M. M., Choi, W. W., & Korttila, K. (1988). Nitrous oxide and human state-dependent memory. *Pharmacology, Biochemistry, and Behavior, 30,* 83–87.

Meyer-Bisch, C. (1996). Epidemiological evaluation of hearing damage related to strongly amplified music (personal cassette players, discotheques, rock concerts): High-definition audiometric survey on 1364 subjects. *Audiology, 35,* 121–142.

Mezzacappa, E. S., Katkin, E. S., & Palmer, S. N. (1999). Epinephrine, arousal, and emotion: A new look at two-factor theory. *Cognition and Emotion, 13,* 181–199.

Miaskowski, C. (1999). The role of sex and gender in pain perception and responses to treatment. In R. J. Gatchel, D. C. Turk, et al. (Eds.), *Psychosocial factors in pain: Critical perspectives* (pp. 401–411). New York: Guilford Press.

Michel, C., & Cabanac, M. (1999). Lipectomy, body weight, and body weight set point in rats. *Physiology and Behavior, 66,* 473–479.

Miczek, K. A., Thompson, M. L., & Shuster, L. (1982). Opioid-like analgesia in defeated mice. *Science, 215,* 1520–1523.

Middlebrooks, J. C., & Green, D. M. (1991). Sound localization by human listeners. *Annual Review of Psychology, 42,* 135–159.

Mignot, E. (1998). Genetic and familial aspects of narcolepsy. *Neurology, 50,* S16–S22.

Mikulincer, M., & Peer-Goldin, I. (1991). Self-congruence and the experience of happiness. *British Journal of Social Psychology, 30,* 21–35.

Milar, K. S. (2000). The first generation of women psychologists and the psychology of women. *American Psychologist, 55,* 616–619.

Miles, C., & Hardman, E. (1998). State-dependent memory produced by aerobic exercise. *Ergonomics, 41,* 20–28.

Miles, J. A., & Greenberg, J. (1993). Using punishment threats to attenuate social loafing effects among swimmers. *Organizational Behavior and Human Decision Processes, 56,* 246–265.

Milgram, S. (1963). Behavioral study of obedience. *Journal of Abnormal and Social Psychology, 67,* 371–378.

Milgram, S. (1964). Issues in the study of obedience: A reply to Baumrind. *American Psychologist, 19,* 848–852.

Milgram, S. (1974). *Obedience to authority.* New York: Harper & Row.

Miller, B. D., & Wood, B. L. (1997). Influence of specific emotional states on autonomic reactivity and pulmonary function in asthmatic children. *Journal of the American Academy of Child and Adolescent Psychiatry, 36,* 669–677.

Miller, E. (1996). Phrenology, neuropsychology, and rehabilitation. *Neuropsychological Rehabilitation, 6,* 245–255.

Miller, E. M. (1994). Intelligence and brain myelination: A hypothesis. *Personality and Individual Differences, 17,* 803–832.

Miller, G. A. (1956). The magical number seven, plus or minus two: Some limits on our capacity for processing information. *Psychological Review, 63,* 81–97.

Miller, G. A. (1990). The place of language in a scientific psychology. *Psychological Science, 1,* 7–14.

Miller, H. L., Chaplin, W. F., & Coombs, D. W. (1990). Cause and correlation: One more time. *Psychological Reports, 66,* 1293–1294.

Miller, J. (1991). Threshold variability in subliminal perception experiments: Fixed threshold estimates reduce power to detect subliminal effects. *Journal of Experimental Psychology: Human Perception and Performance, 17,* 841–851.

Miller, K. J., Gleaves, D. H., Hirsch, T. G., Green, B. A., Snow, A. C., & Corbett, C. C. (2000). Comparisons of body image dimensions by race/ethnicity and gender in a university population. *International Journal of Eating Disorders, 27,* 310–316.

Miller, L. K. (1999). The Savant syndrome: Intellectual impairment and exceptional skill. *Psychological Bulletin, 125,* 31–46.

Miller, N. E. (1985). The value of behavioral research on animals. *American Psychologist, 40,* 423–440.

Miller, T. Q., Smith, T. W., Turner, C. W., Guijarro, M. L., & Hallet, A. J. (1996). Meta-analytic review of research on hostility and physical health. *Psychological Bulletin, 119,* 322–348.

Miller, T. Q., Turner, C. W., Tindale, R. S., Posavac, E. J., & Dugoni, B. L. (1991). Reasons for the trend toward null findings in research on Type A behavior. *Psychological Bulletin, 110,* 469–485.

Miller, W. C. (1999). How effective are traditional dietary and exercise interventions for weight loss? *Medicine and Science in Sports and Exercise, 31,* 1129–1134.

Millon, T. (2000). Sociocultural conceptions of the borderline personality. *Psychiatric Clinics of North America, 23,* 123–136.

Mills, S., & Raine, A. (1994). Neuroimaging and aggression. *Journal of Offender Rehabilitation, 21,* 145–158.

Mimeault, V., & Morin, C. M. (1999). Self-help treatment for insomnia: Bibliotherapy with and without professional guidance. *Journal of Consulting and Clinical Psychology, 67,* 511–519.

Mineka, S., & Cook, M. (1993). Mechanisms involved in the observational conditioning of fear. *Journal of Experimental Psychology General, 122,* 23–38.

Mineka, S., Mystkowski, M. L., Hladek, D., & Rodriguez, B. I. (1999). The effects of changing contexts on return of fear following exposure therapy for spider fear. *Journal of Consulting and Clinical Psychology, 67,* 599–604.

Mino, Y., Inoue, S., Tanaka, S., & Tsuda, T. (1997). Expressed emotion among families and course of schizophrenia in Japan: A 2–year cohort study. *Schizophrenia Research, 24,* 333–339.

Mio, J. S., & Graesser, A. C. (1991). Humor, language, and metaphor. *Metaphor and Symbolic Activity, 6,* 87–102.

Mirsky, A. F., Yardley, S. L., Jones, B. P., & Walsh, D. (1995). Analysis of the attention deficit in schizophrenia: A study of patients and their relatives in Ireland. *Journal of Psychiatric Research, 29,* 23–42.

Mischel, W. (1968). *Personality and assessment.* New York: Wiley.

Mischel, W., & Peake, P. J. (1982). Beyond déjà vu in the search for cross-situational consistency. *Psychological Review, 89,* 730–755.

Miserandino, M. (1991). Memory and the seven dwarfs. *Teaching of Psychology, 18,* 169–171.

Misra, G., Sahoo, F. M., & Puhan, B. N. (1997). Cultural bias in testing: India. *European Review of Applied Psychology, 47,* 309–317.

Mita, T. H., Dermer, M., & Knight, J. (1977). Reversed facial images and the mere-exposure hypothesis. *Journal of Personality and Social Psychology, 35,* 597–601.

Mitchell, P., & Taylor, L. M. (1999). Shape constancy and theory of mind: Is there a link? *Cognition, 70,* 167–190.

Modestin, J., Ammann, R., & Wurmle, O. (1995). Season of birth: Comparison of patients with schizophrenia, affective disorders and alcoholism. *Acta Psychiatrica Scandinavica, 91,* 140–143.

Modigliani, A., & Rochat, F. (1995). The role of interaction sequences and the timing of resistance in shaping obedience and defiance to authority. *Journal of Social Issues, 51,* 107–123.

Mohanty, A. K., & Perreaux, C. (1997). Language acquisition and bilingualism. In J. W. Berry, P. R. Dasen, & T. S. Saraswathi (Eds.), *Handbook of cross-cultural psychology: Vol. 2. Basic processes and human development* (2nd ed., pp. 217–253). Boston: Allyn & Bacon.

Mohr, D. C. (1995). Negative outcome in psychotherapy: A critical review. *Clinical Psychology: Science and Practice, 2,* 1–27.

Molina, M., & Jouen, F. (1998). Modulation of the palmar grasp behavior in neonates according to texture property. *Infant Behavior and Development, 21,* 659–666.

Moniz, E. (1937/1994). Prefrontal leucotomy in the treatment of mental disorders. *American Journal of Psychiatry, 151,* 237–239.

Monroe, S. M. (1982). Life events and disorder: Event-symptom associations and the course of disorder. *Journal of Abnormal Psychology, 91,* 14–24.

Monte, C. F. (1980). *Beneath the mask: An introduction to theories of personality.* New York: Holt, Rinehart & Winston.

Montour, K. (1977). William James Sidis: The broken twig. *American Psychologist, 32,* 265–279.

Moore, C., & Engel, S. A. (1999). Visual perception: Mind and brain see eye to eye. *Current Biology, 9,* R74–R76.

Moore, J. (1990). On mentalism, privacy, and behaviorism. *Journal of Mind and Behavior, 11,* 19–36.

Moore, J. (1996). On the relation between behaviorism and cognitive psychology. *Journal of Mind and Behavior, 17,* 345–367.

Moore, T. E. (1995). Subliminal self-help auditory tapes: An empirical test of perceptual consequences. *Canadian Journal of Behavioural Science, 27,* 9–20.

Moorhead, G., Ference, R., & Neck, C. P. (1991). Group decision fiascoes continue: Space shuttle *Challenger* and a revised groupthink framework. *Human Relations, 44,* 539–550.

Moran, M. G. (1991). Psychological factors affecting pulmonary and rheumatologic diseases: A review. *Psychosomatics, 32,* 14–23.

Morawski, J. G. (1982). Assessing psychology's moral heritage through our neglected utopias. *American Psychologist, 37,* 1082–1095.

Moreland, R. L., & Zajonc, R. B. (1982). Exposure effects in person perception: Familiarity, similarity, and attraction. *Journal of Experimental Social Psychology, 18,* 395–415.

Moretti, M. M., & Higgins, E. T. (1990). Relating self-discrepancy to self-esteem: The contribution of discrepancy beyond actual-self ratings. *Journal of Experimental Social Psychology, 26,* 108–123.

Morgan, C., & Murray, H. A. (1935). A method of investigating fantasies. *Archives of Neurology and Psychiatry, 4,* 310–329.

Morgan, W. G. (1995). Origin and history of the thematic apperception test images. *Journal of Personality Assessment, 65,* 237–254.

Morisse, D., Batra, L., Hess, L., & Silverman, R. (1996). A demonstration of a token economy for the real world. *Applied and Preventive Psychology, 5,* 41–46.

Moritz, S., Andresen, B., Domin, F., Martin, T., Probsthein, E., et al. (1999). Increased automatic spreading activation in healthy subjects with elevated scores in a scale assessing schizophrenic language disturbances. *Psychological Medicine, 29,* 161–170.

Morley, J. E., & Levine, A. S. (1980). Stress-induced eating is mediated through endogenous opiates. *Science, 209,* 1259–1261.

Morris, S. (1980, April). Interview: James Randi. *Omni,* pp. 76–78, 104, 106, 108.

Morris, W., & Morris, M. (1985). *Harper dictionary of contemporary usage.* New York: Harper & Row.

Morrison, A. R. (1983, April). A window on the sleeping brain. *Scientific American,* pp. 94–102.

Morrongiello, B. A., Fenwick, K. D., & Chance, G. (1990). "Sound localization acuity in very young infants: An observer-based testing procedure": Correction. *Developmental Psychology, 26,* 1003.

Morse, C. K. (1999). Age and variability in Francis Galton's data. *Journal of Genetic Psychology, 160,* 99–104.

Mortensen, P. B., Pedersen, C. B., Westergaard, T., Wohlfahrt, J., et al. (1999). Effects of family history and place and season of birth on the risk of schizophrenia. *New England Journal of Medicine, 340,* 603–608.

Moruzzi, G., & Magoun, H. W. (1949). Brain-stem reticular formation and activation of the EEG. *Electroencephalography and Clinical Neurophysiology, 1,* 455–473.

Morvay, Z. (1999). Horney, Zen, and the real self: Theoretical and historical connections. *American Journal of Psychoanalysis, 59,* 25–35.

Moscovitch, M., & Behrmann, M. (1994). Coding of spatial information in the somatosensory system: Evidence from patients with neglect following parietal lobe damage. *Journal of Cognitive Neuroscience, 6,* 151–155.

Mowday, R. T., Steers, R. M., & Porter, L. W. (1979). The measurement of organizational commitment. *Journal of Vocational Behavior, 14,* 224–247.

Mowrer, O. H., & Mowrer, W. M. (1938). Enuresis: A method for its study and treatment. *American Journal of Orthopsychiatry, 8,* 436–559.

Muchinsky, P. M. (2000). *Psychology applied to work: An introduction to industrial and organizational psychology.* Belmont, CA: Wadsworth.

Muehlbach, M. J., & Walsh, J. K. (1995). The effects of caffeine on simulated night-shift work and subsequent daytime sleep. *Sleep, 18,* 22–29.

Mueller, C. G. (1979). Some origins of psychology as a science. *Annual Review of Psychology, 30,* 9–29.

Mueller, R.-A., Rothermel, R. D., Behen, M. E., et al. (1998). Differential patterns of language and motor reorganization following early left hemisphere lesion. *Archives of Neurology, 55,* 1113–1119.

Muir-Broaddus, J., King, T., Downey, D., & Petersen, M. (1998). Conservation as a predictor of individual differences in children's susceptibility to leading questions. *Psychonomic Bulletin and Review, 5,* 454–458.

Mullen, B., Anthony, T., Salas, E., & Driskell, J. E. (1994). Group cohesiveness and quality of decision making: An integration of tests of the groupthink hypothesis. *Small Group Research, 25,* 189–204.

Mullen, B., Futrell, D., Stairs, D., Tice, D. M., et al. (1986). Newscasters' facial expressions and voting behavior of viewers: Can a smile elect a president? *Journal of Personality and Social Psychology, 51,* 291–295.

Mulligan, T., & Moss, C. R. (1991). Sexuality and aging in male veterans: A cross-sectional study of interest, ability, and activity. *Archives of Sexual Behavior, 20,* 17–25.

Mullington, J., & Broughton, R. (1993). Scheduled naps in the management of daytime sleepiness in narcolepsy-cataplexy. *Sleep, 16,* 444–456.

Mumby, D. G., Cameli, L., & Glenn, M. J. (1999). Impaired allocentric spatial working memory and intact retrograde memory after thalamic damage caused by thiamine deficiency in rats. *Behavioral Neuroscience, 113,* 42–50.

Mumenthaler, M. S., Taylor, J. L., O'Hara, R., & Yesavage, J. A. (1999). Gender differences in moderate drinking effects. *Alcohol Research and Health, 23,* 55–61.

Munakata, Y., McClelland, J. L., Johnson, M. H., & Siegler, R. S. (1997). Rethinking infant knowledge: Toward an adaptive process account of successes and failures in object permanence tasks. *Psychological Review, 104,* 686–713.

Münsterberg, H. (1908). *On the witness stand.* New York: Doubleday.

Muris, P., Merckelbach, H., Gadet, B., & Moulaert, V. (2000). Fears, worries and scary dreams in 4– to 12–year-old children: Their content, developmental pattern, and origins. *Journal of Clinical Child Psychology, 29,* 43–52.

Murphy, K. J., & Regan, C. M. (1998). Contributions of cell adhesion molecules to altered synaptic weightings during memory consolidation. *Neurobiology of Learning and Memory, 70,* 73–81.

Murray, H. A. (1938). *Explorations in personality.* New York: Oxford University Press.

Murray, J. B. (1990). Review of research on the Myers-Briggs Type Indicator. *Perceptual and Motor Skills, 70,* 1187–1202.

Murray, J. B. (1995). Evidence for acupuncture's analgesic effectiveness and proposals for the physiological mechanisms involved. *Journal of Psychology, 129,* 443–461.

Murray, R. P., Johnston, J. J., Dolce, J. J., & Lee, W. W. (1995). Social support for smoking cessation and abstinence: The Lung Health Study. *Addictive Behaviors, 20,* 159–170.

Murray, S. L., Holmes, J. G., & Griffin, D. W. (1996). The self-fulfilling nature of positive illusions in romantic relationships: Love is not blind, but prescient. *Journal of Personality and Social Psychology, 71,* 1155–1180.

Murstein, B. (1972). Physical attractiveness and marital choice. *Journal of Personality and Social Psychology, 22,* 8–12.

Myers, D. G. (2000). The funds, friends, and faith of happy people. *American Psychologist, 55,* 56–67.

Myerscough, R., & Taylor, S. (1985). The effects of marijuana on human physical aggression. *Journal of Personality and Social Psychology, 49,* 1541–1546.

Na, E. U., & Loftus, E. F. (1998). Attitudes toward law and prisoners, conservative authoritarianism, attribution, and internal-external locus of control: Korean and American law students and undergraduates. *Journal of Cross-Cultural Psychology, 29,* 595–615.

Nadel, L., & Jacobs, W. J. (1998). Traumatic memory is special. *Current Directions in Psychological Science, 7,* 154–156.

Nadel, L., & Moscovitch, M. (1998). Hippocampal contributions to cortical plasticity. *Neuropharmacology, 37,* 431–439.

Naka, M., Itsukushima, Y., & Itoh, Y. (1996). Eyewitness testimony after three months: A field study on memory for an incident in everyday life. *Japanese Psychological Research, 38,* 14–24.

Nakano, T., Shimomura, T., Takahashi, K., & Ikawa, S. (1993). Platelet substance P and 5–hydroxytryptamine in migraine and tension-type headache. *Headache, 33,* 528–532.

Nakao, M., Nomura, S., Shimosawa, T., Fujita, T., & Kuboki, T. (2000). Blood pressure biofeedback treatment of white-coat hypertension. *Journal of Psychosomatic Research, 48,* 161–169.

Nakayama, K. (1994). James J. Gibson: An appreciation. *Psychological Review, 101,* 329–335.

NAS calls tests fair but limited. (1982, April). *APA Monitor,* p. 2.

Nash, M. (1987). What, if anything, is regressed about hypnotic age regression? A review of the empirical literature. *Psychological Bulletin, 102,* 42–52.

Nation, K., & Snowling, M. J. (2000). Factors influencing syntactic awareness skills in normal readers and poor comprehenders. *Applied Psycholinguistics, 21,* 229–241.

National Institute of Mental Health. (1998). The NIMH Multisite HIV Prevention Trial: Reducing HIV sexual risk behavior. *Science, 280,* 1889–1894.

Natsoulas, T. (1999–2000). The stream of consciousness: XX: A non-ecological conception. *Imagination, Cognition and Personality, 19,* 71–90.

Navarro, M., Fernandex-Ruiz, J. J., de Miguel, R., & Hernandez, M. L. (1993). Motor disturbances induced by an acute dose of d-sup-9-tetrahydro-cannabinol: Possible involvement of nigrostriatal dopaminergic alterations. *Pharmacology, Biochemistry, and Behavior, 45,* 291–298.

Navon, D. (1974). Forest before trees: The precedence of global features in visual perception. *Cognitive Psychology, 9,* 353–383.

Nayak, S., Shiflett, S. C., Eshun, S., & Levine, F. M. (2000). Culture and gender effects in pain beliefs and the prediction of pain tolerance. *Cross-Cultural Research, 34,* 135–151.

Nazzi, T., Floccia, C., & Bertoncini, J. (1998). Discrimination of pitch contours by neonates. *Infant Behavior and Development, 21,* 779–784.

Neher, A. (1996). Jung's theory of archetypes: A critique. *Journal of Humanistic Psychology, 36,* 61–91.

Neisser, U. (1981). John Dean's memory: A case study. *Cognition, 9,* 1–22.

Neisser, U. (1984). Interpreting Harry Bahrick's discovery: What confers immunity against forgetting? *Journal of Experimental Psychology: General, 113,* 32–35.

Neisser, U., & Becklen, R. (1975). Selective looking: Attending to visually specified events. *Cognitive Psychology, 7,* 480–494.

Neisser, U., Boodoo, G., Bouchard, T. J., Jr, Boykin, A. W., Brody, N., et al. (1996). Intelligence: Knowns and unknowns. *American Psychologist, 51,* 77–101.

Nejime, Y., & Moore, B. C. J. (1998). Evaluation of the effect of speech rate slowing on speech intelligibility in noise using a simulation of cochlear hearing loss. *Journal of the Acoustical Society of America, 103,* 572–576.

Nelson, J. C. (1999). A review of the efficacy of serotonergic and noradrenergic reuptake inhibitors for treatment of major depression. *Biological Psychiatry, 46,* 1301–1308.

Nelson, K. E. (1977). Facilitating children's syntax acquisition. *Developmental Psychology, 18,* 101–107.

Nelson, P. L. (1994–1995). Cannabis amotivational syndrome and personality trait absorption: A review and reconceptualization. *Imagination, Cognition, and Personality, 14,* 43–58.

Nelson, T. O., Leonesio, R. J., Shimamura, A. P., Landwehr, R. F., & Narens, L. (1982). Overlearning and the feeling of knowing. *Journal of Experimental Psychology: Learning, Memory, and Cognition, 8,* 279–288.

Nemechek, S., & Olson, K. R. (1999). Five-factor personality similarity and marital adjustment. *Social Behavior and Personality, 27,* 309–318.

Nettelbeck, T. (1998). Jensen's chronometric research: Neither simple nor sufficient but a good place to start. *Intelligence, 26,* 233–241.

Neubauer, A. C., Riemann, R., Mayer, R., & Angleitner, A. (1997). Intelligence and reaction times in the Hick, Sternberg and Posner paradigms. *Personality and Individual Differences, 22,* 885–894.

Nevo, O. (1985). Does one ever really laugh at one's own expense? *Journal of Personality and Social Psychology, 49,* 799–807.

Newcomb, A. F., Bukowski, W. M., & Pattee, L. (1993). Children's peer relations: A meta-analytic review of popular, rejected, neglected, controversial, and average sociometric status. *Psychological Bulletin, 113,* 99–128.

Newcomer, J. W., Craft, S., Fucetola, R., et al. (1999). Glucose-induced increase in memory performance in patients with schizophrenia. *Schizophrenia Bulletin, 25,* 321–335.

Newell, P. T., & Cartwright, R. D. (2000). Affect and cognition in dreams: A critique of the cognitive role in adaptive dream functioning and support for associative models. *Psychiatry: Interpersonal and Biological Processes, 63,* 34–44.

Newman, B., O'Grady, M. A., Ryan, C. S., & Hemmes, N. S. (1993). Pavlovian conditioning of the tickle response of human subjects: Temporal and delay conditioning. *Perceptual and Motor Skills, 77,* 779–785.

Newman, E. A., & Hartline, P. H. (1982, March). The infrared "vision" of snakes. *Scientific American,* pp. 116–124, 127.

Newman, J., & Layton, B. D. (1984). Overjustification: A self-perception perspective. *Personality and Social Psychology Bulletin, 10,* 419–425.

Newton, T., & Keenan, T. (1991). Further analyses of the dispositional argument in organizational behavior. *Journal of Applied Psychology, 76,* 781–787.

Ng, W.-J., & Lindsay, R. C. L. (1994). Cross-race facial recognition: Failure of the contact hypothesis. *Journal of Cross-Cultural Psychology, 25,* 217–232.

NICHD Early Child Care Research Network. (1997). The effects of infant child care on infant-mother attachment security: Results of the NICHD study of early child care. *Child Development, 68,* 860–879.

Nicholson, I. A. M. (1998). Gordon Allport, character, and the "culture of personality," 1897–1937. *History of Psychology, 1,* 52–68.

Nicholson, N., Cole, S. G., & Rocklin, T. (1985). Conformity in the Asch situation: A comparison between contemporary British and U.S. university students. *British Journal of Social Psychology, 24,* 59–63.

Nickerson, R. S., & Adams, M. J. (1979). Long-term memory for a common object. *Cognitive Psychology, 11,* 287–307.

Nicol, S. E., & Gottesman, I. I. (1983). Clues to the genetics and neurobiology of schizophrenia. *American Scientist, 71,* 398–404.

Nicoll, R. A., & Madison, D. V. (1982). General anesthetics hyperpolarize neurons in the vertebrate nervous system. *Science, 217,* 1055–1057.

Nides, M. A., Rakos, R. F., Gonzales, D., & Murray, R. P. (1995). Predictors of initial smoking cessation and relapse through the first 2 years of the Lung Health Study. *Journal of Consulting and Clinical Psychology, 63,* 60–69.

Nides, M., Rand, C., Dolce, J., & Murray, R. (1994). Weight gain as a function of smoking cessation and 2–mg nicotine gum use among middle-aged smokers with mild lung impairment in the first 2 years of the Lung Health Study. *Health Psychology, 13,* 354–361.

Niedeggen, M., & Roesler, F. (1999). N400 effects reflect activation spread during retrieval of arithmetic facts. *Psychological Science, 10,* 271–276.

Nielsen, M., & Day, R. H. (1999). William James and the evolution of consciousness. *Journal of Theoretical and Philosophical Psychology, 19,* 90–113.

Nielsen, T. A. (1993). Changes in the kinesthetic content of dreams following somatosensory stimulation of leg muscles during REM sleep. *Dreaming, 3,* 99–113.

Niles, S. (1998). Achievement goals and means: A cultural comparison. *Journal of Cross-Cultural Psychology, 29,* 656–667.

Nishimura, H., Hashikawa, K., Doi, K., Iwaki, T., Watanabe, Y., Kusuoka, H., Nishimura, T., & Kubo, T. (1999). Sign language "heard" in the auditory cortex. *Nature, 397,* 116.

Nishith, P., Mechanic, M. B., & Resick, P. A. (2000). Prior interpersonal trauma: The contribution to current PTSD symptoms in female rape victims. *Journal of Abnormal Psychology, 109,* 20–25.

Nissen, M. J., Knopman, D. S., & Schacter, D. L. (1987). Neurochemical dissociation of memory systems. *Neurology, 37,* 789–794.

Noels, K. A., Clement, R., & Pelletier, L. G. (1999). Perceptions of teachers' communicative style and students' intrinsic and extrinsic motivation. *Modern Language Journal, 83,* 23–34.

Noice, H., Noice, T., Perrig-Chiello, P., & Perrig, W. (1999). Improving memory in older adults by instructing them in professional actors' learning strategies. *Applied Cognitive Psychology, 13,* 315–328.

Nolen-Hoeksema, S. (2000). The role of rumination in depressive disorders and mixed anxiety/depressive symptoms. *Journal of Abnormal Psychology, 109,* 504–511.

Nolen-Hoeksema, S., & Girgus, J. S. (1994). The emergence of gender differences in depression during adolescence. *Psychological Bulletin, 115,* 424–443.

Nolen-Hoeksema, S., & Morrow, J. (1993). Effects of rumination and distraction on naturally occurring depressed mood. *Cognition and Emotion, 7,* 561–570.

Norman, R. M., & Malla, A. K. (1993). Stressful life events and schizophrenia: I. A review of the research. *British Journal of Psychiatry, 162,* 161–166.

Norris, F. J., & Uhl, G. A. (1993). Chronic stress as a mediator of acute stress: The case of Hurricane Hugo. *Journal of Applied Social Psychology, 23,* 1263–1284.

Norris, N. P. (1978). Fragile subjects. *American Psychologist, 33,* 962–963.

O'Connell, A. N. (1990). Karen Horney (1885–1952). In A. N. O'Connell & N. F. Russo (Eds.), *Women in psychology: A bio-bibliographic sourcebook* (pp. 184–185). New York: Greenwood Press.

O'Connell, A. N., & Russo, N. F. (Eds.). (1990). *Women in psychology: A bio-bibliographic sourcebook.* New York: Greenwood.

O'Connor, K., Todorov, C., Robillard, S., Borgeat, F., & Brault, M. (1999). Cognitive-behaviour therapy and medication in the treatment of obsessive-compulsive disorder: A controlled study. *Canadian Journal of Psychiatry, 44,* 64–71.

O'Leary, A. (1985). Self-efficacy and health. *Behaviour Research and Therapy, 23,* 437–451.

O'Leary, K. D., & Smith, D. A. (1991). Marital interactions. *Annual Review of Psychology, 42,* 191–212.

O'Neil, W. M. (1995). American behaviorism: A historical and critical analysis. *Theory and Psychology, 5,* 285–305.

O'Shea, R. P., Govan, D. G., & Sekuler, R. (1997). Blur and contrast as pictorial depth cues. *Perception, 26,* 599–612.

Obrocki, J., Buchert, R., Vaeterlein, O., et al. (1999). Ecstasy: Long-term effects on the human central nervous system revealed by positron-emission tomography. *British Journal of Psychiatry, 175,* 186–188.

Ockene, J. K., Mermelstein, R. J., Bonollo, D. S., et al. (2000). Relapse and maintenance issues for smoking cessation. *Health Psychology, 19,* 17–31.

Oden, G. C. (1984). Dependence, independence, and emergence of word features. *Journal of Experimental Psychology: Human Perception and Performance, 10,* 394–405.

Oden, M. H. (1968). The fulfillment of promise: 40-year followup of the Terman gifted group. *Genetic Psychology Monographs, 77,* 3–93.

Oesterman, K., Bjoerkqvist, K., Lagerspetz, K. M. J., et al. (1998). Cross-cultural evidence of female indirect aggression. *Aggressive Behavior, 24,* 1–8.

Ogloff, J. R., & Otto, R. K. (1991). Are research participants truly informed? Readability of informed consent forms used in research. *Ethics and Behavior, 1,* 239–252.

Ohayon, M. M., Guilleminault, C., & Priest, R. G. (1999). Night terrors, sleepwalking, and confusional arousals in the general population. *Journal of Clinical Psychiatry, 60,* 268–276.

Ohira, H., & Kurono, K. (1993). Facial feedback effects on impression formation. *Perceptual and Motor Skills, 77,* 1251–1258.

Ohman, A., Erixon, G., & Lofberg, I. (1975). Phobias and preparedness: Phobic versus neutral pictures as conditioned stimuli for human autonomic responses. *Journal of Abnormal Psychology, 84,* 41–45.

Oishi, S., Diener, E. F., Lucas, R. E., & Suh, E-M. (1999). Cross-cultural variations in predictors of life satisfaction: Perspectives from needs and values. *Personality and Social Psychology Bulletin, 25,* 980–990.

Oka, S., Chapman, C. R., & Jacobson, R. C. (2000). Phasic pupil dilation response to noxious stimulation: Effects of conduction distance, sex, and age. *Journal of Psychophysiology, 14,* 97–105.

Okagaki, L., & Sternberg, R. J. (1993). Parental beliefs and children's school performance. *Child Development, 64,* 36–56.

Okogbaa, O., Shell, R. L., & Filipusic, D. (1994). On the investigation of the neurophysiological correlates of knowledge worker mental fatigue using the EEG signal. *Applied Ergonomics, 25,* 355–365.

Olds, J. (1956, October). Pleasure centers in the brain. *Scientific American,* pp. 105–116.

Olds, J., & Milner, P. (1954). Positive reinforcement produced by electrical stimulations of septal area and other regions of rat brain. *Journal of Comparative and Physiological Psychology, 47,* 419–427.

Oliver, M. B., & Hyde, J. S. (1993). Gender differences in sexuality: A meta-analysis. *Psychological Bulletin, 114,* 29–51.

Oller, D. K., & Eilers, R. E. (1988). The role of audition in infant babbling. *Child Development, 59,* 441–449.

Olmo, R. J., & Stevens, G. L. (1984, August). Chess champs: Introverts at play. *Psychology Today,* pp. 72, 74.

Olympia, D. E., Sheridan, S. M., Jenson, W. R., & Andrews, D. (1994). Using student-managed interventions to increase homework completion and accuracy. *Behavior Analysis in School Psychology, 27,* 85–99.

Onstad, S., Skre, I., Torgerson, S., & Kringlen, E. (1991). Twin concordance for DSM-III-R schizophrenia. *Acta Psychiatrica Scandinavica, 83,* 395–401.

Oppliger, P. A., & Sherblom, J. C. (1992). Humor: Incongruity, disparagement, and David Letterman. *Communication Research Reports, 9,* 99–108.

Orne, M. T. (1951). The mechanisms of hypnotic age regression: An experimental study. *Journal of Abnormal and Social Psychology, 46,* 213–225.

Orne, M. T., & Evans, F. J. (1965). Social control in the psychological experiment: Antisocial behavior and hypnosis. *Journal of Personality and Social Psychology, 1,* 189–200.

Orwell, G. (1949). *1984.* New York: Harcourt Brace Jovanovich.

Osberg, T. M. (1993). Psychology is not just common sense: An introductory psychology demonstration. *Teaching of Psychology, 20,* 110–111.

Otero, G. A. (1997). Poverty, cultural disadvantage and brain development: A study of pre-school children in Mexico. *Electroencephalography and Clinical Neurophysiology, 102,* 512–516.

Ottaviani, F., Di Girolamo, S., Briglia, G., et al. (1997). Tonotopic organization of human auditory cortex analyzed by SPECT. *Audiology, 36,* 241–248.

Ouimet, J., & De Man, A. F. (1998). Correlates of attitudes toward the application of eugenics to the treatment of people with intellectual disabilities. *Social Behavior and Personality, 26,* 69–74.

Overton, D. A. (1991). Historical context of state dependent learning and discriminative drug effects. *Behavioural Pharmacology, 2,* 253–264.

Owens, R. A. (1976). Background data. In M. D. Dunnette (Ed.), *Handbook of industrial and organizational psychology.* Chicago: Rand McNally. (p. 199)

Pacini, R., Muir, F., & Epstein, S. (1998). Depressive realism from the perspective of cognitive-experiential self-theory. *Journal of Personality and Social Psychology, 74,* 1056–1068.

Page, S., & Tyrer, J. (1995). Gender and prediction of Gilligan's justice and care orientations. *Journal of College Student Psychotherapy, 10,* 43–56.

Paik, H., & Comstock, G. (1994). The effects of television violence on antisocial behavior: A meta-analysis. *Communication Research, 21,* 516–546.

Paikoff, R. L., & Brooks-Gunn, J. (1991). Do parent-child relationships change during puberty? *Psychological Bulletin, 110,* 47–66.

Palmer, C. A., & Hazelrigg, M. (2000). The guilty but mentally ill verdict: A review and conceptual analysis of intent and impact. *Journal of the American Academy of Psychiatry and the Law, 28,* 47–54.

Palmer, J. A., Honorton, C., & Utts, J. (1989). Reply to the National Research Council study on parapsychology. *Journal of the American Society for Psychical Research, 83,* 31–49.

Palmieri, T. J., & Nosofsky, R. M. (2001). Central tendencies, extreme points, and prototype enhancement effects in ill-defined perceptual categorization. *Quarterly Journal of Experimental Psychology: Human Experimental Psychology, 54A,* 197–235.

Palomaeki, K., Alku, P., Maekinen, V., May, P., & Tiitinen, H. (2000). Sound localization in the human brain: Neuromagnetic observations. *Neuroreport, 11,* 1535–1538.

Panksepp, J., & Bekkedal, M. Y. V. (1997). The affective cerebral consequence of music: Happy vs sad effects on the EEG and clinical implications. *International Journal of Arts Medicine, 5,* 18–27.

Paradis, M. (1998). The other side of language: Pragmatic competence. *Journal of Neurolinguistics, 11,* 1–10.

Parellada, E., Catafau, A. M., Bernardo, M., Lomena, F., Catarineu, S., & Gonzalez-Monclus, E. (1998). The resting and activation issue of hypofrontality: A single photon emission computed tomography study in neuroleptic-naive and neuroleptic-free schizophrenic female patients. *Biological Psychiatry, 44,* 787–790.

Paris, J. (1998). Personality disorders in sociocultural perspective. *Journal of Personality Disorders, 12,* 289–301.

Park, D. C., Smith, A. D., & Cavanaugh, J. C. (1990). Metamemories of memory researchers. *Memory and Cognition, 18,* 321–327.

Park, W. W. (2000). A comprehensive empirical investigation of the relationships among variables of the groupthink model. *Journal of Organizational Behavior, 21,* 873–887.

Parker, K. C. H., Hanson, R. K., & Hunsley, J. (1988). MMPI, Rorschach, and WAIS: A meta-analytic comparison of reliability, stability, and validity. *Psychological Bulletin, 103,* 367–373.

Parker, S. (1990). A note on the growth of the use of statistical tests in perception and psychophysics. *Bulletin of the Psychonomic Society, 28,* 565–566.

Parrott, A. C. (1995). Smoking cessation leads to reduced stress, but why? *International Journal of the Addictions, 30,* 1509–1516.

Parsons, M. W., & Gold, P. E. (1992). Glucose enhancement of memory in elderly humans: An inverted-U dose-response curve. *Neurobiology of Aging, 13,* 401–404.

Parten, M. B. (1932). Social participation among pre-school children. *Journal of Abnormal and Social Psychology, 27,* 243–269.

Patterson, D. R., Adcock, R. J., & Bombardier, C. H. (1997). Factors predicting hypnotic analgesia in clinical burn pain. *International Journal of Clinical and Experimental Hypnosis, 45,* 377–395.

Patterson, F. G., Patterson, L. H., & Brentari, D. K. (1987). Language in child, chimp, and gorilla. *American Psychologist, 42,* 270–272.

Patton, J. E., Routh, D. K., & Stinard, T. A. (1986). Where do children study? Behavioral observations. *Bulletin of the Psychonomic Society, 24,* 439–440.

Paulsen, F. (1899/1963). *Immanuel Kant: His life and doctrine.* New York: Ungar.

Paunovic, N. (1999). Exposure counterconditioning (EC) as a treatment for severe PTSD and depression with an illustrative case. *Journal of Behavior Therapy and Experimental Psychiatry, 30,* 105–117.

Pavlov, I. P. (1928). *Lectures on conditioned reflexes.* New York: Liveright.

Pazzagli, A., & Monti, M. R. (2000). Dysphoria and aloneness in borderline personality disorder. *Psychopathology, 33,* 220–226.

Pear, J. J., & Crone-Todd, D. E. (1999). Personalized system of instruction in cyberspace. *Journal of Applied Behavior Analysis, 32,* 205–209.

Pears, R., & Bryant, P. E. (1990). Transitive inferences by young children about spatial position. *British Journal of Psychology, 81,* 497–510.

Peeters, M. C. W., Buunk, B. P., & Schaufeli, W. B. (1995). A micro-analysis exploration of the cognitive appraisal of daily stressful events at work: The role of controllability. *Anxiety, Stress and Coping, 8,* 127–139.

Penfield, W. (1975). *The mystery of the mind.* Princeton, NJ: Princeton University Press.

Pengilly, J. W., & Dowd, E. T. (2000). Hardiness and social support as moderators of stress. *Journal of Clinical Psychology, 56,* 813–820.

Peretz, I., Kolinsky, R., Tramo, M., & Labrecque, R. (1994). Functional dissociations following bilateral lesions of auditory cortex. *Brain, 117,* 1283–1301.

Perlis, M., Aloia, M., Millikan, A., Boehmler, J., Smith, M., Greenblatt, D., & Giles, D. (2000). Behavioral treatment of insomnia: A clinical case series study. *Journal of Behavioral Medicine, 23,* 149–161.

Perlman, D. (1999, October 15). Odds on the Big One. *San Francisco Chronicle,* p. A1.

Perls, F. (1973). *The Gestalt approach and eyewitness to therapy.* Palo Alto, CA: Science & Behavior Books.

Perri, M. G., Martin, A. D., Leermakers, E. A., & Sears, S. F. (1997). Effects of group- versus home-based exercise in the treatment of obesity. *Journal of Consulting and Clinical Psychology, 65,* 278–285.

Persad, E. (1990). Electroconvulsive therapy in depression. *Canadian Journal of Psychiatry, 35,* 175–182.

Pert, C. B., & Snyder, S. H. (1973). Opiate receptor: Demonstration in nervous tissue. *Science, 179,* 1031–1034.

Peter, B. (1997). Hypnosis in the treatment of cancer pain. *Australian Journal of Clinical and Experimental Hypnosis, 25,* 40–52.

Peters, R., & McGee, R. (1982). Cigarette smoking and state-dependent memory. *Psychopharmacology, 76,* 232–235.

Peters, R. D. (1994). Better Beginnings, Better Futures: A community-based approach to primary prevention. *Canadian Journal of Community Mental Health, 13,* 183–188.

Peterson, C., & Barrett, L. C. (1987). Explanatory style and academic performance among university freshmen. *Journal of Personality and Social Psychology, 53,* 603–607.

Peterson, C., Seligman, M. E. P., & Vaillant, G. E. (1988). Pessimistic explanatory style is a risk factor for physical illness: A 35-year longitudinal study. *Journal of Personality and Social Psychology, 55,* 23–27.

Peterson, C., Seligman, M. E. P., Yurko, K. H., Martin, L. R., & Friedman, H. S. (1998). Catastrophizing and untimely death. *Psychological Science, 9,* 127–130.

Peterson, C. C. (1996). The ticking of the social clock: Adults' beliefs about the timing of transition events. *International Journal of Aging and Human Development, 42,* 189–203.

Peterson, J. L., Coates, T. J., Catania, J., & Hauck, W. W. (1996). Evaluation of an HIV risk reduction intervention among African-American homosexual and bisexual men. *AIDS, 10,* 319–325.

Peterson, L. R., & Peterson, M. (1959). Short-term retention of individual verbal items. *Journal of Experimental Psychology, 58,* 193–198.

Peterson, M. A., & Gibson, B. S. (1994). Must figure-ground organization precede object recognition? An assumption in peril. *Psychological Science, 5,* 253–259.

Petrill, S. A., & Wilkerson, B. (2000). Intelligence and achievement: A behavioral genetic perspective. *Educational Psychology Review, 12,* 185–199.

Pettersen, L., Yonas, A., & Fisch, R. O. (1980). The development of blinking in response to impending collision in preterm, full-term, and postterm infants. *Infant Behavior and Development, 3,* 155–165.

Petty, R. E., & Cacioppo, J. T. (1990). Involvement and persuasion: Tradition versus integration. *Psychological Bulletin, 107,* 367–374.

Petty, R. E., Cacioppo, J. T., & Goldman, R. (1981). Personal involvement as a determinant of argument-based persuasion. *Journal of Personality and Social Psychology, 41,* 847–855.

Pfeffer, K., & Barnecutt, P. (1996). Children's auditory perception of movement of traffic sounds. *Child: Care, Health and Development, 27,* 129–137.

Phelps, M. E., & Mazziotta, J. C. (1985). Positron-emission tomography: Human brain function and biochemistry. *Science, 228,* 799–809.

Philipp, E., Pirke, K. M., Kellner, M. B., & Krieg, J. C. (1991). Disturbed cholecystokinin secretion in patients with eating disorders. *Life Sciences, 48,* 2443–2450.

Phillips, L. (2000). Recontextualizing Kenneth B. Clark: An Afrocentric perspective on the paradoxical legacy of a model psychologist-activist. *History of Psychology, 3,* 142–167.

Phillips, R. D., Wagner, S. H., Fells, C. A., & Lynch, M. (1990). Do infants recognize emotion in facial expressions? Categorical and "metaphorical" evidence. *Infant Behavior and Development, 13,* 71–84.

Phinney, J. S., Ong, A., & Madden, T. (2000). Cultural values and intergenerational value discrepancies in immigrant and non-immigrant families. *Child Development, 71,* 528–539.

Piaget, J. (1932). *The moral judgment of the child.* New York: Harcourt, Brace & World.

Piaget, J. (1952). *The origins of intelligence in children.* New York: International Universities Press.

Piat, M. (2000). The NIMBY phenomenon: Community residents' concerns about housing for deinstitutionalized people. *Health and Social Work, 25,* 127–138.

Piedmont, R. L., Hill, D. C., & Blanco, S. (1999). Predicting athletic performance using the five-factor model of personality. *Personality and Individual Differences, 27,* 769–777.

Pierce, E. F., & Daleng, M. L. (1998). Distortion of body image among elite female dancers. *Perceptual and Motor Skills, 87,* 769–770.

Pierce, E. F., Eastman, N. W., Tripathi, H. L., & Olson, K. G. (1993). b-Endorphin response to endurance exercise: Relationship to exercise dependence. *Perceptual and Motor Skills, 77,* 767–770.

Pieters, R. G. M., & Bijmolt, T. H. A. (1997). Consumer memory for television advertising: A field study of duration, serial position, and competition effects. *Journal of Consumer Research, 23,* 362–372.

Piliavin, J. A., Callero, P. L., & Evans, E. E. (1982). Addiction to altruism: Opponent-process theory and habitual blood donation. *Journal of Personality and Social Psychology, 43,* 1200–1213.

Piner, K. E., & Kahle, L. R. (1984). Adapting to the stigmatizing label of mental illness: Foregone but not forgotten. *Journal of Personality and Social Psychology, 47,* 805–811.

Pines, M. (1981, September). The civilizing of Genie. *Psychology Today,* pp. 28–34.

Pinkofsky, H. B. (1997). Mnemonics for *DSM-IV* personality disorders. *Psychiatric Services, 48,* 1197–1198.

Piper, A. (1993). Tricyclic antidepressants versus electroconvulsive therapy: A review of the evidence for efficacy in depression. *Annals of Clinical Psychiatry, 5,* 13–23.

Pittenger, D. J. (1996). Reconsidering the overjustification effect: A guide to critical resources. *Teaching of Psychology, 23,* 234–236.

Plant, E. A., Hyde, J. S., Keltner, D., & Devine, P. G. (2000). The gender stereotyping of emotion. *Psychology of Women Quarterly, 24,* 81–92.

Platz, S. J., & Hosch, H. M. (1988). Cross-racial/ethnic eyewitness identification: A field study. *Journal of Applied Social Psychology, 18,* 972–984.

Plomin, R. (1994). Nature, nurture, and social development. *Social Develooment, 3,* 37–53.

Plomin, R., & Crabbe, J. (2000). DNA. *Psychological Bulletin, 126,* 806–828.

Plomin, R., Corley, R., Caspi, A., Fulker, D. W., & DeFries, J. (1998). Adoption results for self-reported personality: Evidence for nonadditive genetic effects? *Journal of Personality and Social Psychology, 75,* 211–218.

Plotkin, W. B. (1979). The alpha experience revisited: Biofeedback in the transformation of psychological state. *Psychological Bulletin, 86,* 1132–1148.

Plous, S. (1991). An attitude survey of animal rights activists. *Psychological Science, 2,* 192–196.

Plous, S. (1998). Signs of change within the animal rights movement: Results from a follow-up survey of activists. *Journal of Comparative Psychology, 112,* 48–54.

Plucker, J. A., Callahan, C. M., & Tomchin, E. M. (1996). Wherefore art thou, multiple intelligences? Alternative assessments for identifying talent in ethnically diverse and low income students. *Gifted Child Quarterly, 40,* 81–92.

Plug, C., & Ross, H., E. (1994). The natural moon illusion: A multifactor angular account. *Perception, 23,* 321–333.

Plutchik, R. (1980, February). A language for the emotions. *Psychology Today,* pp. 68–78.

Poincaré, H. (1948, August). Mathematical creation. *Scientific American,* pp. 14–17.

Polivy, J. (1998). The effects of behavioral inhibition: Integrating internal cues, cognition, behavior, and affect. *Psychological Inquiry, 9,* 181–204.

Polster, E., & Polster, M. (1993). Frederick Perls: Legacy and invitation. *Gestalt Journal, 16,* 23–25.

Polygenis, D., Wharton, S., Malmberg, C., Sherman, N., Kennedy, D., Koren, G., & Einarson, T. R. (1998). Moderate alcohol consumption during pregnancy and the incidence of fetal malformations: A meta-analysis. *Neurotoxicology and Teratology, 20,* 61–67.

Pomerleau, O. F. (1995). Individual differences in sensitivity to nicotine: Implications of genetic research on nicotine dependence. *Behavior Genetics, 25,* 161–177.

Poole, D. A., & White, L. T. (1993). Two years later: Effect of question repetition and retention interval on the eyewitness testimony of children and adults. *Developmental Psychology, 29,* 844–853.

Poole, J. H., Tobias, F. C., & Vinogradov, S. (2000). The functional relevance of affect recognition errors in schizophrenia. *Journal of the International Neuropsychological Society, 6,* 649–658.

Poppen, P. J. (1994). Adolescent contraceptive use and communication: Changes over a decade. *Adolescence, 29,* 503–514.

Popplestone, J. A., & McPherson, M. W. (1976). Ten years at the Archives of the History of American Psychology, *American Psychologist 31,* 533–534.

Populin, L. C., & Yin, T. C. T. (1998). Pinna movements of the cat during sound localization. *Journal of Neuroscience, 18,* 4233–4243.

Porac, C., & Coren, S. (1981). *Lateral preferences and human behavior.* New York: Springer-Verlag.

Postman, L. (1985). Human learning and memory. In G. A. Kimble & K. Schlesinger (Eds.), *Topics in the history of psychology (*Vol. 1, pp. 69–134). Hillsdale, NJ: Erlbaum.

Postmes, T., & Spears, R. (1998). Deindividuation and antinormative behavior: A meta-analysis. *Psychological Bulletin, 123,* 238–259.

Poston, W. S., II, & Winebarger, A. A. (1996). The misuse of behavioral genetics in prevention research, or for whom the "Bell Curve" tolls. *Journal of Primary Prevention, 17,* 133–147.

Potegal, M., Hebert, M., DeCoster, M., & Meyerhoff, J. L. (1996). Brief, high-frequency stimulation of the corticomedial amygdala induces a delayed and prolonged increase of aggressiveness in male Syrian golden hamsters. *Behavioral Neuroscience, 110,* 401–412.

Potgieter, J. R., & Venter, R. E. (1995). Relationship between adherence to exercise and scores on extraversion and neuroticism. *Perceptual and Motor Skills, 81,* 520–522.

Poulson, R. L. (1990). Mock juror attribution of criminal responsibility: Effects of race and the guilty but mentally ill (GBMI) verdict option. *Journal of Applied Social Psychology, 20,* 1596–1611.

Powell, D. J., & Fuller, R. W. (1983). Marijuana and sex: Strange bedpartners. *Journal of Psychoactive Drugs, 15,* 269–280.

Powell, J. L., & Drucker, A. D. (1997). The role of peer conformity in the decision to ride with an intoxicated driver. *Journal of Alcohol and Drug Education, 43,* 1–7.

Powell, R. A. (2000). "Memories of childhood abuse: Dissociation, amnesia, and corroboration": Comment. *American Journal of Psychiatry, 157,* 1347–1348.

Prados, J., Chamizo, V. D., & MacKintosh, N. J. (1999). Latent inhibition and perceptual learning in a swimming-pool navigation task. *Journal of Experimental Psychology: Animal Behavior Processes, 25,* 37–44.

Prasinos, S., & Tittler, B. I. (1981). The family relationships of humor-oriented adolescents. *Journal of Personality, 47,* 295–305.

Pratkanis, A. R. (1992). The cargo-cult science of subliminal persuasion. *Skeptical Inquirer, 16,* 260–272.

Pratt, M. W., Norris, J. E., Arnold, M. L., & Filyer, R. (1999). Generativity and moral development as predictors of value-socialization narratives for young persons across the adult life span: From lessons learned to stories shared. *Psychology and Aging, 14,* 414–426.

Pratto, F., & Hegarty, P. (2000). The political psychology of reproductive strategies. *Psychological Science, 11,* 57–62.

Premack, D. (1965). Reinforcement theory. In D. Levine (Ed.), *Nebraska Symposium on motivation* (pp. 123–188). Lincoln: University of Nebraska Press.

Prentice-Dunn, S., & Rogers, R. W. (1982). Effects of public and private self-awareness on deindividuation and aggression. *Journal of Personality and Social Psychology, 43,* 503–513.

Pressman, E. K., DiPietro, J. A., Costigan, K. A., Shupe, A. K., & Johnson, T. R. B. (1998). Fetal neurobehavioral development: Associations with socioeconomic class and fetal sex. *Developmental Psychobiology, 33,* 79–91.

Pressnitzer, D., McAdams, S., Winsberg, S., & Fineberg, J. (2000). Perception of musical tension for nontonal orchestral timbres and its relation to psychoacoustic roughness. *Perception and Psychophysics, 62,* 66–80.

Price, R., & Gottesman, I. I. (1991). Body fat in identical twins reared apart: Roles for genes and environment. *Behavior Genetics, 21,* 1–7.

Price-Williams, E., Gordon, W., & Ramirez, M. (1969). Skill and conservation: A study of pottery-making children. *Developmental Psychology, 1,* 769.

Priester, J. R., & Petty, R. E. (1995). Source attributions and persuasion: Perceived honesty as a determinant of message scrutiny. *Personality and Social Psychology Bulletin, 21,* 637–654.

Pritchard, W. S., Robinson, J. H., deBethizy, J. D., & Davis, R. A. (1995). Caffeine and smoking: Subjective, performance, and psychophysiological effects. *Psychophysiology, 32,* 19–27.

Prochaska, J. O. (1984). *Systems of psychotherapy: A transtheoretical approach.* Homewood, IL: Dorsey.

Program power. (1981, April). *Scientific American,* pp. 83–85.

Prud'homme, M. J. L., Cohen, D. A. D., & Kalaska, J. F. (1994). Tactile activity in primate primary somatosensory cortex during active arm movements: Cytoarchitectonic distribution. *Journal of Neurophysiology, 71,* 173–181.

"Psychic abscam." (1983, March). *Discover,* pp. 10, 13.

Pullum, G. K. (1991). *The great Eskimo vocabulary hoax,* Chicago: University of Chicago Press.

Pulsifer, M. B. (1996). The neuropsychology of mental retardation. *Journal of the International Neuropsychological Society, 2,* 159–176.

Punamacki, R. L., & Joustie, M. (1998). The role of culture, violence, and personal factors affecting dream content. *Journal of Cross-Cultural Psychology, 29,* 320–342.

Purdy, J. E., Harriman, A., & Molitorisz, J. (1993). Contributions to the history of psychology: XCV. Possible relations between theories of evolution and animal learning. *Psychological Reports, 73,* 211–223.

Purghe, F., & Coren, S. (1992). Subjective contours 1900–1990: Research trends and bibliography. *Perception and Psychophysics, 51,* 291–304.

Purnine, D. M., Carey, K. B., Maisto, S. A. & Carey, M. P. (2000). Assessing positive and negative symptoms in outpatients with schizophrenia and mood disorders. *Journal of Nervous and Mental Disease, 188,* 653–661.

Quigley, N., Green, J. F., Morgan, D., Idzikowski, C., & King, D. J. (2000). The effect of sleep deprivation on memory and psychomotor function in healthy volunteers. *Human Psychopharmacology: Clinical and Experimental, 15,* 171–177.

Rabin, J., & Wiley, R. (1994). Switching from forward-looking infrared to night vision goggles: Transitory effects on visual resolution. *Aviation, Space, and Environmental Medicine, 65,* 327–329.

Racagni, G., & Brunello, N. (1999). Physiology to functionality: The brain and neurotransmitter activity. *International Clinical Psychopharmacology, 14,* S3–S7.

Rachman, S. (1991). Neo-conditioning and the classical theory of fear acquisition. *Clinical Psychology Review, 11,* 155–173.

Rachman, S. J. (1993). Statistically significant difference or probable nonchance difference. *American Psychologist, 48,* 1093.

Raesaenen, S., Pakaslahti, A., Syvaelahti, E., Jones, P. B., & Isohanni, M. (2000). Sex differences in schizophrenia: A review. *Nordic Journal of Psychiatry, 54,* 37–45.

Ragland, D. R., & Brand, R. J. (1988). Type A behavior and mortality from coronary heart disease. *New England Journal of Medicine, 318,* 65–69.

Raine, A., Lencz, T., Bihrle, S., LaCasse, L., & Colletti, P. (2000). Reduced prefrontal gray matter volume and reduced autonomic activity in antisocial personality disorder. *Archives of General Psychiatry, 57,* 119–127.

Rainey, D. W. (1994). Assaults on umpires: A statewide survey. *Journal of Sport Behavior, 17,* 148–155.

Raloff, J. (1982). Noise can be hazardous to your health. *Science News, 121,* 377–381.

Ramón y Cajal, S. (1937/1966). *Recollections of my life.* Cambridge, MA: MIT Press.

Randall, J. L. (1998). Physics, philosophy and precognition: Some reflections. *Journal of the Society for Psychical Research, 63,* 1–11.

Rao, U., Poland R. E., Lutchmansingh, P., Ott, G. E., McCracken, J. T., & Keh-Ming, L. (1999). Relationship between ethnicity and sleep patterns in normal controls: Implications for psychopathology and treatment. *Journal of Psychiatric Research, 33,* 419–426.

Rapp, D. (1988). The reception of Freud by the British press: General interest and literary magazines, 1920–1925. *Journal of the History of the Behavioral Sciences, 24,* 191–201.

Raskin, D. C., & Podlesny, J. A. (1979). Truth and deception: A reply to Lykken. *Psychological Bulletin, 86,* 54–59.

Raslear, T. G. (1996, January). *Driver behavior at rail-highway grade crossings: A signal detection theory analysis.* U.S. Department of Transportation Monograph, No. DOT/FRA/ORD-95/14.2, pp. 2–46.

Rauch, S. L., Whalen, P. J., Shin, L. M., et al. (2000). Exaggerated amygdala response to masked facial stimuli in post-traumatic stress disorder: A functional MRI study. *Biological Psychiatry, 47,* 769–776.

Raufaste, E., Eyrolle, H., & Marine, C. (1998). Pertinence generation in radiological diagnosis: Spreading activation and the nature of expertise. *Cognitive Science, 22,* 517–546.

Ravelli, G. P., Stein, Z. A., & Susser, M. W. (1976). Obesity in young men after famine exposure in utero in early infancy. *New England Journal of Medicine, 295,* 349–353.

Rawdon, V. A., Willis, F. N., & Ficken, E. J. (1995). Locus of control in young adults in Russia and the United States. *Perceptual and Motor Skills, 80,* 599–604.

Rawlings, D., & Ciancarelli, V. (1997). Music preference and the five-factor model of the NEO Personality Inventory. *Psychology of Music, 25,* 120–132.

Ray, O. (1983). *Drugs, society, and human behavior.* St. Louis: Mosby.

Read, M. S. (1982). Malnutrition and behavior. *Applied Research in Mental Retardation, 3,* 279–291.

Reason, J. (2000). The Freudian slip revisited. *Psychologist, 13,* 610–611.

Redler, L. (2000). R. D. Laing's contribution to the "treatment" of "schizophrenia": Responsible responses to suffering and malaise. *Psychoanalytic Review, 87,* 561–589.

Reed, D. R., Bachmanov, A. A., Beauchamp, G. K., & Tordoff, M. G. (1997). Heritable variation in food preferences and their contribution to obesity. *Behavior Genetics, 27,* 373–387.

Reed, T. E. (1993). Effect of enriched (complex) environment on nerve conduction velocity: New data and review of implications for the speed of information processing. *Intelligence, 17,* 533–540.

Reese, E. P. (1986). Learning about teaching from teaching about learning: Presenting behavioral analysis in an introductory survey course. In V. P. Makosky (Ed.), *The G. Stanley Hall Lecture Series* (Vol. 6, pp. 65–127). Washington, DC: American Psychological Association.

Reese, H. W., & Fremouw, W. J. (1984). Normal and normative ethics in behavioral sciences. *American Psychologist, 39,* 863–876.

Regan, P. C., Kocan, E. R., & Whitlock, T. (1998). Ain't love grand! A prototype analysis of the concept of romantic love. *Journal of Social and Personal Relationships, 15,* 411–420.

Reilly, R. R., & Chao, G. R. (1982). Validity and fairness of some alternative employee selection procedures. *Personnel Psychology, 35,* 1–62.

Reinecke, M. A., Ryan, N. E., & DuBois, D. L. (1998). Cognitive-behavioral therapy of depression and depressive symptoms during adolescence: A review and meta-analysis. *Journal of the American Academy of Child and Adolescent Psychiatry, 37,* 26–34.

Reisenzein, R. (1983). The Schachter theory of emotion: Two decades later. *Psychological Bulletin, 94,* 239–264.

Reitman, J. S. (1974). Without surreptitious rehearsal, information in short-term memory decays. *Journal of Verbal Learning and Verbal Behavior, 13,* 365–377.

Reneman, L., Booij, J., Schmand, B., van den Brink, W., & Gunning, B. (2000). Memory disturbances in "Ecstasy" users are correlated with an altered brain serotonin neurotransmission. *Psychopharmacology, 148,* 322–324.

Renn, J. A., & Calvert, S. L. (1993). The relation between gender schemas and adults' recall of stereotyped and counter-stereotyped televised information. *Sex Roles, 28,* 449–459.

Renner, J. W., Abraham, M. R., Grzybowski, E. B., & Marek, E. A. (1990). Understandings and misunderstandings of eighth graders of four physics concepts found in textbooks. *Journal of Research in Science Teaching, 27,* 35–54.

Rennie, D. L. (1994). Clients' accounts of resistance in counselling: A qualitative analysis. *Canadian Journal of Counseling, 28,* 43–57.

Rescorla, R. A. (1968). Probability of shock in the presence and absence of CS in fear conditioning. *Journal of Comparative and Physiological Psychology, 66,* 1–5.

Rescorla, R. A., & Holland, P. C. (1982). Behavioral studies of associative learning in animals. *Annual Review of Psychology, 33,* 265–308.

Reuter-Lorenz, P. A., & Miller, A. C. (1998). The cognitive neuroscience of human laterality: Lessons from the bisected brain. *Current Directions in Psychological Science, 7,* 15–20.

Reynaert, C., Janne, P., Bosly, A., & Staquet, P. (1995). From health locus of control to immune control: Internal locus of control has a buffering effect on natural killer cell activity decrease in major depression. *Acta Psychiatrica Scandinavica, 92,* 294–300.

Reyner, L. A., & Horne, J. A. (2000). Early morning driver sleepiness: Effectiveness of 200 mg caffeine. *Psychophysiology, 37,* 251–256.

Reynolds, G. P. (1999) Dopamine receptors, antipsychotic action and schizophrenia. *Journal of Psychopharmacology, 13,* 202–203.

Rhodes, M. G., & Anastasi, J. S. (2000). The effects of a levels-of-processing manipulation on false recall. *Psychonomic Bulletin and Review, 7,* 158–162.

Rhodes, N., & Wood, W. (1992). Self-esteem and intelligence affect influenceability: The mediating role of message reception. *Psychological Bulletin, 111,* 156–171.

Rice, M. L. (1989). Children's language acquisition. *American Psychologist, 44,* 149–156.

Rieber, R. W. (Ed.). (1980). *Wilhelm Wundt and the making of a scientific psychology.* New York: Plenum Press.

Rieckert, J., & Moeller, A. T. (2000). Rational-emotive behavior therapy in the treatment of adult victims of childhood sexual abuse. *Journal of Rational-Emotive and Cognitive Behavior Therapy, 18,* 87–102.

Riehl, J., Honda, K., Kwan, M., Hong, J., Mignot, E., & Nishino, S. (2000). Chronic oral administration of CG-3703, a thyrotropin releasing hormone analog, increases wake and decreases cataplexy in canine narcolepsy. *Neuropsychopharmacology, 23,* 34–45.

Riggio, R. E. (1999). *Introduction to industrial/organizational psychology* (3rd ed.). New York: Addison Wesley Longman.

Riggs, J. M. (1998). Social roles we choose and don't choose: Impressions of employed and unemployed parents. *Sex Roles, 39,* 431–443.

Riggs, L. A. (1985). Sensory processes: Vision. In G. A. Kimble & K. Schlesinger (Eds.), *Topics in the history of psychology* (Vol. 1, pp. 165–220). Hillsdale, NJ: Erlbaum.

Riley, J. L., Robinson, M. E., Wise, E. A., Myers, C. D., & Rillingim, R. B. (1998). Sex differences in the perception of noxious experimental stimuli: A meta-analysis. *Pain, 74,* 181–187.

Rilling, M. (1996). The mystery of the vanished citations: James McConnell's forgotten 1960s quest for planarian learning, a biochemical engram, and celebrity. *American Psychologist, 51,* 589–598.

Rilling, M. (2000). John Watson's paradoxical struggle to explain Freud. *American Psychologist, 55,* 301–312.

Rinaldi, R. C. (1987). Patient-therapist personality similarity and the therapeutic relationship. *Psychotherapy in Private Practice, 5,* 11–29.

Riordan, C. A., & Tedeschi, J. T. (1983). Attraction in aversive environments: Some evidence for classical conditioning and negative reinforcement. *Journal of Personality and Social Psychology, 44,* 683–692.

Rittenhouse, C. D., Stickgold, R., & Hobson, J. A. (1994). Constraint on the transformation of characters, objects, and settings in dream reports. *Consciousness and Cognition, 3,* 100–113.

Rivera-Tovar, L. A., & Jones, R. T. (1990). Effect of elaboration on the acquisition and maintenance of cardiopulmonary resuscitation. *Journal of Pediatric Psychology, 15,* 123–138.

Rivinus, T. M. (1990). The deadly embrace: The suicidal impulse and substance use and abuse in the college student. *Journal of College Student Psychotherapy, 4,* 45–77.

Robert, M. (1990). Observational learning in fish, birds, and mammals: A classified bibliography spanning over 100 years of research. *Psychological Record, 40,* 289–311.

Roberts, A. H. (1985). Biofeedback: Research, training, and clinical roles. *American Psychologist, 40,* 938–941.

Roberts, J. E., & Schuele, C. M. (1990). Otitis media and later academic performance: The linkage and implications for intervention. *Topics in Language Disorders, 11,* 43–62.

Roberts, M. C., & Fanurik, D. (1986). Rewarding elementary school children for their use of safety belts. *Health Psychology, 5,* 185–196.

Roberts, R. E., Phinney, J. S., Masse, L. C., Chen, Y. R., Roberts, C. R., & Romero, A. (1999). The structure of ethnic identity of young adolescents from diverse ethnocultural groups. *Journal of Early Adolescence, 19,* 301–322.

Roberts, R. E. L., & Bengtson, V. L. (1996). Attachment styles, self-esteem, and patterns of seeking feedback from romantic partners. *Social Psychology Quarterly, 59,* 96–106.

Robins, L. N., Helzer, J. E., Weissman, M. M., et al. (1984). Lifetime prevalence of specific psychiatric disorders in three sites. *Archives of General Psychiatry, 41,* 949–958.

Robins, R. W., Gosling, S. D., & Craik, K. H. (1999). An empirical analysis of trends in psychology. *American Psychologist, 54,* 117–128.

Robinson, F. P. (1970). *Effective study.* New York: Harper & Row.

Robinson, M. D. (1998). Running from William James' bear: A review of preattentive mechanisms and their contribu-tions to emotional experience. *Cognition and Emotion, 12,* 667–696.

Rock, I., Gopnik, A., & Hall, S. (1994). Do young children reverse ambiguous figures? *Perception, 23,* 635–644.

Rockwell, T. (1979). Pseudoscience or pseudocriticism? *Journal of Parapsychology, 43,* 221–231.

Rodgers, J. E. (1982, June). The malleable memory of eyewitnesses. *Science, 82,* pp. 32–35.

Rodin, J. (1981). Current status of the internal-external hypothesis for obesity: What went wrong? *American Psychologist, 36,* 361–372.

Rodin, J. (1985). Insulin levels, hunger, and food intake: An example of feedback loops in body weight regulation. *Health Psychology, 4,* 1–23.

Roethlisberger, F. J., & Dickson, E. J. (1939). *Management and the worker.* Cambridge, MA: Harvard University Press.

Rogers, C. R. (1957). The necessary and sufficient conditions of therapeutic personality change. *Journal of Consulting Psychology, 21,* 95–103.

Rogers, C. R. (1985). Toward a more human science of the person. *Journal of Humanistic Psychology, 25,* 7–24.

Rogers, L. J. (2000). Evolution of hemispheric specialization: Advantages and disadvantages. *Brain and Language, 73,* 236–253.

Rogers, R., Duncan, J. C., Lynett, E., & Sewell, K. W. (1994). Prototypical analysis of antisocial personality disorder: *DSM-IV* and beyond. *Law and Human Behavior, 18,* 471–484.

Rogers, R. L., Meyer, J. S., & Mortel, K. F. (1990). After reaching retirement age physical activity sustains cerebral perfusion and cognition. *Journal of the American Geriatrics Society, 38,* 123–128.

Rogge, R. D., & Bradbury, T. N. (1999). Till violence does us part: The differing roles of communication and aggression in predicting adverse marital outcomes. *Journal of Consulting and Clinical Psychology, 67,* 340–351.

Rogoff, B., & Chavajay, P. (1995). What's become of research on the cultural basis of cognitive development? *American Psychologist, 50,* 459–477.

Roig, M. (1993). Summarizing parapsychology in psychology textbooks: A rejoinder to Kalat and Kohn. *Teaching of Psychology, 20,* 174–175.

Rokeach, M. (1964/1981). *The three Christs of Ypsilanti.* New York: Columbia University Press.

Rollman, G. B. (1998). Culture and pain. In S. S. Kazarian & D. R. Evans (Eds.), *Cultural clinical psychology: Theory, research, and practice* (pp. 267–286). New York: Oxford University Press.

Rondall, J. A. (1994). Pieces of minds in psycholinguistics: Steven Pinker, Kenneth Wexler, and Noam Chomsky. *International Journal of Psychology, 29,* 85–104.

Ronn, L. C. B., Berezin, V., & Bock, E. (2000). The neural cell adhesion molecule in synaptic plasticity and ageing. *International Journal of Developmental Neuroscience, 18,* 193–199.

Rosch, E. (1975). Cognitive representation of semantic categories. *Journal of Experimental Psychology: General, 104,* 192–233.

Rose, D. J., & Clark, S. (2000). Can the control of bodily orientation be significantly improved in a group of older adults with a history of falls? *Journal of the American Geriatrics Society, 48,* 275–282.

Rose, J. E., & Fantino, E. (1978). Conditioned reinforcement and discrimination in second-order schedules. *Journal of the Experimental Analysis of Behavior, 29,* 393–418.

Rosenhan, D. L. (1973). On being sane in insane places. *Science, 179,* 250–258.

Rosenkoetter, L. I. (1999). The television situation comedy and children's prosocial behavior. *Journal of Applied Social Psychology, 29,* 979–993.

Rosenthal, R. (1995). Ethical issues in psychological science: Risk, consent, and scientific quality. *Psychological Science, 6,* 322–323.

Rosenthal, R., & Fode, K. L. (1963). The effect of experimenter bias on the performance of the albino rat. *Behavioral Science, 8,* 183–189.

Rosenthal, R., & Jacobson, L. (1968). *Pygmalion in the classroom.* New York: Holt, Rinehart & Winston.

Ross, E. (1999, June 18). Einstein's brain was exceptional. *Philadelphia Inquirer,* p. A1.

Ross, E. D., Thompson, R. D., & Yenkosky, J. (1997). Lateralization of affective prosody in brain and the callosal integration of hemispheric language functions. *Brain and Language, 56,* 27–54.

Rossi, A. F., Rittenhouse, C. D., & Paradiso, M. A. (1996). The representation of brightness in primary visual cortex. *Science, 273,* 1104–1107.

Rossi, A. M., & Seiler, W. J. (1989–1990). The comparative effectiveness of systematic desensitization and an integrative approach in treating public speaking anxiety: A literature review and a preliminary investigation. *Imagination, Cognition, and Personality, 9,* 49–66.

Rossi, F. (1988, November 8). Stress test. *Philadelphia Inquirer,* pp. 1–E, 10–E.

Rotenberg, K. J., Kim, L. S., & Herman-Stahl, M. (1998). The role of primary and secondary appraisals in the negative emotions and psychological maladjustment of children of divorce. *Journal of Divorce and Remarriage, 29,* 43–66.

Rotenberg, V. S., & Arshavsky, V. V. (1997). Right and left brain hemispheres activation in the representatives of two different cultures. *Homeostasis in Health and Disease, 38,* 49–57.

Roth, T. (1995). An overview of the report of the National Commission on Sleep Disorders Research. *European Psychiatry, 10,* 109s-113s.

Rothbaum, B. O., Hodges, L., Watson, B. A., & Kessler, G. D. (1996). Virtual reality exposure therapy in the treatment of fear of flying: A case report. *Behaviour Research and Therapy, 34,* 477–481.

References

Rothbaum, F., & Tsang, B. Y. P. (1998). Lovesongs in the United States and China: On the nature of romantic love. *Journal of Cross-Cultural Psychology, 29,* 306–319.

Rothbaum, F., Weisz, J., Pott, M., Miyake, K., & Morelli, G. (2000). Attachment and culture: Security in the United States and Japan. *American Psychologist, 55,* 1093–1104.

Rothstein, H. R., Schmidt, F. L., Erwin, F. W., Owens, W. A., & Sparks, C. P. (1990). Biographical data in employment selection: Can validities be made generalizable? *Journal of Applied Psychology, 75,* 175–184.

Rotter, J. B. (1966). Generalized expectancies for internal versus external control of reinforcement. *Psychological Monographs, 80,* 1–28.

Rotton, J., & Kelly, I. W. (1985). Much ado about the full moon: A meta-analysis of lunar-lunacy research. *Psychological Bulletin, 97,* 286–306.

Roug, L., Landberg, I., & Lundberg, L. J. (1989). Phonetic development in early infancy: A study of four Swedish children during the first eighteen months of life. *Journal of Child Language, 16,* 19–40.

Rouillon, F. (1997). Epidemiology of panic disorder. *Human Psychopharmacology: Clinical and Experimental, 12,* S7–S12.

Routh, D. K. (1969). Conditioning of vocal response differentiation in infants. *Developmental Psychology, 1,* 219–226.

Rowan, A., & Shapiro, K. J. (1996). Animal rights, a bitten apple. *American Psychologist, 51,* 1183–1184.

Rowsell, H. C. (1988). The status of animal experimentation in Canada. *International Journal of Psychology, 23,* 377–381.

Roy-Byrne, P. P., Uhde, T. W., Holcomb, H. H., & Thompson, K. (1987). Effects of diazepam on cognitive processes in normal subjects. *Psychopharmacology, 91,* 30–33.

Rubin, J. R., Provenzano, F. J., & Luria, Z. (1974). The eye of the beholder: Parents' views on sex of newborns. *American Journal of Orthopsychiatry, 44,* 512–519.

Rubin, P. (1994). Positive and negative symptoms' relation to structural and functional brain changes in schizophrenic patients. *Nordic Journal of Psychiatry, 48,* 23–27.

Rubin, Z. (1985). Deceiving ourselves about deception: Comment on Smith and Richardson's "Amelioration of deception and harm in psychological research." *Journal of Personality and Social Psychology, 48,* 252–253.

Ruch, W., & Forabosco, G. (1996). A cross-cultural study of humor appreciation: Italy and Germany. *Humor, 9,* 1–18.

Ruch, W., McGhee, P. E., & Hehl, F. J. (1990). Age differences in the enjoyment of incongruity-resolution and nonsense humor during adulthood. *Psychology and Aging, 5,* 348–355.

Ruda, M. A. (1982). Opiates and pain pathways: Demonstration of enkephalin synapses on dorsal horn projection neurons. *Science, 215,* 1523–1525.

Rudolph, K. D., & Hammen, C. (1999). Age and gender as determinants of stress exposure, generation, and reactions in youngsters: A transactional perspective. *Child Development, 70,* 660–677.

Ruffin, C. L. (1993). Stress and health: Little hasslers vs. major life events. *Australian Psychologist, 28,* 201–208.

Ruffman, T. K., & Olson, D. R. (1989). Children's ascriptions of knowledge to others. *Developmental Psychology, 25,* 601–606.

Rule, B. G., & Nesdale, A. R. (1976). Emotional arousal and aggressive behavior. *Psychological Bulletin, 83,* 851–863.

Rumbaugh, D. M., Gill, T. V., & von Glasersfeld, E. C. (1973). Reading and sentence completion by a chimpanzee (*Pan*). *Science, 182,* 731–733.

Rummel, A., & Feinberg, R. (1988). Cognitive evaluation theory: A meta-analytic review of the literature. *Social Behavior and Personality, 16,* 147–164.

Runco, M. A. (1993). Divergent thinking, creativity, and giftedness. *Gifted Child Quarterly, 37,* 16–22.

Rury, J. L. (1988). Race, region, and education: An analysis of Black and White scores on the 1917 Army Alpha Intelligence Test. *Journal of Negro Education, 57,* 51–65.

Ruscio, J., Whitney, D. M., & Amabile, T. M. (1998). Looking inside the fishbowl of creativity: Verbal and behavioral predictors of creative performance. *Creativity Research Journal, 11,* 243–263.

Rushton, J. P. (1997). Race, IQ, and the APA report on *The Bell Curve. American Psychologist, 52,* 69–70.

Rushton, J. P., Fulker, D. W., Neale, M. C., et al. (1986). Altruism and aggression: The heritability of individual differences. *Journal of Personality and Social Psychology, 50,* 1192–1198.

Russ, S. W., Robins, A. L., & Christiano, B. A. (1999). Pretend play: Longitudinal prediction of creativity and affect in fantasy in children. *Creativity Research Journal, 12,* 129–139.

Russell, G. L., Fujino, D. C., Sue, S., Cheung, M.-K., & Snowden, L. R. (1996). The effects of therapist-client ethnic match in the assessment of mental health functioning. *Journal of Cross-Cultural Psychology, 27,* 598–615.

Russell, J. A., & Fehr, B. (1987). Relativity in the perception of emotion in facial expressions. *Journal of Experimental Psychology: General, 116,* 223–237.

Russell, M. J. (1976). Human olfactory communication. *Nature, 260,* 520–522.

Rutkowski, G. K., Gruder, C. L., & Romer, D. (1983). Group cohesiveness, social norms, and bystander intervention. *Journal of Personality and Social Psychology, 44,* 545–552.

Ryan, J. J., Sattler, J. M., & Lopez, S. J. (2000). Age effects in Wechsler Adult Intelligence Scale-III subtests. *Archives of Clinical Neuropsychology, 15,* 311–317.

Ryan, K. M., & Kanjorski, J. (1998). The enjoyment of sexist humor, rape attitudes, and relationship aggression in college students. *Sex Roles, 38,* 743–756.

Ryan, R. H., & Geiselman, R. E. (1991). Effects of biased information on the relationship between eyewitness confidence and accuracy. *Bulletin of the Psychonomic Society, 29,* 7–9.

Ryan, R. M., Frederick, C. M., Lepes, D., Rubio, N., & Sheldon, K. M. (1997). Intrinsic motivation and exercise adherence. *International Journal of Sport Psychology, 28,* 335–354.

Rychlak, J. F. (1988). *The psychology of rigorous humanism.* New York: New York University Press.

Sabatini, B. L., & Regehr, W. G. (1999). Timing of synaptic transmission. *Annual Review of Psychology, 61,* 521–542.

Sable, P. (1997). Attachment, detachment and borderline personality disorder. *Psychotherapy, 34,* 171–181.

Sachdev, P. (2000). The current status of tardive dyskinesia. *Australian and New Zealand Journal of Psychiatry, 34,* 355–369.

Sackeim, H. A. (1994). Central issues regarding the mechanisms of action of electroconvulsive therapy: Directions for future research. *Psychopharmacology Bulletin, 30,* 281–308.

Sacks, O. (1985). *The man who mistook his wife for a hat and other clinical tales.* New York: Summit.

Sadeh, A., Raviv, A., & Gruber, R. (2000). Sleep patterns and sleep disruptions in school-age children. *Developmental Psychology, 36,* 291–301.

Salgado, J. F. (1997). The five factor model of personality and job performance in the European Community. *Journal of Applied Psychology, 82,* 30–43.

Salmon, D. P., Butters, N., & Chan, A. S. (1999). The deterioration of semantic memory in Alzheimer's disease. *Canadian Journal of Experimental Psychology, 53,* 108–116.

Salthouse, T. A. (1991). Mediation of adult age differences in cognition by reductions in working memory and speed of processing. *Psychological Science, 2,* 179–183.

Samelson, F. (1981). Struggle for scientific authority: The reception of Watson's behaviorism, 1913–1920. *Journal of the History of the Behavioral Sciences, 17,* 399–425.

Samelson, F. (1992). Rescuing the reputation of Sir Cyril Burt. *Journal of the History of the Behavioral Sciences, 28,* 221–233.

Samelson, F. (1997). On the uses of history: The case of *The Bell Curve. Journal of the History of the Behavioral Sciences, 33,* 129–133.

Samms, M., Hari, R., Rif, J., & Knuutila, J. (1993). The human auditory sensory memory trace persists about 10 sec: Neuromagnetic evidence. *Journal of Cognitive Neuroscience, 5,* 363–370.

Samuels, J., & Nestadt, G. (1997). Epidemiology and genetics of obsessive-compulsive disorder. *International Review of Psychiatry, 9,* 61–72.

Sand, P., Kavvadias, D., Feineis, D., Riederer, P., et al. (2000). Naturally occurring benzodiazepines: Current status of research and clinical implications. *Journal of Clinical Psychopharmacology, 20,* 12–18.

Sanghvi, C. (1995). Efficacy of study skills training in managing study habits and test anxiety of high test anxious students. *Journal of the Indian Academy of Applied Psychology, 21,* 71–75.

Sarason, S. (1984). If it can be studied or developed, should it be? *American Psychologist, 39,* 477–485.

Saraswathi, T. S. (1998). Many deities, same god: Towards convergence in cultural and cross-cultural psychology. *Culture and Psychology, 4,* 147–160.

Sarbin, T. R. (1997). On the futility of psychiatric diagnostic manuals (*DSMs*) and the return of personal agency. *Applied and Preventive Psychology, 6,* 233–243.

Sarter, M., Berntson, G. G., & Cacioppo, J. T. (1996). Brain imaging and cognitive neuroscience: Toward strong inference in attributing function to structure. *American Psychologist, 51,* 13–21.

Satir, V., Bitter, J. R., & Krestensen, K. K. (1988). Family reconstruction: The family within—A group experience. *Journal for Specialists in Group Work, 13,* 200–208.

Sato, T., & Beidler, L. M. (1997). Broad tuning of rat taste cells for four basic taste stimuli. *Chemical Senses, 22,* 287–293.

Saudino, K. J., Gagne, J. R., Grant, J., et al. (1999). Genetic and environmental influences on personality in adult Russian twins. *International Journal of Behavioral Development, 23,* 375–389.

Saunders, C. (1996). Hospice. *Mortality, 1,* 317–322.

Saunders, D. M., Fisher, W. A., Hewitt, E. C., & Clayton, J. P. (1985). A method for empirically assessing volunteer selection effects: Recruitment procedures and responses to erotica. *Journal of Personality and Social Psychology, 49,* 1703–1712.

Savage-Rumbaugh, E. S. (1990). Language acquisition in a nonhuman species: Implications for the innateness debate. *Developmental Psychobiology, 23,* 599–620.

Savage-Rumbaugh, E. S., McDonald, K., Sevcik, R. A., Hopkins, W. D., & Rupert, E. (1986). Spontaneous symbol acquisition and communicative use by pygmy chimpanzees (*Pan paniscus*). *Journal of Experimental Psychology: General, 115,* 211–235.

Savage-Rumbaugh, E. S., Murphy, J., Sevcik, R. A., & Brakke, K. E. (1993). Language comprehension in ape and child. *Monographs of the Society for Research in Child Development, 58* (3/4), v-221.

Savage-Rumbaugh, E. S., Rumbaugh, D. M., Smith, S. T., & Lawson, J. (1980). Reference: The linguistic essential. *Science, 210,* 922–925.

Sawyer, T. F. (2000). Francis Cecil Sumner: His views and influence on African American higher education. *History of Psychology, 3,* 122–141.

Saxe, L., & Ben-Shakhar, G. (1999). Admissibility of polygraph tests: The application of scientific standards post-Daubert. *Psychology, Public Policy, and Law, 5,* 203–223.

Saxena, S., & Rauch, S. L. (2000). Functional neuroimaging and the neuroanatomy of obsessive-compulsive disorder. *Psychiatric Clinics of North America, 23,* 563–586.

Scarborough, E., & Furumoto, L. (1987). *Untold lives: The first generation of American women psychologists.* New York: Columbia University Press.

Scarr, S. (1998). American child care today. *American Psychologist, 53,* 95–108.

Scarr, S., & Carter-Saltzman, L. (1979). Twin method: Defense of a critical assumption. *Behavior Genetics, 9,* 527–542.

Scarr, S., & Weinberg, R. A. (1976). IQ test performance of black children adopted by white families. *American Psychologist, 31,* 726–739.

Scarr, S., & Weinberg, R. A. (1983). The Minnesota Adoption Studies: Genetic differences and malleability. *Child Development, 54,* 260–267.

Schaal, B., Marlier, L., & Soussignan, R. (1998). Olfactory function in the human fetus: Evidence from selective neonatal responsiveness to the odor of amniotic fluid. *Behavioral Neuroscience, 112,* 1438–1449.

Schachter, S. (1971). Some extraordinary facts about obese humans and rats. *American Psychologist, 26,* 129–144.

Schachter, S. (1982). Recidivism and self-cure of smoking and obesity. *American Psychologist, 37,* 436–444.

Schachter, S., & Singer, J. E. (1962). Cognitive, social and physiological determinants of emotional state. *Psychological Review, 69,* 379–399.

Schacter, D. L. (1983). Amnesia observed: Remembering and forgetting in a natural environment. *Journal of Abnormal Psychology, 92,* 236–242.

Schacter, D. L. (1992). Understanding implicit memory: A cognitive neuroscience approach. *American Psychologist, 47,* 559–569.

Schacter, D. L., Norman, K. A., & Koutstaal, W. (1998). The cognitive neuroscience of constructive memory. *Annual Review of Psychology, 49,* 289–318.

Schaefer, G. B., & Bodensteiner, J. B. (1999). Developmental anomalies of the brain in mental retardation. *International Review of Psychiatry, 11,* 47–55.

Schafe, G. E., Sollars, S. I., & Bernstein, I. L. (1995). The CS-US interval and taste aversion learning: A brief look. *Behavioral Neuroscience, 109,* 799–802.

Schaie, K. W. (1989). Perceptual speed in adulthood: Cross-sectional and longitudinal studies. *Psychology and Aging, 4,* 443–453.

Schaie, K. W., & Hertzog, C. (1983). Fourteen-year cohort-sequential analyses of adult intellectual development. *Developmental Psychology, 19,* 531–543.

Schaie, K. W., Labouvie, G. V., & Barrett, T. J. (1973). Selective attrition effects in a 14–year study of adult intelligence. *Journal of Gerontology, 28,* 328–334.

Schaller, M., & Cialdini, R. B. (1988). The economics of empathic helping: Support for a mood management motive. *Journal of Experimental Social Psychology, 24,* 163–181.

Schaubroeck, J., Lam, S. S. K., & Xie, J. L. (2000). Collective efficacy versus self-efficacy in coping responses to stressors and control: A cross-cultural study. *Journal of Applied Psychology, 85,* 512–525.

Scheffler, T. S., & Naus, P. J. (1999). The relationship between fatherly affirmation and a woman's self-esteem, fear of intimacy, comfort with womanhood and comfort with sexuality. *Canadian Journal of Human Sexuality, 8,* 39–45.

Schein, E. H. (1956). Some observations on Chinese methods of handling prisoners of war. *Public Opinion Quarterly, 20,* 321–327.

Scherer, K. R. (1997). Profiles of emotion-antecedent appraisal: Testing theoretical predictions across cultures. *Cognition and Emotion, 11,* 113–150.

Scherer, K. R., & Ceschi, G. (1997). Lost luggage: A field study of emotion-antecedent appraisal. *Motivation and Emotion, 21,* 211–235.

Schiffman, S. S., Sattely-Miller, E. A., Suggs, M. S., & Graham, B. G. (1995). The effect of pleasant odors and hormone status on mood of women at midlife. *Brain Research Bulletin, 36,* 19–29.

Schiffman, S. S., Suggs, M. S., & Sattely-Miller, E. A. (1995). Effect of pleasant odors on mood of males at midlife: Comparison of African-American and European-American men. *Brain Research Bulletin, 36,* 31–37.

Schilling, R. F., & Weaver, G. E. (1983). Effects of extraneous verbal information on memory for telephone numbers. *Journal of Applied Psychology, 68,* 559–564.

Schlegel, P. A., & Roth, A. (1997). Tuning of electroreceptors in the blind cave salamander. *Proteus anguinus L. Brain, Behaviour, and Evolution, 49,* 132–136.

Schleifer, S. J., Keller, S. E., Camerino, M., Thornton, J. C., & Stein, M. (1983). Suppression of lymphocytic stimulation following bereavement. *Journal of the American Medical Association, 250,* 374–377.

Schmeidler, G. R. (1985). Belief and disbelief in psi. *Parapsychology Review, 16,* 1–4.

Schmeidler, G. R. (1997). Psi-conducive experimenters and psi-permissive ones. *European Journal of Parapsychology, 13,* 83–94.

Schmidt, H. G., & Boshuizen, H. P. (1993). On acquiring expertise in medicine. *Educational Psychology Review, 5,* 205–221.

Schmidt, N. B., Lerew, D. R., & Jackson, R. J. (1999). Prospective evaluation of anxiety sensitivity in the pathogenesis of panic: Replication and extension. *Journal of Abnormal Psychology, 108,* 532–537.

Schmidt, S. R., & Bohannon, J. N. (1988). In defense of the flashbulb-memory hypothesis: A comment on McCloskey, Wible, and Cohen (1988). *Journal of Experimental Psychology: General, 117,* 332–335.

Schmidtke, A., Weinacker, B., Apter, A., Batt, A., et al. (1999). Suicide rates in the world: Update. *Archives of Suicide Research, 5,* 81–89.

Schmitt-Rodermund, E., & Vondracek, F. W. (1999). Breadth of interests, exploration, and identity development in adolescence. *Journal of Vocational Behavior, 55,* 298–317.

Schneider, C. J. (1987). Cost effectiveness of biofeedback and behavioral medicine treatments: A review of the literature. *Biofeedback and Self-Regulation, 12,* 71–92.

Schneider, H. G., & Shugar, G. J. (1990). Audience and feedback effects in computer learning. *Computers in Human Behavior, 6,* 315–321.

Schneider-Rosen, K., & Burke, P. B. (1999). Multiple attachment relationships within families: Mothers and fathers with two young children. *Developmental Psychology, 35,* 436–444.

Schoen, L. M. (1996). Mnemopoly: Board games and mnemonics. *Teaching of Psychology, 23,* 30–32.

Schooler, C., Mulatu, M. S., & Oates, G. (1999). The continuing effects of substantively complex work on the intellectual functioning of older workers. *Psychology and Aging, 14,* 483–506.

Schrag, A. E., Brooks, D. J., Brunt, E., et al. (1998). The safety of ropinirole, a selective nonergoline dopamine agonist, in patients with Parkinson's disease. *Clinical Neuropharmacology, 21,* 169–175.

Schredl, M. (2000). Gender differences in dream recall. *Journal of Mental Imagery, 24,* 169–176.

Schreiner, C. E. (1998). Spatial distribution of responses to simple and complex sounds in the primary auditory cortex. *Audiology and Neuro-Otology, 3,* 104–122.

Schretlen, D., Pearlson, G. D., Anthony, J. C., Aylward, E. H., Augustine, A. M., Davis, A., & Barta, P. (2000). Elucidating the contributions of processing speed, executive ability, and frontal lobe volume to normal age-related differences in fluid intelligence. *Journal of the International Neuropsychological Society, 6,* 52–61.

Schrut, A. H. (1994). The Oedipus complex: Some observations and questions regarding its validity and universal existence. *Journal of the American Academy of Psychoanalysis, 22,* 727–751.

Schull, W. J., Norton, S., & Jensh, R. P. (1990). Ionizing radiation and the developing brain. *Neurotoxicology and Teratology, 12,* 249–260.

Schulz, P., & Kaspar, C.-H. (1994). Neuroendocrine and psychological effects of restricted environmental stimulation technique in a flotation tank. *Biological Psychology, 37,* 161–175.

Schulz, R., & Curnow, C. (1988). Peak performance and age among superathletes: Track and field, swimming, baseball, tennis, and golf. *Journal of Gerontology, 43,* 113–120.

Schuster, B., Forsterling, F., & Weiner, B. (1989). Perceiving the causes of success and failure: A cross-cultural examination of attributional concepts. *Journal of Cross-Cultural Psychology, 20,* 191–213.

Schuster, D. T. (1990). Fulfillment of potential, life satisfaction, and competence: Comparing four cohorts of gifted women at midlife. *Journal of Educational Psychology, 82,* 471–478.

Schwartz, B. L., & Smith, S. M. (1997). The retrieval of related information influences tip-of-the-tongue states. *Journal of Memory and Language, 36,* 68–86.

Schwartz, B. L., Travis, D. M., Castro, A. M., & Smith, S. M. (2000). The phenomenology of real and illusory tip-of-the-tongue states. *Memory and Cognition, 28,* 18–27.

Schwartz, J. C., Diaz, J., Pilon, C., & Sokoloff, P. (2000). Possible implications of the dopamine D-sub-3 receptor in schizophrenia and in antipsychotic drug actions. *Brain Research Reviews, 31,* 277–287.

Schweitzer, P. K., Muehlbach, M. J., & Walsh, J. K. (1992). Countermeasures for night work performance deficits: The effect of napping or caffeine on continuous performance at night. *Work and Stress, 6,* 355–365.

Schwolow, R., Wilckens, E., & Roth, N. (1988). Effect of transcutaneous nerve stimulation (TENS) on dental pain: Comparison of psychophysical and neurophysiological data and application in dentistry. *Activitas Nervosa Superior, 30,* 129–130.

Schyns, P. (1998). Cross-national differences in happiness: Economic and cultural factors explored. *Social Indicators, 43,* 3–26.

Scopesi, A., Zanobini, M., & Carossino, P. (1997). Childbirth in different cultures: Psychophysical reactions of women delivering in U.S., German, French, and Italian hospitals. *Journal of Reproductive and Infant Psychology, 15,* 9–30.

Scott, K. G., & Carran, D. T. (1987). The epidemiology and prevention of mental retardation. *American Psychologist, 42,* 801–804.

Scott, M. S., Deuel, L. L. S., Jean-Francois, B., & Urbano, R. C. (1996). Identifying cognitively gifted ethnic minority children. *Gifted Child Quarterly, 40,* 147–153.

Scoville, W. B., & Milner, B. (1957). Loss of recent memory after bilateral hippocampal lesions. *Journal of Neurology, Neurosurgery, and Psychiatry, 20,* 11–21.

Scully, J. A., Tosi, H., & Banning, K. (2000). Life events checklists: Revisiting the Social Readjustment Rating Scale after 30 years. *Educational and Psychological Measurement, 60,* 864–876.

Sears, D. O. (1986). College sophomores in the laboratory: Influences of a narrow data base on social psychology's view of human nature. *Journal of Personality and Social Psychology, 51,* 515–530.

Sechrest, L. (1984). Review of the development and application of social language theory: Selected papers. *Journal of the History of the Behavioral Sciences, 20,* 228–230.

Sedlacek, K., & Taub, E. (1996). Biofeedback treatment of Raynaud's disease. *Professional Psychology: Research and Practice, 27,* 548–553.

Segall, M. H., Dasen, P. R., Berry, J. W., & Poortinga, Y. H. (1990). *Human behavior in global perspective: An introduction to cross-cultural psychology.* New York: Pergamon Press.

Seidlitz, L., & Diener, E. (1998). Sex differences in the recall of affective experiences. *Journal of Personality and Social Psychology, 74,* 262–271.

Seifert, L. S. (1996). On the use of concept formation tasks to educate naive observers about the visual arts. *Visual Arts Research, 22,* 11–19.

Self, D. J., & Baldwin, D. C., Jr. (1998). Does medical education inhibit the development of moral reasoning in medical students? A cross-sectional study. *Academic Medicine, 73,* S91–S93.

Seligman, L., & Hardenburg, S. A. (2000). Assessment and treatment of paraphilias. *Journal of Counseling and Development, 78,* 107–113.

Seligman, M. E. P. (1970). On the generality of the laws of learning. *Psychological Review, 77,* 406–418.

Seligman, M. E. P. (1989). Research in clinical psychology: Why is there so much depression today? In I. S. Cohen (Ed.), *The G. Stanley Hall Lecture Series* (Vol. 9, pp. 75–96). Washington, DC: American Psychological Association.

Seligman, M.E.P., & Maier, S. F. (1967). Failure to escape traumatic shock. *Journal of Experimental Psychology, 74,* 1–9.

Selten, J. P., Slaets, J., & Kahn, R. (1998). Prenatal exposure to influenza and schizophrenia in Surinamese and Dutch Antillean immigrants to the Netherlands. *Schizophrenia Research, 30,* 101–103.

Selye, H. (1936). A syndrome produced by diverse nocuous agents. *Nature, 138,* 32.

Serebriakoff, V. (1985). *Mensa: The society for the highly intelligent.* New York: Stein & Day.

Seroussi, D.-E. (1995). Heuristic hypotheses in problem solving: An example of conceptual issues issues about scientific procedures. *Science Education, 79,* 595–609.

Setlow, B. (1997). Georges Ungar and memory transfer. *Journal of the History of the Neurosciences, 6,* 181–192.

Seyfarth, R. M., Cheney, D. L., & Marler, P. (1980). Monkey responses to three different alarm calls: Evidence of predator classification and semantic communication. *Science, 210,* 801–803.

Seymour, G. O., Stahl, J. M., Levine, S. L., & Ingram, J. L. (1994). Modifying law enforcement training simulators for use in basic research. *Behavior Research Methods, Instruments and Computers, 26,* 266–268.

Seymour, T. L., Seifert, C. M., Shafto, M. G., & Mosmann, A. L. (2000). Using response time measures to assess "guilty knowledge." *Journal of Applied Psychology, 85,* 30–37.

Sforza, E., & Lugaresi, E. (1995). Daytime sleepiness and nasal continuous positive airway pressure therapy in obstructive sleep apnea syndrome patients: Effects of chronic treatment and one-night therapy withdrawal. *Sleep, 18,* 195–201.

Shadish, W. R., Navarro, A. M., Matt, G. E., & Phillips, G. (2000). The effects of psychological therapies under clinically representative conditions: A meta-analysis. *Psychological Bulletin, 126,* 512–529.

Shaffer, D. R., & Bazzini, D. G. (1997). What do you look for in a prospective date? Reexamining the preferences of men and women who differ in self-monitoring propensities. *Personality and Social Psychology Bulletin, 23,* 605–616.

Shaffer, J. W., Graves, P. L., Swank, R. T., & Pearson, T. A. (1987). Clustering of personality traits in youth and the subsequent development of cancer among physicians. *Journal of Behavioral Medicine, 10,* 441–447.

Shafran, R., Watkins, E., & Charman, T. (1996). Guilt in obsessive-compulsive disorder. *Journal of Anxiety Disorders, 10,* 509–516.

Shah, M., & Jeffery, R. W. (1991). Is obesity due to overeating and inactivity, or to a defective metabolic rate? A review. *Annals of Behavioral Medicine, 13,* 73–81.

Shammi, P., & Stuss, D. T. (1999). Humour appreciation: A role of the right frontal lobe. *Brain, 122,* 657–666.

Shanab, M. E., & Yahya, K. A. (1977). A behavioral study of obedience in children. *Journal of Personality and Social Psychology, 35,* 530–536.

Shanker, S. G., Savage-Rumbaugh, E. S., & Taylor, T. J. (1999). Kanzi: A new beginning. *Animal Learning and Behavior, 27,* 24–25.

Shapiro, C. M., Bortz, R., Mitchell, D., Bartel, P., & Jooste, P. (1981). Slow-wave sleep: A recovery period after exercise. *Science, 214,* 1253–1254.

Shapiro, D. A. (1995). Finding out how psychotherapies help people change. *Psychotherapy Research, 5,* 1–21.

Shapiro, J. K. (1995). Dr. Kohlberg goes to Washington: Using Congressional debates to teach moral development. *Teaching of Psychology, 22,* 245–247.

Shapiro, K. L., Caldwell, J., & Sorensen, R. E. (1997). Personal names and the attentional blink: A visual "cocktail party" effect. *Journal of Experimental Psychology: Human Perception and Performance, 23,* 504–514.

Sharpe, D., Adair, J. G., & Roese, N. J. (1992). Twenty years of deception research: A decline in subjects' trust? *Personality and Social Psychology Bulletin, 18,* 585–590.

Shaughnessy, M. F., & Nystul, M. S. (1985). Preventing the greatest loss—Suicide. *Creative Child and Adult Quarterly, 10,* 164–169.

Shavitt, S., Swan, S., Lowrey, T. M., & Wanke, M. (1994). The interaction of endorser attractiveness and involvement in persuasion depends on the goal that guides message processing. *Journal of Consumer Psychology, 3,* 137–162.

Shaw, J. S., III, Garcia, L. A., & McClure, K. A. (1999). A lay perspective on the accuracy of eyewitness testimony. *Journal of Applied Social Psychology, 29,* 52–71.

Shea, M. T., Elkin, I., Imber, S. D., & Sotsky, S. M. (1992). Course of depressive symptoms over follow-up: Findings from the National Institute of Mental Health Treatment of Depression Collaborative Research Program. *Archives of General Psychiatry, 49,* 782–787.

Sheehan, P. W., & Tilden, J. (1983). Effects of suggestibility and hypnosis on accurate and distorted retrieval from memory. *Journal of Experimental Psychology: Learning, Memory, and Cognition, 9,* 283–293.

Sheiner, E. K., Sheiner, E., Shoham-Vardi, I., Mazor, M., & Katz, M. (1999). Ethnic differences influence caregiver's estimates of pain during labour. *Pain, 81,* 299–305.

Shell, D. F., Colvin, C., & Bruning, R. H. (1995). Self-efficacy, attribution, and outcome expectancy mechanisms in reading and writing achievement: Grade-level and achievement-level differences. *Journal of Educational Psychology, 87,* 386–398.

Shepperd, J. A., & Taylor, K. M. (1999). Social loafing and expectancy-value theory. *Personality and Social Psychology Bulletin, 25,* 1147–1158.

Sher, L., Goldman, D., Ozaki, N., & Rosenthal, N. E. (1999). The role of genetic factors in the etiology of seasonal affective disorder and seasonality. *Journal of Affective Disorders, 53,* 203–210.

Shergill, S. S., Bullmore, E., Simmons, A., Murray, R., & McGuire, P. (2000). Functional anatomy of auditory verbal imagery in schizophrenic patients with auditory hallucinations. *American Journal of Psychiatry, 157,* 1691–1693.

Shettleworth, S. J., & Juergensen, M. R. (1980). Reinforcement of the organization of behavior in golden hamsters: Brain stimulation reinforcement for seven action patterns. *Journal of Experimental Psychology: Animal Behavior Processes, 6,* 352–375.

Shevell, S. K., & He, J. C. (1997). The visual photopigments of simple deuteranomalous trichromats inferred from color matching. *Vision Research, 37,* 1115–1127.

Shevrin, H., & Dickman, S. (1980). The psychological unconscious: A necessary assumption for all psychological theory? *American Psychologist, 35,* 421–434.

Shields, S. A. (1975). Functionalism, Darwinism, and the psychology of women: A study in social myth. *American Psychologist, 30,* 739–754.

Shields, S. A. (1982). The variability hypothesis. *Signs, 7,* 769–797.

Shiffman, S., Paty, J. A., Gnys, M., & Kassel, J. D. (1995). Nicotine withdrawal in chippers and regular smokers: Subjective and cognitive effects. *Health Psychology, 14,* 301–309.

Shiffrin, R. M., & Atkinson, R. C. (1969). Storage and retrieval processes in long-term memory. *Psychological Review, 76,* 179–193.

Shih, M., Pittinsky, T. L., & Ambady, N. (1999). Stereotype susceptibility: Identity salience and shifts in quantitative performance. *Psychological Science, 10,* 80–83.

Shioiri, T., Murashita, J., Kato, T., & Fujii, K. (1996). Characteristic clinical features and clinical course in 270 Japanese outpatients with panic disorder. *Journal of Anxiety Disorders, 10,* 163–172.

Shiraishi, T. (1990). CCK as a central satiety factor: Behavioral and electrophysiological evidence. *Physiology and Behavior, 48,* 879–885.

Shirom, A., Melamed, S., & Nir-Dotan, M. (2000). The relationships among objective and subjective environmental stress levels and serum uric acid: The moderating effect of perceived control. *Journal of Occupational Health Psychology, 5,* 374–385.

Shneidman, E. (1987, March). At the point of no return. *Psychology Today,* pp. 54–58.

Shneidman, E. (1994). Clues to suicide reconsidered. *Suicide and Life-Threatening Behavior, 24,* 395–397.

Shook, N. J., Gerrity, D. A., Jurich, J., & Segrist, A. E. (2000). Courtship violence among college students: A comparison of verbally and physically couples. *Journal of Family Violence, 15,* 1–22.

Shostrom, E. L. (1962). *Personal orientation inventory.* San Diego: EDITS.

Shotland, R. L., & Straw, M. J. (1976). Bystander response to an assault: When a man attacks a woman. *Journal of Personality and Social Psychology, 34,* 990–999.

Shouse, M. N., Staba, R. J., Saquib, S. F., & Farber, P. R. (2000). Monoamines and sleep: Microdialysis findings in pons and amygdala. *Brain Research, 860,* 181–189.

Shrivastava, A. K., & Rao, S. (1997). Brain, mind, and behavior: Culture and environmental perspective. *International Medical Journal, 4,* 145–148.

Shulz, D. E., Sosnik, R., Ego, V., Haidarliu, S., & Ahissar, E. (2000). A neuronal annalogue of state-dependent learning. *Nature, 403,* 549–552.

Siegel, J. M., & Brown, J. D. (1988). A prospective study of stressful circumstances, illness symptoms, and depressed mood among adolescents. *Developmental Psychology, 24,* 715–721.

Siegel, S., & Allan, L. G. (1996). The widespread influence of the Rescorla-Wagner model. *Psychonomic Bulletin and Review, 3,* 314–321.

Siegel, S., Baptista, M. A. S., & Kim, J. (2000). Pavlovian psychopharmacology: The associative basis of tolerance. *Experimental and Clinical Psychopharmacology, 8,* 276–293.

Sierra-Honigmann, A. M., Carbone, K. M., & Yolken, R. H. (1995). Polymerase chain reaction (PCR) search for viral nucleic acid sequences in schizophrenia. *British Journal of Psychiatry, 166,* 55–60.

Siever, M. D. (1994). Sexual orientation and gender as factors in socioculturally acquired vulnerability to body dissatisfaction and eating disorders. *Journal of Consulting and Clinical Psychology, 62,* 252–260.

Signorella, M. L., Bigler, R. S., & Liben, L. S. (1997). A meta-analysis of children's memories for own-sex and other-sex information. *Journal of Applied Developmental Psychology, 18,* 429–445.

Silinsky, E. M. (1989). Adenosine derivatives and neuronal function. *Seminars in the Neurosciences, 1,* 155–165.

Silove, D., Manicavasagar, V., Curtis, J., & Blaszczynski, A. (1996). Is early separation anxiety a risk factor for adult panic disorder? A critical review. *Comprehensive Psychiatry, 37,* 167–179.

Silva, J. M., III, & Weinberg, R. S. (1984). *Psychological foundations of sport*. Champaign, IL: Human Kinetics.

Silverstein, L. B., & Auerbach, C. F. (1999). Deconstructing the essential father. *American Psychologist, 54*, 397–407.

Silverthorne, Z. A., & Quinsey, V. L. (2000). Sexual partner age preferences of homosexual and heterosexual men and women. *Archives of Sexual Behavior, 29*, 67–76.

Simmons, R. W., Smith, K., Erez, E., Burke, J. P., & Pozos, R. E. (1998). Balance retraining in a hemiparetic patients using center of gravity biofeedback: A single-case study. *Perception and Motor Skills, 87*, 603–609.

Simon, N. (1979). Kaspar Hauser's recovery and autopsy: A perspective on neurological and sociological requirements for language development. *Annual Progress in Child Psychiatry and Child Development*, 215–224.

Simonoff, E., Bolton, P., & Rutter, M. (1996). Mental retardation: Genetic findings, clinical implications and research agenda. *Journal of Child Psychology and Psychiatry and Allied Disciplines, 37*, 259–280.

Simonton, D. K. (1988). Age and outstanding achievement: What do we know after a century of research? *Psychological Bulletin, 104*, 251–267.

Simonton, D. K. (1999). Creativity and genius. In L. Pervin & O. John (Eds.), *Handbook of personality theory and research* (2nd ed., pp. 629–652). New York: Guilford Press.

Simonton, D. K. (2000). Creativity: Cognitive, personal, developmental, and social aspects. *American Psychologist, 55*, 151–158.

Singer, A. G., & Macrides, F. (1990). Aphrodisin: Pheromone or transducer? *Chemical Senses, 15*, 199–203.

Singer, J. D., Fuller, B., Keiley, M. K., & Wolf, A. (1998). Early child-care selection: Variation by geographic location, maternal characteristics, and family structure. *Developmental Psychology, 34*, 1129–1144.

Singer, J. L., & Kolligian, J., Jr. (1987). Personality: Developments in the study of private experience. *Annual Review of Psychology, 38*, 533–574.

Singh, R., & Ho, S. Y. (2000). Attitudes and attraction: A new test of the attraction, repulsion and similarity-dissimilarity asymmetry hypotheses. *British Journal of Social Psychology, 39*, 197–211.

Siris, S. G. (2000). Endogenous stressors and schizophrenic heterogeneity. *Psychiatric Annals, 30*, 645–648.

Skinner, B. F. (1938). *The behavior of organisms*. New York: Appleton-Century-Crofts.

Skinner, B. F. (1945, October). Baby in a box. *Ladies Home Journal*, pp. 30–31.

Skinner, B. F. (1948). *Walden Two*. New York: Macmillan.

Skinner, B. F. (1956). A case history in scientific method. *American Psychologist, 11*, 221–233.

Skinner, B. F. (1957). *Verbal behavior*. New York: Appleton-Century-Crofts.

Skinner, B. F. (1960). Pigeons in a pelican. *American Psychologist, 15*, 28–37.

Skinner, B. F. (1974). *About behaviorism*. New York: Knopf.

Skinner, B. F. (1984). The shame of American education. *American Psychologist, 39*, 947–954.

Skinner, B. F. (1986). What is wrong with daily life in the Western world? *American Psychologist, 41*, 220–222.

Skinner, B. F. (1989). Teaching machines. *Science, 243*, 1535.

Skinner, N. F. (1983). Switching answers on multiple-choice questions: Shrewdness or shibboleth? *Teaching of Psychology, 10*, 220–222.

Slater, A. (1992). The visual constancies in early infancy. *Irish Journal of Psychology, 13*, 412–425.

Slife, B. D., & Fisher, A. M. (2000). Modern and postmodern approaches to the free will/determinism dilemma in psychotherapy. *Journal of Humanistic Psychology, 40*, 80–107.

Sliwinski, M., & Buschke, H. (1999). Cross-sectional and longitudinal relationships among age, cognition, and processing speed. *Psychology and Aging, 14*, 18–33.

Smart, D. W., & Smart, J. F. (1997). *DSM-IV* and culturally sensitive diagnosis: Some observations for counselors. *Journal of Counseling and Development, 75*, 392–398.

Smith, A. L., & Tart, C. T. (1998). Cosmic consciousness experience and psychedelic experiences: A first-person comparison. *Journal of Consciousness Studies, 5*, 97–107.

Smith, B. D., Cranford, D., & Mann, M. (2000). Gender, cynical hostility and cardiovascular function: Implications for differential cardiovascular disease risk? *Personality and Individual Differences, 29*, 659–670.

Smith, B. H. (1997). An analysis of blocking in odorant mixtures: An increase but not a decrease in intensity of reinforcement produces unblocking. *Behavioral Neuroscience, 111*, 57–69.

Smith, B. M., Schumaker, J. B., Schaefer, J., & Sherman, J. A. (1982). Increasing participation and improving the quality of discussion in seventh-grade social studies classes. *Journal of Applied Behavior Analysis, 15*, 97–110.

Smith, C. (1996). Sleep states, memory processes and synaptic plasticity. *Behavioural Brain Research, 78*, 49–56.

Smith, D. (1982). Trends in counseling and psychotherapy. *American Psychologist, 37*, 802–809.

Smith, D. G., Standing, L., & de Man, A. (1992). Verbal memory elicited by ambient odor. *Perceptual and Motor Skills, 74*, 339–343.

Smith, D. V., & Margolis, F. L. (1999). Taste processing: Whetting our appetites. *Current Biology, 9*, R453–R455.

Smith, G. L., Large, M. M., Kavanagh, D. J., Karayanidis, F., et al. (1998). Further evidence for a deficit in switching attention in schizophrenia. *Journal of Abnormal Psychology, 107*, 390–398.

Smith, H. F. (1995). Introduction: Gedo and Freud on working through. *Journal of the American Psychoanalytic Association, 43*, 331–392.

Smith, H. V. (1992). Is there a magical number 7±2? The role of exposure duration and information content in immediate recall. *Irish Journal of Psychology, 13*, 85–97.

Smith, J., & Baltes, M. M. (1998). The role of gender in very old age: Profiles of functioning and everyday life patterns. *Psychology and Aging, 13*, 676–695.

Smith, J. W., & Frawley, P. J. (1993). Treatment outcome of 600 chemically dependent patients treated in a multimodal inpatient program including aversion therapy and pentothal interviews. *Journal of Substance Abuse Treatment, 10*, 359–369.

Smith, L. C., Friedman, S., & Nevid, J. (1999). Clinical and sociocultural differences in African American and European American patients with panic disorder and agoraphobia. *Journal of Nervous and Mental Disease, 187*, 549–560.

Smith, L. T. (1974). The interanimal transfer phenomenon: A review. *Psychological Bulletin, 81*, 1078–1095.

Smith, M. C. (1983). Hypnotic memory enhancement of witnesses: Does it work? *Psychological Bulletin, 94*, 387–407.

Smith, M. L., Glass, G. V., & Miller, T. I. (1980). *The benefits of psychotherapy*. Baltimore: Johns Hopkins University Press.

Smith, M. V. (1996). Linguistic relativity: On hypotheses and confusions. *Communication and Cognition, 29*, 65–90.

Smith, P. F. (1995). Cannabis and the brain: Recent developments. *New Zealand Journal of Psychology, 24*, 5–12.

Smith, R. H., Diener, E., & Wedell, D. H. (1989). Intrapersonal and social comparison determinants of happiness: A range-frequency analysis. *Journal of Personality and Social Psychology, 56*, 317–325.

Smith, S. M. (1984). A comparison of two techniques for reducing context-dependent forgetting. *Memory and Cognition, 12*, 477–482.

Smith, S. M., & Vela, E. (1992). Environmental context-dependent eyewitness recognition. *Applied Cognitive Psychology, 6*, 125–139.

Smith, S. S., & Richardson, D. (1983). Amelioration of deception and harm in psychological research: The important role of debriefing. *Journal of Personality and Social Psychology, 44*, 1075–1082.

Smolak, L., Murnen, S. K., & Ruble, A. E. (2000). Female athletes and eating problems: A meta-analysis. *International Journal of Eating Disorders, 27*, 371–380.

Snarey, J. R., Reimer, J., & Kohlberg, L. (1985). Development of social-moral reasoning among kibbutz adolescents: A longitudinal cross-cultural study. *Developmental Psychology, 21*, 3–17.

Sno, H. N., Schalken, H. F., & de Jonghe, F. (1992). Empirical research on déjà vu experiences: A review. *Behavioural Neurology, 5*, 155–160.

Snow, C. E. (1981). The uses of imitation. *Journal of Child Language, 8*, 205–212.

Snow, D. S. (2000). The emotional basis of linguistic and nonlinguistic intonation: Implications for hemispheric specialization. *Developmental Neuropsychology, 17*, 1–28.

Snow, W. G., & Sheese, S. (1985). Lateralized brain damage, intelligence, and memory: A failure to find sex differences. *Journal of Consulting and Clinical Psychology, 33*, 940–941.

Snyder, B. K., Roghmann, K. J., & Sigal, L. H. (1993). Stress and psychosocial factors: Effects on primary cellular immune response. *Journal of Behavioral Medicine, 16*, 143–161.

Snyder, M. (1983). The influence of individuals on situations: Implications for understanding the links between personality and social behavior. *Journal of Personality, 51*, 497–516.

Snyder, P. J. (2000). Darwin's contribution to neuropsychology in the twenty-first century. *Brain and Cognition, 42*, 41–43.

Snyder, R. F. (2000). The relationship between learning styles/multiple intelligences and academic achievement of high school students. *High School Journal, 83*, 11–20.

Snyderman, M., & Herrnstein, R. J. (1983). Intelligence tests and the Immigration Act of 1924. *American Psychologist, 38*, 986–995.

Sobal, J., & Stunkard, A. J. (1989). Socioeconomic status and obesity: A review of the literature. *Psychological Bulletin, 105*, 260–275.

Solcova, I., & Sykora, J. (1995). Relation between psychological hardiness and physiological response. *Homeostasis in Health and Disease, 36*, 30–34.

Solomon, C. R., & Serres, F. (1999). Effects of parental verbal aggression on children's self-esteem and school marks. *Child Abuse and Neglect, 23*, 339–351.

Solomon, P. R., & Morse, D. L. (1981). Teaching the principles of operant conditioning through laboratory experience: The rat olympics. *Teaching Psychology, 8*, 111–112.

Solomon, R. L. (1980). The opponent-process theory of acquired motivation: The costs of pleasure and the benefits of pain. *American Psychologist, 35*, 691–712.

Solomon, S., & Guglielmo, K. M. (1985). Treatment of headache by transcutaneous electrical stimulation. *Headache, 25*, 12–15.

Solowij, N., Michie, P. T., & Fox, A. M. (1995). Differential impairments of selective attention due to frequency and duration of cannabis use. *Biological Psychiatry, 37*, 731–739.

Sommer, B., Avis, N., Meyer, P., Ory, M., Madden, T., Kagawa-Singer, M., Mouton, C., Rasor, N. O., & Adler, S. (1999). Attitudes toward menopause and aging across ethnic/racial groups. *Psychosomatic Medicine, 61*, 868–875.

Sommers, S. (1984). Reported emotions and conventions of emotionality among college students. *Journal of Personality and Social Psychology, 46*, 207–215.

Sonoo, M., Tsai-Shozawa, Y., Aoki, M., Nakatani, T., Hatanaka, Y., Mochizuki, A., Sawada, M., Kobayashi, K., & Shimizu, T. (1999). N18 in median somatosensory evoked potentials: A new indicator of medullary function for the diagnosis of brain death. *Journal of Neurology, Neurosurgery and Psychiatry, 67,* 374–378.

Sonstroem, R. J., & Bernardo, P. (1982). Intraindividual pregame state anxiety and basketball performance: A re-examination of the inverted-U curve. *Journal of Sport Psychology, 4,* 235–245.

Soresi, S., & Nota, L. (2000). A social skill training program for persons with Down's syndrome. *European Psychologist, 5,* 34–43.

Spangenberg, E. R., Crowley, A. E., & Henderson, P. W. (1996). Improving the store environment: Do olfactory cues affect evaluations and behaviors? *Journal of Marketing, 60,* 67–80.

Spangenberg, J., & Nel, E. M. (1983). The effect of equal-status contact on ethnic attitudes. *Journal of Social Psychology, 121,* 173–180.

Spangler, W. D. (1992). Validity of questionnaire and TAT measures of need for achievement: Two meta-analyses. *Psychological Bulletin, 112,* 140–154.

Spanos, N. P., & Hewitt, E. C. (1980). The hidden observer in hypnotic analgesia: Discovery or experimental creation? *Journal of Personality and Social Psychology, 49,* 1201–1214.

Spanos, N. P., Burgess, C. A., Burgess, M. F., Samuels, C., & Blois, W. O. (1999). Creating false memories of infancy with hypnotic and non-hypnotic procedures. *Applied Cognitive Psychology, 13,* 201–218.

Spanos, N. P., McNeil, C., & Stam, H. J. (1982). Hypnotically "reliving" a prior burn: Effects on blister formation and localized skin temperature. *Journal of Abnormal Psychology, 91,* 303–305.

Spanos, N., Weekes, J. R., & Bertrand, L. (1985). Multiple personality: A social psychological perspective. *Journal of Abormal Psychology, 94,* 362–376.

Sparks, G. G., & Pellechia, M. (1997). The effect of news stories about UFOs on readers' UFO beliefs: The role of confirming or disconfirming testimony from a scientist. *Communication Reports, 10,* 165–172.

Sparks, G. G., Pellechia, M., & Irvine, C. (1999). The repressive coping style and fright reactions to mass media. *Communication Research, 26,* 176–192.

Speisman, J. C., Lazarus, R. S., Mordkoff, A., & Davison, L. (1964). Experimental reduction of stress based on ego-defense theory. *Journal of Abnormal and Social Psychology, 68,* 367–380.

Spelke, E. S. (1998). Nativism, empiricism, and the origins of knowledge. *Infant Behavior and Development, 21,* 181–200.

Spengler, F., Godde, B., & Dinse, H. R. (1995). Effects of aging on topographic organization of somatosensory cortex. *Neuroreport, 6,* 469–473.

Sperling, G. (1960). The information available in brief visual presentations. *Psychological Monographs, 74* (498).

Sperry, R. W. (1982). Some effects of disconnecting the cerebral hemispheres. *Science, 217,* 1223–1226.

Spiegel, A. D., & Suskind, P. B. (1998). Chloroform-induced insanity defense confounds lawyer Lincoln. *History of Psychiatry, 8,* 487–500.

Spiegel, T. A. (1999). Rate of intake, bites, and chews—the interpretation of lean-obese differences. *Neuroscience and Biobehavioral Reviews, 24,* 229–237.

Spillmann, J., & Spillmann, L. (1993). The rise and fall of Hugo Münsterberg. *Journal of the History of the Behavioral Sciences, 29,* 322–338.

Spinella, M., Znamensky, V., Moroz, M., et al. (1999). Actions of NMDA and cholinergic receptor antagonists in the rostral ventromedial medulla upon beta-endorphin analgesia elicited from the ventrolateral periaqueductal gray. *Brain Research, 829,* 151–159.

Spitzer, R. L. (1975). On pseudoscience in science, logic in remission, and psychiatric diagnosis: A critique of Rosenhan's "On being sane in insane places." *Journal of Abnormal Psychology, 84,* 442–452.

Sprecher, S. (1989). The importance to males and females of physical attractiveness, earning potential, and expressiveness in initial attraction. *Sex Roles, 21,* 591–607.

Springer, S. P., & Deutsch, G. (1998). *Left brain, right brain* (5th ed.). New York: Freeman.

Staats, A. W. (1994). Psychological behaviorism and behaviorizing psychology. *Behavior Analyst, 17,* 93–114.

Stack, S., & Eshleman, J. R. (1998). Marital status and happiness: A 17–nation study. *Journal of Marriage and the Family, 60,* 527–536.

Stairs, A. (1992). Self-image, world-image: Speculations on identity from experiences with Inuit. *Ethos, 20,* 116–126.

Stajkovic, A. D., & Luthans, F. (1998). Self-efficacy and work-related performance: A meta-analysis. *Psychological Bulletin, 124,* 240–261.

Stankov, L., & Roberts, R. D. (1997). Mental speed is not the "basic" process of intelligence. *Personality and Individual Differences, 22,* 69–84.

Stanwick, M. (1998). A skeptic's appraisal of "A skeptical view of parapsychology," by Montague Keen. *Journal of the Society for Psychical Research, 62,* 257–263.

Stark, E. (1981, September). Pigeon patrol. *Science 81,* pp. 85–86.

Staw, B. M., & Ross, J. (1985). Stability in the midst of change: A dispositional approach to job attitudes. *Journal of Applied Psychology, 70,* 469–480.

Steblay, N.-M., & Bothwell, R. K. (1994). Evidence for hypnotically refreshed testimony: The view from the laboratory. *Law and Human Behavior, 18,* 635–651.

Steele, C. M. (1997). A threat in the air: How stereotypes shape intellectual identity and performance. *American Psychologist, 52,* 613–629.

Steele, C. M., & Aronson, J. (1995). Stereotype threat and the intellectual test performance of African Americans. *Journal of Personality and Social Psychology, 69,* 797–811.

Steele, C. M., & Josephs, R. A. (1990). Alcohol myopia: Its prized and dangerous effects. *American Psychologist, 45,* 921–933.

Steenland, K., & Deddens, J. A. (1997). Effect of travel and rest on performance of professional basketball players. *Sleep, 20,* 366–369.

Steers, R. M., & Porter, L. W. (Eds.) (1991). *Motivation and work behavior* (5th ed.). New York: McGraw-Hill.

Steers, R. M., & Rhodes, S. R. (1978). Major influences on employee attendance: A process model. *Journal of Applied Psychology, 63,* 391–407.

Stein, D. J. (2000). Neurobiology of the obsessive-compulsive spectrum disorders. *Biological Psychiatry, 47,* 296–304.

Stein, D. M., & Lambert, M. J. (1995). Graduate training in psychotherapy: Are therapy outcomes enhanced? *Journal of Consulting and Clinical Psychology, 63,* 182–196

Stein, J. A., & Newcomb, M. D. (1999). Adult outcomes of adolescent conventional and agentic orientations: A 20–year longitudinal study. *Journal of Early Adolescence, 19,* 39–65.

Stein, M. B., Jang, K. L., & Livesley, W. J. (1999). Heritability of anxiety sensitivity: A twin study. *American Journal of Psychiatry, 156,* 246–251.

Steinberg, L., Lamborn, S. D., Dornbusch, S. M., & Darling, N. (1992). Impact of parenting practices on adolescent achievement: Authoritative parenting, school achievement, and encouragement to succeed. *Child Development, 63,* 1266–1281.

Steiner, S. S., & Dince, W. M. (1981). Biofeedback efficacy studies: A critique of critiques. *Biofeedback and Self-Regulation, 6,* 275–288.

Steinkamp, F., Milton, J., & Morris, R. L. (1998). A meta-analysis of forced-choice experiments comparing clairvoyance and precognition. *Journal of Parapsychology, 62,* 193–218.

Stelmack, R. M. (1990). Biological bases of extraversion: Psychophysiological evidence. *Journal of Personality, 58,* 293–311.

Stelmack, R. M., & Stalikas, A. (1991). Galen and the humour theory of temperament. *Personality and Individual Differences, 12,* 255–263.

Stemberger, R. T., Turner, S. M., Beidel, D. C., & Calhoun, K. S. (1995). Social phobia: An analysis of possible developmental factors. *Journal of Abnormal Psychology, 104,* 526–531.

Stephan, W. G., Ybarra, O., & Bachman, G. (1999). Prejudice toward immigrants. *Journal of Applied Social Psychology, 29,* 2221–2237.

Stephan, W. G., Ybarra, O., Martinez, C. M., Schwarzwald, J., & Tur-Kaspa, M. (1998). Prejudice toward immigrants to Spain and Israel: An integrated threat theory analysis. *Journal of Cross-Cultural Psychology, 29,* 559–576.

Stephens, J. P. (2000). Is this informed consent? *Psychological Bulletin, 24,* 154.

Steptoe, A., Cropley, M., Griffith, J., & Kirschbaum, C. (2000). Job strain and anger expression predict early morning elevations in salivary cortisol. *Psychosomatic Medicine, 62,* 286–292.

Steptoe, A., Moses, J., Edwards, S., & Mathews, A. (1993). Exercise and responsivity to mental stress: Discrepancies between the subjective and physiological effects of aerobic training. *International Journal of Sport Psychology, 24,* 110–129.

Sternberg, R. J. (1996). The sound of silence: A nation responds to its gifted. *Roeper Review, 18,* 168–172.

Sternberg, R. J. (1999). A triarchic approach to the understanding and assessment of intelligence in multicultural populations. *Journal of School Psychology, 37,* 145–159.

Sternberg, R. J. (2000). Patterns of giftedness: A triarchic analysis. *Roeper Review, 22,* 231–235.

Sternberg, R. J., & Clinkenbeard, P. B. (1995). The triarchic model applied to identifying, teaching, and assessing gifted children. *Roeper Review, 17,* 255–260.

Sternberg, R. J., & Wagner, R. K. (1993). The *g*-ocentric view of intelligence and job performance is wrong. *Current Directions in Psychological Science, 2,* 1–5.

Sternberg, R. J., Torff, B., & Grigorenko, E. L. (1998). Teaching triarchically improves school achievement. *Journal of Educational Psychology, 90,* 374–384.

Stessman, J., Maaravi, Y., Hammerman-Rozenberg, R., & Cohen, A. (2000). The effects of physical activity on mortality in the Jerusalem 70–year-olds longitudinal study. *Journal of the American Geriatrics Society, 48,* 499–504.

Stewart, J. W., Garfinkel, R., Nunes, E. V., Donovan, S., & Klein, D. F. (1998). Atypical features and treatment response in the National Institute of Mental Health Treatment of Depression Collaborative Research Program. *Journal of Clinical Psychopharmacology, 18,* 429–434.

Stilwell, N. A., Wallick, M. M., Thal, S. E., & Burleson, J. A. (2000). Myers-Briggs type and medical specialty choice: A new look at an old question. *Teaching and Learning in Medicine, 12,* 14–20.

Stolerman, I. P., & Jarvis, M. J. (1995). The scientific case that nicotine is addictive. *Psychopharmacology, 117,* 2–10.

Stone, A. A., & Brownell, K. D. (1994). The stress-eating paradox: Multiple daily measurements in adult males and females. *Psychology and Health, 9,* 425–436.

Stone, A. A., Bovbjerg, D. H., Neale, J. M., & Napoli, A. (1992). Development of common cold symptoms following experimental rhinovirus infection is related to prior stressful life events. *Behavioral Medicine, 18,* 115–120.

Stone, A. A., Smyth, J. M., Kaell, A., & Hurewitz, A. (2000). Structured writing about stressful events: Exploring potential psychological mediators of positive health effects. *Health Psychology, 19,* 619–624.

Stone, N. J., & Moroney, W. F. (1998). Teaching undergraduate human factors: The need, the activities, and the benefits. *Teaching of Psychology, 25,* 185–189.

Storck, L. E. (1997). Cultural psychotherapy: A consideration of psychosocial class and cultural differences in group treatment. *Group, 21,* 331–349.

Stoving, R. K., Hangaard, J., Hansen-Nord, M., & Hagen, C. (1999). A review of endocrine changes in anorexia nervosa. *Journal of Psychiatric Research, 33,* 139–152.

Strack, F., Schwarz, N., Chassein, B., & Kern, D. (1990). Salience of comparison standards and the activation of social norms: Consequences for judgements of happiness and their communication. *British Journal of Social Psychology, 29,* 303–314.

Strassman, R. J. (1984). Adverse reactions to psychedelic drugs: A review of the literature. *Journal of Nervous and Mental Disease, 172,* 577–595.

Strauman, T. J., & Higgins, E. T. (1988). Self-discrepancies as predictors of vulnerability to distinct syndromes of chronic emotional distress. *Journal of Personality, 56,* 246–253.

Straus, M. A. (1991). Discipline and deviance: Physical punishment of children and violence and other crime in adulthood. *Social Problems, 38,* 133–154.

Straus, M. A., & Kantor, G. K. (1994). Corporal punishment of adolescents by parents: A risk factor in the epidemiology of depression, suicide, alcohol abuse, child abuse, and wife beating. *Adolescence, 29,* 543–561.

Straus, M. A., & Stewart, J. H. (1999). Corporal punishment by American parents: National data on prevalence, chronicity, severity, and duration, in relation to child and family characteristics. *Clinical Child and Family Psychology Review, 2,* 55–70.

Streitmatter, J. (1993). Gender differences in identity development: An examination of longitudinal data. *Adolescence, 28,* 55–66.

Stretch, R. H. (1991). Psychological readjustment of Canadian Vietnam veterans. *Journal of Consulting and Clinical Psychology, 59,* 188–189.

Stricker, E. M., & McCann, M. J. (1985). Visceral factors in the control of food intake. *Brain Research Bulletin, 14,* 687–692.

Stricker, E. M., & Verbalis, J. G. (1987). Biological bases of hunger and satiety. *Annals of Behavioral Medicine, 9,* 3–8.

Striegel-Moore, R. H., Silberstein, L. R., & Rodin, J. (1986). Toward an understanding of risk factors in bulimia. *American Psychologist, 41,* 246–263.

Stroebe, M. S. (1994). The broken heart phenomenon: An examination of the mortality of bereavement. *Journal of Community and Applied Social Psychology, 4,* 47–61.

Stroebe, W., Stroebe, M. S., & Abakoumkin, G. (1999). Does differential social support cause sex differences in bereavement outcome? *Journal of Community and Applied Social Psychology, 9,* 1–12.

Stuart, G. L., Treat, T. A., & Wade, W. A. (2000). Effectiveness of an empirically based treatment for panic disorder delivered in a service clinic setting: 1 year follow-up. *Journal of Consulting and Clinical Psychology, 68,* 506–512.

Studebaker, C. A., & Penrod, S. D. (1997). Pretrial publicity: The media, the law, and common sense. *Psychology, Public Policy, and Law, 3,* 428–460.

Stunkard, A. J., Stinnett, J. L., & Smoller, J. W. (1986). Psychological and social aspects of the surgical treatment of obesity. *American Journal of Psychiatry, 143,* 417–429.

Sue, D. W., Bingham, R. P., Porché-Burke, & Vasquez, M. (1999). The diversification of psychology: A multicultural revolution. *American Psychologist, 54,* 1061–1069.

Sue, S. (1998). In search of cultural competence in psychotherapy and counseling. *American Psychologist, 53,* 440–448.

Sue, S. (1999). Science, ethnicity, and bias: Where have we gone wrong? *American Psychologist, 54,* 1070–1077.

Suedfeld, P., & Borrie, R. A. (1999). Health and therapeutic applications of chamber and flotation restricted environmental stimulation therapy (REST). *Psychology and Health, 14,* 545–566.

Suh, E., Diener, E., & Fujita, F. (1996). Events and subjective well-being. Only recent events matter. *Journal of Personality and Social Psychology, 70,* 1091–1102.

Super, C. M., & Harkness, S. (1997). The cultural structuring of child development. In J. W. Berry, P. R. Dasen, & T. S. Saraswathi (Eds.), *Handbook of cross-cultural psychology: Vol. 2. Basic processes and human development* (2nd ed., pp. 1–39). Boston: Allyn & Bacon.

Sussan, T. A. (1990). How to handle the process litigation effectively under the Education for All Handicapped Children Act of 1975. *Journal of Reading, Writing, and Learning Disabilities International, 6,* 63–70.

Sussman, S. (1998). The first asylums in Canada: A response to neglectful community care and current trends. *Canadian Journal of Psychiatry, 43,* 260–264.

Svirsky, M. A., Robbins, A. M., Kirk, K. I., Pisoni, D. B., & Miyamoto, R. T. (2000). Language development in profoundly deaf children with cochlear implants. *Psychological Science, 11,* 153–158.

Swain, J. J., Allard, G. B., & Holborn, S. W. (1982). The good toothbrushing game: A school-based dental hygiene program for increasing the toothbrushing effectiveness of children. *Journal of Applied Behavior Analysis, 15,* 171–176.

Swann, W. B., Jr., Hixon, J. G., & De La Ronde, C. (1992). Embracing the bitter "truth": Negative self-concepts and marital commitment. *Psychological Science, 3,* 118–121.

Swayze, V. W. (1995). Frontal leukotomy and related psychosurgical procedures in the era before antipsychotics (1935–1954): A historical overview. *American Journal of Psychiatry, 152,* 505–515.

Sweat, J. A., & Durm, M. W. (1993). Psychics: Do police departments really use them? *Skeptical Inquirer, 17,* 148–158.

Sweeney, P. D., Anderson, K., & Bailey, S. (1986). Attributional style in depression: A meta-analytic review. *Journal of Personality and Social Psychology, 50,* 974–991.

Swendsen, J. D., Tennen, H., Carney, M. A., Affleck, G., Willard, A., & Hromi, A. (2000). Mood and alcohol consumption: An experience sampling test of the self-medication hypothesis. *Journal of Abnormal Psychology, 109,* 198–204.

Swenson, C. R. (1994). Freud's "Anna O.": Social work's Bertha Pappenheim. *Clinical Social Work Journal, 22,* 149–163.

Swiezy, N. B., Matson, J. L., & Box, P. (1992). The Good Behavior Game: A token reinforcement system for preschoolers. *Child and Family Behavior Therapy, 14,* 21–32.

Swihart, G., Yuille, J., & Porter, S. (1999). The role of state-dependent memory in "red-outs." *International Journal of Law and Psychiatry, 22,* 199–212.

Swindale, N. V. (1982). The development of columnar systems in the mammalian visual cortex: The role of innate and environmental factors. *Trends in Neurosciences, 5,* 235–241.

Swindale, N. V. (2000). How many maps are there in visual cortex? *Cerebral Cortex, 10,* 633–643.

Taddese, A., Nah, S.-Y., & McCleskey, E. W. (1995). Selective opioid inhibition of small nociceptive neurons. *Science, 270,* 1366–1369.

Tafarodi, R. W., & Walters, P. (1999). Individualism-collectivism, life events, and self-esteem: A test of two trade-offs. *European Journal of Social Psychology, 29,* 797–814.

Tajfel, H. (1981). *Human groups and social categories: Studies in social psychology.* London: Cambridge University Press.

Tajfel, H., & Billig, M. (1974). Familarity and categorization in intergroup behavior. *Journal of Experimental Social Psychology, 10,* 159–170.

Takagi, M., Toda, H., Yoshizawa, T., & Hara, N. (1992). Ocular convergence-related neuronal responses in the lateral suprasylvian area of alert cats. *Neuroscience Research, 15,* 229–234.

Takahata, Y., Hasegawa, T., & Nishida, T. (1984). Chimpanzee predation in the Mahale Mountains from August 1979 to May 1982. *International Journal of Primatology, 5,* 213–233.

Takeuchi, D. T., Sue, S., & Yeh, M. (1995). Return rates and outcomes from ethnicity-specific mental health programs. *American Journal of Public Health, 85,* 638–643.

Taleb, M., Rouillon, F., Petitjean, F., & Gorwood, P. (1996). Cross-cultural study of schizophrenia. *Psychopathology, 29,* 85–94.

Taller, A. M., Asher, D. M., Pomeroy, K. L., & Eldadah, B. A. (1996). Search for viral nucleic acid sequences in brain tissues of patients with schizophrenia using nested polymerase chain reaction. *Archives of General Psychiatry, 53,* 32–40.

Tam, W.-C. C., & Sewell, K. W. (1995). Seasonality of birth in schizophrenia in Taiwan. *Schizophrenia Bulletin, 21,* 117–127.

Tang, S. H., & Hall, V. C. (1995). The overjustification effect: A meta-analysis. *Applied Cognitive Psychology, 9,* 365–404.

Tankard, J. W. (1984). *The statistical pioneers.* Cambridge, MA: Schenkman.

Task Force on the Use of Laboratory Tests in Psychiatry. (1985). Tricyclic antidepressants—blood level measurements and clinical outcome: An APA task force report. *American Journal of Psychiatry, 142,* 155–162.

Tateyama, M., Asai, M., Kamisada, M., & Hashimoto, M. (1993). Comparison of schizophrenic delusions between Japan and Germany. *Psychopathology, 26,* 151–158.

Tateyama, M., Kudo, I., Hashimoto, M. Abe, Y., et al. (1999). Is paranoid schizophrenia the most common subtype? Comparison of subtype diagnoses by Japanese and European psychiatrists, using summaries of the same patients. *Psychopathology, 32,* 98–106.

Tauer, C. A. (1994). The NIH trials of growth hormone for short stature. *IRB: A Review of Human Subjects Research, 16,* 1–9.

Taulbee, P. (1983). Solving the mystery of anxiety. *Science News, 124,* 45.

Taylor, B. A., Levin, L., & Jasper, S. (1999). Increasing play-related statements in children with autism toward their siblings: Effects of video modeling. *Journal of Development and Physical Disabilities, 11,* 253–264.

Taylor, C. R., & Stern, B. B. (1997). Asian-Americans: Television advertising and the "model minority" stereotype. *Journal of Advertising, 26,* 47–61.

Taylor, S., & Goritsas, E. (1994). Dimensions of identity diffusion. *Journal of Personality Disorders, 8,* 229–239.

Taylor, S. E., & Brown, J. D. (1988). Illusion and well-being: A social psychological perspective on mental health. *Psychological Bulletin, 103,* 193–210.

Taylor, S. E., Kemeny, M. E., Reed, G. M., Bower, J. E., & Gruenewald, T. L. (2000). Psychological resources, positive illusions, and health. *American Psychologist, 55,* 99–109.

Taylor, S. E., Klein, L. C., Lewis, B. P., et al. (2000). Biobehavioral responses to stress in females: Tend-and-befriend, not fight-or-flight. *Psychological Review, 107,* 411–429.

Teasdale, N., Forget, R., Bard, C., & Paillard, J. (1993). The role of proprioceptive information for the production of isometric forces and for handwriting tasks. *Acta Psychologica, 82,* 179–191.

Teichman, Y., & Teichman, M. (1990). Interpersonal view of depression: Review and integration. *Journal of Family Psychology, 3,* 349–367.

Teigen, K. H. (1994). Yerkes-Dodson: A law for all seasons. *Theory and Psychology, 4,* 525–547.

Tellegen, A., Lykken, D. T., Bouchard, T. J., Jr., Wilcox, K. J., Segal, N. L., & Rich, S. (1988). Personality similarity in twins reared apart and together. *Journal of Personality and Social Psychology, 54,* 1031–1039.

Templeton, L. M., & Wilcox, S. A. (2000). A tale of two representations: The misinformation effect and children's developing theory of mind. *Child Development, 71*, 402–416.

Teng, E., & Squire, L. R. (1999). Memory for places learned long ago is intact after hippocampal damage. *Nature, 400*, 675–677.

Terrace, H. S. (1985). In the beginning was the "name." *American Psychologist, 40*, 1011–1028.

Terrace, H. S., Petitto, L. A., Sanders, R. J., & Bever, T. G. (1979). Can an ape create a sentence? *Science, 206*, 891–902.

Thakker, J., & Ward, T. (1998). Culture and classification: The cross-cultural application of the *DSM-IV. Clinical Psychology Review, 18*, 501–529.

Thakker, J., Ward, T., & Strongman, K. T. (1999). Mental disorder and cross-cultural psychology: A constructivist perspective. *Clinical Psychology Review, 19*, 843–874.

Thase, M. E., Greenhouse, J. B., Frank, E., et al. (1997). Treatment of major depression with psychotherapy or psychotherapy-pharmacotherapy combinations. *Archives of General Psychiatry, 54*, 1009–1015.

Theorell, T., Blomkvist, V., Jonsson, H., & Schulman, S. (1995). Social support and the development of immune function in human immunodeficiency virus infection. *Psychosomatic Medicine, 57*, 32–36.

Thomas, E. (1988). Forebrain mechanisms in the relief of fear: The role of the lateral septum. *Psychobiology, 16*, 36–44.

Thomas, H. (1993). A theory explaining sex differences in high mathematical ability has been around for some time. *Behavioral and Brain Sciences, 16*, 187–189.

Thomas, R. E., Vaidya, S. C., Herrick, R. T., & Congleton, J. (1993). The effects of biofeedback on carpal tunnel syndrome. *Ergonomics, 36*, 353–361.

Thomas, T. N. (1997). Sleepwalking disorder and *mens rea*: A review and case report. *Journal of Forensic Sciences, 42*, 17–24.

Thompson, B. (1994). The pivotal role of replication in psychological research: Empirically evaluating the replicability of sample results. *Journal of Personality, 62*, 157–176.

Thompson, J. K., Coovert, M. D., Richards, K. J., & Johnson, S. (1995). Development of body image, eating disturbance, and general psychological functioning in female adolescents: Covariance structure modeling and longitudinal investigations. *International Journal of Eating Disorders, 18*, 221–236.

Thompson, L. (1995, June 12). Search for a gay gene. *Time*, pp. 60–61.

Thompson, P. B., & Lambert, J. V. (1995). Touch sensitivity through latex examination gloves. *Journal of General Psychology, 122*, 47–58.

Thompson, S. M. (2000). Synaptic plasticity: Building memories to last. *Current Biology, 10*, R218–R221.

Thorndike, E. L. (1898). Animal intelligence: An experimental study of the associative processes in animals. *Psychological Review Monograph Supplement, 2* (8).

Thorndike, E. L. (1961). Edward Lee Thorndike. In C. Murchison (Ed.), *A history of psychology in autobiography* (Vol. 1, pp. 263–270). New York: Russell & Russell.

Throne, L. C., Bartholomew, J. B., Craig, J., & Farrar, R. P. (2000). Stress reactivity in fire fighters: An exercise intervention. *International Journal of Stress Management, 7*, 235–246.

Thurstone, L. L. (1938). *Primary mental abilities.* Chicago: University of Chicago Press.

Tiefer, L. (1995). *Sex is not a natural act and other essays.* Boulder, CO: Westview Press.

Tierney, A. J. (2000). Egas Moniz and the origins of psychosurgery: A review commemorating the 50th anniversary of Moniz's Nobel Prize. *Journal of the History of the Neurosciences, 9*, 22–36.

Till, B. D., & Priluck, R. L. (2000). Stimulus generalization in classical conditioning: An initial investigation and extension. *Psychology and Marketing, 17*, 55–72.

Tilley, A. J., & Empson, J. A. (1978). REM sleep and memory consolidation. *Biological Psychology, 6*, 293–300.

Timberlake, W., & Farmer-Dougan, V. A. (1991). Reinforcement in applied settings: Figuring out ahead of time what will work. *Psychological Bulletin, 110*, 379–391.

Timberlake, W., & Melcer, T. (1988). Effects of poisoning on predatory and ingestive behavior toward artificial prey in rats (*Rattus norvegicus*). *Journal of Comparative Psychology, 102*, 182–187.

Timmann, D., Watts, S., & Hare, J. (1999). Failure of cerebellar patients to time finger opening precisely causes ball high-low inaccuracy in overarm throws. *Journal of Neurophysiology, 82*, 103–114.

Timney, B., & Keil, K. (1996). Horses are sensitive to pictorial depth cues. *Perception, 25*, 1121–1128.

Tolman, E. C. (1932). *Purposive behavior in animals and man.* New York: Appleton-Century-Crofts.

Tolman, E. C., & Honzik, C. H. (1930). Introduction and removal of reward, and maze performance in rats. *University of California Publications in Psychology, 4*, 257–275.

Tomlinson-Keasey, C. (1990). The working lives of Terman's gifted women. In H. Y. Grossman & N. L. Chester (Eds.), *The experience and meaning of work in women's lives* (pp. 213–240). Hillsdale, NJ: Erlbaum.

Topp, L., Hando, J., Dillon, P., Roche, A., & Solowij, N. (1999). Ecstasy use in Australia: Patterns of use and associated harm. *Drug and Alcohol Dependence, 55*, 105–115.

Torrey, E. F., Miller, J., Rawlings, R., & Yolken, R. H. (1997). Seasonality of births in schizophrenia and bipolar disorder: A review of the literature. *Schizophrenia Research, 28*, 1–38.

Torri, G., Cecchettin, M., Bellometti, S., & Galzigna, L. (1995). Analgesic effect and beta-endorphin and substance P levels in plasma after short-term administration of a ketoprofen-lysine salt or acetylsalicylic acid in patients with osteoarthrosis. *Current Therapeutic Research, 56*, 62–69.

Toth, L. A., & Krueger, J. M. (1990). Somnogenic, pyrogenic thermatologic effects of experimental pasteurellosis in rabbits. *American Journal of Physiology, 258*, R536–R542.

Toufexis, A. (1990, December 17). Drowsy America. *Time*, pp. 78–85.

Toukmanian, S. G., & Brouwers, M. C. (1998). Cultural aspects of self-disclosure and psychotherapy. In S. S. Kazarian & D. R. Evans (Eds.), *Cultural clinical psychology: Theory, research, and practice* (pp. 106–124). New York: Oxford University Press.

Tran, Y., Craig, A., & McIsaac, P. (2001). Extraversion-introversion and 8–13 Hz waves in frontal cortical regions. *Personality and Individual Differences, 30*, 205–215.

Tranel, D. (1995). Where did my arm go? *Contemporary Psychology, 40*, 885–887.

Tranel, D., & Damasio, A. R. (1985). Knowledge without our awareness: An automatic index of facial recognition by prosopagnosics. *Science, 228*, 1453–1454.

Trappey, C. (1996). A meta-analysis of consumer choice and subliminal advertising. *Psychology and Marketing, 13*, 517–530.

Trask, P. C., & Sigmon, S. T. (1999). Ruminating and distracting: The effects of sequential tasks on depressed mood. *Cognitive Therapy and Research, 23*, 231–246.

Treffert, D. A. (1989). *Extraordinary people: Understanding savant syndrome.* New York: Harper & Row.

Triandis, H. C. (1990). Theoretical concepts that are applicable to the analysis of ethnocentrism. In R. W. Brislin (Ed.), *Applied cross-cultural psychology* (pp. 34–55). Newbury Park, CA: Sage.

Trice, A. D., & Ogden, E. P. (1987). Informed consent: 9. Effects of the withdrawal clause in longitudinal research. *Perceptual and Motor Skills, 65*, 135–138.

Trierweiler, S. J., Neighbors, H. W., Munday, C., et al. (2000). Clinician attributions associated with the diagnosis of schizophrenia in African American and non-African American patients. *Journal of Consulting and Clinical Psychology, 68*, 171–175.

Trijsburg, R. W., Jelicic, M., van den Broek, W. W., & Plekker, A. E. M. (1996). Exposure and participant modelling in a case of injection phobia. *Psychotherapy and Psychosomatics, 65*, 57–61.

Tripathy, S. P., Levi, D. M., Ogmen, H., & Harden, C. (1995). Perceived length across the physiological blind spot. *Visual Neuroscience, 12*, 385–402.

Triplett, N. (1898). The dynamogenic factors in pacemaking and competition. *American Journal of Psychology, 9*, 507–553.

Troster, H., & Bambring, M. (1992). Early social-emotional development in blind infants. *Child Care, Health and Development, 18*, 207–227.

Trotter, R. J. (1981). Psychiatry for the 80's. *Science News, 119*, 348–349.

Trounson, R. (2000, March 1). Eichmann rationalizes his Nazi role in jail notebooks. *Los Angeles Times*, (pp. A1 et seq.).

Tsai, D. C., & Pike, P. L. (2000). Effects of acculturation on the MMPI-2 scores of Asian American students. *Journal of Personality Assessment, 74*, 216–230.

Tsai, G. E., Condie, D., Wu, M.-T., & Chang, I.-W. (1999). Functional magnetic resonance imaging of personality switches in a woman with dissociative identity disorder. *Harvard Review of Psychiatry, 7*, 119–122.

Tsuang, M. (2000). Schizophrenia: Genes and environment. *Biological Psychiatry, 47*, 210–220.

Tubbs, M. E. (1986). Goal setting: A meta-analytic examination of the empirical evidence. *Journal of Applied Psychology, 71*, 474–483.

Tucker, W. H. (1997). Re-considering Burt: Beyond a reasonable doubt. *Journal of the History of the Behavioral Sciences, 33*, 145–162.

Tulsky, F. N. (1986, March 28). $988,000 is awarded in suit over lost psychic power. *Philadelphia Inquirer*, p. 1–A.

Tulving, E. (1985). How many memory systems are there? *American Psychologist, 40*, 385–398.

Tulving, E. (1993). What is episodic memory? *Current Directions in Psychological Science, 2*, 67–70.

Tulving, E., & Markowitsch, H. J. (1998). Episodic and declarative memory: Role of the hippocampus. *Hippocampus, 8*, 198–204.

Tulving, E., & Thomson, D. M. (1973). Encoding specificity and retrieval processes in episodic memory. *Psychological Review, 80*, 352–373.

Turgeon, L., Marchand, A., & Dupuis, G. (1998). Clinical features in panic disorder with agoraphobia: A comparison of men and women. *Journal of Anxiety Disorders, 12*, 539–553.

Turk, C. L., Heimberg, R. G., Orsillo, S. M., Holt, C. S., et al. (1998). An investigation of gender differences in social phobia. *Journal of Anxiety Disorders, 12*, 209–223.

Turkheimer, E. (1991). Individual and group differences in adoption studies of IQ. *Psychological Bulletin, 110*, 392–405.

Turkheimer, E. (1998). Heritability and biological explanation. *Psychological Review, 105*, 782–791.

Turnbull, C. M. (1961). Some observations regarding the experiences of the Bambuti Pygmies. *American Journal of Psychology, 74*, 304–308.

Turner, S. M., Beidel, D. C., & Costello, A. (1987). Psychopathology in the offspring of anxiety disorder patients. *Journal of Consulting and Clinical Psychology, 55*, 229–235.

Twisk, J. W. R., Snel, J., Kemper, H. C. G., & van Mechelen, W. (1999). Changes in daily hassles and life events and the relationship with coronary heart disease risk factors: A 2–year longitudinal study in 27–29–yr-old males and females. *Journal of Psychosomatic Research, 46,* 229–240.

Tyson, P. D., & Sobschak, K. B. (1994). Perceptual responses to infant crying after EEG biofeedback assisted stress management training: Implications for physical child abuse. *Child Abuse and Neglect, 18,* 933–943.

Ujita, H., Yokota, T., Tanikawa, N., & Mutoh, K. (1996). Computer-aided instruction systems for plant operators. *International Journal of Human-Computer Studies, 45,* 397–412.

Ullman, M., Krippner, S., & Vaughan, A. (1973). *Dream telepathy.* New York: Macmillan.

Ullmann, L. P., & Krasner, L. (1975). *Psychological approaches to abnormal behavior.* Englewood Cliffs, NJ: Prentice Hall.

Ulrich, R. E., Stachnik, T. J., & Stainton, N. R. (1963). Student acceptance of generalized personality interpretations. *Psychological Reports, 13,* 831–834.

Unger, G., Desiderio, D. M., & Parr, W. (1972). Isolation, identification and synthesis of a specific-behavior-inducing brain peptide. *Nature, 238,* 198–202.

Urban, M. O., Coutinho, S. V., & Gebhardt, G. F. (1999). Involvement of excitatory amino acid receptors and nitric oxide in the rostral ventromedial medulla in modulating secondary hyperalgesia produced by mustard oil. *Pain, 81,* 45–55.

Usher, J. A., & Neisser, U. (1993). Childhood amnesia and the beginnings of memory for four early life events. *Journal of Experimental Psychology: General, 122,* 155–165.

Vaillant, G. E., & Milofsky, E. (1980). Natural history of male psychological health: 9. Empirical evidence for Erikson's model of the life cycle. *American Journal of Psychiatry, 137,* 1348–1359.

Valacich, J. S., & Schwenk, C. (1995). Devil's advocate and dialectical inquiry effects on face-to-face and computer-mediated group decision making. *Organizational Behavior and Human Decision Processes, 63,* 158–173.

Valentine, C. W. (1930). The innate bases of fear. *Journal of Genetic Psychology, 37,* 485–497.

Vallerand, R. J., & Losier, G. F. (1999). An integrative analysis of intrinsic and extrinsic motivation in sport. *Journal of Applied Sport Psychology, 11,* 142–169.

van Beek, N., & Griez, E. (2000). Reactivity to a 35% CO-sub-2 challenge in health first-degree relative of patients with panic disorder. *Biological Psychiatry, 47,* 830–835.

Van Boven, R. B., Hamilton, R. H., Kauffman, T., Keenan, J. P., & Pascual-Leone, A. (2000). Tactile spatial resolution in blind Braille readers. *Neurology, 54,* 2230–2236.

van Dam-Baggen, R., & Kraaimaat, F. W. (2000). Social skills training in two subtypes of psychiatric inpatients with generalized social phobia. *Scandinavian Journal of Behaviour Therapy, 29,* 14–21.

Van de Water, T. J. (1997). Psychology's entrepeneurs and the marketing of industrial psychology. *Journal of Applied Psychology, 82,* 486–499.

van der Kolk, B. A. (2000). Trauma, neuroscience, and the etiology of hysteria: An exploration of the relevance of Breuer and Freud's 1893 article in light of modern science. *Journal of the American Academy of Psychoanalysis, 28,* 237–262.

van der Linden, G. J. H., Stein, D. J., & van Balkom, A. J. L. M. (2000). The efficacy of the selective serotonin reuptake inhibitors for social anxiety disorder (social phobia): A meta-analysis of randomized controlled trials. *International Clinical Psychopharmacology, 15,* S15–S23.

van der Pompe, G., Antoni, M. H., & Heijnen, C. J. (1998). The effects of surgical stress and psychological stress on the immune function of operative cancer patients. *Psychology and Health, 13,* 1015–1026.

van der Valk, J. C., Verhulst, F. C., Neale, M. C., & Boomsma, D. I. (1998). Longitudinal genetic analysis of problem behaviors in biologically related and unrelated adoptees. *Behavior Genetics, 28,* 365–380.

van Dixhoorn, J. (1998). Cardiorespiratory effects of breathing and relaxation instruction in myocardial infarction patients. *Biological Psychology, 49,* 123–135.

Van Doornen, L. J. P., & van Blokland, R. (1987). Serum-cholesterol: Sex specific psychological correlates during rest and stress. *Journal of Psychosomatic Research, 31,* 239–249.

Van Eerde, W., & Thierry, H. (1996). Vroom's expectancy models and work-related criteria: A meta-analysis. *Journal of Applied Psychology, 81,* 575–586.

Van Horn, K. R., Arnone, A., Nesbitt, K., et al. (1997). Physical distance and interpersonal characteristics in college students' romantic relationships. *Personal Relationships, 4,* 25–34.

van IJzendoorn, M. H., & De Wolff, M. S. (1997). In search of the absent father: Meta-analysis of infant-father attachment. A rejoinder to our discussants. *Child Development, 68,* 604–609.

van Lankveld, J. J. D. M. (1998). Bibliotherapy in the treatment of sexual dysfunctions: A meta-analysis. *Journal of Consulting and Clinical Psychology, 66,* 702–708.

Vance, E. B., & Wagner, N. N. (1976). Written descriptions of orgasm: A study of sex differences. *Archives of Sexual Behavior, 5,* 87–98.

VandenBos, G. R. (1996). Outcome assessment of psychotherapy. *American Psychologist, 51,* 1005–1006.

VanderZee, K., Buunk, B., & Sanderman, R. (1996). The relation between social comparison processes and personality. *Personality and Individual Differences, 20,* 551–565.

Vargas, E. A., & Vargas, J. S. (1991). Programmed instruction: What it is and how to do it. *Journal of Behavioral Education, 1,* 235–251.

Vecera, S. P., & O'Reilly, R. C. (1998). Figure-ground organization and object recognition processes: An interactive account. *Journal of Experimental Psychology: Human Perception and Performance, 24,* 441–462.

Vein, A. M., Sidorov, A. A., Martazaev, M. S., & Karlov, A. V. (1991). Physical exercise and nocturnal sleep in healthy humans. *Human Physiology, 17,* 391–397.

Veissier, I. (1993). Observational learning in cattle. *Applied Animal Behaviour Science, 35,* 235–243.

Vernon, P. A. (1998). From the cognitive to the biological: A sketch of Arthur Jensen's contributions to the study of g. *Intelligence, 26,* 267–271.

Veroff, J., Depner, C., Kulka, R., & Douvan, E. (1980). Comparison of American motives: 1957 versus 1976. *Journal of Personality and Social Psychology, 39,* 1249–1262.

Vigliocco, G., Vinson, D. P., Martin, R. C., & Garrett, M. F. (1999). Is "count" and "mass" information available when the noun is not? An investigation of tip of the tongue states and anomia. *Journal of Memory and Language, 40,* 534–558.

Vincent, K. R. (1991). Black/white IQ differences: Does age make the difference? *Journal of Clinical Psychology, 47,* 266–270.

Viney, W. (1989). The cyclops and the twelve-eyed toad: William James and the unity-disunity problem in psychology. *American Psychologist, 44,* 1261–1265.

Viney, W. (1990). The tempering effect of determinism in the legal system: A response to Rychlak and Rychlak. *New Ideas in Psychology, 8,* 31–42.

Viney, W. (1993). *A history of psychology: Ideas and context.* Boston: Allyn & Bacon.

Vita, A., Dieci, M., Silenzi, C., et al. (2000). Cerebral ventricular enlargement as a generalized feature of schizophrenia: A distribution analysis on 502 subjects. *Schizophrenia Research, 44,* 25–34.

Vittorio Caprara, G., Barbaranelli, C., Bermudez, J., Maslach, C., & Ruch, W. (2000). Multivariate methods for the comparison of factor structures in cross-cultural research: An illustration with the Big Five Questionnaire. *Journal of Cross-Cultural Psychology, 31,* 437–464.

Vlaander, G. P., & Van Rooijen, L. (1985). Independence and conformity in Holland: Asch's experiment three decades later. *Gedrag: Tijdschrift voor Psychologie, 13,* 49–55.

Voeller, B. (1991). AIDS and heterosexual anal intercourse. *Archives of Sexual Behavior, 20,* 233–276.

Vogler, G. P., Mcclearn, G. E., Snieder, H., & Boomsma, D. I. (1997). Genetics and behavioral medicine: Risk factors for cardiovascular disease. *Behavioral Medicine, 22,* 141–149.

Vokey, J. R., & Read, J. D. (1985). Subliminal messages: Between the devil and the media. *American Psychologist, 40,* 1231–1239.

Vollenweider, F. X., Gamma, A., Liechti, M., & Huber, T. (1998). Psychological and cardiovascular effects and short-term sequelae of MDMA ("Ecstasy") in MDMA-naive healthy volunteers. *Neuropsychopharmacology, 19,* 241–251.

Volling, B. L., & Feagans, L. V. (1995). Infant day care and children's social competence. *Infant Behavior and Development, 18,* 177–188.

von Mayrhauser, R. T. (1989). Making intelligence functional: Walter Dill Scott and applied psychological testing in World War I. *Journal of the History of the Behavioral Sciences, 25,* 60–72.

Vosburg, S. K. (1998). The effects of positive and negative mood on divergent-thinking performance. *Creativity Research Journal, 11,* 165–172.

Voss, K., Markiewicz, D., & Doyle, A. B. (1999). Friendship, marriage and self-esteem. *Journal of Social and Personal Relationships, 16,* 103–122.

Voyer, D., Voyer, S., & Bryden, M. P. (1995). Magnitude of sex differences in spatial abilities: A meta-analysis and consideration of critical variables. *Psychological Bulletin, 117,* 250–270.

Vrij, A. (1997). Wearing black clothes: The impact of offenders' and suspects' clothing on impression formation. *Applied Cognitive Psychology, 11,* 47–53.

Vroom, V. H. (1964). *Work and motivation.* New York: Wiley.

Vuksic-Mihaljevic, Z., Mandic, N., Barkic, J., & Mrdenovic, S. (1998). A current psychodynamic understanding of panic disorder. *British Journal of Medical Psychology, 71,* 27–45.

Wadden, T. A., Vogt, R. A., Foster, G. D., & Anderson, D. A. (1998). Exercise and the maintenance of weight loss: 1–year follow-up of a controlled clinical trial. *Journal of Counsulting and Clinical Psychology, 66,* 429–433.

Wade, T., Martin, N. G., Neale, M. C., Tiggemann, M., Treloar, S. A., Bucholz, K. K., Madden, P. A. F., & Heath, A. C. (1999). The structure of genetic and environmental risk factors for three measures of disordered eating. *Psychological Medicine, 29,* 925–934.

Wade, T. D., Bulik, C. M., Neale, M., & Kendler, K. S. (2000). Anorexia nervosa and major depression: Shared genetic and environmental risk factors. *American Journal of Psychiatry, 157,* 469–471.

Wagstaff, G. F., & Frost, R. (1996). Reversing and breaching posthypnotic amnesia and hypnotically created pseudomemories. *Contemporary Hypnosis, 13,* 191–197.

Wagstaff, G. F., Vella, M., & Perfect, T. (1992). The effect of hypnotically elicited testimony on jurors' judgments of guilt and innocence. *Journal of Social Psychology, 132,* 591–595.

Wahlsten, D. (1999). Single-gene influences on behavior. *Annual Review of Psychology, 50,* 599–624.

Wahlund, L.-O. (1996). Magnetic resonance imaging and computed tomography in Alzheimer's disease. *Acta Neurologica Scandinavica Supplementum, 94,* 50–53.

Waid, W. M., & Orne, M. T. (1982). The physiological detection of deception. *American Scientist, 70,* 402–409.

Waid, W. M., Wilson, S. K., & Orne, M. T. (1981). Cross-modal physiological effects of electrodermal ability in the detection of deception. *Journal of Personality and Social Psychology, 40,* 1118–1125.

Walcott, D. M. (2000). Repressed memory still lacks scientific reliability. *Journal of the American Academy of Psychiatry and the Law, 28,* 243–244.

Walczyk, J. J. (2000). The interplay between automatic and control processes in reading. *Reading Research Quarterly, 35,* 554–566.

Wald, G. (1964). The receptors of human color vision. *Science, 145,* 1007–1017.

Waldhauser, F., Saletu, B., & Trinchard, L. I. (1990). Sleep laboratory investigations on hypnotic properties of melatonin. *Psychopharmacology, 100,* 222–226.

Waldrop, M. M. (1984). Artificial intelligence in parallel. *Science, 225,* 608–610.

Walen, H. R., & Lachman, M. E. (2000). Social support and strain from partner, family, and friends: Costs and benefits for men and women in adulthood. *Journal of Social and Personal Relationships, 17,* 5–30.

Walker, E., Hoppes, E., Emory, E., Mednick, S., & Schulsinger, F. (1981). Environmental factors related to schizophrenia in psychophysiologically labile high-risk males. *Journal of Abnormal Psychology, 90,* 313–320.

Walker, L. J. (1986). Experiential and cognitive sources of moral development in adulthood. *Human Development, 29,* 113–124.

Walker, L. J. (1989). A longitudinal study of moral reasoning. *Child Development, 60,* 157–166.

Walker, M. B., & Andrade, M. G. (1996). Conformity in the Asch task as a function of age. *Journal of Social Psychology, 136,* 367–372.

Wall, T. N., & Hayes, J. A. (2000). Depressed clients' attributions of responsibility for the causes of and solutions to their problems. *Journal of Counseling and Development, 78,* 81–86.

Wallabaum, A. B., Rzewnicki, R., Steele, H., & Suedfeld, P. (1991). Progressive muscle relaxation and restricted environmental stimulation therapy for chronic tension headache: A pilot study. *International Journal of Psychosomatics, 38,* 33–39.

Wallace, A. (1986). *The prodigy.* New York: Dutton.

Wallace, C. S., Kilman, V. L., Withers, G. S., & Greenough, W. T. (1992). Increases in dendritic length in occipital cortex after 4 days of differential housing in weanling rats. *Behavioral and Neural Biology, 58,* 64–68.

Wallach, H., & Marshall, F. J. (1986). Shape constancy in pictorial representation. *Perception and Psychophysics, 39,* 233–235.

Waller, N. G., & Ross, C. A. (1997). The prevalence and biometric structure of pathological dissociation in the general population: Taxometric and behavior genetic findings. *Journal of Abnormal Psychology, 106,* 499–510.

Waller, N. G., Kojetin, B. A., Bouchard, T. J., & Lykken, D. T. (1990). Genetic and environmental influences on religious interests, attitudes, and values: A study of twins reared apart and together. *Psychological Science, 1,* 138–142.

Wallin, U., & Hansson, K. (1999). Anorexia nervosa in teenagers: Patterns of family function. *Nordic Journal of Psychiatry, 53,* 29–35.

Wallis, C. (1984, June 11). Unlocking pain's secrets. *Time,* pp. 58–66.

Walsh, J. (1983). Wide world of reports. *Science, 214,* 640–641.

Walsh, J. J., Wilding, J. M., & Eysenck, M. W. (1994). Stress responsivity: The role of individual differences. *Personality and Individual Differences, 16,* 385–394.

Walsleben, J. A., Norman, R. G., Novak, R. D., O'Malley, E. B., Rapoport, D. M., & Strohl, K. P. (1999). Sleep habits of Long Island Rail Road commuters. *Sleep, 22,* 728–734.

Walters, G. C., & Grusec, J. E. (1977). *Punishment.* San Francisco: Freeman.

Waltz, D. L. (1982, October). Artificial intelligence. *Scientific American,* pp. 118–133.

Wanberg, C. R., & Banas, J. T. (2000). Predictors and outcomes of openness to changes in a reorganizing workplace. *Journal of Applied Psychology, 85,* 132–142.

Wang, A. G. (2000). Storm phobia: A North Atlantic phenomenon. *Nordic Journal of Psychiatry, 54,* 67–68.

Wang, C. L., Briston, T., Mowen, J. C., & Chakraborty, G. (2000). Alternative modes of self-construal: Dimensions of connectedness-separateness and advertising appeals to the cultural and gender-specific self. *Journal of Consumer Psychology, 9,* 107–115.

Wang, J. Q., Mao, L., & Han, J.-S. (1992). Comparison of the antinociceptive effects induced by electroacupuncture and transcutaneous electrical nerve stimulation in the rat. *International Journal of Neuroscience, 65,* 117–129.

Wang, M. Q., Nicholson, M. E., Mahoney, B. S., & Li, Y. (1993). *Perceptual and Motor Skills, 77,* 83–88.

Wang, W., & Viney, L. L. (1997). The psychosocial development of children and adolescents in the People's Republic of China: An Eriksonian approach. *International Journal of Psychology, 32,* 139–153.

Wang, W., Wu, Y. X., Peng, Z. G., Lu, S. W., Yu, L., Wang, G. P., Fu, X. M., & Wang, Y. H. (2000). Test of sensation seeking in a Chinese sample. *Personality and Individual Differences, 28,* 169–179.

Wankel, L. M. (1993). The importance of enjoyment to adherence and psychological benefits from physical activity [Special Issue: Exercise and psychological well being]. *International Journal of Sport Psychology, 24,* 151–169.

Wann, D. L., & Schrader, M. P. (2000). Controllability and stability in the self-serving attributions of sport spectators. *Journal of Social Psychology, 140,* 160–168.

Wanzer, M. B., & Frymier, A. B. (1999). The relationship between student perceptions of instructor humor and student's reports of learning. *Communication Education, 48,* 48–62.

Ward, N. J., & Parkes, A. (1994). Head-up displays and their automotive application: An overview of human factors issues affecting safety. *Accident Analysis and Prevention, 26,* 703–717.

Ward, R., & Spitze, G. (1996). Will the children ever leave? Parent-child coresidence history and plans. *Journal of Family Issues, 17,* 514–539.

Warwick-Evans, L. A., Symons, N., Fitch, T., & Burrows, L. (1998). Evaluating sensory conflict and postural instability: Theories of motion sickness. *Brain Research Bulletin, 47,* 465–469.

Washburn, D. A., & Rumbaugh, D. M. (1997). Faster is smarter, so why are we slower? A comparative perspective on intelligence and processing speed. *American Psychologist, 52,* 1147–1148.

Washburn, M. F. (1908). *The animal mind: A textbook of comparative psychology.* New York: Macmillan.

Wasserman, E. A. (1997). What's elementary about associative learning? *Annual Review of Psychology, 48,* 573–607.

Waters, E., Merrick, S., Treboux, D., Crowell, J., & Albersheim, L. (2000). Attachment security in infancy and early adulthood: A 20-year longitudinal study. *Child Development, 71,* 684–689.

Waters, E., Weinfield, N. S., & Hamilton, C. E. (2000). The stability of attachment security from infancy to adolescence and early adulthood: General discussion. *Child Development, 71,* 703–706.

Waters, R. S., Samulack, D. D., Dykes, R. W., & McKinley, P. A. (1990). Topographic organization of baboon primary motor cortex: Face, hand, forelimb, and shoulder representation. *Somatosensory and Motor Research, 7,* 485–514.

Watson, D. C. (2001). Procrastination and the five-factor model: A facet level analysis. *Personality and Individual Differences, 30,* 149–158.

Watson, J. B. (1913). Psychology as the behaviorist views it. *Psychological Review, 20,* 158–177.

Watson, J. B. (1930). *Behaviorism.* New York: W. W. Norton.

Watson, J. B., & Rayner, R. (1920). Conditioned emotional reactions. *Journal of Experimental Psychology, 3,* 1–14.

Watt, S. J., & Bradshaw, M. F. (2000). Binocular cues are important in controlling the grasp but not the reach in natural prehension movements. *Neuropsychologia, 38,* 1473–1481.

Watten, R. G., Lie, I., & Birketvedt, O. (1994). The influence of long-term visual near-work on accommodation and vergence: A field study. *Journal of Human Ergology, 23,* 27–39.

Watters, P. A., Martin, F., & Schreter, Z. (1997). Caffeine and cognitive performance: The nonlinear Yerkes-Dodson Law. *Human Psychopharmacology Clinical and Experimental, 12,* 249–257.

Watts, B. L. (1982). Individual differences in circadian activity rhythms and their effects on roommate relationships. *Journal of Personality, 50,* 374–384.

Watts, R. E., & Critelli, J. W. (1997). Roots of contemporary cognitive theories in the individual psychology of Alfred Adler. *Journal of Cognitive Psychotherapy, 11,* 147–156.

Wax, M. L., (1999). The angel of dreams: Toward an ethnology of dream interpreting. *Journal of the American Academy of Psychoanalysis, 27,* 417–429.

Weaver, C. A. (1993). Do you need a "flash" to form a flashbulb memory? *Journal of Experimental Psychology: General, 122,* 39–46.

Weaver, J. B., Masland, J. L., Kharazmi, S., & Zillman, D. (1985). Effect of alcoholic intoxication on the appreciation of different types of humor. *Journal of Personality and Social Psychology, 49,* 781–787.

Webb, W. B. (1981). An essay on consciousness. *Teaching of Psychology, 8,* 15–19.

Webb, W. B. (1985). Sleep and dreaming. In G. A. Kimble & K. Schlesinger (Eds.), *Topics in the history of psychology* (Vol. 2, pp. 191–217). Hillsdale, NJ: Erlbaum.

Webb, W. B. (1992). *Sleep: The gentle tyrant* (2nd ed.). Boston: Anker.

Webb, W. B., & Agnew, H. W., Jr. (1974). Sleeping and waking in a time-free environment. *Aerospace Medicine, 45,* 617–622.

Weber, M. M., & Engstrom, E. J. (1997). Kraepelin's "diagnostic cards": The confluence of clinical research and preconceived categories. *History of Psychiatry, 8,* 375–385.

Weber, R., & Crocker, J. (1983). Cognitive processes in the revision of stereotype beliefs. *Journal of Personality and Social Psychology, 45,* 961–977.

Webster, S., & Coleman, S. R. (1992). The reception of Clark L. Hull's behavior theory, 1943–1960. *Psychological Reports, 70,* 1063–1071.

Wechsler, D. (1958). *Measurement and appraisal of adult intelligence.* Baltimore: Williams & Wilkins.

Weekes, J. R., Lynn, S. J., Green, J. P., & Brentar, J. T. (1992). Pseudomemory in hypnotized and task-motivated subjects. *Journal of Abnormal Psychology, 101,* 356–360.

Weidman, N. (1997). Heredity, intelligence and neuropsychology—why *The Bell Curve* is good science. *Journal of the History of the Behavioral Sciences, 33,* 141–144.

Weigel, R. H., Vernon, D. T. A., & Tognacci, L. N. (1974). Specificity of the attitude as a determinant of attitude-behavior congruence. *Journal of Personality and Social Psychology, 30,* 724–728.

Weinberg, R. A., Scarr, S., & Waldman, I. D. (1992). The Minnesota Transracial Adoption Study: A follow-up of IQ test performance at adolescence. *Intelligence, 16,* 117–135.

Weinberger, J., & Silverman, L. H. (1990). Testability and empirical verification of psychoanalytic dynamic propositions through subliminal psychodynamic activation. *Psychoanalytic Psychology, 7,* 299–339.

Weiner, B. (1985). An attributional theory of achievement motivation and emotion. *Psychological Review, 92,* 548–573.

Weiner, B., Figueroa-Munoz, A., & Kakihara, C. (1991). The goals of excuses and communication strategies related to causal perceptions. *Personality and Social Psychology Bulletin, 17,* 4–13.

Weiner, D. B. (1992). Philippe Pinel's "Memoir on Madness" of December 11, 1794: A fundamental text of modern psychiatry. *American Journal of Psychiatry, 149,* 725–732.

Weiner, R. D. (2000). Retrograde amnesia with electroconvulsive therapy: *Characteristics Archives of General Psychiatry, 57,* 591–592.

Weinstein, N. D. (1984). Reducing unrealistic optimism about illness susceptibility. *Health Psychology, 3,* 431–457.

Weintraub, S., Daffner, K. R., Ahern, G. L., & Price, B. H. (1996). Right sided hemispatial neglect and bilateral cerebral lesions. *Journal of Neurology, Neurosurgery and Psychiatry, 60,* 342–344.

Weisberg, R. W. (1992). Metacognition and insight during problem solving: Comment on Metcalfe. *Journal of Experimental Psychology: Learning, Memory, and Cognition, 18,* 426–431.

Weisburd, S. (1984). Whales and dolphins use magnetic "roads." *Science News, 126,* 391.

Weisman, J. (1988, November 19–25). Remembering JFK: Our first TV president. *TV Guide,* pp. 2–4, 6–8.

Weiss, S. J., Panlilio, L. V., & Schindler, C. W. (1993). Single-incentive selective associations produced solely as a function of compound-stimulus conditioning context. *Journal of Experimental Psychology: Animal Behavior Processes, 19,* 284–294.

Weissenborn, R., & Duka, T. (2000). State-dependent effects of alcohol on explicit memory: The role of semantic associations. *Psychopharmacology, 149,* 98–106.

Weissman, M. M., Bland, R. C., Canino, G. J., Greenwald, S., et al. (1996). The cross-national epidemiology of social phobia: A preliminary report. *International Clinical Psychopharmacology, 11,* 9–14.

Weisz, J. R., Weiss, B., Han, S. S., & Granger, D. A. (1995). Effects of psychotherapy with children and adolescents revisited: A meta-analysis of treatment outcome studies. *Psychological Bulletin, 117,* 450–468.

Weitzenhoffer, A. M., & Hilgard, E. R. (1962). *Stanford Scale of Hypnotic Susceptibility, Form C.* Palo Alto, CA: Consulting Psychologists Press.

Weldon, E., & Gargano, G. M. (1988). Cognitive loafing: The effects of accountability and shared responsibility on cognitive effort. *Personality and Social Psychology Bulletin, 14,* 159–171.

Wellisch, D., Kagawa-Singer, M., Reid, S. L., et al. (1999). An exploratory study of social support: A cross-cultural comparison of Chinese-, Japanese-, and Anglo-American breast cancer patients. *Psycho-Oncology, 8,* 207–219.

Wells, G. L., & Lindsay, R. C. L. (1985). Methodological notes on the accuracy-confidence relation in eyewitness identification. *Journal of Applied Psychology, 70,* 413–419.

Wenderoth, P. (1994). On the relationship between the psychology of visual perception and the neurophysiology of vision. *Australian Journal of Psychology, 46,* 1–6.

Wertheimer, M. (1978). Humanistic psychology and the humane but tough-minded psychologist. *American Psychologist, 33,* 739–745.

Wertheimer, M., & King, D. B. (1994). Max Wertheimer's American sojourn, 1933–1943. *History of Psychology Newsletter, 26,* 3–15.

Wesp, R., & Montgomery, K. (1998). Developing critical thinking through the study of paranormal phenomena. *Teaching of Psychology, 25,* 275–278.

Westheimer, G. (1999). Gestalt theory reconfigured: Max Wertheimer's anticipation of recent developments in visual neuroscience. *Perception, 28,* 5–15.

Wetter, D. W., Fiore, M. C., Young, T. B., McClure, J. B., et al. (1999). Gender differences in response to nicotine replacement therapy: Objective and subjective indexes of tobacco withdrawal. *Experimental and Clinical Psychopharmacology, 7,* 135–144.

Wetter, D. W., Kenford, S. L., Smith, S. S., Fiore, M. C., et al. (1999). Gender differences in smoking cessation. *Journal of Consulting and Clinical Psychology, 67,* 555–562.

Wever, E. G., & Bray, C. W. (1937). The perception of low tones and the resonance volley theory. *Journal of Psychology, 3,* 101–114.

Wheeler, R. E., Davidson, R. J., & Tomarken, A. J. (1993). Frontal brain asymmetry and emotional reactivity: A biological substrate of affective style. *Psychophysiology, 30,* 82–89.

Wheldall, K., & Benner, H. (1993). Conservation without conversation revisited: A replication and elaboration of the Wheldall-Poborca findings on the nonverbal assessment of conservation of liquid quantity. *Educational Psychology, 13,* 49–58.

White, G. L., Fishbein, S., & Rutstein, J. (1981). Passionate love and the misattribution of arousal. *Journal of Personality, 41,* 56–62.

White, J. W., & Humphrey, J. A. (1994). Women's aggression in heterosexual conflicts. *Aggressive Behavior, 20,* 195–202.

White, J. W., & Kowalski, R. M. (1994). Deconstructing the myth of the nonaggressive woman: A feminist analysis. *Psychology of Women Quarterly, 18,* 487–508.

White, S. H. (1990). Child study at Clark University. *Journal of the History of the Behavioral Sciences, 26,* 131–150.

White, S. H. (1994). Hilgard's vision of psychology's history. *Psychological Science, 5,* 192–194.

Whitehurst, G. J., Falco, F. L., Lonigan, C. J., et al. (1988). Accelerating language development through picture book reading. *Developmental Psychology, 24,* 552–559.

Whitlock, F. A. (1987). Addiction. In R. L. Gregory (Ed.), *Oxford companion to the mind* (pp. 3–5). New York: Oxford University Press.

Whitney, D. J., & Schmitt, N. (1997). Relationship between culture and responses to biodata employment items. *Journal of Applied Psychology, 82,* 113–129.

Whorf, B. L. (1956). Science and linguistics. In J. B. Carroll (Ed.), *Language, thought, and reality: Selected writings of Benjamin Lee Whorf* (pp. 202–219). Cambridge, MA: MIT Press.

Whyte, G. (1998). Recasting Janis's group-think model: The key role of collective efficacy in decision fiascoes. *Organizational Behavior and Human Decision Processes, 73,* 185–209.

Wickelgren, I. (1998). Obesity: How big a problem? *Science, 280,* 1364–1367.

Wicker, F. W., Barron, W. L., & Willis, A. C. (1980). Disparagement humor: Dispositions and resolutions. *Journal of Personality and Social Psychology, 39,* 701–709.

Widiger, T. A., & Clark, L. A. (2000). Toward *DSM-V* and the classification of psychopathology. *Psychological Bulletin, 126,* 946–963.

Widiger, T. A., & Trull, T. J. (1991). Diagnosis and clinical assessment. *Annual Review of Psychology, 42,* 109–133.

Wiebe, D. J., & McCallum, D. M. (1986). Health practices and hardiness as mediators in the stress-illness relationship. *Health Psychology, 5,* 425–438.

Wiederman, M. W. (1999). A classroom demonstration of potential biases in the subjective interpretation of projective tests. *Teaching of Psychology, 26,* 37–39.

Wiederman, M. W., & Kendall, E. (1999). Evolution, sex, and jealousy: Investigation with a sample from Sweden. *Evolution and Human Behavior, 20,* 121–128.

Wiederman, M. W., & Pryor, T. L. (2000). Body dissatisfaction, bulimia, and depression among women: The mediating role of drive for thinness. *International Journal of Eating Disorders, 27,* 90–95.

Wiederman, M. W., Sansone, R. A., & Sansone, L. A. (1998). Disordered eating and perceptions of childhood abuse among women in a primary care setting. *Psychology of Women Quarterly, 22,* 493–497.

Wieling, E., & Marshall, J. P. (1999). Cross-cultural supervision in marriage and family therapy. *Contemporary Family Therapy, 21,* 317–329.

Wiggs, C. L., Weisberg, J., & Martin, A. (1999). Neural correlates of semantic and episodic memory retrieval. *Neuropsychologia, 37,* 103–118.

Wightman, D. C., & Lintern, G. (1984, August). *Part-task training of tracking in manual control.* NAVTRAEQUIPCEN (Technical Report 81–C–0105–2).

Wilborg, I. M., & Dahl, A. A. (1997). The recollection of parental rearing styles in patients with panic disorder. *Acta Psychiatrica Scandinavica, 96,* 58–63.

Wilder, D. A., Simon, A. F., & Faith, M. (1996). Enhancing the impact of counter-stereotypic information: Dispositional attributions for deviance. *Journal of Personality and Social Psychology, 71,* 276–287.

Wilkins, P. (2000). Unconditional positive regard reconsidered. *British Journal of Guidance and Counselling, 28,* 23–36.

Williams, C. D. (1959). The elimination of tantrum behavior by extinction procedures. *Journal of Abnormal and Social Psychology, 59,* 269.

Williams, J., Merritt, J., Rittenhouse, C., & Hobson, J. A. (1992). Bizarreness in dreams and fantasies: Implications for the activation-synthesis hypothesis. *Consciousness and Cognition: An International Journal, 1,* 172–185.

Williams, R. B., Jr., Kuhn, C. M., Melosh, W., White, A. D., & Schonberg, S. M. (1982). Type A behavior and elevated physiological and neuroendocrine responses to cognitive tasks. *Science, 218,* 483–485.

Williams, S. L., Brakke, K. E., & Savage-Rumbaugh, E. S. (1997). Comprehension skills of language-competent and nonlanguage-competent apes. *Language and Communication, 17,* 301–317.

Williams, T. J., Pepitone, M. E., Christensen, S. E., Cooke, B. M., Huberman, A. D., et al. (2000). Finger length patterns and human sexual orientation. *Nature, 404,* 455–456.

Wilson, C., Boni, D., & Hogg, A. (1997). The effectiveness of task clarification, positive reinforcement and corrective feedback in changing courtesy among police staff. *Journal of Organizational Behavior Management, 17,* 65–99.

Wilson, E. J., & Sherrell, D. L. (1993). Source effects in communication and persuasion research: A meta-analysis of effect size. *Journal of the Academy of Marketing Science, 21,* 101–112.

Wilson, E. O. (1975). *Sociobiology: The new synthesis.* Cambridge, MA: Harvard University Press.

Wilson, P., Lincoln, R., & Kocsis, R. (1997). Validity, utility and ethics of profiling for serial violent and sexual offenders. *Psychiatry, Psychology and Law, 4,* 1–11.

Wilson, T. C. (1996). Cohort and prejudice: Whites' attitudes toward Blacks, Hispanics, Jews and Asians. *Public Opinion Quarterly, 60,* 253–274.

Winefield, A. H. (1982). Methodological difficulties in demonstrating learned helplessness in humans. *Journal of General Psychology, 107,* 255–266.

Winn, K. I., Crawford, D. W., & Fischer, J. L. (1991). Equity and commitment in romance versus friendship. *Journal of Social Behavior and Personality, 6,* 301–314.

Winner, E. (1997). Exceptionally high intelligence and schooling. *American Psychologist, 52,* 1070–1081.

Winner, E. (2000). The origins and ends of giftedness. *American Psychologist, 55,* 159–169.

Winningham, R. G., Hyman, I. E., Jr., & Dinnel, D. L. (2000). Flashbulb memories? The effects of when the initial memory report was obtained. *Memory, 8,* 209–216.

Winton, W. M. (1990). Jamesian aspects of misattribution research. *Personality and Social Psychology Bulletin, 16,* 652–664.

Wittchen, H. U., Zhao, S., Kessler, R. C., & Eaton, W. W. (1994). *DSM-III-R* generalized anxiety disorder in the National Comorbidity Survey. *Archives of General Psychiatry, 51,* 355–364.

Wixted, J. T. (1991). Conditions and consequences of maintenance rehearsal. *Journal of Experimental Psychology: Learning, Memory, and Cognition, 17,* 963–973.

Wixted, J. T., & Ebbesen, E. B. (1991). On the form of forgetting. *Psychological Science, 2,* 409–415.

Wogalter, M. S., & Laughery, K. R. (1996). WARNING! Sign and label effectiveness. Current directions in *Psychological Science, 5,* 33–37.

Wojcikiewicz, A., & Orlick, T. (1987). The effects of post-hypnotic suggestion and relaxation with suggestion on competitive fencing anxiety and performance. *International Journal of Sport Psychology, 18,* 303–313.

Wolfe, D. A., Mendes, M. G., & Factor, D. (1984). A parent-administered program to reduce children's television viewing. *Journal of Applied Behavior Analysis, 17,* 267–272.

Wolfe, J. (1936). Effectiveness of token rewards for chimpanzees. *Comparative Psychology Monographs, 12* (No. 5).

Wolff, A. L., & O'Driscoll, G. A. (1999). Motor deficits and schizophrenia: The evidence from neuroleptic-naieve patients and populations at risk. *Journal of Psychiatry and Neuroscience, 24,* 304–314.

Wolff, M., Alsobrook, J. P., II, & Pauls, D. L. (2000). Genetic aspects of obsessive-compulsive disorder. *Psychiatric Clinics of North America, 23,* 535–544.

Wollen, K. A., Weber, A., & Lowry, D. H. (1972). Bizarreness versus interaction of mental images as determinants of learning. *Cognitive Psychology, 3,* 518–523.

Wolpe, J. (1958). *Psychotherapy by reciprocal inhibition.* Stanford, CA: Stanford University Press.

Wolpe, J. (1988). Obituary: Mary Cover Jones 1896–1987. *Journal of Behavior Therapy and Experimental Psychiatry, 19,* 34.

Wolpin, M., Marston, A., Randolph, C., & Clothier, A. (1992). Individual difference correlates of reported lucid dreaming frequency and control. *Journal of Mental Imagery, 16,* 231–236.

Wonderlic, E. F. (1983). *Wonderlic Personnel test.* Northfield, IL: Wonderlic.

Wood, J. M., Bootzin, R. R., Kihlstrom, J. F., & Schacter, D. L. (1992). Implicit and explicit memory for verbal information presented during sleep. *Psychological Science, 3,* 236–239.

Wood, J. M., Bootzin, R. R., Rosenhan, D., Nolen-Hoeksema, S., & Jourden, F. (1992). Effects of the 1989 San Francisco earthquake on frequency and content of nightmares. *Journal of Abnormal Psychology, 101,* 219–224.

Wood, N., & Cowan, N. (1995). The cocktail party phenomenon revisited: How frequent are attention shifts to one's name in an irrelevant auditory channel? *Journal of Experimental Psychology: Learning, Memory, and Cognition, 21,* 255–260.

Wood, W., & Eagly, A. H. (1981). Stages in the analysis of persuasive messages: The role of causal attributions and message comprehension. *Journal of Experimental and Social Psychology, 40,* 246–259.

Wood, W., & Eagly, A. H. (2000). A call to recognize the breadth of evolutionary perspectives: Sociocultural theories and evolutionary psychology. *Psychological Inquiry, 11,* 52–55.

Woodruff-Pak, D. S. (1993). Eyeblink classical conditioning in H. M.: Delay and trace paradigms. *Behavioral Neuroscience, 107,* 911–925.

Woods, C. J. P. (1996). Gender differences in moral development and acquisition: A review of Kohlberg's and Gilligan's models of justice and care. *Social Behavior and Personality, 24,* 375–384.

Woolley, H. T. (1910). A review of recent literature on the psychology of sex. *Psychological Bulletin, 7,* 335–342.

Worringham, C. J., & Messick, D. M. (1983). Social facilitation of running: An unobtrusive study. *Journal of Social Psychology, 121,* 23–29.

Wright, I. C., Rabe-Hesketh, S., Woodruff, P. W. R., David, A. S., et al. (2000). Meta-analysis of regional brain volumes in schizophrenia. *American Journal of Psychiatry, 157,* 16–25.

Wright, J., Clum, G. A., Roodman, A., & Febbraro, G. A. M. (2000). A bibliotherapy approach to relapse prevention in individuals with panic attacks. *Journal of Anxiety Disorders, 14,* 483–499.

Wu, H., Wang, J., Cacioppo, J. T., Glaser, R., Kiecolt-Glaser, J. K., & Malarkey, W. B. (1999). Chronic stress associated with spousal caregiving of patients with Alzheimer's dementia is associated with downregulation of B-lymphocyte GH mRNA. *Journals of Gerontology, 54A,* M212–M215.

Wurtz, R. H., Goldberg, M. E., & Robinson, D. L. (1982, June). Brain mechanisms of visual attention. *Scientific American,* pp. 124–135.

Wyatt, J. W. (1993). Identical twins, emergenesis, and environments. *American Psychologist, 48,* 1294–1295.

Wyatt, J. W., Posey, A., Walker, W., & Seamonds, C. (1984). Natural levels of similarities between identical twins and between unrelated people. *Skeptical Inquirer, 9,* 62–66.

Wynn, K. (1995). Infants possess a system of numerical knowledge. *Current Directions in Psychological Science, 4,* 172–177.

Yamagishi, T., Kikuchi, M., & Kosugi, M. (1999). Trust, gullibility, and social intelligence. *Asian Journal of Social Psychology, 2,* 145–161.

Yamaguchi, H. (1988). Effects of actor's and observer's roles on causal attribution by Japanese subjects for success and failure in competitive situations. *Psychological Reports, 63,* 619–626.

Yancher, S. C. (1997). William James and the challenge of methodological pluralism. *Journal of Mind and Behavior, 18,* 425–442.

Yang, A. (1997). Trends: Attitudes toward homosexuality. *Public Opinion Quarterly, 61,* 477–507.

Yarmey, A. D. (1973). I recognize your face but I can't remember your name: Further evidence on the tip-of-the-tongue phenomenon. *Memory and Cognition, 1,* 287–290.

Yerkes, R. M., & Dodson, J. D. (1908). The relation of strength of stimulus to rapidity of habit-formation. *Journal of Comparative Neurology and Psychology, 18,* 459–482.

Young, L. D., Richter, J. E., Bradley, L. A., & Anderson, K. O. (1987). Disorders of the upper gastrointestinal system: An overview. *Annals of Behavioral Medicine, 9 (3),* 7–12.

Youngren, M. A., & Lewinsohn, P. M. (1980). The functional relation between depression and problematic interpersonal behavior. *Journal of Abnormal Psychology, 89,* 333–341.

Yu, S., & Ho, I. K. (1990). Effects of acute barbiturate administration, tolerance and dependence on brain GABA system: Comparison to alcohol and benzodiazepines. *Alcohol, 7,* 261–272.

Yutrzenka, B. A., Todd-Bazemore, E., & Caraway, S. J. (1999). Four Winds: The evolution of culturally inclusive clinical psychology training for Native Americans. *International Review of Psychiatry, 11,* 129–135.

Zadra, A. L., & Pihl, R. O. (1997). Lucid dreaming as a treatment for recurrent nightmares. *Psychotherapy and Psychosomatics, 66,* 50–55.

Zadra, A. L., O'Brien, S. A., & Donderi, D. C. (1998). Dream content, dream recurrence, and well-being: A replication with a younger sample. *Imagination, Cognition, and Personality, 17,* 293–311.

Zajonc, R. B. (1965). Social facilitation. *Science, 149,* 269–274.

Zajonc, R. B. (1984). On the primacy of affect. *American Psychologist, 39,* 117–123.

Zajonc, R. B. (1985). Emotion and facial efference: A theory revisited. *Science, 228,* 15–21.

Zaldivar, R. A. (1986, June 10). Panel faults NASA on shuttle. *Philadelphia Inquirer,* pp. 1A, 12A.

Zanarini, M. C., Frankenburg, F. R., Reich, D. B., Marino, M. F., et al. (2000). Biparental failure in the childhood experiences of borderline patients. *Journal of Personality Disorders, 14,* 264–273.

Zebrowitz, L. A., Tenenbaum, D. R., & Goldstein, L. H. (1991). The impact of job applicants' facial maturity, gender, and academic achievement on hiring recommendations. *Journal of Applied Social Psychology, 21,* 525–548.

Zehr, D. (2000). Portrayals of Wundt and Titchener in introductory psychology texts: A content analysis. *Teaching of Psychology, 27,* 122–126.

Zentall, T. R., Sutton, J. E., & Sherburne, L. M. (1996). True imitative learning in pigeons. *Psychological Science, 7,* 343–346.

Zhang, J., & Thomas, D. L. (1994). Modernization theory revisited: A cross-cultural study of adolescent conformity to significant others in mainland China, Taiwan, and the USA. *Adolescence, 29,* 885–903.

Zigler, E. (1999). Head Start is not child care. *American Psychologist, 54,* 142.

Zigler, E., Abelson, W. D., Trickett, P. K., & Seitz, V. (1982). Is an intervention program necessary in order to improve economically disadvantaged children's IQ scores? *Child Development, 33,* 340–348.

Zimmer, J. W., & Hocevar, D. J. (1994). Effects of massed versus distributed practice of test taking on achievement and test anxiety. *Psychological Reports, 74,* 915–919.

Zimmerman, M. (1983). Methodological issues in the assessment of life events: A review of issues and research. *Clinical Psychology Review, 3,* 339–370.

Zisook, S., Byrd, D., Kuck, J., & Jeste, D. V. (1995). Command hallucinations in outpatients with schizophrenia. *Journal of Clinical Psychiatry, 56,* 462–465.

Zisook, S., Shuchter, S. R., Irwin, M., & Darko, D. F. (1994). Bereavement, depression, and immune function. *Psychiatry Research, 52,* 1–10.

Ziv, A. (1987). The effect of humor on aggression catharsis in the classroom. *Journal of Psychology, 121,* 359–364.

Zlotnick, C., Elkin, I., & Shea, M. T. (1998). Does the gender of a patient or the gender of a therapist affect the treatment of patients with major depression? *Journal of Consulting and Clinical Psychology, 66,* 655–659.

Zlotnick, C., Kohn, R., Keitner, G., Della G., & Sheri A. (2000). The relationship between quality of interpersonal relationships and major depressive disorder: Findings from the National Comorbidity Survey. *Journal of Affective Disorders, 59,* 205–215.

Zoellner, L. A., Foa, E. B., Brigidi, B. D., & Przeworski, A. (2000). Are trauma victims susceptible to "false memories?" *Journal of Abnormal Psychology, 109,* 517–524.

Zola-Morgan, S. M., & Squire, L. R. (1990). The primate hipppocampal formation: Evidence for a time-limited role in memory storage. *Science, 250,* 288–290.

Zucker, G. S., & Weiner, B. (1993). Conservatism and perceptions of poverty: An attributional analysis. *Journal of Applied Social Psychology, 23,* 925–943.

Zuckerman, M., Joireman, J., Kraft, M., & Kuhlman, D. M. (1999). Where do motivational and emotional traits fit within three-factor models of personality. *Personality and Individual Differences, 26,* 487–504.

Zuniga, J. R., Davis, S. H., Englehardt, R. A., & Miller, I. J. (1993). Taste performance on the anterior human tongue varies with fungiform taste bud density. *Chemical Senses, 18,* 449–460.

Zuwerink, J. R., & Devine, P. G. (1996). Attitude importance and resistance to persuasion: It's not just the thought that counts. *Journal of Personality and Social Psychology, 70,* 931–944.

Zwislocki, J. J. (1981). Sound analysis in the ear: A history of discoveries. *American Scientist, 69,* 184–192.

Credits

Photographs

About the Author

Phillip Lloyd Powell; p. vii top

Chapter 1

Opener: *Recognition*\ by Charles Olson, 1993. Acrylic/Canvas 84" x 60", Collection of the Artist and Denise Bibro Fine Art; **p. 3:** ©James Keivom/Liaison Agency; **p. 5:** ©The Granger Collection; **p. 6, p. 8 top, p. 9:** National Library of Medicine; **p. 8 bottom:** ©Dover Publications, Inc.; **p. 10 top:** Howard University/ Photo, Scurlock Studios; **p. 10 bottom:** ©Culver Pictures; **p. 11:** ©Archives of the History of American Psychology, University of Akron, Akron, OH; **p. 12:** ©Archives of the History of American Psychology, Seymour Wapner Gift, Permission Clark University Archives; **p. 15:** Courtesy Evan Caulkins; **p. 14:** Courtesy Laurel Furumoto; **p. 16 top:** ©Christopher S. Johnson/Stock, Boston; **p. 16 bottom:** ©The Wellcome Library; **p. 17:** ©Corbis/Bettmann; **p. 18:** Courtesy Dr. Herbert A. Simon; **p. 19:** Courtesy Roger Sperry; **p. 20:** Courtesy Dr. William E. Cross, Jr.; **Figure 1.2a-b:** ©Lawrence Migdale/Photo Researchers; **Figure 1.3a-b:** ©David Frazier Photolibrary; **Figure 1.3c:** ©Bill Auth/Uniphoto

Chapter 2

Opener: *Tuscan Evening* by Vincent Ceglia, 1995. Courtesy, Vincent Ceglia; **p. 27:** ©1995, Newsweek, Inc. All rights reserved. Reprinted by permission; **p. 28:** ©David Frazier Photolibrary; **p. 31:** ©Ariel Skelley/Stock Market; **p. 35 top:** ©Penelope Breese/Gamma Liaison; **p. 35 bottom:** ©Olivier Blaise/Gamma/Liaison Agency; **p. 36:** ©Photofest; **p. 37:** ©Corbis/Bettmann; **p. 38:** ©Laura Dwight; **p. 40:** ©John Terrance Turner/FPG; **p. 42:** Courtesy Robert Rosenthal; **p. 44:** Courtesy Stanley Sue; **p. 51:** Courtesy Dr. Diana Baumrind; **p. 53:** ©Paul Conklin; **p. 53:** ©Matt Meadows/Peter Arnold

Chapter 3

Opener: *Listen to Living* by Roberto Sebastian Antonio Matta Echaurren. 1941. Oil on Canvas, 29 1/2 x 37 3/8" (74.9 x 94.9 cm). The Museum of Modern Art, New York. Inter-American Fund. Photograph © 1997 The Museum of Modern Art, New York. © 2001 Artists Rights Society (ARS), New York/SIAE, Rome; **p. 57:** ©The Granger Collection; **Figure 3.1 (all):** Wurtz, Goldberg & Robinson, Scientific American, June 1982; **p. 64:** ©G. Pace/Sygma; **Figure 3.4:** ©Biophoto Associates/Photo Researchers; **p. 70:** ©Historical Pictures/Stock Montage; **p. 71:** ©Don M. Goode/Photo Researchers; **p. 72:** ©Mark Wilson/Liaison Agency; **p. 73 top:** Courtesy Candace Pert, photo by Jules Asher; **p. 73 bottom:** ©AP/Wide World Photos; **p. 74:** ©A. Glauberman/Photo Researchers; **Figure 3.7:** Courtesy of Drs. Michael Phelps and John Mazziotta, UCLA School of Medicine; **Figure 3.8:** ©Scott Camazine/Photo Researchers; **Figure 3.9:** ©The McGraw-Hill Companies, Inc. /Karl Rubin photographer; **p. 84 top:** With Permission of Dr. William Feindel, Montreal Neurological Institute; **p. 84 bottom:** ©Corbis/Bettmann; **p. 85:** National Library of Medicine; **p. 86:** ©Dr. Francis Schiller; **p. 88 top:** ©Courtesy Stanley Coren; **p. 88 bottom:** ©Courtesy Diane Halpern; **Figure 3.15:** Courtesy of Drs. Michael Phelps and John Mazziotta, UCLA School of Medicine; **Figure 3.16:** ©Fred Hossler/Visuals Unlimited; **p. 91:** Courtesy Jerre Levy

Chapter 4

Opener: *Children at Shore* by Edward Potthast. Courtesy, Dr. Spencer H. Gross, Pamela G. Fisher, and Lawrence E. Gross; **p. 95:** ©Bettmann/Corbis Images; **p. 96:** ©Archives of the History of American Psychology, University of Akron, Akron, OH; **Figure 4.1a-d:** ©Petit Format/Photo Researchers; **Figure 4.2:** Courtesy University of Washington; **Figure 4.4, p. 101:** Courtesy Tiffany Field; **Figure 4.5 (both):** ©Enrico Ferorelli; **Figure 4.6 (both):** ©Laura Dwight; **p. 104 bottom:** ©Yves De Braine/Black Star; **Figure 4.7 (both):** ©Laura Dwight; **Figure 4.8:** Harlow Primate Laboratory, University of Wisconsin; **p. 107:** ©Daniel Grogan; **p. 109:** ©David Frazier PhotoLibrary; **p. 110 (both):** ©Laura Dwight; **p. 110 bottom:** ©Courtesy Eleanor Maccoby; **p. 111:** Courtesy Joel and Alexandre Vitart; **p. 112:** ©Harvard University Archives; **p. 114 top left:** ©Bettmann/Corbis Images; **p. 114 top right:** ©David Turnley/Corbis Images; **p. 114 bottom:** ©Keith Carter Photography; **p. 116:** ©David Young-Wolff/Photo Edit; **p. 117:** ©Corbis/Bettmann; **p. 119 top:** ©Lisa Law/The Image Works; **p. 119 bottom:** ©Topham/The Image Works; **p. 120:** ©Bill Bachmann/Photo Network/PictureQuest; **p. 123:** ©Bob Daemmrich/Image Works; **p. 125:** ©Barbara Stitzer/Photo Edit; **p. 128:** ©Bob Daemmrich/ The Image Works; **p. 129 top:** ©Corbis/Bettmann; **p. 129 bottom:** ©NASA

Chapter 5

Opener: *Fall Plowing* by Grant Wood, 1932. Courtesy of the John Deere Art Collection; **Figure 5.1:** From Dallenbach, K. M. (1951). A Puzzle Picture with a New Principle of Concealment. American Journal of Psychology, 54, 431–433; **p. 135:** ©Fred Whitehead/Animals Animals; **p. 137:** ©Corbis/Bettmann; **p. 143:** ©Rob Tringali, Jr./Sportschrome; **p. 144:** ©Villafuerte/TexaStock; **Figure 5.9a-b:** Fritiz Goro/LIFE Magazine ©1944 Time, Inc.; **Figure 5.12:** Courtesy Kaiser Porcelain, Ltd.; **Figure 5.17a:** ©Digital Stock/Animals; **Figure 5.17b-c:** ©Digital Stock/Roads & Structures; **Figure 5.17d:** ©Digital Stock/Flowers; **Figure 5.17e-f:** ©Jean-Claude LeJeune; **Figure 5.18:** ©Van Bucher/Photo Researchers; **Figure 5.19a:** ©Arthur Sirdofsky; **Figure 5.20 (both):** ©Mark Antman/The Image Works; **p. 161:** ©AP/Wide World Photos; **p. 162:** ©Personality Photos; **p. 163:** Courtesy Linda Bartoshuk; **Figure 5.27:** ©Christopher Springmann;

p. 166 top: Courtesy Ronald Melzack; **p. 166 bottom:** ©Willie Hill, Jr./The Image Works; **p. 168:** ©David Frazier Photolibrary; **p. 171:** ©The Granger Collection

Chapter 6

Opener: Henri Rousseau. *The Sleeping Gypsy.* 1897. Oil on canvas, 51" x 6'7". Collection, The Museum of Modern Art, New York. Gift of Mrs. Simon Guggenheim; **p. 177:** AP/Wide World Photos; **p. 184:** ©Susan Leavines/Photo Researchers; **Figure 6.4:** ©Richard T. Nowitz/Photo Researchers; **p. 187:** ©D. Wells/The Image Works; **p. 190:** ©Tom Burton/Orlando Sentinel; **p. 193:** Henry Fuseli, "The Nightmare," 1781. Founders Society Purchase with funds from Mr. and Mrs. Bert L. Smokler and Mr. and Mrs. Lawrence A. Fleischman. Photograph @ 1986 The Detroit Institute of Arts; **p. 195 top:** ©Bettmann/Corbis Images; **p. 195B:** ©Rush-Presbyterian-St. Luke's Medical Center, Photo by Rona Talcott; **p. 197:** ©AP/Gary C. Klein/Wide World Photos; **p. 198:** ©Bettmann/Corbis Images; **p. 201:** Courtesy E. R. Hilgard; Stanford University; **p. 204:** ©Stanford News Service, photo by L. A. Cicero; **p. 206 (all):** Ronald K. Siegel; **p. 207:** ©Bettmann/Corbis Images

Chapter 7

Opener: Henry O. Tanner. *"The Banjo Lesson"* (1893), oil on canvas, 4'1/2" x 3'11". Hampton University Museum, Hampton, VA; **p. 212:** ©Bettmann/Corbis Images; **p. 215:** ©Michael Newman/Photo Edit; **p. 217:** Courtesy of Professor Benjamin Harris; **p. 219:** Photo by Irwin Bernstein; **p. 220:** ©Archives of the History of American Psychology, University of Akron, Akron, OH; **p. 221:** ©Richard Wood/Index Stock Imagery; **Figure 7.4a-d:** Robert W. Kelley/Life Magazine © 1952 Time Inc.; **p. 224:** ©Jeff Greenberg/Unicorn Stock Photos; **p. 225:** ©Arni Katz/Unicorn Stock Photos; **p. 228:** ©Rita Nannini/Photo Researchers; **p. 229:** ©AP/Wide World Photos; **p. 230:**

©Skjold Photography; **p. 231 top:** ©Russ Kinne/Comstock; **p. 231B:** Courtesy Neal Miller; **p. 234:** Courtesy Robert Rescorla; **Figure 7.6 (all), p. 237 bottom:** Courtesy of Albert Bandura

Chapter 8

Opener: Salvador Dali. *The Persistence of Memory,* 1931, oil on canvas, 9 1/2 x 13". Collection, The Museum of Modern Art, New York. Given anonymously. ©1997 Demart Pro Arte (R), Geneva. © 2001 Salvador Dali, Gala-Salvador Dali Foundation / Artists Rights Society (ARS), NY; **p. 241:** ©Sylvia Johnson/Woodfin Camp & Associates; **p. 244:** Courtesy Dr. George Sperling; **p. 249:** Courtesy Endel Tulving; **p. 252:** Courtesy Ulric Neisser; **p. 254:** ©Archives of the History of American Psychology, University of Akron, Akron, OH; **p. 257, p. 261 (both):** ©Bettmann/Corbis Images; **p. 265:** Courtesy Elizabeth Loftus. Photo by Alex-Mares-Manton; **p. 269:** ©Archives of the History of American Psychology, University of Akron, Akron, OH; **p. 270:** Courtesy V.A. Medical Center, San Diego; **p. 272:** ©Mimi Forsyth/Monkmeyer Press

Chapter 9

Opener: *Buste D'Homme Au Chapeau* by Pablo Picasso, Spanish, Christie's Images, London/Superstock. © 2001 Estate of Pablo Picasso/Artists Rights Society (ARS), NY; **p. 277:** Museum of Modern Art Film Stills Library; **Figure 9.2a (both):** ©Giraudon/Art Resource, NY; **Figure 9.2b (top):** ©Erich Lessing/Art Resource, NY; **Figure 9.2b (bottom):** ©Giraudon/Art Resource, NY; **Figure 9.2c (both):** ©2001 Succession H. Matisse, Paris/Artists Rights Society (ARS), NY; **p. 280 bottom left:** ©Archives of the History of American Psychology, University of Akron, Akron, OH; **Figure 9.3 (all):** ©Superstock; **Figure 9.4 (all):** ©Norman Baxley/@1984/Discover Magazine; **p. 284:** ©Robert Kusel; **p. 285:** Courtesy Dr. Teresa M. Amabile; **p. 287 top:** Courtesy Amos Tversky; **p. 287B:** Courtesy Daniel Kahneman; **p. 288:** ©Reuters/Barbara L. Johnson/Archive Photos; **p. 289:** ©Bachman/Uniphoto; **p. 292 top:** ©Ira Wyman/Sygma; **p. 292B:** ©Skjold Photography; **p. 293:** Courtesy Noam Chomsky; **p. 294:** ©Kent & Donna Dannen; **p. 297:**

©The Granger Collection; **p. 298:** ©Susan Kuklin/Photo Researchers; **p. 299 top left:** ©Dr. Ronald Cohn/Gorilla Foundation; **p. 299 top right, center right, bottom right:** ©Language Research Center/Georgia State University

Chapter 10

Opener: *Shakespeare in his Study* by Michelle Puleo. American/Superstock; **p. 303:** ©Liaison Agency; **p. 304 top:** ©Archives of the History of American Psychology, University of Akron, Akron, OH; **p. 304 bottom (both):** ©University College London; **p. 305 (both):** ©Bettmann/Corbis Images; **p. 310:** ©Jeff Greenberg/Photo Edit; **p. 311:** ©Bettmann/Corbis Images; **p. 312:** Courtesy News and Publication Service, Stanford University; **p. 313:** ©Margot Ganitsas/The Image Works; **p. 317a:** ©Kolvoord/TexaStock; **p. 317b:** ©Bettmann/Corbis Images; **p. 317c:** ©AP/Wide World Photos; **p. 317d:** ©Dave Samble/Sygma; **p. 317 bottom right:** ©Archives of the History of American Psychology, University of Akron, Akron, OH; **p. 318:** ©Archives of the History of American Psychology, University of Akron, Akron, OH; **p. 319 left:** ©Edward L. Miller/Stock Boston; **p. 319 right:** ©Philip Jon Bailey/Index Stock Imagery; **p. 322:** Courtesy Dr. Sandra Scarr; **p. 323:** ©Paul Conklin/Uniphoto

Chapter 11

Opener: ©1998 Romare Bearden Foundation/Licensed by VAGA, New York, NY; **p. 327 top:** Courtesy Michael Gardner; **p. 327B:** ©The Philadelphia Inquirer/Charles Fox; **p. 328:** ©Archives of the History of American Psychology, University of Akron, Akron, OH; **p. 329:** Courtesy Edward O. Wilson; **p. 330:** ©Kindra Clineff/Index Stock Imagery; **p. 331:** From Teitelbaum, P. Appetyite, Proceedings of the American Philosophical Society, 1964, 108, 464–473; **p. 334:** Courtesy Judith Rodin; **p. 338:** ©Bettmann/Corbis Images; **p. 339:** Reprinted by permission of The Kinsey Institute for Research in Sex, Gender, and Reproduction, Inc./Photo: Dellenback; **p. 340a:** ©AP/Wide World Photos; **p. 340b:** ©Rufus F. Folkks/Corbis Images; **p. 340c:** ©Neal Preston/Corbis Images; **p. 340d:** ©Bettmann/Corbis Images; **p. 345 left:** ©Tom Bol/Outside

Images/PictureQuest; **p. 345R:** ©Ken Fisher/STONE; **Figure 11.7:** Reprinted by permission of the publisher from THEMATIC APPERCEPTION TEST by Henry A. Murray, Cambridge, Mass.: Harvard University Press, Copyright ©1943 by the Presidents and Fellows of Harvard College, ©1971 by Henry A. Murray; **p. 346a:** ©Dana Fineman/Sygma; **p. 346b:** ©Micheline Pelletier/Sygma; **p. 346c:** ©Paula Lerner/Woodfin Camp & Associates; **p. 346d:** ©Wide World Photos

Chapter 12

Opener: *Tahitian Idyll* by Paul Gaugin. French. Narodni Gallery, Prague, Czechoslovakia/Superstock; **p. 351:** Courtesy Los Alamos National Laboratory; **p. 356:** Courtesy Dr. David T. Lykken; **p. 357:** ©Dr. Richard J. Davidson, William James Professor of Psychology and Psychiatry. Courtesy of University of Wisconsin News Service; **p. 358:** ©Henry Diltz/Corbis Images; **p. 359:** ©David Burnett/Contact Stock Images; **p. 360 left:** ©Dave Bartruff/Stock Boston; **p. 360 center:** Digital Stock/Indigenous People; **p. 360 right:** Digital Stock/Babies & Children; **p. 361:** Courtesy Robert Plutchik; **p. 362:** Courtesy Prof. Edward Diener; **p. 363:** ©AP/Wide World Photos; **p. 364 left:** ©Mitchell Gerber/Corbis Images; **p. 364 center, right:** ©AP/Wide World Photos; **p. 368:** ©Corel/Winter Sports; **p. 369:** ©Mark Antman/The Image Works; **p. 370:** Courtesy Office of Public Information, Columbia University

Chapter 13

Opener: *Girl Before a Mirror,* by Pablo Picasso. Boisgeloup, March 1932. 64 x 51 1/4" (162.3 x 130.2 cm). Oil on canvas. The Museum of Modern Art, New York. Gift of Mrs. Simon Guggenheim. Photograph © 1997 The Museum of Modern Art, New York; **p. 375:** ©AP/Wide World Photos; **p. 376:** ©Mary Evans Picture Library; **Figure 13.2(2):** ©Mark M. Walker/Index Stock Imagery; **Figure 13.2(3):** ©MacDonald/ Index Stock Imagery; **p. 379 bottom:** ©Bettmann/Corbis Images; **p. 380 left:** ©Y. Karsh/Woodfin Camp & Associates; **p. 380 center:** C. G. Jung, The Archetypes and the Collective Unconscious, Bollingen Series XXm, 1969, Princeton University Press; **p. 380 right:** C. G. Jung, The Archetypes and the Collective

Unconscious, Bollingen Series XXm, 1969, Princeton University Press; **p. 381 top:** ©Bettmann/Corbis Images; **p. 381 bottom:** ©The Granger Collection; **p. 383a:** Museum of Modern Art Film Stills Archive; **p. 383b-c:** ©Personality Photos; **p. 383 top:** ©Bettmann/Corbis Images; **p. 384:** ©Archives of the History of American Psychology, University of Akron, Akron, OH; **p. 387:** Courtesy Walter Mischel; **p. 388:** ©Personality Photos; **p. 390:** ©Courtesy Julian Rotter; **p. 392:** National Library of Medicine; **p. 393 top:** Courtesy Hazel Markus; **p. 393 bottom:** Courtesy Shinobu Kitayama; **p. 396:** Courtesy Dr. Thomas J. Bourchard, Jr.; **p. 397 (both):** ©Enrico Ferorelli

Chapter 14

Opener: *Vincent van Gogh.* Self Portrait Dedicated to Paul Gauguin. 1888. oil on canvas, 60.3 x 49.4 cm. Courtesy of the Fogg Art Museum, Harvard University Art Museums, Cambridge, MA. Bequest - Collection of Maurice Wertheim, Class of 1906; **p. 401:** ©Bettmann/Corbis Images; **p. 403:** ©AP/Wide World Photos; **p. 407:** ©Bettmann/Corbis Images; **p. 409:** Courtesy Samuel Turner; **p. 410:** ©Scala/Art Resource, NY; **p. 411:** ©Jean Gaumy/Magnum Photos; **p. 414a-c:** Museum of Modern Art Film Stills Archive; **p. 414d:** ©AP/Wide World Photos; **p. 415a, c:** ©Corbis/Bettmann; **p. 415b:** ©Kathy Banks/Sygma; **p. 416:** Courtesy Susan Nolen-Hoeksema; **Figure 14.2:** Courtesy of Drs. Lewis Baxter and Michael Phelps, UCLA School of Medicine; **p. 419:** ©Reuters/Lee Celano/Archive Photos; **p. 420 (all):** ©Derek Bayes/Life Magazine ©Time Warner; **p. 421:** ©Grunnitus/Monkmeyer Press; **Figure 14.4 top:** ©Alexander Tsiaras/Science Source/Photo Researchers; **Figure 14.4 bottom:** Courtesy Dr. Daniel R. Weinberger **TA14.8:** © 2001 The Munich Museum/The Munch-Ellingsen Group/Artists Rights Society (ARS), NY

Chapter 15

Opener: *The Armour* by Gayle Ray. American/Superstock; **p. 429:** ©Sigmund Freud Copyrights/Mary Evans Picture Library; **p. 430:** Courtesy National Museum of Denmark; **Figure 15.1a-b:** ©Bettmann/Corbis Images; **Figure 15.1c:** National Library of Medicine; **p. 431 top:** ©The Granger Collection;

p. 431: ©Bettmann/Corbis Images; p. 432: ©R. Sidney/Image Works; p. 434 top left: Courtesy Joseph Wolpe; p. 434 top right: ©Archives of the History of American Psychology, University of Akron, Akron, OH; p. 434 bottom: ©Jacques M. Chenet/Woodfin Camp & Associates; p. 438: Courtesy Aaron T. Beck; p. 440: ©Esalen Institute/Paul Herbert, photographer; p. 442: ©Karen R. Preuss/The Image Works; Figure 15.3: ©Will McIntyre/Photo Researchers; p. 446: ©Mark Antman/The Image Works; p. 448: Courtesy Lester Luborsky;

Chapter 16

Opener: *Summer* by Eric Isenburger. Private Collection/Superstock; p. 455: ©Kelly-Mooney Photography/Corbis Images; p. 458: ©Sygma; p. 460 top: ©AP/Wide World Photos; p. 460 bottom: ©Tomas Del Amo/Index Stock/Profiles West; Figure 16.1(1): ©Lund, RBP/Custom Medical Stock Photo; Figure 16.1(2): ©Roseman/Custom Medical Stock Photo; p. 462: Courtesy Dr. Redford Williams; p. 463 top: Courtesy Karen Matthews; p. 463 bottom: ©Meckes/Ottawa/Photo Researchers; p. 467: Courtesy Dr. Shelley Taylor; p. 470: Courtesy Janice Kiecolt-Glaser; p. 471 left: ©Ralph Domingue/Globe Photos; p. 471 right: ©Bill Nation/Sygma; Figure 16.5 left: ©Scala/Art Resource, NY; p. 472: ©yDave Luchansky/Online USA/Newsmakers/Liaison Agency; Figure 16.5 center: ©AP/Wide World Photos; Figure 16.5 right: ©Mopnika Graff/Image Works;

Chapter 17

Opener: *Boulevard des Capucines* by Claude Monet. 1873. Oil on canvas. 31 3/4" x 23 13/16". The Nelson-Atkins Museum of Art, Kansas City, Missouri. Purchase: Kenneth A. and Helen F. Spencer Foundation Acquisition Fund; p. 479: ©AP/Wide World Photos; p. 480: Courtesy Bernard Weiner; p. 482 top: ©Hangarter/The Picture Cube; p. 482 bottom: ©Alan Carey/The Image Works; p. 484 top: Courtesy Ellen Berscheid; p. 484 bottom: Courtesy Elaine Hatfield; p. 485: ©AP/Wide World Photos; p. 486: ©Skjold Photography; p. 488: ©AP/Wide World Photos; p. 489: ©Pacha/Corbis Images; p. 490: ©AP/Wide World Photos; p. 491 left: ©Rick Friedman/Index Stock Imagery; p. 491 right: ©Larry Kolvoord/The

Image Works; p. 492: Courtesy Northside Center for Child Development, NYC; p. 493: Courtesy Yale University, Office of Public Information; p. 494 top: ©AP/Wide World Photos; p. 494 bottom: ©Bob Daemmrich/The Image Works; Figure 17.1a-b: ©William Vandivert/TimePix; p. 496: Courtesy Florence M. Asch; Figure 17.2 (both): From film OBEDIENCE copyright 1965 Stanley Milgram; distributed by Penn State Media Sales. Photo courtesy Mrs. Alexandra Milgram; p. 498: Courtesy Alexandra Milgram/Photo by Eric Kroll; p. 499: Courtesy Prof. Robert Cialdini; p. 500: Courtesy Bibb Latane; p. 501: ©Bill Perry/Gannett News Service; p. 502: ©AP/Wide World Photos; p. 503: Courtesy University of Wisconsin, Madison; p. 504: ©AP/Wide World Photos; p. 520: Property of AT&T Archives. Reprinted with permission of AT&T; p. 526: Courtesy Edwin Locke.

Line Art, Excerpts

Chapter 1

p. 12: Copyright © The New Yorker Collection 1979 Dana Fradon from cartoonbank.com. All Rights Reserved. Figure 1.1: Source: Data from National Science Foundation, *Special Analyses of the Data from 1973-1991: Survey of Doctoral Recipients,* 1994.

Chapter 2

Figure 2.2: Source: Data from Rosenthal and Fode, "The Effect of Experimenter Bias on the Performance of the Albino Rat" in *Behavioral Science,* 8:183–189, 1963.

Chapter 3

p. 60: Copyright © The New Yorker Collection RMA. Robert Mankoff from cartoonbank.com. All Rights Reserved. p. 61: Copyright © The New Yorker Collection 1983 Lee Lorenz from cartoonbank.com. All Rights Reserved. Figure 3.5: From Kurt Schlesinger and Philip M. Groves, *Psychology: A Dynamic Science.* Copyright © 1976 Wm. C. Brown Communications, Inc., Dubuque, Iowa. Reprinted by permission of the author. Figure 3.14: From S. Coren and D. Halpern, "Left Handedness: A Marker for Decreased Survival Fitness" in *Psychological Bulletin,* 109: 91. Copyright © 1991

by the American Psychological Association. Reprinted with permission.

Chapter 5

Figure 5.2: From John W. Santrock, *Psychology: The Science of Mind and Behavior,* 3d ed. Copyright © 1991 The McGraw-Hill Companies, Inc. All Rights Reserved. Reprinted by permission. Figure 5.3: From David Shier, et al., *Hole's Human Anatomy & Physiology,* 7th ed. Copyright © 1996 The McGraw-Hill Companies, Inc. All Rights Reserved. Reprinted by permission. Figure 5.8: From G. Wald and P. K. Brown, "Human Color Vision and Color Blindness" in *Cold Spring Harbor Laboratory Symposia on Quantitative Biology,* 30:351. Copyright © 1965 Cold Spring Harbor. Reprinted by permission. Figure 5.16: From *American Journal of Psychology.* Copyright 1977 by the Board of Trustees of the University of Illinois. Used with permission of the University of Illinois Press. Figure 5.18: From Benjamin B. Lahey, *Psychology: An Introduction,* 3d ed. Copyright © 1989 The McGraw-Hill Companies, Inc. All Rights Reserved. Reprinted by permission. Figure 5.9b: From Benjamin B. Lahey, *Psychology: An Introduction,* 3rd ed., Copyright © 1989 The McGraw-Hill Companies, Inc., All Rights Reserved. Figure 5.22: From Seeley, Stephens, and Tate, *Anatomy and Physiology,* 4th ed., Copyright © 1998 The McGraw-Hill Companies, Inc., All Rights Reserved. Figure 5.23: From John W. Santrock, *Psychology: The Science of Mind and Behavior,* 3d ed. Copyright © 1991 The McGraw-Hill Companies, Inc. All Rights Reserved. Reprinted by permission. p. 172: Reprinted with permission of General Media Communications, Inc.

Chapter 6

Figure 6.5: From R. D. Cartwright, *A Primer on Sleep and Dreaming.* Copyright © 1978 Addison-Wesley Publishing Company, Reading, MA. Reprinted by permission of the author. Figure 6.6: From Spanos and Hewitt, *Journal of Personality and Social Psychology,* 39:1209. Copyright © 1980 by the American Psychological Association. Reprinted with permission. Figure 6.7: From Spanos & Hewitt, *Journal of Personality and Social Psychology,* 39:1209. Copyright © 1980 by the American Psychology Association. Reprinted with permission.

Chapter 7

Figure 7.3: Source: Data from Ilene L. Bernstein, "Learned Taste Aversions in Children Receiving Chemotherapy" in *Science,* 200:1302–1303, American Association for the Advancement of Science, 1978. Figure 7.5: From Benjamin B. Lahey, *Psychology: An Introduction,* 5th ed. Copyright © 1995 The McGraw-Hill Companies, Inc. All Rights Reserved. Reprinted by permission.

Chapter 8

Figure 8.2: G. Sperling, *Psychological Monographs,* 74 (whole no. 498), 1960. Figure 8.3: Source: L. R. Peterson and M. J. Peterson, "Short-Term Retention of Individual Items" in *Journal of Experimental Psychology,* 58:193–198, 1959. Figure 8.4: From R. S. Nickerson and M. J. Adams, *Cognitive Psychology,* 11:297. Copyright © 1979 Academic Press, reproduced with permission of publisher. Figure 8.5: Source: Data from F. I. M. Craik and E. Tulving, *Journal of Experimental Psychology: General,* 104:268–294, American Psychological Association, 1975. Figure 8.7: From A. M. Collins and E. F. Loftus, "A Spreading Activation Theory of Semantic Processing" in *Psychological Review,* 82:407–428. Copyright © 1975 by the American Psychological Association. Reprinted with permission. Figure 8.9: Source (top): Hermann Ebbinghaus, *Uber das Cedachnis (On Memory),* 1885. Figure 8.10: Source: J. G. Jenkins and K. M. Dallenbach, "Obliviscence During Sleeping and Waking" in *American Journal of Psychology,* 35:605–612, 1924. Figure 8.12: Adapted from D. R. Godden and A. D. Baddeley, "Context-Dependent Memory in Two Natural Environments: On Land and Under Water" in *British Journal of Psychology,* 66:325–331. Copyright © 1975 British Psychological Society, Leicester, England. Reprinted by permission. Figure 8.14: From G. H. Bower and M. C. Clark, "Narrative Stories as Mediators for Serial Learning" in *Psychonomic Science,* 14:181–182. Copyright © 1969 The Psychonomic Society, Inc. Reprinted by permission of the Psychonomic Society, Inc.

Chapter 9

Figure 9.1: From Benjamin B. Lahey, *Psychology: An Introduction,* 3d ed.

Table 9.1: Data from S.A. Mednick, "The Associative Basis of the Creative Process," *Psychological Review,* 69:220–232, American Psychology. **Figure 9.5:** Source: Abraham S. Luchins, "Mechanization in Problem-Solving: The Effect of Einstellung" in *Psychological Monographs,* 6 (whole no. 248), 1942. **Figure 9.16:** Source: L. Carmichael, et al., "An Experimental Study of the Effect of Language on the Reproduction of Visually Perceived Form" in *Journal of Experimental Psychology,* 15:73–86, 1932.

Chapter 10

Figure 10.2: Item A5 from Raven's Standard Progressive Matrices. Copyright J.C. Raven Ltd. Reprinted with permission of Campbell, Thomson & McLaughlin Ltd. **Figure 10.3:** From J. L. Horn and G. Donaldson, "On the Myth of Intellectual Decline in Adulthood" in *American Psychologist,* 31:701–719. Copyright © 1976 by the American Psychological Association. Reprinted with permission. **Figure 10.4:** Source: Data from T. J. Bouchard, et al., "Familial Studies of Intelligence: A Review" in *Science,* 212:1055–1059, AAAS, 1981.

Chapter 11

Figure 11.3: Data from A. J. Stunkard, *New England Journal of Medicine,* 314:193–198, Massachusetts Medical Society, 1986. **Figure 11.4:** From A. J. Stunkard, et al., "Use of the Danish Adoption Register for the Study of Obesity and Thinness" in The Genetics of Neurological and Psychiatric Disorders, S. Kety (ed.), 1980, 1983, page 119. Reprinted with permission of Lippincott, Williams and Wilkins Publishing. **Figure 11.5:** From W. H. Masters and V. E. Johnson, Copyright © 1966 Masters and Johnson Institute. Reprinted by permission.

Chapter 12

Figure 12.6: From R. L. Solomon, "The Opponent-Process Theory of Acquired Motivation: The Costs of Pleasure and Benefits of Pain" in *American Psychologist,* 35:691–712. Copyright © 1980 by the American Psychological Association. Reprinted with permission. **Figure 12.8:** From J. C. Speisman, et al., "Experimental Reduction of Stress Based on Ego-Defense Theory" in *Journal of Abnormal and Social Psychology,* 68:367–380. Copyright © 1964 by the American Psychological Association. Reprinted with permission. **Figure 12.13:** Source: Data from B.

Kleinmuntz and J. Szucko, "A Field Study of the Fallibility of Polygraph Lie Detection" in *Nature,* 308:449–450, Macmillan Magazine Ltd., 1984.

Chapter 13

Figure 13.3: Courtesy of Hans J. Eysneck.

Chapter 14

Figure 14.1: Source: Data from L. N. Robins, et al., "Lifetime Prevalence of Specific Psychiatric Disorders in Three Sites" in *Archives of General Psychiatry,* 41:949–958, American Medical Association, 1984. **Figure 14.3:** Source: Data from I. I. Gottesman and J. Shields, *Schizophrenia: The Epigenetic Puzzle,* Cambridge University Press, 1982. **p. 409:** Copyright © The New Yorker Collection 1986 Bill Woodman from cartoonbank.com. All Rights Reserved.

Chapter 15

Table 15.1: From A. Ellis, *Growth Through Reason,* pages 247–248. Science & Behavior Books, Inc., Palo Alto, California, 1971. Reprinted by permission. **Table 15.2:** From *On Being A Person.* Copyright © 1961 by Carl R. Rogers. Reprinted by permission of Houghton Mifflin Company. All rights reserved. **Figure**

15.6: Source: Data from Mary Lee Smith, et al., *The Benefits of Psychotherapy,* The John Hopkins University Press, 1981. **Figure 15.7:** From K. I. Howard, et al., "The Dose-Effect Relationship In Psychotherapy" in *American Psychologist,* p. 160. Copyright © 1986 by the American Psychological Association. Reprinted with permission.

Chapter 17

Figure 17.1: Source (line art): Solomon E. Asch , "Studies of Independence and Conformity: A Minority of One Against a Unanimous Majority" in *Psychological Monographs,* 90 (whole no. 416), 1956. **Figure 17.13:** From J. M. Darley and B. Latane, "Bystander Intervention in Emergencies: Diffusion of Responsibility" in *Journal of Personality and Social Psychology,* 8:377–383. Copyright © 1968 by the American Psychological Association. Reprinted with permission. **Figure 17.11:** From E. Donnerstein and L. Berkowitz, "Victim Reactions in Aggressive Erotic Films as a Factor in Violence against Women" in *Journal of Personality and Social Psychology,* 41:710–724. Copyright © 1981 by the American Psychological Association. Reprinted with permission.

Name Index

Franko, D. L., 446
Frasciello, L. M., 336
Frawley, P. J., 435
Fredrikson, M., 410
Freedman, J. L., 40
Freeman, A., 382
Freivalds, A., 142
Fremouw, W. J., 50
French, D., 232
French, S., 362
Freud, A., 17, 117
Freud, S., 11–13, 106, 111, 125, 192, 194, 205, 257, 270, 364, 375–379, 380, 383, 404, 405, 431, 432, 442, 502
Freund, A. M., 129
Frick, W. B., 17
Fridrich, P., 495
Friedman, M., 461
Friedman, R. C., 342
Friedman, S., 411
Friesen, W. V., 359, 360, 366
Fritsch, G., 82
Fritzsche, B. A., 501
Froming, W. J., 393
Frost, J. A., 87
Frost, R., 258
Fry, J. M., 191
Frymier, A. B., 363
Fuchs-Beauchamp, K. D., 284
Fudin, R., 182
Fujita, F., 362
Fujita, K., 155, 156
Fuld, K., 154
Fulker, D. W., 319
Fuller, R. W., 207
Fultz, J., 499
Funder, D. C., 388
Funtowicz, M. N., 408
Furnham, A., 384, 473
Furstenberg, F. F., Jr., 110, 119
Furumoto, L., 14, 15
Fyrberg, 51

G

Gabriel, P., 137
Gabrieli, J. D. E., 249
Gacy, J. W., 402, 425
Gaffan, E. A., 451
Gage, P., 76, 85
Gaillard, A. W. K., 494
Galanter, E., 135
Galef, B. G., Jr., 222, 237
Galen, 395, 463
Gall, F. J., 75–76
Gallacher, J. E. J., 469
Gallup, G. G., Jr., 53
Galton, F., 7, 32, 33, 39, 46, 62, 120, 304–305, 311, 317
Galvani, L., 68

Gamaro, G. D., 273
Ganchrow, J. R., 360
Gandhi, M., 330
Ganellen, R. J., 416
Gangestad, S., 388
Gannon, L., 39
Gansberg, M., 499
Garcia, J., 211, 218, 220
Garcia, L. A., 263
Garcia, M. P., 475
Garcia-Vera, M. P., 469
Gardner, B. T., 298
Gardner, C. O., 396
Gardner, H., 18, 316
Gardner, R., 188–189
Gardner, R. A., 298
Garfinkel, P. E., 336
Gargano, G. M., 494
Garmon, L. C., 114
Garnefski, N., 437
Garonzik, R., 87
Garske, J. P., 450
Gastil, J., 296
Gathercole, 266
Gauthier, J., 232
Gavin, M. R., 232
Gawin, F. H., 205
Gay, P., 11
Gay, V., 5
Gazzaniga, M. S., 91
Gebbardt, G. F., 80
Geen, R. G., 386, 502
Gehrig, P., 244
Geiselman, R. E., 263
Gelb, S. A., 318
Gempeler, J., 245
Genovese, K., 499, 501
Gentilomo, A., 248
George, C., 108
Gerhart, B., 527
Gescheider, G. A., 165
Geschwind, N., 86
Gesn, P. R., 121
Gessa, G. L., 72
Gettman, L. R., 472
Gfellner, B. M., 119
Ghaderi, A., 384
Ghizzani, A., 336
Gibbons, B., 164
Gibson, B. S., 147
Gibson, E. J., 101, 102
Gibson, H. B., 497
Gibson, J. J., 147
Gibson, J. T., 199
Gidron, Y., 463
Giesler, G. J., 166
Giladi, E. E., 361
Gilbert, H. M., 474
Gilbreth, F., 520
Gilbreth, L., 520

Gill, D., 129, 154, 290
Gill, T. V., 298
Gillam, B., 147
Gillberg, C., 412
Gilligan, C., 114, 118
Gilliland, 490
Gilliland, K., 384
Gilovich, T., 287
Girgus, J. S., 417
Gisiner, R., 297
Glanz, J., 78, 79
Glanzman, D. L., 269
Glaser, 463
Glaser, R. A., 463, 464
Glass, G. V., 49, 448, 449
Glassman, R. B., 246
Gleaves, D. H., 414
Gleitman, H., 495
Glenn, J. H., 129, 493
Glenn, M. J., 270
Glennon, R. A., 206
Glick, P., 491
Gliedman, J., 290
Gloor, P., 77
Gluck, M. A., 278
Glucksberg, S., 283
Glueckauf, R. L., 441
Gobet, F., 246
Goble, A. K., 138
Goddard, H. H., 305, 318
Godden, D. R., 259, 260
Godemont, M., 430
Godin, G., 472
Goebel, 330
Goebel, B. L., 129
Goh, V. H. H., 183
Goisman, R. M., 451
Gold, P. E., 273
Goldberg, L. R., 151
Goldberg, M. A., 166
Goldberg, M. E., 58
Goldbloom, D. S., 336
Goldfried, M. R., 433
Goldin-Meadow, S., 293
Goldman, D. L., 430
Goldman, H. H., 446
Goldman, R., 490
Goldman-Rakic, P. S., 72
Goldschmidt, L., 99
Goldstein, A., 358
Goldstein, B. D., 166
Goldstein, I. L., 282, 525
Goldstein, L. H., 491
Goldstein, S. R., 224
Golombok, S., 66, 342
Gonzales, M. H., 486
Good, R. H., III, 22
Goodale, M. A., 180
Goodall, J., 35, 36
Goode, B., 165
Goodman, G. S., 264

Gopaul-McNicol, S., 440
Gopnik, A., 147
Goran, M. I., 333
Gordon, B. N., 262
Gordon, C. M., 185
Gordon, E., 78
Gordon, I. E., 152
Gordon, P. M., 474
Gordon, W., 105
Gorey, K. M., 33
Gorman, K. S., 314
Gosling, S. D., 18
Gosselin, J. Y., 424
Gosselin, P., 359
Gosset, W. S., 514
Goswami, M., 191
Gotlib, I. H., 416
Gottesman, 422
Gottesman, I. I., 62, 332
Gottesman, I. L., 422
Gottlieb, B. H., 442
Gould, S. J., 318, 319, 321
Gouzoulis, M. E., 207
Govan, D. G., 151
Grace, M. S., 139
Graesser, A. C., 363
Graham, M. J., 116
Graham, T., 121
Granholm, E., 250
Grant, H. M., 259
Gravitz, M. A., 263
Gray, J. T., 237
Gray, M. M., 108
Gray-Little, B., 492
Green, D. M., 162
Green, J. A., 232
Green, J. P., 265
Green, J. T., 270
Greenberg, J., 494
Greenberg, L. S., 433
Greenberg, R. P., 195, 433
Greene, D., 347
Greene, E., 264
Greene, R. L., 248
Greenglass, E. R., 126
Greenlees, I. A., 486
Greeno, J. G., 235
Greenough, A., 331
Greenough, W. T., 99
Greenwald, A. G., 136
Greenwood, J. D., 278
Gregg, E., 502
Grey, W., 173
Griez, E., 410
Griffin, D. W., 482
Griffin, M. J., 136
Griggs, R. A., 170
Grigorenko, E. L., 316
Grimshaw, G. M., 277
Grissom, R. J., 448

Gross, 194
Gross, A. M., 202
Grossberg, S., 150
Grosser, B. I., 164
Grossman, G. H., 183
Grouios, G., 87
Grove, W. M., 425
Gruber, R., 186
Gruder, C. L., 500
Grunberg, N. E., 357
Grunewald, A., 150
Grusec, J. E., 227
Guarino, M., 495
Guarnaccia, P. J. J., 406, 419
Guglielmo, K. M., 167
Guilford, J. P., 284
Guilleminault, C., 185, 193
Guion, R. M., 528
Guion, S. G., 292
Gulevich, G., 188
Gump, B. B., 462
Gunderson, V. M., 156
Gunnell, D. J., 418
Gunther, L. M., 234
Gur, R. E., 423
Gurin, J., 473
Gustavson, A. R., 211
Gustavson, C. R., 211
Guyll, M., 462

H

Haaga, D. A. F., 416
Haber, R. N., 150
Habib, R., 271
Hackett, R. D., 528
Hadjikhani, N., 140
Hafdahl, A. R., 492
Hager, M., 341
Hagerty, 330
Hagopian, L. P., 223, 229, 435
Hahn, C. G., 445
Haidt, J., 361
Haier, R. J., 421
Haight, B. K., 129
Haimowitz, C., 441
Halasz, J., 444
Hales, S., 67
Hall, 207
Hall, C., 503
Hall, C. S., 193
Hall, D., 224
Hall, G. C. N., 49, 386
Hall, G. S., 12, 96, 118
Hall, M., 189
Hall, S., 147
Hall, V. C., 347
Hallenbeck, B. A., 237
Haller, J., 444
Halpern, C. T., 502

Halpern, D. F., 49, 87–89, 120, 121, 123, 125
Halpern, L., 161
Hamburg, D. A., 455
Hamburger, Y., 492
Hamer, 339
Hamill, R., 287
Hamilton, C. E., 107
Hamilton, T. K., 418
Hammen, C., 404, 457
Hammer, M. C., 115
Hammersmith, S. J., 342
Hampson, E., 122
Han, J. S., 167
Han, M. H., 425
Han, S., 148
Hanna, E., 237
Hanna, G., 121
Hansen, C. H., 360
Hansen, I., 211
Hansen, R. D., 360
Hanson, R. K., 386, 458
Hansson, K., 336
Harbach, H., 74
Harbin, D., 143
Harbin, G., 143
Hardaway, R. A., 182
Hardenburg, S. A., 338
Hardman, E., 260
Hardy, C. J., 494
Hare, J., 80
Hare, R. D., 425
Hariri, A. R., 357
Harkness, S., 108
Harlow, H. F., 106
Harlow, J. M., 85
Harman, M. J., 441
Harmon-Jones, E., 487
Harper, D. C., 168
Harper, S., 316
Harriman, A., 212
Harris, B., 217
Harris, E., 3
Harris, J. A., 502
Harris, L. J., 89, 268
Harris, M. J., 42, 43
Harris, R. J., 251
Harris, R. L., 128
Harrison, A. A., 486
Harrison, D. W., 232
Harrison, L. K., 363
Harrison, P. J., 334, 336
Hart, D., 279
Hartley, J., 279
Hartung, C. M., 408
Hartup, W. W., 110
Harvey, A. G., 191
Harvey, E. N., 184
Harvey, M., 57
Harvey, T., 76
Hasegawa, T., 36

Hashemi, A. H., 423
Hasher, L., 251
Haslam, N., 342
Hassett, J., 68
Hassin, R., 395
Hatfield, E., 484, 486
Hatfield, G., 11
Hathaway, S. R., 385
Hattori, N., 430
Hatzichristou, D. G., 282
Hauck, C., 198
Hausenblas, H. A., 494
Hauser, K., 277
Hawkes, 489
Hawking, S., 317
Hawkins, M. J., 394
Hawkins, W. E., 394
Hayashi, S., 439
Hayden, T., 387
Hayes, A. F., 391
Hayes, C., 297
Hayes, D. S., 267
Hayes, J. A., 416
Hayes, K., 297
Hayes, R. L., 80
Hayflick, L., 124
Hayhoe, M. M., 141
Hayman, L. A., 81
Haywood, C. S., 357
Haywood, H. C., 309
Hazelrigg, M., 404
Hazelrigg, P. J., 44
He, J. C., 146
He, Z. X., 419
Hearne, K. M., 170
Hearnshaw, L. S., 5, 319
Hearst, E., 220
Heath, A. C., 187
Heath, D. T., 127
Heatherton, T. F., 336
Heaton, P., 303
Heavey, L., 303
Hebb, D. O., 343, 344
Hechinger, N., 165
Heckhausen, J., 328
Hedges, L. V., 33, 308
Heffner, H. E., 159
Hegarty, P., 59
Hehl, F. J., 364
Heider, B., 133
Heider, F., 480
Heijnen, C. J., 463
Heine, S. H., 394
Heiser, J. F., 72
Heiser, P., 189
Heitzmann, C. A., 468
Hellekant, G., 164
Helmholtz, H. von, 6, 144–145, 147, 159
Henderlite, S. E., 329
Henderson, P. W., 162

Hendrick, C., 44
Hendriks, 385
Hendrix, J., 115
Hendrix, S., 129
Henle, M., 11
Henley, S. H., 382
Hennig, J., 74, 358
Hennrikus, D. J., 475
Henriksen, L., 108
Hensley, D. L., 251
Hepper, P. G., 87
Herbert, T. B., 463
Herbert, W., 271, 386, 404
Herek, G. M., 490
Hering, E., 145
Herkenhahn, M., 207
Herman, C. P., 333, 336
Herman, D., 446
Herman, L. M., 297
Herman-Stahl, M., 371
Hermelin, B., 303
Hernandez, J. M., 169
Herning, R. I., 77
Heron, W., 344
Herrnstein, R. J., 318, 320
Hershberger, S., 340
Hertz, H., 156
Hertzog, C., 124
Herz, R. S., 163
Herzog, H. A., Jr., 53
Herzog, T. A., 217
Herzog, T. R., 363
Heslegrave, R., 425
Hetherington, A. W., 331
Hewitt, E. C., 200, 201
Hewitt, J. K., 333
Hewlett, B. S., 106
Heyes, C. M., 237
Hicks, R. A., 88, 188
Higashiyama, A., 150
Higgins, E. T., 393, 394, 409, 417
Higgins, J. E., 469
Higgins, J. J., 310
Higgins, S. T., 475
Highet, A., 382
Hilgard, E. R., 7, 18, 197, 199
Hill, J. O., 333
Hill, R. D., 269
Hillbrand, M., 390
Hillerbrand, J., 161
Hillson, T. R., 364
Hinchy, J., 234
Hines, M., 98, 122
Hines, T. M., 183
Hippocrates, 75, 395, 429, 465
Hirata, Y., 158
Hirsch, H. V. B., 155
Hiscock, M., 87, 180
Hitchcock, C. H., 229

Mitchell, P., 152
Mitchell, T. R., 527
M'Naghten, D., 403
Modestin, J., 422
Modigliani, A., 498
Moeller, A. T., 437
Moeller, G. H., 345
Moffitt, T. E., 116
Mohanty, A. K., 292
Mohr, D. C., 451
Molina, B., 380
Molina, M., 101
Molitorisz, J., 212
Molk, H., 403
Mondale, W., 359
Moniz, E., 442
Monroe, M., 473
Monroe, S. M., 457
Montanes, P., 245
Monte, C. F., 380
Montesquieu, C., 362
Montgomery, G. H., 166, 197
Montgomery, K., 171
Monti, M. R., 425
Monti, T. C., 446
Montomoli, M., 336
Montour, K., 311
Moore, B. C. J., 135
Moore, B. V., 520
Moore, C., 143
Moore, J., 10, 278
Moore, T. E., 136
Moore-Ede, M. C., 184
Moorhead, G., 493
Moran, M. G., 460
Morawski, J. G., 10
Moreland, R. L., 483
Moreno, F. A., 415
Moretti, M. M., 393
Morgan, C., 346, 381
Morgan, D. W., 457
Morgan, W. G., 381
Morin, C. M., 447
Morisse, D., 230
Moritz, S., 252
Morley, J. E., 334
Moroney, W. F., 23
Morris, M., 378
Morris, R. L., 170
Morris, S., 171, 250
Morris, W., 378
Morrison, A. R., 190
Morrison, T., 346
Morrongiello, B. A., 101
Morrow, J., 417
Morse, C. K., 304
Morse, D. L., 223
Mortel, K. F., 124
Mortensen, P. B., 422
Moruzzi, G., 81
Morvay, Z., 381

Moscone, G., 403
Moscovitch, M., 81–82
Moskowitz, J. T., 466
Moss, C. R., 97
Mother Teresa, 383
Mount, 384
Mowday, R. T., 527
Mowrer, O. H., 214
Mowrer, W. M., 214
Muchinsky, P. M., 521, 527
Muehlbach, M. J., 204
Mueller, C. G., 10
Mueller, R. A., 89
Muir, F., 416
Muir-Broaddus, J., 105
Mulatu, M. S., 124
Mulhall, D. J., 303
Mullen, B., 359, 493
Müller-Lyer, F., 154
Mulligan, T., 97
Mullington, J., 191
Mumby, D. G., 270
Mumenthaler, M. S., 202
Munakata, Y., 103
Munch, E., 419
Münsterberg, H., 9–10, 15, 261, 520
Muris, P., 88, 193
Murphy, K. J., 270
Murray, B., 383
Murray, C., 320
Murray, H. A., 345, 346, 381
Murray, J. B., 166, 385
Murray, S. L., 482
Mustein, B., 486
Myers, D. G., 361
Myers, D. M., 261
Myers, I. B., 385
Myerscough, R., 207
Mylander, C., 293

N

Na, E. U., 480
Nadel, L., 81–82, 413
Nah, S. Y., 166
Naka, M., 262
Nakano, T., 73
Nakao, M., 231
Nakayama, K., 147
Nasby, W., 393
Naseema, A. M., 204
Nash, M., 201
Nason, S., 258
Nathan, 406
Nathan, P. E., 31
Nation, K., 290
Natsoulas, T., 178
Nava, F., 72
Navarro, A. M., 450
Navarro, M., 207

Navon, D., 148
Nayak, S., 166
Nazzi, T., 101
Neale, J. M., 420
Neave, N. J., 39
Neck, C. P., 493
Neggers, Y. H., 463
Neher, A., 382
Neisser, U., 179, 252, 253, 270, 307, 320
Nejime, Y., 135
Nel, E. M., 492
Nelson, C. E., 484
Nelson, K. E., 293
Nelson, P. L., 207
Nelson, T. O., 266
Nemechek, S., 384
Nemeroff, C. B., 445
Nesdale, A. R., 503
Nestadt, G., 409
Nettelbeck, T., 314
Neubauer, A. C., 314
Neufeld, R. W. J., 450
Nevid, J., 411
Nevo, O., 363
Newcomb, A. F., 110
Newcomb, M. D., 126
Newcomb, T., 503
Newcomer, J. W., 72
Newell, P. T., 195
Newman, B., 213
Newman, J., 347
Newport, E. L., 292
Newton, T., 527
Nezlek, 347
Ng, W. J., 262
Nicholson, I. A. M., 383
Nicholson, J., 524
Nicholson, N., 496
Nickerson, R. S., 247
Nicol, 422
Nicol, C. J., 237
Nicoll, R. A., 69
Nides, M. A., 475
Niedeggen, M., 252
Nielsen, T. A., 194
Nielsen-Gammon, E., 228
Nightingale, F., 45
Niles, S., 348
Ninomiya, Y., 164
Nir-Dotan, M., 467
Nisbett, R. E., 287, 347, 481
Nishida, T., 36
Nishimura, H., 158
Nishith, P., 457
Nissen, M. J., 272
Nixon, R., 253, 489
Noels, K. A., 347
Noice, H., 265
Nokes, T., 237
Nolen-Hoeksema, S., 416, 417

Noonan, M. J., 229
Norenzayan, A., 481
Norman, K. A., 253
Norman, R. M., 422
Normann, R. A., 144
Norris, 458
Norris, N. P., 50
Norton, J., 401
Norton, S., 99, 310
Nosofsky, R. M., 279
Nota, L., 441
Nowell, A., 308
Nwosu, C. M., 466
Nystul, M. S., 419

O

Oates, G., 124
O'Brien, E. J., 388
O'Brien, S. A., 193
O'Brien, W. H., 466
Obrocki, J., 78
Ockene, J. K., 475
O'Connell, A. N., 14, 15, 381
O'Connor, K., 438
Oden, G. C., 148
Oden, M. H., 312
O'Driscoll, G. A., 421
Oesterman, K., 503
Ogden, E. P., 50
Ogilvie, R., 194
Ogloff, J. R., 50
Oh, K. S., 411
O'Hara, M., 448
O'Hara, R., 253
Ohayon, M. M., 185, 193
Ohira, H., 369
Ohman, A., 412
Ohrwall, H., 164
Oishi, S., 362
Oka, S., 140
Okogbaa, O., 78
Olds, J., 81
O'Leary, A., 470
O'Leary, K. D., 126
Oliver, M. B., 119, 339
Ollendick, T. H., 412
Oller, D. K., 291
Olmo, R. J., 384
Olmsted, M. P., 333
Olson, D. R., 104
Olson, J. M., 491
Olson, K. R., 384
Olympia, D. E., 22
O'Neil, W. M., 10
Ong, A., 119
Onstad, S., 421
Opper, C., 74, 358
Oppliger, P. A., 363
O'Reilly, R. C., 147, 270
Orlick, T., 198

Rajagopal, M. R., 204
Raloff, J., 160
Ramalingam, S., 260
Ramey, C., 309
Ramirez, M., 105
Ramón y Cajal, S., 70, 270
Rand, T., 171
Randall, J. L., 171
Randi, 171
Ranson, S. W., 331
Rao, S., 79
Rao, U., 186
Rapp, D., 376
Raskin, D. C., 355
Raslear, T. G., 135
Rather, D., 359
Rauch, S. L., 409, 458
Raufaste, E., 252
Rautiainen, J., 182
Ravelli, G. P., 333
Raviv, A., 186
Rawdon, V. A., 390
Rawlings, D., 385
Ray, A., 340
Ray, F., 198
Ray, O., 204, 205
Rayner, R., 216
Raynor, D. A., 468
Read, J. D., 137
Read, M. S., 310
Reagan, R., 111, 171, 359
Reason, J., 181, 376
Redd, W. H., 197
Redler, L., 424
Reed, D. R., 332
Reed, T. E., 100
Reekum, R., 425
Reese, E. P., 211, 226
Reese, H. W., 50
Reese, L., 390
Reeve, C., 64
Regan, C. M., 270
Regan, P. C., 279
Regehr, W. G., 70
Reidelberger, R. D., 331
Reilly, R. R., 309
Reimer, J., 113, 114
Reinecke, M. A., 438
Reisenzein, R., 370
Reitman, J. S., 246
Rejeski, W. J., 502
Remy-St. Louis, G., 166
Reneman, L., 207
Renn, J. A., 111
Renner, J. W., 117
Rennie, D. L., 432
Rescorla, R. A., 215, 234
Resick, P. A., 457
Reuter-Lorenz, P. A., 91
Reynaert, C., 467
Reyner, L. A., 188, 204

Reynolds, C. R., 308
Reynolds, G. P., 72
Reynolds, K. D., 333
Reynolds, S., 406
Rhine, J. B., 171
Rhodes, M. G., 248
Rhodes, N., 490
Rhodes, S. R., 528
Rhue, J. W., 197
Ricciardelli, L. A., 334
Rice, M. L., 291
Richardson, B., 351, 352
Richardson, D., 51
Richardson, G. A., 99
Richelson, E., 272
Ridenour, 386
Rieber, R. W., 178
Riecken, H. W., 487
Rieckert, J., 437
Riehl, J., 191
Riggio, R. E., 523
Riggs, J. M., 481
Riggs, L. A., 141, 144
Riley, J. L., 166
Rilling, M., 12, 272
Rinaldi, R. C., 450
Ringelmann, M., 494
Riordan, C. A., 485
Risha, H., 404
Rittenhouse, C. D., 143, 196
Ritter, B., 436
Rivera-Tovar, L. A., 248
Rivet, K. M., 394
Rivinus, T. M., 419
Rizzo, M., 84
Robers, C., 439
Robert, M., 237
Roberts, A. H., 232
Roberts, J. E., 157, 418
Roberts, L., 460
Roberts, M. C., 228
Roberts, R. D., 314, 317
Roberts, R. E., 118
Roberts, R. E. L., 393
Robins, A. L., 284
Robins, L. N., 408
Robins, R. W., 18
Robinson, D. L., 58
Robinson, F. P., 265
Robinson, L. A., 416
Robinson, M. D., 366
Rocchetti, G., 383
Rochat, F., 498
Rock, C., 364
Rock, I., 147, 154
Rocklin, T., 496
Rockwell, 173
Rodgers, J. E., 261
Rodin, J., 332, 334, 336, 467
Roesch, R., 404
Roese, N. J., 51

Roesler, F., 252
Roethlisberger, F. J., 521
Rogers, C. R., 17–18, 405,
    439, 441
Rogers, L. J., 86
Rogers, R., 386, 425
Rogers, R. L., 124
Rogers, R. W., 504
Rogge, R. D., 126
Roghmann, K. J., 459
Rogoff, B., 117
Roig, M., 172
Rokeach, M., 420
Rollman, G. B., 166
Romer, D., 500
Romney, D. M., 111
Ronan, K. R., 344
Rondall, J. A., 293
Ronn, L. C. B., 98
Rook, 115
Roosevelt, E., 330, 392
Roosevelt, F., 37
Rorschach, H., 381
Rosch, E., 279, 295
Rose, D. J., 232
Rose, J. E., 234
Rosenhan, D. L., 407
Rosenkoetter, L. I., 236
Rosenman, R. H., 461
Rosenthal, R., 42, 43, 50, 359
Roskies, E., 472
Ross, C. A., 412
Ross, D. F., 262
Ross, E. D., 76, 89
Ross, H. E., 154
Ross, J., 527
Ross, R. R., 44
Rossi, A. F., 143
Rossi, A. M., 434
Rossi, F., 456
Rotenberg, K. J., 371
Rotenberg, V. S., 86
Roth, A., 134
Roth, N., 167
Roth, T., 191
Rothbaum, B. O., 434
Rothbaum, F., 106, 486
Rothstein, H. R., 523
Rotter, J. B., 390
Rotton, J., 404
Roug, L., 291
Rouillon, F., 410
Routh, D. K., 293, 343
Rouw, R., 133
Rovine, M. J., 61
Rowan, A., 53
Rowsell, H. C., 52
Royal, K. E., 484
Roy-Byrne, P. P., 260
Rozin, P., 335, 495
Rubin, E., 147

Rubin, J. R., 111
Rubin, P., 423
Rubin, Z., 51
Ruch, W., 363, 364
Ruda, M. A., 166
Rudolph, D., 457
Rudolph, K. D., 457
Ruffin, C. L., 458
Ruffman, T. K., 104
Rule, B. G., 503
Rumbaugh, D. M., 298,
    299, 314
Rummel, A., 347
Runco, M. A., 285
Rury, J. L., 319
Ruscio, J., 284
Rush, B., 430
Rushton, J. P., 320, 502
Russ, S. W., 284
Russell, G. L., 450
Russell, J. A., 356
Russell, M. J., 164
Russo, N. F., 14, 15
Rutherford, E., 159
Rutkowski, G. K., 500
Rutledge, T. R., 369
Rutstein, J., 485
Rutter, M., 310
Ryalls, B. O., 251
Ryan, E. R., 394
Ryan, J. J., 124
Ryan, K. M., 365
Ryan, N. E., 438
Ryan, R. H., 263
Ryan, R. M., 347, 472
Rychlak, J. F., 18

S

Sabatini, B. L., 70
Sabini, J., 495
Sable, P., 425
Sachdev, P., 445
Sackeim, H. A., 443
Sacks, O., 76–77, 133, 168
Sadeh, A., 186
Sahoo, F. M., 308
Saletu, B., 49
Salgado, J. F., 523
Saliers, E., 340
Salmon, D. P., 250, 270
Salthouse, T. A., 125
Saltz, E., 382
Samelson, F., 320, 321
Samms, M., 245
Samuels, J., 409
Sand, P., 444
Sanderman, R., 362
Sanders, P., 292
Sanford, E. C., 14–15
Sanghvi, C., 265

Subject Index

Avoidance learning, 226
Awareness, perception without, 179–181
Axons, 67–68

B

Backmasking, 137
Backward chaining, 223
Backward conditioning, 215
Barbiturates, 203–204
"Barnum effect," 375
Basal metabolic rate, obesity and, 333
Basic anxiety, 381
Basic hostility, 381
Basic research, 21
Basilar membrane, 157–158
Bedwetting, classical conditioning to control, 214
Behavior
    attitudes and, 487–488
    hypnosis and, 198–199
    television's influence on, 236, 237
Behavioral aggregation, 388
Behavioral contingencies, 221
Behavioral genetics, 19, 60–63, 396, 397
    adoption studies and, 62
    family studies and, 61–62
    twin studies and, 62–63
Behavioral neuroscience, 22, 56–92. *See also* Brain; Neuron(s)
    communication systems and, 63–66
    heredity and, 57–63
Behavioral orientation, to therapy, 433–437
Behavioral perspective, 16
Behavioral preparedness, 233
Behavioral viewpoint
    on psychological disorders, 405
    on schizophrenia, 424
Behaviorism, 10
Behavior modification, 230
Behavior therapy, 433
Benzodiazepines, 444
Beta rhythm, 77
Beta waves, 184
Bias(es)
    in causal attribution, 480–481
    cultural, intelligence testing and, 308
    experimenter, 42–44
    in-group, 491
    participant, 42
    response, 135
Bibliotherapy, 447
Binet-Simon scale, 305

Binocular cues, 149, 150
Biodata, validation of, 523
Biofeedback, 230–232
Biological rhythms, 183
    sleep-wake cycle and, 183–184
Biomedical model, of health and illness, 456
Biopsychological approach to personality, 395–398
    heredity and, 396, 397
    personality assessment and, 396
    status of, 396, 398
Biopsychological factors, phobias and, 411–412
Biopsychological orientation to therapy, 442–445
Biopsychological perspective, 18–19
    on mood disorders, 415
    on psychological disorders, 404
    on schizophrenia, 421–423
Biopsychosocial model of health and illness, 455
Bipolar cells, 140, 141
Bipolar disorder, 417–418
Blindsight, 180
Blind spot, 141
Blocking, classical conditioning and, 234
B-lymphocytes, 464
Bodily-kinesthetic intelligence, 316
Body senses, 168–170
Borderline personality disorders (BPD), 424–425
Bottom-up processing, 147
Brain, 63, 74–92
    clinical case studies of, 76–77
    dreaming as by-product of random activity of, 196
    emotion and, 356–357
    experimental manipulation of, 77
    functions of, 79–91
    hemispheric specialization of. *See* Hemispheric specialization
    hunger and, 331
    imaging of, 78–79
    phrenology and, 75–76
    psychoactive drug effects on, 203
    recording electrical activity of, 77–78
    sexual orientation and, 341
    vision and, 142–144
Brain stem, 79–81
Brainwashing, 344
Brightness, of light, 139
Brightness constancy, 152
Broca's aphasia, 86
Broca's area, 85–86

Bulimia nervosa, 336
Bystander intervention, 499–501

C

Caffeine, 204
Cancer, stress and, 463
Cannabis sativa, 206–207
Cannon-Bard theory of emotion, 367
Cardinal traits, 383–384
Cardiovascular disease, stress and, 460–463
Case studies, 36
Castration anxiety, 378
Catatonic schizophrenia, 421
Catharsis, 376, 429, 502
Causal attribution, 480–481
Causation, 39
    correlation versus, 39–40
Cell-adhesion molecules, 98
Cell body, of neuron, 67
Central tendency error, 524
Central tendency measures, 45–46, 511
Central traits, 384
Cerebellum, 80
Cerebral cortex, 82–86
    association areas of, 84–85
    hemispheric specialization and, 86–91
    language areas of, 85–86, 87
    motor areas of, 82–83
    sensory areas of, 84
Cerebral hemispheres, 82
Cerebral palsy, 310
Cerebrum, 82
C fibers, 166
Chaining, 223
Challenger accident, 493
Chemical senses, 162–165
Child abuse, recovered memories of, 258–259
Child psychology, 96
Child rearing
    operant conditioning for, 228
    parenting styles and, 107–108
    sexual orientation and, 342
Children. *See also* Adolescent development; Infant/child development
    as eyewitnesses, 262, 264
    gender role concepts of, 296
Chimpanzees
    language in, 297–298
    naturalistic observation of, 35–36
Chloride, resting potential and, 68–70
Cholecystokinin, hunger and, 331
Choleric temperament, 395

Chromosomes, 60
Chunks, 246
Circadian rhythms, 183
Civil Rights Act of 1964, 523
Civil Rights Act of 1991, 523–524
Clairvoyance, 170
Classical conditioning, 212–220
    acquisition in, 213–215
    applications of, 216–218, 219
    backward, 215
    biological constraints on, 218, 220
    cognitive factors in, 234
    delayed, 214–215
    extinction in, 215–216
    higher-order, 213–214
    of immune response, 464–465
    simultaneous, 215
    stimulus generalization and stimulus discrimination in, 215
    therapies based on, 433–435
    trace, 215
Client-centered therapy, 439, 440
Clinical case studies, of brain, 76–77
Clinical psychology, 22
Closure, principle of, 147
Cocaine, 205
Cochlea, 157
Cochlear implants, 160
Codes of ethics, 50
Coefficient of correlation, 46–47
Cognition, hypnosis and, 198
Cognitive abilities, gender differences in, 120–121
Cognitive appraisal, stress response and, 466
Cognitive-appraisal theory of emotion, 369, 371
Cognitive-behavioral approach to personality, 389–391
    personality assessment and, 390
    social-cognitive theory and, 389–390
    status of, 390–391
Cognitive choice theories of motivation, 526
Cognitive development
    during adolescence, 116–117
    during adulthood, 124–125
    during infancy and childhood, 101, 103–105
    Piaget's stages of, 103–105, 116–117
Cognitive dissonance theory, 487–488
Cognitive-evaluation theory, 347
Cognitive learning, 233–238